Oxford
Mini Thesaurus

FOURTH EDITION

Edited by

Sara Hawker
Lucy Hollingworth

OXFORD
UNIVERSITY PRESS

OXFORD
UNIVERSITY PRESS

Great Clarendon Street, Oxford OX2 6DP

Oxford University Press is a department of the University of Oxford.
It furthers the University's objective of excellence in research, scholarship,
and education by publishing worldwide in

Oxford New York

Auckland Cape Town Dar es Salaam Hong Kong Karachi
Kuala Lumpur Madrid Melbourne Mexico City Nairobi
New Delhi Shanghai Taipei Toronto

With offices in

Argentina Austria Brazil Chile Czech Republic France Greece
Guatemala Hungary Italy Japan Poland Portugal Singapore
South Korea Switzerland Thailand Turkey Ukraine Vietnam

Oxford is a registered trade mark of Oxford University Press
in the UK and in certain other countries

British Library Cataloguing in Publication Data

Data available

Library of Congress Cataloging in Publication Data

Data available

ISBN 978-0-19-921364-1 (OUP Main edition)

ISBN 978-0-19-923954-2 (Daily Mail Edition)

10 9 8 7 6

Typeset in Argo and Arial
by SPI Publisher Services, Pondicherry, India
Printed and bound in Italy
by L.E.G.O. S.p.A., Lavis (TN)

8497844951654224

Introduction

A thesaurus contains lists of words that have the same or a similar meaning to another word. It can help you to express yourself more clearly, find a word that is on the tip of your tongue, or avoid repeating a word that you have already used. It can also be a very useful resource for crossword puzzles and other word games.

The fourth edition of the *Oxford Mini Thesaurus* has been completely revised and redesigned to make it the clearest and most helpful quick-reference thesaurus available. The lists of alternative words (known as 'synonyms') are arranged in order of their closeness in meaning to the entry word, with the closest one given first and printed in **bold** type to make it easy to find the sense you are looking for.

New to this edition are the Word Link features, which contain extra vocabulary linked to a selection of key main entries. At the Word Link for **bird**, for example, you will find the terms **ornithology** (the study of birds) and **avian** (relating to birds). The Wordfinder section in the centre of the book provides still more sources of vocabulary to help with puzzle-solving, in the form of handy lists of animals, plants, clothes, types of food, and more.

Guide to the thesaurus

The *Oxford Mini Thesaurus* is designed to be as easy to use and understand as possible. Here is an explanation of the main features that you will find.

Entry word (known as a *headword*)

colourful adj. **1 bright**, vivid, vibrant, brilliant, radiant, gaudy, garish, multicoloured, psychedelic; informal jazzy. **2** *a colourful account*: **vivid**, graphic, lively, animated, dramatic, fascinating, interesting, stimulating, scintillating, evocative.
OPPOSITES drab, dull.

Numbered sense of the entry word

Example of use

Word closest in meaning to the entry word (in bold type)

Words meaning the opposite of the entry word

horse n. **mount**, charger, cob, nag, hack, colt, stallion, mare, filly; N. Amer. bronco; Austral./NZ moke; informal gee-gee.

Label showing the level of English in which the following synonym is used

Labels showing the region of the world in which the following synonyms are used

WORD LINKS
relating to horses: equine;
relating to horse riding: equestrian

Word link providing extra vocabulary related to the entry word

Different parts of speech of entry word

root n. **1 source**, origin, cause, reason, basis, foundation, bottom, seat. **2** *his Irish roots:* **origins**, beginnings, family, birth, heritage.
▶v. **rummage**, hunt, search, rifle, delve, forage, dig, poke.
□ **root out** eradicate, eliminate, weed out, destroy, wipe out, stamp out, abolish, end, put a stop to.

Phrase for which synonyms are given

Labels

Most of the synonyms in the *Oxford Mini Thesaurus* are part of standard English, but some are used only in certain contexts or types of writing. These are grouped at the end of their sense, preceded by one of the following labels, as appropriate:

informal	normally used only in speech or informal writing or email (e.g. *barmy* or *gawp*)
formal	normally used only in writing, especially in official documents (e.g. *dwelling*)
dated	no longer used by most people (e.g. *navvy*)
old use	not in ordinary use today, though sometimes used to give an old-fashioned effect (e.g. *comely*)
historical	only used today to refer to things that are no longer part of modern life (e.g. *alms*)
literary	found only or mainly in works of literature (e.g. *plenteous*)
technical:	normally used only in technical language (e.g. *occlude*)
derogatory	meant to convey a low opinion or to insult someone (e.g. *pleb*)

Geographical labels

English is spoken throughout the world, and while most of the words used in standard British English will be the same as those used in other varieties, there are some words which are only found in one type of English. If a word has the geographical label Brit. in this thesaurus, this means that it is used in standard British English but not in American English, although it may be found in other varieties such as Australian English.

The labels US and N. Amer., on the other hand, mean that the word is typically American and is not standard in British English, though it may be found elsewhere.

Subject labels

These are used to show that a word or sense is connected with a particular subject or specialist activity such as Medicine or Computing.

Abbreviations used in the thesaurus

adj.	adjective	Austral.	Australian
adv.	adverb	Brit.	British
conj.	conjunction	Canad.	Canadian
det.	determiner	N. Amer.	North American
n.	noun	NZ	New Zealand
pl. n.	plural noun	US	United States
prep.	preposition		
pron.	pronoun		
v.	verb		

Trademarks

This thesaurus includes some words which have, or are asserted to have, proprietary status as trademarks or otherwise. Their inclusion does not imply that they have acquired for legal purposes a non-proprietary or general significance, nor any other judgement concerning their legal status. In cases where the editorial staff have some evidence that a word has proprietary status this is indicated in the entry for that word by the label trademark, but no judgement concerning the legal status of such words is made or implied thereby.

abandon v. **1** *he abandoned his wife*: **desert**, leave, turn your back on, cast aside, finish with, jilt, throw over; informal pack in, quit; informal walk/run out on, dump, ditch; literary forsake. **2** *she had abandoned painting*: **give up**, stop, have done with; informal pack in, quit; Brit. jack in. **3** *they abandoned the car*: **leave (behind)**, vacate, dump, quit, evacuate, discard, jettison. **4** *the party abandoned those policies*: **renounce**, relinquish, dispense with, discard, give up, drop; informal ditch, scrap, junk; formal forswear.
– OPPOSITES keep.
• n. **uninhibitedness**, recklessness, lack of restraint, lack of inhibition.
– OPPOSITES self-control.

abate v. **subside**, die down/away/out, lessen, ease (off), let up, decrease, diminish, fade, weaken.
– OPPOSITES intensify.

abbreviate v. **shorten**, reduce, cut, contract, condense, compress, abridge, summarize, precis.
– OPPOSITES lengthen, expand.

abbreviation n. **short form**, contraction, acronym, initialism.

abdicate v. **resign**, retire, stand down, step down, renounce the throne.

abdomen n. **stomach**, belly, gut, middle; informal tummy, guts.

WORD LINKS
relating to the abdomen:
abdominal, ventral

abdominal adj. **gastric**, intestinal, stomach, duodenal, visceral, coeliac, ventral.

abduct v. **kidnap**, carry off, seize, capture, run away/off with, take hostage; informal snatch.

aberration n. **anomaly**, deviation, abnormality, irregularity, variation, freak, oddity, peculiarity, curiosity, mistake.

abhor v. **hate**, detest, loathe, despise, shudder at; formal abominate.
– OPPOSITES love, admire.

abhorrent adj. **hateful**, detestable, loathsome, abominable, repellent, repugnant, repulsive, revolting, vile, odious, disgusting, horrible, horrid, horrifying, awful, heinous.
– OPPOSITES admirable.

abide v. **1** (informal) *I can't abide smoke*: **stand**, bear; Brit. informal stick. **2** *one memory will abide*: **continue**, remain, survive, last, persist, live on.
□ **abide by** comply with, obey, observe, follow, keep to, adhere

a to, stick to, go along with, heed, accept.

abiding adj. **enduring**, lasting, everlasting, perpetual, eternal, unending, permanent.

ability n. **1 capacity**, capability, power, potential, faculty, facility, wherewithal, means. **2 talent**, skill, aptitude, expertise, savoir faire, prowess, accomplishment, competence, proficiency, flair, gift, knack, genius; informal know-how.
– OPPOSITES inability.

able adj. **intelligent**, clever, talented, skilful, skilled, expert, accomplished, gifted, proficient, apt, adroit, adept, capable, competent.
– OPPOSITES incompetent.

abnormal adj. **unusual**, uncommon, atypical, untypical, unexpected, unrepresentative, irregular, anomalous, deviant, aberrant, freak, strange, odd, peculiar, eccentric, bizarre, weird, unnatural, perverted, twisted, warped; informal funny, freaky, kinky.
– OPPOSITES normal.

abnormality n. **deformity**, defect, malformation, oddity, strangeness, irregularity, anomaly, deviation, aberration.

abolish v. **put an end to**, get rid of, scrap, cancel, end, remove, dissolve, stop, ban; informal do away with, axe, ditch.

abominable adj. **loathsome**, detestable, hateful, obnoxious, despicable, contemptible, disgusting, revolting, repellent, repulsive, repugnant, abhorrent, reprehensible, atrocious, execrable, foul, vile, wretched, horrible, awful, dreadful, appalling, nauseating; informal terrible, shocking, God-awful; Brit. informal beastly.
– OPPOSITES good, admirable.

abort v. the crew aborted the take-off: **halt**, stop, end, call off, abandon, discontinue, terminate; informal pull the plug on.

abortion n. **termination**, miscarriage.

abortive adj. **unsuccessful**, failed, vain, ineffective, ineffectual, unproductive, futile, useless, unavailing.
– OPPOSITES successful.

abound v. **be plentiful**, be abundant, be numerous, be thick on the ground; informal grow on trees, be two/ten a penny.

about prep. **regarding**, concerning, referring to, with regard to, with respect to, relating to, on, dealing with, on the subject of.
• adv. **approximately**, roughly, around, in the region of, circa, of the order of, or so, or thereabouts, more or less; Brit. getting on for; N. Amer. informal in the ballpark of.

above prep. **1 over**, higher (up) than, on top of, on. **2 superior to**, senior to, over, higher (up) than, more powerful than, in charge of, commanding.
– OPPOSITES below.
• adv. **overhead**, on/at the top,

high up, on high, up above, (up) in the sky.

▫ **above all** most importantly, most of all, chiefly, primarily, first and foremost, essentially, in essence, at bottom; informal at the end of the day, when all is said and done.

abrasion n. **1** graze, cut, scrape, scratch, gash, laceration. **2** erosion, wearing away/down.

abrasive adj. **1** rough, coarse, harsh, scratchy, chafing. **2** curt, brusque, sharp, harsh, caustic, grating.
– OPPOSITES gentle.

abridge v. shorten, cut (down), edit, abbreviate, condense, compress, truncate, prune, summarize, precis, synopsize; (**abridged**) concise.
– OPPOSITES extend.

abridgement n. summary, synopsis, precis, abstract, outline, résumé, digest, cut-down version.

abroad adv. overseas, out of the country, to/in foreign parts, to/ in a foreign country/land.

abrupt adj. **1** sudden, rapid, quick, hasty, unexpected, unanticipated, unforeseen, precipitate. **2** curt, brusque, blunt, short, rude, sharp, terse, brisk, unceremonious.
– OPPOSITES gradual, gentle.

abscond v. run away, run off, escape, bolt, flee, make off, take flight, take off, decamp; informal scarper, vamoose, do a bunk, do a runner.

absence n. **1** non-attendance, absenteeism, truancy, leave, holiday, vacation, sabbatical. **2** lack, want, non-existence, unavailability, scarcity, shortage, dearth.
– OPPOSITES presence.

absent adj. **1** away, off, out, elsewhere, off duty, on holiday, on leave, playing truant; informal AWOL. **2** non-existent, lacking, missing. **3** distracted, preoccupied, inattentive, vague, absorbed, dreamy, faraway, blank, empty, vacant.
– OPPOSITES present.

▫ **absent yourself** stay away, be absent, go away, leave, withdraw.

absent-minded adj. forgetful, distracted, scatterbrained, preoccupied, inattentive, vague; informal with a mind/memory like a sieve.

absolute adj. **1** absolute silence | an absolute disgrace: complete, total, utter, out-and-out, outright, perfect, pure, thorough, unqualified, unreserved, downright, unmitigated, sheer, unadulterated. **2** absolute power: unlimited, unrestricted, unrestrained, infinite, total, supreme, unconditional. **3** an absolute ruler: autocratic, dictatorial, all-powerful, omnipotent, supreme.
– OPPOSITES partial, qualified, limited.

absolutely adv. completely, totally, utterly, perfectly, entirely, wholly, fully, quite, thoroughly, unreservedly, definitely,

a certainly, unquestionably, undoubtedly, without (a) doubt, without question, in every way/respect, one hundred per cent.

absorb v. **1 soak up**, suck up, draw up/in, take up/in, mop up. **2 engross**, captivate, occupy, preoccupy, engage, rivet, grip, hold, immerse, involve, enthral, spellbind, fascinate.

absorbent adj. **spongy**, sponge-like, porous, permeable.

absorbing adj. **fascinating**, interesting, captivating, gripping, engrossing, compelling, compulsive, enthralling, riveting, spellbinding; informal unputdownable.
– OPPOSITES boring.

absorption n. **1 soaking up**, sucking up. **2 involvement**, immersion, raptness, preoccupation, captivation, fascination, enthralment.

abstain v. **refrain**, desist, forbear, give up, renounce, avoid, eschew, forgo, go/do without, refuse, decline; informal cut out.

abstemious adj. **moderate**, restrained, temperate, self-disciplined, self-restrained, self-denying, sober, austere, ascetic, puritanical, spartan.
– OPPOSITES self-indulgent.

abstinence n. **self-denial**, self-restraint, teetotalism, temperance, sobriety, abstemiousness.

abstract adj. **theoretical**, conceptual, intellectual, metaphysical, philosophical, academic.

– OPPOSITES actual, concrete.
• n. **summary**, synopsis, precis, résumé, outline, abridgement; N. Amer. wrap-up.

abstruse adj. **obscure**, arcane, esoteric, rarefied, recondite, difficult, hard, cryptic, over/above your head, incomprehensible, unfathomable, impenetrable.

absurd adj. **irrational**, illogical, inappropriate, ridiculous, ludicrous, farcical, comical, stupid, idiotic, asinine, hare-brained, foolish, silly, pointless, senseless, preposterous; informal crazy, cockeyed; Brit. informal barmy, daft.
– OPPOSITES sensible.

abundance n. **plenty**, plentifulness, plethora, profusion, exuberance, riot, cornucopia, superabundance.
– OPPOSITES scarcity.

abundant adj. **plentiful**, copious, ample, profuse, large, huge, great, bumper, prolific, overflowing, teeming, superabundant; informal galore.
– OPPOSITES scarce.

abuse v. **1 misuse**, exploit, take advantage of. **2 mistreat**, maltreat, ill-treat, hurt, harm, beat, molest, interfere with. **3 insult**, be rude to, swear at, shout at, vilify, curse.
• n. **1 misuse**, exploitation. **2 mistreatment**, maltreatment, ill-treatment, molestation. **3 insults**, expletives, swear words, swearing, name-calling, invective, vilification, curses.

abusive adj. **1 insulting**, rude, offensive, derogatory, defamatory, slanderous, libellous. **2 violent**, brutal, cruel, harsh, oppressive.
– OPPOSITES polite.

abysmal adj. **terrible**, dreadful, awful, appalling, frightful, atrocious, disgraceful, deplorable, lamentable; informal rotten, pathetic, pitiful, woeful, useless, lousy, dire, poxy, the pits; Brit. informal chronic, shocking.

abyss n. **chasm**, crevasse, gulf, pit, void.

academic adj. **1 educational**, scholastic. **2 scholarly**, learned, literary, intellectual, erudite, high-brow, bookish, studious. **3 theoretical**, hypothetical, notional, speculative, conjectural, irrelevant, beside the point.
• n. **scholar**, intellectual, don, professor, man/woman of letters, thinker; informal egghead; Brit. informal boffin.

academy n. **college**, school, university, institute.

accelerate v. **1 speed up**, go faster, gain momentum, increase speed, pick up speed, gather speed. **2 hasten**, quicken, speed up, further, advance, expedite; informal crank up.
– OPPOSITES decelerate, delay.

accent n. **1 pronunciation**, intonation, enunciation, articulation, inflection. **2 emphasis**, stress, priority, importance, prominence.

accentuate v. **focus attention on**, draw attention to, point up, underline, underscore, accent, highlight, spotlight, foreground, bring to the fore, emphasize, stress.

accept v. **1 receive**, take, get, obtain, acquire, pick up. **2 agree to**, accede to, consent to, acquiesce in, concur with, endorse, comply with, go along with, defer to, put up with, recognize, acknowledge, admit. **3 believe**, trust, credit, be convinced of, have faith in; informal buy, swallow.
– OPPOSITES reject.

acceptable adj. **satisfactory**, adequate, reasonable, fair, good enough, sufficient, tolerable, passable.

acceptance n. **1 receipt**, receiving, taking. **2 respect**, acknowledgement, belief, toleration, consent, agreement, assent, compliance, acquiescence.

accepted adj. **recognized**, acknowledged, established, traditional, orthodox, agreed, approved, customary, normal, standard.
– OPPOSITES unorthodox.

access n. **1** *a side access:* **entrance**, entry, approach, path, drive, way in. **2** *they were denied access:* **admission**, admittance, entry.

accessible adj. **approachable**, attainable, reachable, obtainable, available, understandable, comprehensible, intelligible; informal get-at-able.

a accessory n. **1 extra**, add-on, addition, supplement, attachment, fitment. **2 accomplice**, abetter, collaborator, co-conspirator, henchman, associate.

accident n. **1 mishap**, misadventure, disaster, tragedy, catastrophe, calamity. **2 crash**, collision, smash, bump, derailment; N. Amer. wreck; informal smash-up, pile-up; Brit. informal shunt. **3 chance**, fate, fortune, luck, good luck, fluke, coincidence.

accidental adj. **1 chance**, coincidental, unexpected, incidental, fortuitous, serendipitous. **2 unintentional**, unintended, unplanned, inadvertent, unwitting, unpremeditated.
– OPPOSITES intentional.

acclaim v. **praise**, applaud, cheer, commend, approve, welcome, hail, celebrate, eulogize; formal laud.
– OPPOSITES criticize.
•n. **praise**, applause, tributes, plaudits, approval, admiration, congratulations, commendation, eulogies.
– OPPOSITES criticism.

acclimatize v. **adjust**, adapt, get used, familiarize yourself, find your feet, get your bearings; N. Amer. acclimate.

accommodate v. **1** *refugees were accommodated in army camps*: **lodge**, house, put up, billet, board. **2** *the cottages accommodate six people*: **hold**, take, have room for, sleep, seat.
3 *we tried to accommodate her*: **help**, assist, oblige, cater for, fit in with, satisfy, meet the needs of.

accommodating adj. **obliging**, cooperative, helpful, amenable, hospitable, flexible.

accommodation n. **housing**, homes, lodging(s), (living) quarters, rooms, billet, shelter, a roof over your head; informal digs, pad; formal residence, dwelling, abode.

accompaniment n. **1** *a musical accompaniment*: **backing**, support, background, soundtrack. **2** *wine is a good accompaniment to cheese*: **complement**, addition, adjunct, accessory, companion.

accompany v. **1 escort**, go with, travel with, keep someone company, chaperone, partner, show, see, usher, conduct. **2 occur with**, go along with with, go together with, attend, be linked with, go hand in hand with. **3** *he accompanied the choir on the piano*: **back**, play along with, support.

accomplice n. **partner in crime**, abetter, accessory, collaborator, co-conspirator, henchman, associate; informal sidekick.

accomplish v. **achieve**, succeed in, realize, attain, manage, bring off, carry through, execute, effect, perform, complete.

accomplished adj. **expert**, skilled, skilful, masterly, virtuoso, master, proficient, polished, practised, consummate, talented, gifted, able, capable; informal mean, nifty, crack, ace.

accomplishment n. **1** achievement, success, act, deed, exploit, effort, feat, coup. **2** talent, skill, gift, ability.

accord v. **1** give, grant, present, award, confer on, bestow on. **2** correspond, agree, tally, match, concur, be in harmony, be in tune.
– OPPOSITES disagree, differ.
• n. **1** *a peace accord:* **pact**, treaty, agreement, settlement, deal, entente, protocol. **2** *the two sides failed to reach accord:* **agreement**, consensus, unanimity, harmony.
– OPPOSITES disagreement.
□ **of your own accord** voluntarily, of your own free will, of your own volition, by choice, willingly, freely, readily.

account n. **1** description, report, version, story, statement, explanation, tale, chronicle, narrative, history, record, log. **2** financial record, ledger, balance sheet, financial statement; (**accounts**) books. **3** *his background is of no account:* **importance**, import, significance, consequence, value.
□ **account for 1** explain, answer for, give reasons for, justify. **2** constitute, make up, comprise, represent, be responsible for, produce.

accountability n. responsibility, liability, answerability.

accountable adj. responsible, liable, answerable, to blame.

accumulate v. gather, collect, amass, stockpile, pile up, build up, store (up), hoard, lay in/up, increase, accrue, run up.
– OPPOSITES disperse.

accumulation n. mass, buildup, pile, collection, stock, store, stockpile, hoard.

accuracy n. correctness, precision, exactness, fidelity, truth, truthfulness, authenticity, realism.

accurate adj. **1** correct, precise, exact, right, factual, literal, faithful, true, truthful, on the mark, authentic, realistic; Brit. informal spot on, bang on; N. Amer. informal on the money, on the button. **2** well aimed, on target, unerring, deadly, true.

accusation n. allegation, charge, indictment, impeachment, claim, assertion, imputation.

accuse v. **1** charge, indict, impeach, prefer charges against, arraign. **2** blame, hold responsible, condemn, criticize, denounce; informal point the finger at.

accustom v. adapt, adjust, acclimatize, habituate, familiarize, become reconciled, get used to, come to terms with, learn to live with; N. Amer. acclimate.

accustomed adj. customary, established, habitual, usual, normal, regular, routine; literary wonted.

a

ache n. **pain**, twinge, pang, soreness, tenderness, irritation, discomfort, burning, throbbing, cramp.
- v. **hurt**, be sore, be painful, be tender, burn, be in pain, throb.

achieve v. **attain**, reach, realize, bring off, pull off, accomplish, carry through, fulfil, complete, succeed in, manage, effect; informal wrap up, swing.

achievement n. **1 attainment**, realization, accomplishment, fulfilment, implementation, completion. **2 feat**, exploit, triumph, coup, accomplishment, act, action, deed, effort, work, handiwork.

acid adj. **1 sour**, acidic, tart, sharp, vinegary. **2 sharp**, sharp-tongued, catty, sarcastic, scathing, cutting, biting, stinging, caustic; informal bitchy.
- OPPOSITES sweet.

acknowledge v. **1 admit**, accept, grant, agree, own, allow, concede, confess, recognize. **2 greet**, salute, address, nod to, wave to, say hello to. **3 answer**, reply to, respond to.
- OPPOSITES deny, ignore.

acquaint v. **familiarize**, make aware of, inform of, advise of, brief; informal fill in on, clue in on.

acquaintance n. **1** a business acquaintance: **contact**, associate, colleague. **2** my acquaintance with George: **association**, relationship. **3** some acquaintance with the language: **familiarity with**, knowledge of,

experience of, awareness of, understanding of, grasp of.

acquire v. **get**, obtain, come by, receive, collect, gain, buy, earn, win, come into, secure, pick up, procure; informal get your hands on, get hold of, land, bag, score.
- OPPOSITES lose.

acquisition n. **purchase**, addition, investment, possession, accession; informal buy.

acquit v. **1 clear**, exonerate, find innocent, absolve, discharge, free, release; informal let off (the hook). **2** the boys acquitted themselves well: **behave**, conduct yourself, perform, act.
- OPPOSITES convict.

acrid adj. **pungent**, bitter, sharp, harsh, stinging, burning.

acrimonious adj. **bitter**, angry, rancorous, harsh, vicious, nasty, bad-tempered, ill-natured.

act v. **1 take action**, take steps, take measures, move. **2 behave**, conduct yourself, react. **3** I'll act as lookout: **function**, work, serve, operate. **4 perform**, play, appear; informal tread the boards.
- n. **1 deed**, action, step, move, gesture, feat, exploit. **2 law**, decree, statute, bill, edict, ruling, order. **3 performance**, turn, routine, number, sketch. **4 pretence**, show, front, facade, masquerade, charade, pose; informal a put-on.

acting adj. **temporary**, interim, caretaker, pro tem, provisional,

stopgap; N. Amer. informal pinch-hitting.
– OPPOSITES permanent.

action n. **1** deed, act, undertaking, feat, exploit, behaviour, conduct, activity. **2 measures**, steps, initiatives, activism, campaigning, pressure. **3 operation**, working, effect, influence, process, power. **4 battle**, combat, hostilities, fighting, conflict, active service. **5 lawsuit**, suit, case, prosecution, litigation, proceedings.

activate v. **start (up)**, switch on, turn on, set going, trigger (off), set off, energize.

active adj. **1 busy**, lively, dynamic, vigorous, sprightly, spry, mobile; informal on the go, full of beans. **2 hard-working**, industrious, tireless, energetic, diligent, enthusiastic, keen, committed, devoted, zealous. **3 working**, operative, functioning, operational, in action, in operation, in force; informal (up and) running.
– OPPOSITES inactive.

activity n. **1 action**, bustle, movement, life, hurly-burly; informal toing and froing, comings and goings. **2 pursuit**, occupation, hobby, pastime, recreation, diversion, venture, undertaking, enterprise, project, scheme.

actor, actress n. performer, player, thespian, star, starlet; Brit. informal luvvy.

actual adj. **real**, true, genuine, authentic, bona fide, confirmed, definite, hard, concrete; informal real live.
– OPPOSITES imaginary.

actually adv. **really**, in (actual) fact, in point of fact, as a matter of fact, in reality, in truth, if truth be told, to tell the truth.

acute adj. **1 severe**, dire, terrible, grave, serious, desperate, urgent, pressing. **2 excruciating**, sharp, severe, stabbing, agonizing, racking, searing. **3 quick**, astute, shrewd, sharp, keen, penetrating, razor-sharp, quick-witted, agile, nimble, intelligent, canny, discerning, perceptive.
– OPPOSITES mild, dull.

adamant adj. **unshakeable**, unwavering, unswerving, immovable, resolute, resolved, determined, firm, dead set.

adapt v. **1** the policy can be adapted: **modify**, alter, change, adjust, remodel, reorganize, customize, tailor; informal tweak. **2** he adapts well to new surroundings: **adjust**, conform, acclimatize, accommodate, get used, get accustomed, habituate yourself.

add v. **1 attach**, append, tack on, join on. **2** they added the figures up: **total**, count (up), reckon up, tally; Brit. tot up.
– OPPOSITES subtract.

□ **add to** increase, augment, magnify, amplify, enhance, intensify, heighten, deepen, exacerbate, aggravate, compound, reinforce. **add up to** amount to, come to, run to, make, total, equal, number.

addict n. **1** abuser; informal junkie, druggy, -head, freak; N. Amer. informal hophead. **2** (informal) enthusiast, fan, lover, devotee, aficionado; informal buff, freak, nut, fanatic.

addicted adj. dependent, obsessed, fixated, fanatical, passionate, a slave to; informal hooked.

addiction n. dependency, dependence, habit, obsession, infatuation, passion, love, mania, enslavement.

addictive adj. habit-forming, compulsive; Brit. informal moreish.

addition n. **1** adding, inclusion, incorporation, introduction. **2** add-on, extra, adjunct, appendage, supplement, rider, addendum, postscript, appendix.
– OPPOSITES subtraction.
□ **in addition** see ADDITION-ALLY.

additional adj. extra, added, supplementary, further, more, spare, other, new, fresh.

additionally adv. also, in addition, besides, too, as well, on top of (that), furthermore, moreover, into the bargain, to boot, to say nothing of.

address n. **1** house, flat, apartment, home, location, whereabouts; formal residence, dwelling, domicile. **2** speech, lecture, talk, presentation, dissertation, sermon, oration.
• v. **speak to**, talk to, give a talk to, lecture, make a speech to, hold forth to.

adept adj. expert, proficient, accomplished, skilful, practised, masterly, consummate.
– OPPOSITES inept.

adequate adj. **1** he has adequate financial resources: sufficient, enough. **2** an adequate service: satisfactory, acceptable, passable, reasonable, tolerable, fair, average, not bad, all right, middling; informal OK.
– OPPOSITES insufficient, inadequate.

adhere v. stick, cling, bond, hold.
□ **adhere to** abide by, stick to, hold to, comply with, conform to, follow, obey, heed, observe, respect, uphold, fulfil.

adherent n. follower, supporter, upholder, defender, advocate, disciple, devotee, member.
– OPPOSITES opponent.

adjacent adj. adjoining, neighbouring, next-door, abutting; formal contiguous.
□ **adjacent to** next to, by the side of, bordering on, beside, alongside, touching.

adjoining adj. connecting, connected, interconnecting, bordering, abutting, attached, adjacent, neighbouring, next-door.

adjourn v. suspend, break off, discontinue, interrupt, recess, postpone, put off/back, defer, delay, hold over.

adjust v. **1** modify, alter, regulate, tune, fine-tune, balance, tailor, customize, rearrange, change, reshape; informal tweak. **2** *she adjusted to her new life:* **adapt**, become accustomed, get used, accommodate, acclimatize, habituate yourself, assimilate, come to terms with, fit in with; N. Amer. acclimate.

adjustable adj. alterable, adaptable, modifiable, variable, convertible, multiway, versatile.

administer v. **1** manage, direct, control, operate, regulate, coordinate, conduct, handle, run, organize, govern, steer. **2** dispense, issue, give out, provide, apply, offer, distribute, deliver, hand out, deal out, dole out.

administration n. **1** management, direction, control, conduct, operation, running, coordination, governance, supervision, regulation. **2** government, regime, executive, cabinet, authority, directorate, council, leadership, management, incumbency, term of office.

administrative adj. managerial, executive, operational, organizational, supervisory, directorial, governmental, regulatory.

administrator n. manager, director, executive, controller, official, coordinator, supervisor.

admirable adj. commendable, praiseworthy, laudable, creditable, exemplary, worthy, deserving, respectable, worthwhile, good, sterling, fine, excellent.
– OPPOSITES deplorable.

admiration n. respect, approval, appreciation, (high) regard, esteem, recognition.
– OPPOSITES scorn.

admire v. **1** respect, think highly of, look up to, have a high opinion of, hold in high regard, rate highly, esteem, prize, approve of. **2** adore, love, worship, be taken with, be attracted to, idolize, hero-worship; informal carry a torch for, have a thing about.
– OPPOSITES despise.

admirer n. fan, devotee, enthusiast, aficionado, supporter, adherent, follower, disciple.

admission n. **1** confession, acknowledgement, acceptance, concession, disclosure, divulgence. **2** admittance, entry, entrance, access, entrée, acceptance, initiation.

admit v. **1** *Paul admitted that he was angry:* **confess**, acknowledge, concede, grant, accept, allow, own, reveal, disclose, divulge. **2** *he admitted the offence:* **confess (to)**, plead guilty to, own up to. **3** let in, accept, receive, initiate, take on.
– OPPOSITES deny.

admittance n. entry, admission, entrance, access, entrée.
– OPPOSITES exclusion.

adolescence n. teenage years, teens, youth, later childhood.

adolescent n. teenager, youth, juvenile; informal teen, teenybopper.
•adj. teenage, young, pubescent,

a

immature, childish, juvenile, infantile, puerile; informal teen.
– OPPOSITES mature.

adopt v. **take on**, embrace, take up, espouse, assume, follow, choose, endorse, approve.
– OPPOSITES abandon.

adore v. **love**, be devoted to, dote on, cherish, treasure, prize, think the world of, admire, look up to, revere, worship.
– OPPOSITES hate.

adorn v. **decorate**, embellish, array, ornament, bedeck, trim, enhance.
– OPPOSITES disfigure.

adrift adj. **1 lost**, off course, drifting, disorientated, confused, (all) at sea, rootless, unsettled. **2** (informal) **loose**, free, detached, unsecured, unfastened.

adult adj. **mature**, grown-up, fully grown, fully developed, of age.
– OPPOSITES immature.

advance v. **1 move forward**, press on, push on, attack, make progress, make headway, gain ground, forge ahead. **2** the move advanced his career: **promote**, further, forward, help, aid, assist, boost. **3** technology has advanced: **progress**, develop, evolve, make strides, move forward (in leaps and bounds), move on. **4 lend**, loan, put up, come up with; Brit. informal sub.
– OPPOSITES retreat.
• n. **1 progress**, (forward) movement, attack. **2 breakthrough**,

development, step forward, (quantum) leap.
• adj. **early**, prior.
□ **in advance** beforehand, before, ahead of time, earlier, previously, in readiness.

advanced adj. **1 state-of-the-art**, modern, sophisticated, up to date, up to the minute, cutting-edge, new, the latest, pioneering, innovative, progressive, trendsetting. **2 higher-level**, higher, tertiary.
– OPPOSITES primitive, elementary.

advantage n. **1 upper hand**, edge, lead, sway, whip hand, superiority, dominance, supremacy. **2 benefit**, value, good/strong point, asset, plus, bonus, boon, blessing, virtue, profit, good.
– OPPOSITES disadvantage.

advantageous adj. **1 superior**, dominant, powerful, fortunate, lucky, favourable. **2 beneficial**, of benefit, helpful, of assistance, useful, of value, profitable, in someone's interests.
– OPPOSITES disadvantageous.

adventure n. **1 exploit**, escapade, undertaking, experience, incident. **2 excitement**, thrills, action, stimulation, risk, danger.

adventurous adj. **1 intrepid**, daring, daredevil, bold, fearless, brave; informal gutsy. **2 risky**, dangerous, perilous, hazardous, exciting.
– OPPOSITES cautious, safe.

adversary n. **opponent**, rival, enemy, antagonist, challenger,

contender, competitor, opposition, competition; literary foe.
- OPPOSITES ally.

adverse adj. **1** *adverse weather:* **unfavourable**, inclement, bad, poor, untoward, inauspicious, unpropitious. **2** *adverse side effects:* **harmful**, dangerous, injurious, detrimental, deleterious, inimical. **3** *an adverse response:* **hostile**, unfavourable, antagonistic, unfriendly, negative.
- OPPOSITES favourable, beneficial.

adversity n. **misfortune**, bad luck, trouble, difficulty, hardship, disaster, suffering, sorrow, misery, woe, trials and tribulations.

advertise v. **publicize**, make public, announce, broadcast, proclaim, trumpet, promote, market; informal push, plug, hype; N. Amer. informal ballyhoo, flack.

advertisement n. **announcement**, commercial, promotion, blurb, write-up; informal ad, push, plug; Brit. informal advert.

advice n. **guidance**, counselling, counsel, help, direction, recommendations, guidelines, suggestions, hints, tips, pointers.

advisable adj. **wise**, sensible, prudent, expedient, politic, in your (best) interests.

advise v. **1 counsel**, give guidance, guide, offer suggestions, give hints/tips/pointers. **2 recommend**, advocate, suggest, urge. **3 inform**, notify, give notice, apprise, warn.

adviser n. **counsellor**, aide, mentor, guide, consultant, confidant, confidante, guru.

advocate n. **champion**, upholder, supporter, apologist, backer, promoter, proponent, campaigner, lobbyist; N. Amer. booster.
- OPPOSITES critic.
- v. **recommend**, champion, uphold, support, back, promote, campaign for, urge, subscribe to, speak for, argue for, lobby for.
- OPPOSITES oppose.

affair n. **1 event**, incident, episode, case, matter, business. **2 business**, concern, matter, responsibility, problem; Brit. informal lookout. **3 (affairs) transactions**, activities, dealings, undertakings, ventures, business. **4 relationship**, romance, fling, dalliance, liaison, involvement, amour; informal hanky-panky; Brit. informal carry-on.

affect[1] v. **1 influence**, have an effect on, have an impact on, act on, change, alter, modify. **2 move**, touch, hit (hard), make an impression on, upset, trouble, distress, disturb, shake (up).

affect[2] v. **put on**, assume, take on, adopt, feign.

affectation n. **pretension**, pretentiousness, affectedness, artificiality, posturing, airs (and graces); Brit. informal side.

affection n. **fondness**, love, liking, soft spot, tenderness,

a

warmth, devotion, caring, attachment, friendship.

affectionate adj. **fond**, loving, adoring, devoted, caring, tender, warm, friendly, demonstrative; informal touchy-feely, lovey-dovey.
– OPPOSITES cold.

affiliate v. **associate**, unite, combine, join (up), join forces, link up, ally, align, amalgamate, merge.

affinity n. **empathy**, rapport, sympathy, accord, harmony, similarity, relationship, bond, closeness, understanding; informal chemistry.
– OPPOSITES aversion.

affirm v. **declare**, state, assert, proclaim, pronounce, attest, swear, maintain, avow.
– OPPOSITES deny.

affirmative adj. **positive**, assenting, consenting, approving, favourable.
– OPPOSITES negative.

afflict v. **trouble**, burden, distress, beset, harass, worry, oppress, torment, plague, bedevil.

affluent adj. **wealthy**, rich, prosperous, well off, well-to-do, of means; informal well heeled, rolling in it, made of money, loaded.
– OPPOSITES poor.

afford v. **1 pay for**, find the money for, run to, stretch to, stand, manage, spare. **2 give**, offer, supply, provide, furnish, yield.

afraid adj. **1 frightened**, scared, terrified, fearful, nervous, petrified, intimidated, cowardly, faint-hearted; informal scared stiff, chicken; N. Amer. informal spooked. **2 reluctant**, hesitant, unwilling, slow, shy. **3** *I'm afraid I'm late:* sorry.
– OPPOSITES brave, confident.

after prep. **following**, subsequent to, at the end of, in the wake of.

aftermath n. **consequences**, after-effects, results, repercussions, upshot.

afterwards adv. **later**, later on, subsequently, then, next, after this/that, in due course.

again adv. **once more**, another time, afresh, anew.

against prep. **opposed to**, in opposition to, hostile to, antagonistic towards, unsympathetic to, at odds with, in disagreement with; informal anti.

age n. **1 old age**, maturity, advancing years, elderliness, seniority, senescence. **2 era**, epoch, period, time, generation.
 •v. **1 mature**, mellow, ripen, soften, season, weather. **2 grow old**, decline, wither, fade

agency n. **business**, organization, company, firm, office, bureau.

agenda n. **programme**, schedule, to-do list, timetable, plan.

agent n. **1 representative**, intermediary, middleman, negotiator, go-between, proxy, broker, emissary, envoy, spokesperson, delegate; informal rep. **2 spy**, secret agent, operative,

mole; N. Amer. informal spook,
G-man.

aggravate v. **1 worsen**, make
worse, exacerbate, inflame,
compound. **2** (informal) **annoy**,
antagonize, irritate, exasperate,
nettle, provoke, get on someone's nerves; Brit. rub up the
wrong way; informal needle, hack
off, get someone's goat; Brit.
informal wind up; N. Amer. informal
tick off.
– OPPOSITES alleviate, improve.

aggregate n. **total**, sum, grand
total, combined score.

aggression n. **hostility**, belliger-
ence, force, violence, attack.

aggressive adj. **1** *aggressive
behaviour:* **violent**, confrontational, antagonistic, combative,
pugnacious. **2** *aggressive foreign
policy:* **warmongering**, warlike,
warring, belligerent, bellicose,
hawkish, militaristic, expan-
sionist; informal gung-ho. **3** *an
aggressive campaign:* **assertive**,
forceful, pushy, vigorous, energetic, dynamic, audacious;
informal in-your-face, feisty.
– OPPOSITES peaceable, peaceful.

agile adj. **1 nimble**, lithe, supple,
graceful, fit, acrobatic, sprightly,
spry. **2 alert**, sharp, acute,
shrewd, astute, perceptive,
quick.
– OPPOSITES clumsy.

agitate v. **1 upset**, fluster, ruffle,
disconcert, unnerve, disquiet,
disturb, distress, unsettle,
worry, perturb, trouble; informal
rattle, faze. **2 shake**, whisk,
beat, stir.

agonizing adj. **excruciating**,
painful, acute, searing, severe,
harrowing, torturous.

agony n. **suffering**, torture, pain,
torment, anguish.

agree v. **1 concur**, see eye to eye,
be in sympathy, be as one, be
unanimous. **2** *they agreed to a
ceasefire:* **consent**, assent, acquiesce, allow, approve; formal accede. **3 match (up)**, correspond,
conform, coincide, fit, tally, be
consistent; informal square.
4 decide on, settle, arrive at,
negotiate, shake hands on.
– OPPOSITES disagree.

agreeable adj. **1** *an agreeable
atmosphere:* **pleasant**, pleasing,
enjoyable, pleasurable, nice,
appealing, relaxing, friendly,
congenial. **2** *an agreeable man:*
likeable, amiable, affable,
pleasant, nice, friendly, good-
natured, sociable, genial. **3 willing**, amenable, in agreement.
– OPPOSITES unpleasant.

agreement n. **1 accord**, con-
currence, consensus, assent,
acceptance, consent, acquiescence. **2 contract**, treaty, pact,
concordat, accord, settlement,
understanding, bargain. **3 correspondence**, consistency,
compatibility, accord, similarity,
resemblance, likeness.
– OPPOSITES discord, dissimilarity.

agricultural adj. **farm**, farming,
agrarian, rural, rustic, countryside.
– OPPOSITES urban.

a **agriculture** n. **farming**, cultivation, husbandry, agribusiness, agronomy.

> **WORD LINKS**
> relating to agriculture: agrarian

aid n. **1** with the aid of his colleagues: **assistance**, support, help, backing, cooperation, a helping hand. **2** humanitarian aid: **relief**, assistance, support, subsidy, funding, donations, grants; historical alms.
– OPPOSITES hindrance.
•v. **help**, assist, be of service, support, encourage, further, boost, promote, facilitate.
– OPPOSITES hinder.

aide n. **assistant**, helper, adviser, supporter, right-hand man/woman, adjutant, deputy, second (in command), lieutenant.

ailing adj. **1** ill, sick, unwell, sickly, poorly, weak, in poor/bad health, infirm. **2** failing, weak, poor, fragile, unstable.
– OPPOSITES healthy.

ailment n. **illness**, disease, disorder, affliction, malady, complaint, infirmity; informal bug, virus.

aim v. **1** he aimed the rifle: **point**, direct, train, sight, line up. **2** she aimed at the target: **take aim**, fix on, zero in on, draw a bead on. **3** this food is aimed at children: **target**, intend, direct, design, tailor, market, pitch. **4** intend, mean, hope, want, plan, propose.
•n. **objective**, object, goal, end, target, design, desire, intention, intent, plan, purpose, ambition, aspiration, wish, dream, hope.

aimless adj. **purposeless**, pointless, directionless, undirected, random.
– OPPOSITES purposeful.

air n. **1** breeze, draught, wind, gust/puff of wind; literary zephyr. **2** an air of defiance: **look**, appearance, impression, aspect, manner, tone, feel, atmosphere, mood.
•v. **1** express, voice, make public, articulate, give vent to, state, declare. **2** ventilate, freshen, refresh, cool.

> **WORD LINKS**
> relating to air: aerial

airless adj. **stuffy**, close, muggy, humid, stifling, suffocating, oppressive, unventilated.
– OPPOSITES airy.

airy adj. **spacious**, uncluttered, light, bright, well ventilated, fresh.
– OPPOSITES airless, stuffy.

aisle n. **passage**, passageway, lane, path, gangway, walkway.

akin adj. **similar**, related, close, near, comparable, equivalent, connected, alike, analogous.
– OPPOSITES unlike.

alarm n. **1** fear, anxiety, apprehension, distress, agitation, consternation, fright, panic, trepidation. **2** warning, danger signal, siren, bell, detector, sensor.
– OPPOSITES calmness, composure.

•v. **frighten**, scare, panic, unnerve, distress, agitate, upset, disconcert, shock, disturb; informal rattle, spook; Brit. informal put the wind up.

alcoholic adj. **intoxicating**, strong, hard, stiff, fermented, brewed, distilled.
•n. **drunkard**, dipsomaniac, drunk, heavy drinker, problem drinker, alcohol-abuser; informal lush, alky, dipso, soak, wino; Austral./NZ informal hophead.

alert adj. **1 vigilant**, watchful, attentive, observant, wide awake, on the lookout, on your guard/ toes; informal keeping your eyes open/peeled. **2 quick-witted**, sharp, bright, quick, perceptive, on your toes; informal on the ball, quick on the uptake, all there, with it.
– OPPOSITES inattentive.
•n. **1 vigilance**, watchfulness, attentiveness, alertness.
2 warning, notification, notice, siren, alarm, signal.
•v. **warn**, notify, inform, apprise, forewarn, put on your guard; informal tip off.

alien adj. **foreign**, unfamiliar, unknown, peculiar, exotic, strange.
– OPPOSITES native, familiar.
•n. **1 foreigner**, non-native, immigrant, émigré, stranger.
2 extraterrestrial, ET; informal little green man.

alienate v. **isolate**, distance, estrange, cut off, turn away, drive apart, set at variance/ odds, drive a wedge between.

alienation n. **isolation**, detachment, estrangement, distance, separation.

alight adj. **burning**, ablaze, on fire, in flames, blazing, lit.

align v. **1 line up**, range, rank, straighten, even up, arrange, co-ordinate. **2** he aligned himself with the workers: **ally**, affiliate, associate, side, join forces, team up, band together, throw in your lot.

alike adj. **similar**, (much) the same, analogous, corresponding, indistinguishable, identical, uniform, interchangeable; informal much of a muchness.
– OPPOSITES different.
•adv. great minds think alike: **similarly**, the same, correspondingly, analogously, identically.
– OPPOSITES differently.

alive adj. **1 active**, in existence, functioning, in operation, operative, on the map. **2 alert**, awake, aware, conscious, mindful, heedful, sensitive.
– OPPOSITES dead, unaware.

allay v. **reduce**, diminish, decrease, lessen, alleviate, assuage, ease, relieve, soothe, soften, calm.
– OPPOSITES increase, intensify.

allegation n. **claim**, assertion, charge, accusation, contention.

allege v. **claim**, assert, accuse, contend, state, declare, maintain.

alleged adj. **reported**, supposed, so-called, claimed,

a professed, purported, ostensible, unproven.
– OPPOSITES confirmed.

allegiance n. **loyalty**, faithfulness, fidelity, obedience, adherence, devotion; historical fealty.
– OPPOSITES disloyalty, treachery.

alleviate v. **ease**, relieve, take the edge off, deaden, dull, lessen, reduce, moderate, allay, assuage, soothe, help, soften.
– OPPOSITES aggravate.

alley n. **passage**, passageway, alleyway, backstreet, lane, path, pathway, walk.

alliance n. **association**, union, league, confederation, federation, syndicate, consortium, cartel, coalition, partnership, relationship, marriage, co-operation.

allied adj. **associated**, united, related, connected, interconnected, linked, cooperating, in league, affiliated, combined, coupled, married.
– OPPOSITES unrelated, independent.

allocate v. **allot**, assign, set aside, earmark, consign, distribute, apportion, share out, dole out, give out.

allocation n. **1 allotment**, assignment, distribution, sharing out, doling out, giving out. **2 allowance**, allotment, consignment, quota, share, ration; informal cut; Brit. informal whack.

allow v. **1 permit**, let, enable, authorize, give leave, license, entitle, consent to, assent to,

acquiesce in, agree to, approve; informal give the go-ahead to, give the thumbs up to, OK, give the green light to; formal accede to. **2 set aside**, allocate, allot, earmark, designate, reserve.
– OPPOSITES prevent, forbid.

allowance n. **1 allocation**, allotment, quota, share, ration, grant, limit. **2 payment**, contribution, grant, handout, subsidy, maintenance.

all right adj. **1 satisfactory**, acceptable, adequate, passable, reasonable; informal so-so, OK. **2 unhurt**, uninjured, unharmed, in one piece, safe (and sound), alive and well; informal OK. **3 permissible**, permitted, allowed, acceptable, legal, lawful, authorized, approved, in order; informal OK, legit, cool.
– OPPOSITES unsatisfactory.
•adv. **satisfactorily**, adequately, fairly well, passably, acceptably, reasonably, well, fine; informal OK.

allude v. **refer**, touch on, suggest, hint, imply, mention (in passing), intimate.

allusion n. **reference**, mention, suggestion, intimation, hint.

ally n. **associate**, colleague, friend, confederate, partner, supporter.
– OPPOSITES enemy, opponent.
•v. **unite**, combine, join (up), join forces, band together, team up, collaborate, side, align yourself.

almost adv. **nearly**, (just) about, practically, virtually, all but, as good as, close to, not quite;

informal **pretty nearly/much/well**; literary **well nigh, nigh on**.

alone adj. & adv. **by yourself**, on your own, unaccompanied, solo, single, isolated, solitary, lonely, deserted, abandoned, friendless; Brit. informal **on your tod**.
– OPPOSITES accompanied.

aloof adj. **distant**, detached, unfriendly, remote, unapproachable, reserved, unforthcoming, uncommunicative; informal **stand-offish**.
– OPPOSITES friendly.

also adv. **too**, as well, besides, in addition, additionally, furthermore, further, moreover, into the bargain, on top (of that), what's more, to boot.

alter v. **change**, make/become different, adjust, adapt, amend, modify, revise, rework, redo, transform; informal **tweak**.

alteration n. **change**, adjustment, adaptation, modification, amendment, transformation.

alternate v. **1 be interspersed**, follow one another, take turns, take it in turns, oscillate, seesaw. **2 rotate**, swap, exchange, interchange.
•adj. **every other**, every second, alternating.

alternative adj. **1 different**, other, second, substitute, replacement, standby, emergency, reserve, backup, auxiliary, fallback; N. Amer. **alternate**. **2 unorthodox**, unconventional, nonconformist, radical, revolutionary, avant-garde; informal **offbeat**, way-out.

•n. **(other) option**, (other) choice, substitute, replacement.

altogether adv. **1 completely**, totally, entirely, absolutely, wholly, fully, thoroughly, utterly, perfectly, one hundred per cent, in all respects. **2 in all**, all told, in total.

always adv. **1** *he's always late*: **every time**, all the time, without fail, consistently, invariably, regularly, habitually, unfailingly. **2** *she's always complaining*: **continually**, continuously, constantly, forever, all the time, day and night; informal **24-7**. **3** *the place will always be dear to me*: **forever**, for good, for evermore, for ever and ever, until the end of time, eternally.
– OPPOSITES never, seldom.

amalgamate v. **combine**, merge, unite, join, fuse, blend, meld, mix, incorporate.
– OPPOSITES separate.

amass v. **gather**, collect, assemble, accumulate, stockpile, hoard.

amateur n. **non-professional**, non-specialist, layman, layperson, dilettante, dabbler.
•adj. **non-professional**, unpaid, non-specialist, lay, unqualified, inexperienced.
– OPPOSITES professional, expert.

amateurish adj. **incompetent**, inept, inexpert, unprofessional, amateur, clumsy, crude, second-rate; Brit. informal **bodged**.

amaze v. **astonish**, astound, surprise, stun, stagger, nonplus,

a

shock, startle, stop someone in their tracks, leave open-mouthed, dumbfound; *informal* bowl over, flabbergast; *Brit. informal* knock for six; **(amazed)** thunderstruck, at a loss for words, speechless; *informal* gob-smacked.

amazement n. **astonishment**, surprise, shock, speechlessness, awe, wonder.

amazing adj. **astonishing**, astounding, surprising, stunning, staggering, breathtaking, awesome, awe-inspiring, sensational, remarkable, spectacular, stupendous, phenomenal, extraordinary, incredible, unbelievable; *informal* mind-blowing; *literary* wondrous.

ambassador n. **envoy**, emissary, representative, diplomat, minister, consul, attaché.

ambiguous adj. **vague**, unclear, ambivalent, double-edged, equivocal, inconclusive, enigmatic, cryptic.
– OPPOSITES clear.

ambition n. **1 drive**, determination, enterprise, initiative, eagerness, motivation, a sense of purpose; *informal* get-up-and-go. **2 aspiration**, desire, dream, intention, goal, aim, objective, plan.

ambitious adj. **1 aspiring**, determined, motivated, energetic, committed, purposeful, power-hungry; *informal* go-ahead, go-getting. **2 challenging**, exacting, demanding, formidable, difficult, hard, tough.

ambush v. **surprise**, waylay, trap, ensnare, attack, jump on, pounce on; *N. Amer.* bushwhack.

amend v. **revise**, alter, change, modify, adapt, adjust, edit, rewrite, redraft, rephrase, reword.

amends pl. n.
□ **make amends for** make up for, atone for, pay for, make good.
□ **make amends to** compensate, recompense, indemnify, make it up to.

amenity n. **facility**, service, resource, convenience, comfort.

amiable adj. **friendly**, affable, amicable, cordial, good-natured, nice, pleasant, agreeable, likeable, genial, good-humoured, companionable.
– OPPOSITES unfriendly, disagreeable.

amnesty n. **pardon**, reprieve, forgiveness, release, discharge; *informal* let-off.

amount n. **quantity**, number, total, aggregate, sum, quota, size, mass, weight, volume.
□ **amount to 1** add up to, come to, run to; *Brit.* tot up to. **2** constitute, comprise, be tantamount to.

ample adj. **1 enough**, sufficient, adequate, plenty of, more than enough, abundant, copious, profuse, lavish, liberal, generous; *informal* galore. **2 spacious**, full, capacious, roomy, voluminous, loose-fitting, baggy, sloppy.
– OPPOSITES insufficient.

amplify v. **1 make louder**, turn up, increase, raise. **2 expand**, enlarge on, elaborate on, develop, flesh out.

amuse v. **1 make someone laugh**, entertain, delight, divert, cheer (up), please, charm, tickle; Brit. informal crack up. **2 occupy**, engage, busy, absorb, engross, entertain.
– OPPOSITES bore.

amusement n. **1 mirth**, merriment, hilarity, glee, delight. **2 entertainment**, pleasure, leisure, relaxation, fun, enjoyment, interest. **3 activity**, entertainment, diversion, pastime, recreation, game, sport.

amusing adj. **funny**, comical, humorous, light-hearted, jocular, witty, droll, entertaining, diverting.

analogy n. **similarity**, parallel, correspondence, likeness, resemblance, correlation, relation, comparison.
– OPPOSITES dissimilarity.

analyse v. **examine**, inspect, survey, study, scrutinize, investigate, probe, explore, evaluate, break down.

analysis n. **examination**, inspection, study, scrutiny, breakdown, investigation, exploration, evaluation.

analytical, **analytic** adj. **systematic**, logical, scientific, methodical, precise, meticulous, rigorous, investigative, enquiring.

anarchy n. **lawlessness**, disorder, chaos, pandemonium, mayhem, riot, revolution.
– OPPOSITES order.

anatomy n. **structure**, make-up, composition, constitution, form, body, physique.

ancestor n. **forefather**, forebear, predecessor, antecedent, progenitor, parent, grandparent.
– OPPOSITES descendant.

ancestry n. **ancestors**, forebears, forefathers, progenitors, antecedents, family tree, lineage, genealogy, parentage, blood.

ancient adj. **1** *ancient civilizations*: **early**, prehistoric, primeval, primordial, primitive, bygone. **2** *an ancient custom*: **old**, ageold, venerable, time-worn, timehonoured, archaic, antique, obsolete. **3** *I feel ancient*: **antiquated**, antediluvian, geriatric; informal out of the ark; Brit. informal past its/your sell-by date, superannuated.
– OPPOSITES contemporary, recent.

anecdote n. **story**, tale, urban myth, narrative, reminiscence; informal yarn.

angelic adj. **innocent**, pure, virtuous, saintly, cherubic, adorable.

anger n. **annoyance**, vexation, temper, indignation, rage, fury, wrath, outrage; literary ire.
•v. **annoy**, irk, vex, enrage, incense, infuriate, rile, provoke, outrage.
– OPPOSITES pacify, placate.

a

angle n. **1 gradient**, slope, slant, inclination. **2 corner**, point, fork, nook, crook, edge. **3 perspective**, point of view, viewpoint, standpoint, position, aspect, slant, direction, approach, tack. •v. **tilt**, slant, twist, swivel, lean, tip, turn.

angry adj. **furious**, irate, vexed, wrathful, irked, enraged, incensed, seething, infuriated, in a temper, fuming, apoplectic, outraged, cross; informal (hopping) mad, up in arms, foaming at the mouth, steamed up, in a paddy; Brit. informal shirty; N. Amer. informal sore.
– OPPOSITES pleased.
□ **get angry** lose your temper, go berserk, flare up; informal hit the roof, go through the roof, go up the wall, see red, go off the deep end, fly off the handle, blow your top, blow a fuse/gasket, lose your rag, flip (your lid), have a fit, foam at the mouth, go ballistic; Brit. informal go spare, do your nut.

anguish n. **agony**, pain, torment, torture, suffering, distress, woe, misery, sorrow, heartache.
– OPPOSITES happiness.

animal n. **1 creature**, beast, (living) thing; (**animals**) wildlife, fauna. *The man was an animal:* **beast**, brute, monster, devil, fiend; informal swine, bastard, pig.

> WORD LINKS
> *relating to animals:* zoological;
> *study of animals:* zoology

animate v. **enliven**, energize, invigorate, liven up, inspire, fire, rouse, stir, galvanize, stimulate, excite, move, revitalize, revive, rejuvenate.
•adj. **living**, alive, live, breathing, sentient.
– OPPOSITES inanimate.

animated adj. **lively**, spirited, energetic, full of life, excited, enthusiastic, eager, alive, vigorous, vibrant, vivacious, exuberant, ebullient, bouncy, bubbly, perky; informal bright-eyed and bushy-tailed, full of beans, bright and breezy, chirpy, chipper.
– OPPOSITES lethargic, lifeless.

animosity n. **hostility**, antipathy, antagonism, rancour, enmity, resentment, hatred, loathing, ill feeling/will, dislike, bad blood, animus.
– OPPOSITES goodwill, friendship.

annihilate v. **destroy**, obliterate, eradicate, wipe out, wipe off the face of the earth; informal rub out, snuff out.
– OPPOSITES create.

announce v. **make public**, make known, report, declare, state, give out, publicize, broadcast, publish, advertise, circulate, proclaim, release, disclose, divulge.

announcement n. **1 statement**, declaration, proclamation, pronouncement, bulletin, communiqué; N. Amer. advisory. **2 declaration**, notification, reporting, publishing, broadcasting, disclosure.

annoy v. **irritate**, bother, vex, make cross, exasperate, irk, anger, antagonize, nettle, rankle with; Brit. rub up the wrong way; informal aggravate, peeve, miff, rile, needle, get (to), bug, hack off, wind up; Brit. informal nark, get on someone's wick; N. Amer. informal tee off, tick off.
- OPPOSITES please.

annoyance n. **irritation**, exasperation, vexation, indignation, anger, displeasure, chagrin.

annoyed adj. **irritated**, cross, angry, vexed, exasperated, irked, piqued, displeased, put out, disgruntled, nettled; informal aggravated, peeved, miffed, riled, hacked off, hot under the collar, narked, shirty; N. Amer. informal ticked off, sore.

annoying adj. **irritating**, infuriating, exasperating, maddening, trying, tiresome, troublesome, irksome, vexing, galling; informal aggravating.

annual adj. **yearly**, once-a-year, year-long, twelve-month.

annually adv. **yearly**, once a year, each year, per annum.

annul v. **declare invalid**, declare null and void, nullify, invalidate, void, repeal, revoke.

anomaly n. **oddity**, peculiarity, abnormality, irregularity, inconsistency, aberration, quirk.

anonymous adj. **unnamed**, nameless, unidentified, unknown, incognito, unsigned.

answer n. **1 reply**, response, rejoinder, reaction, retort,

riposte; informal comeback.
2 solution, remedy, way out, explanation.
- OPPOSITES question.
- v. **reply**, respond, rejoin, retort, riposte.
☐ **answer for** pay for, be punished for, suffer for, make amends for.

answerable adj. **accountable**, responsible, liable.

antagonistic adj. **hostile**, opposed, antipathetic, ill-disposed, resistant, in disagreement; informal anti.

antagonize v. **provoke**, intimidate, alienate, anger, annoy, irritate.
- OPPOSITES pacify.

anthem n. **hymn**, song, chorale, chant, psalm, canticle.

anthology n. **collection**, selection, compendium, compilation, miscellany, treasury.

anticipate v. **1 expect**, foresee, predict, be prepared for, bargain on, reckon on; N. Amer. informal figure on. **2 look forward to**, await, long for, can't wait for.

anticipation n. **expectation**, expectancy, prediction, hope, excitement, suspense.

anticlimax n. **let-down**, disappointment, comedown, non-event, disillusionment, bathos; Brit. damp squib; informal washout.

antics pl. n. **capers**, pranks, larks, high jinks, skylarking, horseplay, clowning; Brit. informal monkey tricks.

antidote n. remedy, cure, solution, countermeasure, corrective.

antipathy n. hostility, antagonism, animosity, aversion, animus, distaste, dislike, hatred, abhorrence, loathing.
– OPPOSITES affinity, liking.

antiquated adj. outdated, outmoded, outworn, behind the times, old, old-fashioned, anachronistic, antediluvian; informal out of the ark, superannuated, clunky.
– OPPOSITES modern.

antique n. collector's item, museum piece, period piece, antiquity.
• adj. antiquarian, old, collectable, vintage, classic.
– OPPOSITES modern.

antisocial adj. 1 antisocial behaviour: objectionable, offensive, unacceptable, disruptive, rowdy. 2 I'm feeling a bit antisocial: unsociable, unfriendly, uncommunicative, reclusive, misanthropic.
– OPPOSITES acceptable, sociable.

anxiety n. worry, concern, apprehension, unease, fear, disquiet, doubts, nervousness, nerves, tension, stress, angst; informal butterflies (in your stomach), the jitters, collywobbles.

anxious adj. 1 worried, concerned, apprehensive, fearful, uneasy, disturbed, fretful, agitated, nervous, on edge, worked up, jumpy, tense, distraught; informal uptight, with butterflies in your stomach, jittery, twitchy;

N. Amer. informal antsy. 2 she was anxious for news: eager, keen, itching, impatient, desperate.
– OPPOSITES unconcerned.

apart adv.
□ apart from except for, but for, aside from, with the exception of, excepting, excluding, bar, barring, besides, other than; informal outside of.

apartment n. 1 flat, suite, penthouse; Austral. home unit. 2 suite (of rooms), rooms, quarters, accommodation.

apathetic adj. uninterested, indifferent, unenthusiastic, unconcerned, unmoved, uninvolved, unemotional, lukewarm, half-hearted, unresponsive, lethargic; informal couldn't-care-less.
– OPPOSITES enthusiastic.

aperture n. opening, hole, gap, slit, slot, vent, crevice, chink, crack; technical orifice.

apologetic adj. sorry, regretful, contrite, remorseful, penitent, repentant.
– OPPOSITES unrepentant.

apologize v. say sorry, express regret, ask forgiveness, ask for pardon, eat humble pie.

apology n. regrets, expression of regret.
□ apology for travesty of, poor imitation of, poor substitute for, pale shadow of; informal excuse for.

appal v. horrify, shock, dismay, distress, outrage, scandalize, disgust, revolt, sicken, nauseate, offend, make someone's blood run cold.

appalling adj. **1** an appalling crime: **horrific**, shocking, horrible, terrible, awful, dreadful, ghastly, hideous, horrendous, frightful, atrocious, abominable, outrageous. **2** your schoolwork is appalling: **dreadful**, terrible, atrocious, deplorable, hopeless, lamentable; informal rotten, crummy, woeful, useless, lousy, abysmal, dire; Brit. informal chronic, shocking.

apparatus n. **equipment**, gear, tackle, mechanism, appliance, device, instrument, machine, tool.

apparent adj. **1** evident, plain, obvious, clear, manifest, visible, discernible, noticeable, perceptible, unmistakable, patent. **2** seeming, ostensible, outward, superficial.
– OPPOSITES unclear, real.

appeal v. **ask**, request, call, petition, plead, entreat, beg, implore, beseech.
□ **appeal to** attract, interest, fascinate, please, tempt, lure, draw; informal float someone's boat.
•n. **1** plea, request, petition, entreaty, cry, call, cri de coeur. **2** attraction, allure, charm, fascination, magnetism, pull.

appealing adj. **attractive**, engaging, alluring, enchanting, captivating, bewitching, fascinating, tempting, enticing, irresistible, charming; Brit. informal tasty.

appear v. **1** become visible, come into view, materialize, turn up, show up. **2** differences were beginning to appear: **be revealed**, emerge, surface, manifest itself, become apparent/evident, come to light, arrive, arise, crop up, show up. **3** they appeared completely devoted: **seem**, look, give the impression of being, come across as, strike someone as.
– OPPOSITES vanish.

appearance n. **1** her dishevelled appearance: **look**, air, aspect, looks, mien, expression, behaviour. **2** an appearance of respectability: **impression**, air, (outward) show, semblance, illusion, facade, front, pretence. **3** occurrence, manifestation, emergence, arrival, development, materialization.

appease v. **placate**, conciliate, pacify, mollify, reconcile, win over; informal sweeten.
– OPPOSITES provoke.

appendix n. **supplement**, addendum, postscript, codicil, coda, epilogue, afterword, tailpiece.

appetite n. **1** hunger, taste, palate, stomach. **2** my appetite for learning: **desire**, liking, hunger, thirst, longing, yearning, passion, enthusiasm, keenness, eagerness; informal yen.

appetizing adj. **mouthwatering**, inviting, tempting, tasty, delicious, flavoursome, toothsome, delectable; informal

a

a scrumptious, scrummy, yummy, moreish.

applaud v. **1** clap, give a standing ovation, put your hands together; *informal* give someone a big hand. **2** praise, congratulate, commend, salute, welcome, celebrate, approve of.
– OPPOSITES boo, criticize.

appliance n. device, machine, instrument, gadget, tool, contraption, apparatus, mechanism, contrivance, labour-saving device; *informal* gizmo.

applicable adj. relevant, appropriate, pertinent, apposite, material, fitting, suitable, apt.
– OPPOSITES inappropriate, irrelevant.

applicant n. candidate, interviewee, contender, entrant, claimant, petitioner, prospective student/employee, job-seeker.

application n. **1** request, appeal, petition, approach, claim, demand. **2** implementation, use, exercise, employment, execution, enactment. **3** hard work, diligence, industry, effort, commitment, dedication, devotion, perseverance, persistence, concentration.

apply v. **1** *300 people applied for the job:* put in, bid, try, audition, seek, solicit, claim, request, ask, petition. **2** *the Act did not apply to Scotland:* be relevant, pertain, appertain, relate, concern, affect, involve, cover, touch, deal with, have a bearing on. **3** implement, put into practice,

introduce. **4** put on, rub in/on, work in, spread, smear on, slap on. **5** exert, administer, use, exercise, employ, utilize, bring to bear.

▫ **apply yourself** work hard, exert yourself, make an effort, be industrious, show dedication, buckle down, persevere, persist, concentrate; *informal* put your back in it, knuckle down, get stuck in.

appoint v. nominate, name, designate, install, commission, engage, co-opt, select, choose, elect, vote in.

appointed adj. **1** scheduled, arranged, prearranged, specified, agreed, designated, set, allotted, fixed. **2** furnished, decorated, fitted out, supplied.

appointment n. **1** meeting, engagement, interview, consultation, rendezvous, date, assignation; *literary* tryst. **2** nomination, naming, designation, installation, commissioning, engagement, co-option, selection, election. **3** job, post, position, situation, place, office.

appraisal n. assessment, evaluation, estimation, judgement, summing-up, consideration.

appreciate v. **1** value, admire, respect, think highly of, think much of, be grateful for, be glad of. **2** recognize, realize, know, be aware of, be conscious of, be sensitive to, understand, sympathize with. **3** increase, gain, grow, rise, go up, soar.
– OPPOSITES disparage, depreciate.

appreciation n. **1 knowledge**, awareness, enjoyment, love, feeling, discrimination, sensitivity. **2 gratitude**, thanks, gratefulness. **3 acknowledgement**, recognition, realization, knowledge, awareness, consciousness, understanding. **4 review**, critique, criticism, analysis, assessment, evaluation, judgement; Brit. informal crit. **5 increase**, gain, growth, rise, inflation, escalation.
– OPPOSITES ingratitude, depreciation.

appreciative adj. **1** *we are appreciative of your support:* **grateful**, thankful, obliged, indebted. **2** *an appreciative audience:* **admiring**, enthusiastic, approving, complimentary.

apprehension n. **1 anxiety**, worry, unease, nervousness, nerves, misgivings, disquiet, concern, trepidation. **2 arrest**, capture, seizure, detention.
– OPPOSITES confidence.

apprehensive adj. **anxious**, worried, uneasy, nervous, concerned, fearful.
– OPPOSITES confident.

apprentice n. **trainee**, learner, probationer, novice, beginner, tyro, starter, pupil, student; informal rookie; N. Amer. informal tenderfoot, greenhorn.
– OPPOSITES veteran.

approach v. **1 move towards**, near, come near, close in on, close with, gain on. **2 speak to**, talk to, sound out, make a proposal to, proposition, appeal to.

3 tackle, address, manage, set about, go about, start work on.
– OPPOSITES leave.
•n. **1 method**, procedure, technique, modus operandi, style, way, strategy, tactic, system, means, line of action. **2 proposal**, submission, application, appeal, plea, request, overture, proposition. **3 advance**, arrival, appearance. **4 driveway**, drive, road, path, entry, way.

approachable adj. **1 friendly**, welcoming, pleasant, agreeable, affable, sympathetic, congenial. **2 accessible**, reachable, attainable; informal get-at-able.
– OPPOSITES aloof, inaccessible.

appropriate adj. **suitable**, proper, fitting, seemly, apt, right, convenient, opportune, relevant, apposite.
– OPPOSITES inappropriate.
•v. **seize**, commandeer, requisition, expropriate, usurp, take over, hijack, steal; informal swipe, nab; Brit. informal pinch, nick.

approval n. **1 acceptance**, agreement, consent, assent, permission, rubber stamp, sanction, blessing, endorsement, ratification, authorization; informal the go-ahead, the green light, the OK, the thumbs up. **2 favour**, liking, appreciation, admiration, regard, esteem, respect.
– OPPOSITES refusal, disapproval.

approve v. **agree to**, accept, consent to, assent to, give your blessing to, bless, ratify, sanction, endorse, authorize,

a validate, pass, rubber-stamp; informal give the go-ahead to, give the green light to, give the OK to, give the thumbs-up to.
– OPPOSITES refuse.
□ **approve of** agree with, hold with, endorse, support, be in favour of, favour, think well of, like, take kindly to, admire.

approximate adj. **estimated**, rough, imprecise, inexact, broad, loose; N. Amer. informal ballpark.
– OPPOSITES precise.
□ **approximate to** roughly equal, come near/close to, approach, border on, verge on, resemble, be similar to.

approximately adv. **roughly**, about, around, circa, round about, more or less, nearly, almost, approaching; Brit. getting on for; informal pushing; N. Amer. informal in the ballpark of.

apt adj. **1 suitable**, fitting, appropriate, relevant, apposite, felicitous; Brit. informal spot on. **2 inclined**, given, likely, liable, prone. **3 clever**, quick, bright, sharp, smart, able, gifted, talented.
– OPPOSITES inappropriate.

aptitude n. **talent**, gift, flair, bent, skill, knack, facility, ability, capability, potential, capacity, faculty.

arbitrary adj. **random**, unpredictable, capricious, subjective, whimsical, wanton, motiveless, irrational, groundless, unjustified.

arbitration n. **adjudication**, judgement, mediation, conciliation, intervention.

arbitrator n. **adjudicator**, arbiter, judge, referee, umpire, mediator, go-between.

arc n. **curve**, arch, bow, curl, crescent, semicircle, half-moon.

arch n. **archway**, vault, span.
▸v. **curve**, arc, bend, bow, crook, hunch.

architect n. **designer**, planner, originator, author, creator, founder, inventor.

architecture n. **building**, planning, design, construction.

archive n. **1** the family archives: **records**, papers, documents, files, annals, chronicles, history. **2** the National Sound Archive: **record office**, registry, repository, museum, library.
▸v. **file**, log, catalogue, document, record, register, store.

ardent adj. **passionate**, fervent, zealous, wholehearted, intense, fierce, enthusiastic, keen, eager, avid, committed, dedicated.
– OPPOSITES apathetic.

arduous adj. **tough**, difficult, hard, heavy, laborious, onerous, taxing, strenuous, backbreaking, demanding, challenging, punishing, gruelling; informal killing; Brit. informal knackering.
– OPPOSITES easy.

area n. **1 district**, zone, region, sector, quarter, locality, neighbourhood; informal neck of the woods; Brit. informal manor; N. Amer.

informal **turf. 2** *the dining area:* **space**, section, part, place, room. **3** *specific areas of knowledge:* **field**, sphere, realm, domain, sector, province, territory.

arena n. **1 stadium**, amphitheatre, ground, field, ring, rink, pitch, court; N. Amer. bowl, park. **2 scene**, sphere, realm, province, domain, forum, territory, world.

argue v. **1 claim**, maintain, insist, contend, assert, hold, reason, allege. **2 quarrel**, disagree, dispute, row, squabble, bicker, have words, cross swords, fight, wrangle.

argument n. **1 quarrel**, disagreement, difference of opinion, squabble, dispute, altercation, fight, wrangle; Brit. row; informal slanging match, tiff, set-to; Brit. informal barney. **2 reasoning**, justification, explanation, case, defence, vindication, evidence, reasons, grounds.

arid adj. **1 dry**, waterless, parched, scorched, desiccated, desert, barren, infertile.
– OPPOSITES wet, fertile.

arise v. **1** *many problems arose:* **come about**, happen, occur, come into being, emerge, crop up, come to light, become apparent, appear, turn up, surface, spring up. **2** *injuries arising from defective products:* **result**, stem, originate, proceed, follow, ensue, be caused by.

aristocrat n. **nobleman**, noblewoman, lord, lady, peer (of the realm), patrician; informal aristo; Brit. informal toff, nob.
– OPPOSITES commoner.

aristocratic adj. **noble**, titled, upper-class, blue-blooded, high-born, patrician; informal upper crust, top drawer; Brit. informal posh.
– OPPOSITES common.

arm v. **equip**, provide, supply, furnish, issue, fit out.

armaments pl. n. **arms**, weapons, weaponry, firearms, guns, ordnance, artillery, munitions, materiel.

armistice n. **truce**, ceasefire, peace, suspension of hostilities.

armoured adj. **armour-plated**, steel-plated, ironclad, bulletproof, bombproof, reinforced, toughened.

arms pl. n. **weapons**, weaponry, firearms, guns, ordnance, artillery, armaments, munitions.

army n. **1 armed force**, military force, land force(s), military, soldiery, infantry, militia, troops, soldiers. **2** *an army of tourists:* **crowd**, swarm, horde, mob, gang, throng, mass, flock, herd, pack.

> **WORD LINKS**
> relating to armies: military, martial

aroma n. **smell**, odour, fragrance, scent, perfume, bouquet, nose.

aromatic adj. **fragrant**, scented, perfumed, fragranced.

around prep. **1 surrounding**, enclosing, on all sides of.

a

2 approximately, about, round about, circa, roughly, more or less, nearly, almost, approaching; Brit. getting on for; N. Amer. informal in the ballpark of.

arouse v. **1 provoke**, trigger, stir up, engender, cause, whip up, rouse, inflame, agitate, incite, galvanize, electrify, stimulate, inspire, fire up. **2 wake (up)**, awaken, bring to/round, rouse.
– OPPOSITES allay.

arrange v. **1 set out**, (put in) order, lay out, align, position, present, display, exhibit, group, sort, organize, tidy. **2 organize**, fix (up), plan, schedule, contrive, determine, agree. **3** *he arranged the piece for a full orchestra*: **adapt**, set, score, orchestrate.

arrangement n. **1 positioning**, presentation, grouping, organization, alignment. **2 preparation**, plan, provision, planning. **3 agreement**, deal, understanding, bargain, settlement, pact. **4** *an arrangement of Beethoven's symphonies*: **adaptation**, orchestration, scoring, interpretation.

array n. **range**, collection, selection, assortment, variety, arrangement, line-up, display, exhibition.
•v. **arrange**, assemble, group, order, range, place, position, set out, lay out, spread out, display, exhibit.

arrest v. **1 detain**, apprehend, seize, capture, take into custody; informal pick up, pull in, collar; Brit. informal nick. **2 stop**,

halt, check, block, curb, prevent, obstruct, stem, slow, interrupt, delay.
– OPPOSITES release.
•n. **detention**, apprehension, seizure, capture.

arresting adj. **striking**, eye-catching, conspicuous, impressive, imposing, spectacular, dramatic, breathtaking, stunning, awe-inspiring.
– OPPOSITES inconspicuous.

arrival n. **1 coming**, appearance, entrance, entry, approach, advent.
– OPPOSITES departure.

arrive v. **come**, turn up, get here/there, make it, appear; informal show (up), roll in/up, blow in.
– OPPOSITES depart, leave.

arrogant adj. **haughty**, conceited, self-important, cocky, supercilious, condescending, full of yourself, overbearing, imperious, proud; informal high and mighty; too big for your boots.
– OPPOSITES modest.

art n. **1 fine art**, design, artwork, aesthetics. **2 skill**, craft, technique, knack, facility, aptitude, talent, flair, mastery, expertise.

article n. **1 object**, thing, item, piece, artefact, device, implement. **2 report**, account, story, essay, feature, item, piece (of writing), column. **3 clause**, section, paragraph, point, item.

articulate adj. **eloquent**, fluent, effective, persuasive, lucid, expressive, silver-tongued, clear, coherent.

– OPPOSITES unintelligible.

•v. **express**, voice, vocalize, put in words, communicate, state.

artificial adj. **1 synthetic**, fake, imitation, mock, ersatz, man-made, manufactured, plastic, simulated, faux; informal pretend. **2 insincere**, feigned, false, unnatural, contrived, put-on, forced, laboured, hollow; informal pretend, phoney.
– OPPOSITES natural, genuine.

artistic adj. **1 creative**, imaginative, inventive, sensitive, perceptive, discerning. **2 attractive**, aesthetic, beautiful, stylish, ornamental, decorative, graceful, subtle, expressive.

ascent n. **1** *the ascent of the Matterhorn:* **climbing**, scaling, conquest. **2** *the ascent grew steeper:* **slope**, incline, gradient, hill, climb.
– OPPOSITES descent, drop.

ascertain v. **find out**, discover, get to know, work out, make out, fathom (out), learn, deduce, divine, establish, determine; informal figure out.

ashamed adj. **1 sorry**, shamefaced, sheepish, guilty, contrite, remorseful, regretful, apologetic, mortified, red-faced, repentant, penitent, rueful, chagrined. **2 reluctant**, loath, unwilling, afraid, embarrassed.
– OPPOSITES proud.

ask v. **1 enquire**, want to know, question, interrogate, quiz. **2** *they'll ask a few questions:* **put (forward)**, pose, raise, submit.

3 request, demand, seek, solicit, apply, petition, call, appeal.
– OPPOSITES answer.

asleep adj. **sleeping**, napping, dozing, drowsing; informal snoozing, dead to the world; humorous in the land of Nod.
– OPPOSITES awake.

aspect n. **1 feature**, facet, side, characteristic, particular, detail. **2 point of view**, position, standpoint, viewpoint, perspective, angle, slant. **3** *his face had a sinister aspect:* **appearance**, look, air, mien, demeanour, expression.

aspiration n. **desire**, hope, dream, wish, longing, yearning, aim, ambition, expectation, goal, target.

aspire v.
□ **aspire to** desire, aim for, hope for, dream of, long for, yearn for, set your heart on, wish for, want, seek, set your sights on.

aspiring adj. **would-be**, hopeful, budding, potential, prospective; informal wannabe.

assassin n. **murderer**, killer, gunman, executioner; informal hit man.

assassinate v. **murder**, kill, eliminate, liquidate, execute; N. Amer. terminate; informal hit.

assault v. **attack**, hit, strike, beat up; informal lay into, rough up, do over.
•n. **1 violence**, battery; Brit. grievous bodily harm, GBH, actual bodily harm, ABH. **2 attack**,

a

strike, onslaught, offensive, charge, push, thrust, raid.

assemble v. **1 gather**, collect, get together, congregate, convene, meet, muster, rally, round up, marshal. **2 construct**, build, erect, set up, make, manufacture, fabricate, put together, connect.
– OPPOSITES disperse, dismantle.

assembly n. **1 gathering**, meeting, congregation, convention, council, rally, group, crowd; informal get-together. **2 construction**, manufacture, building, fabrication, erection.

assert v. **1 declare**, state, maintain, contend, argue, claim, insist. **2** *you should assert your rights:* **insist on**, stand up for, uphold, defend, press/push for.

assertion n. **declaration**, contention, statement, claim, opinion, protestation.

assertive adj. **confident**, self-confident, bold, decisive, forceful, insistent, emphatic, determined, strong-willed, commanding, pushy; informal feisty.
– OPPOSITES timid.

assess v. **evaluate**, judge, gauge, rate, estimate, appraise, weigh up, calculate, value, work out, determine; informal size up.

asset n. **1 benefit**, advantage, blessing, good/strong point, strength, forte, virtue, recommendation, attraction, resource. **2** *the seizure of all their assets:* **property**, resources, estate,

holdings, funds, valuables, possessions, effects, belongings.
– OPPOSITES liability.

assign v. **1 allocate**, give, set, charge with, entrust with. **2 appoint**, promote, delegate, nominate, commission, post, co-opt; Military detail. **3 earmark**, designate, set aside, reserve, appropriate, allot, allocate.

assignation n. **rendezvous**, date, appointment, meeting; literary tryst.

assignment n. **task**, job, duty, responsibility, mission, errand, undertaking, commission.

assist v. **1 help**, aid, lend a (helping) hand to, support, back (up), work with, cooperate with. **2** *the aim was to assist cashflow:* **facilitate**, aid, ease, promote, boost, speed, benefit, encourage, further.
– OPPOSITES hinder.

assistance n. **help**, aid, a (helping) hand, support, backing, reinforcement.
– OPPOSITES hindrance.

assistant n. **helper**, aide, deputy, second (in command), number two, right-hand man/woman, PA, auxiliary, attendant, henchman; informal sidekick, gofer; Brit. informal dogsbody, skivvy.

associate v. **1 link**, connect, relate, bracket, identify, equate. **2 mix**, keep company, mingle, socialize, go around, have dealings; informal hobnob, hang out/around/round.

– OPPOSITES avoid.

•n. **partner**, colleague, co-worker, workmate, collaborator, comrade, ally; informal crony.

associated adj. **related**, connected, linked, similar, corresponding, attendant, accompanying, incidental.
– OPPOSITES unrelated.

association n. **1 alliance**, consortium, coalition, union, league, guild, syndicate, federation, confederation, cartel, cooperative, partnership. **2 relationship**, relation, interrelation, connection, interconnection, interdependence, link, bond.

assorted adj. **various**, miscellaneous, mixed, varied, diverse, different, sundry.
– OPPOSITES uniform.

assortment n. **variety**, mixture, array, mix, miscellany, selection, medley, melange, ragbag, potpourri.

assume v. **1 presume**, suppose, take it (as given), take for granted, take as read, conclude, infer, think, fancy, imagine, surmise, believe, understand, gather, suspect; N. Amer. figure. **2 affect**, adopt, put on. **3 accept**, shoulder, bear, undertake, take on/up. **4 seize**, take (over), appropriate, wrest, usurp.

assumed adj. **false**, fictitious, fake, bogus, invented, made-up; informal pretend, phoney.
– OPPOSITES genuine.

assumption n. **supposition**, presumption, inference, conjecture, belief, surmise, hypothesis, theory, suspicion, guess.

assurance n. **1 promise**, word (of honour), pledge, vow, oath, undertaking, guarantee, commitment. **2 confidence**, self-confidence, self-assurance, self-possession, nerve, poise; informal cool. **3 insurance**, indemnity, protection, security, cover.

assure v. **1 reassure**, convince, satisfy, persuade. **2 promise**, guarantee, swear, confirm, certify, vow, give your word. **3 ensure**, secure, guarantee, seal, clinch; informal sew up.

assured adj. **1 confident**, self-confident, self-assured, self-possessed, poised, composed, imperturbable, unruffled; informal unflappable, together. **2 guaranteed**, certain, sure, secure, reliable, dependable; informal sure-fire.
– OPPOSITES nervous, uncertain.

astonish v. **amaze**, astound, stagger, startle, stun, surprise, confound, dumbfound, nonplus, take aback, leave open-mouthed; informal flabbergast, bowl over; Brit. informal knock for six.

astonishing adj. **amazing**, astounding, staggering, surprising, breathtaking, remarkable, extraordinary, incredible, unbelievable, phenomenal; informal mind-boggling.
– OPPOSITES unremarkable.

astound v. **amaze**, astonish, stagger, surprise, startle, stun, confound, dumbfound, take aback, leave open-mouthed; informal flabbergast, bowl over; Brit. informal knock for six.

astounding adj. **amazing**, astonishing, staggering, surprising, breathtaking, remarkable, extraordinary, incredible, unbelievable, phenomenal; informal mind-boggling.
– OPPOSITES unremarkable.

astute adj. **shrewd**, sharp, acute, quick, clever, intelligent, bright, smart, canny, perceptive, perspicacious; informal quick on the uptake.
– OPPOSITES stupid.

asylum n. **refuge**, sanctuary, shelter, protection, immunity, a safe haven.

athletic adj. **muscular**, fit, strapping, well built, strong, sturdy, powerful, brawny, burly.

atmosphere n. **1 air**, sky; literary the heavens, the ether. **2** a relaxed atmosphere: **ambience**, spirit, air, mood, feel, feeling, character, tone, aura, quality, environment, climate; informal vibe.

> WORD LINKS
> study of the atmosphere:
> meteorology

atrocious adj. **1 wicked**, cruel, brutal, barbaric, vicious, monstrous, vile, inhuman, fiendish. **2 appalling**, awful, dreadful, terrible, miserable; informal abysmal, dire, rotten, lousy; Brit. informal shocking.
– OPPOSITES admirable, superb.

atrocity n. **1** a number of atrocities: **outrage**, horror, violation, abuse, crime. **2** scenes of hardship and atrocity: **wickedness**, cruelty, brutality, barbarity, viciousness, savagery, inhumanity.

attach v. **1 fasten**, fix, affix, join, secure, stick, connect, tie, link, couple, pin, hitch. **2** they attach importance to research: **ascribe**, assign, attribute, accredit, impute. **3** the medical officer attached to HQ: **assign**, appoint, allocate, second.
– OPPOSITES detach.

attached adj.
□ **attached to** fond of, devoted to, keen on; informal mad about, crazy about.

attachment n. **1 bond**, closeness, devotion, loyalty, fondness for, love for, affection for, feeling for, sympathy for. **2 accessory**, fitting, extension, add-on.

attack v. **1 assault**, beat up, set upon, mug, charge, pounce on, raid, rush, storm; informal lay into, do over, work over, rough up; Brit. informal duff up. **2 criticize**, censure, condemn, denounce, revile, vilify, impugn, disparage; informal knock, slam, lay into; Brit. informal slate, slag off, rubbish.
– OPPOSITES defend, praise.
•n. **1 assault**, onslaught, offensive, strike, blitz, raid, incursion, sortie, foray, charge, invasion. **2 criticism**, censure,

condemnation, vilification, disparagement; Brit. informal slating. **3** fit, seizure, spasm, convulsion, paroxysm, bout, episode.
– OPPOSITES defence, praise.

attacker n. **assailant**, assaulter, mugger, aggressor, raider, invader.
– OPPOSITES victim.

attain v. achieve, accomplish, reach, obtain, gain, secure, get, win, earn, realize, fulfil; informal clinch, bag, wrap up.

attempt v. **try**, strive, aim, venture, endeavour, seek, have a go, bid.
• n. **try**, effort, endeavour, venture, bid, go; informal crack, shot, stab.

attend v. **1 be present at**, sit in on, take part in, appear at, turn up at, visit, go to; informal show up at. **2 pay attention**, listen, be attentive, concentrate.
□ **attend to 1** deal with, see to, look after, manage, organize, sort out, handle, take care of, tackle. **2** care for, look after, minister to, see to, tend, treat, help.

attendance n. **1 presence**, appearance, attention. **2 audience**, turnout, house, gate, crowd.
– OPPOSITES absence.

attendant n. **assistant**, aide, companion, escort, steward, equerry, servant, retainer, valet, maid.
• adj. **accompanying**, associated,

concomitant, related, connected, resulting, consequent.

attention n. **1 consideration**, contemplation, deliberation, thought, study, observation, mind, investigation, action. **2 awareness**, notice, scrutiny, eye, gaze. **3** medical attention: **care**, ministrations, treatment, therapy, relief, aid, assistance.

attentive adj. **1** an attentive pupil: **alert**, perceptive, observant, acute, aware, heedful, focused, studious, diligent, conscientious, earnest. **2** the most attentive of husbands: **considerate**, conscientious, thoughtful, kind, caring, solicitous, understanding, sympathetic.
– OPPOSITES inattentive.

attic n. **loft**, roof space, garret.

attitude n. **1 view**, viewpoint, outlook, perspective, stance, standpoint, position, frame of mind, approach, opinion. **2** an attitude of prayer: **posture**, position, pose, stance.

attract v. **1 appeal to**, fascinate, charm, captivate, interest, tempt, entice, lure, bewitch, beguile, seduce. **2 draw**, pull, magnetize.
– OPPOSITES repel.

attraction n. **1 appeal**, attractiveness, pull, desirability, fascination, allure, charisma, charm. **2** the town's main attractions: **entertainment**, activity, diversion, amenity, service. **3** magnetic attraction: **pull**, draw, force.
– OPPOSITES repulsion.

a **attractive** adj. **1** good-looking, beautiful, pretty, handsome, lovely, stunning, striking, desirable, gorgeous, prepossessing, fetching; Scottish & N. English bonny; informal drop-dead gorgeous, hunky; Brit. informal fit; N. Amer. informal cute; old use comely. **2** appealing, inviting, tempting, pleasing, interesting.
– OPPOSITES unattractive, ugly.

attribute v. ascribe, assign, accredit, credit, put down, chalk up, pin on.
• n. quality, characteristic, trait, feature, element, aspect, property, sign, hallmark, mark.

audible adj. perceptible, discernible, detectable, distinct, clear.
– OPPOSITES inaudible, faint.

audience n. **1** spectators, listeners, viewers, onlookers, crowd, throng, gallery, congregation, turnout. **2** meeting, interview, consultation, conference, hearing, reception.

augment v. increase, add to, supplement, enhance, build up, raise, boost, up, hike up, enlarge, swell, expand, extend.
– OPPOSITES decrease, reduce.

august adj. distinguished, respected, eminent, venerable, illustrious, prestigious, renowned, celebrated, honoured, acclaimed, esteemed.

aura n. atmosphere, ambience, air, quality, character, mood, feeling; informal vibe.

auspicious adj. favourable, promising, encouraging, fortunate, opportune, timely, advantageous, good.
– OPPOSITES inauspicious, unfavourable.

austere adj. **1** severe, stern, strict, harsh, dour, grim, cold, frosty, unfriendly. **2** spartan, frugal, ascetic, puritanical, abstemious, strict, simple, hard. **3** an austere building: plain, simple, basic, functional, unadorned, bleak, bare, clinical.
– OPPOSITES easy-going, ornate.

authentic adj. **1** genuine, real, bona fide, true, legitimate; informal pukka, kosher; Austral./NZ informal dinkum. **2** accurate, factual, true, truthful, reliable, trustworthy, honest, faithful.
– OPPOSITES fake, unreliable.

authenticate v. verify, validate, prove, substantiate, corroborate, confirm, support, back up.
– OPPOSITES disprove.

author n. **1** writer, novelist, poet, playwright, dramatist, columnist, reporter, wordsmith; informal scribe, scribbler. **2** creator, originator, founder, father, architect, designer, producer.

authoritarian adj. strict, autocratic, dictatorial, despotic, tyrannical, domineering, imperious, illiberal, undemocratic; informal bossy.
– OPPOSITES democratic, liberal.
• n. disciplinarian, autocrat, dictator, despot, tyrant.
– OPPOSITES democrat, liberal.

authoritative adj. **1** reliable, dependable, trustworthy, accurate, authentic, valid, definitive, classic. **2 commanding**, masterful, assertive, self-assured, self-confident.
– OPPOSITES unreliable.

authority n. **1** *a rebellion against those in authority*: **power**, command, control, charge, dominance, jurisdiction, rule; *informal* clout. **2** *the authority to arrest drug traffickers*: **right**, authorization, power, mandate, prerogative, licence. **3** *they need parliamentary authority*: **permission**, authorization, consent, sanction, assent, approval, clearance; *informal* the go-ahead. **4** (**the authorities**) **officials**, officialdom, government, administration, establishment, police; *informal* the powers that be. **5 expert**, specialist, professional, master, connoisseur, pundit, doyen(ne), guru.

authorize v. **1** *they authorized further action*: **permit**, sanction, allow, approve, consent to, assent to; *informal* give the go-ahead to, OK. **2** *the troops were authorized to fire*: **empower**, give authority, mandate, commission, entitle.
– OPPOSITES forbid.

authorized adj. **approved**, sanctioned, accredited, recognized, licensed, certified, official, legal, legitimate.
– OPPOSITES unauthorized, unofficial.

automatic adj. **1 mechanized**, powered, mechanical, automated, computerized, electronic, robotic. **2 instinctive**, involuntary, unconscious, reflex, knee-jerk, subconscious, spontaneous, impulsive, unthinking, mechanical; *informal* gut. **3 inevitable**, unavoidable, inescapable, certain.
– OPPOSITES manual, conscious, deliberate.

autonomous adj. **self-governing**, independent, sovereign, free.
– OPPOSITES dependent.

autonomy n. **self-government**, self-rule, home rule, self-determination, independence, sovereignty, freedom.
– OPPOSITES dependence.

auxiliary adj. **additional**, supplementary, extra, reserve, backup, emergency, fallback, second.

available adj. **obtainable**, accessible, to/at hand, to be had, on sale, untaken, unsold, free, vacant, unoccupied; *informal* up for grabs, on tap.

avalanche n. *an avalanche of enquiries*: **barrage**, flood, deluge, torrent, wave, onslaught.

avant-garde adj. **experimental**, modern, cutting-edge, progressive, unorthodox, unconventional; *informal* edgy, offbeat, way-out.
– OPPOSITES conservative, traditional.

a

avarice n. **greed**, acquisitiveness, covetousness, materialism.
– OPPOSITES generosity.

average n. **mean**, median,
mode, norm, standard, rule, par.
•adj. **1** *the average temperature:*
mean, median. **2** *a woman of
average height:* **normal**, standard, typical, ordinary, common,
regular.
– OPPOSITES abnormal, unusual.
□ **on average** normally,
usually, ordinarily, generally,
typically, for the most part, as a
rule, by and large, overall, on the
whole.

averse adj. **opposed**, hostile,
antagonistic, resistant, disinclined, reluctant, loath; informal
anti.
– OPPOSITES keen.

aversion n. **dislike**, hatred,
loathing, abhorrence, distaste,
antipathy, hostility, reluctance,
disinclination.
– OPPOSITES liking.

avert v. **1 turn aside**, turn away,
shift, redirect. **2 prevent**, avoid,
stave off, ward off, head off,
forestall.

avid adj. **keen**, eager, enthusiastic, ardent, passionate, zealous,
devoted.
– OPPOSITES apathetic.

avoid v. **1 keep away from**, steer
clear of, give a wide berth to.
2 evade, dodge, sidestep,
escape, run away from; informal
duck, wriggle out of, get out of.
3 *book early to avoid disappointment:* **prevent**, preclude, stave
off, forestall, head off, ward off.

4 *avoid alcohol:* **refrain from**,
abstain from, desist from, steer
clear of, eschew.
– OPPOSITES confront, face.

await v. **1 wait for**, expect, look
forward to, anticipate. **2 be in
store for**, lie ahead of, be waiting for, be round the corner.

awake v. **wake up**, wake,
awaken, waken, stir, come to,
come round, rouse, call.
•adj. **1 sleepless**, wide awake,
restless, insomniac. **2** *too few are
awake to the dangers:* **aware of**,
conscious of, mindful of, alert to.
– OPPOSITES asleep, oblivious.

awaken v. **1** see AWAKE.
2 arouse, kindle, bring out,
trigger, stir up, stimulate,
revive.

award v. **give**, grant, accord,
confer on, bestow on, present
to, decorate with.
•n. **1 prize**, trophy, medal, decoration, reward; informal gong.
2 grant, scholarship, endowment; Brit. bursary.

aware adj. **1** *she is aware of the
dangers:* **conscious of**, mindful
of, informed about, acquainted
with, familiar with, alive to, alert
to; informal wise to, in the know
about. **2** *environmentally aware:*
sensitive, enlightened, knowledgeable, (well) informed;
informal clued-up; Brit. informal
switched-on.
– OPPOSITES ignorant.

awareness n. **consciousness**,
recognition, realization, perception, understanding, grasp,

appreciation, knowledge, familiarity.

away adv. **elsewhere**, abroad, gone, off, out, absent, on holiday, on vacation.

awe n. **wonder**, wonderment, admiration, reverence, respect, fear, dread.

awesome adj. **breathtaking**, awe-inspiring, magnificent, amazing, stunning, staggering, imposing, formidable, intimidating; informal mind-boggling, mind-blowing, brilliant.
– OPPOSITES unimpressive.

awful adj. **1** the place smells awful: **disgusting**, terrible, dreadful, ghastly, horrible, vile, foul, revolting, repulsive, repugnant, sickening, nauseating; informal gross; Brit. informal beastly. **2** an awful book: **dreadful**, terrible, frightful, atrocious, lamentable; informal crummy, pathetic, rotten, woeful, lousy, appalling, abysmal, dismal, dire; Brit. informal rubbish. **3** I feel awful: **ill**, unwell, sick, nauseous, off colour, poorly; informal grotty, ropy; Austral./NZ informal crook.
– OPPOSITES delightful, excellent, well.

awfully adv. **1** (informal) an awfully nice man: **very**, extremely, really, immensely, exceedingly, thoroughly, dreadfully, terrifically, terribly, exceptionally, remarkably, extraordinarily; N. English right; informal seriously; Brit. informal jolly, dead, well; N. Amer. informal real, mighty;

informal, dated frightfully. **2** we played awfully: **terribly**, dreadfully, atrociously, appallingly; informal abysmally, diabolically.

awkward adj. **1 difficult**, tricky, cumbersome, unwieldy; Brit. informal fiddly. **2 unreasonable**, uncooperative, unhelpful, difficult, obstructive, contrary, perverse, obstinate, stubborn; Brit. informal bloody-minded, bolshie; N. Amer. informal balky. **3** an awkward time: **inconvenient**, inappropriate, inopportune, difficult. **4** he put her in an awkward position: **embarrassing**, uncomfortable, unenviable, delicate, tricky, problematic, troublesome, humiliating, compromising; informal sticky. **5** she felt awkward: **uncomfortable**, uneasy, tense, nervous, edgy, self-conscious, embarrassed. **6** his awkward movements: **clumsy**, ungainly, uncoordinated, graceless, inelegant, gauche, gawky, stiff, unskilful, inept, blundering; informal ham-fisted, cack-handed; Brit. informal all (fingers and) thumbs.
– OPPOSITES easy, amenable, convenient, graceful.

axe n. **hatchet**, chopper, cleaver; historical battleaxe.
•v. **1 cancel**, withdraw, drop, scrap, cut, discontinue, end; informal ditch, dump, pull the plug on. **2 dismiss**, make redundant, lay off, get rid of; informal sack, fire.

axle n. **shaft**, spindle, rod.

Bb

babble v. **prattle**, rattle on, gabble, chatter, jabber, twitter, burble, blather; informal yatter, blabber, jaw, gas, shoot your mouth off; Brit. informal witter, rabbit, chunter, natter, waffle.

baby n. **infant**, newborn, child; Scottish & N. English bairn; technical neonate; informal sprog, tot; literary babe.
- adj. **miniature**, mini, little, toy, pocket, midget, dwarf; Scottish wee; N. Amer. vest-pocket; informal teeny, teensy, tiddly, bite-sized; Brit. informal titchy.

babyish adj. **childish**, infantile, juvenile, puerile, immature.
- OPPOSITES mature.

back n. **1** spine, backbone, spinal column, vertebral column. **2** rear, end, rear end, tail end; Nautical stern. **3** reverse, other side, underside; informal flip side.
- OPPOSITES front.
- v. **1** sponsor, finance, fund, subsidize, underwrite; informal pick up the bill for. **2** support, endorse, sanction, approve of, give your blessing to, smile on, favour, advocate, promote, champion; informal throw your weight behind. **3** bet on, gamble on, stake money on. **4** reverse, draw back, step back, pull back, retreat, withdraw.
- OPPOSITES oppose, advance.
- adj. **1** rear, rearmost, hind, hindmost, posterior. **2** past, old, previous, earlier.
- OPPOSITES front, future.
- □ **back down** give in, concede defeat, surrender, yield, submit, climb down. **back out of** renege on, withdraw from, pull out of, fail to honour. **back up 1** substantiate, corroborate, confirm, support, bear out, endorse, lend weight to. **2** support, stand by, side with, take someone's part.

WORD LINKS

relating to the back: dorsal, lumbar;
lying on your back: supine

---

backbone n. **1** spine, spinal column, vertebral column, vertebrae. **2** mainstay, cornerstone, foundation. **3** strength of character, strength of will, firmness, resolution, resolve, grit, determination, fortitude, mettle, spirit.

backer n. **1** sponsor, investor, underwriter, financier, patron, benefactor; informal angel. **2** supporter, defender, advocate, promoter; N. Amer. booster.

backfire v. **rebound**, boomerang, come back, fail; informal blow up in someone's face.

background n. **1** backdrop, backcloth, surrounding(s), setting, scene, framework. **2** social

circumstances, family circumstances, environment, class, culture, tradition. **3 experience**, record, history, past, training, education.
– OPPOSITES foreground.

backing n. **1 support**, endorsement, approval, blessing, assistance, aid, help. **2 sponsorship**, finance, funding, subsidy, patronage.

backlash n. **adverse reaction**, counterblast, repercussion, comeback, retaliation, reprisal.

backup n. **help**, support, assistance, aid, reserve, reinforcements.
• adj. **reserve**, spare, substitute, replacement, standby, fallback, emergency.

backward adj. **1 rearward**, towards the rear, behind you, reverse. **2 retrograde**, regressive, for the worse, in the wrong direction, downhill, negative. **3 underdeveloped**, undeveloped, primitive. **4 hesitant**, reticent, reluctant, shy, diffident, timid, self-effacing, unassertive.
– OPPOSITES forward, advanced.

backwards adv. **towards the rear**, rearwards, behind you.
– OPPOSITES forwards.

bad adj. **1** *bad workmanship*: **unsatisfactory**, substandard, poor, inferior, second-rate, second-class, inadequate, deficient, imperfect, defective, faulty, shoddy, negligent, disgraceful, awful, terrible, appalling, dreadful, frightful,

atrocious, abysmal; informal crummy, rotten, pathetic, useless, woeful, lousy, diabolical; Brit. informal duff, rubbish. **2** *the alcohol had a bad effect*: **harmful**, damaging, detrimental, injurious, hurtful, destructive, deleterious, inimical. **3** *the bad guys*: **wicked**, evil, sinful, criminal, immoral, corrupt, villainous; informal crooked, bent. **4** *you bad girl!* **naughty**, badly behaved, disobedient, wayward, wilful, defiant, unruly, undisciplined. **5** *bad news*: **unpleasant**, disagreeable, unwelcome, unfavourable, unfortunate, grim, distressing, gloomy. **6** *a bad time to arrive*: **unfavourable**, inauspicious, unpropitious, inopportune, unfortunate, disadvantageous, inappropriate, unsuitable. **7** *a bad accident*: **serious**, severe, grave, critical, acute. **8** *the meat's bad*: **rotten**, off, decayed, putrid, rancid, curdled, sour, mouldy. **9** *a bad knee*: **injured**, wounded, diseased; informal gammy; Brit. informal knackered; Austral./NZ informal crook.
– OPPOSITES good, beneficial, virtuous, favourable.

badge n. **1 brooch**, pin, emblem, crest, insignia; N. Amer. button. **2** *a badge of success*: **sign**, symbol, indication, signal, mark, hallmark, trademark.

badger v. **pester**, harass, hound, harry, nag, bother, go on at; informal hassle, bug.

badly adv. **1 poorly**, unsatisfactorily, inadequately, incorrectly,

b

faultily, defectively, shoddily, amateurishly, carelessly, incompetently, inexpertly. **2 unfavourably**, ill, critically, disapprovingly. **3 naughtily**, disobediently, wilfully, mischievously. **4 cruelly**, wickedly, unkindly, harshly, shamefully, unfairly, unjustly, wrongly. **5 unfavourably**, unsuccessfully, adversely, unfortunately. **6 severely**, seriously, gravely, acutely, critically.
– OPPOSITES well.

bad-tempered adj. **irritable**, irascible, tetchy, testy, grumpy, grouchy, crotchety, in a (bad) mood, cantankerous, curmudgeonly, ill-tempered, ill-humoured, peevish, cross, fractious, petulant, pettish, crabby, quarrelsome, dyspeptic; informal snappish, on a short fuse; Brit. informal shirty, stroppy, ratty; N. Amer. informal cranky, ornery.
– OPPOSITES good-humoured, affable.

baffle v. **puzzle**, perplex, bewilder, mystify, confuse; informal flummox, stump, beat, fox.

bag n. **suitcase**, case, valise, holdall, grip, rucksack, haversack, satchel, handbag.
•v. **1 catch**, land, capture, trap, net, snare. **2 get**, secure, obtain, acquire, pick up, win, achieve; informal land, net.

baggage n. **luggage**, suitcases, cases, bags, belongings.

baggy adj. **loose**, roomy, generously cut, sloppy, voluminous, full.
– OPPOSITES tight.

bail n. **surety**, security, indemnity, bond, guarantee, pledge.
□ **bail out 1 eject**, parachute to safety. **2 rescue**, save, relieve, finance, help (out), aid.

bait n. **enticement**, lure, decoy, snare, trap, inducement, siren, carrot, attraction; informal come-on.
•v. **taunt**, tease, goad, pick on, torment, persecute, harass; informal needle; Brit. informal wind up.

balance n. **1 stability**, equilibrium, steadiness, footing. **2 fairness**, justice, impartiality, parity, equity, evenness, uniformity, comparability. **3 remainder**, outstanding amount, rest, residue, difference.
– OPPOSITES instability, bias.
•v. **1 steady**, stabilize, poise, level. **2 counterbalance**, balance out, offset, counteract, compensate for, make up for. **3 correspond**, agree, tally, match up, coincide. **4 weigh (up)**, compare, evaluate, consider, assess.

bald adj. **1 hairless**, smooth, shaven, depilated. **2 plain**, simple, direct, blunt, unadorned, unvarnished, unembellished, stark; informal upfront.
– OPPOSITES hairy.

ball n. **sphere**, globe, orb, globule, spheroid.

ballot n. **vote**, poll, election, referendum, show of hands, plebiscite.

ban v. **prohibit**, forbid, veto, proscribe, outlaw, make illegal,

bar, debar, prevent, exclude, banish.
– OPPOSITES permit, admit.
•n. **prohibition**, embargo, veto, boycott, bar, proscription, moratorium, injunction.

banal adj. **unoriginal**, unimaginative, uninspired, trite, hackneyed, clichéd, platitudinous, commonplace, stereotyped, overused, stale, boring, dull, obvious, predictable, tired, pedestrian; informal corny, old hat.
– OPPOSITES original.

band¹ n. **1 loop**, wristband, headband, ring, hoop, circlet, belt, sash, girdle, strap, strip, tape, circle. **2 stripe**, strip, line, belt, bar, streak, border, swathe.

band² n. **1 gang**, group, mob, pack, troop, troupe, company, set, party, crew, body, team; informal bunch. **2 pop group**, ensemble, group, orchestra; informal combo.

bandage n. **dressing**, covering, plaster, compress, gauze, lint.
•v. **bind**, dress, cover, strap (up).

bandit n. **robber**, thief, raider, mugger, pirate, outlaw, hijacker, looter, marauder, gangster; literary brigand; historical rustler, highwayman, footpad.

bang n. **1 crash**, crack, thud, thump, bump, boom, blast, clap, report, explosion. **2 blow**, bump, knock, hit, smack, crack, thump; informal bash, whack.
•v. **1 hit**, strike, beat, thump, hammer, knock, rap, pound, thud, punch, bump, smack, crack, slap, slam; informal bash,

whack, clobber, clout, wallop.
2 crash, boom, pound, explode, detonate, burst, blow up.

banish v. **1 exile**, expel, deport, eject, repatriate, transport, extradite, evict, throw out, exclude, shut out, ban. **2 dispel**, dismiss, disperse, scatter, dissipate, drive away, chase away, shut out.

bank¹ n. **1 edge**, shore, side, embankment, levee, margin, verge, brink. **2 slope**, rise, incline, gradient, ramp, mound, pile, heap, ridge, hillock, knoll, bar, shoal, mass, drift. **3 array**, row, line, tier, group, series.
•v. **1 pile up**, heap up, stack up, amass. **2 tilt**, lean, tip, slant, incline, angle, list, camber, pitch.

bank² n. **store**, reserve, stock, stockpile, supply, pool, fund, cache, hoard, deposit.
•v. **deposit**, pay in, save.

bankrupt adj. **insolvent**, ruined; Brit. in administration, in receivership; informal bust, broke, belly up, wiped out.
– OPPOSITES solvent.

banner n. **1 placard**, sign, poster, notice. **2 flag**, standard, ensign, colour(s), pennant, pennon, banderole.

banquet n. **feast**, dinner; informal spread, blowout; Brit. informal nosh-up, slap-up meal.

banter n. **repartee**, witty conversation, raillery, wordplay, cut and thrust, badinage, persiflage.
•v. **joke**, jest; informal josh, wisecrack.

b

b

baptize v. **1 christen. 2** *they were baptized into the church:* **admit**, initiate, enrol, recruit. **3 name**, call, dub.

bar n. **1 rod**, stick, pole, batten, shaft, rail, spar, strut, cross-piece, beam. **2 block**, slab, cake, tablet, wedge, ingot. **3 counter**, table, buffet. **4 inn**, tavern, hostelry; Brit. pub, public house; Brit. informal local, boozer. **5 obstacle**, impediment, hindrance, obstruction, block, hurdle, barrier.
– OPPOSITES aid.
•v. **1 bolt**, lock, fasten, secure, block, barricade, obstruct.
2 prohibit, debar, preclude, forbid, ban, exclude, obstruct, prevent, hinder, block, stop.

barbarian n. **savage**, heathen, brute, beast, philistine, boor, yahoo, oaf, lout, vandal; Brit. informal yob.

barbaric adj. **1 cruel**, brutal, barbarous, brutish, savage, vicious, wicked, ruthless, vile, inhuman. **2 uncultured**, uncivilized, barbarian, philistine, boorish, loutish; Brit. informal yobbish.
– OPPOSITES civilized.

bare adj. **1 naked**, unclothed, undressed, uncovered, stripped, with nothing on, nude; informal without a stitch on, in the altogether; Brit. informal starkers; Scottish informal in the scud; N. Amer. informal buck naked. **2 empty**, unfurnished, clear, undecorated, unadorned, bleak, austere. **3 basic**, essential, fundamental, plain, straightforward,

simple, unembellished, pure, stark, bald, cold, hard.
– OPPOSITES dressed.

barely adv. **hardly**, scarcely, only just, narrowly, by the skin of your teeth, by a hair's breadth; informal by a whisker; Brit. informal at a push.

bargain n. **1 agreement**, arrangement, understanding, deal, contract, pact. **2 good value**; informal good buy, cheap buy, snip, steal, giveaway.
•v. **haggle**, negotiate, discuss terms, deal, barter.
□ **bargain for/on** expect, anticipate, be prepared for, allow for, plan for, reckon with, envisage, foresee, predict, count on, reckon on; N. Amer. informal figure on. **into the bargain** in addition, as well, also, moreover, besides, on top, to boot, for good measure.

bark¹ v. **1 woof**, yap. **2 shout**, snap, bawl, yell, roar, bellow, thunder; informal holler.
– OPPOSITES whisper.

bark² n. **rind**, skin, peel, covering.

barracks pl. n. **garrison**, camp, encampment, depot, billet, quarters, fort, cantonment.

barrage n. **1 bombardment**, gunfire, shelling, salvo, volley, fusillade; historical broadside. **2 deluge**, stream, storm, torrent, onslaught, flood, spate, tide, avalanche, hail, blaze. **3 dam**, barrier, weir, dyke, embankment, wall.

b

barrel n. cask, keg, butt, vat, tun, drum, hogshead, firkin.

> **WORD LINKS**
> *person who makes barrels:*
> cooper

barren adj. **unproductive**, infertile, unfruitful, sterile, arid, desert, waste, lifeless, empty.
– OPPOSITES fertile.

barricade n. barrier, roadblock, blockade, obstacle, obstruction.
•v. **seal up**, close up, block off, shut off/up, defend, protect, fortify, occupy.

barrier n. **1 fence**, railing, barricade, hurdle, bar, blockade, roadblock. **2** *a barrier to international trade:* **obstacle**, obstruction, hurdle, stumbling block, bar, impediment, hindrance, curb.

barter v. **1 swap**, trade, exchange, sell. **2 haggle**, bargain, negotiate, deal.

base[1] n. **1 foundation**, bottom, foot, support, stand, pedestal, plinth, rest. **2 basis**, foundation, bedrock, starting point, source, origin, root(s), core, key component. **3 headquarters**, camp, site, station, settlement, post, centre.
– OPPOSITES top.
•v. **1 found**, build, construct, form, ground; (**be based on**) derive from, spring from, stem from, depend on. **2 locate**, situate, position, install, station, site.

base[2] adj. **sordid**, ignoble, low, mean, immoral, unscrupulous, unprincipled, dishonest, dishonourable, shameful, shabby, contemptible, despicable.
– OPPOSITES noble.

bashful adj. **shy**, reserved, diffident, inhibited, retiring, reticent, reluctant, shrinking, self-effacing, unassertive, timid, nervous, self-conscious.
– OPPOSITES bold, confident.

basic adj. **1 fundamental**, essential, vital, primary, principal, cardinal, elementary, intrinsic, central, pivotal, critical, key, focal. **2 plain**, simple, unsophisticated, straightforward, adequate, spartan, stark, severe, austere, limited, meagre, rudimentary, patchy, sketchy, minimal, crude, makeshift; informal bog-standard.
– OPPOSITES unimportant, luxurious.

basically adv. **fundamentally**, essentially, first and foremost, primarily, at heart, at bottom, intrinsically, inherently, principally, chiefly, above all, mostly, mainly, on the whole, by and large; informal at the end of the day.

basics pl. n. **fundamentals**, essentials, first principles, foundations, preliminaries, groundwork, essence, basis, core; informal nitty-gritty, brass tacks, nuts and bolts, ABC.

basin n. **bowl**, dish, pan, container, receptacle, vessel.

basis n. **1** *the basis of his method:* **foundation**, support, base, reasoning, rationale, defence,

b

reason, grounds, justification. **2** *the basis of discussion:* **starting point**, base, point of departure, beginning, premise, fundamental point/principle, cornerstone, core, heart. **3** *on a part-time basis:* **footing**, condition, status, position, arrangement.

bask v. **1** laze, lie, lounge, relax, sprawl, loll, luxuriate. **2** revel, wallow, delight, take pleasure, enjoy, relish, savour.

bass adj. low, deep, resonant, sonorous, rumbling, booming, resounding.
– OPPOSITES high.

batch n. group, quantity, lot, bunch, cluster, raft, set, collection, bundle, pack, consignment, shipment.

bathe v. **1** swim, take a dip. **2** clean, rinse, wet, soak, steep. **3** envelop, cover, flood, fill, wash, pervade, suffuse.

baton n. stick, rod, staff, wand, truncheon, club, mace.

batter v. beat up, hit repeatedly, pummel, pound, rain blows on, buffet, belabour, thrash; *informal* knock about/around, lay into, do over.

battle n. **1** *he was killed in the battle:* **fight**, engagement, armed conflict, clash, struggle, skirmish, fray, war, campaign, crusade, warfare, combat, action, hostilities; *informal* scrap, dogfight, shoot-out. **2** *a legal battle:* **conflict**, clash, struggle, disagreement, argument, dispute, tussle.
• v. fight, combat, contend with, resist, withstand, stand up to, confront, war, feud, struggle, strive, work.

battlefield n. battleground, field of battle, field of operations, combat zone, lines, front, theatre of war.

bawdy adj. ribald, indecent, risqué, racy, earthy, rude, suggestive, titillating, naughty, improper, indelicate, vulgar, crude, smutty; *informal* raunchy.

bawl v. **1** shout, yell, roar, bellow, screech, scream, shriek, bark, thunder; *informal* holler. **2** cry, sob, weep, wail, whine, howl; *Scottish informal* greet.
– OPPOSITES whisper.

bay[1] n. cove, inlet, gulf, sound, bight, basin, fjord.

bay[2] n. alcove, recess, niche, nook, opening, inglenook.

bazaar n. **1** market, marketplace, souk, mart. **2** fete, fair, fund-raiser; *Brit.* jumble sale, bring-and-buy sale, car boot sale; *N. Amer.* rummage sale, tag sale.

be v. **1** exist, live, be alive, breathe, be extant. **2** occur, happen, take place, come about, arise, fall; *literary* come to pass, befall, betide. **3** be situated, be located, be found, be present, be set, be positioned, be placed, be installed, sit, lie.

beach n. sands, seaside, seashore, coast; *literary* strand, littoral.
• v. land, ground, strand, run ashore.

beached adj. **stranded**, run aground, ashore, marooned, high and dry, stuck.
– OPPOSITES afloat.

beacon n. **signal**, light, fire, danger signal, bonfire, lighthouse.

bead n. **1 ball**, pellet, pill, globule, sphere, spheroid, orb, round; (**beads**) necklace, rosary, chaplet. **2** beads of sweat: **droplet**, drop, drip, blob, pearl, dot.

beaker n. **cup**, tumbler, glass, mug, drinking vessel.

beam n. **1 plank**, timber, joist, rafter, lintel, spar, girder, support. **2 ray**, shaft, stream, streak, pencil, flash, gleam, glint. **3 grin**, smile.
– OPPOSITES frown.
•v. **1 broadcast**, transmit, relay, disseminate, direct, send, aim. **2 shine**, radiate, glare, gleam. **3 grin**, smile.
– OPPOSITES frown.

bear[1] v. **1 carry**, bring, transport, move, convey, take, fetch; informal tote. **2 display**, be marked with, show, carry, exhibit. **3 withstand**, support, sustain, stand, take, carry, hold up, cope with, handle. **4 harbour**, foster, entertain, cherish, nurse. **5** I can't bear sport: **endure**, tolerate, put up with, stand, abide, countenance, stomach; informal hack, swallow; Brit. informal stick, wear; formal brook. **6 give birth to**, bring forth, deliver, have, produce, spawn. **7 produce**, yield, give, provide, supply.
□ **bear fruit** yield results, succeed, be effective, be profitable,

work; informal pay off, do the trick. **bear out** confirm, corroborate, substantiate, endorse, vindicate, give credence to, support, justify, prove. **bear up** remain cheerful, cope, manage, get by, muddle through. **bear with** be patient with, make allowances for, tolerate, put up with, endure.

bear[2] n.

WORD LINKS
relating to bears: ursine
---

bearable adj. **tolerable**, endurable, supportable, sustainable.

bearer n. **1 carrier**, porter. **2 bringer**, messenger, agent, conveyor, emissary.

bearing n. **1 posture**, stance, carriage, gait, demeanour, manner, mien, air, aspect, attitude, style; Brit. deportment. **2** this has no bearing on the matter: **relevance**, pertinence, connection, relation, relationship, import, significance, application. **3 direction**, orientation, course, trajectory, heading, tack, path. **4** I lost my bearings: **orientation**, sense of direction, whereabouts, location, position.
– OPPOSITES irrelevance.

beast n. **1 creature**, animal; N. Amer. informal critter. **2 monster**, brute, savage, barbarian, animal, swine, ogre, fiend, sadist, demon, devil.

beat v. **1 hit**, strike, batter, thump, bang, hammer, punch, knock, thrash, pound, pummel, slap, rain blows on, assault;

b

b

informal wallop, belt, bash, whack, clout, clobber. **2 throb**, pulse, pulsate, pump, palpitate, pound, thump, thud, hammer, drum. **3 flap**, flutter, thrash, wave, vibrate. **4 whisk**, mix, blend, whip. **5 defeat**, conquer, vanquish, trounce, rout, overpower, overcome; informal lick, thrash, whip. **6 exceed**, surpass, better, improve on, eclipse, transcend, top, trump, cap.
‣ n. **1 rhythm**, pulse, metre, time, measure, cadence, stress, accent. **2 pounding**, banging, thumping, thudding, hammering, crashing. **3 pulse**, pulsation, vibration, throb, palpitation, reverberation, pounding, thump, thud, hammering, drumming. **4 circuit**, round, route, path.
▫ **beat off** repel, fight off, fend off, stave off, repulse, drive away/back, push back. **beat up** assault, attack, mug; informal knock about/around, do over, work over, rough up; Brit. informal duff up.

beautiful adj. **attractive**, pretty, handsome, good-looking, fetching, lovely, charming, graceful, elegant, appealing, winsome, ravishing, gorgeous, stunning, glamorous; Scottish & N. English bonny; informal tasty, knockout, drop-dead gorgeous; Brit. informal smashing; N. Amer. informal cute, foxy; Austral./NZ informal beaut, spunky; old use comely.
– OPPOSITES ugly.

beautify v. **adorn**, embellish, enhance, decorate, ornament,

prettify, glamorize; informal do up, tart up.

beauty n. **1 attractiveness**, prettiness, good looks, loveliness, appeal, winsomeness, charm, grace, elegance, exquisiteness, glamour; literary pulchritude. **2 belle**, vision, goddess, picture, Venus; informal babe, looker, lovely, stunner, knockout, bombshell, bit of all right.
– OPPOSITES ugliness.

because conj. **since**, as, seeing that, in view of the fact that, in that.
▫ **because of** on account of, as a result of, as a consequence of, owing to, due to, thanks to, by virtue of; formal by reason of.

beckon v. **1 gesture**, signal, wave, gesticulate, motion. **2 entice**, invite, tempt, lure, charm, attract, draw, call.

become v. **1** she became rich: **grow**, get, turn, come to be, get to be. **2** he became a tyrant: **turn into**, change into, be transformed into, be converted into. **3** he became Foreign Secretary: **be appointed**, be assigned as, be nominated, be elected. **4 suit**, flatter, look good on, set off; informal do something to.
▫ **become of** happen to, be the fate of, be the lot of, overtake.

becoming adj. **flattering**, fetching, attractive, pretty, elegant, handsome, well chosen, stylish, fashionable, tasteful.

bed n. **1 couch**, berth, billet, cot; informal the sack. **2** a flower bed:

b

patch, plot, border, strip.
3 base, foundation, footing, support, basis.
•v. **embed**, set, fix, insert, inlay, implant, bury, plant.
□ **go to bed** retire; informal hit the sack, hit the hay, turn in.

bedraggled adj. **dishevelled**, disordered, untidy, unkempt, tousled; N. Amer. informal mussed.
– OPPOSITES neat.

before prep. **1 prior to**, previous to, earlier than, preparatory to, in advance of, ahead of, pre-.
2 in front of, in the presence of.
3 in preference to, rather than, sooner than.
– OPPOSITES after.
•adv. **previously**, before now/then, until now/then, up to now/then, earlier, formerly, hitherto, in the past.
– OPPOSITES afterwards, later.

beforehand adv. **in advance**, in readiness, ahead of time, betimes, before now/then, earlier (on), previously, already, sooner.
– OPPOSITES afterwards.

beg v. **1 ask for money**, seek charity; informal sponge, cadge, scrounge, bum. **2** we begged for mercy: **plead for**, request, ask for, appeal for, call for, sue for, solicit, seek. **3** he begged her not to go: **implore**, entreat, plead with, appeal to, pray to, call on, petition; literary beseech.

beggar n. **tramp**, vagrant, vagabond, mendicant; N. Amer. hobo; informal scrounger, sponger, cadger, freeloader; Brit. informal

dosser; N. Amer. informal bum; Austral./NZ informal bagman.

begin v. **1 start**, commence, set about, go about, embark on, launch into, get down to, take up, initiate, set in motion, get going, get off the ground, lead off, institute, inaugurate, open; informal get cracking on, kick off.
2 appear, arise, become apparent, spring up, crop up, turn up, come into existence, originate, start, commence, develop.
– OPPOSITES finish, end.

beginner n. **novice**, learner, starter, (raw) recruit, newcomer, tyro, fresher, probationer, apprentice, trainee; N. Amer. informal rookie, new kid (on the block), tenderfoot, greenhorn.
– OPPOSITES expert, veteran.

beginning n. **1 start**, commencement, creation, birth, inception, conception, origination, origin, genesis, germ, emergence, rise, dawn, launch, onset, outset, day one; informal kick-off. **2 opening**, start, commencement, first part, introduction, preamble.
– OPPOSITES end, conclusion.

begrudge v. **envy**, resent, grudge, be jealous of, be envious of, mind, object to.

behalf n.
□ **on behalf of 1** representing, as a representative of, as a spokesperson for, for, in the name of, in place of, on the authority of. **2** in the interests of, in support of, for, for the

benefit of, for the good of, for the sake of.

behave v. **1** *she behaved badly*: **act**, conduct yourself, acquit yourself. **2** *the children behaved themselves*: **act correctly**, be good, be well behaved, mind your manners; informal mind your Ps and Qs.
- OPPOSITES misbehave.

behaviour n. **conduct**, actions, manners, ways, deportment, bearing, etiquette.

behind prep. **1 at the back of**, at the rear of, beyond, on the far side of; N. Amer. in back of. **2 after**, following, at the back/rear of, hard on the heels of, in the wake of. **3 responsible for**, at the bottom of, the cause of, the perpetrator of, the organizer of, to blame for, guilty of. **4 supporting**, backing, for, on the side of, in agreement with; informal rooting for.

being n. **1 existence**, living, life, reality, lifeblood, vital force. **2 soul**, spirit, nature, essence, psyche, heart, bosom, breast. **3 creature**, life form, organism, living thing, individual, person, human.

belated adj. **late**, overdue, behindhand, delayed, tardy, unpunctual.
- OPPOSITES early.

beleaguered adj. **1 besieged**, blockaded, surrounded, encircled, hemmed in, under attack. **2 troubled**, harassed, hard-pressed, in difficulties,

under pressure, in a tight corner; informal up against it.

belief n. **1 opinion**, view, conviction, judgement, thinking, idea, theory, thought, feeling. **2 faith**, trust, reliance, confidence, credence. **3 ideology**, principle, ethic, tenet, doctrine, teaching, dogma, creed, credo.
- OPPOSITES disbelief, doubt.

believe v. **1** *I don't believe you*: **trust**, have confidence in, consider honest, consider truthful. **2** *do you believe that story?* **accept**, be convinced by, give credence to, credit, trust, put confidence in; informal swallow, buy, go for. **3 think**, be of the opinion that, have an idea that, imagine, assume, presume, take it, understand, gather; informal reckon, figure.
- OPPOSITES doubt.
□ **believe in** have faith in, trust in, have every confidence in, cling to, set (great) store by, value, be convinced by, be persuaded by; informal swear by, rate.

believer n. **disciple**, follower, supporter, adherent, devotee, upholder, worshipper.
- OPPOSITES infidel, sceptic.

belittle v. **disparage**, denigrate, run down, deprecate, play down, trivialize, minimize; informal do down, pooh-pooh.

belligerent adj. **1 hostile**, aggressive, threatening, antagonistic, pugnacious, bellicose, truculent, confrontational,

bellow → benefactor

contentious, militant, combative, argumentative; informal spoiling for a fight; Brit. informal stroppy, bolshie; N. Amer. informal scrappy. **2** *the belligerent states*: **warring**, combatant, fighting, battling.
– OPPOSITES peaceable.

bellow v. **roar**, shout, bawl, thunder, boom, bark, yell, shriek, howl, scream; informal holler.
– OPPOSITES whisper.

belly n. **stomach**, abdomen, paunch, middle, midriff, girth; informal tummy, gut, insides.

belong v. **1 be owned by**, be the property of, be held by, be in the hands of. **2 be a member of**, be in, be affiliated to, be allied to, be associated with. **3 be part of**, be attached to, go with. **4 fit in**, be suited to; informal go, click.

belongings pl. n. **possessions**, effects, worldly goods, chattels, property; informal gear, tackle, kit, things, stuff, bits and pieces; Brit. informal clobber.

beloved adj. **darling**, dear, precious, adored, cherished, treasured, prized, valued, idolized.
•n. **sweetheart**, love, darling, dearest, lover, girlfriend, boyfriend; informal steady, baby, angel, honey, pet.

below prep. **1 beneath**, under, underneath, lower than. **2 less than**, lower than, under, not as much as, smaller than. **3 inferior to**, subordinate to, under, beneath.
– OPPOSITES above, over.

belt n. **1 sash**, girdle, band, strap, cummerbund. **2 region**, strip, stretch, zone, area, district, sector, territory.

bemused adj. **bewildered**, confused, puzzled, perplexed, baffled, mystified, nonplussed, dumbfounded, at sea, at a loss; informal flummoxed, bamboozled, fazed.

bench n. **1 seat**, form, pew, stall, settle. **2 workbench**, worktop, counter.

benchmark n. **standard**, point of reference, guide, guideline, norm, touchstone, yardstick, barometer, model, gauge, criterion, specification.

bend v. **1 curve**, crook, flex, angle, hook, bow, arch, buckle, warp, contort, distort, deform, twist. **2 turn**, curve, incline, swing, veer, fork, change course, curl, loop. **3 stoop**, bow, crouch, hunch, lean down/over.
– OPPOSITES straighten.
•n. **curve**, turn, corner, kink, angle, arc, twist.

beneath prep. **1 under**, underneath, below, at the foot of, at the bottom of, lower than. **2 inferior to**, below, lower than, subordinate to. **3 unworthy of**, unbecoming to, degrading to.
– OPPOSITES above.
•adv. **underneath**, below, further down, lower down.
– OPPOSITES above.

benefactor n. **patron**, supporter, backer, sponsor, donor, contributor, subscriber; informal angel.

b

beneficial adj. **advantageous**, favourable, helpful, useful, of assistance, valuable, salutary, worthwhile, fruitful, productive, profitable, rewarding, gainful.
– OPPOSITES disadvantageous.

beneficiary n. **recipient**, payee, heir, heiress, inheritor.

benefit n. **1 good**, sake, welfare, well-being, advantage, comfort, ease, convenience, help, aid, assistance, service. **2 advantage**, profit, plus point, boon, blessing, reward; informal perk. **3 social security payment**, welfare, charity; informal the dole.
– OPPOSITES detriment, disadvantage.
▪ v. **1 help**, be advantageous to, be beneficial to, profit, do good to, be of service to, serve, be useful to, be helpful to, aid, assist. **2 profit**, gain, reap reward, make the most of, exploit, turn to your advantage, put to good use.
– OPPOSITES disadvantage, harm.

benevolent adj. **kind**, kindly, kind-hearted, good-natured, compassionate, caring, altruistic, humanitarian, philanthropic, beneficent, well meaning, benign.
– OPPOSITES unkind.

benign adj. **1 kindly**, kind, warm-hearted, good-natured, friendly, genial, tender-hearted, gentle, sympathetic, compassionate, caring, well disposed, benevolent. **2 mild**, temperate, gentle, balmy, soft, pleasant, favourable, healthy. **3** (Medicine) **harm-**less, non-malignant, non-cancerous.
– OPPOSITES unkind, malignant.

bent adj. **1 twisted**, crooked, warped, contorted, deformed, misshapen, out of shape, bowed, arched, curved, angled, hooked, kinked; N. Amer. informal pretzeled. **2 corrupt**, dishonest, fraudulent, criminal, untrustworthy.
– OPPOSITES straight.
▪ n. **inclination**, leaning, tendency, talent, gift, flair, aptitude, facility, skill.
□ **bent on** intent on, determined on, set on, insistent on, resolved on.

bequeath v. **leave**, will, hand down, pass on, entrust, make over, grant, transfer, give, bestow on, confer on.

bequest n. **legacy**, estate, inheritance, endowment, settlement.

bereavement n. **death in the family**, loss, passing (away), demise; formal decease.

berserk adj. **mad**, crazy, insane, out of your mind, hysterical, frenzied, crazed, demented, maniacal, manic, frantic, raving, wild, out of control, amok, on the rampage; informal off your head, off the deep end, ape, bananas, bonkers; Brit. informal spare; N. Amer. informal postal.

berth n. **1 bunk**, bed, cot, couch, hammock. **2 mooring**, dock, pier, jetty, quay.
▪ v. **dock**, moor, land, tie up, make fast.

b

beseech v. **implore**, beg, entreat, plead with, appeal to, call on, importune, pray to, ask, petition.

beside prep. **alongside**, by/at the side of, next to, parallel to, abreast of, adjacent to, next door to, neighbouring.
□ **beside yourself** distraught, overcome, out of your mind, frantic, desperate, distracted, at your wits' end, frenzied, hysterical.

besides prep. **in addition to**, as well as, over and above, on top of, apart from, other than, aside from, not counting, excluding, leaving aside; N. Amer. informal outside of.

besiege v. **1 lay siege to**, beleaguer, blockade. **2 surround**, mob, harass, pester, badger. **3 overwhelm**, bombard, inundate, deluge, flood, swamp, snow under.

best adj. **finest**, premier, greatest, top, foremost, leading, pre-eminent, supreme, superlative, unrivalled, second to none, without equal, unsurpassed, unparalleled, unbeatable, optimum, ultimate, incomparable, record-breaking; informal star, number-one, a cut above the rest, top-drawer.
•n. only the best will do: **finest**, choicest, top, cream, choice, prime, elite, crème de la crème, flower, jewel in the crown; informal tops, pick of the bunch.
– OPPOSITES worst.

bestow v. **confer on**, grant, accord, afford, endow with,
present, award, give, donate, entrust with, vouchsafe.

bet v. **1 wager**, gamble, stake, risk, venture, hazard, chance; Brit. informal punt, have a flutter. **2** (informal) **be certain**, be sure, be convinced, be confident, expect, predict, guess.
•n. **1 wager**, gamble, stake, ante; Brit. informal punt, flutter. **2** (informal) your best bet is to go early: **option**, choice, alternative, course of action, plan.

betray v. **1 be disloyal to**, be unfaithful to, break faith with, play someone false, inform on/against, give away, denounce, sell out, stab in the back; informal split on, rat on, stitch up, do the dirty on, sell down the river; Brit. informal grass on, shop, sneak on; N. Amer. informal rat out, drop a/the dime on, finger; Austral. /NZ informal dob in, point the bone at. **2 reveal**, disclose, divulge, tell, give away, leak, bring out into the open.

betrayal n. **disloyalty**, treachery, bad faith, breach of faith, breach of trust, faithlessness, duplicity, deception, double-dealing, stab in the back, double-cross, sell-out.
– OPPOSITES loyalty.

better adj. **1 superior**, finer, of higher quality, preferable; informal a cut above, streets ahead, head and shoulders above, ahead of the pack/field. **2 healthier**, fitter, stronger, well again, cured, healed, recovered,

recovering, on the road to recovery, on the mend.
– OPPOSITES worse, inferior.
•v. 1 **surpass**, improve on, beat, exceed, top, cap, trump, eclipse. 2 **improve**, ameliorate, raise, advance, further, lift, upgrade, enhance.
– OPPOSITES worsen.

between prep. 1 **in the middle of**, with one on either side, among; old use betwixt. 2 **connecting**, linking, joining, uniting, allying.

beware v. **watch out**, look out, mind out, be alert, be on your guard, keep your eyes open/peeled, keep an eye out, take care, be careful, be cautious, watch your step, guard against.

bewilder v. **baffle**, mystify, bemuse, perplex, puzzle, confuse; informal flummox, faze, stump, beat.

bewildered adj. **baffled**, mystified, bemused, perplexed, puzzled, confused, nonplussed, at sea, at a loss, disorientated; informal flummoxed, bamboozled; N. Amer. informal discombobulated.

bewitch v. **captivate**, enchant, entrance, enrapture, charm, beguile, delight, fascinate, enthral, cast a spell on.

beyond prep. 1 **on the far side of**, on the other side of, further away from, behind, past, after. 2 **later than**, past, after. 3 **greater than**, more than, exceeding, in excess of, above, upwards of.

bias n. **prejudice**, partiality, favouritism, partisanship, unfairness, one-sidedness, discrimination, leaning, tendency, inclination.
– OPPOSITES impartiality.
•v. **prejudice**, influence, colour, sway, predispose, distort, skew, slant.

biased adj. **prejudiced**, partial, partisan, one-sided, bigoted, discriminatory, distorted, warped, twisted, skewed.
– OPPOSITES impartial.

bid v. **offer**, put up, tender, proffer, propose.
•n. 1 **offer**, tender, proposal. 2 **attempt**, effort, endeavour, try; informal crack, go, shot, stab.

bidding n. **command**, order, direction, instruction, decree, injunction, demand, beck and call.

big adj. 1 **large**, sizeable, substantial, considerable, great, huge, immense, enormous, extensive, colossal, massive, mammoth, vast, gigantic, giant, spacious; informal jumbo, whopping, thumping, bumper, mega; Brit. informal whacking, ginormous; formal commodious. 2 **well built**, sturdy, brawny, burly, broad-shouldered, muscular, bulky, hulking, strapping, hefty, tall, huge, fat, stout; informal hunky, beefy. 3 **elder**, older, grown-up, adult, mature, grown. 4 **important**, significant, major, momentous, weighty, far-reaching, key, vital, crucial. 5 *that was big of you*: **generous**,

kind, kindly, caring, compassionate, loving.
- OPPOSITES small, minor.

bigoted adj. **prejudiced**, biased, partial, one-sided, sectarian, discriminatory, opinionated, dogmatic, intolerant, narrow-minded, blinkered, illiberal.
- OPPOSITES open-minded.

bill n. **1 invoice**, account, statement, list of charges; humorous the damage; N. Amer. check; informal tab. **2 draft law**, proposal, measure. **3 programme**, line-up; N. Amer. playbill.
4 (N. Amer.) **banknote**, note; US informal greenback. **5 poster**, advertisement, notice, announcement, flyer, leaflet, handbill; informal ad; Brit. informal advert.
•v. **1 invoice**, charge, debit.
2 advertise, announce, schedule, programme, timetable; N. Amer. slate. **3** *he was billed as the new Sean Connery*: **describe**, call, style, label, dub, promote, talk up; informal hype.

billow v. **1 puff out**, balloon (out), swell, fill (out). **2 swirl**, spiral, roll, undulate, eddy, pour, flow.

bind v. **1 tie up**, fasten together, secure, make fast, attach, rope, lash, tether. **2 bandage**, dress, cover, wrap, strap up, tape up. **3 trim**, hem, edge, border, fringe.
- OPPOSITES untie.

binding adj. **irrevocable**, unalterable, inescapable, unbreakable, contractual, compulsory, obligatory, mandatory, incumbent.

binge n. (informal) **bout**, spell, fling, spree, orgy, drinking bout; informal bender, session; Scottish informal skite; N. Amer. informal jag.

bird n. **fowl**, chick, fledgling, nestling.

> WORD LINKS
> *relating to birds:* avian;
> *study of birds:* ornithology

birth n. **1 childbirth**, delivery, nativity. **2 beginning(s)**, emergence, genesis, dawn, dawning, rise, start. **3 ancestry**, lineage, blood, descent, parentage, family, extraction, origin, stock.
- OPPOSITES death, end.
□ **give birth to** have, bear, produce, be delivered of, bring into the world; informal drop.

> WORD LINKS
> *before birth:* antenatal;
> *after birth:* post-natal;
> *branch of medicine concerned with birth:* obstetrics

bit n. **piece**, portion, section, part, chunk, lump, hunk, fragment, scrap, shred, crumb, grain, speck, spot, drop, pinch, dash, morsel, mouthful, bite, sample, iota, jot, whit, atom, particle, trace, touch, suggestion, hint, tinge; informal smidgen, tad.

bite v. **1 chew**, sink your teeth into, munch, crunch, champ. **2 grip**, hold, get a purchase. **3 take effect**, work, act, have results.
•n. **1 chew**, munch, nibble, gnaw, nip, snap. **2 mouthful**,

piece, bit, morsel, snack.
3 piquancy, pungency, spiciness, tang, zest; informal kick, punch, zing.

biting adj. **1 vicious**, harsh, cruel, savage, cutting, sharp, bitter, scathing, caustic, acerbic, acid, acrimonious, spiteful, venomous, vitriolic; informal bitchy, catty. **2 freezing**, icy, arctic, bitter, piercing, penetrating, raw.
– OPPOSITES mild.

bitter adj. **1 sharp**, acid, acrid, tart, sour, vinegary. **2 acrimonious**, hostile, angry, rancorous, spiteful, vicious, vitriolic, savage, ferocious, nasty. **3** *a bitter woman*: **resentful**, embittered, aggrieved, spiteful, jaundiced, sullen, sour. **4 freezing**, icy, arctic, biting, piercing, penetrating, raw.
– OPPOSITES sweet, mild.

bizarre adj. **strange**, peculiar, odd, funny, fantastic, extraordinary, curious, outlandish, eccentric, unconventional, unorthodox, weird, outré, surreal; informal wacky, oddball, way out, freaky; N. Amer. informal wacko.
– OPPOSITES normal.

black adj. **1 dark**, pitch-black, coal-black, jet-black, ebony, inky, sable. **2** *a black day*: **tragic**, dark, disastrous, calamitous, catastrophic, cataclysmic, fateful. **3** *a black mood*: **miserable**, unhappy, sad, wretched, heartbroken, grief-stricken, sorrowful, anguished, desolate, des-

pairing, disconsolate, downcast, dejected, gloomy; informal blue.
4 macabre, cynical, unhealthy, ghoulish, weird, morbid, gruesome; informal sick.
– OPPOSITES white, bright.
□ **black out** faint, lose consciousness, pass out, swoon.

blacklist v. **boycott**, ostracize, avoid, embargo, ignore, refuse to employ.

blackmail n. **extortion**, demanding money with menaces, threats, intimidation.
▸v. **1 extort money from**, threaten, hold to ransom, intimidate. **2 coerce**, pressure, force, dragoon; informal lean on, twist someone's arm.

blame v. **1 hold responsible**, hold accountable, condemn, accuse, find/consider guilty. **2** *they blame youth crime on unemployment*: **attribute to**, ascribe to, impute to, lay at the door of, put down to; informal pin.
– OPPOSITES absolve.
▸n. **responsibility**, guilt, accountability, liability, culpability, fault.

blameless adj. **innocent**, guiltless, above reproach, irreproachable, unimpeachable, in the clear, exemplary, impeccable, unblemished; informal squeaky clean.
– OPPOSITES guilty.

bland adj. **1 uninteresting**, dull, boring, tedious, monotonous, ordinary, run-of-the-mill, drab, dreary, unexciting, lacklustre,

flat, stale, trite. **2 tasteless**, flavourless, plain, insipid, weak, watery, thin, wishy-washy.
– OPPOSITES interesting, tangy.

blank adj. **1 empty**, unmarked, unused, clear, free, bare, clean, plain. **2 expressionless**, deadpan, wooden, stony, impassive, inscrutable, glazed, fixed, lifeless.
– OPPOSITES expressive.
• n. **space**, gap, void.

blanket n. *a blanket of cloud:* **covering**, layer, coating, carpet, cloak, mantle, veil, pall, shroud.
• v. **cover**, coat, carpet, cloak, shroud, swathe, envelop.

blasé adj. **indifferent**, unconcerned, casual, nonchalant, offhand, uninterested, unimpressed, unmoved, uncaring; *informal* laid-back.

blasphemous adj. **sacrilegious**, profane, irreligious, irreverent, impious, ungodly, godless.
– OPPOSITES reverent.

blasphemy n. **profanity**, sacrilege, irreligion, irreverence, taking the Lord's name in vain, impiety, desecration.
– OPPOSITES reverence.

blast n. **1 explosion**, detonation, discharge, burst. **2 gust**, rush, gale, squall, flurry. **3** *the shrill blast of the trumpets:* **blare**, wail, roar, screech, shriek, hoot, honk, beep.
• v. **1 blow up**, bomb, blow (to pieces), dynamite, explode, fire, shoot, blaze, let fly, discharge.

2 blare, boom, roar, thunder, bellow, shriek, screech.

blatant adj. **flagrant**, glaring, obvious, undisguised, open, overt, outright, naked, shameless, barefaced, unashamed, brazen.
– OPPOSITES discreet, inconspicuous.

blaze n. **1 fire**, flames, conflagration, inferno, holocaust. **2** *a blaze of light:* **glare**, flash, burst, flare, streak, radiance, brilliance, beam, glitter.
• v. **1 burn**, be alight, be on fire, be in flames. **2 shine**, flash, glare, gleam, glitter, glisten. **3 fire**, shoot, blast, let fly.

bleach v. **turn white**, whiten, turn pale, blanch, lighten, fade.
– OPPOSITES darken.

bleak adj. **1 bare**, exposed, desolate, stark, desert, lunar, open, empty, windswept. **2 unpromising**, unfavourable, dim, gloomy, black, grim, discouraging, disheartening, depressing, dismal.
– OPPOSITES lush, promising.

bleary adj. **blurry**, unfocused, fogged, clouded, misty, watery, rheumy.
– OPPOSITES clear.

blemish n. **imperfection**, flaw, defect, fault, discoloration, stain, scar, mark, spot.
• v. **mar**, spoil, impair, disfigure, deface, mark, stain, scar, blight, tarnish.
– OPPOSITES enhance.

blend v. **1 mix**, mingle, combine, merge, fuse, amalgamate, stir,

b

whisk, fold in. **2 harmonize**, go (well), fit (in), be in tune, be compatible, coordinate, match, complement, suit.
•n. **mixture**, mix, melange, combination, synthesis, compound, amalgam, fusion, alloy.

bless v. **1 consecrate**, sanctify, dedicate to God, make holy; formal hallow. **2 endow**, bestow, furnish, give, favour, confer on. **3 sanction**, consent to, endorse, agree to, approve, back, support; informal give the green light to, OK.
– OPPOSITES curse, oppose.

blessed adj. **holy**, sacred, hallowed, consecrated, sanctified, ordained, canonized, beatified.
– OPPOSITES cursed.

blessing n. **1 benediction**, dedication, consecration, grace, invocation, intercession. **2 sanction**, endorsement, approval, consent, assent, agreement, backing, support; informal the green light, OK. **3 advantage**, godsend, boon, benefit, help, bonus, plus, stroke of luck, windfall.
– OPPOSITES condemnation.

blight n. **1** *potato blight:* **disease**, canker, infestation, fungus, mildew, mould. **2** *the blight of aircraft noise:* **curse**, scourge, affliction, plague, menace, misfortune, bane, trouble, nuisance, pest.
•v. **ruin**, wreck, spoil, mar, frustrate, disrupt, undo, scotch, destroy, shatter, devastate, demolish; informal mess up, foul up,

put paid to, put the kibosh on, stymie; Brit. informal scupper.

blind adj. **1 sightless**, unsighted, visually impaired, unseeing. **2 uncritical**, unreasoned, unthinking, unquestioning, mindless, undiscerning, indiscriminate. **3** *blind to the realities of the situation:* **unaware of**, oblivious to, ignorant of, unmindful of, heedless of, insensible to, indifferent to.
•n. **screen**, shade, sunshade, curtain, awning, canopy, louvre, jalousie, shutter.

blindly adv. **1 impetuously**, impulsively, recklessly, heedlessly. **2 uncritically**, unquestioningly, unthinkingly, mindlessly, indiscriminately.

bliss n. **joy**, happiness, pleasure, delight, ecstasy, elation, rapture, euphoria, seventh heaven.
– OPPOSITES misery.

blitz n. **bombing**, air raid, air strike, bombardment, barrage, attack, assault.

bloated adj. **swollen**, distended, bulging, puffed out, inflated, dilated.

blob n. **drop**, droplet, globule, bead, bubble, spot, dab, blotch, blot, dot, smudge; informal splodge.

bloc n. **group**, alliance, coalition, federation, confederation, league, union, axis, association.

block n. **1 chunk**, hunk, lump, wedge, cube, brick, ingot, slab, piece. **2 building**, complex, structure, development.

b

3 obstacle, bar, barrier, impediment, hindrance, check, hurdle.
•v. **1 clog**, stop up, choke, plug, bung up, obstruct, gum up, dam up, congest, jam. **2 hinder**, hamper, obstruct, impede, inhibit, halt, stop, bar, check, prevent, fend off, hold off, repel.
– OPPOSITES clear, aid.
□ **block out** keep out, exclude, stop, conceal, blot out, blank out, obliterate.

blockage n. **obstruction**, stoppage, block, jam, congestion, bottleneck.

blonde, **blond** adj. **fair**, light, yellow, flaxen, golden.
– OPPOSITES dark.

blood n. **1 lifeblood**, gore, vital fluid. **2 ancestry**, lineage, descent, parentage, family, birth, extraction, origin, stock.

> **WORD LINKS**
> branch of medicine concerned with blood: haematology

bloodshed n. **slaughter**, massacre, killing, wounding, carnage, butchery, bloodletting, bloodbath.

bloodthirsty adj. **murderous**, homicidal, violent, vicious, barbarous, barbaric, savage, brutal, cut-throat.

bloody adj. **1 bloodstained**, blood-soaked, gory, bleeding. **2 vicious**, ferocious, savage, fierce, brutal, cruel, murderous, gory.

bloom v. **1 flower**, blossom, open, mature. **2 flourish**, thrive, prosper, progress, burgeon; informal be in the pink.
– OPPOSITES wither, decline.

blossom n. **flower**, bloom, bud.
•v. **1 bloom**, flower, open, mature. **2 develop**, grow, mature, progress, evolve, burgeon, flourish, thrive, prosper, bloom.
– OPPOSITES wither, decline.

blot n. **1 patch**, dab, smudge, blotch, mark, dot, spot; Brit. informal splodge. **2 blemish**, taint, stain, blight, flaw, fault. **3** a blot on the landscape: **eyesore**, monstrosity, carbuncle, mess; informal sight.
□ **blot out 1 conceal**, hide, obscure, exclude, obliterate, shadow, eclipse. **2 erase**, blank out, wipe out, eradicate.

blow¹ v. **1 gust**, puff, flurry, blast, roar, bluster, rush, storm. **2 sweep**, carry, toss, drive, push, force, drift, flutter, waft, float, glide, whirl. **3** he blew the trumpet: **sound**, blast, toot, play, pipe, trumpet.
□ **blow out extinguish**, put out, snuff, douse, quench, smother. **blow up 1 explode**, detonate, go off, ignite, erupt, bomb, blast, destroy. **2 inflate**, pump up, fill up, puff up, swell, expand, distend.

blow² n. **1 stroke**, knock, bang, hit, punch, thump, smack, crack, rap; informal whack, bash, clout, wallop. **2 upset**, disaster, setback, misfortune, disappointment, calamity, catastrophe, thunderbolt, bombshell, shock, surprise, jolt.

b

blue adj. azure, cobalt, sapphire, navy, indigo, sky-blue, ultramarine, aquamarine, turquoise, cyan.

blueprint n. **plan**, design, diagram, drawing, sketch, layout, model, template, pattern, example, guide, prototype, pilot.

bluff[1] n. **trick**, deception, fraud, ruse, pretence, sham, fake, hoax, charade; informal put-on.
•v. **pretend**, sham, fake, feign, lie, deceive, delude, mislead, trick, fool, hoodwink, dupe, hoax; informal con, kid, have on.

bluff[2] adj. **plain-spoken**, straightforward, blunt, direct, no-nonsense, frank, open, candid, forthright, unequivocal; informal upfront.
– OPPOSITES guarded.

blunder n. **mistake**, error, gaffe, slip, oversight, faux pas; informal slip-up, boo-boo; Brit. informal clanger, boob, howler; N. Amer. informal blooper.
•v. **1 make a mistake**, err, miscalculate, bungle, trip up; informal slip up, screw up, blow it, goof; Brit. informal boob. **2 stumble**, lurch, stagger, flounder, grope.

blunt adj. **1** *a blunt knife*: **dull**, worn. **2** *a broad leaf with a blunt tip*: **rounded**, flat, stubby. **3 straightforward**, frank, plain-spoken, candid, direct, bluff, forthright, unequivocal, brusque, abrupt, curt, bald, brutal, harsh, stark; informal upfront.
– OPPOSITES sharp, subtle.

v. **dull**, deaden, dampen, numb, take the edge off, weaken, allay, diminish, lessen.
– OPPOSITES intensify.

blur v. **cloud**, fog, obscure, dim, make hazy, make fuzzy, soften, dull, numb, deaden, mute.

blurred adj. **indistinct**, fuzzy, hazy, misty, foggy, clouded, cloudy, faint, unclear, vague, indefinite, unfocused.
– OPPOSITES sharp, clear.

blurt v.
☐ **blurt out** burst out with, exclaim, call out, divulge, disclose, reveal, betray, let slip, give away; informal blab, let on, spill the beans.

blush v. **redden**, go pink, go red, flush, colour, burn up.
•n. **flush**, rosiness, redness, pinkness, bloom, high colour, glow.

blustery adj. **stormy**, gusty, blowy, windy, squally, wild.
– OPPOSITES calm.

board n. **1 plank**, beam, panel, slat, batten, timber. **2 committee**, council, panel, directorate, commission.
•v. **1 get on**, go aboard, enter, mount, ascend, embark, catch. **2 lodge**, live, reside, stay, be housed; N. Amer. room; informal put up.

boast v. **1 brag**, crow, swagger, swank, show off, blow your own trumpet, sing your own praises; informal talk big, lay it on thick; Austral./NZ informal skite. **2** *the hotel boasts a fine restaurant:* **have**, possess, own, enjoy, pride yourself/itself on, offer.

•n. **1 brag**, exaggeration, overstatement; informal swank; Austral. /NZ informal skite. **2 pride**, joy, pride and joy, apple of someone's eye, wonder, delight.

boastful adj. **bragging**, swaggering, bumptious, swollen-headed, puffed up, full of yourself, cocky, conceited, arrogant; informal swanky, big-headed.
– OPPOSITES modest.

bob v. **move up and down**, bounce, toss, sway, wobble, jiggle, joggle, jolt, jerk.

bodily adj. **physical**, corporeal, corporal, mortal, material, tangible, concrete, real, actual, incarnate.
– OPPOSITES spiritual, mental.
•adv. **forcefully**, forcibly, violently, completely, entirely.

body n. **1 figure**, frame, form, physique, anatomy, skeleton. **2 torso**, trunk. **3 corpse**, carcass, skeleton, remains; informal stiff; Medicine cadaver. **4 main part**, core, heart, hub. **5 association**, organization, assembly, delegation, committee, executive, company, society, corporation, group.

> WORD LINKS
> *relating to the body:* corporal, corporeal

bog n. **marsh**, swamp, mire, quagmire, morass, slough, fen, wetland.
□ **bog down** mire, stick, entangle, ensnare, embroil,

hamper, hinder, impede, obstruct, swamp, overwhelm.

bogus adj. **fake**, spurious, false, fraudulent, sham, counterfeit, forged, feigned; informal phoney, pretend.
– OPPOSITES genuine.

boil¹ v. **simmer**, bubble, stew, seethe, froth, foam.

boil² n. **swelling**, spot, pimple, blister, gathering, pustule, carbuncle, abscess.

boisterous adj. **lively**, animated, exuberant, spirited, noisy, loud, rowdy, unruly, wild, uproarious, unrestrained, uninhibited, uncontrolled, rough, disorderly, riotous; informal rumbustious.
– OPPOSITES restrained.

bold adj. **1 daring**, intrepid, brave, courageous, valiant, valorous, fearless, dauntless, audacious, daredevil, adventurous, heroic, plucky; informal gutsy, spunky. **2 striking**, vivid, bright, strong, eye-catching, prominent, gaudy, lurid, garish.
– OPPOSITES timid, faint.

bolster v. **strengthen**, reinforce, boost, fortify, support, prop up, buoy up, shore up, buttress, maintain, help, augment, increase.

bolt n. **1** *the bolt on the door:* **bar**, lock, catch, latch, fastener. **2** *nuts and bolts:* **pin**, rivet, peg, screw.
•v. **1** *he bolted the door:* **lock**, bar, latch, fasten, secure. **2** *the lid was bolted down:* **pin**, rivet, screw, fasten, fix. **3 dash**, dart,

run, sprint, hurtle, rush, fly, shoot; informal tear, scoot, leg it. **4 gobble**, gulp, wolf, guzzle, devour; informal demolish, polish off, shovel down; N. Amer. informal scarf, snarf.

bomb n. **explosive**, incendiary (device), missile, projectile.
•v. **blow up**, blast, shell, blitz, strafe, pound, bombard, attack, assault, destroy, demolish.

bombard v. **1 shell**, pound, blitz, strafe, bomb, batter, blast, pelt. **2 swamp**, inundate, flood, deluge, snow under, overwhelm.

bombardment n. **assault**, attack, bombing, shelling, strafing, blitz, air raid, cannonade, fusillade, barrage, broadside.

bonanza n. **windfall**, godsend, blessing, bonus, stroke of luck; informal jackpot.

bond n. **1 friendship**, relationship, fellowship, partnership, association, affiliation, alliance, attachment, tie, connection, link. **2 promise**, pledge, vow, oath, word (of honour), guarantee, assurance, agreement, contract, pact, deal.
•v. **join**, fasten, fix, affix, attach, secure, bind, stick, fuse.

bonus n. **1 advantage**, plus, benefit, extra, boon, blessing, godsend, stroke of luck, attraction. **2 gratuity**, handout, gift, present, reward, prize, incentive; informal perk, sweetener.
– OPPOSITES disadvantage.

bony adj. **skinny**, thin, lean, gaunt, scrawny, spare, skin and bone, skeletal, emaciated, underweight.
– OPPOSITES plump.

book n. **1 volume**, tome, publication, title, novel, treatise, manual. **2 notepad**, notebook, pad, exercise book, logbook, ledger, journal, diary; Brit. jotter, pocketbook; N. Amer. scratch pad.
•v. **reserve**, prearrange, order; informal bag.
◻ **book in** register, check in, enrol.

> **WORD LINKS**
> list of books: bibliography

booklet n. **pamphlet**, brochure, leaflet, tract; N. Amer. folder, mailer.

boom n. **1 roar**, rumble, thunder, crashing, drumming, pounding, echoing, resonance, reverberation. **2 increase**, growth, advance, boost, escalation, improvement, upsurge, upturn.
– OPPOSITES slump.
•v. **1 roar**, rumble, thunder, crash, roll, clap, explode, bang, resound, blare, echo, resonate, reverberate. **2 shout**, yell, bellow, roar, thunder, bawl; informal holler. **3 flourish**, thrive, prosper, burgeon, progress, improve, pick up, expand.

boorish adj. **coarse**, uncouth, rude, vulgar, uncivilized, unrefined, oafish, ignorant, uncultured, philistine, rough, thuggish, loutish, Neanderthal; Brit. informal yobbish; Austral. informal ocker.
– OPPOSITES refined.

b

boost v. **increase**, raise, escalate, improve, strengthen, inflate, push up, promote, advance, foster, stimulate, encourage, facilitate, help, assist, aid; informal hike, bump up.
– OPPOSITES decrease.
• n. **1** *a boost to your morale:* **uplift**, lift, spur, encouragement, help, inspiration, stimulus, fillip; informal shot in the arm. **2** *a boost in sales:* **increase**, expansion, upturn, upsurge, rise, escalation, improvement, advance, growth, boom; informal hike.
– OPPOSITES decrease.

boot v. **kick**, punt, tap, propel, drive, knock.

booth n. **1 stall**, stand, kiosk. **2** *a phone booth:* **cubicle**, kiosk, box, compartment, enclosure, cabin.

booty n. **loot**, plunder, haul, spoils, ill-gotten gains, pickings; informal swag.

border n. **1 edge**, margin, perimeter, circumference, periphery, rim, fringe, verge, sides. **2 frontier**, boundary, borderline, perimeter.
• v. **1 surround**, enclose, encircle, edge, fringe, bound, flank. **2 edge**, fringe, hem, trim, pipe, finish. **3 adjoin**, abut, be next to, be adjacent to, touch.
□ **border on** verge on, approach, come close to, be comparable to, approximate to, be tantamount to.

bore¹ v. **drill**, pierce, perforate, puncture, punch, tunnel, burrow, mine, dig, gouge, sink.

bore² v. **weary**, pall on, tire, fatigue, send to sleep, leave cold; informal turn off.
– OPPOSITES interest.
• n. **tedious person/thing**, tiresome person/thing, bother, nuisance, pest, annoyance, trial, thorn in your flesh/side; informal drag, pain (in the neck), headache, hassle.

boredom n. **tedium**, ennui, apathy, weariness, dullness, monotony, repetitiveness, flatness, dreariness.
– OPPOSITES interest, excitement.

boring adj. **tedious**, dull, dreary, monotonous, repetitive, uneventful, unimaginative, characterless, featureless, colourless, lifeless, uninteresting, unexciting, lacklustre, humdrum, mind-numbing, soul-destroying, wearisome, tiresome; informal deadly; Brit. informal samey; N. Amer. informal dullsville.
– OPPOSITES interesting, exciting.

borrow v. **1 loan**, lease, hire; informal cadge, scrounge, bum, touch someone for; N. Amer. informal mooch; Austral./NZ informal bludge. **2 adopt**, take on, acquire, embrace, copy, imitate.
– OPPOSITES lend.

boss (informal) n. **head**, chief, principal, director, president, chief executive, chair, manager, supervisor, foreman, overseer, controller, employer, owner, proprietor; Brit. informal gaffer, governor; N. Amer. informal head honcho.
• v. **order around**, dictate to,

b

bully, push around/about, call the shots, lay down the law; informal bulldoze, walk all over, railroad.

bossy adj. (informal) **domineering**, pushy, overbearing, imperious, officious, high-handed, authoritarian, dictatorial, autocratic; informal high and mighty.
– OPPOSITES submissive.

bother v. **1** no one bothered her: **disturb**, trouble, inconvenience, pester, badger, harass, molest, plague; informal hassle, bug; N. English informal mither; N. Amer. informal ride. **2** don't bother about me: **mind**, care, worry, concern yourself, trouble yourself. **3** something was bothering him: **worry**, trouble, concern, perturb, disturb, disquiet; informal rattle.
▪ n. **1** trouble, effort, exertion, inconvenience, fuss, pains; informal hassle. **2** nuisance, pest, palaver, rigmarole, job, trial, bind, bore, drag, inconvenience, trouble; informal headache, pain (in the neck). **3** a spot of bother in the public bar: **disorder**, fighting, trouble, disturbance, commotion, uproar; informal hoo-ha, aggro, argy-bargy, kerfuffle.

bottle n. flask, carafe, decanter, pitcher, flagon, magnum, demijohn, phial.
□ **bottle up** suppress, repress, restrain, hold in, smother, contain, conceal, hide; informal keep a lid on.

bottom n. **1** foot, lowest part, base, foundation. **2** underside,

underneath, undersurface, underbelly. **3** floor, bed, depths. **4** farthest point, extremity, far end. **5** (Brit.) buttocks, rear (end), rump, seat, derrière; informal behind, backside; Brit. informal bum, jacksie; N. Amer. informal butt, fanny; humorous posterior.
– OPPOSITES top, surface.
▪ adj. lowest, last, bottommost.
– OPPOSITES top.

bounce v. **1** rebound, spring back, ricochet; N. Amer. carom. **2** bound, leap, jump, spring, bob, hop, skip, gambol, trip, prance.
▪ n. **1** springiness, resilience, elasticity, give. **2** vitality, vigour, energy, vivacity, liveliness, animation, sparkle, verve, spirit; informal get-up-and-go, pep, zing.

bound[1] adj. **1** tied, restrained, fixed, fastened, secured. **2** certain, sure, very likely, destined. **3** bound by the Official Secrets Act: **constrained**, obliged, compelled, required, obligated.
– OPPOSITES free.

bound[2] v. leap, jump, spring, vault, bounce, hop, skip, dance, prance, gambol, gallop.

bound[3] v. **1** limit, restrict, confine, circumscribe, demarcate, delimit. **2** enclose, surround, encircle, circle, border, close in/off, hem in.

boundary n. **1** border, frontier, borderline, partition, dividing line. **2** the boundary of his estate: **limits**, confines, bounds, margins, edges, fringes, border, periphery, perimeter.

boundless adj. limitless, untold, immeasurable, abundant, inexhaustible, endless, infinite, interminable, unfailing, ceaseless, everlasting.
– OPPOSITES limited.

bouquet n. 1 posy, nosegay, spray, corsage, buttonhole, garland, wreath, arrangement. 2 aroma, nose, smell, fragrance, perfume, scent, odour.

bourgeois adj. middle-class, conservative, conformist, conventional, propertied, provincial, suburban, small-town.
– OPPOSITES proletarian.

bout n. 1 spell, period, stretch, stint, session, burst, flurry, spurt. 2 attack, fit, spasm. 3 contest, fight, match, round, competition, meeting, encounter.

bow¹ v. 1 incline your head, bend, stoop, bob, curtsy, kneel, genuflect. 2 *the mast bowed in the wind*: **bend**, buckle, curve, flex. 3 *the government bowed to foreign pressure*: **give in**, submit, yield, surrender, succumb, capitulate.
•n. nod, bob, obeisance, curtsy, genuflection, salaam.

bow² n. prow, front, stem, nose, head.

bowels pl. n. 1 intestines, entrails, viscera, innards, digestive system; Medicine gut; informal guts, insides. 2 interior, inside, core, belly, depths, recesses; informal innards.

bowl¹ v. throw, pitch, hurl, toss, lob, fling, roll, launch, propel; informal chuck, sling, bung.

bowl² n. dish, basin, pot, crock, vessel, receptacle.

box¹ n. 1 carton, pack, packet, case, crate, chest, coffer, casket. 2 *a telephone box*: **booth**, kiosk, cubicle, compartment, cabin, hut.
•v. pack, package, parcel, encase, bundle, crate.

box² v. fight, spar, battle, brawl; informal scrap.

boxer n. fighter, pugilist, prize-fighter; informal bruiser, scrapper.

boy n. lad, youth, young man, stripling; Scottish & N. English laddie.

boycott v. shun, snub, spurn, avoid, ostracize, blacklist, blackball, reject, veto, send to Coventry.
•n. ban, veto, embargo, prohibition, moratorium, sanction, restriction, avoidance, rejection.

boyfriend n. lover, sweetheart, beloved, darling, partner; informal fella, fancy man; N. Amer. informal squeeze; dated beau; literary swain.

brace n. prop, strut, stay, support, bracket.
•v. 1 support, shore up, prop up, hold up, buttress, reinforce. 2 steady, secure, stabilize, poise, fix. 3 *brace yourself for disappointment*: **prepare**, get ready, gear up, nerve, steel, fortify; informal psych yourself up.

bracing adj. invigorating, refreshing, stimulating, energizing, exhilarating, restorative, rejuvenating.

bracket n. **1 support**, prop, stay, batten, rest, mounting, rack, frame. **2 group**, category, grade, classification, division.

brag v. **boast**, crow, swagger, swank, show off, blow your own trumpet, sing your own praises; informal talk big.

brain n. **intelligence**, intellect, brainpower, cleverness, wit(s), reasoning, wisdom, judgement, understanding, sense; informal nous, grey matter; N. Amer. informal smarts.

> WORD LINKS
> relating to the brain: cerebral

brake n. **curb**, check, restraint, constraint, control, limit.
• v. **slow (down)**, decelerate, reduce speed.
– OPPOSITES accelerate.

branch n. **1 bough**, limb, arm, offshoot, twig. **2 division**, subdivision, section, subsection, department, unit, sector, wing, office, bureau, agency, subsidiary.
• v. **1 fork**, divide, split, bifurcate. **2** narrow paths branched off the road: **diverge**, split off, fan out, radiate.

brand n. **1 make**, line, label, marque, trade name, trademark, proprietary name. **2 type**, kind, sort, variety, class, category, genre, style, ilk; N. Amer. stripe.
• v. **1 mark**, stamp, burn, sear. **2 stigmatize**, characterize, label, mark out, denounce, discredit, vilify.

brandish v. **flourish**, wave, shake, wield, swing, swish.

brash adj. **1 self-assertive**, pushy, cocky, self-confident, arrogant, bold, audacious, brazen. **2 garish**, gaudy, loud, flamboyant, showy, tasteless; informal flashy, tacky.
– OPPOSITES meek.

brave adj. **courageous**, intrepid, bold, plucky, heroic, fearless, daring, audacious, dauntless, valiant, valorous, doughty, indomitable, stout-hearted; informal game, gutsy.
– OPPOSITES cowardly.
• v. **endure**, put up with, bear, withstand, weather, suffer, face, confront, defy.

bravery n. **courage**, boldness, heroism, intrepidity, nerve, daring, fearlessness, audacity, pluck, valour; informal guts; Brit. informal bottle.

brawl n. **fight**, skirmish, scuffle, tussle, fray, melee, fracas, fisticuffs; informal scrap, set-to; Brit. informal punch-up.

brawny adj. **strong**, muscular, muscly, well built, powerful, strapping, burly, sturdy; informal beefy, hulking.
– OPPOSITES puny, weak.

brazen adj. **bold**, shameless, unashamed, unrepentant, unabashed, defiant, impudent, impertinent, cheeky, barefaced, blatant, flagrant.

breach n. **1 contravention**, violation, infringement, infraction, transgression. **2 break**, rupture,

split, crack, fracture, opening, gap, hole, fissure. **3 rift**, severance, estrangement, parting, parting of the ways, split, falling-out, schism.
•v. **1 break (through)**, burst, rupture. **2 contravene**, break, violate, infringe, defy, disobey, flout.

breadth n. **1 width**, broadness, thickness, span, diameter. **2 range**, extent, scope, depth, reach, compass, scale.

break v. **1 shatter**, smash, crack, snap, fracture, fragment, splinter, split, burst; informal bust. **2 stop working**, break down, give out, go wrong, malfunction, crash; informal go kaput, conk out; Brit. informal pack up. **3 violate**, contravene, infringe, breach, defy, flout, disobey. **4** the film broke box-office records: **beat**, surpass, exceed, better, cap, top, outdo, eclipse. **5** he tried to break the news gently: **reveal**, disclose, divulge, impart, tell, announce, release.
– OPPOSITES repair, obey.
•n. **1 interval**, interruption, gap, disruption, stoppage, cessation, halt, stop. **2 rest**, respite, recess, pause, intermission; informal breather, time out. **3 gap**, opening, space, hole, breach, chink, crack, fracture, fissure, tear, split.
☐ **break down 1 stop working**, give out, go wrong, malfunction, crash; informal go kaput, conk out; Brit. informal pack up. **2 fail**, collapse, founder, fall through.

3 burst into tears, lose control, be overcome, go to pieces; informal crack up, lose it. **4 analyse**, categorize, classify, sort, itemize, organize, divide, separate, split. **break off 1 snap off**, pull off, sever, detach. **2 end**, terminate, stop, cease, call a halt to, suspend, discontinue; informal pull the plug on. **break out 1 escape**, abscond, flee, get free. **2 flare up**, start suddenly, erupt, burst out. **break up 1 end**, finish, stop, terminate, adjourn; N. Amer. recess. **2 disperse**, scatter, disband, part company. **3 split up**, separate, part (company), divorce.

breakdown n. **1 failure**, collapse, disintegration, foundering. **2 nervous breakdown**, collapse. **3 malfunction**, failure, crash. **4 analysis**, itemization, classification, examination, investigation, explanation.

break-in n. **burglary**, robbery, theft, raid, breaking and entering; informal smash-and-grab.

breakthrough n. **advance**, development, step forward, success, improvement, discovery, innovation, revolution, quantum leap.
– OPPOSITES setback.

breast n. **chest**, bosom, bust; informal boobs, knockers.

breath n. **inhalation**, exhalation, gulp of air, puff, gasp; Medicine respiration.

breathe v. **1 inhale**, exhale, respire, draw breath, puff, pant, blow, gasp, wheeze; Medicine

b

inspire, expire. **2** whisper, murmur, purr, sigh.

WORD LINKS
relating to breathing:
respiratory

breathless adj. **1** out of breath, panting, puffing, gasping, wheezing, winded; informal out of puff. **2** eager, agog, openmouthed, excited, on the edge of your seat, on tenterhooks.

breathtaking adj. spectacular, magnificent, awe-inspiring, awesome, astonishing, amazing, stunning, thrilling; informal sensational, out of this world.

breed v. **1** reproduce, produce offspring, procreate, multiply, mate. **2** bring up, rear, raise, nurture. **3** cause, produce, bring about, give rise to, occasion, arouse, stir up, generate, foster.
•n. **1** *a breed of cow:* variety, stock, strain, race, species. **2** *a new breed of journalist:* type, kind, sort, variety, class, genre, generation.

breeding n. **(good) manners**, gentility, refinement, cultivation, polish, urbanity; informal class.

breeze n. gentle wind, puff of air, gust, draught; literary zephyr.

breezy adj. **1** windy, fresh, brisk, blowy, blustery, gusty. **2** jaunty, cheerful, cheery, brisk, carefree, easy, casual, relaxed, informal, light-hearted, upbeat.

brevity n. **conciseness**, concision, succinctness, pithiness, incisiveness, shortness, compactness.

brew v. **1** ferment, make, prepare, infuse; Brit. informal mash. **2** develop, loom, be imminent, be on the horizon, be in the offing, be just around the corner.
•n. **1** *home brew:* beer, ale. **2** *a hot reviving brew:* drink, beverage, infusion. **3** mixture, mix, blend, combination, amalgam, cocktail.

bribe v. buy off, pay off, suborn; informal grease someone's palm, keep someone sweet, square; Brit. informal nobble.
•n. **inducement**; informal bung, backhander, pay-off, kickback, sweetener.

bribery n. corruption; N. Amer. payola; informal palm-greasing, graft, hush money.

WORD LINKS
susceptible to bribery: venal

bridge n. **1** viaduct, flyover, overpass, aqueduct. **2** link, connection, bond, tie.
•v. span, cross (over), extend across, traverse, arch over, straddle.

WORD LINKS
relating to bridges: pontine

brief adj. **1** concise, succinct, short, pithy, compact, thumbnail, potted, condensed, to the point, terse, summary. **2** short, flying, fleeting, hasty, hurried, quick, cursory, perfunctory, temporary, short-lived, ephemeral, transient, transitory.
– OPPOSITES long.
•n. **1** *my brief is to reorganize the project:* instructions, directions,

directive, remit, mandate. **2** *a barrister's brief:* **case**, summary, argument, contention, dossier.
•v. **inform**, tell, update, notify, advise, prepare, prime, instruct; informal fill in, put in the picture.

briefly adv. **1 concisely**, succinctly, tersely. **2 momentarily**, temporarily, fleetingly. **3** *briefly, the plot is as follows:* **in short**, to cut a long story short, in brief, in a word, in a nutshell, in essence.

briefs pl. n. **underpants**, pants, knickers, bikini briefs; N. Amer. shorts; informal panties; Brit. informal kecks.

brigade n. **squad**, team, group, band, party, crew, force, outfit.

bright adj. **1 shining**, brilliant, dazzling, glaring, sparkling, flashing, glittering, gleaming, glistening, shimmering, radiant, glowing, luminous, shiny, glossy, lustrous. **2 sunny**, cloudless, clear, fair, fine. **3** *bright colours:* **vivid**, brilliant, intense, strong, vibrant, bold, gaudy, lurid, garish. **4 clever**, intelligent, quick-witted, smart, canny, astute, perceptive, ingenious; informal brainy.
– OPPOSITES dull, cloudy, dark, stupid.

brighten v. **1 illuminate**, light up, lighten. **2 cheer up**, perk up, liven up, rally, feel heartened; informal buck up.

brilliance n. **1 brightness**, vividness, intensity, sparkle, glitter, blaze, luminosity, radiance. **2 genius**, intelligence, talent, ability, prowess, skill,

expertise, aptitude, flair, wisdom, intellect. **3 splendour**, magnificence, grandeur, resplendence, glory.
– OPPOSITES dullness, stupidity.

brilliant adj. **1 bright**, shining, sparkling, blazing, dazzling, vivid, intense, glaring, luminous, radiant. **2 clever**, bright, intelligent, smart, able, talented, gifted, skilful, astute; informal brainy. **3** *her brilliant career:* **superb**, glorious, illustrious, successful, impressive, remarkable, exceptional, excellent, outstanding, distinguished.
– OPPOSITES dim, stupid, undistinguished.

brim n. **1 peak**, visor, shield. **2 rim**, lip, brink, edge.
•v. **be full (up)**, overflow, run over, well over.

bring v. **1 fetch**, carry, bear, take, convey, transport, shift. **2 escort**, conduct, guide, lead, usher. **3 cause**, produce, create, bring about, generate, precipitate, occasion, provoke, lead to, give rise to, result in.
◻ **bring in** introduce, launch, inaugurate, initiate, institute. **bring off** achieve, accomplish, bring about, succeed in, pull off, carry off, manage. **bring out** launch, establish, begin, start, found, set up, market, publish, issue. **bring up 1** rear, raise, nurture, look after. **2** mention, raise, broach, introduce, air, suggest.

brink n. **1 edge**, verge, margin, rim, lip, border, boundary. **2** on *the brink of war:* **verge**, threshold, point, edge.

brisk adj. **1 quick**, rapid, fast, swift, speedy, hurried, energetic, lively; informal nippy. **2 no-nonsense**, businesslike, decisive, brusque, abrupt, short, sharp, curt, blunt, terse; informal snappy.
– OPPOSITES leisurely.

bristle n. **1 hair**, whisker; (**bristles**) stubble, five o'clock shadow. **2 spine**, prickle, quill, barb.
•v. **1 rise**, stand up, stand on end. **2 take offence**, bridle, take umbrage, be offended. **3 be crowded**, be full, be packed, be jammed, be covered, overflow; informal be thick, be chock-full.

brittle adj. **breakable**, fragile, crisp, crumbly, delicate.
– OPPOSITES flexible.

broach v. **bring up**, raise, introduce, mention, touch on, air.

broad adj. **1 wide**, extensive, vast, immense, great, spacious, expansive, sizeable, sweeping. **2 comprehensive**, inclusive, extensive, wide, all-embracing, unlimited. **3** *a broad outline:* **general**, non-specific, rough, approximate, basic, loose, vague.
– OPPOSITES narrow, limited.

broadcast v. **1 transmit**, relay, air, beam, show, televise, screen. **2 report**, announce, publicize, advertise, make public, proclaim, spread, circulate, promulgate.
•n. **transmission**, programme, show, telecast, production.

broaden v. **1** *her smile broadened:* **widen**, expand, stretch (out), spread. **2** *the government tried to broaden its political base:* **expand**, enlarge, extend, widen, swell, increase, add to, develop.
– OPPOSITES narrow, restrict.

broad-minded adj. **liberal**, tolerant, freethinking, indulgent, progressive, permissive, unshockable, unprejudiced, unbiased.
– OPPOSITES intolerant.

brochure n. **booklet**, prospectus, catalogue, pamphlet, leaflet, circular, mailshot; N. Amer. folder.

broken adj. **1 smashed**, shattered, fragmented, splintered, crushed, snapped, in bits, in pieces, cracked, split, fractured; informal in smithereens. **2 faulty**, damaged, defective, not working, malfunctioning, out of order, broken down, down; informal kaput, bust, acting up; Brit. informal knackered. **3 interrupted**, disturbed, fitful, disrupted, discontinuous, intermittent. **4 halting**, hesitating, faltering, imperfect.

broken-hearted adj. **heartbroken**, grief-stricken, desolate, devastated, inconsolable, miserable, wretched, forlorn, heavy-hearted, woeful.
– OPPOSITES overjoyed.

broker n. **dealer**, agent, middleman, intermediary, mediator, factor, liaison, stockbroker.
•v. **arrange**, organize, orches-

b

trate, work out, settle, clinch, negotiate, mediate.

brood n. **offspring**, young, family, litter, clutch, progeny.
• v. **think**, ponder, contemplate, meditate, ruminate, muse, worry, dwell on, fret, agonize.

brook n. **stream**, rill; N. English beck; Scottish & N. English burn; N. Amer. & Austral./NZ creek.

brotherly adj. **fraternal**, friendly, comradely, affectionate, amicable, kind, devoted, loyal.

brow n. **1 forehead**, temple. **2 summit**, peak, top, crest, crown, head, pinnacle, apex.

browbeat v. **bully**, intimidate, force, coerce, compel, dragoon, bludgeon, pressure, pressurize, tyrannize, terrorize; informal bulldoze, railroad.

brown adj. **1 hazel**, chestnut, chocolate, coffee, brunette, sepia, mahogany, tan, café au lait, caramel. **2 tanned**, suntanned, bronzed, swarthy.
• v. **grill**, toast, singe, sear, barbecue, sauté.

browse v. **look through**, scan, skim, glance, peruse, thumb, leaf, flick, dip into.

bruise n. **contusion**, bump, swelling, lump, mark, injury, welt.
• v. **contuse**, injure, mark, discolour, make black and blue, blemish, damage, spoil.

brush¹ n. **1 broom**, sweeper, besom, whisk. **2 clean**, sweep, wipe, dust. **3** *a brush with the*

law: **encounter**, clash, confrontation, conflict, altercation, incident; informal run-in, to-do; Brit. informal spot of bother.
• v. **1 sweep**, clean, buff, polish, scrub. **2 groom**, comb, neaten, tidy, smooth, arrange. **3** *his lips brushed her cheek:* **touch**, stroke, caress, skim, sweep, graze, contact, kiss.
□ **brush aside** disregard, ignore, dismiss, shrug off, wave aside, reject, spurn, laugh off, make light of; informal pooh-pooh. **brush up (on)** revise, read up, go over, improve, polish up, enhance, hone, perfect; informal bone up on; Brit. informal swot up (on).

brush² n. **undergrowth**, scrub, brushwood, shrubs, bushes; N. Amer. underbrush, chaparral.

brusque adj. **curt**, abrupt, blunt, short, sharp, brisk, peremptory, gruff, discourteous, impolite, rude.
– OPPOSITES polite.

brutal adj. **savage**, violent, cruel, vicious, ferocious, barbaric, wicked, murderous, bloodthirsty, cold-blooded, callous, ruthless, heartless, merciless, sadistic, inhuman.
– OPPOSITES gentle.

bubbly adj. **1 fizzy**, sparkling, effervescent, gassy, aerated, carbonated, frothy, foamy. **2 vivacious**, animated, ebullient, lively, high-spirited, bouncy, merry, happy, cheerful, sunny; informal chirpy.
– OPPOSITES still.

buckle n. clasp, clip, catch, hasp, fastener.
- •v. **1 fasten**, do up, hook, secure, clasp, clip. **2 bend**, warp, twist, distort, contort, deform, crumple, collapse, give way.

budding adj. **promising**, up-and-coming, rising, in the making, aspiring, future, fledgling, developing.

budge v. **1 move**, shift, stir, go. **2 persuade**, convince, influence, sway, bend.

budget n. **1 financial plan**, forecast. **2** *the defence budget*: allowance, allocation, quota, funds, resources, capital.
- •v. **allocate**, allot, allow, earmark, designate, set aside.

buff[1] v. **polish**, burnish, shine, smooth, rub.

buff[2] n. (informal) **enthusiast**, fan, devotee, lover, admirer, expert, aficionado, authority; informal freak, nut, addict.

buffer n. **cushion**, bulwark, shield, barrier, guard, safeguard.

buffet[1] n. **1 cold table**, self-service meal, smorgasbord. **2 cafe**, cafeteria, snack bar, canteen, restaurant.

buffet[2] v. **batter**, pound, lash, strike, hit, beat.

bug n. **1** (informal) **illness**, disease, sickness, disorder, upset, ailment, infection, virus; Brit. informal lurgy. **2 insect**, minibeast; informal creepy-crawly, beastie. **3 listening device**, hidden microphone, wire, wiretap, tap. **4 fault**, error, defect, flaw, virus; informal glitch, gremlin.
- •v. **eavesdrop on**, spy on, tap, monitor.

build v. **construct**, erect, put up, assemble, make, create, fashion, model, shape.
- OPPOSITES demolish, dismantle.
- •n. **physique**, frame, body, figure, form, shape, stature, proportions; informal vital statistics.
- □ **build up 1** increase, grow, mount up, intensify, strengthen. **2** boost, strengthen, increase, improve, augment, raise, enhance, swell. **3** accumulate, amass, collect, gather.

building n. **structure**, construction, edifice, pile, property, premises, establishment.

> WORD LINKS
> relating to building:
> architectural

build-up n. **increase**, growth, expansion, enlargement, escalation, accumulation, development.

bulbous adj. **bulging**, round, fat, rotund, swollen, distended, bloated.

bulge n. **swelling**, bump, lump, hump, protrusion, protuberance.
- •v. **swell**, stick out, project, protrude, stand out, puff out, balloon (out), fill out, distend.

bulk n. **1 size**, volume, dimensions, proportions, mass, scale. **2 majority**, mass, generality, main part, lion's share, preponderance.

bulky adj. **unwieldy**, cumbersome, unmanageable, awkward, ponderous, outsize, oversized; informal hulking.

bullet n. **ball**, shot, pellet; informal slug; (**bullets**) lead.

bulletin n. **1 report**, dispatch, story, newsflash, statement, announcement, message, communication, communiqué. **2 newsletter**, news-sheet, proceedings, newspaper, magazine, gazette, review.

bully n. **persecutor**, oppressor, tyrant, tormentor, intimidator, bully boy, thug.
•v. **1** *the others bully him:* **persecute**, oppress, tyrannize, browbeat, intimidate, dominate, terrorize; informal push around/about. **2** *she was bullied into helping:* **coerce**, pressure, press, push, prod, browbeat, dragoon, strong-arm; informal bulldoze, railroad, lean on.

bump n. **1 jolt**, crash, smash, smack, crack, bang, thud, thump, clang, knock, clunk, boom; informal whack, wallop. **2 swelling**, lump, bulge, injury, contusion, hump, knob.
•v. **1 hit**, crash into, smash into, slam into, bang, knock, run into, plough into, ram, collide with, strike; N. Amer. impact. **2 bounce**, jolt, jerk, rattle, shake.

bumper adj. **exceptional**, large, abundant, rich, bountiful, good, plentiful, record, successful; informal whopping.
– OPPOSITES meagre.

bumpy adj. **1 uneven**, rough, rutted, pitted, potholed, lumpy, rocky. **2 bouncy**, rough, uncomfortable, jolting, lurching, jerky, jarring, bone-shaking.
– OPPOSITES smooth.

bunch n. **1 bouquet**, posy, nosegay, spray, wreath, garland. **2 cluster**, clump, knot, group, bundle.
•v. **cluster**, huddle, gather, congregate, collect, amass, group, crowd.

bundle n. **collection**, roll, clump, wad, parcel, sheaf, bale, pile, stack, heap, mass, bunch; informal load, wodge.
•v. **1 tie**, parcel, wrap, swathe, roll, fold, bind, pack. **2** *he was bundled into a van:* **push**, shove, thrust, throw, propel, jostle, manhandle.

bungle v. **mishandle**, mismanage, mess up, spoil, ruin; informal blow, botch, fluff, make a hash of, screw up; Brit. informal make a pig's ear of; N. Amer. informal goof up.

bungling adj. **incompetent**, blundering, amateurish, inept, unskilful, clumsy, awkward, bumbling; informal ham-fisted, cack-handed.

buoy n. **float**, marker, beacon.

buoyant adj. **1 floating**, floatable. **2 cheerful**, cheery, happy, light-hearted, carefree, joyful, bubbly, bouncy, sunny, upbeat.
– OPPOSITES gloomy.

burden n. **responsibility**, onus, obligation, duty, liability,

trouble, care, problem, difficulty, worry, strain.
• v. oppress, trouble, worry, weigh down, overload, encumber, saddle, tax, afflict.

bureau n. **1** desk, writing table, secretaire. **2 department**, agency, office, division, branch, section, station, unit.

bureaucracy n. **1 red tape**, rules and regulations, protocol, officialdom, paperwork. **2 civil service**, government, administration, establishment, system, powers that be, authorities.

bureaucrat n. **official**, administrator, civil servant, minister, functionary, mandarin; derogatory apparatchik.

burgeon v. **grow**, increase, rocket, mushroom, expand, escalate, swell, boom, flourish, thrive, prosper.

burglar n. **housebreaker**, thief, intruder, robber, raider, looter.

burglary n. **housebreaking**, breaking and entering, break-in, theft, raid, stealing, robbery, larceny, looting; informal smash-and-grab; N. Amer. informal heist.

burgle v. **rob**, loot, steal from, raid.

burial n. **funeral**, interment, committal, inhumation, entombment, obsequies, exequies.
– OPPOSITES exhumation.

burly adj. **strapping**, well built, strong, muscular, muscly, hefty, sturdy, brawny; informal hunky, beefy.
– OPPOSITES puny.

burn v. **1 be on fire**, be alight, blaze, go up (in smoke), be in flames, smoulder, glow. **2 set fire to**, set alight, set light to, kindle, ignite, touch off, incinerate, cremate; informal torch. **3 scorch**, singe, sear, char, blacken, brand.

burning adj. **1 on fire**, blazing, flaming, fiery, glowing, red-hot, smouldering. **2** a burning desire: **intense**, passionate, deep-seated, profound, strong, ardent, fervent, urgent, fierce, consuming. **3** burning issues: **important**, crucial, critical, vital, essential, pivotal, urgent, pressing, compelling.

burrow n. **warren**, tunnel, hole, dugout, lair, set, den, earth.
• v. **tunnel**, dig, excavate, mine, bore, channel.

burst v. **1** one balloon burst: **split (open)**, rupture, break, tear. **2** a shell burst: **explode**, blow up, detonate, go off. **3** smoke burst through the hole: **gush**, erupt, surge, rush, stream, flow, pour, spurt, jet. **4** he burst into the room: **charge**, plunge, barge, plough, hurtle, career, rush, dash, tear.
• n. **1 rupture**, puncture, breach, split, blowout. **2 explosion**, detonation, blast, eruption, bang. **3** a burst of gunfire: **volley**, salvo, barrage, hail, rain. **4** a burst of activity: **outbreak**, eruption, flare-up, blaze, attack, fit, rush, storm, surge, spurt.

bury v. **1 inter**, lay to rest, entomb. **2 hide**, conceal, cover,

enfold, sink. **3** *the bullet buried itself in the wood:* **embed**, sink, implant, submerge, lodge.
– OPPOSITES exhume.

bush n. **1 shrub**, thicket; (**bushes**) undergrowth, shrubbery. **2 wilds**, wilderness, backwoods; N. Amer. backcountry; Austral./NZ outback, backblocks; N. Amer. informal boondocks.

bushy adj. **thick**, shaggy, curly, fuzzy, bristly, fluffy, woolly.

business n. **1 work**, occupation, profession, career, employment, job, position. **2 trade**, commerce, dealing, traffic, dealings, transactions, negotiations. **3 firm**, company, concern, enterprise, venture, organization, operation, undertaking; informal **outfit**. **4** *it's none of your business:* **concern**, affair, responsibility, duty. **5** *an odd business:* **affair**, matter, case, circumstance, situation, event, incident.

businesslike adj. **professional**, efficient, organized, slick, methodical, systematic, orderly, structured, disciplined, practical, pragmatic.

businessman, businesswoman n. **executive**, entrepreneur, industrialist, merchant, dealer, trader, manufacturer, tycoon, employer, broker, buyer, seller, tradesman, retailer, supplier.

bust n. **1 bosom**, breasts, chest; informal **boobs**, knockers. **2 sculp-** ture, carving, effigy, statue, head and shoulders.

bustle v. **rush**, dash, hurry, scurry, scuttle, scamper, scramble; informal scoot, beetle, buzz.
• n. **activity**, action, liveliness, excitement, tumult, commotion, hubbub, hurly-burly, whirl; informal toing and froing.

bustling adj. **busy**, crowded, swarming, teeming, humming, buzzing, hectic, lively.

busy adj. **1** *I'm very busy:* **hard at work**, involved, rushed off your feet, hard-pressed, pushed; informal on the go, hard at it; Brit. informal on the hop. **2** *I'm sorry, she's busy:* **unavailable**, engaged, occupied, absorbed, engrossed, immersed, preoccupied, working; informal tied up. **3** *a busy day:* **hectic**, active, lively, full, eventful, energetic, tiring.
– OPPOSITES idle, free, quiet.
• v. **occupy**, involve, engage, concern, absorb, engross, immerse, distract.

but conj. **1 however**, nevertheless, nonetheless, even so, yet, still. **2 whereas**, conversely.
• prep. **except (for)**, apart from, other than, besides, aside from, with the exception of, bar.
▫ **but for** except for, if it were not for, notwithstanding, barring.

butt[1] v. **ram**, headbutt, bump, poke, prod, push, shove, thrust.
▫ **butt in** interrupt, intrude, break in, cut in, interfere, put

your oar in; informal poke your nose in; Brit. informal chip in.

b
c

butt² n. target, victim, object, dupe, laughing stock.

butt³ n. **1** stock, end, handle, hilt, haft. **2** stub, end, stump; informal fag end, dog end.

buttocks pl. n. bottom, rear (end), rump, seat, derrière, cheeks; informal behind, backside; Brit. informal bum; N. Amer. informal butt, fanny; humorous posterior.

buttress v. strengthen, shore up, reinforce, fortify, support, bolster, underpin, cement, uphold, defend, back up.

buy v. purchase, acquire, obtain, get, pick up, snap up, invest in; informal get hold of, score.
– OPPOSITES sell.

• n. (informal) purchase, deal, bargain, investment, acquisition.

buyer n. purchaser, customer, consumer, shopper, investor; (buyers) clientele, market.

buzz n. hum, murmur, drone, whirr.

bypass n. ring road, detour, diversion, alternative route; Brit. relief road.
• v. **1 go round**, go past, make a detour round, avoid. **2** ignore, sidestep, avoid, evade, escape, elude, skirt, dodge, circumvent, get round, go over the head of, pass over; informal short-circuit, duck.

bystander n. onlooker, passerby, observer, spectator, eyewitness.

Cc

cab n. taxi, taxi cab; Brit. minicab, hackney carriage; N. Amer. hack.

cabin n. **1** berth, stateroom, compartment. **2** hut, log cabin, shanty, shack, chalet; Scottish bothy; N. Amer. cabana.

cabinet n. cupboard, bureau, chest of drawers.

cable n. **1** a thick cable moored the ship: rope, cord, line, guy; Nautical hawser. **2** electric cables: wire, lead, cord, power line; Brit. flex.

cache n. hoard, store, stockpile, stock, supply, reserve, arsenal; informal stash.

cadence n. rhythm, tempo, metre, beat, pulse, intonation, modulation, lilt.

cafe n. snack bar, cafeteria, coffee bar/shop, tea room/shop, bistro, brasserie; N. Amer. diner, lunchroom.

cafeteria n. self-service restaurant, canteen, cafe, buffet, refectory, mess hall.

cage n. **enclosure**, pen, pound, coop, hutch, birdcage, aviary.
•v. **confine**, shut in/up, pen, coop up, enclose.

cagey adj. (informal) **secretive**, guarded, tight-lipped, reticent, evasive; informal playing your cards close to your chest.

cajole v. **persuade**, wheedle, coax, talk into, prevail on; informal sweet-talk, soft-soap.

cake n. **1 bun**, pastry, gateau, slice. **2 bar**, tablet, block, slab, lump, wedge.
•v. **boots caked with mud: coat**, encrust, plaster, cover.

calamity n. **disaster**, catastrophe, tragedy, cataclysm, accident, misfortune, misadventure.

calculate v. **1 compute**, work out, reckon, figure, add up/together, count up, tally, total; Brit. tot up. **2 intend**, mean, design.

calculated adj. **deliberate**, premeditated, planned, pre-planned, preconceived, intentional, intended.
– OPPOSITES unintentional.

calculating adj. **cunning**, crafty, wily, sly, scheming, devious, disingenuous.

calculation n. **1 computation**, reckoning, adding up, counting up, working out; Brit. totting up. **2 assessment**, judgement, forecast, projection, prediction.

calendar n. **schedule**, diary, programme, timetable, agenda.

calibre n. **1 quality**, standard, level, merit, distinction, stature, excellence, ability, expertise, talent, capability. **2 bore**, diameter, gauge.

call v. **1 cry**, cry out, shout, yell, sing out, exclaim, shriek, scream, roar; informal holler. **2 wake (up)**, awaken, rouse; Brit. informal knock up. **3 phone**, telephone, give someone a call; Brit. ring up, give someone a ring; informal call up, give someone a buzz; Brit. informal give someone a bell. **4 summon**, send for, order. **5 pay a visit to**, visit, call/drop/look in on, drop/stop by, pop into, nip over to. **6 convene**, summon, assemble. **7 name**, christen, baptize, designate, style, term, dub. **8 describe as**, regard as, look on as, think of as, consider to be.
•n. **1 cry**, shout, yell, exclamation, shriek, scream, roar; informal holler. **2 the call of the barn owl: cry**, song. **3 phone call**, telephone call; Brit. ring; informal buzz; Brit. informal bell. **4 appeal**, plea, request. **5 there's no call for that kind of language: need**, necessity, reason, justification, excuse. **6 there's no call for expensive wine: demand**, desire, market. **7 attraction**, appeal, lure, allure, pull, draw.
□ **call for 1 require**, need, necessitate, make necessary, demand, be grounds for, justify, warrant. **2 ask for**, request, seek, apply for, appeal for, demand, insist on, order. **call off** cancel,

c

abandon, scrap, drop, axe; informal scrub; N. Amer. informal redline. **call up** enlist, recruit, conscript; US draft.

calling n. **profession**, occupation, job, vocation, career, métier, work, line of work, employment, trade, craft.

callous adj. **heartless**, unfeeling, uncaring, cold, cold-hearted, hard, hardbitten, as hard as nails, hard-hearted, insensitive, unsympathetic.
– OPPOSITES kind, compassionate.

calm adj. **1 relaxed**, composed, self-possessed, serene, tranquil, unruffled, unperturbed, unflustered, untroubled, unexcitable, level-headed, unemotional, phlegmatic, imperturbable; informal unflappable, laid-back. **2 windless**, still, quiet, tranquil, smooth.
– OPPOSITES excited, nervous, stormy.
• n. **1** his usual calm deserted him: **composure**, coolness, calmness, self-possession, sangfroid, serenity, tranquillity; informal cool, unflappability. **2** calm prevailed: **tranquillity**, stillness, quiet, peace.
□ **calm down 1** soothe, pacify, placate, mollify; Brit. quieten (down). **2** compose yourself, regain your composure, control yourself, pull yourself together, simmer down, cool down/off, take it easy; Brit. calm down; informal get a grip, keep your shirt on; N. Amer. informal decompress.

camouflage n. **disguise**, mask, screen, cover, cloak, front, facade, blind, concealment, subterfuge.
• v. **disguise**, hide, conceal, mask, screen, cover (up).

camp n. **1 campsite**, encampment, camping ground, bivouac, base, settlement. **2 faction**, wing, group, lobby, caucus, bloc.

campaign n. **1** Napoleon's Russian campaign: **operation(s)**, manoeuvre(s), offensive, attack, war, battle, crusade. **2** the campaign to reduce vehicle emissions: **effort**, drive, push, struggle, movement, crusade, operation, strategy.
• v. **fight**, battle, push, press, strive, struggle, lobby, agitate.

cancel v. **1 call off**, abandon, scrap, drop, axe; informal scrub; N. Amer. informal redline. **2 annul**, invalidate, declare null and void, void, revoke, rescind, retract, withdraw.
□ **cancel out** neutralize, negate, nullify, wipe out, balance (out), make up for, compensate for, offset.

cancer n. **(malignant) growth**, tumour, malignancy; technical carcinoma, sarcoma.

WORD LINKS
causing cancer: carcinogenic; branch of medicine concerned with cancer: oncology

candid adj. **frank**, forthright, direct, blunt, outspoken, plainspoken, open, honest, truthful,

sincere; informal upfront; N. Amer. informal on the up and up.
– OPPOSITES guarded.

candidate n. **applicant**, contender, competitor, entrant, claimant, nominee, interviewee, examinee, possible; Brit. informal runner.

canny adj. **shrewd**, astute, smart, sharp, discerning, discriminating, perceptive, clever, judicious, wise.
– OPPOSITES foolish.

canopy n. **awning**, shade, sunshade, covering.

canvass v. **1 campaign**, electioneer. **2 poll**, question, survey, interview, consult.

canyon n. **ravine**, gorge, gully, chasm, abyss, gulf; N. Amer. gulch, coulee.

cap n. **1 lid**, top, stopper, cork, bung; N. Amer. stopple. **2 limit**, ceiling, curb, check.
▸v. **1 top**, crown, cover, coat, tip. **2 limit**, restrict, curb, control, peg.

capability n. **ability**, capacity, power, potential, competence, aptitude, faculty, skill, talent, flair; informal know-how.
– OPPOSITES inability.

capable adj. **able**, competent, effective, proficient, accomplished, experienced, skilful, talented, gifted; informal useful.
– OPPOSITES incapable, incompetent.

capacity n. **1 volume**, size, dimensions, measurements, proportions. **2 ability**, capability,

power, potential, competence, aptitude, faculty, skill, talent, flair. **3 role**, function, position, post, job, office.

cape[1] n. **cloak**, mantle, shawl, poncho, pashmina.

cape[2] n. **headland**, promontory, point, head, horn, mull, peninsula.

capital n. **money**, finance(s), funds, cash, wherewithal, means, assets, wealth, resources.

capitalism n. **private enterprise**, free enterprise, the free market, private ownership.
– OPPOSITES communism.

capitalize v.
□ **capitalize on** take advantage of, profit from, make the most of, exploit, develop; informal cash in on.

capitulate v. **surrender**, give in, yield, concede defeat, give up (the struggle), submit, lay down your arms, throw in the towel/sponge.
– OPPOSITES resist.

capricious adj. **fickle**, volatile, unpredictable, temperamental, mercurial, impulsive, changeable, unreliable, erratic, wayward, whimsical, flighty.
– OPPOSITES consistent.

capsize v. **overturn**, turn over, turn upside down, upend, flip/tip over, keel over, turn turtle.

capsule n. **1 pill**, tablet, lozenge, pastille; informal tab. **2 module**, craft, probe.

captain n. **1** *the ship's captain:* **commander**, master; informal skipper. **2** *the team captain:* **leader**, head, chief; informal boss, skipper.

caption n. **title**, heading, legend, description.

captivate v. **enthral**, charm, enchant, bewitch, fascinate, beguile, entrance, delight, attract, allure.
– OPPOSITES bore.

captive n. **prisoner**, convict, detainee, hostage, prisoner of war, internee.
•adj. **confined**, caged, incarcerated, locked up, jailed, imprisoned, interned, detained.
– OPPOSITES free.

captivity n. **imprisonment**, incarceration, confinement, detention, internment.
– OPPOSITES freedom.

capture v. **1** catch, apprehend, seize, arrest, take prisoner, take into custody, detain. **2** occupy, invade, conquer, seize, take.
– OPPOSITES release, liberate.
•n. **arrest**, apprehension, detention, seizure.

car n. **1** motor, motor car, automobile; informal wheels; N. Amer. informal auto. **2** carriage, coach; Brit. saloon.

carcass n. **corpse**, dead body, remains; Medicine cadaver; informal stiff.

care n. **1** safe keeping, supervision, custody, charge, protection, responsibility, guardianship. **2** discretion,

caution, sensitivity, thought, regard, consideration. **3** worry, anxiety, trouble, concern, stress, pressure, strain.
– OPPOSITES neglect, carelessness.
•v. be concerned, worry (yourself), trouble/concern yourself, bother, mind, be interested; informal give a damn/hoot.
□ care for **1** love, be fond of, be devoted to, treasure, adore, dote on, think the world of, worship. **2** look after, take care of, tend, attend to, minister to, nurse.

career n. **profession**, occupation, vocation, calling, life's work, employment.
•v. **hurtle**, rush, shoot, race, speed, charge, hare, fly; informal belt, tear; Brit. informal bucket.

carefree adj. **unworried**, untroubled, blithe, nonchalant, happy-go-lucky, free and easy, easy-going, relaxed; informal laid-back.
– OPPOSITES troubled.

careful adj. **1** *be careful on the stairs:* **cautious**, alert, attentive, watchful, vigilant, wary, on your guard, circumspect. **2** *careful with money:* **prudent**, thrifty, economical, sparing, frugal. **3** *careful consideration of the facts:* **attentive**, conscientious, painstaking, meticulous, diligent, assiduous, scrupulous, methodical.
– OPPOSITES careless.

careless adj. **1** *careless motorists:* **inattentive**, negligent,

heedless, irresponsible, impetuous, reckless. **2** *careless work*: **shoddy**, slapdash, slipshod, scrappy, slovenly, sloppy, negligent, lax, slack, disorganized, hasty, hurried. **3** *a careless remark*: **thoughtless**, insensitive, indiscreet, unguarded, incautious, inadvertent.
– OPPOSITES careful.

caress v. **stroke**, touch, fondle, brush, feel, skim.

caretaker n. **janitor**, attendant, porter, custodian, concierge; N. Amer. superintendent.
•adj. **temporary**, acting, provisional, substitute, interim, stand-in, fill-in, stopgap; N. Amer. informal pinch-hitting.

cargo n. **freight**, load, haul, consignment, delivery, shipment, goods, merchandise.

caricature n. **cartoon**, parody, satire, lampoon, burlesque; informal send-up, take-off.
•v. **parody**, satirize, lampoon, make fun of, mock, ridicule; informal send up, take off.

carnage n. **slaughter**, massacre, murder, butchery, bloodbath, bloodletting, holocaust.

carnival n. **festival**, fiesta, fete, fair, gala, Mardi Gras.

carp v. **complain**, find fault, quibble, grumble, grouse, whine; informal nit-pick, gripe, moan, bitch, whinge.

carpenter n. **woodworker**, joiner, cabinetmaker; Brit. informal chippy.

carriage n. **1** *a railway carriage*: **coach**, car; Brit. saloon. **2** *a horse and carriage*: **wagon**, coach. **3** **posture**, bearing, gait; Brit. deportment.

carry v. **1** **convey**, transfer, transport, move, take, bring, bear, fetch; informal cart, hump, lug. **2** **transmit**, conduct, relay, communicate, convey, beam, send. **3** **approve**, pass, accept, endorse, ratify. **4** **be audible**, travel, reach, be heard.
☐ **carry on** continue, keep (on), go on, persist in; informal stick with/at. **carry out** conduct, perform, execute, implement. **2** keep, honour, fulfil, observe, abide by, comply with, adhere to, stick to.

carton n. **box**, package, cardboard box, case, container, pack, packet.

cartoon n. **1** **animation**, animated film, comic strip, graphic novel. **2** **caricature**, parody, lampoon, satire; informal take-off, send-up.

cartridge n. **cassette**, magazine, canister, case, container.

carve v. **1** **sculpt**, cut, hew, whittle, chisel, shape, fashion. **2** **engrave**, incise, score, cut. **3** **slice**, cut up, chop.
☐ **carve up** divide, break up, partition, apportion, subdivide, split up, share out.

cascade n. **waterfall**, cataract, falls, rapids, white water, flood, torrent.
•v. **pour**, gush, surge, spill, stream, flow, issue, spurt, jet.

c

case[1] n. **1** *a classic case of over-reaction:* **instance**, example, occurrence, occasion, demonstration, illustration. **2** *is that the case?* **situation**, position, state of affairs, circumstances, conditions, facts; Brit. state of play; informal score. **3** **assignment**, job, project, investigation, exercise. **4** *he lost his case:* **lawsuit**, legal action, trial, legal proceedings, litigation. **5** *the case against animal testing:* **argument**, defence, justification, vindication, exposition, thesis.

case[2] n. **1** **container**, box, canister, holder. **2** **casing**, cover, sheath, envelope, sleeve, jacket, shell. **3** (Brit.) **suitcase**, travel bag, valise; (**cases**) luggage, baggage. **4** **cabinet**, cupboard.

cash n. **1** **money**, currency, bank notes, coins, change; N. Amer. bills; informal dough, loot; Brit. informal dosh, brass; N. Amer. informal dinero. **2** **finance**, money, resources, funds, assets, means, wherewithal.

cashier n. **clerk**, teller, banker, treasurer, bursar, purser.

cask n. **barrel**, keg, butt, tun, vat, drum, hogshead; historical firkin.

cast v. **1** **throw**, toss, fling, pitch, hurl, lob; informal chuck, sling, bung. **2** **direct**, shoot, throw, fling, send. **3** **register**, record, enter, file. **4** **emit**, give off, throw, send out, radiate. **5** **mould**, fashion, form, shape, forge.
• n. **1** **mould**, die, matrix, shape, casting, model. **2** **actors**, performers, players, company,

troupe, dramatis personae, characters.

caste n. **class**, rank, level, order, stratum, echelon, status.

castle n. **fortress**, fort, stronghold, fortification, keep, citadel, palace, chateau, tower.

casual adj. **1** *a casual attitude:* **unconcerned**, uncaring, indifferent, lackadaisical, nonchalant, offhand, flippant, easygoing, free and easy, blithe, carefree, devil-may-care; informal laid-back. **2** *a casual remark:* **offhand**, spontaneous, unthinking, unconsidered, impromptu, throwaway, unguarded; informal off-the-cuff. **3** *a casual glance:* **cursory**, perfunctory, superficial, passing, fleeting. **4** *casual work:* **temporary**, freelance, irregular, occasional. **5** *a casual meeting:* **chance**, accidental, unplanned, unintended, unexpected, unforeseen. **6** *a casual atmosphere:* **relaxed**, friendly, informal, easy-going, free and easy; informal laid-back.
– OPPOSITES serious, deliberate, formal.

casualty n. **victim**, sufferer, fatality, death, loss, wounded person, injured person.

cat n. **feline**, tomcat, tom, kitten; informal pussy (cat), puss, kitty; Brit. informal moggie, mog.

┌─────────────────────────┐
│ **WORD LINKS** │
│ *relating to cats:* feline │
└─────────────────────────┘

catalogue n. **directory**, register, index, list, listing, record, schedule, archive, inventory.

•v. **classify**, categorize, index, list, archive, record, itemize.

catastrophe n. **disaster**, calamity, cataclysm, ruin, tragedy, fiasco, debacle.

catch v. **1 seize**, grab, snatch, grasp, grip, clutch, intercept, trap, receive, get. **2 capture**, apprehend, seize, arrest, take prisoner, trap, snare, net; informal nab, collar; Brit. informal nick. **3 become trapped**, become entangled, snag, jam, wedge, lodge, get stuck. **4 discover**, find, come across, stumble on, chance on, surprise. **5 contract**, go/come down with, be taken ill with, develop, pick up, succumb to.

– OPPOSITES drop, release.

•n. **1 haul**, net, bag, yield. **2 latch**, lock, fastener, clasp, hasp. **3 snag**, disadvantage, drawback, stumbling block, hitch, complication, problem, trap, trick.

□ **catch on** (informal) **1 become popular**, take off, boom, flourish, thrive. **2 comprehend**, understand, learn, see the light; informal cotton on, latch on.

catching adj. (informal) **infectious**, contagious, communicable; dated infective.

catchy adj. **memorable**, unforgettable, haunting, appealing, popular.

– OPPOSITES forgettable.

categorical adj. **unqualified**, unconditional, unequivocal, absolute, explicit, unambiguous, definite, direct, emphatic, positive, out-and-out.

category n. **class**, classification, group, grouping, bracket, heading, set, type, sort, kind, grade, order, rank.

cater v.

□ **cater for 1 provide** (food) **for**, feed, serve, cook for. **2** *a resort catering for older holidaymakers:* serve, provide for, meet the needs/wants of, accommodate. **3** *we cater for all tastes:* take into account, take into consideration, allow for, consider, bear in mind, make provision for, have regard for.

cattle pl. n. **cows**, oxen, herd, livestock.

> **WORD LINKS**
> *relating to cattle:* bovine

cause n. **1** *the cause of the fire:* **source**, root, origin, beginning, starting point, originator, author, creator, agent. **2** *there is no cause for alarm:* **reason**, grounds, justification, call, need, necessity, occasion, excuse. **3** *raising money for good causes:* **principle**, ideal, belief, conviction, object, aim, objective, purpose, charity.

•v. **bring about**, give rise to, lead to, result in, create, produce, generate, engender, spawn, bring on, precipitate, prompt, provoke, trigger, make happen, induce, inspire, promote, foster.

caustic adj. **1 corrosive**, acid, burning. **2 sarcastic**, cutting, biting, mordant, sharp, scathing, sardonic, scornful, trenchant, acerbic, vitriolic.

caution n. **1** care, attention, alertness, circumspection, discretion, prudence. **2** warning, admonishment, injunction, reprimand, rebuke; informal telling-off, dressing-down; Brit. informal ticking-off.
•v. **1** advisers cautioned against tax increases: advise, warn, counsel, urge. **2** he was cautioned by the police: warn, admonish, reprimand; informal tell off; Brit. informal tick off.

cautious adj. careful, attentive, alert, judicious, circumspect, prudent, tentative, guarded.
– OPPOSITES reckless.

cave n. **cavern**, grotto, pothole, chamber, gallery, hollow.

> WORD LINKS
> exploration of caves:
> speleology, potholing;
> (N. Amer.) spelunking

cavity n. space, chamber, hollow, hole, pocket, gap, crater, pit.

cease v. stop, come/bring to an end, come/bring to a halt, end, halt, conclude, terminate, finish, wind up, discontinue, suspend, break off.
– OPPOSITES start, continue.

ceaseless adj. continual, constant, continuous, incessant, unending, endless, never-ending, interminable, non-stop, unremitting, relentless, unrelenting, sustained, persistent, eternal, perpetual.
– OPPOSITES intermittent.

celebrate v. **1** commemorate, observe, mark, keep, honour, remember. **2** enjoy yourself, make merry, have fun, have a good time, have a party; N. Amer. step out; informal party, whoop it up, have a ball. **3** perform, observe, officiate at, preside at.

celebrated adj. acclaimed, admired, highly rated, esteemed, exalted, vaunted, eminent, great, distinguished, prestigious, illustrious, notable.
– OPPOSITES unsung.

celebration n. **1** commemoration, observance, marking, keeping. **2** merrymaking, jollification, revelry, revels, festivities; informal partying. **3** party, function, gathering, festivities, festival, fete, carnival, jamboree; informal do, bash, rave; Brit. informal rave-up. **4** performance, observance, officiation, solemnization.

celebrity n. **1** fame, prominence, renown, stardom, popularity, distinction, prestige, stature, repute, reputation. **2** famous person, VIP, personality, big name, household name, star, superstar; informal celeb, megastar.
– OPPOSITES obscurity.

celestial adj. **1** (in) space, heavenly, astronomical, extra-terrestrial, stellar, planetary. **2** heavenly, holy, saintly, divine, godly, godlike, ethereal, angelic.

celibate adj. unmarried, single, chaste, pure, virginal.

cell n. **1 room**, cubicle, chamber, dungeon, compartment, lock-up. **2 unit**, squad, detachment, group.

cellar n. **basement**, vault, crypt.

cement n. **adhesive**, glue, fixative, gum, paste.

cemetery n. **graveyard**, churchyard, burial ground, necropolis, garden of remembrance, mass grave; Scottish kirkyard.

censor v. **cut**, edit, expurgate, sanitize, clean up, ban, delete.

censorious adj. **critical**, overcritical, hypercritical, disapproving, condemnatory, judgemental, moralistic, fault-finding, reproachful.

censure v. **condemn**, criticize, attack, reprimand, rebuke, admonish, upbraid, reproach.
– OPPOSITES defend, praise.
•n. **condemnation**, criticism, attack, reprimand, rebuke, admonishment, reproof, disapproval, reproach.
– OPPOSITES approval, praise.

central adj. **1** *a central position*: **middle**, centre, halfway, midway, mid. **2** *central London*: **inner**, innermost, middle, mid. **3 main**, chief, principal, primary, foremost, key, crucial, vital, essential, basic, fundamental, core; informal number-one.
– OPPOSITES side, outer.

centralize v. **concentrate**, consolidate, amalgamate, condense, unify, focus.
– OPPOSITES devolve.

centre n. **middle**, nucleus, heart, core, hub.
– OPPOSITES edge.
•v. *the story centres on a doctor*: **focus**, concentrate, pivot, revolve, be based.

ceremonial adj. **formal**, official, state, public, ritual, ritualistic, stately, solemn.
– OPPOSITES informal.

ceremony n. **1 rite**, ritual, observance, service, event, function. **2 pomp**, protocol, formality, formalities, niceties, decorum, etiquette, pageantry, ceremonial.

certain adj. **1** *I'm certain he's guilty*: **sure**, confident, positive, convinced, in no doubt, satisfied. **2** *it is certain that more changes are in the offing*: **unquestionable**, sure, definite, beyond question, indubitable, undeniable, indisputable. **3** *they are certain to win*: **sure**, bound, destined. **4** *certain defeat*: **inevitable**, assured, unavoidable, inescapable, inexorable. **5** *there is no certain cure*: **reliable**, dependable, foolproof, guaranteed, sure, infallible; informal sure-fire.
– OPPOSITES doubtful, unlikely, possible.

certainly adv. **definitely**, surely, assuredly, unquestionably, beyond/without question, undoubtedly, without doubt, indubitably, undeniably, irrefutably, indisputably.

certainty n. **1 confidence**, sureness, conviction, assurance. **2 inevitability**, foregone

conclusion; informal sure thing; Brit. informal (dead) cert.
– OPPOSITES doubt, possibility.

certificate n. **guarantee**, document, authorization, authentication, accreditation, credentials, testimonial.

certify v. **1 verify**, guarantee, attest, validate, confirm, endorse. **2 accredit**, recognize, license, authorize, approve.

cessation n. **end**, termination, halt, finish, stoppage, conclusion, winding up, pause, suspension.
– OPPOSITES start, resumption.

chain n. **1 fetters**, shackles, irons, manacles, handcuffs; informal cuffs, bracelets. **2 series**, succession, string, sequence, train, course.
•v. **secure**, fasten, tie, tether, hitch, restrain, shackle, fetter, manacle, handcuff.

chairman, **chairwoman** n. **chair**, chairperson, president, chief executive, leader, master of ceremonies, MC.

challenge n. **1 dare**, provocation, offer. **2 problem**, difficult task, test, trial.
•v. **1 question**, dispute, take issue with, call into question, protest against, oppose. **2 dare**, defy, invite, throw down the gauntlet to. **3 test**, tax, strain, make demands on, stretch.

challenging adj. **demanding**, testing, taxing, exacting, hard, difficult, stimulating.
– OPPOSITES easy.

champion n. **1 winner**, title-holder, gold medallist, prizewinner; informal champ, number one. **2 advocate**, proponent, promoter, supporter, defender, upholder, backer; N. Amer. booster.
•v. **advocate**, promote, defend, uphold, support, espouse, stand up for, campaign for, lobby for, fight for.
– OPPOSITES oppose.

chance n. **1 possibility**, prospect, probability, likelihood, risk, threat, danger. **2** I gave her a chance to answer: **opportunity**, opening, occasion, window; N. Amer. & Austral./NZ show; Brit. informal look-in. **3** he took an awful chance: **risk**, gamble, leap in the dark. **4 coincidence**, accident, fate, destiny, providence, happenstance, good fortune, luck, fluke.
– OPPOSITES certainty.
•adj. **accidental**, fortuitous, fluky, coincidental.
□ **by chance** by accident, fortuitously, accidentally, coincidentally, unintentionally, inadvertently.

change v. **1 alter**, make/become different, adjust, adapt, amend, modify, revise, vary, transform, metamorphose, evolve. **2 exchange**, substitute, swap, switch, replace, alternate.
•n. **1 alteration**, modification, variation, revision, amendment, adjustment, adaptation, metamorphosis, transformation, evolution. **2 replacement**,

exchange, substitution, swap, switch.

changeable adj. **variable**, varying, changing, fluctuating, irregular, erratic, inconsistent, unstable, unsettled, inconstant, fickle, capricious, temperamental, volatile, mercurial, unpredictable.
– OPPOSITES constant.

channel n. **1 strait(s)**, sound, narrows, passage. **2 duct**, gutter, conduit, trough, sluice, drain. **3 means**, medium, instrument, mechanism, agency, vehicle, route, avenue.
•v. **convey**, transmit, conduct, direct, relay, pass on, transfer.

chant n. **shout**, cry, call, slogan, chorus, refrain.
•v. **shout**, chorus, repeat, call.

chaos n. **disorder**, disorganization, confusion, mayhem, bedlam, pandemonium, havoc, turmoil, anarchy, lawlessness; Brit. a shambles; informal all hell broken loose.
– OPPOSITES order.

chaotic adj. **disorderly**, disorganized, in confusion, in turmoil, topsy-turvy, anarchic, lawless; Brit. informal shambolic.

chap n. (Brit.) **man**, boy, individual, character; informal fellow, guy, geezer; Brit. informal bloke, lad; N. Amer. informal dude, hombre.

chapter n. **1 section**, part, division, topic, stage, episode. **2 period**, phase, page, stage, epoch, era.

character n. **1 personality**, nature, quality, disposition, temperament, mentality, make-up, spirit, identity, tone, feel. **2 integrity**, honour, moral strength/fibre, strength, backbone, resolve, grit, will power; informal guts; Brit. informal bottle. **3 reputation**, (good) name, standing, position, status. **4 eccentric**, oddity, crank, original, individualist, madcap, nonconformist; informal oddball. **5 person**, man, woman, soul, creature, individual, customer; informal cookie; Brit. informal bod, guy. **6 letter**, figure, symbol, mark, device, sign, hieroglyph.

characteristic n. **attribute**, feature, quality, property, trait, aspect, idiosyncrasy, peculiarity, quirk.
•adj. **typical**, usual, normal, distinctive, representative, particular, special, peculiar, idiosyncratic.
– OPPOSITES abnormal.

characterize v. **1 distinguish**, mark, typify, set apart. **2 portray**, depict, present, represent, describe, categorize, class, brand.

charade n. **pretence**, act, masquerade, show, facade, pantomime, farce, travesty, mockery, parody.

charge v. **1 ask**, demand, bill, invoice. **2 accuse**, indict, arraign, prosecute, try, put on trial; N. Amer. impeach. **3 entrust**, burden, encumber, saddle, tax. **4 attack**, storm, assault, assail, descend on; informal lay into, tear into. **5 rush**, storm, stampede, push, plough, launch yourself, go headlong; informal steam; N. Amer. informal barrel. **6** *charge your glasses!* **fill (up)**, top up, load (up), arm.

•n. **1 fee**, payment, price, rate, tariff, fare, levy. **2 accusation**, allegation, indictment, arraignment; N. Amer. impeachment. **3 attack**, assault, offensive, onslaught, drive, push. **4** *the child was in her charge:* **care**, protection, safe keeping, control, custody, hands.

charisma n. **charm**, presence, (force of) personality, strength of character, (animal) magnetism, appeal, allure.

charismatic adj. **charming**, magnetic, compelling, inspiring, captivating, mesmerizing, appealing, alluring, glamorous.

charitable adj. **1 philanthropic**, generous, open-handed, giving, munificent, benevolent, altruistic, unselfish, public-spirited, humanitarian, non-profit-making. **2 magnanimous**, generous, liberal, tolerant, sympathetic, understanding, lenient, indulgent, forgiving.
– OPPOSITES commercial, mean.

charity n. **1 voluntary organization**, charitable institution, fund, trust, foundation. **2 aid**, financial assistance, welfare, relief, donations, handouts, gifts, largesse; historical alms. **3 philanthropy**, humanitarianism, altruism, public-

spiritedness, social conscience, benevolence. **4 goodwill**, compassion, consideration, concern, kindness, sympathy, indulgence, tolerance, leniency.

charm n. **1 appeal**, attraction, fascination, beauty, loveliness, allure, seductiveness, magnetism, charisma; informal pulling power. **2 spell**, incantation, formula; N. Amer. mojo, hex. **3 talisman**, trinket, amulet, mascot, fetish.

•v. **1 delight**, please, win (over), attract, captivate, lure, fascinate, enchant, beguile. **2 coax**, cajole, wheedle; informal sweet-talk, soft-soap.

charming adj. **delightful**, pleasing, endearing, lovely, adorable, appealing, attractive, good-looking, alluring, winning, fetching, captivating, enchanting, entrancing.

chart n. **graph**, table, diagram, plan, map; Computing graphic.
•v. **1 plot**, tabulate, graph, record, register, represent. **2 follow**, trace, outline, describe, detail, record, document.

charter n. **1** *a Royal charter:* **authority**, authorization, sanction, dispensation, permit, licence, warrant. **2** *the UN Charter:* **constitution**, code, principles.
•v. **hire**, lease, rent, book.

chase v. **1 pursue**, run after, follow, hunt, track, trail; informal tail. **2** *she chased away the dogs:* **drive**, send, scare; informal send packing. **3** *she chased away all*

thoughts of him: **dispel**, banish, dismiss, drive away, shut out, put out of your mind.
•n. **pursuit**, hunt, trail.

chat n. **talk**, conversation, gossip; informal jaw, gas, confab; Brit. informal natter, chinwag.
•v. **talk**, gossip; informal gas, jaw, chew the rag/fat; Brit. informal natter, have a chinwag; N. Amer. informal shoot the breeze/bull.

chatter v. **prattle**, chat, gossip, jabber, babble; informal yatter; Brit. informal natter, chunter, rabbit on.
•n. **prattle**, chat, gossip, patter, jabber, babble; informal chit-chat, yattering; Brit. informal nattering, chuntering, rabbiting on.

chatty adj. **talkative**, communicative, effusive, gossipy, loquacious, voluble; informal mouthy, gabby.
– OPPOSITES taciturn.

cheap adj. **1 inexpensive**, low-priced, low-cost, economical, competitive, affordable, reasonable, budget, economy, bargain, cut-price, reduced, discounted; informal dirt cheap. **2 poor-quality**, second-rate, substandard, inferior, vulgar, shoddy, trashy, tawdry; informal tacky; Brit. informal naff. **3 despicable**, contemptible, immoral, unscrupulous, unprincipled, cynical.
– OPPOSITES expensive.

cheat v. **swindle**, defraud, deceive, trick, dupe, hoodwink, double-cross, gull; informal rip off, diddle, con, pull a fast one on; N. Amer. informal sucker.
•n. **swindler**, fraudster, confidence trickster, double-dealer, double-crosser, fraud, fake, charlatan; informal con artist.

check v. **1 examine**, inspect, look at/over, scrutinize, study, investigate, probe, look into, enquire into; informal check out, give something a/the once-over. **2 make sure**, confirm, verify. **3 halt**, stop, arrest, bar, obstruct, foil, thwart, curb, block.
•n. **1 examination**, inspection, scrutiny, perusal, study, investigation, test, check-up; informal once-over. **2 control**, restraint, constraint, curb, limitation.
□ **check in** register, book in, report. **check out** pay the bill, settle up, leave.

cheek n. **impudence**, impertinence, insolence, rudeness, disrespect; informal brass neck, lip, mouth, chutzpah; Brit. informal backchat; N. Amer. informal sass, back talk.

cheeky adj. **impudent**, impertinent, insolent, rude, disrespectful; informal brass-necked, lippy, mouthy, fresh; N. Amer. informal sassy, nervy.
– OPPOSITES respectful, polite.

cheer v. **1 applaud**, hail, salute, shout for, clap, put your hands together for, bring the house down; informal holler for, give someone a big hand; N. Amer. informal ballyhoo. **2 please**, raise/lift someone's spirits, brighten, buoy up, hearten, gladden, perk up, encourage; informal buck up.
– OPPOSITES boo, depress.

•n. **hurrah**, hurray, whoop, bravo, shout; (**cheers**) acclaim, applause, ovation.
– OPPOSITES boo.

□ **cheer up** perk up, brighten up, rally, revive, bounce back, take heart; informal buck up.

cheerful adj. **1 happy**, jolly, merry, bright, sunny, joyful, in good/high spirits, buoyant, cheery, animated, smiling, good-humoured; informal chipper, chirpy, full of beans. **2 pleasant**, attractive, agreeable, bright, sunny, friendly, welcoming.
– OPPOSITES sad, gloomy.

cheerless adj. **gloomy**, dreary, dull, dismal, bleak, drab, sombre, dark, dim, dingy, funereal, austere, stark, unwelcoming, uninviting, depressing.

chemist n. **pharmacist**, dispenser; N. Amer. druggist; old use apothecary.

cherish v. **1 adore**, love, dote on, be devoted to, revere, think the world of, care for, look after, protect, keep safe. **2 treasure**, prize, hold dear. **3 harbour**, entertain, nurse, cling to, foster.
– OPPOSITES hate.

chest n. **1 breast**, upper body, torso, trunk, front. **2 box**, case, casket, crate, trunk, coffer, strongbox.

> WORD LINKS
> relating to the chest: pectoral, thoracic

chew v. **munch**, champ, chomp, crunch, gnaw, bite, masticate.

chic adj. **stylish**, smart, elegant, sophisticated, fashionable; informal trendy; Brit. informal swish; N. Amer. informal kicky, tony.
– OPPOSITES unfashionable.

chief n. **1** a Highland chief: **leader**, chieftain, head, ruler, master, commander. **2** the chief of the central bank: **head**, chief executive, chief executive officer, CEO, president, chairman, chairwoman, principal, governor, director, manager; informal boss, (head) honcho; Brit. informal gaffer, guv'nor.
•adj. **1 head**, leading, principal, premier, highest, supreme, arch. **2 main**, principal, primary, prime, first, cardinal, central, key, crucial, essential; informal number-one.
– OPPOSITES subordinate, minor.

chiefly adv. **mainly**, in the main, primarily, principally, predominantly, mostly, for the most part, usually, typically, commonly, generally, on the whole, largely.

child n. **youngster**, baby, infant, toddler, minor, juvenile, junior, descendant; Scottish & N. English bairn; informal kid, kiddie, nipper, tiny, tot; derogatory brat.

> WORD LINKS
> branch of medicine concerned with children: paediatrics

childbirth n. **labour**, delivery, birthing; old use confinement.

childhood n. **youth**, early years/life, infancy, babyhood, boyhood, girlhood, minority.
– OPPOSITES adulthood.

childish adj. **immature**, babyish, infantile, juvenile, puerile, silly.
– OPPOSITES mature.

childlike adj. **youthful**, innocent, unsophisticated, naive, trusting, artless, unaffected, uninhibited, natural, spontaneous.
– OPPOSITES adult.

chill n. **1 coldness**, chilliness, coolness, nip. **2 cold**, dose of flu, fever. **3 shiver**, frisson.
– OPPOSITES warmth.
•v. **scare**, frighten, petrify, terrify, alarm, make someone's blood run cold; informal scare the pants off; Brit. informal put the wind up.
•adj. **cold**, chilly, cool, fresh, wintry, frosty, icy, arctic, bitter, freezing; informal nippy; Brit. informal parky.
– OPPOSITES warm.

chilly adj. **1 cold**, cool, crisp, fresh, wintry, frosty, icy; informal nippy; Brit. informal parky. **2 unfriendly**, unwelcoming, cold, cool, frosty; informal stand-offish.
– OPPOSITES warm.

china n. **crockery**, dishes, plates, cups and saucers, tableware, porcelain, dinnerware, dinner service, tea service.

chink n. **gap**, crack, space, hole, aperture, fissure, cranny, cleft, split, slit.

chip n. **1 fragment**, sliver, splinter, shaving, shard, flake. **2 nick**, crack, scratch. **3 counter**, token; N. Amer. check.
•v. **1 nick**, crack, scratch. **2 chip off the old plaster: cut**, hack, chisel, carve, hew, whittle.

chivalrous adj. **gallant**, gentlemanly, honourable, respectful, considerate, courteous, polite, gracious, well mannered.
– OPPOSITES rude.

choice n. **1** *freedom of choice:* **selection**, choosing, picking, pick, preference, decision, say, vote. **2** *you have no other choice:* **option**, alternative, course of action. **3** *an extensive choice:* **range**, variety, selection, assortment.
•adj. **superior**, first-class, first-rate, prime, premier, grade A, best, finest, select, quality, top, top-quality, high-grade, prize; informal A1, top-notch.
– OPPOSITES inferior.

choke v. **1 gag**, retch, cough, fight for breath. **2 suffocate**, asphyxiate, smother, stifle, strangle, throttle; informal strangulate. **3 clog (up)**, bung up, stop up, block, obstruct.

choose v. **1 select**, pick (out), opt for, plump for, settle on, prefer, decide on, fix on, elect, adopt. **2 wish**, want, desire, please, like.

choosy adj. (informal) **fussy**, finicky, fastidious, over-particular, hard to please; informal picky, pernickety; N. Amer. informal persnickety.

chop v. **cut (up)**, cube, dice, hew, split, fell; N. Amer. hash. □ **chop off** cut off, sever, lop, shear.

choppy adj. **rough**, turbulent, heavy, heaving, stormy, tempestuous, squally.
– OPPOSITES calm.

C

chore n. task, job, duty, errand, burden; informal hassle.

christen v. **1** *she was christened Sara:* **baptize**, name, give the name of, call. **2** *a group christened 'The Magic Circle':* **call**, name, dub, style, term, label, nickname.

chronic adj. **1** *a chronic illness:* **persistent**, long-standing, long-term, incurable. **2** *chronic economic problems:* **constant**, continuing, persistent, long-lasting, severe, serious, acute, grave, dire. **3** *a chronic liar:* **inveterate**, hardened, dyed-in-the-wool, incorrigible, compulsive; informal pathological.
– OPPOSITES acute, temporary.

chronicle n. record, account, history, annals, archive(s), log, diary, journal.
•v. **record**, write down, set down, document, report.

chubby adj. plump, tubby, flabby, rotund, portly, chunky; Brit. informal podgy; N. Amer. informal zaftig, corn-fed.
– OPPOSITES skinny.

chuck v. (informal) **1** throw, toss, fling, hurl, pitch, cast, lob; informal sling, bung. **2** throw away, throw out, discard, dispose of, get rid of, dump, bin, jettison; informal ditch, junk; N. Amer. informal trash. **3** give up, leave, resign from; informal quit, pack in; Brit. informal jack in. **4** jilt, finish with, break off with, leave; informal dump, ditch, give someone the elbow; Brit. informal give someone the push.

chuckle v. laugh, chortle, giggle, titter, snigger.

chum n. (informal) friend, companion, playmate, classmate, schoolmate, workmate; informal pal, crony; Brit. informal mate; N. Amer. informal buddy.
– OPPOSITES enemy.

chunk n. lump, hunk, wedge, block, slab, square, nugget, brick, cube; informal wodge; N. Amer. informal gob.

churlish adj. rude, ill-mannered, discourteous, ungracious, impolite, inconsiderate, surly, sullen.
– OPPOSITES polite.

churn v. disturb, stir up, agitate, beat.

cinema n. **1** the movies, the pictures, multiplex; informal the flicks. **2** *British cinema:* films, film, movies, pictures, motion pictures.

circa prep. approximately, (round) about, around, in the region of, roughly, something like, or so, or thereabouts, more or less; informal as near as dammit; N. Amer. informal in the ballpark of.
– OPPOSITES exactly.

circle n. **1** ring, band, hoop, circlet, halo, disc. **2** group, set, crowd, band, company, clique, coterie, club, society; informal gang, bunch.
•v. **1** *seagulls circled above:* **wheel**, revolve, rotate, whirl, spiral. **2** *satellites circling the earth:* **go round**, travel round, circumnavigate, orbit. **3** *the*

abbey was circled by a wall: **surround**, encircle, ring, enclose.

circuit n. **1** *two circuits of the track:* **lap**, turn, round, circle. **2** (Brit.) *a racing circuit:* **track**, racetrack, course, route, stadium.

circuitous adj. **roundabout**, indirect, winding, meandering, twisting, tortuous.
– OPPOSITES direct.

circular adj. **round**, ring-shaped.
•n. **leaflet**, pamphlet, handbill, flyer, advertisement, notice.

circulate v. **1 spread**, communicate, disseminate, make known, make public, broadcast, publicize, distribute. **2 socialize**, mingle, mix, wander, stroll.

circumspect adj. **cautious**, wary, careful, chary, guarded, on your guard; informal cagey.
– OPPOSITES unguarded.

circumstances pl. n. **situation**, conditions, state of affairs, position, the lie of the land, (turn of) events, factors, facts, background, environment, context.

cite v. **quote**, mention, refer to, allude to, instance, specify, name.

citizen n. **1** *a British citizen:* **subject**, national, passport holder. **2** *the citizens of Edinburgh:* **inhabitant**, resident, native, townsman, townswoman, taxpayer; formal denizen.

city n. **town**, municipality, metropolis, conurbation, urban area; Scottish burgh; informal big smoke; N. Amer. informal burg.

┌─────────────────────────────┐
│ WORD LINKS   │
│ *relating to cities:* urban, civic, │
│ metropolitan   │
└─────────────────────────────┘

civic adj. **municipal**, city, town, urban, metropolitan, public, community.

civil adj. **1 secular**, non-religious, lay. **2 non-military**, civilian. **3 polite**, courteous, well mannered, gentlemanly, chivalrous, ladylike.
– OPPOSITES religious, military, rude.

civilization n. **1 human development**, advancement, progress, enlightenment, culture, refinement, sophistication. **2 culture**, society, nation, people.

civilize v. **enlighten**, improve, educate, instruct, refine, cultivate, socialize.

civilized adj. **1** *civilized society:* **advanced**, developed, sophisticated, enlightened, educated, cultured, cultivated. **2** *civilized behaviour:* **polite**, courteous, well mannered, civil, refined, polished.
– OPPOSITES unsophisticated, rude.

claim v. **1 assert**, declare, profess, protest, maintain, insist, contend, allege. **2 request**, ask for, apply for, demand.
•n. **1 assertion**, declaration, profession, protestation, insistence, contention, allegation. **2 application**, request, demand.

clamour n. **noise**, din, racket, rumpus, uproar, shouting, commotion, hubbub; Brit. row; informal hullabaloo.

clamp v. **fasten**, secure, fix, attach, clench, grip, hold, press, clasp, screw, bolt.

clan n. **family**, house, dynasty, tribe.

clandestine adj. **secret**, covert, furtive, surreptitious, stealthy, cloak-and-dagger, underhand; informal hush-hush.

clap v. **applaud**, give someone a round of applause, put your hands together; informal give someone a (big) hand; N. Amer. informal give it up.
• n. **1 round of applause**, handclap; informal hand. **2 crack**, peal, crash, bang, boom.

clarify v. **make clear**, shed/throw light on, illuminate, elucidate, explain, interpret, spell out, clear up.
– OPPOSITES confuse.

clarity n. **1** the clarity of his explanation: **lucidity**, precision, coherence, transparency, simplicity. **2** the clarity of the image: **sharpness**, clearness, crispness, definition. **3** the clarity of the water: **transparency**, clearness, limpidity, translucence.

clash n. **1 fight**, battle, confrontation, skirmish, engagement, encounter, conflict. **2 argument**, altercation, confrontation, quarrel, disagreement, dispute; informal run-in, slanging match. **3 crash**, clang, bang, clatter, clangour.
• v. **1 fight**, battle, confront,

skirmish, contend, come to blows. **2 disagree**, differ, wrangle, dispute, cross swords, lock horns, be at loggerheads. **3 conflict**, coincide, overlap. **4 bang**, strike, clang, crash.

clasp v. **grasp**, grip, clutch, hold, squeeze, seize, grab, embrace, hug.
• n. **1 fastener**, catch, clip, pin, buckle. **2 grasp**, grip, squeeze, embrace, hug.

class n. **1 kind**, sort, type, variety, genre, category, grade, rating, classification. **2 group**, grouping, rank, stratum, level, echelon, status, caste.
• v. **classify**, categorize, group, grade, order, rate, bracket, designate, label, rank.

classic adj. **1 definitive**, authoritative, outstanding, first-rate, first-class, best, finest, excellent, superior, masterly. **2 typical**, archetypal, quintessential, model, representative, perfect, prime, textbook. **3 timeless**, traditional, simple, elegant, understated.
• n. **definitive example**, model, epitome, paradigm, exemplar, masterpiece, master work.

classification n. **categorization**, classifying, grouping, grading, ranking, organization, sorting, codification.

classify v. **categorize**, group, grade, rank, order, organize, sort, type, codify, bracket.

classy adj. (informal) **stylish**, high-class, superior, exclusive, chic, elegant, smart, sophisticated;

Brit. upmarket; N. Amer. high-toned; informal posh, ritzy, plush, swanky; Brit. informal swish.

clause n. section, paragraph, article, passage, subsection, chapter, condition, proviso, rider.

claw n. talon, nail, pincer.
- v. scratch, lacerate, tear, rip, scrape, dig into.

clean adj. **1** washed, scrubbed, cleansed, cleaned, laundered, spotless, unstained, unsullied, unblemished, immaculate, pristine, disinfected, sterilized, sterile, aseptic, decontaminated. **2** blank, empty, clear, plain, unused, new, pristine, fresh, unmarked. **3** pure, clear, fresh, unpolluted, uncontaminated.
- OPPOSITES dirty, polluted.
- v. wash, cleanse, wipe, sponge, scrub, mop, rinse, scour, swab, shampoo, launder, dry-clean.
- OPPOSITES dirty.

cleanse v. **1** clean (up), wash, bathe, rinse, disinfect. **2** cleansing the environment of traces of lead: rid, clear, free, purify, purge.

clear adj. **1** understandable, comprehensible, intelligible, plain, uncomplicated, explicit, lucid, coherent, simple, straightforward, unambiguous, clear-cut. **2** obvious, evident, plain, sure, definite, unmistakable, manifest, indisputable, unambiguous, patent, incontrovertible, visible, conspicuous, overt, blatant, glaring. **3** transparent, limpid, translucent,

crystal clear, pellucid. **4** bright, cloudless, unclouded, blue, sunny, starry. **5** unobstructed, passable, open, unrestricted, unhindered.
- OPPOSITES incoherent, vague, cloudy.
- v. **1** disappear, go away, stop, die away, fade, wear off, lift, settle, evaporate, dissipate, decrease, lessen, shift. **2** unblock, unstop, clean out. **3** evacuate, vacate, empty, leave. **4** remove, strip, take away, carry away, tidy away/up. **5** go over, pass over, sail over, jump (over), vault (over), leap (over). **6** acquit, declare innocent, find not guilty, absolve, exonerate; informal let off (the hook).
- □ **clear up 1** tidy (up), put in order, straighten up, clean up, fix. **2** solve, resolve, straighten out, find an/the answer to, get to the bottom of, explain; informal crack, figure out, suss out.

clearance n. **1** removal, clearing, demolition. **2** authorization, permission, consent, approval, leave, sanction, licence, dispensation; informal the go-ahead. **3** space, room (to spare), headroom, margin, leeway.

clear-cut adj. definite, distinct, precise, specific, explicit, unambiguous, unequivocal, black and white.
- OPPOSITES vague.

clearly adv. **1** intelligibly, plainly, distinctly, comprehensibly, legibly, audibly. **2** obviously, evidently, patently, unquestionably, undoubtedly, without doubt, plainly, undeniably.

c **cleft** n. **split**, crack, fissure, crevice.

clench v. **grip**, grasp, grab, clutch, clasp, clamp, hold tightly, seize, squeeze.

clergyman, clergywoman n. **priest**, cleric, minister, preacher, chaplain, padre, father, pastor, vicar, rector, parson, curate; Scottish kirkman.

clerical adj. **1 office**, desk, administrative, secretarial, white-collar. **2 ecclesiastical**, church, priestly, religious, spiritual, holy.

clever adj. **1 intelligent**, bright, smart, astute, quick-witted, shrewd, talented, gifted, capable, able, competent; informal brainy. **2** *a clever scheme*: **ingenious**, canny, cunning, crafty, artful, slick, neat. **3** *she was clever with her hands*: **skilful**, dexterous, adroit, adept, deft, nimble, handy, skilled, talented, gifted.
– OPPOSITES stupid.

cliché n. **platitude**, hackneyed phrase, commonplace, banality, truism, stock phrase; informal old chestnut.

click v. **1 clack**, snick, snap, clink. **2 become clear**, fall into place, make sense, dawn on someone, register, get through, sink in. **3 take to each other**, get along, be compatible, be like-minded, see eye to eye, be on the same

wavelength; informal hit it off. **4 go down well**, prove popular, be a hit, succeed, resonate, work, take off.

client n. **customer**, buyer, purchaser, shopper, patient, patron; Brit. informal punter.

cliff n. **precipice**, rock face, crag, bluff, ridge, escarpment, scar, scarp.

climate n. **1 (weather) conditions**, weather. **2 atmosphere**, mood, spirit, ethos, feeling, ambience, environment.

climax n. **peak**, pinnacle, height, high point, top, zenith, culmination.
– OPPOSITES anticlimax, nadir.

climb v. **1 ascend**, mount, scale, scramble up, clamber up, shin up, conquer. **2 rise**, ascend, go up, gain height, soar, rocket. **3** *the road climbs steeply*: **slope (upwards)**, rise, go uphill, incline.
– OPPOSITES descend.
□ **climb down** back down, retreat, give in, backtrack, eat your words, eat humble pie, do a U-turn; N. Amer. informal eat crow.

clinch v. **1** *he clinched the deal*: **secure**, settle, conclude, close, confirm, seal, finalize, wrap up; informal sew up. **2** *these findings clinched the matter*: **settle**, decide, determine, resolve.

cling v. **stick**, adhere, hold.
□ **cling (on) to** hold on, clutch, grip, grasp, clasp, hang on, embrace, hug.

clinical adj. **1 detached**, impersonal, dispassionate, indifferent, uninvolved, distant, remote, aloof, cold. **2 plain**, stark, austere, spartan, bleak, bare, functional, basic, institutional.
– OPPOSITES emotional.

clip¹ n. **fastener**, clasp, hasp, catch, hook, buckle, lock.
•v. **fasten**, attach, fix, join, pin, staple, tack.

clip² v. **1 trim**, prune, cut, snip, crop, shear, lop. **2 hit**, strike, graze, glance off, nudge, scrape.
•n. **1 extract**, excerpt, snippet, fragment, trailer. **2 trim**, cut, crop, haircut.

clique n. **coterie**, set, circle, ring, in-crowd, group, gang, fraternity.

cloak n. **1 cape**, robe, wrap, mantle. **2** *a cloak of secrecy:* **cover**, veil, mantle, shroud, screen, blanket.
•v. **conceal**, hide, cover, veil, shroud, mask, obscure, cloud, envelop, swathe, surround.

clog v. **block**, obstruct, congest, jam, choke, bung up, plug, stop up.

close¹ adj. **1 near**, nearby, adjacent, neighbouring, adjoining, abutting, at hand. **2 neck and neck**, even, nip and tuck. **3 intimate**, dear, bosom, close-knit, inseparable, devoted, faithful, special, firm. **4** *a close resemblance:* **noticeable**, marked, distinct, pronounced, strong. **5 careful**, detailed, thorough, minute, searching, painstaking, meticulous, rigorous. **6 humid**,

muggy, stuffy, airless, heavy, sticky, sultry, stifling.
– OPPOSITES far, distant.

close² v. **1** *she closed the door:* **shut**, pull to, push to, slam. **2** *close the hole:* **block**, stop up, plug, seal, bung up, clog up, choke, obstruct. **3 end**, conclude, finish, terminate, wind up. **4 shut down**, close down, cease production, cease trading, be wound up, go out of business; informal fold, go to the wall, go bust. **5 clinch**, settle, secure, seal, confirm, pull off, conclude, finalize; informal wrap up.
– OPPOSITES open, start.
•n. **end**, finish, conclusion.
– OPPOSITES beginning.

closet n. **cupboard**, wardrobe, cabinet, locker.
•adj. **secret**, covert, private, surreptitious, clandestine.
•v. **shut away**, sequester, seclude, cloister, confine, isolate.

clot n. **lump**, clump, mass, thrombosis; informal glob; Brit. informal gob.
•v. **coagulate**, set, congeal, thicken, solidify.

cloth n. **1 fabric**, material, textile(s), stuff. **2 rag**, wipe, duster, flannel; Austral. washer.

clothe v. **dress**, attire, robe, garb, costume, swathe, deck (out), turn out, fit out, rig (out); informal get up.

clothes pl. n. **clothing**, garments, attire, garb, dress, wear, costume, wardrobe; informal gear,

c

togs; Brit. informal clobber; N. Amer. informal threads; formal apparel.

WORD LINKS
relating to clothes: sartorial; person who sells or makes clothes: clothier, couturier, tailor

clothing n. see CLOTHES.

cloud n. a cloud of exhaust smoke: **mass**, billow, mantle, blanket, pall.
• v. **confuse**, muddle, obscure.

cloudy adj. **1** overcast, dark, grey, black, leaden, murky, gloomy, sunless, starless. **2** murky, muddy, milky, dirty, turbid.
– OPPOSITES clear, sunny.

clown n. **1** joker, comedian, comic, wag, wit, jester. **2** fool, idiot, buffoon, dolt, ignoramus; informal moron, ass, numbskull, halfwit, fathead; Brit. informal prat, berk, twit, twerp.

club[1] n. **1** society, association, group, circle, league, guild, union. **2** nightclub, bar; informal disco. **3** team, squad, side.

club[2] n. stick, cudgel, truncheon, bludgeon, baton, mace, bat; N. Amer. blackjack, nightstick; Brit. informal cosh.
• v. **hit**, beat, strike, cudgel, bludgeon, batter; informal clout, clobber; Brit. informal cosh.

clue n. **hint**, indication, sign, signal, pointer, lead, tip, evidence.

clump n. **1** a clump of trees: **cluster**, thicket, group, bunch. **2** a clump of earth: **lump**, clod, mass, chunk.

clumsy adj. **1** awkward, uncoordinated, ungainly, graceless, lumbering, inelegant, inept, unskilful, accident-prone, all fingers and thumbs; informal cack-handed, ham-fisted, butter-fingered; N. Amer. informal klutzy. **2** unwieldy, cumbersome, bulky, awkward.
– OPPOSITES graceful.

cluster n. **bunch**, clump, mass, knot, group, clutch, huddle, crowd.
• v. **congregate**, gather, collect, group, assemble, huddle, crowd.

clutch v. **grip**, grasp, clasp, cling to, hang on to, clench, hold, grab, snatch.

clutter n. **disorder**, chaos, mess, disarray, untidiness, confusion, litter, rubbish, junk.
• v. **litter**, mess up, be strewn, be scattered, cover, bury.

coach[1] n. **1** a journey by coach: **bus**; dated omnibus, charabanc. **2** a railway coach: **carriage**, wagon; N. Amer. car.

coach[2] n. **instructor**, trainer, teacher, tutor, mentor, guru.
• v. **instruct**, teach, tutor, school, educate, drill, train.

coagulate v. **congeal**, clot, thicken, solidify, harden, set, dry.

coalition n. **alliance**, union, partnership, bloc, federation, league, association, confederation, consortium, syndicate, amalgamation, merger.

coarse adj. **1 rough**, scratchy, prickly, wiry, harsh. **2** *coarse manners*: **uncouth**, oafish, loutish, boorish, rude, impolite, ill-mannered, vulgar, common, rough. **3** *a coarse remark*: **vulgar**, crude, rude, off colour, lewd, smutty, indelicate.
– OPPOSITES soft, refined, polite.

coast n. **shore**, coastline, seashore, seaboard, shoreline, seaside; literary strand.
•v. **freewheel**, cruise, taxi, drift, glide, sail.

WORD LINKS
relating to a coast or seashore: littoral

coat n. **1 fur**, hair, wool, fleece, hide, pelt, skin. **2 layer**, covering, coating, skin, film, deposit.
•v. **cover**, surface, plate, spread, daub, smear, plaster, cake.

coax v. **persuade**, wheedle, cajole, get round, inveigle, manoeuvre; informal sweet-talk, soft-soap, twist someone's arm.

cocky adj. **arrogant**, conceited, overconfident, swollen-headed, self-important, full of yourself, egotistical, presumptuous, boastful; informal too big for your boots.
– OPPOSITES modest.

code n. **1 cipher**. **2 convention**, etiquette, protocol, ethic. **3 law(s)**, rules, regulations, constitution, system.

coerce v. **pressure**, press, push, constrain, force, compel, oblige, browbeat, bully, threaten, intimidate, dragoon, twist

someone's arm; informal railroad, steamroller, lean on.

cogent adj. **convincing**, persuasive, compelling, strong, forceful, powerful, potent, effective, sound, telling, coherent, clear, lucid, logical, well argued.

coherent adj. **logical**, reasoned, rational, sound, cogent, consistent, clear, lucid, articulate, intelligible.
– OPPOSITES muddled.

coil v. **wind**, loop, twist, curl, spiral, twine, wrap.

coin v. **invent**, create, make up, conceive, originate, think up, dream up.

WORD LINKS
relating to coins: numismatic

coincide v. **1 occur simultaneously**, happen together, co-occur, coexist. **2 tally**, correspond, agree, accord, match up, be compatible, dovetail, mesh; informal square.
– OPPOSITES differ.

coincidence n. **accident**, chance, providence, happenstance, fate, luck, fortune, fluke.

coincidental adj. **accidental**, chance, fluky, random, fortuitous, unintentional, unplanned.

cold adj. **1 chilly**, chill, cool, freezing, icy, wintry, frosty, raw, bitter; informal nippy; Brit. informal parky. **2 unfriendly**, inhospitable, unwelcoming, cool, frigid, frosty, distant, formal, stiff.
– OPPOSITES hot, warm.

collaborate v. **1 cooperate**, join forces, work together, combine,

pool resources, club together.
2 fraternize, conspire, collude, cooperate, consort.

collaborator n. **1 co-worker**, partner, associate, colleague, confederate, assistant. **2 sympathizer**, traitor, quisling, fifth columnist.

collapse v. **1 cave in**, fall in, subside, fall down, give (way), crumple, crumble, disintegrate. **2 faint**, pass out, black out, lose consciousness. **3 go to pieces**, break down, be overcome; informal crack up. **4 fail**, break down, fall through, fold, founder; informal flop, fizzle out.
•n. **1 cave-in**, disintegration. **2 breakdown**, failure.

colleague n. **co-worker**, fellow worker, workmate, teammate, associate, partner, collaborator, ally, confederate.

collect v. **1** he collected up the rubbish: **gather**, accumulate, assemble, amass, stockpile, pile up, heap up, store (up), hoard, save. **2** a crowd soon collected: **gather**, assemble, meet, muster, congregate, convene, converge. **3 fetch**, pick up, go/come and get, call for, meet.
– OPPOSITES distribute, disperse.

collected adj. **calm**, cool, self-possessed, self-controlled, composed, poised, serene, tranquil, relaxed; informal laid-back.
– OPPOSITES excited.

collection n. **1 hoard**, pile, heap, stock, store, stockpile, accumulation, reserve, supply, bank, pool, fund; informal stash.

2 group, crowd, body, gathering, knot, cluster. **3 anthology**, compilation, miscellany, treasury. **4 appeal**; informal whip-round.

collective adj. **common**, shared, joint, combined, mutual, communal, pooled, united, allied, cooperative, collaborative.
– OPPOSITES individual.

collide v. **crash**, hit, strike, run into, bump into.

collision n. **crash**, accident, smash; N. Amer. wreck; informal pile-up; Brit. informal shunt, prang.

colloquial adj. **informal**, conversational, everyday, familiar, popular, casual, idiomatic, slangy, vernacular.
– OPPOSITES formal.

colonize v. **settle (in)**, people, populate, occupy, take over, invade.

colony n. **territory**, dependency, protectorate, satellite, settlement, outpost, province.

colossal adj. **huge**, massive, enormous, gigantic, giant, mammoth, vast, immense, monumental, mountainous; informal monster, whopping, humongous; Brit. informal ginormous.
– OPPOSITES tiny.

colour n. **1 hue**, shade, tint, tone, coloration. **2 paint**, pigment, colourant, dye, stain.
•v. **1 tint**, dye, stain, tinge. **2 influence**, affect, taint, warp, skew, distort.

WORD LINKS
relating to colour: chromatic

colourful adj. **1 bright**, vivid, vibrant, brilliant, radiant, gaudy, garish, multicoloured, psychedelic; *informal* jazzy. **2** *a colourful account:* **vivid**, graphic, lively, animated, dramatic, fascinating, interesting, stimulating, scintillating, evocative.
– OPPOSITES drab, dull.

column n. **1 pillar**, post, support, upright, pier, pile. **2 article**, piece, feature. **3 line**, file, queue, procession, convoy; *informal* crocodile.

comb v. **1 groom**, brush, untangle, smooth, straighten, neaten, tidy, arrange. **2 search**, scour, explore, sweep.

combat n. **battle**, fighting, action, hostilities, conflict, war, warfare.
• v. **fight**, battle, tackle, attack, counter, resist.

combative adj. **aggressive**, pugnacious, antagonistic, quarrelsome, argumentative, hostile, truculent, belligerent; *informal* spoiling for a fight.
– OPPOSITES conciliatory.

combination n. **mixture**, mix, blend, fusion, amalgamation, amalgam, merger, marriage, synthesis.

combine v. **1 mix**, blend, fuse, amalgamate, integrate, merge, marry. **2 unite**, collaborate, join forces, get together, team up.

come v. **1** *come and listen:* **approach**, advance, draw close/

closer, draw near/nearer. **2** *they came last night:* **arrive**, get here/there, make it, appear, turn up, materialize; *informal* show (up), roll up. **3** *they came to a stream:* **reach**, arrive at, get to, come across, run across, happen on, chance on, come upon, stumble on, end up at; *informal* wind up at. **4** *she comes from Belgium:* **be from**, be a native of, hail from, live in, reside in. **5 happen**, occur, take place, come about, fall, crop up.
– OPPOSITES go, leave.
□ **come about** happen, occur, take place, transpire, fall, arise. **come across** meet, run into, run across, come upon, chance on, stumble on, happen on, discover, encounter, find; *informal* bump into. **come on** progress, develop, shape up, take shape, come along, turn out, improve.

comeback n. **return**, recovery, resurgence, rally, upturn; *Brit.* fightback.

comedian n. **1 comic**, comedienne, funny man/woman, humorist, stand-up; *N. Amer.* tummler. **2 joker**, wit, wag, comic, clown; *informal* laugh, hoot.

comedy n. **humour**, fun, hilarity, funny side, laughs, jokes.
– OPPOSITES tragedy.

comfort n. **1 ease**, repose, luxury, prosperity. **2 consolation**, condolence, sympathy, commiseration, support, reassurance, cheer.

c

– OPPOSITES discomfort.

• v. **console**, support, reassure, soothe, calm, cheer, hearten.

– OPPOSITES distress, depress.

comfortable adj. **1** affluent, prosperous, well-to-do, pleasant, luxurious, opulent. **2** cosy, snug, warm, pleasant, agreeable, homely; informal comfy. **3** loose, loose-fitting, roomy, casual; informal comfy.

comforting adj. soothing, reassuring, calming, heartening, cheering.

– OPPOSITES upsetting.

comic adj. **humorous**, funny, amusing, hilarious, comical, zany, witty, droll.

– OPPOSITES serious.

• n. **comedian**, comedienne, funny man/woman, humorist, wit, joker.

comical adj. **1** funny, humorous, droll, witty, comic, amusing, entertaining; informal wacky. **2** absurd, silly, ridiculous, laughable, ludicrous, preposterous, foolish; informal crazy.

– OPPOSITES serious.

coming adj. forthcoming, imminent, impending, approaching.

• n. **approach**, advance, advent, arrival, appearance, emergence.

command v. **1** order, tell, direct, instruct, call on, require, charge, enjoin, ordain; old use bid. **2** be in charge of, be in command of, head, lead, control, direct, manage, supervise, oversee; informal head up.

• n. **1** order, instruction, direction, directive, injunction,

decree, edict, dictate, mandate, commandment, fiat. **2** he had 160 men under his command: **authority**, control, charge, power, direction, dominion, guidance, leadership, rule, government, management, supervision, jurisdiction. **3** knowledge, mastery, grasp, comprehension, understanding.

commander n. **leader**, head, chief, overseer, director, controller; informal boss, skipper, head honcho; Brit. informal gaffer, guv'nor.

commanding adj. **dominant**, controlling, superior, powerful, advantageous, favourable.

commemorate v. **celebrate**, remember, recognize, acknowledge, observe, mark, pay tribute to, pay homage to, honour, salute.

commence v. **begin**, inaugurate, start, initiate, launch into, open, get the ball rolling, get going, get under way, get off the ground, set about, embark on; informal kick off.

– OPPOSITES conclude.

commend v. **1** praise, compliment, congratulate, applaud, salute, honour, sing the praises of, pay tribute to. **2** recommend, endorse, vouch for, speak for, support, back.

– OPPOSITES criticize.

commendable adj. admirable, praiseworthy, creditable, laudable, meritorious, exemplary, honourable, respectable.

– OPPOSITES reprehensible.

comment n. **1 remark**, observation, statement, pronouncement, judgement, reflection, opinion, view. **2 discussion**, debate, interest. **3 note**, annotation, commentary, footnote, gloss, explanation.
• v. **remark**, observe, say, state, note, point out, mention, interject; formal opine.

commentary n. **1 narration**, description, report, review, voice-over. **2 explanation**, elucidation, interpretation, analysis, assessment, review, criticism, notes, comments.

commentator n. **1 reporter**, narrator, journalist, newscaster. **2 analyst**, pundit, critic, columnist, leader-writer, opinion-former, monitor, observer.

commerce n. **trade**, trading, business, dealing, buying and selling, traffic, trafficking.

commercial adj. **1 trade**, trading, business, mercantile, sales. **2 profit-making**, materialistic, mercenary.

commission n. **1 percentage**, share, premium, fee, bonus, royalty; informal cut, rake-off, slice; Brit. informal whack. **2 contract**, engagement, assignment, booking, job. **3 committee**, board, council, panel, body.
• v. **1 engage**, contract, book, employ, hire, recruit, take on, retain, appoint. **2 order**, place an order for, pay for.

commit v. **1 carry out**, do, perpetrate, engage in, execute,

accomplish, be responsible for; informal pull off. **2 entrust**, consign, assign, deliver, hand over. **3 consign**, send, confine.

commitment n. **1 responsibility**, obligation, duty, liability, engagement, tie. **2 dedication**, devotion, allegiance, loyalty. **3 promise**, vow, pledge, undertaking.

committed adj. **devoted**, dedicated, staunch, loyal, faithful, devout, firm, steadfast, unwavering, passionate, ardent, sworn.
– OPPOSITES apathetic.

common adj. **1** *a common occurrence*: **frequent**, regular, everyday, normal, usual, ordinary, familiar, standard, commonplace, average, unexceptional, typical. **2** *a common belief*: **widespread**, general, universal, popular, mainstream, prevalent, rife, established, conventional, accepted. **3 collective**, communal, shared, community, public, popular, general. **4 uncouth**, vulgar, coarse, rough, uncivilized, unsophisticated, unrefined, inferior, plebeian; informal plebby.
– OPPOSITES unusual, rare.

commonplace adj. see **COMMON** sense 1.

common sense n. **good sense**, native wit, good judgement, level-headedness, prudence, wisdom; informal horse sense, nous; Brit. informal common; N. Amer. informal smarts.
– OPPOSITES stupidity.

commotion n. disturbance, uproar, disorder, confusion, rumpus, fuss, furore, hue and cry, stir, storm, chaos, havoc, pandemonium.

communal adj. 1 *a communal kitchen*: **shared**, joint, common, public, general. 2 *they farm on a communal basis*: **collective**, cooperative, community.
– OPPOSITES private, individual.

communicate v. 1 **liaise**, be in touch, be in contact, have dealings, talk, speak, interface. 2 **convey**, tell, relay, transmit, impart, pass on, report, recount, relate. 3 **transmit**, spread, transfer, pass on.

communication n. 1 **contact**, dealings, relations, connection, correspondence, dialogue, conversation. 2 **message**, statement, announcement, report, dispatch, bulletin, disclosure, communiqué, letter, correspondence.

communicative adj. **forthcoming**, expansive, expressive, unreserved, vocal, outgoing, frank, open, candid, talkative, chatty.

communist n. & adj. **collectivist**, Bolshevik, Marxist, Maoist, Soviet; informal, derogatory red, Commie.

community n. **society**, population, populace, people, public, residents, inhabitants, citizens.

compact¹ adj. 1 **dense**, tightly packed, compressed, thick, tight, firm, solid. 2 **neat**, small, handy, portable. 3 **concise**, succinct, condensed, brief, pithy, to the point, short and sweet; informal snappy.
– OPPOSITES loose, bulky, lengthy.
•v. **compress**, condense, pack down, tamp (down), flatten.

compact² n. **treaty**, pact, accord, agreement, contract, bargain, deal, settlement.

companion n. **comrade**, fellow, partner, associate, escort, compatriot, confederate, friend; informal pal, chum, crony; Brit. informal mate; N. Amer. informal buddy.

company n. 1 **firm**, business, corporation, establishment, agency, office, house, institution, concern, enterprise, consortium, syndicate; informal outfit. 2 **companionship**, fellowship, society, presence. 3 **unit**, section, detachment, corps, squad, platoon.

comparable adj. 1 **similar**, close, near, approximate, equivalent, proportionate. 2 *nobody is comparable with him*: **equal to**, as good as, in the same league as, on a level with, a match for.
– OPPOSITES incomparable.

compare v. 1 **contrast**, balance, set against, weigh up. 2 **liken**, equate, class with, bracket with. 3 **be as good as**, be comparable to, bear comparison with, be the equal of, match up to, be on a par with, be in the same league as, come close to, rival.

comparison n. resemblance, likeness, similarity, correspondence.

compartment n. bay, locker, recess, alcove, cell, cubicle, pod, pigeonhole, cubbyhole.

compass n. scope, range, extent, reach, span, breadth, ambit, limits, parameters, bounds.

compassion n. sympathy, empathy, understanding, fellow feeling, pity, care, concern, sensitivity, kindness.
– OPPOSITES indifference, cruelty.

compassionate adj. sympathetic, understanding, pitying, caring, sensitive, warm, loving, kind.
– OPPOSITES unsympathetic, uncaring.

compatible adj. well matched, (well) suited, like-minded, in tune, in harmony, in keeping, consistent, consonant; informal on the same wavelength.

compel v. force, pressure, coerce, dragoon, press, push, oblige, require, make; informal lean on, railroad, put the screws on.

compelling adj. 1 enthralling, captivating, gripping, riveting, spellbinding, mesmerizing, absorbing. 2 convincing, persuasive, cogent, irresistible, powerful, strong.
– OPPOSITES boring, weak.

compensate v. 1 recompense, repay, pay back, reimburse, remunerate, indemnify. 2 balance (out), counterbalance, counteract, offset, make up for, cancel out.

compensation n. recompense, repayment, reimbursement, remuneration, redress, amends, damages; N. Amer. informal comp.

compete v. 1 take part, participate, be a contestant, play, enter, go in for. 2 they had to compete with other firms: contend, vie, battle, jockey, go head to head, pit yourself against, challenge, take on.

competence n. 1 my technical competence: ability, capability, proficiency, accomplishment, expertise, skill, prowess; informal know-how. 2 the competence of the system: adequacy, suitability, fitness.

competent adj. 1 able, capable, proficient, adept, accomplished, skilful, skilled, expert. 2 fit, suitable, suited, appropriate, qualified, empowered, authorized.

competition n. 1 contest, tournament, championship, match, game, heat. 2 rivalry, competitiveness, conflict; informal keeping up with the Joneses. 3 opposition, rivals, other side, field, enemy.

competitive adj. 1 a competitive player: ambitious, zealous, keen, combative, aggressive; informal go-ahead. 2 a highly competitive industry: ruthless, aggressive, fierce, cut-throat; informal dog-eat-dog. 3 competitive prices: reasonable, moderate, keen, low, cheap, budget, bargain, rock-bottom, bargain-basement.

competitor n. **1 contestant**, contender, challenger, participant, entrant, player. **2 rival**, challenger, opponent, competition, opposition.

compile v. **assemble**, put together, make up, collate, compose, organize, arrange, gather, collect.

complacency n. **smugness**, self-satisfaction, self-congratulation, self-regard.

complacent adj. **smug**, self-satisfied, self-congratulatory, resting on your laurels, pleased with yourself.

complain v. **protest**, grumble, whine, bleat, carp, cavil, grouse, make a fuss, object, find fault; informal whinge, gripe, moan, bitch.

complaint n. **1 protest**, objection, grievance, grouse, grumble, criticism; informal gripe, whinge. **2 disorder**, disease, illness, sickness, ailment, infection, condition, problem, upset, trouble.

complement n. **1 accompaniment**, companion, addition, supplement, accessory, finishing touch. **2 amount**, contingent, capacity, allowance, quota.
•v. **accompany**, go with, round off, set off, suit, harmonize with, enhance, complete.

complementary adj. **harmonious**, compatible, corresponding, matching, reciprocal.

complete adj. **1 entire**, whole, full, total, uncut, unabridged, unexpurgated. **2 finished**, ended, concluded, completed; informal wrapped up, sewn up. **3 absolute**, utter, out-and-out, total, downright, prize, perfect, unqualified, unmitigated, sheer; N. Amer. full-bore.
– OPPOSITES partial, unfinished.
•v. **1 finish**, end, conclude, finalize, wind up, clinch; informal wrap up. **2 finish off**, round off, top off, crown, cap, add the finishing touch.

completely adv. **totally**, entirely, wholly, thoroughly, fully, utterly, absolutely, perfectly, downright.

complex adj. **1 compound**, composite, multiplex. **2 complicated**, involved, intricate, convoluted, elaborate, difficult; Brit. informal fiddly.
– OPPOSITES simple.
•n. **1 network**, system, nexus, web. **2** (informal) **obsession**, fixation, preoccupation, neurosis; informal hang-up, thing.

complexion n. **1 skin**, skin colour/tone, colouring. **2 kind**, nature, character, colour, persuasion, outlook.

complicate v. **make (more) difficult**, make complicated, mix up, confuse, muddle, obscure.
– OPPOSITES simplify.

complicated adj. **complex**, involved, intricate, convoluted, elaborate, difficult, knotty,

tortuous, labyrinthine, Byzantine; Brit. informal fiddly.
- OPPOSITES simple, straightforward.

complication n. **difficulty**, problem, obstacle, hurdle, stumbling block, snag, catch, hitch; Brit. spanner in the works; informal headache.

compliment n. **tribute**, accolade, commendation, pat on the back; (**compliments**) praise, acclaim, admiration, flattery, congratulations.
- OPPOSITES criticism, insult.
- v. **praise**, pay tribute to, flatter, commend, acclaim, applaud, salute, congratulate.
- OPPOSITES criticize.

complimentary adj. **1 flattering**, appreciative, congratulatory, admiring, approving, favourable, glowing. **2 free (of charge)**, gratis; informal on the house.
- OPPOSITES critical.

comply v. **obey**, observe, abide by, adhere to, conform to, follow, respect, go along with.
- OPPOSITES disobey.

component n. **part**, piece, bit, element, constituent, ingredient, unit, module.

compose v. **1 write**, devise, make up, think up, produce, invent, pen, author. **2 organize**, arrange, construct, set out. **3 make up**, constitute, form, comprise.
□ **compose yourself** calm down, control yourself, regain your composure, pull yourself

together, steady yourself; informal get a grip.

composed adj. **calm**, collected, cool (as a cucumber), self-possessed, poised, serene, relaxed, at ease, unruffled, unperturbed; informal unflappable, together, laid-back.

composition n. **make-up**, **1** constitution, configuration, structure, formation, anatomy, organization. **2 work (of art)**, creation, opus, piece. **3 writing**, creation, formulation, compilation. **4 essay**, paper, study, piece of writing; N. Amer. theme. **5 arrangement**, layout, proportions, balance, symmetry.

composure n. **self-control**, self-possession, calm, equanimity, equilibrium, serenity, tranquillity, poise, presence of mind, sangfroid, placidness, impassivity; informal cool.

compound n. **amalgam**, blend, mixture, mix, alloy.
- adj. **composite**, complex, multiple.
- OPPOSITES simple.
- v. **1 mix**, combine, blend. **2 aggravate**, exacerbate, worsen, add to, augment, intensify, heighten, increase.

comprehend v. **understand**, grasp, see, take in, follow, make sense of, fathom; informal work out, figure out, get.

comprehensible adj. **intelligible**, understandable, lucid, coherent, accessible, self-explanatory, clear, plain, straightforward.
- OPPOSITES incomprehensible.

comprehension n. under-standing, grasp, mastery, con-ception, knowledge, awareness.
– OPPOSITES ignorance.

comprehensive adj. **inclusive**, all-inclusive, complete, full, thorough, extensive, all-embracing, blanket, exhaustive, detailed, sweeping, wholesale, broad, wide-ranging.
– OPPOSITES limited.

compress v. **1 squeeze**, press, squash, crush, compact. **2 shorten**, abridge, condense, abbreviate, contract, telescope, summarize, precis.
– OPPOSITES expand, pad out.

comprise v. **1** the country comprises twenty states: **consist of**, be made up of, be composed of, contain. **2** this breed comprises half the herd: **make up**, consti-tute, form, account for.

compromise n. **agreement**, understanding, settlement, terms, deal, trade-off, bargain, middle ground.
•v. **1 meet each other halfway**, come to an understanding, make a deal, make concessions, find a happy medium, strike a balance. **2 undermine**, weaken, damage, harm, jeopardize, prejudice.

compulsion n. **1** he is under no compulsion to go: **obligation**, pressure, coercion. **2 urge**, impulse, need, desire, drive, obsession, fixation, addiction.

compulsive adj. **1** a compulsive desire: **irresistible**, uncontroll-able, compelling, overwhelm-ing. **2** compulsive eating: **obsessive**, obsessional, addictive, uncontrollable. **3 inveterate**, chronic, incor-rigible, incurable, hopeless, persistent, habitual; informal pathological. **4 fascinating**, compelling, gripping, riveting, engrossing, enthralling, captivating.

compulsory adj. **obligatory**, mandatory, required, requisite, necessary, binding, enforced, prescribed.
– OPPOSITES optional.

compute v. **calculate**, work out, reckon, determine, evaluate, add up, total.

comrade n. **companion**, friend, colleague, associate, partner, ally; Brit. informal mate; N. Amer. informal buddy.

conceal v. **1** clouds concealed the sun: **hide**, screen, cover, obscure, block out, blot out, mask. **2** he concealed his true feelings: **keep secret**, hide, dis-guise, mask, veil, bottle up; informal keep a/the lid on.
– OPPOSITES reveal, confess.

concede v. **1 admit**, acknow-ledge, accept, allow, grant, recognize, own, confess, agree. **2 surrender**, yield, give up, relinquish, hand over.
– OPPOSITES deny.

conceit n. **vanity**, pride, arrogance, egotism, self-importance, narcissism, self-admiration.
– OPPOSITES humility.

conceited → concession

conceited adj. **vain**, proud, arrogant, egotistic, self-important, narcissistic, full of yourself, swollen-headed, boastful, cocky, self-satisfied, smug; *informal* big-headed, stuck-up.

conceivable adj. **imaginable**, possible, plausible, credible, believable, feasible.

conceive v. **1 think up**, think of, dream up, devise, formulate, design, create, develop; *informal* cook up. **2 imagine**, envisage, visualize, picture.

concentrate v. **1 focus on**, pay attention to, give your attention to, put your mind to, keep your mind on, be absorbed in, be engrossed in, be immersed in. **2 collect**, gather, congregate, converge, mass, rally.
- OPPOSITES indifference.

concentrated adj. **1 strenuous**, concerted, intensive, all-out, intense. **2 condensed**, reduced, undiluted, strong.
- OPPOSITES half-hearted, diluted.

concentration n. **close attention**, attentiveness, application, single-mindedness, absorption.
- OPPOSITES inattention.

concept n. **idea**, notion, conception, abstraction, theory, hypothesis.

conception n. **1 pregnancy**, fertilization, impregnation, insemination. **2 inception**, genesis, origination, creation, invention, beginning, origin. **3 plan**, idea, notion, scheme, project, proposal, intention, aim.

concern v. **1 be about**, deal with, cover, relate to, pertain to. **2 affect**, involve, be relevant to, apply to, have a bearing on, impact on. **3 worry**, disturb, trouble, bother, perturb, unsettle.
- n. **1 anxiety**, worry, disquiet, apprehensiveness, unease, misgiving. **2 care**, consideration, solicitude, sympathy. **3 responsibility**, business, affair, duty, job; *informal* bailiwick; *Brit. informal* lookout. **4** *issues of concern to women*: **interest**, importance, relevance, significance. **5 firm**, business, company, enterprise, operation, corporation; *informal* outfit.

concerned adj. **1 worried**, anxious, upset, troubled, uneasy, bothered. **2 interested**, involved, affected, implicated.
- OPPOSITES unconcerned.

concerning prep. **about**, regarding, relating to, with reference to, referring to, with regard to, as regards, touching, in connection with, re, apropos.

concerted adj. **1** *a concerted effort:* **strenuous**, vigorous, intensive, all-out, intense, concentrated. **2** *a concerted action:* **joint**, united, collaborative, collective, combined, cooperative.

concession n. **1 compromise**, accommodation, trade-off, sop. **2 reduction**, cut, discount, deduction, rebate; *informal* break. **3 right**, privilege, licence, permit, franchise, warrant.

concise adj. **succinct**, pithy, brief, abridged, condensed, abbreviated, compact, potted.
– OPPOSITES lengthy.

conclude v. **1 finish**, end, come/bring to an end, draw to a close, close, wind up, terminate, stop, cease; informal wrap up. **2 settle**, clinch, finalize, tie up; informal sew up. **3 deduce**, infer, gather, judge, decide, surmise; N. Amer. figure.
– OPPOSITES begin.

conclusion n. **1 end**, ending, finish, close. **2 settlement**, clinching, completion, arrangement. **3 deduction**, inference, interpretation, judgement, verdict.
– OPPOSITES beginning.

conclusive adj. **incontrovertible**, undeniable, indisputable, irrefutable, unquestionable, convincing, certain, decisive, definitive, definite, positive, categorical, unequivocal.
– OPPOSITES unconvincing.

concoct v. **make up**, dream up, fabricate, invent, devise, formulate, hatch, brew; informal cook up.

concrete adj. **1 solid**, material, real, physical, tangible. **2 definite**, specific, firm, positive, conclusive, definitive.
– OPPOSITES abstract, imaginary.

concur v. **agree**, be in agreement, accord, be in sympathy, see eye to eye, be of the same mind, be of the same opinion.
– OPPOSITES disagree.

condemn v. **1 censure**, criticize, denounce, deplore, decry; informal slam; Brit. informal slate, slag off. **2 his illness condemned him to a lonely childhood: doom**, destine, damn, sentence.
– OPPOSITES praise.

condense v. **abridge**, compress, summarize, shorten, cut, abbreviate, edit.
– OPPOSITES expand.

condescend v. **1 patronize**, talk down to, look down your nose at, look down on. **2 he condescended to see us: deign**, stoop, lower yourself, demean yourself, consent.

condescending adj. **patronizing**, supercilious, superior, disdainful, lofty, haughty; informal snooty, stuck-up; Brit. informal toffee-nosed.

condition n. **1 state**, shape, order, fitness, health, form; Brit. informal nick, fettle. **2 circumstances**, surroundings, environment, situation, state of affairs, position. **3 disorder**, problem, complaint, illness, disease, ailment, malady. **4 stipulation**, constraint, prerequisite, precondition, requirement, term, proviso.
• v. **train**, teach, educate, guide, accustom, adapt, habituate, mould.

conditional adj. **qualified**, dependent, contingent, with reservations, limited, provisional, provisory.

condone v. **disregard**, accept, allow, let pass, turn a blind eye

to, overlook, forget, forgive, pardon, excuse.
- OPPOSITES condemn.

conducive adj. favourable, beneficial, advantageous, opportune, encouraging, promising, convenient, good, helpful, instrumental.
- OPPOSITES unfavourable.

conduct n. 1 **behaviour**, actions, deeds, doings, exploits. 2 **management**, running, direction, control, supervision, regulation, administration, organization, coordination, handling.
•v. 1 **manage**, direct, run, administer, organize, coordinate, orchestrate, handle, carry out/on. 2 **escort**, guide, lead, usher, steer. 3 **transmit**, convey, carry, channel.
□ **conduct yourself** behave, act, acquit yourself, bear yourself.

confer v. 1 **bestow**, present, grant, award, honour with. 2 **consult**, talk, speak, converse, have a chat, deliberate, compare notes.

conference n. **meeting**, congress, convention, seminar, discussion, council, forum, summit.

confess v. 1 **admit**, acknowledge, reveal, disclose, divulge, own up, plead guilty, accept the blame; informal come clean. 2 *I confess I don't know:* **acknowledge**, admit, concede, grant, allow, own.
- OPPOSITES deny.

confide v. reveal, disclose, divulge, impart, declare, vouchsafe, tell, confess.

confidence n. 1 **trust**, belief, faith, credence. 2 **self-assurance**, self-confidence, self-possession, assertiveness, self-belief, conviction.
- OPPOSITES distrust, doubt.

confident adj. 1 **sure**, certain, positive, convinced, in no doubt, satisfied. 2 **self-assured**, assured, self-confident, positive, assertive, self-possessed.

confidential adj. **private**, personal, intimate, quiet, secret, sensitive, classified, restricted; informal hush-hush.

confine v. 1 **enclose**, incarcerate, imprison, intern, hold captive, cage, lock up, coop up. 2 **restrict**, limit.

confirm v. 1 **corroborate**, verify, prove, substantiate, justify, vindicate, bear out. 2 **affirm**, reaffirm, assert, assure someone, repeat. 3 **ratify**, approve, endorse, validate, sanction, authorize.
- OPPOSITES contradict, deny.

confiscate v. **impound**, seize, commandeer, requisition, appropriate, expropriate, take, sequestrate.

conflict n. 1 **dispute**, quarrel, squabble, disagreement, clash, feud, discord, friction, strife, antagonism, hostility. 2 **war**, campaign, fighting, engagement, struggle, hostilities, warfare, combat. 3 *a conflict between*

work and home life: **clash**, incompatibility, friction, mismatch, variance, contradiction.
- OPPOSITES agreement, peace, harmony.
•v. **clash**, be incompatible, be at odds, differ, diverge, disagree, collide.

conflicting adj. contradictory, incompatible, inconsistent, irreconcilable, contrary, opposite, opposing, clashing.

conform v. 1 visitors have to conform to our rules: **comply with**, abide by, obey, observe, follow, keep to, stick to, adhere to, uphold, heed, accept, go along with. 2 **fit in** behave (yourself), toe the line, obey the rules; informal play by the rules.
- OPPOSITES flout, rebel.

confound v. baffle, bewilder, mystify, bemuse, perplex, puzzle, confuse, dumbfound, throw; informal flabbergast, flummox.

confront v. 1 challenge, square up to, face (up to), come face to face with, meet, accost, stand up to, tackle. 2 **face**, bedevil, beset, plague, bother, trouble, threaten. 3 they must confront these issues: **tackle**, address, face (up to), get to grips with, grapple with, deal with, sort out.
- OPPOSITES evade.

confrontation n. conflict, clash, fight, battle, encounter, head-to-head; informal set-to, run-in, dust-up, showdown.

confuse v. 1 **bewilder**, baffle, mystify, bemuse, perplex, puzzle, nonplus; informal flummox,

faze. 2 the authors have confused the issue: **complicate**, muddle, blur, obscure, cloud. 3 some confuse strokes with heart attacks: **mix up**, muddle up, mistake for.
- OPPOSITES enlighten, simplify.

confused adj. 1 puzzled, bemused, bewildered, perplexed, baffled, mystified; informal flummoxed. 2 disorientated, bewildered, muddled, addled, befuddled, demented, senile. 3 a confused recollection: **vague**, unclear, indistinct, imprecise, blurred, hazy, dim. 4 disorderly, disorganized, untidy, jumbled, mixed up, chaotic, topsy-turvy, tangled; informal higgledy-piggledy; Brit. informal shambolic.
- OPPOSITES clear, lucid.

confusion n. 1 bewilderment, bafflement, perplexity, puzzlement, bemusement, mystification, befuddlement, disorientation, uncertainty. 2 disorder, disarray, muddle, mess, chaos, mayhem, pandemonium, turmoil; informal shambles.
- OPPOSITES clarity, order.

congeal v. coagulate, clot, thicken, cake, set, gel.

congenial adj. agreeable, pleasant, friendly, amicable, amiable, nice.
- OPPOSITES unfriendly, unpleasant.

congested adj. blocked, clogged, choked, jammed, obstructed, crowded, overcrowded, overflowing,

packed; informal snarled up, gridlocked.
– OPPOSITES clear.

congratulate v. **compliment**, wish someone happiness, pay tribute to, pat on the back, take your hat off to, praise, applaud, salute, honour.
– OPPOSITES criticize.

congratulations pl. n. **best wishes**, compliments, greetings, felicitations.

congregate v. **assemble**, gather, collect, come together, convene, rally, muster, meet, cluster, group.
– OPPOSITES disperse.

conjure v. **1 produce**, magic, summon. **2** *the picture that his words conjured up:* **bring to mind**, call to mind, evoke, summon up, suggest.

connect v. **1 attach**, join, fasten, fix, link, hook (up), secure, hitch, stick. **2 associate**, link, couple, identify, relate to.
– OPPOSITES detach.

connection n. **1 link**, relationship, relation, interconnection, interdependence, association, bond, tie, tie-in, correspondence. **2** *he has the right connections:* **contact**, friend, acquaintance, ally, colleague, associate, relation.

connive v. **1 ignore**, overlook, disregard, pass over, take no notice of, turn a blind eye to. **2 conspire**, collude, collaborate, plot, scheme.

conniving adj. **scheming**, cunning, calculating, devious, wily, sly, artful, manipulative, Machiavellian, deceitful.

connotation n. **overtone**, undertone, undercurrent, implication, nuance, hint, echo, association.

conquer v. **1 defeat**, beat, vanquish, triumph over, overcome, overwhelm, overpower, overthrow, subdue, subjugate. **2** *Peru was conquered by Spain:* **seize**, take (over), appropriate, capture, occupy, invade, annex, overrun. **3 overcome**, get the better of, control, master, deal with, cope with, rise above; informal lick.

conquest n. **1 defeat**, overthrow, subjugation. **2 seizure**, takeover, capture, occupation, invasion, annexation.

conscience n. **moral sense**, morals, sense of right and wrong, standards, values, principles, ethics, beliefs, scruples, qualms.

conscientious adj. **diligent**, industrious, punctilious, painstaking, dedicated, careful, meticulous, thorough, attentive, hard-working, rigorous, scrupulous.
– OPPOSITES casual.

conscious adj. **1 aware**, awake, responsive; informal with us. **2 deliberate**, purposeful, knowing, considered, calculated, wilful, premeditated.
– OPPOSITES unaware, unconscious.

consecutive adj. **successive**, succeeding, in succession, running, in a row, straight; informal on the trot.

consensus n. **1 agreement**, unanimity, harmony, accord, unity, solidarity. *the consensus was that they should act:* **general opinion**, common view.
– OPPOSITES disagreement.

consent n. **1 agreement**, assent, acceptance, approval, permission, authorization, sanction; informal go-ahead, green light, OK.
– OPPOSITES dissent.
•v. **agree**, assent, submit, allow, sanction, approve, go along with.
– OPPOSITES forbid, refuse.

consequence n. **1 result**, upshot, outcome, effect, repercussion, ramification, product, end result. **2** *the past is of no consequence:* **importance**, import, significance, account, value, concern.
– OPPOSITES cause.

consequent adj. **resulting**, resultant, ensuing, consequential, following, subsequent.

consequently adv. **as a result**, as a consequence, so, thus, therefore, accordingly, hence, for this/that reason, because of this/that.

conservation n. **preservation**, protection, safe keeping, husbandry, upkeep, maintenance, repair, restoration.

conservative adj. **1 right-wing**, reactionary, traditionalist, old-fashioned, dyed-in-the-wool, hidebound, unadventurous, set in your ways; informal stick-in-the-mud. **2 conventional**, sober, modest, sensible, restrained; informal square.
– OPPOSITES socialist, radical.

conserve v. **preserve**, protect, save, safeguard, keep, look after, sustain, husband.
– OPPOSITES squander.

consider v. **1 think about**, contemplate, reflect on, mull over, ponder, deliberate on, chew over, meditate on, ruminate on, evaluate, weigh up, appraise, take account of, bear in mind; informal size up. **2 deem**, think, believe, judge, rate, count, find, regard as, hold to be, reckon to be, view as, see as.

considerable adj. **sizeable**, substantial, appreciable, significant, plentiful, goodly; informal tidy.
– OPPOSITES paltry.

considerably adv. **greatly**, (very) much, a great deal, a lot, lots, significantly, substantially, appreciably, markedly, noticeably; informal plenty.

considerate adj. **attentive**, thoughtful, solicitous, kind, unselfish, caring, polite, sensitive.

consideration n. **1 thought**, deliberation, reflection, contemplation, examination, inspection, scrutiny, analysis, discussion, attention. **2 factor**, issue, matter, concern, aspect, feature. **3 attentiveness**, concern, care, thoughtfulness, solicitude, understanding, respect, sensitivity.

considering prep. **bearing in mind**, taking into consideration, taking into account, in view of, in the light of.

consist v.
□ **consist of** be composed of, be made up of, be formed of, comprise, include, contain.

consistent adj. **1 constant**, regular, uniform, steady, stable, even, unchanging. **2** *her injuries were consistent with a knife attack:* **compatible**, in tune, in line, corresponding to, conforming to, consonant with.
– OPPOSITES irregular, incompatible.

consolation n. **comfort**, solace, sympathy, pity, commiseration, relief, encouragement, reassurance.

console v. **comfort**, sympathize with, commiserate with, show compassion for, help, support, cheer (up), hearten, encourage, reassure, soothe.
– OPPOSITES upset.

consolidate v. **1 strengthen**, secure, stabilize, reinforce, fortify. **2 combine**, unite, merge, integrate, amalgamate, fuse, synthesize.

consort v.
□ **consort with** associate with, keep company with, mix with, socialize with, fraternize with, have dealings with.

conspicuous adj. **obvious**, evident, apparent, visible, noticeable, clear, plain, marked, patent, blatant.
– OPPOSITES inconspicuous.

conspiracy n. **plot**, scheme, intrigue, plan, collusion.

conspire v. **1 plot**, scheme, intrigue, manoeuvre, plan. **2 combine**, unite, join forces, work together.

constant adj. **1** *constant noise:* **continuous**, persistent, sustained, ceaseless, unceasing, perpetual, incessant, neverending, eternal, endless, nonstop. **2** *a constant speed:* **consistent**, regular, steady, uniform, even, invariable, unvarying, unchanging. **3 faithful**, loyal, devoted, true, fast, firm, unswerving.
– OPPOSITES intermittent, variable, fickle.

consternation n. **dismay**, distress, disquiet, discomposure, surprise, alarm, fear, fright, shock.

constitute v. **1 comprise**, make up, form, account for. **2 amount to**, be tantamount to, be equivalent to, represent. **3 establish**, inaugurate, found, create, set up.

constitution n. **1 composition**, make-up, structure, construction, arrangement, configuration, formation, anatomy. **2 health**, condition, strength, stamina, build, physique.

constraint n. **1 restriction**, limitation, curb, check, restraint, control. **2 inhibition**,

uneasiness, embarrassment, self-consciousness, awkwardness.
- OPPOSITES freedom, ease.

constrict v. narrow, tighten, compress, contract, squeeze, strangle.
- OPPOSITES expand, dilate.

construct v. 1 build, erect, put up, set up, assemble, fabricate. 2 formulate, create, form, put together, devise, compose, work out, frame.
- OPPOSITES demolish.

construction n. 1 structure, building, edifice, work. 2 interpretation, explanation, analysis, reading, meaning; informal take.

constructive adj. useful, helpful, productive, positive, practical, valuable, profitable, worthwhile.

consult v. 1 seek advice from, ask, call (on), turn to; informal pick someone's brains. 2 confer, talk things over, communicate, deliberate, compare notes. 3 refer to, look at, check.

consultant n. adviser, expert, specialist, authority.

consultation n. 1 discussion, talk(s), dialogue, debate, negotiation, deliberation. 2 meeting, talk, discussion, interview, audience, hearing.

consume v. 1 eat, devour, swallow, gobble up, wolf down, guzzle, drink. 2 use (up), expend, deplete, exhaust, spend. 3 destroy, demolish, lay waste, raze, devastate, gut, ruin, wreck. 4 eat up, devour, grip, overwhelm, absorb, obsess, preoccupy.

consumer n. buyer, purchaser, customer, shopper, user.

contact n. 1 communication, correspondence, connection, relations, dealings, touch. 2 connection, link, acquaintance, associate, friend.
-v. get in touch with, communicate with, approach, notify, speak to, write to, come forward; informal get hold of.

contagious adj. infectious, communicable, transmittable, transmissible; informal catching.

contain v. 1 hold, carry, enclose, accommodate, have room for. 2 include, comprise, incorporate, involve, consist of, be made up of, be composed of. 3 restrain, control, curb, rein in, suppress, stifle, swallow, bottle up, keep in check.

container n. receptacle, vessel, holder, repository.

contaminate v. pollute, taint, poison, stain, adulterate, defile, debase, corrupt.
- OPPOSITES purify.

contemplate v. 1 look at, gaze at, stare at, view, regard, examine, inspect, observe, survey, study, eye. 2 think about, ponder, reflect on, consider, mull over, muse on, dwell on, deliberate over, meditate on, ruminate on, chew over. 3 envisage, consider, think about, have in mind, intend, plan, propose.

contemplative adj. **thoughtful**, pensive, reflective, meditative, ruminative, introspective, brooding, deep/lost in thought.

contemporary adj. **1** *contemporary sources:* **of the time**, contemporaneous, concurrent, coexisting, coeval. **2** *contemporary society:* **modern**, present-day, present, current. **3** *a very contemporary design:* **modern**, up to date, up to the minute, fashionable, recent; informal trendy.
– OPPOSITES former, old-fashioned.

contempt n. **scorn**, disdain, derision, disgust, disrespect.
– OPPOSITES respect.

contemptible adj. **despicable**, detestable, beneath contempt, reprehensible, deplorable, unspeakable, disgraceful, shameful, ignominious, abject, low, mean, cowardly, discreditable, worthless, shabby, cheap.
– OPPOSITES admirable.

contemptuous adj. **scornful**, disdainful, derisive, mocking, sneering, scoffing, condescending, dismissive.
– OPPOSITES respectful.

contend v. **1 compete**, vie, battle, tussle, struggle, jostle, strive. **2 assert**, maintain, hold, claim, argue, insist, allege.
□ **contend with** cope with, struggle with, grapple with, deal with, take on, handle.

content[1] adj. **satisfied**, contented, pleased, gratified, fulfilled, happy, glad, cheerful, at ease, at peace, relaxed, comfortable, untroubled.
– OPPOSITES dissatisfied.
•v. **satisfy**, comfort, gratify, gladden, please, soothe, placate, appease, mollify.

content[2] n. **1 amount**, proportion, level. **2 constituents**, ingredients, components. **3 subject matter**, theme, argument, thesis, message, substance, material, ideas.

contented adj. see **CONTENT**[1].

contentious adj. **controversial**, debatable, disputed, open to debate, moot, vexed.

contentment n. **contentedness**, content, satisfaction, fulfilment, happiness, pleasure, cheerfulness, ease, comfort, well-being, peace.

contest n. **1 competition**, match, tournament, rally, race, game, bout. **2 fight**, battle, tussle, struggle, competition, race.
•v. **1** *he will contest the seat:* **compete for**, contend for, vie for, fight for. **2** *the parties contesting the election:* **compete in**, take part in, fight, enter. **3 oppose**, challenge, take issue with, question, call into question, object to.
– OPPOSITES accept.

contestant n. **competitor**, participant, player, contender, candidate, entrant.

context n. **circumstances**, conditions, frame of reference, factors, state of affairs, situation, background, scene, setting.

contingency n. eventuality, possibility, chance event, incident, occurrence, accident, emergency.

continual adj. **1** *continual breakdowns*: **frequent**, regular, repeated, constant, recurrent, recurring, habitual. **2** *continual pain*: **constant**, continuous, unremitting, unrelenting, non-stop, sustained, chronic, uninterrupted, incessant, ceaseless, unceasing, never-ending, unbroken, perpetual.
– OPPOSITES occasional, temporary.

continue v. **1** **carry on**, go on, keep on, persist, persevere, proceed, pursue, keep at; *informal* stick at. **2** *we hope to continue this relationship*: **maintain**, keep up, sustain, keep going, keep alive, preserve, perpetuate. **3** *his willingness to continue in office*: **remain**, stay, carry on, keep going. **4** *we continued our conversation*: **resume**, pick up, take up, carry on with, return to, revisit.
– OPPOSITES stop.

continuous adj. continual, persistent, sustained, ceaseless, unceasing, unremitting, unrelenting, perpetual, incessant, never-ending, eternal, endless, non-stop, unbroken, uninterrupted.
– OPPOSITES intermittent.

contort v. **twist**, bend out of shape, distort, misshape, warp, buckle, deform.

contract n. agreement, arrangement, commitment, settlement, understanding, compact, covenant, deal, bargain.
▸v. **1** **shrink**, diminish, reduce, decrease, dwindle, decline. **2** **tighten**, tense, flex, constrict, draw in. **3** **engage**, take on, hire, commission, employ. **4** **catch**, pick up, come/go down with, develop.
– OPPOSITES expand, relax, lengthen.

contraction n. **1** **shrinking**, shrinkage, decline, decrease, diminution, dwindling. **2** **tightening**, tensing, flexing. **3** **abbreviation**, short form, shortening.

contradict v. **1** **deny**, refute, rebut, dispute, challenge, counter. **2** **argue with**, go against, challenge, oppose.
– OPPOSITES confirm, agree with.

contradiction n. **1** **conflict**, clash, disagreement, inconsistency, mismatch. **2** **denial**, refutation, rebuttal, countering.
– OPPOSITES agreement, confirmation.

contradictory adj. **inconsistent**, incompatible, irreconcilable, opposed, opposite, contrary, conflicting, at variance.

contraption n. device, gadget, apparatus, machine, appliance, mechanism, invention, contrivance; *informal* gizmo, widget; *Brit. informal* gubbins.

contrary adj. **1** **opposite**, opposing, contradictory, clashing,

conflicting, antithetical, incompatible, irreconcilable. **2 perverse**, awkward, difficult, uncooperative, obstinate, pigheaded, intractable; Brit. informal bloody-minded, stroppy; N. Amer. informal balky.
– OPPOSITES compatible, accommodating.
•n. **opposite**, reverse, converse, antithesis.

contrast n. **1 difference**, dissimilarity, disparity, divergence, variance, distinction, comparison. **2 opposite**, antithesis, foil, complement.
– OPPOSITES similarity.
•v. **1 differ**, be at variance, be contrary, conflict, be at odds, disagree, clash. **2 compare**, juxtapose, measure, distinguish, differentiate.
– OPPOSITES resemble, liken.

contribute v. **give**, donate, put up, grant, provide, supply; informal chip in; Brit. informal stump up.
□ **contribute to** play a part in, be instrumental in, have a hand in, be conducive to, make for.

contribution n. **gift**, donation, offering, present, handout, grant, subsidy.

contributor n. **donor**, benefactor, supporter, backer, patron, sponsor.

contrite adj. **remorseful**, repentant, penitent, regretful, sorry, apologetic, rueful, sheepish, hangdog, ashamed, shamefaced.

contrive v. **1 create**, engineer, manufacture, devise, concoct, construct, fabricate, hatch. **2 manage**, find a way, engineer a way, arrange.
– OPPOSITES fail.

contrived adj. **forced**, strained, laboured, overdone, unnatural, artificial, false, affected.
– OPPOSITES natural.

control n. **1 power**, authority, command, dominance, sway, management, direction, leadership, rule, government, sovereignty, supremacy. **2 limit**, limitation, restriction, restraint, check, curb, regulation. **3 self-control**, self-restraint, composure, calm; informal cool.
•v. **1 run**, manage, direct, preside over, supervise, command, rule, govern, lead, dominate. **2** she struggled to control her temper: **restrain**, keep in check, curb, hold back, suppress, repress. **3** public spending was controlled: **limit**, restrict, curb, cap.

controversial adj. **disputed**, contentious, moot, debatable, arguable, vexed.

controversy n. **dispute**, disagreement, argument, debate, contention, quarrel, war of words, storm; Brit. informal row.

convalesce v. **recuperate**, get better, recover, get well, get back on your feet.

convene v. **1** he convened a meeting: **summon**, call, order. **2** the committee convened:

assemble, gather, meet, come together; formal foregather.

convenience n. **1 advantage**, benefit, expedience, suitability. **2 ease of use**, usefulness, utility, accessibility, availability.
– OPPOSITES inconvenience.

convenient adj. **1 suitable**, favourable, advantageous, appropriate, opportune, timely, expedient. **2 nearby**, handy, well situated, practical, useful, accessible.

convention n. **1 custom**, usage, practice, tradition, etiquette, protocol. **2 agreement**, accord, protocol, pact, treaty. **3 conference**, meeting, congress, assembly, gathering.

conventional adj. **1 orthodox**, traditional, established, accepted, customary, received, prevailing, normal, standard, regular, ordinary, usual, typical. **2 conservative**, traditional, conformist, old-fashioned; informal square, stick-in-the-mud. **3 unoriginal**, formulaic, predictable, unadventurous, run-of-the-mill, routine, pedestrian.
– OPPOSITES unorthodox, original.

converge v. meet, intersect, cross, connect, link up, join, merge.
– OPPOSITES diverge.
□ **converge on** meet at, arrive at, close in on, bear down on, descend on, approach, move towards.

conversation n. discussion, talk, chat, gossip, tête-à-tête,

exchange, dialogue; Brit. informal chinwag, natter.

conversion n. change, transformation, metamorphosis, alteration, adaptation, modification, redevelopment, rebuilding, remodelling.

convert v. **1 change**, transform, alter, adapt, turn, modify, redevelop, remodel, rebuild, reorganize, metamorphose. **2 win over**, convince, persuade, claim, redeem, save, reform, re-educate, proselytize, evangelize.

convey v. **1 transport**, carry, bring, take, fetch, move. **2 communicate**, pass on, impart, relate, relay, transmit, send. **3 express**, get across/over, put across/over, communicate, indicate.

convict v. find guilty, sentence.
– OPPOSITES acquit.
•n. **prisoner**, inmate, criminal, offender, felon; informal jailbird, con, (old) lag.

conviction n. **1 beliefs**, opinions, views, persuasion, ideals, position, stance, values. **2 assurance**, confidence, certainty.
– OPPOSITES diffidence.

convince v. **1** he convinced me I was wrong: **assure**, persuade, satisfy, prove to. **2** I convinced her to marry me: **persuade**, induce, prevail on, talk into, talk round, win over, coax, cajole.

convincing adj. **1 persuasive**, powerful, strong, forceful, compelling, cogent, plausible, irresistible, telling. **2** a convincing

win: resounding, emphatic, decisive, conclusive.
- OPPOSITES unconvincing.

convivial adj. **friendly**, genial, affable, amiable, congenial, agreeable, cordial, warm, sociable, outgoing, gregarious, cheerful.

convoy n. **group**, fleet, cavalcade, motorcade, cortège, caravan, line.

cook v. **prepare**, make, put together; informal fix, rustle up; Brit. informal knock up.

> **WORD LINKS**
> relating to cooking: culinary

cool adj. **1 chilly**, chill, bracing, cold, brisk, crisp, fresh; informal nippy; Brit. informal parky. **2 unenthusiastic**, lukewarm, tepid, indifferent, uninterested, apathetic. **3 unfriendly**, distant, remote, aloof, cold, chilly, frosty, unwelcoming; informal standoffish. **4 calm**, collected, composed, self-possessed, poised, serene, relaxed, at ease, unruffled, unperturbed; informal unflappable, together, laid-back.
- OPPOSITES warm, enthusiastic, friendly.
  - •n. **1 chill**, chilliness, coldness, coolness. **2** (informal) **self-control**, control, composure, self-possession, calmness, aplomb, poise.
- OPPOSITES warmth.
  - •v. **chill**, refrigerate, freeze.
- OPPOSITES warm.

cooperate v. **1 collaborate**, work together, pull together,

join forces, team up, unite, combine, pool resources. **2 assist**, help, lend a hand, be of service, do your bit; informal play ball.

cooperation n. **1 collaboration**, joint action, combined effort, teamwork, give and take, compromise. **2 assistance**, help.

cooperative adj. **1 collaborative**, collective, combined, joint, shared, united, concerted. **2 helpful**, eager to help, obliging, accommodating, willing.

coordinate v. **organize**, arrange, order, synchronize, bring together, orchestrate.

cope v. **1 manage**, survive, look after yourself, fend for yourself, shift for yourself, get by/through, hold your own. **2** his inability to cope with the situation: **deal with**, handle, manage, address, face (up to), confront, tackle, get to grips with.

copious adj. **abundant**, plentiful, ample, profuse, extensive, generous, lavish, liberal, overflowing, in abundance, numerous, many; informal galore; literary plenteous.
- OPPOSITES sparse.

copy n. **1 duplicate**, facsimile, photocopy; trademark Xerox. **2 replica**, reproduction, imitation, likeness, forgery, fake, counterfeit.
  - •v. **1 duplicate**, photocopy, xerox, photostat, reproduce. **2 reproduce**, replicate, forge, fake, counterfeit. **3 imitate**,

reproduce, emulate, mimic; informal rip off.

cord n. string, thread, line, rope, cable, wire, twine, yarn.

cordon n. barrier, line, chain, ring, circle.

☐ **cordon off** close off, seal off, fence off, separate off, isolate, enclose, encircle, surround.

core n. 1 *the earth's core:* centre, interior, middle, nucleus. 2 *the core of the argument:* heart, nucleus, nub, kernel, meat, essence, crux, pith, substance; informal nitty-gritty.

corner n. 1 bend, curve, turn, junction; Brit. hairpin bend. 2 district, region, area, quarter; informal neck of the woods.
•v. 1 surround, trap, hem in, pen in, cut off. 2 gain control of, take over, dominate, monopolize, capture; informal sew up.

corporation n. company, firm, business, concern, operation, conglomerate, group, chain, multinational.

corpse n. dead body, carcass, remains; informal stiff; Medicine cadaver.

correct adj. 1 right, accurate, exact, true, perfect; informal spot on. 2 proper, decent, right, respectable, decorous, seemly, suitable, appropriate, accepted.
– OPPOSITES wrong, improper.
•v. rectify, amend, put right, set right, amend, remedy, repair, reform, cure.

correction n. rectification, righting, amendment, repair, remedy, cure.

correctly adv. 1 accurately, right, properly, exactly, precisely. 2 properly, decorously, with decorum, decently, fittingly, appropriately, well.

correspond v. 1 be consistent, correlate, agree, accord, coincide, tally, tie in, match; informal square. 2 *a rank corresponding to a British sergeant:* be equivalent, be analogous, be comparable, equate. 3 exchange letters, write, communicate.

correspondence n. 1 parallel, correlation, agreement, consistency, conformity, similarity, resemblance, comparability. 2 letters, messages, mail, post, communication.

correspondent n. reporter, journalist, columnist, writer, contributor, commentator.

corresponding adj. equivalent, related, parallel, matching, comparable, analogous.

corrupt adj. 1 dishonest, unscrupulous, criminal, fraudulent, illegal, unlawful; informal crooked; Brit. informal bent. 2 immoral, depraved, degenerate, debauched, vice-ridden, perverted, dissolute.
– OPPOSITES honest, ethical, pure.
•v. deprave, pervert, lead astray, debauch, defile, pollute, sully.

corruption n. 1 dishonesty, unscrupulousness, double-dealing, fraud, misconduct, bribery, venality; N. Amer. payola; informal graft, sleaze. 2 immorality, depravity, vice, degeneracy,

perversion, debauchery, wickedness, evil, sin.
- OPPOSITES honesty, morality.

cosmetic adj. **superficial**, surface, skin-deep, outward, external.
- OPPOSITES fundamental.

cosmopolitan adj. **1 multicultural**, multiracial, international, worldwide, global. **2 sophisticated**, cultivated, cultured, worldly, suave, urbane.

cost n. **1 price**, fee, tariff, fare, toll, levy, charge, payment, value, rate, outlay; humorous damage. **2 sacrifice**, loss, toll, harm, damage, price. **3** we need to cover our costs: **expenses**, outgoings, overheads, expenditure, spend, outlay.
•v. **1 be priced at**, sell for, be valued at, fetch, come to, amount to; informal set someone back, go for. **2 price**, value, put a price/value/figure on.

costly adj. **1 expensive**, dear, high-cost, overpriced; informal steep, pricey. **2 catastrophic**, disastrous, calamitous, ruinous, damaging, harmful, deleterious.
- OPPOSITES cheap.

costume n. **clothes**, garments, outfit, ensemble, dress, clothing, attire, garb, uniform, livery; formal apparel.

cosy adj. **1 snug**, comfortable, warm, homely, welcoming, safe, sheltered, secure; informal comfy. **2 intimate**, relaxed, informal, friendly.

cottage n. **lodge**, chalet, cabin, shack, shanty; (in Russia) dacha; Scottish bothy; Austral. informal weekender.

cough v. **hack**, hawk, bark, clear your throat.
•n. **bark**, hack; informal frog in your throat.

council n. **1** the town council: **authority**, government, administration, executive, chamber, assembly; Brit. corporation. **2** the Schools Council: **committee**, board, commission, assembly, panel, synod.

counsel n. **1 advice**, guidance, counselling, recommendations, suggestions, direction. **2 barrister**, lawyer; Scottish advocate; N. Amer. attorney, counselor(-at-law).
•v. **advise**, recommend, advocate, encourage, warn, caution, guide.

count v. **1 add up**, reckon up, total, tally, compute; Brit. tot up. **2 include**, take into account/consideration, take account of, allow for. **3 consider**, think, feel, regard, look on as, view as, hold to be, judge, deem. **4 matter**, be important, be of consequence, be significant, signify, carry weight, rate.
□ **count on** rely on, depend on, bank on, be sure of, have confidence in, believe in, put your faith in, take for granted, take as read.

counter v. **1 respond to**, parry, hit back at, answer. **2 oppose**, dispute, argue against/with, contradict, challenge, contest.
- OPPOSITES support.

c

c

□ **counter to** against, in opposition to, contrary to, at variance with, in defiance of, in conflict with, at odds with.

counteract v. **offset**, counterbalance, cancel (out), work against, countervail, neutralize, nullify, prevent.

counterfeit adj. **fake**, pirate, bogus, forged, imitation; informal phoney.
– OPPOSITES genuine.
▪v. **fake**, forgery, copy, reproduction, imitation, fraud, sham; informal phoney.
– OPPOSITES original.
▪v. **fake**, forge, copy, reproduce, imitate, falsify.

counterpart n. **equivalent**, opposite number, peer, equal, parallel, complement, analogue, match, twin, mate, fellow.

countless adj. **innumerable**, numerous, untold, legion, numberless, limitless, incalculable; informal umpteen; N. Amer. informal gazillions of.
– OPPOSITES few.

country n. **1 nation**, state, kingdom, realm, land, territory, province. **2 people**, public, population, populace, citizens, nation; Brit. informal Joe Public. **3 terrain**, land, territory, landscape, countryside, scenery, surroundings, environment. **4 countryside**, provinces, rural areas, backwoods, hinterland; Austral./NZ outback, bush, back country; informal sticks.

countryside n. see **COUNTRY** senses 3, 4.

county n. **shire**, province, territory, region, district, area.

coup n. **1 takeover**, coup d'état, overthrow, palace revolution, rebellion, uprising. **2 success**, triumph, feat, masterstroke, accomplishment, achievement, scoop.

couple n. **1 pair**, duo, twosome, two, brace. **2 husband and wife**, twosome, partners, lovers; informal item.
▪v. **1 combine**, accompany, ally, mix, incorporate, add to. **2 connect**, attach, join, fasten, fix, link, secure, hook (up).
– OPPOSITES detach.

coupon n. **voucher**, token, ticket, slip.

courage n. **bravery**, pluck, valour, fearlessness, nerve, daring, audacity, boldness, grit, heroism, gallantry; informal guts; Brit. informal bottle.
– OPPOSITES cowardice.

courageous adj. **brave**, plucky, fearless, intrepid, valiant, heroic, undaunted, dauntless; informal gutsy, have-a-go.
– OPPOSITES cowardly.

course n. **1 route**, way, track, path, line, trail, trajectory, bearing, heading. **2 procedure**, plan (of action), course of action, practice, approach, technique, policy, strategy, tactic. **3 racecourse**, racetrack, track. **4 course of study**, curriculum, syllabus, classes, lectures, studies. **5 programme**, series, sequence, system, schedule, regime.

•v. **flow**, pour, stream, run, rush, gush, cascade, flood, roll.

◻ **of course** naturally, as you would expect, needless to say, as a matter of course, obviously, it goes without saying.

court n. **1 court of law**, law court, bench, bar, tribunal, assizes. **2 household**, retinue, entourage, train, courtiers, attendants.

•v. **1 cultivate**, flatter, curry favour with, wine and dine; informal butter up. **2 seek**, pursue, go after, strive for, solicit. **3 risk**, invite, attract, bring on yourself. **4** (dated) **woo**, go out with, date, go steady with.

> WORD LINKS
> relating to a court of law:
> forensic

courteous adj. **polite**, well mannered, civil, respectful, well behaved, gracious, obliging, considerate.
– OPPOSITES rude.

courtesy n. **politeness**, good manners, civility, respect, grace, consideration, thought.

cove n. **bay**, inlet, fjord.

cover v. **1 protect**, shield, shelter, hide, conceal, mask, screen, veil, obscure, spread over, extend over, overlay. **2 cake**, coat, encrust, plaster, smother, blanket, carpet, shroud. **3 deal with**, consider, take in, include, involve, incorporate, embrace.
– OPPOSITES reveal.

•n. **1** a protective cover: **covering**, sleeve, wrapping, wrapper, envelope, sheath, housing,

jacket, casing, cowling, canopy. **2** a manhole cover: **lid**, top, cap. **3** a book cover: **binding**, jacket, dust jacket, dust cover, wrapper. **4 coating**, coat, covering, layer, carpet, blanket, film, sheet, veneer, crust, skin, cloak, mantle, veil, pall, shroud. **5 shelter**, protection, refuge, sanctuary.

covert adj. **secret**, furtive, clandestine, surreptitious, stealthy, cloak-and-dagger, backstairs, hidden, concealed, private, undercover, underground; informal hush-hush.
– OPPOSITES overt.

covet v. **desire**, yearn for, crave, have your heart set on, long for, hanker after/for, hunger after/for, thirst for.

coward n. **mouse**, baby; informal chicken, scaredy-cat, yellow-belly, sissy; Brit. informal big girl's blouse; N. Amer. informal pantywaist.

cowardly adj. **faint-hearted**, lily-livered, spineless, craven, timid, timorous, fearful; informal yellow, chicken, gutless, yellow-bellied.
– OPPOSITES brave.

cower v. **cringe**, shrink, flinch, crouch, blench.

coy adj. **demure**, shy, modest, bashful, diffident, self-effacing, shrinking.
– OPPOSITES brazen.

crack n. **1** a crack in the glass: **split**, break, chip, fracture, rupture. **2** a crack between two rocks: **space**, gap, crevice, fissure, cleft, cranny, chink. **3 bang**, report, explosion, detonation, clap, crash. **4** *a crack on the head:* **blow**, bang, hit, knock, rap, bump, smack, slap; informal bash, whack, clout.

-v. **1 break**, split, fracture, rupture, snap. **2 break down**, give way, cave in, go to pieces, give in, yield, succumb. **3 hit**, strike, smack, slap, beat, thump, knock, rap; informal bash, whack, clobber, clout, clip. **4** (informal) **decipher**, interpret, decode, break, solve.

cradle n. **1 crib**, Moses basket, cot, carrycot. **2 birthplace**, fount, fountainhead, source, spring, origin.
-v. **hold**, support, cushion, pillow, nurse, rest.

craft n. **1 activity**, occupation, trade, profession, work, line of work, job. **2 cunning**, craftiness, guile, wiliness, artfulness, deviousness, slyness, trickery, duplicity, dishonesty, deceit, deceitfulness, deception, intrigue, subterfuge, wiles, ploys, ruses, schemes, tricks. **3 vessel**, ship, boat, aircraft, spacecraft.

craftsman, **craftswoman** n. **artisan**, artist, skilled worker, technician, expert, master.

crafty adj. **cunning**, wily, sly, artful, devious, tricky, scheming, calculating, shrewd, canny, dishonest, deceitful.
– OPPOSITES honest.

cram v. **1** *wardrobes crammed with clothes:* **fill**, stuff, pack, jam, fill to overflowing, overload, crowd, throng. **2** *he crammed his clothes into a case:* **push**, thrust,

shove, force, ram, jam, stuff, pack, pile, squash, squeeze, compress. **3 revise**, study; informal swot, mug up, bone up.

cramp n. **spasm**, pain, shooting pain, twinge, pang, convulsion.
-v. **hinder**, impede, inhibit, hamper, constrain, hamstring, interfere with, restrict, limit, slow.

cramped adj. **1 poky**, uncomfortable, confined, restricted, constricted, small, tiny, narrow, crowded, congested. **2 small**, crabbed, illegible, unreadable, indecipherable.
– OPPOSITES spacious.

crash v. **1** *the car crashed into a tree:* **smash into**, collide with, be in collision with, hit, strike, ram, cannon into, plough into, meet head-on; N. Amer. impact. **2** *he crashed his car:* **smash**, wreck; Brit. write off; Brit. informal prang; N. Amer. informal total. **3 fall**, drop, plummet, plunge, sink, dive, tumble. **4** (informal) **fail**, fold, collapse, go under, go bankrupt; informal go bust, go to the wall.
-n. **1 accident**, collision, smash; N. Amer. wreck; Brit. informal pile-up; Brit. informal shunt, prang. **2 bang**, smash, smack, crack, bump, thud, explosion. **3 failure**, collapse, liquidation, bankruptcy.

crate n. **packing case**, chest, tea chest, box, container.

crater n. **hollow**, bowl, basin, hole, cavity, depression, dip; Geology caldera.

crave v. **long for**, yearn for, hanker after, desire, want, hunger for, thirst for, pine for; informal be dying for.

craving n. **longing**, yearning, desire, hankering, hunger, thirst, appetite.

crawl v. **1 creep**, worm your way, go on all fours, wriggle, slither, squirm. **2** (informal) **grovel**, kowtow, pander, toady, bow and scrape, fawn; informal suck up, lick someone's boots.

craze n. **fad**, fashion, trend, vogue, enthusiasm, mania, passion, rage; informal thing.

crazy adj. (informal) **1 mad**, insane, out of your mind, deranged, demented, crazed, lunatic, unbalanced, unhinged; informal mental, off your head, round the bend; Brit. informal barmy, crackers, barking (mad), potty, round the twist. **2** *a crazy idea:* **stupid**, foolish, idiotic, silly, absurd, ridiculous, ludicrous, preposterous, asinine; informal cockeyed, half-baked; Brit. informal barmy, daft. **3** *he's crazy about her:* **passionate**, very keen, enamoured, infatuated, smitten, enthusiastic, fanatical; informal wild, mad, nuts; Brit. informal potty.
– OPPOSITES sane, sensible.

cream n. **1 lotion**, ointment, moisturizer, cosmetic, salve, rub. **2 best**, finest, pick, flower, crème de la crème, elite.
– OPPOSITES dregs.
•adj. **off-white**, creamy, ivory.

creamy adj. **smooth**, thick, velvety, rich, buttery.

crease n. **fold**, line, crinkle, ridge, furrow, groove, corrugation, wrinkle, crow's foot.
•v. **crumple**, wrinkle, crinkle, line, scrunch up, rumple, ruck up, pucker.

create v. **1 produce**, generate, bring into being, make, fashion, build, construct. **2 bring about**, give rise to, lead to, result in, cause, breed, generate, engender, produce. **3 establish**, found, initiate, institute, constitute, inaugurate, launch, set up, form.
– OPPOSITES destroy, abolish.

creation n. **1 establishment**, formation, foundation, initiation, institution, inauguration, constitution, setting up. **2 the world**, the universe, the cosmos, nature, the natural world. **3 work**, work of art, production, opus, oeuvre, achievement, concoction, invention; informal brainchild.
– OPPOSITES abolition, destruction.

creative adj. **inventive**, imaginative, innovative, experimental, original, artistic, inspired, visionary.
– OPPOSITES unimaginative.

creator n. **maker**, producer, author, designer, deviser, originator, inventor, architect.

creature n. **animal**, beast, brute, living thing, living being; N. Amer. informal critter.

credentials pl. n. **1 suitability**, eligibility, attributes, qualifications, record, experience, background. **2 documents**, identity papers, ID, passport, testimonial, reference, certification.

c **credibility** n. **plausibility**, believability, credence, trustworthiness, reliability, dependability, integrity.

credible adj. **believable**, plausible, conceivable, persuasive, convincing, tenable, probable, possible, feasible, reasonable.

credit n. **praise**, commendation, acclaim, acknowledgement, recognition, kudos, glory, respect, appreciation.
•v. **1** (Brit.) you wouldn't credit it! **believe**, accept, give credence to, trust, have faith in. **2 ascribe to**, attribute to, put down to.

credulous adj. **gullible**, naive, easily taken in, impressionable, unsuspecting, unsuspicious, innocent, inexperienced, unsophisticated, wide-eyed.
– OPPOSITES suspicious.

creed n. **1** people of many creeds: **faith**, religion, belief, religious persuasion. **2** his personal creed: **beliefs**, principles, articles of faith, tenets, ideology, credo, doctrines, teachings.

creek n. **inlet**, bay, estuary, fjord; Scottish firth.

creep v. **tiptoe**, steal, sneak, slink, edge, inch, skulk, prowl.

creepy adj. (informal) **frightening**, eerie, disturbing, sinister, weird, menacing, threatening; informal spooky, scary.

crest n. **1 tuft**, comb, plume, crown. **2 summit**, peak, top,
ridge, pinnacle, brow, crown, apex. **3 insignia**, emblem, coat of arms, arms, badge, device, regalia.

crestfallen adj. **downhearted**, downcast, despondent, disappointed, disconsolate, disheartened, discouraged, dispirited, dejected, sad, dismayed, unhappy, forlorn.
– OPPOSITES cheerful.

crevice n. **crack**, fissure, interstice, cleft, chink, cranny, slit, split.

crew n. **1** the ship's crew: **company**, complement, sailors, hands. **2** a film crew: **team**, squad, company, unit, party, gang.

crime n. **1 offence**, unlawful act, illegal act, felony, violation, misdemeanour. **2 lawbreaking**, delinquency, wrongdoing, criminality, misconduct, illegality, villainy, vice.

criminal n. **1 lawbreaker**, felon, offender, malefactor, villain, delinquent, culprit, miscreant, wrongdoer; informal crook.
•adj. **1 unlawful**, illegal, illicit, lawless, delinquent, corrupt, felonious, nefarious; informal crooked; Brit. informal bent.
2 (informal) **deplorable**, shameful, reprehensible, disgraceful, inexcusable, outrageous, scandalous.
– OPPOSITES lawful.

cringe v. **1 cower**, shrink, recoil, shy away, flinch, quail, blench, tremble, quiver, quake. **2 wince**, shudder, squirm, feel embarrassed/mortified.

cripple v. **1 disable**, paralyse, immobilize, incapacitate, handicap. **2 damage**, weaken, hamper, paralyse, ruin, destroy, wipe out, bring to a standstill, put out of action, put out of business.

crippled adj. **disabled**, paralysed, incapacitated, physically handicapped, lame, immobilized, bedridden, confined to a wheelchair; euphemistic physically challenged.

crisis n. **1 emergency**, disaster, catastrophe, calamity, meltdown, predicament, plight, dire straits. **2 critical point**, turning point, crossroads, head, point of no return, moment of truth; informal crunch.

crisp adj. **1 crunchy**, crispy, brittle, breakable, dry. **2 invigorating**, brisk, cool, fresh, refreshing, exhilarating.
- OPPOSITES soft.

criterion n. **standard**, measure, gauge, test, benchmark, yardstick, touchstone, barometer.

critic n. **1 reviewer**, commentator, analyst, judge, pundit, expert. **2 detractor**, attacker, fault-finder.

critical adj. **1 disapproving**, disparaging, scathing, faultfinding, judgemental, negative, unfavourable, censorious, picky; informal nit-picking, picky. **2 serious**, grave, precarious, touch-and-go, in the balance, desperate, dire, acute, life-and-death. **3 crucial**, vital,

essential, all-important, paramount, fundamental, key, pivotal.
- OPPOSITES complimentary.

criticism n. **1 fault-finding**, censure, condemnation, disapproval, disparagement; informal flak, a bad press, panning; Brit. informal stick. **2 evaluation**, assessment, appraisal, appreciation, analysis, critique, judgement, commentary.
- OPPOSITES praise.

criticize v. **find fault with**, censure, condemn, attack, disparage, denigrate, run down; informal knock, pan, pull to pieces; Brit. informal slag off, slate, rubbish; N. Amer. informal trash.
- OPPOSITES praise.

crook n. see **CRIMINAL**.

crooked adj. **1 winding**, twisting, zigzag, meandering, tortuous, serpentine. **2 bent**, twisted, misshapen, deformed, malformed, contorted, warped, bowed, distorted. **3 lopsided**, askew, awry, off-centre, out of true, at an angle, slanting, squint; Scottish agley; Brit. informal skew-whiff, wonky. **4** (informal) **dishonest**, criminal, illegal, unlawful, nefarious, fraudulent, corrupt; informal shady; Brit. informal bent.
- OPPOSITES straight.

crop n. **harvest**, yield, fruits, produce, vintage.
▸v. **1 cut**, clip, trim, shear, shave, lop off, chop off, hack off, dock. **2 graze on**, browse on, feed on, nibble, eat.

❑ **crop up** happen, occur, arise, turn up, pop up, emerge, materialize, surface, appear, come to light.

cross n. **1** *we all have our crosses to bear:* **burden**, trouble, worry, trial, tribulation, affliction, curse, misfortune, woe; informal hassle, headache. **2** *a cross between a yak and a cow:* **mixture**, blend, combination, amalgam, hybrid, cross-breed, mongrel.
•v. **1 travel across**, traverse, negotiate, navigate, cover. **2 intersect**, meet, join, connect. **3 oppose**, resist, defy, obstruct, contradict, argue with, stand up to. **4 hybridize**, cross-breed, interbreed, cross-fertilize, cross-pollinate.
•adj. **angry**, annoyed, irate, vexed, irritated, in a bad mood, put out, exasperated; informal hot under the collar, peeved; Brit. informal shirty, ratty; N. Amer. informal sore, ticked off.
– OPPOSITES pleased.
❑ **cross out** delete, strike out, score out, cancel, obliterate.

crossing n. **1 junction**, crossroads, intersection, interchange, level crossing. **2 journey**, passage, voyage.

crouch v. **squat**, bend (down), hunker down, hunch over, stoop, duck, cower.

crow v. **boast**, brag, blow your own trumpet, swagger, swank, gloat.

crowd n. **1 horde**, throng, mass, multitude, host, army, herd, swarm, troop, mob, rabble; informal gaggle. **2** *they're a nice crowd:* **group**, set, circle, clique; informal gang, bunch, crew, lot. **3** *a capacity crowd:* **audience**, spectators, listeners, viewers, house, turnout, attendance, gate, congregation.
•v. **1 cluster**, flock, swarm, mill, throng, huddle, gather, assemble, congregate, converge. **2 surge**, throng, push, jostle, elbow your way, squeeze, pile, cram.

crowded adj. **packed**, full, filled to capacity, full to bursting, congested, overflowing, teeming, swarming, thronged, populous, overpopulated, busy; informal jam-packed, stuffed, chock-a-block, chock-full, bursting at the seams, full to the gunwales, wall-to-wall, mobbed; Austral./NZ informal chocker.
– OPPOSITES deserted.

crown n. **1 coronet**, diadem, tiara, circlet. **2 monarch**, sovereign, king, queen, emperor, empress, monarchy, royalty. **3 top**, crest, summit, peak, pinnacle, tip, brow, apex.
•v. *the post at Harvard crowned his career:* **round off**, cap, be the climax of, be the culmination of, top off, complete, perfect.

crucial adj. **1 pivotal**, critical, key, decisive, life-and-death. **2 all-important**, of the utmost importance, of the essence, critical, paramount, essential, vital.
– OPPOSITES insignificant, unimportant.

crude adj. **1 unrefined**, unpurified, unprocessed, untreated, coarse, raw, natural. **2 primitive**, simple, basic, homespun, rudimentary, rough and ready, makeshift, improvised, unsophisticated. **3 vulgar**, rude, dirty, naughty, smutty, indecent, obscene, coarse; informal blue.
– OPPOSITES refined.

cruel adj. **1** a cruel man: **brutal**, savage, inhuman, barbaric, vicious, sadistic, monstrous, callous, ruthless, merciless, heartless, pitiless, implacable, unkind, inhuman. **2** her death was a cruel blow: **harsh**, severe, bitter, heartbreaking, heart-rending, painful, agonizing, traumatic.
– OPPOSITES compassionate.

cruise n. (boat) **trip**, voyage, sail.
▪v. **1 sail**, voyage. **2 drive slowly**, drift; informal mosey, tootle; Brit. informal pootle.

crumb n. **fragment**, bit, morsel, particle, speck, scrap, shred, atom, trace, mite, jot, ounce; informal smidgen, tad.

crumble v. **1 disintegrate**, fall apart, fall to pieces, collapse, decompose, break up, decay, become dilapidated, deteriorate, degenerate. **2 break up**, crush, fragment, pulverize.

crumple v. **1 crush**, scrunch up, screw up, squash, squeeze. **2 crease**, wrinkle, crinkle, rumple. **3 collapse**, give way, cave in, go to pieces, break down, crumble.

crunch v. **munch**, chomp, champ, bite into, crush, grind.

crusade n. **campaign**, drive, push, movement, effort, struggle, battle, war, offensive.
▪v. **campaign**, fight, battle, do battle, strive, struggle, agitate, lobby.

crush v. **1 squash**, squeeze, press, pulp, mash, mangle, pulverize. **2 crease**, crumple, rumple, wrinkle, scrunch up. **3 suppress**, put down, quell, stamp out, repress, subdue, extinguish. **4 demoralize**, deflate, flatten, squash, devastate, shatter, mortify, humiliate.
▪n. **crowd**, throng, horde, swarm, press, mob.

crust n. **covering**, layer, coating, surface, topping, sheet, film, skin, shell, scab.

cry v. **1 weep**, shed tears, sob, wail, snivel, whimper; Scottish greet; informal blub, blubber; Brit. informal grizzle. **2 call**, shout, exclaim, sing out, yell, bawl, bellow, roar; informal holler.
– OPPOSITES laugh.
▪n. **call**, shout, exclamation, yell, bawl, bellow, roar; informal holler.
□ **cry off** (informal) **back out**, pull out, cancel, withdraw, change your mind; informal get cold feet, cop out.

crypt n. **tomb**, vault, burial chamber, sepulchre, catacomb.

cryptic adj. **enigmatic**, mysterious, mystifying, puzzling, obscure, abstruse, arcane, unintelligible.
– OPPOSITES clear.

cuddle v. **1** hug, embrace, clasp, hold in your arms, caress, pet, fondle; informal canoodle, smooch. **2** snuggle, nestle, curl, nuzzle.

cudgel n. club, truncheon, bludgeon, baton, shillelagh, mace; N. Amer. blackjack, nightstick; Brit. informal cosh. •v. club, bludgeon, beat, batter, bash; Brit. informal cosh.

cue n. signal, sign, indication, prompt, reminder.

culminate v. **come to a climax**, come to a head, climax, end, finish, conclude, build up to, lead up to.

culmination n. climax, peak, pinnacle, high point, height, summit, zenith, apotheosis, apex, apogee.

culpable adj. **to blame**, guilty, at fault, in the wrong, answerable, accountable, responsible. – OPPOSITES innocent.

culprit n. guilty party, offender, wrongdoer, miscreant, criminal, lawbreaker, felon, delinquent; informal baddy, crook.

cult n. **1** sect, group, movement. **2** obsession, fixation, idolization, devotion, worship, veneration.

cultivate v. **1** farm, work, till, plough, dig. **2** grow, raise, rear, tend, plant, sow. **3** woo, court, curry favour with, ingratiate yourself with; informal get in someone's good books. **4** improve, better, refine, educate, develop, enrich.

cultivated adj. see **CULTURED**.

cultural adj. **1** social, lifestyle, sociological, anthropological, racial, ethnic. **2** aesthetic, artistic, intellectual, educational, civilizing.

culture n. **1** *a lover of culture:* **the arts**, high art. **2** *a man of culture:* **education**, cultivation, enlightenment, discernment, discrimination, taste, refinement, sophistication. **3** civilization, society, way of life, lifestyle, customs, traditions, heritage, values. **4** philosophy, ethic, outlook, approach, rationale.

cultured adj. cultivated, artistic, enlightened, civilized, educated, well read, learned, discerning, discriminating, refined, sophisticated; informal arty. – OPPOSITES ignorant.

cunning adj. **1** crafty, wily, artful, devious, Machiavellian, sly, scheming, canny, dishonest, deceitful. **2** clever, shrewd, astute, canny, ingenious, imaginative, enterprising, inventive, resourceful, creative, original, inspired, brilliant. – OPPOSITES honest, stupid. •n. **1** guile, craftiness, deviousness, trickery, duplicity. **2** ingenuity, imagination, inventiveness, enterprise, resourcefulness.

curator n. custodian, keeper, conservator, guardian, caretaker.

curb n. restraint, restriction, check, brake, control, limit. •v. restrain, hold back, keep in check, control, rein in, contain; *informal* keep a lid on.

cure v. **1** heal, restore to health, make well/better. **2** rectify, remedy, put/set right, right, fix, mend, repair, solve, sort out, eliminate, end. **3** preserve, smoke, salt, dry, pickle.
• n. remedy, medicine, medication, antidote, treatment, therapy.

curiosity n. **1** interest, inquisitiveness, attention, spirit of inquiry. **2** oddity, curio, novelty, rarity.

curious adj. **1** intrigued, interested, eager, inquisitive. **2** strange, odd, peculiar, funny, unusual, queer, bizarre, weird, eccentric, extraordinary, abnormal, anomalous.
– OPPOSITES uninterested, normal.

curl v. spiral, coil, wreathe, twirl, swirl, wind, curve, twist (and turn), snake, corkscrew, twine, entwine, wrap.
• n. **1** ringlet, corkscrew, kink, lock. **2** *a curl of smoke:* spiral, coil, twirl, swirl, twist, corkscrew.

curly adj. wavy, curling, curled, frizzy, kinky, corkscrew.
– OPPOSITES straight.

currency n. **1** money, legal tender, cash, banknotes, notes, coins; N. Amer. bills. **2** popularity, circulation, exposure, acceptance, prevalence.

current adj. **1** contemporary, present-day, modern, topical, live, burning. **2** prevalent, com-

mon, accepted, in circulation, popular, widespread. **3** valid, usable, up to date. **4** incumbent, present, in office, in power, reigning.
– OPPOSITES past, former.
• n. **1** flow, stream, draught, jet, tide. **2** course, progress, progression, flow, tide, movement.

curse n. jinx, malediction; N. Amer. hex; *formal* imprecation, anathema. **2** affliction, burden, misery, ordeal, evil, scourge. **3** swear word, expletive, oath, profanity, four-letter word, dirty word, obscenity; *informal* cuss word.
• v. **1** afflict, trouble, plague, bedevil. **2** swear, take the Lord's name in vain, blaspheme; *informal* cuss, turn the air blue, eff and blind.

cursed adj. damned, doomed, ill-fated, ill-starred, jinxed.

cursory adj. brief, hasty, hurried, quick, rapid, passing, perfunctory, desultory, casual.
– OPPOSITES thorough.

curt adj. terse, brusque, abrupt, clipped, blunt, short, sharp, rude, ungracious; *informal* snappy.
– OPPOSITES expansive.

curtail v. reduce, shorten, cut, cut down, decrease, trim, restrict, limit, curb, rein in/back, cut short, truncate; *informal* slash.
– OPPOSITES increase, extend.

curve n. bend, turn, loop, arc, arch, bow, curvature.
• v. bend, turn, loop, wind, meander, snake, arc, arch.

curved adj. **bent**, arched, bowed, rounded, crescent.
- OPPOSITES straight.

cushion n. *a cushion against inflation:* **protection**, buffer, shield, defence, bulwark.
•v. 1 *cushioned from the outside world:* **protect**, shield, shelter, cocoon. 2 *cushion the blow:* **soften**, lessen, diminish, mitigate, alleviate, take the edge off, dull, deaden.

custody n. **care**, guardianship, charge, supervision, safe keeping, responsibility, protection.
□ **in custody** in prison, in jail, imprisoned, incarcerated, under lock and key, on remand; informal behind bars, doing time, inside; Brit. informal banged up.

custom n. 1 *local customs:* **tradition**, practice, usage, way, convention, formality, ritual, mores. 2 *it was his custom to sleep in a chair:* **habit**, practice, routine, way; formal wont.

customary adj. **usual**, traditional, normal, conventional, habitual, familiar, accepted, accustomed, routine, established, time-honoured, prevailing.
- OPPOSITES unusual.

customer n. **consumer**, buyer, purchaser, patron, client, shopper; Brit. informal punter.

cut v. 1 **gash**, slash, lacerate, slit, wound, scratch, graze, nick. 2 **slice**, chop, dice, cube, carve; N. Amer. hash. 3 **carve**, engrave, incise, etch, score, chisel, whittle. 4 **reduce**, cut back/down on, decrease, lessen, mark down,

discount, lower; informal slash. 5 **shorten**, abridge, condense, abbreviate, truncate, edit, censor. 6 **delete**, remove, take out, excise.
•n. 1 **gash**, slash, laceration, incision, wound, scratch, graze, nick. 2 **piece**, joint, fillet, section. 3 (informal) **share**, portion, quota, percentage; informal slice (of the cake). 4 **reduction**, cutback, decrease, lessening; N. Amer. rollback. 5 **style**, design, line, fit.

cutback n. **reduction**, cut, decrease, economy, saving; N. Amer. rollback.
- OPPOSITES increase.

cute adj. **endearing**, adorable, lovable, sweet, lovely, appealing, engaging, delightful, dear; informal twee; Brit. informal dinky.

cutting n. **clipping**, article, piece, column, paragraph.
•adj. **hurtful**, wounding, barbed, sharp, scathing, caustic, sarcastic, snide, spiteful, malicious, vicious, cruel; informal bitchy.

cycle n. 1 *the cycle of birth, death, and rebirth:* **circle**, round, pattern, rhythm, loop. 2 *a cycle of three plays:* **series**, sequence, set, succession, run.

cynic n. **sceptic**, doubter, doubting Thomas, pessimist, prophet of doom.
- OPPOSITES idealist, optimist.

cynical adj. **sceptical**, doubtful, distrustful, suspicious, disbelieving, pessimistic, negative, world-weary, disillusioned, disenchanted, jaundiced.
- OPPOSITES idealistic, optimistic.

Dd

dab v. pat, press, touch, blot, swab, daub, wipe.
•n. **drop**, spot, smear, splash, bit.

dabble v. **toy with**, dip into, flirt with, tinker with, play with.

daft adj. (Brit. informal) **absurd**, preposterous, ridiculous, ludicrous, idiotic, stupid, foolish, asinine, senseless, inane; informal crazy, cockeyed, half-baked; Brit. informal barmy.
– OPPOSITES sensible.

daily adj. **everyday**, day-to-day; formal quotidian.
•adv. **every day**, once a day, day after day.

dainty adj. **1 delicate**, fine, elegant, exquisite, graceful. **2 fastidious**, fussy, particular, finicky; informal choosy, picky; Brit. informal faddy.
– OPPOSITES unwieldy.

dam n. **barrage**, barrier, wall, embankment, barricade, obstruction.
•v. **block (up)**, obstruct, bung up, close, hold back.

damage n. **1 harm**, destruction, vandalism, injury, ruin, devastation. **2** *she won £4,000 damages*: **compensation**, recompense, restitution, redress, reparation(s); N. Amer. informal comp.
•v. **harm**, injure, deface, spoil, impair, vandalize, ruin, destroy, wreck; N. Amer. informal trash.

– OPPOSITES repair.

damaging adj. **harmful**, detrimental, injurious, hurtful, destructive, ruinous, deleterious.
– OPPOSITES beneficial.

damn v. **condemn**, censure, criticize, attack, denounce.
– OPPOSITES praise.

damning adj. **incriminating**, damaging, condemnatory, conclusive, irrefutable.

damp adj. **moist**, humid, muggy, clammy, sweaty, dank, wet, rainy, drizzly, showery, misty, foggy, dewy.
– OPPOSITES dry.
•n. **moisture**, liquid, wet, wetness, dampness, humidity.

dampen v. **1 moisten**, damp, wet, soak. **2 lessen**, decrease, diminish, reduce, moderate, cool, suppress, stifle, inhibit.
– OPPOSITES dry, heighten.

dance v. **1 sway**, twirl, whirl, pirouette, gyrate, jive; informal bop, trip the light fantastic; N. Amer. informal get down. **2** *the girls danced round me*: **caper**, cavort, frolic, skip, prance, gambol, leap, hop, jig, bounce.
•n. **ball**; N. Amer. prom, hoedown; informal disco, rave, hop, bop.

danger n. **1 peril**, hazard, risk, jeopardy, endangerment, menace. **2 possibility**, chance,

risk, probability, likelihood, threat.
– OPPOSITES safety.

dangerous adj. **1 menacing**, threatening, treacherous. **2 hazardous**, perilous, risky, unsafe, unpredictable, precarious, insecure; informal dicey, hairy; Brit. informal dodgy.
– OPPOSITES harmless, safe.

dangle v. **hang**, swing, droop, wave, trail, stream.

dank adj. **damp**, musty, chilly, clammy.
– OPPOSITES dry.

dapper adj. **smart**, spruce, trim, debonair, neat, well dressed, elegant; informal snappy, natty; N. Amer. informal spiffy, fly.
– OPPOSITES scruffy.

dare v. **1 be brave enough**, have the courage, venture, have the nerve, risk, take the liberty of; N. Amer. take a flyer; informal stick your neck out. **2 challenge**, defy, invite, bid, provoke, goad.
•n. **challenge**, invitation, wager, bet.

daring adj. **bold**, audacious, intrepid, fearless, brave, heroic, dashing; informal gutsy.
– OPPOSITES cowardly, timid.
•n. **boldness**, audacity, temerity, fearlessness, bravery, courage, pluck; informal nerve, guts; Brit. informal bottle; N. Amer. informal moxie.
– OPPOSITES cowardice.

dark adj. **1** a dark room: **dingy**, gloomy, shadowy, murky, grey, poorly lit, inky, black. **2** dark hair: **brunette**, dark brown, sable, jet-black, ebony. **3** dark skin: **swarthy**, dusky, olive, black, ebony. **4** dark thoughts: **gloomy**, dismal, negative, downbeat, bleak, grim, fatalistic, black. **5** a dark look: **angry**, forbidding, threatening, ominous, moody, brooding, sullen, scowling, glowering. **6** dark deeds: **evil**, wicked, sinful, bad, iniquitous, ungodly, vile, foul, monstrous; informal dirty, shady, crooked.
– OPPOSITES bright, light, blonde, pale.
•n. **night**, night-time, darkness, nightfall, blackout.

darken v. **grow dark**, make dark, blacken, grow dim, cloud over, lour.
– OPPOSITES lighten.

darkness n. **1** lights shone in the darkness: **blackness**, dark, gloom, dimness, murk, shadow, shade. **2** darkness fell: **night**, night-time, dark. **3** the forces of darkness: **evil**, wickedness, sin, ungodliness, the Devil.

darling n. **1 dear**, dearest, love, sweetheart, beloved; informal honey, angel, pet, sweetie, baby, poppet. **2 favourite**, idol, hero, heroine; Brit. informal blue-eyed boy/girl.
•adj. **1 dear**, dearest, precious, beloved. **2 adorable**, charming, cute, sweet, enchanting, dear, delightful; Scottish & N. English bonny.

dart v. **1 dash**, rush, tear, shoot, sprint, bound, scurry, scamper, informal **scoot**, whip. **2 direct**, cast, throw, shoot, send, flash.

dash v. **1 rush**, race, run, sprint, career, charge, shoot, hurtle, hare, fly, speed, zoom; informal tear, belt; Brit. informal bomb; N. Amer. informal barrel. **2 hurl**, smash, fling, slam, throw, toss, cast; informal chuck, sling. **3 shatter**, destroy, wreck, ruin, demolish, scotch, frustrate, thwart; informal put paid to; Brit. informal scupper.
- OPPOSITES dawdle.
•n. **1 rush**, race, run, sprint, bolt, dart, leap, charge, bound. **2 pinch**, touch, sprinkle, taste, spot, drop, dab, splash; informal smidgen, tad.

dashing adj. **debonair**, stylish, dapper, devil-may-care, raffish, flamboyant, swashbuckling.

data n. **facts**, figures, statistics, details, particulars, information.

date n. **1 day**, occasion, time, year, age, period, era, epoch. **2 appointment**, meeting, engagement, rendezvous, commitment, assignation; literary tryst. **3** (informal) **partner**, escort, girlfriend, boyfriend.
•v. **1 age**, grow old, become dated, show its age, be of its time. **2** (informal) **go out with**, take out, go with, see; informal go steady with; dated woo.
□ **date from** be from, originate in, come from, belong to, go back to.

WORD LINKS
relating to dates: chronological

dated adj. **old-fashioned**, outdated, outmoded, unfashionable, passé, behind the times, archaic, obsolete, antiquated; informal old hat, out of the ark.
- OPPOSITES modern.

daunt v. **discourage**, deter, demoralize, put off, dishearten, intimidate, overawe, awe.

daunting adj. **intimidating**, forbidding, challenging, formidable, unnerving, disconcerting, discouraging, disheartening, demoralizing, dismaying, scary, frightening, alarming.

dawdle v. **linger**, take your time, be slow, waste time, dally, amble, stroll, trail, move at a snail's pace; informal dilly-dally.
- OPPOSITES hurry.

dawn n. **1 daybreak**, sunrise, first light, daylight, cockcrow, first thing; N. Amer. sunup. **2 beginning**, start, birth, inception, genesis, emergence, advent, appearance, arrival, rise, origin.
- OPPOSITES dusk.
•v. **1** *Thursday dawned crisp and sunny:* **begin**, break, arrive, emerge. **2** *a bright new future has dawned:* **begin**, start, commence, be born, appear, arrive, emerge, arise, rise, unfold, develop. **3** *the reality dawned on him:* **become evident**, register, cross someone's mind, suggest itself, occur to, come to, strike, hit.

day n. **1 daytime**, daylight (hours), waking hours. **2 period**, time, date, age, era, generation.
- OPPOSITES night.

d

WORD LINKS
relating to the day: diurnal

daze v. dumbfound, stupefy, stun, shock, stagger, bewilder, take aback, nonplus; informal flabbergast; Brit. informal knock for six.
•n. stupor, trance, haze, spin, whirl, muddle, jumble.

dazzle v. 1 blind, confuse, disorient. 2 overwhelm, overcome, impress, move, stir, touch, awe, overawe; informal bowl over, blow away, knock out.

dead adj. 1 passed on, passed away, departed, late, lost, perished, fallen, killed, lifeless, extinct; informal six feet under, pushing up daisies; formal deceased. 2 obsolete, extinct, defunct, disused, abandoned, superseded, vanished, archaic, ancient. 3 not working, out of order, inoperative, inactive, broken, defective; informal kaput, conked out, on the blink, bust; Brit. informal knackered. 4 boring, uninteresting, unexciting, uninspiring, dull, flat, quiet, sleepy, slow, lifeless; informal one-horse; N. Amer. informal dullsville.
– OPPOSITES alive, living, lively.
•adv. 1 completely, absolutely, totally, utterly, deadly, perfectly, entirely, quite, thoroughly. 2 directly, exactly, precisely, immediately, right, straight, due.

deaden v. 1 numb, dull, blunt, alleviate, mitigate, diminish, reduce, lessen, ease, soothe, relieve, assuage. 2 muffle, mute, smother, stifle, damp (down), soften, cushion.
– OPPOSITES intensify, amplify.

deadline n. time limit, finishing date, target date, cut-off point.

deadlock n. stalemate, impasse, checkmate, stand-off, standstill, gridlock.

deadly adj. 1 fatal, lethal, mortal, life-threatening, noxious, toxic, poisonous. 2 *deadly enemies:* mortal, irreconcilable, implacable, bitter, sworn. 3 *his aim is deadly:* unerring, unfailing, perfect, true, accurate; Brit. informal spot on.
– OPPOSITES harmless.

deafening adj. ear-splitting, thunderous, crashing, uproarious, almighty, booming.
– OPPOSITES low, soft.

deal n. agreement, understanding, pact, bargain, covenant, contract, treaty, arrangement, compromise, settlement, terms.
•v. 1 trade in, buy and sell, purvey, supply, market, traffic in. 2 distribute, give out, share out, divide out, hand out, pass out, pass round, dispense, allocate.
□ deal with 1 cope with, handle, manage, treat, take care of, take charge of, take in hand, sort out, tackle, take on, control. 2 concern, be about, have to do with, discuss, consider, cover, tackle, explore, investigate, examine.

dealer n. trader, merchant, salesman/woman, seller, vendor, purveyor, pedlar, distributor, supplier, shopkeeper, retailer, wholesaler, tradesman, tradesperson; Brit. stockist.

dear adj. **1** *a dear friend*: **beloved**, precious, close, intimate, bosom. **2** *her pictures were too dear to part with*: **precious**, treasured, valued, prized, cherished, special. **3 endearing**, adorable, lovable, appealing, engaging, charming, captivating, lovely, delightful, sweet, darling. **4 expensive**, costly, high-priced, overpriced, exorbitant, extortionate; Brit. over the odds; informal pricey.
– OPPOSITES disagreeable, cheap.
•n. **darling**, dearest, love, beloved, sweetheart, precious; informal sweetie, sugar, honey, baby, pet, poppet.

dearly adv. **very much**, a great deal, greatly, profoundly, deeply.

dearth n. **lack**, scarcity, shortage, shortfall, deficiency, insufficiency, inadequacy, absence.
– OPPOSITES surfeit.

death n. **1 dying**, demise, end, passing, loss of life; formal decease. **2 end**, finish, termination, extinction, extinguishing, collapse, destruction.
– OPPOSITES life, birth.

> **WORD LINKS**
> *causing death:* fatal, lethal, mortal

deathly adj. **deathlike**, ghostly, ghastly, ashen, white, pale, pallid.

debacle n. **fiasco**, failure, catastrophe, disaster.

debase v. **degrade**, devalue, demean, cheapen, prostitute, discredit, drag down, tarnish, blacken, disgrace, dishonour, shame.
– OPPOSITES enhance.

debatable adj. **arguable**, questionable, open to question, disputable, controversial, contentious, doubtful, dubious, uncertain, borderline, moot.

debate n. **discussion**, argument, dispute, talks.
•v. **1 discuss**, talk over/through, talk about, thrash out, argue, dispute. **2 consider**, think over/about, chew over, mull over, weigh up, ponder, deliberate.

debauched adj. **dissolute**, dissipated, degenerate, decadent, profligate, immoral, lecherous, lewd, licentious.
– OPPOSITES wholesome.

debris n. **ruins**, remains, rubble, wreckage, detritus, refuse, rubbish, waste, scrap, flotsam and jetsam.

debt n. **1 bill**, account, dues, arrears, charges. **2 indebtedness**, obligation, gratitude, appreciation.

decay v. **1 decompose**, rot, putrefy, go bad, go off, spoil, fester, perish. **2 deteriorate**, degenerate, decline, go downhill, slump, slide, go to rack and ruin, go to seed; informal go to the dogs.
•n. **1 decomposition**, putrefaction, rot. **2 deterioration**,

degeneration, decline, weakening, crumbling, disintegration, collapse.

deceit n. **deception**, deceitfulness, duplicity, double-dealing, lies, fraud, cheating, trickery.
– OPPOSITES honesty.

deceitful adj. **dishonest**, untruthful, insincere, false, disingenuous, untrustworthy, unscrupulous, unprincipled, two-faced, duplicitous, fraudulent, double-dealing; informal sneaky, tricky, crooked; Brit. informal bent.
– OPPOSITES honest.

deceive v. **trick**, cheat, defraud, swindle, hoodwink, hoax, dupe, take in, mislead, delude, fool; informal con, pull the wool over someone's eyes; N. Amer. informal sucker, goldbrick.

decency n. **1 propriety**, decorum, good taste, respectability, morality, virtue, modesty. **2 courtesy**, politeness, good manners, civility, consideration, thoughtfulness.

decent adj. **1** *a decent burial:* **proper**, correct, right, appropriate, suitable, respectable, decorous, modest, seemly, accepted; informal pukka. **2** *a job with decent pay:* **satisfactory**, reasonable, fair, acceptable, adequate, sufficient, not bad, all right, tolerable, passable, suitable; informal OK. **3** (Brit. informal) **kind**, generous, thoughtful, considerate, obliging, courteous, polite, well mannered, neighbourly,

hospitable, pleasant, agreeable, amiable.
– OPPOSITES improper, unsatisfactory.

deception n. **1 deceit**, duplicity, double-dealing, fraud, cheating, trickery, guile, bluff, lying, pretence, treachery. **2 trick**, sham, fraud, pretence, hoax, ruse, scheme, dodge, cheat, swindle; informal con, set-up, scam.

deceptive adj. **misleading**, confusing, illusory, distorted, ambiguous.

decide v. **1 resolve**, determine, make up your mind, choose, opt, plan, aim, intend, have in mind, set your sights on. **2 settle**, resolve, determine, work out, answer; informal sort out. **3 adjudicate**, arbitrate, judge, pronounce on, give a verdict on, rule on.

decidedly adv. **distinctly**, clearly, markedly, obviously, noticeably, unmistakably, patently, manifestly, definitely, positively.

decision n. **1 resolution**, conclusion, settlement, choice, option, selection. **2 verdict**, finding, ruling, judgement, adjudication, sentence.

decisive adj. **1 resolute**, firm, strong-minded, strong-willed, determined, purposeful. **2 deciding**, conclusive, determining, key, pivotal, critical, crucial.

declaration n. **1 announcement**, statement, communication, pronouncement,

proclamation; N. Amer. advisory.
2 assertion, profession, affirmation, acknowledgement,
revelation, disclosure, confirmation, testimony, avowal,
protestation.

declare v. **1 announce**, proclaim, state, reveal, air, voice,
articulate, express, vent, set
forth, publicize, broadcast.
2 assert, profess, affirm, maintain, state, contend, claim,
argue, insist, avow.

decline v. **1 turn down**, reject,
brush aside, refuse, rebuff,
spurn, repulse, dismiss, pass up,
say no; informal give something a
miss. **2 decrease**, reduce, less-
en, diminish, dwindle, contract,
shrink, fall off, tail off, drop, fall,
go down. **3 deteriorate**, degenerate, decay, crumble, collapse,
slump, slip, slide, go downhill,
worsen; informal go to the dogs.
– OPPOSITES accept, increase,
improve.
•n. **1 reduction**, decrease,
downturn, downswing, diminution, ebb, drop, slump, plunge.
2 deterioration, degeneration,
degradation, shrinkage, erosion.
– OPPOSITES rise, improvement.

decompose v. decay, rot,
putrefy, go bad, go off, spoil,
perish, deteriorate, degrade,
break down.

decor n. decoration, furnishing,
colour scheme.

decorate v. **1 ornament**, adorn,
trim, embellish, garnish, furnish,
enhance. **2 paint**, wallpaper,
paper, refurbish, renovate,

redecorate; informal do up, give
something a facelift, give something a makeover. **3 give a
medal to**, honour, cite, reward.

decoration n. **1 ornamentation**, adornment, trimming,
embellishment, beautification.
2 ornament, bauble, trinket,
knick-knack. **3 medal**, award,
prize; Brit. informal gong.

decorative adj. **ornamental**,
fancy, ornate, attractive, pretty,
showy.
– OPPOSITES functional.

decorum n. **1 propriety**, seem-
liness, decency, good taste,
correctness, politeness, good
manners. **2 etiquette**, protocol,
good form, custom, convention.
– OPPOSITES impropriety.

decrease v. lessen, reduce,
drop, diminish, decline, dwindle,
fall off, plummet, plunge.
– OPPOSITES increase.
•n. **reduction**, drop, decline,
downturn, cut, cutback,
diminution.
– OPPOSITES increase.

decree n. **1** a presidential decree:
order, command, command-
ment, edict, proclamation, law,
statute, act. **2** a court decree:
judgement, verdict, adjudication, finding, ruling, decision.
•v. **order**, direct, command, rule,
dictate, pronounce, proclaim,
ordain.

decrepit adj. dilapidated, rickety, run down, tumbledown,
ramshackle, derelict, ruined, in
(a state of) disrepair, gone to

d

rack and ruin, on its last legs, decayed, crumbling.

dedicate v. **1 commit**, devote, pledge, give (up), sacrifice, set aside. **2 inscribe**, address, offer. **3 devote**, assign, bless, consecrate, sanctify.

dedicated adj. **1 committed**, devoted, enthusiastic, keen, staunch, firm, steadfast, loyal, faithful. **2 specialized**, custombuilt, customized, purposebuilt, exclusive.
– OPPOSITES half-hearted.

dedication n. **1 commitment**, devotion, loyalty, allegiance, application, resolve, conscientiousness, perseverance, persistence. **2 inscription**, message.
– OPPOSITES apathy.

deduce v. **conclude**, reason, work out, infer, understand, assume, presume, surmise, reckon; informal figure out, put two and two together; Brit. informal suss out.

deduct v. **subtract**, take away, take off, debit, dock, stop; informal knock off.
– OPPOSITES add.

deduction n. **1 subtraction**, removal, debit. **2 stoppage**, tax, expenses, rebate, discount, concession. **3 conclusion**, inference, supposition, hypothesis, assumption, presumption, suspicion.

deed n. **1 act**, action, feat, exploit, achievement, accomplishment, endeavour. **2 document**, contract, instrument.

deep adj. **1 cavernous**, yawning, gaping, huge, extensive, bottomless, fathomless. **2 intense**, heartfelt, wholehearted, deep-seated, sincere, genuine, earnest, enthusiastic, great. **3 profound**, serious, intelligent, intellectual, learned, wise, scholarly. **4** *he was deep in concentration*: **rapt**, absorbed, engrossed, preoccupied, intent, immersed, lost, gripped. **5 obscure**, complex, mysterious, unfathomable, opaque, abstruse, esoteric, enigmatic. **6 low-pitched**, low, bass, rich, resonant, booming, sonorous. **7 dark**, intense, rich, strong, vivid.
– OPPOSITES shallow, superficial, high.

deeply adv. **profoundly**, greatly, enormously, extremely, very, strongly, intensely, keenly, acutely, thoroughly, completely, entirely, seriously.

deface v. **vandalize**, disfigure, spoil, ruin, damage; N. Amer. informal trash.

defeat v. **1 beat**, conquer, win against, triumph over, get the better of, vanquish, rout, trounce, overcome, overpower; informal lick, thrash. **2 thwart**, frustrate, foil, ruin, scotch, derail; informal put paid to, stymie; Brit. informal scupper.
▪ n. **loss**, conquest, rout; informal thrashing, hiding, drubbing, licking.
– OPPOSITES victory.

defect n. **fault**, flaw, imperfection, deficiency, deformity, blemish, mistake, error.

defective adj. **faulty**, flawed, imperfect, unsound, inoperative, malfunctioning, out of order, broken; informal on the blink; Brit. informal duff.
– OPPOSITES perfect.

defence n. **1 protection**, guarding, security, fortification, resistance. **2 armaments**, weapons, weaponry, arms, the military, the armed forces. **3 justification**, vindication, explanation, mitigation, excuse, alibi, denial, rebuttal, plea, pleading, argument, case.
– OPPOSITES attack, prosecution.

defenceless adj. **vulnerable**, helpless, powerless, weak, undefended, unprotected, unguarded, unarmed, exposed, open to attack

defend v. **1 protect**, guard, safeguard, secure, shield, fortify, watch over. **2 justify**, vindicate, explain, argue for, support, back, stand by, make a case for, stick up for.
– OPPOSITES attack, criticize.

defender n. **1 protector**, guardian, guard, custodian. **2 supporter**, upholder, backer, champion, advocate, apologist.

defensive adj. **1 defending**, protective. **2 self-justifying**, oversensitive, prickly, paranoid, neurotic; informal twitchy.

defer v. **postpone**, put off, delay, hold over/off, put back, shelve, suspend; N. Amer. table; informal put on ice, put on the back burner.

defiance n. **resistance**, opposition, non-compliance, disobedience, insubordination, rebellion, disregard, contempt, insolence.
– OPPOSITES obedience.

defiant adj. **disobedient**, resistant, obstinate, uncooperative, non-compliant, recalcitrant, insubordinate; Brit. informal stroppy, bolshie.
– OPPOSITES cooperative.

deficiency n. **1 lack**, insufficiency, shortage, inadequacy, deficit, shortfall, scarcity, dearth. **2 defect**, fault, flaw, failing, weakness, shortcoming, limitation.
– OPPOSITES surplus, strength.

deficit n. **shortfall**, deficiency, shortage, debt, arrears, loss.
– OPPOSITES surplus.

define v. **1 explain**, give the meaning of, spell out, expound, interpret, describe. **2 determine**, establish, fix, specify, designate, decide, stipulate, set out.

definite adj. **specific**, explicit, express, precise, exact, clear, clear-cut, unambiguous, certain, sure, positive, conclusive, decisive, firm, unequivocal, unmistakable, proven, decided, marked, distinct, identifiable.
– OPPOSITES vague, ambiguous.

definitely adv. **certainly**, surely, for sure, unquestionably, without doubt, undoubtedly, undeniably, clearly, positively, absolutely, unmistakably.

definition n. **1** meaning, sense, interpretation, explanation, description. **2** clarity, sharpness, focus, crispness, resolution.

definitive adj. **1** conclusive, final, unqualified, absolute, categorical, positive, definite. **2** authoritative, best, ultimate, classic, standard, recognized, accepted, exhaustive.

deflect v. divert, turn away, draw away, distract, fend off, parry, stave off.

deformed adj. misshapen, distorted, malformed, contorted, out of shape, twisted, crooked, warped, buckled, gnarled, disfigured, mutilated, mangled.

defraud v. swindle, cheat, rob, deceive, dupe, hoodwink, double-cross, trick; informal con, do, sting, diddle, rip off, shaft, pull a fast one on, put one over on, sell a pup to; N. Amer. informal sucker, snooker, stiff; Austral. informal pull a swifty on.

deft adj. skilful, adept, adroit, dexterous, agile, nimble, handy, able, capable, skilled, proficient, accomplished, expert, polished, slick, professional.
– OPPOSITES clumsy.

defy v. disobey, flout, disregard, ignore, break, violate, contravene, breach, challenge, fly in the face of, confront.
– OPPOSITES obey.

degenerate adj. corrupt, perverted, decadent, dissolute, dissipated, debauched, immoral, unprincipled, disreputable.

• v. deteriorate, decline, worsen, slip, slide, go downhill; informal go to the dogs.
– OPPOSITES improve.

degrade v. demean, debase, humiliate, humble, belittle, mortify, dehumanize, brutalize.
– OPPOSITES dignify.

degree n. level, standard, grade, stage, mark, amount, extent, measure, intensity, strength, proportion.

deign v. condescend, stoop, lower yourself, demean yourself, humble yourself, consent.

dejected adj. downcast, downhearted, despondent, disconsolate, dispirited, crestfallen, disheartened, depressed; informal down in the mouth, down in the dumps.
– OPPOSITES cheerful.

delay v. **1** detain, hold up, make late, slow up/down, bog down, hinder, hamper, impede, obstruct. **2** linger, drag your feet, hold back, dawdle, waste time, stall, hesitate, dither, shilly-shally; informal dilly-dally. **3** postpone, put off, defer, hold over, adjourn, reschedule.
– OPPOSITES hurry, advance.

• n. **1** hold-up, wait, interruption, stoppage. **2** *the delay of his trial:* postponement, deferral, adjournment.

delegate n. representative, envoy, emissary, commissioner, agent, deputy.

• v. assign, entrust, pass on, hand on/over, turn over, devolve.

delegation n. deputation, mission, commission, contingent, legation.

delete v. remove, cut (out), take out, edit out, excise, cancel, cross out, strike out, obliterate, rub out, erase.
– OPPOSITES add.

deliberate adj. **1** intentional, calculated, conscious, intended, planned, wilful, premeditated. **2** careful, cautious, measured, regular, even, steady. **3** methodical, systematic, careful, painstaking, meticulous, thorough.
– OPPOSITES accidental, hasty.
•v. think, think about/over, ponder, consider, contemplate, reflect on, muse on, meditate on, ruminate on, mull over; N. Amer. think on.

deliberately adv. **1** intentionally, on purpose, purposely, by design, knowingly, wittingly, consciously, wilfully. **2** carefully, cautiously, slowly, steadily, evenly.

deliberation n. thought, consideration, reflection, contemplation, discussion.

delicacy n. **1** fineness, delicateness, fragility, thinness, lightness, flimsiness. **2** difficulty, trickiness, sensitivity, ticklishness, awkwardness. **3** care, sensitivity, tact, discretion, diplomacy, subtlety. **4** treat, luxury, titbit, speciality.

delicate adj. **1** delicate embroidery: fine, intricate, dainty, exquisite, graceful. **2** a delicate shade of blue: subtle, soft, pale, muted, pastel, light. **3** delicate china cups: fragile, dainty. **4** his wife is very delicate: sickly, unhealthy, frail, feeble, weak. **5** a delicate issue: difficult, tricky, sensitive, ticklish, awkward, touchy, embarrassing; informal sticky, dicey. **6** the matter needs delicate handling: careful, sensitive, tactful, diplomatic, discreet, kid-glove, subtle. **7** a delicate mechanism: sensitive, light, precision.
– OPPOSITES coarse, strong, robust.

delicious adj. delectable, mouth-watering, appetizing, tasty, flavoursome; informal scrumptious, moreish; N. Amer. informal finger-licking.
– OPPOSITES unpalatable.

delight v. charm, enchant, captivate, entrance, thrill, entertain, amuse, divert; informal send, tickle pink, bowl over.
– OPPOSITES dismay, disgust.
•n. pleasure, happiness, joy, glee, excitement, amusement, bliss, ecstasy.
– OPPOSITES displeasure.
□ **delight in** love, relish, savour, adore, lap up, take pleasure in, enjoy, revel in.

delighted adj. pleased, glad, happy, thrilled, overjoyed, ecstatic, elated, on cloud nine, walking on air, in seventh heaven, jumping for joy, gleeful, cock-a-hoop; informal over the moon, tickled pink, as pleased as Punch, on top of the world, as happy as Larry; Brit. informal chuffed; N. English informal made up; Austral. informal wrapped.

delightful adj. **1** a delightful evening: **lovely**, enjoyable, amusing, entertaining, pleasant, pleasurable. **2** a delightful girl: **charming**, enchanting, captivating, bewitching, appealing, sweet, endearing, cute, adorable, delectable.

deliver v. **1 bring**, take, convey, carry, transport, send, distribute, dispatch, ship. **2 state**, utter, give, read, broadcast, pronounce, announce, declare, proclaim, hand down, return. **3 administer**, deal, inflict, give; informal land.

delivery n. **1 conveyance**, carriage, transportation, transport, distribution, dispatch, shipping. **2 consignment**, load, shipment. **3 speech**, pronunciation, enunciation, articulation, elocution.

delusion n. **misapprehension**, misconception, false impression, misunderstanding, mistake, error, misconstruction, illusion, fantasy, fancy.

delve v. **1 rummage**, search, hunt, scrabble about, root about, ferret, fish about, dig, rifle through. **2 investigate**, enquire, probe, explore, research, look into, go into.

demand n. **1** I gave in to her demands: **request**, call, command, order, dictate. **2** the demands of a young family: **requirement**, need, claim, commitment, imposition. **3 market**, call, appetite, desire.

▸v. **1 call for**, ask for, request, push for, press for, seek, claim, insist on. **2 order**, command, enjoin, require. **3 ask**, enquire, question, query. **4 require**, need, necessitate, call for, involve, entail. **5 insist on**, stipulate, expect, look for.

demanding adj. **1 difficult**, challenging, taxing, exacting, tough, hard, onerous, formidable, arduous, gruelling, backbreaking, punishing. **2 nagging**, trying, tiresome, hard to please, high-maintenance.
– OPPOSITES easy.

demeaning adj. **degrading**, humiliating, shameful, undignified, menial; informal infra dig.

demeanour n. **manner**, air, attitude, appearance, look, mien, bearing, carriage, behaviour, conduct.

demise n. **1 death**, dying, passing, end. **2 end**, break-up, disintegration, fall, downfall, collapse, overthrow.
– OPPOSITES birth.

democratic adj. **elected**, representative, parliamentary, popular, egalitarian, self-governing.

demolish v. **1 knock down**, pull down, tear down, destroy, flatten, raze to the ground, dismantle, level, bulldoze, blow up. **2 destroy**, ruin, wreck, overturn, explode, drive a coach and horses through; informal shoot full of holes.
– OPPOSITES build.

demonstrate v. **1 indicate**, prove, show, establish, confirm, verify. **2 reveal**, manifest, indicate, illustrate, signify, signal, denote, show, display, exhibit. **3 protest**, march, parade, picket, strike.

demonstration n. **1 exhibition**, presentation, display. **2 manifestation**, indication, sign, mark, proof, testimony. **3 protest**, march, rally, mass lobby, sit-in; informal demo.

demonstrative adj. **expressive**, open, forthcoming, communicative, unreserved, emotional, effusive, affectionate, loving, warm, friendly, approachable; informal touchy-feely.
- OPPOSITES reserved.

demoralized adj. **dispirited**, disheartened, downhearted, dejected, downcast, low, depressed, dismayed, daunted, discouraged.

demure adj. **modest**, reserved, shy, unassuming, decorous, decent, proper.
- OPPOSITES brazen.

den n. **1 lair**, burrow, hole, shelter, hiding place, hideout. **2 study**, studio, workshop, retreat, sanctuary, hideaway; informal hidey-hole.

denial n. **1 contradiction**, rebuttal, repudiation, refutation, disclaimer. **2 refusal**, withholding.

denomination n. **1 religious group**, sect, cult, movement, persuasion, order, creed, school, church. **2 value**, unit, size.

denote v. **indicate**, be a mark of, signify, signal, designate, symbolize, represent.

denounce v. **1 condemn**, attack, censure, decry, stigmatize, deprecate, disparage, revile, damn. **2 expose**, betray, inform on, incriminate, implicate, cite, accuse.

dense adj. **1** *a dense forest:* **thick**, crowded, compact, solid, tight, overgrown, impenetrable, impassable. **2** *dense smoke:* **thick**, heavy, opaque, murky. **3** (informal) **stupid**, brainless, foolish, obtuse, simple-minded, empty-headed, obtuse; informal thick, dim, dopey.
- OPPOSITES sparse, thin.

dent n. **knock**, indentation, dint, depression, hollow, crater, pit; N. Amer. informal ding.
•v. **knock**, dint, mark; N. Amer. informal ding.

deny v. **1 contradict**, rebut, repudiate, refute, challenge, contest. **2 refuse**, turn down, reject, rebuff, decline, veto, dismiss; informal give the thumbs down to.
- OPPOSITES confirm, allow, accept.

depart v. **1 leave**, go away, withdraw, absent yourself, quit, exit, decamp, retreat, retire, make off; informal make tracks, take off, split; Brit. informal sling your hook. **2 deviate**, diverge, digress, stray, veer, differ, vary.
- OPPOSITES arrive.

department n. **division**, section, sector, unit, branch, wing, office, bureau, agency, ministry.

d

departure n. **1 leaving**, going, leave-taking, withdrawal, exit. **2 deviation**, divergence, digression, shift, variation. **3 change**, innovation, novelty.

d depend v. **1** *her career depends on this:* **be dependent on**, hinge on, hang on, rest on, rely on. **2** *my family depends on me:* **rely on**, lean on, count on, bank on, trust (in), pin your hopes on.

dependable adj. **reliable**, trustworthy, trusty, faithful, loyal, stable, sensible, responsible.

dependent adj. **1 addicted**, reliant; informal hooked. **2 reliant**, needy, helpless, infirm, invalid, incapable, debilitated, disabled.
– OPPOSITES independent.
□ **dependent on 1 conditional** on, contingent on, based on, subject to, determined by, influenced by. **2 reliant** on, relying on, counting on, sustained by.

depict v. **1 portray**, show, represent, picture, illustrate, reproduce, render. **2 describe**, detail, relate, present, set forth, set out, outline.

deplete v. **reduce**, decrease, diminish, exhaust, use up, consume, expend, drain, empty.
– OPPOSITES augment.

deplore v. **1 abhor**, find unacceptable, frown on, disapprove of, take a dim view of, take exception to, condemn, denounce. **2 regret**, lament, mourn, bemoan, bewail, complain about, grieve over, sigh over.
– OPPOSITES applaud.

deploy v. **1 position**, station, post, place, install, locate, base. **2 use**, utilize, employ, take advantage of, exploit, call on.

deport v. **expel**, banish, extradite, repatriate.
– OPPOSITES admit.

depose v. **overthrow**, unseat, dethrone, topple, remove, supplant, displace, oust.

deposit n. **1 layer**, covering, coating, blanket, accumulation, sediment. **2 seam**, vein, lode, layer, stratum, bed. **3 down payment**, advance payment, prepayment, instalment, retainer, security.
▸v. **1 put down**, place, set down, unload, rest, drop; informal dump, park, plonk; N. Amer. informal plunk. **2 leave (behind)**, precipitate, dump, wash up, cast up. **3 lodge**, bank, house, store, stow.

depot n. **1 terminal**, terminus, station, garage, headquarters, base. **2 storehouse**, warehouse, store, repository, depository, cache, arsenal, armoury, dump.

depress v. **1 sadden**, dispirit, cast down, get down, dishearten, demoralize, crush, weigh down on. **2 slow down**, weaken, impair, inhibit, restrict. **3 reduce**, lower, cut, cheapen, discount, deflate, depreciate, devalue. **4 press**, push, hold down.
– OPPOSITES cheer, boost, raise.

depressed adj. **1 sad**, unhappy, miserable, gloomy, dejected, downhearted, downcast, down,

despondent, dispirited, low, morose, dismal, desolate; *informal* blue, down in the dumps, down in the mouth. **2 weak**, inactive, flat, slow, slack, sluggish, stagnant. **3 poverty-stricken**, poor, disadvantaged, deprived, needy, distressed, run down.
- OPPOSITES cheerful.

depressing adj. dismal, sad, unhappy, sombre, gloomy, grave, bleak, black, melancholy, dreary, grim, cheerless.

depression n. **1 unhappiness**, sadness, melancholy, melancholia, misery, sorrow, gloom, despondency, low spirits. **2 recession**, slump, decline, downturn. **3 hollow**, indentation, dent, cavity, dip, pit, crater, basin, bowl.

deprivation n. **1 poverty**, impoverishment, privation, hardship, destitution, need, want. **2 dispossession**, withholding, withdrawal, removal, seizure.
- OPPOSITES prosperity.

deprive v. dispossess, strip, divest, relieve, rob, cheat out of.

deprived adj. disadvantaged, underprivileged, poverty-stricken, impoverished, poor, destitute, needy.
- OPPOSITES privileged.

depth n. **1 deepness**, drop, height. **2 extent**, range, scope, breadth, width. **3 profundity**, wisdom, understanding, intelligence, discernment, penetration, insight, awareness.

4 intensity, richness, vividness, strength, brilliance.

deputize v. **stand in**, sit in, fill in, cover, substitute, replace, take someone's place, take over, hold the fort, step into the breach.

deputy n. **second in command**, number two, assistant, aide, proxy, stand-in, replacement, substitute, representative, reserve.

derelict adj. **dilapidated**, ramshackle, run down, tumbledown, in ruins, falling down, disused, abandoned, deserted.
•n. **tramp**, vagrant, down and out, homeless person, drifter, beggar; *informal* dosser, bag lady.

derision n. **mockery**, ridicule, jeers, sneers, taunts, disdain, disparagement, denigration, insults.

derogatory adj. **disparaging**, disrespectful, demeaning, critical, pejorative, negative, unfavourable, uncomplimentary, unflattering, insulting, defamatory, slanderous, libellous.
- OPPOSITES complimentary.

descend v. **1 go down**, come down, drop, fall, sink, dive, plummet, plunge, nosedive. **2 slope**, dip, slant, go down, fall away. **3 alight**, disembark, get down, get off, dismount.
- OPPOSITES climb, board.
☐ **descend on** flock to, besiege, surround, take over, invade, swoop on, occupy.

descent n. **1** dive, drop, fall, plunge, nosedive. **2 slope**, incline, dip, drop, gradient. **3 decline**, slide, fall, degeneration, deterioration. **4 ancestry**, parentage, ancestors, family, extraction, origin, derivation, birth, lineage, stock, blood, roots, origins.

describe v. **1 report**, recount, relate, narrate, tell of, set out, detail, give a rundown of. **2** portray, depict, paint, define, characterize, call, label, class, brand. **3 mark out**, delineate, outline, trace, draw.

description n. **1 account**, report, narrative, story, portrayal, portrait, sketch, details. **2 designation**, labelling, naming, dubbing, characterization, definition, classification, branding. **3 sort**, variety, kind, type.

desert[1] v. **1 abandon**, leave, jilt, leave high and dry, leave in the lurch, leave behind, strand, maroon; *informal* walk/run out on, dump, ditch; *literary* forsake. **2 abscond**, defect, run away, decamp, flee, turn tail, take French leave; *Military* go AWOL.

desert[2] n. **wasteland**, wastes, wilderness, dust bowl.

deserted adj. **1 abandoned**, jilted, cast aside, neglected, stranded, marooned, forlorn; *literary* forsaken. **2 empty**, uninhabited, unoccupied, abandoned, evacuated, desolate, lonely, godforsaken.
– OPPOSITES populous.

deserve v. **merit**, earn, warrant, rate, justify, be worthy of, be entitled to.

deserved adj. **well earned**, merited, warranted, justified, rightful, due, fitting, just, proper.

deserving adj. **worthy**, commendable, praiseworthy, admirable, estimable, creditable.

design n. **1 plan**, blueprint, drawing, sketch, outline, map, plot, diagram, draft. **2 pattern**, motif, device, style, theme, layout.
•v. **1 invent**, create, think up, come up with, devise, formulate, conceive; *informal* dream up. **2 intend**, aim, mean.

designate v. **1 appoint**, nominate, delegate, select, choose, pick, elect, name, identify, assign. **2 classify**, class, label, tag, name, call, term, dub.

desirable adj. **1 attractive**, sought-after, in demand, popular, enviable; *informal* to die for, must-have. **2 advantageous**, advisable, wise, sensible, recommended, beneficial, preferable. **3 (sexually) attractive**, beautiful, pretty, appealing, seductive, alluring, irresistible; *informal* sexy.
– OPPOSITES unattractive.

desire n. **1 wish**, want, aspiration, yearning, longing, craving, hankering, hunger; *informal* yen, itch. **2 lust**, passion, sensuality, sexuality, libido, lasciviousness.
•v. **want**, wish for, long for, yearn for, crave, hanker after, be

desperate for, be bent on, covet, aspire to.

desolate adj. **1** bleak, stark, bare, dismal, grim, wild, inhospitable, deserted, uninhabited, empty, abandoned, godforsaken, isolated, remote. **2** miserable, unhappy, despondent, depressed, disconsolate, devastated, despairing, inconsolable, wretched, broken-hearted.

despair n. desperation, anguish, unhappiness, despondency, depression, misery, wretchedness, hopelessness.
– OPPOSITES hope, joy.
• v. lose hope, give up, lose heart, be discouraged, be despondent, be demoralized.

despatch v. & n. see DISPATCH.

desperate adj. **1** despairing, hopeless, anguished, distressed, wretched, desolate, forlorn, distraught, at your wits' end, at the end of your tether. **2** last-ditch, last-gasp, eleventh-hour, do-or-die, final, frantic, frenzied, wild. **3** grave, serious, critical, acute, urgent, pressing, drastic, extreme.

desperation n. hopelessness, despair, distress, anguish, agony, torment, misery.

despise v. detest, hate, loathe, abhor, deplore, scorn, disdain, deride, sneer at, revile, spurn, shun.
– OPPOSITES adore, respect.

despite prep. in spite of, notwithstanding, regardless of, in the face of, in the teeth of, undeterred by, for all, even with.

destined adj. **1** fated, ordained, predestined, doomed, meant, intended. **2** computers destined for Pakistan: **heading**, bound, en route, scheduled, headed.

destiny n. **1** future, fate, fortune, doom, lot. **2** providence, fate, God, the stars, luck, fortune, chance, karma, kismet.

destitute adj. penniless, poor, impoverished, poverty-stricken, impecunious, indigent, down and out; Brit. on the breadline; informal (flat) broke, on your uppers; Brit. informal stony broke, skint; formal penurious.
– OPPOSITES rich.

destroy v. **1** demolish, knock down, level, raze to the ground, fell, blow up. **2** spoil, ruin, wreck, blight, devastate, wreak havoc on. **3** kill, put down, put to sleep, slaughter, cull. **4** annihilate, wipe out, obliterate, eliminate, eradicate, liquidate, exterminate; informal take out; N. Amer. informal waste.
– OPPOSITES build.

destruction n. **1** devastation, carnage, ruin, chaos, wreckage. **2** the destruction of the countryside: **wrecking**, ruining, annihilation, obliteration, elimination, eradication, devastation. **3** killing, slaughter, extermination, culling.
– OPPOSITES preservation.

destructive adj. devastating, ruinous, damaging, harmful, detrimental, injurious, hurtful, deleterious.

d

detach v. **disconnect**, separate, unfasten, disengage, uncouple, isolate, remove, loose, unhitch, unhook, free, pull off, cut off, break off, split off, sever.
– OPPOSITES attach, join.

detached adj. **1 disconnected**, separated, separate, unfastened, disengaged, uncoupled, isolated, loosened, unhitched, unhooked, free, severed, cut off. **2 dispassionate**, disinterested, objective, outside, neutral, unbiased, impartial.

detachment n. **1 objectivity**, dispassion, disinterest, neutrality, impartiality. **2 unit**, squad, detail, troop, contingent, task force, party, platoon.

detail n. **1 feature**, respect, particular, characteristic, specific, aspect, fact, point, element. **2 triviality**, technicality, nicety, fine point. **3 unit**, detachment, squad, troop, contingent, outfit, task force, party, platoon.
• v. **describe**, relate, catalogue, list, spell out, itemize, identify, specify.

detailed adj. **comprehensive**, full, complete, thorough, exhaustive, all-inclusive, elaborate, minute, precise, itemized, blow-by-blow.
– OPPOSITES general.

detain v. **1 hold**, take into custody, confine, imprison, intern, arrest, apprehend, seize; informal pick up; Brit. informal nick. **2 delay**, hold up, make late, keep, slow up/down, hinder.
– OPPOSITES release.

detect v. **1 notice**, perceive, discern, become aware of, note, make out, spot, recognize, identify, catch, sense. **2 discover**, uncover, turn up, unearth, dig up, root out, expose. **3 catch**, hunt down, track down, find out, expose, reveal, unmask, smoke out.

detective n. **investigator**, police officer; informal private eye, sleuth; N. Amer. informal gumshoe.

detention n. **custody**, imprisonment, incarceration, internment, captivity, remand, arrest, quarantine.
– OPPOSITES release.

deter v. **1 discourage**, dissuade, put off, scare off, dishearten, demoralize, daunt, intimidate. **2 prevent**, stop, avert, stave off, ward off.
– OPPOSITES encourage.

deteriorate v. **worsen**, decline, degenerate, fail, go downhill, wane.
– OPPOSITES improve.

determination n. **resolution**, resolve, will power, strength of character, dedication, single-mindedness, perseverance, persistence, tenacity, staying power, doggedness; informal guts.

determine v. **1 control**, decide, regulate, direct, dictate, govern. **2 resolve**, decide, make up your mind, choose, elect, opt. **3 specify**, set, fix, decide on, settle, establish, ordain, prescribe, decree. **4 ascertain**, find out, discover, learn, establish, calculate, work out; informal figure out.

determined adj. **resolute**, purposeful, adamant, single-minded, unswerving, unwavering, persevering, persistent, tenacious, dedicated, dogged.
– OPPOSITES irresolute.

deterrent n. **disincentive**, discouragement, damper, curb, check, restraint, inhibition.
– OPPOSITES incentive.

detest v. **hate**, abhor, loathe, regard with disgust, be unable to bear, have an aversion to, find intolerable, disdain, despise.
– OPPOSITES love.

detrimental adj. **harmful**, damaging, injurious, hurtful, inimical, deleterious, destructive, pernicious, undesirable, unfavourable.
– OPPOSITES beneficial.

devastate v. **1 destroy**, ruin, wreck, lay waste, ravage, demolish, raze to the ground, level, flatten. **2 shatter**, shock, stun, daze, dumbfound, traumatize, distress; informal knock sideways; Brit. informal knock for six.

devastation n. **destruction**, ruin, desolation, wreckage, ruins.

develop v. **1 grow**, expand, spread, advance, progress, evolve, mature. **2 initiate**, instigate, set in motion, originate, invent, form. **3 expand**, augment, broaden, supplement, reinforce, enhance, refine,

improve, polish, perfect. **4 start**, begin, emerge, erupt, break out, arise, break, unfold.

development n. **1 evolution**, growth, expansion, enlargement, spread, progress. **2 event**, change, circumstance, incident, occurrence. **3 estate**, complex, site.

deviate v. **diverge**, digress, drift, stray, veer, swerve, get sidetracked, branch off, differ, vary.

device n. **1 implement**, gadget, utensil, tool, appliance, apparatus, instrument, machine, mechanism, contrivance, contraption; informal gizmo. **2 ploy**, tactic, move, stratagem, scheme, manoeuvre, plot, trick, ruse.

devil n. **1 Satan**, Beelzebub, Lucifer, the Prince of Darkness; informal Old Nick. **2 evil spirit**, demon, fiend. **3 brute**, beast, monster, fiend, villain, sadist, barbarian, ogre.

> **WORD LINKS**
> relating to the Devil: diabolical, diabolic, satanic

devious adj. **1 underhand**, dishonest, crafty, cunning, conniving, scheming, sneaky, furtive; informal crooked, shady; Brit. informal dodgy. **2 circuitous**, roundabout, indirect, meandering, tortuous.
– OPPOSITES honest, direct.

devise v. **conceive**, think up, dream up, work out, formulate, concoct, hatch, contrive, design, invent, coin; informal cook up.

devoid adj.
□ **devoid of** empty of, free of, bereft of, lacking, deficient in, without, wanting in; informal minus.

devote v. **dedicate**, allocate, assign, allot, commit, give (over), consign, pledge, set aside, earmark, reserve.

devoted adj. **dedicated**, committed, devout, loyal, faithful, true, staunch, steadfast, fond, loving.

devotee n. **enthusiast**, fan, lover, aficionado, admirer, supporter, disciple; informal buff, freak, nut, fanatic.

devotion n. **1 loyalty**, fidelity, commitment, allegiance, dedication, fondness, love, care. **2 piety**, spirituality, godliness, holiness, sanctity.

devour v. **1 gobble**, guzzle, gulp down, bolt, wolf; informal polish off; Brit. informal scoff. **2 consume**, engulf, envelop.

devout adj. **dedicated**, devoted, committed, loyal, sincere, fervent, pious, reverent, God-fearing, dutiful, churchgoing.

diagnose v. **identify**, determine, distinguish, recognize, interpret, detect, pinpoint.

diagnosis n. **1 identification**, detection, recognition, determination, discovery, pinpointing. **2 opinion**, judgement, verdict, conclusion.

diagonal adj. **crosswise**, crossways, slanting, slanted, oblique, angled, cornerways, cornerwise.

diagram n. **drawing**, representation, plan, outline, figure, chart, graph.

dialogue n. **conversation**, talk, discussion, chat, tête-à-tête, exchange, debate, conference, consultation; informal confab.

diary n. **1 appointment book**, engagement book, personal organizer; trademark Filofax. **2 journal**, memoir, chronicle, log, logbook, history, annal, record, weblog, blog; N. Amer. daybook.

dictate v. **1 prescribe**, lay down, impose, set down, order, command, decree, ordain, direct. **2 determine**, control, govern, decide, influence, affect.
□ **dictate to** give orders to, order about/around, lord it over; informal boss about/around, push about/around.

dictator n. **autocrat**, despot, tyrant, absolute ruler.
– OPPOSITES democrat.

dictatorial adj. **domineering**, autocratic, authoritarian, oppressive, imperious, overweening, overbearing, peremptory; informal bossy, high-handed.

dictionary n. **lexicon**, glossary, vocabulary.

WORD LINKS
writing of dictionaries:
lexicography

die v. **1 pass away**, pass on, perish; informal give up the ghost, kick the bucket, croak, bite the dust; Brit. informal snuff it, peg out,

pop your clogs; N. Amer. informal buy the farm. **2 lessen**, subside, drop, ease (off), let up, moderate, abate, fade, peter out, wane, ebb. **3** (informal) *the engine died:* **fail**, cut out, give out, break down, informal conk out, go kaput; Brit. informal pack up.
- OPPOSITES live.

diet n. **1** *a healthy diet:* **food**, nutrition, eating habits. **2** *she's on a diet:* **dietary regime**, regimen, restricted diet, fast.
•v. **be on a diet**, slim, lose weight, watch your weight; N. Amer. reduce; N. Amer. informal slenderize.

differ v. **1** *the second set of data differed from the first:* **contrast with**, be different to, vary from, deviate from, conflict with, run counter to, be at odds with, contradict. **2** disagree, conflict, be at variance/odds, be in dispute, not see eye to eye.
- OPPOSITES resemble, agree.

difference n. **1** dissimilarity, contrast, distinction, differentiation, variance, variation, divergence, disparity, contradiction. **2 disagreement**, difference of opinion, dispute, argument, quarrel; Brit. row. **3** *I'll pay the difference:* **balance**, remainder, rest.
- OPPOSITES similarity.

different adj. **1 dissimilar**, unlike, contrasting, differing, varying, disparate, poles apart, incompatible, mismatched; informal like chalk and cheese. **2 changed**, altered, transformed, new, unfamiliar, unknown, strange. **3 distinct**, separate, individual, independent. **4** (informal) **unusual**, out of the ordinary, unfamiliar, novel, new, fresh, original, unconventional, exotic.
- OPPOSITES similar, ordinary.

difficult adj. **1** *a difficult job:* **laborious**, strenuous, arduous, hard, tough, demanding, punishing, gruelling, back-breaking, exhausting, tiring; informal hellish, killing, no picnic. **2** *a difficult problem:* **hard**, complicated, complex, puzzling, perplexing, baffling, problematic, thorny, ticklish. **3** *a difficult child:* **troublesome**, tiresome, trying, exasperating, awkward, demanding, contrary, recalcitrant, uncooperative, fussy.
- OPPOSITES easy, simple, cooperative.

difficulty n. **1** strain, stress, trouble, problems, struggle; informal hassle. **2 problem**, complication, snag, hitch, obstacle, hurdle, stumbling block, pitfall; Brit. spanner in the works; informal headache. **3** *he got into difficulties:* **trouble**, predicament, plight, hard times; informal fix, scrape, jam.
- OPPOSITES ease.

diffident adj. **shy**, bashful, modest, self-effacing, unassuming, meek, unconfident, insecure, unassertive, timid, shrinking, reticent.
- OPPOSITES confident.

dig v. **1** *she began to dig the soil*: **turn over**, work, break up. **2** *he dug a hole*: **excavate**, dig out, quarry, hollow out, scoop out, bore, burrow, mine. **3** *poke*, prod, jab, stab, shove, ram, push, thrust, drive, stick. **4** *delve*, probe, search, enquire, look, investigate, research.
▪ n. **1** poke, prod, jab, stab, shove, push. **2** (*informal*) **snide remark**, cutting remark, jibe, taunt, sneer, insult; *informal* wisecrack, put-down.
□ **dig up** exhume, disinter, unearth.

digest v. **assimilate**, absorb, take in, understand, comprehend, grasp.
▪ n. **summary**, synopsis, abstract, precis, résumé, summation.

dignified adj. **stately**, noble, majestic, distinguished, regal, imposing, impressive, grand, solemn, formal, ceremonious, decorous, sedate.

dignity n. **1 stateliness**, nobility, majesty, impressiveness, grandeur, magnificence, ceremoniousness, formality, decorum, propriety, respectability, worthiness, integrity, solemnity, gravitas. **2 self-respect**, pride, self-esteem, self-worth.

dilapidated adj. **run down**, tumbledown, ramshackle, in disrepair, shabby, battered, rickety, crumbling, in ruins, ruined, decaying, decrepit, neglected, uncared-for, gone to rack and ruin.

dilemma n. **quandary**, predicament, catch-22, vicious circle, plight, conflict; *informal* fix, tight spot/corner; (**in a dilemma**) between the devil and the deep blue sea, between a rock and a hard place.

diligent adj. **industrious**, hardworking, assiduous, conscientious, particular, punctilious, meticulous, painstaking, rigorous, careful, thorough, sedulous.
– OPPOSITES lazy.

dilute v. **1** *dilute the bleach with water*: **make weaker**, water down, thin, doctor, adulterate; *informal* cut. **2** *the original plans have been diluted*: **tone down**, moderate, weaken, water down, compromise.

dim adj. **1** *the dim light*: **faint**, weak, feeble, soft, pale, dull, subdued, muted. **2** *long dim corridors*: **dark**, badly lit, dingy, dismal, gloomy, murky. **3** *a dim figure*: **indistinct**, ill-defined, vague, shadowy, nebulous, blurred, fuzzy. **4** *dim memories*: **vague**, imprecise, imperfect, unclear, indistinct, sketchy, hazy. **5** see **STUPID**.
– OPPOSITES bright, distinct, clear.
▪ v. **1** turn down, lower, soften, subdue. **2** fade, dwindle, dull.
– OPPOSITES brighten.

dimension n. **1 size**, measurements, proportions, extent, length, width, breadth, depth. **2 aspect**, feature, element, angle, facet, side.

diminish v. **1 subside**, lessen, decline, reduce, decrease, dwindle, fade, slacken off, let up. **2** *new laws diminished the courts' authority:* **reduce**, decrease, lessen, curtail, cut, limit, curb.
– OPPOSITES increase.

din n. **noise**, racket, rumpus, cacophony, hubbub, uproar, commotion, clangour, clatter, clamour; Brit. row; informal hullabaloo.
– OPPOSITES silence.

dine v. **eat**, have dinner, have lunch.

dingy adj. **gloomy**, dark, dull, dim, dismal, dreary, drab, sombre, grim, cheerless, dirty, grimy, shabby, seedy, run down.
– OPPOSITES bright.

dinner n. **main meal**, lunch, evening meal, supper, feast, banquet; Brit. tea.

dip v. **1 immerse**, submerge, plunge, dunk, bathe, sink. **2 sink**, set, drop, fall, descend. **3 decrease**, fall, drop, fall off, decline, diminish, dwindle, slump, plummet, plunge. **4 slope down**, descend, go down, drop (away), fall away.
– OPPOSITES rise, increase.
▪ n. **1 swim**, bathe, paddle. **2 slope**, incline, decline, descent, hollow, depression, basin. **3 decrease**, fall, drop, downturn, decline, falling-off, slump, reduction.
▫ **dip into 1** draw on, use, spend. **2** browse through, skim through, look through, flick through.

diplomacy n. **1 statesmanship**, statecraft, negotiation(s), discussion(s), talks. **2 tact**, tactfulness, sensitivity, discretion.

diplomat n. **ambassador**, attaché, consul, chargé d'affaires, envoy, emissary.

diplomatic adj. **tactful**, sensitive, subtle, delicate, polite, discreet, judicious, politic.
– OPPOSITES tactless.

dire adj. **terrible**, dreadful, appalling, frightful, awful, grim, sore, alarming, acute, grave, serious, urgent, pressing, wretched, desperate, parlous.

direct adj. **1 straight**, short, quick. **2 non-stop**, through, unbroken, uninterrupted. **3 frank**, candid, straightforward, open, blunt, plain-spoken, outspoken, forthright, no-nonsense, matter-of-fact; informal upfront.
▪ v. **1 manage**, govern, run, administer, control, conduct, handle, be in charge of, preside over, lead, head, rule. **2 aim**, target, address to, intend for, mean for, design for. **3 give directions**, show the way, point someone in the direction of. **4 instruct**, tell, command, order, require; old use bid.

direction n. **1 way**, route, course, line, bearing, orientation. **2 running**, management, administration, conduct, handling, supervision, superintendence, command, rule, leadership. **3 instruction**, order,

d

command, rule, regulation, requirement.

directive n. **instruction**, direction, command, order, injunction, decree, dictum, edict.

directly adv. **1** *they flew directly to New York:* **straight**, as the crow flies. **2** *directly after breakfast:* **immediately**, right (away), straight (away), without delay, promptly. **3** *the houses directly opposite:* **exactly**, right, immediately, diametrically; *informal* bang. **4** **frankly**, candidly, openly, bluntly, forthrightly, without beating about the bush.

director n. **manager**, head, chief, principal, leader, governor, president, chair, chief executive; *informal* boss, gaffer.

dirt n. **1** **grime**, filth, muck, dust, mud, pollution; *Brit. informal* gunge. **2** *a dirt road:* **earth**, soil, clay, loam.

dirty adj. **1** **soiled**, grimy, grubby, filthy, mucky, stained, unwashed, greasy, muddy, dusty, polluted, contaminated, foul, unhygienic; *Brit. informal* manky, grotty. **2** **obscene**, indecent, rude, naughty, vulgar, smutty, coarse, crude, filthy, off colour, pornographic, explicit, X-rated; *informal* blue; *euphemistic* adult. **3** **malevolent**, hostile, black, angry, disapproving.
– OPPOSITES clean.
– v. **soil**, stain, muddy, blacken, mess (up), mark, spatter, smudge, smear, splatter, sully, pollute, foul.

disability n. **handicap**, incapacity, impairment, infirmity, defect, abnormality, condition, disorder, affliction.

disable v. **1** **incapacitate**, put out of action, debilitate, handicap, cripple, lame, maim, immobilize, paralyse. **2** **deactivate**, defuse, disarm, make safe.

disabled adj. **handicapped**, incapacitated, infirm, crippled, lame, paralysed, immobilized, bedridden; *euphemistic* physically challenged, differently abled.
– OPPOSITES able-bodied.

disadvantage n. **1** **drawback**, snag, downside, fly in the ointment, catch, nuisance, handicap, trouble, *informal* minus. **2** **detriment**, prejudice, harm, loss, hurt.
– OPPOSITES advantage.

disagree v. **1** be of a different opinion, not see eye to eye, take issue, challenge, contradict, differ, dissent, be in dispute, clash. **2** **differ**, be dissimilar, be different, be at variance/odds, vary, contradict each other, conflict. **3** *the food disagreed with her:* **make ill**, make unwell, upset, nauseate.
– OPPOSITES agree.

disagreeable adj. **unpleasant**, distasteful, off-putting, unpalatable, nasty, objectionable, disgusting, horrible, offensive, repulsive, obnoxious, odious, repellent, revolting, vile, foul.
– OPPOSITES pleasant.

disagreement n. **dissent**, difference of opinion, controversy, discord, division, dispute, quarrel.
- OPPOSITES agreement.

disappear v. **1 vanish**, be lost to view/sight, recede, fade away, melt away, clear. **2 die out**, cease to exist, end, go, pass away, pass into oblivion, vanish, perish.
- OPPOSITES materialize.

disappoint v. **let down**, fail, dissatisfy, upset, dismay, sadden, disenchant, disillusion, shatter someone's illusions.

disappointed adj. **upset**, saddened, let down, displeased, dissatisfied, disheartened, downhearted, discouraged, crestfallen, disenchanted, disillusioned; informal choked, cut up; Brit. informal gutted, as sick as a parrot.
- OPPOSITES delighted.

disappointment n. **1 sadness**, sorrow, regret, dismay, displeasure, dissatisfaction, disenchantment, disillusionment. **2 let-down**, non-event, anticlimax; Brit. damp squib; informal washout.
- OPPOSITES delight.

disapproval n. **disfavour**, objection, dislike, dissatisfaction, distaste, displeasure, criticism, censure, condemnation, denunciation.
- OPPOSITES approval.

disapprove v.
□ **disapprove of** object to, have a poor opinion of, take exception to, dislike, take a dim view of, look askance at, frown on, be against, not believe in, deplore, censure, condemn, denounce.

disarm v. **1 lay down your arms**, demobilize, disband, demilitarize. **2 defuse**, disable, deactivate, make safe. **3 win over**, charm, persuade, soothe, mollify, appease, placate.
- OPPOSITES arm, antagonize.

disarmament n. **demilitarization**, demobilization, disbandment, decommissioning, arms reduction, arms limitation.

disarming adj. **winning**, charming, irresistible, persuasive, soothing, conciliatory, mollifying.

disarray n. **disorder**, confusion, chaos, untidiness, disorganization, a mess, a muddle, a shambles.
- OPPOSITES tidiness.

disaster n. **1 catastrophe**, calamity, cataclysm, tragedy, act of God, accident. **2 misfortune**, mishap, misadventure, setback, reversal, stroke of bad luck, blow. **3 failure**, fiasco, catastrophe; informal flop, washout, dead loss.
- OPPOSITES success.

disastrous adj. **catastrophic**, calamitous, cataclysmic, tragic, devastating, ruinous, terrible, awful.

disbelief n. **incredulity**, incredulousness, scepticism, doubt, cynicism, suspicion, distrust, mistrust.

discard v. dispose of, throw away/out, get rid of, toss out, jettison, dispense with, scrap, reject, drop; informal ditch, bin, junk; Brit. informal get shot of; N. Amer. informal trash.
– OPPOSITES keep.

discharge v. **1 dismiss**, eject, expel, throw out, make redundant, release, let go; Military cashier; informal sack, fire. **2 free**, set free, release, let out, liberate. **3 emit**, give off, let out, send out, exude, leak, secrete, excrete, release. **4 fire**, shoot, let off, set off, loose off, trigger, launch. **5 unload**, offload, put off, remove. **6 carry out**, perform, execute, conduct, fulfil, complete.
– OPPOSITES recruit, imprison.
•n. **1 dismissal**, release, removal, ejection, expulsion; Military cashiering; informal the sack, the boot. **2 leak**, leakage, emission, secretion, excretion, suppuration, pus. **3 carrying out**, performance, execution, conduct, fulfilment, accomplishment, completion.

disciple n. **follower**, adherent, believer, admirer, devotee, acolyte, apostle, supporter, advocate.

discipline n. **1 control**, regulation, direction, order, authority, strictness. **2 good behaviour**, order, control, obedience. **3 field (of study)**, branch of knowledge, subject, area, speciality. •v. **1 train**, drill, teach, school, coach. **2 punish**, penalize, bring

to book, reprimand, rebuke; Brit. informal carpet.

disclose v. **reveal**, make known, divulge, tell, impart, communicate, pass on, release, make public, broadcast, publish.
– OPPOSITES conceal.

discolour v. **stain**, mark, soil, dirty, streak, smear, tarnish, spoil.

discomfort n. **1 pain**, aches and pains, soreness, aching, twinge, pang, throb, cramp. **2 inconvenience**, difficulty, problem, trial, tribulation, hardship. **3 embarrassment**, discomfiture, unease, awkwardness, discomposure, confusion, nervousness, distress, anxiety.

disconnect v. **1 detach**, disengage, uncouple, unhook, unhitch, undo, unfasten, unyoke. **2 separate**, cut off, divorce, sever, isolate, dissociate, remove. **3 deactivate**, shut off, turn off, switch off, unplug.
– OPPOSITES attach, connect.

discontent n. **dissatisfaction**, disaffection, grievances, unhappiness, displeasure, resentment, envy, restlessness, unrest, unease.
– OPPOSITES satisfaction.

discontented adj. **dissatisfied**, disgruntled, disaffected, unhappy, aggrieved, displeased, resentful, envious, restless, frustrated; informal fed up.
– OPPOSITES satisfied.

discordant adj. **tunelesss**, inharmonious, off-key, dissonant,

harsh, jarring, grating, jangly, jangling, strident, shrill, cacophonous.
- OPPOSITES harmonious.

discount n. **reduction**, deduction, markdown, price cut, concession, rebate.
•v. **1 disregard**, pay no attention to, take no notice of, dismiss, ignore, overlook; informal poohpooh. **2 reduce**, mark down, cut, lower; informal knock down.

discourage v. **1 dissuade**, deter, put off, talk out of. **2 dishearten**, dispirit, demoralize, disappoint, put off, unnerve, daunt, intimidate. **3 prevent**, deter, stop, avert, inhibit, curb.
- OPPOSITES encourage.

discover v. **1 find**, locate, come across/upon, stumble on, chance on, uncover, unearth, turn up. **2 find out**, learn, realize, ascertain, work out, recognize; informal figure out; Brit. informal twig.

discovery n. **1 finding**, location, uncovering, unearthing. **2 realization**, recognition, revelation, disclosure. **3 breakthrough**, finding, find, innovation.

discredit v. **1 bring into disrepute**, disgrace, dishonour, blacken the name of, put/show in a bad light, compromise, smear, tarnish; N. Amer. slur. **2 disprove**, invalidate, explode, refute; informal debunk.
- OPPOSITES honour, prove.
•n. **dishonour**, disgrace, shame, humiliation, ignominy.

discreet adj. **tactful**, circumspect, diplomatic, judicious, sensitive, careful, cautious, strategic.

discrepancy n. **difference**, disparity, variation, deviation, divergence, disagreement, inconsistency, mismatch, conflict.
- OPPOSITES correspondence.

discretion n. **1 tact**, diplomacy, delicacy, sensitivity, good sense, prudence, circumspection. **2** at the discretion of the council: **choice**, option, preference, disposition, pleasure, will, inclination.

discriminate v. **1 differentiate**, distinguish, draw a distinction, tell the difference, tell apart, separate. **2** policies that discriminate against women: **be biased**, be prejudiced, treat differently, treat unfairly, put at a disadvantage, victimize, pick on.

discriminating adj. **discerning**, perceptive, judicious, selective, tasteful, refined, sensitive, cultivated, cultured.
- OPPOSITES indiscriminate.

discrimination n. **1 prejudice**, bias, bigotry, intolerance, favouritism, partisanship. **2 discernment**, judgement, perceptiveness, (good) taste, refinement, sensitivity, cultivation.
- OPPOSITES impartiality.

discuss v. **1 talk over**, talk about, talk through, debate, confer about. **2 examine**, explore, study, analyse, go into, deal with, consider, tackle.

d

discussion n. **1 conversation**, talk, chat, dialogue, conference, debate, exchange of views, consultation, deliberation; informal confab. **2 examination**, exploration, study, analysis, treatment, consideration.

disdain n. **contempt**, scorn, derision, disrespect, condescension, superciliousness, hauteur, haughtiness.
– OPPOSITES respect.
• v. **scorn**, deride, regard with contempt, sneer at, look down your nose at, look down on, despise.

disease n. **illness**, sickness, ill health, infection, ailment, malady, disorder, condition, problem; informal bug, virus; Brit. informal lurgy.

WORD LINKS
relating to disease: pathological

diseased adj. **unhealthy**, ill, sick, unwell, ailing, infected, septic, rotten, bad.

disgrace n. **1 dishonour**, shame, discredit, ignominy, disrepute, infamy, scandal, stigma, humiliation, loss of face. **2 scandal**, discredit, reproach, stain, blemish, blot, black mark, outrage, affront.
– OPPOSITES honour, credit.
• v. **shame**, bring shame on, dishonour, discredit, stigmatize, taint, sully, tarnish, stain, blacken.
– OPPOSITES honour.

disgraceful adj. **shameful**, scandalous, contemptible, dishonourable, discreditable, disreputable, reprehensible, blameworthy, unworthy, ignoble.
– OPPOSITES admirable.

disgruntled adj. **dissatisfied**, discontented, fed up, put out, aggrieved, resentful, displeased, unhappy, disappointed, annoyed; informal hacked off, browned off; Brit. informal cheesed off, narked; N. Amer. informal sore, ticked off.
– OPPOSITES contented.

disguise v. **camouflage**, conceal, hide, cover up, mask, screen, veil, paper over.
– OPPOSITES expose.

disgust n. **revulsion**, repugnance, aversion, distaste, abhorrence, loathing, hatred.
– OPPOSITES delight.
• v. **revolt**, repel, repulse, sicken, nauseate, horrify, appal, shock, turn someone's stomach, scandalize, outrage, offend, affront; N. Amer. informal gross out.
– OPPOSITES delight.

disgusting adj. **1** *the food was disgusting:* **revolting**, repulsive, sickening, nauseating, stomach-turning, off-putting; N. Amer. vomitous; informal gross, sick-making. **2** *I find racism disgusting:* **outrageous**, objectionable, abhorrent, repellent, loathsome, offensive, appalling, shocking, horrifying, scandalous, monstrous, detestable; informal sick.
– OPPOSITES delightful.

dish n. **1** bowl, plate, platter, salver, pot. **2** recipe, meal, course, fare.
□ **dish out** distribute, dispense, issue, hand out/round, give out, pass round, deal out, dole out, allocate.

dishevelled adj. untidy, unkempt, scruffy, messy, disarranged, rumpled, bedraggled, tousled, tangled, windswept; N. Amer. informal mussed (up).
- OPPOSITES tidy.

dishonest adj. fraudulent, cheating, underhand, devious, treacherous, unfair, dirty, criminal, illegal, unlawful, false, untruthful, deceitful, lying, corrupt, dishonourable, untrustworthy, unscrupulous; informal crooked, shady, sharp; Brit. informal bent; Austral./NZ informal shonky.
- OPPOSITES honest.

dishonourable adj. disgraceful, shameful, discreditable, ignoble, reprehensible, shabby, shoddy, despicable, contemptible, base, low.
- OPPOSITES honest.

disintegrate v. break up, crumble, break apart, fall apart, fall to pieces, collapse, fragment, shatter, splinter.

disinterested adj. unbiased, unprejudiced, impartial, neutral, detached, objective, dispassionate, non-partisan.

dislike v. find distasteful, regard with distaste, be averse to, have an aversion to, disapprove of, object to, take exception to, have no taste for, hate, despise.
- OPPOSITES like.
•n. distaste, aversion, disfavour, antipathy, disgust, abhorrence, hatred.
- OPPOSITES liking.

disloyal adj. unfaithful, faithless, false, untrue, inconstant, two-faced, double-dealing, double-crossing, deceitful, treacherous, subversive, seditious, unpatriotic; informal back-stabbing, two-timing; literary perfidious.

dismal adj. **1** a dismal look: gloomy, glum, melancholy, morose, doleful, woebegone, forlorn, dejected, downcast. **2** a dismal hall: dim, dingy, dark, gloomy, dreary, drab, dull.
- OPPOSITES cheerful, bright.

dismantle v. take apart, take to pieces/bits, pull to pieces, disassemble, break up, strip (down).
- OPPOSITES build.

dismay n. alarm, distress, concern, surprise, consternation, disquiet.
- OPPOSITES pleasure, relief.
•v. concern, distress, disturb, worry, alarm, disconcert, take aback, unnerve, unsettle.
- OPPOSITES encourage.

dismiss v. **1** give someone their notice, discharge, lay off, make redundant; informal sack, fire. **2** send away, let go, release, disband, discharge. **3** banish, set aside, put out of your mind, brush aside, reject, repudiate, spurn; informal pooh-pooh.

disobedient adj. naughty, insubordinate, defiant, unruly,

wayward, badly behaved, delinquent, rebellious, mutinous, troublesome, wilful.
– OPPOSITES obedient.

disobey v. **defy**, go against, flout, contravene, infringe, transgress, violate, disregard, ignore, pay no heed to.

disorder n. **1 untidiness**, mess, disarray, chaos, confusion, clutter, jumble, a muddle, a shambles. **2 unrest**, disturbance, turmoil, mayhem, violence, fighting, fracas, rioting, lawlessness, anarchy, breach of the peace. **3 disease**, infection, complaint, condition, affliction, malady, sickness, illness, ailment.
– OPPOSITES tidiness, peace.

disorderly adj. **1 untidy**, disorganized, topsy-turvy, at sixes and sevens, messy, jumbled, cluttered, in disarray, chaotic; informal like a bomb's hit it, higgledy-piggledy; Brit. informal shambolic. **2 unruly**, riotous, disruptive, troublesome, disobedient, lawless.
– OPPOSITES tidy, peaceful.

disorganized adj. **unmethodical**, unsystematic, undisciplined, unstructured, haphazard, chaotic, muddled, hit-or-miss, sloppy, slapdash, slipshod; Brit. informal shambolic.
– OPPOSITES organized.

disown v. reject, cast off/aside, abandon, renounce, repudiate, deny, turn your back on, wash your hands of, disinherit.

dispatch v. **1 send (off)**, post, mail, forward. **2 deal with**, finish, conclude, settle, discharge, perform. **3 kill**, put to death, massacre, wipe out, exterminate, eliminate, murder, assassinate, execute.
•n. **message**, report, communication, communiqué, bulletin, statement, letter, news, intelligence.

dispel v. banish, drive away/off, chase away, scatter, eliminate, dismiss, allay, ease, quell.

dispense v. **1 distribute**, pass round, hand out, dole out, dish out, share out. **2 administer**, deliver, issue, deal out, mete out. **3 dispensing medicines: prepare**, make up, supply, provide. ☐ **dispense with 1** waive, omit, drop, leave out, forgo, do away with; informal give something a miss. **2** get rid of, throw away/out, dispose of, discard; informal ditch, scrap, dump, chuck out/away; Brit. informal get shot of.

disperse v. **1 break up**, split up, disband, scatter, leave, go their separate ways, drive away/off, chase away. **2 dissipate**, dissolve, melt away, fade away, clear, lift. **3 scatter**, distribute, spread, disseminate.
– OPPOSITES assemble, gather.

displace v. **1 dislodge**, dislocate, move out of place/position, shift. **2 replace**, take the place of, supplant, supersede, oust, remove, depose.

display v. **1 exhibit**, show, arrange, array, present, lay out,

displease → dissent

set out. **2 show off**, parade, highlight, reveal, showcase. **3 manifest**, be evidence of, reveal, demonstrate, show.
– OPPOSITES conceal.
•n. **1 exhibition**, exposition, array, arrangement, presentation, demonstration, spectacle, show, parade. **2 manifestation**, expression, show, proof, demonstration, evidence.

displease v. annoy, irritate, anger, incense, irk, vex, nettle, put out, upset, exasperate.

dispose v.
□ **dispose of** throw away, throw out, get rid of, discard, jettison, scrap; informal dump, junk, ditch, chuck (out/away); Brit. informal get shot of; N. Amer. informal trash.

disposition n. **1 temperament**, nature, character, constitution, make-up, mentality. **2 arrangement**, positioning, placement, configuration, set-up, line-up, layout.

disprove v. refute, prove false, rebut, debunk, give the lie to, demolish; informal shoot full of holes, blow out of the water.

dispute n. **1 debate**, discussion, argument, controversy, disagreement, dissent, conflict. **2 quarrel**, argument, altercation, squabble, falling-out, disagreement, difference of opinion, clash; Brit. row.
– OPPOSITES agreement.
•v. **1 debate**, discuss, exchange views, quarrel, argue, disagree, clash, fall out, wrangle, bicker, squabble. **2 challenge**, contest, question, call into question, quibble over, contradict, argue about, disagree with, take issue with.
– OPPOSITES accept.

disqualify v. rule out, bar, exclude, prohibit, debar, preclude.

disregard v. ignore, take no notice of, pay no attention to, discount, overlook, turn a blind eye to, shut your eyes to, gloss over, brush off/aside, shrug off.
– OPPOSITES heed.
•n. **indifference**, non-observance, inattention, heedlessness, neglect, contempt.
– OPPOSITES attention.

disrupt v. interrupt, disturb, interfere with, play havoc with, upset, unsettle, obstruct, impede, hold up, delay.

disruptive adj. troublesome, disturbing, upsetting, unsettling, unruly, badly behaved, rowdy, disorderly, undisciplined, unmanageable, uncontrollable, uncooperative.
– OPPOSITES well behaved.

dissatisfied adj. discontented, disappointed, disaffected, displeased, disgruntled, aggrieved, unhappy.
– OPPOSITES contented.

dissent v. disagree, differ, demur, be at variance/odds, take issue, protest, object.
– OPPOSITES agree, conform.
•n. **disagreement**, difference of opinion, argument, dispute,

d

resistance, objection, protest, opposition.
- OPPOSITES agreement, conformity.

dissident n. **dissenter**, objector, protester, rebel, revolutionary, subversive, agitator, refusenik.
- OPPOSITES conformist.
•adj. **dissenting**, opposing, objecting, protesting, rebellious, revolutionary, subversive, nonconformist.
- OPPOSITES conformist.

dissimilar adj. **different**, differing, unalike, variant, diverse, divergent, heterogeneous, disparate, unrelated, distinct, contrasting.

dissociate v. **separate**, detach, disconnect, sever, cut off, divorce, isolate, alienate.
- OPPOSITES associate.

dissolve v. **1 break down**, liquefy, melt, deliquesce, disintegrate. **2 disband**, disperse, bring to an end, end, terminate, discontinue, break up, close down, wind up/down, suspend, adjourn. **3 annul**, nullify, void, invalidate, revoke.

dissuade v. **discourage**, deter, prevent, stop, talk out of, persuade against, advise against, argue out of.
- OPPOSITES encourage.

distance n. **1 interval**, space, span, gap, extent, length, range, reach. **2 aloofness**, remoteness, detachment, unfriendliness, reserve, reticence, formality; informal stand-offishness.
- OPPOSITES proximity.

distant adj. **1 faraway**, far-off, far-flung, remote, out of the way, outlying. **2 bygone**, remote, ancient, prehistoric. **3 vague**, faint, dim, indistinct, sketchy, hazy. **4 aloof**, reserved, remote, detached, unapproachable, unfriendly; informal standoffish. **5 distracted**, absent, faraway, detached, vague.
- OPPOSITES near, close, recent.

distasteful adj. **unpleasant**, disagreeable, displeasing, undesirable, objectionable, offensive, unsavoury, unpalatable.
- OPPOSITES agreeable.

distinct adj. **1** *two distinct categories*: **discrete**, separate, different, unconnected, distinctive, contrasting. **2** *the tail has distinct black tips*: **clear**, well defined, unmistakable, easily distinguishable, recognizable, visible, obvious, pronounced, prominent, striking.
- OPPOSITES similar.

distinction n. **1 difference**, contrast, variation, division, differentiation, discrepancy. **2 merit**, worth, greatness, excellence, quality, repute, renown, honour, credit.
- OPPOSITES similarity.

distinctive adj. **distinguishing**, characteristic, typical, individual, particular, peculiar, unique, exclusive, special.
- OPPOSITES common.

distinctly adv. **1 decidedly**, markedly, definitely, unmistakably, manifestly, patently.

2 clearly, plainly, intelligibly, audibly.

distinguish v. **1 differentiate**, tell apart, discriminate between, tell the difference between. **2 discern**, see, perceive, make out, detect, recognize, identify. **3 separate**, set apart, make distinctive, make different, single out, mark off.

distinguished adj. **eminent**, famous, renowned, prominent, great, well known, esteemed, respected, notable, illustrious, acclaimed, celebrated.
– OPPOSITES unknown, obscure.

distorted adj. **1 twisted**, warped, contorted, buckled, deformed, malformed, misshapen, disfigured, crooked, out of shape. **2 misrepresented**, perverted, twisted, falsified, misreported, misstated, garbled, inaccurate, biased, prejudiced.

distract v. **divert**, sidetrack, draw away, lead astray, disturb, put off.

distracted adj. **preoccupied**, inattentive, vague, abstracted, absent-minded, faraway, in a world of your own, troubled, harassed, worried; informal miles away, not with it.
– OPPOSITES attentive.

distraction n. **1 diversion**, interruption, disturbance, interference. **2 amusement**, entertainment, diversion, recreation, pastime, leisure pursuit.

distraught adj. **distressed**, frantic, fraught, overcome, over-

wrought, beside yourself, out of your mind, desperate, hysterical, worked up, at your wits' end; informal in a state.
– OPPOSITES calm.

distress n. **1 anguish**, suffering, pain, agony, torment, heartache, heartbreak, sorrow, sadness, unhappiness. **2** *a ship in distress*: **danger**, peril, difficulty, trouble, jeopardy, risk.
– OPPOSITES happiness.
▪ v. **upset**, pain, trouble, worry, perturb, disturb, disquiet, agitate, torment.
– OPPOSITES comfort.

distribute v. **1 give out**, deal out, dole out, dish out, hand out/round, share out, divide up/up, parcel out, apportion, allocate, allot. **2** *the newsletter is distributed free*: **circulate**, issue, deliver, disseminate, publish.
– OPPOSITES collect.

distribution n. **1** *the distribution of aid*: **giving out**, dealing out, doling out, handing out/round, issuing, allocation, sharing out, dividing up/out, parcelling out. **2** *centres of food distribution*: **supply**, delivery, dispersal, transportation.

district n. **area**, region, quarter, sector, zone, territory, locality, neighbourhood, community.

distrust n. **mistrust**, suspicion, wariness, scepticism, doubt, cynicism, misgivings, qualms.
– OPPOSITES trust.
▪ v. **mistrust**, be suspicious of, be wary of, be chary of, regard with suspicion, suspect, be

sceptical of, doubt, be unsure of/about, have misgivings about.
- OPPOSITES trust.

disturb v. **1** interrupt, intrude on, butt in on, barge in on, distract, disrupt, bother, trouble, pester, harass. **2** move, rearrange, mix up, interfere with, mess up. **3** perturb, trouble, concern, worry, upset, fluster, disconcert, dismay, alarm, distress, unsettle.
- OPPOSITES calm, reassure.

disturbance n. **1** disruption, distraction, interference, inconvenience, upset, annoyance, irritation, intrusion. **2** riot, fracas, brawl, street fight, free-for-all, commotion, disorder.
- OPPOSITES order.

disturbed adj. **1** disrupted, interrupted, fitful, intermittent, broken. **2** troubled, distressed, upset, distraught, unbalanced, unstable, disordered, dysfunctional, maladjusted, neurotic, unhinged; informal screwed up.
- OPPOSITES uninterrupted.

ditch n. trench, trough, channel, dyke, drain, gutter, gully, watercourse.

dive v. **1** plunge, plummet, nosedive, jump, fall, drop, pitch. **2** leap, jump, lunge, throw/fling yourself, go headlong.
-n. **1** plunge, nosedive, jump, fall, drop, swoop. **2** lunge, spring, jump, leap.

diverge v. **1** separate, part, fork, divide, split, bifurcate, go in different directions. **2** differ, be

different, be dissimilar, disagree, be at variance/odds, conflict, clash.
- OPPOSITES converge, agree.

diverse adj. various, sundry, varied, varying, miscellaneous, assorted, mixed, diversified, divergent, different, differing, distinct, unlike, dissimilar.
- OPPOSITES similar.

diversion n. **1** detour, deviation, alternative route, re-routing, redirection. **2** distraction, disturbance, smokescreen; informal red herring. **3** entertainment, amusement, pastime, delight, fun, recreation, pleasure.

diversity n. variety, miscellany, assortment, mixture, mix, range, array, multiplicity, variation, difference.
- OPPOSITES uniformity.

divert v. **1** re-route, redirect, change the course of, deflect, channel. **2** distract, sidetrack, disturb, draw away, put off. **3** amuse, entertain, distract, delight, enchant, interest, fascinate, absorb, engross, rivet, grip.

divide v. **1** he divided his kingdom into four: split (up), cut up, carve up, dissect, bisect, halve, quarter. **2** a curtain divided her cabin from the galley: separate, segregate, partition, screen off, section off, split off. **3** diverge, separate, part, branch (off), fork, split (in two). **4** share out, ration out, parcel out, deal out, dole out, dish out, distribute. **5** disunite, drive apart, drive a wedge

between, break up, split (up),
separate, isolate, alienate.
- OPPOSITES unify, converge,
unite.

divine[1] adj. **godly**, angelic, heavenly, celestial, holy, sacred.
- OPPOSITES mortal.

divine[2] v. **guess**, surmise, deduce, infer, discern, discover, perceive; informal figure (out); Brit. informal suss.

division n. **1** the division of the island: **dividing (up)**, breaking up, break-up, carving up, splitting, dissection, partitioning, separation, segregation. **2** the division of his estates: **sharing out**, dividing up, parcelling out, dishing out, allocation, allotment, splitting up, carving up. **3** dividing line, divide, boundary, border, demarcation line, gap, gulf. **4 section**, subsection, subdivision, category, class, group, grouping, set. **5 department**, branch, arm, wing. **6 disunity**, disunion, conflict, discord, disagreement, alienation, isolation.
- OPPOSITES unification.

divorce n. **1 dissolution**, annulment, decree nisi, separation. **2** the divorce between the church and people: **separation**, division, split, gulf, disunity, alienation, schism.
- OPPOSITES marriage.
•v. **1 split up**, get a divorce, separate. **2** religion cannot be divorced from morality: **separate**, divide, detach, isolate, alienate, set apart, cut off.

divulge v. **disclose**, reveal, tell, communicate, pass on, publish, give away, let slip.
- OPPOSITES conceal.

dizzy adj. **giddy**, light-headed, faint, unsteady, shaky, muzzy, wobbly; informal woozy.

do v. **1** she does most of the work: **carry out**, undertake, discharge, execute, perform, accomplish, achieve, bring about, engineer; informal pull off. **2** they can do as they please: **act**, behave, conduct yourself. **3 suffice**, be adequate, be satisfactory, fill/fit the bill, serve. **4** a portrait I am doing: **make**, create, produce, work on, design, manufacture.
□ **do away with** abolish, get rid of, eliminate, discontinue, stop, end, terminate, drop, abandon, give up; informal scrap.
do without forgo, dispense with, abstain from, refrain from, eschew, give up, cut out, renounce, manage without.

docile adj. **compliant**, obedient, pliant, submissive, deferential, unassertive, cooperative, amenable, accommodating, biddable.
- OPPOSITES disobedient, wilful.

dock[1] n. **harbour**, marina, port, wharf, quay, pier, jetty, landing stage.
•v. **moor**, berth, put in, tie up, anchor.

dock[2] v. **1 deduct**, subtract, remove, debit, take off/away; informal knock off. **2 reduce**, cut, decrease. **3 cut off**, cut short, shorten, crop, lop.

doctor n. **physician**, medical practitioner, general practitioner, GP, clinician, consultant; informal doc, medic; Brit. informal quack.
- v. **1 adulterate**, tamper with, lace; informal spike. **2 falsify**, tamper with, interfere with, alter, change, forge, fake; Brit. informal fiddle.

doctrine n. **creed**, credo, dogma, belief, teaching, ideology, tenet, maxim, canon, principle.

document n. **paper**, certificate, deed, form, contract, agreement, report, record.
- v. **record**, register, report, log, chronicle, authenticate, verify.

dodge v. **1** he dodged the police: **elude**, evade, avoid, escape, run away from, lose, shake (off); informal give someone the slip. **2** the minister tried to dodge the debate: **avoid**, evade, get out of, back out of, sidestep; informal duck, wriggle out of. **3 dart**, duck, dive, swerve, veer.
- n. a clever dodge | a tax dodge: **ruse**, scheme, tactic, stratagem, ploy, subterfuge, trick, hoax, cheat, deception, fraud; informal scam; Brit. informal wheeze.

dog n. **hound**, canine, man's best friend, mongrel; informal pooch, mutt; Austral. informal bitzer.
- v. **plague**, beset, bedevil, blight, trouble.

WORD LINKS
relating to dogs: canine

dogged adj. **tenacious**, determined, resolute, stubborn, obstinate, purposeful, persistent, persevering, single-minded, tireless.
- OPPOSITES half-hearted.

dogmatic adj. **opinionated**, assertive, insistent, emphatic, adamant, doctrinaire, authoritarian, imperious, dictatorial, uncompromising.

dole v.
□ **dole out** deal out, share out, divide up, allocate, distribute, dispense, hand out, give out, dish out.

domain n. **1 realm**, kingdom, empire, dominion, province, territory, land. **2 field**, area, sphere, discipline, province, world.

domestic adj. **1 family**, home, household. **2 domesticated**, homely, home-loving. **3 tame**, pet, domesticated; Brit. house-trained. **4 national**, state, home, internal.

dominant adj. **1 ruling**, governing, controlling, presiding, commanding. **2 assertive**, authoritative, forceful, domineering, commanding, controlling, pushy. **3 main**, principal, prime, chief, primary, central, key, crucial, core.
- OPPOSITES subservient, subsidiary.

dominate v. **1 control**, influence, command, be in charge of, rule, govern, direct. **2 overlook**, command, tower above/over, loom over.

domination n. **control**, power, command, authority, dominion, rule, supremacy, superiority, ascendancy, sway, mastery.

domineering adj. **overbearing**, authoritarian, imperious, high-handed, peremptory, auto-cratic, dictatorial, despotic, strict, harsh; informal bossy.

don v. **put on**, get dressed in, dress (yourself) in, get into, slip into/on, change into.

donate v. **give**, contribute, gift, subscribe, grant, present, endow; informal chip in, stump up.

donation n. **gift**, contribution, subscription, present, handout, grant, offering.

donor n. **giver**, contributor, benefactor, benefactress, sub-scriber, supporter, backer, patron, sponsor.
– OPPOSITES beneficiary.

doom n. **destruction**, downfall, ruin, extinction, annihilation, death, nemesis.
•v. **destine**, fate, predestine, preordain, mean, condemn, sentence.

doomed adj. **ill-fated**, ill-starred, cursed, jinxed, damned; literary star-crossed.

dose n. **measure**, portion, draught, dosage.

dot n. **spot**, speck, fleck, speckle, full stop, decimal point.
•v. **1 spot**, fleck, mark, spatter. **2 scatter**, pepper, sprinkle, strew, spread.

dote v.
□ **dote on** adore, love dearly, be devoted to, idolize, treasure, cherish, worship.

double adj. **dual**, duplex, twin, binary, duplicate, coupled, matching, twofold, in pairs.
– OPPOSITES single.
•n. **lookalike**, twin, clone, dupli-cate, exact likeness, replica, copy, facsimile, doppelgänger; informal spitting image, dead ringer.

doubt n. **1 uncertainty**, indeci-sion, hesitation, irresolution, hesitancy, vacillation, lack of conviction. **2 scepticism**, dis-trust, mistrust, suspicion, cyni-cism, wariness, reservations, misgivings, suspicions.
– OPPOSITES certainty, trust.
•v. **disbelieve**, distrust, mistrust, suspect, be suspicious of, have misgivings about.
□ **in doubt 1** doubtful, uncer-tain, unconfirmed, unknown, undecided, unresolved, in the balance, up in the air; informal iffy. **2** irresolute, hesitant, doubtful, unsure, uncertain, in two minds, undecided, in a quandary/ dilemma. **no doubt** doubtless, undoubtedly, indubitably, with-out (a) doubt, unquestionably, undeniably, clearly, plainly, obviously, patently.

doubtful adj. **1 hesitant**, in doubt, unsure, uncertain, in two minds, in a quandary, in a dilemma. **2 in doubt**, uncertain, open to question, unsure, debat-able, up in the air, inconclusive,

d

unconfirmed. **3 unlikely**, improbable. **4 distrustful**, mistrustful, sceptical, suspicious, having reservations, wary, chary, leery. **5 questionable**, dubious, suspect, suspicious.
– OPPOSITES confident, certain.

doubtless adv. **undoubtedly**, no doubt, unquestionably, indisputably, undeniably, certainly, surely, of course.

douse v. **1 drench**, soak, saturate, wet. **2 extinguish**, put out, quench, smother.

dowdy adj. **unfashionable**, frumpy, old-fashioned, shabby, frowzy; Brit. informal mumsy.
– OPPOSITES fashionable.

downfall n. **ruin**, ruination, undoing, defeat, overthrow, destruction, annihilation, end, collapse, fall, crash, failure.
– OPPOSITES rise.

downgrade v. **demote**, reduce, relegate.
– OPPOSITES promote.

downright adj. **complete**, total, absolute, utter, thorough, out-and-out, outright, sheer, arrant, pure.
•adv. **thoroughly**, utterly, positively, profoundly, really, completely, totally, entirely.

drab adj. **1 colourless**, grey, dull, washed out, dingy, dreary, dismal, cheerless, gloomy, sombre. **2 uninteresting**, dull, boring, tedious, monotonous, dry, dreary.
– OPPOSITES bright, interesting.

draft n. **1 version**, sketch, attempt, effort, outline, plan.

2 cheque, order, money order, bill of exchange.

drag v. **haul**, pull, tug, heave, lug, draw, trail.
•n. **1 pull**, resistance, tug. **2** (informal) **bore**, nuisance, bother, trouble, pest, annoyance, trial; informal pain (in the neck), bind, headache, hassle.

drain v. **1** a valve for draining the tank: **empty (out)**, void, clear (out), evacuate, unload. **2** drain off any surplus liquid: **draw off**, extract, siphon off, pour out, pour off, bleed, tap, filter, discharge. **3** the water drained away: **flow**, pour, trickle, stream, run, rush, gush, flood, surge, leak, ooze, seep, dribble. **4 use up**, exhaust, deplete, consume, expend, get through, sap, milk, bleed. **5 drink**, gulp (down), guzzle, quaff, swallow, finish off, toss off; informal sink, down, swig, swill (down), knock back.
– OPPOSITES fill.
•n. **1 sewer**, channel, ditch, culvert, duct, pipe, gutter. **2 strain**, pressure, burden, load, demand.

drama n. **1 play**, show, piece, theatrical work, stage show, dramatization. **2 acting**, the theatre, the stage, dramatic art, stagecraft, dramaturgy. **3 incident**, scene, spectacle, crisis, disturbance, row, commotion, excitement, thrill, sensation, dramatics, theatrics, histrionics.

dramatic adj. **1 theatrical**, thespian, dramaturgical. **2 considerable**, substantial, significant, remarkable,

extraordinary, exceptional, phenomenal. **3 exciting**, stirring, action-packed, sensational, spectacular, startling, unexpected, tense, gripping, riveting, thrilling, hair-raising, lively. **4 striking**, impressive, imposing, spectacular, breathtaking, dazzling, sensational, awesome, awe-inspiring, remarkable. **5 exaggerated**, theatrical, ostentatious, actressy, stagy, showy, melodramatic.
- OPPOSITES unremarkable, boring.

dramatize v. **1 adapt**, turn into a play/film. **2 exaggerate**, overdo, overstate, magnify, amplify, inflate, sensationalize, embroider, colour, aggrandize, embellish, elaborate; informal blow up (out of all proportion).

drape v. **wrap**, cover, envelop, shroud, wind, swathe, festoon, hang.

drastic adj. **extreme**, serious, desperate, radical, far-reaching, momentous, substantial.
- OPPOSITES moderate.

draught n. **1 current of air**, wind, breeze, gust, puff, waft. **2 gulp**, drink, swallow, mouthful; informal swig.

draw v. **1 sketch**, outline, rough out, illustrate, render, represent, trace, portray, depict. **2 pull**, haul, drag, tug, heave, lug, tow; informal yank. **3 move**, go, come, proceed, progress, pass, drive, inch, roll, glide, cruise, sweep. **4 pull out**, take out, produce,

fish out, extract, withdraw, unsheathe. **5 attract**, win, capture, catch, engage, lure, entice, bring in.
• n. **1 raffle**, lottery, sweepstake, sweep, tombola, ballot. **2 tie**, dead heat, stalemate. **3 attraction**, lure, allure, pull, appeal, temptation, charm, fascination.
□ **draw on** call on, have recourse to, turn to, look to, exploit, use, employ, utilize, bring into play. **draw out** prolong, protract, drag out, spin out, string out, extend, lengthen. **draw up** compose, formulate, frame, write down, draft, prepare, think up, devise, work out, create, invent, design.

drawback n. **disadvantage**, snag, downside, catch, hitch, pitfall, fly in the ointment, weak spot/point, weakness, imperfection; informal minus.
- OPPOSITES benefit.

drawing n. **sketch**, picture, illustration, representation, portrayal, depiction, diagram, outline.

WORD LINKS
relating to drawing: graphic

dread v. **fear**, be afraid of, worry about, be anxious about, shudder at the thought of.
• n. **fear**, apprehension, trepidation, anxiety, panic, alarm, terror, disquiet, unease.

dreadful adj. **1** a dreadful accident: **terrible**, frightful, horrible, grim, awful, horrifying,

shocking, distressing, appalling, harrowing, ghastly, gruesome, fearful, horrendous, tragic. **2** *a dreadful meal*: **very bad**, frightful, shocking, awful, abysmal, dire, atrocious, disgraceful, deplorable; informal woeful, rotten, lousy, ropy; Brit. informal duff, rubbish. **3** *a dreadful flirt*: **outrageous**, shocking, real, awful, terrible, inordinate, incorrigible.
– OPPOSITES wonderful, excellent.

dream n. **1** daydream, reverie, trance, daze, stupor. **2 ambition**, aspiration, hope, goal, aim, objective, intention, desire, wish, daydream, fantasy. **3 delight**, joy, marvel, wonder, gem, treasure.
– OPPOSITES nightmare.
•v. **1** fantasize, daydream, wish, hope, long, yearn, hanker. **2 daydream**, be in a trance, be lost in thought, be preoccupied, be abstracted, stare into space, •be in cloud cuckoo land.
☐ **dream up** think up, invent, concoct, devise, hatch, come up with.

dreary adj. dull, uninteresting, tedious, boring, unexciting, unstimulating, uninspiring, soul-destroying, monotonous, uneventful.
– OPPOSITES exciting.

drench v. soak, saturate, wet through, douse, steep, flood, drown.

dress n. **1** *a long blue dress*: **frock**, gown, robe, shift. **2** *full evening dress*: **clothes**, clothing, garments, garb, attire, costume,

outfit; informal get-up, gear; Brit. informal clobber; formal apparel.
•v. **1 clothe**, attire, deck out, garb; informal get up. **2 decorate**, trim, adorn, arrange, prepare. **3 bandage**, cover, bind, wrap.
– OPPOSITES undress.

> **WORD LINKS**
> relating to dress: sartorial

dribble v. **1** drool, slaver, slobber. **2** trickle, drip, roll, run, drizzle, ooze, seep, leak.

drift v. **1 be carried**, be borne, float, bob, glide, coast, waft. **2 wander**, meander, stray, stroll, dawdle, float, roam. **3 stray**, digress, wander, deviate, get sidetracked. **4 pile up**, bank up, heap up, accumulate, gather, amass.
•n. **1 movement**, shift, flow, transfer, gravitation. **2 gist**, meaning, sense, significance, thrust, import, tenor, intention, direction. **3 pile**, heap, bank, mound, mass, accumulation.

drill n. **1 training**, instruction, coaching, teaching, (physical) exercises; informal square-bashing. **2 procedure**, routine, practice, programme, schedule, method, system.
•v. **1 bore**, pierce, puncture, perforate. **2 train**, instruct, coach, teach, discipline, exercise.

drink v. **1 swallow**, gulp (down), quaff, guzzle, imbibe, sip, drain; informal swig, down, knock back. **2 take alcohol**, tipple, indulge, carouse; informal hit the bottle, booze; Brit. informal bevvy.

•n. **1 beverage**, liquid refreshment; Brit. informal bevvy. **2 alcohol**, intoxicating liquor, spirits; informal booze, the hard stuff, the bottle, grog. **3 swallow**, gulp, mouthful, draught, sip; informal swig, slug.

drip v. **drop**, dribble, leak, trickle, run, splash, sprinkle.
•n. **drop**, dribble, spot, trickle, splash, bead.

drive v. **1 operate**, handle, manage, pilot, steer, work. **2 go by car**, motor. **3 run**, chauffeur, give someone a lift, take, ferry, transport, convey. **4 power**, propel, move, push. **5 hammer**, screw, ram, sink, plunge, thrust, knock. **6 force**, compel, prompt, precipitate, oblige, coerce, pressure, spur, prod.
•n. **1 excursion**, outing, trip, jaunt, tour, ride, run, journey; informal spin. **2 motivation**, ambition, single-mindedness, determination, will power, dedication, doggedness, tenacity, enthusiasm, zeal, commitment, energy, vigour; informal get-up-and-go. **3 campaign**, crusade, movement, effort, push, initiative.

droop v. **hang down**, wilt, dangle, sag, flop, sink, slump, drop.

drop v. **1 let fall**, let go of, release. **2 fall**, descend, plunge, plummet, dive, sink, dip, tumble. **3 decrease**, lessen, reduce, fall, decline, dwindle, sink, slump. **4 abandon**, give up, discontinue, finish with, renounce, reject, forgo, relinquish, dispense with, leave out; informal dump, pack in, quit.
– OPPOSITES rise, increase.
•n. **1 droplet**, blob, globule, bead. **2 small amount**, little, bit, dash, spot, dribble, sprinkle, trickle, splash, mouthful; informal smidgen, tad. **3 decrease**, reduction, decline, fall-off, downturn, slump. **4 cliff**, precipice, slope, descent, incline.
□ **drop off** fall asleep, doze (off), nap, drowse; informal nod off, drift off, snooze, take forty winks. **drop out** leave, give up, withdraw, retire, pull out, abandon something, fall by the wayside; informal quit, pack in, jack in.

drug n. **1 medicine**, medication, remedy, cure, antidote. **2 narcotic**, stimulant, hallucinogen; informal dope, gear.
•v. **1 anaesthetize**, poison, knock out; informal dope. **2 tamper with**, lace, poison; informal dope, spike, doctor.

WORD LINKS
branch of medicine concerned with drugs: pharmacology; shop selling drugs: pharmacy, (Brit.) chemist, (N. Amer.) drugstore

drum n. **canister**, barrel, cylinder, tank, bin, can.
•v. **1 tap**, beat, rap, thud, thump, tattoo, thrum. **2 instil**, drive, din, hammer, drill, implant, ingrain, inculcate.
□ **drum up** round up, gather, collect, summon, attract, canvass, solicit, petition.

drunk adj. **intoxicated**, inebriated, drunken, tipsy, under the influence; informal tight, merry, plastered, sloshed, pickled, tanked (up), ratted, three sheets to the wind, squiffy; Brit. informal legless, paralytic, Brahms and Liszt, tiddly; N. Amer. informal loaded.
- OPPOSITES sober.
　•n. **drunkard**, alcoholic, dipsomaniac, inebriate; informal boozer, soak, wino, alky.

dry adj. **1** arid, parched, waterless, dehydrated, desiccated, withered, shrivelled, wizened. **2 dull**, uninteresting, boring, unexciting, tedious, dreary, monotonous, unimaginative, sterile; informal deadly. **3 wry**, subtle, laconic, ironic, sardonic, sarcastic, cynical.
- OPPOSITES wet, moist.
　•v. **1 parch**, scorch, bake, sear, dehydrate, desiccate, wither, shrivel. **2 wipe**, towel, rub dry, drain.
- OPPOSITES wet, moisten.

dual adj. **double**, twofold, duplex, binary, twin, matching, paired, coupled.
- OPPOSITES single.

dub v. **name**, call, nickname, label, christen, term, tag.

dubious adj. **1 doubtful**, uncertain, unsure, hesitant, sceptical, suspicious; informal iffy. **2 suspicious**, suspect, untrustworthy, unreliable, questionable; informal shady; Brit. informal dodgy.
- OPPOSITES certain, trustworthy.

duck v. **1 bob down**, bend down, stoop, crouch, squat, hunch down, hunker down. **2** (informal) **shirk**, dodge, evade, avoid, elude, escape, sidestep.

duct n. **tube**, channel, canal, vessel, conduit, pipe, outlet, inlet, flue, shaft, vent.

due adj. **1** their fees were due: **owing**, owed, payable, outstanding, overdue, unpaid, unsettled. **2** the chancellor's statement is due today: **expected**, anticipated, scheduled, awaited, required. **3 deserved**, merited, warranted, justified, owing, appropriate, fitting, right, rightful, proper. **4 proper**, correct, suitable, appropriate, adequate, sufficient.
　•n. **fee**, subscription, charge, payment, contribution, levy.
　•adv. **directly**, straight, exactly, precisely, dead.
　□ **due to 1** her death was due to an infection: **attributable to**, caused by, because of, down to. **2** the train was cancelled due to staffshortages: **because of**, owing to, on account of, as a consequence of, as a result of, thanks to.

duel n. **1 single combat**, fight, confrontation, head-to-head; informal shoot-out. **2 contest**, match, game, meet, encounter, clash.

dull adj. **1 uninteresting**, boring, tedious, monotonous, unimaginative, uneventful, featureless, colourless, lifeless, unexciting, uninspiring, flat,

bland, stodgy, dreary; informal deadly; N. Amer. informal dullsville.
2 overcast, cloudy, gloomy, dark, dismal, dreary, sombre, grey, murky, sunless.
3 drab, dreary, sombre, dark, subdued, muted. **4 muffled**, muted, quiet, soft, faint, indistinct, stifled. **5 unintelligent**, stupid, slow, brainless, mindless, foolish, idiotic; informal dense, dim, half-witted, thick.
– OPPOSITES interesting, bright.
– v. **lessen**, decrease, diminish, reduce, dampen, blunt, deaden, allay, ease.
– OPPOSITES intensify.

duly adv. **1 properly**, correctly, appropriately, suitably, fittingly. **2 at the right time**, on time, punctually.

dumb adj. **1 mute**, speechless, tongue-tied, silent, at a loss for words. **2** (informal) **stupid**, unintelligent, ignorant, dense, brainless, foolish, slow, dull, simple; informal thick, dim; Brit. informal daft.
– OPPOSITES talkative, clever.

dummy n. **1 mannequin**, model, figure.
• adj. **simulated**, practice, trial, mock, make-believe; informal pretend.

dump n. **1 tip**, rubbish dump, dumping ground. **2** (informal) **hovel**, slum; informal hole, pigsty.
• v. **1 put down**, set down, deposit, place, shove, unload, drop, throw down; informal stick, park, plonk; Brit. informal bung.
2 dispose of, get rid of, throw

away/out, discard, bin, jettison; informal ditch, junk.

dune n. **bank**, mound, hillock, hummock, knoll, ridge, heap, drift.

duplicate n. **copy**, photocopy, facsimile, reprint, replica, reproduction, clone; trademark Xerox, photostat.
• adj. **matching**, identical, twin, corresponding, equivalent.
• v. **1 copy**, photocopy, photostat, xerox, reproduce, replicate, reprint, run off. **2 repeat**, do again, redo, replicate.

durable adj. **1 hard-wearing**, wear-resistant, heavy-duty, tough, long-lasting, strong, sturdy, robust, utilitarian.
2 lasting, long-lasting, longterm, enduring, persistent, abiding, permanent, undying, everlasting.
– OPPOSITES delicate, short-lived.

duration n. **length**, time, period, term, span, extent, stretch.

dusk n. **twilight**, nightfall, sunset, sundown, evening, close of day, semi-darkness, gloom; literary gloaming.
– OPPOSITES dawn.

dust n. **dirt**, grime, grit, powder, particles.
• v. **1 wipe**, clean, brush, sweep. **2 dust the cake with icing sugar**: **sprinkle**, scatter, powder, dredge, cover.

dusty adj. **1 dirty**, grimy, grubby. **2 powdery**, crumbly, chalky, granular, soft, gritty.

dutiful adj. **conscientious**, responsible, dedicated, devoted, attentive, obedient, deferential.
– OPPOSITES remiss.

duty n. **1** *a sense of duty:* **responsibility**, obligation, commitment, allegiance, loyalty. **2** *it was his duty to attend the king:* **job**, task, assignment, mission, function, role. **3** **tax**, levy, tariff, excise, toll, rate.

dwarf v. **1** **dominate**, tower over, loom over, overshadow. **2** **overshadow**, outshine, surpass, exceed, outclass, outstrip, outdo, top.

dwell v. (formal) **reside**, live, be housed, lodge, stay; informal put up; formal abide.
□ **dwell on** linger over, mull over, muse on, brood about/over, think about, be preoccupied by, obsess about, harp on about.

dwindle v. **diminish**, decrease, reduce, lessen, shrink, wane.
– OPPOSITES increase.

dye n. **colouring**, dyestuff, pigment, tint, stain, wash.
•v. **colour**, tint, pigment, stain, wash.

dying adj. **1** **terminally ill**, at death's door, on your deathbed, fading fast, not long for this world, moribund, in extremis. **2** **declining**, vanishing, fading, waning; informal on the way out.

dynamic adj. **energetic**, spirited, active, lively, vigorous, forceful, high-powered, aggressive, enterprising; informal go-getting, go-ahead.

dynasty n. **family**, house, line, lineage, regime, empire.

Ee

each adv. **apiece**, per person, per head, per capita.

eager adj. **1** **keen**, enthusiastic, avid, ardent, zealous, highly motivated, committed, earnest. **2** *we were eager for news:* **anxious**, impatient, agog, longing, yearning, wishing, hoping; informal itching, dying, raring.
– OPPOSITES apathetic.

ear n. *he has an ear for a good song:* **appreciation**, feel, instinct, intuition, sense.

WORD LINKS
relating to the ear: aural

early adj. **1** **advance**, initial, preliminary, first. **2** **untimely**, premature, unseasonable. **3** **primitive**, ancient, prehistoric, primeval. **4** **prompt**, timely, quick, speedy.
– OPPOSITES late, overdue.
•adv. **1** **in advance**, in good time, ahead of schedule, with time to spare, before the last moment.

2 prematurely, before the usual time, too soon, ahead of schedule.
– OPPOSITES late.

earmark v. set aside, keep (back), reserve, designate, assign, allocate.

earn v. **1 be paid**, take home, gross, receive, get, make, collect, bring in; informal pocket, bank. **2 deserve**, merit, warrant, justify, be worthy of, gain, win, secure, obtain.
– OPPOSITES lose.

earnest adj. **1 serious**, solemn, grave, sober, humourless, staid, intense. **2 devout**, heartfelt, wholehearted, sincere, impassioned, fervent, intense.
– OPPOSITES frivolous, half-hearted.

earnings pl. n. **income**, pay, wages, salary, stipend, remuneration, fees, revenue, yield, profit, takings, proceeds.

earth n. **1 world**, globe, planet. **2 land**, ground, terra firma, floor. **3 soil**, clay, dust, dirt, loam, ground, turf.

> **WORD LINKS**
> relating to the earth: terrestrial; study of the earth: geography, geology

earthly adj. **worldly**, temporal, mortal, human, material, carnal, fleshly, bodily, physical, corporeal, sensual.
– OPPOSITES spiritual, heavenly.

earthquake n. **(earth) tremor**, shock, convulsion; informal quake.

> **WORD LINKS**
> relating to earthquakes: seismic; study of earthquakes: seismology

earthy adj. **1 down-to-earth**, unsophisticated, unrefined, simple, plain, unpretentious, natural. **2 bawdy**, ribald, racy, rude, crude, coarse, indelicate, indecent; informal raunchy; Brit. informal fruity.

ease n. **1 effortlessness**, no trouble, simplicity. **2 naturalness**, casualness, informality, composure, nonchalance, insouciance. **3 affluence**, wealth, prosperity, luxury, plenty, comfort, enjoyment, well-being.
– OPPOSITES difficulty.
•v. **1 relieve**, alleviate, soothe, moderate, dull, deaden, numb. **2** the rain eased off: **let up**, abate, subside, die down, slacken off, diminish, lessen. **3 calm**, quieten, pacify, soothe, comfort, console. **4 slide**, slip, squeeze, guide, manoeuvre, inch, edge.
– OPPOSITES aggravate, intensify.

easily adv. **effortlessly**, comfortably, simply, without difficulty, readily, without a hitch.

easy adj. **1 uncomplicated**, undemanding, effortless, painless, trouble-free, simple, straightforward, elementary, plain sailing; informal a piece of cake, child's play, a cinch. **2 natural**, casual, informal, unceremonious, unreserved, unaffected, easy-going, amiable, affable, genial, good-humoured,

e

carefree, nonchalant, unconcerned; informal laid-back.
3 quiet, tranquil, serene, peaceful, untroubled, contented, relaxed, comfortable, secure, safe; informal cushy. **4** *an easy pace*: leisurely, unhurried, comfortable, undemanding, easy-going, gentle, sedate, moderate, steady.
– OPPOSITES difficult, demanding.

easy-going adj. relaxed, even-tempered, placid, happy-go-lucky, carefree, imperturbable, undemanding, patient, tolerant, lenient, broad-minded, understanding; informal laid-back, unflappable.
– OPPOSITES intolerant.

eat v. **1 consume**, devour, swallow, partake of, munch, chomp; informal tuck into, put away.
2 have a meal, feed, snack, breakfast, lunch, dine; informal graze.

eavesdrop v. listen in, spy, overhear; informal snoop, earwig.

ebb v. **1 recede**, go out, retreat.
2 diminish, dwindle, wane, fade (away), peter out, decline, flag.
– OPPOSITES flow, increase.

ebullient adj. **exuberant**, buoyant, cheerful, cheery, merry, jolly, sunny, jaunty, animated, sparkling, vivacious, irrepressible; informal bubbly, bouncy, upbeat, chirpy, full of beans.
– OPPOSITES depressed.

eccentric adj. **unconventional**, abnormal, anomalous, odd, strange, peculiar, weird, bizarre, outlandish, idiosyncratic, quirky; informal oddball, kooky, cranky.

– OPPOSITES conventional.
•n. **oddity**, free spirit, misfit; informal oddball, weirdo.

echo n. **reverberation**, reflection, ringing, repetition, repeat.
•v. **1 reverberate**, resonate, resound, reflect, ring, vibrate.
2 repeat, restate, reiterate, imitate, parrot, mimic, reproduce, recite.

eclipse v. **outshine**, overshadow, surpass, exceed, outclass, outstrip, outdo, transcend.

economic adj. **1 financial**, monetary, budgetary, commercial, fiscal. **2 profitable**, money-making, lucrative, remunerative, fruitful, productive.
– OPPOSITES unprofitable.

economical adj. **1 cheap**, inexpensive, low-cost, budget, economy, cut-price, bargain.
2 thrifty, provident, prudent, sensible, frugal.
– OPPOSITES expensive, spendthrift.

economize v. **save (money)**, cut costs, cut back, make cutbacks, retrench, scrimp.

economy n. **1 wealth**, financial resources, financial management. **2 thrift**, thriftiness, prudence, careful budgeting, economizing, saving, restraint, frugality.
– OPPOSITES extravagance.

ecstasy n. **rapture**, bliss, joy, elation, euphoria, rhapsodies.
– OPPOSITES misery.

ecstatic adj. **enraptured**, elated, euphoric, rapturous, joyful, overjoyed, blissful; informal over the moon, on top of the world.

eddy n. swirl, whirlpool, vortex.
- v. swirl, whirl, spiral, wind, twist.

edge n. **1 border**, boundary, extremity, fringe, margin, side, lip, rim, brim, brink, verge, perimeter. **2 sharpness**, severity, bite, sting, sarcasm, malice, spite, venom. **3 advantage**, lead, head start, the whip hand, the upper hand, dominance.
– OPPOSITES middle.
- v. **1 border**, fringe, skirt, surround, enclose, encircle, bound. **2 trim**, decorate, finish, border, fringe. **3 creep**, inch, work your way, ease yourself, sidle, steal.

edgy adj. **tense**, nervous, on edge, anxious, apprehensive, uneasy, unsettled, twitchy, jumpy, nervy, keyed up, restive; informal uptight, wired.
– OPPOSITES calm.

edit v. correct, check, copy-edit, improve, polish, modify, adapt, revise, rewrite, reword, shorten, condense, cut, abridge.

edition n. **issue**, number, volume, printing, impression, publication, programme, version.

educate v. teach, school, tutor, instruct, coach, train, inform, enlighten.

educated adj. **informed**, literate, schooled, tutored, well read, learned, knowledgeable, enlightened, intellectual, academic, erudite, scholarly, cultivated, cultured.
– OPPOSITES uneducated.

education n. **1 teaching**, schooling, tuition, tutoring, instruction, coaching, training, guidance, enlightenment. **2 learning**, knowledge, literacy, scholarship, enlightenment.

educational adj. **1 academic**, scholastic, learning, teaching, pedagogic. **2 instructive**, instructional, educative, informative, illuminating, enlightening; formal edifying.

eerie adj. **uncanny**, sinister, ghostly, unnatural, unearthly, supernatural, other-worldly, strange, abnormal, weird, freakish; informal creepy, scary, spooky.

effect n. **1** the effect of these changes: **result**, consequence, upshot, outcome, repercussions, end result, aftermath. **2** the effect of the drug: **impact**, action, effectiveness, power, potency, strength, success. **3** the dead man's effects: **belongings**, possessions, worldly goods, chattels, property; informal things, stuff; Brit. informal clobber.
– OPPOSITES cause.
- v. **achieve**, accomplish, carry out, manage, bring off, execute, conduct, engineer, perform, do, cause, bring about, produce.

effective adj. **1 successful**, effectual, potent, powerful, helpful, beneficial, advantageous, valuable, useful. **2 convincing**, compelling, strong, forceful, persuasive, plausible, credible, logical, reasonable, cogent. **3 operative**, in force, in effect,

valid, official, legal, binding.
4 virtual, practical, essential,
actual.
– OPPOSITES ineffective.

effervescent adj. **fizzy**, sparkling, carbonated, aerated, gassy,
bubbly.
– OPPOSITES still.

efficiency n. **1 economy**, productivity, cost-effectiveness, organization, order, orderliness,
regulation. **2 competence**,
capability, ability, proficiency,
expertise, skill, effectiveness.
– OPPOSITES inefficiency,
incompetence.

efficient adj. **1 economic**, productive, effective, cost-effective,
streamlined, organized, methodical, systematic, orderly.
2 competent, capable, able,
proficient, skilful, skilled, effective, productive, organized,
businesslike.
– OPPOSITES inefficient,
incompetent.

effort n. **1 attempt**, try,
endeavour; informal shot, stab,
bash. **2 achievement**, accomplishment, feat, undertaking,
enterprise, work, result, outcome. **3 exertion**, energy, work,
application; informal elbow
grease; Brit. informal graft.

egg n. **ovum**, gamete; (**eggs**)
roe, spawn.
□ **egg on** urge, goad, incite,
provoke, push, drive, spur on,
prod.

WORD LINKS
egg-shaped: ovoid

egotistic, **egoistic** adj. **self-
centred**, selfish, egocentric,
self-interested, self-seeking,
self-absorbed, self-obsessed,
narcissistic, vain, conceited, self-
important, boastful.

eject v. **1 emit**, spew out, discharge, disgorge, give off, send
out, belch, vent. **2 expel**, throw
out, remove, oust, evict, banish;
informal kick out, turf out, boot
out.

elaborate adj. **1 complicated**,
complex, intricate, involved,
detailed. **2 ornate**, decorated,
embellished, adorned, ornamented, fancy, fussy, busy.
– OPPOSITES simple, plain.
•v. **expand on**, enlarge on, add
to, flesh out, develop, fill out,
amplify.

elastic adj. **1 stretchy**, elasti-
cated, springy, flexible, pliable,
supple. **2 adaptable**, flexible,
adjustable, accommodating,
variable, fluid, versatile.
– OPPOSITES rigid.

elated adj. **thrilled**, delighted,
overjoyed, ecstatic, euphoric,
jubilant, rapturous, in raptures,
walking on air, on cloud nine, in
seventh heaven; informal on top
of the world, over the moon,
tickled pink.
– OPPOSITES miserable.

elder adj. **older**, senior.
•n. **leader**, patriarch, father.

elderly adj. **aged**, old, ageing,
long in the tooth, grey-haired, in
your dotage; informal getting on,
over the hill.
– OPPOSITES youthful.

elect v. **1 vote in**, vote for, return, cast your vote for, choose, pick, select. **2 choose**, decide, opt, prefer, vote.

election n. ballot, vote, poll; Brit. by-election; US primary.

WORD LINKS
study of elections: psephology

electric adj. *the atmosphere was electric:* **exciting**, charged, electrifying, thrilling, dramatic, dynamic, stimulating, galvanizing.

electrify v. **excite**, thrill, stimulate, arouse, rouse, inspire, stir (up), exhilarate, galvanize, fire (with enthusiasm), fire someone's imagination, invigorate, animate; N. Amer. light a fire under.

elegance n. **1 style**, grace, taste, sophistication, refinement, dignity, poise. **2 neatness**, simplicity, aptness.

elegant adj. **1 stylish**, graceful, tasteful, sophisticated, classic, chic, smart, poised, cultivated, polished, cultured. **2** *an elegant solution:* **neat**, simple, apt.
– OPPOSITES inelegant.

element n. **1 component**, constituent, part, section, portion, piece, segment, aspect, factor, feature, facet, ingredient, strand, detail, member. **2 trace**, touch, hint, smattering, soupçon. **3** (**elements**) **weather**, climate, weather conditions.

elementary adj. **1** *an elementary astronomy course:* **basic**, rudimentary, preparatory, introductory. **2** *a lot of the work is elementary:* **easy**, simple, straightforward, uncomplicated, undemanding, painless, child's play, plain sailing; informal a piece of cake.
– OPPOSITES advanced, difficult.

elevate v. **1 raise**, lift (up), raise up/aloft, hoist, hike up, haul up. **2 promote**, upgrade, move up, raise; informal kick upstairs.
– OPPOSITES lower, demote.

elevated adj. **1 raised**, overhead, in the air, high up. **2 lofty**, grand, fine, sublime, inflated, pompous, bombastic. **3 high**, high-ranking, lofty, exalted, grand, noble.

elicit v. **obtain**, draw out, extract, bring out, evoke, induce, prompt, generate, trigger, provoke.

eligible adj. **1 entitled**, permitted, allowed, qualified, able. **2 desirable**, suitable, available, single, unmarried, unattached.

eliminate v. **1 remove**, get rid of, put an end to, do away with, end, stop, eradicate, destroy, stamp out. **2 knock out**, exclude, rule out, disqualify.

elite n. **best**, pick, cream, crème de la crème, flower, high society, beautiful people, aristocracy, ruling class.
– OPPOSITES dregs.

eloquent adj. **articulate**, fluent, expressive, persuasive, well expressed, effective, lucid, vivid.
– OPPOSITES inarticulate.

elude v. **evade**, avoid, get away from, dodge, escape from, lose, shake off, give the slip to, slip away from, throw off the scent.

elusive adj. **1 difficult to find**, evasive, slippery. **2 indefinable**, intangible, impalpable, fugitive, fleeting, transitory, ambiguous.

emaciated adj. **thin**, skeletal, bony, gaunt, wasted, thin as a rake, scrawny, skinny, scraggy, skin and bone, starved, cadaverous, shrivelled, shrunken, withered.
– OPPOSITES fat.

embargo n. **ban**, bar, prohibition, stoppage, veto, moratorium, restriction, block, boycott.
•v. **ban**, bar, prohibit, stop, outlaw, blacklist, restrict, block, boycott.
– OPPOSITES allow.

embark v. **board (ship)**, go on board, go aboard; informal hop on, jump on.
– OPPOSITES disembark.
□ **embark on** begin, start, undertake, set out on, take up, turn your hand to, get down to, enter into, venture into, launch into, plunge into, engage in.

embarrass v. **humiliate**, shame, put someone to shame, abash, mortify, fluster, discomfit; informal show up.

embarrassed adj. **humiliated**, mortified, red-faced, blushing, abashed, shamed, ashamed, shamefaced, self-conscious, uncomfortable, discomfited, disconcerted, flustered; informal with egg on your face.

embarrassing adj. **humiliating**, shameful, mortifying, ignomini-ous, awkward, uncomfortable, compromising; informal cringe-worthy, cringe-making, toe-curling.

embarrassment n. **1 humiliation**, mortification, shame, shamefacedness, awkwardness, self-consciousness, discomfort, discomfiture. **2 difficulty**, predicament, plight, problem, mess; informal bind, pickle, fix.

embellish v. **decorate**, adorn, ornament, beautify, enhance, trim, garnish, gild, deck, bedeck, festoon, emblazon.

embezzle v. **misappropriate**, steal, thieve, pilfer, purloin, appropriate, siphon off, pocket; informal filch; Brit. informal pinch, nick.

emblem n. **symbol**, representation, token, image, figure, mark, sign, crest, badge, device, insignia, coat of arms, shield, logo, trademark.

embody v. **1 personify**, manifest, symbolize, represent, express, epitomize, stand for, typify, exemplify. **2 incorporate**, include, contain.

embrace v. **1 hug**, take/hold in your arms, hold, cuddle, clasp to your bosom, squeeze, clutch, enfold. **2 welcome**, welcome with open arms, accept, take on board, take up, take to your heart, adopt, espouse. **3 include**, take in, comprise, contain, incorporate, encompass, cover, subsume.
•n. **hug**, cuddle, squeeze, clinch, caress.

emerge v. **1 appear**, come out, come into view, become visible, surface, materialize, issue, come forth. **2 become known**, become apparent, be revealed, come to light, come out, turn up, transpire, unfold, turn out, prove to be the case.

emergence n. **appearance**, arrival, coming, materialization, advent, inception, dawn, birth, origination, start, development.

emergency n. **crisis**, disaster, catastrophe, calamity, plight; informal panic stations.
•adj. **1 urgent**, crisis, extraordinary. **2 reserve**, standby, backup, fallback.

emigrate v. **move abroad**, move overseas, leave your country, migrate, relocate, resettle.
– OPPOSITES immigrate.

eminent adj. **illustrious**, distinguished, renowned, esteemed, pre-eminent, notable, noted, noteworthy, great, prestigious, important, outstanding, celebrated, prominent, well known, acclaimed, exalted.
– OPPOSITES unknown.

emission n. **discharge**, release, outpouring, outflow, outrush, leak.

emit v. **1 discharge**, release, give out/off, pour out, radiate, leak, ooze, disgorge, eject, belch, spew out, exude. **2 utter**, voice, let out, produce, give vent to, come out with.

emotion n. **1 feeling**, sentiment, reaction, response, instinct, intuition. **2 passion**, strength of feeling, heart.

emotional adj. **1 passionate**, hot-blooded, ardent, fervent, warm, responsive, excitable, temperamental, demonstrative, sensitive. **2 poignant**, moving, touching, affecting, powerful, stirring, emotive, impassioned, dramatic; informal tear-jerking.
– OPPOSITES cold, clinical.

emphasis n. **1 prominence**, importance, significance, value, stress, weight, accent, attention, priority. **2** the emphasis is on the word 'little': **stress**, accent, weight, beat.

emphasize v. **stress**, underline, highlight, focus attention on, point up, lay stress on, draw attention to, spotlight, foreground.
– OPPOSITES understate.

emphatic adj. **forceful**, firm, vehement, wholehearted, energetic, vigorous, direct, insistent, certain, definite, out-and-out, decided, categorical, unqualified, unconditional, unequivocal, unambiguous, absolute, explicit, downright, outright, clear.

empire n. **1 kingdom**, realm, domain, territory, commonwealth, power. **2 business**, firm, company, corporation, multinational, conglomerate, group, consortium, operation.

> **WORD LINKS**
> relating to an empire: **imperial**

employ v. **1 hire**, engage, recruit, take on, sign up, appoint,

retain. **2 occupy**, engage, involve, keep busy, tie up. **3 use**, utilize, make use of, apply, exercise, practise, put into practice, exert, bring into play, bring to bear, draw on, resort to, turn to, have recourse to.
- OPPOSITES dismiss.

employed adj. **working**, in work, in employment, holding down a job, earning, salaried, waged.
- OPPOSITES unemployed.

employee n. **worker**, member of staff, blue-collar worker, white-collar worker, workman, labourer, hand; **(employees)** personnel, staff, workforce.

employment n. **work**, labour, service, job, post, position, situation, occupation, profession, trade, business, line of work.

empower v. **1 authorize**, entitle, permit, allow, license, enable. **2 emancipate**, unshackle, set free, liberate, enfranchise.
- OPPOSITES forbid.

empty adj. **1 vacant**, unoccupied, uninhabited, bare, clear, free. **2 meaningless**, hollow, idle, vain, futile, worthless, useless, ineffectual. **3 futile**, pointless, purposeless, worthless, meaningless, fruitless, valueless, of no value, senseless.
- OPPOSITES full, occupied.
- v. **1 unload**, unpack, clear, evacuate, drain. **2 remove**, take out, extract, tip out, pour out.
- OPPOSITES fill, replace.

emulate v. **imitate**, copy, mirror, echo, follow, model yourself on, take a leaf out of someone's book.

enable v. **allow**, permit, let, equip, empower, make able, fit, authorize, entitle, qualify.
- OPPOSITES prevent.

enact v. **1 make law**, pass, approve, ratify, validate, sanction, authorize. **2 act out**, perform, appear in, stage, mount, put on, present.
- OPPOSITES repeal.

enchanting adj. **captivating**, charming, delightful, adorable, lovely, attractive, appealing, engaging, fetching, irresistible, fascinating.

enclose v. **1 surround**, circle, ring, encircle, bound, close in, wall in. **2 include**, insert, put in, send.

> **WORD LINKS**
> *fear of enclosed spaces:*
> claustrophobia

enclosure n. **compound**, pen, fold, stockade, ring, paddock, yard, run, coop; N. Amer. corral.

encompass v. **include**, cover, embrace, incorporate, take in, contain, comprise, involve, deal with.

encounter v. **1 experience**, run into, meet, come up against, face, be faced with, confront, suffer. **2 meet**, run into, come across/upon, stumble across/on, chance on, happen on; informal bump into.
- n. **1 meeting**, chance meeting. **2 battle**, fight, skirmish, clash,

scuffle, confrontation, struggle; informal run-in, set-to, scrap.

encourage v. **1 hearten**, cheer, buoy up, uplift, inspire, motivate, spur on, stir, fire up, stimulate, embolden; informal buck up. **2** *she encouraged him to go:* **persuade**, coax, urge, press, push, pressure, prod, egg on. **3 support**, back, promote, further, foster, nurture, cultivate, strengthen, stimulate.
– OPPOSITES discourage.

encouragement n. **1 support**, cheering up, inspiration, motivation, stimulation, morale-boosting; informal a shot in the arm. **2 persuasion**, coaxing, urging, prodding, prompting, inducement, incentive, carrot. **3 backing**, sponsorship, support, promotion, furtherance, fostering, nurture, cultivation, stimulation.

encouraging adj. **1 promising**, hopeful, auspicious, favourable, heartening, reassuring, cheering, comforting, welcome, pleasing, gratifying. **2 supportive**, understanding, helpful, positive, enthusiastic.

end n. **1 conclusion**, termination, ending, finish, close, resolution, climax, finale, culmination, denouement. **2 extremity**, limit, edge, border, boundary, periphery, point, tip, head, top, bottom. **3 aim**, goal, purpose, objective, object, target, intention, aspiration, wish, desire, ambition.

– OPPOSITES beginning, means.
•v. **1 finish**, conclude, terminate, close, stop, cease, culminate, climax. **2 break off**, call off, bring to an end, put an end to, stop, finish, terminate, discontinue, cancel.
– OPPOSITES begin.

endanger v. **jeopardize**, risk, put at risk, put in danger, be a danger to, threaten, compromise, imperil.
– OPPOSITES safeguard.

endearing adj. **charming**, appealing, attractive, engaging, winning, captivating, enchanting, cute, sweet, delightful, lovely.

endeavour v. **try**, attempt, seek, strive, struggle, labour, toil, work.
•n. **1 attempt**, try, bid, effort. **2 undertaking**, enterprise, venture, exercise, activity, exploit, deed, act, action, move.

ending n. **end**, finish, close, conclusion, resolution, summing-up, denouement, finale.
– OPPOSITES beginning.

endless adj. **1 unlimited**, limitless, infinite, inexhaustible, boundless, unbounded, ceaseless, unending, everlasting, constant, continuous, interminable, unfailing, perpetual, eternal, never-ending. **2 countless**, innumerable, numerous, a multitude of; informal umpteen, no end of; literary myriad.
– OPPOSITES limited, few.

endorse v. **support**, back, agree with, approve (of), favour,

subscribe to, recommend, champion, uphold, sanction.
- OPPOSITES oppose.

endorsement n. support, backing, approval, seal of approval, agreement, recommendation, patronage, sanction.

endow v. **1** finance, fund, pay for, subsidize, sponsor. **2** *he was endowed with great strength*: **provide**, supply, furnish, equip, favour, bless, grace.

endowment n. gift, present, grant, funding, award, donation, contribution, subsidy, sponsorship, bequest, legacy.

endurance n. **1** toleration, tolerance, forbearance, patience, acceptance, resignation, stoicism. **2** resistance, durability, permanence, longevity, strength, toughness, stamina, staying power, fortitude.

endure v. **1** undergo, go through, live through, experience, cope with, deal with, face, suffer, tolerate, put up with, brave, bear, withstand. **2** last, live, live on, go on, survive, abide, continue, persist, remain.

enemy n. opponent, adversary, rival, antagonist, combatant, challenger, competitor, opposition, competition, the other side; *literary* foe.
- OPPOSITES friend, ally.

energetic adj. **1** *an energetic woman*: **active**, lively, dynamic, spirited, animated, bouncy, bubbly, sprightly, tireless, indefatigable, enthusiastic; *informal*

full of beans. **2** *energetic exercises*: **vigorous**, strenuous, brisk, hard, arduous, demanding, taxing, tough, rigorous. **3** *an energetic advertising campaign*: **forceful**, vigorous, aggressive, hard-hitting, high-powered, all-out, determined, bold, intensive; *informal* in-your-face.
- OPPOSITES lethargic.

energy n. vitality, vigour, strength, stamina, animation, spirit, verve, enthusiasm, zest, exuberance, dynamism, drive; *informal* punch, bounce, oomph, go, get-up-and-go.

enforce v. **1** impose, apply, administer, carry out, implement, bring to bear, put into effect. **2** force, compel, coerce, exact.

engage v. **1** capture, catch, arrest, grab, draw, attract, gain, hold, grip, absorb, occupy. **2** employ, hire, recruit, take on, enrol, appoint. **3** *the chance to engage in a wide range of pursuits*: **participate in**, join in, take part in, partake in/of, enter into, embark on. **4** attack, fall on, take on, clash with, encounter, meet, fight, do battle with.
- OPPOSITES lose, dismiss.

engagement n. **1** appointment, meeting, arrangement, commitment, date, assignation, rendezvous. **2** participation, involvement. **3** battle, fight, clash, confrontation, encounter, conflict, skirmish, action, hostilities.

engaging adj. charming, attractive, appealing, pleasing, pleasant, agreeable, likeable,

lovable, sweet, winning, fetching; Scottish & N. English bonny.
– OPPOSITES unappealing.

engender v. cause, give rise to, bring about, occasion, lead to, result in, produce, create, generate, arouse, rouse, inspire, provoke, kindle, trigger, spark, stir up, whip up.

engine n. motor, generator, machine, turbine.

engineer n. 1 *a structural engineer:* designer, planner, builder. 2 *a repair engineer:* mechanic, repairer, technician, maintenance man, operator, driver.
•v. bring about, arrange, pull off, bring off, contrive, manoeuvre, negotiate, organize, orchestrate, plan, mastermind.

engraving n. etching, print, plate, picture, illustration, inscription.

engrossed adj. absorbed, involved, interested, occupied, preoccupied, immersed, caught up, riveted, gripped, rapt, fascinated, intent, captivated, enthralled.

engulf v. swamp, inundate, flood, deluge, immerse, swallow up, submerge, bury, envelop, overwhelm.

enhance v. improve, add to, strengthen, boost, increase, intensify, heighten, magnify, amplify, inflate, build up, supplement, augment.
– OPPOSITES diminish.

enjoy v. 1 like, be fond of, take pleasure in, be keen on, delight

in, relish, revel in, adore, lap up, savour, luxuriate in, bask in; *informal* get a thrill out of. 2 benefit from, be blessed with, be favoured with, be endowed with, possess, own, boast.
– OPPOSITES dislike, lack.
□ **enjoy yourself** have fun, have a good time, make merry, celebrate, revel; *informal* party, have a whale of a time, let your hair down.

enjoyable adj. entertaining, amusing, delightful, pleasant, congenial, convivial, agreeable, pleasurable, satisfying.
– OPPOSITES disagreeable.

enjoyment n. pleasure, fun, entertainment, amusement, recreation, relaxation, happiness, merriment, joy, satisfaction, liking.

enlarge v. 1 extend, expand, grow, add to, amplify, augment, magnify, build up, stretch, widen, broaden, lengthen, elongate, deepen, thicken. 2 swell, distend, bloat, bulge, dilate, blow up, puff up.
– OPPOSITES reduce, shrink.
□ **enlarge on** elaborate on, expand on, add to, flesh out, add detail to, develop, fill out, embellish, embroider.

enlighten v. inform, tell, make aware, open someone's eyes, illuminate; *informal* put someone in the picture.

enlightened adj. informed, aware, sophisticated, liberal, open-minded, broad-minded,

educated, knowledgeable, civilized, refined, cultured.
– OPPOSITES benighted.

enlightenment n. insight, understanding, awareness, education, learning, knowledge, illumination, awakening, instruction, teaching, open-mindedness, broad-mindedness, culture, refinement, cultivation, civilization.

enlist v. 1 join up, enrol, sign up for, volunteer, register. 2 recruit, call up, enrol, sign up, conscript, mobilize; US draft. 3 obtain, engage, secure, win, get.
– OPPOSITES discharge, demobilize.

enormity n. 1 wickedness, vileness, heinousness, baseness, depravity, outrageousness. 2 immensity, hugeness, size, extent, magnitude.

enormous adj. huge, vast, immense, gigantic, giant, massive, colossal, mammoth, tremendous, extensive, mighty, monumental, mountainous; informal mega, monster, whopping; Brit. informal ginormous.
– OPPOSITES tiny.

enough det. sufficient, adequate, ample, abundant, the necessary; informal plenty of.
– OPPOSITES insufficient.
• pron. sufficient, plenty, an adequate amount, as much as necessary, a sufficiency, an ample supply, your fill.

enquire, inquire v. 1 ask, query, question. 2 investigate,

probe, look into, make enquiries, research, examine, explore, delve into; informal check out.

enquiry, inquiry n. 1 question, query. 2 investigation, probe, examination, exploration, inquest, hearing.

enrage v. anger, infuriate, incense, madden, inflame, antagonize, provoke; informal drive mad/crazy, make someone see red, make someone's blood boil.
– OPPOSITES placate.

enraged adj. furious, infuriated, irate, incensed, raging, incandescent, fuming, seething, beside yourself; informal mad, livid, foaming at the mouth.

enrich v. enhance, improve, better, add to, augment, supplement, complement, refine.

enrol v. 1 register, sign on/up, put your name down, apply, volunteer, enter, join. 2 accept, admit, take on, sign on/up, recruit, engage.

ensemble n. 1 group, band, company, troupe, cast, chorus, corps; informal combo. 2 whole, unit, body, set, collection, combination, composite, package. 3 outfit, costume, suit; informal get-up.

ensue v. result, follow, develop, succeed, emerge, arise, proceed, stem.

ensure v. 1 make sure, make certain, see to it, check, confirm, establish, verify. 2 secure, guarantee, assure, certify.

entail v. **involve**, necessitate, require, need, demand, call for, mean, imply, cause, give rise to, occasion.

enter v. **1 go into**, come into, get into, set foot in, gain access to. **2 penetrate**, pierce, puncture, perforate. **3 join**, enrol in/for, enlist in, volunteer for, sign up for. **4 go in for**, register for, enrol for, sign on/up for, compete in, take part in, participate in. **5 record**, write, put down, take down, note, jot down, register, log. **6 key (in)**, type (in), tap in.
– OPPOSITES leave.

enterprise n. **1 undertaking**, endeavour, venture, exercise, activity, operation, task, business, project, scheme. **2 initiative**, resourcefulness, imagination, ingenuity, inventiveness, originality, creativity. **3 business**, company, firm, venture, organization, operation, concern, establishment; informal outfit.

enterprising adj. **resourceful**, entrepreneurial, imaginative, ingenious, inventive, creative, adventurous, bold; informal go-ahead.

entertain v. **1 amuse**, please, charm, cheer, interest, engage, occupy. **2 receive**, play host/hostess to, throw a party for, wine and dine, feed, fete. **3 consider**, contemplate, think of, hear of, countenance.
– OPPOSITES bore, reject.

entertainment n. **amusement**, pleasure, leisure, recreation, relaxation, fun, enjoyment, diversion, interest.

enthralling adj. **fascinating**, entrancing, enchanting, bewitching, captivating, delightful, absorbing, engrossing, compelling, riveting, gripping, exciting; informal unputdownable.

enthusiasm n. **keenness**, eagerness, passion, fervour, zeal, zest, gusto, energy, vigour, fire, spirit, interest, commitment, devotion; informal get-up-and-go.
– OPPOSITES apathy.

enthusiast n. **fan**, devotee, supporter, follower, aficionado, lover, admirer; informal buff.

enthusiastic adj. **keen**, eager, avid, ardent, fervent, passionate, zealous, excited, wholehearted, committed, devoted, fanatical, earnest.
– OPPOSITES apathetic.

entice v. **tempt**, lure, attract, appeal to, invite, persuade, beguile, coax, woo, lead on; seduce; informal sweet-talk.

entire adj. **whole**, complete, total, full.

entirely adv. **1 absolutely**, completely, totally, wholly, utterly, quite, altogether, thoroughly. **2 solely**, only, exclusively, purely, merely, just, alone.

entitle v. **1 qualify**, make eligible, authorize, allow, permit, enable, empower. **2 name**, title, call, label, designate, dub.

entity n. being, creature, individual, organism, life form, body, object, article, thing.

entrance¹ n. **1** entry, way in, access, approach, door, portal, gate, opening, mouth, foyer, lobby, porch; N. Amer. entryway. **2** appearance, arrival, entry, coming. **3** admission, admittance, (right of) entry, entrée, access.
– OPPOSITES exit, departure.

entrance² v. enchant, bewitch, beguile, captivate, mesmerize, hypnotize, spellbind, transfix, enthral, engross, absorb, fascinate, stun, electrify, charm, delight; informal bowl over, knock out.

entrant n. competitor, contestant, contender, participant, candidate, applicant.

entreat v. implore, beg, plead with, pray, ask, request, bid, enjoin, appeal to, call on; literary beseech.

entrenched, intrenched adj. ingrained, established, fixed, firm, deep-seated, deep-rooted, unshakeable, ineradicable.

entrust v. **1** charge, give someone the responsibility for, present. **2** assign, confer on, bestow on, vest in, delegate, give, grant, vouchsafe.

entry n. **1** appearance, arrival, entrance, coming. **2** entrance, way in, access, approach, door, portal, gate, entrance hall, foyer, lobby; N. Amer. entryway. **3** admission, admittance, entrance,

access. **4** item, record, note, memo, memorandum. **5** submission, application, entry form.
– OPPOSITES departure, exit.

envelop v. surround, cover, enfold, engulf, encircle, cocoon, sheathe, swathe, enclose, cloak, veil, shroud.

envious adj. jealous, covetous, desirous, grudging, begrudging, resentful; informal green with envy.

environment n. **1** situation, setting, milieu, background, backdrop, context, conditions, ambience, atmosphere. **2** the natural world, nature, the earth, the ecosystem, the biosphere, Mother Nature, wildlife, flora and fauna, the countryside.

> **WORD LINKS**
> study of the environment:
> ecology

environmentalist n. conservationist, ecologist, naturelover, green; informal eco-warrior, tree-hugger.

envisage v. **1** foresee, predict, forecast, anticipate, expect, think likely. **2** imagine, contemplate, picture, conceive of, think of.

envoy n. ambassador, emissary, diplomat, representative, delegate, spokesperson, agent, intermediary, mediator; informal go-between.

envy n. jealousy, covetousness, resentment, bitterness.
•v. **1** be envious of, be jealous

of, be resentful of. **2 covet**, desire, aspire to, wish for, want, long for, yearn for, hanker after, crave.

ephemeral adj. **transitory**, transient, fleeting, passing, short-lived, momentary, brief, short, temporary, impermanent, short-term.
– OPPOSITES permanent.

epidemic n. **1 outbreak**, plague, pandemic. **2 spate**, rash, wave, eruption, plague, outbreak, craze, upsurge.

episode n. **1 incident**, event, occurrence, chapter, experience, occasion, interlude, adventure, exploit. **2 instalment**, chapter, passage, part, portion, section, programme, show. **3 period**, spell, bout, attack, phase; informal dose.

epitome n. **personification**, embodiment, incarnation, essence, quintessence, archetype, paradigm, exemplar, model.

epoch n. **era**, age, period, time, aeon.

equal adj. **1 identical**, uniform, alike, like, the same, matching, equivalent, corresponding. **2 impartial**, non-partisan, fair, just, equitable, unprejudiced, non-discriminatory. **3 evenly matched**, even, balanced, level, nip and tuck, neck and neck; informal level pegging.
– OPPOSITES different, unequal.
• n. **equivalent**, peer, fellow, like, counterpart, match, parallel.
• v. **1 be equal to**, be equivalent to, be the same as, come to,

amount to, make, total, add up to. **2 match**, reach, parallel, be level with.

equality n. **fairness**, equal rights, equal opportunities, impartiality, even-handedness, justice.

equanimity n. **composure**, calm, level-headedness, self-possession, presence of mind, serenity, tranquillity, imperturbability, equilibrium, poise, aplomb, sangfroid, nerve; informal cool.
– OPPOSITES anxiety.

equate v. **1** he equates criticism with treachery: **identify**, compare, bracket, class, associate, connect, link, relate. **2 equalize**, balance, even out/up, level, square, tally, match.

equilibrium n. **balance**, stability, poise, symmetry, harmony.
– OPPOSITES imbalance.

equip v. **1** the boat was equipped with a flare gun: **provide**, furnish, supply, issue, kit out, stock, provision, arm. **2** the course will equip them for the workplace: **prepare**, qualify, ready, suit, train.

equipment n. **apparatus**, paraphernalia, tools, utensils, implements, hardware, gadgetry, things; informal stuff, gear.

equivalent adj. **comparable**, corresponding, commensurate, similar, parallel, analogous.
• n. **counterpart**, parallel, alternative, analogue, twin, opposite number.

equivocal adj. **ambiguous**, indefinite, non-committal, vague, imprecise, inexact, inexplicit, hazy, unclear, ambivalent, uncertain, unsure.
– OPPOSITES definite.

era n. **age**, epoch, period, time, date, day, generation.

eradicate v. **eliminate**, get rid of, remove, obliterate, extinguish, exterminate, destroy, annihilate, kill, wipe out.

erase v. **delete**, rub out, wipe off, blank out, expunge, excise, remove, obliterate.

erect adj. **upright**, straight, vertical, perpendicular, standing (on end), bristling, stiff.
• v. **build**, construct, put up, assemble, put together, fabricate, raise.
– OPPOSITES demolish, dismantle.

erode v. **wear away**, abrade, grind down, crumble, weather, undermine, weaken, deteriorate, destroy.

erosion n. **wearing away**, abrasion, attrition, weathering, dissolution, deterioration, disintegration, destruction.

erotic adj. **sexually arousing**, sexually stimulating, titillating, suggestive, pornographic, sexually explicit; informal blue, X-rated; euphemistic adult.

errand n. **task**, job, chore, assignment, mission.

erratic adj. **unpredictable**, inconsistent, changeable, variable, inconstant, irregular, fitful,
unstable, varying, fluctuating, unreliable.
– OPPOSITES consistent.

error n. **mistake**, inaccuracy, miscalculation, blunder, slip, oversight, misconception, delusion, misprint; Brit. informal boob.

erupt v. **fighting erupted: break out**, flare up, blow up, explode, burst out.

eruption n. **1 discharge**, explosion, lava flow, pyroclastic flow. **2 outbreak**, flare-up, upsurge, outburst, explosion, wave, spate.

escalate v. **1 increase rapidly**, soar, rocket, shoot up, spiral; informal go through the roof. **2 grow**, develop, mushroom, increase, heighten, intensify, accelerate.
– OPPOSITES plunge, subside.

escape v. **1 run away**, run off, get away, break out, break free, bolt, make your getaway, slip away, abscond; informal vamoose, skedaddle, fly the coop; Brit. informal do a runner, do a bunk. **2 he escaped his pursuers: get away from**, elude, avoid, dodge, shake off; informal give someone the slip. **3 they cannot escape their duties: avoid**, evade, elude, cheat, sidestep, circumvent, steer clear of, shirk. **4 leak (out)**, spill (out), seep (out), discharge, flow (out), pour (out).
• n. **1 getaway**, breakout, flight. **2 leak**, spill, seepage, discharge, outflow, outpouring.

escort n. **guard**, bodyguard, protector, minder, attendant,

chaperone, entourage, retinue, protection, convoy.
•v. **1 conduct**, accompany, guide, usher, shepherd, take, lead. **2 partner**, accompany, chaperone.

esoteric adj. **abstruse**, obscure, arcane, rarefied, recondite, abstract, enigmatic, cryptic, complex, complicated, incomprehensible, impenetrable, mysterious.

especially adv. **1 mainly**, mostly, chiefly, particularly, principally, largely, primarily. **2** *a committee formed especially for the purpose:* **expressly**, specially, specifically, exclusively, just, particularly, explicitly. **3** *he is especially talented:* **exceptionally**, particularly, unusually, extraordinarily, uncommonly, uniquely, remarkably, outstandingly.

essay n. **article**, composition, paper, dissertation, thesis, discourse, study, assignment, treatise, piece, feature; N. Amer. theme.

essence n. **1 nature**, heart, core, substance, basis, principle, quintessence, soul, spirit, reality; informal nitty-gritty. **2 extract**, concentrate, elixir, juice, oil.

essential adj. **1 crucial**, key, vital, indispensable, all-important, critical, imperative. **2 basic**, inherent, fundamental, quintessential, intrinsic, underlying, characteristic, innate, primary.
– OPPOSITES unimportant, incidental.
•n. **1 necessity**, prerequisite;

informal must. **2** (**essentials**) **fundamentals**, basics, rudiments, first principles, foundations, essence, basis, core, kernel, crux; informal nitty-gritty, nuts and bolts.

establish v. **1 set up**, start, initiate, institute, found, create, inaugurate. **2 prove**, demonstrate, show, indicate, determine, confirm.

established adj. **accepted**, traditional, orthodox, set, fixed, official, usual, customary, common, normal, general, prevailing, accustomed, familiar, expected, conventional, standard.

establishment n. **1 foundation**, institution, formation, inception, creation, installation, inauguration. **2 business**, firm, company, concern, enterprise, venture, organization, operation; informal outfit. **3 institution**, place, premises, institute. **4** *criticism of the Establishment:* **the authorities**, the powers that be, the system, the ruling class.

estate n. **1 property**, grounds, garden(s), park, parkland, land(s), territory. **2** *an industrial estate:* **area**, development, complex. **3 plantation**, farm, holding, forest, vineyard; N. Amer. ranch. **4 assets**, capital, wealth, riches, holdings, fortune, property, effects, possessions, belongings.

esteem n. **respect**, admiration, acclaim, appreciation,

recognition, honour, reverence, estimation, regard.
•v. **respect**, admire, value, regard highly, appreciate, like, prize, treasure, revere.

estimate v. **1 calculate**, approximate, guess, evaluate, judge, assess, weigh up. **2 consider**, believe, reckon, deem, judge, rate.
•n. **calculation**, approximation, estimation, guess, assessment, evaluation, costing, quotation, valuation; informal guesstimate.

estrangement n. **alienation**, disaffection, parting, separation, divorce, break-up, split, breach.

etch v. **engrave**, carve, inscribe, incise, score, mark, scratch.

etching n. **engraving**, print, plate.

eternal adj. **everlasting**, never-ending, endless, perpetual, undying, immortal, abiding, permanent, enduring, constant, continual, continuous, sustained, uninterrupted, unbroken, non-stop, round-the-clock.

eternity n. **1 ever**, all time, perpetuity. **2** (informal) **a long time**, an age, ages, a lifetime, hours, years, forever.

ethical adj. **moral**, morally correct, right-minded, principled, good, just, honourable, fair.

ethics pl. n. **morals**, morality, values, principles, ideals, standards (of behaviour).

ethnic adj. **racial**, race-related, national, cultural, folk, tribal, ethnological.

euphoria n. **elation**, happiness, joy, delight, glee, excitement, exhilaration, jubilation, exultation, ecstasy, bliss, rapture.
– OPPOSITES misery.

evacuate v. **1 remove**, move out, take away. **2 leave**, vacate, abandon, move out of, quit, withdraw from, retreat from, flee. **3** police evacuated the area: **clear**, empty.

evade v. **1 elude**, avoid, dodge, escape from, steer clear of, sidestep, lose, leave behind, shake off; informal give someone the slip. **2 avoid**, dodge, sidestep, bypass, skirt round, fudge; informal duck, cop out of.
– OPPOSITES confront.

evaluate v. **assess**, judge, gauge, rate, estimate, appraise, weigh up; informal size up.

evaporate v. **1 vaporize**, dry up. **2 end**, pass (away), fizzle out, peter out, wear off, vanish, fade, disappear, melt away.
– OPPOSITES condense, materialize.

evasive adj. **equivocal**, prevaricating, elusive, ambiguous, non-committal, vague, unclear, oblique.

even adj. **1 flat**, smooth, uniform, level, plane. **2 uniform**, constant, steady, stable, consistent, unvarying, unchanging, regular. **3 all square**, drawn, tied, level, neck and neck, nip and tuck; Brit. level pegging; informal even-steven(s).
– OPPOSITES bumpy, irregular, unequal.

evening n. dusk, twilight, nightfall, sunset, sundown, night.

event n. **1** occurrence, happening, incident, affair, occasion, phenomenon, function, gathering; informal do. **2** competition, contest, tournament, match, fixture, race, game, sport, discipline.

eventful adj. busy, action-packed, full, lively, active, hectic.
– OPPOSITES dull.

eventual adj. final, ultimate, resulting, ensuing, consequent, subsequent.

eventually adv. in the end, in due course, by and by, in time, after a time, finally, at last, ultimately, in the long run, at the end of the day, one day, some day, sometime, sooner or later.

ever adv. **1 at any time**, at any point, on any occasion, under any circumstances, on any account, until now. **2 always**, forever, eternally, continually, constantly, endlessly, perpetually, incessantly.

everlasting adj. eternal, endless, never-ending, perpetual, undying, abiding, enduring, infinite.
– OPPOSITES transient, occasional.

everybody pron. everyone, every person, each person, all, one and all, all and sundry, the whole world, the public.
– OPPOSITES nobody.

everyday adj. **1 daily**, day-to-day, ongoing, frequent, quotidian. **2 commonplace**, ordinary,

common, usual, regular, familiar, conventional, routine, run-of-the-mill, standard, stock, household, domestic; Brit. common or garden.
– OPPOSITES unusual.

everyone pron. see EVERYBODY.

everywhere adv. all over, all around, in every nook and cranny, far and wide, near and far, high and low, [here, there, and everywhere], the world over, worldwide; informal all over the place; Brit. informal all over the shop; N. Amer. informal all over the map.
– OPPOSITES nowhere.

evict v. expel, eject, remove, dislodge, turn out, throw out, drive out, dispossess; informal chuck out, kick out, boot out, throw someone out on their ear; Brit. informal turf out.

evidence n. **1 proof**, confirmation, verification, substantiation, corroboration. **2 testimony**, witness statement, declaration, submission; Law deposition, affidavit. **3 signs**, indications, marks, traces, suggestions, hints.

evident adj. obvious, apparent, noticeable, conspicuous, visible, discernible, clear, plain, manifest, patent; informal as clear as day.

evidently adv. **1 obviously**, clearly, plainly, unmistakably, manifestly, patently. **2 seemingly**, apparently, as far as one can tell, from all appearances, on the face of it, it seems, it appears.

evil adj. **1** *an evil deed:* wicked, bad, wrong, immoral, sinful, vile, iniquitous, villainous, vicious, malicious, malevolent, demonic, diabolical, fiendish, dark, monstrous. **2** *an evil spirit:* harmful, bad, malign. **3** unpleasant, disagreeable, nasty, horrible, foul, filthy, vile.
– OPPOSITES good, virtuous.
•n. **1** *the evil in our midst:* wickedness, badness, wrongdoing, sin, sinfulness, immorality, vice, iniquity, corruption, villainy. **2** *nothing but evil will result:* harm, pain, misery, sorrow, suffering, trouble, disaster, misfortune, woe.
– OPPOSITES good.

evoke v. bring to mind, put someone in mind of, conjure up, summon (up), invoke, elicit, induce, kindle, awaken, arouse.

evolution n. **1** development, progress, rise, expansion, growth. **2** natural selection, Darwinism, adaptation, development.

evolve v. develop, progress, advance, grow, expand, spread.

exacerbate v. aggravate, worsen, inflame, compound, intensify, increase, heighten, magnify, add to.
– OPPOSITES reduce.

exact adj. **1** *an exact description:* precise, accurate, correct, faithful, close, true, literal, strict, perfect. **2** *an exact record keeper:* careful, meticulous, painstaking, punctilious, conscientious, scrupulous.

– OPPOSITES inaccurate, careless.
•v. **1** demand, require, impose, extract, compel, force, wring. **2** inflict, impose, administer, mete out, wreak.

exacting adj. demanding, stringent, testing, challenging, arduous, laborious, hard, taxing, gruelling, punishing, tough.
– OPPOSITES easy, easy-going.

exactly adv. **1** precisely, entirely, absolutely, completely, totally, just, quite, in every respect. **2** accurately, precisely, unerringly, faultlessly, perfectly, faithfully.

exaggerate v. overstate, overemphasize, overestimate, inflate, embellish, embroider, elaborate, overplay, dramatize; Brit. informal blow out of all proportion.
– OPPOSITES understate.

examination n. **1** *items spread out for examination:* scrutiny, inspection, perusal, study, investigation, consideration, analysis. **2** *a medical examination:* inspection, check-up, assessment, appraisal, test, scan. **3** *a school examination:* test, exam, assessment; N. Amer. quiz.

examine v. **1** inspect, scrutinize, investigate, look at, study, appraise, analyse, review, survey; informal check out. **2** test, quiz, question, assess, appraise.

example n. **1** specimen, sample, instance, case, illustration. **2** precedent, lead, model, pattern, ideal, standard. **3** warning, lesson, deterrent, disincentive.

exasperate v. **infuriate**, anger, annoy, irritate, madden, provoke, irk, vex, gall, get on someone's nerves; Brit. rub up the wrong way; informal aggravate, rile, bug, hack off; Brit. informal nark, get on someone's wick; N. Amer. informal tee off, tick off.

excavate v. **unearth**, dig up, uncover, reveal, disinter, exhume, dig out, quarry, mine.

exceed v. **be more than**, be greater than, be over, go beyond, top, surpass.

excel v. **shine**, be excellent, be outstanding, be skilful, be talented, stand out, be second to none.

excellence n. **distinction**, quality, superiority, brilliance, greatness, calibre, eminence.

excellent adj. **very good**, outstanding, superb, exceptional, marvellous, wonderful, splendid; informal terrific, fantastic.
– OPPOSITES inferior.

except prep. **excluding**, not including, excepting, except for, omitting, not counting, but, besides, apart from, aside from, barring, bar, other than; informal outside of.

exception n. **anomaly**, irregularity, deviation, special case, peculiarity, abnormality, oddity.

exceptional adj. **1** the drought was exceptional: **unusual**, abnormal, atypical, out of the ordinary, rare, unprecedented, unexpected, surprising. **2** her exceptional ability: **outstanding**,

extraordinary, remarkable, special, phenomenal, prodigious.
– OPPOSITES normal, average.

excerpt n. **extract**, part, section, piece, portion, clip, citation, quotation, quote, line, passage, fragment.

excess n. **1 surplus**, surfeit, overabundance, superabundance, superfluity, glut. **2 remainder**, leftovers, extra, rest, residue. **3 overindulgence**, intemperance, immoderation, profligacy, extravagance, self-indulgence.
– OPPOSITES lack, restraint.
• adj. excess oil: **surplus**, superfluous, redundant, unwanted, unneeded, extra.

excessive adj. **1 immoderate**, intemperate, overindulgent, unrestrained, uncontrolled, extravagant. **2 exorbitant**, extortionate, unreasonable, outrageous, uncalled for, inordinate, unwarranted, disproportionate; informal over the top.

exchange n. **1 interchange**, trade, trading, swapping, traffic, trafficking. **2 conversation**, dialogue, chat, talk, discussion.
• v. **trade**, swap, switch, change.

excitable adj. **temperamental**, volatile, mercurial, emotional, sensitive, highly strung, tempestuous, hot-headed, fiery.
– OPPOSITES placid.

excite v. **1 thrill**, exhilarate, animate, enliven, rouse, stir, stimulate, galvanize. **2 provoke**, stir up, rouse, arouse, kindle, trigger, spark off, incite, cause.
– OPPOSITES bore.

e

excitement n. **1** *the excitement of seeing a leopard in the wild*: **thrill**, pleasure, delight, joy; *informal* kick, buzz. **2** *the excitement in her eyes*: **exhilaration**, elation, animation, enthusiasm, eagerness, anticipation.

e **exciting** adj. **thrilling**, exhilarating, stirring, rousing, stimulating, intoxicating, electrifying, invigorating, gripping, compelling, powerful, dramatic.

exclaim v. **cry out**, declare, proclaim, blurt out, call out, shout, yell.

exclude v. **1 keep out**, deny access to, shut out, bar, ban, prohibit. **2 rule out**, preclude. **3 be exclusive of**, not include.
– OPPOSITES admit, include.

exclusive adj. **1 select**, chic, high-class, elite, fashionable, stylish, elegant, premier; Brit. upmarket; *informal* posh, classy; Brit. *informal* swish. **2 sole**, unshared, unique, individual, personal, private. **3** *prices exclusive of VAT*: **not including**, excluding, leaving out, omitting, excepting.
– OPPOSITES inclusive.

excruciating adj. **agonizing**, severe, acute, intense, violent, racking, searing, piercing, stabbing, unbearable, unendurable; *informal* splitting, killing.

excursion n. **outing**, trip, jaunt, expedition, journey, tour, day out, drive, run; *informal* spin.

excuse v. **1 forgive**, pardon. **2 justify**, defend, condone, forgive, overlook, disregard,

ignore, tolerate, explain, mitigate. **3 let off**, release, relieve, exempt, absolve, free.
– OPPOSITES punish, condemn.
▪ n. **1 justification**, defence, reason, explanation, mitigating circumstances, mitigation. **2 pretext**, pretence; Brit. get-out; *informal* story, alibi.

execute v. **1 carry out**, accomplish, bring off/about, implement, achieve, complete, engineer; *informal* pull off. **2 put to death**, kill, hang, behead, electrocute, shoot.

execution n. **1 implementation**, carrying out, performance, accomplishment, bringing off/about, attainment, realization. **2 killing**. capital punishment, the death penalty.

executive adj. **administrative**, managerial, decision-making, law-making, governing, controlling.
▪ n. **1 director**, manager, senior official, administrator; *informal* boss, exec, suit. **2 administration**, management, directorate, government, authority.

exemplary adj. **perfect**, ideal, model, faultless, flawless, impeccable, irreproachable.
– OPPOSITES deplorable.

exemplify v. **typify**, epitomize, be an example of, be representative of, symbolize, illustrate, demonstrate.

exempt adj. **free**, not liable, not subject, immune, excepted, excused, absolved.
▪ v. **excuse**, free, release,

exclude, grant immunity, spare, absolve; informal let off.

exemption n. immunity, exception, dispensation, indemnity, exclusion, freedom, release, relief, absolution.

exercise n. **1 physical activity**, a workout, working out, movement, training. **2 task**, piece of work, problem, assignment, practice. **3 manoeuvre**, operation, deployment.
•v. **1 work out**, do exercises, train. **2 use**, employ, make use of, utilize, practise, apply. **3 concern**, occupy, worry, trouble, bother, disturb, prey on someone's mind.

exert v. **bring to bear**, apply, use, utilize, deploy.
□ **exert yourself** work hard, labour, toil, make an effort, endeavour, slog away, push yourself.

exhaust v. **1 tire out**, wear out, overtire, fatigue, weary, drain; informal take it out of someone, shatter; Brit. informal knacker; N. Amer. informal poop, tucker out. **2 use up**, get through, consume, finish, deplete, spend, empty, drain; informal blow.
– opposites invigorate, replenish.

exhausting adj. tiring, wearying, taxing, wearing, draining, arduous, strenuous, onerous, demanding, gruelling; informal killing; Brit. informal knackering.

exhaustion n. tiredness, fatigue, weariness, debility, enervation.

exhibit v. **1 put on display**, show, display, unveil, present. **2 show**, reveal, display, manifest, indicate, demonstrate, express, evince, evidence.
•n. **item**, piece, artefact, display, collection.

exhibition n. **1 exposition**, display, show, showing, presentation. **2 display**, show, demonstration, manifestation, expression.

exhilarating adj. thrilling, exciting, invigorating, stimulating, intoxicating, electrifying.

exhort v. urge, encourage, call on, enjoin, charge, press, bid, appeal to, entreat, implore; literary beseech.

exile n. **1 banishment**, expulsion, deportation, eviction, isolation. **2 expatriate**, émigré, deportee, displaced person, refugee.

exist v. **1 live**, be alive, be, be present. **2 prevail**, occur, be found, be in existence, be the case; formal obtain. **3 survive**, subsist, live, support yourself, manage, make do, get by, scrape by, make ends meet, eke out a living.

existence n. **1 survival**, continuation. **2 way of life**, life, lifestyle, situation.
□ **in existence** existing, alive, surviving, remaining, extant, existent, in circulation, current.

exit n. **1 way out**, door, escape route, egress. **2 turning**, turn-off, junction. **3 departure**,

leaving, withdrawal, going, retreat, flight, exodus, escape.
- OPPOSITES entrance, arrival.
•v. **leave**, go out, depart, withdraw, retreat.
- OPPOSITES enter.

exonerate v. **absolve**, clear, acquit, find innocent, discharge; formal exculpate.
- OPPOSITES convict.

exorbitant adj. **extortionate**, excessive, prohibitive, outrageous, unreasonable, inflated; Brit. over the odds; informal steep, stiff, a rip-off; Brit. informal daylight robbery.
- OPPOSITES cheap.

exotic adj. **1** *exotic birds:* **foreign**, non-native, alien, tropical. **2** *exotic places:* **foreign**, faraway, far-off, far-flung, distant. **3** *striking*, colourful, eye-catching, unusual, unconventional, extravagant, outlandish.

expand v. **1** *metals expand when heated:* **enlarge**, increase in size, swell, lengthen, stretch, spread, thicken, fill out. **2** *the company is expanding:* **grow**, enlarge, increase in size, extend, augment, broaden, widen, develop, diversify, build up, branch out, spread.
- OPPOSITES contract.
□ **expand on** elaborate on, enlarge on, go into detail about, flesh out, develop.

expanse n. **area**, stretch, sweep, tract, swathe, belt, region, sea, carpet, blanket, sheet.

expansion n. **1** *expansion and contraction:* **enlargement**,

swelling, lengthening, elongation, stretching, thickening. **2** *the expansion of the company:* **growth**, increase in size, enlargement, extension, development, diversification, spread.
- OPPOSITES contraction.

expect v. **1 suppose**, presume, imagine, assume, surmise; informal guess, reckon; N. Amer. informal figure. **2 anticipate**, envisage, await, look for, hope for, look forward to, contemplate, bargain for/on, predict, forecast. **3 require**, ask for, call for, want, insist on, demand.

expectation n. **1 supposition**, assumption, presumption, conjecture, calculation, prediction, hope. **2 anticipation**, expectancy, eagerness, excitement, suspense.

expedient adj. **convenient**, advantageous, useful, beneficial, helpful, practical, pragmatic, politic, prudent, judicious.
•n. **measure**, means, method, stratagem, scheme, plan, move, tactic, manoeuvre, device, contrivance, ploy, ruse.

expedition n. **journey**, voyage, tour, safari, trek, mission, quest, hike, trip.

expel v. **throw out**, bar, ban, debar, drum out, banish, exile, deport, evict; informal chuck out.
- OPPOSITES admit.

expense n. **cost**, expenditure, spending, outlay, outgoings, payment, price, charge, fees, overheads, tariff, bill.
- OPPOSITES income, profit.

expensive adj. **costly**, dear, high-priced, overpriced, exorbitant, extortionate; informal steep, stiff, pricey.
– OPPOSITES cheap.

experience n. **1 skill**, practical knowledge, understanding, familiarity, involvement, participation, contact, acquaintance, exposure, background, track record, history; informal know-how. **2 incident**, occurrence, event, happening, episode, adventure.
▸v. **undergo**, go through, encounter, face, meet, come across, come up against, come into contact with.

experienced adj. **knowledgeable**, skilful, skilled, expert, proficient, trained, competent, capable, seasoned, practised, mature, veteran.

experiment n. **test**, investigation, trial, examination, observation, research, assessment, evaluation, appraisal, analysis, study.
▸v. **carry out experiments**, test, trial, try out, assess, appraise, evaluate.

experimental adj. **1 exploratory**, investigational, trial, test, pilot, speculative, tentative, preliminary. **2 new**, innovative, creative, radical, avant-garde, alternative, unorthodox, unconventional, cutting-edge.

expert n. **specialist**, authority, professional, pundit, maestro, virtuoso, master, wizard, connoisseur, aficionado; informal ace,

pro, hotshot; Brit. informal dab hand; N. Amer. informal maven.
– OPPOSITES amateur.
▸adj. **skilful**, skilled, adept, accomplished, experienced, practised, knowledgeable, talented, masterly, virtuoso; informal ace, crack, mean.
– OPPOSITES incompetent.

expertise n. **skill**, prowess, proficiency, competence, knowledge, ability, aptitude, capability; informal know-how.

expire v. **1 run out**, become invalid, become void, lapse, end, finish, stop, terminate. **2 die**, pass away, breathe your last; informal kick the bucket, croak; Brit. informal snuff it, peg out; N. Amer. informal buy the farm.

explain v. **1 describe**, make clear, spell out, put into words, define, elucidate, expound, clarify, throw light on. **2 account for**, give a reason for, excuse.

explanation n. **1 clarification**, description, statement, interpretation, definition, commentary. **2 account**, reason, justification, answer, excuse, defence, vindication.

explicit adj. **1 clear**, plain, straightforward, crystal clear, precise, exact, specific, unequivocal, unambiguous, detailed. **2 graphic**, candid, full-frontal, uncensored.
– OPPOSITES vague.

explode v. **1 blow up**, detonate, go off, burst, erupt. **2 lose your temper**, blow up; informal fly off the handle, hit the roof, blow your top; Brit. informal go spare; N. Amer. informal blow your lid/stack. **3 increase rapidly**, mushroom, snowball, escalate, burgeon, rocket. **4 disprove**, refute, rebut, repudiate, debunk, give the lie to; informal shoot full of holes, blow out of the water.

exploit v. **1 utilize**, make use of, turn/put to good use, make the most of, capitalize on, benefit from; informal cash in on. **2 take advantage of**, abuse, impose on, treat unfairly, misuse, illtreat; informal walk (all) over. •n. **feat**, deed, act, adventure, stunt, escapade, achievement.

exploration n. investigation, study, survey, research, inspection, examination, scrutiny, observation.

explore v. **1 travel through**, tour, survey, scout, reconnoitre. **2 investigate**, look into, consider, examine, research, survey, scrutinize, study, review; informal check out.

explosion n. **1 detonation**, eruption, bang, blast, boom. **2 outburst**, flare-up, outbreak, eruption, storm, rush, surge, fit, paroxysm. **3 sudden increase**, mushrooming, snowballing, escalation, multiplication, burgeoning, rocketing.

explosive adj. **1 volatile**, inflammable, flammable, combustible, incendiary. **2 fiery**, stormy, violent, volatile, passionate, tempestuous, turbulent, touchy, irascible. **3 tense**, highly

charged, overwrought, dangerous, perilous, hazardous, sensitive, delicate, unstable, volatile. •n. **bomb**, charge, incendiary (device).

expose v. **1** at low tide the rocks are exposed: **reveal**, uncover, lay bare. **2** he was exposed to radiation: **lay open**, subject, put at risk of, put in jeopardy of, leave unprotected from. **3** they were exposed to new ideas: **introduce to**, bring into contact with, make aware of, familiarize with, acquaint with. **4 uncover**, reveal, unveil, unmask, detect, find out, denounce, condemn; informal blow the whistle on.
– OPPOSITES cover, protect.

exposure n. **1 frostbite**, cold, hypothermia. **2 uncovering**, revelation, disclosure, unveiling, unmasking, discovery, detection. **3 publicity**, advertising, public attention, media interest; informal hype.

express[1] v. **communicate**, convey, indicate, show, demonstrate, reveal, put across/over, get across/over, articulate, put into words, voice, give voice to, state, air, give vent to.

express[2] adj. **rapid**, swift, fast, high-speed, non-stop, direct.

express[3] adj. **1 explicit**, clear, direct, plain, distinct, unambiguous, categorical. **2 sole**, specific, particular, special, specified.
– OPPOSITES vague.

expression n. **1 utterance**, uttering, voicing, declaration, articulation. **2 indication**, demonstration, show, exhibition, token, illustration. **3 look**, appearance, air, manner, countenance, mien. **4 idiom**, phrase, turn of phrase, term, proverb, saying, adage, maxim. **5 emotion**, feeling, spirit, passion, intensity, style.

expressive adj. **1 eloquent**, meaningful, demonstrative, suggestive. **2 emotional**, passionate, poignant, moving, stirring, emotionally charged, lyrical.
- OPPOSITES undemonstrative.

expulsion n. **1 removal**, debarment, dismissal, exclusion, ejection, banishment, eviction. **2 discharge**, ejection, excretion, voiding, evacuation, elimination, passing.
- OPPOSITES admission.

exquisite adj. **1 beautiful**, lovely, elegant, fine, delicate, fragile, dainty, subtle. **2** *exquisite taste:* **discriminating**, discerning, sensitive, fastidious, refined.

extend v. **1 expand**, enlarge, increase, lengthen, widen, broaden. **3 continue**, carry on, stretch, reach. **3 widen**, expand, broaden, augment, supplement, increase, add to, enhance, develop. **4 prolong**, lengthen, increase, stretch out, protract, spin out, string out. **5 hold out**, reach out, hold forth, stretch out, outstretch, offer, give, proffer.
- OPPOSITES reduce, shorten.

□ **extend to** include, take in, incorporate, encompass.

extension n. **1 addition**, add-on, adjunct, annex, wing. **2 expansion**, increase, enlargement, widening, broadening, deepening, augmentation, enhancement, development, growth. **3 prolongation**, lengthening, increase.

extensive adj. **1 large**, sizeable, substantial, considerable, ample, great, vast. **2 comprehensive**, thorough, exhaustive, broad, wide, wide-ranging, catholic.

extent n. **1 area**, size, expanse, length, proportions, dimensions. **2 degree**, scale, level, magnitude, scope, size, reach, range.

exterior adj. **outer**, outside, outermost, outward, external.
- OPPOSITES interior.
▪ n. **outside**, external surface, outward appearance, facade.
- OPPOSITES interior.

external adj. **outer**, outside, outermost, outward, exterior.
- OPPOSITES internal.

extinct adj. **1 vanished**, lost, gone, died out, wiped out, destroyed. **2 inactive**.
- OPPOSITES living, dormant.

extinction n. **dying out**, disappearance, vanishing, extermination, destruction, elimination, eradication, annihilation.

extinguish v. **douse**, quench, put out, stamp out, smother, snuff out.
- OPPOSITES light.

extol v. **praise**, wax lyrical about, sing the praises of, acclaim, applaud, celebrate, eulogize, rave about, enthuse over; formal laud.
– OPPOSITES criticize.

extort v. **extract**, exact, wring, wrest, screw, squeeze.

extortionate adj. **exorbitant**, excessive, outrageous, unreasonable, inordinate, inflated; Brit. informal daylight robbery.

extra adj. **additional**, more, added, supplementary, further, auxiliary, ancillary, subsidiary, secondary.
•adv. **exceptionally**, particularly, specially, especially, extremely.
•n. **addition**, supplement, bonus, adjunct, addendum, add-on.

extract v. **1 take out**, draw out, pull out, remove, withdraw, release, extricate. **2 wrest**, exact, wring, screw, squeeze, obtain by force, extort. **3 squeeze out**, press out, obtain.
– OPPOSITES insert.
•n. **1 excerpt**, passage, citation, quotation. **2 distillation**, distillate, concentrate, essence, juice.

extraordinary adj. **1** an extraordinary coincidence: **remarkable**, exceptional, amazing, astonishing, astounding, sensational, stunning, incredible, unbelievable, phenomenal; informal fantastic. **2** extraordinary speed: **very great**, tremendous, enormous, immense, prodigious, stupendous, monumental.
– OPPOSITES unremarkable.

extravagant adj. **1 spendthrift**, profligate, wasteful, prodigal,

lavish. **2 excessive**, immoderate, exaggerated, gushing, unrestrained, effusive, fulsome. **3 ornate**, elaborate, fancy, overelaborate, ostentatious, exaggerated; informal flashy.
– OPPOSITES thrifty, moderate.

extreme adj. **1** extreme danger: **utmost**, (very) great, greatest (possible), maximum, great, acute, enormous, severe, serious. **2** extreme measures: **drastic**, serious, desperate, dire, radical, far-reaching, draconian; Brit. swingeing. **3 radical**, extremist, immoderate, fanatical, revolutionary, subversive, militant. **4 dangerous**, hazardous, risky, high-risk; informal white-knuckle. **5 furthest**, farthest, utmost, remotest, ultra-.
– OPPOSITES slight, moderate.
•n. **opposite**, antithesis, side of the coin, (opposite) pole, limit, extremity, contrast.

extremely adv. **very**, exceptionally, especially, extraordinarily, tremendously, immensely, hugely, supremely, highly, mightily; informal awfully, terribly, seriously; Brit. informal jolly; N. Amer. informal mighty.
– OPPOSITES slightly.

extremist n. **fanatic**, radical, zealot, fundamentalist, hardliner, militant, activist.
– OPPOSITES moderate.

extrovert adj. **outgoing**, extroverted, sociable, gregarious, lively, ebullient, exuberant, uninhibited, unreserved.
– OPPOSITES introverted.

exuberant adj. **ebullient**, buoyant, cheerful, high-spirited, cheery, lively, vivacious, enthusiastic, irrepressible, energetic, animated, full of life, sparkling; informal bubbly, bouncy, full of beans.

eye v. **look at**, observe, view, gaze at, stare at, regard, contemplate, survey, scrutinize, consider, glance at, watch; informal check out, size up; N. Amer. informal eyeball.

> **WORD LINKS**
> *relating to the eye:* ocular, ophthalmic, optic;
> *branch of medicine dealing with the eye:* ophthalmology

eyewitness n. **observer**, onlooker, witness, bystander, passer-by.

Ff

fable n. **parable**, allegory, myth, legend, story, tale.

fabric n. **1 cloth**, material, textile, stuff. **2 structure**, construction, make-up, organization, framework, essence.

fabricate v. **falsify**, fake, counterfeit, invent, make up.

fabulous adj. **1 stupendous**, prodigious, phenomenal, exceptional, fantastic, breathtaking, staggering, unthinkable, unimaginable, incredible, undreamed of. **2** (informal) *a fabulous time:* see **EXCELLENT**.

facade n. **1 front**, frontage, face, elevation, exterior, outside. **2 show**, front, appearance, pretence, simulation, affectation, act, charade, mask, veneer.

face n. **1 countenance**, physiognomy, features, profile; literary visage, lineaments. **2 expression**, look, appearance, mien,

air. **3** *he made a face:* **grimace**, scowl, wince, frown, pout. **4 side**, aspect, surface, plane, facet, wall, elevation.
•v. **1 look on to**, front on to, look towards, look over/across, overlook, be opposite (to). **2 accept**, get used to, adjust to, learn to live with, cope with, deal with, come to terms with, become resigned to. **3 beset**, worry, trouble, confront, torment, plague, bedevil. **4 brave**, face up to, encounter, meet (head-on), confront. **5 cover**, clad, veneer, surface, dress, laminate, coat, line.

facelift n. **renovation**, redecoration, refurbishment, revamp, makeover.

facet n. **aspect**, feature, factor, side, dimension, strand, component, element.

facetious adj. flippant, flip, glib, frivolous, tongue-in-cheek, joking, jokey, jocular, playful.
– OPPOSITES serious.

facilitate v. make easier, ease, make possible, smooth the way for, enable, assist, help (along), aid, promote, hasten, speed up.
– OPPOSITES impede.

facility n. **1** *a wealth of local facilities*: amenity, resource, service, benefit, convenience, equipment. **2** *a medical facility*: establishment, centre, station, location, premises, site, post, base. **3** ease, effortlessness, skill, adroitness, smoothness, fluency, slickness.

fact n. **1** *a fact we cannot ignore*: reality, actuality, certainty, truth, verity, gospel. **2** *every fact was double-checked*: detail, particular, finding, point, factor, feature, characteristic, aspect; (facts) information, data.
– OPPOSITES lie, fiction.

faction n. **1** clique, coterie, caucus, bloc, camp, group, grouping, splinter group. **2** infighting, dissent, dispute, discord, strife, conflict, friction, argument, disagreement, disunity, schism.

factor n. element, part, component, ingredient, strand, constituent, feature, facet, aspect, characteristic, consideration, influence, circumstance.

factory n. works, plant, yard, mill, facility, workshop, shop.

factual adj. truthful, true, accurate, authentic, historical, genuine, true-to-life, correct, exact.
– OPPOSITES fictitious.

faculty n. **1** power, capability, capacity, facility; (faculties) senses, wits, reason, intelligence. **2** department, school.

fad n. craze, vogue, trend, fashion, mode, mania, rage.

fade v. **1** grow pale, become bleached, become washed out, lose colour, discolour, blanch. **2** (grow) dim, grow faint, fail, dwindle, die away, wane, disappear, vanish, decline, melt away. **3** decline, die out, diminish, decay, crumble, collapse, fail.
– OPPOSITES brighten.

fail v. **1** be unsuccessful, fall through, fall flat, collapse, founder, backfire, miscarry, come unstuck; informal flop, bomb. **2** be unsuccessful in, not make the grade; informal flunk. **3** let down, disappoint, desert, abandon, betray, be disloyal to. **4** break (down), stop working, cut out, crash, malfunction, go wrong; informal conk out; Brit. informal pack up. **5** deteriorate, degenerate, decline, fade. **6** collapse, crash, go under, go bankrupt, cease trading, be wound up; informal fold, go bust.
– OPPOSITES succeed, pass, improve.

failing n. fault, shortcoming, weakness, imperfection, deficiency, defect, flaw, frailty.
– OPPOSITES strength.

failure n. **1** lack of success, defeat, collapse, foundering.

2 fiasco, debacle, catastrophe, disaster; informal flop, washout, dead loss. **3 loser**, under-achiever, ne'er-do-well, disappointment; informal no-hoper, dud. **4 negligence**, dereliction, omission, oversight. **5 breakdown**, malfunction, crash. **6 collapse**, crash, bankruptcy, insolvency, liquidation, closure.
– OPPOSITES success.

faint adj. **1 indistinct**, vague, unclear, indefinite, ill-defined, imperceptible, pale, light, faded. **2 quiet**, muted, muffled, stifled, feeble, weak, low, soft, gentle. **3 slight**, slender, slim, small, tiny, remote, vague. **4 dizzy**, giddy, light-headed, unsteady; informal woozy.
– OPPOSITES clear, loud, strong.
•v. **pass out**, lose consciousness, black out, keel over, swoon.
•n. **blackout**, fainting fit, loss of consciousness, coma, swoon.

faintly adv. **1 indistinctly**, softly, gently, weakly, in a whisper. **2 slightly**, vaguely, somewhat, quite, fairly, rather, a little, a bit, a touch, a shade.

fair¹ adj. **1 just**, equitable, honest, impartial, unbiased, unprejudiced, neutral, even-handed. **2 fine**, dry, bright, clear, sunny, cloudless. **3 blond(e)**, yellow, golden, flaxen, light. **4 pale**, light, pink, white, creamy. **5 reasonable**, passable, tolerable, satisfactory, acceptable, respectable, decent, all right, good enough, pretty good.
– OPPOSITES inclement, dark, poor.

fair² n. **1 fete**, gala, festival, carnival. **2 market**, bazaar, exchange, sale. **3 exhibition**, display, show, exposition.

fairly adv. **1 justly**, equitably, impartially, without bias, without prejudice, even-handedly, equally. **2 reasonably**, passably, tolerably, adequately, moderately, quite, relatively, comparatively; informal pretty. **3 positively**, really, simply, absolutely.

fairy n. sprite, pixie, elf, imp, brownie, puck, leprechaun.

faith n. **1 trust**, belief, confidence, conviction, reliance. **2 religion**, belief, creed, church, persuasion, ideology, doctrine.
– OPPOSITES mistrust.

faithful adj. **1 loyal**, constant, true, devoted, staunch, steadfast, dedicated, committed, trusty, dependable, reliable. **2 accurate**, precise, exact, true, strict, realistic, authentic.
– OPPOSITES disloyal, treacherous.

fake n. **1 forgery**, counterfeit, copy, sham, fraud, hoax, imitation; informal phoney, rip-off. **2 charlatan**, quack, sham, fraud, impostor; informal phoney.
•adj. **1 counterfeit**, forged, fraudulent, sham, pirated, false, bogus; informal phoney, dud. **2 imitation**, artificial, synthetic, simulated, reproduction, replica, ersatz, man-made, dummy, false, mock; informal pretend.

3 feigned, faked, put-on, assumed, invented, affected.
- OPPOSITES genuine, real, authentic.

•v. **1 forge**, counterfeit, falsify, copy, pirate. **2 feign**, pretend, simulate, put on, affect.

fall v. **1 drop**, descend, plummet, plunge, sink, dive, tumble, cascade. **2 topple over**, tumble over, fall down/over, collapse. **3 subside**, recede, drop, retreat, fall away, go down, sink. **4 decrease**, decline, diminish, fall off, drop off, lessen, dwindle, plummet, plunge, slump, sink. **5 die**, perish, lose your life, be killed, be slain, be lost; informal bite the dust, buy it. **6 surrender**, yield, submit, give in, capitulate, succumb, be taken, be overwhelmed. **7 occur**, take place, happen, come about.
- OPPOSITES rise.

•n. **1 tumble**, trip, spill, topple. **2 decline**, fall-off, drop, decrease, cut, dip, reduction, slump; informal crash. **3 downfall**, collapse, failure, decline, destruction, overthrow, demise. **4 surrender**, capitulation, yielding, submission, defeat. **5 descent**, slope, slant.
- OPPOSITES rise.

□ **fall back** retreat, withdraw, back off, draw back, pull back, move away. **fall back on** resort to, turn to, look to, call on, have recourse to. **fall for** (informal) **1** fall in love with, take a fancy to, be smitten by, be attracted to. **2** be deceived by, be duped by, be fooled by, be taken in by;

informal go for, buy, swallow. **fall out** quarrel, argue, fight, squabble, bicker; Brit. row. **fall through** fail, be unsuccessful, come to nothing, miscarry, go awry, collapse, founder, come to grief.

false adj. **1 incorrect**, untrue, wrong, inaccurate, untruthful, fictitious, fabricated, invented, made up, trumped up, counterfeit, forged, fraudulent. **2 disloyal**, faithless, unfaithful, untrue, inconstant, treacherous, double-crossing, deceitful, dishonest, duplicitous. **3 fake**, artificial, imitation, synthetic, simulated, reproduction, replica, ersatz, man-made, dummy, mock; informal pretend.
- OPPOSITES correct, faithful, genuine.

falsify v. forge, fake, counterfeit, fabricate, alter, change, doctor, tamper with, manipulate, misrepresent, misreport, distort.

falter v. hesitate, delay, drag your feet, stall, waver, vacillate, be indecisive, be irresolute; Brit. hum and haw; informal sit on the fence.

fame n. renown, celebrity, stardom, popularity, prominence, distinction, esteem, eminence, repute.
- OPPOSITES obscurity.

familiar adj. **1 well known**, recognized, accustomed, everyday, day-to-day, habitual, customary, routine. **2** *are you familiar with the subject?* **acquainted**, conversant, versed, knowledgeable, well informed, au fait; informal well up on. **3 overfamiliar**, presumptuous, disrespectful, forward, bold, impudent, impertinent.

familiarity n. **1** *a familiarity with politics*: **acquaintance**, awareness, knowledge, experience, insight, understanding, comprehension. **2 overfamiliarity**, presumption, forwardness, boldness, cheek, impudence, impertinence, disrespect. **3 closeness**, intimacy, friendliness, friendship.

family n. **1 relatives**, relations, (next of) kin, clan, tribe; informal folks. **2 children**, little ones, youngsters; informal kids. **3 species**, order, class, genus, phylum.

famine n. **1 food shortage**, hunger, starvation, malnutrition. **2 shortage**, scarcity, lack, dearth, deficiency, insufficiency, shortfall.
- OPPOSITES plenty.

famished adj. **ravenous**, hungry, starving, starved, empty, unfed; informal peckish.
- OPPOSITES replete.

famous adj. **well known**, prominent, famed, popular, renowned, noted, eminent, distinguished, celebrated, illustrious, legendary.
- OPPOSITES unknown.

fan n. **enthusiast**, devotee, admirer, lover, aficionado, supporter, follower, disciple, adherent; informal buff.

fanatic n. **extremist**, militant, dogmatist, bigot, zealot, radical, diehard; informal maniac.

fanatical adj. **1 zealous**, extremist, extreme, militant, gung-ho, dogmatic, radical, diehard, intolerant, single-minded, blinkered, inflexible, uncompromising. **2 enthusiastic**, eager, keen, fervent, passionate, obsessive, obsessed, fixated, compulsive; informal wild, nuts, crazy; Brit. informal potty.

fancy v. **1** (Brit. informal) **wish for**, want, desire, long for, yearn for, crave, thirst for, hanker after, dream of, covet. **2** (Brit. informal) **be attracted to**, find attractive, be infatuated with, be taken with; informal have a crush on, carry a torch for. **3 imagine**, believe, think, be under the impression; informal reckon.
• adj. **elaborate**, ornate, ornamental, decorative, embellished, intricate, ostentatious, showy, flamboyant, lavish, expensive; informal flashy, snazzy, posh, classy; Brit. informal swish.
- OPPOSITES plain.
• n. **1 whim**, foible, urge, whimsy, fascination, fad, craze, enthusiasm, passion, caprice. **2 fantasy**, dreaming, imagination, creativity.

fantastic adj. **1 fanciful**, extravagant, extraordinary, irrational, wild, absurd, far-fetched, unthinkable, implausible, improbable, unlikely; informal crazy. **2 strange**, weird, bizarre, outlandish, grotesque, surreal,

fantasy → fashionable

exotic. **3** (informal) **marvellous**, wonderful, sensational, outstanding, superb, excellent; informal terrific, fabulous; Brit. informal brilliant; Austral./NZ informal bonzer.
- OPPOSITES ordinary.

fantasy n. **1 imagination**, fancy, invention, make-believe, creativity, vision, daydreaming, reverie. **2 dream**, daydream, pipe dream, fanciful notion, wish, fond hope, delusion; informal pie in the sky.
- OPPOSITES realism.

far adv. **1 a long way**, a great distance, a good way, afar. **2 much**, considerably, markedly, greatly, significantly, substantially, appreciably, by a long way, by a mile, easily.
•adj. **1 distant**, faraway, far-off, remote, out of the way, far-flung, outlying. **2 further**, opposite.
- OPPOSITES near.

farce n. **mockery**, travesty, parody, sham, pretence, charade, joke; informal shambles.
- OPPOSITES tragedy.

fare n. **1 price**, cost, charge, fee, toll, tariff. **2 food**, meals, cooking, cuisine.
•v. **get on**, get along, cope, manage, do, survive; informal make out.

farewell exclam. **goodbye**, so long, adieu, au revoir, ciao; informal bye, cheerio, see you (later); Brit. informal ta-ta, cheers.
•n. **goodbye**, adieu, leave-

taking, parting, departure, send-off.

farm n. **smallholding**, farmstead, plantation, estate, farmland; Brit. grange, croft; Scottish steading; N. Amer. ranch; Austral./NZ station.
•v. **breed**, rear, keep, raise, tend.
□ **farm out** contract out, outsource, subcontract, delegate.

farming n. **agriculture**, cultivation, husbandry; Brit. crofting.

fascinating adj. **interesting**, captivating, engrossing, absorbing, enchanting, enthralling, spellbinding, riveting, engaging, compelling, compulsive, gripping, charming, attractive, intriguing, diverting, entertaining.
- OPPOSITES boring

fascination n. **interest**, preoccupation, passion, obsession, compulsion, allure, lure, charm, attraction, appeal, pull, draw.

fashion n. **1 vogue**, trend, craze, rage, mania, fad, style, look, convention, mode; informal thing. **2 clothes**, clothing design, couture; informal the rag trade. **3 manner**, way, method, style, approach, mode.
•v. **construct**, build, make, manufacture, cast, shape, form, mould, sculpt, forge, hew, carve.

fashionable adj. **in vogue**, in fashion, popular, up to date, up to the minute, modern, all the rage, trendsetting, stylish, chic, modish; informal trendy, classy, cool; N. Amer. informal tony.

fast¹ adj. **1 speedy**, quick, swift, rapid, high-speed, accelerated, express, blistering, breakneck, hasty, hurried; informal nippy, scorching, supersonic; Brit. informal cracking. **2 secure**, fastened, tight, firm, closed, shut, immovable. **3 loyal**, devoted, faithful, firm, steadfast, staunch, true, boon, bosom, inseparable.
– OPPOSITES slow, loose.
▸adv. **1 quickly**, rapidly, swiftly, speedily, briskly, at full tilt, hastily, hurriedly, in a hurry; informal double quick, nippily; N. Amer. informal lickety-split. **2 securely**, firmly, tight. **3** *he's fast asleep:* **deeply**, sound, completely.

fast² v. **eat nothing**, go without food, go hungry, starve yourself, go on hunger strike.

fasten v. **1 bolt**, lock, secure, make fast, chain, seal. **2 attach**, fix, affix, clip, pin, tack, stick, join. **3 tie (up)**, tether, hitch, truss, fetter, lash, anchor, strap, rope.
– OPPOSITES unlock, untie.

fat adj. **1 obese**, overweight, plump, stout, chubby, portly, flabby, paunchy, pot-bellied, corpulent; informal tubby; Brit. informal podgy. **2 fatty**, greasy, oily. **3 thick**, big, chunky, substantial, sizeable.
– OPPOSITES thin, slim, lean.
▸n. **1 blubber**, fatty tissue, adipose tissue, cellulite. **2 oil**, grease, lard, suet, butter, margarine.

fatal adj. **1 deadly**, lethal, mortal, death-dealing, terminal, incurable, untreatable, inoperable.

2 disastrous, devastating, ruinous, catastrophic, calamitous, dire.
– OPPOSITES harmless, beneficial.

fate n. **1 destiny**, providence, the stars, chance, luck, serendipity, fortune, karma, kismet. **2 future**, destiny, outcome, end, lot. **3 death**, demise, end, sentence.
▸v. **predestine**, preordain, destine, mean, doom.

father n. **1** informal **dad**, daddy, pop, pa, old man; informal, dated pater. **2 originator**, initiator, founder, inventor, creator, author, architect.
▸v. **sire**, spawn, breed, give life to.

> **WORD LINKS**
> *relating to a father:* paternal;
> *killing of your father:* patricide

fatigue n. **tiredness**, weariness, exhaustion.
– OPPOSITES energy.
▸v. **tire out**, exhaust, wear out, drain, weary, overtire; informal knock out, take it out of; Brit. informal knacker.

fatty adj. **greasy**, fat, oily, creamy, rich.

fault n. **1** *he has his faults:* **defect**, failing, imperfection, blemish, flaw, shortcoming, weakness, weak point, vice. **2** *engineers have located the fault:* **defect**, flaw, imperfection, bug, error, mistake, inaccuracy, oversight; informal glitch. **3 responsibility**, liability, culpability, guilt.
– OPPOSITES strength.
▸v. **find fault with**, criticize,

attack, condemn; informal knock; Brit. informal slag off.

□ **at fault** to blame, blameworthy, culpable, responsible, guilty, in the wrong.

faultless adj. perfect, flawless, without fault, error-free, impeccable, accurate, precise, exact, correct, exemplary.
– OPPOSITES flawed.

faulty adj. **1** malfunctioning, broken, damaged, defective, not working, out of order; informal on the blink, acting up; Brit. informal playing up. **2** flawed, unsound, defective, inaccurate, incorrect, erroneous, wrong.
– OPPOSITES working, sound.

favour n. **1** good turn, service, good deed, act of kindness, courtesy. **2** approval, approbation, goodwill, kindness, benevolence.
– OPPOSITES disservice, disapproval.
•v. **1** advocate, recommend, approve of, be in favour of, support, back, champion, campaign for, press for, lobby for, promote; informal push for. **2** prefer, go for, choose, opt for, select, pick, plump for, like better, be biased towards. **3** benefit, be to the advantage of, help, assist, aid, advance, be of service to.
– OPPOSITES oppose.
□ **in favour of** on the side of, pro, for, giving support to, approving of, sympathetic to.

favourable adj. **1** approving, positive, complimentary, full of praise, flattering, glowing,

enthusiastic, kind, good; informal rave. **2** advantageous, beneficial, in your favour, good, right, suitable, appropriate, auspicious, promising, encouraging. **3** positive, affirmative, assenting, approving, encouraging, reassuring.
– OPPOSITES critical, unfavourable.

favourite adj. favoured, preferred, chosen, choice, best-loved, dearest, pet.
•n. **first choice**, pick, preference, pet, darling, the apple of your eye; informal golden boy, teacher's pet; Brit. informal blue-eyed boy/girl; N. Amer. informal fair-haired boy/girl.

fear n. **1** terror, fright, fearfulness, horror, alarm, panic, trepidation, dread, anxiety, angst, apprehension, nervousness. **2** phobia, aversion, antipathy, dread, nightmare, horror, terror; informal hang-up.
•v. **1** be afraid of, be fearful of, be scared of, be apprehensive of, dread, live in fear of, be terrified of. **2** suspect, be afraid, have a sneaking suspicion, be inclined to think, have a hunch.

fearful adj. **1** afraid, scared, frightened, scared stiff, scared to death, terrified, petrified, nervous, apprehensive, uneasy, anxious, timid; informal jittery. **2** terrible, dreadful, awful, appalling, frightful, ghastly, horrific, horrible, shocking, gruesome.
– OPPOSITES unafraid.

fearless adj. **brave**, courageous, bold, audacious, intrepid, valiant, plucky, heroic, daring, unafraid; informal gutsy.
– OPPOSITES timid, cowardly.

feasible adj. **practicable**, practical, workable, achievable, attainable, realizable, viable, realistic, possible; informal doable.
– OPPOSITES impracticable.

feast n. **banquet**, dinner, treat; informal spread; Brit. informal beanfeast, slap-up meal.
•v. **gorge**, dine, binge; (**feast on**) devour, consume, partake of, eat your fill of; informal stuff your face with, pig out on.

feat n. **achievement**, accomplishment, coup, triumph, undertaking, enterprise, venture, exploit, operation, exercise, endeavour, effort.

feather n. **plume**, quill; (**feathers**) plumage, down.

feature n. **1 characteristic**, attribute, quality, property, trait, hallmark, aspect, facet, factor, ingredient, component, element. **2** *her delicate features*: **face**, countenance, physiognomy; informal mug; Brit. informal mush, phizog; literary lineaments, visage. **3 centrepiece**, special attraction, highlight, focal point, focus, conversation piece. **4 article**, piece, item, report, story, column.
•v. **1 present**, promote, make a feature of, spotlight, highlight, showcase, foreground. **2 star**, appear, participate.

federation n. **confederation**, confederacy, association, league, alliance, coalition, union, syndicate, guild, consortium.

fee n. **payment**, wage, salary, price, charge, bill, tariff, rate; (**fees**) remuneration, dues, earnings, pay; formal emolument.

feeble adj. **1 weak**, weakened, debilitated, enfeebled, frail, decrepit, infirm, delicate, sickly, ailing, unwell, poorly. **2 ineffective**, unconvincing, implausible, unsatisfactory, poor, weak, flimsy, lame. **3 cowardly**, fainthearted, spineless, timid, timorous, fearful, unassertive, weak, ineffectual; informal sissy, chicken; Brit. informal wet. **4 faint**, dim, weak, pale, soft, subdued, muted.
– OPPOSITES strong.

feed v. **1 cater for**, provide for, cook for, dine, nourish. **2 eat**, graze, browse, crop. **3 supply**, provide, give, deliver.
•n. **fodder**, food, provender.

feel v. **1 touch**, stroke, caress, fondle, finger, paw, handle. **2** *she felt a breeze on her back*: **perceive**, sense, detect, discern, notice, be aware of, be conscious of. **3** *he will not feel any pain*: **experience**, undergo, go through, bear, endure, suffer. **4 grope**, fumble, scrabble. **5 believe**, think, consider it right, be of the opinion, hold, maintain, judge; informal reckon, figure.
•n. **1 texture**, finish, touch, consistency. **2 atmosphere**,

ambience, aura, mood, feeling, air, impression, spirit; informal vibes. **3 aptitude**, knack, flair, bent, talent, gift, ability.

feeling n. **1 sensation**, sense, perception, awareness, consciousness. **2 (sneaking) suspicion**, notion, inkling, hunch, impression, intuition, instinct, funny feeling, fancy, idea. **3 love**, affection, fondness, tenderness, warmth, emotion, passion, desire. **4 mood**, (tide of) opinion, attitude, sentiment, emotion, belief, views, consensus. **5 compassion**, sympathy, empathy, fellow feeling, concern, pity, sorrow, commiseration. **6** *he hurt her feelings*: **sensibilities**, sensitivities, self-esteem, pride. **7 atmosphere**, ambience, aura, air, mood, impression, spirit; informal vibes. **8 aptitude**, knack, flair, bent, talent, feel, gift, ability.

felicitous adj. **apt**, well chosen, fitting, suitable, appropriate, apposite, pertinent, germane, relevant.
– OPPOSITES inappropriate.

fell v. **1 cut down**, chop down, hack down, saw down, clear. **2 knock down**, knock to the ground, floor, strike down, knock out; informal deck, flatten, lay out.

fellow n. **1** (informal) **man**, boy, person, individual, character; informal guy, lad; Brit. informal chap, bloke; N. Amer. informal dude. **2 companion**, friend, comrade, partner, associate, co-worker,

colleague; informal pal, buddy; Brit. informal mate.

fellowship n. **1 companionship**, comradeship, camaraderie, friendship, sociability, solidarity. **2 association**, organization, society, club, league, union, guild, alliance, fraternity, brotherhood.

feminine adj. **womanly**, ladylike, soft, gentle, tender, delicate, pretty.
– OPPOSITES masculine.

fence n. **barrier**, paling, railing, enclosure, barricade, stockade.
•v. **1 enclose**, surround, encircle. **2 confine**, pen in, coop up, shut in/up; N. Amer. corral.

fend v.
□ **fend off** ward off, head off, stave off, hold off, repel, repulse, resist, fight off. **fend for yourself** take care of yourself, look after yourself, shift for yourself, cope alone, stand on your own two feet, get by.

ferocious adj. **1** *ferocious animals*: **fierce**, savage, wild, predatory, ravening, aggressive, dangerous. **2** *a ferocious attack*: **brutal**, vicious, violent, bloody, barbaric, savage, frenzied.
– OPPOSITES gentle, mild.

ferry v. **transport**, convey, carry, run, ship, shuttle.

fertile adj. **1 productive**, fruitful, fecund, rich, lush. **2 creative**, inventive, innovative, visionary, original, ingenious, prolific.
– OPPOSITES barren.

fertilizer n. **plant food**, dressing, manure, muck, guano, compost.

fervent → fiction

fervent adj. **impassioned**, passionate, intense, vehement, ardent, sincere, heartfelt, enthusiastic, zealous, fanatical, wholehearted, avid, eager, keen, committed, dedicated, devout.
– OPPOSITES apathetic.

fervour n. **passion**, ardour, intensity, zeal, vehemence, emotion, warmth, avidity, eagerness, keenness, enthusiasm, excitement, animation, vigour, energy, fire, spirit.
– OPPOSITES apathy.

festival n. **celebration**, festivity, fete, fair, gala, carnival, fiesta, jamboree, feast day, holiday, holy day.

festive adj. **jolly**, merry, joyous, joyful, happy, jovial, lighthearted, cheerful, jubilant, celebratory.

festoon v. **decorate**, adorn, ornament, trim, deck (out), hang, loop, drape, swathe, garland, wreathe, bedeck; informal do up/out, get up.

fetch v. **1 go and get**, go for, call for, summon, pick up, collect, bring, carry, convey, transport. **2 sell for**, bring in, raise, realize, yield, make, command; informal go for.

fetching adj. **attractive**, appealing, sweet, pretty, lovely, delightful, charming, captivating, enchanting; Scottish & N. English bonny; Brit. informal fit.

feud n. **vendetta**, conflict, quarrel, row, rivalry, hostility, strife.
•v. **quarrel**, fight, clash, argue, squabble, dispute.

fever n. **1 feverishness**, high temperature; Medicine pyrexia; informal temperature. **2 excitement**, mania, frenzy, agitation, passion.

> **WORD LINKS**
> having a fever: febrile

feverish adj. **1 febrile**, fevered, hot, burning. **2 frenzied**, frenetic, hectic, agitated, excited, restless, nervous, worked up, overwrought, frantic, furious, hysterical, wild, uncontrolled, unrestrained.

few det. **not many**, hardly any, scarcely any, a small number of, a handful of, a couple of, one or two.
– OPPOSITES many.
•adj. **scarce**, scant, meagre, sparse, in short supply, thin on the ground, few and far between.
– OPPOSITES plentiful.

fiasco n. **failure**, disaster, catastrophe, debacle, farce, mess; informal flop, washout, shambles; Brit. informal cock-up.
– OPPOSITES success.

fibre n. **thread**, strand, filament, wisp, yarn.

fickle adj. **capricious**, flighty, giddy, changeable, volatile, mercurial, erratic, unpredictable, unreliable, unsteady.
– OPPOSITES constant.

fiction n. **1 novels**, stories, literature, creative writing. **2 fabrication**, invention, lie, fib, tall story, untruth, falsehood, fantasy, nonsense.
– OPPOSITES fact.

fictitious adj. **false**, fake, fabricated, bogus, spurious, assumed, affected, adopted, invented, made up; informal pretend, phoney.
– OPPOSITES genuine.

fiddle n. **fraud**, swindle, confidence trick; informal racket, scam.
• v. **1 fidget**, play, toy, finger, handle. **2 adjust**, tinker, play about/around, fool about/around, meddle, interfere, tamper; informal tweak, mess about/around; Brit. informal muck about/around. **3 falsify**, manipulate, massage, rig, distort, misrepresent, doctor, tamper with, interfere with; informal fix, cook (the books).

fidelity n. **1 faithfulness**, loyalty, constancy, allegiance, commitment, devotion. **2 accuracy**, exactness, precision, correctness, strictness, closeness, authenticity.
– OPPOSITES disloyalty.

fidget v. **1 wriggle**, squirm, twitch, jiggle, shuffle, be agitated; informal be jittery. **2 play**, fuss, toy, twiddle, fool about/around; informal fiddle, mess about/around.

fidgety adj. **restless**, restive, on edge, uneasy, nervous, nervy, keyed up, anxious, agitated; informal jittery, twitchy.

field n. **1 meadow**, pasture, paddock, grassland; literary lea, mead, greensward. **2 pitch**, ground; Brit. informal park. **3 area**, sphere, discipline, province, department, domain, territory, branch, subject. **4 scope**, range, sweep, reach, extent. **5 competitors**, entrants, competition, applicants, candidates, runners.
• v. **1 catch**, stop, retrieve, return, throw back. **2 deal with**, handle, cope with, answer, reply to, respond to.

fiendish adj. **1 wicked**, cruel, vicious, evil, malevolent, villainous, brutal, savage, barbaric, barbarous, inhuman, murderous, ruthless, merciless. **2 cunning**, clever, ingenious, crafty, canny, wily, devious. **3 difficult**, complex, challenging, complicated, intricate.

fierce adj. **1 ferocious**, savage, vicious, aggressive. **2 aggressive**, cut-throat, keen, intense, strong, relentless, dog-eat-dog. **3 intense**, powerful, vehement, passionate, impassioned, fervent, ardent. **4 powerful**, strong, violent, forceful, stormy, howling, raging, tempestuous.
– OPPOSITES gentle, mild.

fiery adj. **1 burning**, blazing, on fire, flaming, ablaze. **2 bright**, brilliant, vivid, intense, rich. **3 passionate**, impassioned, excitable, spirited, quick-tempered, volatile, explosive, impetuous.

fight v. **1 brawl**, exchange blows, scuffle, grapple, wrestle, tussle, spar; informal scrap; Brit. informal have a punch-up; N. Amer. informal rough-house. **2 do battle**, serve your country, go to war, take up arms, engage, meet, clash, skirmish. **3 wage**, engage in, conduct, prosecute, undertake.

fighter → fill

4 quarrel, argue, bicker, squabble, fall out, feud, wrangle; Brit. row; informal scrap. **5 campaign**, strive, battle, struggle, crusade, agitate, lobby, push, press. **6 oppose**, contest, confront, challenge, appeal against, take a stand against, dispute, resist. **7 repress**, restrain, suppress, stifle, smother, hold back, fight back, keep in check, curb, choke back; informal keep the lid on, cork up.

•n. **1 brawl**, scuffle, disturbance, fisticuffs, fracas, melee, skirmish, clash, tussle; informal scrap, dust-up; Brit. informal punch-up; N. Amer. informal rough house; dated affray. **2 boxing match**, bout, match, contest. **3 battle**, engagement, conflict, struggle, war, campaign, crusade, action, hostilities. **4 argument**, quarrel, squabble, wrangle, disagreement, falling-out, dispute, feud; Brit. row; informal tiff, spat, scrap; Brit. informal barney, ding-dong. **5 struggle**, battle, campaign, push, effort. **6** she had no fight left in her: **will**, resistance, spirit, pluck, grit, strength, backbone, determination, resolution, resolve.

fighter n. **1 soldier**, fighting man/woman, warrior, combatant, serviceman, servicewoman; (**fighters**) troops, personnel, militia. **2 boxer**, pugilist, prizefighter, wrestler.

figurative adj. **metaphorical**, non-literal, symbolic, allegorical, representative, emblematic.
– OPPOSITES literal.

figure n. **1 statistic**, number, quantity, amount, level, total, sum; (**figures**) data, statistics. **2 digit**, numeral, character, symbol. **3 price**, cost, amount, value, valuation. **4 shape**, outline, form, silhouette, proportions, physique, build, frame. **5 person**, personage, individual, character, personality, celebrity. **6 shape**, pattern, design, motif. **7 diagram**, illustration, drawing, picture, plate.
•v. he figures in many myths: **feature**, appear, be featured, be mentioned, be referred to.
□ **figure out** (informal) **work out**, fathom, puzzle out, decipher, make sense of, think through, get to the bottom of, understand, comprehend, see, grasp, get the hang of; informal twig, crack; Brit. informal suss out.

file[1] n. **1 folder**, portfolio, binder. **2 dossier**, document, record, report, data, information, documentation, archives.
•v. **1 categorize**, classify, organize, put in order, order, arrange, catalogue, store, archive. **2 bring**, press, lodge.

file[2] n. **line**, column, row, queue, string, chain, procession; Brit. informal crocodile.
•v. **walk in a line**, queue, march, parade, troop.

file[3] v. **smooth**, buff, rub down, polish, shape, scrape, abrade, rasp, manicure.

fill v. **1 fill up**, top up, charge. **2 crowd into**, throng, pack (into), occupy, squeeze into,

cram (into). **3 stock**, pack, load, supply, replenish. **4 block up**, stop (up), plug, seal, caulk. **5 pervade**, permeate, suffuse, penetrate, infuse. **6 occupy**, hold, take up.
– OPPOSITES empty, clear, leave.

filling n. **stuffing**, padding, wadding, filler, contents.
•adj. **substantial**, hearty, ample, satisfying, square, heavy, stodgy.

film n. **1 layer**, coat, coating, covering, cover, skin, patina, tissue. **2 movie**, picture, feature film, motion picture, video, DVD. **3 cinema**, movies, the pictures, films, the silver screen, the big screen.
•v. **1 photograph**, record on film, shoot, capture on film, video. **2 cloud**, mist, haze, blur.

filter n. **strainer**, sifter, sieve, gauze, mesh, net.
•v. **1 sieve**, strain, sift, clarify, purify, refine, treat. **2 seep**, percolate, leak, trickle, ooze, leach.

filth n. **dirt**, muck, grime, mud, sludge, slime, excrement, excreta, ordure, sewage, pollution.

filthy adj. **1 dirty**, mucky, grimy, foul, squalid, sordid, soiled, stained, polluted, contaminated, unwashed. **2 obscene**, rude, vulgar, dirty, smutty, improper, coarse, bawdy, lewd; informal blue. **3 bad**, foul, irritable, grumpy, grouchy, cross; informal snappy; Brit. informal shirty, stroppy; N. Amer. informal cranky, ornery.
– OPPOSITES clean, pleasant.

final adj. **1 last**, closing, concluding, finishing, end, ultimate, eventual. **2 irrevocable**, unalterable, absolute, conclusive, irrefutable, incontrovertible, indisputable, unchallengeable, binding.
– OPPOSITES first, provisional.

finale n. **climax**, culmination, end, ending, finish, close, conclusion, termination, denouement.
– OPPOSITES opening.

finally adv. **1 eventually**, ultimately, in the end, after a long time, at (long) last, in the long run, in the fullness of time. **2 lastly**, last, in conclusion. **3 conclusively**, irrevocably, decisively, definitively, for ever, for good, once and for all.

finance n. **1 financial affairs**, money matters, economics, commerce, business, investment. **2 funds**, money, capital, cash, resources, assets, reserves, funding.
•v. **fund**, pay for, back, capitalize, endow, subsidize, invest in, sponsor; N. Amer. informal bankroll.

financial adj. **monetary**, money, economic, pecuniary, fiscal, banking, commercial, business, investment.

find v. **1 locate**, spot, pinpoint, unearth, obtain, search out, track down, root out, come across/upon, run across/into, chance on, happen on, stumble on, encounter; informal bump into. **2 discover**, invent, come up with, hit on. **3 realize**, become aware, discover, observe, notice, note, learn. **4 consider**, think, feel to be, look on as, view as, see as, judge, deem, regard as. **5 judge**, deem, rule, declare, pronounce.

– OPPOSITES lose.

▪n. **1 discovery**, acquisition. **2 bargain**, godsend, boon, catch, asset; informal good buy. ▫ **find out** discover, become aware of, learn, detect, discern, observe, notice, note, get/come to know, realize, bring to light; informal figure out, cotton on, tumble; Brit. informal twig, suss.

fine¹ adj. **1 fine wines: good**, choice, select, excellent, first-class, first-rate, great, exceptional, outstanding, splendid, magnificent, exquisite, superb, wonderful, superlative, prime, quality, special, superior, of distinction, premium, classic, vintage; informal A1, top-notch. **2 a fine fellow: worthy**, admirable, praiseworthy, laudable, upright, upstanding, respectable. **3 all right**, acceptable, suitable, good (enough), passable, satisfactory, adequate, reasonable, tolerable; informal OK. **4 healthy**, well, good, all right, (fighting) fit, blooming, thriving, in good shape/condition; informal OK, in fine fettle, in the pink. **5 fair**, dry, bright, clear, sunny, cloudless, balmy. **6 keen**, quick, alert, sharp, razor-sharp, acute, bright, brilliant, astute, clever, intelligent. **7 elegant**, stylish, expensive, smart, chic, fashionable, fancy, sumptuous, lavish, opulent;

informal flashy. **8 flyaway**, wispy, delicate, thin, light. **9 sheer**, light, lightweight, thin, flimsy, diaphanous, filmy, see-through. **10 subtle**, ultra-fine, nice, hair-splitting.

fine² n. **penalty**, forfeit, damages, fee, excess charge.

finger n. **digit**.

▪v. **touch**, feel, handle, stroke, rub, caress, fondle, toy with, play (about/around) with, fiddle with.

finish v. **1 complete**, end, conclude, close, terminate, wind up, round off, achieve, accomplish, fulfil; informal wrap up, sew up. **2 consume**, eat, devour, drink, finish off, polish off, use (up), exhaust, empty, drain, get through; informal down. **3 end**, come to an end, stop, conclude, come to a close, cease.

– OPPOSITES start.

▪n. **1 end**, ending, completion, conclusion, close, termination, finale, denouement. **2 surface**, texture, coating, covering, lacquer, glaze, veneer, gloss, patina, sheen, lustre.

– OPPOSITES start.

▫ **finish off 1 kill**, execute, terminate, exterminate, liquidate, get rid of; informal wipe out, bump off, dispose of; N. Amer. informal waste. **2 overwhelm**, overcome, defeat, get the better of, bring down; informal drive to the wall.

finite adj. **limited**, restricted, determinate, fixed.

– OPPOSITES infinite.

f

fire n. **1 blaze**, conflagration, inferno, flames, burning, combustion. **2 dynamism**, energy, vigour, animation, vitality, exuberance, zest, elan, passion, zeal, spirit, verve, vivacity, enthusiasm; informal go, get-up-and-go, oomph. **3 gunfire**, firing, shooting, bombardment, shelling, volley, salvo, hail.
•v. **1 launch**, shoot, discharge, let fly with. **2 shoot**, discharge, let off, set off. **3** (informal) **dismiss**, discharge, give someone their notice, lay off, let go; informal sack. **4 stimulate**, stir up, excite, awaken, rouse, inflame, animate, inspire, motivate.
□ **catch fire** ignite, catch light, burst into flames, go up in flames. **set on fire** ignite, light, set fire to, set alight.

WORD LINKS
crime of setting fire to property: arson;
obsessive desire to set fire to things: pyromania

firm[1] adj. **1 hard**, solid, unyielding, resistant, compacted, compressed, dense, stiff, rigid, set. **2 secure**, stable, steady, strong, fixed, fast, tight, immovable, rooted, stationary, motionless. **3 resolute**, determined, decided, resolved, steadfast, adamant, emphatic, insistent, single-minded, wholehearted, unfaltering, unwavering, unflinching, unswerving, unbending, committed. **4 close**, good, boon, intimate, inseparable, dear, special, constant, devoted, loving, faithful, long-standing, steady, steadfast. **5 definite**, fixed, settled, decided, cut-and-dried, established, confirmed, agreed.
– OPPOSITES soft, unstable.

firm[2] n. **business**, company, concern, enterprise, organization, corporation, conglomerate, office, bureau, agency, consortium; informal outfit, operation.

first adj. **1 earliest**, initial, opening, introductory. **2 fundamental**, basic, rudimentary, primary, key, cardinal, central, chief, vital, essential. **3 foremost**, principal, highest, greatest, paramount, top, main, overriding, central, core; informal number-one. **4 top**, best, prime, premier, winning, champion.
– OPPOSITES last.
•adv. **at first**, to begin with, first of all, at the outset, initially.
•n. **novelty**, innovation, departure, break with tradition.

fish v. **1 go fishing**, angle, trawl. **2 search**, delve, look, hunt, grope, fumble, ferret, rummage.
□ **fish out** pull out, haul out, remove, extricate, extract, retrieve, rescue, save.

WORD LINKS
relating to fish: piscine;
study of fish: ichthyology

fit[1] adj. **1 suitable**, appropriate, suited, apposite, fitting, good enough, apt. **2 competent**, able, capable, ready,

prepared, equipped. **3 healthy**, well, in good health, in (good) shape, in trim, in good condition, fighting fit, athletic, muscular, strapping, strong, robust, hale and hearty.
- OPPOSITES unsuitable, incapable.
- v. **1 lay**, install, put in position, place, fix, arrange. **2 equip**, provide, supply, fit out, furnish. **3 join**, connect, piece together, attach, unite, link. **4 be appropriate to**, suit, match, correspond to, tally with, go with, accord with. **5 qualify**, prepare, make ready, train.
- □ **fit in** conform, be in harmony, blend in, be in line, be assimilated.

fit² n. **1 convulsion**, spasm, paroxysm, seizure, attack. **2 outbreak**, outburst, attack, bout, spell. **3 tantrum**, frenzy; informal paddy.

fitness n. **1 good health**, strength, robustness, vigour, athleticism, toughness, stamina. **2 suitability**, capability, competence, ability, aptitude, readiness, preparedness.

fitting n. **1 attachment**, part, piece, component, accessory, apparatus. **2 furnishings**, furniture, fixtures, fitments, equipment.
- adj. **apt**, appropriate, suitable, apposite, fit, proper, right, seemly, correct.
- OPPOSITES unsuitable.

fix v. **1 fasten**, attach, affix, secure, connect, couple, link, install,

stick, glue, pin, nail, screw, bolt, clamp, clip. **2 lodge**, stick, embed. **3 focus**, direct, level, point, train. **4 repair**, mend, put right, get working, restore. **5 arrange**, organize, contrive, manage, engineer; informal swing, wangle. **6** (informal) **arrange**, put in order, adjust, style, groom, comb, brush; informal do. **7** (informal) **prepare**, cook, make, get; informal rustle up; Brit. informal knock up. **8 decide on**, select, choose, settle, set, arrange, establish, allot, designate, name, appoint, specify. **9** (informal) **rig**, tamper with, skew, influence; informal fiddle.
- n. (informal) **1 predicament**, plight, difficulty, awkward situation, corner, tight spot, mess; informal pickle, jam, hole, scrape, bind. **2 fraud**, swindle, trick, charade, sham; informal set-up, fiddle.

fixation n. **obsession**, preoccupation, mania, addiction, compulsion; informal thing, bug, bee in your bonnet.

fixed adj. **predetermined**, set, established, arranged, specified, decided, agreed, determined, confirmed, prescribed, definite, defined, explicit, precise.

fizz v. **bubble**, sparkle, effervesce, froth.
- n. **1 bubbles**, sparkle, fizziness, effervescence, gassiness, froth. **2 crackle**, buzz, hiss, white noise.

fizzy adj. **sparkling**, effervescent, carbonated, gassy, bubbly, frothy.
- OPPOSITES still, flat.

flag[1] n. **banner**, standard, ensign, pennant, streamer, colours; Brit. pendant.
▸v. **indicate**, identify, point out, mark, label, tag, highlight.
□ **flag down** hail, wave down, stop, halt.

flag[2] v. **1** tire, grow tired, wilt, weaken, grow weak, droop. **2** fade, decline, wane, ebb, diminish, decrease, lessen, dwindle.
− OPPOSITES revive.

flagrant adj. **blatant**, glaring, obvious, conspicuous, barefaced, shameless, brazen, undisguised.

flair n. **1** aptitude, talent, gift, instinct, ability, facility, knack, skill. **2** style, elegance, panache, dash, elan, poise, taste; informal class.

flake n. **sliver**, wafer, shaving, paring, chip, fragment, scrap, shred.
▸v. **peel (off)**, chip, blister, come off.

flamboyant adj. **1** ostentatious, exuberant, confident, lively, animated, vibrant, vivacious. **2** colourful, bright, vibrant, vivid, dazzling, bold, showy, gaudy, garish, loud; informal jazzy, flashy.
− OPPOSITES restrained.

flame n. **1** fire, blaze, conflagration, inferno. **2** (informal) **sweetheart**, boyfriend, girlfriend, lover, partner.
□ **in flames** on fire, burning, alight, flaming, blazing.

flank n. **1** side, haunch, quarter, thigh. **2** side, wing, sector, face, aspect.

▸v. **edge**, bound, line, border, fringe.

flap v. **1** ducks flapped their wings: **beat**, flutter, agitate, vibrate, wag, thrash, flail. **2** the flag flapped in the breeze: **flutter**, wave, fly, blow, swing, ripple, stir.
▸n. **1** beat, stroke, flutter, movement. **2** (informal) **panic**, fluster; informal state, stew, tizzy; N. Amer. informal twit.

flare n. **1** blaze, flame, flash, burst, flicker. **2** signal, beacon, rocket, light, torch.
▸v. **1** blaze, flash, flare up, flame, burn, flicker. **2** spread, splay, broaden, widen, dilate.

flash v. **1** shine, flare, blaze, gleam, glint, sparkle, burn, blink, wink, flicker, shimmer, twinkle, glimmer, glisten. **2** (informal) **show off**, flaunt, flourish, display, parade. **3** zoom, streak, tear, shoot, dash, dart, fly, whistle, hurtle, rush, bolt, race, speed, career; informal belt, zap; Brit. informal bomb; N. Amer. informal barrel.
▸n. **flare**, blaze, burst, gleam, glint, sparkle, flicker, shimmer, twinkle, glimmer.

flashy adj. (informal) **ostentatious**, flamboyant, showy, conspicuous, extravagant, expensive, vulgar, tasteless, brash, garish, loud, gaudy; informal snazzy, fancy, swanky, flash, glitzy.
− OPPOSITES understated.

flat[1] adj. **1** level, horizontal, smooth, even, plane. **2** calm, still, glassy, smooth, placid, like a millpond. **3** stretched out,

prone, spreadeagled, prostrate, supine, recumbent. **4 monotonous**, toneless, lifeless, droning, boring, dull, tedious, uninteresting, unexciting. **5 inactive**, slow, sluggish, slack, quiet, depressed. **6** (Brit.) **run down**, dead, used up, expired. **7 deflated**, punctured, burst, blown. **8 fixed**, set, invariable, regular, constant. **9 outright**, direct, absolute, definite, positive, straight, plain, explicit, categorical.
- OPPOSITES sloping, rough, uneven.
•adv. **stretched out**, outstretched, spreadeagled, sprawling, prone, prostrate.

flat² n. apartment, suite, penthouse, rooms.

flatten v. **1 level**, even out, smooth out, make/become flat. **2 squash**, compress, press down, crush, compact, trample. **3 demolish**, raze (to the ground), tear down, knock down, destroy, wreck, devastate.
- OPPOSITES crumple.

flatter v. **1 compliment**, praise, express admiration for, fawn on, humour, wheedle, blarney; informal sweet-talk, soft-soap, butter up, play up to. **2 honour**, gratify, please, delight; informal tickle pink. **3 suit**, become, look good on, go well with; informal do something for.
- OPPOSITES insult, offend.

flattering adj. **1 complimentary**, praising, favourable, admiring, appreciative, fulsome,

honeyed, obsequious, ingratiating, sycophantic. **2 pleasing**, gratifying, an honour. **3 becoming**, enhancing.
- OPPOSITES unflattering.

flattery n. praise, adulation, compliments, blandishments, honeyed words, fawning, blarney; informal sweet talk, soft soap, buttering up.

flaunt v. **show off**, display, make a great show of, put on show/display, parade, draw attention to, brag about, crow about, vaunt; informal flash.

flavour n. **1 taste**, savour, tang, smack. **2 flavouring**, seasoning, taste, tang, relish, bite, piquancy, spice. **3 character**, quality, feel, feeling, ambience, atmosphere, air, mood, tone, spirit. **4 impression**, suggestion, hint, taste.
- v. **season**, spice (up), add piquancy to, ginger up, enrich, infuse.

flaw n. **defect**, blemish, fault, imperfection, deficiency, weakness, weak spot/point, failing; Computing bug; informal glitch.
- OPPOSITES strength.

flawed adj. **1 faulty**, defective, unsound, imperfect, blemished, broken, cracked, scratched; Brit. informal duff. **2 unsound**, distorted, inaccurate, incorrect, erroneous, fallacious, wrong.
- OPPOSITES flawless.

flawless adj. **perfect**, unblemished, unmarked, unimpaired, whole, intact, sound, unbroken, undamaged, mint, pristine,

impeccable, immaculate, accurate, correct, faultless, error-free, exemplary, model, ideal, copybook.
– OPPOSITES flawed.

flee v. **run away**, run off, run for it, make off, take off, take to your heels, make a break for it, bolt, beat a (hasty) retreat, make a quick exit, escape; informal beat it, clear off/out, skedaddle, scram; Brit. informal scarper.

fleet n. **navy**, naval force, (naval) task force, armada, flotilla, squadron, convoy.

fleeting adj. **brief**, short-lived, quick, momentary, cursory, transient, ephemeral, passing, transitory.
– OPPOSITES lasting.

flesh n. **1 tissue**, skin, muscle, fat, meat, body. **2 pulp**, marrow, meat. **3** the pleasures of the flesh: **the body**, human nature, physicality, sensuality, sexuality.

flexibility n. **1 pliability**, suppleness, elasticity, stretchiness, springiness, spring, resilience, bounce; informal give. **2 adaptability**, adjustability, versatility, open-endedness, freedom, latitude. **3 willingness to compromise**, give and take, amenability, cooperation, tolerance.
– OPPOSITES rigidity.

flexible adj. **1 bendy**, pliable, supple, pliant, plastic, elastic, stretchy, springy, resilient, bouncy. **2 adaptable**, adjustable, variable, versatile, open-

ended, open. **3 accommodating**, amenable, willing to compromise, cooperative, tolerant.
– OPPOSITES rigid, inflexible.

flick n. **jerk**, snap, flip, whisk.
•v. **1 click**, snap, flip, jerk, throw. **2 swish**, twitch, wave, wag, waggle, shake.
▫ **flick through** thumb through, leaf through, flip through, skim, scan, look through, browse through, dip into, glance at/through.

flicker v. **1 glimmer**, flare, dance, gutter, twinkle, sparkle, wink, flash. **2 flutter**, quiver, tremble, shiver, shudder, jerk, twitch.

flight n. **1 aviation**, flying, air transport, aeronautics. **2 flock**, swarm, cloud, throng. **3 escape**, getaway, hasty departure, exit, exodus, breakout, bolt, disappearance; Brit. informal flit.

flimsy adj. **1 insubstantial**, fragile, frail, rickety, ramshackle, makeshift, jerry-built, shoddy. **2 thin**, light, fine, filmy, floaty, diaphanous, sheer, delicate, gossamer, gauzy. **3 weak**, feeble, poor, inadequate, insufficient, thin, unsubstantial, unconvincing, implausible.
– OPPOSITES sturdy.

flinch v. **1 wince**, start, shudder, quiver, jerk. **2** he never flinched from his duty: **shrink from**, recoil from, shy away from, dodge, evade, avoid, duck, baulk at.

fling v. **throw**, hurl, toss, sling, launch, pitch, lob; informal chuck, heave.
•n. **1 good time**, party, spree,

fun and games; informal binge, bash, night on the town. **2 affair**, love affair, relationship, romance, liaison, entanglement, involvement.

flip v. **1 overturn**, turn over, tip over, roll (over), upturn, capsize, upend, invert, knock over, keel over, topple over, turn turtle. **2 flick**, click, throw, push, pull. □ **flip through** thumb through, leaf through, flick through, skim through, scan, look through, browse through, dip into, glance at/through, peruse, run your eye over.

flippant adj. **frivolous**, facetious, tongue-in-cheek, disrespectful, irreverent, cheeky; informal flip, saucy; N. Amer. informal sassy.
– OPPOSITES serious.

flirt n. **tease**, coquette, heart-breaker.
□ **flirt with 1** tease, lead on, toy with. **2** dabble in, toy with, trifle with, play with, tinker with, dip into, scratch the surface of.

float v. **1 stay afloat**, stay on the surface, be buoyant, be buoyed up. **2 hover**, levitate, be suspended, hang, defy gravity. **3 drift**, glide, sail, slip, slide, waft. **4 launch**, offer, sell, introduce.
– OPPOSITES sink.

floating adj. **1 uncommitted**, undecided, undeclared, wavering; informal sitting on the fence. **2 unsettled**, transient, temporary, migrant, wandering, nomadic, migratory, itinerant.

flock n. **1 herd**, drove. **2 flight**, swarm, cloud, gaggle, skein.
• v. **1** *people flocked around her:* **gather**, collect, congregate, assemble, converge, mass, crowd, throng, cluster, swarm. **2** *tourists flock to the place:* **stream**, go in large numbers, swarm, crowd, troop.

flog v. **whip**, thrash, lash, scourge, birch, cane, beat.

flood n. **1 inundation**, deluge, torrent, overflow, flash flood; Brit. spate. **2 gush**, outpouring, torrent, rush, stream, surge, cascade. **3 succession**, series, string, barrage, volley, battery, avalanche, torrent, stream, storm.
• v. **1** *the town was flooded:* **inundate**, swamp, deluge, immerse, submerge, drown, engulf. **2** *the river could flood:* **overflow**, burst its banks, brim over, run over. **3 glut**, swamp, saturate, oversupply. **4 pour**, stream, flow, surge, swarm, pile, crowd.

floor n. **1 ground**, flooring. **2 storey**, level, deck, tier, stage.
• v. **1 knock down**, knock over, fell; informal deck, lay out. **2** (informal) **baffle**, defeat, confound, perplex, puzzle, disconcert; informal throw, beat, stump.

flop v. **1 collapse**, slump, crumple, sink, drop. **2 hang (down)**, dangle, droop, sag, loll. **3** (informal) **be unsuccessful**, fail, fall flat, founder; informal bomb; N. Amer. informal tank.
• n. (informal) **failure**, disaster, fiasco, debacle, catastrophe; Brit.

f

damp squib; informal washout, also-ran.
– OPPOSITES success.

floppy adj. **limp**, flaccid, slack, flabby, relaxed, drooping, droopy, loose, flowing.
– OPPOSITES erect, stiff.

flounder v. **1** *floundering in the water:* **struggle**, thrash, flail, twist and turn, splash, stagger, stumble, reel, lurch, blunder. **2** *she floundered, not knowing what to say:* **struggle**, be out of your depth, be confused; informal scratch your head, be flummoxed, be fazed, be floored.

flourish v. **1** *ferns flourish in the shade:* **grow**, thrive, prosper, do well, burgeon, increase, multiply, proliferate, run riot. **2** *the arts flourished:* **thrive**, prosper, bloom, be in good health, be vigorous, be in its heyday, make progress, advance, expand; informal go places. **3 brandish**, wave, shake, wield, swing, display, show off.
– OPPOSITES wither, decline.

flout v. **defy**, refuse to obey, disobey, break, violate, fail to comply with, fail to observe, contravene, infringe, breach, commit a breach of, transgress against, ignore, disregard; informal cock a snook at.
– OPPOSITES observe.

flow v. **1 pour**, run, course, circulate, stream, swirl, surge, sweep, gush, cascade, roll, rush, trickle, seep, ooze, dribble. **2 result**, proceed, arise, follow,

ensue, stem, originate, emanate, spring.
•n. **movement**, motion, current, circulation, stream, swirl, surge, gush, rush, spate, tide, trickle, ooze.

flower n. & v. **bloom**, blossom.

WORD LINKS
relating to flowers: floral;
person who sells flowers: florist

fluctuate v. **vary**, change, shift, alter, waver, swing, oscillate, alternate, rise and fall.

fluent adj. **articulate**, eloquent, silver-tongued, communicative, natural, effortless.
– OPPOSITES inarticulate.

fluid n. **liquid**, solution, liquor, gas, vapour.
•adj. **1 free-flowing**, runny, liquid, liquefied, melted, molten, gaseous. **2 smooth**, fluent, flowing, effortless, easy, continuous, graceful, elegant.
– OPPOSITES solid.

flurry n. **1 swirl**, whirl, eddy, shower, gust. **2 burst**, outbreak, spurt, fit, spell, bout, rash, eruption.

flush v. **1 blush**, redden, go pink, go red, go crimson, go scarlet, colour (up). **2 rinse**, wash, sluice, swill, cleanse, clean; Brit. informal sloosh. **3 chase**, force, drive, dislodge, expel.
•n. **blush**, colour, rosiness, pinkness, ruddiness, bloom.
– OPPOSITES pallor.

flutter v. **1** *butterflies fluttered around:* **flit**, hover, dance. **2** *a* *robin fluttered its wings:* **flap**, beat, quiver, agitate, vibrate, ruffle. **3** *she fluttered her eyelashes:* **flicker**, bat. **4** *flags fluttered:* **flap**, wave, ripple, undulate, quiver, fly.

fly v. **1 wing**, glide, soar, wheel, take wing, take to the air, hover, swoop. **2 pilot**, operate, control, manoeuvre, steer. **3** *the ship flew a French flag:* **display**, show, exhibit, hoist, raise, wave. **4 dash**, race, rush, bolt, zoom, dart, speed, hurry, career, hurtle; *informal* tear.

foam n. **froth**, spume, surf, spray, fizz, effervescence, bubbles, head, lather, suds.
• v. **froth**, fizz, effervesce, bubble, lather, ferment, boil, seethe.

focus n. **1 centre**, focal point, central point, centre of attention, hub, pivot, nucleus, heart, cornerstone, linchpin. **2 subject**, theme, concern, subject matter, topic, point, essence, gist.
• v. **bring into focus**, aim, point, turn.
▫ **focus on** concentrate, centre, zero in, zoom in, address yourself to, pay attention to, pinpoint, revolve around.

fog n. **mist**, smog, murk, haze; *informal* pea-souper.

foggy adj. **1 misty**, smoggy, hazy, murky. **2** *a foggy memory:* **muddled**, confused, dim, hazy, shadowy, cloudy, blurred, obscure, vague, indistinct, unclear.
– OPPOSITES clear.

foil¹ v. **thwart**, frustrate, stop, defeat, block, prevent, obstruct, hinder, snooker, scotch; *informal* put paid to; *Brit. informal* scupper.
– OPPOSITES assist.

foil² n. **contrast**, complement, antithesis.

fold v. **1 double**, crease, turn, bend, tuck, pleat. **2 fail**, collapse, founder, go bankrupt, cease trading, be wound up, be shut (down); *informal* crash, go bust, go under, go to the wall, go belly up.
• n. **crease**, knife-edge, wrinkle, crinkle, pucker, furrow, pleat.

folk n. (*informal*) **1 people**, individuals, (men, women, and children), (living) souls, citizenry, inhabitants, residents, populace, population. **2 relatives**, relations, family, people; *informal* peeps.

follow v. **1 come behind**, come after, go behind, go after, walk behind. **2 accompany**, go along with, go around with, travel with, escort, attend; *informal* tag along with. **3 shadow**, trail, stalk, track; *informal* tail. **4 obey**, comply with, conform to, adhere to, stick to, keep to, act in accordance with, abide by, observe. **5 understand**, comprehend, take in, grasp, fathom, see; *informal* make head or tail of, figure out; *Brit. informal* suss out. **6 be a fan of**, be a supporter of, support, watch, keep up with.
– OPPOSITES lead, flout.

follower n. **1 disciple**, apostle, defender, champion, believer,

worshipper. **2 fan**, enthusiast, admirer, devotee, lover, supporter, adherent.
– OPPOSITES leader, opponent.

following n. admirers, supporters, backers, fans, adherents, devotees, public, audience.
– OPPOSITES opposition.
•adj. **next**, ensuing, succeeding, subsequent, successive.
– OPPOSITES preceding.

folly n. foolishness, foolhardiness, stupidity, idiocy, lunacy, madness, rashness, recklessness, irresponsibility.
– OPPOSITES wisdom.

fond adj. **1** she was fond of dancing: keen on, partial to, enthusiastic about, attached to; informal into. **2 adoring**, devoted, doting, loving, caring, affectionate, indulgent. **3 unrealistic**, naive, foolish, over-optimistic, absurd, vain.
– OPPOSITES indifferent, uncaring.

fondle v. caress, stroke, pat, pet, finger, tickle, play with.

food n. nourishment, sustenance, nutriment, fare, cooking, cuisine, foodstuffs, refreshments, meals, provisions, rations; informal eats, grub, nosh; literary viands; dated victuals.

> WORD LINKS
> *relating to food:* alimentary

fool n. **1 idiot**, ass, halfwit, blockhead, dunce, simpleton; informal nincompoop, clod, dimwit, dummy, fathead, numbskull; Brit. informal nitwit, twit, clot, berk, prat, pillock, wally, dork, twerp, charlie; N. Amer. informal schmuck; Austral./NZ informal drongo. **2** she made a fool of me: laughing stock, dupe, gull; informal stooge, sucker, mug, fall guy; N. Amer. informal sap.
– OPPOSITES genius.
•v. **1 deceive**, trick, hoax, dupe, take in, mislead, delude, hoodwink, bluff, gull; informal bamboozle, take for a ride, have on; N. Amer. informal sucker; Austral. informal pull a swifty on. **2 pretend**, make believe, put on an act, act, sham, fake, joke, jest; informal kid; Brit. informal have on.

foolish adj. **stupid**, idiotic, senseless, mindless, unintelligent, thoughtless, imprudent, unwise, ill-advised, rash, reckless, foolhardy; informal dumb, dim, dim-witted, half-witted, moronic, thick, hare-brained; Brit. informal barmy, daft, potty.
– OPPOSITES sensible, wise.

foolproof adj. **infallible**, dependable, reliable, trustworthy, certain, sure, guaranteed, safe, sound, tried and tested, watertight, airtight, flawless, perfect; informal sure-fire.

foot n. **1 paw**, hoof, trotter, pad. **2 bottom**, base, lowest part, end, foundation.

> WORD LINKS
> *medical treatment of the feet:* chiropody, podiatry

footing n. **1** a solid financial footing: basis, base, foundation. **2** on an equal footing: standing,

forbid → foresight

status, position, condition, arrangement, basis, relationship, terms.

forbid v. **prohibit**, ban, outlaw, make illegal, veto, proscribe, embargo, bar, debar, rule out.
– OPPOSITES permit.

forbidden adj. **prohibited**, verboten, taboo, illegal, illicit, against the law.

forbidding adj. **threatening**, ominous, menacing, sinister, daunting, off-putting.

force n. **1 strength**, power, energy, might, effort. **2 coercion**, compulsion, constraint, duress, pressure, oppression, harassment, intimidation, violence; informal arm-twisting. **3 power**, potency, weight, effectiveness, persuasiveness, validity, strength, significance, influence, authority; informal punch.
4 body, group, outfit, party, team, detachment, unit, squad.
•v. **1 compel**, coerce, make, constrain, oblige, impel, drive, pressure, pressurize, press-gang, bully; informal lean on, twist someone's arm. **2 break open**, knock/smash/break down, kick in. **3 propel**, push, thrust, shove, drive, press, pump.
□ **in force** effective, in operation, operative, valid, current, binding.

forced adj. **1 enforced**, compulsory, obligatory, mandatory, involuntary, imposed, required. **2 strained**, unnatural, artificial, false, feigned, simulated, contrived, laboured, affected, hollow; informal phoney, pretend, put on.
– OPPOSITES voluntary, natural.

forceful adj. **1 dynamic**, energetic, assertive, authoritative, vigorous, powerful, strong, pushy; informal in-your-face, go-ahead, feisty. **2 convincing**, cogent, compelling, strong, powerful, persuasive, coherent.
– OPPOSITES weak.

forecast v. **predict**, prophesy, foretell, foresee.
•n. **prediction**, prophecy, prognostication, prognosis.

foreign adj. **alien**, overseas, non-native, imported, distant, external, far-off, exotic, strange.
– OPPOSITES domestic, native.

foreigner n. **alien**, non-native, stranger, outsider, immigrant, settler, newcomer, incomer.
– OPPOSITES native, national.

> **WORD LINKS**
> irrational dislike or fear of foreigners: xenophobia

foremost adj. **leading**, principal, premier, prime, top, greatest, best, supreme, pre-eminent, outstanding, most important, most notable; N. Amer. ranking; informal number-one.
– OPPOSITES minor.

foresee v. **anticipate**, expect, envisage, predict, forecast, foretell, prophesy.

foresight n. **forethought**, planning, far-sightedness, vision, anticipation, prudence, care, caution; N. Amer. forehandedness.
– OPPOSITES hindsight.

foretell v. predict, forecast, prophesy, foresee, anticipate, envisage, warn of.

forever adv. **1 for always**, evermore, for ever and ever, for good, for all time, until the end of time, eternally; N. Amer. forevermore; informal until the cows come home. **2 always**, continually, constantly, perpetually, incessantly, endlessly, persistently, repeatedly, regularly; informal 24-7.

forfeit v. **lose**, be deprived of, surrender, relinquish, sacrifice, give up, renounce, forgo.
•n. **penalty**, sanction, punishment, penance, fine, confiscation, loss, forfeiture, surrender.

forge v. **1 hammer out**, beat out, fashion. **2 build**, construct, form, create, establish, set up. **3 fake**, falsify, counterfeit, copy, imitate, pirate.

forged adj. **fake**, false, counterfeit, imitation, copied, pirate, bogus; informal phoney, dud.
– OPPOSITES genuine.

forgery n. **fake**, counterfeit, fraud, imitation, replica, copy, pirate copy; informal phoney.

forget v. **1 fail to remember**, be unable to remember. **2 leave behind**, fail to take/bring, travel/leave home without. **3** I forgot to close the door: **neglect**, fail, omit.
– OPPOSITES remember.

forgetful adj. **1 absent-minded**, amnesiac, vague, scatter-brained, disorganized, dreamy, abstracted, with a mind/memory like a sieve; informal scatty.

2 forgetful of the time: **heedless**, careless, inattentive to, negligent about, oblivious to, unconcerned about, indifferent to.

forgive v. **1 pardon**, excuse, exonerate, absolve. **2 excuse**, overlook, disregard, ignore, make allowances for, turn a blind eye to, condone, indulge, tolerate.
– OPPOSITES blame, resent.

forgiveness n. **pardon**, absolution, exoneration, indulgence, clemency, mercy, reprieve, amnesty; informal let-off.
– OPPOSITES punishment.

forgiving adj. **merciful**, lenient, compassionate, magnanimous, humane, soft-hearted, forbearing, tolerant, indulgent, understanding.
– OPPOSITES merciless, vindictive.

forgo, forego v. **do without**, go without, give up, waive, renounce, surrender, relinquish, part with, drop, sacrifice, abstain from, refrain from, eschew, cut out; informal swear off; formal forswear, abjure.

fork v. **split**, branch, divide, separate, part, diverge, go in different directions, bifurcate.

forlorn adj. **1 unhappy**, sad, miserable, sorrowful, dejected, despondent, disconsolate, wretched, down, downcast, dispirited, downhearted, crestfallen, depressed, melancholy, gloomy, glum, mournful, despairing, doleful, woebegone; informal blue, down in the mouth, down in the dumps, fed up.

2 hopeless, useless, futile, pointless, purposeless, vain, unavailing.
– OPPOSITES happy.

form n. **1 shape**, configuration, formation, structure, construction, arrangement, appearance, exterior, outline, format, layout, design. **2 body**, shape, figure, frame, physique, anatomy; informal vital statistics. **3 manifestation**, appearance, embodiment, incarnation, semblance, shape, guise. **4 kind**, sort, type, class, category, variety, genre, brand, style. **5 questionnaire**, document, coupon, slip. **6 class**, year; N. Amer. grade. **7 condition**, fettle, shape, health; Brit. informal nick.
▸v. **1 make**, construct, build, manufacture, fabricate, assemble, put together, create, fashion, shape. **2 formulate**, devise, conceive, work out, think up, lay, draw up, put together, produce, fashion, concoct, forge, hatch; informal dream up. **3 set up**, establish, found, launch, create, institute, start, inaugurate. **4 materialize**, come into being/existence, emerge, develop, take shape, gather, accumulate, collect, amass. **5 arrange**, draw up, line up, assemble, organize, sort, order. **6 comprise**, make, make up, constitute, compose, add up to.
– OPPOSITES dissolve, disappear.

formal adj. **1 ceremonial**, ritualistic, ritual, official, conventional, traditional, stately, solemn, ceremonious. **2 aloof**, reserved, remote, detached, unapproachable, stiff, stuffy, correct, proper; informal standoffish. **3 official**, legal, authorized, approved, certified, endorsed, sanctioned, licensed, recognized.
– OPPOSITES informal, casual, unofficial.

formality n. **1 ceremony**, ritual, protocol, decorum, solemnity. **2 aloofness**, reserve, remoteness, detachment, unapproachability, stiffness, stuffiness, correctness; informal standoffishness.
– OPPOSITES informality.

format n. **design**, style, appearance, look, form, shape, size, arrangement, plan, structure, scheme, composition, configuration.

formation n. **1** *the formation of the island*: **emergence**, genesis, development, evolution, shaping, origin. **2** *the formation of a new government*: **establishment**, setting up, institution, foundation, creation, inauguration. **3 configuration**, arrangement, grouping, pattern, array, alignment, order.
– OPPOSITES destruction, dissolution.

former adj. **1 one-time**, erstwhile, sometime, ex-, previous, preceding, earlier, prior, last; formal quondam. **2 earlier**, old, past, bygone, olden, long ago, gone by, long past, of old. **3 first-mentioned**, first.
– OPPOSITES future, current, latter.

formerly adv. **previously**, earlier, before, until now/then, once, once upon a time, at one time, in the past.

formidable adj. **1 intimidating**, daunting, indomitable, forbidding, alarming, frightening, awesome, fearsome; humorous redoubtable. **2 accomplished**, masterly, virtuoso, expert, impressive, powerful, terrific, superb; informal tremendous, nifty, crack, ace, wizard, magic, mean, wicked, deadly.

formula n. **1 form of words**, set expression, rubric, phrase, saying. **2 recipe**, prescription, blueprint, plan, policy, method, procedure.

formulate v. **1 devise**, conceive, work out, think up, lay, draw up, form, concoct, contrive, forge, hatch, prepare, develop. **2 express**, phrase, word, define, specify, put into words, frame, couch, put, articulate, say.

fort n. **fortress**, castle, citadel, bunker, stronghold, fortification, bastion.

forte n. **strength**, strong point, speciality, strong suit, talent, skill, gift; informal thing.

forthcoming adj. **1 coming**, upcoming, approaching, imminent, impending, future. **2 communicative**, talkative, chatty, informative, expansive, expressive, frank, open, candid.
– OPPOSITES past, current, reticent.

forthright adj. **frank**, direct, straightforward, honest, candid, open, sincere, outspoken, straight, blunt, plain-spoken, no-nonsense, bluff, matter-of-fact, to the point; informal upfront.
– OPPOSITES secretive, evasive.

fortify v. **1 strengthen**, secure, barricade, protect, buttress, shore up. **2 invigorate**, strengthen, energize, enliven, animate, vitalize, buoy up; informal pep up, buck up.
– OPPOSITES weaken.

fortitude n. **courage**, bravery, endurance, resilience, mettle, strength of character, backbone, grit; informal guts; Brit. informal bottle.

fortress n. **fort**, castle, citadel, bunker, stronghold, fortification.

fortunate adj. **1 lucky**, favoured, blessed, leading a charmed life, in luck; Brit. informal born with a silver spoon in your mouth, jammy. **2 favourable**, advantageous, happy.
– OPPOSITES unfavourable, unlucky.

fortunately adv. **luckily**, as luck would have it, happily, mercifully, thankfully.

fortune n. **1 chance**, accident, coincidence, serendipity, destiny, providence; N. Amer. happenstance. **2 luck**, fate, destiny, predestination, the stars, karma, kismet, lot. **3** *an upswing in their fortunes:* **circumstances**, state

forum → fracas

of affairs, condition, position, situation. **4 wealth**, money, riches, assets, resources, means, possessions, property, estate.

forum n. **meeting**, assembly, gathering, rally, conference, seminar, convention, symposium.

forward adv. **1 ahead**, forwards, onwards, onward, on, further. **2 towards the front**, out, forth, into view, up.
– OPPOSITES backwards, back.
•adj. **1 onward**, advancing. **2 front**, advance, foremost, leading. **3 future**, forward-looking, for the future, anticipatory. **4 bold**, brazen, cheeky, shameless, familiar, overfamiliar, presumptuous; informal fresh.
– OPPOSITES backward, rear.
•v. **1 send on**, post on, redirect, readdress, pass on. **2 send**, dispatch, transmit, carry, convey, deliver, ship.

foster v. **1 encourage**, promote, further, nurture, help, aid, assist, support, back. **2 bring up**, rear, raise, care for, take care of, look after, provide for.

foul adj. **1 disgusting**, revolting, repulsive, repugnant, abhorrent, loathsome, offensive, sickening, nauseating; informal ghastly, gruesome, gross. **2 contaminated**, polluted, infected, tainted, impure, filthy, dirty, unclean. **3 vulgar**, crude, coarse, filthy, dirty, obscene, indecent, naughty, offensive; informal blue.
– OPPOSITES pleasant.

•v. **1 dirty**, pollute, contaminate, poison, taint, sully. **2 tangle up**, entangle, snarl, catch, entwine.

found v. **establish**, set up, start, begin, get going, institute, inaugurate, launch.

foundation n. **1 footing**, foot, base, substructure, underpinning. **2 justification**, grounds, evidence, basis. **3 institution**, establishment, charitable body, agency.

founder¹ n. **originator**, creator, (founding) father, architect, developer, pioneer, author, inventor, mastermind.

founder² v. **1 sink**, go to the bottom, go down, be lost at sea. **2 fail**, be unsuccessful, fall flat, fall through, collapse, backfire, meet with disaster; informal flop, bomb.
– OPPOSITES succeed.

fountain n. **1 jet**, spray, spout, spurt, cascade, water feature. **2 source**, fount, well, reservoir, fund, mine.

foyer n. **entrance hall**, hallway, entry, porch, reception area, atrium, concourse, lobby, anteroom; N. Amer. entryway.

fracas n. **disturbance**, brawl, melee, rumpus, skirmish, struggle, scuffle, scrum, clash, fisticuffs, altercation; informal scrap, dust-up, set-to, shindy, shindig; Brit. informal punch-up, bust-up, ruck; N. Amer. informal rough house; Law, dated affray.

fraction n. **1** *a fraction of the population:* tiny part, fragment, snippet, snatch. **2** *he moved a fraction closer:* bit, little, touch, soupçon, trifle, mite, shade, jot; informal smidgen, tad.
– OPPOSITES whole.

fractious adj. **grumpy**, bad-tempered, irascible, irritable, crotchety, grouchy, cantankerous, tetchy, testy, ill-tempered, peevish, cross, pettish, waspish, crabby, crusty; Brit. informal shirty, stroppy, narky, ratty; N. Amer. informal cranky, ornery.

fracture n. **break**, crack, split, rupture, fissure.
•v. **break**, crack, split, rupture, snap, shatter, fragment, splinter.

fragile adj. **1** breakable, delicate, brittle, flimsy, dainty, fine. **2** tenuous, shaky, insecure, vulnerable, flimsy. **3** weak, delicate, frail, debilitated, ill, unwell, poorly, sickly.
– OPPOSITES sturdy, robust.

fragment n. **1** piece, bit, particle, speck, chip, shard, sliver, splinter, flake. **2** snatch, snippet, scrap, bit.
•v. **break up**, crack open, shatter, splinter, fracture, disintegrate, fall to pieces, fall apart.

fragrance n. **1** sweet smell, scent, perfume, bouquet, aroma, nose. **2** perfume, scent, eau de toilette.

fragrant adj. **sweet-scented**, sweet-smelling, scented, perfumed, aromatic.
– OPPOSITES smelly.

frail adj. **1** *a frail old lady:* weak, delicate, feeble, infirm, ill, unwell, sickly, poorly. **2** *a frail structure:* fragile, easily damaged, delicate, flimsy, insubstantial, unsteady, unstable, rickety.
– OPPOSITES strong, robust.

frame n. **1** framework, structure, substructure, skeleton, casing, chassis, shell. **2** body, figure, form, shape, physique, anatomy, build.
•v. **1** mount, set in a frame. **2** formulate, draw up, draft, shape, compose, put together, form, devise.
□ **frame of mind** mood, state of mind, humour, temper, disposition.

framework n. **1** frame, structure, skeleton, chassis, support, scaffolding. **2** structure, shape, fabric, order, scheme, system, organization, anatomy; informal make-up.

frank adj. **1** candid, direct, forthright, plain, plain-spoken, straight, to the point, matter-of-fact, open, honest; informal up-front. **2** undisguised, open, unconcealed, naked, unmistakable, clear, obvious, transparent, patent, evident.
– OPPOSITES evasive.

frankly adv. **1** to be frank, to be honest, to tell the truth, in all honesty. **2** candidly, directly, plainly, straightforwardly, forthrightly, openly, honestly, without beating about the bush, bluntly.

frantic adj. **panic-stricken**, panicky, beside yourself, at your wits' end, distraught, overwrought, worked up, frenzied, frenetic, fraught, feverish, desperate; informal in a state, tearing your hair out; Brit. informal having kittens, in a flat spin.
– OPPOSITES calm.

fraternity n. **1 brotherhood**, fellowship, kinship, friendship, mutual support, solidarity, community. **2 profession**, community, trade, set, circle. **3** (N. Amer.) **society**, club, association, group.

fraud n. **1 deception**, sharp practice, cheating, swindling, trickery, embezzlement, deceit, double-dealing, chicanery. **2 swindle**, racket, deception, trick, cheat, hoax; informal scam, con, rip-off, sting, fiddle; N. Amer. informal hustle. **3 impostor**, fake, sham, charlatan, swindler, fraudster, confidence trickster; informal phoney.

fraudulent adj. **dishonest**, cheating, swindling, corrupt, criminal, deceitful, double-dealing, duplicitous; informal crooked, shady, dirty; Brit. informal bent, dodgy; Austral./NZ informal shonky.
– OPPOSITES honest.

fraught adj. **1** a world fraught with danger: **full of**, filled with, rife with. **2 anxious**, worried, stressed, upset, distraught, overwrought, worked up, agitated, distressed, desperate, frantic, panic-stricken, panicky,

beside yourself, at your wits' end, at the end of your tether.

frayed adj. **1 worn**, threadbare, tattered, ragged, the worse for wear; informal tatty; N. Amer. informal raggedy. **2 strained**, fraught, tense, edgy, stressed.

freak n. **1 aberration**, abnormality, oddity, monster, monstrosity, mutant, chimera. **2 anomaly**, aberration, rarity, oddity, one-off, fluke, twist of fate. **3** (informal) **eccentric**, misfit, oddity, crank; informal oddball, weirdo, nut; Brit. informal nutter; N. Amer. informal wacko, kook. **4** (informal) **enthusiast**, fan, devotee, lover, aficionado; informal nut, fanatic, addict, maniac.
•adj. **unusual**, anomalous, aberrant, atypical, unrepresentative, irregular, exceptional, isolated.

free adj. **1 free of charge**, without charge, for nothing, complimentary, gratis; informal for free, on the house. **2** free of any pressures: **without**, unencumbered by, unaffected by, clear of, rid of, exempt from, not liable to, safe from, immune to, excused. **3 unoccupied**, not busy, available, off duty, off work, on holiday, on leave, at leisure, with time to spare. **4 vacant**, empty, available, unoccupied, not in use. **5 independent**, self-governing, self-determining, sovereign, autonomous, democratic. **6 on the loose**, at liberty, at large, on loose, unrestrained. **7** you are free to leave: **able**, in a position, allowed, permitted.

8 unobstructed, unimpeded, unrestricted, unhampered, clear, open. **9** *she was free with her money*: **generous**, liberal, open-handed, unstinting.
– OPPOSITES busy, occupied, confined.
•v. **1 release**, set free, let go, liberate, set loose, untie. **2 extricate**, release, get out, cut free, pull free, rescue.
– OPPOSITES confine, trap.

freedom n. **1 liberty**, liberation, release, deliverance. **2 independence**, self-government, self-determination, self-rule, home rule, sovereignty, autonomy, democracy. **3** *freedom from political accountability*: **exemption**, immunity, dispensation, impunity. **4 right**, entitlement, privilege, prerogative, discretion, latitude, elbow room, licence, free rein, a free hand, carte blanche.
– OPPOSITES captivity, obligation.

freely adv. **1 openly**, candidly, frankly, directly, without beating about the bush, without mincing your words. **2 voluntarily**, willingly, readily, of your own accord, of your own free will, without being told to.

freeze v. **1 ice over**, ice up, solidify. **2 stand still**, stop dead in your tracks, go rigid, become motionless, become paralysed. **3 fix**, hold, peg, set, limit, restrict, cap.
– OPPOSITES thaw.

freezing adj. **1 icy**, bitter, chill, frosty, glacial, arctic, wintry,

sub-zero, raw, biting. **2 frozen**, numb with cold, chilled to the bone/marrow.
– OPPOSITES balmy, hot.

freight n. **goods**, cargo, merchandise.

frenzied adj. **frantic**, wild, frenetic, hectic, feverish, fevered, mad, crazed, manic, furious, uncontrolled.
– OPPOSITES calm.

frenzy n. **hysteria**, madness, mania, delirium, wild excitement, fever, lather, passion, panic, fury, rage.

frequent adj. **recurrent**, recurring, repeated, periodic, continual, habitual, regular, successive, numerous, several.
– OPPOSITES occasional.
•v. **visit**, patronize, spend time in, visit regularly, haunt; informal hang out at.
– OPPOSITES avoid.

frequently adv. **often**, all the time, habitually, regularly, customarily, routinely, again and again, repeatedly, recurrently, continually; N. Amer. oftentimes.

fresh adj. **1 new**, modern, original, novel, different, innovative. **2 recently made**, just picked, crisp, raw, natural, unprocessed. **3 refreshed**, rested, restored, energetic, vigorous, invigorated, lively, sprightly, bright, alert, bouncing, perky; informal full of beans, bright-eyed and bushy-tailed. **4 bracing**, brisk, strong, invigorating, chilly, cool; informal nippy; Brit. informal parky. **5 cool**, crisp,

refreshing, invigorating, pure, clean, clear. **6** (informal) **impudent**, impertinent, insolent, presumptuous, forward, cheeky, disrespectful, rude; informal mouthy, saucy, lippy; N. Amer. informal sassy.
– OPPOSITES stale, old.

fret v. worry, be anxious, distress yourself, upset yourself, concern yourself, agonize, lose sleep.

friction n. **1 rubbing**, chafing, grating, rasping, scraping, resistance, drag, abrasion. **2 discord**, disagreement, dissension, dispute, conflict, hostility, animosity, antipathy, antagonism, resentment, acrimony, bitterness, bad feeling.
– OPPOSITES harmony.

friend n. **companion**, comrade, confidant, confidante, familiar, intimate, soul mate, playmate, playfellow, ally, associate; informal pal, chum; Brit. informal mate; N. Amer. informal buddy, amigo, compadre, homeboy.
– OPPOSITES enemy.

friendly adj. **1** a friendly woman: **amiable**, companionable, sociable, gregarious, comradely, neighbourly, hospitable, easy to get on with, affable, genial, cordial, warm, affectionate, convivial; informal chummy, pally; Brit. informal matey. **2** friendly conversation: **amicable**, cordial, pleasant, easy, relaxed, casual, informal, close, intimate, familiar.
– OPPOSITES hostile.

friendship n. **1** lasting friendships: **relationship**, attachment, association, bond, tie, link, union. **2** ties of friendship: **friendliness**, affection, camaraderie, comradeship, companionship, fellowship, closeness, affinity, unity, intimacy.
– OPPOSITES hostility.

fright n. **1 fear**, terror, horror, alarm, panic, dread, trepidation, dismay, nervousness. **2 scare**, shock, surprise, turn, jolt, start.

frighten v. **scare**, startle, alarm, terrify, petrify, shock, chill, panic, unnerve, intimidate; informal spook; Brit. informal put the wind up.

frightening adj. **terrifying**, horrifying, alarming, startling, chilling, spine-chilling, hair-raising, blood-curdling, disturbing, unnerving, intimidating, daunting, eerie, sinister, fearsome, nightmarish, menacing; informal scary, spooky, creepy.

frightful adj. **horrible**, horrific, ghastly, horrendous, awful, dreadful, terrible, nasty; informal horrid.

fringe n. **1 edge**, border, margin, extremity, perimeter, periphery, rim, limits, outskirts. **2 edging**, border, trimming, frill, flounce, ruffle.
– OPPOSITES middle.
• adj. **alternative**, avant-garde, experimental, innovative, left-field, radical.
– OPPOSITES mainstream.

frisky adj. **lively**, bouncy, bubbly, perky, active, energetic, animated, playful, coltish, skittish, spirited, high-spirited, in high spirits, exuberant; informal full of beans.

frivolous adj. flippant, glib, facetious, joking, jokey, lighthearted, fatuous, inane; informal flip.

– OPPOSITES serious.

front n. 1 fore, foremost part, forepart, nose, head, bow, prow, foreground. 2 frontage, face, facing, facade. 3 head, beginning, start, top, lead. 4 appearance, air, face, manner, exterior, veneer, (outward) show, act, pretence. 5 cover, blind, disguise, facade, mask, cloak, screen, smokescreen, camouflage.

– OPPOSITES back.

•adj. leading, lead, first, foremost.

– OPPOSITES back, last.

◻ in front ahead, to/at the fore, at the head, up ahead, in the lead, leading, coming first, at the head of the queue; informal up front.

frontier n. border, boundary, borderline, dividing line, perimeter, limit, edge.

frosty adj. 1 cold, freezing, frozen, icy, bitter, chill, wintry, arctic; informal nippy; Brit. informal parky. 2 unfriendly, cold, frigid, icy, glacial, inhospitable, unwelcoming, forbidding, hostile, stony.

– OPPOSITES warm, friendly.

froth n. foam, head, bubbles, frothiness, fizz, effervescence, lather, suds.

•v. bubble, fizz, effervesce, foam, lather, churn, seethe.

frown v. scowl, glower, glare, lour, make a face, look daggers, give someone a black look, knit your brows; informal give someone a dirty look.

– OPPOSITES smile.

◻ frown on disapprove of, take a dim view of, take exception to, object to, look askance at, not take kindly to.

frugal adj. 1 thrifty, economical, careful, cautious, prudent, provident, sparing, abstemious, austere, self-denying, ascetic, spartan. 2 meagre, scanty, scant, paltry, skimpy, plain, simple, spartan, inexpensive, cheap, economical.

– OPPOSITES extravagant, lavish.

fruitful adj. productive, constructive, useful, worthwhile, helpful, beneficial, valuable, rewarding, profitable, advantageous.

– OPPOSITES barren, futile.

fruition n. fulfilment, realization, actualization, materialization, achievement, attainment, accomplishment, success, completion, consummation, conclusion, close, finish, perfection, maturity.

fruitless adj. futile, vain, in vain, to no avail, to no effect, idle, pointless, useless, worthless, hollow, ineffectual, ineffective, unproductive, unrewarding, profitless, unsuccessful, unavailing, abortive.

– OPPOSITES fruitful, productive.

frustrate v. **1 thwart**, defeat, foil, block, stop, counter, spoil, check, forestall, scotch, derail, snooker; informal stymie; Brit. informal scupper. **2 exasperate**, infuriate, discourage, dishearten, disappoint.
– OPPOSITES further, satisfy.

fudge v. **evade**, avoid, dodge, skirt, duck, gloss over, cloud, hedge, beat about the bush, equivocate.

fuel v. **1 power**, fire, drive, run. **2 fan**, feed, stoke up, inflame, intensify, stimulate, encourage, provoke, incite, sustain.

fugitive n. **escapee**, runaway, deserter, absconder, refugee.

fulfil v. **1 achieve**, attain, realize, make happen, succeed in, bring to completion, bring to fruition, satisfy. **2 carry out**, perform, accomplish, execute, do, discharge, conduct. **3 meet**, satisfy, comply with, conform to, fill, answer.

fulfilled adj. **satisfied**, content, contented, happy, pleased, at peace.
– OPPOSITES discontented.

full adj. **1 filled**, brimming, brimful, packed, loaded, crammed, crowded, bursting, overflowing, congested; informal jam-packed, wall-to-wall, chock-a-block, chock-full, awash. **2 replete**, full up, satisfied, sated, satiated; informal stuffed. **3 eventful**, interesting, exciting, lively, action-packed, busy, active. **4 comprehensive**, thorough, exhaustive, all-inclusive, all-encompassing, all-embracing, in-depth, complete, entire, whole, unabridged, uncut. **5 plump**, rounded, buxom, shapely, ample, curvaceous, voluptuous; informal busty, curvy, well endowed; N. Amer. informal zaftig. **6 loose-fitting**, loose, baggy, voluminous, roomy, capacious, billowing.
– OPPOSITES empty.

fully adv. **completely**, entirely, wholly, totally, perfectly, quite, altogether, thoroughly, in all respects, (up) to the hilt.
– OPPOSITES partly.

fumble v. **grope**, fish, scrabble, feel.

fume n. **smoke**, vapour, gas, exhaust, pollution.
•v. **be furious**, seethe, be livid, be incensed, boil, be beside yourself, spit; informal foam at the mouth, see red.

fumigate v. **disinfect**, purify, sterilize, sanitize, decontaminate, cleanse, clean out.

fun n. **1 enjoyment**, entertainment, amusement, pleasure, jollification, merrymaking, recreation, leisure, relaxation, a good time; informal living it up, a ball. **2 merriment**, cheerfulness, jollity, joviality, high spirits, mirth, laughter, hilarity, lightheartedness, levity. **3** *he became a figure of fun:* **ridicule**, derision, mockery, scorn, contempt.
– OPPOSITES boredom.
•adj. (informal) **enjoyable**, entertaining, amusing, pleasurable, pleasant, agreeable, convivial.

f

□ **make fun of** tease, poke fun at, ridicule, mock, laugh at, parody, caricature, satirize; informal take the mickey out of, send up; N. Amer. informal goof on.

function n. 1 **purpose**, task, use, role. 2 **responsibility**, duty, role, province, activity, assignment, task, job, mission. 3 **social event**, party, social occasion, affair, gathering, reception, soirée; N. Amer. levee; informal do, bash.
• v. 1 **work**, go, run, be in working/running order, operate. 2 **act**, serve, operate, perform, do duty.

functional adj. 1 **practical**, useful, utilitarian, workaday, serviceable, no-frills. 2 **working**, in working order, functioning, in service, in use, going, running, operative; informal up and running.

fund n. 1 **collection**, kitty, reserve, pool, purse, savings, coffers. 2 **money**, cash, wealth, means, assets, resources, savings, capital, reserves, the wherewithal; informal dosh; Brit. informal lolly.
• v. **finance**, pay for, back, capitalize, subsidize, endow, invest in, sponsor; N. Amer. informal bankroll.

fundamental adj. **basic**, underlying, core, rudimentary, root, primary, prime, cardinal, principal, chief, key, central, vital, essential.

– OPPOSITES secondary, incidental.

fundamentally adv. **essentially**, in essence, basically, at heart, at bottom, deep down, profoundly, primarily, above all.

funeral n. **burial**, interment, entombment, committal, laying to rest, cremation.

funny adj. 1 **amusing**, humorous, witty, comic, comical, hilarious, hysterical, riotous, uproarious, farcical; informal rib-tickling, priceless. 2 **strange**, peculiar, odd, weird, bizarre, curious, freakish, quirky, unusual. 3 **suspicious**, suspect, dubious, untrustworthy, questionable; informal fishy; Brit. informal dodgy.

– OPPOSITES serious.

furious adj. 1 **very angry**, enraged, infuriated, irate, incensed, fuming, ranting, raving, seething, outraged; informal hopping mad, wild, livid, beside yourself. 2 **fierce**, heated, passionate, fiery, tumultuous, turbulent, tempestuous, violent, stormy, acrimonious.

– OPPOSITES pleased, calm.

furnish v. 1 **fit out**, appoint, equip; Brit. informal do out. 2 *they furnished us with waterproofs:* **supply**, provide, equip, issue, kit out; informal fix up.

furore n. **commotion**, uproar, outcry, fuss, upset, brouhaha, stir; informal to-do, hoo-ha, hullabaloo.

further adv. see FURTHERMORE.
• adj. **additional**, more, extra,

supplementary, new, fresh.
• v. **promote**, advance, forward, develop, facilitate, aid, assist, help, boost, encourage.
– OPPOSITES impede.

furthermore adv. moreover, further, what's more, also, additionally, in addition, besides, as well, too, on top of that, into the bargain.

furthest adj. most distant, remotest, farthest, furthermost, farthermost, outer, outermost, extreme.
– OPPOSITES nearest.

furtive adj. surreptitious, secretive, secret, clandestine, hidden, covert, conspiratorial, cloak-and-dagger, sneaky; informal shifty.
– OPPOSITES open.

fury n. **1** rage, anger, wrath, outrage; literary ire. **2** ferocity, violence, turbulence, tempestuousness, savagery, severity, intensity, vehemence, force.

fuss n. **1** commotion, excitement, stir, confusion, disturbance, brouhaha, uproar, furore, storm in a teacup; informal hoo-ha, to-do, song and dance, performance. **2** protest, complaint, objection, argument; Brit. row. **3** trouble, bother, inconvenience, effort, exertion, labour; informal hassle.

• v. **worry**, fret, be agitated, be worked up, make a big thing out of it, make a mountain out of a molehill; informal flap, be in a tizzy.

fussy adj. **1** particular, finicky, fastidious, hard to please, faddish; informal pernickety, choosy, picky; Brit. informal faddy; N. Amer. informal persnickety. **2** over-elaborate, ornate, fancy, busy, cluttered.

futile adj. fruitless, vain, pointless, useless, ineffectual, forlorn, hopeless.
– OPPOSITES useful.

future n. **1** plans for the future: time to come, what lies ahead, the hereafter. **2** her future lay in acting: destiny, fate, fortune, prospects, chances.
– OPPOSITES past.

• adj. **1** later, to come, following, forthcoming, ensuing, succeeding, subsequent, coming, impending, approaching. **2** her future husband: to be, destined, intended, planned, prospective.
– OPPOSITES previous, past.

fuzzy adj. **1** frizzy, fluffy, woolly, downy. **2** blurred, indistinct, unclear, out of focus, misty. **3** unclear, imprecise, unfocused, nebulous, vague, hazy, loose, woolly.
– OPPOSITES smooth, sharp, clear.

Gg

gadget n. **device**, appliance, apparatus, instrument, implement, tool, utensil, contrivance, contraption, machine, mechanism, invention; informal gizmo.

gaffe n. **blunder**, mistake, error, slip, faux pas, indiscretion, solecism; informal slip-up, howler, boo-boo; Brit. informal boob, clanger; N. Amer. informal blooper.

gag¹ v. **1 silence**, muzzle, suppress, stifle, censor, curb, restrain. **2 retch**, heave.

gag² n. (informal) **joke**, quip, jest, witticism; informal crack, wisecrack, one-liner.

gain v. **1 obtain**, get, secure, acquire, come by, procure, attain, achieve, earn, win, capture; informal land. **2** they stood to gain from the deal: **profit**, make money, benefit, do well out of. **3** she gained weight: **put on**, increase in, build up. **4** they're gaining on us: **catch up (with)**, catch, reduce someone's lead, narrow the gap.
– OPPOSITES lose.
• n. **1 profit**, earnings, income, yield, return, reward, advantage, benefit; informal take. **2 increase**, addition, rise, increment, advance.
– OPPOSITES loss.

gainful adj. **profitable**, paid, well paid, remunerative, lucrative,

moneymaking, rewarding, fruitful, worthwhile, useful, productive, constructive, beneficial, advantageous, valuable.

gait n. **walk**, step, stride, pace, tread, way of walking, bearing, carriage; Brit. deportment.

gala n. **festival**, fair, fete, carnival, pageant, jubilee, jamboree, celebration.

gale n. **1 high wind**, blast, squall, storm, tempest, hurricane, tornado, cyclone, whirlwind, typhoon. **2 peal**, howl, hoot, shriek, roar, fit, paroxysm.

gallant adj. **1 brave**, courageous, valiant, bold, plucky, daring, fearless, intrepid, heroic, stouthearted; informal gutsy, spunky. **2 chivalrous**, gentlemanly, courteous, polite, attentive, respectful, gracious, considerate, thoughtful.
– OPPOSITES cowardly, discourteous.

gamble v. **1 bet**, place a bet, wager, hazard; Brit. informal punt, have a flutter. **2 take a chance**, take a risk; N. Amer. take a flyer; informal stick your neck out; Brit. informal chance your arm.
• n. I took a gamble: **risk**, chance, leap in the dark, speculation, lottery, pot luck.

game n. **1 pastime**, diversion, entertainment, amusement, distraction, recreation, sport, activity. **2 match**, contest, fixture, meeting, tie, clash. •adj. **willing**, prepared, ready, disposed, interested, eager, keen, enthusiastic.

gang n. **band**, group, crowd, pack, horde, throng, mob, herd, swarm, troop; informal bunch, gaggle, load.

gangster n. **hoodlum**, racketeer, thug, villain, criminal, Mafioso; informal mobster, crook, tough; N. Amer. informal hood.

gaol n. see **JAIL**.

gap n. **1 opening**, aperture, space, breach, chink, slit, crack, crevice, cleft, cavity, hole, interstice. **2 pause**, intermission, interval, interlude, break, breathing space, breather, respite, hiatus, lull; N. Amer. recess. **3 omission**, blank, lacuna. **4 the gap between rich and poor: chasm**, gulf, separation, contrast, difference, disparity, divergence, imbalance.

gape v. **1 stare**, goggle, gaze, ogle; informal rubberneck; Brit. informal gawp. **2 open**, yawn, part, split.

gaping adj. **wide**, broad, vast, yawning, cavernous.

garbage (N. Amer.) n. **1 waste**, refuse, rubbish, detritus, litter, junk, scrap, scraps, leftovers, remains; N. Amer. trash. **2 nonsense**, rubbish, balderdash, claptrap, twaddle, dross; informal hogwash, baloney, tripe, bilge, bull, bunk, poppycock, rot,

piffle; Brit. informal tosh, codswallop.

garble v. **mix up**, muddle, jumble, confuse, obscure, distort.

garden n. park, estate, grounds.

> **WORD LINKS**
> relating to gardens: horticultural

garish adj. **gaudy**, lurid, loud, harsh, showy, glittering, brash, tasteless, vulgar; informal flashy.
– **OPPOSITES** drab, tasteful.

garments pl. n. **clothes**, clothing, dress, garb, wardrobe, costume, attire; informal gear, togs; Brit. informal clobber; N. Amer. informal threads; formal apparel.

garnish v. **decorate**, adorn, ornament, trim, dress, embellish. •n. **decoration**, adornment, ornament, embellishment, enhancement, finishing touch.

garrison n. **1 troops**, forces, militia, soldiers, force, detachment, unit. **2 base**, camp, station, barracks, fort, command post. •v. **station**, post, deploy, base, site, place, billet.

garrulous adj. **talkative**, loquacious, voluble, verbose, chatty, gossipy, effusive, expansive, forthcoming, conversational, communicative; informal mouthy, having the gift of the gab.
– **OPPOSITES** taciturn.

gash n. **cut**, laceration, slash, slit, split, wound, injury. •v. **cut**, lacerate, slash, slit, split, wound, injure.

g

gasp v. **1 catch your breath**, gulp, draw in your breath. **2 pant**, puff, puff and blow, wheeze, breathe hard/heavily, choke, fight for breath.
• n. **gulp**, pant, puff.

gate n. **barrier**, turnstile, gateway, doorway, entrance, exit, door, portal; N. Amer. entryway.

gather v. **1 congregate**, assemble, meet, collect, get together, convene, muster, rally, converge. **2 summon**, call together, bring together, assemble, convene, rally, round up, muster, marshal. **3 harvest**, reap, crop, pick, pluck, collect. **4 understand**, believe, be led to believe, conclude, infer, assume, take it, surmise, hear, learn, discover. **5 pleat**, pucker, tuck, fold, ruffle.
- OPPOSITES disperse.

gathering n. **assembly**, meeting, convention, rally, council, congress, congregation, audience, crowd, group, throng, mass; informal get-together.

gauche adj. **awkward**, gawky, inelegant, graceless, ungraceful, clumsy, ungainly, maladroit, inept, unsophisticated.
- OPPOSITES elegant, sophisticated.

gaudy adj. **garish**, lurid, loud, glaring, harsh, showy, glittering, ostentatious, tasteless; informal flashy, tacky.
- OPPOSITES drab, tasteful.

gauge n. **meter**, measure, indicator, dial, scale, display.
• v. **1 measure**, calculate, compute, work out, determine, ascertain, count, weigh, quantify, put a figure on. **2 assess**, evaluate, determine, estimate, form an opinion of, appraise, weigh up, judge, guess; informal size up.

gaunt adj. **haggard**, drawn, thin, lean, skinny, spindly, spare, bony, angular, raw-boned, pinched, hollow-cheeked, scrawny, scraggy, as thin as a rake, cadaverous, skeletal, emaciated, skin and bone, wasted, withered; informal like a bag of bones.
- OPPOSITES plump.

gaze v. **stare**, gape, look fixedly, goggle, eye, scrutinize, ogle; informal rubberneck; Brit. informal gawp; N. Amer. informal eyeball.
• n. **stare**, gape, fixed look, regard, scrutiny.

gear n. **1 equipment**, apparatus, paraphernalia, tools, utensils, implements, instruments, rig, tackle; informal clobber. **2** (informal) **belongings**, possessions, effects, paraphernalia, bits and pieces; informal things, stuff, kit; Brit. informal clobber, gubbins. **3** (informal) **clothes**, clothing, garments, outfits, attire, garb, wardrobe; informal togs; Brit. informal clobber, kit; N. Amer. informal threads; formal apparel.

gem n. **1 jewel**, precious stone, semi-precious stone; informal rock, sparkler. **2 masterpiece**, classic, treasure, prize, find; informal one in a million, the bee's knees.

genealogy n. **lineage**, line (of descent), family tree, bloodline, pedigree, ancestry, heritage, parentage, family, stock, blood, roots.

general adj. **1** *suitable for general use*: **widespread**, common, extensive, universal, wide, popular, public, mainstream. **2** *a general pay increase*: **comprehensive**, overall, across the board, blanket, global, universal, mass, wholesale. **3** *usual*, customary, habitual, traditional, normal, conventional, typical, standard, regular, accepted, prevailing, routine, established, everyday. **4** *a general description*: **broad**, rough, loose, approximate, unspecific, vague, imprecise, inexact.
- OPPOSITES restricted, unusual, detailed.

generally adv. **1 normally**, in general, as a rule, by and large, mainly, mostly, for the most part, predominantly, on the whole, usually. **2 widely**, commonly, extensively, universally, popularly.

generate v. **create**, make, produce, engender, spawn, precipitate, prompt, provoke, trigger, spark off, stir up, induce.

generation n. **1 age**, age group, peer group. **2 crop**, batch, wave, range.

generosity n. **liberality**, lavishness, magnanimity, bounty, munificence, open-handedness, largesse, unselfishness, altruism, charity.

- OPPOSITES meanness, selfishness.

generous adj. **1 liberal**, lavish, magnanimous, giving, open-handed, bountiful, unselfish, ungrudging, free, unstinting, munificent; literary bounteous. **2 plentiful**, copious, ample, liberal, large, abundant, rich.
- OPPOSITES mean, selfish, meagre.

genesis n. **origin**, source, root, beginning, start.

genial adj. **friendly**, affable, cordial, amiable, warm, easy-going, approachable, sympathetic, good-natured, good-humoured, cheerful, hospitable, companionable, sociable, convivial, outgoing, gregarious; informal chummy, pally; Brit. informal matey.
- OPPOSITES unfriendly.

genius n. **1 brilliance**, intelligence, intellect, ability, cleverness, brains. **2 talent**, gift, flair, aptitude, facility, knack, ability, expertise, capacity, faculty. **3 brilliant person**, mastermind, Einstein, intellectual, brain, prodigy; informal egghead, bright spark; Brit. informal brainbox, clever clogs; N. Amer. informal brainiac.

genre n. **category**, class, classification, group, set, type, sort, kind, variety.

genteel adj. **refined**, respectable, well mannered, courteous, polite, proper, correct, seemly, well bred, ladylike, gentlemanly, dignified, gracious.
- OPPOSITES uncouth.

g

gentle adj. **1 kind**, tender, sympathetic, considerate, understanding, compassionate, humane, mild, placid, serene. **2 light**, soft, quiet, low. **3 gradual**, slight, easy, slow, imperceptible.
– OPPOSITES brutal, strong, loud, steep.

genuine adj. **1 authentic**, real, actual, original, bona fide, true; informal pukka, the real McCoy, the real thing, kosher; Austral./NZ informal dinkum. **2 sincere**, honest, truthful, straightforward, direct, frank, candid, open, natural; informal straight, upfront.
– OPPOSITES bogus, insincere.

germ n. **1 microbe**, microorganism, bacillus, bacterium, virus; informal bug. **2** the germ of an idea: **start**, beginnings, seed, embryo, bud, root, origin, source.

gesture n. **1 signal**, sign, motion, indication, gesticulation. **2 action**, act, deed, move.
•v. **signal**, motion, gesticulate, wave, indicate, give a sign.

get v. **1 obtain**, acquire, come by, receive, gain, earn, win, be given; informal get hold of, score. **2 become**, grow, turn, go. **3 fetch**, collect, go/come for, call for, pick up, bring, deliver, convey. **4 capture**, catch, arrest, apprehend, seize; informal collar, grab, pick up; Brit. informal nick. **5 contract**, develop, go down with, catch, fall ill with. **6 hear**, catch, make out, follow, take in. **7 understand**, comprehend, grasp, see, fathom, follow.

8 arrive, reach, make it, turn up, appear, present yourself, come along; informal show up. **9 persuade**, induce, prevail on, influence, talk into. **10 prepare**, get ready, cook, make; informal fix, rustle up; Brit. informal knock up.
– OPPOSITES give.
▫ **get across** communicate, get over, impart, convey, transmit, make clear, express. **get along** be friendly, be compatible, get on, agree, see eye to eye; informal hit it off. **get away** escape, run away/off, break free, bolt, flee, make off, take off, decamp; informal skedaddle, scarper; Brit. informal do a bunk, do a runner. **get by** manage, cope, survive, exist, subsist, muddle through/along, scrape by, make ends meet, make do; informal make out. **get out of** evade, dodge, shirk, avoid, escape, sidestep; informal wriggle out of. **get round** cajole, persuade, wheedle, coax, prevail on, win over, bring round, sway, inveigle; informal sweet-talk, butter up. **get up** get out of bed, rise, stir, rouse yourself; informal surface.

ghastly adj. **1 terrible**, frightful, horrible, grim, awful, horrifying, shocking, appalling, gruesome, horrendous, monstrous. **2** (informal) **unpleasant**, objectionable, disagreeable, distasteful, awful, terrible, dreadful, frightful, detestable, vile; informal horrible, horrid.
– OPPOSITES pleasant.

ghost n. spectre, phantom, wraith, spirit, presence, apparition; informal spook.

> **WORD LINKS**
> relating to a ghost: spectral

ghostly adj. supernatural, unearthly, spectral, phantom, unnatural, eerie, weird, uncanny; informal spooky.

giant n. colossus, mammoth, monster, leviathan, ogre.
– OPPOSITES dwarf.
• adj. huge, colossal, massive, enormous, gigantic, mammoth, vast, immense, monumental, mountainous, titanic, towering, gargantuan; informal mega, monster, whopping; Brit. informal ginormous.
– OPPOSITES miniature.

giddy adj. 1 dizzy, light-headed, faint, unsteady, wobbly, reeling; informal woozy. 2 flighty, silly, frivolous, skittish, irresponsible, scatty; informal dizzy.

gift n. 1 present, handout, donation, offering, bonus, award, endowment; informal prezzie. 2 talent, flair, aptitude, facility, knack, bent, ability, skill, capacity, faculty.

gifted adj. talented, skilled, accomplished, expert, able, proficient, intelligent, clever, bright, brilliant, precocious; informal crack, ace.
– OPPOSITES inept.

gigantic adj. huge, enormous, vast, giant, massive, colossal, mammoth, immense, monumental, mountainous, gargantuan; informal mega, monster, whopping, humongous; Brit. informal ginormous.
– OPPOSITES tiny.

giggle v. & n. titter, snigger, chuckle, chortle, laugh.

girl n. young woman, young lady, miss; Scottish & N. English lass, lassie; Irish colleen; informal chick; Brit. informal bird; N. Amer. informal gal, broad, dame, babe; Austral./NZ informal sheila.

girlfriend n. sweetheart, lover, partner, significant other, girl, woman; informal steady; Brit. informal bird; N. Amer. informal squeeze.

give v. 1 donate, contribute, present with, award, grant, bestow, hand (over), bequeath, leave, make over. 2 convey, pass on, impart, communicate, transmit, send, deliver, relay. 3 sacrifice, give up, relinquish, devote, dedicate. 4 organize, arrange, lay on, throw, host, hold, have. 5 perform, execute, make, do. 6 utter, let out, emit, produce, make.
– OPPOSITES receive, take.
□ give away betray, inform on; informal split on, rat on; Brit. informal grass on, shop; N. Amer. informal finger; Austral./NZ informal dob in. give in/up capitulate, concede defeat, admit defeat, give up, surrender, yield, submit. give off emit, produce, send out, throw out, discharge, release. give up stop, cease, discontinue, desist from, abstain from, cut out, renounce, forgo; informal quit; Brit. informal jack in.

g

glad adj. **1 pleased**, happy, gratified, delighted, thrilled, overjoyed; informal over the moon; Brit. informal chuffed; N. English informal made up. **2** I'd be glad to help: **willing**, eager, happy, pleased, delighted, ready, prepared.
– OPPOSITES dismayed, reluctant.

gladly adv. **with pleasure**, happily, cheerfully, willingly, readily, eagerly, freely, ungrudgingly.

glamorous adj. **1 beautiful**, elegant, chic, stylish, fashionable. **2 exciting**, glittering, glossy, colourful, exotic; informal glitzy, jet-setting.
– OPPOSITES dowdy, dull.

glamour n. **1** she had undeniable glamour: **beauty**, allure, elegance, chic, style, charisma, charm, magnetism. **2** the glamour of TV: **allure**, attraction, fascination, charm, magic, romance, excitement, thrill; informal glitz, glam.

glance v. **1 look briefly**, look quickly, peek, peep, glimpse, catch a glimpse. **2** I glanced through the report: **read quickly**, scan, skim, leaf, flick, flip, thumb, browse.

glare v. **scowl**, glower, look daggers, frown, lour; informal give someone a dirty look.
• n. **1 scowl**, glower, angry stare, frown, black look; informal dirty look. **2 blaze**, dazzle, shine, beam, brilliance.

glaring adj. **1 dazzling**, blinding, blazing, strong, harsh. **2 obvious**, conspicuous, unmistak-

able, inescapable, unmissable, striking, flagrant, blatant.

glaze v. **cover**, coat, varnish, lacquer, polish.
• n. **coating**, topping, varnish, lacquer, polish.

gleam v. **shine**, glint, glitter, shimmer, glimmer, sparkle, twinkle, flicker, wink, glisten, flash.
• n. **flash**, glimmer, glint, shimmer, twinkle, sparkle, flicker, beam, ray, shaft.

glide v. **1** a gondola glided past: **slide**, slip, sail, float, drift, flow. **2** seagulls gliding over the waves: **soar**, wheel, plane, fly.

glimpse n. **glance**, brief/quick look, sighting, sighting, peek, peep.
• v. **catch sight of**, sight, spot, notice, discern, spy, pick out, make out.

glitter v. **sparkle**, twinkle, glint, shimmer, glimmer, wink, flash, shine.
• n. **sparkle**, twinkle, glint, shimmer, glimmer, flicker, flash.

global adj. **1 worldwide**, international, world, intercontinental, universal. **2 comprehensive**, overall, general, all-inclusive, all-encompassing, universal, broad.

gloom n. **1 darkness**, dark, murk, shadows, shade. **2 despondency**, depression, dejection, melancholy, unhappiness, sadness, misery, woe, despair.
– OPPOSITES light, happiness.

gloomy adj. **1 dark**, shadowy, murky, sunless, dim, dingy. **2 despondent**, depressed,

downcast, downhearted, dejected, dispirited, disheartened, demoralized, crestfallen, glum, melancholy; informal down in the mouth, down in the dumps.
3 pessimistic, depressing, downbeat, disheartening, disappointing, unfavourable, bleak, black.
– OPPOSITES bright, cheerful.

glorious adj. **wonderful**, marvellous, magnificent, superb, sublime, spectacular, lovely, fine, delightful; informal stunning, fantastic, terrific, tremendous, sensational, heavenly, divine, gorgeous, fabulous, awesome.
– OPPOSITES undistinguished.

glory n. **1 honour**, distinction, prestige, fame, renown, kudos, eminence, acclaim, celebrity, praise, recognition. **2 magnificence**, splendour, grandeur, majesty, greatness, nobility, opulence, beauty, elegance.
– OPPOSITES shame.
•v. *we gloried in our independence:* **delight**, triumph, revel, rejoice, exult, relish, savour, be proud of; informal get a kick out of.

gloss n. **shine**, sheen, lustre, gleam, patina, polish, brilliance, shimmer.
□ **gloss over** conceal, cover up, hide, disguise, mask, veil, play down, minimize, understate.

glossy adj. **shiny**, gleaming, lustrous, brilliant, glistening, glassy, polished, lacquered, glazed.
– OPPOSITES dull.

glow v. **1 shine**, gleam, glimmer, flicker, flare. **2 smoulder**, burn.
•n. **radiance**, light, gleam, glimmer.

glowing adj. **1 bright**, radiant, incandescent, luminous, smouldering; literary lambent. **2 rosy**, pink, red, ruddy, flushed, blushing, burning. **3 vivid**, vibrant, bright, brilliant, rich, intense, radiant. **4 complimentary**, favourable, enthusiastic, admiring, rapturous, fulsome; informal rave.

glue n. **adhesive**, gum, paste, cement; N. Amer. mucilage; N. Amer. informal stickum.
•v. **stick**, gum, paste, fix, seal, cement.

glum adj. **gloomy**, downcast, dejected, despondent, crestfallen, disheartened, depressed, doleful, miserable, woebegone; informal fed up, down in the dumps, down in the mouth.
– OPPOSITES cheerful.

go v. **1** *he's gone into town:* **travel**, move, proceed, make your way, journey, advance, progress, pass. **2** *the road goes to London:* **lead**, stretch, reach, extend. **3 leave**, depart, take yourself off, go away, withdraw, absent yourself, exit, set off, start out, get under way, be on your way; Brit. make a move; informal make tracks. **4 be used up**, be spent, be exhausted, be consumed. **5 become**, get, turn, grow. **6 turn out**, work out, develop, progress, result, end (up); informal pan out. **7 match**, harmonize, blend, be complementary,

g

coordinate, be compatible.
8 function, work, run, operate.
• n. (informal) **1** here, have a go: **try**, attempt, effort, bid; informal shot, stab, crack. **2 turn**, opportunity, chance, stint, spell, time.

□ **go down 1** sink, founder. **2** decrease, fall, drop, decline, plummet, plunge, slump.
go in for take part in, participate in, engage in, get involved in, join in, enter into, undertake, practise, pursue, espouse, adopt, embrace. **go into** investigate, examine, enquire into, look into, research, probe, explore, delve into, consider, review, analyse.
go off 1 explode, detonate, blow up. **2** (Brit.) go bad, go stale, go sour, turn, spoil, go rancid. **go on 1** last, continue, carry on, run on, proceed, endure, persist, take. **2** talk at length, ramble, rattle on, chatter, prattle; Brit. informal witter, rabbit. **3** happen, take place, occur, transpire; N. Amer. informal go down. **go out 1** be turned off, be extinguished, stop burning. **2** see, take out, be someone's boyfriend/girlfriend, be in a relationship with; informal date, go with. **go through 1** undergo, experience, face, suffer, live through, endure. **2** search, look, hunt, rummage, rifle. **3** examine, study, scrutinize, inspect, look over, scan, check.

goal n. **objective**, aim, end, target, intention, plan, purpose, ambition, aspiration.

gobble v. **guzzle**, bolt, gulp, devour, wolf; informal tuck into, put away, demolish; Brit. informal scoff; N. Amer. informal scarf (down/up).

god n. **deity**, goddess, divine being, divinity, immortal.

<table>
<tr><td colspan="2">WORD LINKS</td></tr>
<tr><td>relating to God or a god:</td><td>divine;</td></tr>
<tr><td>study of God:</td><td>theology</td></tr>
</table>

golden adj. **blonde**, yellow, fair, flaxen.
– OPPOSITES dark.

gone adj. **1 away**, absent, off, out, missing. **2 past**, over (and done with), no more, done, finished, ended, forgotten. **3 used up**, consumed, finished, spent, depleted.

good adj. **1 fine**, superior, excellent, superb, outstanding, magnificent, exceptional, marvellous, wonderful, first-rate, first-class, quality; informal great, ace, terrific, fantastic, fabulous, class, awesome, wicked; Brit. informal brilliant. **2 virtuous**, righteous, upright, upstanding, moral, ethical, principled, law-abiding, blameless, honourable, decent, respectable, trustworthy; informal squeaky clean. **3 well behaved**, obedient, dutiful, polite, courteous, respectful. **4 capable**, able, proficient, adept, adroit, accomplished, skilful, talented, masterly, expert; informal mean, wicked, nifty; N. Amer. informal crackerjack. **5 close**, intimate, dear, bosom, special, best, firm, loyal.

6 enjoyable, pleasant, agreeable, pleasurable, delightful, lovely, amusing. **7** *it was good of you to come*: **kind**, generous, charitable, gracious, noble, altruistic, unselfish. **8 convenient**, suitable, appropriate, fitting, fit, opportune, timely, favourable. **9** *milk is good for you*: **wholesome**, healthy, nourishing, nutritious, beneficial. **10 tasty**, appetizing, flavoursome, palatable, succulent; *informal* scrumptious, scrummy, yummy; *Brit. informal* moreish. **11 valid**, genuine, authentic, legitimate, sound, bona fide, convincing, compelling. **12 fine**, fair, dry, bright, clear, sunny, cloudless, calm, warm, mild.
– OPPOSITES bad, wicked, naughty.
•n. **1 virtue**, righteousness, goodness, morality, integrity, honesty, truth, honour. **2** *it's for your own good*: **benefit**, advantage, profit, gain, interest, welfare, well-being.
– OPPOSITES wickedness, disadvantage.
◻ **for good** forever, permanently, for always, (for) evermore, for ever and ever; *N. Amer.* forevermore; *informal* for keeps.
goodbye exclam. **farewell**, adieu, au revoir, ciao, adios; *informal* bye, bye-bye, so long, see you (later); *Brit. informal* cheerio, cheers, ta-ta.
good-looking adj. **attractive**, beautiful, pretty, handsome, lovely, stunning, striking, arresting, gorgeous, prepossessing,

fetching; *Scottish & N. English* bonny; *informal* tasty, easy on the eye; *Brit. informal* fit; *N. Amer. informal* cute, foxy; *old use* comely.
– OPPOSITES ugly.

goodness n. **1 virtue**, good, righteousness, morality, integrity, rectitude, honesty, honour, decency, respectability, nobility, worth, merit. **2 kindness**, humanity, benevolence, tenderness, warmth, affection, love, goodwill, sympathy, compassion, care, concern, understanding, generosity, charity.
goods pl. n. **merchandise**, wares, stock, commodities, produce, products, articles.
goodwill n. **kindness**, compassion, goodness, benevolence, consideration, charity, decency, neighbourliness.
– OPPOSITES hostility.
gorge n. **ravine**, canyon, gully, defile, couloir, chasm, gulf; *S. English* chine; *N. English* gill; *N. Amer.* gulch, coulee.
◻ **gorge yourself** stuff yourself, guzzle, overindulge; *informal* pig yourself, pig out, stuff your face.
gorgeous adj. **1 good-looking**, attractive, beautiful, pretty, handsome, lovely, stunning; *Scottish & N. English* bonny; *informal* fanciable, tasty, hot; *Brit. informal* fit; *N. Amer. informal* cute, foxy; *old use* comely. **2 spectacular**, splendid, superb, wonderful, grand, impressive, awe-inspiring, awesome, stunning, breathtaking; *informal* sensational,

fabulous, fantastic. **3 resplendent**, magnificent, sumptuous, luxurious, elegant, dazzling, brilliant.

- **OPPOSITES** ugly, drab.

gossip n. **1 news**, rumours, scandal, hearsay, tittle-tattle; informal dirt, buzz; N. Amer. informal scuttlebutt. **2 chat**, talk, conversation, chatter, heart-to-heart, tête-à-tête; informal jaw, gas; Brit. informal natter, chinwag; N. Amer. informal gabfest. **3 gossipmonger**, busybody, scandalmonger, rumourmonger, muckraker.

•v. **1 talk**, whisper, tell tales, spread rumours; informal dish the dirt. **2** *people sat around gossiping*: **chat**, talk, converse; informal gas, chew the fat, chew the rag, jaw; Brit. informal natter, chinwag; N. Amer. informal shoot the breeze.

gourmet n. **gastronome**, epicure, epicurean, connoisseur; informal foodie.

govern v. **1 rule**, preside over, control, be in charge of, command, run, head, manage, oversee, supervise. **2 determine**, decide, control, constrain, regulate, direct, rule, dictate, shape, affect.

government n. **administration**, executive, regime, authority, council, powers that be, cabinet, ministry.

governor n. **leader**, ruler, chief, head, administrator, principal, director, chairman, chairwoman, chair, superintendent, commissioner, controller; informal boss.

gown n. **dress**, frock, robe, habit, costume.

grab v. **seize**, grasp, snatch, take hold of, grip, clasp, clutch, catch.

grace n. **1 elegance**, poise, finesse, polish, fluency, smoothness, suppleness. **2** *he had the grace to apologize*: **courtesy**, decency, (good) manners, politeness, respect. **3** *he fell from grace*: **favour**, approval, approbation, acceptance, esteem, regard, respect.

- **OPPOSITES** awkwardness.

•v. **adorn**, embellish, decorate, ornament, enhance.

graceful adj. **elegant**, fluid, fluent, easy, polished, supple.

gracious adj. **courteous**, polite, civil, well mannered, tactful, diplomatic, kind, considerate, thoughtful, obliging, accommodating, hospitable.

grade n. **1** *hotels within the same grade*: **category**, class, classification, ranking, quality, grouping, group, bracket. **2** *his job is of the lowest grade*: **rank**, level, standing, position, class, status, order, echelon. **3 mark**, score, assessment, evaluation, appraisal. **4** (N. Amer.) **year**, form, class.

•v. **classify**, class, categorize, bracket, sort, group, arrange, pigeonhole, rank, evaluate, rate, value.

gradient n. **slope**, incline, hill, rise, ramp, bank; N. Amer. grade.

gradual adj. **1 slow**, steady, measured, unhurried, cautious, piecemeal, step-by-step, bit-

by-bit, progressive, continuous. **2 gentle**, moderate, slight, easy.
– OPPOSITES abrupt, steep.

gradually adv. **slowly**, steadily, slowly but surely, cautiously, gently, gingerly, piecemeal, bit by bit, by degrees, progressively, systematically.

graft n. **transplant**, implant.
•v. **1 splice**, join, insert, fix. **2 transplant**, implant.

grain n. **1 kernel**, seed. **2 granule**, particle, speck, bit, scrap, crumb, fragment, morsel. **3 trace**, hint, tinge, suggestion, shadow, soupçon, ounce, iota, jot, scrap, shred; informal smidgen. **4 texture**, weave, pattern, nap.

grand adj. **1 magnificent**, imposing, impressive, awe-inspiring, splendid, resplendent, majestic, monumental, palatial, stately; Brit. upmarket; N. Amer. upscale; informal fancy, posh; Brit. informal swish. **2 ambitious**, bold, epic, big, extravagant. **3 august**, distinguished, illustrious, eminent, venerable, dignified, proud. **4** (informal) **excellent**, marvellous, splendid, first-class, first-rate, wonderful, outstanding; informal superb, terrific, great, super; Brit. informal brilliant.
– OPPOSITES humble, poor.

grandeur n. **splendour**, magnificence, glory, resplendence, majesty, greatness, stateliness, pomp, ceremony.

grant v. **1** he granted them leave of absence: **allow**, permit, agree to, accord, afford, vouchsafe.

2 he granted them £20,000: **give**, award, bestow on, confer on, present with, endow with. **3 admit**, accept, concede, allow, appreciate, recognize, acknowledge, confess.
– OPPOSITES refuse, deny.
•n. **award**, bursary, endowment, scholarship, allowance, subsidy, contribution, handout, donation, gift.

graphic adj. **1 visual**, pictorial, illustrative, diagrammatic. **2 vivid**, explicit, detailed, realistic, descriptive, powerful, colourful, lurid, shocking.
– OPPOSITES vague.

grapple v. **1 wrestle**, struggle, tussle, scuffle, battle. **2 deal**, cope, get to grips, tackle, confront, face.

grasp v. **1 grip**, clutch, clasp, clench, squeeze, catch, seize, grab, snatch. **2 understand**, comprehend, take in, see, apprehend, assimilate, absorb; informal get, take on board; Brit. informal twig.
•n. **1 grip**, hold, squeeze. **2 reach**, scope, power, range, sights. **3 understanding**, comprehension, awareness, grip, knowledge, mastery, command.

grasping adj. **greedy**, acquisitive, avaricious, rapacious, mercenary, materialistic; informal tight-fisted, tight, money-grubbing.

grate v. **1 shred**, pulverize, mince, grind, crush, crumble. **2 grind**, rub, rasp, scrape, jar, creak.

g

grateful adj. **thankful**, appreciative, indebted, obliged, in someone's debt, beholden.

gratitude n. **thanks**, gratefulness, thankfulness, appreciation, indebtedness, recognition, acknowledgement.

grave[1] n. **tomb**, burial place, last resting place, vault, mausoleum, sepulchre.

grave[2] adj. **1 serious**, important, weighty, profound, significant, momentous, critical, urgent, pressing, dire, terrible, dreadful. **2 solemn**, serious, sober, unsmiling, grim, sombre, dour.
– OPPOSITES trivial, light-hearted.

graveyard n. **cemetery**, churchyard, burial ground, necropolis, garden of remembrance; Scottish kirkyard.

gravity n. **1 seriousness**, importance, significance, weight, consequence, magnitude, acuteness, urgency, dreadfulness. **2 solemnity**, seriousness, sobriety, severity, grimness, sombreness, dourness.

graze[1] v. **feed**, eat, crop, nibble, browse.

graze[2] v. **1 scrape**, skin, scratch, chafe, scuff, rasp. **2 touch**, brush, shave, skim, kiss, scrape, clip, glance off.
•n. **scratch**, scrape, abrasion.

grease n. **oil**, fat, lubricant.

greasy adj. **oily**, fatty, buttery, oleaginous, slippery, slick, slimy, slithery; informal slippy.

great adj. **1 considerable**, substantial, significant, serious, exceptional, extraordinary. **2 large**, big, extensive, expansive, broad, wide, vast, immense, huge, enormous, massive; informal humongous, whopping; Brit. informal ginormous. **3 prominent**, eminent, distinguished, illustrious, celebrated, acclaimed, admired, esteemed, renowned, famous, well known, leading, top, major. **4 magnificent**, imposing, impressive, awe-inspiring, grand, splendid, majestic. **5 expert**, skilful, skilled, adept, accomplished, talented, fine, masterly, master, brilliant, virtuoso, marvellous, outstanding, first-class, superb; informal crack, class. **6 keen**, eager, enthusiastic, devoted, ardent, fanatical, passionate, dedicated, committed. **7 enjoyable**, delightful, lovely, excellent, marvellous, wonderful, fine, splendid; informal terrific, fantastic, fabulous, super, cool; Brit. informal brilliant.
– OPPOSITES little, small, minor, modest.

greatly adv. **very much**, extremely, considerably, substantially, significantly, markedly, seriously, materially, enormously, vastly, immensely, tremendously, mightily.

greatness n. **1 eminence**, distinction, celebrity, fame, prominence, renown, importance. **2 brilliance**, genius, prowess, talent, expertise, mastery, artistry, skill, proficiency, flair.

greed n. **1** avarice, acquisitiveness, covetousness, materialism, mercenariness; informal money-grubbing. **2** gluttony, hunger, voracity, self-indulgence; informal piggishness. **3** desire, appetite, hunger, thirst, craving, longing, yearning, hankering; informal itch.
– OPPOSITES generosity, temperance, indifference.

greedy adj. **1** gluttonous, ravenous, voracious; informal piggish, piggy. **2** avaricious, acquisitive, covetous, grasping, materialistic, mercenary; informal money-grubbing.

green adj. **1** olive green, pea green, emerald green, lime green, avocado, pistachio, bottle green, Lincoln green, jade. **2** verdant, grassy, leafy. **environmental**, ecological, conservationist, eco-, eco-friendly. **4** inexperienced, callow, raw, unseasoned, untried, naive, innocent, unworldly; informal wet behind the ears.

greet v. **1** say hello to, address, salute, hail, welcome, meet, receive. **2** *the decision was greeted with outrage*: receive, respond to, react to, take.

greeting n. **1** hello, salutation, welcome, reception. **2** best wishes, good wishes, congratulations, compliments, regards, respects.
– OPPOSITES farewell.

grey adj. **1** silvery, gunmetal, slate, charcoal, smoky. **2** cloudy, overcast, dull, dark, sunless, murky, gloomy, cheerless. **3** pale, wan, ashen, pasty, pallid, colourless, waxen. **4** characterless, colourless, nondescript, flat, bland, dull, boring, tedious, monotonous. **5** *a grey area*: ambiguous, doubtful, unclear, uncertain, indefinite, debatable.

grief n. sorrow, misery, sadness, anguish, pain, distress, heartache, heartbreak, agony, woe, desolation.
– OPPOSITES joy.

grievance n. complaint, objection, grumble, grouse, ill feeling, bad feeling, resentment; informal gripe.

grieve v. **1** mourn, sorrow, cry, sob, weep. **2** sadden, upset, distress, pain, hurt, wound, break someone's heart.
– OPPOSITES rejoice.

grim adj. **1** stern, forbidding, uninviting, unsmiling, dour, formidable. **2** dreadful, ghastly, horrible, terrible, awful, appalling, frightful, shocking, grisly, gruesome, depressing, distressing, upsetting. **3** bleak, dismal, dingy, wretched, miserable, depressing, cheerless, joyless, gloomy, uninviting.
– OPPOSITES amiable, pleasant.

grin v. & n. smile, beam, smirk.

grind v. **1** crush, pound, pulverize, mill, crumble. **2** rub, grate, scrape. **3** sharpen, whet, hone, put an edge on, mill, machine, polish, smooth.
•n. **drudgery**, toil, labour,

g

donkey work, exertion, chores; informal slog.

grip v. **1 grasp**, clutch, clasp, take hold of, clench, cling to, grab, seize, squeeze. **2 engross**, enthral, absorb, rivet, spellbind, fascinate, mesmerize.
•n. **1 grasp**, hold. **2 traction**, purchase, friction, adhesion. **3 control**, power, hold, stranglehold, clutches, influence.

gripping adj. **engrossing**, enthralling, absorbing, riveting, captivating, spellbinding, fascinating, compelling, thrilling, exciting, action-packed, dramatic.
– OPPOSITES boring.

groan v. **1 moan**, cry. **2 complain**, grumble, moan, mutter; informal grouse, bellyache, bitch, whinge. **3 creak**, grate, rasp.
•n. **1 moan**, cry. **2 complaint**, grumble, grievance, moan, muttering; informal grouse, gripe, whinge. **3 creaking**, creak, grating, grinding.

groom v. **1 curry**, brush, clean, rub down. **2 brush**, comb, arrange, do; informal fix. **3 prepare**, prime, condition, coach, train, drill, teach, school.

groove n. **furrow**, channel, trench, trough, rut, gutter, canal, hollow, indentation.

grope v. **fumble**, scrabble, fish, ferret, rummage, feel, search, hunt.

gross adj. **1** (informal) **disgusting**, repulsive, revolting, foul, nasty, obnoxious, sickening, nauseat-

ing, stomach-churning. **2 thorough**, complete, utter, out and out, shameful, serious, unacceptable, flagrant, blatant, obvious, barefaced, shameless, brazen. **3 total**, full, overall, combined, before deductions, before tax.
– OPPOSITES pleasant, net.
•v. **earn**, make, bring in, take, get, receive; informal rake in.

grotesque adj. **1 misshapen**, deformed, distorted, twisted, monstrous, hideous, freakish, unnatural, abnormal, strange; informal weird. **2 outrageous**, monstrous, shocking, appalling, preposterous, ridiculous, ludicrous, unbelievable, incredible.

ground n. **1 floor**, earth, terra firma; informal deck. **2 earth**, soil, turf, land, terrain. **3 stadium**, pitch, field, arena, track; Brit. informal park. **4** the mansion's grounds: **estate**, gardens, park, land, property, surroundings, territory. **5** grounds for dismissal: **reason**, cause, basis, foundation, justification, rationale, argument, occasion, excuse, pretext.
•v. **1 base**, found, establish, root, build, form. **2** she was well grounded in the classics: **teach**, instruct, coach, tutor, educate, school, train, drill.

group n. **1 category**, class, classification, grouping, cluster, set, batch, type, sort, kind, variety, family. **2 crowd**, party, body, band, company, gathering, congregation, assembly, collection,

cluster, clump, knot, flock, pack, troop, gang; informal bunch.
3 band, ensemble, act; informal line-up, combo, outfit.
▸v. **1 categorize**, classify, class, catalogue, sort, bracket, pigeonhole. **2 assemble**, collect, organize, place, arrange, range, line up, lay out.

grovel v. **1 prostrate yourself**, lie, kneel, cringe. **2 be obsequious**, fawn on, kowtow, bow and scrape, toady, dance attendance on, ingratiate yourself with; informal crawl, creep, suck up to, lick someone's boots.

grow v. **1 enlarge**, get bigger, get larger, get taller, expand, increase in size, extend, spread, swell, multiply, snowball, mushroom, balloon, build up, mount up, pile up. **2 sprout**, germinate, spring up, develop, bud, bloom, flourish, thrive, run riot. **3 cultivate**, produce, propagate, raise, rear, farm. **4 become**, get, turn, begin to be.
– OPPOSITES shrink, decline.

grown-up adj. **adult**, mature, of age, fully grown, independent.
▸n. **adult**, woman, man, grown man/woman.
– OPPOSITES child.

growth n. **1 enlargement**, increase in size, expansion, extension, swelling, multiplication, mushrooming, snowballing, rise, escalation, build-up, development. **2 tumour**, malignancy, cancer, lump, swelling.

grubby adj. **dirty**, grimy, filthy, mucky, unwashed, stained, soiled; informal cruddy, yucky; Brit. informal manky.
– OPPOSITES clean.

grudge n. **grievance**, resentment, bitterness, rancour, ill will, animosity, antipathy, antagonism; informal a chip on your shoulder.

gruelling adj. **exhausting**, tiring, taxing, draining, demanding, exacting, difficult, arduous, strenuous, back-breaking, punishing, crippling; informal murderous; Brit. informal knackering.

gruesome adj. **grisly**, ghastly, frightful, horrid, horrifying, hideous, horrible, grim, awful, dreadful, terrible, horrific; informal sick, sick-making, gross.
– OPPOSITES pleasant.

grumble v. **complain**, grouse, whine, mutter, carp, make a fuss; informal moan, bellyache, bitch, whinge; N. English informal mither.
▸n. **complaint**, grouse, grievance, protest; informal grouch, moan, whinge, beef, gripe.

grumpy adj. **bad-tempered**, crabby, tetchy, touchy, irascible, cantankerous, curmudgeonly, surly, fractious; informal grouchy; Brit. informal ratty; N. Amer. informal cranky, ornery.
– OPPOSITES good-humoured.

guarantee n. **1 warranty**. **2 promise**, assurance, word (of honour), pledge, vow, oath, commitment. **3 collateral**, security, surety, bond.
▸v. **1 promise**, swear, pledge, vow, give your word, give an

g

assurance, give an undertaking.
2 underwrite, stand surety.

guard v. **protect**, defend, shield, secure, cover, mind, stand guard over, watch, keep an eye on.
•n. **1 sentry**, sentinel, nightwatchman, protector, defender, guardian, lookout, watch. **2 warder**, warden, keeper, jailer; informal screw. **3 cover**, shield, screen, fender, bumper, buffer.

guarded adj. **cautious**, careful, circumspect, wary, chary, reluctant, non-committal; informal cagey.

guardian n. **protector**, defender, preserver, custodian, warden, guard, keeper, curator, caretaker, steward, trustee.

> **WORD LINKS**
> relating to a guardian: tutelary

guerrilla n. **rebel**, irregular, partisan, freedom fighter, revolutionary, terrorist.

guess v. **1 estimate**, reckon, judge, speculate, conjecture, hypothesize, surmise. **2** (informal) **suppose**, think, imagine, expect, suspect, dare say; informal reckon.
•n. **hypothesis**, theory, conjecture, surmise, estimate, belief, opinion, supposition, speculation, suspicion, impression, feeling.

guest n. **1 visitor**, caller, company. **2 client**, customer, resident, boarder, lodger, patron, diner, holidaymaker, tourist.
– OPPOSITES host.

guidance n. **1 advice**, counsel, instruction, suggestions, tips, hints, pointers, guidelines. **2 direction**, control, leadership, management, supervision.

guide n. **1 escort**, attendant, courier, leader, usher. **2 outline**, template, example, exemplar, model, pattern, guideline, yardstick, precedent. **3 guidebook**, travel guide, vade mecum, companion, handbook, manual, directory, A to Z, instructions, directions; informal bible.
•v. **1 lead**, conduct, show, usher, shepherd, direct, steer, pilot, escort. **2 direct**, steer, manage, conduct, run, be in charge of, govern, preside over, supervise, oversee. **3 advise**, counsel, direct.

guild n. **association**, society, union, league, organization, company, fellowship, club, order, lodge.

guilt n. **1 culpability**, blameworthiness, responsibility. **2 remorse**, shame, regret, contrition, self-reproach, a guilty conscience.
– OPPOSITES innocence.

guilty adj. **1 culpable**, to blame, at fault, in the wrong, responsible. **2 ashamed**, guilt-ridden, conscience-stricken, remorseful, sorry, contrite, repentant, penitent, regretful, rueful, shamefaced.
– OPPOSITES innocent.

gulf n. **1 bay**, inlet, cove, bight, fjord, estuary, sound; Scottish

firth. 2 gap, divide, separation, difference, contrast.

gullible adj. **credulous**, naive, easily deceived, impressionable, unsuspecting, ingenuous, innocent, inexperienced, green; informal wet behind the ears.
– OPPOSITES suspicious.

gulp v. **1 swallow**, quaff, swill down; informal swig, down, knock back. **2 gobble**, guzzle, devour, bolt, wolf; informal shovel down; Brit. informal scoff. **3** *she gulped back her tears:* **choke back**, fight/hold back, suppress, stifle, smother.
•n. **mouthful**, swallow, draught; informal swig.

gum n. **glue**, adhesive, paste, cement; N. Amer. mucilage; N. Amer. informal stickum.
•v. **stick**, glue, paste, cement, attach.

gun n. **firearm**, side arm, handgun, weapon; informal shooter; N. Amer. informal piece, shooting iron.

gunman n. **armed criminal**, assassin, sniper, terrorist, gunfighter; informal hit man, gunslinger; N. Amer. informal shootist.

guru n. **1 spiritual teacher**, tutor, sage, mentor, spiritual leader, master. **2 expert**, authority, pundit, leading light, master, specialist.
– OPPOSITES disciple.

gush v. **surge**, stream, spout, spurt, jet, rush, pour, spill, cascade, flood; Brit. informal sloosh.
•n. **surge**, stream, spout, spurt, jet, rush, outpouring, spill, outflow, cascade, flood, torrent.

gushing adj. **effusive**, over-enthusiastic, extravagant, fulsome, lavish, unrestrained; informal over the top.

gust n. **flurry**, blast, puff, blow, rush, squall.

gut n. **1 stomach**, belly, abdomen, paunch, intestines, viscera; informal tummy, insides, innards. **2** (informal) *he has a lot of guts:* **courage**, bravery, backbone, nerve, pluck, spirit, daring, grit, fearlessness, determination; Brit. informal bottle; N. Amer. informal moxie.
•adj. (informal) **instinctive**, intuitive, deep-seated, involuntary, spontaneous, unthinking, knee-jerk.
•v. **1 clean (out)**, disembowel, draw; formal eviscerate. **2 strip**, empty, devastate, lay waste, ravage, ruin, wreck.

WORD LINKS
relating to the gut: visceral

---

gutter n. **drain**, trough, trench, ditch, sluice, sewer, channel, conduit, pipe.

guy n. (informal) **man**, fellow; informal lad; Brit. informal chap, bloke, geezer; N. Amer. informal dude, hombre.

guzzle v. **1 gobble**, bolt, wolf, devour; informal tuck into, shovel down, hoover up; Brit. informal scoff; N. Amer. informal snarf, scarf. **2 gulp down**, quaff, swill; informal knock back, swig, slug, neck.

gyrate v. **rotate**, revolve, wheel, turn, whirl, circle, pirouette, twirl, swirl, spin, swivel.

Hh

habit n. **1 custom**, practice, routine, way; formal **wont**. **2** (informal) **addiction**, dependence, craving, fixation.

habitual adj. **1 constant**, persistent, continual, continuous, perpetual, non-stop, endless, never-ending; informal **eternal**. **2 inveterate**, confirmed, compulsive, incorrigible, hardened, ingrained, chronic, regular. **3 customary**, accustomed, regular, usual, normal, characteristic; literary **wonted**.
– OPPOSITES occasional.

hack v. **cut**, chop, hew, lop, saw, slash.

hackneyed adj. **overused**, overdone, overworked, worn out, time-worn, stale, tired, threadbare, trite, banal, clichéd.
– OPPOSITES original.

haggard adj. **drawn**, tired, exhausted, drained, careworn, gaunt, pinched, hollow-cheeked, hollow-eyed.

haggle v. **barter**, bargain, negotiate, wrangle.

hail¹ n. **barrage**, volley, shower, stream, salvo.

hail² v. **1 call out to**, shout to, address, greet, salute, say hello to. **2 flag down**, wave down. **3 acclaim**, praise, applaud. **4** he hails from Australia: **come**, be, be a native of.

hair n. **1 head of hair**, shock of hair, mane, mop, locks, tresses, curls. **2 hairstyle**, haircut; informal **hairdo**. **3 fur**, wool, coat, fleece, pelt, mane.

hairdresser n. **hairstylist**, coiffeur, coiffeuse, barber.

hairy adj. **1 shaggy**, bushy, long-haired, woolly, furry, fleecy. **2 bearded**, unshaven, stubbly, bristly; formal **hirsute**. **3** (informal) **risky**, dangerous, perilous, hazardous, tricky; informal **dicey**; Brit. informal **dodgy**.

half-hearted adj. **unenthusiastic**, cool, lukewarm, tepid, apathetic.
– OPPOSITES enthusiastic.

halfway adj. **midway**, middle, mid, central, centre, intermediate.
• adv. **midway**, in the middle, in the centre, part of the way.

hall n. **1 entrance hall**, hallway, entry, entrance, lobby, foyer, vestibule, atrium. **2 assembly room**, meeting room, chamber, auditorium, theatre, house.

hallucination n. **delusion**, illusion, figment of the imagination, mirage, chimera, fantasy.

halt v. **1** halt at the barrier: **stop**, come to a halt, come to a stop, come to a standstill, pull up, draw up. **2** a strike halted production: **stop**, bring to a stop,

put a stop to, suspend, arrest, check, curb, stem, staunch, block, stall.
- •n. **1 stop**, standstill. **2 stoppage**, break, pause, interval, interruption.
- OPPOSITES start.

halting adj. **hesitant**, faltering, hesitating, stumbling, stammering, stuttering, broken, imperfect.
- OPPOSITES fluent.

hammer v. **beat**, batter, bang, pummel, pound, knock, thump.

hamper v. **hinder**, obstruct, impede, inhibit, delay, slow down, hold up, interfere with, handicap, hamstring.
- OPPOSITES help.

hand n. **1 fist**, palm; informal paw, mitt. **2 handwriting**, writing, script. **3 worker**, employee, workman, labourer, operative, craftsman.
- •v. **pass**, give, present, let someone have.

WORD LINKS
relating to the hands: manual

handbook n. **manual**, instructions, ABC, A to Z, companion, guide, guidebook, vade mecum.

handcuff v. **manacle**, shackle, clap/put someone in irons; informal cuff.
- •n. (**handcuffs**) manacles, shackles, irons; informal cuffs, bracelets.

handful n. **few**, small number, small amount, small quantity,

sprinkling, smattering, one or two, some, not many.
- OPPOSITES lot.

handicap n. **1 disability**, infirmity, defect, impairment, affliction. **2 impediment**, hindrance, obstacle, barrier, constraint, disadvantage, stumbling block.
- OPPOSITES benefit, advantage.
- •v. **hamper**, impede, hinder, impair, hamstring, restrict, constrain.
- OPPOSITES help.

handle v. **1 hold**, pick up, grasp, grip, lift, finger. **2 control**, drive, steer, operate, manoeuvre. **3 deal with**, manage, tackle, take care of, look after, take charge of, attend to, see to, sort out. **4 trade in**, deal in, buy, sell, supply, peddle, traffic in.
- •n. **grip**, haft, hilt, stock, shaft.

handsome adj. **1 good-looking**, attractive, striking; informal hunky, dishy, tasty, fanciable; Brit. informal fit; N. Amer. informal cute. **2 substantial**, considerable, sizeable, princely, generous, lavish, ample, bumper; informal tidy, whopping; Brit. informal ginormous.
- OPPOSITES ugly.

handy adj. **1 useful**, convenient, practical, neat, easy to use, user-friendly, functional. **2 ready**, to hand, within reach, accessible, readily available, nearby, at the ready. **3 skilful**, skilled, dexterous, deft, adept, proficient.

hang v. **1** *lights hung from the trees:* **be suspended**, dangle, swing, sway, hover, float. **2** *hang the picture at eye level:* **suspend**, put up, pin up, display. **3 decorate**, adorn, drape, festoon, deck out. **4 send to the gallows**, execute, lynch; *informal* string up.

hang-up n. neurosis, phobia, preoccupation, fixation, obsession, inhibition, mental block; *informal* complex, thing, issue, bee in your bonnet.

hanker v. **yearn**, long, wish, hunger, thirst, lust, ache; *informal* itch.

haphazard adj. **random**, disorderly, indiscriminate, chaotic, hit-and-miss, aimless, chance; *informal* higgledy-piggledy.
– OPPOSITES methodical.

hapless adj. **unfortunate**, unlucky, unhappy, wretched, miserable.
– OPPOSITES lucky.

happen v. **1 occur**, take place, come about, arise, develop, result, transpire; *N. Amer. informal* go down; *literary* come to pass. **2** *I happened to be in London:* **chance**, have the good/bad luck.

happening n. **occurrence**, event, incident, episode, affair.

happily adv. **1 cheerfully**, contentedly, cheerily, merrily, joyfully. **2 gladly**, willingly, readily, freely. **3 fortunately**, luckily, thankfully, mercifully, as luck would have it.

happiness n. **pleasure**, contentment, well-being, satisfaction, cheerfulness, good spirits, merriment, joy, joyfulness, delight, elation, jubilation.
– OPPOSITES sadness.

happy adj. **1 cheerful**, cheery, merry, joyful, jovial, jolly, carefree, in good spirits, in a good mood, pleased, contented, content, satisfied, gratified, delighted, sunny, radiant, elated, jubilant; *literary* blithe. **2 glad**, pleased, delighted, more than willing. **3 fortunate**, lucky, timely, convenient.
– OPPOSITES sad, unhappy, unfortunate.

harass v. **persecute**, intimidate, hound, pester, bother; *informal* hassle, bug; *N. Amer. informal* ride.

harassed adj. **stressed**, hard-pressed, careworn, worried, troubled; *informal* hassled.
– OPPOSITES carefree.

harassment n. **persecution**, intimidation, victimization, trouble, bother; *informal* hassle.

harbour n. **port**, dock, haven, marina, mooring, wharf, anchorage, waterfront.
–v. **1 shelter**, conceal, hide, shield, protect, give asylum to. **2 bear**, hold, nurse, foster.

hard adj. **1 firm**, solid, rigid, stiff, unbreakable, unyielding, compacted, compressed, tough, strong. **2 arduous**, strenuous, tiring, exhausting, back-breaking, gruelling, heavy, laborious, demanding, uphill; *Brit. informal* knackering. **3 industrious**, diligent, assiduous, conscientious, energetic, keen, enthusiastic, indefatigable. **4 difficult**, puzzling, complicated, complex, intricate, knotty, thorny, problematic.

5 harsh, unpleasant, grim, austere, difficult, bad, bleak, tough. **6 forceful**, heavy, strong, sharp, violent, powerful.
– OPPOSITES soft, easy, gentle.
•adv. **1 forcefully**, roughly, heavily, sharply, violently. **2 diligently**, industriously, assiduously, conscientiously, energetically, doggedly; informal like mad, like crazy. **3 closely**, intently, critically, carefully, searchingly.

harden v. **1 solidify**, set, stiffen, thicken, cake, congeal. **2 toughen**, desensitize, inure, season, train, numb.
– OPPOSITES soften.

hardened adj. **inveterate**, seasoned, habitual, chronic, compulsive, confirmed, incorrigible.

hardly adv. **scarcely**, barely, only just, just.

hardship n. **difficulty**, privation, destitution, poverty, austerity, need, distress, suffering, adversity.
– OPPOSITES prosperity, ease.

hardware n. **equipment**, apparatus, gear, paraphernalia, tackle, kit, machinery.

hardy adj. **robust**, healthy, fit, strong, sturdy, tough, rugged.
– OPPOSITES delicate.

harm n. **injury**, damage, mischief, detriment, disservice.
– OPPOSITES good.
•v. **1 hurt**, injure, wound, lay a finger on, mistreat, ill-treat, maltreat. **2 damage**, spoil, affect, undermine, ruin.

– OPPOSITES heal, help.

harmful adj. **damaging**, injurious, detrimental, dangerous, unhealthy, unwholesome, hurtful, destructive, hazardous.
– OPPOSITES beneficial.

harmless adj. **1 safe**, innocuous, gentle, mild, non-toxic. **2 inoffensive**, innocuous, innocent, blameless, gentle.
– OPPOSITES harmful, objectionable.

harmonious adj. **1 melodious**, tuneful, musical, sweet-sounding, mellifluous, dulcet, euphonious. **2 friendly**, amicable, cordial, amiable, congenial, peaceful, in harmony, in tune. **3 balanced**, coordinated, pleasing, tasteful.
– OPPOSITES discordant, hostile.

harmonize v. **1 coordinate**, go together, match, blend, mix, balance, tone in, be compatible, be harmonious, suit each other, set each other off. **2 standardize**, coordinate, integrate, synchronize, make consistent, bring into line, systematize.
– OPPOSITES clash.

harmony n. **1 tunefulness**, euphony, melodiousness, unison. **2 accord**, agreement, peace, friendship, fellowship, cooperation, understanding, rapport, unity.
– OPPOSITES dissonance, disagreement.

harrowing adj. **distressing**, traumatic, upsetting, shocking, disturbing, painful, agonizing.

h

harry v. harass, hound, torment, pester, worry, badger, nag, plague; informal hassle, bug.

harsh adj. **1** grating, rasping, strident, raucous, discordant, jarring, dissonant. **2** garish, loud, glaring, gaudy, lurid. **3** cruel, savage, barbarous, merciless, inhumane, ruthless, brutal, hard-hearted, unfeeling, unrelenting. **4** severe, stringent, firm, stiff, stern, rigorous, uncompromising, draconian. **5** rude, discourteous, unfriendly, sharp, bitter, unkind, critical, disparaging. **6** austere, grim, spartan, hard, inhospitable. **7** cold, freezing, icy, bitter, hard, severe, bleak.
– OPPOSITES kind, mild, gentle.

harvest n. crop, yield, vintage, produce.
•v. **gather**, bring in, reap, pick, collect.

hassle (informal) n. **inconvenience**, bother, nuisance, trouble, annoyance, irritation, fuss; informal aggravation, headache, pain in the neck.
•v. **harass**, pester, be on at, badger, hound, bother, nag, torment; informal bug; N. English informal mither.

haste n. speed, hurriedness, swiftness, rapidity, quickness, briskness, alacrity; old use celerity.
– OPPOSITES delay.
□ **in haste** quickly, rapidly, fast, speedily, in a rush, in a hurry.

hasten v. **1** hurry, rush, dash, race, fly, speed; informal zip, hare, scoot, hotfoot it; N. Amer. informal hightail. **2** speed up, bring on, precipitate, advance.
– OPPOSITES dawdle, delay.

hasty adj. hurried, rash, impetuous, impulsive, reckless, precipitate, spur-of-the-moment.
– OPPOSITES considered.

hate v. **1** loathe, detest, despise, dislike, abhor, shrink from, be unable to bear/stand; formal abominate. **2** be sorry, be reluctant, be loath.
•n. hatred, loathing, abhorrence, abomination, aversion, disgust.
– OPPOSITES love.

hatred n. see HATE.

haul v. drag, pull, heave, lug, hump.
•n. booty, loot, plunder, spoils, stolen goods; informal swag.

haunt v. torment, disturb, trouble, worry, plague, prey on.
•n. meeting place, stamping ground, spot, venue; informal hang-out; N. Amer. stomping ground.

haunted adj. **1** possessed, cursed, jinxed, eerie. **2** tormented, anguished, tortured, obsessed, troubled, worried.

haunting adj. evocative, affecting, stirring, powerful, poignant, memorable.

have v. **1** own, be in possession of, be blessed with, boast, enjoy. **2** comprise, consist of, contain, include, incorporate, be composed of, be made up of. **3** eat, drink, take. **4** organize, hold,

give, throw, put on, lay on.
5 *I have to get up at six:* **must**, be obliged to, be required to, be compelled to, be forced to, be bound to.
□ **have on 1** be wearing, be dressed in, be clothed in, be decked out in, sport. **2** (Brit. informal) play a trick on, play a joke on, pull someone's leg; Brit. informal wind up; N. Amer. informal put on.

haven n. refuge, retreat, shelter, sanctuary, oasis.

havoc n. chaos, mayhem, bedlam, pandemonium, a shambles.

hazard n. danger, risk, peril, menace, jeopardy, threat.

hazardous adj. risky, dangerous, unsafe, perilous, fraught with danger, high-risk; informal dicey; Brit. informal dodgy.
– OPPOSITES safe.

haze n. mist, fog, cloud, vapour.

hazy adj. **1** misty, foggy, smoggy, murky. **2** vague, dim, nebulous, blurred, fuzzy.

head n. **1** skull, cranium; informal nut. **2** brain(s), mind, intellect, intelligence, grey matter; Brit. informal loaf; N. Amer. informal smarts. **3** *a head for business:* **aptitude**, talent, gift, capacity. **4** leader, chief, controller, governor, superintendent, commander, captain, director, manager, principal, president; informal boss; Brit. informal gaffer, guv'nor. **5** front, beginning, start, top.
• adj. **chief**, principal, leading, main, first, top, highest.

•v. **command**, control, lead, manage, direct, supervise, superintend, oversee, preside over.
□ **head off 1** intercept, divert, redirect, re-route, turn away. **2** forestall, avert, stave off, nip in the bud, prevent, avoid, stop.

headache n. **1** sore head, migraine. **2** (informal) **problem**, worry, hassle, pain in the neck, bind.

heading n. title, caption, legend, rubric, headline.

headlong adv. **1** head first, on your head. **2** without thinking, precipitously, impetuously, rashly, recklessly, hastily.
– OPPOSITES cautiously.
• adj. breakneck, whirlwind, reckless, precipitous.

headquarters pl. n. head office, HQ, base, nerve centre, mission control.

heady adj. **1** potent, intoxicating, strong. **2** exhilarating, exciting, stimulating, thrilling, intoxicating.

heal v. **1** cure, make better, restore to health, treat. **2** get better, be cured, recover, recuperate, mend, be on the mend. **3** put right, repair, resolve, reconcile, settle; informal patch up.

health n. **1** well-being, fitness, good condition, strength, robustness, vigour. **2** *her poor health forced her to retire:* **condition**, state of health, physical shape, constitution.
– OPPOSITES illness.

WORD LINKS
good for the health: salubrious

healthy adj. **1** well, fit, in good shape, in fine fettle, in tip-top condition, strong, fighting fit; informal in the pink. **2** wholesome, good for you, health-giving, nutritious, nourishing, invigorating, sanitary, hygienic.

heap n. pile, stack, mound, mountain.
•v. pile (up), stack (up), make a mound of.

hear v. **1** make out, catch, get, perceive, overhear. **2** learn, find out, discover, gather, glean. **3** try, judge, adjudicate on.

hearing n. **1** earshot, hearing distance. **2** trial, court case, enquiry, inquest, tribunal.

WORD LINKS
relating to hearing: auditory, aural

heart n. **1** emotions, feelings, sentiments, soul, mind. **2** compassion, sympathy, humanity, fellow feeling(s), empathy, understanding, soul, goodwill. **3** enthusiasm, spirit, determination, resolve, nerve; Brit. informal bottle. **4** centre, middle, hub, core. **5** essence, crux, core, nub, root, meat, substance, kernel; informal nitty-gritty.
□ **at heart** deep down, basically, fundamentally, essentially, in essence, intrinsically. **by heart** from memory, off pat, word for word, verbatim, parrot-fashion, word-perfect.

WORD LINKS
relating to the heart: cardiac; *relating to the heart's arteries:* coronary; *branch of medicine concerning the heart:* cardiology

heartache n. anguish, suffering, distress, unhappiness, grief, misery, sorrow, sadness, heart-break, pain, hurt, woe.
– OPPOSITES happiness.

heartbreaking adj. distressing, upsetting, disturbing, heart-rending, tragic, painful, sad, agonizing, harrowing.
– OPPOSITES comforting.

heartfelt adj. sincere, genuine, from the heart, earnest, profound, deep, wholehearted, honest.
– OPPOSITES insincere.

heartily adv. **1** wholeheartedly, warmly, profoundly, eagerly, enthusiastically. **2** thoroughly, completely, absolutely, exceedingly, downright; N. Amer. quite; informal seriously; Brit. informal jolly; N. Amer. informal real, mighty.

heartless adj. unfeeling, unsympathetic, unkind, uncaring, hard-hearted, cold, callous, cruel, merciless, pitiless, inhuman.
– OPPOSITES compassionate.

hearty adj. **1** exuberant, jovial, ebullient, cheerful, lively, loud, animated, vivacious, energetic, spirited. **2** wholehearted, heartfelt, sincere, genuine, real. **3** robust, healthy, hardy, fit, vigorous, sturdy, strong.

4 substantial, large, ample, satisfying, filling, generous.

heat n. **1 warmth**, hotness, high temperature. **2 passion**, intensity, vehemence, fervour, excitement, agitation, anger.
– OPPOSITES cold, apathy.
– v. **1 warm (up)**, reheat, cook, keep warm. **2 get hot**, get warm, warm up; Brit. informal hot up.
– OPPOSITES cool.

> WORD LINKS
> relating to heat: thermal

heated adj. **1 vehement**, passionate, impassioned, animated, lively, acrimonious, angry, bitter, furious, fierce. **2 excited**, animated, worked up, wound up, keyed up; informal het up.

heave v. **1 haul**, pull, drag, tug; informal yank. **2** (informal) **throw**, fling, cast, hurl, lob, pitch; informal chuck, sling. **3 let out**, breathe, give, emit, utter. **4 rise and fall**, roll, swell, surge, churn, seethe. **5 retch**, vomit, cough up; Brit. be sick; N. Amer. get sick; informal throw up, puke, chunder, chuck up, hurl, spew; N. Amer. informal barf.

heaven n. **1 paradise**, the hereafter, the next world, the afterworld, nirvana, Zion, Elysium. **2 bliss**, ecstasy, rapture, contentment, happiness, delight, joy, paradise.
– OPPOSITES hell.

> WORD LINKS
> relating to heaven: celestial

heavenly adj. **1 divine**, angelic, holy, celestial. **2 celestial**, cosmic, stellar, sidereal. **3** (informal) **delightful**, wonderful, glorious, sublime, exquisite, beautiful, lovely, gorgeous, enchanting; informal divine, super, fantastic, fabulous.

heavily adv. **1 laboriously**, slowly, ponderously, awkwardly, clumsily. **2 decisively**, conclusively, roundly, soundly, utterly, completely, thoroughly. **3 excessively**, immoderately, copiously, intemperately. **4 densely**, closely, thickly. **5 deeply**, extremely, greatly, exceedingly, tremendously, profoundly.

heavy adj. **1 weighty**, hefty, substantial, ponderous, solid, dense, cumbersome, unwieldy. **2 forceful**, hard, strong, violent, powerful, mighty, sharp, severe. **3 strenuous**, hard, physical, difficult, arduous, demanding, back-breaking, gruelling. **4 intense**, fierce, relentless, severe, serious. **5 substantial**, filling, stodgy, rich, big.
– OPPOSITES light.

hectic adj. **frantic**, frenetic, frenzied, feverish, manic, busy, active, fast and furious.
– OPPOSITES leisurely.

heed v. **pay attention to**, take notice of, take note of, listen to, consider, take to heart, take into account, obey, adhere to, abide by, observe.
– OPPOSITES disregard.
– n. **attention**, notice, note, regard, thought.

h

hefty adj. **1** burly, sturdy, strapping, bulky, strong, muscular, big, solid, well built; informal hulking, beefy. **2 powerful**, violent, hard, forceful, mighty. **3 substantial**, sizeable, considerable, stiff, large, heavy; informal whopping.
– OPPOSITES light.

height n. **1 tallness**, stature, elevation, altitude. **2** *mountain heights*: **summit**, top, peak, crest, crown, tip, cap, pinnacle. **3** *the height of their fame*: **highest point**, peak, zenith, pinnacle, climax.
– OPPOSITES width, nadir.

WORD LINKS
fear of heights: acrophobia

heighten v. **intensify**, increase, enhance, add to, augment, boost, strengthen, deepen, magnify, reinforce.
– OPPOSITES reduce.

heinous adj. **odious**, wicked, evil, atrocious, monstrous, abominable, detestable, despicable, horrific, terrible, awful, abhorrent, loathsome, hideous, unspeakable, execrable.
– OPPOSITES admirable.

heir, heiress n. **successor**, next in line, inheritor, beneficiary, legatee.

hell n. **1 the underworld**, the netherworld, eternal damnation, perdition, hellfire, fire and brimstone, the Inferno, Hades. **2 misery**, torture, agony, purgatory, torment, a nightmare.
– OPPOSITES heaven, bliss.

WORD LINKS
relating to hell: infernal

help v. **1 assist**, aid, abet, lend a hand, give assistance, come to the aid of, be of service, do someone a favour, do someone a service, do someone a good turn, rally round, pitch in. **2 support**, contribute to, give money to, donate to, promote, boost, back. **3 relieve**, soothe, ease, alleviate, improve, lessen. **4** *he could not help laughing*: **resist**, avoid, refrain from, keep from, stop.
– OPPOSITES hinder, impede.
• n. **1 assistance**, aid, support, succour, benefit, use, advantage, service. **2 relief**, alleviation, improvement, healing.
– OPPOSITES hindrance.

helper n. **assistant**, aide, deputy, auxiliary, supporter, second, mate, right-hand man/woman, attendant.

helpful adj. **1 obliging**, of assistance, supportive, cooperative, accommodating, neighbourly, eager to please. **2 useful**, beneficial, valuable, constructive, informative, instructive. **3 handy**, useful, convenient, practical, easy-to-use, serviceable; informal neat, nifty.
– OPPOSITES useless.

helping n. **portion**, serving, piece, slice, share, plateful; informal dollop.

helpless adj. **dependent**, incapable, powerless, paralysed,

defenceless, vulnerable, exposed, unprotected.
– OPPOSITES independent.

hence adv. **consequently**, as a consequence, for this reason, therefore, so, accordingly, as a result, that being so.

herd n. **drove**, flock, pack, fold, swarm, mass, crowd, horde.

hereditary adj. **1 inherited**, bequeathed, handed down, passed down, family, ancestral. **2 genetic**, inborn, inherited, inbred, innate, in the family, in the blood, in the genes.

heritage n. **1 tradition**, history, past, background, culture, customs. **2 ancestry**, lineage, descent, extraction, parentage, roots, heredity, birth.

hermit n. **recluse**, loner, ascetic; *historical* anchorite, anchoress; *old use* eremite.

hero n. **1 star**, superstar, megastar, idol, celebrity, favourite, darling; *informal* celeb. **2 main character**, starring role, male protagonist, (male) lead, leading man; *informal* good guy.
– OPPOSITES villain.

heroic adj. **brave**, courageous, valiant, intrepid, bold, fearless, daring; *informal* gutsy, spunky.
– OPPOSITES cowardly.

heroine n. **1 star**, superstar, megastar, idol, celebrity, favourite, darling; *informal* celeb. **2 main character**, female protagonist, lead, leading lady, prima donna, diva.

heroism n. **bravery**, courage, valour, daring, fearlessness,

pluck; *informal* guts, spunk; *Brit. informal* bottle; *N. Amer. informal* moxie.
– OPPOSITES cowardice.

hesitant adj. **1 uncertain**, undecided, unsure, doubtful, dubious, ambivalent, in two minds, wavering, vacillating, irresolute, indecisive; *Brit.* havering, humming and hawing; *informal* iffy. **2 timid**, diffident, shy, bashful, insecure, nervous.
– OPPOSITES certain, decisive, confident.

hesitate v. **1 pause**, delay, wait, stall, be uncertain, be unsure, be doubtful, be indecisive, vacillate, waver; *Brit.* haver, hum and haw; *informal* dilly-dally. **2** *don't hesitate to ask*: **be reluctant**, be unwilling, be disinclined, scruple, have misgivings about, have qualms about, think twice about.

hidden adj. **1 concealed**, secret, invisible, unseen, camouflaged. **2 obscure**, unclear, concealed, cryptic, arcane, mysterious, secret, covert, abstruse, deep.
– OPPOSITES visible, obvious.

hide v. **1 conceal**, secrete, put out of sight, cache; *informal* stash. **2 conceal yourself**, secrete yourself, take cover, lie low, go to ground; *informal* hole up. **3 obscure**, block out, blot out, obstruct, cloud, shroud, veil, eclipse, camouflage. **4 keep secret**, conceal, cover up, keep quiet about, hush up, suppress, disguise, mask; *informal* keep a/the lid on.
– OPPOSITES reveal.

hideaway n. **retreat**, refuge, hiding place, hideout, safe house, den, bolt-hole; informal hidey-hole.

hideous adj. **1 ugly**, repulsive, repellent, unsightly, revolting, grotesque. **2 horrific**, terrible, appalling, awful, dreadful, frightful, horrible, horrendous, horrifying, shocking, sickening, gruesome, ghastly.
– OPPOSITES beautiful, pleasant.

hiding n. (informal) **beating**, thrashing, whipping, drubbing; informal licking, belting, pasting, walloping.

hierarchy n. **ranking**, order, pecking order, grading, ladder, scale.

high adj. **1 tall**, lofty, towering, giant, big, multi-storey, high-rise, elevated. **2 high-ranking**, leading, top, prominent, senior, influential, powerful, important, exalted; N. Amer. ranking. **3 inflated**, excessive, unreasonable, expensive, exorbitant, extortionate, informal steep, stiff. **4 high-pitched**, shrill, piercing, squeaky, penetrating, soprano, treble, falsetto.
– OPPOSITES low, deep.
•adv. **at a great height**, high up, way up, at altitude, in the sky, aloft, overhead, to a great height.
– OPPOSITES low.

highlight n. **high point**, climax, peak, pinnacle, height, zenith, summit, focus, feature.
•v. **spotlight**, call attention to, focus on, underline, show up,

bring out, accentuate, accent, stress, emphasize.
– OPPOSITES play down.

hijack v. **commandeer**, seize, take over, appropriate, expropriate.

hike n. **1 walk**, trek, tramp, trudge, slog, march, ramble. **2 increase**, rise.
•v. **1 walk**, trek, tramp, trudge, slog, march, ramble, backpack. **2 increase**, raise, up, put up, push up; informal jack up, bump up.

hilarious adj. **very funny**, hysterical, uproarious, rib-tickling; informal side-splitting, priceless, a scream, a hoot.

hill n. **high ground**, hillock, hillside, rise, mound, knoll, hummock, fell, mountain; Scottish brae.

hinder v. **hamper**, impede, inhibit, thwart, foil, delay, interfere with, slow down, hold back, hold up, restrict, handicap, hamstring.
– OPPOSITES facilitate.

hindrance n. **impediment**, obstacle, barrier, obstruction, handicap, hurdle, restraint, restriction, encumbrance, complication, delay, drawback, setback, difficulty, inconvenience, hitch, stumbling block, fly in the ointment, hiccup; Brit. spanner in the works.
– OPPOSITES aid, help.

hint n. **1 clue**, inkling, suggestion, indication, sign, signal, intimation. **2 tip**, suggestion,

pointer, guideline, recommendation. **3 trace**, touch, suspicion, suggestion, dash, soupçon; informal smidgen, tad.
•v. **imply**, insinuate, intimate, suggest, refer to, drive at, mean; informal get at.

hire v. **1 rent**, lease, charter.
2 employ, engage, recruit, appoint, take on, sign up.
– OPPOSITES dismiss.

hiss v. **1 fizz**, whistle, wheeze.
2 jeer, catcall, whistle, hoot.
– OPPOSITES cheer.
•n. **1 fizz**, whistle, wheeze.
2 jeer, catcall, whistle, abuse, derision.
– OPPOSITES cheer.

historic adj. **significant**, notable, important, momentous, memorable, groundbreaking; informal earth-shattering.

historical adj. **1 documented**, recorded, chronicled, authentic, factual, actual. **2 past**, bygone, ancient, old, former.

history n. **1 the past**, former times, the olden days, yesterday, antiquity. **2 chronicle**, archive, record, report, narrative, account, study. **3 background**, past, life story, experiences, record.

hit v. **1 strike**, smack, slap, beat, punch, thump, thrash, batter, club, pummel, cuff, swat; informal whack, wallop, bash, clout, belt, clobber; Brit. informal slosh, slug, sock one on; N. Amer. informal slug; Austral./NZ informal quilt. **2 crash into**, run into, smash into, knock into, bump into, plough into,

collide with, meet head-on.
3 devastate, affect badly, upset, shatter, crush, traumatize; informal knock sideways; Brit. informal knock for six.
•n. **1 blow**, slap, smack, thump, punch, knock, bang; informal whack, wallop, bash, clout, belt; N. Amer. informal slug. **2 success**, sell-out, winner, triumph, sensation, best-seller; informal smash hit, chart-topper, crowd-puller.
– OPPOSITES failure.
□ **hit back** retaliate, respond, reply, react, counter. **hit it off** (informal) get on (well), get along, be compatible, be on the same wavelength, see eye to eye, take to each other; informal click. **hit on** discover, come up with, think of, conceive of, dream up, invent, devise.

hitch v. **1 pull**, lift, raise; informal yank. **2 harness**, yoke, couple, fasten, connect, attach.
•n. **problem**, difficulty, snag, setback, obstacle, complication; informal glitch, hiccup.

hoard n. **cache**, stockpile, store, collection, supply, reserve; informal stash.
•v. **stockpile**, store up, put aside, put by, lay by, set aside, cache, save, squirrel away; informal salt away.
– OPPOSITES squander.

hoarse adj. **rough**, harsh, croaky, throaty, gruff, husky, grating, rasping.

hoax n. **practical joke**, prank, trick, deception, fraud; informal con, spoof, wind-up, scam.

hobble v. limp, shamble, totter, dodder, stagger, stumble.

hobby n. pastime, leisure activity, sideline, diversion, relaxation, recreation, amusement.

hoist v. raise, lift, haul up, heave up, winch up, pull up, elevate.
• n. **crane**, winch, pulley, windlass.

hold v. 1 clasp, clutch, grasp, grip, clench, cling to, hold on to, embrace, hug, squeeze. 2 detain, imprison, lock up, keep behind bars, confine, intern, incarcerate. 3 take, contain, accommodate, fit, have room for. 4 maintain, consider, take the view, believe, think, feel, deem, be of the opinion, rule, decide; informal reckon. 5 convene, call, summon, conduct, organize, run.
– OPPOSITES release.
• n. 1 grip, grasp, clasp, clutch. 2 influence, power, control, grip, dominance, authority, sway.

holder n. 1 bearer, owner, possessor, keeper. 2 container, receptacle, case, cover, housing, sheath.

hold-up n. 1 delay, setback, hitch, snag, difficulty, problem, glitch, hiccup, traffic jam, tailback; informal snarl-up. 2 robbery, raid, armed robbery, mugging; informal stick-up; N. Amer. informal heist.

hole n. 1 opening, aperture, orifice, gap, space, interstice, fissure, vent, chink, breach, crack, rupture, puncture. 2 pit, crater, depression, hollow,

cavern, cave, chamber. 3 burrow, lair, den, earth, sett.

holiday n. vacation, break, rest, recess, time off, leave, day off, festival, feast day.

hollow adj. 1 empty, hollowed out, void. 2 sunken, deep-set, concave, depressed, recessed. 3 worthless, meaningless, empty, profitless, fruitless, pointless, pyrrhic. 4 insincere, false, deceitful, hypocritical, sham, untrue.
– OPPOSITES solid, convex.
• n. 1 hole, pit, cavity, crater, trough, depression, indentation, dip. 2 valley, vale, dale, dell.
• v. gouge, scoop, dig, cut, excavate, channel.

holy adj. 1 saintly, godly, pious, religious, devout, God-fearing, spiritual. 2 sacred, consecrated, hallowed, sanctified, venerated, revered.
– OPPOSITES sinful, irreligious.

homage n. respect, honour, reverence, worship, admiration, esteem, adulation, tribute.
– OPPOSITES contempt.

home n. 1 residence, house, accommodation, property, quarters, lodgings, address, place; informal pad; formal abode, dwelling. 2 homeland, native land, home town, birthplace, roots, fatherland, mother country, motherland. 3 institution, hospice, shelter, refuge, retreat, asylum, hostel.
• adj. **domestic**, internal, local, national.
– OPPOSITES foreign, international.

homeless adj. of no fixed abode, without a roof over your head, on the streets, vagrant, sleeping rough, destitute.

homely adj. 1 (Brit.) cosy, comfortable, snug, welcoming, friendly; informal comfy. 2 (N. Amer.) unattractive, plain, unprepossessing, ugly; Brit. informal no oil painting.

homicide n. murder, manslaughter, killing, slaughter, butchery, assassination.

honest adj. 1 an honest man: upright, honourable, principled, virtuous, good, decent, law-abiding, trustworthy, scrupulous, ethical, upstanding, right-minded. 2 I haven't been honest with you: truthful, sincere, candid, frank, open, forthright, straight; informal upfront.
– OPPOSITES dishonest.

honestly adv. 1 fairly, lawfully, legally, legitimately, honourably, decently, ethically; informal on the level. 2 sincerely, genuinely, truthfully, truly, wholeheartedly, to be honest, to be frank, in all honesty, in all sincerity.

honesty n. 1 integrity, uprightness, honour, righteousness, virtue, goodness, probity, trustworthiness. 2 sincerity, candour, frankness, directness, truthfulness, truth, openness, straightforwardness.
– OPPOSITES dishonesty, insincerity.

honorary adj. 1 titular, nominal, in name only, unofficial, token.

2 (Brit.) unpaid, unsalaried, voluntary, volunteer.

honour n. 1 integrity, honesty, uprightness, morality, probity, principles, high-mindedness, decency, scrupulousness, fairness, justness. 2 distinction, privilege, glory, kudos, cachet, prestige. 3 reputation, good name, character, repute, image, standing, status. 4 privilege, pleasure, compliment.
– OPPOSITES shame.
▸v. 1 respect, esteem, admire, look up to, value, cherish, revere, venerate. 2 applaud, acclaim, praise, salute, recognize, celebrate, pay tribute to. 3 fulfil, observe, keep, obey, heed, follow, carry out, keep to, abide by, adhere to, comply with, conform to, be true to.
– OPPOSITES disobey, break.

honourable adj. 1 honest, moral, principled, righteous, decent, respectable, virtuous, good, upstanding, upright, noble, fair, trustworthy, law-abiding. 2 illustrious, distinguished, eminent, great, glorious, prestigious.
– OPPOSITES dishonourable.

hook n. 1 peg, nail. 2 fastener, clasp, hasp, clip.
▸v. 1 attach, hitch, fasten, fix, secure, catch, clasp. 2 catch, land, net, take, bag.

hooked adj. curved, hook-shaped, aquiline, angular, bent. □ hooked on (informal) addicted to, dependent on, obsessed with, fanatical about, enthusiastic about; informal mad about.

hooligan n. **lout**, thug, tearaway, vandal, delinquent, ruffian, troublemaker; Austral. larrikin; informal tough, bruiser; Brit. informal yob, yobbo, lager lout; Scottish informal ned.

hoop n. **ring**, band, circle, wheel, circlet, loop.

hop v. & n. **jump**, bound, spring, bounce, skip, leap, prance, caper.

hope n. **1 aspiration**, desire, wish, expectation, ambition, aim, plan, dream. **2 optimism**, expectation, confidence, faith, belief.
– OPPOSITES pessimism.
•v. **1 expect**, anticipate, look for, be hopeful of, dream of. **2 aim**, intend, be looking, have the intention, have in mind, plan.

hopeful adj. **1 optimistic**, full of hope, confident, sanguine, positive, buoyant, bullish, upbeat. **2 promising**, encouraging, heartening, reassuring, favourable, optimistic.
– OPPOSITES pessimistic, discouraging.

hopefully adv. **1 optimistically**, full of hope, confidently, buoyantly, expectantly. **2 all being well**, if all goes well, God willing, with luck, touch wood, fingers crossed.

hopeless adj. **1 forlorn**, beyond hope, lost, irreparable, irreversible, incurable, impossible,

futile. **2 bad**, poor, awful, terrible, dreadful, appalling, atrocious, incompetent; informal pathetic, useless, lousy, rotten; Brit. informal rubbish.
– OPPOSITES competent.

hopelessly adv. **utterly**, completely, irretrievably, impossibly, extremely, totally.

horde n. **crowd**, mob, pack, gang, troop, army, swarm, mass, throng.

horizontal adj. **level**, flat, parallel.
– OPPOSITES vertical.

horrible adj. **1 dreadful**, awful, terrible, shocking, appalling, horrifying, horrific, horrendous, grisly, ghastly, gruesome, harrowing, unspeakable, abhorrent. **2** (informal) **nasty**, horrid, disagreeable, obnoxious, disgusting, hateful, odious, objectionable, insufferable.
– OPPOSITES pleasant.

horrific adj. **dreadful**, horrendous, horrible, terrible, atrocious, horrifying, shocking, appalling, harrowing, hideous, grisly, ghastly, sickening.

horrify v. **shock**, appal, outrage, scandalize, offend, disgust, revolt, nauseate, sicken.

horror n. **1 terror**, fear, fright, alarm, panic. **2 dismay**, consternation, alarm, distress, disgust, shock.
– OPPOSITES delight, satisfaction.

horse n. **mount**, charger, cob, nag, hack, colt, stallion, mare,

filly; N. Amer. bronco; Austral./NZ
moke; informal gee-gee.

> **WORD LINKS**
> *relating to horses:* equine;
> *relating to horse riding:*
> equestrian

hospitable adj. **welcoming**,
friendly, sociable, cordial, gracious, accommodating, warm.

hospital n. **infirmary**, clinic,
sanatorium, hospice; Brit.
cottage hospital; Military field
hospital.

hospitality n. **friendliness**,
neighbourliness, sociability,
welcome, warmth, kindness,
cordiality, generosity.

host n. **presenter**, compère,
anchor, anchorman, anchor-
woman, announcer.
– OPPOSITES guest.
• v. **present**, introduce, compère, front, anchor.

hostage n. **captive**, prisoner,
detainee, internee.

hostile adj. **1 unfriendly**, unkind,
unsympathetic, antagonistic,
aggressive, confrontational,
belligerent. **2 unfavourable**,
adverse, bad, harsh, grim, inhospitable, forbidding. **3** they
are hostile to the idea: **opposed**,
averse, antagonistic, ill-
disposed, unsympathetic, antipathetic, against; informal anti.
– OPPOSITES friendly, favourable.

hostility n. **1 antagonism**, unfriendliness, malevolence,
venom, hatred, aggression, bel-
ligerence. **2 opposition**, antagonism, animosity, antipathy.

3 *a cessation of hostilities:*
fighting, armed conflict, combat, warfare, war, bloodshed,
violence.

hot adj. **1** hot food: **heated**,
sizzling, roasting, boiling,
scorching, scalding, red-hot. **2** a
hot day: **very warm**, balmy,
summery, tropical, scorching,
searing, blistering, sweltering,
torrid, sultry; informal boiling,
baking, roasting. **3 spicy**, peppery, fiery, strong, piquant,
powerful. **4 fierce**, intense,
keen, competitive, cut-throat,
ruthless, aggressive, violent.
5 (informal) she's hot on local
history: **knowledgeable**, well
informed, au fait, well up, well
versed; informal clued up.
– OPPOSITES cold, mild.

hotly adv. **vehemently**, vigorously, strenuously, fiercely,
heatedly.

hound v. **pursue**, chase, stalk,
harry, harass, pester, badger,
torment.

house n. **1 residence**, home;
informal pad; Brit. informal gaff; formal
dwelling, abode, habitation,
domicile. **2 family**, clan, tribe,
dynasty, line, bloodline, lineage.
3 firm, business, company, corporation, enterprise, establishment, institution, concern,
organization, operation; informal
outfit. **4 assembly**, legislative
body, chamber, council, parliament, congress, senate.
• v. **1 accommodate**, give someone a roof over their head, lodge,
quarter, board, billet, take in,

sleep, put up. **2 contain**, hold, store, cover, protect, enclose.

household n. **family**, house, occupants, clan, tribe; informal brood.
•adj. **domestic**, family, everyday, workaday.

housing n. **1 accommodation**, houses, homes, living quarters; formal dwellings. **2 casing**, covering, case, cover, holder, fairing, sleeve.

hovel n. **shack**, slum, shanty, hut; informal dump, hole.

hover v. **1 hang**, be poised, be suspended, float, fly, drift. **2 wait**, linger, loiter.

however adv. **nevertheless**, nonetheless, even so, but, for all that, despite that, in spite of that.

howl n. **1 baying**, cry, bark, yelp, yowl. **2 wail**, cry, yell, yelp, bellow, roar, shout, shriek, scream, screech.
•v. **1 bay**, cry, bark, yelp, yowl. **2 wail**, cry, yell, bawl, bellow, shriek, scream, screech, caterwaul, ululate; informal holler.

hub n. **centre**, core, heart, focus, focal point, nucleus, kernel, nerve centre.
– OPPOSITES periphery.

huddle v. **1 crowd**, cluster, gather, bunch, throng, flock, collect, group, congregate. **2 curl up**, snuggle, nestle, hunch up.
– OPPOSITES disperse.
•n. **group**, cluster, bunch, collection; informal gaggle.

hue n. **colour**, shade, tone, tint, tinge.

hug v. **embrace**, cuddle, squeeze, clasp, clutch, hold tight.
•n. **embrace**, cuddle, squeeze, bear hug.

huge adj. **enormous**, vast, immense, massive, colossal, prodigious, gigantic, gargantuan, mammoth, monumental, giant, towering, mountainous; informal mega, monster, astronomical; Brit. informal ginormous.
– OPPOSITES tiny.

hull n. **framework**, body, shell, frame, skeleton, structure.

hum v. **1 purr**, drone, murmur, buzz, whirr, throb. **2 be busy**, be active, be lively, buzz, bustle, be a hive of activity, throb.
•n. **murmur**, drone, purr, buzz.

human adj. **1 mortal**, flesh and blood, fallible, weak, frail, imperfect, vulnerable, physical, bodily, fleshly. **2 compassionate**, humane, kind, considerate, understanding, sympathetic.
•n. **person**, human being, Homo sapiens, man, woman, individual, mortal, (living) soul, earthling; (**humans**) the human race, humanity, humankind, mankind, people.

> WORD LINKS
> study of humankind:
> anthropology

humane adj. **compassionate**, kind, considerate, understanding, sympathetic, tolerant,

forbearing, forgiving, merciful, humanitarian, charitable.
- OPPOSITES cruel.

humanitarian adj. **1 compassionate**, humane, unselfish, altruistic, generous. **2 charitable**, philanthropic, public-spirited, socially concerned.
•n. **philanthropist**, altruist, benefactor, social reformer, good Samaritan, do-gooder.

humanity n. **1 humankind**, mankind, man, people, the human race, Homo sapiens. **2 compassion**, brotherly love, fellow feeling, humaneness, kindness, consideration, understanding, sympathy, tolerance.

humble adj. **1 meek**, deferential, respectful, submissive, self-effacing, unassertive, modest, unassuming, self-deprecating. **2 lowly**, poor, undistinguished, mean, common, ordinary, simple, modest.
- OPPOSITES proud, arrogant.
•v. **humiliate**, demean, lower, degrade, debase, mortify, shame.

humdrum adj. **mundane**, dull, dreary, boring, tedious, monotonous, prosaic, routine, ordinary, everyday, run-of-the-mill, workaday, pedestrian.

humid adj. **muggy**, close, sultry, sticky, steamy, clammy, heavy.
- OPPOSITES dry, fresh.

humiliate v. **embarrass**, mortify, humble, shame, disgrace, chasten, deflate, crush, squash, demean, take down a peg or two; informal show up, put down,

cut down to size; N. Amer. informal make someone eat crow.
- OPPOSITES dignify.

humiliating adj. **embarrassing**, mortifying, humbling, ignominious, inglorious, shaming, undignified, chastening, demeaning, degrading, deflating.

humiliation n. **embarrassment**, mortification, shame, indignity, ignominy, disgrace, dishonour, degradation, discredit, loss of face, blow to your pride.

humility n. **modesty**, humbleness, meekness, respect, deference, diffidence.
- OPPOSITES pride.

humorous adj. **amusing**, funny, comic, comical, entertaining, diverting, witty, jocular, light-hearted, hilarious.
- OPPOSITES serious.

humour n. **1 comedy**, funny side, hilarity, absurdity, ludicrousness, satire, irony. **2 jokes**, jests, quips, witticisms, funny remarks, wit, comedy; informal gags, wisecracks. **3 mood**, temper, disposition, spirits.
- OPPOSITES seriousness.
•v. **indulge**, accommodate, pander to, cater to, give in to, go along with, flatter, mollify, placate.

hunch n. **feeling**, guess, suspicion, impression, inkling, idea, notion, fancy, intuition; informal gut feeling.

hunger n. **1 lack of food**, starvation, malnutrition, undernourishment. **2 desire**, craving,

longing, yearning, hankering, appetite, thirst; informal itch.
□ **hunger after/for** desire, crave, long for, yearn for, pine for, ache for, hanker after, thirst for, lust for; informal itch for, be dying for, be gagging for.

hungry adj. **1 ravenous**, famished, starving, starved, malnourished, undernourished, underfed; informal peckish. **2** *they are hungry for success*: **eager**, keen, avid, longing, yearning, aching, greedy, craving, desirous of, hankering after; informal itching, dying, gagging.
– OPPOSITES full.

hunk n. **chunk**, wedge, block, slab, lump, square, gobbet; Brit. informal wodge.

hunt v. **1 chase**, stalk, pursue, course, track, trail. **2 search**, seek, look high and low, scour the area.
•n. **1 chase**, pursuit. **2 search**, quest.

hurdle n. **obstacle**, difficulty, problem, barrier, bar, snag, stumbling block, impediment, obstruction, complication, hindrance.

hurl v. **throw**, toss, fling, launch, pitch, cast, lob; informal chuck, sling, bung.

hurricane n. **cyclone**, typhoon, tornado, storm, windstorm, whirlwind, gale, tempest; Austral. willy-willy; N. Amer. informal twister.

hurried adj. **1 quick**, fast, swift, rapid, speedy, brisk, cursory, perfunctory, brief, short,

fleeting. **2 hasty**, rushed, precipitate, spur-of-the-moment.
– OPPOSITES slow.

hurry v. **1 be quick**, hurry up, hasten, speed up, run, dash, rush, race, scurry, scramble, scuttle, sprint; informal get a move on, step on it, get a wiggle on, hightail it, hotfoot it; Brit. informal get your skates on. **2 hustle**, hasten, push, urge.
– OPPOSITES dawdle, delay.
•n. **rush**, haste, speed, urgency, hustle and bustle.

hurt v. **1 be painful**, ache, be sore, be tender, smart, sting, burn, throb; informal be agony. **2 injure**, wound, damage, disable, bruise, cut, gash, graze, scrape, scratch. **3 distress**, pain, wound, sting, upset, sadden, devastate, grieve, mortify.
•n. **distress**, pain, suffering, grief, misery, anguish, upset, sadness, sorrow.
•adj. **1 injured**, wounded, bruised, grazed, cut, gashed, sore, painful, aching. **2 pained**, aggrieved, offended, distressed, upset, sad, mortified; informal miffed.

hurtful adj. **upsetting**, distressing, wounding, unkind, cruel, nasty, mean, malicious, spiteful.

hush v. **silence**, quieten (down), shush, gag, muzzle; informal shut up.
•n. **silence**, quiet, stillness, peace, calm, tranquillity.
– OPPOSITES noise.
□ **hush up** keep secret, conceal, hide, suppress, cover up, keep

quiet about, sweep under the carpet.

hut n. **shack**, shanty, cabin, shelter, shed, lean-to, hovel; Scottish bothy; N. Amer. cabana.

hybrid n. **cross**, cross-breed, mixture, blend, combination, composite, fusion, amalgam. • adj. **composite**, cross-bred, interbred, mixed, blended, compound.

hygiene n. **cleanliness**, sanitation, sterility, purity, disinfection.

hygienic adj. **sanitary**, clean, germ-free, disinfected, sterilized, sterile, antiseptic, aseptic. – OPPOSITES insanitary.

hypocritical adj. **sanctimonious**, pious, self-righteous, holier-than-thou, superior, insincere, two-faced.

hysteria n. **frenzy**, feverishness, hysterics, agitation, mania, panic, alarm, distress. – OPPOSITES calm.

hysterical adj. **1 overwrought**, overemotional, out of control, frenzied, frantic, wild, beside yourself, manic, delirious; informal in a state. **2** (informal) **very funny**, hilarious, uproarious, ribtickling; informal side-splitting, priceless, a scream, a hoot. – OPPOSITES calm.

h
i

I

ice n. **1 icicles**, black ice, frost, permafrost, hoar (frost); literary rime. **2 ice cream**, water ice, sorbet; N. Amer. sherbet. **3 coldness**, coolness, frostiness, iciness, hostility, unfriendliness.

WORD LINKS
relating to ice: glacial

icy adj. **1 iced (over)**, frozen, frosty, slippery, treacherous; literary rimy. **2 freezing**, chill, biting, bitter, raw, arctic. **3 unfriendly**, hostile, forbidding, cold, chilly, frosty, stern.

idea n. **1 concept**, notion, conception, thought. **2 plan**, scheme, design, proposal, proposition, suggestion, aim, intention, objective, goal. **3 thought**, theory, view, opinion, feeling, belief. **4 sense**, feeling, suspicion, fancy, inkling, hunch, notion. **5 estimate**, approximation, guess, conjecture; informal guesstimate.

ideal adj. **perfect**, faultless, exemplary, classic, archetypal, quintessential, model, ultimate, utopian, fairy-tale. • n. **1** an ideal to aim at: **model**, pattern, archetype, exemplar, example, perfection, epitome, last word. **2** liberal ideals: **principle**, standard, value, belief, conviction, ethos.

idealistic adj. **Utopian**, visionary, romantic, quixotic, unrealistic, impractical.

identical adj. **(exactly) the same**, indistinguishable, twin, duplicate, interchangeable, alike, matching.
– OPPOSITES different.

identification n. **1 recognition**, singling out, pinpointing, naming. **2 determination**, establishing, ascertainment, discovery, diagnosis. **3 ID**, papers, documents, credentials, card, pass, badge.

identify v. **1 recognize**, pick out, spot, point out, pinpoint, put your finger on, name. **2 determine**, establish, ascertain, make out, discern, distinguish. **3** *we identify sport with glamour*: **associate**, link, connect, relate. **4** *he identified with the team captain*: **empathize**, sympathize, understand, relate to, feel for.

identity n. **individuality**, self, personality, character, originality, distinctiveness, uniqueness.

ideology n. **belief**; doctrine, creed, theory.

idiomatic adj. **colloquial**, everyday, conversational, vernacular, natural.

idiosyncrasy n. **peculiarity**, oddity, eccentricity, mannerism, quirk, characteristic.

idiot n. **fool**, ass, halfwit, blockhead, dunce, simpleton; informal nincompoop, clod, dimwit, dummy, fathead, numbskull; Brit. informal nitwit, twit, clot, berk,

prat, pillock, wally, dork, twerp, charlie, moron; N. Amer. informal schmuck; Austral./NZ informal drongo.
– OPPOSITES genius.

idle adj. **1 lazy**, indolent, slothful, shiftless, work-shy. **2 unemployed**, jobless, out of work, redundant, unoccupied; Brit. informal on the dole. **3 unoccupied**, spare, empty, unfilled. **4 frivolous**, trivial, trifling, minor, insignificant, unimportant, empty, meaningless, vain.
– OPPOSITES industrious, busy.

idol n. **1 icon**, effigy, statue, figurine, totem. **2 hero**, heroine, star, superstar, icon, celebrity, darling; informal pin-up, heartthrob.

idolize v. **hero-worship**, worship, revere, venerate, look up to, exalt; informal put on a pedestal.

if conj. **provided**, providing, on condition that, presuming, supposing, assuming, as long as, in the event that.

ignite v. **1 catch fire**, burst into flames, explode. **2 light**, set fire to, set alight, kindle.
– OPPOSITES extinguish.

ignorance n. **1 lack of knowledge**, lack of education, unenlightenment. **2 unfamiliarity**, incomprehension, inexperience, innocence.
– OPPOSITES education, knowledge.

ignorant adj. **1 uneducated**, unschooled, illiterate, uninformed,

unenlightened, inexperienced, unsophisticated. **2 unaware**, unconscious, unfamiliar, unacquainted, uninformed; informal in the dark.
- OPPOSITES educated, knowledgeable.

ignore v. **1 snub**, look right through, cold-shoulder, take no notice of, pay no attention to, cut (dead); informal blank. **2 disregard**, take no account of, fail to observe, disobey, defy, overlook, brush aside, turn a blind eye to.
- OPPOSITES acknowledge, obey.

ill adj. **1 unwell**, sick, poorly, peaky, indisposed, nauseous, queasy; informal rough, under the weather; Brit. informal grotty; Austral./NZ informal crook. **2 ill effects**: **harmful**, damaging, detrimental, deleterious, adverse, injurious, destructive, dangerous.
- OPPOSITES well, beneficial.
•n. **problem**, trouble, difficulty, misfortune, trial, tribulation; informal headache, hassle.
•adv. **1 barely**, scarcely, hardly, only just. **2 inadequately**, insufficiently, poorly, badly.

illegal adj. **unlawful**, illicit, illegitimate, criminal, fraudulent, corrupt, dishonest, outlawed, banned, forbidden, prohibited, proscribed, unlicensed, unauthorized; informal crooked, shady; Brit. informal bent, dodgy.
- OPPOSITES legal.

illegible adj. **unreadable**, indecipherable, unintelligible.

illegitimate adj. **illegal**, unlawful, illicit, criminal, felonious, fraudulent, corrupt, dishonest; informal crooked, shady; Brit. informal bent, dodgy.
- OPPOSITES legal, legitimate.

illicit adj. **illegal**, unlawful, criminal, outlawed, banned, forbidden, prohibited, proscribed, unlicensed, unauthorized, improper, disapproved of.
- OPPOSITES legal.

illness n. **sickness**, poor health, disease, ailment, disorder, complaint, indisposition, malady, affliction, infection; informal bug, virus.
- OPPOSITES health.

illogical adj. **irrational**, unreasonable, erroneous, invalid, spurious, fallacious, specious.

illuminating adj. **informative**, enlightening, revealing, explanatory, instructive, helpful, educational.
- OPPOSITES confusing.

illumination n. **light**, lighting, radiance, gleam, glow, glare.

illusion n. **1 delusion**, misapprehension, misconception, false impression, mistaken impression, fantasy, dream, fancy. **2 appearance**, impression, semblance. **3 mirage**, hallucination, apparition, figment of the imagination, trick of the light.

illusory adj. **false**, imagined, imaginary, fanciful, unreal, sham, fallacious.
- OPPOSITES real.

illustrate v. **1 decorate**, ornament, accompany, support.

i

2 explain, elucidate, clarify, demonstrate, show, point up; informal get across/over.

illustration n. **1 picture**, drawing, sketch, figure, plate, image, print. **2 example**, sample, case, instance, exemplification, demonstration.

image n. **1 likeness**, depiction, portrayal, representation, painting, picture, portrait, drawing, photograph. **2 conception**, impression, perception, notion, idea. **3 persona**, profile, face.

> **WORD LINKS**
> *study of images:* iconography

imaginary adj. **unreal**, nonexistent, fictional, pretend, make-believe, invented, made-up, illusory.
– OPPOSITES real.

imagination n. **1 mind's eye**, fancy. **2 creativity**, vision, inventiveness, resourcefulness, ingenuity, originality.

imaginative adj. **creative**, visionary, inventive, resourceful, ingenious, original, innovative.

imagine v. **1 visualize**, envisage, picture, see in your mind's eye, dream up, think up/of, conceive. **2 assume**, presume, expect, take it (as read), suppose.

imbue v. **permeate**, saturate, suffuse, inject, inculcate, fill.

imitate v. **1 copy**, emulate, follow, echo, ape, parrot; informal rip off. **2 mimic**, do an impression of, impersonate, parody, caricature; informal take off, send up.

imitation n. **1 copy**, simulation, reproduction, replica, forgery. **2 emulation**, copying. **3 impersonation**, impression, parody, caricature; informal take-off, send-up, spoof.
• adj. **artificial**, synthetic, mock, fake, simulated, man-made, manufactured, substitute, ersatz.
– OPPOSITES real.

immaculate adj. **1 clean**, spotless, shining, shiny, gleaming, perfect, pristine, mint, flawless, faultless, unblemished; informal tip-top, A1. **2** *his immaculate record:* **impeccable**, unsullied, spotless, unblemished, untarnished; informal squeaky clean.
– OPPOSITES dirty, damaged.

immature adj. **childish**, babyish, infantile, juvenile, puerile, callow.

immediate adj. **1 instant**, instantaneous, prompt, swift, speedy, rapid, quick. **2 current**, present, urgent, pressing. **3 nearest**, close, next-door, adjacent, adjoining.
– OPPOSITES delayed.

immediately adv. **1 straight away**, at once, right away, instantly, (right) now, directly, forthwith, there and then; informal pronto. **2 directly**, right, exactly, precisely, squarely, just, dead; informal slap bang; N. Amer. informal smack dab.
– OPPOSITES later.

immense adj. **huge**, massive, vast, enormous, gigantic, colossal, monumental, towering,

giant, mammoth; informal monster, whopping (great); Brit. informal ginormous.
– OPPOSITES tiny.

immerse v. **1 dip**, submerge, dunk, duck, sink. **2 absorb**, engross, occupy, engage, involve, bury, preoccupy; informal lose.

immigrant n. **newcomer**, settler, incomer, migrant, non-native, foreigner, alien, expatriate.
– OPPOSITES native.

imminent adj. **near**, close (at hand), impending, approaching, coming, forthcoming, on the way, expected, looming.
– OPPOSITES distant.

immobile adj. **motionless**, still, stock-still, static, stationary, rooted to the spot, rigid, frozen, transfixed.

immodest adj. **indecorous**, improper, indecent, indelicate, immoral, forward, bold, brazen, shameless.

immoral adj. **wicked**, bad, wrong, unethical, unprincipled, unscrupulous, dishonest, corrupt, sinful, impure.
– OPPOSITES moral, ethical.

immortal adj. **1 undying**, deathless, eternal, everlasting, imperishable, indestructible. **2 timeless**, perennial, classic, time-honoured, enduring, evergreen.
– OPPOSITES mortal, ephemeral.

immovable adj. **1 fixed**, secure, set firm, set fast, stuck, jammed, stiff. **2 motionless**, unmoving, stationary, still, stock-still,
rooted to the spot, transfixed, paralysed, frozen.
– OPPOSITES mobile.

immune adj. **resistant**, not subject, not liable, not vulnerable, protected from, safe from, secure against.
– OPPOSITES susceptible, liable.

immunity n. **1 resistance**, protection, defence. **2 exemption**, exception, freedom, indemnity, privilege, prerogative, licence, impunity, protection .
– OPPOSITES susceptibility, liability.

immunize v. **vaccinate**, inoculate, inject.

impact n. **1 collision**, crash, smash, bump, knock. **2 effect**, influence, consequences, repercussions, ramifications.
•v. **1 crash into**, smash into, collide with, hit, strike, smack into, bang into. **2** *interest rates impacted on spending:* **affect**, influence, hit, have an effect, make an impression.

impair v. **weaken**, damage, harm, undermine, diminish, reduce, lessen, decrease.
– OPPOSITES improve, enhance.

impart v. **communicate**, pass on, convey, transmit, relay, relate, tell, make known, report, announce.

impartial adj. **unbiased**, unprejudiced, neutral, non-partisan, disinterested, detached, dispassionate, objective.
– OPPOSITES biased, partisan.

impasse n. **deadlock**, dead end, stalemate, stand-off, standstill.

impatient adj. **1 restless**, agitated, nervous, anxious. **2 anxious**, eager, keen; informal itching, dying. **3 irritated**, annoyed, angry, tetchy, snappy, cross, curt, brusque.
– OPPOSITES patient.

impeccable adj. **flawless**, faultless, unblemished, spotless, stainless, perfect, exemplary, irreproachable; informal squeaky clean.
– OPPOSITES imperfect.

impede v. **hinder**, obstruct, hamper, hold back/up, delay, interfere with, disrupt, retard, slow (down).
– OPPOSITES facilitate.

impediment n. **1 hindrance**, obstruction, obstacle, barrier, bar, block, check, curb, restriction. **2 defect**, impairment, stammer, stutter, lisp.

impending adj. **imminent**, close (at hand), near, approaching, coming, brewing, looming, threatening.

impenetrable adj. **1 unbreakable**, indestructible, solid, thick, unyielding. **2 impassable**, dense, thick, overgrown. **3 incomprehensible**, unfathomable, unintelligible, baffling, bewildering, confusing, opaque.

imperative adj. **vital**, crucial, critical, essential, pressing, urgent.

imperceptible adj. **unnoticeable**, undetectable, indiscernible, invisible, inaudible, impalpable, slight, small, subtle, faint.

imperfect adj. **faulty**, flawed, defective, inferior, second-rate, shoddy, substandard, damaged, blemished, torn, broken, cracked, scratched; Brit. informal duff.

imperious adj. **peremptory**, high-handed, overbearing, domineering, authoritarian, dictatorial, authoritative, bossy, arrogant; informal pushy, high and mighty.

impersonal adj. **aloof**, distant, remote, detached, unemotional, unsentimental, cold, cool, indifferent, unconcerned, formal, stiff, businesslike, matter-of-fact; informal starchy, standoffish.

impersonate v. **imitate**, mimic, do an impression of, ape, parody, caricature, satirize, lampoon, masquerade as, pose as, pass yourself off as; informal take off, send up.

impertinent adj. **rude**, insolent, impolite, ill-mannered, disrespectful, impudent, cheeky, presumptuous, forward.
– OPPOSITES polite, respectful.

impetuous adj. **impulsive**, rash, hasty, reckless, foolhardy, imprudent, ill-considered, spontaneous, impromptu, spur-of-the-moment.

impetus n. **1 momentum**, drive, thrust, energy, force, power, push. **2 motivation**, stimulus, incentive, inspiration, driving force.

implant v. **1 insert**, embed, bury, inject, transplant, graft.

2 instil, inculcate, introduce, plant, sow.

implausible adj. unlikely, improbable, questionable, doubtful, debatable, unconvincing, far-fetched.
– OPPOSITES convincing.

implement n. **1 tool**, utensil, instrument, device, apparatus, gadget, contraption, appliance; informal gizmo.
•v. **execute**, apply, put into effect, put into practice, carry out/through, perform, enact, fulfil.
– OPPOSITES abolish, cancel.

implicate v. incriminate, involve, connect, embroil, enmesh.

implication n. **1 suggestion**, inference, insinuation, innuendo, intimation, imputation. **2 consequence**, result, ramification, repercussion, reverberation, effect. **3 incrimination**, involvement, connection, entanglement, association.

implicit adj. **1 implied**, inferred, understood, hinted at, suggested, unspoken, unstated, tacit, taken for granted. **2 inherent**, latent, underlying, inbuilt, incorporated. **3 absolute**, complete, total, wholehearted, utter, unqualified, unconditional, unshakeable, unquestioning, firm.
– OPPOSITES explicit.

implore v. plead with, beg, entreat, appeal to, ask, request, call on, exhort, urge.

imply v. **1 insinuate**, suggest, infer, hint, intimate, give someone to understand, make out. **2 involve**, entail, mean, point to, signify, indicate, presuppose.

impolite adj. rude, bad-mannered, ill-mannered, discourteous, uncivil, disrespectful, insolent, impudent, impertinent, cheeky; informal lippy.

import v. bring in, buy in, ship in.
– OPPOSITES export.
•n. **1 importance**, significance, consequence, momentousness, magnitude, substance, weight, note, gravity, seriousness. **2 meaning**, sense, essence, gist, drift, message, thrust, substance, implication.
– OPPOSITES insignificance.

importance n. **1 significance**, momentousness, moment, import, consequence, note, weight, seriousness, gravity. **2 status**, eminence, prestige, worth, influence, power, authority.
– OPPOSITES insignificance.

important adj. **1 significant**, consequential, momentous, of great import, major, valuable, necessary, crucial, vital, essential, pivotal, decisive, far-reaching, historic. **2 powerful**, influential, well connected, high-ranking, prominent, eminent, notable, distinguished, esteemed, respected, great, prestigious.
– OPPOSITES insignificant.

impose v. he imposed his ideas on everyone: **foist**, force, inflict,

press, saddle someone with. **2 levy**, charge, apply, enforce, set, establish, institute, introduce, bring into effect.
– OPPOSITES abolish.
□ **impose on** take advantage of, exploit, take liberties with, bother, trouble, disturb, inconvenience, put out, put to trouble.

imposing adj. **impressive**, spectacular, striking, dramatic, commanding, arresting, awesome, formidable, splendid, grand, majestic.
– OPPOSITES modest.

imposition n. **1 imposing**, foisting, forcing, inflicting. **2 levying**, charging, application, enforcement, enforcing, setting, establishment, introduction. **3 burden**, encumbrance, liberty, bother, worry; informal hassle.

impossible adj. **1 out of the question**, impracticable, non-viable, unworkable. **2 unattainable**, unachievable, unobtainable, hopeless, impracticable, unworkable. **3 unbearable**, intolerable, unendurable. **4** (informal) **unreasonable**, difficult, awkward, intolerable, unbearable, exasperating, maddening, infuriating.
– OPPOSITES possible.

impostor n. **impersonator**, deceiver, hoaxer, fraudster, fake, fraud; informal phoney.

impound v. **confiscate**, appropriate, take possession of, seize, commandeer, expropriate, requisition, take over.

impracticable adj. **unworkable**, unfeasible, non-viable, unachievable, unattainable, impractical.
– OPPOSITES practicable.

impractical adj. **1 unrealistic**, unworkable, unfeasible, non-viable, ill-thought-out, absurd, idealistic, fanciful, romantic, starry-eyed, pie-in-the-sky; informal cockeyed, crackpot, crazy. **2 unsuitable**, not sensible, inappropriate, unserviceable.
– OPPOSITES realistic, practical.

imprecise adj. **1 vague**, loose, indistinct, inaccurate, non-specific, sweeping, broad, general, hazy, fuzzy, woolly, nebulous, ambiguous, equivocal, uncertain. **2 inexact**, approximate, rough; N. Amer. informal ballpark.
– OPPOSITES exact.

impress v. **make an impression on**, have an impact on, influence, affect, move, stir, rouse, excite, inspire, dazzle, awe.
– OPPOSITES disappoint.
□ **impress on** emphasize to, stress to, bring home to, instil in, inculcate into, drum into.

impression n. **1 feeling**, sense, fancy, (sneaking) suspicion, inkling, intuition, hunch, notion, idea. **2 opinion**, view, image, picture, perception, reaction, judgement, verdict, estimation. **3 impact**, effect, influence. **4 indentation**, dent, mark, outline, imprint. **5 impersonation**, imitation, caricature; informal take-off.

impressionable adj. **easily influenced**, suggestible, susceptible, persuadable, pliable, malleable, pliant, ingenuous, trusting, naive, gullible.

impressive adj. **magnificent**, majestic, imposing, splendid, spectacular, grand, awe-inspiring, stunning, breathtaking.

imprint v. **stamp**, print, impress, mark, emboss.
•n. **impression**, print, mark, stamp, indentation.

imprison v. **incarcerate**, send to prison, jail, lock up, put away, intern, detain, hold prisoner, hold captive; *informal* send down; *Brit. informal* bang up.

imprisonment n. **custody**, incarceration, internment, confinement, detention, captivity; *informal* time; *Brit. informal* porridge.

improbable adj. **1 unlikely**, doubtful, dubious, debatable, questionable, uncertain. **2 unconvincing**, unbelievable, implausible, unlikely.

impromptu adj. **unrehearsed**, unprepared, unscripted, extempore, extemporized, improvised, spontaneous, unplanned; *informal* off-the-cuff.

improper adj. **1 unacceptable**, unprofessional, irregular, unethical, dishonest. **2 unseemly**, unfitting, unbecoming, unladylike, ungentlemanly, inappropriate, indelicate, indecent, immodest, indecorous, immoral. **3 indecent**, risqué, suggestive,

naughty, dirty, filthy, vulgar, crude, rude, obscene, lewd; *informal* blue, raunchy, steamy.
– OPPOSITES proper, seemly.

improve v. **1 make better**, ameliorate, upgrade, refine, enhance, boost, build on, raise. **2 get better**, advance, progress, develop, make headway, make progress, pick up, look up, move forward. **3 recover**, get better, recuperate, rally, revive, be on the mend.
– OPPOSITES worsen, deteriorate.

improvement n. **advance**, development, upgrade, refinement, enhancement, betterment, amelioration, boost, augmentation, rally, recovery, upswing.

improvise v. **1 extemporize**, ad-lib; *informal* speak off the cuff, play it by ear, busk it, wing it. **2 contrive**, devise, throw together, cobble together, rig up; *informal* whip up, rustle up; *Brit. informal* knock up.

impulse n. **1 urge**, instinct, drive, compulsion, itch, whim, desire, fancy, notion. **2 spontaneity**, impetuosity, recklessness, rashness.

impulsive adj. **1 hasty**, sudden, quick, precipitate, impetuous, impromptu, spontaneous, snap, unplanned, unpremeditated, thoughtless, rash, reckless. **2 impetuous**, instinctive, passionate, intuitive, emotional, devil-may-care.
– OPPOSITES cautious, premeditated.

inaccurate adj. **inexact**, imprecise, incorrect, wrong, erroneous, faulty, imperfect, defective, unreliable, false, mistaken, untrue; Brit. informal adrift.

inactivity n. **inaction**, inertia, idleness, non-intervention, negligence, apathy, indolence, laziness, slothfulness.
– OPPOSITES action.

inadequate adj. **1 insufficient**, deficient, poor, scant, scarce, sparse, in short supply, paltry, meagre. **2 incapable**, incompetent, ineffective, inefficient, inept, unfit; informal not up to scratch.

inadvertently adv. **accidentally**, by accident, unintentionally, by mistake, mistakenly, unwittingly.
– OPPOSITES intentionally.

inappropriate adj. **unsuitable**, unfitting, unseemly, unbecoming, improper, out of place/keeping, inapposite; informal out of order.

inaudible adj. **unclear**, indistinct, faint, muted, soft, low, muffled, whispered, muttered, murmured, mumbled.

inaugurate v. **1 initiate**, begin, start, institute, launch, get going, get under way, establish, bring in, usher in; informal kick off. **2 install**, instate, swear in, invest, ordain, crown.

incapable adj. **incompetent**, inept, inadequate, ineffective, ineffectual, unfit, unqualified; informal not up to it.
– OPPOSITES competent.

incense v. **enrage**, infuriate, anger, madden, outrage, exasperate, antagonize, provoke; informal make someone see red.
– OPPOSITES placate.

incensed adj. **enraged**, furious, infuriated, irate, raging, incandescent, fuming, seething, beside yourself, outraged; informal mad, hopping mad, wild, livid.

incentive n. **inducement**, motivation, motive, reason, stimulus, spur, impetus, encouragement, carrot; informal sweetener.
– OPPOSITES deterrent.

incident n. **1 event**, occurrence, episode, happening, affair, business, adventure, exploit, escapade. **2 disturbance**, commotion, clash, confrontation, scene, accident, fracas, contretemps; Brit. row. **3** the journey was not without incident: **excitement**, adventure, drama, crisis, danger.

incidental adj. **1 secondary**, subsidiary, minor, peripheral, background, by-the-by, unimportant, insignificant, tangential. **2 chance**, accidental, random, fluky, fortuitous, serendipitous, coincidental, unlooked-for.
– OPPOSITES essential.

incidentally adv. **1 by the way**, by the by, in passing, speaking of which; informal as it happens. **2 by chance**, by accident, accidentally, fortuitously, by a fluke, by happenstance.

incite v. **1 stir up**, whip up, encourage, stoke up, fuel, kindle, inflame, instigate, provoke, excite, trigger, spark off. **2 provoke**, encourage, urge, goad, spur on, egg on, drive, prod, prompt, induce; informal put up to.
– OPPOSITES discourage, deter.

inclination n. **tendency**, propensity, leaning, predisposition, predilection, impulse, bent, liking, taste, penchant, preference.
– OPPOSITES aversion.

incline v. **1 predispose**, lead, make, dispose, prejudice, prompt, induce. **2** *I incline to the opposite view*: **tend**, lean, swing, veer, gravitate, be drawn, prefer, favour, go for. **3 bend**, bow, nod, bob, lower, dip.
•n. **slope**, gradient, pitch, ramp, bank, ascent, rise, hill, dip, descent; N. Amer. grade.

inclined adj. **1 disposed**, minded, of a mind. **2 prone**, given, in the habit of, liable, apt.

include v. **1 incorporate**, comprise, encompass, cover, embrace, take in, number, contain. **2 allow for**, count, take into account, take into consideration. **3 add**, insert, put in, append, enter.
– OPPOSITES exclude, leave out.

inclusive adj. **all-in**, comprehensive, overall, full, all-round, umbrella, catch-all, all-encompassing.
– OPPOSITES exclusive, limited.

income n. **earnings**, salary, wages, pay, remuneration, revenue, receipts, takings, profits,

proceeds, yield, dividend; N. Amer. take.
– OPPOSITES expenditure, outgoings.

incoming adj. **1 arriving**, approaching, inbound, inward, returning, homeward. **2 new**, next, future, elect, designate.
– OPPOSITES outward, outgoing.

incompatible adj. **mismatched**, unsuited, poles apart, irreconcilable, inconsistent, conflicting, opposed, opposite, contradictory, at odds, at variance.
– OPPOSITES harmonious, consistent.

incompetent adj. **inept**, unskilled, inexpert, amateurish, unprofessional, bungling, blundering, clumsy; informal useless, not up to it.

incomplete adj. **1 unfinished**, uncompleted, partial, half-finished. **2 deficient**, insufficient, partial, sketchy, fragmentary, scrappy, bitty.
– OPPOSITES completed, full.

incomprehensible adj. **unintelligible**, impenetrable, unclear, indecipherable, unfathomable, abstruse, difficult, involved; Brit. informal double Dutch.
– OPPOSITES intelligible, clear.

inconsistent adj. **1 erratic**, changeable, unpredictable, variable, unstable, fickle, unreliable, volatile; informal up and down. **2 incompatible**, conflicting, at odds, at variance, irreconcilable, out of keeping, contrary.

i

inconvenience n. **trouble**, nuisance, bother, problem, disruption, difficulty, disturbance; informal aggravation, hassle, headache, pain, pain in the neck. • v. **trouble**, bother, put out, put to any trouble, disturb, impose on.

inconvenient adj. **awkward**, difficult, inopportune, badly timed, unsuitable, inappropriate, unfortunate.

incorporate v. **1 absorb**, include, subsume, assimilate, integrate, swallow up. **2 include**, contain, embrace, build in, offer, boast. **3 blend**, mix, combine, fold in, stir in.

incorrect adj. **1 wrong**, erroneous, mistaken, untrue, false, fallacious, flawed; informal wide of the mark. **2 inappropriate**, unsuitable, unacceptable, improper, unseemly; informal out of order.
– OPPOSITES correct

increase v. **1 grow**, get bigger, get larger, enlarge, expand, swell, rise, climb, mount, intensify, strengthen, extend, spread, widen. **2 add to**, make larger, make bigger, augment, supplement, top up, build up, extend, raise, swell, inflate, intensify, heighten; informal up, bump up. • n. **growth**, rise, enlargement, expansion, extension, increment, gain, addition, augmentation, surge; informal hike.
– OPPOSITES decrease.

incredible adj. **1 unbelievable**, unconvincing, far-fetched, implausible, improbable, inconceivable, unimaginable. **2 wonderful**, marvellous, spectacular, remarkable, phenomenal, prodigious, breathtaking; informal fantastic, terrific.

incur v. **bring on yourself**, expose yourself to, lay yourself open to, run up, earn, sustain, experience.

indecent adj. **1 obscene**, dirty, filthy, rude, naughty, vulgar, smutty, pornographic; informal blue; euphemistic adult. **2 unseemly**, improper, unbecoming, inappropriate.

independence n. **1 self-government**, self-rule, home rule, self-determination, sovereignty, autonomy. **2 impartiality**, neutrality, disinterestedness, detachment, objectivity.

independent adj. **1 self-governing**, self-ruling, self-determining, sovereign, autonomous, non-aligned, free. **2 separate**, different, unconnected, unrelated, discrete. **3 private**, non-state-run, private-sector, fee-paying, privatized, deregulated, denationalized. **4 impartial**, unbiased, unprejudiced, neutral, disinterested, uninvolved, detached, dispassionate, objective, non-partisan.
– OPPOSITES related, biased.

independently adv. **alone**, on your own, separately, individually, unaccompanied, solo, unaided, unassisted, without help, by your own efforts, under your own steam, single-handedly.

index n. **list**, listing, inventory, catalogue, register, directory, database.

indicate v. **1 point to**, be a sign of, be evidence of, demonstrate, show, testify to, be symptomatic of, denote, mark, signal, reflect, signify, suggest, imply. **2 state**, declare, make known, communicate, announce, put on record. **3 specify**, designate, stipulate, show.

indication n. **sign**, signal, indicator, symptom, mark, demonstration, pointer, guide, hint, clue, omen, warning.

indicator n. **measure**, gauge, meter, barometer, guide, index, mark, sign, signal.

indictment n. **charge**, accusation, arraignment, prosecution, citation, summons; N. Amer. impeachment.

indifference n. **detachment**, lack of concern, disinterest, lack of interest, nonchalance, boredom, unresponsiveness, impassivity, coolness.
– OPPOSITES concern.

indifferent adj. **1 detached**, unconcerned, uninterested, uncaring, casual, nonchalant, offhand, unenthusiastic, unimpressed, unmoved, impassive, cool. **2 mediocre**, ordinary, average, middle-of-the-road, uninspired, undistinguished, unexceptional, pedestrian, forgettable,

amateurish; informal no great shakes, not up to much.
– OPPOSITES enthusiastic, brilliant.

indignant adj. **aggrieved**, affronted, displeased, resentful, angry, annoyed, offended, exasperated; informal peeved, irked, put out; Brit. informal narked; N. Amer. informal sore.

indirect adj. **1 incidental**, secondary, subordinate, ancillary, collateral, concomitant, contingent. **2 roundabout**, circuitous, meandering, winding, tortuous. **3 oblique**, implicit, implied.

individual adj. **1 single**, separate, discrete, independent, lone. **2 unique**, characteristic, distinctive, distinct, particular, idiosyncratic, peculiar, personal, special. **3 original**, exclusive, different, unusual, novel, unorthodox, out of the ordinary.
– OPPOSITES multiple, shared, ordinary.
• n. **person**, human being, soul, creature, character; informal type, sort, customer.

individually adv. **separately**, singly, one by one, one at a time, independently.

induce v. **1 persuade**, convince, prevail on, get, make, prompt, encourage, cajole into, talk into. **2 bring about**, cause, produce, create, give rise to, generate, engender.
– OPPOSITES dissuade.

indulge v. **1 satisfy**, gratify, fulfil, feed, yield to, give in to, go along with. **2 pamper**, spoil, overindulge, coddle, molly-

i

coddle, cosset, pander to, wait on hand and foot.

indulgence n. **1 satisfaction**, gratification, fulfilment. **2 self-gratification**, self-indulgence, overindulgence, intemperance, excess, extravagance, hedonism. **3 extravagance**, luxury, treat, non-essential, extra, frill. **4 pampering**, coddling, mollycoddling, cosseting. **5 tolerance**, forbearance, understanding, compassion, sympathy, leniency.
– OPPOSITES asceticism, intolerance.

indulgent adj. **generous**, permissive, easy-going, liberal, tolerant, forgiving, forbearing, lenient, kind, kindly, soft-hearted.
– OPPOSITES strict.

industrialist n. **manufacturer**, factory owner, captain of industry, magnate, tycoon.

industry n. **1 manufacturing**, production, construction, trade, commerce. **2 business**, trade, field, line of business, profession. **3 activity**, energy, effort, endeavour, hard work, industriousness, diligence, application.

ineffective adj. **1 unsuccessful**, unproductive, unprofitable, ineffectual, unavailing, to no avail, fruitless, futile. **2 ineffectual**, inefficient, inadequate, incompetent, incapable, unfit, inept; informal useless, hopeless.
– OPPOSITES effective.

inefficient adj. **1 ineffective**, ineffectual, incompetent, inept, disorganized. **2 uneconomical**, wasteful, unproductive, time-wasting, slow, unsystematic.

inequality n. **imbalance**, inequity, inconsistency, disparity, discrepancy, dissimilarity, difference, bias, prejudice, discrimination, unfairness.

inevitable adj. **unavoidable**, inescapable, inexorable, assured, certain, sure.
– OPPOSITES avoidable.

inevitably adv. **unavoidably**, necessarily, automatically, naturally, as a matter of course, of necessity, inescapably, certainly, surely; informal like it or not.

inexpensive adj. **cheap**, affordable, low-cost, economical, competitive, reasonable, budget, economy, bargain, cut-price, reduced.

inexperienced adj. **inexpert**, untrained, unqualified, unskilled, unseasoned, naïve, new, callow, immature; informal wet behind the ears, wide-eyed.

infamous adj. **notorious**, disreputable, scandalous.
– OPPOSITES reputable.

infancy n. **beginnings**, early days, early stages, emergence, dawn, outset, birth, inception.
– OPPOSITES end.

infant n. **baby**, newborn, young child, tiny tot, little one; Medicine neonate; Scottish & N. English bairn, wean; informal tiny, sprog.

infect v. **contaminate**, pollute, taint, foul, poison, blight.

infection n. **1 disease**, virus, illness, ailment, disorder, sickness, informal **bug. 2 contamination**, poison, bacteria, germs; Medicine sepsis.

infectious adj. **communicable**, contagious, transmittable, transmissible, transferable; informal **catching.**

inferior adj. **1 second-class**, lower-ranking, subordinate, junior, minor, lowly, humble, menial, beneath someone. **2 second-rate**, mediocre, substandard, low-grade, unsatisfactory, shoddy, poor; informal **crummy, lousy.**
– OPPOSITES superior.
• n. **subordinate**, junior, underling, minion.

infertility n. **barrenness**, sterility, childlessness.

infested adj. **overrun**, swarming, teeming, crawling, alive, plagued.

infiltrate v. **penetrate**, insinuate yourself into, worm your way into, sneak into, slip into, creep into, invade.

infiltrator n. **spy**, secret agent, plant, intruder, interloper, subversive, informer, mole, fifth columnist; N. Amer. informal **spook.**

infinite adj. **boundless**, unbounded, unlimited, limitless, never-ending, incalculable, untold, countless, uncountable, innumerable, numberless, immeasurable.
– OPPOSITES limited.

inflame v. **1 enrage**, incense, anger, madden, infuriate, exasperate, provoke, antagonize; informal **make someone see red.**

2 aggravate, exacerbate, intensify, worsen, compound.
– OPPOSITES placate.

inflamed adj. **swollen**, red, hot, burning, itchy, sore, painful, tender, infected.

inflate v. **1 blow up**, pump up, fill, puff up/out, dilate, distend, swell, bloat. **2 increase**, raise, boost, escalate, put up; informal **hike up, jack up.**
– OPPOSITES deflate, lower.

inflated adj. **1 high**, sky-high, excessive, unreasonable, outrageous, exorbitant, extortionate; Brit. over the odds; informal **steep. 2 exaggerated**, immoderate, overblown, overstated.
– OPPOSITES low, modest.

inflict v. **1 give**, administer, deal out, mete out, exact, wreak. **2 impose**, force, thrust, foist.

influence n. **1 effect**, impact, control, spell, hold. **2** a good influence on her: **example to**, role model for, inspiration to. **3 power**, authority, sway, leverage, weight, pull; informal **clout.**
• v. **1 affect**, have an impact on, determine, guide, control, shape, govern, decide, change, alter. **2 sway**, bias, prejudice, manipulate, persuade, induce.

influential adj. **powerful**, controlling, important, authoritative, leading, significant, instrumental, guiding.

inform v. **1 tell**, notify, apprise, advise, impart to, communicate to, let someone know, brief, enlighten, send word to. **2** he

informed on two colleagues:
betray, give away, denounce, incriminate; report; informal rat, squeal, split, snitch, tell, blow the whistle; Brit. informal grass, shop; N. Amer. informal finger; Austral./NZ informal dob in.

informal adj. **1 unofficial**, casual, relaxed, easy-going, low-key. **2 colloquial**, vernacular, idiomatic, popular, familiar, everyday; informal slangy, chatty. **3 casual**, relaxed, comfortable, everyday; informal comfy.
– OPPOSITES formal.

information n. **facts**, particulars, details, figures, statistics, data, knowledge, intelligence; informal info, gen.

informative adj. **instructive**, illuminating, enlightening, revealing, explanatory, factual, educational, edifying.

informed adj. **knowledgeable**, enlightened, educated, briefed, up to date, up to speed, in the picture, in the know, au fait; informal clued up.
– OPPOSITES ignorant.

infuriate v. **enrage**, incense, provoke, anger, madden, exasperate; informal make someone see red; Brit. informal wind up.
– OPPOSITES please.

ingenious adj. **inventive**, creative, imaginative, original, innovative, pioneering, resourceful, enterprising, inspired, clever.
– OPPOSITES unimaginative.

ingredient n. **constituent**, component, element, item, part, strand, unit, feature, aspect, attribute.

inhabit v. **live in**, occupy, settle, people, populate, colonize.

inhabitant n. **resident**, occupant, occupier, settler, local, native; (**inhabitants**) population, populace, people, public, community, citizenry, townsfolk, townspeople.

inhale v. **breathe in**, draw in, suck in, sniff in, drink in, gasp.
– OPPOSITES exhale.

inherit v. **be bequeathed**, be left, be willed, come into, succeed to, assume, take over.

inheritance n. **legacy**, bequest, endowment, birthright, heritage, patrimony.

> WORD LINKS
> relating to inheritance:
> hereditary

inhibit v. **impede**, hinder, hamper, hold back, discourage, interfere with, obstruct, slow down, retard.
– OPPOSITES assist, allow.

inhibited adj. **reserved**, reticent, guarded, self-conscious, insecure, withdrawn, repressed, undemonstrative, shy, diffident, bashful; informal uptight.

initial adj. **beginning**, opening, commencing, starting, first, earliest, primary, preliminary, preparatory, introductory, inaugural.
– OPPOSITES final.

initially adv. **at first**, at the start, at the outset, in/at the beginning, to begin with, to start with, originally.

initiate v. **1** begin, start (off), commence, institute, inaugurate, launch, instigate, establish, set up. **2** *he was initiated into a religious cult*: introduce, admit, induct, install, swear in, ordain, invest.
– OPPOSITES end, expel.

initiative n. **1** enterprise, resourcefulness, inventiveness, imagination, ingenuity, originality, creativity. **2** advantage, upper hand, edge, lead, start. **3** scheme, plan, strategy, measure, proposal, step, action.

inject v. **1** administer, take; *informal* shoot (up), mainline, fix. **2** inoculate, vaccinate. **3** insert, introduce, feed, push, force, shoot. **4** introduce, instil, infuse, imbue, breathe.

injection n. **1** inoculation, vaccination, immunization, booster; *informal* jab, shot. **2** addition, introduction, investment, dose, infusion, insertion.

injunction n. order, ruling, direction, directive, command, instruction, mandate.

injure v. **1** hurt, wound, damage, harm, disable, break; *Medicine* traumatize. **2** damage, mar, spoil, weaken, ruin, blight, blemish, tarnish, blacken.

injured adj. **1** hurt, wounded, damaged, sore, bruised, broken, fractured; *Medicine* traumatized; *Brit. informal* gammy. **2** upset, hurt, wounded, offended, reproachful, pained, aggrieved.
– OPPOSITES healthy.

injury n. **1** wound, bruise, cut, gash, scratch, graze; *Medicine* trauma, lesion. **2** harm, hurt, damage, pain, suffering. **3** offence, abuse, injustice, disservice, affront, insult.

injustice n. **1** unfairness, onesidedness, inequity, bias, prejudice, discrimination, intolerance, exploitation, corruption. **2** wrong, offence, crime, sin, outrage, scandal, disgrace, affront.

inland adj. interior, inshore, internal, upcountry.
– OPPOSITES coastal.

inlet n. **1** cove, bay, bight, creek, estuary, fjord, sound; *Scottish* firth. **2** vent, flue, shaft, duct, channel, pipe.

inmate n. **1** patient, inpatient, resident, occupant. **2** prisoner, convict, captive, detainee, internee.

inner adj. **1** central, innermost; *N. Amer.* downtown. **2** internal, interior, inside, innermost. **3** hidden, secret, deep, underlying, veiled.
– OPPOSITES outer.

innocence n. **1** guiltlessness, blamelessness. **2** naivety, credulity, inexperience, gullibility, ingenuousness.

innocent adj. **1** guiltless, blameless, clean, irreproachable, above reproach, honest, upright, law-abiding. **2** harmless, innocuous, safe, inoffensive, unobjectionable. **3** naive, ingenuous, trusting, credulous, impressionable, easily led,

inexperienced, unsophisticated, artless.
- OPPOSITES guilty.

innovation n. **change**, alteration, upheaval, reorganization, restructuring, novelty, departure.

innovative adj. **original**, new, novel, fresh, unusual, experimental, inventive, ingenious, pioneering, groundbreaking, revolutionary, radical.

inquest n. **enquiry**, investigation, probe, examination, review, hearing.

inquire, inquiring, inquiry see ENQUIRE etc.

insane adj. **1 mad**, of unsound mind, certifiable, psychotic, schizophrenic, unhinged; informal crazy, raving mad, bonkers, loony, round the bend; Brit. informal crackers, off your trolley; N. Amer. informal nutso. **2 stupid**, idiotic, nonsensical, absurd, ridiculous, ludicrous, preposterous; informal crazy, mad; Brit. informal daft, barmy.
- OPPOSITES sane.

insect n. **bug**; informal creepy-crawly; Brit. informal minibeast.

> WORD LINKS
> *study of insects:* entomology

insecure adj. **1 unconfident**, uncertain, unsure, doubtful, diffident, hesitant, self-conscious, anxious, fearful. **2 unprotected**, unguarded, vulnerable, unsecured. **3 unstable**, rickety, wobbly, shaky, unsteady, precarious.
- OPPOSITES confident, stable.

insecurity n. **lack of confidence**, uncertainty, self-doubt, diffidence, hesitancy, nervousness, self-consciousness, anxiety, worry, unease.

insert v. **put**, place, push, thrust, slide, slip, load, fit, slot, install; informal pop, stick, bung.
- OPPOSITES extract, remove.

inside n. **1 interior**, centre, core, middle, heart. **2 (insides) stomach**, gut, bowels, intestines; informal tummy, belly, guts.
• adj. **1 inner**, interior, internal, innermost. **2 confidential**, classified, restricted, privileged, private, secret, exclusive; informal hush-hush.
- OPPOSITES outside.

insight n. **intuition**, perception, understanding, comprehension, appreciation, judgement, discernment, vision, imagination, wisdom; informal nous.

insignificant adj. **unimportant**, trivial, trifling, negligible, inconsequential, of no account, paltry, petty, insubstantial; informal piddling.

insincere adj. **false**, fake, hollow, artificial, feigned, pretended, put-on, disingenuous, hypocritical, cynical; informal phoney, pretend.

insist v. **1 stand firm**, stand your ground, be resolute, be determined, hold out, persist, be emphatic, lay down the law, not take no for an answer; informal stick to your guns, put your foot down. **2 demand**, command, order, require. **3 maintain**, assert, protest, swear, declare, repeat.

insistent adj. **persistent**, determined, tenacious, unyielding, dogged, unrelenting, importunate, relentless, inexorable.

inspect v. **examine**, check, scrutinize, investigate, vet, test, monitor, survey, study, look over; informal check out, give something a/the once-over.

inspection n. **examination**, check-up, survey, scrutiny, exploration, investigation; informal once-over, going-over.

inspector n. **examiner**, scrutineer, investigator, surveyor, assessor, supervisor, monitor, watchdog, ombudsman, auditor.

inspiration n. **1 stimulus**, motivation, encouragement, influence, spur, fillip; informal shot in the arm. **2 creativity**, invention, innovation, ingenuity, imagination, originality, insight, vision. **3 bright idea**, revelation; informal brainwave; N. Amer. informal brainstorm.

inspire v. **1 stimulate**, motivate, encourage, influence, move, spur, energize, galvanize. **2 give rise to**, lead to, bring about, prompt, spawn, engender. **3 arouse**, awaken, prompt, induce, ignite, trigger, kindle, produce, bring out.

inspired adj. **outstanding**, wonderful, marvellous, excellent, magnificent, exceptional, first-

class, virtuoso, superlative; informal tremendous, superb, awesome, out of this world; Brit. informal brilliant.

inspiring adj. **inspirational**, encouraging, heartening, uplifting, stirring, rousing, electrifying, moving.

instability n. **unreliability**, uncertainty, unpredictability, insecurity, volatility, capriciousness, changeability, variability, inconsistency, mutability.
– OPPOSITES stability.

install v. **1 put**, place, station, site, insert. **2 swear in**, induct, inaugurate, invest, appoint, ordain, consecrate, anoint, enthrone, crown. **3 ensconce**, position, settle, seat, plant, sit (down); informal plonk, park.
– OPPOSITES remove.

instalment n. **1 payment**, repayment, tranche, portion. **2 part**, episode, chapter, issue, programme, section, segment, volume.

instance n. **example**, occasion, occurrence, case, illustration, sample.

instant adj. **1 immediate**, instantaneous, on-the-spot, prompt, swift, speedy, rapid, quick; informal snappy. **2 prepared**, pre-cooked, microwaveable.
– OPPOSITES delayed.
•n. **moment**, minute, second, split second, trice, twinkling of an eye, flash; informal jiffy.

instantly adv. **immediately**, at once, straight away, right away, instantaneously, forthwith, there and then, here and now, this/that minute, this/that second.

instead adv. **as an alternative**, in lieu, alternatively, rather, on second thoughts; N. Amer. alternately.

instinct n. **1 inclination**, urge, drive, compulsion, intuition, feeling, sixth sense, nose. **2 talent**, gift, ability, aptitude, skill, flair, feel, knack.

instinctive adj. **intuitive**, natural, instinctual, innate, inborn, inherent, unconscious, subconscious, automatic, reflex, kneejerk; informal gut.

institute n. **organization**, establishment, institution, foundation, centre, academy, school, college, university, society, association, federation, body. ▪v. **set up**, inaugurate, found, establish, organize, initiate, set in motion, get under way, get off the ground, start, launch. – OPPOSITES abolish, end.

institution n. **1 establishment**, organization, institute, foundation, centre, academy, school, college, university, society, association, body. **2 (residential) home**, hospital, asylum, prison. **3** the institution of marriage: **practice**, custom, convention, tradition.

institutional adj. **organized**, established, bureaucratic, conventional, procedural, formal, formalized, systematic, systematized, structured, regulated.

instruct v. **1 order**, direct, command, tell, mandate; old use bid. **2 teach**, coach, train, educate, tutor, guide, school, show.

instruction n. **1 order**, command, directive, direction, decree, injunction, mandate, commandment; old use bidding. **2** read the instructions: **directions**, handbook, manual, guide, advice, guidance. **3 tuition**, teaching, coaching, schooling, lessons, classes, lectures, training, drill, guidance.

instructor n. **trainer**, coach, teacher, tutor, adviser, counsellor, guide.

instrument n. **1 implement**, tool, utensil, device, apparatus, gadget. **2 gauge**, meter, indicator, dial, display. **3 agent**, cause, agency, channel, medium, means, vehicle.

instrumental adj. □ **be instrumental in** play a part in, contribute to, be a factor in, have a hand in, promote, advance, further.

insufficient adj. **inadequate**, deficient, poor, scant, scanty, not enough, too little, too few.

insulate v. **1 wrap**, sheathe, cover, encase, enclose, lag, soundproof. **2 protect**, save, shield, shelter, screen, cushion, cocoon.

insult v. **abuse**, be rude to, call someone names, slight, disparage, discredit, malign, defame, denigrate, offend, hurt, humiliate; informal bad-mouth; Brit. informal slag off.

– OPPOSITES compliment.

• **n.** jibe, affront, slight, slur, barb, indignity, abuse, aspersions; informal dig, put-down.

insulting adj. **abusive**, rude, offensive, disparaging, belittling, derogatory, deprecating, disrespectful, uncomplimentary; informal bitchy, catty.

insurance n. **indemnity**, assurance, protection, security, cover, safeguard, warranty.

insure v. **provide insurance for**, indemnify, cover, assure, protect, underwrite, warrant.

intact adj. **whole**, entire, complete, unbroken, undamaged, unscathed, unblemished, unmarked, in one piece.
– OPPOSITES damaged.

integral adj. **1 essential**, fundamental, component, basic, intrinsic, inherent, vital, necessary. **2 built-in**, inbuilt, integrated, inboard, fitted. **3 unified**, integrated, comprehensive, holistic, joined-up, all-embracing.
– OPPOSITES peripheral, supplementary.

integrate v. **combine**, amalgamate, merge, unite, fuse, blend, consolidate, meld, mix, incorporate, assimilate, homogenize, desegregate.
– OPPOSITES separate.

integrity n. **1 honesty**, probity, rectitude, uprightness, fairness, honour, sincerity, truthfulness, trustworthiness. **2 unity**, coherence, cohesion, solidity. **3 soundness**, strength, sturdiness, solidity, durability, stability, rigidity.
– OPPOSITES dishonesty.

intellect n. **mind**, brain(s), intelligence, reason, judgement, grey matter, brain cells.

intellectual adj. **1 mental**, cerebral, rational, conceptual, theoretical, analytical, logical, cognitive. **2 learned**, academic, erudite, bookish, highbrow, scholarly, donnish.

intelligence n. **1 intellect**, cleverness, brainpower, judgement, reasoning, acumen, wit, insight, perception. **2 information**, facts, details, particulars, data, knowledge.

intelligent adj. **clever**, bright, quick-witted, smart, astute, sharp, insightful, perceptive, penetrating, educated, knowledgeable, enlightened; informal brainy.

intelligible adj. **comprehensible**, understandable, accessible, digestible, user-friendly, clear, coherent, plain, unambiguous.

intend v. **plan**, mean, have in mind, aim, propose, hope, expect, envisage.

intense adj. **1 extreme**, great, acute, fierce, severe, high, exceptional, extraordinary, harsh, strong, powerful, violent; informal serious. **2 passionate**, impassioned, zealous, vehement, fervent, earnest, eager, committed.
– OPPOSITES mild, apathetic.

intensify v. **escalate**, increase, step up, raise, strengthen, reinforce, pick up, build up, heighten, deepen, extend, expand, amplify, magnify, aggravate, exacerbate, worsen, inflame, compound.
– OPPOSITES abate.

intensity n. **1 strength**, power, force, severity, ferocity, fierceness, harshness, violence. **2 passion**, ardour, fervour, vehemence, fire, emotion, eagerness.

intensive adj. **thorough**, thoroughgoing, in-depth, rigorous, exhaustive, vigorous, detailed, minute, meticulous, painstaking, methodical, extensive.
– OPPOSITES cursory.

intent n. **aim**, intention, purpose, objective, goal.
•adj. **1** *he was intent on proving his point*: **bent**, set, determined, insistent, resolved, hell-bent, keen, committed to, determined to. **2 attentive**, absorbed, engrossed, fascinated, enthralled, rapt, focused, concentrating, preoccupied.
– OPPOSITES distracted.

intention n. **aim**, purpose, intent, objective, goal.

intentional adj. **deliberate**, done on purpose, wilful, calculated, conscious, intended, planned, meant, knowing.

inter v. **bury**, lay to rest, consign to the grave, entomb.
– OPPOSITES exhume.

intercept v. **stop**, head off, cut off, catch, seize, block, interrupt.

intercourse n. **1 dealings**, relations, relationships, contact, interchange, communication, networking. **2 sexual intercourse**, sex, sexual relations, mating, copulation, fornication; technical coitus.

interdict n. **prohibition**, ban, bar, veto, embargo, moratorium, injunction.

interest n. **1 attentiveness**, attention, regard, notice, curiosity, enjoyment, delight. **2** *this will be of interest*: **concern**, consequence, importance, import, significance, note, relevance, value. **3 hobby**, pastime, leisure pursuit, amusement, recreation, diversion, passion. **4 stake**, share, claim, investment, involvement, concern.
– OPPOSITES boredom.
•v. **appeal to**, be of interest to, attract, intrigue, amuse, divert, entertain, arouse someone's curiosity, whet someone's appetite; informal tickle someone's fancy.

interested adj. **1 attentive**, fascinated, riveted, gripped, captivated, agog, intrigued, curious, keen, eager. **2 concerned**, involved, affected.

interesting adj. **absorbing**, engrossing, fascinating, riveting, gripping, compelling, captivating, engaging, enthralling, appealing, entertaining, stimulating, diverting, intriguing.

interfere v. **butt in**, barge in, intrude, meddle, tamper, encroach; informal poke your nose in, stick your oar in.

□ **interfere with** impede, obstruct, stand in the way of, hinder, inhibit, restrict, constrain, hamper, handicap, disturb, disrupt, influence, affect, confuse.

interference n. **1 intrusion**, intervention, involvement, meddling, prying. **2 disruption**, disturbance, static, noise.

interior adj. **1 inside**, inner, internal, inland, upcountry, central. **2 internal**, home, domestic, national, state, civil, local. **3 inner**, mental, spiritual, psychological, private, personal, secret.
• n. **1 inside**, depths, recesses, bowels, belly, heart. **2 centre**, heartland.
– OPPOSITES exterior.

intermediary n. mediator, go-between, negotiator, arbitrator, peacemaker, middleman, broker.

intermediate adj. halfway, in-between, middle, mid, midway, intervening, transitional.

intermittent adj. sporadic, irregular, fitful, spasmodic, discontinuous, isolated, random, patchy, scattered, occasional, periodic.
– OPPOSITES continuous.

internal adj. **1 inner**, interior, inside, central. **2 domestic**, home, interior, civil, local, national, state.
– OPPOSITES external, foreign.

international adj. global, worldwide, world, intercontin-

ental, universal, cosmopolitan, multiracial, multinational.
– OPPOSITES national, local.

interpret v. **1 explain**, elucidate, expound, clarify. **2 understand**, construe, take (to mean), see, regard. **3 decipher**, decode, translate, understand.

interpretation n. **1 explanation**, elucidation, exposition, clarification, analysis. **2 meaning**, understanding, explanation, inference. **3 rendition**, execution, presentation, performance, reading, playing, singing.

interrupt v. **1 cut in (on)**, break in (on), barge in (on), intrude, intervene; informal butt in (on), chime in (on); Brit. informal chip in (on). **2 suspend**, discontinue, adjourn, break off, stop, halt; informal put on ice.

interruption n. **1 cutting in**, barging in, interference, intervention, intrusion, disturbance; informal butting in. **2 suspension**, breaking off, discontinuance, stopping.

interval n. intermission, interlude, break, recess, time out.

intervene v. intercede, involve yourself, get involved, step in, interfere, intrude.

interview n. meeting, discussion, interrogation, cross-examination, debriefing, audience, talk, chat; informal grilling.
• v. talk to, question, quiz, interrogate, cross-examine, debrief, poll, canvass, sound out; informal grill, pump.

4

interviewer n. **questioner**, interrogator, examiner, assessor, journalist, reporter, inquisitor.

intimacy n. **closeness**, togetherness, rapport, attachment, familiarity, friendliness, affection, warmth.
– OPPOSITES formality.

intimate[1] adj. **1 close**, bosom, dear, cherished, fast, firm. **2 friendly**, warm, welcoming, hospitable, relaxed, informal, cosy, comfortable. **3 personal**, private, confidential, secret, inward. **4 detailed**, thorough, exhaustive, deep, in-depth, profound.
– OPPOSITES distant, formal, cold.

intimate[2] v. **1 announce**, state, make known, disclose, reveal, divulge, let it be known. **2 imply**, suggest, hint at, indicate, insinuate.

intimidate v. **frighten**, menace, scare, terrorize, threaten, browbeat, bully, harass, hound; informal lean on.

intricate adj. **complex**, complicated, convoluted, tangled, elaborate, ornate, detailed.
– OPPOSITES simple.

intrigue v. **interest**, fascinate, arouse someone's curiosity, attract, engage.
• n. **plotting**, conniving, scheming, machination, doubledealing, subterfuge.

intriguing adj. **interesting**, fascinating, absorbing, engaging.

introduce v. **1 institute**, initiate, launch, inaugurate, establish, found, bring in, set in motion, start, begin, get going. **2 present**, make known, acquaint with. **3 insert**, inject, put, force, shoot, feed. **4 instil**, infuse, inject, add.
– OPPOSITES end, remove.

introduction n. **1 institution**, establishment, initiation, launch, inauguration, foundation. **2 presentation**, meeting, audience. **3 foreword**, preface, preamble, prologue, prelude; informal intro.
– OPPOSITES ending, epilogue.

introductory adj. **1 opening**, initial, starting, initiatory, first, preliminary. **2 elementary**, basic, rudimentary, entry-level.
– OPPOSITES final, advanced.

intrude v. **encroach**, impinge, trespass, infringe, invade, violate, disturb, disrupt.

intruder n. **trespasser**, interloper, invader, infiltrator, burglar, housebreaker; informal gatecrasher.

intuition n. **1 instinct**, feeling, insight, sixth sense. **2 hunch**, feeling in your bones, inkling, sneaking suspicion, premonition; informal gut feeling.

intuitive adj. **instinctive**, innate, inborn, inherent, natural, unconscious, subconscious; informal gut.

invade v. **1 occupy**, conquer, capture, seize, take (over), annex, overrun, storm. **2 intrude on**, violate, encroach on, infringe on, trespass on, disturb, disrupt.
– OPPOSITES leave, liberate.

invader n. attacker, conqueror, raider, marauder, occupier, intruder, trespasser.

invalid[1] adj. **ill**, sick, ailing, infirm, incapacitated, bedridden, frail, sickly, poorly.
– OPPOSITES healthy.
•v. **disable**, incapacitate, hospitalize, put out of action, lay up.

invalid[2] adj. **1 void**, null and void, not binding, illegitimate, inapplicable. **2 false**, fallacious, spurious, unsound, wrong, untenable.

invaluable adj. **indispensable**, irreplaceable, all-important, crucial, vital, worth its weight in gold.
– OPPOSITES dispensable.

invariably adv. **always**, at all times, without fail, without exception, consistently, habitually, unfailingly.

invasion n. **1 occupation**, conquering, capture, seizure, annexation, takeover. **2 violation**, infringement, interruption, encroachment, disturbance, disruption, breach.
– OPPOSITES withdrawal.

invent v. **1 originate**, create, design, devise, develop. **2 make up**, fabricate, concoct, hatch, contrive, dream up; informal cook up.

invention n. **1 origination**, creation, development, design, discovery. **2 innovation**, contraption, contrivance, device, gadget. **3 fabrication**, concoction, (piece of) fiction,

story, tale, lie, untruth, falsehood, fib.

inventive adj. **creative**, original, innovative, imaginative, resourceful, unusual, fresh, novel, new, groundbreaking, unorthodox, unconventional.
– OPPOSITES unimaginative.

inventor n. **originator**, creator, designer, deviser, developer, author, architect, father.

inventory n. **list**, listing, catalogue, record, register, checklist, log, archive.

invest v. **put in**, plough in, put up, advance, expend, spend; informal lay out.
☐ **invest in** put money into, sink money into, plough money into, fund, back, finance, underwrite.

investigate v. **enquire into**, look into, go into, probe, explore, scrutinize, analyse, study, examine; informal check out, suss out.

investigation n. **examination**, enquiry, study, inspection, exploration, analysis, research, scrutiny, probe, review.

investigator n. **researcher**, examiner, analyst, inspector, scrutineer, detective.

investment n. **1 investing**, speculation, outlay, funding, backing, financing, underwriting. **2 stake**, payment, outlay, venture, proposition.

invidious adj. **1 unpleasant**, awkward, difficult, undesirable, unenviable. **2 unfair**, unjust, unwarranted.

invigorate v. **revitalize**, energize, refresh, revive, enliven, liven up, perk up, wake up, animate, galvanize, fortify, rouse, exhilarate; informal buck up, pep up.
– OPPOSITES tire.

invincible adj. **invulnerable**, indestructible, unconquerable, unbeatable, indomitable, unassailable, impregnable.
– OPPOSITES vulnerable.

invisible adj. **unseen**, imperceptible, undetectable, inconspicuous, unnoticed, unobserved, hidden, out of sight.
– OPPOSITES visible.

invitation n. **request**, call, summons; informal invite.

invite v. **1 ask**, summon. **2 ask for**, request, call for, appeal for, solicit, seek. **3 cause**, induce, provoke, ask for, encourage, lead to, bring on yourself, arouse.

inviting adj. **tempting**, enticing, alluring, attractive, appealing, appetizing, mouth-watering, intriguing, seductive.
– OPPOSITES repellent.

invoke v. **1 cite**, refer to, resort to, have recourse to, turn to. **2 pray to**, call on, appeal to. **3 bring forth**, bring out, elicit, conjure up, generate.

involuntary adj. **1 reflex**, automatic, instinctive, unintentional, uncontrollable. **2 compulsory**, obligatory, mandatory, forced, prescribed.
– OPPOSITES deliberate, optional.

involve v. **1 entail**, require, necessitate, demand, call for. **2 include**, take in, incorporate, encompass, comprise, cover.
– OPPOSITES preclude, exclude.

involved adj. **1** *social workers involved in the case*: **associated**, connected, concerned. **2** *he had been involved in burglaries*: **implicated**, caught up, mixed up. **3 complicated**, intricate, complex, elaborate, convoluted, confusing. **4 engrossed**, absorbed, immersed, caught up, preoccupied, intent.

involvement n. **1 participation**, collaboration, collusion, complicity, association, connection, entanglement. **2 attachment**, friendship, intimacy, commitment.

inwards adv. **inside**, towards the inside, into the interior, inward, within.

iota n. **(little) bit**, mite, speck, scrap, shred, ounce, jot.

iron adj. **1 ferric**, ferrous. **2 uncompromising**, unrelenting, unyielding, unbending, rigid, steely.
– OPPOSITES flexible.
□ **iron out 1 resolve**, straighten out, sort out, clear up, put right, solve, rectify; informal fix. **2 eliminate**, eradicate, reconcile, resolve.

ironic adj. **1 sarcastic**, sardonic, satirical, dry, wry, double-edged, mocking, derisive, scornful; Brit. informal sarky. **2 paradoxical**, funny, strange.

irony n. **1 sarcasm**, mockery, ridicule, derision, scorn; Brit. informal sarkiness. **2 paradox**.

irrational adj. **unreasonable**, illogical, groundless, baseless, unfounded, unjustifiable.
– OPPOSITES rational, logical.

irrefutable adj. **indisputable**, undeniable, unquestionable, incontrovertible, incontestable, beyond question, beyond doubt, conclusive, definite, definitive, decisive.

irregular adj. **1 uneven**, crooked, misshapen, lopsided, asymmetrical, twisted. **2 rough**, bumpy, uneven, pitted, rutted, lumpy, knobbly, gnarled. **3 inconsistent**, unsteady, uneven, fitful, patchy, variable, varying, changeable, inconstant, erratic, unstable, spasmodic, intermittent. **4 improper**, illegitimate, unethical, unprofessional; informal shady, dodgy. **5 guerrilla**, underground, paramilitary, partisan, mercenary, terrorist.
• n. **guerrilla**, paramilitary, resistance fighter, partisan, mercenary, terrorist.

irrelevant adj. **beside the point**, immaterial, unconnected, unrelated, peripheral, extraneous.

irreparable adj. **irreversible**, irrevocable, irrecoverable, unrepairable, beyond repair.

irrepressible adj. **ebullient**, exuberant, buoyant, breezy, jaunty, high-spirited, vivacious, animated, full of life, lively; informal bubbly, bouncy, peppy, chipper, chirpy, full of beans.

irresistible adj. **1 captivating**, enticing, alluring, enchanting, fascinating, seductive. **2 un-**controllable, overwhelming, overpowering, ungovernable, compelling.

irresponsible adj. **reckless**, rash, careless, unwise, imprudent, ill-advised, injudicious, hasty, impetuous, foolhardy, foolish, unreliable, undependable, untrustworthy.

irreverent adj. **disrespectful**, impertinent, cheeky, flippant, rude, discourteous.
– OPPOSITES respectful.

irrevocable adj. **irreversible**, unalterable, unchangeable, immutable, final, binding, permanent, set in stone.

irritable adj. **bad-tempered**, short-tempered, irascible, tetchy, testy, grumpy, grouchy, crotchety, cantankerous, fractious, curmudgeonly.
– OPPOSITES good-humoured.

irritate v. **1 annoy**, bother, vex, make cross, exasperate, infuriate, anger, madden; Brit. rub up the wrong way; informal aggravate, peeve, rile, needle, get (to), bug, hack off; Brit. informal nark, get on someone's wick; N. Amer. informal tee off, tick off. **2 inflame**, hurt, chafe, scratch, scrape, rub.
– OPPOSITES delight, soothe.

irritation n. **annoyance**, exasperation, vexation, indignation, anger, displeasure, chagrin.
– OPPOSITES delight.

island n. **isle**, islet, atoll; Brit. holm; (**islands**) archipelago.

WORD LINKS
relating to an island: insular

isolate v. **separate**, segregate, detach, cut off, shut away, alienate, distance, cloister, seclude, cordon off, seal off, close off, fence off.
– OPPOSITES integrate.

isolated adj. **1 remote**, out of the way, outlying, off the beaten track, in the back of beyond, godforsaken, inaccessible, cut-off; informal in the middle of nowhere, in the sticks; N. Amer. informal jerkwater. **2 solitary**, lonely, secluded, reclusive, hermit-like; N. Amer. lonesome. **3 unique**, lone, solitary, unusual, exceptional, untypical, freak; informal one-off.
– OPPOSITES accessible.

isolation n. **1 solitariness**, loneliness, friendlessness. **2 remoteness**, inaccessibility.
– OPPOSITES contact.

issue n. **1 matter**, question, point at issue, affair, case, subject, topic, problem, situation. **2 edition**, number, instalment, copy, impression. **3 issuing**, release, publication, distribution.

•v. **1 release**, put out, deliver, publish, broadcast, circulate, distribute. **2 supply**, provide, furnish, arm, equip, fit out, rig out, kit out; informal fix up.
□ **take issue with** disagree with, challenge, dispute, (call into) question.

itch n. **1 tingling**, irritation, itchiness, prickle. **2** (informal) **longing**, yearning, craving, ache, hunger, thirst, urge, hankering; informal yen.
•v. **1 tingle**, be irritated, be itchy, sting, hurt, be sore. **2** (informal) **long**, yearn, ache, burn, crave, hanker for/after, hunger, thirst, be eager, be desperate; informal be dying.

item n. **1 thing**, article, object, piece, element, constituent, component, ingredient. **2 issue**, matter, affair, case, subject, topic, question, point. **3 report**, article, piece, write-up, bulletin, feature, review.

itinerary n. **route**, plan, schedule, timetable, programme.

Jj

jab v. & n. **poke**, prod, dig, elbow, nudge, thrust, stab, push.

jacket n. **wrapping**, wrapper, sleeve, cover, covering, sheath.

jagged adj. **spiky**, barbed, ragged, rough, uneven, irregular, serrated.

– OPPOSITES smooth.

jail n. **prison**, lock-up, detention centre; N. Amer. penitentiary, jailhouse; informal clink, cooler, the slammer, inside; Brit. informal nick; N. Amer. informal can, pen, slam, pokey.

v. **imprison**, incarcerate, lock up, put away, detain; informal send down, press, push, put behind bars, put inside; Brit. informal bang up.
– OPPOSITES acquit, release.

jam v. 1 **stuff**, shove, force, ram, thrust, press, push, wedge, stick, cram. 2 **crowd**, pack, pile, press, squeeze, sandwich, cram, throng, mob, fill, block, clog, congest. 3 **stick**, become stuck, catch, seize (up).
•n. **tailback**, hold-up, queue, congestion, bottleneck; N. Amer. gridlock; informal snarl-up.

jar¹ n. **pot**, container, crock.

jar² v. 1 **jolt**, jerk, shake, vibrate. 2 **grate**, set someone's teeth on edge, irritate, annoy, get on someone's nerves. 3 **clash**, conflict, contrast, be incompatible, be at variance, be at odds.
– OPPOSITES soothe.

jargon n. **slang**, idiom, cant, argot, gobbledegook; informal lingo, -speak, -ese.

jaunt n. **trip**, outing, excursion, tour, drive, ride, run; informal spin, junket.

jaws pl. n. **mouth**, maw, muzzle, mandibles; informal chops.

jealous adj. 1 **envious**, covetous, resentful, grudging, green with envy. 2 **suspicious**, distrustful, possessive, proprietorial, overprotective. 3 **protective**, vigilant, watchful, mindful, careful.
– OPPOSITES trusting.

jealousy n. **envy**, resentment, bitterness; humorous the greeneyed monster.

jeer v. **taunt**, mock, ridicule, deride, insult, abuse, heckle, cat-

call (at), boo (at), whistle at, scoff at, sneer at; Brit. barrack.
– OPPOSITES applaud, cheer.
•n. **taunt**, sneer, insult, shout, jibe, boo, catcall, derision, teasing, scoffing, abuse, scorn, heckling, catcalling; Brit. barracking.
– OPPOSITES applause, cheer.

jeopardize v. **threaten**, endanger, imperil, risk, compromise, prejudice.
– OPPOSITES safeguard.

jeopardy n. **danger**, peril, risk.

jerk n. 1 **yank**, tug, pull, wrench. 2 **jolt**, lurch, bump, judder, jump, bounce, jounce, shake.
•v. 1 **yank**, tug, pull, wrench, wrest, drag, snatch. 2 **jolt**, lurch, bump, judder, bounce, jounce.

jerky adj. **convulsive**, spasmodic, fitful, twitchy, shaky.
– OPPOSITES smooth.

jet n. 1 **stream**, spurt, spray, fountain, rush, spout, gush, surge, burst. 2 **nozzle**, head, spout.

jettison v. **dump**, drop, ditch, throw out, get rid of, discard, dispose of, scrap.

jetty n. **pier**, landing (stage), quay, wharf, dock, breakwater, groyne, mole; N. Amer. levee.

jewel n. 1 **gem**, gemstone, (precious) stone; informal sparkler, rock. 2 **showpiece**, pride (and joy), cream, crème de la crème, jewel in the crown, prize, pick.

jibe n. **taunt**, sneer, jeer, insult, barb; informal dig, put-down.

jilt v. **leave**, walk out on, throw over, finish with, break up with, stand up, leave at the altar; informal chuck, ditch, dump, drop, run out on, give someone the push/elbow, give someone the big E.

jingle n. & v. **clink**, chink, tinkle, jangle, ring.

jinx n. **curse**, spell, the evil eye, black magic, voodoo, bad luck; N. Amer. hex.
• v. **curse**, cast a spell on; Austral. point the bone at; N. Amer. hex.

job n. **1 position**, post, situation, appointment, occupation, profession, trade, career, work, vocation, calling, métier. **2 task**, piece of work, assignment, mission, project, undertaking, operation, duty, chore, errand, responsibility, charge, role, function; informal department.

jobless adj. **unemployed**, out of work, unwaged, redundant, laid off; Brit. informal on the dole; Canad. informal on pogey; Austral./NZ informal on the wallaby track.
– OPPOSITES employed.

jog v. **1 run**, trot, lope. **2 nudge**, prod, poke, push, bump, jar.

join v. **1** the two parts are joined with clay: **connect**, unite, couple, fix, affix, attach, fasten, stick, glue, fuse, weld, amalgamate, bond, link, yoke, merge, secure, make fast, tie, bind. **2** the path joins a major road: **meet**, touch, reach. **3** he joined the search party: **help in**, participate in, get involved in, contribute to, enlist in, join up, sign up, band together, get together, team up.
– OPPOSITES separate, leave.

joint n. **join**, junction, intersection, link, connection, weld, seam, coupling.
• adj. **common**, shared, communal, collective, mutual, cooperative, collaborative, concerted, combined, united, allied.
– OPPOSITES separate.

jointly adv. **together**, in partnership, in cooperation, cooperatively, in conjunction, in combination, mutually, in league.

joke n. **1 witticism**, jest, quip, pun; informal gag, wisecrack, crack, funny, one-liner. **2 trick**, prank, stunt, hoax, jape; informal leg-pull, spoof, wind-up. **3** (informal) **laughing stock**, figure of fun, Aunt Sally. **4** (informal) **farce**, travesty.
• v. **tell jokes**, jest, banter, quip; informal wisecrack, josh.

joker n. **comedian**, comedienne, comic, humorist, wit, jester, prankster, practical joker, clown.

jolly adj. **cheerful**, happy, cheery, good-humoured, jovial, merry, sunny, joyful, light-hearted, in high spirits, buoyant, bubbly, genial; informal chipper, chirpy, perky; literary blithe.
– OPPOSITES miserable.

jolt v. **1 push**, jar, bump, knock, bang, shake, jog. **2 bump**, bounce, jerk, rattle, lurch, shudder, judder, jounce. **3 startle**, surprise, shock, stun, shake; informal rock, knock sideways.
• n. **bump**, bounce, shake, jerk, lurch, jounce.

jostle v. **1 push**, shove, elbow, barge into, bang into, bump against, knock against. **2** *photographers jostled for position:* **struggle**, vie, jockey, scramble, fight.

journal n. **1 periodical**, magazine, gazette, review, newsletter, news-sheet, bulletin, newspaper, paper, daily, weekly, monthly, quarterly. **2 diary**, log, logbook, weblog, blog, chronicle, history, yearbook; N. Amer. daybook.

journalist n. **reporter**, correspondent, columnist; Brit. pressman; informal news hound, hack, hackette, stringer, journo.

journey n. **trip**, expedition, tour, trek, travels, voyage, cruise, ride, drive, crossing, passage, flight, odyssey, pilgrimage, safari, globetrotting; old use peregrinations.
•v. **travel**, go, voyage, sail, cruise, fly, hike, trek, ride, drive, make your way.

jovial adj. **cheerful**, jolly, happy, cheery, jocular, good-humoured, convivial, genial, good-natured, affable, outgoing, smiling, merry, sunny; literary blithe.
– OPPOSITES miserable.

joy n. **delight**, pleasure, jubilation, triumph, exultation, rejoicing, happiness, elation, euphoria, bliss, ecstasy, rapture.
– OPPOSITES misery.

joyful adj. **1 cheerful**, happy, jolly, merry, sunny, joyous, cheery, smiling, jovial, mirthful, gleeful, pleased, delighted,

thrilled, jubilant, elated, ecstatic; informal over the moon, on cloud nine. **2** *joyful news:* **pleasing**, happy, good, cheering, gladdening, welcome, gratifying, heart-warming.
– OPPOSITES sad.

jubilant adj. **overjoyed**, exultant, triumphant, joyful, cock-a-hoop, elated, thrilled, gleeful, euphoric, ecstatic; informal over the moon, on cloud nine.
– OPPOSITES despondent.

jubilee n. **anniversary**, commemoration, celebration, festival.

judge n. **1 justice**, magistrate, recorder, sheriff; N. Amer. jurist; Brit. informal beak. **2 adjudicator**, referee, umpire, arbiter, assessor, examiner, moderator, scrutineer.
•v. **1 conclude**, decide, consider, believe, think, deduce, infer, gauge, estimate, guess, surmise, conjecture, regard as, rate as, class as; informal reckon, figure. **2** *she was judged innocent:* **pronounce**, decree, rule, find. **3 adjudicate**, arbitrate, moderate, referee, umpire. **4 assess**, evaluate, appraise, examine, review.

judgement n. **1 sense**, discernment, perception, discrimination, understanding, powers of reasoning, reason, logic. **2 opinion**, view, estimate, appraisal, conclusion, diagnosis, assessment, impression, conviction, perception, thinking. **3** *a court judgement:* **verdict**, decision, adjudication, ruling, pronouncement, decree, finding, sentence.

judgemental adj. critical, censorious, disapproving, disparaging, deprecating, negative, overcritical.

judicious adj. wise, sensible, prudent, shrewd, astute, canny, discerning, sagacious, strategic, politic, expedient.
– OPPOSITES ill-advised.

jug n. pitcher, ewer, crock, jar, urn, carafe, flask, flagon, decanter; N. Amer. creamer.

juice n. liquid, fluid, sap, extract, concentrate, essence.

juicy adj. **1** succulent, tender, moist, ripe. **2** (informal) sensational, fascinating, intriguing, exciting, graphic, lurid.
– OPPOSITES dry.

jumble n. heap, muddle, mess, tangle, confusion, disarray, chaos, hotchpotch; N. Amer. hodgepodge; informal shambles.
•v. mix up, muddle up, disorganize, disorder, tangle, confuse.

jump v. **1** leap, spring, bound, vault, hop, skip, caper, dance, prance. **2** pre-tax profits jumped: rise, go up, shoot up, soar, surge, climb, increase; informal skyrocket. **3** the noise made her jump: start, jolt, flinch, recoil, shudder.
•n. **1** leap, spring, bound, hop, skip. **2** rise, leap, increase, upsurge, upswing; informal hike. **3** start, jerk, spasm, shudder.

jumper n. (Brit.) sweater, pullover, jersey; informal woolly.

jumpy adj. (informal) nervous, on edge, edgy, tense, anxious, restless, fidgety, keyed up, overwrought; informal jittery, uptight, het up; N. Amer. informal antsy.
– OPPOSITES calm.

junction n. crossroads, intersection, interchange, T-junction, turn, turn-off, exit; Brit. roundabout; N. Amer. turnout, cloverleaf.

junior adj. younger, minor, subordinate, lower, lesser, low-ranking, inferior, secondary.
– OPPOSITES senior, older.

junk n. (informal) rubbish, clutter, odds and ends, bric-a-brac, refuse, litter, scrap, waste, debris; N. Amer. trash.

just adj. **1** a just society: fair, fair-minded, equitable, even-handed, impartial, unbiased, objective, neutral, disinterested, unprejudiced, honourable, upright, decent, principled. **2** a just reward: deserved, well deserved, well earned, merited, rightful, due, proper, fitting, appropriate, defensible, justified, justifiable.
– OPPOSITES unfair.
•adv. **1** exactly, precisely, absolutely, completely, totally, entirely, perfectly, utterly, thoroughly; informal dead. **2** narrowly, only just, by a hair's breadth, by the skin of your teeth, barely, scarcely, hardly; informal by a whisker.

justice n. **1** fairness, justness, fair play, fair-mindedness, equity, right, even-handedness, honesty, morality. **2** the justice of his case: validity, justification, soundness, well-foundedness, legitimacy. **3 judge**, magistrate, recorder, sheriff; N. Amer. jurist.

> **WORD LINKS**
> *relating to a system of justice:*
> judicial

justifiable adj. **valid**, legitimate, warranted, well founded, justified, just, reasonable, tenable, defensible, sound, warrantable.
– OPPOSITES unjustifiable, unwarranted.

justification n. **grounds**, reason, basis, rationale, premise, vindication, explanation, defence, argument, case.

justify v. **1 give grounds for**, give reasons for, explain, account for, defend, vindicate, excuse, exonerate. **2 warrant**, be good reason for.

jut v. **stick out**, project, protrude, bulge out, overhang, beetle.

juvenile adj. **1 young**, teenage, adolescent, junior. **2 childish**, immature, puerile, infantile, babyish.
– OPPOSITES adult, mature.
• n. **child**, youngster, teenager, adolescent, minor, junior; informal kid.
– OPPOSITES adult.

Kk

keel v.
□ **keel over 1** capsize, turn turtle, turn upside down, founder, overturn, turn over, tip over. **2** collapse, faint, pass out, black out, swoon.

keen adj. **1** *I'm keen to help:* **eager**, anxious, intent, impatient, determined; informal raring, itching, dying. **2** *a keen bird-watcher:* **enthusiastic**, avid, ardent, fervent, conscientious, committed, dedicated. **3** *a girl he was keen on:* **attracted to**, interested in, fond of, taken with, smitten with, enamoured of; informal struck on. **4** *a keen mind:* **acute**, penetrating, astute, incisive, sharp, perceptive,

piercing, razor-sharp, shrewd, discerning, clever, intelligent, brilliant, bright, smart, wise, insightful. **5** *a keen sense of duty:* **intense**, acute, fierce, passionate, burning, fervent, strong, powerful.
– OPPOSITES reluctant, unenthusiastic.

keep v. **1** *I kept the forms:* **retain**, hold on to, save, store, put by/aside, set aside; informal hang on to. **2** *keep calm:* **remain**, stay. **3** *he keeps going on about it:* **persist in**, keep on, carry on, continue, insist on. **4** *keep the rules:* **comply with**, obey, observe, conform to, abide by, adhere to, stick to, heed, follow,

j
k

carry out, act on, make good, honour, keep to, stand by.
5 *keeping the old traditions:* **preserve**, keep alive/up, carry on, perpetuate, maintain, uphold.
6 *he stole to keep his family:* **provide for**, support, feed, maintain, sustain, take care of, look after. **7** *she keeps rabbits:* **breed**, rear, raise, tend, farm, own.
•n. **maintenance**, upkeep, sustenance, board (and lodging), food, livelihood.

keeper n. **curator**, custodian, guardian, conservator, administrator, overseer, steward, caretaker, attendant, concierge.

keeping n. **care**, custody, charge, guardianship, possession, trust, protection.
□ **in keeping with** consistent with, in harmony with, in accord with, in agreement with, in line with, in character with, compatible with, appropriate to, befitting, suitable for.

key n. **1** *the key to the mystery:* **answer**, clue, solution, explanation, basis, foundation. **2** *the key to success:* **means**, way, route, path, passport, secret, formula.
•adj. **crucial**, central, essential, indispensable, pivotal, critical, vital, principal, prime, major, leading, main, important.

kick v. **boot**, punt.
•n. (informal) *I get a kick out of driving:* **thrill**, excitement, stimulation, tingle, frisson; informal buzz, high; N. Amer. informal charge.

□ **kick off** (informal) start, commence, begin, get going, get off the ground, get under way, open, set in motion, launch, initiate, introduce, inaugurate.

kid n. (informal) **child**, youngster, baby, toddler, tot, infant, boy, girl, minor, juvenile, adolescent, teenager, youth, stripling; Scottish bairn; informal kiddie, nipper, kiddiewink; Brit. informal sprog; N. Amer. informal rug rat; Austral./NZ ankle-biter; derogatory brat.

kidnap v. **abduct**, carry off, capture, seize, snatch, take hostage.

kill v. **murder**, assassinate, eliminate, terminate, dispatch, execute, slaughter, exterminate, butcher, massacre; informal bump off, do away with, do in, top, take out, blow away; N. Amer. informal rub out, waste; literary slay.

killer n. **murderer**, assassin, butcher, gunman, terminator, executioner; informal hit man.

killing n. **murder**, assassination, homicide, manslaughter, execution, slaughter, massacre, butchery, bloodshed, carnage, extermination, genocide.

kin n. **relatives**, relations, family, kith and kin, kindred, kinsfolk, kinsmen, kinswomen, people; informal folks.

kind¹ n. **sort**, type, variety, style, form, class, category, genre, genus, species.

kind² adj. **kindly**, good-natured, kind-hearted, warm-hearted, caring, affectionate, loving,

kindle → knock

warm, considerate, obliging, compassionate, sympathetic, understanding, benevolent, benign, altruistic, unselfish, generous, charitable, philanthropic, helpful, thoughtful, humane; Brit. informal decent.
– OPPOSITES unkind.

kindle v. **1 light,** ignite, set light to, set fire to; informal torch. **2 rouse,** arouse, wake, awaken, stimulate, inspire, stir (up), excite, fire, trigger, activate, spark off.
– OPPOSITES extinguish.

kindly adj. **benevolent,** kind, kind-hearted, warm-hearted, generous, good-natured, gentle, warm, compassionate, caring, loving, benign, well meaning, considerate.
– OPPOSITES unkind, cruel.

kindness n. **kindliness,** affection, warmth, gentleness, concern, care, consideration, altruism, unselfishness, compassion, sympathy, benevolence, generosity.
– OPPOSITES unkindness.

king n. **ruler,** sovereign, monarch, Crown, His Majesty, emperor, prince, potentate.

kingdom n. **realm,** domain, dominion, country, empire, land, territory, nation, (sovereign) state, province.

kiss v. informal peck, smooch, canoodle, neck, pet; Brit. informal snog; N. Amer. informal buss; formal osculate.
•n. informal peck, smack, smacker,

smooch; Brit. informal snog; N. Amer. informal buss.

kit n. **1 equipment,** tools, implements, instruments, gadgets, utensils, appliances, gear, tackle, hardware, paraphernalia; informal things, stuff; Military accoutrements. **2** (informal) **clothes,** clothing, garments, outfit, dress, costume, attire, garb, strip; informal gear, get-up, rig-out. **3** a tool kit: **set,** selection, collection, pack. □ **kit out** equip, fit (out/up), furnish, supply, provide, issue, dress, clothe, attire, rig out, deck out; informal fix up.

knack n. **1 gift,** talent, flair, instinct, genius, ability, capability, capacity, aptitude, bent, facility, trick; informal the hang of something. **2 tendency,** habit, liability, propensity.

knickers pl. n. (Brit.) **underpants,** briefs; Brit. pants; informal panties, undies; Brit. informal smalls; dated drawers; historical bloomers.

knife v. **stab,** hack, gash, slash, lacerate, cut, bayonet, wound.

knit v. **unite,** unify, bond, fuse, coalesce, merge, meld, blend, join, link.

knob n. **lump,** bump, protrusion, protuberance, bulge, swelling, knot, nodule, boss.

knock v. **1 bang,** tap, rap, thump, pound, hammer, beat, strike, hit; informal bash. **2 collide with,** bump into, run into, crash into, smash into, plough into; N. Amer. impact.
•n. **tap,** rap, rat-tat, knocking,

k

bang, banging, pounding, hammering, thump, thud.
□ **knock down 1** fell, floor, flatten, knock over, run over/down. **2** demolish, pull down, tear down, destroy, raze, level, flatten, bulldoze. **knock out** knock unconscious, floor, prostrate; informal lay out, KO, fell.

knot n. *a knot of people:* cluster, group, band, huddle, bunch, circle, ring.
▪ v. **tie**, fasten, secure, bind, do up.

knotted adj. **tangled**, matted, snarled, unkempt, tousled; informal mussed up.

know v. **1** *she doesn't know I'm here:* **be aware**, realize, be conscious, be cognizant. **2** *I know the rules:* **be familiar with**, be conversant with, be acquainted with, be versed in, have a grasp of, understand, comprehend; informal be clued up on. **3** *do you know her?* **be acquainted with**, have met, be familiar with; Scottish ken.

know-how n. (informal) **expertise**, skill, proficiency, knowledge, understanding, mastery, technique; informal savvy.

knowing adj. **significant**, meaningful, expressive, suggestive, eloquent, superior.

knowledge n. **1 understanding**, comprehension, grasp, command, mastery, familiarity, acquaintance; informal know-how. **2 learning**, erudition, education, scholarship, schooling, wisdom. **3 awareness**, consciousness, realization, cognition, apprehension, perception, appreciation, cognizance.
– OPPOSITES ignorance.

WORD LINKS
relating to knowledge: gnostic

knowledgeable adj. **1 well informed**, learned, well read, (well) educated, erudite, scholarly, cultured, cultivated, enlightened. **2** *he's knowledgeable about art:* **conversant with**, familiar with, well acquainted with, au fait with, up on, up to date with, abreast of; informal clued up on.
– OPPOSITES ignorant.

known adj. **recognized**, well known, widely known, noted, celebrated, notable, notorious, acknowledged.

kudos n. **prestige**, cachet, glory, honour, status, standing, distinction, admiration, respect, esteem.

label n. **1 tag**, ticket, tab, sticker, marker, docket. **2 description**, designation, name, epithet, nickname, sobriquet, title.
•v. **1 tag**, ticket, mark, stamp. **2 categorize**, classify, class, describe, designate, identify, mark, stamp, brand, call, name, term, dub.

laborious adj. **1 arduous**, hard, heavy, difficult, strenuous, gruelling, punishing, exacting, tough, onerous, challenging, painstaking, time-consuming. **2 laboured**, strained, forced, stiff, stilted, unnatural, artificial, ponderous.
– OPPOSITES easy, effortless.

labour n. **1 work**, toil, exertion, effort, industry, drudgery; informal slog, grind; old use travail. **2 workers**, employees, labourers, workforce, staff. **3 childbirth**, birth, delivery; technical parturition.
•v. **work (hard)**, toil, slave (away), struggle, strive, exert yourself, endeavour, try hard; informal slog away, plug away.

laboured adj. **1** laboured breathing: **strained**, difficult, forced, laborious. **2** a laboured metaphor: **contrived**, forced, unconvincing, unnatural, artificial, overdone.
– OPPOSITES natural, easy.

labourer n. **workman**, worker, manual worker, blue-collar worker, (hired) hand, roustabout, drudge, menial; Austral./NZ rouseabout; dated navvy.

labyrinthine adj. **1 maze-like**, winding, twisting, serpentine, meandering. **2 complicated**, intricate, complex, involved, tortuous, convoluted, elaborate, confusing, puzzling, mystifying, bewildering, baffling.

lace v. **1 fasten**, do up, tie up, secure, knot. **2 flavour**, mix, blend, fortify, strengthen, season, spice (up), liven up, doctor, adulterate; informal spike.

laceration n. **gash**, cut, wound, injury, tear, slash, scratch, scrape, abrasion, graze.

lack n. **absence**, want, need, deficiency, dearth, shortage, shortfall, scarcity, paucity.
– OPPOSITES abundance.
•v. **be without**, be in need of, be short of, be deficient in, be low on, be pressed for, need; informal be strapped for.

lacklustre adj. **uninspired**, uninspiring, unimaginative, dull, humdrum, colourless, bland, insipid, flat, dry, lifeless, tame, prosaic, dreary, tedious.
– OPPOSITES inspired.

lad n. (informal) **1 boy**, schoolboy, youth, youngster, juvenile, stripling; informal kid, nipper; Scottish informal laddie; derogatory brat. **2 (young) man**, fellow; informal guy, geezer; Brit. informal chap, bloke; N. Amer. informal dude, hombre.

laden adj. **loaded**, burdened, weighed down, overloaded, piled high, full, packed, stuffed, crammed; informal chock-full, chock-a-block.

lady n. **1 woman**, female, girl; Scottish & N. English lass, lassie; N. Amer. informal dame, broad; Austral. informal sheila. **2 noblewoman**, aristocrat, duchess, countess, peeress, viscountess, baroness.

ladylike adj. **genteel**, polite, refined, well bred, cultivated, polished, decorous, proper, respectable, well mannered, cultured, sophisticated, elegant; Brit. informal posh.

lag v. **fall behind**, trail, bring up the rear, dawdle, hang back, delay, loiter, linger, dally, straggle.

laid-back adj. (informal) **relaxed**, easy-going, free and easy, casual, nonchalant, blasé, cool, calm, unconcerned, leisurely, unhurried; informal unflappable.
– OPPOSITES uptight.

lake n. **pool**, pond, tarn, reservoir, lagoon, waterhole; Scottish loch; Anglo-Irish lough; N. Amer. bayou.

lame adj. **1 limping**, hobbling, crippled, disabled, incapacitated; informal gammy. **2 feeble**, weak, thin, flimsy, poor, unconvincing, implausible, unlikely.

lament v. **1 mourn**, grieve, sorrow, weep, cry, wail, keen. **2 complain about**, bewail, bemoan, deplore.
– OPPOSITES celebrate, welcome.

lamentable adj. **deplorable**, regrettable, terrible, awful, wretched, woeful, dire, disastrous, desperate, grave, appalling, dreadful, pitiful, shameful, unfortunate; formal egregious.
– OPPOSITES wonderful.

land n. **1 dry land**, terra firma, coast, coastline, shore. **2 grounds**, fields, property, acres, acreage, estate, real estate. **3 country**, nation, state, realm, kingdom, province, region, territory, area, domain.
• v. **1 disembark**, go ashore, debark, alight, get off, berth, dock, moor, (drop) anchor, tie up, put in, touch down, come to rest. **2** (informal) **get**, obtain, acquire, secure, gain, net, win, achieve, attain, bag, carry off.
– OPPOSITES embark, take off.

> **WORD LINKS**
> *relating to land:* terrestrial

landlord, landlady n. **1 owner**, proprietor, lessor, householder, landowner. **2 licensee**, innkeeper, hotelier; Brit. publican; humorous mine host.
– OPPOSITES tenant.

landmark n. **1 feature**, sight, monument, building. **2** *a landmark in Indian history:* **turning point**, milestone, watershed.

landscape n. **scenery**, country, countryside, topography, terrain, view, panorama.

landslide n. **1 landslip**, rockfall, mudslide, avalanche. **2 decisive victory**, runaway victory, overwhelming majority; informal whitewash.

lane n. **road**, street, track, trail, alley, alleyway, passage, path.

language n. **1 speech**, speaking, talk, discourse, communication, words, vocabulary. **2 tongue**, mother tongue, native tongue, dialect, patois; informal lingo. **3 wording**, phrasing, phraseology, style, vocabulary, terminology, expressions, turn of phrase, parlance.

WORD LINKS
relating to language: linguistic

languish v. **1 deteriorate**, decline, go downhill, wither, droop, wilt, fade. **2 waste away**, rot, be abandoned, be neglected, be forgotten, suffer.
– OPPOSITES thrive.

lap[1] v. **1 drink**, lick up, sup, swallow, slurp, gulp. **2 splash**, wash, swish, slosh, break, plash; literary purl.
□ **lap up** relish, revel in, savour, delight in, wallow in, glory in, enjoy.

lap[2] n. **circuit**, leg, circle, round, stretch.

lapse n. **1 failure**, slip, error, mistake, blunder, fault, omission; informal slip-up. **2 decline**, fall, deterioration, degeneration, backsliding, regression. **3 interval**, gap, pause, interlude, lull, hiatus, break.
•v. **1 expire**, run out, (come to

an) end, cease, stop, terminate. **2 revert**, relapse, drift, slide, slip, sink.

large adj. **big**, great, sizeable, substantial, considerable, huge, extensive, voluminous, vast, prodigious, massive, immense, enormous, colossal, king-size(d), heavy, mammoth, gigantic, giant, fat, stout, strapping, bulky, burly; informal jumbo, mega, whopping.
– OPPOSITES small.

largely adv. **mostly**, mainly, to a large/great extent, chiefly, predominantly, primarily, principally, for the most part, in the main, on the whole.

lash v. **1 beat against**, dash against, pound, batter, hammer against, strike, hit, drum. **2 fasten**, bind, tie (up), tether, hitch, knot, rope.
□ **lash out 1** criticize, attack, condemn, censure; informal lay into, dis; Brit. informal slag off, have a go at. **2** hit out at, strike, let fly at, take a swing at, set on, turn on, round on, attack; informal lay into, pitch into.

last[1] adj. **1 final**, closing, concluding, end, ultimate, terminal, later, latter. **2 rearmost**, hindmost, endmost, furthest (back). **3 previous**, preceding, prior, former, latest, most recent.
– OPPOSITES first, next.

last[2] v. **1** *the hearing lasted for six days:* **continue**, go on, carry on, keep on/going, take. **2** *he won't last long as manager:* **survive**, endure, hold on/out, keep

going, persevere, persist, stay, remain; informal stick it out, hang on, go the distance.
– OPPOSITES end.

lasting adj. **enduring**, long-lasting, long-lived, abiding, continuing, long-term, permanent, durable, stable, secure, long-standing, eternal, undying, everlasting, unending, never-ending.
– OPPOSITES passing, ephemeral.

late adj. **1 behind schedule**, tardy, overdue, delayed, belated, behindhand. **2 dead**, departed, lamented, passed on/away; formal deceased. **3 recent**, fresh, new, up to date, latter-day, current.
– OPPOSITES punctual, early.

lately adv. **recently**, not long ago, of late, latterly, in recent times.

latent adj. **dormant**, untapped, undiscovered, hidden, concealed, undeveloped, unrealized, unfulfilled, potential.

later adj. **subsequent**, following, succeeding, future, upcoming, to come, ensuing, next.
– OPPOSITES earlier, preceding.
• adv. **subsequently**, eventually, then, next, later on, afterwards, at a later date, in the future, in due course, by and by, in a while, in time; formal thereafter.

latest adj. **most recent**, newest, up to the minute, current, state-of-the-art, cutting-edge; informal in, with it, trendy, hip, hot, happening, cool.
– OPPOSITES old.

latitude n. **freedom**, scope, leeway, (breathing) space, flexibility, liberty, independence, free rein, licence.
– OPPOSITES restriction.

latter adj. **1 later**, closing, end, concluding, final. **2 last-mentioned**, second, last, final.
– OPPOSITES earlier, former.

laudable adj. **praiseworthy**, commendable, admirable, worthy, deserving, creditable, estimable, exemplary.
– OPPOSITES shameful.

laugh v. **chuckle**, chortle, guffaw, giggle, titter, snigger, roar, split your sides; informal be in stitches, be rolling in the aisles, crease up, fall about, crack up; Brit. informal kill yourself.
• n. **1 chuckle**, chortle, guffaw, giggle, titter, snigger, roar, shriek. **2** (informal) **joke**, prank, jest; informal lark, hoot, scream.
□ **laugh at** ridicule, mock, deride, scoff at, jeer at, sneer at, jibe at, make fun of, poke fun at, taunt, tease; informal take the mickey out of. **laugh off** dismiss, make a joke of, make light of, shrug off, brush aside; informal pooh-pooh.

laughter n. **1 laughing**, chuckling, chortling, guffawing, giggling, tittering, sniggering. **2 amusement**, entertainment, humour, mirth, merriment, gaiety, hilarity, jollity, fun.

launch v. **1 propel**, fire, shoot, throw, hurl, fling, pitch, lob, let fly; informal chuck, heave, sling. **2 start**, begin, initiate, put in place, set up, inaugurate, introduce; informal kick off.

lavatory n. **toilet**, WC, convenience, privy, latrine; Brit. cloakroom; N. Amer. washroom, bathroom, rest room, men's/ladies' room, comfort station; Brit. informal loo, bog, the Ladies, the Gents, khazi; N. Amer. informal can, john; Austral./NZ informal dunny.

lavish adj. **1 sumptuous**, luxurious, gorgeous, costly, expensive, opulent, grand, splendid, rich, fancy; informal posh, bling-bling. **2 generous**, liberal, bountiful, unstinting, unsparing, free, munificent, extravagant, abundant, copious, plentiful, prolific, excessive, wasteful, prodigal; literary plenteous.
– OPPOSITES meagre, frugal.
▸v. **shower**, heap, pour, deluge, throw at, squander, dissipate.
– OPPOSITES begrudge, stint.

law n. **1 regulation**, statute, act, bill, decree, edict, rule, ruling, dictum, command, order, directive, dictate, diktat, fiat, by-law; (**laws**) legislation, constitution, code; N. Amer. formal ordinance. **2 principle**, rule, precept, commandment, belief, creed, credo, maxim, tenet, doctrine, canon.

> **WORD LINKS**
> *relating to laws:* legal, legislative

lawful adj. **legitimate**, legal, licit, permissible, permitted, allowable, allowed, rightful, sanctioned, authorized, warranted; informal legit.

– OPPOSITES illegal.

lawyer n. solicitor, barrister, advocate, counsel, Queen's Counsel, QC; N. Amer. attorney, counselor(-at-law); informal brief, legal eagle.

lax adj. **slack**, slipshod, negligent, remiss, careless, sloppy, slapdash, offhand, casual.
– OPPOSITES strict.

lay¹ v. **1 put (down)**, place, set (down), deposit, rest, position, shove; informal stick, dump, park, plonk; Brit. informal bung. **2** *we laid plans for the voyage:* **devise**, arrange, prepare, work out, hatch, design, plan, scheme, plot, conceive, put together, draw up, produce, develop, formulate; informal cook up. **3** *I'd lay money on it:* **bet**, wager, gamble, stake.
▫ **lay down 1** relinquish, surrender, give up, abandon. **2** formulate, set down, draw up, frame, ordain, dictate, decree, enact, pass, decide, determine. **lay in** stock up with, stockpile, store (up), amass, hoard, put aside/away/by, garner, squirrel away; informal salt away, stash away. **lay off 1** make redundant, dismiss, let go, discharge, give notice to; informal sack, fire. **2** (informal) give up, stop, refrain from, abstain from, desist from, cut out; informal pack in, leave off, quit. **lay on** provide, supply, furnish, line up, organize, prepare, produce, make available; informal fix up.

lay² adj. **1** *a lay preacher:* **non-ordained**, non-clerical. **2** *science* *books for a lay audience:* **non-expert**, non-professional, non-specialist, non-technical, amateur, unqualified, untrained.

layer n. **sheet**, stratum, level, tier, seam, coat, coating, film, covering, blanket, skin.

layout n. **arrangement**, design, plan, formation, format, configuration, composition, organization, geography, structure.

laze v. **relax**, unwind, loaf around/about, lounge around/about, loll around/about, lie around/about, take it easy, idle; *informal* hang around, chill (out), veg (out).

lazy adj. **1 idle**, indolent, slothful, bone idle, work-shy, shiftless. **2 slow**, slow-moving, languid, leisurely, lethargic, sluggish, torpid.
– OPPOSITES industrious.

lead v. **1 guide**, conduct, show (the way), usher, escort, steer, shepherd, accompany, see, take. **2** *what led you to believe him?* **cause**, induce, prompt, move, persuade, drive, make. **3 control**, preside over, head, command, govern, run, manage, rule, be in charge of; *informal* head up. **4 be ahead**, be winning, be in front, be in the lead, be first, outrun, outstrip, outpace, leave behind, outdo, outclass, beat. **5** *I want to lead a normal life:* **live**, have, spend, follow, pass, enjoy.
– OPPOSITES follow.
•n. **1 first place**, winning position, vanguard. **2** *a 3–0 lead:*

margin, advantage, gap, edge. **3 example**, model, pattern, standard, guidance, direction, role model. **4 leading role**, starring role, title role, principal role. **5 leash**, tether, rope, chain. **6 clue**, pointer, hint, tip, tip-off, suggestion, indication.
•adj. **leading**, first, top, foremost, front, pole, head, chief, principal, premier.
□ **lead to** result in, cause, bring on/about, give rise to, create, produce, occasion, effect, generate, contribute to, promote, provoke, stir up, spark off.

leader n. **chief**, head, principal, commander, captain, controller, superior, chairman, chair, director, manager, superintendent, supervisor, overseer, master, mistress, prime minister, president, premier, governor, ruler, monarch, sovereign; *informal* boss, skipper, gaffer, guv'nor, number one.
– OPPOSITES follower, supporter.

leadership n. **1** *the leadership of the Party:* **control**, rule, command, dominion, headship, directorship, premiership, chairmanship, governorship, captaincy. **2** *firm leadership:* **guidance**, direction, authority, management, supervision, government.

leading adj. **main**, chief, top, front, major, prime, principal, foremost, key, central, dominant, greatest, pre-eminent, star.
– OPPOSITES subordinate, minor.

leaf n. **1** (**leaves**) foliage, greenery. **2 page**, sheet, folio.
•v. I leafed through a magazine: flick, flip, thumb, skim, browse, glance, riffle, scan, run your eye over, peruse.

leaflet n. **pamphlet**, booklet, brochure, handbill, circular, flyer, handout; N. Amer. folder, dodger.

league n. **1 alliance**, confederation, confederacy, federation, union, association, coalition, consortium, affiliation, cooperative, partnership, fellowship, syndicate. **2 class**, group, category, level, standard.
□ **in league** collaborating, cooperating, in alliance, allied, conspiring, hand in glove; informal in cahoots.

leak v. **1 seep**, escape, ooze, drip, dribble, drain, run. **2 disclose**, divulge, reveal, make public, tell, expose, release, let slip.
•n. **1 hole**, opening, puncture, perforation, gash, slit, break, crack, chink, fissure, rupture, tear. **2 escape**, leakage, discharge, seepage. **3 disclosure**, revelation, exposé.

lean¹ v. **1 rest**, recline, be propped. **2 slant**, incline, bend, tilt, slope, tip, list. **3** (**lean towards**) tend towards, incline towards, gravitate towards, favour, prefer, have a preference for, have an affinity with.
4 (**lean on**) depend on, rely on, count on, bank on, trust in, have faith in.

lean² adj. **1 thin**, slim, slender, skinny, spare, angular, spindly, wiry, lanky. **2 meagre**, sparse, poor, mean, inadequate, insufficient, paltry.
– OPPOSITES fat, abundant.

leaning n. **inclination**, tendency, bent, propensity, penchant, preference, predisposition, predilection, proclivity.

leap v. **1 jump**, vault, spring, bound, hop, clear. **2 rise**, soar, rocket, skyrocket, shoot up, escalate.
•n. **rise**, surge, upsurge, escalation, upswing, upturn.

learn v. **1 master**, grasp, take in, absorb, assimilate, digest, familiarize yourself with; informal get the hang of. **2 memorize**, learn by heart, learn parrot-fashion, get off pat. **3 discover**, find out, become aware, be informed, hear, understand, gather; informal get wind of.

learned adj. **scholarly**, erudite, knowledgeable, widely read, cultured, intellectual, academic, literary, bookish, highbrow; informal brainy.
– OPPOSITES ignorant.

learner n. **beginner**, novice, starter, trainee, apprentice, pupil, student, fledgling, neophyte, tyro; informal rookie, greenhorn.
– OPPOSITES expert, veteran.

learning n. **study**, knowledge, education, schooling, tuition, teaching, scholarship, erudition, understanding, wisdom.
– OPPOSITES ignorance.

lease v. **rent (out)**, hire (out), charter (out), let (out), sublet.

leave[1] v. **1 go away**, depart, withdraw, retire, take your leave, pull out, quit, decamp, flee, escape, abandon, desert, vacate; informal vamoose, push off, shove off, clear out/off, split, make tracks, do a bunk. **2 set off**, set sail, get going. **3 abandon**, desert, jilt, leave in the lurch, leave high and dry, throw over; informal dump, ditch, walk/run out on. **4 resign**, retire, step down, give up, drop out; informal quit, jack in. **5 leave behind**, forget, lose, mislay. **6 entrust**, hand over, pass on, refer, delegate. **7 bequeath**, will, endow, hand down.
– OPPOSITES arrive.
□ **leave out** miss out, omit, overlook, forget, skip, exclude, drop, pass over.

leave[2] n. **1 permission**, consent, authorization, sanction, dispensation, approval, clearance, blessing, agreement, assent; informal the go-ahead, the green light. **2 holiday**, vacation, break, furlough, sabbatical, leave of absence; informal vac.

lecherous adj. **lustful**, licentious, lascivious, libidinous, lewd, salacious, prurient; informal randy; formal concupiscent.

lecture n. **1 speech**, talk, address, discourse, presentation, oration. **2 reprimand**, scolding, rebuke, reproach; informal dressing-down, telling-off, talking-to, tongue-lashing.
•v. **1 talk**, speak, discourse, hold forth, teach; informal spout, sound off. **2 reprimand**, scold, rebuke, reproach, take to task, berate, upbraid, remonstrate with, castigate; informal tell off, bawl out; Brit. informal tick off, carpet.

leeway n. **freedom**, scope, latitude, space, room, liberty, flexibility, licence, free hand, free rein.

left adj. **left-hand**, sinistral; Nautical port; Heraldry sinister.
– OPPOSITES right.

left-wing adj. **socialist**, communist, leftist, Labour; informal Commie, lefty, red, pinko.
– OPPOSITES right-wing, conservative.

leg n. **1 limb**, member, shank; informal pin, peg. **2 part**, stage, section, phase, stretch, lap.

legacy n. **bequest**, inheritance, endowment, gift, birthright, estate, heirloom.

legal adj. **1 lawful**, legitimate, legalized, valid, permissible, permitted, sanctioned, authorized, licensed, allowed, allowable, above board, acceptable, constitutional; informal legit. **2** the legal system: **judicial**, juridical, forensic.
– OPPOSITES illegal.

legend n. **1 myth**, saga, epic, folk tale, folk story, fable; (**legends**) lore, folklore, mythology. **2 celebrity**, star, superstar, icon, phenomenon, luminary, giant, hero; informal celeb, megastar. **3 caption**, inscription, dedication, slogan, heading, title.

legendary adj. **1 fabled**, mythical, traditional, fairy-tale, storybook, mythological, fictional, fictitious. **2 famous**, celebrated, famed, renowned, acclaimed, illustrious, esteemed, honoured, exalted, venerable, eminent, distinguished, great.

legion n. **horde**, throng, multitude, crowd, mass, mob, gang, swarm, flock, herd, army.

legislation n. **law**, rules, rulings, regulations, acts, bills, statutes; N. Amer. formal ordinances.

legislature n. **parliament**, senate, congress, council, chamber, house.

legitimate adj. **1** *the legitimate use of such weapons*: **legal**, lawful, authorized, permitted, sanctioned, approved, licensed; informal legit. **2** *the legitimate heir*: **rightful**, lawful, genuine, authentic, real, true, proper; informal kosher. **3** *a legitimate excuse*: **valid**, sound, admissible, acceptable, well founded, justifiable, reasonable, sensible, just, fair, bona fide.
– OPPOSITES illegal, invalid.

leisure n. **free time**, spare time, time off, rest, recreation, relaxation, R & R.
– OPPOSITES work.

leisurely adj. **unhurried**, relaxed, easy, gentle, sedate, comfortable, restful, undemanding, slow.
– OPPOSITES hurried.

lend v. **1 loan**, advance; Brit. informal sub. **2 add**, impart, give,

bestow, confer, provide, supply, furnish, contribute.
– OPPOSITES borrow.

length n. **1 extent**, distance, span, reach, area, expanse, range. **2 period**, duration, stretch, span, term. **3** *a length of silk*: **piece**, strip, section, swatch.
□ **at length 1** in detail, in depth, thoroughly, for a long time, for ages, for hours, interminably, endlessly. **2** eventually, in time, finally, at (long) last, in the end, ultimately.

lengthen v. **extend**, elongate, increase, prolong, draw out, protract, spin out.
– OPPOSITES shorten.

lengthy adj. **(very) long**, longlasting, protracted, extended, long-drawn-out, prolonged, interminable, time-consuming, long-winded.
– OPPOSITES short.

lenient adj. **merciful**, forgiving, forbearing, tolerant, charitable, humane, indulgent, magnanimous, clement.
– OPPOSITES severe.

lessen v. **1 reduce**, decrease, minimize, moderate, diminish, allay, assuage, alleviate, dull, deaden, take the edge off. **2 decrease**, decline, subside, slacken, abate, fade, die down, let up, ease off, tail off, drop (off/away), dwindle, ebb, wane, recede.
– OPPOSITES increase.

lesser adj. **1 less important**, minor, secondary, subsidiary, peripheral. **2 subordinate**,

inferior, second-class, subservient, lowly, humble.
– OPPOSITES greater, superior.

lesson n. **1 class**, session, seminar, tutorial, lecture, period. **2 warning**, deterrent, caution, example, message, moral.

let v. **1 allow**, permit, give permission to, give leave to, authorize, license, empower, enable, entitle; informal give the go-ahead to, OK. **2 rent (out)**, lease, hire (out), sublet.
– OPPOSITES prevent, prohibit.
□ **let down** fail, disappoint, disillusion, abandon, desert, leave in the lurch. **let go** release, loose your hold on, relinquish. **let off 1 detonate**, discharge, explode, set off, fire (off), launch. **2** (informal) **pardon**, forgive, acquit, absolve, exonerate, clear, vindicate; informal let someone off the hook. **3 excuse**, exempt, spare. **let out 1 release**, liberate, (set) free, let go, discharge, set/turn loose. **2 utter**, emit, give (vent to), produce, issue, express, voice, release. **3 reveal**, make known, tell, disclose, mention, divulge, let slip, give away, let it be known, blurt out. **let up** (informal) **1 lessen**, decrease, subside, abate, ease, moderate, die down, diminish, tail off. **2 relax**, ease up, slow down, pause, break (off), take a break, rest, stop.

let-down n. **disappointment**, anticlimax, comedown, nonevent, fiasco; informal washout, damp squib.

lethal adj. **fatal**, deadly, mortal, terminal, life-threatening, murderous, poisonous, toxic, noxious, venomous, dangerous.
– OPPOSITES harmless, safe.

lethargic adj. **sluggish**, inert, inactive, slow, lifeless, languid, listless, apathetic, weary, tired, fatigued, enervated.
– OPPOSITES energetic.

letter n. **1 character**, sign, symbol, figure. **2 message**, note, line, missive, dispatch, communication; formal epistle; **(letters) correspondence**, post, mail.

WORD LINKS
relating to letter-writing:
epistolary

level adj. **1** a level surface: **flat**, smooth, even, uniform, plane, flush, horizontal. **2** a level voice: **steady**, even, uniform, regular, constant, unchanging. **3** the scores were level: **equal**, even, drawn, tied, all square, neck and neck, level pegging, on a par, evenly matched; informal even-stevens, nip and tuck.
– OPPOSITES uneven, unequal.
•n. **1 rank**, position, degree, grade, stage, standard, class, group, set, classification. **2** a high level of employment: **quantity**, amount, extent, measure, degree, volume.
•v. **1 even out**, even out, flatten, smooth (out). **2 raze (to the ground)**, demolish, flatten, bulldoze, destroy. **3 equalize**, equal, even (up), make level.

4 aim, point, direct, train, focus, turn.

□ **on the level** (informal) genuine, straight, honest, above board, fair, true, sincere, straightforward; informal upfront; N. Amer. informal on the up and up.

lever n. **handle**, arm, switch, crowbar, bar, jemmy.
•v. **prise**, force, wrench; N. Amer. pry; informal jemmy.

leverage n. **1 force**, purchase, grip, hold, anchorage. **2** more leverage in negotiations: **influence**, power, authority, weight, sway, pull, control, say, advantage, pressure; informal clout, muscle, teeth.

levy v. **impose**, charge, exact, raise, collect.
•n. **tax**, tariff, toll, excise, duty.

liability n. **1 responsibility**, accountability. **2** (**liabilities**) **obligations**, debts, arrears, dues, commitments. **3** he became a liability on and off the field: **hindrance**, handicap, nuisance, inconvenience, embarrassment, impediment, disadvantage, millstone, encumbrance, burden.
– OPPOSITES asset.

liable adj. **1 responsible**, accountable, answerable, blameworthy, at fault. **2 likely**, inclined, tending, apt, prone, given, subject, susceptible, vulnerable, exposed, in danger of, at risk of.

liaise v. **cooperate**, collaborate, communicate, network, interface, link up; informal hook up.

liaison n. **1 cooperation**, contact, association, connection, collaboration, communication, alliance, partnership. **2 love affair**, relationship, romance, attachment, fling.

liar n. **fibber**, deceiver, perjurer, dissembler, faker, hoaxer, impostor.

libel n. **defamation** (of character), character assassination, calumny, misrepresentation, scandalmongering, slur, smear; informal mud-slinging.
•v. **defame**, malign, blacken someone's name, sully someone's reputation, smear, cast aspersions on, drag someone's name through the mud/mire, denigrate, traduce; N. Amer. slur.

libellous adj. **defamatory**, denigratory, disparaging, derogatory, false, untrue, insulting, scurrilous.

liberal adj. **1 tolerant**, unprejudiced, broad-minded, open-minded, permissive, free (and easy), easy-going, libertarian, indulgent, lenient. **2** a liberal social agenda: **progressive**, advanced, modern, forward-looking, forward-thinking, enlightened, reformist, radical; informal go-ahead. **3** a liberal interpretation of the law: **flexible**, broad, loose, rough, free, non-literal. **4 abundant**, copious, ample, plentiful, lavish, generous, open-handed, unsparing, unstinting, free, munificent.
– OPPOSITES reactionary, strict.

liberate v. **(set) free**, release, let out, let go, set loose, save, rescue, emancipate; historical enfranchise.
– OPPOSITES imprison, enslave.

liberty n. **freedom**, independence, immunity, self-determination, autonomy, emancipation, sovereignty, self-government, self-rule, self determination, civil liberties, human rights.
– OPPOSITES slavery.
□ **at liberty 1 free**, loose, on the loose, at large, on the run, out. **2 able**, free, entitled, permitted.

licence n. **1 permit**, certificate, document, documentation, authorization, warrant, credentials, pass, papers. **2 franchise**, consent, sanction, warrant, charter, concession. **3 freedom**, free rein, latitude, independence, scope, carte blanche; informal a blank cheque.

license v. **permit**, allow, authorize, give authority to, give permission to, certify, accredit, empower, entitle, enable, sanction.
– OPPOSITES ban.

lid n. **cover**, top, cap, covering, stopper.

lie[1] n. **untruth**, falsehood, fib, fabrication, deception, invention, (piece of) fiction, falsification, white lie; informal tall story, whopper; humorous terminological inexactitude.
– OPPOSITES truth.
▪ v. **tell a lie**, fib, dissemble, perjure yourself.

WORD LINKS
telling lies: mendacious

---

lie[2] v. **1** *he was lying on the bed:* **recline**, lie down, be recumbent, be prostrate, be supine, be prone, be stretched out, sprawl, rest, repose, lounge, loll. **2** *her bag lay on the chair:* **be**, be situated, be positioned, be located, be placed, be found, be sited, be arranged, rest.
– OPPOSITES stand.

life n. **1 existence**, being, living, animation, sentience, creation, viability. **2 living creatures**, fauna, flora, the ecosystem, the biosphere, the ecosphere. **3 way of life**, lifestyle, situation, fate, lot. **4 lifetime**, lifespan, days, time (on earth), existence. **5 vitality**, animation, liveliness, vivacity, verve, high spirits, exuberance, zest, enthusiasm, energy, vigour, dynamism, elan, gusto, bounce, spirit, fire. **6 biography**, autobiography, history, chronicle, account, memoirs, diary.
– OPPOSITES death.

WORD LINKS
having life: animate, vital

---

lifeless adj. **1 dead**, stiff, cold, inert, inanimate; formal deceased. **2 barren**, sterile, bare, desolate, stark, bleak, arid, infertile, uninhabited. **3 lacklustre**, apathetic, lethargic, uninspired, dull, colourless, characterless, wooden.
– OPPOSITES alive, lively.

lifelike adj. **realistic**, true to life, faithful, detailed, vivid, graphic, natural, naturalistic, representational.

lifestyle n. **way of life**, life, situation, conduct, behaviour, ways, habits, mores.

lifetime n. **lifespan**, life, days, time (on earth), existence, career.

lift v. **1 raise**, hoist, heave, haul up, heft, elevate, hold high, pick up, grab, take up, winch up, jack up; informal heave. **2** *the fog had lifted:* **clear**, rise, disperse, dissipate, disappear, vanish, dissolve. **3** *the ban has been lifted:* **cancel**, remove, withdraw, revoke, rescind, end, stop, terminate.
• n. *the goal will give his confidence a lift:* **boost**, fillip, impetus, encouragement, spur, push; informal shot in the arm.
□ **lift off** take off, become airborne, be launched, take to the air, blast off.

light¹ n. **1 illumination**, brightness, shining, gleam, brilliance, radiance, luminosity, luminescence, incandescence, blaze, glare, glow, lustre; literary refulgence, effulgence. **2 lamp**, lantern, torch, beacon, candle, bulb. **3 daylight**, daytime, day, sunlight.
– OPPOSITES darkness.
• adj. **1 bright**, well lit, sunny. **2 pale**, pastel, delicate, subtle, faded, bleached.
– OPPOSITES dark.
• v. **1 set fire to**, ignite, kindle.

2 illuminate, irradiate, floodlight; literary illumine.

light² adj. **1 lightweight**, portable, underweight. **2 flimsy**, thin, lightweight, floaty, gauzy, diaphanous, filmy. **3** *a light dinner:* **small**, modest, simple, insubstantial, frugal. **4** *light duties:* **easy**, simple, undemanding, untaxing; informal cushy. **5** *a light touch:* **gentle**, delicate, dainty, soft, faint, careful, sensitive, subtle. **6** *light entertainment:* **undemanding**, middle-of-the-road, mainstream, lightweight, lowbrow, mass-market, superficial, frivolous, trivial.
– OPPOSITES heavy.

lighten¹ v. **1 brighten**, light up, illuminate, irradiate; literary illumine. **2 bleach**, whiten, blanch.
– OPPOSITES darken.

lighten² v. **1 reduce**, lessen, decrease, diminish, ease, alleviate, relieve. **2 cheer (up)**, brighten, gladden, lift, boost, buoy (up), revive, restore, revitalize.
– OPPOSITES increase.

light-hearted adj. **carefree**, cheerful, cheery, happy, merry, glad, playful, blithe, bright, entertaining, amusing, diverting; informal upbeat; dated gay, sportive.
– OPPOSITES miserable.

lightly adv. **1 softly**, gently, faintly, delicately. **2 sparingly**, sparsely, moderately, slightly, subtly. **3** carelessly, airily, readily, heedlessly, uncaringly, unthinkingly, thoughtlessly, flippantly.

lightweight adj. **1** thin, light, filmy, flimsy, insubstantial, summery. **2** trivial, insubstantial, superficial, shallow, undemanding, frivolous.
– OPPOSITES heavy, serious.

like[1] v. **1** be fond of, have a soft spot for, care about, think well/highly of, admire, respect; be attracted to, fancy, be keen on, be taken with; informal rate. **2** enjoy, have a taste for, care for, be partial to, take pleasure in, be keen on, appreciate, love, adore, relish; informal have a thing about, be into, be mad about, be hooked on. **3** *feel free to say what you like:* choose, please, wish, want, see/think fit, care to, will.
– OPPOSITES hate.

like[2] prep. **1** similar to, the same as, identical to, akin to, resembling. **2** in the manner of, in the same way/manner as, in a similar way to. **3** such as, for example, for instance, namely, in particular, viz. **4** characteristic of, typical of, in character with.
– OPPOSITES unlike.

likeable adj. pleasant, friendly, agreeable, affable, amiable, genial, personable, nice, good-natured, engaging, appealing, endearing, convivial, congenial.
– OPPOSITES unpleasant.

likelihood n. probability, chance, prospect, possibility, odds, risk, threat, danger, hope, promise.

likely adj. **1** probable, possible, odds-on, expected, anticipated; informal on the cards. **2** plausible, reasonable, feasible, acceptable, believable, credible, tenable. **3** suitable, promising, appropriate.
– OPPOSITES unlikely, implausible.

liken v. compare, equate, set beside.
– OPPOSITES contrast.

likeness n. **1** resemblance, similarity, similitude, correspondence. **2** representation, image, depiction, portrayal, picture, drawing, sketch, painting, portrait, photograph, study.
– OPPOSITES dissimilarity.

likewise adv. **1** also, equally, in addition, too, as well, to boot, besides, moreover, furthermore. **2** the same, similarly, correspondingly.

liking n. fondness, love, affection, penchant, soft spot, attachment, taste, passion, preference, partiality, predilection, weakness.
– OPPOSITES dislike.

limb n. **1** arm, leg, wing, appendage; old use member. **2** branch, bough.

limelight n. attention, interest, scrutiny, the public eye, publicity, prominence, the spotlight, fame, celebrity.
– OPPOSITES obscurity.

limit n. **1** boundary (line), border, frontier, bound, edge,

perimeter, margin. **2 maximum**, ceiling, cap, cut-off point.
•v. **restrict**, curb, cap, (hold in) check, restrain, circumscribe, regulate, control, govern, ration.

limitation n. **1 restriction**, curb, restraint, control, check. **2 imperfection**, flaw, defect, failing, shortcoming, weak point, deficiency, frailty, weakness.
– OPPOSITES strength.

limited adj. restricted, circumscribed, finite, small, tight, slight, in short supply, short, meagre, scanty, sparse, inadequate, insufficient, paltry, poor, minimal.
– OPPOSITES limitless, ample.

limp¹ v. hobble, hop, lurch, stagger, shuffle, totter, shamble.

limp² adj. soft, flaccid, loose, slack, lax, floppy, drooping, droopy, sagging.
– OPPOSITES firm.

line n. **1 stroke**, dash, score, underline, underscore, slash, stripe, strip, band, belt; Brit. oblique. **2 wrinkle**, furrow, crease, crinkle, crow's foot. **3** *the Bentley's classic lines:* **contour**, outline, configuration, shape, design, profile, silhouette. **4** *the county line:* **boundary**, limit, border, frontier, touchline, margin, perimeter. **5 cord**, rope, cable, wire, thread, string. **6 file**, rank, column, string, train, procession, row, queue; Brit. informal crocodile. **7 course**, direction, route, track, path, trajectory.
•v. **1 furrow**, wrinkle, crease,

score. **2 border**, edge, fringe, bound.
□ **in line 1** in a queue, in a row, in a file. **2** in agreement, in accord, in accordance, in harmony, in step, in compliance. **3** level, aligned, alongside, abreast, side by side. **line up** assemble, get together, organize, prepare, arrange, fix up, lay on, book, schedule, timetable.

lineage n. **ancestry**, family, parentage, birth, descent, extraction, genealogy, roots, origins.

lined adj. **1 ruled**, feint, striped, banded. **2 wrinkled**, wrinkly, furrowed, wizened.

line-up n. **1 cast**, bill, programme. **2 team**, squad, side, configuration.

linger v. **1 wait (around)**, stand (around), remain, loiter; informal stick around, hang around. **2 persist**, continue, remain, stay, endure, carry on, last.

lining n. backing, facing, padding, insulation.

link n. **connection**, relationship, association, linkage, tie-up, tie, bond, attachment, affiliation.
•v. **1 join**, connect, fasten, attach, bind, secure, fix, tie, couple, yoke. **2** *the evidence linking him with the body:* **associate**, connect, relate, bracket.
– OPPOSITES separate.

lion n.

> **WORD LINKS**
> relating to lions: leonine

lip n. edge, rim, brim, border, verge, brink.

liquid n. **fluid**, moisture, solution, liquor, juice, sap.
•adj. **fluid**, liquefied, melted, molten, thawed, dissolved, runny.
– OPPOSITES solid.

liquor n. **1 alcohol**, spirits, drink; informal booze, the hard stuff, hooch, moonshine. **2 stock**, broth, bouillon, juice, liquid.

list[1] n. **catalogue**, inventory, record, register, roll, file, index, directory, checklist.
•v. **record**, register, enter, itemize, enumerate, catalogue, file, log, minute, categorize, inventory, classify, group, sort, rank, index.

list[2] v. **lean (over)**, tilt, tip, heel (over), pitch, incline, slant, slope, bank, careen, cant.

listen v. **1 pay attention**, be attentive, attend, concentrate, keep your ears open, prick up your ears; informal be all ears. **2 heed**, take heed of, take notice/note of, bear in mind, take into consideration/account.

listless adj. **lethargic**, lifeless, enervated, languid, inactive, inert, sluggish, apathetic, passive, supine, indifferent, uninterested, impassive.
– OPPOSITES energetic.

literal adj. **1 strict**, technical, original, true. **2 word for word**, verbatim, exact, accurate, faithful.
– OPPOSITES figurative.

literary adj. **1 artistic**, poetic, dramatic. **2 scholarly**, intellec-

tual, academic, bookish, erudite, well read, cultured.

literate adj. **1 (well) educated**, well read, widely read, scholarly, learned, knowledgeable, cultured, cultivated.
– OPPOSITES ignorant.

literature n. **1 writing**, poetry, drama, plays, prose. **2 publications**, reports, studies, material, documentation, leaflets, pamphlets, brochures, handouts, publicity, advertising; informal bumf.

lithe adj. **agile**, graceful, supple, flexible, lissom, loose-limbed, nimble.
– OPPOSITES clumsy.

litigation n. **legal proceedings**, legal action, case, lawsuit, suit, prosecution, indictment.

litter n. **rubbish**, refuse, junk, waste, debris, detritus; N. Amer. trash, garbage.
•v. **cover**, clutter up, mess up, be scattered/strewn around.

little adj. **1 small**, compact, miniature, tiny, minute, minuscule, toy, baby, undersized, dwarf, midget; Scottish wee; informal teeny-weeny; Brit. informal titchy, dinky; N. Amer. informal vest-pocket. **2 short**, small, slight, petite, diminutive, tiny, elfin; Scottish wee; informal pint-sized. **3 young**, younger, baby. **4 brief**, short, quick, hasty, cursory. **5 minor**, unimportant, insignificant, trivial, trifling, petty, paltry, inconsequential, negligible.
– OPPOSITES big, large, elder, major.

• adv. **1 hardly**, barely, scarcely, not much, only slightly. **2 rarely**, seldom, infrequently, hardly (ever), scarcely ever, not much.
– OPPOSITES well, often.
▫ **a little 1** some, a bit of, a touch of, a dash of, a taste of, a spot of, a hint of, a dribble of, a splash of, a pinch of, a sprinkling of, a speck of; *informal* a smidgen of, a tad of. **2** a short time, a while, a bit, an interval, a short period, a minute, a moment, a second, an instant; *informal* a sec, a mo, a jiffy. **3** slightly, somewhat, a little bit, quite, to some degree.

live¹ v. **1 exist**, be alive, be, have life, breathe, draw breath, walk the earth. **2 reside**, have your home, lodge, inhabit, occupy; *Scottish* stay; *formal* dwell; *old use* abide, bide. **3** *she had lived a difficult life*: **experience**, spend, pass, lead, have, go through, undergo. **4** *he lived by scavenging*: **survive**, make a living, eke out a living, subsist, support yourself, sustain yourself, make ends meet, keep body and soul together.
– OPPOSITES die.

live² adj. **1 living**, alive, conscious, animate, vital. **2** *a live rail*: **electrified**, charged, powered up, active, switched on. **3** *a live grenade*: **unexploded**, explosive, active, primed. **4** *a live issue*: **topical**, current, controversial, hot, burning, pressing, important, relevant.
– OPPOSITES dead, inanimate.

livelihood n. **(source of) income**, living, subsistence, bread and butter, job, work, employment, occupation.

lively adj. **1 energetic**, active, animated, dynamic, full of life, outgoing, spirited, sprightly, high-spirited, vivacious, enthusiastic, vibrant, buoyant, exuberant, boisterous, effervescent, cheerful; *informal* chirpy, full of beans. **2 busy**, crowded, bustling, hectic, buzzing, vibrant, colourful. **3** *a lively debate*: **stimulating**, interesting, vigorous, animated, spirited, heated.
– OPPOSITES quiet, dull.

livid adj. (informal) **furious**, enraged, very angry, infuriated, irate, incensed, fuming, ranting, raving, seething, beside yourself, outraged; *informal* hopping mad, wild.

living n. **1 livelihood**, (source of) income, subsistence, keep, daily bread, bread and butter, job, work, employment, occupation. **2 way of life**, lifestyle, life, conduct, behaviour, activities, habits.
• adj. **1 alive**, live, animate, sentient, breathing, existing. **2** *a living language*: **current**, contemporary.
– OPPOSITES dead, extinct.

load n. **1 cargo**, freight, consignment, delivery, shipment, goods, pack, bundle, parcel. **2** *a heavy teaching load*: **commitment**, responsibility, duty, obligation, burden, onus.

•v. **1 fill (up)**, pack, stock, stack, stow, store, bundle, place, put, deposit, pile, stuff, cram; old use lade. **2 burden**, weigh down, saddle, oppress, charge, over-burden, overwhelm, encumber, tax, strain, trouble, worry. **3** *he loaded the gun:* prime, charge, set up, prepare. **4** *load the cassette into the camcorder:* insert, put, place, slot, slide.

loaded adj. **1 full**, filled, laden, packed, stuffed, crammed, brimming, stacked; informal chock-full, chock-a-block. **2** *a politically loaded word:* **charged**, emotive, sensitive, delicate.

loaf v. laze, lounge, loll, idle; informal hang around; Brit. informal hang about, mooch about/around; N. Amer. informal bum around.

loan n. credit, advance, mort-gage, overdraft, Brit. informal sub.
•v. lend, advance.

loath adj. reluctant, unwilling, disinclined, averse, opposed, resistant.
– OPPOSITES eager, willing.

loathe v. hate, detest, abhor, despise, abominate, not be able to bear/stand, execrate.
– OPPOSITES love.

loathing n. hatred, hate, de-testation, abhorrence, abomin-ation, antipathy, aversion, dislike, disgust, repugnance.

loathsome adj. hateful, detest-able, abhorrent, repulsive, odi-ous, repugnant, repellent, dis-gusting, revolting, sickening,

nauseating, abominable, despicable, contemptible, reprehensible, vile, horrible, nasty, obnoxious, gross, foul, execrable; informal horrid; literary noisome.

lobby n. **1 entrance (hall)**, hall-way, hall, vestibule, foyer, re-ception. **2** *the anti-hunt lobby:* **pressure group**, interest group, movement, campaign, crusade, faction, camp, ginger group.
•v. **1 approach**, contact, peti-tion, appeal to, pressurize, im-portune. **2 campaign**, crusade, press, push, ask, call, demand, promote, advocate, champion.

local adj. **1** *the local council:* **dis-trict**, regional, town, municipal, provincial, parish. **2** *a local restaurant:* **neighbourhood**, nearby, near, at hand, close by, handy, convenient. **3** *a local infection:* **confined**, restricted, contained, localized.
– OPPOSITES national, widespread.
•n. resident, native, inhabitant, parishioner.
– OPPOSITES outsider.

locate v. **1 find**, pinpoint, track down, unearth, sniff out, smoke out, search out, uncover, run to earth. **2 situate**, site, position, place, base, put, build, establish, station.

location n. position, place, situ-ation, site, locality, locale, spot, whereabouts, scene, setting, area, environment, venue, address; technical locus.

lock¹ n. bolt, catch, fastener, clasp, hasp, latch.

• v. **1 bolt**, fasten, secure, padlock, latch, chain. **2 join**, interlock, link, engage, combine, connect, couple. **3 become stuck**, stick, jam, seize. **4 clasp**, clench, grasp, embrace, hug, squeeze.
– OPPOSITES unlock, open.
□ **lock up** imprison, jail, incarcerate, intern, send to prison, put behind bars, put under lock and key, cage, pen, coop up; informal send down, put away, put inside.

lock² n. strand, tress, curl, ringlet, hank, tuft, wisp, coil, tendril.

locker n. cupboard, cabinet, chest, safe, box, case, coffer, storeroom.

lodge n. **1 gatehouse**, cottage, house, cabin, hut. **2** *a Masonic lodge*: **section**, branch, wing, group; N. Amer. chapter.
• v. **1 submit**, register, enter, put forward, advance, lay, present, tender, proffer, put on record, record, table, file. **2** *the bullet lodged in his back*: **become embedded**, get stuck, stick, catch, get caught, wedge. **3 reside**, board, stay, live, stop; N. Amer. room; literary sojourn. **4 deposit**, put, bank, stash, store, stow, put away.

lodging n. accommodation, rooms, chambers, living quarters, a roof over your head, housing, shelter; informal digs; N. Amer. informal crib; formal residence, dwelling, abode.

lofty adj. **1 tall**, high, towering. **2** *lofty ideals*: **noble**, exalted,

high, high-minded, worthy, grand, fine, elevated. **3** *lofty disdain*: **haughty**, arrogant, disdainful, supercilious, condescending, patronizing, scornful, contemptuous, self-important, conceited, snobbish; informal stuck-up, snooty; Brit. informal toffee-nosed.
– OPPOSITES low, short.

log n. record, register, logbook, journal, diary, minutes, ledger, account, tally.
• v. **1 register**, record, note, write down, put in writing, enter, file. **2** *the pilot had logged 95 hours*: **attain**, achieve, chalk up, make, do, go, cover, clock up.

logic n. **1 reason**, judgement, rationality, wisdom, sense, good sense, common sense, sanity. **2** *the logic of their argument*: **reasoning**, rationale, argument.

logical adj. **1 reasoned**, rational, sound, cogent, valid, coherent, clear, systematic, orderly, methodical, analytical, consistent. **2** *the logical outcome*: **natural**, reasonable, sensible, understandable, predictable, unsurprising, likely.
– OPPOSITES illogical

logo n. design, symbol, emblem, trademark, motif, monogram.

loiter v. linger, wait, skulk, loaf, lounge, idle; informal hang about/around; Brit. informal mooch about/around.

lone adj. **1 solitary**, single, solo, unaccompanied, sole, isolated. **2** *a lone parent*: **single**, unmarried,

separated, divorced,
widowed.

loneliness n. **1 isolation**, friendlessness, abandonment, rejec-
tion; N. Amer. lonesomeness.
2 solitariness, solitude, alone-
ness, separation, seclusion.

lonely adj. **1 isolated**, alone,
friendless, with no one to turn
to, abandoned, rejected, unloved, unwanted; N. Amer. lonesome. **2 deserted**, uninhabited,
desolate, solitary, isolated, remote, out of the way, off the
beaten track, secluded, in the
back of beyond, godforsaken;
informal in the middle of nowhere.

long¹ adj. **lengthy**, extended,
prolonged, protracted, long-
lasting, drawn-out, endless,
lingering, interminable.
– OPPOSITES short, brief.

long² v. *I longed for the holidays:*
yearn, pine, ache, hanker for/
after, hunger, thirst, itch, be
eager, be desperate, crave,
dream of; informal be dying.

longing n. **yearning**, craving,
ache, burning, hunger, thirst,
hankering, desire, wish, hope,
aspiration; informal yen, itch.

long-standing adj. **well established**, time-honoured, traditional, abiding, enduring.
– OPPOSITES new, recent.

long-suffering adj. **patient**,
forbearing, tolerant, uncomplaining, philosophical, stoical,
forgiving.

long-winded adj. **verbose**,
wordy, lengthy, long, prolix,

interminable, rambling, tortuous, meandering, repetitious,
repetitive; Brit. informal waffly.
– OPPOSITES concise, succinct.

look v. **1 glance**, gaze, stare,
gape, peer, peep, peek, watch,
observe, view, regard, examine,
inspect, eye, scan, scrutinize,
survey, study, contemplate,
take in, ogle, leer at; informal take
a gander, rubberneck, get a load
of; Brit. informal gawp; N. Amer.
informal eyeball. **2 seem (to be)**,
appear (to be), come across/
over as.
▸ n. **1 glance**, examination, study,
inspection, scrutiny, peep, peek,
glimpse; informal eyeful, once-
over, squint; Brit. informal dekko,
butcher's, shufti. **2 expression**,
mien, countenance. **3 appearance**, air, style, effect, ambience, impression, aspect,
manner, demeanour.
□ **look after** take care of, care
for, attend to, minister to, tend,
mind, keep an eye on, keep safe,
guard, supervise, be responsible
for, protect, nurse, babysit.
look down on disdain, scorn,
look down your nose at, sneer
at, despise. **look for** search for,
hunt, try to find, seek, cast
about/around for, forage for.
look into investigate, enquire
into, go into, probe, explore,
follow up, research, study,
examine; informal check out;
N. Amer. informal scope out. **look
like** resemble, bear a resemblance to, look similar to, take
after; informal be the (spitting)

image of, be a dead ringer for. **look out** beware, watch out, mind out, be on your guard, be alert, be wary, be vigilant, be careful, take care, be cautious, pay attention, keep your eyes open/peeled, keep an eye out, watch your step. **look over** inspect, examine, scrutinize, cast an eye over, take stock of, vet, view, peruse, read through; *informal* give something a/the once-over; N. Amer. check out; N. Amer. *informal* eyeball. **look up** improve, get better, pick up, come along/on, progress, make progress, make headway, perk up, rally, take a turn for the better. **look up to** admire, think highly of, hold in high regard, respect, esteem, venerate, revere, idolize.

lookalike n. double, twin, clone, living image, doppelgänger, replica; *informal* spitting image, dead ringer.

lookout n. **1** watchman, watch, guard, sentry, sentinel, observer. **2** (*Brit. informal*) *that's your lookout:* **problem**, concern, business, affair, responsibility, worry; *informal* pigeon.

loom v. **1** emerge, appear, materialize, take shape. **2** be imminent, be on the horizon, impend, threaten, brew, be just around the corner.

loop n. coil, ring, circle, noose, spiral, curl, bend, curve, arc, twirl, whorl, twist, helix.
‣v. **1** coil, wind, twist, snake, spiral, curve, bend, turn.

2 fasten, tie, join, connect, knot, bind.

loophole n. flaw, discrepancy, inconsistency, ambiguity, omission, excuse, escape clause; *Brit.* get-out.

loose adj. **1** not secure, unsecured, unattached, untied, detached, wobbly, unsteady, dangling, free. **2** free, at large, at liberty, on the loose. **3** baggy, roomy, oversized, voluminous, shapeless, sloppy. **4** *a loose interpretation:* vague, imprecise, approximate, broad, general, rough, liberal.
– OPPOSITES secure, tight.
– v. **1** free, let loose, release, untie, unchain, unfasten, unleash, relax. **2** relax, slacken, loosen.
– OPPOSITES confine, tighten.

loosen v. **1** undo, slacken, unfasten, detach, release, disconnect. **2** weaken, relax, slacken, loose, let go.
– OPPOSITES tighten.

loot n. booty, spoils, plunder, haul, *informal* swag, boodle.
‣v. plunder, pillage, ransack, sack, rifle, rob, strip, gut.

lopsided adj. crooked, askew, awry, off-centre, uneven, out of true, asymmetrical, tilted, at an angle, slanting; *Scottish* agley; *informal* cockeyed; *Brit. informal* skew-whiff, wonky.
– OPPOSITES even, level.

lord n. **1** noble, nobleman, peer, aristocrat. **2** master, ruler, leader, chief, superior, monarch, sovereign, king, emperor, prince, governor, commander.

lorry n. **truck**, wagon, van, juggernaut, trailer, HGV; dated pantechnicon.

lose v. **1 mislay**, misplace, be unable to find, lose track of. **2 escape from**, evade, elude, dodge, avoid, give someone the slip, shake off, throw off, leave behind, outdistance, outrun. **3 waste**, squander, let pass, miss; informal pass up, blow. **4 be defeated**, be beaten; informal come a cropper, go down.
– OPPOSITES find, seize, win.

loser n. (informal) **failure**, underachiever, dead loss, write-off, has-been, informal also-ran, non-starter, no-hoper.

loss n. **1 mislaying**, deprivation, forfeiture, erosion, reduction, depletion. **2 death**, demise, passing away, bereavement. **3 casualty**, fatality, victim, death toll. **4 deficit**, debit, debt.
– OPPOSITES recovery, profit.
□ **at a loss** baffled, mystified, puzzled, perplexed, bewildered, confused, stumped, stuck; informal flummoxed, beaten.

lost adj. **1 missing**, mislaid, misplaced, gone astray. **2 stray**, off course, going round in circles, adrift, at sea. *a lost opportunity:* **missed**, wasted, squandered, gone by the board; informal down the drain. **3 lost traditions:** **bygone**, past, former, old, vanished, forgotten, dead. **5 lost species and habitats:** **extinct**, died out, defunct, vanished,

gone, destroyed, wiped out, exterminated. **6 lost in thought:** **engrossed**, absorbed, rapt, immersed, deep, intent, engaged, wrapped up.

lot pron. (**a lot/lots**) **a large amount**, a good/great deal, an abundance, a wealth, a profusion, plenty, many, a great many, a large number, a considerable number; informal hundreds, loads, masses, heaps, piles, stacks, tons, oodles; Brit. informal lashings.
• adv. (**a lot**) **a great deal**, a good deal, much, often, frequently, regularly.
• n. **1** (informal) **group**, crowd, circle, crew; informal bunch, gang, mob. **2 an auction lot:** **item**, article, batch, group, bundle, parcel. **3 his lot in life:** **fate**, destiny, fortune, situation, circumstances, plight, predicament.

lotion n. **ointment**, cream, balm, rub, moisturizer, lubricant, embrocation, liniment, salve, unguent.

lottery n. **raffle**, (prize) draw, sweepstake, sweep, tombola, lotto, pools.

loud adj. **1 noisy**, blaring, booming, roaring, thunderous, resounding, sonorous, powerful, stentorian, deafening, ear-splitting, piercing, shrill, raucous; Music forte, fortissimo. **2 vociferous**, clamorous, insistent, vehement, emphatic. **3 garish**, gaudy, lurid, showy, flamboyant, ostentatious, vulgar, tasteless; informal flashy.
– OPPOSITES quiet.

loudly adv. **at the top of your voice**, noisily, stridently, vociferously, shrilly.

lounge v. laze, lie, loll, recline, relax, rest, take it easy, sprawl, slump, slouch, loaf, idle.
•n. **living room**, sitting room, front room, drawing room; dated parlour.

lout n. **hooligan**, ruffian, thug, boor, oaf, rowdy; informal tough, bruiser; Brit. informal yob, yobbo.

lovable adj. **adorable**, dear, sweet, cute, charming, lovely, likeable, engaging, endearing, winning, winsome.
– OPPOSITES hateful, loathsome.

love n. **1 adoration**, devotion, affection, fondness, tenderness, attachment, warmth, passion, desire, lust, yearning, infatuation, besottedness. **2 liking**, taste, zeal, zest, enthusiasm, keenness, fondness, weakness, partiality, predilection, penchant. **3 compassion**, care, regard, concern, altruism, unselfishness, philanthropy, benevolence, humanity.
4 beloved, loved one, dearest, darling, sweetheart, sweet, angel, honey.
– OPPOSITES hatred.
•v. **1 be in love with**, adore, be devoted to, be infatuated with, be smitten with, be besotted with, idolize, worship, think the world of, dote on, care for, hold dear, cherish; informal be mad/crazy about, carry a torch for.
2 like, delight in, relish, enjoy, have a soft spot for, have a

weakness for, be addicted to, be taken with; informal have a thing about, be hooked on, get a kick out of.
– OPPOSITES hate.

love affair n. **relationship**, affair(e), romance, liaison, fling, amour, entanglement, involvement, intrigue; Brit. informal carry-on.

lovely adj. **1 beautiful**, pretty, attractive, good-looking, handsome, adorable, charming, engaging, enchanting, gorgeous, alluring, ravishing, glamorous; Scottish & N. English bonny; informal tasty, drop-dead gorgeous; Brit. informal fit; N. Amer. informal cute, foxy; old use comely. **2 delightful**, marvellous, magnificent, stunning, splendid, wonderful, superb, pleasant, enjoyable; informal terrific, fabulous, heavenly, divine, amazing, glorious.
– OPPOSITES ugly, horrible.

lover n. **1 boyfriend**, **girlfriend**, beloved, sweetheart, inamorato/a, mistress, partner, gigolo; informal bit on the side, fancy man, fancy woman; dated beau; literary swain; old use paramour. **2 devotee**, admirer, fan, enthusiast, aficionado; informal buff, nut.

loving adj. **affectionate**, fond, devoted, adoring, doting, caring, tender, warm, close, amorous, passionate.
– OPPOSITES cold, cruel.

low adj. **1 short**, small, little, squat, stubby, stunted. **2 cheap**, economical, moderate, reasonable, affordable, modest, bargain, bargain-basement, rock-bottom. **3 scarce**, scant, meagre, sparse, few, little, reduced, depleted, diminished. **4 inferior**, substandard, poor, low-grade, unsatisfactory, inadequate, second-rate. **5 quiet**, soft, faint, gentle, muted, subdued, muffled, hushed. **6 bass**, low-pitched, deep, rumbling, booming, sonorous. **7 depressed**, dejected, despondent, downhearted, downcast, down, miserable, dispirited, gloomy, glum, flat; *informal* fed up, down in the dumps, blue.
– OPPOSITES high, expensive, loud.

lower[1] adj. **1 subordinate**, inferior, lesser, junior, minor, secondary, subsidiary, subservient. **2** *her lower lip:* **bottom**, nether, bottommost, under.
– OPPOSITES upper.

lower[2] v. **1 let down**, take down, drop, let fall. **2 soften**, modulate, quieten, hush, tone down, muffle, turn down, mute. **3 reduce**, decrease, lessen, bring down, cut, slash.
– OPPOSITES raise, increase.

low-key adj. **restrained**, modest, understated, muted, subtle, quiet, low-profile, inconspicuous, unobtrusive, discreet.
– OPPOSITES ostentatious, obtrusive.

lowly adj. **humble**, low, low-ranking, common, ordinary, plain, modest, simple, obscure.
– OPPOSITES aristocratic, exalted.

loyal adj. **faithful**, true, true-blue, devoted, constant, steadfast, staunch, dependable, reliable, trustworthy, trusty, patriotic, unswerving.
– OPPOSITES disloyal, treacherous.

loyalty n. **allegiance**, faithfulness, fidelity, obedience, adherence, devotion, steadfastness, staunchness, dedication, commitment, patriotism; *old use* fealty.
– OPPOSITES disloyalty, treachery.

lucid adj. **1 clear**, crystal-clear, intelligible, comprehensible, cogent, coherent, articulate. **2 rational**, sane, in possession of your faculties, compos mentis, clear-headed, sober; *informal* all there.
– OPPOSITES confused.

luck n. **1 good fortune**, good luck, stroke of luck, fluke; *informal* lucky break. **2 fortune**, fate, serendipity, chance, accident, a twist of fate.
– OPPOSITES bad luck, misfortune.

luckily adv. **fortunately**, happily, providentially, by good fortune, as luck would have it, mercifully, thankfully.

lucky adj. **1 fortunate**, in luck, favoured, charmed, successful; *Brit. informal* jammy. **2 providential**, fortunate, timely, opportune, serendipitous, chance, fortuitous, accidental.
– OPPOSITES unlucky.

lucrative adj. **profitable**, gainful, remunerative, moneymaking, well paid, rewarding, worthwhile.
– OPPOSITES unprofitable.

ludicrous adj. **absurd**, ridiculous, farcical, laughable, risible, preposterous, mad, insane, idiotic, stupid, asinine, nonsensical; informal crazy.
– OPPOSITES sensible.

luggage n. **baggage**, bags, suitcases, cases.

lukewarm adj. a lukewarm response: **indifferent**, cool, half-hearted, apathetic, tepid, unenthusiastic, uninterested, non-committal.
– OPPOSITES warm.

lull v. **soothe**, calm, quiet, still, assuage, allay, ease, quell.
▪ n. **1** pause, respite, interval, break, suspension, breathing space, hiatus; informal let-up, breather. **2** the lull before the storm: **calm**, stillness, quiet, tranquillity, peace, silence, hush.

lumber¹ v. **trundle**, stump, clump, plod, stumble, shamble, shuffle, trudge.

lumber² v. (Brit. informal) **burden**, saddle, encumber, land.

lumbering adj. **clumsy**, awkward, slow, blundering, bumbling, ponderous, ungainly; informal clodhopping.
– OPPOSITES nimble, agile.

luminous adj. **shining**, bright, brilliant, radiant, dazzling, glowing, luminescent, phosphorescent, fluorescent, incandescent.
– OPPOSITES dark.

lump n. **1** chunk, hunk, piece, block, wedge, slab, ball, knob, pat, clod, clump, nugget, gobbet. **2** swelling, bump, bulge, protuberance, protrusion, growth, nodule, tumour.
▪ v. it's more convenient to lump them together: **combine**, put, group, bunch, throw.

lunatic n. **maniac**, psychopath, madman, madwoman, idiot; informal loony, nutcase, headcase, psycho; Brit. informal nutter; N. Amer. informal screwball.
▪ adj. **stupid**, foolish, idiotic, insane, absurd, ridiculous, ludicrous, preposterous, asinine; informal crazy, mad; Brit. informal barmy, daft.

lung n.

> WORD LINKS
> relating to the lungs:
> pulmonary

lunge n. Darren made a lunge at his attacker: **thrust**, dive, rush, charge, grab.
▪ v. he lunged at her with a knife: **thrust**, dive, spring, launch yourself, rush.

lurch v. **1** stagger, stumble, sway, reel, roll, totter, weave. **2** swing, list, roll, pitch, veer, swerve.

lure v. **tempt**, entice, attract, induce, coax, persuade, inveigle, seduce, beguile, draw.
– OPPOSITES deter, put off.
▪ n. the lure of the stage: **temptation**, attraction, pull, draw, appeal, inducement,

allure, fascination, interest, glamour.

lurid adj. **1 bright**, vivid, glaring, fluorescent, gaudy, loud. **2** *lurid details*: **sensational**, colourful, salacious, graphic, explicit, prurient, shocking, gruesome, gory, grisly; informal juicy.

lurk v. **skulk**, loiter, lie in wait, hide.

lush adj. **1 profuse**, abundant, luxuriant, flourishing, rich, riotous, vigorous, dense, thick, rampant. **2 luxurious**, sumptuous, palatial, opulent, lavish, elaborate, extravagant, fancy; informal plush, posh, swanky, bling-bling; Brit. informal swish; N. Amer. informal swank.
– OPPOSITES sparse, austere.

lust n. **1 desire**, longing, passion, libido, sex drive, sexuality, lecherousness, lasciviousness; Brit. informal randiness. **2 greed**, desire, craving, eagerness, longing, yearning, hunger, thirst, appetite, hankering.
□ **lust for/after** crave, desire, want, long for, yearn for, dream of, hanker for/after, hunger for, thirst for, ache for.

luxurious adj. **opulent**, sumptuous, grand, palatial, magnificent, extravagant, fancy, de luxe, expensive; Brit. upmarket; informal plush, posh, classy, swanky, bling-bling; Brit. informal swish; N. Amer. informal swank.
– OPPOSITES plain, basic.

luxury n. **1 opulence**, sumptuousness, grandeur, magnificence, splendour, luxuriousness, affluence. **2 indulgence**, extravagance, treat, extra, frill.
– OPPOSITES simplicity, necessity.

lying n. **dishonesty**, fabrication, fibbing, perjury, untruthfulness, mendacity, misrepresentation, deceit, duplicity.
– OPPOSITES honesty.
•adj. **dishonest**, untruthful, false, mendacious, deceitful, duplicitous, double-dealing, two-faced.
– OPPOSITES honest.

lyrical adj. **1 expressive**, emotional, deeply felt, personal. **2 enthusiastic**, effusive, rapturous, ecstatic, euphoric, passionate, impassioned.
– OPPOSITES unenthusiastic.

Wordfinder

Contents

Animals

Birds

albatross	booby	capercaillie	coot
auk	bowerbird	caracara	cormorant
avocet	brambling	cassowary	corncrake
barnacle goose	budgerigar	chaffinch	crane
barn owl	bullfinch	chicken	crossbill
bird of paradise	bunting	chiffchaff	crow
bittern	bustard	chough	cuckoo
blackbird	butcher-bird	coal tit	curlew
blackcap	buzzard	cockatiel	dabchick
bluebird	Canada goose	cockatoo	dipper
blue tit	canary	condor	dodo

Wordfinder

dotterel	heron	osprey	shag
dove	hobby	ostrich	shearwater
duck	hoopoe	ouzel	shelduck
dunlin	hornbill	owl	shrike
dunnock	house martin	oystercatcher	skua
eagle	hummingbird	parakeet	skylark
egret	ibis	parrot	snipe
eider duck	jackdaw	partridge	sparrow
emu	jay	peacock	sparrowhawk
falcon	kestrel	peewit	spoonbill
fantail	kingfisher	pelican	starling
fieldfare	kite	penguin	stonechat
finch	kittiwake	peregrine	stork
flamingo	kiwi	falcon	sunbird
flycatcher	kookaburra	petrel	swallow
fulmar	lammergeier	pheasant	swan
gannet	lapwing	pigeon	swift
goldcrest	lark	pipit	tern
golden eagle	linnet	plover	thrush
goldfinch	lovebird	ptarmigan	tit
goose	lyrebird	puffin	toucan
goshawk	macaw	quail	turkey
great tit	magpie	raven	vulture
grebe	mallard	red kite	wagtail
greenfinch	martin	redpoll	warbler
grouse	merlin	redstart	waxwing
guillemot	moa	redwing	weaver bird
guineafowl	mockingbird	rhea	woodcock
gull	moorhen	roadrunner	woodlark
harrier	mynah bird	robin	woodpecker
hawfinch	nightingale	rook	wren
hawk	nightjar	sandpiper	yellowhammer
hen	nuthatch	seagull	

Crustaceans

barnacle	crayfish	langoustine	shrimp
crab	hermit crab	lobster	spider crab
crawfish	krill	prawn	woodlouse

Dinosaurs

allosaurus	deinonychus	megalosaurus	sauropod
ankylosaur	diplodocus	pliosaur	seismosaurus
apatosaurus	dromaeosaur	protoceratops	stegosaurus
brachiosaurus	duck-billed	pteranodon	theropod
brontosaurus	dinosaur	pterodactyl	triceratops
carnosaur	hadrosaur	raptor	tyrannosaurus
coelurosaur	iguanodon	saurischian	velociraptor

Fish

anchovy	dogfish	hoki	pipefish
angelfish	dorado	huss	piranha
anglerfish	dory	John Dory	plaice
archerfish	Dover sole	koi carp	pollack
barbel	eel	lamprey	porbeagle
barracouta	fighting fish	lanternfish	puffer fish
barracuda	filefish	lemon sole	rabbitfish
bass	flatfish	loach	rainbow trout
beluga	flathead	lumpsucker	ray
blenny	flounder	lungfish	roach
bluefin	flying fish	mackerel	sailfish
boxfish	garfish	mako	salmon
bream	goby	manta	sardine
brill	goldfish	marlin	sawfish
brisling	gourami	minnow	scorpionfish
bullhead	grayling	monkfish	sea horse
carp	great white	moray eel	shad
catfish	shark	mudskipper	shark
charr	grouper	mullet	skate
chub	gudgeon	needlefish	skipjack tuna
clownfish	guppy	nurse shark	skipper
cod	gurnard	oarfish	smelt
coelacanth	haddock	orfe	snapper
coley	hake	parrotfish	sockeye
conger eel	halfbeak	perch	salmon
dab	halibut	pike	sole
dace	hammerhead	pilchard	sprat
damselfish	herring	pilotfish	stargazer

stickleback
stingray
stonefish
sturgeon
sunfish
surgeonfish
swordfish

swordtail
tarpon
tench
tetra
thresher
tope
triggerfish

trout
tuna
turbot
weever
whaler shark
whitebait
whitefish

whiting
wobbegong
wrasse
zander

Insects and Arachnids

ant
aphid
bedbug
bee
beetle
blackfly
black widow
blowfly
bluebottle
bombardier
  beetle
borer
botfly
bumblebee
butterfly
caddis fly
chafer
chigger
cicada
cockchafer
cockroach
crane fly
cricket

daddy-long-
  legs
damselfly
death-watch
  beetle
dragonfly
earwig
firefly
flea
fluke
fly
froghopper
gadfly
glow-worm
gnat
grasshopper
greenbottle
greenfly
harvestman
honeybee
hornet
horsefly
housefly

hoverfly
lacewing
ladybird
leafcutter ant
leafhopper
leaf miner
leatherjacket
leech
locust
louse
mantis
May bug
mayfly
mealy bug
midge
mite
mosquito
moth
pond skater
praying mantis
sandfly
sawfly
scarab

scorpion
silverfish
spider
springtail
stag beetle
stick insect
tarantula
termite
thrips
thunderbug
thunderfly
tick
tsetse fly
warble fly
wasp
water boatman
weevil
whirligig
whitefly
witchetty grub

Mammals

aardvark
alpaca
angora
anteater

antelope
ape
armadillo
ass

aurochs
baboon
badger
bandicoot

bat
bear
beaver
beluga

Wordfinder

bison
blue whale
boar
bobcat
bottlenose
  dolphin
buffalo
bushbaby
camel
capuchin
  monkey
capybara
caribou
cat
chamois
cheetah
chimpanzee
chinchilla
chipmunk
civet
coati
colobus
cougar
cow
coyote
coypu
deer
dingo
dog
dolphin
donkey
dormouse
dromedary
duck-billed
  platypus
dugong
echidna
eland
elephant

elk
ermine
fallow deer
fennec
ferret
flying fox
fox
gazelle
gemsbok
gerbil
gibbon
giraffe
gnu
goat
gopher
gorilla
grampus
grizzly bear
guinea pig
hamster
hare
hartebeest
hedgehog
hippopotamus
hog
horse
howler monkey
humpback
  whale
hyena
hyrax
ibex
impala
jackal
jaguar
kangaroo
killer whale
kinkajou
koala

kudu
langur
lemming
lemur
leopard
lion
llama
loris
lynx
macaque
manatee
mandrill
margay
marmoset
marten
meerkat
mink
minke whale
mole
mongoose
monkey
moose
mouse
mule
muntjac
musk ox
narwhal
ocelot
okapi
opossum
orang-utan
orca
oryx
otter
ox
panda
pangolin
panther
peccary

phalanger
pig
pine marten
pipistrelle
platypus
polar bear
polecat
porcupine
porpoise
possum
potto
puma
rabbit
raccoon
rat
reindeer
rhinoceros
roe deer
rorqual
sea cow
seal
sea lion
serval
sheep
shrew
skunk
sloth
sperm whale
spider monkey
springbok
squirrel
stoat
tapir
tiger
vampire bat
vervet monkey
vole
wallaby
walrus

wapiti	water buffalo	wildcat	wombat
warthog	weasel	wildebeest	yak
waterbuck	whale	wolverine	zebra

Reptiles and Amphibians

adder	crocodile	loggerhead	sidewinder
alligator	frog	turtle	skink
anaconda	galliwasp	mamba	slow-worm
axolotl	gecko	moloch	snake
basilisk	gharial	monitor lizard	taipan
boa constrictor	Gila monster	natterjack toad	terrapin
bullfrog	grass snake	newt	toad
caiman	iguana	puff adder	tortoise
cane toad	Komodo	python	turtle
chameleon	dragon	rattlesnake	viper
cobra	leatherback	rinkhals	
constrictor	lizard	salamander	

Shellfish and Other Molluscs

abalone	limpet	ormer	sea slug
argonaut	mitre	oyster	slug
auger shell	murex	paua	snail
clam	mussel	periwinkle	squid
cockle	nautilus	piddock	triton
conch	nerite	quahog	whelk
cowrie	nudibranch	razor shell	winkle
cuttlefish	octopus	scallop	

Male and Female Animals

antelope: *buck, doe*
badger: *boar, sow*
bear: *boar, sow*
bird: *cock, hen*
buffalo: *bull, cow*
cat: *tom, queen*
cattle: *bull, cow*
chicken: *cock, hen*

deer: *stag, doe*
dog: *dog, bitch*
donkey: *jackass, jenny*
duck: *drake, duck*
elephant: *bull, cow*
ferret: *jack, gill*
fish: *cock, hen*
fox: *dog, vixen*

goat: *billy goat, nanny*
goose: *gander, goose*
hare: *buck, doe*
horse: *stallion, mare*
kangaroo: *buck, doe*
leopard: *leopard, leopardess*
lion: *lion, lioness*

otter: *dog, bitch*
pheasant: *cock, hen*
pig: *boar, sow*
rabbit: *buck, doe*

seal: *bull, cow*
sheep: *ram, ewe*
swan: *cob, pen*
tiger: *tiger, tigress*

whale: *bull, cow*
wolf: *dog, bitch*
zebra: *stallion, mare*

Young Animals

calf (*antelope, buffalo, camel, cattle, elephant, elk, giraffe, rhinoceros, seal, whale*)
chick (*chicken, hawk, pheasant*)
colt (*male horse*)
cub (*badger, bear, fox, leopard, lion, tiger, walrus, wolf*)
cygnet (*swan*)
duckling (*duck*)
eaglet (*eagle*)

elver (*eel*)
eyas (*hawk*)
fawn (*caribou, deer*)
filly (*female horse*)
foal (*horse, zebra*)
fry (*fish*)
gosling (*goose*)
joey (*kangaroo, wallaby, possum*)
kid (*goat, roe deer*)
kit (*beaver, ferret, fox, mink, weasel*)
kitten (*cat, cougar, rabbit, skunk*)

lamb (*sheep*)
leveret (*hare*)
owlet (*owl*)
parr (*salmon*)
piglet (*pig*)
pup (*dog, rat, seal, wolf*)
puppy (*coyote, dog*)
smolt (*salmon*)
squab (*pigeon*)
tadpole (*frog, toad*)
whelp (*dog, wolf*)

Collective Names for Animals

band (*gorillas*)
bask (*crocodiles*)
bellowing (*bullfinches*)
bevy (*roe deer, quails, larks, pheasants*)
bloat (*hippopotami*)
brood (*chickens*)
bury (*rabbits*)
busyness (*ferrets*)
charm (*finches*)
cloud (*gnats*)
covey (*partridges*)
crash (*rhinoceros*)
cry (*hounds*)

descent (*woodpeckers*)
down (*hares*)
drove (*bullocks*)
exaltation (*larks*)
flight (*birds*)
flock (*sheep*)
gaggle (*geese on land*)
herd (*cattle, elephants*)
hive (*bees*)
hover (*trout*)
kennel (*dogs*)
kindle (*kittens*)

knot (*toads*)
labour (*moles*)
leap (*leopards*)
litter (*kittens, pigs*)
mob (*kangaroos*)
murder (*crows*)
murmuration (*starlings*)
muster (*peacocks, penguins*)
obstinacy (*buffalo*)
pack (*hounds, grouse*)
pandemonium (*parrots*)
parade (*elephants*)

parliament (*owls*)
pod (*seals*)
pride (*lions*)
rookery (*rooks*)
safe (*ducks*)
school (*whales,
dolphins, porpoises*)
shoal (*fish*)
shrewdness (*apes*)

siege (*herons*)
skein (*geese in flight*)
skulk (*foxes*)
sloth (*bears*)
span (*mules*)
stare (*owls*)
string (*horses*)
stud (*mares*)
swarm (*bees, flies*)

tiding (*magpies*)
trip (*goats*)
troop (*baboons*)
turmoil (*porpoises*)
turn (*turtles*)
unkindness (*ravens*)
watch (*nightingales*)
yoke (*oxen*)
zeal (*zebras*)

Chemical Elements

*Metal

*actinium (Ac)
*aluminium (Al)
*americium (Am)
*antimony (Sb)
argon (Ar)
arsenic (As)
astatine (At)
*barium (Ba)
*berkelium (Bk)
*beryllium (Be)
*bismuth (Bi)
bohrium (Bh)
boron (B)
bromine (Br)
*cadmium (Cd)
*caesium (Cs)
*calcium (Ca)
*californium (Cf)
carbon (C)
*cerium (Ce)
chlorine (Cl)
*chromium (Cr)
*cobalt (Co)
*copper (Cu)

*curium (Cm)
darmstadtium (Ds)
dubnium (Db)
*dysprosium (Dy)
einsteinium (Es)
*erbium (Er)
*europium (Eu)
fermium (Fm)
fluorine (F)
*francium (Fr)
*gadolinium (Gd)
*gallium (Ga)
germanium (Ge)
*gold (Au)
*hafnium (Hf)
hassium (Hs)
helium (He)
*holmium (Ho)
hydrogen (H)
*indium (In)
iodine (I)
*iridium (Ir)
*iron (Fe)
krypton (Kr)

*lanthanum (La)
*lawrencium (Lr)
*lead (Pb)
*lithium (Li)
*lutetium (Lu)
*magnesium (Mg)
*manganese (Mn)
meitnerium (Mt)
*mendelevium (Md)
*mercury (Hg)
*molybdenum (Mo)
*neodymium (Nd)
neon (Ne)
*neptunium (Np)
*nickel (Ni)
*niobium (Nb)
nitrogen (N)
*nobelium (No)
*osmium (Os)
oxygen (O)
*palladium (Pd)
phosphorus (P)
*platinum (Pt)
*plutonium (Pu)

*polonium (Po)
*potassium (K)
*praseodymium (Pr)
*promethium (Pm)
*protactinium (Pa)
*radium (Ra)
radon (Rn)
*rhenium (Re)
*rhodium (Rh)
roentgenium (Rg)
*rubidium (Rb)
*ruthenium (Ru)
rutherfordium (Rf)

*samarium (Sm)
*scandium (Sc)
seaborgium (Sg)
selenium (Se)
silicon (Si)
*silver (Ag)
*sodium (Na)
*strontium (Sr)
sulphur (S)
*tantalum (Ta)
*technetium (Tc)
tellurium (Te)
*terbium (Tb)

*thallium (Tl)
*thorium (Th)
*thulium (Tm)
*tin (Sn)
*titanium (Ti)
*tungsten (W)
*uranium (U)
*vanadium (V)
*xenon (Xe)
*ytterbium (Yb)
*yttrium (Y)
*zinc (Zn)
*zirconium (Zr)

Clothing

Clothes

anorak
apron
ballgown
bandeau
basque
bell-bottoms
belt
Bermuda
  shorts
bib
bikini
blazer
bloomers
blouse
blouson
boa
bodice
body
body stocking
bolero

bomber jacket
bow tie
bra
braces
breeches
burka/burkha/
  burqa
burnous
cagoule
cape
capri pants
cardigan
cargo pants
carpenter
  trousers
catsuit
chador
chinos
churidars
coat

combat
  trousers
corset
cravat
crinoline
crop top
culottes
cummerbund
dhoti
dinner jacket
dirndl
djellaba
dolman
donkey jacket
doublet
dress
dressing gown
dress shirt
duffel coat
dungarees

flannels
flares
fleece
flying jacket
frock coat
gilet
glove
gown
greatcoat
guernsey
gymslip
hipsters
hoody/hoodie
hose
hot pants
housecoat
hula skirt
jacket
jeans
jerkin

jersey
jilbab
jodhpurs
jogging pants
jumper
jumpsuit
kaftan
kagoul
kameez
kilt
kimono
knickers
lederhosen
leggings
leg warmers
leotard
loincloth
lumberjacket
mac
mackintosh/
  macintosh
maillot
mantilla
mantle
mini
miniskirt
mitten
morning coat
muff
muffler
nightdress
nightshirt

oilskins
overalls
overcoat
palazzo pants
pantaloons
panties
pants
pantyhose
parka
pedal pushers
peignoir
pencil skirt
peplum
petticoat
pinafore
pinafore dress
plus fours
polo neck
polo shirt
poncho
pullover
pyjamas
raincoat
reefer jacket
robe
roll-neck
ruff
safari jacket
sailor suit
salopettes
sari
sarong

sash
scarf
serape/sarape
shawl
sheath dress
sheepskin
shell suit
shift
shirt dress
shirtwaister
shorts
skinny-rib
ski pants
skirt
slacks
slip
smock
smoking jacket
sock
stirrup pants
stock
stocking
stole
suit
sundress
suspenders
sweater
sweatpants
sweatshirt
swimming
  costume
swimsuit

T-shirt
tabard
tailcoat
tails
tank top
tee
tie
tights
toga
top
topcoat
tracksuit
trench coat
trews
trousers
trouser suit
trunks
tunic
turtleneck
tutu
tux/tuxedo
twinset
ulster
underpants
underskirt
veil
vest
V-neck
waistcoat
windcheater
yashmak

Footwear

beetle-crusher
boot
bootee
brogue

clog
court shoe
cowboy boot
deck shoe

desert boot
Dr Martens
  (trademark)
espadrille

flip-flop
galosh
gumboot
high-low

hobnail boot	mule	sabot	trainer
jackboot	overshoe	sandal	wader
jelly shoe	Oxford	shoe	wedge
lace-up	patten	slingback	wellington
loafer	peep-toe	slip-on	boot
moccasin	platform	slipper	
moon boot	plimsoll	sneaker	
mukluk	pump	stiletto	

Headgear

balaclava	cowl	Juliet cap	stovepipe hat
bandeau	crash helmet	keffiyeh	tam-o'-shanter
baseball cap	crown	kepi	tarboosh
beanie	deerstalker	mantilla	ten-gallon hat
bearskin	derby	mitre	tiara
beret	diadem	mob cap	top hat
biretta	Dolly Varden	mortar board	topi
boater	fedora	nightcap	topper
bobble hat	fez	panama	toque
bonnet	flat cap	pillbox hat	tricorne
bowler	garland	pork-pie hat	trilby
busby	glengarry	skullcap	turban
cap	hard hat	slouch hat	veil
chaplet	headband	snood	wimple
circlet	headscarf	sola topi	wreath
cloche	helmet	sombrero	
cloth cap	hijab	sou'wester	
coif	homburg	Stetson	
coronet	hood	(trademark)	

Food and Drink

Bread and Bread Rolls

bagel	bap	brioche	ciabatta
baguette	bloomer	bun	cob
bannock	bridge roll	chapatti	cornbread

cottage loaf	fruit loaf	muffin	poppadom
crumpet	granary bread	nan/naan	pumpernickel
farl	(trademark)	paratha	puri
flatbread	hoagie	pikelet	rye
focaccia	malt loaf	pitta	soda bread
French stick	matzo	pone	sourdough

Cakes, Biscuits, and Desserts

angel cake	cassata	eclair	lardy cake
apfelstrudel	charlotte	egg custard	macaroon
baba	charlotte russe	Eve's pudding	Madeira cake
baked Alaska	cheesecake	fairy cake	madeleine
Bakewell tart	clafoutis	fancy	marble cake
baklava	cobbler	flapjack	meringue
banana split	compote	Florentine	milk pudding
banoffi/	cookie	flummery	millefeuille
banoffee pie	cream cracker	fool	mince pie
Bath bun	cream puff	fortune cookie	Mississippi
Battenberg	crème brûlée	frangipane	mud pie
beignet	crème caramel	fruit cocktail	mousse
biscotti	crêpe	fruit salad	muffin
Black Forest	crêpe Suzette	garibaldi	oatcake
gateau	crispbread	gateau	pancake
blancmange	crumble	Genoa cake	panettone
bombe	crumpet	gingerbread	panforte
bourbon	cupcake	ginger nut	parfait
brack	custard cream	ginger snap	parkin
brandy snap	custard pie	granita	pavlova
bread pudding	custard tart	halwa	peach Melba
bread-and-	Danish pastry	hot cross bun	petit four
butter	devil's food	ice cream	plum duff
pudding	cake	jelly	plum pudding
Brown Betty	digestive	junket	popover
brownie	doughnut	Knickerbocker	pound cake
bun	drop scone	Glory	profiterole
butterfly cake	dumpling	kulfi	queen of
cabinet	Dundee cake	lady's finger	puddings
pudding	Eccles cake	langue de chat	ratafia

rice pudding
rock cake
roly-poly
rusk
Sachertorte
sago pudding
Sally Lunn
sandwich
savarin
scone
seed cake
shortbread

shortcake
simnel cake
sorbet
soufflé
sponge
spotted dick
stollen
strudel
summer
  pudding
sundae
Swiss roll

syllabub
tart
tarte Tatin
tartlet
tartufo
tipsy cake
tiramisu
torte
treacle tart
trifle
turnover
tutti-frutti

upside-down
  cake
Victoria sponge
waffle
water biscuit
water ice
whip
yogurt
yule log
zabaglione

Cheeses

asiago
Bel Paese
  (trademark)
blue vinny
Boursin
  (trademark)
Brie
Caerphilly
Camembert
Chaumes
Cheddar
Cheshire
chèvre
cottage cheese
cream cheese

Danish blue
Derby
Dolcelatte
  (trademark)
Double
  Gloucester
Edam
Emmental
feta
fontina
Gloucester
Gorgonzola
Gouda
Gruyère
halloumi

havarti
Jarlsberg
  (trademark)
Lancashire
Leicester
Limburger
Manchego
mascarpone
Monterey Jack
mozzarella
paneer/panir
Parmesan
Parmigiano
  Reggiano
pecorino

Port Salut
provolone
Red Leicester
ricotta
Romano
Roquefort
  (trademark)
sage Derby
scamorza
Stilton
  (trademark)
taleggio
Tilsit
Wensleydale

Fruit and Nuts

almond
apple
apricot
avocado
banana
betel nut
bilberry

blackberry
blackcurrant
blueberry
boysenberry
Brazil nut
breadfruit
butternut

cantaloupe
Cape
  gooseberry
carambola
cashew
cherimoya
cherry

chestnut
Chinese
  gooseberry
citron
clementine
cloudberry
cobnut

coconut
cola nut
cowberry
crab apple
cranberry
currant
damson
date
elderberry
fig
filbert
galia melon
gooseberry
gourd
grape
grapefruit
greengage
groundnut
guava
hazelnut

honeydew
  melon
huckleberry
jackfruit
jujube
kiwi fruit
kumquat
lemon
lime
loganberry
loquat
lychee
macadamia
mandarin
mango
melon
monkey nut
mulberry
nectarine
olive
orange

ortanique
papaya
passion fruit
pawpaw
peach
peanut
pear
pecan
persimmon
pineapple
pine nut
pistachio
plum
pomegranate
pomelo
prickly pear
pumpkin
quince
rambutan
raspberry
redcurrant

salmonberry
sapodilla
satsuma
serviceberry
sharon fruit
sloe
star anise
starfruit
strawberry
tamarillo
tangerine
tayberry
tiger nut
Ugli fruit
  (trademark)
walnut
water chestnut
watermelon
whortleberry

Meat

bacon
beef
brawn
chicken
duck
game
gammon
goose

ham
haslet
lamb
luncheon meat
mince
mutton
offal
oxtail

ox-tongue
Parma ham
pâté
pork
prosciutto
rabbit
sausage
steak

sweetbreads
tripe
turkey
veal
venison

Pasta

agnolotti
angel hair
cannelloni
capellini
conchiglie

ditalini
farfalle
fettuccine
fusilli
lasagne

linguine
macaroni
noodles
orecchiette
orzo

pappardelle
penne
radiatori
ravioli
rigatoni

spaghetti	tagliolini	tortelloni
spaghettini	tortelli	vermicelli
tagliatelle	tortellini	ziti

Vegetables

aduki/adzuki	celeriac	lamb's lettuce	runner bean
bean	celery	leek	salsify
alfalfa	chard	lentil	samphire
artichoke	chervil	lettuce	savoy cabbage
asparagus	chickpea	lima bean	shallot
aubergine	chicory	lollo rosso	snow pea
bamboo shoots	Chinese leaves	mache	soybean
bean	corn on the cob	mangetout	spinach
beet	cos lettuce	marrow	spring greens
beetroot	courgette	marrowfat pea	spring onion
black bean	cress	mooli	squash
black-eyed	cucumber	mung bean	string bean
bean	eggplant	mushroom	sugar pea
borlotti bean	endive	okra	sugar snap pea
breadfruit	fennel	onion	swede
broad bean	flageolet	pak choi	sweetcorn
broccoli	French bean	parsnip	sweet pepper
Brussels sprout	garlic	pea	sweet potato
butter bean	gherkin	pepper	tomato
butternut	globe artichoke	petits pois	turnip
squash	gourd	pimiento	vegetable
cabbage	haricot bean	pinto bean	spaghetti
calabrese	iceberg lettuce	plantain	water chestnut
cannellini bean	Jerusalem	potato	watercress
capsicum	artichoke	pumpkin	waxpod
carrot	kale	radicchio	yam
cassava	kidney bean	radish	zucchini
cauliflower	kohlrabi	rocket	

Alcoholic Drinks

absinthe	ale	aquavit	beer
advocaat	amaretto	Armagnac	bitter
alcopop	amontillado	barley wine	bock

bourbon
brandy
brown ale
burgundy
Calvados
cassis
cava
champagne
chartreuse
cherry brandy
cider
claret
cocktail
cognac
crème de
  menthe
curaçao
fino
genever
gin
ginger wine

grappa
hock
ice beer
Irish coffee
Irish whiskey
kirsch
kümmel
kvass
lager
light ale
liqueur
Madeira
malmsey
malt whisky
manzanilla
maraschino
Marsala
mead
mescal
mild
milk stout

moscato
muscat
muscatel
oloroso
ouzo
pale ale
perry
Pils
Pilsner/Pilsener
port
porter
poteen
raki
ratafia
retsina
rum
rye
sack
sake
sangria
schnapps

Scotch whisky
scrumpy
Sekt
shandy
sherry
single malt
slivovitz
sloe gin
spritzer
spumante
stout
tequila
triple sec
vermouth
vinho verde
vodka
whiskey/
  whisky
wine

Non-alcoholic Drinks

barley water
bitter lemon
buttermilk
cafe au lait
caffè latte
caffè
  macchiato
camomile tea
cappuccino
cherryade
citron pressé
club soda
  (trademark)
cocoa
coffee

cola
cordial
cream soda
dandelion and
  burdock
decaffeinated
  coffee
espresso
filter coffee
fruit juice
ginger ale
ginger beer
green tea
horchata
hot chocolate

iced tea
Indian tea
lassi
latte
lemonade
limeade
malted milk
maté
milkshake
mineral water
mint tea
mocha
mochaccino
orangeade
prairie oyster

pressé
root beer
sarsaparilla
seltzer
sherbet
smoothie
soda water
squash
St Clements
tea
tisane
tonic water
yerba maté

Plants

Flowering Plants and Shrubs

acacia
acanthus
aconite
African violet
agapanthus
aloe
alstroemeria
alyssum
amaranth
amaryllis
anemone
aquilegia
arrowgrass
arum lily
asphodel
aspidistra
aster
astilbe
aubretia
avens
azalea
balsam
banksia
bedstraw
begonia
belladonna
bellflower
bergamot
betony
bilberry
bindweed
bird's-foot
  trefoil

blackthorn
bluebell
boneset
borage
bougainvillea
bramble
broom
bryony
buddleia
bugloss
bulrush
burdock
burnet
busy Lizzie
buttercup
cactus
calceolaria
calendula
camellia
camomile
campanula
campion
candytuft
Canterbury bell
carnation
catmint
ceanothus
celandine
chickweed
chicory
Chinese lantern
chives
choisya

chokeberry
Christmas
  cactus
Christmas rose
chrysanthe-
  mum
cicely
cinquefoil
clematis
clove pink
clover
cockscomb
coltsfoot
columbine
comfrey
convolvulus
coreopsis
cornflower
corydalis
cotoneaster
cottonweed
cow parsley
cowslip
cranesbill
crocus
cuckoo pint
cyclamen
daffodil
dahlia
daisy
damask rose
dandelion
daphne

deadly
  nightshade
delphinium
dianthus
dill
dittany
dock
dog rose
duckweed
echinacea
edelweiss
eglantine
elder
evening
  primrose
eyebright
feverfew
figwort
firethorn
flax
forget-me-not
forsythia
foxglove
frangipani
freesia
fritillary
fuchsia
furze
gardenia
gentian
geranium
gerbera
gladiolus

gloxinia
golden rod
gorse
grape hyacinth
groundsel
guelder rose
gypsophila
harebell
hawkweed
hawthorn
heartsease
heather
hebe
helianthemum
helianthus
heliotrope
hellebore
hemlock
heuchera
hibiscus
hogweed
holly
hollyhock
honesty
honeysuckle
hosta
hyacinth
hydrangea
iris
jacaranda
japonica
jasmine
jonquil
kingcup
knapweed
knotgrass
laburnum
lady's mantle
lady's tresses

larkspur
lavatera
lavender
lemon balm
lilac
lily
lily of the valley
lobelia
London pride
loosestrife
lords and ladies
lotus
lovage
love-in-a-mist
love-lies-
   bleeding
lungwort
lupin
madonna lily
magnolia
mahonia
mallow
mandrake
marguerite
marigold
marshwort
may
mayflower
meadow rue
meadow
   saffron
meadowsweet
Michaelmas
   daisy
milfoil
mimosa
mint
mistletoe
mock orange

montbretia
morning glory
musk rose
myrtle
narcissus
nasturtium
nettle
nicotiana
nigella
night-scented
   stock
nightshade
old man's
   beard
oleander
orchid
ox-eye daisy
oxlip
pansy
Parma violet
parsley
pasque flower
passion flower
pelargonium
pennyroyal
penstemon
peony
peppermint
periwinkle
petunia
phlox
pimpernel
pink
pitcher plant
plantain
plumbago
poinsettia
polyanthus
poppy

potentilla
prickly pear
primrose
primula
privet
pulsatilla
pyracantha
pyrethrum
ragwort
ramsons
red-hot poker
rhododendron
rock rose
rose
rosebay
   willowherb
rose of Sharon
safflower
St John's wort
salvia
samphire
saxifrage
scabious
scarlet
   pimpernel
scilla
sedum
shamrock
shrimp plant
snapdragon
snowdrop
soapwort
sorrel
speedwell
spikenard
spiraea
spurge
spurrey
squill

starwort
stock
stonecrop
streptocarpus
sunflower
sweet pea
sweet william
tansy
teasel

thistle
thrift
toadflax
tradescantia
trefoil
tulip
valerian
Venus flytrap
verbena

veronica
vervain
vetch
viburnum
violet
viper's bugloss
wallflower
water lily
willowherb

wintergreen
wisteria
witch hazel
wolfsbane
woodruff
wormwood
yarrow
yucca
zinnia

Trees and Shrubs

acacia
acer
alder
almond
apple
apricot
araucaria
ash
aspen
azalea
balsa
bamboo
banksia
banyan
baobab
basswood
bay tree
beech
beefwood
bergamot
birch
blackthorn
bottlebrush
bottle tree
bo tree
box
box elder

bristlecone
  pine
broom
buckeye
buckthorn
butternut
cacao
calabash
camellia
candleberry
candlenut
carambola
carob
cassava
cassia
casuarina
cedar
cherimoya
cherry
chestnut
cinnamon
citron
coco de mer
coconut palm
cola
coolibah
copper beech

cork oak
coromandel
crab apple
cypress
dogwood
dragon tree
ebony
elder
elm
eucalyptus
euonymus
ficus
fig
filbert
fir
firethorn
flame tree
frangipani
fuchsia
gean
ginkgo
gorse
grapefruit
greengage
guava
gum tree
hawthorn

hazel
hickory
holly
holm oak
honeysuckle
hornbeam
horse chestnut
hydrangea
ilex
iroko
ironbark
ironwood
jacaranda
jackfruit
jack pine
japonica
jasmine
juniper
kalmia
kapok
kermes oak
laburnum
larch
laurel
lemon
Leyland cypress
leylandii

lilac
lime
linden
lodgepole pine
logwood
macadamia
magnolia
mahogany
maidenhair
  tree
mango
mangosteen
mangrove
maple
mastic
may
mimosa
mirabelle
monkey puzzle
mountain ash
mulberry
mulga
myrtle
nutmeg

nux vomica
oak
oleaster
olive
osier
pagoda tree
palm
papaya
paperbark
pawpaw
pear
persimmon
pine
pistachio
pitch pine
plane
plum
pomegranate
pomelo
poplar
privet
pussy willow
quassia
quince

rambutan
red cedar
redwood
rhododendron
robinia
rosewood
rowan
rubber plant
rubber tree
sallow
sandalwood
sapele
sapodilla
sassafras
satinwood
senna
sequoia
service tree
silver birch
Sitka cypress
slippery elm
smoke tree
soapberry
spindle

spruce
star anise
stinkwood
storax
sumac
sycamore
tamarind
tamarisk
tea
teak
tea tree
thuja
tulip tree
tulipwood
umbrella tree
viburnum
walnut
weeping willow
wellingtonia
whitebeam
willow
witch hazel
wych elm
yew

Mm

machine n. **1** device, appliance, apparatus, engine, gadget, mechanism, tool, instrument, contraption. **2** *an efficient publicity machine:* **organization**, system, structure, machinery; informal set-up.

machinery n. **1** equipment, apparatus, plant, hardware, gear, gadgetry, technology. **2** *the machinery of local government:* **workings**, organization, system, structure; informal set-up.

macho adj. manly, male, masculine, virile, red-blooded; informal butch, laddish.

mad adj. **1** insane, crazy, out of your mind, deranged, demented, crazed, lunatic, unbalanced, unhinged, psychotic, non compos mentis; informal mental, off your head, round the bend, nuts, nutty, off your rocker, bonkers, loony, loopy, batty, cuckoo; Brit. informal barmy, crackers, barking (mad), potty, round the twist. **2** (informal) angry, furious, infuriated, enraged, fuming, incensed, beside yourself; informal livid, spare; N. Amer. informal sore. **3** *a mad scheme:* **foolish**, insane, stupid, lunatic, idiotic, foolhardy, absurd, ludicrous, silly, asinine, wild, crackbrained, senseless, preposterous; informal crazy, crackpot; Brit. informal daft. **4** (informal) *he's mad about her:* **passionate**, fanatical, ardent, fervent, devoted, infatuated; informal crazy, dotty, nuts, wild, hooked; Brit. informal potty; N. Amer. informal nutso. **5** *a mad dash to get ready:* **frenzied**, frantic, frenetic, feverish, hysterical, wild, hectic, manic.
– **OPPOSITES** sane, sensible.

madden v. infuriate, exasperate, irritate, incense, anger, enrage, provoke, make someone see red, inflame; informal aggravate, make someone's blood boil; Brit. informal nark; N. Amer. informal tee off, tick off.
– **OPPOSITES** calm.

madman, madwoman n. lunatic, maniac, psychotic, psychopath; informal loony, nut, nutcase, head case, psycho; Brit. informal nutter; N. Amer. informal screwball.

madness n. **1** insanity, mental illness, dementia, derangement, lunacy, mania, psychosis. **2** folly, foolishness, idiocy, stupidity, foolhardiness. **3** bedlam, mayhem, chaos, pandemonium, uproar, turmoil.
– **OPPOSITES** sanity.

magazine n. journal, periodical, supplement, fanzine; informal glossy, mag.

magic n. **1 sorcery**, witchcraft, wizardry, necromancy, enchantment, the supernatural, occultism, the occult, black magic, the black arts, voodoo, hoodoo. **2 conjuring (tricks)**, sleight of hand, legerdemain, illusion; formal prestidigitation. **3 allure**, excitement, fascination, charm, glamour.

magical adj. **1 supernatural**, magic, mystical, other-worldly. **2 enchanting**, entrancing, spellbinding, bewitching, fascinating, captivating, alluring, enthralling, charming, lovely, delightful, beautiful, amazing; informal heavenly, gorgeous.

magician n. **1 sorcerer**, sorceress, witch, wizard, warlock, enchanter, enchantress, necromancer; formal thaumaturge. **2 conjuror**, illusionist; formal prestidigitator.

magnanimous adj. generous, charitable, benevolent, beneficent, big-hearted, openhanded, munificent, philanthropic, noble, unselfish, altruistic.
– OPPOSITES mean.

magnetic adj. **attractive**, irresistible, seductive, charismatic, hypnotic, alluring, fascinating, captivating.

magnificent adj. **1 splendid**, spectacular, impressive, striking, glorious, superb, majestic, awe-inspiring, breathtaking, sublime, resplendent, sumptuous, grand, imposing, monumental, palatial, opulent, luxurious, lavish, rich, dazzling, beautiful. **2 excellent**, outstanding, marvellous, brilliant, wonderful, virtuoso, fine, superb.
– OPPOSITES uninspiring, ordinary.

magnify v. **enlarge**, increase, augment, extend, expand, boost, enhance, maximize, amplify, intensify; informal blow up.
– OPPOSITES reduce, minimize.

magnitude n. **1 size**, extent, immensity, vastness, hugeness, enormity. **2 importance**, import, significance, consequence.

mail n. **post**, letters, correspondence, email.
• v. **send**, post, dispatch, forward, ship, email.

maim v. **injure**, wound, cripple, disable, incapacitate, mutilate, disfigure, mangle.

main adj. **principal**, chief, head, leading, foremost, most important, major, dominant, central, focal, key, prime, primary, first, fundamental, predominant, pre-eminent, paramount.
– OPPOSITES subsidiary, minor.

mainly adv. **mostly**, for the most part, in the main, on the whole, largely, by and large, to a large extent, predominantly, chiefly, principally, primarily.

maintain v. **1 preserve**, conserve, keep, retain, keep going, prolong, perpetuate, sustain, carry on, continue. **2 look after**, service, care for, take care of, support, provide for, keep. **3 insist**, declare, assert, protest,

affirm, profess, avow, claim, contend, argue; formal aver.
- OPPOSITES discontinue.

maintenance n. **1** preservation, conservation, prolongation, continuation. **2** servicing, service, repair, running repairs, care. **3** support, upkeep, alimony, allowance.

majestic adj. stately, dignified, distinguished, magnificent, grand, splendid, glorious, impressive, regal, noble, awe-inspiring, monumental, palatial, imposing.
- OPPOSITES modest.

majesty n. stateliness, dignity, magnificence, pomp, grandeur, splendour, glory, impressiveness, nobility.

major adj. **1** greatest, best, finest, most important, chief, main, prime, principal, leading, foremost, outstanding, preeminent. **2** crucial, vital, important, big, significant, considerable, weighty, serious, key, utmost, great, paramount, prime.
- OPPOSITES minor, trivial.

majority n. **1** most, bulk, mass, best part, lion's share, (main) body, preponderance, predominance. **2** coming of age, age of consent, adulthood, seniority.
- OPPOSITES minority.

make v. **1** construct, build, erect, assemble, put together, manufacture, produce, fabricate, create, form, forge, fashion, model, improvise. **2** force, compel, coerce, press, drive, dragoon,

pressurize, oblige, require; informal railroad, steamroller. **3** cause, create, bring about, produce, generate, give rise to, effect. **4** they made him chairman: **appoint**, designate, name, nominate, select, elect, vote in. **5** he's made a lot of money: **acquire**, obtain, gain, get, secure, win, earn. **6** he made the tea: **prepare**, concoct, cook, whip up, brew; informal fix.
- OPPOSITES destroy.
•n. **brand**, marque, label, type, sort, kind, variety.
□ **make for** contribute to, produce, promote, facilitate, foster. **make off** run away, run off, take to your heels, flee, take off, take flight, bolt; informal clear off, beat it, split, scram; Brit. informal scarper, do a runner. **make out 1** see, discern, distinguish, detect, observe, recognize. **2** understand, grasp, follow, work out, interpret, decipher, make head or tail of, catch. **make peace** make up, bury the hatchet, forgive and forget, shake hands. **make up 1** comprise, form, compose, constitute, account for. **2** invent, fabricate, concoct, think up; informal cook up. **make up for** offset, counterbalance, counteract, cancel out, compensate for, atone for, make amends for.

make-believe n. fantasy, pretence, daydreaming, invention, fabrication, charade, play-acting, masquerade.
•adj. **imaginary**, imagined,

m

made-up, fanciful, fictitious; informal pretend.
– OPPOSITES real, actual.

maker n. creator, manufacturer, constructor, builder, producer.

makeshift adj. temporary, provisional, stopgap, standby, rough and ready, improvised, ad hoc.

make-up n. **1** cosmetics, greasepaint; informal warpaint, slap. **2** composition, constitution, structure, configuration, arrangement. **3** character, nature, temperament, personality, mentality, persona.

makings pl. n. qualities, characteristics, ingredients, potential, capacity, capability, stuff.

maladjusted adj. disturbed, unstable, neurotic, dysfunctional; informal mixed up, screwed up.

male adj. masculine, manly, virile, macho.
– OPPOSITES female.

malfunction v. break down, fail, stop working, crash, go down; informal conk out, go kaput; Brit. informal play up, pack up.

malice n. spite, malevolence, ill will, vindictiveness, vengefulness, malignity, animus, enmity, rancour.
– OPPOSITES benevolence.

malicious adj. spiteful, malevolent, vindictive, vengeful, resentful, malign, nasty, hurtful, cruel, catty, venomous, poisonous, barbed; informal bitchy.
– OPPOSITES benevolent.

maltreat v. ill-treat, mistreat, abuse, ill-use, mishandle, misuse, persecute, harm, hurt, injure.

man n. **1** male, gentleman, fellow, youth; informal guy, gent, geezer; Brit. informal bloke, chap, lad; N. Amer. informal dude, hombre. **2** human being, human, person, mortal, individual, soul. **3** the human race, Homo sapiens, humankind, humanity, human beings, humans, people, mankind.
•v. **1** staff, crew, occupy. **2** operate, work, use.

> **WORD LINKS**
> *relating to men:* male, masculine, virile

manage v. **1** be in charge of, run, head, direct, control, preside over, lead, govern, rule, command, supervise, oversee, administer; informal head up. **2** accomplish, achieve, carry out, perform, undertake, deal with, cope with, get through. **3** cope, get along/on, make do, survive, get by, muddle through/along, make ends meet; informal make out, hack it.

manageable adj. **1** achievable, doable, practicable, feasible, reasonable, attainable, viable. **2** compliant, tractable, pliant, biddable, docile, amenable, accommodating, acquiescent.

management n. **1** administration, running, managing, organization, direction, leadership, control, governance, rule, com-

mand, supervision, guidance, operation. **2 managers**, employers, directors, board, directorate, executive, administration; informal bosses, top brass.
– OPPOSITES employees.

manager n. **executive**, head, supervisor, principal, director, superintendent, foreman, forewoman, overseer, organizer, administrator; informal boss, chief, governor; Brit. informal gaffer, guv'nor, honcho.

mandate n. **1 authority**, approval, ratification, endorsement, sanction, authorization. **2 instruction**, directive, decree, command, order, injunction.

mandatory adj. **obligatory**, compulsory, binding, required, requisite, necessary.
– OPPOSITES optional.

mania n. **obsession**, compulsion, fixation, fetish, fascination, preoccupation, passion, enthusiasm, desire, urge, craving, craze, fad, rage; informal thing.

maniac n. **lunatic**, madman, madwoman, psychopath; informal loony, nutcase, nut, head case, headbanger, psycho, sicko; Brit. informal nutter; N. Amer. informal screwball.

manifest v. **display**, show, exhibit, demonstrate, betray, present, reveal; formal evince.
– OPPOSITES hide.
•adj. **obvious**, clear, plain, apparent, evident, patent, distinct, definite, blatant, overt, glaring,

transparent, conspicuous, undisguised.

manifestation n. **1 display**, demonstration, show, exhibition, presentation. **2 sign**, indication, evidence, symptom, testimony, proof, mark, reflection, example, instance.

manipulate v. **1 operate**, work, handle, turn, pull, push, twist, slide. **2 control**, influence, use to your advantage, exploit, twist.

mankind n. **the human race**, humankind, humanity, human beings, humans, Homo sapiens, people, man, men and women.

manly adj. **virile**, masculine, strong, all-male, red-blooded, muscular, muscly, strapping, well built, rugged, tough, powerful, brawny; informal hunky.
– OPPOSITES effeminate.

man-made adj. **artificial**, synthetic, manufactured, imitation, ersatz, simulated, mock, fake, faux.
– OPPOSITES natural, real.

manner n. **1 way**, fashion, mode, means, method, methodology, system, style, approach, technique, procedure, process. **2** *her unfriendly manner*: **behaviour**, attitude, demeanour, air, aspect, mien, bearing, conduct. **3 (manners) social graces**, politeness, Ps and Qs, etiquette, protocol, decorum, propriety, civility.

mannerism n. **idiosyncrasy**, quirk, oddity, foible, trait, peculiarity, habit, characteristic.

manoeuvre v. **1 steer**, guide, drive, negotiate, jockey, navigate, pilot, direct, move, work. **2 manipulate**, contrive, manage, engineer, fix, organize, arrange, orchestrate, choreograph, stage-manage; informal wangle, pull strings.
•n. **1 operation**, exercise, move, movement, action. **2 stratagem**, tactic, gambit, ploy, trick, dodge, ruse, scheme, device, plot, machination, artifice, subterfuge, intrigue.

mansion n. **country house**, stately home, hall, manor house; informal pile.
– OPPOSITES hovel.

manual n. **handbook**, instructions, guide, companion, ABC, guidebook, vade mecum; informal bible.
•adj. **physical**, labouring, blue-collar, hand.

manufacture v. **1 make**, produce, mass-produce, build, construct, assemble, put together, turn out, process. **2 make up**, invent, fabricate, concoct, hatch, dream up, think up, contrive; informal cook up.
•n. **production**, making, manufacturing, mass production, construction, building, assembly.

manufacturer n. **maker**, producer, builder, constructor, industrialist.

many det. & adj. **numerous**, a lot of, plenty of, countless, innumerable, scores of, untold, copious, abundant; informal lots of, umpteen, loads of, masses of, stacks of, heaps of, oodles of, a slew of; literary myriad.
– OPPOSITES few.

map n. **plan**, chart, A to Z, atlas.
•v. **chart**, plot, draw, record.

> WORD LINKS
> making of maps: cartography

mar v. **spoil**, impair, detract from, disfigure, blemish, scar, deface, ruin, damage, wreck, taint, tarnish.
– OPPOSITES enhance.

march v. **1 stride**, walk, troop, step, pace, tread, slog, tramp, hike, trudge, parade, file. **2 stalk**, strut, flounce, storm, stomp, sweep.
•n. **1 walk**, trek, slog, route march, hike. **2 parade**, procession, cortège, demonstration; informal demo.

margin n. **1 edge**, side, verge, border, perimeter, brink, brim, rim, fringe, boundary, periphery, extremity. **2 leeway**, latitude, scope, room, space, allowance.

marginal adj. **slight**, small, tiny, minute, insignificant, minimal, negligible.
– OPPOSITES considerable.

marine adj. **1 seawater**, sea, saltwater, aquatic. **2 maritime**, nautical, naval, seafaring, seagoing, ocean-going.

mariner n. **sailor**, seaman, seafarer; informal matelot, sea dog, old salt; dated tar.

marital adj. **matrimonial**, conjugal, married, wedded, nuptial.

maritime adj. **naval**, marine, nautical, seafaring, seagoing, sea, ocean-going, oceanic, coastal.

mark n. **1 blemish**, streak, spot, fleck, blot, stain, smear, speck, smudge, blotch, bruise, scratch, scar, dent, chip, nick; informal splodge. **2 sign**, token, symbol, emblem, badge, indication, characteristic, feature, trait, attribute, quality, hallmark, indicator, symptom, proof. **3 grade**, grading, rating, score, percentage.
 ▸v. **1 discolour**, stain, smear, smudge, streak, dirty, scratch, scar, dent; informal splodge. **2 label**, identify, flag, tag, initial, highlight, name, brand. **3 celebrate**, observe, recognize, acknowledge, keep, honour, commemorate, remember, solemnize. **4 represent**, signify, indicate, herald. **5 characterize**, distinguish, identify, typify. **6 assess**, evaluate, appraise, correct; N. Amer. grade.

marked adj. **noticeable**, pronounced, decided, distinct, striking, clear, unmistakable, obvious, conspicuous, notable.
 – OPPOSITES imperceptible.

market n. **shopping centre**, marketplace, bazaar, souk, fair; N. Amer. mart.

 ▸v. **sell**, retail, merchandise, trade, advertise, promote.

maroon v. **strand**, cast away, cast ashore, abandon, desert, leave behind, leave.

marriage n. **1 matrimony**, wedlock, wedding, nuptials, union, match. **2** *a marriage of jazz, pop, and gospel*: **union**, fusion, mixture, mix, blend, amalgamation, combination, hybrid.
 – OPPOSITES divorce, separation.

> **WORD LINKS**
> *relating to marriage*: marital, matrimonial, nuptial, conjugal

marry v. **1 get married**, wed, become man and wife; informal tie the knot, walk down the aisle, get spliced, get hitched. **2** *the show marries poetry with art*: **join**, unite, combine, fuse, mix, blend, merge, amalgamate.
 – OPPOSITES divorce, separate.

marsh n. **swamp**, marshland, bog, morass, mire, quagmire, slough, fen.

marshal v. **assemble**, gather (together), collect, muster, call together, draw up, line up, array, organize, group, arrange, deploy, position, summon, round up.

martial adj. **military**, soldierly, warlike, fighting, militaristic; informal gung-ho.

marvel v. **be amazed**, be astonished, be in awe, wonder; informal be gobsmacked.
 ▸n. **wonder**, miracle, sensation, spectacle, phenomenon, prodigy.

m

marvellous adj. **excellent**, splendid, wonderful, magnificent, superb, sensational, glorious, sublime, lovely, delightful; informal super, great, amazing, fantastic, terrific, tremendous, fabulous, cracking, awesome, divine, ace, wicked; Brit. informal smashing, brilliant.
– OPPOSITES commonplace, awful.

masculine adj. **1 virile**, macho, manly, male, muscular, muscly, strong, strapping, well built, rugged, robust, brawny, powerful, red-blooded, vigorous; informal hunky, laddish. **2 mannish**, unfeminine, unladylike; informal butch.
– OPPOSITES feminine, effeminate.

mash v. **pulp**, crush, purée, cream, pound, beat.

mask n. **pretence**, semblance, veil, screen, front, facade, veneer, disguise, cover, cloak, camouflage.
•v. **hide**, conceal, disguise, cover up, obscure, screen, cloak, camouflage.

mass n. **1** a mass of fallen leaves: **pile**, heap, accumulation, aggregation, mat, tangle. **2** a mass of cyclists: **crowd**, horde, throng, host, troop, army, herd, flock, swarm, mob, pack, flood, multitude. **3** the mass of the population: **majority**, most, preponderance, greater part, best/better part, bulk, body.
•adj. **widespread**, general, extensive, large-scale, wholesale, universal, indiscriminate.
•v. **assemble**, gather together, collect, rally.

massacre n. **slaughter**, mass murder, mass execution, ethnic cleansing, genocide, holocaust, annihilation, liquidation, extermination, carnage, butchery, bloodbath, bloodletting.
•v. **slaughter**, butcher, murder, kill, annihilate, exterminate, execute, liquidate, eliminate, mow down.

massage n. **rub**, rub-down, kneading.
•v. **1 rub**, knead, manipulate, pummel, work. **2 alter**, tamper with, manipulate, doctor, falsify, juggle, fiddle with, tinker with, distort, rig; informal cook, fiddle.

massive adj. **huge**, enormous, vast, immense, mighty, great, colossal, tremendous, gigantic, mammoth, monumental, giant, mountainous; informal monster, whopping, astronomical, mega; Brit. informal whacking, ginormous.
– OPPOSITES tiny.

master n. **1** (historical) **lord**, liege, ruler, sovereign, monarch. **2 expert**, genius, maestro, virtuoso, authority; informal ace, wizard, whizz, hotshot, pro; Brit. informal dab hand; N. Amer. informal maven, crackerjack. **3 teacher**, schoolteacher, schoolmaster, tutor, instructor. **4 guru**, teacher, leader, guide, mentor.
– OPPOSITES servant, pupil.
•v. **1 overcome**, conquer, beat,

quell, suppress, control, triumph over, subdue, vanquish, subjugate, curb, check, defeat, get the better of; informal lick. **2** *he'd mastered the technique:* **learn**, become proficient in, pick up, grasp, understand; informal get the hang of.
• adj. **expert**, adept, proficient, skilled, skilful, deft, dexterous, adroit, practised, experienced, masterly, accomplished; informal crack, ace; N. Amer. informal crackerjack.
– OPPOSITES amateur.

masterful adj. **commanding**, powerful, imposing, magisterial, authoritative.
– OPPOSITES weak.

masterly adj. **expert**, adept, skilful, skilled, adroit, proficient, deft, dexterous, accomplished, polished, consummate.
– OPPOSITES inept.

mastermind n. **genius**, intellect, informal brain(s).
• v. **plan**, control, direct, be in charge of, run, conduct, organize, arrange, preside over, orchestrate, stage-manage, engineer, manage, coordinate.

masterpiece n. **magnum opus**, chef-d'œuvre, masterwork, pièce de résistance, tour de force, classic.

mastery n. **1 proficiency**, ability, capability, knowledge, understanding, comprehension, command, grasp. **2 control**, domination, command, supremacy, superiority, power, authority,

jurisdiction, dominion, sovereignty.

mat n. **rug**, carpet, doormat, runner.

match n. **1 contest**, competition, game, tournament, tie, fixture, meet, friendly, (local) derby, bout, fight. **2** *an exact match:* **lookalike**, double, twin, duplicate, mate, companion, counterpart, pair, replica, copy, doppelgänger; informal spitting image, dead ringer.
• v. **1 go with**, coordinate with, complement, suit, set off. **2 correspond**, tally, agree, coincide, square. **3 equal**, compare with, be in the same league as, touch, rival, compete with; informal hold a candle to.

matching adj. **corresponding**, equivalent, parallel, analogous, complementary, paired, twin, identical, alike.
– OPPOSITES different, clashing.

mate n. **1** (Brit. informal) **friend**, companion, schoolmate, classmate, workmate; informal pal, chum; N. Amer. informal buddy, amigo, compadre. **2 partner**, husband, wife, spouse, consort, lover; informal better half, other half. **3** *a plumber's mate:* **assistant**, helper, apprentice.
• v. **breed**, couple, copulate, pair.

material n. **1 matter**, substance, stuff, constituents. **2 fabric**, cloth, textiles. **3 information**, data, facts, facts and figures, statistics, evidence, details, particulars, background; informal info.

m

•adj. **1 physical**, corporeal, fleshly, bodily, tangible, mundane, worldly, earthly, secular, temporal, concrete, real. **2** *information material to the enquiry*: **relevant**, pertinent, applicable, germane, vital, essential, key.
– OPPOSITES spiritual.

materialize v. **1 happen**, occur, come about, take place, transpire; informal come off; literary come to pass. **2 appear**, turn up, arrive, emerge, surface, pop up; informal show up, fetch up.

maternal adj. **motherly**, protective, caring, nurturing, maternalistic.

matrimonial adj. **marital**, conjugal, married, wedded, nuptial; literary connubial.

matted adj. **tangled**, knotted, tousled, dishevelled, uncombed, unkempt, ratty.

matter n. **1 material**, stuff, substance. **2 affair**, business, situation, concern, incident, episode, subject, topic, issue, question, point at issue, case.
•v. **be important**, make any difference, be of consequence, be relevant, count, signify.

matter-of-fact adj. **unemotional**, practical, down-to-earth, sensible, realistic, unsentimental, pragmatic, businesslike, commonsensical, level-headed, hard-headed, no-nonsense, straightforward.

mature adj. **1 adult**, of age, fully grown, in your prime. **2 grown-up**, sensible, responsible, adult.

3 ripe, ripened, mellow, seasoned, ready.
– OPPOSITES immature.
•v. **1 grow up**, come of age, reach adulthood. **2 ripen**, mellow, age. **3 develop**, grow, bloom, blossom, evolve.

maturity n. **1 adulthood**, coming of age, manhood, womanhood. **2 responsibility**, sense, wisdom.

maul v. **savage**, attack, claw, scratch, lacerate, mangle, tear.

maverick n. **individualist**, nonconformist, free spirit, original, eccentric, rebel, dissenter, dissident.
– OPPOSITES conformist.

maxim n. **saying**, adage, aphorism, proverb, motto, saw, axiom, dictum, precept, epigram.

maximum adj. **greatest**, highest, biggest, largest, top, most, utmost, supreme.
•n. **upper limit**, limit, utmost, greatest, most, peak, pinnacle, height, ceiling, top.
– OPPOSITES minimum.

maybe adv. **perhaps**, possibly, for all you know; N. English happen; literary perchance.

mayhem n. **chaos**, havoc, bedlam, pandemonium, uproar, turmoil, a riot, anarchy; informal a madhouse.

maze n. **labyrinth**, network, warren, web, tangle, confusion, jungle.

meadow n. **field**, paddock, pasture; literary lea, mead.

m

meagre adj. **inadequate**, scant, paltry, limited, restricted, sparse, negligible, skimpy, slender, pitiful, miserly, niggardly; informal measly, stingy.
– OPPOSITES abundant.

meal n. snack, feast, banquet; informal spread, blowout; Brit. informal nosh-up; formal repast.

WORD LINKS
relating to meals: prandial

mean[1] v. **1 signify**, denote, indicate, convey, designate, show, express, spell out, stand for, represent, symbolize, imply, suggest, intimate, portend. **2 intend**, aim, plan, have in mind, set out, want. **3** *this will mean war:* entail, involve, necessitate, lead to, result in, give rise to, bring about, cause, engender, produce.

mean[2] adj. **1 miserly**, niggardly, parsimonious, penny-pinching, cheese-paring; informal tightfisted, stingy, tight; N. Amer. informal cheap. **2 unkind**, nasty, unpleasant, spiteful, malicious, unfair, shabby, horrible, despicable, contemptible, obnoxious, vile, loathsome, base, low; informal rotten.
– OPPOSITES generous, kind.

meaning n. **1 significance**, sense, signification, import, gist, thrust, drift, implication, message. **2 definition**, sense, explanation, interpretation, connotation.

WORD LINKS
relating to meaning: semantic

meaningful adj. **1 significant**, relevant, important, telling, expressive, eloquent, pointed, pregnant, revealing, suggestive. **2 sincere**, deep, serious, earnest, significant, important.

meaningless adj. **unintelligible**, incomprehensible, incoherent, senseless, pointless.

means pl. n. **1 method**, way, manner, course, agency, channel, avenue, procedure, process, methodology, expedient. **2 money**, resources, capital, income, finance, funds, cash, the wherewithal, assets, wealth, riches, affluence, fortune.

meanwhile, meantime adv. **1 for now**, for the moment, for the present, for the time being, in the meanwhile, in the meantime, in the interim. **2 at the same time**, simultaneously, concurrently.

measure v. **quantify**, gauge, size, count, weigh, evaluate, assess, determine, calculate, compute.
•n. **1 action**, act, course of action, deed, procedure, step, expedient, initiative, programme. **2 statute**, act, bill, law. **3 ruler**, tape measure, gauge, meter, scale. **4** *sales are a measure of their success:* yardstick, test, standard, barometer, touchstone, benchmark.

measured adj. **1 regular**, steady, even, rhythmic, unfaltering, slow, dignified, stately, sedate, leisurely, unhurried. **2 careful**, thoughtful, considered, reasoned, calculated.

measurement n. **1** quantification, evaluation, assessment, calculation, computation, mensuration. **2** size, dimension, proportions, value, amount, quantity.

meat n. **flesh**.

WORD LINKS
meat-eating: carnivorous

mechanical adj. **1** mechanized, machine-driven, automated, automatic. **2** automatic, knee-jerk, unthinking, instinctive, habitual, routine, unemotional, unfeeling.
– OPPOSITES manual.

m **mechanism** n. **1** apparatus, machine, machinery, appliance, device, instrument, tool, contraption, gadget; informal gizmo. **2** *a complaints mechanism:* procedure, process, system, method, means, medium, channel.

meddle v. **1** interfere, intrude, intervene, pry; informal poke your nose in. **2** fiddle, interfere, tamper, mess about; Brit. informal muck about.

mediate v. arbitrate, conciliate, moderate, make peace, intervene, intercede, act as an intermediary, negotiate, liaise, referee.

mediation n. arbitration, conciliation, reconciliation, intervention, intercession, negotiation, shuttle diplomacy.

mediator n. arbitrator, arbiter, negotiator, conciliator, peacemaker, go-between, middleman, intermediary, moderator, honest broker, liaison officer, umpire, referee, adjudicator, judge.

medicinal adj. curative, healing, remedial, therapeutic, restorative, health-giving.

medicine n. medication, drug, prescription, treatment, remedy, cure, nostrum, panacea, cure-all.

WORD LINKS
relating to medicines: pharmaceutical

mediocre adj. average, ordinary, undistinguished, uninspired, indifferent, unexceptional, unexciting, unremarkable, run-of-the-mill, pedestrian, prosaic, lacklustre, forgettable, amateurish; informal so-so.
– OPPOSITES excellent.

meditate v. contemplate, think, consider, ponder, muse, reflect, deliberate, ruminate, brood, mull over.

medium n. *a medium of expression:* means, method, avenue, channel, vehicle, organ, instrument, mechanism.
•adj. average, middling, medium-sized, middle-sized, moderate, normal, standard.

meek adj. submissive, obedient, compliant, tame, biddable, acquiescent, timid, quiet, mild, gentle, docile, shy, diffident, unassuming, self-effacing.
– OPPOSITES assertive.

meet v. **1 encounter**, come face to face with, run into, run across, come across/upon, chance on, happen on, stumble across; informal bump into. **2 get to know**, be introduced to, make the acquaintance of. **3 assemble**, gather, congregate, convene; formal foregather. **4 converge**, connect, touch, link up, intersect, cross, join.

meeting n. **1 gathering**, assembly, conference, congregation, convention, forum, summit, rally, consultation, audience, interview, conclave; informal get-together. **2 encounter**, contact, appointment, assignation, rendezvous; literary tryst. **3** the meeting of land and sea: **convergence**, confluence, conjunction, union, intersection, crossing. **4** an athletics meeting: **event**, tournament, meet, rally, competition, match, game, contest.

melancholy adj. **sad**, sorrowful, unhappy, gloomy, despondent, dejected, disconsolate, downcast, downhearted, woebegone, glum, miserable, morose, depressed, dispirited, mournful, doleful, lugubrious; informal down in the dumps, blue.
– OPPOSITES cheerful.
• n. **sadness**, sorrow, unhappiness, depression, despondency, dejection, gloom, misery; informal the blues.
– OPPOSITES happiness.

mellow adj. **1 sweet-sounding**, dulcet, melodious, mellifluous, soft, smooth, rich. **2 genial**, affable, amiable, good-humoured, good-natured, pleasant, relaxed, easy-going.
– OPPOSITES harsh, rough.

melodious adj. **tuneful**, melodic, musical, mellifluous, dulcet, sweet-sounding, harmonious, euphonious, lyrical.
– OPPOSITES discordant.

melodramatic adj. **exaggerated**, histrionic, extravagant, overdramatic, overdone, sensationalized, overemotional, theatrical, stagy; informal hammy.

melody n. **tune**, air, strain, theme, song, refrain.

melt v. **1 liquefy**, thaw, defrost, soften, dissolve; technical deliquesce. **2 vanish**, disappear, fade, evaporate.
– OPPOSITES freeze, solidify.

member n. **subscriber**, associate, fellow, representative.

memento n. **souvenir**, keepsake, reminder, remembrance, token, memorial.

memoir n. **1 account**, history, record, chronicle, narrative, story, portrayal, depiction, portrait, profile. **2 (memoirs) autobiography**, life story, journal, diary.

memorable adj. **unforgettable**, momentous, significant, historic, remarkable, notable, noteworthy, important, outstanding, arresting, indelible, catchy, haunting.

memorial n. **1 monument**, cenotaph, mausoleum, statue,

m

plaque, cairn, shrine, tombstone. **2 tribute**, testimonial, remembrance, memento.

memorize v. **commit to memory**, remember, learn (by heart), become word-perfect in, get/have off pat.

memory n. **1 recollection**, remembrance, reminiscence, recall. **2 commemoration**, remembrance, honour, tribute, recognition, respect.

> **WORD LINKS**
> *helping the memory:*
> mnemonic

menace n. **1 threat**, intimidation, malevolence, oppression. **2 danger**, peril, risk, hazard, threat. **3 nuisance**, pest, troublemaker, mischief-maker.
 •v. **1 threaten**, endanger, put at risk, jeopardize, imperil. **2 intimidate**, threaten, terrorize, frighten, scare, terrify.

menacing adj. **threatening**, ominous, intimidating, frightening, forbidding, hostile, sinister, baleful.
 – OPPOSITES friendly.

mend v. **repair**, fix, restore, sew (up), stitch, darn, patch, renew, renovate; informal patch up.
 – OPPOSITES break.

menial adj. **unskilled**, lowly, humble, low-grade, low-status, humdrum, routine, boring, dull.

mental adj. **1 intellectual**, cerebral, cognitive, rational. **2 psychiatric**, psychological, behavioural.
 – OPPOSITES physical.

mentality n. **way of thinking**, mind set, mind, psychology, attitude, outlook, make-up, disposition, character.

mentally adv. **psychologically**, intellectually, in your mind, in your head, inwardly, internally.

mention v. **1 allude to**, refer to, touch on, bring up, raise, broach. **2 state**, say, observe, remark, indicate, disclose, divulge, reveal.
 •n. **reference**, allusion, comment, citation; informal namecheck, plug.

mentor n. **adviser**, counsellor, guide, guru, consultant, confidant(e), trainer, teacher, tutor, instructor.

menu n. **bill of fare**, tariff, carte du jour, set menu, table d'hôte.

mercenary adj. **grasping**, greedy, acquisitive, avaricious, materialistic, venal; informal money-grubbing.

merchandise n. **goods**, wares, stock, commodities, produce, products.

merchant n. **trader**, tradesman, dealer, wholesaler, broker, agent, seller, retailer, supplier, buyer, vendor, distributor.

merciful adj. **forgiving**, compassionate, pitying, forbearing, lenient, humane, mild, kind, soft-hearted, tender-hearted, sympathetic, humanitarian, liberal, generous, magnanimous.
 – OPPOSITES cruel.

merciless adj. **ruthless**, remorseless, pitiless, unforgiving, im-

placable, inexorable, relentless, inhumane, inhuman, unfeeling, severe, cold-blooded, hard-hearted, stony-hearted, heartless, harsh, callous, cruel, brutal.
– OPPOSITES compassionate.

mercy n. **pity**, compassion, leniency, clemency, charity, forgiveness, forbearance, kindness, sympathy, indulgence, tolerance, generosity, magnanimity.
– OPPOSITES ruthlessness, cruelty.

merely adv. **only**, purely, solely, simply, just, but.

merge v. **1 join (together)**, join forces, unite, affiliate, team up. **2 amalgamate**, bring together, join, consolidate, conflate, unite, unify, combine, incorporate, integrate. **3 mingle**, blend, fuse, mix, intermix, intermingle, coalesce.
– OPPOSITES separate.

merger n. **amalgamation**, combination, union, fusion, coalition, affiliation, unification, incorporation, consolidation, link-up, alliance.
– OPPOSITES split.

merit n. **1 excellence**, quality, calibre, worth, value, distinction, eminence. **2 good point**, strong point, advantage, benefit, value, asset, plus.
– OPPOSITES fault, disadvantage.
•v. **deserve**, warrant, justify, earn, rate, be worthy of, be entitled to, have a right to, have a claim to.

merry adj. **cheerful**, cheery, in high spirits, sunny, smiling, light-hearted, lively, carefree, joyful, joyous, jolly, convivial, festive, gleeful, happy, laughing; informal chirpy.
– OPPOSITES miserable.

mesh n. **netting**, net, grille, screen, lattice, gauze.
•v. **1 engage**, connect, lock, interlock. **2 harmonize**, fit together, match, dovetail, connect, interconnect.

mess n. **1 untidiness**, disorder, disarray, clutter, muddle, jumble, chaos; informal shambles; Brit. informal tip. **2 plight**, predicament, tight spot, tight corner, difficulty, trouble, quandary, dilemma, problem, muddle, mix-up; informal jam, fix, pickle, hole.
□ **mess about/around** potter about, fiddle about/around, play about/around, fool about/around, fidget, toy, trifle, tamper, tinker, interfere, meddle, monkey about/around; Brit. informal muck about/around.

mess up 1 dirty, clutter up, jumble, dishevel, rumple; N. Amer. informal muss up. **2 bungle**, spoil, make a mess of, ruin; informal botch, make a hash of, muck up, foul up, screw up, muff.

message n. **1 communication**, news, note, memo, email, letter, missive, report, bulletin, communiqué, dispatch. **2** the message of his teaching: **meaning**, sense, import, idea, point, thrust, moral, gist, essence, implication.

messenger n. **courier**, postman, runner, dispatch rider, envoy, emissary, agent, go-between.

messy adj. **1** dirty, filthy, grubby, soiled, grimy, mucky, muddy, stained, smeared, smudged, dishevelled, scruffy, unkempt, rumpled, matted, tousled. **2** untidy, disordered, in a muddle, chaotic, confused, disorganized, in disarray, cluttered, in a jumble; informal like a bomb's hit it; Brit. informal shambolic. **3** a messy legal battle: **complex**, tangled, confused, convoluted, unpleasant, nasty, bitter, acrimonious.
– OPPOSITES clean, tidy.

metaphor n. figure of speech, image, trope, analogy, comparison, symbol.

method n. **1** procedure, technique, system, practice, routine, modus operandi, process, strategy, tactic, approach, way, manner, mode. **2** there's no method in his approach: **order**, organization, structure, form, system, logic, planning, design, consistency.
– OPPOSITES disorder.

methodical adj. orderly, well ordered, well organized, well planned, efficient, businesslike, systematic, structured, logical, disciplined, consistent, scientific.

meticulous adj. careful, conscientious, diligent, scrupulous, punctilious, painstaking, thorough, studious, rigorous, detailed, perfectionist, fastidious.
– OPPOSITES careless.

midday n. noon, twelve noon, high noon, noonday.
– OPPOSITES midnight.

middle n. **1** centre, midpoint, halfway point, dead centre, hub, eye, heart, core, kernel. **2** midriff, waist, belly, stomach; informal tummy.
– OPPOSITES edge.
· adj. central, mid, mean, medium, median, midway, halfway, equidistant.

might n. strength, force, forcefulness, power, vigour, energy, brawn.

mighty adj. powerful, forceful, strong, hard, heavy, violent, vigorous, hefty.
– OPPOSITES feeble.

migrant n. immigrant, emigrant, nomad, itinerant, traveller, transient, wanderer, drifter.
· adj. travelling, wandering, drifting, nomadic, itinerant, transient.

mild adj. **1** gentle, tender, soft, sympathetic, peaceable, good-natured, quiet, placid, docile, meek. **2** a mild punishment: **lenient**, light. **3** warm, balmy, temperate, clement. **4** bland, tasteless, insipid.
– OPPOSITES harsh, strong, severe.

militant adj. hard-line, extreme, extremist, committed, zealous, fanatical, radical.
· n. activist, extremist, partisan, radical, zealot.

military adj. fighting, service, army, armed, defence, martial.

– OPPOSITES civilian.
- n. **(armed) forces**, services, militia, army, navy, air force, marines.

militate v.
□ **militate against** work against, hinder, discourage, be prejudicial to, be detrimental to.

milk v. **exploit**, take advantage of, suck dry; informal bleed, squeeze, fleece.

WORD LINKS
relating to milk: lactic

mill n. **factory**, plant, works, workshop, shop, foundry.
- v. **grind**, pulverize, powder, granulate, pound, crush, press.
□ **mill around/about** wander, drift, swarm, crowd, fill, pack, throng.

mimic v. **imitate**, copy, impersonate, do an impression of, ape, caricature, parody; informal send up, take off.
- n. **impersonator**, impressionist; informal copycat.

mince v. **grind**, chop up, cut up, dice, crumble; N. Amer. hash.

mind n. **1 brain**, intelligence, intellect, brains, brainpower, wits, understanding, reasoning, judgement, sense, head; informal grey matter; N. Amer. informal smarts. **2 attention**, thoughts, concentration. **3 sanity**, mental faculties, senses, wits, reason, reasoning, judgement. **4 intellect**, thinker, brain, scholar, genius.
- v. **1 object**, care, be bothered, be annoyed, be upset, take

offence, disapprove, look askance; informal give/care a damn. **2 be careful of**, watch out for, look out for, beware of. **3 look after**, take care of, keep an eye on, watch, attend to, care for.

WORD LINKS
relating to the mind: mental

mindless adj. **1 stupid**, idiotic, brainless, asinine, witless, empty-headed; informal dumb, dopey, dim, half-witted, fat-headed, boneheaded. **2 unthinking**, thoughtless, senseless, gratuitous, wanton, indiscriminate. **3 mechanical**, routine, tedious, boring, monotonous, mind-numbing.

mine n. **1 pit**, colliery, excavation, quarry. **2** *a mine of information:* **store**, storehouse, reservoir, repository, gold mine, treasure house, treasury.
- v. **quarry**, excavate, dig, extract.

mingle v. **1 mix**, blend, intermingle, intermix, interweave, interlace, combine, merge, fuse, unite, join, amalgamate. **2 socialize**, circulate, associate, fraternize, get together; informal hobnob.
– OPPOSITES separate.

miniature adj. **small**, mini, little, small-scale, baby, toy, pocket, diminutive; informal pint-sized; Scottish wee; N. Amer. vest-pocket.
– OPPOSITES giant.

minimal adj. **very little**, very small, minimum, the least

m

(possible), nominal, token, negligible.
– OPPOSITES maximum.

minimize v. **1 keep down**, keep to a minimum, reduce, decrease, cut (down), lessen, curtail, prune; informal slash. **2 belittle**, make light of, play down, underrate, downplay, undervalue.
– OPPOSITES maximize, exaggerate.

minimum n. **lowest level**, lower limit, rock bottom, least, lowest.
• adj. **minimal**, least, smallest, least possible, slightest, lowest.
– OPPOSITES maximum.

minister n. **1 member of the government**, member of the cabinet, Secretary of State. **2 clergyman**, clergywoman, cleric, pastor, vicar, rector, priest, parson, curate; informal reverend, padre.
• v. *doctors ministered to the injured:* **tend**, care for, take care of, look after, nurse, treat, attend to, see to, help.

ministry n. **1 department**, bureau, agency, office. **2 the priesthood**, holy orders, the church.

minor adj. **1 slight**, small, unimportant, insignificant, inconsequential, negligible, trivial, trifling, paltry, petty; N. Amer. nickel-and-dime; informal piffling. **2** *a minor poet:* **little known**, unknown, lesser, unimportant, obscure; N. Amer. minor-league; informal small-time; N. Amer. informal two-bit.

– OPPOSITES major, important.
• n. **child**, infant, youth, adolescent, teenager, boy, girl; informal kid.
– OPPOSITES adult.

mint v. **coin**, stamp, strike, cast, make, manufacture.

minute[1] n. **1 moment**, short time, little while, second, instant; informal sec, jiffy; Brit. informal tick, mo, two ticks. **2 (minutes) record(s)**, proceedings, log, notes, transcript, summary.

minute[2] adj. **1 tiny**, minuscule, microscopic, miniature; Scottish wee; informal teeny, teeny-weeny; Brit. informal titchy, tiddly. **2** *minute detail:* **exhaustive**, painstaking, meticulous, rigorous, thorough.
– OPPOSITES huge.

miracle n. **wonder**, marvel, sensation, phenomenon.

miraculous adj. **amazing**, astounding, remarkable, extraordinary, incredible, unbelievable, sensational, phenomenal, inexplicable.

mirror n. **looking glass**; Brit. glass.
• v. **reflect**, match, reproduce, imitate, copy, mimic, echo, parallel.

misbehave v. **behave badly**, be naughty, be disobedient, get up to mischief, get up to no good, be rude; informal carry on, act up.

miscellaneous adj. **various**, varied, different, assorted, mixed, sundry, diverse, disparate, heterogeneous.

mischief n. **naughtiness**, bad behaviour, misbehaviour, misconduct, disobedience, wrongdoing; informal monkey business, shenanigans.

mischievous adj. **1 naughty**, bad, badly behaved, troublesome, disobedient, rascally. **2 playful**, wicked, impish, roguish.
– OPPOSITES well behaved.

misconduct n. **1 wrongdoing**, criminality, unprofessionalism, malpractice, negligence, impropriety; formal maladministration. **2 misbehaviour**, bad behaviour, mischief, misdeeds, naughtiness.

miser n. **penny-pincher**, Scrooge; informal skinflint, cheapskate; N. Amer. informal tightwad.
– OPPOSITES spendthrift.

miserable adj. **1 unhappy**, sad, sorrowful, melancholy, dejected, depressed, downhearted, downcast, despondent, disconsolate, wretched, glum, gloomy, forlorn, woebegone, mournful; informal blue, down in the dumps. **2 their miserable surroundings:** dreary, dismal, gloomy, drab, wretched, depressing, grim, cheerless, bleak, desolate.
– OPPOSITES cheerful, lovely.

miserly adj. **mean**, parsimonious, close-fisted, penny-pinching, cheese-paring, grasping, niggardly; informal stingy, tight, tight-fisted; N. Amer. informal cheap.
– OPPOSITES generous.

misery n. **unhappiness**, distress, wretchedness, suffering, angst, anguish, anxiety, torment, pain, grief, heartache, heartbreak, despair, despondency, dejection, depression, gloom, sorrow; informal the blues.
– OPPOSITES contentment, pleasure.

misfortune n. **problem**, difficulty, setback, trouble, adversity, (stroke of) bad luck, misadventure, mishap, blow, failure, accident, disaster, trial, tribulation.

misguided adj. **unwise**, foolish, ill-advised, ill-judged, ill-considered, injudicious, imprudent, unsound, mistaken, misplaced.
– OPPOSITES wise.

mislay v. **lose**, misplace, be unable to find.
– OPPOSITES find.

mislead v. **deceive**, delude, take in, lie to, fool, hoodwink, misinform; informal lead up the garden path, take for a ride; N. Amer. informal give someone a bum steer.

misleading adj. **deceptive**, confusing, deceiving, equivocal, false.
– OPPOSITES clear, straightforward.

miss v. **1 go wide of**, fall short of, pass, overshoot. **2 avoid**, beat, evade, escape, dodge, sidestep, elude, circumvent, bypass. **3 pine for**, yearn for, ache for, long for. **4 fail to attend**, be absent from, play truant from,

m

cut, skip, omit; Brit. informal skive off.
- OPPOSITES hit, catch.
  □ **miss out** leave out, exclude, miss (off), fail to mention, pass over, skip, omit, ignore.

missing adj. **1 lost**, mislaid, misplaced, absent, gone (astray), unaccounted for. **2 absent**, lacking, wanting.
- OPPOSITES present.

mission n. **1 assignment**, commission, expedition, journey, trip, undertaking, operation, project. **2** her mission in life: **vocation**, calling, goal, aim, quest, purpose, function, task, job, labour, work, duty.

missionary n. **evangelist**, apostle, proselytizer, preacher.

mist n. **haze**, fog, smog, murk, cloud, vapour, steam, spray, condensation.

mistake n. **error**, fault, inaccuracy, omission, slip, blunder, miscalculation, misunderstanding, oversight, misinterpretation, gaffe, faux pas, solecism; informal slip-up, boo-boo, howler; Brit. informal boob, clanger; N. Amer. informal goof.
  □ **make a mistake** make an error, go wrong, err, blunder, miscalculate. **mistake for** confuse with, mix up with, take for.

mistaken adj. **1 inaccurate**, wrong, erroneous, incorrect, off beam, false, fallacious, unfounded, misguided. **2 misinformed**, wrong, in error, under a

misapprehension, barking up the wrong tree.
- OPPOSITES correct.

mistimed adj. **ill-timed**, badly timed, inopportune, inappropriate, untimely.

mistreat v. **ill-treat**, maltreat, abuse, knock about/around, hit, beat, molest, injure, harm, hurt, misuse.

mistrust v. **be suspicious of**, be sceptical of, be wary of, be chary of, distrust, have doubts about, have misgivings about, have reservations about, suspect.

misty adj. **hazy**, foggy, cloudy, blurred, vague, indistinct.
- OPPOSITES clear.

misunderstand v. **misapprehend**, misinterpret, misconstrue, misconceive, mistake, misread, be mistaken, get the wrong idea; informal get (hold of) the wrong end of the stick.

misunderstanding n. **1 misinterpretation**, misreading, misapprehension, misconception, false impression. **2 disagreement**, difference (of opinion), dispute, falling-out, quarrel, argument, clash.

misuse v. **put to wrong use**, misapply, misemploy, abuse, squander, waste, dissipate, misappropriate, embezzle.

mix v. **1 blend**, mingle, combine, jumble, fuse, unite, join, amalgamate, incorporate, meld, homogenize; technical admix; literary commingle. **2 associate**, socialize, keep company, con-

mixed → model

sort, mingle, circulate; Brit. rub shoulders; N. Amer. rub elbows; informal hang out/around, hobnob.
– **OPPOSITES** separate.
• n. **mixture**, blend, combination, compound, fusion, union, amalgamation, medley, selection, assortment, variety.

mixed adj. **1** assorted, varied, variegated, miscellaneous, disparate, diverse, diversified, motley, sundry, jumbled, heterogeneous. **2** *mixed reactions*: **ambivalent**, equivocal, contradictory, conflicting, confused, muddled.
– **OPPOSITES** homogeneous.

mixture n. **1** blend, mix, brew, combination, concoction, composition, compound, alloy, amalgam. **2** assortment, miscellany, medley, blend, variety, mixed bag, mix, diversity, collection, selection, hotchpotch, ragbag; N. Amer. hodgepodge.

mix-up n. confusion, muddle, misunderstanding, mistake, error.

moan v. **1** groan, wail, whimper, sob, cry. **2** complain, grouse, grumble, whine, carp; informal gripe, grouch, bellyache, bitch, beef, whinge.

mob n. crowd, horde, multitude, rabble, mass, throng, gathering, assembly.
• v. **surround**, crowd round, besiege, jostle.

mobile adj. **1** able to move, able to walk, walking; informal up and about. **2** *a mobile library*:

travelling, transportable, portable, movable, itinerant, peripatetic.
– **OPPOSITES** immobile.

mobilize v. **1** *mobilize the troops*: **marshal**, deploy, muster, rally, call up, assemble, mass, organize, prepare. **2** *mobilizing support for the party*: **generate**, arouse, awaken, excite, stimulate, stir up, encourage, inspire, whip up.

mock v. ridicule, jeer at, sneer at, deride, make fun of, laugh at, scoff at, tease, taunt; informal take the mickey out of; N. Amer. informal goof on, rag on.
• adj. **imitation**, artificial, manmade, simulated, synthetic, ersatz, fake, reproduction, pseudo, false, spurious; informal pretend.
– **OPPOSITES** genuine.

mocking adj. **sneering**, derisive, contemptuous, scornful, sardonic, ironic, sarcastic, satirical.

mode n. **1** manner, way, means, method, system, style, approach. **2** *the camera is in manual mode*: **function**, position, operation, setting, option.

model n. **1** replica, copy, representation, mock-up, dummy, imitation, duplicate, reproduction, facsimile. **2** prototype, archetype, type, paradigm, version, mould, template, framework, pattern, design, blueprint. **3** fashion model, supermodel, mannequin; informal clothes horse.
• adj. **1** replica, toy, miniature, dummy, imitation, duplicate,

m

reproduction, facsimile. **2 ideal**, perfect, exemplary, classic, flawless, faultless, nonpareil.

moderate adj. **1 average**, modest, medium, middling, tolerable, passable, adequate, fair; informal OK, so-so, bog-standard, fair-to-middling. **2** *moderate prices*: **reasonable**, within reason, acceptable, affordable, inexpensive, fair, modest. **3** *moderate views*: **middle-of-the-road**, non-extremist, liberal, pragmatic.
– OPPOSITES immoderate, extreme.
• v. **1 die down**, abate, let up, calm down, lessen, decrease, diminish, recede, weaken, subside. **2 curb**, control, check, temper, restrain, subdue, tame, lessen, decrease, lower, reduce, diminish, alleviate, allay, appease, ease, soothe, calm, tone down.
– OPPOSITES increase.

moderately adv. **somewhat**, quite, fairly, reasonably, comparatively, relatively, to some extent, tolerably, adequately; informal pretty.

modern adj. **1 present-day**, contemporary, present, current, twenty-first-century, latter-day, recent. **2 fashionable**, up to date, trendsetting, stylish, chic, à la mode, the latest, new, newest, newfangled, advanced; informal trendy, cool, in, funky.
– OPPOSITES past, old-fashioned.

modernize v. **update**, bring up to date, streamline, rationalize,

overhaul, renovate, remodel, refashion, revamp.

modest adj. **1 humble**, self-deprecating, self-effacing, unassuming, shy, diffident, reserved, bashful. **2** *modest success*: **moderate**, fair, limited, tolerable, passable, adequate, satisfactory, acceptable, unexceptional. **3** *a modest house*: **small**, ordinary, simple, plain, humble, inexpensive, unostentatious, unpretentious. **4** *her modest dress*: **demure**, decent, seemly, decorous, proper.
– OPPOSITES conceited, grand, indecent.

modesty n. **humility**, self-effacement, shyness, bashfulness, self-consciousness, reserve.

modification n. **change**, adjustment, alteration, adaptation, refinement, revision, amendment; informal tweak.

modify v. **1 change**, alter, adjust, adapt, amend, revise, refine; informal tweak. **2 moderate**, temper, soften, tone down, qualify.

moist adj. **1 damp**, steamy, humid, muggy, clammy, dank, wet, soggy, sweaty, sticky. **2 succulent**, juicy, soft, tender.
– OPPOSITES dry.

moisten v. **dampen**, wet, damp, water, humidify.

moisture n. **wetness**, wet, water, liquid, condensation, steam, vapour, dampness, damp, humidity.

moment n. **1 little while**, short time, bit, minute, instant, (split) second; informal sec, jiffy; Brit. informal tick, mo, two ticks.
2 point (in time), stage, juncture, instant, time, hour, second, minute, day.

momentary adj. **brief**, short, short-lived, fleeting, passing, transitory, transient, ephemeral.
– OPPOSITES lengthy.

momentous adj. **important**, significant, historic, critical, crucial, decisive, pivotal, consequential, far-reaching; informal earth-shattering.
– OPPOSITES insignificant.

momentum n. **impetus**, energy, force, driving force, power, strength, thrust, speed, velocity.

monarch n. **sovereign**, ruler, Crown, crowned head, potentate, king, queen, emperor, empress, prince, princess.

monastery n. **friary**, abbey, priory, cloister.

monetary adj. **financial**, fiscal, pecuniary, money, cash, capital, economic, budgetary.

money n. **cash**, hard cash, means, wherewithal, funds, capital, finances, notes, coins, change, currency, specie; informal dough, bread, loot; Brit. informal dosh, brass, lolly, spondulicks, the readies; N. Amer. informal dinero.

monitor n. **1 detector**, scanner, recorder, sensor, security camera, CCTV. **2** UN monitors: **observer**, watchdog, overseer,

supervisor, scrutineer. **3** a computer monitor: **screen**, display, VDU.
▸v. **observe**, watch, track, keep an eye on, keep under surveillance, record, note, oversee; informal keep tabs on.

monkey n. **simian**, primate, ape.
□ **monkey with** tamper with, fiddle with, interfere with, meddle with, tinker with, play with; informal mess with; Brit. informal muck about with.

monotonous adj. **tedious**, boring, uninteresting, unexciting, dull, repetitive, repetitious, unvarying, unchanging, mechanical, mind-numbing, soul-destroying; informal deadly.
– OPPOSITES interesting.

monster n. **1 giant**, mammoth, demon, dragon, colossus, leviathan. **2 fiend**, animal, beast, devil, demon, barbarian, savage, brute; informal swine.

monstrous adj. **1 grotesque**, hideous, ugly, ghastly, gruesome, horrible, horrific, horrifying, grisly, disgusting, repulsive, dreadful, frightening, terrible, terrifying. **2 appalling**, wicked, abominable, terrible, horrible, dreadful, vile, outrageous, unspeakable, despicable, vicious, savage, barbaric, inhuman.
– OPPOSITES beautiful, humane.

monument n. **memorial**, statue, pillar, cairn, column, obelisk, cross, cenotaph, tomb, mausoleum, shrine.

monumental adj. **1 huge**, enormous, gigantic, massive, colos-

m

sal, mammoth, immense, tremendous, mighty, stupendous. **2 significant**, important, majestic, memorable, remarkable, noteworthy, momentous, grand, awe-inspiring, heroic, epic.
– OPPOSITES tiny.

mood n. **1 frame of mind**, state of mind, humour, temper. **2 bad mood**, temper, bad temper, sulk, low spirits, the doldrums, the blues; Brit. informal paddy. **3 atmosphere**, feeling, spirit, ambience, aura, character, flavour, feel, tone.

moody adj. **temperamental**, emotional, volatile, capricious, erratic, bad-tempered, petulant, sulky, sullen, morose.
– OPPOSITES cheerful.

moon v. **1 waste time**, loaf, idle; Brit. informal mooch. **2 mope**, pine, brood, daydream.

WORD LINKS
relating to the moon: lunar

moor¹ v. **tie (up)**, secure, make fast, berth, dock.

moor² n. **upland**, heath, moorland; Brit. fell, wold.

mop n. a tousled mop of hair: **shock**, mane, tangle, mass.

moral adj. **1 ethical**, good, virtuous, righteous, upright, upstanding, high-minded, principled, honourable, honest, just, noble. **2 moral support: psychological**, emotional, mental.
– OPPOSITES immoral, unethical.
• n. **1 lesson**, message, meaning, significance, import, point,

teaching. **2** he's got no morals: **moral code**, code of ethics, values, principles, standards, (sense of) morality, scruples.

morale n. **confidence**, self-confidence, self-esteem, spirit(s), team spirit, esprit de corps, motivation.

morality n. **1 ethics**, rights and wrongs, whys and wherefores. **2 virtue**, good behaviour, righteousness, uprightness, morals, standards, principles, honesty, integrity, propriety, honour, decency.

morbid adj. **ghoulish**, macabre, unhealthy, gruesome, unwholesome; informal sick.
– OPPOSITES wholesome.

more det. **extra**, further, added, additional, supplementary, increased, new.
– OPPOSITES less, fewer.

moreover adv. **besides**, furthermore, what's more, in addition, also, as well, too, to boot, additionally, on top of that, into the bargain.

morning n. **1 before lunch**, a.m.; literary morn; Nautical & N. Amer. forenoon. **2 dawn**, daybreak, sunrise, first light; N. Amer. sunup.

mortal adj. **1** all men are mortal: **perishable**, physical, bodily, corporeal, human, fleshly, earthly, impermanent, transient, ephemeral. **2** a mortal blow: **fatal**, lethal, deadly, deathdealing, murderous, terminal. **3** mortal enemies: **deadly**, sworn,

irreconcilable, bitter, implacable, unrelenting, remorseless.
– OPPOSITES eternal.
• n. **human (being)**, person, man, woman, earthling.

mortuary n. morgue, funeral parlour; Brit. chapel of rest.

mostly adv. **1 mainly**, for the most part, on the whole, in the main, largely, chiefly, predominantly, principally, primarily. **2 usually**, generally, in general, as a rule, ordinarily, normally, customarily, typically, most of the time, almost always.

mother n. matriarch, materfamilias; informal ma; Brit. informal mum, mummy; N. Amer. informal mom, mommy; Brit. informal, dated mater.
• v. **look after**, care for, take care of, nurse, protect, tend, raise, rear, pamper, coddle, cosset, fuss over.

WORD LINKS
relating to a mother: maternal;
killing of your mother: matricide

motherly adj. maternal, maternalistic, protective, caring, loving, affectionate, nurturing.

motif n. **1 design**, pattern, decoration, figure, shape, device, emblem, ornament. **2 theme**, idea, concept, subject, topic, leitmotif.

motion n. **1 movement**, locomotion, progress, passage, transit, course, travel, orbit. **2 gesture**, movement, signal, sign, indication, wave, nod, gesticulation. **3 proposal**, proposition, recommendation.

• v. **gesture**, signal, direct, indicate, wave, beckon, nod.

WORD LINKS
relating to motion: kinetic

motivate v. **prompt**, drive, move, inspire, stimulate, influence, activate, impel, propel, push, spur (on), encourage, incentivize.

motivation n. **motive**, motivating force, incentive, stimulus, stimulation, inspiration, inducement, incitement, spur.

motive n. **reason**, motivation, motivating force, rationale, grounds, cause, basis.

motto n. **slogan**, maxim, saying, proverb, aphorism, adage, saw, axiom, formula, catchphrase.

mould n. **1 cast**, die, matrix, form, shape, template, pattern, frame. **2** *an actress in the Hollywood mould:* **pattern**, form, type, style, tradition, school.
• v. **1 shape**, form, fashion, model, work, construct, make, create, sculpt, cast. **2 determine**, direct, control, guide, influence, shape, form, fashion, make.

mound n. **1 heap**, pile, stack, mountain. **2 hillock**, hill, knoll, rise, hummock, hump; Scottish brae.

mount v. **1 go up**, ascend, climb (up), scale. **2** *mount a horse:* **get on to**, bestride, climb on to, leap on to, hop on to. **3** *mount an exhibition:* **put on**, present, install, organize, stage, set up, prepare, launch, set in motion.

m

4 increase, grow, rise, escalate, soar, spiral, shoot up, rocket, climb, accumulate, build up, multiply.
– OPPOSITES descend, dismount, fall.
•n. **setting**, backing, support, mounting, frame, stand.

mountain n. **1 peak**, summit; (**mountains**) range, massif, sierra; Scottish ben. **2 lot**; informal heap, pile, stack, slew, lots, loads, tons, masses.

mourn v. **1 grieve for**, sorrow over, lament for, weep for. **2 deplore**, bewail, bemoan, rue, regret.

mourning n. grief, grieving, sorrowing, lamentation.

m **mouth** n. **1 lips**, jaws, muzzle; informal trap, chops, kisser; Brit. informal gob; N. Amer. informal puss. **2 entrance**, opening. **3 estuary**, delta, firth, outlet, outfall.

WORD LINKS
relating to the mouth: oral

move v. **1 go**, walk, step, proceed, progress, advance, budge, stir, shift, change position. **2 carry**, transfer, shift, push, pull, lift, slide. **3 progress**, advance, develop, evolve, change, happen. **4 act**, take steps, do something, take measures; informal get moving. **5 relocate**, move house, move away/out, change address, go (away), decamp. **6 affect**, touch, impress, shake, upset, disturb. **7 inspire**, prompt, stimulate, motivate, provoke, influence,

rouse, induce, incite. **8 propose**, submit, suggest, advocate, recommend, urge.
•n. **1 movement**, motion, action, gesture. **2 relocation**, change of house/address, transfer, posting. **3 initiative**, step, action, measure, manoeuvre, tactic, stratagem. **4 turn**, go; Scottish shot.

movement n. **1 motion**, move, gesture, sign, signal, action. **2 transportation**, shifting, conveyance, moving, transfer. **3 group**, party, faction, wing, lobby, camp. **4 campaign**, crusade, drive, push, initiative.

WORD LINKS
relating to movement: kinetic

movie n. film, picture, motion picture, feature film; informal flick.

moving adj. **1 in motion**, operating, operational, working, on the move, active, movable, mobile. **2 touching**, poignant, heart-warming, heart-rending, affecting, emotional, inspiring, inspirational, stimulating, stirring.
– OPPOSITES stationary, fixed.

mow v. **cut**, trim, crop, clip, shear.

much det. **a lot of**, a great/good deal of, a great/large amount of, plenty of, ample, abundant, plentiful; informal lots of, loads of, heaps of, masses of, tons of, stacks of.
– OPPOSITES little.
•adv. **1 greatly**, a great deal, a lot, considerably, appreciably.
2 often, frequently, many times,

regularly, habitually, routinely, usually, normally, commonly.
• pron. **a lot**, a great/good deal, plenty; informal lots, loads, heaps, masses, tons.

muck n. **1 dirt**, grime, filth, mud, mess; Brit. informal gunge. **2 dung**, manure, excrement, droppings, ordure.

mud n. **dirt**, sludge, ooze, silt, clay, mire, soil.

muddle v. **1 confuse**, mix up, jumble (up), disarrange, disorganize, disorder, mess up. **2 bewilder**, confuse, bemuse, perplex, puzzle, baffle, mystify.
• n. **mess**, confusion, jumble, tangle, chaos, disorder, disarray, disorganization.

muddy adj. **1 marshy**, boggy, swampy, waterlogged, squelchy, squishy, mucky, slimy, wet, soft. **2 dirty**, filthy, mucky, grimy, soiled. **3 murky**, cloudy, turbid.
– OPPOSITES clean, clear.

muffle v. **1 wrap (up)**, swathe, enfold, envelop, cloak. **2 deaden**, dull, dampen, mute, soften, quieten, mask, stifle, smother.

mug n. **beaker**, cup, tankard, glass, stein.
• v. **assault**, attack, set upon, beat up, rob; informal jump.

muggy adj. **humid**, close, sultry, sticky, oppressive, airless, stifling, suffocating, stuffy.
– OPPOSITES fresh.

mull v.
□ **mull over** ponder, consider, think over/about, reflect on,

contemplate, chew over; formal cogitate on.

multicoloured adj. **kaleidoscopic**, psychedelic, colourful, many-hued, jazzy, variegated.
– OPPOSITES monochrome.

multiple adj. **numerous**, many, various, different, diverse, several, manifold.
– OPPOSITES single.

multiply v. **increase**, grow, accumulate, proliferate, mount up, mushroom, snowball.
– OPPOSITES decrease.

mumble v. **mutter**, murmur, talk under your breath.

mundane adj. **humdrum**, dull, boring, tedious, monotonous, tiresome, unexciting, uninteresting, uneventful, unremarkable, routine, ordinary.
– OPPOSITES extraordinary.

municipal adj. **civic**, civil, metropolitan, urban, city, town, borough, council.

murder n. **killing**, homicide, assassination, extermination, execution, slaughter, butchery, massacre, manslaughter; literary slaying.
• v. **kill**, put to death, assassinate, execute, butcher, slaughter, massacre, wipe out; informal bump off; N. Amer. informal ice, waste; literary slay.

murderer n. **killer**, assassin, serial killer, butcher; informal hit man, hired gun.

murderous adj. **homicidal**, brutal, violent, savage, ferocious, fierce, vicious, bloodthirsty,

m

barbarous, barbaric, fatal, lethal, deadly.

murky adj. **1 dark**, gloomy, grey, leaden, dull, dim, overcast, cloudy, clouded, sunless, dismal, dreary, bleak. **2 dirty**, muddy, cloudy, turbid.
– OPPOSITES bright, clear.

murmur n. **1 whisper**, mutter, mumble, undertone. **2 hum**, buzz, drone.
•v. **mutter**, mumble, whisper, talk under your breath, talk sotto voce.

muscle n. **1 strength**, power, brawn; informal beef, beefiness. **2** financial muscle: **influence**, power, strength, might, force, forcefulness, weight; informal clout.
□ **muscle in** (informal) interfere, force your way in, impose yourself, encroach; informal horn in.

muscular adj. **strong**, brawny, muscly, well built, burly, strapping, sturdy, powerful, athletic; informal hunky, beefy.

muse v. **ponder**, consider, think over/about, mull over, reflect on, contemplate, turn over in your mind, chew over.

musical adj. **tuneful**, melodic, melodious, harmonious, sweet-sounding, dulcet, euphonious, mellifluous.
– OPPOSITES discordant.

must v. **ought to**, should, have (got) to, need to, be obliged to, be required to, be compelled to.

muster v. **1 assemble**, rally, raise, summon, gather, call up, call to arms, recruit, conscript; US draft. **2 congregate**, assemble, gather (together), come together, collect, convene, mass, rally. **3** she mustered her courage: **summon (up)**, screw up, call up, rally.

mutation n. **1 alteration**, change, transformation, metamorphosis, transmutation. **2 mutant**, freak (of nature), deviant, monstrosity, monster.

mute adj. **1 silent**, speechless, dumb, speaking, tight-lipped, taciturn; informal mum. **2 wordless**, silent, dumb, unspoken.
– OPPOSITES voluble, spoken.

muted adj. **1 muffled**, faint, indistinct, quiet, soft, low, distant, faraway. **2 subdued**, pastel, delicate, subtle, understated, restrained.

mutilate v. **1 disfigure**, maim, mangle, dismember, slash, hack up. **2 vandalize**, damage, slash, deface, violate, desecrate.

mutinous adj. **rebellious**, insubordinate, subversive, seditious, insurgent, insurrectionary, disobedient, restive.

mutiny n. **insurrection**, rebellion, revolt, riot, uprising, insurgence, insubordination.
•v. **rise up**, rebel, revolt, riot, strike.

mutter v. **1 murmur**, talk under your breath, talk sotto voce, mumble, whisper. **2 grumble**,

m

complain, grouse, carp, whine; informal moan, whinge.

mutual adj. **reciprocal**, reciprocated, requited, returned, common, joint, shared.

mysterious adj. **1 puzzling**, strange, peculiar, curious, funny, odd, weird, queer, bizarre, mystifying, inexplicable, baffling, perplexing, arcane, esoteric, cryptic, obscure. **2 secretive**, inscrutable, impenetrable, enigmatic, reticent, evasive.

mystery n. **1 puzzle**, enigma, conundrum, riddle, secret, paradox, question mark, closed book. **2 secrecy**, obscurity, uncertainty.

mystic, mystical adj. **spiritual**, religious, transcendental, paranormal, other-worldly, supernatural, occult, metaphysical.

mystify v. **bewilder**, puzzle, perplex, baffle, confuse, confound, bemuse, throw; informal flummox, stump, bamboozle.

myth n. **1 folk tale**, folk story, legend, fable, saga, lore, folklore. **2 misconception**, fallacy, old wives' tale, fairy story, fiction; informal cock and bull story.

Nn

nadir n. **low point**, all-time low, bottom, rock bottom; informal the pits.
– OPPOSITES zenith.

nag v. **1 harass**, keep on at, go on at, badger, chivvy, hound, plague, criticize, find fault with, moan at, grumble at, henpeck; informal hassle; N. Amer. informal ride. **2 trouble**, worry, bother, torment, niggle, prey on your mind; informal bug.

nail n. **tack**, pin, brad, hobnail, spike, staple, rivet.
•v. **fasten**, fix, attach, secure, affix, pin, tack, hammer.

naive adj. **innocent**, unsophisticated, artless, inexperienced, unworldly, trusting, gullible, credulous, immature, callow, raw, green; informal wet behind the ears.
– OPPOSITES worldly.

naked adj. **nude**, bare, in the nude, stark naked, stripped, unclothed, undressed; informal without a stitch on, in your birthday suit, in the raw/buff, in the altogether; Brit. informal starkers; N. Amer. informal buck naked.
– OPPOSITES dressed.

name n. **title**, designation, tag, nickname, sobriquet, epithet, label, honorific; informal moniker, handle; formal appellation, denomination, cognomen.
•v. **1 call**, dub, label, style, term, title, baptize, christen.

2 nominate, designate, select, pick, decide on, choose.

> **WORD LINKS**
> *relating to names:* onomastic

namely adv. **that is (to say)**, to be specific, specifically, viz., to wit, in other words.

nap n. **sleep**, catnap, siesta, doze, lie-down, rest; informal snooze, forty winks, shut-eye; Brit. informal kip, zizz.

narcotic n. **drug**, sedative, opiate, painkiller, analgesic, palliative.
• adj. **soporific**, sedative, calming, painkilling, pain-relieving, analgesic, anodyne.

narrate v. **tell**, relate, recount, recite, describe, chronicle, report, present.

n **narrative** n. **account**, chronicle, history, description, record, report, story, tale.

narrator n. **storyteller**, chronicler, commentator, presenter, author.
– OPPOSITES listener, audience.

narrow adj. **1 slender**, slim, small, slight, attenuated, tapering, thin, tiny. **2 confined**, cramped, tight, restricted, limited, constricted, small, tiny, inadequate, insufficient.
– OPPOSITES wide, broad.
• v. **reduce**, restrict, limit, decrease, diminish, taper, contract, shrink, constrict.
– OPPOSITES widen.

narrowly adv. **(only) just**, barely, scarcely, hardly, by a hair's breadth; informal by a whisker.

narrow-minded adj. **intolerant**, illiberal, reactionary, conservative, parochial, provincial, insular, small-minded, petty, blinkered, inward-looking, hidebound, prejudiced, bigoted.
– OPPOSITES tolerant.

nasty adj. **1 unpleasant**, disagreeable, disgusting, vile, foul, abominable, revolting, repulsive, repellent, horrible, obnoxious, unsavoury, loathsome, noxious, foul-smelling, smelly, stinking, rank, fetid, malodorous; informal ghastly, horrid, yucky; N. Amer. informal lousy; literary noisome. **2 unkind**, unpleasant, unfriendly, disagreeable, rude, spiteful, malicious, mean, vicious, malevolent, hurtful. **3** *a nasty accident*: **serious**, dangerous, bad, awful, dreadful, terrible, severe, painful.
– OPPOSITES nice, pleasant.

nation n. **country**, state, land, realm, kingdom, republic, people, race, tribe.

national adj. **1** *national politics*: **state**, public, federal, governmental. **2** *a national strike*: **nationwide**, countrywide, general, widespread.
– OPPOSITES local, international.
• n. **citizen**, subject, native, resident, inhabitant, voter, passport holder.

nationalism n. **patriotism**, allegiance, xenophobia, chauvinism, jingoism, flag-waving.

nationwide adj. national, countrywide, state, general, widespread, extensive.
– OPPOSITES local.

native n. inhabitant, resident, local, citizen, national, countryman.
– OPPOSITES foreigner.
•adj. **1** *native species:* **indigenous**, original, local, domestic. **2** *native wit:* **innate**, inborn, natural, inherent, intrinsic.

natural adj. **1** unprocessed, organic, pure, unrefined, additive-free, green, GM-free. **2** *a natural occurrence:* **normal**, ordinary, everyday, usual, regular, common, commonplace, typical, routine, standard, logical, understandable, (only) to be expected, predictable. **3** *a natural leader:* **born**, instinctive, congenital, pathological. **4** *his natural instincts:* **innate**, inborn, inherent, native, inherited, hereditary. **5** *she seemed very natural:* **unaffected**, spontaneous, uninhibited, relaxed, unselfconscious, genuine, open, artless, guileless, unpretentious, unstudied.
– OPPOSITES abnormal, artificial, affected.

naturally adv. of course, as might be expected, needless to say, obviously, clearly, it goes without saying.

nature n. **1 the natural world**, the environment, Mother Earth, the universe, the cosmos, wildlife, the countryside, the land. **2 character**, personality, disposition, temperament, make-up, psyche. **3** kind, sort, type, variety, category, class, genre, order, quality, complexion; N. Amer. stripe.

naughty adj. **1 badly behaved**, disobedient, bad, wayward, defiant, unruly, insubordinate, wilful, delinquent, undisciplined, refractory, disruptive, mischievous, impish. **2 indecent**, risqué, rude, racy, vulgar, dirty, filthy, smutty, crude, coarse.
– OPPOSITES well behaved, clean.

nausea n. sickness, biliousness, queasiness, vomiting, retching.

nautical adj. maritime, marine, naval, seafaring, seagoing, sailing.

navigate v. steer, pilot, guide, direct, captain; informal skipper.

navy n. fleet, flotilla, armada.

near adj. **1 close**, nearby, (close/near) at hand, a stone's throw away, neighbouring, within reach, accessible, handy, convenient; informal within spitting distance. **2 imminent**, in the offing, on its way, coming, impending, looming.
– OPPOSITES far, distant.

nearby adj. **not far away**, not far off, close at hand, close by, near, within reach, neighbouring, local, accessible, convenient, handy.
– OPPOSITES distant.

nearly adv. almost, just about, more or less, practically, virtually, all but, as good as, not far off, to all intents and purposes, not quite; informal pretty well.

n

neat adj. **1 tidy**, orderly, well ordered, in (good) order, spick and span, uncluttered, shipshape, straight, trim. **2 smart**, spruce, dapper, trim, well groomed, well turned out; informal natty. **3** *his neat footwork:* **skilful**, deft, dexterous, adroit, adept, expert, nimble, elegant, graceful, accurate; informal nifty. **4** *a neat solution:* **clever**, ingenious, inventive, imaginative. **5** *neat gin:* **undiluted**, straight, pure.
– OPPOSITES untidy.

necessarily adv. **as a consequence**, as a result, automatically, as a matter of course, certainly, incontrovertibly, inevitably, unavoidably, inescapably, of necessity.

n necessary adj. **1 obligatory**, required, requisite, compulsory, mandatory, imperative, needed, essential, vital, indispensable, de rigueur; formal needful. **2** *a necessary consequence:* **inevitable**, unavoidable, inescapable, inexorable.

necessity n. **1 essential**, prerequisite, requisite, sine qua non; informal must-have. **2** *political necessity forced him to resign:* **force of circumstance**, obligation, need, exigency.

need v. **require**, be in need of, want, be crying out for, demand, call for, necessitate, entail, involve, lack, be without, be short of.
• n. **1** *there's no need to apologize:* **necessity**, requirement, call,

demand. **2** *basic human needs:* **requirement**, necessity, want, requisite, prerequisite, desideratum. **3** *my hour of need:* **difficulty**, trouble, distress, crisis, emergency, urgency, extremity.

needed adj. **necessary**, required, called for, wanted, desired, lacking.
– OPPOSITES optional.

needless adj. **unnecessary**, unneeded, uncalled for, gratuitous, pointless, superfluous, redundant, excessive.
– OPPOSITES necessary.

needy adj. **poor**, deprived, disadvantaged, underprivileged, in need, hard up, poverty-stricken, impoverished, destitute, penniless; informal broke, strapped (for cash); Brit. informal skint; dated needful.
– OPPOSITES wealthy.

negative adj. **1 pessimistic**, defeatist, gloomy, critical, cynical, fatalistic, dismissive, unenthusiastic, apathetic, unresponsive. **2 harmful**, bad, adverse, damaging, detrimental, unfavourable, disadvantageous.
– OPPOSITES positive, optimistic, favourable.

neglect v. **1 fail to look after**, leave alone, abandon, ignore, pay no attention to, let slide, not attend to, be remiss about, be lax about, shirk. **2 fail**, omit, forget.
– OPPOSITES cherish, remember.
• n. **1 disrepair**, dilapidation, shabbiness, abandonment, disuse. **2 negligence**,

dereliction (of duty), careless-ness, laxity, slackness, irres-ponsibility.
- OPPOSITES care.

neglected adj. **1** *neglected animals:* **uncared for**, abandoned, mistreated, maltreated. **2** *a neglected cottage:* **derelict**, dilapidated, tumbledown, ram-shackle, untended. **3** *a neglected masterpiece:* **disregarded**, for-gotten, overlooked, ignored, unrecognized, unnoticed, un-sung, underrated.

negligent adj. **neglectful**, re-miss, careless, lax, irresponsible, inattentive, thoughtless, uncar-ing, unmindful, forgetful, slack, sloppy; N. Amer. derelict.
- OPPOSITES dutiful.

negligible adj. **trivial**, trifling, insignificant, unimportant, of no account, minor, inconsequen-tial, minimal, small, slight, infinitesimal, minuscule.
- OPPOSITES significant.

negotiate v. **1** **discuss (terms)**, talk, consult, confer, debate, compromise, bargain, haggle. **2** **arrange**, broker, work out, thrash out, complete, close, conclude, agree on. **3** **get round**, get past, get over, clear, cross, surmount, overcome, deal with, cope with.

negotiation n. **1** **discussion(s)**, talks, conference, debate, dia-logue, consultation. **2** **arrange-ment**, brokering, settlement, conclusion, completion.

negotiator n. **mediator**, arbi-trator, moderator, go-between,

middleman, intermediary, rep-resentative, spokesperson, broker.

neighbourhood n. **1** **district**, area, locality, locale, quarter, community; informal neck of the woods; N. Amer. informal hood. **2** **vicinity**, environs.

neighbouring adj. **adjacent**, adjoining, bordering, connect-ing, next-door, nearby, in the vicinity.
- OPPOSITES remote.

neighbourly adj. **obliging**, helpful, friendly, kind, consider-ate, amicable, sociable, hospit-able, companionable, civil, cordial.
- OPPOSITES unfriendly.

nerve n. **1** **confidence**, assur-ance, courage, bravery, deter-mination, will power, spirit, grit; informal guts; Brit. informal bottle; N. Amer. informal moxie. **2** **audacity**, cheek, effrontery, gall, temerity, presumption, impudence, im-pertinence, arrogance; informal face, front, brass neck, chutz-pah. **3** **(nerves) anxiety**, ten-sion, nervousness, stress, worry, cold feet, apprehension; informal butterflies (in your stomach), collywobbles, jitters, the heebie-jeebies.

WORD LINKS
relating to nerves in the body:
neural

nervous adj. **anxious**, worried, apprehensive, on edge, edgy, tense, stressed, agitated, un-easy, restless, worked up, keyed

n

up, overwrought, jumpy, on tenterhooks, highly strung, nervy, excitable, neurotic; *informal* jittery, twitchy, in a state, uptight, wired, trepidatious; *N. Amer. informal* squirrelly.
- OPPOSITES relaxed, calm.

nestle v. **snuggle**, cuddle, huddle, nuzzle, settle, burrow.

net¹ n. **netting**, mesh, tulle, fishnet, lace, openwork.
•v. **catch**, capture, trap, snare; *informal* nab, bag, collar, bust; *Brit. informal* nick.

net² adj. **after tax**, after deductions, take-home, final.
- OPPOSITES gross.
•v. **earn**, make, clear, take home, bring in, pocket, realize.

network n. **web**, lattice, net, matrix, mesh, criss-cross, grid, maze, labyrinth, warren, tangle.

neurotic adj. **highly strung**, oversensitive, nervous, tense, paranoid, obsessive, fixated, hysterical, overwrought, irrational.
- OPPOSITES stable, calm.

neutral adj. **1 impartial**, unbiased, unprejudiced, objective, open-minded, non-partisan, even-handed, disinterested, dispassionate, detached, non-aligned, unaffiliated, uninvolved. **2 inoffensive**, bland, unobjectionable, unexceptionable, anodyne, uncontroversial, safe, harmless, innocuous. **3 pale**, light, colourless, indeterminate, drab, insipid, nondescript, dull.
- OPPOSITES biased, provocative.

neutralize v. **counteract**, offset, counterbalance, balance, cancel out, nullify, negate.

never-ending adj. **incessant**, continuous, ceaseless, constant, continual, perpetual, uninterrupted, unbroken, steady, unremitting, relentless, persistent, interminable, non-stop, endless, unending.

nevertheless adv. **nonetheless**, even so, however, still, yet, in spite of that, despite that, be that as it may, notwithstanding.

new adj. **1 recent**, up to date, the latest, current, state-of-the-art, contemporary, advanced, cutting-edge, modern, avant-garde. **2 unused**, brand new, pristine, fresh. **3 different**, another, alternative, additional, extra, supplementary, further, unfamiliar, unknown, strange. **4 reinvigorated**, restored, revived, improved, refreshed, regenerated.
- OPPOSITES old, second-hand.

newcomer n. **1 incomer**, immigrant, settler, stranger, outsider, foreigner, alien; *informal* new kid on the block, johnny-come-lately; *Austral. informal* blow-in. **2 beginner**, novice, learner, trainee, apprentice, probationer; *informal* rookie, newbie; *N. Amer. informal* tenderfoot.

newly adv. **recently**, only just, lately, freshly, not long ago.

news n. **report**, story, account, announcement, press release, communication, communiqué, bulletin, intelligence, information, word, revelation, disclosure, exposé; Brit. stop press; informal scoop; literary tidings.

newspaper n. paper, journal, gazette, news-sheet, tabloid, broadsheet, periodical; Brit. red top; informal rag.

next adj. **1** following, succeeding, subsequent, ensuing, upcoming, to come. **2** neighbouring, adjacent, adjoining, next-door, bordering, connected, closest, nearest; formal contiguous, proximate.
– OPPOSITES previous.
• adv. afterwards, after, then, later, subsequently; formal thereafter.

nice adj. **1** have a nice time: enjoyable, pleasant, agreeable, good, pleasurable, satisfying, entertaining, amusing; informal lovely, great; N. Amer. informal neat. **2** nice people: pleasant, likeable, agreeable, personable, good-natured, congenial, amiable, affable, genial, friendly, charming, delightful, engaging, sympathetic, polite, courteous, well mannered, civil, kind, obliging, helpful. **3** nice weather: fine, dry, sunny, warm, mild, clement. **4** a nice distinction: subtle, fine, slight, delicate, precise.
– OPPOSITES unpleasant, nasty.

niche n. **1** recess, alcove, nook, cranny, hollow, bay, cavity, pigeonhole. **2** position, slot, place, vocation, calling, métier, station, job, level.

nick n. cut, scratch, incision, notch, chip, dent, indentation.
• v. cut, scratch, graze, chip, dent.

nickname n. pet name, diminutive, endearment, tag, label, sobriquet, epithet; informal handle, moniker.

night n. night-time, (hours of) darkness, dark.
– OPPOSITES day.

> **WORD LINKS**
> *occurring or active at night:* nocturnal

nightfall n. sunset, sundown, dusk, twilight, evening, dark; literary eventide.
– OPPOSITES dawn.

nightmare n. ordeal, trial, hell, misery, agony, torture, murder, purgatory, disaster; informal the pits.

nil n. nothing, none, nought, zero; Tennis love; Cricket a duck.

nimble adj. **1** agile, light, quick, lithe, skilful, deft, dexterous, adroit, sprightly, spry; informal nippy. **2** a nimble mind: quick, alert, lively, astute, perceptive, penetrating, discerning, shrewd, sharp, intelligent, bright, smart, clever, brilliant; informal quick on the uptake.
– OPPOSITES clumsy.

nip v. & n. bite, nibble, peck, pinch, tweak.

no adv. absolutely not, of course not, under no circumstances, not at all, never; informal nope, no way, not a chance, not on your

n

life; Brit. informal no fear; old use nay.
– OPPOSITES yes.

noble adj. **1 aristocratic**, blue-blooded, patrician, high-born, titled. **2 worthy**, righteous, good, honourable, virtuous, upright. **3 magnificent**, splendid, grand, impressive, stately, imposing, dignified, proud, striking, majestic.
– OPPOSITES humble, lowly.
•n. **aristocrat**, nobleman, noblewoman, lord, lady, peer (of the realm), peeress, patrician; informal aristo.
– OPPOSITES commoner.

nod v. **1 incline**, bob, bow, dip. **2 signal**, gesture, gesticulate, motion, sign, indicate.

noise n. **sound**, din, hubbub, clamour, racket, uproar, tumult, commotion, pandemonium; Brit. row; informal hullabaloo.
– OPPOSITES silence.

noisy adj. **1 raucous**, rowdy, strident, clamorous, vociferous, boisterous. **2 loud**, blaring, booming, deafening, thunderous, ear-splitting, piercing, cacophonous, tumultuous.
– OPPOSITES quiet, soft.

nominal adj. **1 in name only**, titular, formal, official, theoretical, supposed, ostensible, so-called, self-styled. **2 token**, symbolic, minimal; Brit. peppercorn.
– OPPOSITES real, considerable.

nominate v. **1 propose**, put forward, put up, submit, present, recommend, suggest. **2 appoint**, choose, decide on, select, designate, assign.

nonchalant adj. **calm**, composed, unconcerned, cool, imperturbable, casual, blasé, offhand, insouciant; informal laid-back.
– OPPOSITES anxious.

non-committal adj. **evasive**, equivocal, guarded, circumspect, reserved; informal cagey.

nonconformist n. **dissenter**, protester, rebel, freethinker, individualist, free spirit, maverick, renegade, schismatic, apostate, heretic.

nondescript adj. **undistinguished**, unremarkable, featureless, unmemorable, ordinary, average, run-of-the-mill, mundane, uninteresting, uninspiring, colourless, bland.
– OPPOSITES distinctive.

non-existent adj. **imaginary**, imagined, unreal, fictional, fictitious, made up, invented, fanciful, mythical, illusory.
– OPPOSITES real.

nonsense n. **1 rubbish**, gibberish, claptrap, balderdash, garbage; informal baloney, bosh, tripe, drivel, gobbledegook, mumbo-jumbo, poppycock, twaddle, guff, tosh, bilge, hogwash, piffle; Brit. informal cobblers, codswallop, double Dutch, rot. **2 mischief**, misbehaviour; informal tomfoolery, monkey business, shenanigans, malarkey; Brit. informal monkey tricks, jiggery-pokery.
– OPPOSITES sense.

non-stop adj. **continuous**, constant, continual, incessant, ceaseless, uninterrupted, unbroken, never-ending, perpetual, round-the-clock, persistent, steady, unremitting, relentless, interminable.
– OPPOSITES intermittent, occasional.
• adv. **continuously**, continually, incessantly, ceaselessly, all the time, constantly, perpetually, persistently, steadily, relentlessly, interminably; informal 24-7.

noon n. **midday**, twelve o'clock, twelve hundred hours, high noon, noonday.

norm n. **standard**, convention, criterion, yardstick, benchmark, touchstone, rule, formula, pattern.
☐ **the norm** normal, usual, the rule, standard, typical, average, par for the course, expected.

normal adj. **1 usual**, standard, ordinary, customary, conventional, habitual, accustomed, typical, common, regular, routine, traditional, commonplace, everyday. **2 ordinary**, average, run-of-the-mill, middle-of-the-road, conventional, mainstream; N. Amer. garden-variety; Brit. informal common or garden, bog-standard. **3 sane**, in your right mind, right in the head, of sound mind, compos mentis; informal all there.
– OPPOSITES unusual, insane.

normally adv. **1 naturally**, conventionally, properly, like everyone else. **2 usually**, ordinarily, as

a rule, generally, in general, mostly, on the whole, typically, habitually.

nose n. **snout**, muzzle, proboscis, trunk; informal beak, conk, schnozz, hooter.
• v. **1 pry**, enquire, poke about/around, interfere (in), meddle (in), stick/poke your nose in; informal snoop; Austral./NZ informal stickybeak. **2 ease**, inch, edge, move, manoeuvre, steer, guide.

> WORD LINKS
> relating to the nose: nasal

nostalgic adj. **wistful**, sentimental, emotional, homesick, regretful, dewy-eyed, maudlin.

nosy adj. (informal) **prying**, inquisitive, curious, spying, eavesdropping, intrusive; informal snooping.

notable adj. **1 noteworthy**, remarkable, outstanding, important, significant, memorable, marked, striking, impressive, momentous, uncommon. **2 prominent**, well known, famous, famed, noted, of note.
– OPPOSITES unremarkable, unknown.
• n. **celebrity**, VIP, dignitary, luminary, star, big name, personage; informal celeb, bigwig.

notably adv. **1 in particular**, particularly, especially, primarily, principally, chiefly. **2 remarkably**, especially, exceptionally, singularly, particularly, peculiarly, distinctly, significantly, unusually, uncommonly, conspicuously.

notch n. nick, cut, incision, score, scratch, slit, snick, slot, groove.

note n. **1** record, entry, reminder, comment, jotting. **2** message, letter, line, missive; informal memo; formal memorandum, epistle. **3** annotation, footnote, marginalia. **4** (Brit.) banknote; N. Amer. bill; US informal greenback. **5** *the note of hopelessness in her voice:* tone, hint, indication, sign, element, suggestion, sense.
•v. **1** bear in mind, be mindful of, consider, take notice of, register, be aware, take in, notice, observe, see, perceive. **2** write down, put down, jot down, take down, scribble, enter, mark, record, register, pencil in.

n notebook n. notepad, exercise book, register, logbook, log, diary, journal, record; Brit. jotter, pocketbook; trademark Filofax.

noted adj. famous, famed, well known, renowned, prominent, notable, important, eminent, great, acclaimed, celebrated, distinguished.
– OPPOSITES unknown.

noteworthy adj. notable, interesting, significant, important, remarkable, striking, memorable, unique, special, unusual.
– OPPOSITES unexceptional.

nothing n. **1** not a thing, zero; N. English nowt; informal zilch, sweet FA, not a dicky bird; N. Amer. informal zip, nada, diddly-squat. **2** zero, nought, nil, 0; Tennis love; Cricket a duck.

notice v. observe, note, see, discern, detect, spot, perceive, make out; Brit. informal clock.
– OPPOSITES overlook.
•n. **1** sign, announcement, advertisement, poster, placard, bill, handbill, flyer. **2** attention, observation, awareness, consciousness, perception, regard, consideration, scrutiny; formal cognizance. **3** *advance notice of the price increase:* notification, warning, information, news, word.

noticeable adj. obvious, evident, apparent, manifest, plain, clear, conspicuous, perceptible, discernible, detectable, observable, visible, appreciable, unmistakable, patent.
– OPPOSITES imperceptible.

notify v. inform, tell, let someone know, advise, apprise, alert, warn.

notion n. idea, impression, belief, opinion, view, concept, conception, understanding, feeling, suspicion, intuition, inkling.

notorious adj. infamous, scandalous, disreputable, of ill repute.

nought n. nil, zero, nothing; Tennis love; Cricket a duck; informal zilch; N. Amer. informal zip, nada.

nourish v. feed, sustain, provide for, care for, nurture.

nourishing adj. nutritious, wholesome, good for you, nutritive, healthy, health-giving, beneficial.
– OPPOSITES unhealthy.

nourishment n. food, nutriment, nutrients, nutrition, sustenance.

novel¹ n. story, tale, narrative, romance, novella.

novel² adj. new, original, unusual, unconventional, unorthodox, different, fresh, imaginative, innovative, unfamiliar, surprising.
– OPPOSITES traditional.

novelty n. **1 originality**, newness, freshness, unconventionality, innovation, unfamiliarity. **2 knick-knack**, trinket, bauble, toy, trifle, ornament; N. Amer. kickshaw.

novice n. beginner, learner, newcomer, fledgling, trainee, probationer, student, pupil, apprentice, tyro, neophyte; informal rookie, newbie; N. Amer. informal tenderfoot, greenhorn.
– OPPOSITES expert, veteran.

now adv. **1 at the moment**, at present, presently, at this moment in time, currently, nowadays, these days, today, in this day and age. **2 at once**, straight away, right away, this minute, this instant, immediately, instantly, directly; informal pronto, asap.

noxious adj. poisonous, toxic, deadly, harmful, dangerous, unhealthy, unpleasant.
– OPPOSITES innocuous.

nuance n. distinction, shade, gradation, refinement, degree, subtlety, nicety.

nucleus n. core, centre, heart, kernel, nub, hub, middle, focus.

nude adj. naked, stark naked, bare, unclothed, undressed, stripped; informal without a stitch on, in your birthday suit, in the raw/buff, in the altogether; Brit. informal starkers; N. Amer. informal buck naked.
– OPPOSITES dressed.

nudge v. prod, elbow, dig, poke, jab, jog, push, touch.
•n. prod, dig (in the ribs), poke, jab, push.

nuisance n. annoyance, inconvenience, bore, bother, irritation, trial, burden, pest; informal pain (in the neck), hassle, bind, drag, headache.

nullify v. annul, render null and void, invalidate, repeal, reverse, rescind, revoke, cancel, neutralize, negate, counteract.

numb adj. **1 without feeling**, without sensation, dead, numbed, desensitized, frozen, anaesthetized, insensible, insensate. **2 dazed**, stunned, stupefied, paralysed, immobilized.
•v. **1 deaden**, desensitize, anaesthetize, immobilize, freeze. **2 daze**, stun, stupefy, paralyse, immobilize.

number n. **1 numeral**, integer, figure, digit, character. **2 quantity**, total, aggregate, tally, quota. **3 song**, piece, tune, track, dance.
•v. **1 add up to**, amount to, total, come to. **2 include**, count, reckon, deem.

WORD LINKS
relating to numbers: numerical

numerous adj. **many**, a number of, a lot of/lots of, several, plenty of, countless, copious, an abundance of, frequent; informal umpteen.
– OPPOSITES few.

nurse v. **1 care for**, take care of, look after, tend, minister to. **2** *they nursed old grievances*: **harbour**, foster, bear, have, hold (on to), retain.

nurture v. **1 bring up**, care for, take care of, look after, tend, rear, raise. **2** *he nurtured my love of art*: **encourage**, promote, stimulate, develop, foster, cultivate, boost, strengthen, fuel.
– OPPOSITES neglect.

nut n. (informal) **1 maniac**, lunatic, madman, madwoman; informal loony, nutcase, head case; Brit. informal nutter; N. Amer. informal screwball. **2 enthusiast**, fan, devotee, aficionado; informal freak, fanatic, addict, buff.

nutritious adj. **nourishing**, nutritive, wholesome, good for you, healthy, health-giving, beneficial.

Oo

oath n. **1 vow**, pledge, promise, affirmation, word (of honour), guarantee. **2 swear word**, expletive, profanity, four-letter word, dirty word, obscenity, curse; formal imprecation.

obedient adj. **compliant**, biddable, acquiescent, good, law-abiding, deferential, governable, docile, submissive.
– OPPOSITES rebellious.

obey v. **1 do as you are told**, defer to, submit to, bow to. **2** *he refused to obey the order*: **carry out**, perform, act on, execute, discharge, implement. **3** *rules have to be obeyed*: **comply with**, adhere to, observe, abide by, act in accordance with, conform to, respect, follow, keep to, stick to.
– OPPOSITES defy, ignore.

object n. **1 thing**, article, item, entity, device, gadget. **2 target**, butt, focus, recipient, victim. **3 objective**, aim, goal, target, purpose, end, plan, point, ambition, intention, idea.
• v. *they objected to the scheme*: **protest about**, oppose, take exception to, take issue with, take a stand against, argue against, quarrel with, condemn, draw the line at, demur at, mind, complain about.
– OPPOSITES approve of, accept.

objection n. **protest**, protestation, complaint, opposition, demurral, counter-argument, disagreement, disapproval, dissent.

objective adj. **1 impartial**, unbiased, unprejudiced, non-partisan, disinterested, neutral, uninvolved, even-handed, fair, dispassionate, detached. **2 factual**, actual, real, empirical, verifiable.
– OPPOSITES subjective, emotional.
•n. **aim**, intention, purpose, target, goal, object, end, idea, plan, ambition.

objectively adv. **impartially**, without bias/prejudice, even-handedly, fairly, dispassionately, with an open mind, without fear or favour.

obligation n. **1 commitment**, duty, responsibility, function, task, job, charge, onus, liability, requirement, debt. **2** *a sense of obligation:* **duty**, compulsion, indebtedness, necessity, pressure, constraint.

obligatory adj. **compulsory**, mandatory, prescribed, required, statutory, enforced, binding, requisite, necessary, imperative, de rigueur.
– OPPOSITES optional.

oblige v. **1 compel**, force, require, make, bind, constrain. **2** *do someone a favour*, accommodate, help, assist, indulge, humour.

obliged adj. **thankful**, grateful, appreciative, beholden, indebted, in someone's debt.

obliging adj. **helpful**, accommodating, cooperative, agreeable, amenable, generous, kind; Brit. informal decent.

obliterate v. **1 destroy**, wipe out, annihilate, demolish; informal zap. **2 hide**, obscure, blot out, block, cover, screen.

oblivious adj. **unaware**, unconscious, heedless, unmindful, insensible, ignorant, blind, deaf, impervious.
– OPPOSITES conscious.

obscene adj. **1 pornographic**, indecent, smutty, dirty, filthy, X-rated, explicit, lewd, rude, vulgar, coarse, scatological; informal blue; euphemistic adult. **2 scandalous**, shocking, outrageous, immoral.

obscure adj. **1 unclear**, uncertain, unknown, mysterious, hazy, vague, indeterminate. **2 abstruse**, oblique, opaque, cryptic, arcane, enigmatic, puzzling, perplexing, baffling, incomprehensible, impenetrable, elliptical. **3 little known**, unknown, unheard of, unsung, minor, unrecognized, forgotten.
– OPPOSITES clear, plain, famous.
•v. **1 hide**, conceal, cover, veil, shroud, screen, mask, cloak, block, obliterate, eclipse. **2 confuse**, complicate, obfuscate, cloud, blur, muddy.
– OPPOSITES reveal, clarify.

observant adj. **alert**, sharp-eyed, eagle-eyed, attentive, watchful; informal beady-eyed, on the ball.
– OPPOSITES inattentive.

observation n. **1 monitoring**, watching, scrutiny, survey, surveillance, attention, study. **2 remark**, comment, opinion, impression, thought, reflection.

o

observe v. **1 notice**, see, note, perceive, discern, spot. **2 watch**, look at, contemplate, view, survey, regard, keep an eye on, scrutinize, keep under surveillance, monitor; informal keep tabs on. **3 remark**, comment, say, mention, declare, announce, state; formal opine. **4 comply with**, abide by, keep, obey, adhere to, heed, honour, fulfil, respect, follow, consent to, accept.

observer n. **spectator**, onlooker, watcher, fly on the wall, viewer, witness.

obsessed adj. **fixated**, possessed, haunted, consumed, infatuated, besotted; informal smitten, hung up.

obsession n. **fixation**, passion, mania, compulsion, fetish, preoccupation, infatuation, hobby horse, phobia, complex, neurosis; informal bee in your bonnet, hang-up, thing.

obsessive adj. **consuming**, all-consuming, compulsive, controlling, fanatical, neurotic, excessive; informal pathological.

obsolete adj. **out of date**, outdated, outmoded, old-fashioned, passé, antiquated, antediluvian, anachronistic, superannuated, archaic, ancient, fossilized, extinct, defunct; informal out of the ark; Brit. informal past its sell-by date.
– OPPOSITES current, modern.

obstacle n. **barrier**, hurdle, stumbling block, obstruction, bar, block, impediment,

hindrance, snag, catch, drawback, hitch, fly in the ointment, handicap, difficulty, problem, disadvantage; Brit. spanner in the works.
– OPPOSITES advantage, aid.

obstinate adj. **stubborn**, pigheaded, mulish, self-willed, unyielding, inflexible, unbending, intransigent, intractable; old use contumacious.
– OPPOSITES compliant.

obstruct v. **1 block (up)**, clog (up), cut off, bung up, choke, dam up; technical occlude. **2 impede**, hinder, interfere with, hamper, block, interrupt, hold up, stand in the way of, frustrate, slow down, delay, bring to a standstill, stop, halt.
– OPPOSITES clear, facilitate.

obstruction n. **obstacle**, barrier, stumbling block, impediment, hindrance, difficulty, check, restriction, blockage, stoppage, congestion, bottleneck, hold-up.

obtain v. **get**, acquire, come by, secure, procure, pick up, gain, earn, achieve, attain; informal get hold of, lay your hands on, land.

obtainable adj. **available**, to be had, in circulation, on the market, on offer, in season, at your disposal, accessible; informal up for grabs, on tap.

obvious adj. **clear**, plain, evident, apparent, patent, manifest, conspicuous, pronounced, prominent, distinct, noticeable, unmistakable, perceptible, visible,

palpable; informal sticking out a mile.
– OPPOSITES imperceptible.

occasion n. **1 time**, instance, juncture, point, moment, experience, case. **2 event**, affair, function, celebration, party, get-together, gathering; informal do, bash.
▸v. **cause**, give rise to, bring about, result in, lead to, prompt, create, engender.

occasional adj. **infrequent**, intermittent, irregular, periodic, sporadic, odd; N. Amer. sometime.
– OPPOSITES regular, frequent.

occasionally adv. **sometimes**, from time to time, (every) now and then, (every) now and again, at times, every so often, (every) once in a while, on occasion, periodically.
– OPPOSITES often.

occult adj. **supernatural**, magic, magical, satanic, mystical, unearthly, esoteric, psychic.
◻ **the occult** the supernatural, magic, black magic, witchcraft, necromancy, the black arts, occultism.

occupant n. **resident**, inhabitant, owner, householder, tenant, leaseholder, lessee; Brit. occupier, owner-occupier.

occupation n. **1 job**, profession, work, line of work, trade, employment, business, career, métier, calling. **2 pastime**, activity, hobby, pursuit, interest, entertainment, recreation. **3 conquest**, capture, invasion, seizure,

annexation, colonization, subjugation.

occupied adj. **1 busy**, working, at work, active; informal tied up, hard at it, on the go. **2 in use**, full, engaged, taken.

occupy v. **1 live in**, inhabit, lodge in, tenant, move into, people, populate, settle; Scottish stay in. **2 engage**, busy, distract, absorb, engross, hold, interest, involve, entertain. **3** *the region was occupied by Japan*: **capture**, seize, conquer, invade, colonize, annex, subjugate.

occur v. **1 happen**, take place, come about, transpire; N. Amer. informal go down. **2 be found**, be present, exist, appear, develop, manifest itself.
◻ **occur to** enter your head, cross your mind, come/spring to mind, strike, dawn on, suggest itself.

occurrence n. **1 event**, incident, happening, phenomenon, circumstance, episode. **2 existence**, instance, appearance, frequency, incidence, prevalence, rate; Statistics distribution.

odd adj. **1 strange**, peculiar, queer, funny, bizarre, eccentric, unconventional, outlandish, unusual, weird, curious, abnormal, puzzling, mystifying, baffling, unaccountable; informal wacky. **2** *odd jobs*: **occasional**, casual, irregular, isolated, sporadic, periodic, miscellaneous, various, varied, sundry. **3** *an odd shoe*: **mismatched**, unmatched,

O

unpaired, single, lone, solitary, extra, leftover, spare.
- OPPOSITES normal, ordinary, regular.

odds pl. n. **likelihood**, probability, chances.

□ **odds and ends** bits and pieces, bits and bobs, stuff, paraphernalia, sundries, bric-a-brac, knick-knacks, oddments; informal junk; Brit. informal odds and sods, clobber, gubbins.

odour n. **smell**, stench, stink, reek, aroma, bouquet, scent, perfume, fragrance; Brit. informal pong, whiff, niff; N. Amer. informal funk; literary redolence.

> **WORD LINKS**
> relating to odour: olfactory

odyssey n. **journey**, voyage, trip, trek, travels, quest, crusade, pilgrimage.

off adj. **1 away**, absent, off duty, on holiday/leave; N. Amer. on vacation. **2 cancelled**, postponed, called off. **3 rotten**, bad, stale, mouldy, sour, rancid, turned, spoiled.

offence n. **1 crime**, illegal act, misdemeanour, felony, infringement, violation, wrongdoing, sin. **2 annoyance**, resentment, indignation, displeasure, bad feeling, animosity.

offend v. **1 upset**, give offence to, affront, hurt someone's feelings, insult, hurt, wound, slight. **2 break the law**, commit a crime, do wrong.

offender n. **wrongdoer**, criminal, lawbreaker, crook, villain,

miscreant, felon, delinquent, malefactor, culprit, guilty party.

offensive adj. **1 insulting**, rude, derogatory, disrespectful, personal, hurtful, upsetting, wounding, abusive. **2 unpleasant**, disagreeable, nasty, distasteful, objectionable, off-putting, dreadful, frightful, obnoxious, abominable, disgusting, repulsive, repellent, vile, foul, horrible, sickening, nauseating; informal ghastly, horrid, gross; Brit. informal beastly. **3 hostile**, attacking, aggressive, invading, incursive, combative, threatening, martial, warlike, belligerent, bellicose.
- OPPOSITES complimentary, pleasant, defensive.
• n. **attack**, assault, onslaught, invasion, push, thrust, charge, raid, incursion, blitz, campaign.

offer v. **1 put forward**, proffer, give, present, come up with, suggest, propose, advance, submit, tender. **2 volunteer**, step/come forward, show willing. **3 bid**, tender, put in a bid/offer of.
- OPPOSITES withdraw, refuse.
• n. **1 proposal**, proposition, suggestion, submission, approach, overture. **2 bid**, tender, bidding price.

offering n. **contribution**, donation, gift, present, sacrifice, tribute.

offhand adj. **casual**, careless, uninterested, indifferent, cool, nonchalant, blasé, insouciant, cavalier, glib, perfunctory, cursory, dismissive.

office n. **1** place of work, workplace, workroom. **2** *the company's Paris office*: branch, division, section, bureau, department. **3** *the office of President*: post, position, appointment, job, occupation, role, situation, function.

officer n. official, functionary, executive.

official adj. **1** authorized, approved, validated, authenticated, certified, accredited, endorsed, sanctioned, licensed, recognized, legitimate, legal, lawful, valid, bona fide, proper; informal kosher. **2** ceremonial, formal, solemn, bureaucratic.
- OPPOSITES unauthorized, informal.
•n. **officer**, executive, functionary, administrator, bureaucrat, mandarin, representative, agent; derogatory apparatchik.

officious adj. self-important, bumptious, self-assertive, overbearing, interfering, intrusive, meddlesome, meddling; informal bossy.

offset v. counteract, balance (out), even out/up, counterbalance, compensate for, make up for, neutralize, cancel (out).

offspring n. children, family, progeny, young, brood, descendants, heirs, successors; informal kids; Brit. informal sprogs, brats.

often adv. frequently, many times, a lot, repeatedly, again and again, time after time, regularly, commonly, generally, ordinarily; N. Amer. oftentimes.
- OPPOSITES seldom.

oily adj. greasy, fatty, buttery, rich, oleaginous.

ointment n. lotion, cream, salve, liniment, embrocation, rub, gel, balm, emollient, unguent.

OK, okay (informal) adj. **1** satisfactory, all right, acceptable, competent, adequate, tolerable, passable, reasonable, decent, fair, not bad, average, middling, moderate, unremarkable, unexceptional; informal so-so, fair-to-middling. **2** permissible, allowable, acceptable, all right, in order, permitted, fitting, suitable, appropriate.
- OPPOSITES unsatisfactory.
•n. **authorization**, (seal of) approval, agreement, consent, assent, permission, endorsement, ratification, sanction, blessing, leave; informal the go-ahead, the green light, the thumbs up, say-so.

old adj. **1** *old people*: elderly, aged, older, senior, venerable, in your dotage, past your prime, long in the tooth, grizzled, ancient, decrepit, doddery, senescent, senile; informal getting on, past it, over the hill. **2** *old clothes*: worn, shabby, threadbare, frayed, patched, tattered, motheaten, ragged; informal tatty. **3** *the old days*: bygone, olden, past, prehistoric, primitive. **4** *old cars*: antique, veteran,

O

vintage, classic. **5** *an old girl-friend:* **former**, previous, earlier, past, ex-, one-time, sometime, erstwhile; formal quondam.
– OPPOSITES young, new, modern current.

WORD LINKS
relating to old people: geriatric

old-fashioned adj. **out of date**, outdated, dated, out of fashion, outmoded, unfashionable, passé, outworn, behind the times, antiquated, antediluvian, archaic, obsolescent, obsolete, superannuated; informal out of the ark, old hat, clunky.
– OPPOSITES modern.

omen n. **portent**, sign, signal, token, forewarning, warning, harbinger, presage, indication; literary foretoken.

ominous adj. **threatening**, menacing, baleful, forbidding, foreboding, fateful, sinister, black, dark, gloomy.
– OPPOSITES promising.

omission n. **1 exclusion**, leaving out, deletion, elimination. **2 negligence**, neglect, dereliction, oversight, lapse, failure.

omit v. **1 leave out**, exclude, miss out, miss, cut, drop, skip. **2 forget**, neglect, overlook, fail.
– OPPOSITES include, remember.

once adv. **1 on one occasion**, one time. **2 formerly**, previously, in the past, once upon a time, in days/times gone by, in the (good) old days, long ago.

• conjunction **as soon as**, the moment, when, after.
◻ **at once 1 immediately**, right away, right now, straight away, instantly, directly, forthwith, without delay, without further ado. **2 at the same time**, (all) together, simultaneously, as a group, in unison.

one-sided adj. **1 biased**, prejudiced, partisan, partial, slanted, distorted, unfair. **2 unequal**, uneven, unbalanced.
– OPPOSITES impartial, equal.

ongoing adj. **in progress**, under way, going on, continuing, proceeding.

onlooker n. **eyewitness**, witness, observer, spectator, bystander; informal rubberneck.

only adv. **1 at best**, at most, just, no more than, hardly, barely, scarcely. **2 exclusively**, solely, purely.
• adj. **sole**, single, one (and only), solitary, lone, unique, exclusive.

onset n. **start**, beginning, commencement, arrival, appearance, inception, day one, outbreak; informal kick-off.
– OPPOSITES end.

onslaught n. **attack**, assault, offensive, advance, charge, blitz, bombardment, barrage.

onus n. **burden**, responsibility, obligation, duty, weight, load.

ooze v. **seep**, discharge, flow, exude, trickle, drip, dribble, drain, leak.

opaque adj. **1 non-transparent**, cloudy, filmy, blurred, smeared,

misty. **2** obscure, unclear, unfathomable, incomprehensible, unintelligible, impenetrable; *informal* as clear as mud.
– OPPOSITES transparent, clear.

open adj. **1** unlocked, unlatched, off the latch, ajar, gaping, yawning. **2** *open countryside* | *open spaces:* unenclosed, rolling, sweeping, wide open, exposed, spacious, uncrowded, uncluttered, undeveloped. **3** *the position is still open:* available, free, vacant, unfilled; *informal* up for grabs. **4** *open to abuse:* vulnerable, subject, susceptible, liable, exposed, an easy target for. **5** *she was very open:* frank, candid, honest, forthcoming, communicative, forthright, direct, unreserved, plain-spoken, outspoken, blunt; *informal* upfront. **6** *open hostility:* overt, manifest, conspicuous, plain, undisguised, unconcealed, clear, naked, blatant, flagrant, barefaced, brazen.
– OPPOSITES shut, closed.
▸v. **1** unfasten, unlock, unbolt, throw wide. **2** unwrap, undo, untie. **3** spread out, unfold, unfurl, unroll, straighten out. **4** begin, start, commence, initiate, set in motion, get going, get under way, get off the ground; *informal* kick off.
– OPPOSITES close, shut.

> WORD LINKS
> *fear of open spaces:*
> agoraphobia

open-air adj. **outdoor**, out-of-doors, outside, alfresco.

opening n. **1** hole, gap, aperture, space, orifice, vent, crack, slit, chink, fissure, cleft, crevice, interstice. **2** beginning, start, commencement, outset; *informal* kick-off. **3** vacancy, position, post, job, opportunity.
▸adj. **first**, initial, introductory, preliminary, maiden, inaugural.
– OPPOSITES final, closing.

openly adv. **1** publicly, blatantly, flagrantly, overtly. **2** frankly, candidly, explicitly, honestly, sincerely, forthrightly, freely.

open-minded adj. **unbiased**, unprejudiced, neutral, objective, disinterested, tolerant, liberal, permissive, broad-minded.
– OPPOSITES prejudiced, narrow-minded.

operate v. **1** work, run, use, handle, control, manage, drive, steer, manoeuvre, function, go, perform. **2** direct, control, manage, run, handle, be in control/charge of.

operation n. **1** functioning, working, running, performance, action. **2** *a military operation:* action, exercise, undertaking, enterprise, manoeuvre, campaign. **3** business, enterprise, company, firm.

operational adj. **running**, up and running, working, functioning, operative, in operation, in use, in action, in working order, serviceable, functional.

operative adj. **running**, up and running, working, functioning, operational, in operation, in use, in action, in effect.

•n. **1 machinist**, operator, mechanic, engineer, worker, workman, (factory) hand. **2 agent**, secret/undercover agent, spy, mole, plant; N. Amer. informal spook.

opinion n. **belief**, thought(s), idea, way of thinking, feeling, mind, view, point of view, viewpoint, standpoint, assessment, estimation, judgement, conviction.

opponent n. **1 rival**, adversary, competitor, enemy, antagonist, combatant, contender, challenger; literary foe. **2 critic**, objector, dissenter.
– OPPOSITES ally, supporter.

opportunity n. **chance**, time, occasion, moment, opening, option, window, possibility, scope, freedom; informal shot, break, look-in.

o **oppose** v. **be against**, object to, be hostile to, disagree with, disapprove of, resist, take a stand against, put up a fight against, fight, counter, challenge, take issue with.
– OPPOSITES support.

opposed adj.
□ **opposed to** against, dead set against, averse to, hostile to, antagonistic to, antipathetic to; informal anti.

opposing adj. **1 conflicting**, contrasting, incompatible, irreconcilable, contradictory, clashing, at variance, at odds, opposed, opposite, enemy, competing.
– OPPOSITES similar, allied.

opposite adj. **1 facing**, face to face with, across from. **2 conflicting**, contrasting, incompatible, irreconcilable, contradictory, at variance, differing, at odds. **3 rival**, opposing, competing, enemy.
•n. **reverse**, converse, antithesis, contrary.
– OPPOSITES same.

opposition n. **1 resistance**, hostility, antagonism, antipathy, objection, dissent, disapproval. **2 opponent(s)**, opposing side, competition, rival(s), adversary.
– OPPOSITES agreement.

oppress v. **persecute**, tyrannize, crush, repress, subjugate, subdue, keep down, rule with a rod of iron.

oppression n. **persecution**, abuse, ill-treatment, tyranny, repression, suppression, subjugation, cruelty, brutality, injustice.
– OPPOSITES freedom.

oppressive adj. **1 harsh**, cruel, brutal, repressive, tyrannical, despotic, draconian, ruthless, merciless, pitiless. **2 muggy**, close, heavy, hot, humid, sticky, airless, stuffy, stifling, sultry.
– OPPOSITES lenient, fresh.

opt v. **choose**, select, pick, decide, elect; (**opt for**) go for, settle on, plump for.

optimistic adj. **1 positive**, confident, hopeful, sanguine, bullish, buoyant, upbeat. **2 encouraging**, promising, reassuring, favourable.
– OPPOSITES pessimistic, depressing.

optimum adj. **best**, most favourable, most advantageous, ideal, perfect, prime, optimal.

option n. **choice**, preference, alternative, selection, possibility.

optional adj. **voluntary**, non-compulsory, elective, discretionary.
– OPPOSITES compulsory.

opulent adj. **luxurious**, sumptuous, palatial, lavishly appointed, rich, splendid, magnificent, grand, fancy; informal plush; Brit. informal swish; N. Amer. informal swank.
– OPPOSITES spartan.

oral adj. **spoken**, verbal, unwritten, vocal, uttered.
– OPPOSITES written.

orbit n. **circuit**, course, path, track, trajectory, rotation, revolution.
▸v. **circle**, go round, revolve round, travel round, circumnavigate.

orchestra n. **ensemble**, group; informal band, combo.

orchestrate v. **organize**, arrange, plan, set up, mobilize, mount, stage, mastermind, coordinate, direct.

ordain v. **1** confer holy orders **on**, admit to the priesthood, appoint, anoint, consecrate. **2** determine, predestine, preordain, predetermine, prescribe, designate.

ordeal n. **trial**, hardship, suffering, nightmare, trauma, hell, torture, torment, agony.

order n. **1** alphabetical order: **sequence**, arrangement, organization, codification, classification, system, series, succession. **2** some semblance of order: **tidiness**, neatness, orderliness, method, symmetry, uniformity, regularity, routine. **3** the police managed to keep order: **peace**, control, law and order, calm. **4** in good order: **condition**, state, repair, shape, situation; Brit. informal nick. **5** I had to obey orders: **command**, instruction, directive, direction, decree, edict, injunction, dictate. **6** the lower orders of society: **class**, level, rank, grade, caste. **7** a religious order: **community**, brotherhood, sisterhood. **8** the Orange Order: **organization**, association, society, fellowship, fraternity, lodge, guild, league, union, club.
– OPPOSITES chaos.
▸v. **1** instruct, tell, command, direct, charge, require, enjoin, ordain, decree, rule. **2** request, apply for, book, reserve, requisition. **3** organize, arrange, sort out, lay out, group, classify, categorize, catalogue.

o

orderly adj. **1** neat, tidy, well ordered, in order, trim, in apple-pie order, shipshape. **2** organized, efficient, methodical, systematic, coherent, structured, logical. **3** well behaved, law-abiding, disciplined, peaceful, peaceable.
– OPPOSITES untidy, unruly.

ordinary adj. **1** usual, normal, standard, typical, common,

customary, habitual, everyday, regular, routine, day-to-day, quotidian. **2 average**, run-of-the-mill, typical, middle-of-the-road, conventional, humdrum, unremarkable, unexceptional, pedestrian, prosaic, workday; informal bog-standard; Brit. informal common or garden; N. Amer. informal garden-variety.
– OPPOSITES unusual.

organ n. newspaper, paper, journal, periodical, magazine, voice, mouthpiece.

organic adj. **1** *organic matter:* **living**, live, animate, biological. **2** *organic vegetables:* **natural**, chemical-free, pesticide-free, bio-. **3** *an organic whole:* **structured**, organized, coherent, integrated, coordinated, ordered, harmonious.

organism n. living thing, being, creature, animal, plant, life form.

organization n. **1 planning**, arrangement, coordination, organizing, running, management. **2 structure**, arrangement, plan, pattern, order, form, format, framework, composition. **3 institution**, body, group, company, concern, firm, business, corporation, conglomerate, consortium, syndicate, agency, association, society; informal outfit.

organize v. **1 order**, arrange, sort, assemble, marshal, put straight, group, classify, collate, categorize, catalogue, codify. **2 arrange**, coordinate, sort out, put together, fix up, set up, lay

on, orchestrate, see to, mobilize.

orient, orientate v. **1** *you need time to orient yourself:* **acclimatize**, familiarize, adjust, accustom, find your feet, get your bearings. **2 aim**, direct, pitch, design, intend. **3 align**, place, position, arrange.

origin n. **1 beginning**, start, genesis, birth, dawning, dawn, emergence, creation, source, basis, cause, root(s), derivation, provenance. **2 descent**, ancestry, parentage, pedigree, lineage, line (of descent), heritage, birth, extraction, family, roots.

original adj. **1 indigenous**, aboriginal, native, first, earliest, early, ur-. **2 authentic**, genuine, actual, true, bona fide. **3 innovative**, creative, imaginative, inventive, new, novel, fresh, unusual, unconventional, unorthodox, groundbreaking, pioneering, unique, distinctive.
•n. **prototype**, source, master.

originally adv. at first, in the beginning, to begin with, initially, in the first place, at the outset.

originate v. **1 arise**, have its origin, begin, start, stem, spring, emerge, emanate. **2 invent**, create, devise, think up, dream up, conceive, formulate, form, develop, produce, mastermind, pioneer.

ornament n. **1 knick-knack**, trinket, bauble, gewgaw; N. Amer. informal kickshaw. **2 decoration**, adornment, embellishment, ornamentation, trimming, accessories, frills.

ornamental adj. **decorative**, fancy, ornate, ornamented, attractive.

ornate adj. **elaborate**, decorated, embellished, adorned, ornamented, rococo, fancy, fussy, ostentatious, showy; informal flashy.
– OPPOSITES plain.

orthodox adj. **1 conventional**, mainstream, conformist, established, traditional, traditionalist, prevalent, popular, conservative, received. **2** *an orthodox Muslim:* **observant**, devout, strict.
– OPPOSITES unconventional.

oscillate v. **1 swing to and fro**, swing back and forth, sway. **2 waver**, swing, fluctuate, alternate, see-saw, yo-yo, vacillate.

ostentatious adj. **showy**, conspicuous, flamboyant, gaudy, brash, vulgar, loud, extravagant, fancy, ornate, rococo; informal flash, flashy, bling-bling, over the top, OTT, glitzy.
– OPPOSITES restrained.

ostracize v. **exclude**, shun, spurn, cold-shoulder, reject, ignore, snub, cut dead, blackball, blacklist; Brit. send to Coventry; informal freeze out; Brit. informal blank.

other adj. **1 alternative**, different, distinct, separate, various. **2 more**, further, additional, extra, fresh, new, added, supplementary.

oust v. **expel**, drive out, force out, eject, get rid of, depose, topple, unseat, overthrow, bring down, overturn, dismiss, dislodge.

outbreak n. **1 eruption**, flare-up, upsurge, rash, wave, spate, burst, flurry. **2 start**, beginning, commencement, onset.

outburst n. **explosion**, flare-up, storm, outpouring, burst, surge, fit, paroxysm, spasm.

outcome n. **result**, end result, net result, consequence, upshot, conclusion, end product; informal pay-off.

outcry n. **protest**, protestation, complaints, objections, furore, hue and cry, fuss, uproar, opposition, dissent; informal hullabaloo, ructions, stink.

outdated adj. **old-fashioned**, out of date, outmoded, out of fashion, unfashionable, dated, passé, old, behind the times, antiquated; informal out, old hat, square, clunky.
– OPPOSITES modern.

outdo v. **surpass**, outshine, overshadow, eclipse, outclass, outmanoeuvre, put in the shade, upstage, exceed, transcend, top, cap, beat, better; informal be a cut above.

outdoor adj. **open-air**, out-of-doors, outside, alfresco.
– OPPOSITES indoor.

outer adj. **1 outside**, outermost, outward, exterior, external, surface. **2 outlying**, distant,

o

remote, faraway, far-flung, furthest.
– OPPOSITES inner.

outfit n. **1 costume**, suit, uniform, ensemble, clothes, clothing, dress, garb; informal get-up, gear; Brit. informal kit. **2** (informal) **organization**, enterprise, company, firm, business, group, body, team; informal set-up.

outgoing adj. **1 extrovert**, uninhibited, unreserved, demonstrative, affectionate, warm, sociable, gregarious, convivial, lively, expansive. **2 departing**, retiring, leaving.
– OPPOSITES introverted, incoming.

outgoings pl. n. **expenses**, expenditure, spending, outlay, payments, costs, overheads.

outing n. **trip**, excursion, jaunt, expedition, day out, tour, drive, ride, run; informal spin, junket.

outlaw n. **fugitive**, bandit, robber.
• v. **ban**, bar, prohibit, forbid, make illegal, proscribe.
– OPPOSITES permit.

outlet n. **1 vent**, way out, outfall, opening, channel, conduit, duct. **2 market**, shop, store.

outline n. **1 silhouette**, profile, shape, contours, form, lines. **2 rough idea**, thumbnail sketch, rundown, summary, synopsis, résumé, precis, gist, bare bones.
• v. **rough out**, sketch out, draft, summarize, precis.

outlook n. **1 point of view**, viewpoint, way of thinking, perspective, attitude, standpoint,

stance, frame of mind. **2 view**, vista, prospect, panorama. **3 prospects**, future, expectations, prognosis.

out of date adj. **1 old-fashioned**, outmoded, outdated, dated, old, passé, behind the times, obsolete, antiquated, anachronistic, antediluvian; informal old hat, clunky. **2 expired**, lapsed, invalid, void.
– OPPOSITES fashionable, valid, current.

output n. **production**, yield, product, productivity, work, result.

outrage n. **1 indignation**, fury, anger, rage, wrath, annoyance; literary ire. **2 scandal**, offence, insult, affront, disgrace, atrocity.
• v. **enrage**, infuriate, incense, anger, scandalize, offend, affront, shock.

outrageous adj. **1 shocking**, disgraceful, scandalous, atrocious, appalling, dreadful, insufferable, intolerable. **2 exaggerated**, improbable, preposterous, ridiculous, unwarranted.

outright adv. **1 completely**, entirely, wholly, totally, categorically, absolutely, utterly, flatly, unreservedly, out of hand. **2 explicitly**, directly, frankly, candidly, bluntly, plainly, to someone's face; Brit. informal straight up. **3 instantly**, instantaneously, immediately, at once, straight away, then and there, on the spot.
• adj. **1 complete**, absolute, out-and-out, downright, utter, sheer, categorical. **2 definite**,

unequivocal, unmistakable, clear.

outset n. **start**, starting point, beginning, inception; informal the word go.
- OPPOSITES end.

outside n. **exterior**, case, skin, shell, covering, facade.
• adj. **1 exterior**, external, outer, outdoor, out-of-doors. **2 independent**, freelance, consultant, external.
• adv. **outdoors**, out of doors, alfresco.
- OPPOSITES inside.

outsider n. **stranger**, visitor, foreigner, alien, interloper, immigrant, incomer, newcomer.

outskirts pl. n. **edges**, fringes, margins, suburbs, suburbia, environs, borders, periphery.

outspoken adj. **forthright**, direct, candid, frank, straightforward, open, straight from the shoulder, plain-spoken, blunt.

outstanding adj. **1 excellent**, marvellous, fine, magnificent, superb, wonderful, superlative, exceptional, pre-eminent, renowned, celebrated; informal great, terrific, tremendous, super; Brit. informal brilliant; N. Amer. informal neat. **2 to be done**, undone, unfinished, incomplete, remaining, pending. **3 unpaid**, unsettled, owing, owed, to be paid, payable, due, overdue; N. Amer. delinquent.

outward adj. **external**, surface, superficial, seeming, apparent, ostensible.
- OPPOSITES inward.

outweigh v. **be greater than**, exceed, be superior to, prevail over, override, supersede, offset, cancel out, outbalance, compensate for.

outwit v. **outsmart**, outmanoeuvre, steal a march on, trick, get the better of; informal pull a fast one on, put one over on.

ovation n. **applause**, round of applause, cheers, bravos, acclaim, standing ovation; informal (big) hand.

over prep. **1 above**, on top of, atop, covering. **2 more than**, above, in excess of, upwards of.
- OPPOSITES under.
• adv. **1 overhead**, past, by. **2 at an end**, finished, ended, no more, a thing of the past; informal finito.

overall adj. **total**, all-inclusive, gross, final, inclusive, complete, entire, blanket.
• adv. **generally (speaking)**, in general, altogether, all in all, on balance, on average, for the most part, in the main, on the whole, by and large.

overbearing adj. **domineering**, dominating, autocratic, tyrannical, despotic, high-handed; informal bossy.

overcast adj. **cloudy**, sunless, dark, grey, black, leaden, heavy, dull, murky.
- OPPOSITES bright.

overcome v. **conquer**, defeat, beat, prevail over, control, get/bring under control, master, get the better of; informal lick, best.

o

• adj. she was overcome with excitement: **overwhelmed**, moved, affected, speechless.

overdue adj. **1 late**, behind schedule, behind time, delayed, tardy. **2 unpaid**, unsettled, owing, owed, payable, due, outstanding, undischarged; N. Amer. delinquent.
– OPPOSITES early, punctual.

overflow v. **spill over**, flow over, brim over, well over, flood.
• n. **surplus**, excess, extra, remainder, overspill.

overhaul v. **service**, maintain, repair, mend, fix up, rebuild, renovate, recondition, refit, refurbish.

overlook v. **1 fail to notice**, fail to spot, miss. **2 disregard**, neglect, ignore, pass over, forget, take no notice of, make allowances for, turn a blind eye to, excuse, pardon, forgive. **3 have a view of**, look over/across, look on to, look out on.

overpower v. **overwhelm**, get the better of, overthrow, subdue, suppress, subjugate, repress, bring someone to their knees.

overpowering adj. **overwhelming**, oppressive, unbearable, unendurable, intolerable, shattering.

override v. **1 disallow**, overrule, countermand, veto, quash, overturn, overthrow, cancel, reverse, rescind, revoke, repeal. **2 outweigh**, supersede, take precedence over, take priority over, cancel out, outbalance.

overriding adj. **most important**, top, first (and foremost), predominant, principal, primary, paramount, chief, main, major, foremost, central, key.

overrule v. **countermand**, cancel, reverse, rescind, repeal, revoke, disallow, override, veto, quash, overturn, overthrow.

overrun v. **invade**, storm, occupy, swarm into, surge into, inundate, overwhelm.

overshadow v. **outshine**, eclipse, surpass, exceed, outclass, outstrip, outdo, upstage; informal be head and shoulders above.

overt adj. **undisguised**, unconcealed, plain (to see), clear, conspicuous, obvious, noticeable, manifest, patent, open, blatant.
– OPPOSITES covert.

overtake v. **1 pass**, go past, pull ahead of; Brit. overhaul. **2 outstrip**, surpass, overshadow, eclipse, outshine, outclass, exceed, top, cap. **3 befall**, happen to, come upon, hit, strike, overwhelm, overcome.

overthrow v. **oust**, remove, bring down, topple, depose, displace, unseat, defeat, conquer.
• n. **removal**, ousting, defeat, fall, collapse, demise.

overture n. **1 preliminary**, prelude, introduction, lead-in, precursor, start, beginning. **2 opening move**, approach, advances, feeler, signal.

overturn v. **1 capsize**, turn turtle, keel over, tip over, topple over, upset, turn over, knock over, upend. **2 cancel**, reverse, rescind, repeal, revoke, countermand, disallow, override, overrule, veto, quash, overthrow.

overweight adj. **fat**, obese, stout, plump, portly, chubby, pot-bellied, flabby; informal tubby; Brit. informal podgy.

overwhelm v. **1 trounce**, rout, beat hollow, conquer, crush; informal thrash, lick, wipe the floor with. **2 overcome**, move, stir, affect, touch, strike, dumbfound, shake, leave speechless; informal bowl over, knock sideways; Brit. informal knock/hit for six.

overwhelming adj. **1 very large**, enormous, immense, inordinate, massive, huge. **2 very strong**, powerful, uncontrollable, irrepressible, irresistible, overpowering, compelling.

owe v. **be in debt (to)**, be indebted (to), be in arrears (to), be under an obligation (to).

owing adj. **unpaid**, to be paid, payable, due, overdue, undischarged, owed, outstanding, in arrears; N. Amer. delinquent.
□ **owing to** because of, as a result of, on account of, due to, as a consequence of, thanks to, in view of.

own adj. **personal**, individual, particular, private, personalized, unique.
•v. **possess**, keep, hold, be the owner of, have to your name.
□ **own up** confess, admit, acknowledge; informal come clean.

owner n. **possessor**, holder, proprietor, homeowner, freeholder, landlord, landlady.

ownership n. **possession**, freehold, proprietorship, title.

o
p

Pp

pace n. **1 step**, stride. **2 gait**, walk, march, tread. **3 speed**, rate, velocity, tempo.
•v. **walk**, step, stride, march, pound.

pacify v. **placate**, appease, calm (down), conciliate, propitiate, assuage, mollify, soothe.
– OPPOSITES enrage.

pack n. **1 packet**, container, package, box, carton, parcel.

2 group, herd, troop, crowd, mob, band, party, set, gang, rabble, horde, throng, huddle, mass, assembly, gathering, host; informal crew, bunch.
•v. **1 fill**, load, stow, store, bundle, stuff, cram. **2 wrap (up)**, package, parcel, swathe, swaddle, encase, envelop, bundle. **3 throng**, crowd, fill,

cram, jam, squash into, squeeze into.

package n. **1 parcel**, packet, box, carton. **2 collection**, bundle, combination, range, complement, raft, platform.
•v. **wrap**, gift-wrap, pack, box, seal.

packed adj. **crowded**, full, filled (to capacity), crammed, jammed, solid, teeming, seething, swarming; informal jam-packed, chock-full, chock-a-block, full to the gunwales, bursting/ bulging at the seams.

packet n. **pack**, carton, container, case, package.

pact n. **agreement**, treaty, entente, protocol, deal, settlement, armistice, truce.

pad¹ n. **1 dressing**, pack, wad. **2 notebook**, notepad, writing pad, jotter; N. Amer. scratch pad.

pad² v. **creep**, sneak, steal, tiptoe, pussyfoot.

padded adj. **cushioned**, insulated, lined, quilted, stuffed, lagged.

padding n. **1 wadding**, cushioning, stuffing, packing, filling, lining. **2 verbiage**, wordiness; Brit. informal waffle.

paddle¹ n. **oar**, scull.
•v. **row**, pull, scull.

paddle² v. **splash (about)**, dabble, wade.

pagan n. & adj. **heathen**, infidel, non-Christian.

page¹ n. **folio**, sheet, side, leaf.

page² n. **1 errand boy**, messenger boy; N. Amer. bellboy, bellhop.

2 attendant, pageboy, trainbearer.
•v. **call (for)**, summon, send for.

pageant n. **parade**, procession, cavalcade, tableau, spectacle, extravaganza, show.

pageantry n. **spectacle**, display, ceremony, magnificence, pomp, splendour, grandeur, show; informal razzle-dazzle, razzmatazz.

pain n. **1 suffering**, agony, torture, torment. **2 ache**, aching, soreness, throbbing, sting, twinge, stab, pang, discomfort, irritation. **3 sorrow**, grief, heartache, heartbreak, sadness, unhappiness, distress, misery, despair, agony, torment, torture. **4** *he took pains to hide his feelings*: **care**, effort, bother, trouble.
•v. **sadden**, grieve, distress, trouble, perturb, oppress, cause anguish to.

> **WORD LINKS**
>
> *pain-relieving drug*: analgesic; *drug that stops you feeling pain*: anaesthetic

painful adj. **1 sore**, hurting, tender, aching, throbbing. **2 disagreeable**, unpleasant, nasty, distressing, upsetting, sad, traumatic, miserable, heartbreaking, agonizing, harrowing.

painfully adv. **distressingly**, disturbingly, uncomfortably, unpleasantly, dreadfully.

painless adj. **1 pain-free**, without pain. **2 easy**, trouble-free, straightforward, simple, uncomplicated; informal child's play.
– OPPOSITES painful, difficult.

painstaking adj. **careful**, meticulous, thorough, assiduous, attentive, conscientious, punctilious, scrupulous, rigorous.
– OPPOSITES slapdash.

paint n. **colouring**, colour, tint, dye, stain, pigment, emulsion, gloss.
▪v. **1 colour**, decorate, whitewash, airbrush, daub, smear. **2 portray**, picture, paint a picture/portrait of, depict, represent.

painting n. **picture**, illustration, portrayal, depiction, representation, image, artwork, canvas, oil, watercolour.

pair n. **set**, brace, couple, duo, two.
▪v. **match**, put together, couple, combine.

palace n. **castle**, château, mansion, stately home, schloss.

palatable adj. **1 edible**, tasty, appetizing, delicious, mouthwatering, toothsome, succulent; informal scrumptious, yummy, scrummy, moreish. **2 pleasant**, acceptable, agreeable, to your liking.
– OPPOSITES disagreeable.

palatial adj. **luxurious**, magnificent, sumptuous, splendid, grand, opulent, lavish, stately, fancy; Brit. upmarket; informal plush, swanky, posh, ritzy; Brit. informal swish.
– OPPOSITES modest.

pale adj. **1 white**, pallid, pasty, wan, colourless, anaemic, washed out, peaky, ashen, sickly; informal like death warmed up. **2 light**, pastel, muted, subtle, soft, faded, bleached, washed out. **3 dim**, faint, weak, feeble.
– OPPOSITES ruddy, dark.
▪v. **turn white**, turn pale, blanch, lose colour.

palpable adj. **1 tangible**, touchable. **2 perceptible**, visible, noticeable, discernible, detectable, observable, unmistakable, transparent, obvious, clear, plain (to see), evident, apparent, manifest, staring you in the face, written all over someone.
– OPPOSITES imperceptible.

paltry adj. **small**, meagre, trifling, insignificant, negligible, inadequate, insufficient, derisory, pitiful, pathetic, miserable, niggardly, beggarly; informal measly, piddling, poxy.
– OPPOSITES considerable.

pamper v. **spoil**, indulge, overindulge, cosset, mollycoddle, coddle, baby, wait on someone hand and foot.

pamphlet n. **brochure**, leaflet, booklet, circular; N. Amer. mailer, folder.

pan¹ n. **saucepan**, pot, bowl, frying pan, skillet.

pan² v. **swing (round)**, sweep, move, turn.

panache n. **flamboyance**, confidence, self-assurance, style, flair, elan, dash, verve, zest, spirit, brio, vivacity, gusto, liveliness, vitality, energy; informal pizzazz, oomph, zip, zing.

P

panel n. **1** console, dashboard, instruments, controls, dials. **2** group, team, body, committee, board.

panic n. alarm, anxiety, fear, fright, trepidation, dread, terror, hysteria, apprehension; informal flap, fluster, cold sweat.
– OPPOSITES calm.
•v. **1** be alarmed, be scared, be afraid, take fright, be hysterical, lose your nerve, get worked up; informal run around like a headless chicken. **2** frighten, alarm, scare, unnerve; Brit. informal put the wind up.

panorama n. view, vista, prospect, scenery, landscape, seascape, cityscape, skyline.

panoramic adj. sweeping, wide, extensive, scenic, commanding.

pant v. breathe heavily, breathe hard, puff and blow, huff and puff, gasp, heave, wheeze.

pants pl. n. **1** (Brit.) underpants, briefs, boxer shorts, boxers, knickers; N. Amer. shorts, undershorts; informal panties; dated drawers, bloomers. **2** (N. Amer.) trousers, slacks; Brit. informal trews, strides, kecks; Austral. informal daks.

paper n. **1** newspaper, journal, gazette, periodical, tabloid, broadsheet, daily, weekly; informal rag. **2** exam, examination, test. **3** essay, article, monograph, thesis, work, dissertation, treatise, study, report, analysis; N. Amer. theme. **4** document, certificate, letter, file, deed, record, archive; **(papers)**

paperwork, documentation. **5** they asked us for our papers: identification, identity card, ID, credentials.

parable n. allegory, moral tale, fable.

parade n. **1** procession, march, cavalcade, motorcade, spectacle, display, pageant, review, tattoo; Brit. march past. **2** promenade, walkway, esplanade, mall; N. Amer. boardwalk; Brit. informal prom.
•v. **1** march, process, file, troop. **2** strut, swagger, stride; N. Amer. sashay. **3** display, exhibit, make a show of, flaunt, show (off), demonstrate.

paradise n. **1** heaven, the promised land, the Elysian Fields. **2** Utopia, Shangri-La, Eden, idyll. **3** bliss, heaven (on earth), ecstasy, delight, joy, happiness.
– OPPOSITES hell.

paradox n. contradiction, self-contradiction, inconsistency, incongruity, conflict, enigma, puzzle, conundrum.

paragraph n. section, division, part, portion, segment, passage, clause.

parallel adj. **1** aligned, side by side, equidistant. **2** similar, analogous, comparable, corresponding, like, equivalent, matching.
– OPPOSITES divergent, different.
•n. **1** counterpart, analogue, equivalent, match, twin, duplicate, mirror. **2** similarity, likeness, resemblance, analogy,

correspondence, comparison, equivalence, symmetry.
– OPPOSITES divergence, difference.

paralyse v. **1** disable, cripple, immobilize, incapacitate; (**paralysed**) Medicine paraplegic, quadriplegic. **2 bring to a standstill**, immobilize, bring to a halt, freeze, cripple, disable.

paralysis n. **1** immobility, powerlessness, incapacity; Medicine paraplegia, quadriplegia. **2** shutdown, immobilization, stoppage, gridlock, standstill, blockage.

parameter n. framework, variable, limit, boundary, limitation, restriction, criterion, guideline.

paramount adj. most important, supreme, chief, overriding, predominant, foremost, prime, primary, principal, main, key, central; informal number-one.

paranoid adj. suspicious, mistrustful, anxious, fearful, insecure, obsessive.

paraphrase v. reword, rephrase, express differently, rewrite, gloss.

parasite n. hanger-on, cadger, leech, passenger; informal freeloader, sponger, scrounger; N. Amer. informal mooch; Austral./NZ informal bludger.

parcel n. **1** package, packet, pack, bundle, box, case, bale.
▸v. **pack (up)**, package, wrap (up), gift-wrap, tie up, bundle up.

parched adj. **1** (bone) dry, dried up/out, arid, desiccated, dehydrated, baked, burned, scorched, withered, shrivelled. **2** dehydrated, dry; informal gasping.

pardon n. **1** forgiveness, absolution. **2** reprieve, amnesty, exoneration, release, acquittal, discharge.
▸v. **1** forgive, absolve. **2** exonerate, acquit, reprieve; informal let off.
– OPPOSITES blame, punish.

parentage n. origins, extraction, birth, family, ancestry, lineage, heritage, pedigree, descent, blood, stock, roots.

parish n. **1** district, community. **2** parishioners, churchgoers, congregation, fold, flock, community.

> WORD LINKS
> relating to a parish: parochial

park n. **1** public garden, recreation ground, playground. **2** parkland, grassland, woodland, garden(s), lawns, grounds, estate.
▸v. **1** leave, position, stop, pull up. **2** (informal) put (down), place, deposit, leave, stick, shove, dump; informal plonk; Brit. informal bung.

parliament n. legislature, assembly, chamber, house, congress, senate, diet.

parliamentary adj. legislative, law-making, governmental, congressional, democratic, elected.

parochial adj. **narrow-minded**, small-minded, provincial, small-town, conservative; N. Amer. informal jerkwater.
– OPPOSITES broad-minded.

parody n. **1 satire**, burlesque, lampoon, pastiche, caricature, imitation; informal spoof, take-off, send-up. **2 distortion**, travesty, misrepresentation, perversion, corruption.

parry v. **1** he parried the blow: **ward off**, fend off, deflect, block. **2** I parried her questions: **evade**, sidestep, avoid, dodge, field.

parson n. **priest**, minister, clergyman, vicar, rector, cleric, chaplain, pastor, curate; informal reverend, padre.

part n. **1 piece**, amount, portion, proportion, percentage, fraction; informal slice, chunk. **2 component**, bit, constituent, element, module, unit. **3 organ**, limb, member. **4 section**, division, volume, chapter, act, scene, instalment. **5 district**, neighbourhood, quarter, section, area, region. **6 role**, character. **7 involvement**, role, function, hand, responsibility, capacity, participation, contribution; informal bit.
– OPPOSITES whole.
▸v. **1 separate**, divide, split, move apart. **2 leave each other**, part company, say goodbye/farewell, say your goodbyes/farewells, go your separate ways, take your leave.
– OPPOSITES join, meet.

□ **part with** give away, give up, relinquish, forgo, surrender, hand over. **take part** participate, join in, get involved, enter, play a part, play a role, be a participant, contribute, have a hand; informal get in on the act.

partial adj. **1 incomplete**, limited, qualified, imperfect, fragmentary, unfinished. **2 biased**, prejudiced, partisan, one-sided, slanted, skewed, coloured, unbalanced.
– OPPOSITES complete, unbiased.
□ **be partial to** like, love, enjoy, be fond of, be keen on, have a soft spot for, have a taste for, have a penchant for.

partially adv. **somewhat**, to a limited extent, to a certain extent, partly, in part, up to a point, slightly.
– OPPOSITES wholly.

participant n. **participator**, contributor, party, member, entrant, competitor, player, contestant, candidate.

participate v. **take part**, join, engage, get involved, share, play a part, play a role, contribute, partake, have a hand in.

participation n. **involvement**, part, contribution, association.

particle n. **(tiny) bit**, (tiny) piece, speck, spot, fragment, sliver, splinter.

particular adj. **1 specific**, individual, certain, distinct, separate, definite, precise. **2 special**, exceptional, unusual, uncommon, notable, noteworthy,

P

remarkable, unique. **3 fussy**, fastidious, finicky, discriminating, selective; *informal* pernickety, choosy, picky; *Brit. informal* faddy.
- OPPOSITES general, indiscriminate.
• n. **detail**, item, point, element, fact, circumstance, feature.

particularly adv. **1 especially**, specially, exceptionally, unusually, remarkably, outstandingly, uncommonly, uniquely. **2 specifically**, explicitly, expressly, in particular, especially, specially.

parting n. **farewell**, leave-taking, goodbye, adieu, departure.

partisan n. **guerrilla**, freedom fighter, resistance fighter, underground fighter, irregular.
• adj. **biased**, prejudiced, one-sided, discriminatory, partial, sectarian, factional.
- OPPOSITES neutral.

partition n. **1 division**, partitioning, separation, break-up. **2 screen**, divider, dividing wall, barrier, panel.
• v. **1 divide**, separate, split up, break up. **2 subdivide**, divide (up), separate, section off, screen off.

partly adv. **in part**, partially, somewhat, a little, up to a point, in some measure, slightly, to some extent.
- OPPOSITES wholly.

partner n. **1 colleague**, associate, co-worker, fellow worker, collaborator, comrade, team-mate. **2 accomplice**, confeder-

ate, accessory, collaborator, fellow conspirator, helper; *informal* sidekick. **3 spouse**, husband, wife, lover, girlfriend, boyfriend, fiancé, fiancée, significant other, live-in lover, mate; *Brit. informal* other half.

partnership n. **1 cooperation**, association, collaboration, coalition, alliance, union, affiliation, connection. **2 company**, association, consortium, syndicate, firm, business, organization.

party n. **1 social gathering**, function, get-together, celebration, reunion, festivity, reception, soirée, social; *informal* bash, do. **2 group**, company, body, gang, band, crowd, pack, contingent; *informal* bunch, crew, load. **3 faction**, group, bloc, camp, caucus, alliance.

pass v. **1 go**, proceed, move, progress, make your way, travel. **2 overtake**, go past/by, pull ahead of, leave behind. **3 elapse**, go by, advance, wear on, roll by, tick by. **4** *he passed the time reading:* **occupy**, spend, fill, use (up), employ, while away. **5 hand**, let someone have, give, reach. **6** *her estate passed to her grandson:* **be transferred**, go, be left, be bequeathed, be handed down/on, be passed on; *Law* devolve. **7 happen**, occur, take place. **8 come to an end**, fade (away), blow over, run its course, die out/down, finish, end, cease. **9 be successful in**, succeed in, get through; *informal* sail through,

scrape through. **10 approve**, vote for, accept, ratify, adopt, agree to, authorize, endorse, legalize, enact; informal OK.
– OPPOSITES fail, reject.
  • n. **permit**, warrant, authorization, licence.
  ◻ **pass out** faint, lose consciousness, black out. **pass up** turn down, reject, refuse, decline, give up, forgo, let pass, miss (out on); informal give something a miss.

passable adj. **1 adequate**, all right, acceptable, satisfactory, not (too) bad, average, tolerable, fair, mediocre, middling, ordinary, indifferent, unremarkable, unexceptional; informal OK, so-so. **2 navigable**, traversable, negotiable, open, clear.

passage n. **1 journey**, voyage, crossing, transit, trip. **2 passing**, progress, advance, course, march, flow. **3 corridor**, hall, hallway. **4 alley**, alleyway, passageway, lane, path, footpath, track, thoroughfare; N. Amer. areaway. **5 extract**, excerpt, quotation, quote.

passenger n. **traveller**, commuter, fare-payer, rider, fare.

passing adj. **1 fleeting**, transient, transitory, ephemeral, brief, short-lived, temporary, momentary. **2 hasty**, rapid, hurried, brief, quick, cursory, superficial, casual, perfunctory, desultory.
  • n. **1 passage**, course, progress, advance. **2 death**, demise, passing away, end, loss.

passion n. **1 intensity**, enthusiasm, fervour, eagerness, zeal, vigour, fire, energy, spirit, fanaticism. **2 love**, desire, ardour, lust, lasciviousness, lustfulness. **3 fascination**, love, mania, obsession, preoccupation, fanaticism, fixation, compulsion, appetite, addiction; informal thing.
– OPPOSITES apathy.

passionate adj. **1 intense**, impassioned, ardent, fervent, vehement, fiery, heated, emotional, heartfelt, excited. **2 very keen**, very enthusiastic, addicted; informal mad, crazy, hooked. **3 amorous**, ardent, hot-blooded, loving, sexy, sensual, erotic, lustful; informal steamy, hot, turned on.
– OPPOSITES apathetic, cool.

passive adj. **1 inactive**, non-active, non-participative, uninvolved. **2 submissive**, acquiescent, unresisting, compliant, docile.
– OPPOSITES active, resistant.

past adj. **1 gone by**, bygone, former, previous, old, of old, olden, long-ago. **2 last**, recent, preceding. **3 previous**, former, foregoing, erstwhile, one-time, sometime, ex-.
– OPPOSITES present, future.
  • n. **history**, background, past life, life story.

paste n. **1 purée**, pulp, mush, spread, pâté. **2 adhesive**, glue, gum; N. Amer. mucilage.
  • v. **stick**, glue, gum, fix, affix.

pastel adj. **pale**, soft, light, delicate, muted.
– OPPOSITES dark, bright.

pastime n. **hobby**, leisure activity, leisure pursuit, recreation, game, amusement, diversion, entertainment, interest.

pastor n. **priest**, minister, parson, clergyman, cleric, chaplain, vicar, rector, curate; informal reverend, padre.

pastoral adj. **1 rural**, country, rustic, agricultural, bucolic; literary Arcadian. **2 priestly**, clerical, ecclesiastical, ministerial.
– OPPOSITES urban, lay.

pasture n. **grassland**, grass, grazing, meadow, field; literary lea.

pat v. & n. **tap**, clap, touch, stroke.

patch n. **1 blotch**, mark, spot, smudge, smear, stain, streak, blemish; informal splodge. **2 plot**, area, piece, strip, tract, parcel, bed; Brit. allotment; N. Amer. lot. **3** (Brit. informal) **period**, time, spell, phase, stretch.
•v. **mend**, repair, sew up, stitch up, cover, reinforce.

patent adj. **1 obvious**, clear, plain, evident, manifest, conspicuous, blatant, barefaced, flagrant. **2 proprietary**, patented, licensed, branded.

path n. **1 footpath**, pathway, track, trail, bridle path, lane, towpath. **2 route**, way, course, direction, orbit, trajectory. **3 course of action**, route, road, avenue, line, approach, tack.

pathetic adj. **1 pitiful**, piteous, moving, touching, poignant,

plaintive, wretched, heart-rending, sad. **2** (informal) **feeble**, woeful, sorry, poor, weak, pitiful, lamentable, deplorable, contemptible.

pathological adj. **1 morbid**, diseased. **2** (informal) **compulsive**, obsessive, inveterate, habitual, persistent, chronic, hardened, confirmed.

patience n. **1 forbearance**, tolerance, restraint, equanimity, understanding, indulgence. **2 perseverance**, persistence, endurance, tenacity, application, doggedness, staying power.

patient adj. **1 forbearing**, uncomplaining, long-suffering, resigned, stoical, tolerant, calm, imperturbable, accommodating, indulgent. **2 persevering**, persistent, tenacious, dogged, determined.
– OPPOSITES impatient.

patriotic adj. **nationalistic**, loyalist, loyal, chauvinistic, jingoistic, flag-waving.
– OPPOSITES traitorous.

patrol n. **1** ships on patrol in the straits: **guard**, watch, vigil. **2 squad**, detachment, party, force.
•v. **guard**, keep watch on, police, make the rounds of, stand guard (over), defend, safeguard.

patron n. **1 sponsor**, backer, benefactor, contributor, subscriber, donor, philanthropist, promoter, friend, supporter; informal angel. **2 customer**, client, consumer, user, visitor, guest; informal regular.

patronage n. **1** sponsorship, backing, funding, financing, assistance, support. **2** custom, trade, business.

patronize v. **1** talk down to, look down on, condescend to, treat like a child. **2** use, buy from, shop at, be a customer/ client of, deal with, frequent, support.

patronizing adj. **condescending**, supercilious, superior, imperious, scornful; informal uppity, high and mighty.

pattern n. **1** design, decoration, motif, device, marking. **2** system, order, arrangement, form, method, structure, scheme, plan, format. **3** model, example, blueprint, criterion, standard, norm, yardstick, touchstone, benchmark.

pause n. break, interruption, lull, respite, breathing space, gap, interlude, adjournment, rest, wait, hesitation; informal let-up, breather.
•v. stop, break off, take a break, adjourn, rest, wait, hesitate; informal take a breather.

pave v. surface, floor, cover, tile, flag.

pavement n. N. Amer. footpath, walkway; N. Amer. sidewalk.

pay v. **1** reward, reimburse, recompense, remunerate. **2** spend, pay out; informal lay out, shell out, fork out, cough up; N. Amer. informal ante up, pony up. **3** dis-

charge, settle, pay off, clear. **4** be profitable, make money, make a profit. **5** be advantageous to, benefit, be of advantage to, be beneficial to. **6** he will pay for his mistakes: suffer, be punished, atone, pay the penalty/price.
•n. salary, wages, payment, earnings, remuneration, fee, reimbursement, income, revenue, stipend, emolument.
□ **pay back 1** get your revenge on, get back at, get even with, settle the score. **2** repay, pay off, give back, return, reimburse, refund. **pay off** pay (in full), settle, discharge, clear, liquidate.

payable adj. due, owed, owing, outstanding, unpaid, overdue; N. Amer. delinquent.

payment n. **1** remittance, settlement, discharge, clearance. **2** instalment, premium. **3** salary, wages, pay, earnings, fees, remuneration, reimbursement, income, stipend, emolument.

peace n. **1** quiet, silence, peace and quiet, hush, stillness, still. **2** serenity, peacefulness, tranquillity, calm, calmness, composure, ease, contentment, rest, repose. **3** treaty, truce, ceasefire, armistice.
– OPPOSITES noise, war.

peaceful adj. **1** tranquil, calm, restful, quiet, still, relaxing, serene, composed, placid, at ease, untroubled, unworried.
2 harmonious, on good terms,

amicable, friendly, cordial, non-violent.
– OPPOSITES noisy.

peacemaker n. arbitrator, arbiter, mediator, negotiator, conciliator, go-between, intermediary.

peak n. **1 summit**, top, crest, pinnacle, cap. **2 mountain**, hill, height. **3 height**, high point, pinnacle, summit, top, climax, culmination, apex, zenith, acme.
• v. **reach its height**, climax, culminate.
• adj. **maximum**, greatest, busiest, highest.

peculiar adj. **1 strange**, unusual, odd, funny, curious, bizarre, weird, eccentric, queer, abnormal, unconventional, outlandish, anomalous, out of the ordinary, unexpected, offbeat. **2** customs peculiar to the area: **distinctive**, exclusive, unique, characteristic, distinct, individual, typical, special.
– OPPOSITES ordinary.

pedant n. dogmatist, purist, literalist, formalist, quibbler, hair-splitter; informal nit-picker.

pedantic adj. finicky, fussy, fastidious, dogmatic, purist, hair-splitting, quibbling; informal nit-picking, pernickety.

peddle v. sell, hawk, tout, trade, deal in, traffic in.

pedestal n. plinth, base, support, mount, stand, pillar, column.
□ **put on a pedestal** idealize, look up to, hold in high regard,

think highly of, admire, esteem, revere, worship.

pedestrian n. walker, person on foot.
• adj. **dull**, boring, tedious, monotonous, unremarkable, uninspired, unimaginative, unexciting, routine, commonplace, ordinary, everyday, run-of-the-mill, mundane, humdrum; informal bog-standard.
– OPPOSITES exciting.

pedigree n. ancestry, lineage, line, descent, genealogy, extraction, parentage, bloodline, family tree.
• adj. **pure-bred**, full-blooded, thoroughbred.

peek v. **1 peep**, look; informal take a gander, have a squint; Brit. informal have a dekko, take a butcher's, take a shufti. **2 appear**, show, peep (out).
• n. **look**, peep, glance, glimpse.

peel v. **1 pare**, skin, hull, shell. **2 flake (off)**, come off, fall off, strip off.
• n. **rind**, skin, covering, zest.

peep v. peek, look, sneak a look, glance; informal squint.
• n. **peek**, look, glance; informal squint, dekko.

peer¹ v. **look closely**, squint, gaze.

peer² n. **1 aristocrat**, lord, lady, noble, nobleman, noblewoman. **2 equal**, fellow, contemporary.

peeve v. (informal) **irritate**, annoy, vex, anger, irk, gall, pique, put out, nettle; informal aggravate, rile, needle, get to, bug, hack

p

off, get someone's goat, get/put someone's back up; N. Amer. informal tee off, tick off.

peg n. pin, nail, dowel.
– v. **1 fix**, pin, attach, fasten, secure. **2 set**, hold, fix, limit, freeze, keep down, hold down.

pen[1] v. **write**, compose, draft, dash off, scribble.

pen[2] n. **enclosure**, fold, pound, compound, stockade, sty, coop; N. Amer. corral.
– v. **confine**, coop, cage, shut, box, lock, trap, imprison, incarcerate.

penalize v. **1 punish**, discipline. **2 handicap**, disadvantage, discriminate against.
– OPPOSITES reward.

penalty n. **punishment**, sanction, fine, forfeit, sentence.
– OPPOSITES reward.

penance n. **atonement**, expiation, amends, punishment, penalty.

penchant n. **liking**, fondness, preference, taste, appetite, partiality, love, passion, weakness, inclination, bent, proclivity, predilection, predisposition.

pending adj. **1 unresolved**, undecided, unsettled, up in the air, ongoing, outstanding; informal on the back burner. **2 imminent**, impending, about to happen, forthcoming, on the way, coming, approaching, looming, near, on the horizon, in the offing.

penetrate v. **1 pierce**, puncture, enter, perforate, stab, gore.

2 permeate, pervade, fill, imbue, suffuse, seep through, saturate. **3 register**, sink in, become clear, fall into place; informal click.

penetrating adj. **1 cold**, cutting, biting, keen, sharp, harsh, raw, freezing, chill, bitter. **2 shrill**, strident, piercing, ear-splitting. **3 intent**, searching, piercing, probing, sharp, keen. **4 perceptive**, insightful, keen, sharp, intelligent, clever, smart, incisive, trenchant, astute.
– OPPOSITES mild, soft.

pension n. **old-age pension**, superannuation, allowance, benefit, support, welfare.

pensioner n. **retired person**, old-age pensioner, OAP, senior citizen; N. Amer. senior, retiree, golden ager.

people pl. n. **1 human beings**, persons, individuals, humans, mortals, living souls, personages, [men, women, and children]; informal folk. **2 citizens**, subjects, electors, voters, taxpayers, residents, inhabitants, public, citizenry, nation, population, populace. **3 the common people**, the proletariat, the masses, the populace, the rank and file; derogatory the hoi polloi; informal, derogatory the proles, the plebs. **4 family**, parents, relatives, relations, folk, kinsfolk, flesh and blood, nearest and dearest; informal folks. **5** (singular) **race**, ethnic group, tribe, clan, nation.

p

•v. **populate**, settle (in), colonize, inhabit, live in, occupy.

> **WORD LINKS**
> *relating to a people*: ethnic;
> *study of people*: anthropology

pepper v. **1 sprinkle**, fleck, dot, spot, stipple. **2 bombard**, pelt, shower, rain down on, strafe, rake, blitz.

perceive v. **1 see**, discern, detect, catch sight of, spot, observe, notice; *literary* espy. **2 regard**, look on, view, consider, think of, judge, deem.

perception n. **1 impression**, idea, conception, notion, thought, belief. **2 insight**, perceptiveness, understanding, intelligence, intuition, incisiveness.

perceptive adj. **insightful**, discerning, sensitive, intuitive, observant, penetrating, intelligent, clever, canny, keen, sharp, astute, shrewd, quick, smart, acute; *informal* on the ball; *N. Amer. informal* heads-up.
– OPPOSITES obtuse.

perch v. **1 sit**, rest, alight, settle, land, roost. **2 put**, place, set, rest, balance.

perennial adj. **lasting**, enduring, abiding, long-lasting, long-lived, perpetual, continuing, continual, recurring.
– OPPOSITES ephemeral.

perfect adj. **1 ideal**, model, faultless, flawless, consummate, exemplary, best, ultimate, copybook. **2 flawless**, mint, as good as new, pristine, immacu-

late, optimum, prime, peak; *informal* tip-top, A1. **3 exact**, precise, accurate, faithful, true; *Brit. informal* spot on; *N. Amer. informal* on the money. **4 absolute**, complete, total, real, out-and-out, thorough, downright, utter; *Brit. informal* right; *Austral./NZ informal* fair.
•v. **improve**, polish (up), hone, refine, brush up, fine-tune.

perfection n. **the ideal**, a paragon, the last word, the ultimate; *informal* the tops, the bee's knees.

perform v. **1 carry out**, do, execute, discharge, conduct, implement; *informal* pull off. **2 function**, work, operate, run, go, respond, behave, act. **3 stage**, put on, present, mount, act, produce. **4 play**, sing, appear.

performance n. **1 show**, production, showing, presentation, staging, concert, recital; *informal* gig. **2 rendition**, interpretation, playing, acting. **3 carrying out**, execution, discharge, completion, fulfilment. **4 functioning**, working, operation, running, behaviour, response.

performer n. **actor**, **actress**, artiste, artist, entertainer, trouper, player, musician, singer, dancer, comic, comedian, comedienne.

perfume n. **1 scent**, fragrance, eau de toilette, toilet water, cologne, eau de cologne. **2 smell**, scent, fragrance, aroma, bouquet, nose.

perhaps adv. **maybe**, for all you know, it could be, it may be, it's

P

possible, possibly, conceivably; N. English happen.

peril n. **danger**, jeopardy, risk, hazard, menace, threat.
– OPPOSITES safety.

perimeter n. **boundary**, border, limits, bounds, edge, margin, fringe(s), periphery.
– OPPOSITES centre.

period n. **1 time**, spell, interval, stretch, term, span, phase, bout; Brit. informal patch. **2 era**, age, epoch, aeon, time, days, years.

periodic adj. **regular**, at fixed intervals, recurrent, recurring, repeated, cyclical, seasonal, occasional, intermittent, sporadic, odd.

periodical n. **journal**, magazine, newspaper, paper, review, newsletter, digest, gazette, organ; informal mag, glossy.

peripheral adj. **secondary**, subsidiary, incidental, tangential, marginal, minor, unimportant, ancillary.
– OPPOSITES central.

perish v. **1 die**, lose your life, be killed, fall, be lost; informal buy it. **2 go bad**, spoil, rot, decay, decompose.

perk n. **fringe benefit**, advantage, bonus, extra, plus; informal freebie.

permanent adj. **lasting**, enduring, indefinite, continuing, constant, perpetual, indelible, irreparable, irreversible, lifelong, perennial, established, standing, long-term, stable, secure.
– OPPOSITES temporary.

permanently adv. **1 forever**, for all time, for good, irreversibly, incurably, irreparably, indelibly; informal for keeps. **2 continually**, constantly, perpetually, always.

permission n. **authorization**, consent, leave, authority, sanction, licence, dispensation, assent, agreement, approval, blessing, clearance; informal the go-ahead, the green light, say-so.
– OPPOSITES ban.

permit v. **allow**, let, authorize, give permission, sanction, grant, license, consent to, assent to, agree to; informal give the go-ahead to, give the green light to.
– OPPOSITES forbid.
•n. **authorization**, licence, pass, ticket, warrant, passport, visa.

perpetual adj. **1 constant**, permanent, uninterrupted, continuous, unremitting, unending, everlasting, eternal, unceasing, without end, persistent, lasting, abiding. **2 interminable**, incessant, ceaseless, endless, relentless, unrelenting, persistent, continual, continuous, nonstop, never-ending, repeated, unremitting, round-the-clock, unabating; informal eternal.
– OPPOSITES temporary, intermittent.

perpetuate v. **keep alive**, keep going, preserve, conserve, sustain, maintain, continue, extend.

perplex v. **puzzle**, baffle, mystify, bemuse, bewilder, confound, confuse, nonplus, disconcert; informal flummox.

perplexing adj. **puzzling**, baffling, mystifying, mysterious, bewildering, confusing, disconcerting, worrying.

persecute v. **1 oppress**, abuse, victimize, ill-treat, mistreat, maltreat, torment, torture. **2 harass**, hound, plague, badger, harry, intimidate, pick on, pester; informal hassle.

persecution n. **1 oppression**, victimization, ill-treatment, mistreatment, abuse, discrimination. **2 harassment**, hounding, intimidation, bullying.

persevere v. **persist**, continue, carry on, go on, keep on, keep going, struggle on, hammer away, be persistent, keep at it, not take no for an answer, be tenacious, plod on, plough on; informal soldier on, hang on, plug away, stick to your guns, stick it out, hang in there.
– OPPOSITES give up.

persist v. **1** *he persisted with his questioning:* **persevere**, continue, carry on, go on, keep on, keep going, hammer away, keep at it; informal plug on, plug away. **2** *the dry weather persists:* **continue**, hold, carry on, last, keep on, remain, linger, stay, endure.
– OPPOSITES give up, stop.

persistence n. **perseverance**, tenacity, determination, staying power, endurance, doggedness, stamina; informal stickability; formal pertinacity.

persistent adj. **1 tenacious**, determined, resolute, dogged, tireless, indefatigable, insistent, unrelenting; formal pertinacious. **2 constant**, continuous, continuing, continual, non-stop, never-ending, steady, uninterrupted, unbroken, interminable, incessant, endless, unending, unrelenting. **3** *a persistent cough:* **chronic**, nagging, frequent, repeated, habitual.
– OPPOSITES irresolute, intermittent.

person n. **human being**, individual, man, woman, human, being, living soul, mortal, creature; informal type, sort, beggar, cookie.
□ **in person** physically, in the flesh, personally, yourself.

personal adj. **1 distinctive**, characteristic, unique, individual, idiosyncratic. **2 in person**, in the flesh, actual, live, physical. **3 private**, intimate. **4 derogatory**, disparaging, belittling, insulting, rude, disrespectful, offensive, pejorative.

personality n. **1 character**, nature, disposition, temperament, make-up, psyche. **2 charisma**, magnetism, character, charm, presence. **3 celebrity**, VIP, star, superstar, big name, somebody, leading light, luminary, notable; informal celeb.

personally adv. **1 in person**, yourself. **2 for my part**, for myself, as far as I am concerned, from my own point of view, subjectively.

personification n. embodiment, incarnation, epitome, quintessence, essence, type, symbol, soul, model, exemplification, exemplar, image, representation.

personnel n. staff, employees, workforce, workers, labour force, manpower, human resources.

perspective n. outlook, view, viewpoint, point of view, standpoint, position, stand, stance, angle, slant, attitude.

persuade v. 1 prevail on, talk into, coax, convince, get, induce, win over, bring round, influence, sway; informal sweet-talk. 2 cause, lead, move, dispose, incline.
– OPPOSITES dissuade, deter.

persuasion n. 1 coaxing, urging, inducement, encouragement; informal sweet-talking. 2 group, grouping, sect, denomination, party, camp, side, faction, school of thought, belief, creed, faith.

persuasive adj. convincing, compelling, effective, telling, forceful, powerful, eloquent, impressive, sound, cogent, valid, strong, plausible, credible.
– OPPOSITES unconvincing.

pertain v. 1 developments pertaining to the economy: concern, relate to, be connected with, be relevant to, apply to, refer to, have a bearing on, affect, involve, touch on. 2 exist, be the case, prevail.

pertinent adj. relevant, to the point, apposite, appropriate, suitable, applicable, material, germane.
– OPPOSITES irrelevant.

perturb v. worry, upset, disturb, unsettle, concern, trouble, disquiet, disconcert, discomfit, unnerve, alarm, bother; informal rattle.
– OPPOSITES reassure.

pervade v. permeate, spread through, fill, suffuse, imbue, penetrate, filter through, infuse, inform.

pervasive adj. prevalent, pervading, extensive, ubiquitous, omnipresent, universal, widespread, general.

perverse adj. 1 awkward, contrary, difficult, unreasonable, uncooperative, unhelpful, obstructive, stubborn, obstinate; Brit. informal bloody-minded, bolshie. 2 illogical, irrational, wrong-headed.

perversion n. 1 distortion, misrepresentation, travesty, twisting, corruption, misuse. 2 deviance, abnormality, depravity.

pervert v. distort, warp, corrupt, subvert, twist, bend, abuse, divert.
•n. deviant, degenerate; informal perv, dirty old man, sicko.

perverted adj. unnatural, deviant, warped, twisted, abnormal, unhealthy, depraved, perverse, aberrant, debased, degenerate; informal sick, kinky.

pessimist n. **defeatist**, fatalist, prophet of doom, alarmist, cynic, sceptic, misery, killjoy, Cassandra; informal doom (and gloom) merchant, wet blanket.
– OPPOSITES optimist.

pessimistic adj. **gloomy**, negative, cynical, defeatist, downbeat, bleak, fatalistic, depressed.
– OPPOSITES optimistic.

pest n. **nuisance**, annoyance, irritant, thorn in your flesh/side, trial, menace, trouble, problem, worry, bother; informal pain in the neck, headache.

pester v. **badger**, hound, harass, plague, annoy, bother, harry, worry; informal hassle, bug.

pet adj. **1 tame**, domesticated, companion; Brit. house-trained; N. Amer. housebroken. **2 favourite**, favoured, cherished, particular, special, personal.
• v. **1 stroke**, caress, fondle, pat, tickle. **2 cuddle**, embrace, caress, kiss; informal canoodle, neck, smooch; Brit. informal snog; N. Amer. informal make out.

peter v.
□ **peter out** fizzle out, fade (away), die away/out, dwindle, diminish, taper off, tail off, trail away/off, wane, ebb, melt away, evaporate, disappear.

petition n. **appeal**, round robin, letter, request, entreaty, application, plea.
• v. **appeal to**, request, ask, call on, entreat, beg, implore, plead with, apply to, press, urge.

petrified adj. **1 terrified**, horrified, scared/frightened out of your wits, scared/frightened to death. **2 ossified**, fossilized, calcified.

petty adj. **1 trivial**, trifling, minor, insignificant, paltry, unimportant, inconsequential, footling, negligible; informal piffling. **2 small-minded**, mean, shabby, spiteful.
– OPPOSITES important, magnanimous.

petulant adj. **peevish**, bad-tempered, querulous, pettish, fretful, irritable, sulky, tetchy, crotchety, testy, fractious; informal grouchy; Brit. informal ratty; N. English informal mardy; N. Amer. informal cranky.
– OPPOSITES good-humoured.

phantom n. **ghost**, apparition, spirit, spectre, wraith; informal spook.

phase n. **stage**, period, chapter, episode, part, step.

phenomenal adj. **remarkable**, exceptional, extraordinary, marvellous, miraculous, wonderful, outstanding, unprecedented; informal fantastic, terrific, tremendous, stupendous.

phenomenon n. **1 occurrence**, event, happening, fact, situation, circumstance, experience, case, incident, episode. **2 marvel**, sensation, wonder, prodigy.

philanderer n. **womanizer**, Casanova, Don Juan, Lothario, flirt, ladies' man, playboy; informal stud, ladykiller.

philanthropic adj. **charitable**, generous, benevolent,

humanitarian, public-spirited, altruistic, magnanimous, unselfish, kind.
– OPPOSITES selfish, mean.

philistine adj. **uncultured**, lowbrow, uncultivated, uncivilized, uneducated, unenlightened, commercial, materialist, bourgeois, ignorant, crass, boorish, barbarian.
•n. **barbarian**, boor, yahoo, materialist.

philosopher n. **thinker**, theorist, theoretician, scholar, intellectual, sage.

philosophical adj. **1 theoretical**, metaphysical. **2 thoughtful**, reflective, pensive, meditative, contemplative, introspective. **3 stoical**, self-possessed, serene, dispassionate, phlegmatic, long-suffering, resigned.

philosophy n. **1 thinking**, thought, reasoning, logic. **2 beliefs**, credo, ideology, ideas, thinking, theories, doctrine, principles, views, outlook.

phobia n. **fear**, dread, horror, terror, aversion, antipathy, revulsion; informal hang-up.

phone n. **telephone**, mobile; N. Amer. cellphone, cell; Brit. informal blower.
•v. **call**, telephone; Brit. ring, give someone a ring; informal call up, give someone a buzz; Brit. informal give someone a bell.

phoney (informal) adj. **bogus**, false, fake, fraudulent, counterfeit, forged, imitation, affected,

insincere; informal pretend; Brit. informal cod.
– OPPOSITES authentic.
•n. **1 impostor**, sham, fake, fraud, charlatan; informal con artist. **2 fake**, imitation, counterfeit, forgery.

photocopy n. **copy**, duplicate, reproduction, facsimile; trademark Xerox, photostat.
•v. **copy**, duplicate, xerox, photostat, reproduce.

photograph n. **picture**, photo, snap, snapshot, shot, print, still, transparency.

photographic adj. **1 pictorial**, graphic, in photographs. **2 detailed**, exact, precise, accurate, vivid.

phrase n. **expression**, construction, term, turn of phrase, idiom, saying.
•v. **express**, put into words, put, word, formulate, couch, frame.

physical adj. **1 bodily**, corporeal, corporal, carnal, fleshly, non-spiritual. **2 manual**, labouring, blue-collar. **3 material**, concrete, tangible, palpable, solid, substantial, real, actual, visible.
– OPPOSITES mental, spiritual.

physician n. **doctor**, medical practitioner, general practitioner, GP, clinician, specialist, consultant; informal doc, medic, quack.

pick v. **1 harvest**, gather (in), collect, pluck. **2 choose**, select, single out, opt for, plump for, elect, decide on, settle on, fix on, name, nominate, identify.

3 *pick a fight:* **provoke**, start, cause, incite, instigate, prompt.
▸n. **best**, finest, choice, choicest, cream, flower, crème de la crème, elite.
□ **pick on** bully, victimize, torment, persecute, taunt, tease; informal get at, needle. **pick out** see, make out, distinguish, discern, spot, perceive, detect, notice, recognize, identify, catch sight of, glimpse. **pick up 1** improve, recover, rally, bounce back, perk up, look up, take a turn for the better, turn the corner, be on the mend, make headway, make progress. **2** lift, take up, raise, hoist, scoop up, gather up, snatch up. **3** arrest, apprehend, detain, take into custody, seize; informal nab, run in; Brit. informal nick. **4** *he picked up the story in the 1950s:* resume, take up, start again, recommence, continue, carry/go on with.

picket n. **1 demonstrator**, striker, protester. **2 demonstration**, picket line, blockade, boycott, strike.

pickup n. **improvement**, recovery, revival, upturn, upswing, rally, resurgence, renewal, turnaround.

picture n. **1 painting**, **drawing**, sketch, watercolour, print, canvas, portrait, illustration, depiction, likeness, representation, image. **2 photograph**, photo, snap, snapshot, shot, frame, exposure, still, print. **3 concept**, idea, impression, image, vision, visualization, notion.

4 personification, embodiment, epitome, essence, quintessence, soul, model.
▸v. **1 depict**, portray, show, represent, draw, sketch, photograph, paint. **2 visualize**, see (in your mind's eye), imagine, remember.

picturesque adj. **attractive**, pretty, beautiful, lovely, scenic, charming, quaint, pleasing, delightful.
– OPPOSITES ugly.

piece n. **1 bit**, slice, chunk, segment, section, lump, hunk, wedge, slab, block, cake, bar, stick, length. **2 component**, part, bit, constituent, element, section, unit, module. **3 item**, article, specimen. **4 share**, portion, slice, quota, part, percentage, amount, quantity, ration, fraction; Brit. informal whack. **5 work (of art)**, artwork, artefact, composition, opus. **6 article**, item, story, report, essay, feature, review, column.

pier n. **jetty**, quay, wharf, dock, landing stage.

pierce v. **penetrate**, puncture, perforate, prick, spike, stab, drill, bore.

piercing adj. **1 shrill**, ear-splitting, high-pitched, penetrating, strident. **2 searching**, probing, penetrating, sharp, keen, shrewd.

pig n. **hog**, boar, sow, porker, swine, piglet.

> WORD LINKS
> *relating to pigs:* porcine

p

pigment n. **colouring**, colour, tint, dye, stain.

pile¹ n. **1 heap**, stack, mound, pyramid, mass, collection, accumulation, assemblage, stockpile, hoard. **2** (informal) **lot**, mountain, reams, abundance; informal load, heap, mass, slew, stack, ton, oodles.
•v. **1 heap**, stack, load, fill, charge. **2 crowd**, clamber, pack, squeeze, scramble, struggle.
□ **pile up** accumulate, amass, grow, mount up, build up, multiply, escalate, soar, spiral, rocket, increase.

pile² n. **nap**, fibres, threads.

pile-up n. **crash**, collision, smash, accident; Brit. RTA; N. Amer. wreck; Brit. informal shunt.

pilgrim n. **traveller**, wayfarer, worshipper, devotee, believer; Islam haji; old use palmer.

pilgrimage n. **journey**, expedition, mission, hajj, visit, trek, trip, odyssey.

pill n. **tablet**, capsule, pellet, lozenge, pastille.

pillar n. **1 column**, post, support, upright, pier, pile, prop, stanchion, obelisk. **2 stalwart**, mainstay, bastion, leading light, worthy, backbone, supporter, upholder, champion.

pilot n. **1 airman**, airwoman, flyer, captain; informal skipper; dated aviator. **2 navigator**, helmsman, steersman, coxswain. **3 trial**, sample, experiment.
•adj. **experimental**, exploratory, trial, test, sample, preliminary.
•v. **navigate**, guide, manoeuvre, steer, control, direct, captain, fly, drive, sail; informal skipper.

pin n. **1 tack**, safety pin, nail, staple, fastener. **2 bolt**, peg, rod, rivet, dowel. **3 badge**, brooch.
•v. **1 attach**, fasten, affix, fix, join, secure, clip, nail. **2 hold**, press, pinion.
□ **pin down** confine, trap, hem in, corner, close in, shut in, pen in. **pin on** blame for, hold responsible for, attribute to, ascribe to, lay something at someone's door; informal stick on.

pinch v. **nip**, tweak, squeeze, grasp, compress.
•n. **1 nip**, tweak, squeeze. **2 bit**, touch, dash, spot, trace, soupçon, speck, taste; informal smidgen, tad.

pine v. **fade**, waste away, weaken, decline, languish, wilt, sicken.
□ **pine for** long for, yearn for, ache for, sigh for, hunger for, thirst for, itch for, carry a torch for, miss, mourn.

pink adj. **rose**, rosy, rosé, pale red, salmon, coral, flushed, blushing.

pinnacle n. **1 height**, peak, high point, top, apex, zenith, acme. **2 peak**, needle, crag, tor.
– OPPOSITES nadir.

pinpoint adj. **pinpoint accuracy**: precise, exact, strict, absolute, complete, scientific.
•v. **identify**, determine, distinguish, discover, find, locate, detect, track down, spot,

diagnose, recognize, pin down, home in on.

pioneer n. **1 settler**, colonist, colonizer, frontiersman, explorer. **2 developer**, innovator, trailblazer, groundbreaker, founding father, architect, creator.
•v. **introduce**, develop, launch, instigate, initiate, spearhead, institute, establish, found.

pious adj. **religious**, devout, God-fearing, churchgoing, holy, godly, saintly, reverent, righteous.
– OPPOSITES irreligious.

pipe n. **tube**, conduit, hose, main, duct, line, channel, pipeline, drain.
•v. **feed**, siphon, channel, run, convey.

piquant adj. **1** *a piquant sauce:* **spicy**, tangy, peppery, hot, tasty, flavoursome, savoury, pungent, sharp, tart, zesty, strong, salty. **2** *a piquant story:* **intriguing**, stimulating, interesting, fascinating, colourful, exciting, lively, spicy, provocative, racy; informal juicy.
– OPPOSITES bland, dull.

pirate n. **raider**, hijacker, freebooter, marauder; historical privateer, buccaneer; old use corsair.
•v. **steal**, copy, plagiarize, poach, appropriate, bootleg; informal crib, lift, rip off.

pit n. **1 hole**, trough, hollow, excavation, cavity, crater, pothole. **2 coal mine**, colliery, quarry, shaft.
•v. **mark**, pockmark, pock, scar, dent, indent.

pitch n. **1 playing field**, ground, sports field, stadium; Brit. park. **2 tone**, key, modulation, frequency. **3 gradient**, slope, slant, angle, tilt, incline. **4 level**, intensity, point, degree, height, extent. **5 patter**, talk; informal spiel, line.
•v. **1 throw**, toss, fling, hurl, cast, lob, flip; informal chuck, sling, heave, bung. **2 fall**, tumble, topple, plunge, plummet. **3 put up**, set up, erect, raise. **4 lurch**, toss, plunge, roll, reel, sway, rock, list.

pitfall n. **hazard**, danger, risk, peril, difficulty, catch, snag, stumbling block, drawback.

pitiful adj. **1 distressing**, sad, piteous, pitiable, pathetic, heart-rending, moving, touching, tear-jerking, plaintive, poignant, forlorn, poor, sorry, wretched, miserable. **2 paltry**, miserable, meagre, trifling, negligible, pitiable, derisory; informal pathetic, measly; Brit. informal poxy. **3 dreadful**, awful, terrible, appalling, lamentable, hopeless, feeble, pitiable, woeful, inadequate, deplorable, laughable; informal pathetic, useless, lousy, abysmal, dire.

pitiless adj. **merciless**, unmerciful, ruthless, cruel, heartless, remorseless, hard-hearted, cold-hearted, harsh, callous, severe, unsparing, unforgiving, unfeeling, uncaring, unsympathetic, uncharitable.
– OPPOSITES merciful.

p

pity n. **1 compassion**, commiseration, condolence, sympathy, fellow feeling, understanding. **2** *it's a pity you can't go*: **shame**, misfortune.
– OPPOSITES indifference.
• v. **feel sorry for**, feel for, sympathize with, empathize with, commiserate with, take pity on, be moved by, bleed for.

pivot n. **fulcrum**, axis, axle, swivel, pin, shaft, hub, spindle, hinge, kingpin.
• v. **1 rotate**, turn, swivel, revolve, spin. **2** *it all pivoted on his response*: **depend**, hinge, turn, centre, hang, rely, rest, revolve around.

placate v. **pacify**, calm, appease, mollify, soothe, win over, conciliate, propitiate, make peace with, humour.
– OPPOSITES provoke.

place n. **1 location**, site, spot, setting, position, situation, area, region, locale, venue. **2 country**, state, area, region, town, city. **3 home**, house, flat, apartment, pied-à-terre, accommodation, property, rooms, quarters; *informal* pad; *formal* residence, abode, dwelling. **4 situation**, position, circumstances. **5 seat**, chair, space. **6 job**, position, post, appointment, situation, employment. **7 status**, position, standing, rank, niche. **8 responsibility**, duty, job, task, role, function, concern, affair, charge.
• v. **1 put (down)**, set (down), lay, deposit, position, plant,

rest, stand, station, situate, leave; *informal* stick, dump, bung, park, plonk, pop; *N. Amer. informal* plunk. **2 rank**, order, grade, class, classify, put. **3 identify**, recognize, remember, put a name to, pin down, locate, pinpoint.
□ **out of place 1** inappropriate, unsuitable, unseemly, improper, untoward, out of keeping, unbecoming. **2** incongruous, out of your element, like a fish out of water, uncomfortable, uneasy. **take place** happen, occur, come about, go on, transpire; *N. Amer. informal* go down. **take the place of** replace, stand in for, substitute for, act for, fill in for, cover for, relieve.

placid adj. **1 even-tempered**, calm, tranquil, equable, unexcitable, serene, mild, composed, self-possessed, poised, easygoing, level-headed, steady, unruffled, unperturbed, phlegmatic; *informal* unflappable. **2 quiet**, calm, tranquil, still, peaceful, undisturbed, restful, sleepy.
– OPPOSITES excitable.

plagiarize v. **copy**, pirate, steal, poach, appropriate; *informal* rip off, crib; *Brit. informal* pinch, nick.

plague n. **1 pandemic**, epidemic, disease, sickness; *dated* contagion; *old use* pestilence. **2 infestation**, invasion, swarm.
• v. **1 afflict**, trouble, torment, beset, dog, curse, bedevil. **2 pester**, harass, badger, bother, torment, harry, hound,

trouble, nag, molest; informal hassle, bug.

plain adj. **1 obvious**, clear, evident, apparent, manifest, unmistakable. **2 intelligible**, comprehensible, understandable, clear, lucid, simple, straightforward, user-friendly. **3 candid**, frank, outspoken, forthright, direct, honest, truthful, blunt, bald, unequivocal; informal upfront. **4 simple**, ordinary, unadorned, homely, basic, modest, unsophisticated, restrained. **5 unattractive**, unprepossessing, ugly, ordinary; N. Amer. homely; Brit. informal no oil painting. **6 sheer**, pure, downright, out-and-out.
- OPPOSITES obscure, fancy, attractive.
•n. **grassland**, flatland, prairie, savannah, steppe, tundra, pampas, veld, plateau.

plaintive adj. **mournful**, sad, pathetic, pitiful, melancholy, sorrowful, unhappy, wretched, woeful, forlorn.

plan n. **1 scheme**, idea, proposal, proposition, project, programme, system, method, strategy, stratagem, formula, recipe. **2 intention**, aim, idea, objective, object, goal, target, ambition. **3 map**, diagram, chart, blueprint, drawing, sketch, impression; N. Amer. plat.
•v. **1 organize**, arrange, work out, outline, map out, prepare, formulate, frame, develop, devise. **2 intend**, aim, propose, mean, hope. **3 design**, draw up a plan for, sketch out, map out; N. Amer. plat.

plane¹ n. **level**, degree, standard, stratum, dimension.
•v. **skim**, glide.

plane² n. **aircraft**, airliner, jet, flying machine; Brit. aeroplane; N. Amer. airplane, ship.

> WORD LINKS
> science of flight: aeronautics

plant n. **1 flower**, vegetable, herb, shrub, bush, weed; **(plants)** vegetation, greenery, flora. **2 spy**, informant, informer, secret agent, mole, infiltrator, operative; N. Amer. informal spook. **3 factory**, works, facility, refinery, mill. **4 machinery**, machines, equipment, apparatus, appliances, gear.
•v. **1 sow**, scatter. **2 place**, put, set, position, situate, settle; informal plonk. **3 instil**, implant, put, place, introduce, fix, establish, lodge.

> WORD LINKS
> study of plants: botany
> plant-eating: herbivorous

plaster v. **1 spread**, smother, smear, cake, coat, bedaub. **2 flatten (down)**, smooth down, slick down.

plastic adj. **1 soft**, pliable, pliant, flexible, malleable, workable, mouldable; informal bendy. **2 artificial**, false, fake, bogus, insincere; informal phoney, pretend.

plate n. **1 dish**, platter, salver; historical trencher; old use charger. **2 plateful**, helping, portion,

p

serving. **3 panel**, sheet, slab.
4 plaque, sign, tablet. **5 picture**,
print, illustration, photograph,
photo.
•v. **cover**, coat, overlay, laminate, gild.

plateau n. upland, mesa, highland, tableland.

platform n. **1 stage**, dais, rostrum, podium, stand. **2 programme**, manifesto, policies,
principles, party line.

platitude n. **cliché**, truism,
commonplace, old chestnut,
banality.

platter n. **plate**, dish, salver,
tray; old use charger.

plausible adj. **credible**, believable, reasonable, likely, possible, conceivable, imaginable,
convincing, persuasive.
– OPPOSITES unlikely.

play v. **1 amuse yourself**, entertain yourself, enjoy yourself,
have fun, relax, occupy yourself,
frolic, romp, cavort; informal mess
about/around. **2 take part in**,
participate in, be involved in,
compete in, do. **3 compete
against**, take on, meet. **4 act
the part of**, take the role of,
appear as, portray, perform.
•n. **1 amusement**, relaxation,
recreation, diversion, leisure,
enjoyment, pleasure, fun.
2 drama, theatrical work, piece,
comedy, tragedy, production,
performance.
□ **play down** make light of,
make little of, gloss over, downplay, understate, soft-pedal, diminish, trivialize. **play up** (Brit.

informal) **1** misbehave, be bad, be
naughty. **2** malfunction, not
work, be defective, be faulty;
informal be on the blink, act up.

player n. **1 participant**, contestant, competitor, contender,
sportsman, sportswoman.
2 musician, performer, artist,
virtuoso, instrumentalist.
3 actor, **actress**, performer,
thespian, entertainer, artiste,
trouper.

playful adj. **1 frisky**, lively, full of
fun, frolicsome, high-spirited,
exuberant, mischievous, impish;
informal full of beans. **2 light-
hearted**, jokey, teasing, humorous, jocular, facetious, frivolous,
flippant.
– OPPOSITES serious.

plea n. **appeal**, entreaty, suppli-
cation, petition, request, call.

plead v. **claim**, use as an excuse,
assert, allege, argue.
□ **plead with** beg, implore, entreat, appeal to, ask.

pleasant adj. **1 enjoyable**,
pleasurable, nice, agreeable,
entertaining, amusing, delightful, charming; informal lovely,
great. **2 friendly**, charming,
agreeable, amiable, nice,
delightful, sweet, genial, cordial, good-natured, personable,
hospitable, polite.

please v. **1 make happy**, give
pleasure to, delight, charm,
amuse, entertain, divert, satisfy,
gratify, humour. **2 like**, want,
wish, desire, see fit, think fit,
choose, will, prefer.
– OPPOSITES annoy.

pleased adj. happy, glad, delighted, gratified, grateful, thankful, content, contented, satisfied, thrilled; informal over the moon, on cloud nine; Brit. informal chuffed; N. English informal made up; Austral. informal wrapped.
– OPPOSITES unhappy.

pleasing adj. **1** good, agreeable, pleasant, pleasurable, satisfying, gratifying, great. **2** friendly, amiable, pleasant, agreeable, affable, nice, genial, likeable, charming, engaging, delightful; informal lovely.

pleasure n. happiness, delight, joy, gladness, glee, satisfaction, gratification, contentment, enjoyment, amusement, fun, entertainment, relaxation, recreation, diversion.

pledge n. promise, vow, undertaking, word, commitment, assurance, oath, guarantee.
•v. promise, vow, undertake, swear, commit yourself, declare, affirm.

plentiful adj. abundant, copious, ample, profuse, rich, lavish, generous, bountiful, bumper, prolific; informal galore.
– OPPOSITES scarce.

plenty pron. a lot of, many, a great deal of, a plethora of, enough, enough and to spare, no lack of, a wealth of; informal loads of, heaps of, stacks of, masses of, oodles of.
•n. prosperity, affluence, wealth, opulence, comfort, luxury, abundance.

plethora n. excess, abundance, superabundance, surplus, glut, surfeit, profusion, enough and to spare.
– OPPOSITES dearth.

pliable adj. **1** flexible, pliant, bendable, supple, workable, plastic; informal bendy. **2** malleable, impressionable, flexible, adaptable, biddable, pliant, tractable, suggestible, persuadable.
– OPPOSITES rigid.

plight n. predicament, difficult situation, dire straits, trouble, difficulty, bind; informal tight corner, tight spot, hole, pickle, jam, fix.

plod v. trudge, walk heavily, clump, stomp, tramp, lumber, slog.

plot n. **1** conspiracy, intrigue, stratagem, plan, machinations. **2** storyline, story, scenario, action, thread, narrative. **3** piece of ground, patch, area, tract, acreage; Brit. allotment; N. Amer. lot, plat.
•v. **1** plan, scheme, arrange, organize, contrive. **2** conspire, scheme, intrigue, connive. **3** mark, chart, map.

plough v. **1** till, furrow, harrow, cultivate, work. **2** crash, smash, career, plunge, bulldoze, hurtle, cannon.

ploy n. ruse, tactic, move, device, stratagem, scheme, trick, gambit, plan, manoeuvre, dodge, subterfuge; Brit. informal wheeze.

pluck v. **1** remove, pick, pull, extract. **2 pull**, tug, clutch, snatch, grab, catch, tweak, jerk; informal yank. **3** strum, pick, thrum, twang.

• n. **courage**, bravery, nerve, daring, spirit, grit; Brit. informal bottle; N. Amer. informal moxie.

plug n. **1** stopper, bung, cork; N. Amer. stopple. **2** (informal) **advertisement**, promotion, commercial, recommendation, mention, good word; informal hype, puff.

• v. **1** stop, seal, close, block, fill. **2** (informal) **publicize**, promote, advertise, mention, bang the drum for, draw attention to; informal hype, push.

plumb v. **explore**, probe, delve into, search, examine, investigate, fathom, penetrate, understand.

• adv. (informal) **right**, exactly, precisely, directly, dead, straight; informal (slap) bang.

plummet v. **plunge**, dive, drop, fall, hurtle, nosedive, tumble.
– OPPOSITES soar.

plump adj. **fat**, chubby, rotund, ample, round, stout, portly, overweight; informal tubby, rolypoly, pudgy; Brit. informal podgy; N. Amer. informal zaftig, corn-fed.
– OPPOSITES thin.

plunder v. **1** pillage, loot, rob, raid, ransack, rifle, strip, sack. **2 steal**, seize, thieve, pilfer, embezzle.

• n. **booty**, loot, stolen goods, spoils, ill-gotten gains; informal swag.

plunge v. **1** dive, jump, throw yourself, immerse yourself. **2 plummet**, nosedive, drop, fall, tumble, descend. **3 charge**, hurtle, career, plough, tear; N. Amer. informal barrel. **4 thrust**, stab, sink, stick, ram, drive, push, shove, force.

plus prep. **as well as**, together with, along with, in addition to, and, added to, not to mention.
– OPPOSITES minus.

• n. **advantage**, good point, asset, pro, benefit, bonus, attraction; informal perk.
– OPPOSITES disadvantage.

plush adj. (informal) **luxurious**, luxury, de luxe, sumptuous, opulent, magnificent, rich, expensive, fancy; Brit. upmarket; informal posh, classy; Brit. informal swish; N. Amer. informal swank.
– OPPOSITES austere.

ply v. **1** engage in, carry on, pursue, conduct, practise. **2 travel**, shuttle, go back and forth. **3** *she plied me with scones:* **provide**, supply, shower. **4** *he plied her with questions:* **bombard**, assail, pester, plague, harass; informal hassle.

pocket n. **1** pouch, compartment. **2 area**, patch, region, cluster.

• adj. **small**, little, miniature, mini, compact, concise, abridged, portable.

• v. **1 acquire**, obtain, gain, get, secure, win, make, earn. **2 steal**, appropriate, purloin, misappropriate, embezzle.

pod n. **shell**, husk, hull, case; N. Amer. shuck.

podium n. **platform**, stage, dais, rostrum, stand.

poem n. **verse**, rhyme, lyric, piece of poetry.

poetic adj. **expressive**, figurative, symbolic, flowery, artistic, imaginative, creative.

poetry n. **poems**, verse, versification, rhyme.

poignant adj. **touching**, moving, sad, affecting, pitiful, pathetic, plaintive.

point n. **1 tip**, (sharp) end, extremity, prong, spike, tine, nib, barb. **2 pinpoint**, dot, spot, speck. **3 place**, position, location, site, spot. **4 time**, stage, juncture, period, phase. **5 level**, degree, stage, pitch, extent. **6 detail**, item, fact, thing, argument, consideration, factor, element, subject, issue, topic, question, matter. **7 heart of the matter**, essence, nub, core, crux; informal nitty-gritty. **8 purpose**, aim, object, objective, goal, intention, use, sense, value, advantage. **9 attribute**, characteristic, feature, trait, quality, property, aspect, side.
•v. **aim**, direct, level, train, focus.
□ **point out** identify, show, draw attention to, indicate, specify, detail, mention. **point to** indicate, suggest, evidence, signal, signify, denote.

pointed adj. **1 sharp**, spiky, spiked, tapering, barbed.

2 cutting, biting, incisive, trenchant, acerbic, caustic, scathing, venomous, sarcastic.

pointer n. **1 indicator**, needle, arrow, hand. **2 indication**, indicator, clue, hint, sign, signal, evidence. **3 tip**, hint, suggestion, guideline, recommendation.

pointless adj. **senseless**, futile, useless, hopeless, unavailing, unproductive, aimless, idle, worthless, valueless.
– OPPOSITES valuable.

poise n. **1 grace**, gracefulness, elegance, balance, control. **2 composure**, equanimity, self-possession, aplomb, self-assurance, self-control, sangfroid, dignity, presence of mind; informal cool.

poised adj. **1 balanced**, suspended, motionless, hanging, hovering. **2 prepared**, ready, braced, geared up, all set, standing by.

poison n. **toxin**, venom.
•v. **pollute**, contaminate, infect, taint, spoil.

┌─ WORD LINKS ──────────
│ study of poisons: toxicology
└────────────────────────

poisonous adj. **1 venomous**, deadly. **2 toxic**, noxious, deadly, fatal, lethal, mortal. **3 malicious**, malevolent, hostile, spiteful, bitter, venomous, malign.
– OPPOSITES harmless.

poke v. **1 prod**, jab, dig, elbow, nudge, shove, jolt, stab, stick. **2** leave the cable poking out: **stick**

P

out, jut out, protrude, project, extend.
•n. **prod**, jab, dig, elbow, nudge.

poky adj. **small**, little, tiny, cramped, confined, restricted, boxy.
– OPPOSITES spacious.

pole n. **post**, pillar, stanchion, stake, support, prop, stick, paling, staff.

police n. **police force**, police service, police officers, policemen, policewomen; Brit. constabulary; informal the cops, the fuzz, the law, the boys in blue; Brit. informal the (Old) Bill; N. Amer. informal the heat.
•v. **1 guard**, watch over, protect, defend, patrol. **2 enforce**, regulate, oversee, supervise, monitor, observe, check.

police officer n. **policeman**, **policewoman**; Brit. constable; N. Amer. patrolman, trooper, roundsman; informal cop; Brit. informal rozzer, bobby; N. Amer. informal uniform.

policy n. **plans**, approach, code, system, guidelines, theory, line, position, stance.

polish v. **1 shine**, wax, buff, rub up/down, gloss, burnish. **2** polish up your essay: **perfect**, refine, improve, hone, enhance, brush up, revise, edit, correct, rewrite, go over, touch up.
•n. **sophistication**, refinement, urbanity, suaveness, elegance, style, grace, finesse; informal class.

polished adj. **1 shiny**, glossy, gleaming, lustrous, glassy,
waxed, buffed, burnished. **2 expert**, accomplished, masterly, skilful, adept, adroit, dexterous, consummate, superlative, superb.
– OPPOSITES dull, inexpert.

polite adj. **1 well mannered**, civil, courteous, respectful, well behaved, well bred, gentlemanly, ladylike, genteel, gracious, tactful, diplomatic. **2 civilized**, refined, cultured, sophisticated, urbane.
– OPPOSITES rude.

politic adj. **wise**, prudent, sensible, shrewd, astute, judicious, expedient, advantageous, beneficial, profitable.
– OPPOSITES unwise.

political adj. **governmental**, government, constitutional, ministerial, parliamentary, diplomatic, legislative, administrative.

politician n. **legislator**, Member of Parliament, MP, representative, minister, statesman, stateswoman, senator, congressman, congresswoman; informal politico.

poll n. **1 vote**, ballot, show of hands, referendum, plebiscite, election. **2 survey**, opinion poll, market research, census.
•v. **1 canvass**, survey, ask, question, interview, ballot. **2 get**, gain, register, record, return.

pollute v. **contaminate**, taint, poison, foul, dirty, soil, infect.
– OPPOSITES purify.

pollution n. **contamination**, impurity, dirt, filth, infection.

pomp n. **ceremony**, solemnity, ritual, display, spectacle, pageantry, show, ostentation, splendour, grandeur, magnificence, majesty, stateliness, glory; informal razzmatazz.

pompous adj. **self-important**, overbearing, sententious, grandiose, affected, pretentious, puffed up, haughty, proud, conceited, supercilious, condescending, patronizing.

ponder v. **think about**, contemplate, consider, review, reflect on, mull over, meditate on, muse on, dwell on.

pontificate v. **hold forth**, expound, declaim, preach, lay down the law, sound off, lecture; informal mouth off.

pool[1] n. **puddle**, pond, lake; literary mere.

pool[2] n. **1 supply**, reserve(s), reservoir, fund, store, bank, stock, cache. **2 fund**, reserve, kitty, pot, bank, purse.
•v. **combine**, group, join, unite, merge, share.

poor adj. **1 poverty-stricken**, penniless, impoverished, impecunious, needy, destitute; Brit. on the breadline; informal hard up, strapped, on your uppers; formal penurious. **2 substandard**, bad, deficient, defective, faulty, imperfect, inferior, unsatisfactory, shoddy, crude, inadequate, unacceptable; informal crummy, rotten; Brit. informal duff. **3 meagre**, scanty, scant, paltry, reduced, modest, sparse, spare, deficient, insubstantial, skimpy,

lean; informal measly, stingy. **4 unfortunate**, unlucky, unhappy, hapless, wretched, luckless, ill-fated, ill-starred.
– OPPOSITES rich.

poorly adv. **badly**, imperfectly, incompetently, crudely, shoddily, inadequately.
•adj. **ill**, unwell, not very well, ailing, indisposed, out of sorts, under par, peaky; Brit. off colour; informal under the weather, rough; Brit. informal ropy, grotty; Scottish informal wabbit; Austral./NZ informal crook.

pop v. **1 go bang**, go off, crack, snap, burst, explode. **2 go**; informal tootle, whip; Brit. informal nip. **3 put**, place, slip, throw, slide, stick, set, lay, position.
•n. **bang**, crack, snap, explosion, report.

populace n. **population**, inhabitants, residents, natives, community, country, (general) public, people, nation, common people, masses, multitude, rank and file; Brit. informal Joe Public; derogatory hoi polloi, common herd, rabble, riff-raff.

popular adj. **1 well liked**, sought-after, in demand, commercial, marketable, fashionable, in vogue, all the rage, hot; informal in, cool, big. **2 non-specialist**, non-technical, amateur, lay person's, general, middle-of-the-road, accessible, simplified, understandable, mass-market. **3 widespread**, general, common, current, prevailing, standard, ordinary, conventional.

populate v. **inhabit**, occupy, people, settle, colonize.

population n. **inhabitants**, residents, people, citizens, public, community, populace, society, natives, occupants.

pornographic adj. **obscene**, indecent, dirty, smutty, filthy, erotic, titillating, sexy, risqué, X-rated, adult.

porous adj. **permeable**, penetrable, absorbent, spongy.
– OPPOSITES impermeable.

port n. **harbour**, docks, marina, haven, seaport.

portable adj. **transportable**, movable, mobile, wireless, lightweight, compact, handy, convenient.

portend v. **presage**, augur, foreshadow, foretell, prophesy, be a sign, warn, be an omen, indicate, herald, signal, bode, promise, threaten, signify, spell, denote.

porter[1] n. **carrier**, bearer; N. Amer. redcap, skycap.

porter[2] n. (Brit.) **doorman**, doorkeeper, commissionaire, gatekeeper, concierge, security officer.

portion n. **1 part**, piece, bit, section, segment. **2 share**, quota, ration, allocation, tranche; Brit. informal whack. **3 helping**, serving, plateful, slice, piece.

portrait n. **1 picture**, likeness, painting, drawing, photograph, image. **2 description**, portrayal,

representation, depiction, impression, account, profile.

portray v. **1 paint**, draw, sketch, picture, depict, represent, illustrate, render, show. **2 describe**, depict, characterize, delineate, put into words. **3 play**, act the part of, take the role of, represent, appear as.

portrayal n. **description**, representation, characterization, depiction, delineation, evocation, interpretation.

pose v. **1 constitute**, present, offer. **2 raise**, ask, put, submit, advance, propose. **3 posture**, attitudinize, put on airs; informal show off, ponce about.
• n. **1 posture**, position, stance, attitude. **2 act**, affectation, show, display, front, airs.
□ **pose as** pretend to be, impersonate, pass yourself off as, masquerade as; formal personate.

poser[1] n. **difficult question**, problem, puzzle, mystery, riddle, conundrum; informal dilemma.

poser[2] n. **exhibitionist**, poseur; informal show-off, pseud.

posh adj. **1** (informal) **smart**, stylish, fancy, high-class, fashionable, chic, luxurious, luxury, exclusive; Brit. upmarket; informal classy, plush, flash; Brit. informal swish; N. Amer. informal swank, tony. **2** (Brit. informal) **upper-class**, aristocratic.

position n. **1 location**, place, situation, spot, site, locality, setting, area, whereabouts, bearings. **2 posture**, stance,

attitude, pose. **3 situation**, state, condition, circumstances, predicament, plight. **4 status**, place, level, rank, standing, stature, prestige, reputation. **5 job**, post, situation, appointment, opening, vacancy, placement. **6 viewpoint**, opinion, outlook, attitude, stand, standpoint, stance, perspective, thinking, policy, feelings.
•v. **put**, place, locate, situate, set, site, stand, station, plant, stick; informal plonk, park.

positive adj. **1 affirmative**, favourable, good, enthusiastic, supportive, constructive, useful, productive, helpful, worthwhile, beneficial. **2 optimistic**, hopeful, confident, cheerful, sanguine, buoyant; informal upbeat. **3** positive economic signs: **good**, promising, favourable, encouraging, heartening, propitious, auspicious. **4 definite**, certain, reliable, concrete, tangible, clear-cut, explicit, firm, decisive, real, actual. **5 convinced**, sure, confident, satisfied.
– OPPOSITES negative, pessimistic.

positively adv. **1 confidently**, definitely, firmly, categorically, with certainty, conclusively. **2 absolutely**, utterly, downright, simply, virtually; informal plain.

possess v. **1 own**, have (to your name), be in possession of. **2 have**, be blessed with, be endowed with, enjoy, boast. **3 take control of**, take over, bewitch, enchant, enslave.

possession n. **1 ownership**, control, hands, keeping, care, custody, charge. **2** she packed her possessions: **belongings**, things, property, worldly goods, goods and chattels, personal effects, stuff, bits and pieces; informal gear, junk; Brit. informal clobber.

possessive adj. **proprietorial**, overprotective, controlling, dominating, jealous, clingy.

possibility n. **1 chance**, likelihood, probability, potentiality, hope, risk, hazard, danger, fear. **2 option**, alternative, choice, course of action, solution. **3 potential**, promise, prospects.

possible adj. **1 feasible**, practicable, viable, attainable, achievable, workable, within reach; informal on, doable. **2 likely**, plausible, imaginable, believable, potential, probable, credible, tenable.
– OPPOSITES impossible, unlikely.

possibly adv. **1 perhaps**, maybe, it is possible, for all you know. **2 conceivably**, under any circumstances, by any means.

post¹ n. **pole**, stake, upright, shaft, prop, support, picket, strut, pillar, stanchion, baluster.
•v. **1 affix**, attach, fasten, display, pin up, put up, stick up. **2 announce**, report, make known, publish.

post² n. (Brit.) **1 mail**; informal snail mail. **2 letters**, correspondence, mail.

post³ n. **1 job**, position, appointment, situation, place, vacancy,

p

opening. **2 assigned position**, station, place, base.
• v. **1 send**, assign, dispatch, consign. **2 put on duty**, mount, station.

poster n. notice, placard, bill, sign, advertisement, playbill.

postpone v. put off, put back, delay, defer, hold over, re-schedule, adjourn, shelve; informal put on ice, put on the back burner.

posture n. **1 position**, pose, attitude, stance, carriage, bearing, comportment; Brit. deportment. **2 attitude**, standpoint, point of view, viewpoint, opinion, position, stance.
• v. **pose**, strike an attitude, attitudinize, strut; informal show off.

potent adj. **1 powerful**, strong, mighty, formidable, influential, dominant. **2 forceful**, convincing, cogent, compelling, persuasive, powerful, strong.
– OPPOSITES weak.

potential adj. possible, likely, prospective, future, probable.
• n. **possibilities**, potentiality, prospects, promise, capability, capacity.

potion n. concoction, mixture, brew, elixir, drink, medicine, tonic, philtre.

potter v. amble, wander, meander, stroll, saunter; informal mosey, tootle, toddle; N. Amer. informal putter.

pottery n. ceramics, crockery, earthenware, terracotta, stoneware, china, porcelain.

pouch n. bag, purse, sack, sac, pocket; Scottish sporran.

pounce v. jump, spring, leap, dive, lunge, swoop, attack.

pound[1] v. **1 beat**, strike, hit, batter, thump, pummel, punch, rain blows on, belabour, hammer; informal bash, clobber, wallop. **2 beat against**, crash against, batter, dash against, lash, buffet. **3 bombard**, bomb, shell. **4 crush**, grind, pulverize, mash, pulp. **5 stomp**, stamp, clomp, clump, tramp, lumber. **6 throb**, thump, thud, hammer, pulse, race.

pound[2] n. enclosure, compound, pen, yard, corral.

pour v. **1 stream**, flow, run, gush, course, jet, spurt, surge, spill. **2 tip**, splash, spill, decant; informal slosh, slop. **3 rain hard**, teem down, pelt down, tip down, rain cats and dogs; informal be chucking it down; Brit. informal bucket down; N. Amer. informal rain pitchforks. **4 crowd**, throng, swarm, stream, flood.

poverty n. **1 pennilessness**, destitution, penury, impoverishment, neediness, hardship, impecuniousness, indigence. **2 scarcity**, deficiency, dearth, shortage, paucity, absence, lack, inadequacy.
– OPPOSITES wealth, abundance.

powdery adj. fine, dry, fine-grained, powder-like, dusty, chalky, floury, sandy, crumbly, friable.

power n. **1** ability, capacity, capability, potential, potentiality, faculty. **2** control, command, authority, dominance, supremacy, ascendancy, mastery, influence, sway, leverage; informal clout, teeth. **3** authority, right, authorization. **4** state, country, nation. **5** strength, might, force, vigour, energy; Brit. informal welly. **6** forcefulness, powerfulness, strength, force, cogency, persuasiveness. **7** driving force, horsepower, acceleration, torque; informal oomph, poke. **8** energy, electricity.
– OPPOSITES weakness.

> WORD LINKS
> obsession with power: megalomania

powerful adj. **1** strong, muscular, muscly, sturdy, strapping, robust, brawny, burly, athletic, manly, well built, solid; informal beefy. **2** intoxicating, hard, strong, stiff, potent. **3** violent, forceful, hard, mighty. **4** intense, keen, fierce, strong, irresistible, overpowering, overwhelming. **5** influential, strong, important, dominant, commanding, formidable. **6** cogent, compelling, convincing, persuasive, forceful, potent.
– OPPOSITES weak, gentle.

powerless adj. **impotent**, helpless, ineffectual, ineffective, useless, defenceless, vulnerable.

practicable adj. **realistic**, feasible, possible, viable, reasonable, workable, achievable; informal doable.

practical adj. **1** empirical, hands-on, actual. **2** feasible, practicable, realistic, viable, workable, possible, reasonable, sensible; informal doable. **3** functional, sensible, utilitarian. **4** realistic, sensible, down-to-earth, businesslike, commonsensical, hard-headed, no-nonsense; informal hard-nosed.
– OPPOSITES theoretical.

practically adv. **1** almost, very nearly, virtually, just about, all but, more or less, as good as, to all intents and purposes; informal pretty well. **2** realistically, sensibly, reasonably, rationally, matter-of-factly.

practice n. **1** application, exercise, use, operation, implementation, execution. **2** custom, procedure, policy, convention, tradition. **3** training, rehearsal, repetition, preparation, dummy run, run-through; informal dry run. **4** profession, career, business, work. **5** business, firm, office, company; informal outfit.

practise v. **1** rehearse, run through, go over/through, work on/at, polish, perfect, refine. **2** train, rehearse, prepare, go through your paces. **3** carry out, perform, observe, follow. **4** work in, pursue a career in, engage in.

practised adj. **expert**, experienced, seasoned, skilled, skilful, accomplished, proficient, talented, able, adept.

p

pragmatic adj. **practical**, matter-of-fact, sensible, down-to-earth, commonsensical, businesslike, hard-headed, no-nonsense; informal hard-nosed.
– OPPOSITES impractical.

praise v. **commend**, applaud, pay tribute to, speak highly of, compliment, congratulate, sing the praises of, rave about.
– OPPOSITES criticize.
•n. **approval**, acclaim, admiration, approbation, plaudits, congratulations, commendation, accolade, compliment, a pat on the back, eulogy.
– OPPOSITES criticism.

praiseworthy adj. **commendable**, admirable, laudable, worthy (of admiration), meritorious, estimable, excellent, exemplary.

prance v. **cavort**, dance, jig, trip, caper, jump, leap, spring, bound, skip, hop, frisk, romp, frolic.

prank n. **(practical) joke**, trick, escapade, stunt, caper, jape, game, hoax; informal lark, leg-pull.

preach v. **1 give a sermon**, sermonize, evangelize, spread the gospel. **2 proclaim**, teach, spread, propagate, expound. **3 advocate**, recommend, advise, urge, teach, counsel.

WORD LINKS
relating to preaching: homiletic

precarious adj. **insecure**, uncertain, unpredictable, risky, hazardous, dangerous, parlous, unsafe, unstable, unsteady,
shaky; informal dicey, iffy; Brit. informal dodgy.
– OPPOSITES safe.

precaution n. **safeguard**, preventive measure, safety measure, insurance; informal backstop.

precede v. **1 go before**, come before, lead up to, pave the way for, herald, introduce, usher in. **2 go ahead of**, go in front of, lead the way.
– OPPOSITES follow.

precedence n. **seniority**, superiority, ascendancy, supremacy. □ **take precedence over** take priority over, outweigh, prevail over, come before.

precedent n. **model**, exemplar, example, pattern, paradigm, criterion, yardstick, standard.

precinct n. **district**, zone, sector, quarter, area.

precious adj. **1 valuable**, costly, expensive, invaluable, priceless. **2 valued**, cherished, treasured, prized, favourite, dear, beloved, special. **3 affected**, pretentious; informal la-di-da; Brit. informal poncey.

precipitate v. **bring about**, bring on, cause, lead to, give rise to, instigate, trigger, spark off, touch off, provoke, hasten, speed up, accelerate.
•adj. **hasty**, overhasty, rash, hurried, rushed, impetuous, impulsive, precipitous, incautious, imprudent, injudicious, ill-advised, reckless.

precipitous adj. **1 steep**, sheer, perpendicular, abrupt, sharp,

431

vertical. **2 sudden**, rapid, swift, abrupt, headlong, speedy, quick, fast.

precise adj. **1 exact**, accurate, correct, specific, detailed, explicit, careful, meticulous, strict, rigorous. **2** *at that precise moment:* **exact**, particular, actual, specific, distinct.
– OPPOSITES inaccurate.

precisely adv. **1 exactly**, sharp, on the dot, promptly; informal bang (on); Brit. informal spot on; N. Amer. informal on the button. **2 just**, exactly, in all respects; informal to a T.

precision n. **exactness**, accuracy, exactitude, correctness, care, meticulousness, scrupulousness, punctiliousness, rigour.

preclude v. **prevent**, make it impossible for, rule out, stop, prohibit, debar, bar, hinder, impede, inhibit, exclude.

preconception n. **preconceived idea**, presupposition, assumption, presumption, prejudgement, prejudice.

predatory adj. **1 predacious**, carnivorous, hunting. **2 exploitative**, wolfish, rapacious, manipulative.

predecessor n. **1 forerunner**, precursor, antecedent. **2 ancestor**, forefather, forebear, antecedent.
– OPPOSITES successor, descendant.

predicament n. **difficulty**, mess, plight, quandary, muddle,

dilemma; informal hole, fix, jam, pickle.

predict v. **forecast**, foretell, prophesy; old use augur.

predictable adj. **foreseeable**, to be expected, anticipated, likely, foreseen, unsurprising, reliable; informal inevitable.

prediction n. **forecast**, prophecy, prognosis, prognostication.

predisposition n. **1 susceptibility**, proneness, tendency, liability, inclination, vulnerability. **2 preference**, predilection, inclination, leaning, bent.

predominantly adv. **mainly**, mostly, for the most part, chiefly, principally, primarily, in the main, on the whole, largely, by and large, typically, generally, usually.

preface n. **introduction**, foreword, preamble, prologue, prelude, front matter; informal intro.
▶v. **precede**, introduce, begin, open, start.

prefer v. **like better**, would rather (have), would sooner (have), favour, be more partial to, choose, select, pick, opt for, go for, plump for.

preferable adj. **better**, best, more desirable, more suitable, advantageous, superior, preferred, recommended.

preferably adv. **ideally**, if possible, for preference, from choice.

preference n. **1 liking**, partiality, fondness, taste, inclination, leaning, bent, penchant, predisposition. **2 priority**, favour, precedence, preferential treatment.

pregnant adj. **1 expecting**, expectant, carrying a child, with child; informal in the family way. **2 meaningful**, significant, suggestive, expressive, charged.

prejudice n. **1 preconceived idea**, preconception. **2 bigotry**, bias, partiality, intolerance, discrimination, unfairness, inequality.
•v. **1 bias**, influence, sway, predispose, make partial, colour. **2 damage**, be detrimental to, be prejudicial to, injure, harm, hurt, spoil, impair, undermine, compromise.

prejudiced adj. **biased**, bigoted, discriminatory, partisan, intolerant, narrow-minded, unfair, unjust, inequitable.
– OPPOSITES impartial.

preliminary adj. **preparatory**, introductory, initial, opening, early, exploratory.
– OPPOSITES final.
•n. **introduction**, preamble, preface, opening remarks, formalities.

prelude n. **preliminary**, overture, opening, preparation, introduction, lead-in, precursor.

premature adj. **1 untimely**, too early, before time, unseasonable. **2 rash**, overhasty, hasty, precipitate, impulsive, impetuous; informal previous.
– OPPOSITES overdue.

premier adj. **leading**, foremost, chief, principal, head, top-ranking, top, prime, primary, first, highest, pre-eminent, senior, outstanding; N. Amer. ranking.
•n. **head of government**, prime minister, PM, president, chancellor.

premiere n. **first performance**, first night, opening night, debut.

premise n. **proposition**, assumption, hypothesis, thesis, presupposition, supposition, presumption, assertion.

premises pl. n. **building(s)**, property, site, office, establishment.

premium n. **1 (regular) payment**, instalment. **2 surcharge**, additional payment, extra.
□ **at a premium** scarce, in great demand, hard to come by, in short supply, thin on the ground, like gold dust.

preoccupation n. **obsession**, fixation, concern, passion, enthusiasm, hobby horse; informal bee in your bonnet.

preoccupied adj. **lost in thought**, deep in thought, oblivious, pensive, distracted, absorbed, engrossed, involved, wrapped up, concerned.

preparation n. **1** *preparations for the party:* **arrangements**, planning, plans, groundwork, spadework, provision. **2 devising**, drawing up, construction, composition, development. **3 mixture**, compound, concoction, solution, medicine, potion.

prepare v. **1 get ready**, put together, draw up, produce, arrange, assemble, construct, compose, formulate. **2 cook**, make, get, concoct; informal fix, rustle up; Brit. informal knock up. **3 get ready**, make preparations, arrange things, make provision. **4 train**, get into shape, practise, get ready, warm up, limber up. **5** *prepare yourself for a shock:* **brace**, ready, tense, steel, steady.

prepared adj. **1 ready**, (all) set, equipped, primed, waiting, poised. **2 willing**, ready, disposed, (favourably) inclined, of a mind, minded.

prescribe v. **1 advise**, recommend, advocate, suggest. **2 stipulate**, lay down, dictate, order, direct, specify, determine.

presence n. **1 existence**, being. **2 attendance**, appearance. **3 aura**, charisma, personality, magnetism.
– OPPOSITES absence.
□ **presence of mind** composure, self-possession, levelheadedness, self-assurance, calmness, alertness, quickwittedness; informal cool, unflappability.

present[1] adj. **1 in attendance**, here, there, near, nearby, at hand, available. **2 in existence**, detectable, occurring, existing, extant, current.
– OPPOSITES absent.
• n. **now**, today, the present

time, the here and now, modern times.
– OPPOSITES past, future.
□ **at present** at the moment, just now, right now, at the present time, currently, at this moment in time.

present[2] v. **1 hand over**, give (out), confer, bestow, award, grant, accord. **2 submit**, set forth, put forward, offer, tender, table. **3 introduce**, make known, acquaint someone with. **4 host**, introduce, compère; N. Amer. informal emcee. **5 represent**, describe, portray, depict.

present[3] n. **gift**, donation, offering, contribution, gratuity, tip, handout; informal prezzie.

presentation n. **1 awarding**, presenting, bestowal, granting. **2 appearance**, arrangement, packaging, layout. **3 demonstration**, talk, lecture, address, speech, show, exhibition, display, introduction, launch, unveiling.

presently adv. **1 soon**, shortly, quite soon, in a short time, in a little while, at any moment/minute/second, before long; N. Amer. momentarily; Brit. informal in a mo. **2 at present**, currently, at the/this moment.

preservation n. **1 conservation**, protection, care. **2 continuation**, conservation, maintenance, upholding, sustaining, perpetuation.

preserve v. **1 conserve**, protect, maintain, care for, look after. **2 continue (with)**, conserve,

keep going, maintain, uphold, sustain, perpetuate, prolong. **3 guard**, protect, keep, defend, safeguard, shelter, shield.
- OPPOSITES attack, abandon.
•n. **1** *jobs which are no longer the preserve of men:* domain, area, field, sphere, orbit, realm, province, territory; informal turf, bailiwick. **2 sanctuary**, (game) reserve, reservation.

preside v.
□ **preside over** be in charge of, be responsible for, head, manage, administer, control, direct, chair, conduct, officiate at, lead, govern, rule, command, supervise, oversee; informal head up his.

press v. **1 push (down)**, depress, hold down, force, thrust, squeeze, compress. **2 iron**, smooth out, flatten. **3 clasp**, hold close, hug, cuddle, squeeze, clutch, grasp, embrace. **4 cluster**, gather, converge, congregate, flock, swarm, crowd. **5 plead**, urge, advance, present, submit, put forward. **6 urge**, put pressure on, pressurize, force, push, coerce, dragoon, steamroller, browbeat; informal lean on, put the screws on, twist someone's arm, railroad, bulldoze. **7** *they pressed for a ban:* call, ask, clamour, push, campaign, demand.
•n. **the media**, the newspapers, journalism, reporters, the fourth estate; Brit. dated Fleet Street.

pressing adj. **1 urgent**, critical, crucial, acute, desperate, serious, grave, life-and-death.

2 important, high-priority, critical, crucial, unavoidable.

pressure n. **1 force**, load, stress, thrust, compression, weight. **2 persuasion**, intimidation, coercion, compulsion, duress, harassment, nagging, badgering. **3 strain**, stress, tension, trouble, difficulty, burden; informal hassle.
•v. **coerce**, push, persuade, force, bulldoze, hound, nag, badger, browbeat, bully, intimidate, dragoon, twist someone's arm; informal railroad, lean on; N. Amer. informal hustle.

pressurize v. **coerce**, pressure, push, persuade, force, bulldoze, hound, nag, badger, browbeat, bully, bludgeon, intimidate, dragoon, twist someone's arm; informal railroad, lean on; N. Amer. informal hustle.

prestige n. **status**, standing, kudos, cachet, stature, reputation, repute, renown, honour, esteem, importance, prominence, distinction.

prestigious adj. **reputable**, distinguished, respected, high-status, esteemed, eminent, highly regarded, renowned, influential.
- OPPOSITES disreputable, obscure.

presume v. **1 assume**, suppose, surmise, imagine, take it, expect. **2 dare**, venture, have the effrontery, be so bold as, go so far as, take the liberty of.

pretence n. **1 make-believe**, acting, faking, play-acting, posturing, deception, trickery.

2 show, semblance, affectation, appearance, outward
appearance, impression, guise,
facade.
– OPPOSITES honesty.

pretend v. put on an act, act,
play-act, put it on, dissemble,
sham, feign, fake, dissimulate,
make believe, put on a false
front, posture, go through the
motions, make as if.
• adj. (informal) mock, fake, sham,
simulated, artificial, false,
pseudo; informal phoney.

pretty adj. attractive, good-
looking, nice-looking, personable, fetching, prepossessing,
appealing, charming, delightful,
cute; Scottish & N. English bonny; old
use fair, comely.
– OPPOSITES plain, ugly.
• adv. (informal) quite, rather,
somewhat, fairly.

prevail v. **1 win**, triumph, be
victorious, carry the day, come
out on top, succeed, rule, reign.
2 exist, be present, be the case,
occur, be prevalent, be in force.

prevailing adj. current, existing,
prevalent, usual, common, general, widespread.

prevalent adj. widespread, frequent, usual, common, current,
popular, general.
– OPPOSITES rare.

prevent v. **stop**, avert, nip in the
bud, foil, inhibit, thwart, prohibit, forbid.
– OPPOSITES allow.

previous adj. **1 preceding**, foregoing, prior, past, last.

2 former, preceding, old, earlier,
ex-, past, last, sometime, one-
time, erstwhile; formal quondam.
– OPPOSITES next.

previously adv. formerly, earlier
(on), before, hitherto, at one
time, in the past.

prey n. **1 quarry**, kill. **2 victim**,
target, dupe; informal sucker; Brit.
informal mug.
– OPPOSITES predator.

price n. **1 cost**, charge, fee, fare,
amount, sum; informal damage.
2 consequence, result, cost,
penalty, toll, sacrifice, downside, drawback, disadvantage,
minus.

priceless adj. invaluable,
beyond price, irreplaceable,
expensive, costly.
– OPPOSITES worthless, cheap.

prick v. pierce, puncture, stab,
perforate, spike, penetrate, jab.
• n. jab, sting, pinprick, stab,
pinhole, wound.

prickly adj. spiky, spiked, thorny,
barbed, spiny, bristly.

pride n. **1 self-esteem**, dignity,
honour, self-respect. **2 pleasure**, joy, delight, gratification,
fulfilment, satisfaction, sense of
achievement. **3 arrogance**, vanity, self-importance, hubris, con-
ceitedness, egotism, snobbery.
– OPPOSITES shame, humility.

priest n. clergyman, clergywoman, minister, cleric, pastor,
vicar, rector, parson, church-
man, churchwoman, father,
curate; N. Amer. dominie;
informal reverend, padre.

P

WORD LINKS
relating to priests: clerical, sacerdotal

primarily adv. **1 first and foremost**, firstly, essentially, in essence, fundamentally, principally, predominantly. **2 mostly**, for the most part, chiefly, mainly, in the main, on the whole, largely, principally, predominantly.

primary adj. **main**, chief, key, prime, central, principal, foremost, first, most important, predominant, paramount; *informal* number-one.
– OPPOSITES secondary.

prime¹ adj. **1 main**, chief, key, primary, central, principal, foremost, first, most important, paramount, major; *informal* number-one. **2 top-quality**, top, best, first-class, superior, choice, select, finest; *informal* tip-top, A1.
– OPPOSITES secondary, inferior.
• n. **heyday**, peak, pinnacle, high point/spot, zenith, flower, bloom, flush.

prime² v. **brief**, fill in, prepare, advise, instruct, coach, drill, train.

primitive adj. **1 ancient**, earliest, first, prehistoric, primordial, primeval. **2 crude**, simple, rough (and ready), basic, rudimentary, makeshift.
– OPPOSITES modern, sophisticated.

prince n. **ruler**, sovereign, monarch, crowned head.

principal adj. **main**, chief, primary, leading, foremost, first, most important, predominant, dominant, pre-eminent, highest, top; *informal* number-one.
– OPPOSITES minor.
• n. **head teacher**, headmaster, headmistress, head, dean, rector, master, mistress, chancellor, vice chancellor, president, provost, warden.

principally adv. **mainly**, mostly, chiefly, for the most part, in the main, on the whole, largely, predominantly, primarily.

principle n. **1 truth**, concept, idea, theory, fundamental, essential, precept, rule, law. **2 doctrine**, belief, creed, credo, code, ethic. **3 morals**, morality, ethics, ideals, standards, integrity, virtue, probity, honour, decency, conscience, scruples.
□ **in principle 1** in theory, theoretically, on paper, ideally. **2** in general, in essence, on the whole, in the main.

print v. **1 publish**, issue, release, circulate, run off, copy, reproduce. **2 imprint**, impress, stamp, mark.
• n. **1 type**, printing, letters, lettering, characters, typeface, font. **2 impression**, handprint, fingerprint, footprint. **3 picture**, engraving, etching, lithograph, woodcut. **4 photograph**, photo, snap, snapshot, picture, still, enlargement, reproduction, copy.

prior adj. **earlier**, previous, preceding, advance, pre-existing.

– OPPOSITES subsequent.

□ **prior to** before, until, up to, previous to, preceding, earlier than, in advance of.

priority n. **1 prime concern**, main consideration, most important thing. **2 precedence**, preference, pre-eminence, predominance, primacy.

prison n. jail, penal institution; N. Amer. jailhouse, penitentiary, correctional facility; informal clink, slammer; Brit. informal nick; N. Amer. informal can, pen.

□ **in prison** behind bars; informal inside, doing time; Brit. informal doing porridge.

prisoner n. **1 convict**, detainee, inmate; informal jailbird, con; Brit. informal lag; N. Amer. informal yardbird. **2 prisoner of war**, POW, internee, captive, hostage.

pristine adj. **immaculate**, perfect, in mint condition, as new, spotless, unspoilt.

– OPPOSITES dirty, spoilt.

privacy n. **seclusion**, solitude, isolation.

private adj. **1 personal**, own, special, exclusive. **2 confidential**, secret, classified, privileged, unofficial, off the record; informal hush-hush. **3 intimate**, personal, secret, innermost, undisclosed, unspoken, unvoiced. **4 reserved**, introverted, self-contained, reticent, retiring, unsociable, withdrawn, solitary, reclusive, secretive. **5 secluded**, undisturbed, out of the way, remote, isolated. **6 independent**, non-state, privatized, commercial, private-enterprise.

– OPPOSITES public, open, official.

▪n. **private soldier**, trooper; Brit. sapper, gunner; US GI; Brit. informal Tommy, squaddie.

□ **in private** in secret, secretly, privately, behind closed doors, in camera, sub rosa.

privilege n. **1 advantage**, benefit, prerogative, entitlement, right, concession, freedom, liberty. **2 honour**, pleasure.

privileged adj. **1 wealthy**, rich, affluent, prosperous, elite, advantaged. **2 confidential**, private, secret, restricted, classified, not for publication, off the record, inside; informal hush-hush.

– OPPOSITES underprivileged, disadvantaged.

prize n. **award**, reward, trophy, medal, cup, winnings, purse, honour.

▪adj. **1 champion**, award-winning, top, best. **2 utter**, complete, total, absolute, real, perfect; Brit. informal right.

probability n. **likelihood**, prospect, expectation, chance(s), odds, possibility.

probable adj. **likely**, odds-on, expected, anticipated, predictable; informal on the cards, a safe bet.

– OPPOSITES unlikely.

probably adv. **in all likelihood**, in all probability, as likely as not, ten to one, the chances are, doubtless.

probation n. **trial**, trial period, apprenticeship, training.

probe n. **investigation**, enquiry, examination, inquest, study.
- v. **1 prod**, poke, dig into, delve into, explore, feel around in, examine. **2 investigate**, enquire into, look into, go into, study, examine, explore.

problem n. **1 difficulty**, worry, complication, snag, hitch, drawback, stumbling block, obstacle, hiccup, setback, catch, dilemma, quandary; informal headache, fly in the ointment. **2 nuisance**, bother; informal drag, pain, hassle. **3 puzzle**, question, poser, riddle, conundrum; informal brain-teaser.

problematic adj. **difficult**, troublesome, tricky, awkward, controversial, ticklish, complicated, complex, knotty.
- OPPOSITES easy, straightforward.

procedure n. **course of action**, method, system, strategy, way, approach, formula, mechanism, technique, routine, drill, practice.

proceed v. **1 begin**, make a start, get going, move. **2 go**, make your way, advance, move, progress, carry on, continue, press on, push on.
- OPPOSITES stop.

proceedings pl. n. **1 events**, activities, action, happenings, goings-on. **2 report**, transactions, minutes, account, story, record(s). **3 legal action**, litigation, suit, lawsuit, case, prosecution.

proceeds pl. n. **profits**, earnings, receipts, returns, takings, income, revenue, profit, yield; Sport gate (money); N. Amer. take.

process n. **1 procedure**, operation, action, activity, exercise, business, job, task, undertaking. **2** a new manufacturing process: **method**, system, technique, means.
- v. **deal with**, attend to, see to, sort out, handle, take care of.

procession n. **parade**, march, march past, cavalcade, motorcade, cortège, column, file; Brit. informal crocodile.

proclaim v. **declare**, announce, pronounce, state, make known, give out, advertise, publish, broadcast, trumpet.

prod v. **1 poke**, jab, stab, dig, nudge, elbow. **2 spur**, stimulate, prompt, push, galvanize, persuade, urge, chivvy, remind.

prodigal adj. **wasteful**, extravagant, spendthrift.
- OPPOSITES thrifty.

prodigy n. **genius**, mastermind, virtuoso, wunderkind; informal whizz-kid, whizz.

produce v. **1 manufacture**, make, construct, build, fabricate, put together, assemble, turn out, create, mass-produce. **2 yield**, grow, give, supply, provide, furnish, bear. **3 give birth to**, bear, deliver, bring forth, bring into the world. **4 create**, fashion, turn out, compose,

write, pen, paint. **5 pull out**, extract, fish out, present, offer, proffer, show. **6 cause**, bring about, give rise to, occasion, generate, lead to, result in, provoke, precipitate, spark off, trigger. **7 stage**, put on, mount, present, exhibit.
•n. **food**, foodstuff(s), products, crops, harvest.

producer n. **1 manufacturer**, maker, builder, constructor. **2 grower**, farmer. **3 impresario**, manager, administrator, promoter, director.

product n. **1 artefact**, commodity; (**products**) goods, ware(s), merchandise, produce. **2 result**, consequence, outcome, effect, upshot.

production n. **1 manufacture**, making, construction, building, fabrication, assembly, creation, mass production. **2 creation**, origination, fashioning, composition, writing. **3 output**, yield, productivity. **4 performance**, staging, presentation, show, piece, play.

productive adj. **1 prolific**, inventive, creative. **2 useful**, constructive, profitable, fruitful, valuable, effective, worthwhile, helpful. **3 fertile**, fruitful, rich, fecund.

productivity n. **efficiency**, work rate, output, yield, production.

profess v. **1 declare**, announce, proclaim, assert, state, affirm, maintain, protest, avow.

2 claim, pretend, purport, affect, make out.

professed adj. **1 claimed**, supposed, ostensible, self-styled, apparent, pretended, purported. **2 declared**, sworn, confirmed, self-confessed.

profession n. **career**, occupation, calling, vocation, métier, line of work, job, business, trade, craft.

professional adj. **1 white-collar**, non-manual, graduate, qualified, chartered. **2 paid**, salaried. **3 expert**, accomplished, skilful, masterly, fine, polished, skilled, proficient, competent, able, businesslike, deft. **4** *he always behaved in a professional way:* **appropriate**, fitting, proper, honourable, ethical.
– OPPOSITES amateur, amateurish.
•n. **expert**, virtuoso, old hand, master, maestro, past master; *informal* pro, ace.

profile n. **1 outline**, silhouette, side view, contour, shape, form, lines. **2 description**, account, study, portrait, rundown, sketch, outline.

profit n. **1 financial gain**, return(s), yield, proceeds, earnings, winnings, surplus; *informal* pay dirt, bottom line. **2 advantage**, benefit, value, use, good; *informal* mileage.
– OPPOSITES loss, disadvantage.
•v. **1 make money**, earn; *informal* rake it in, clean up, make a killing; *N. Amer. informal* make a fast buck. **2 benefit**, be advantageous to, be of use to, do some-

one good, help, be of service to, serve.
– OPPOSITES lose.

profitable adj. **1 moneymaking**, profit-making, paying, lucrative, commercial, successful, money-spinning, gainful. **2 beneficial**, useful, advantageous, valuable, productive, worthwhile, rewarding, fruitful, illuminating, informative, well spent.

profound adj. **1 heartfelt**, intense, keen, extreme, acute, severe, sincere, earnest, deep, deep-seated, overpowering, overwhelming. **2 far-reaching**, radical, extensive, sweeping, exhaustive, thoroughgoing. **3 wise**, learned, intelligent, scholarly, discerning, penetrating, perceptive, astute, thoughtful, insightful.
– OPPOSITES superficial.

programme n. **1 schedule**, agenda, calendar, timetable, order (of the day), line-up. **2 scheme**, plan, package, strategy, initiative, proposal. **3 broadcast**, production, show, presentation, transmission, performance. **4 course**, syllabus, curriculum.
•v. **arrange**, organize, schedule, plan, map out, timetable, line up; N. Amer. slate.

progress n. **1 (forward) movement**, advance, going, headway, passage. **2 development**, advance, advancement, headway, step forward, improvement, growth.
•v. **1 go**, make your way, move,

proceed, advance, go on, continue, make headway, work your way. **2 develop**, make progress, advance, make headway, move on, get on, gain ground, improve, get better, come on, come along, make strides.
– OPPOSITES regress.
☐ **in progress** under way, going on, ongoing, happening, occurring, taking place, proceeding, continuing.

progression n. **1 progress**, advancement, movement, passage, development, evolution, growth. **2 succession**, series, sequence, string, stream, chain, train, row, cycle.

progressive adj. **1 continuing**, continuous, ongoing, gradual, step-by-step, cumulative. **2 modern**, liberal, advanced, forward-thinking, enlightened, pioneering, reforming, reformist, radical; informal go-ahead.
– OPPOSITES conservative.

prohibit v. **1 forbid**, ban, bar, proscribe, make illegal, outlaw, disallow, veto. **2 prevent**, stop, rule out, preclude, make impossible.
– OPPOSITES allow.

prohibition n. **ban**, bar, veto, embargo, boycott, injunction, moratorium, interdict.

project n. **1 scheme**, plan, programme, enterprise, undertaking, venture, proposal, idea, concept. **2 assignment**, piece of work, task.
•v. **1 forecast**, predict, expect, estimate, calculate, reckon.

2 stick out, jut (out), protrude, extend, stand out, bulge out.
3 cast, throw, send, shed, shine.

projection n. **1 forecast**, prediction, prognosis, expectation, estimate. **2 outcrop**, outgrowth, overhang, ledge, shelf, prominence, protrusion, protuberance.

proliferate v. **increase**, grow, multiply, rocket, mushroom, snowball, burgeon, spread, expand, run riot.
– OPPOSITES decrease, dwindle.

prolific adj. **1 plentiful**, abundant, bountiful, profuse, copious, luxuriant, rich, lush, fruitful. **2 productive**, fertile, creative, inventive.
– OPPOSITES meagre.

prolong v. **lengthen**, extend, drag out, draw out, protract, spin out, carry on, continue, keep up, perpetuate.
– OPPOSITES shorten.

prominence n. **1 fame**, celebrity, eminence, importance, distinction, greatness, prestige, stature, standing. **2** the press gave prominence to the reports: **wide coverage**, importance, precedence, weight, a high profile, top billing.

prominent adj. **1 important**, well known, leading, eminent, distinguished, notable, noteworthy, noted, illustrious, celebrated, famous, renowned; N. Amer. major-league. **2 jutting (out)**, protruding, projecting, protuberant, standing out, sticking out, proud, bulging.

3 conspicuous, noticeable, obvious, unmistakable, eye-catching, pronounced, salient, striking, dominant, obtrusive.
– OPPOSITES unimportant, inconspicuous.

promise n. **1 word (of honour)**, assurance, pledge, vow, guarantee, oath, bond, undertaking, agreement, commitment, contract. **2 potential**, ability, talent, aptitude, possibility.
• v. **1 give your word**, swear, pledge, vow, undertake, give an undertaking, guarantee, warrant, contract, give an assurance, commit yourself. **2 indicate**, lead someone to expect, point to, be a sign of, betoken, give hope of, augur, herald, portend, presage.

promising adj. **1 good**, encouraging, favourable, hopeful, auspicious, propitious, bright, rosy, heartening. **2 talented**, gifted, budding, up-and-coming, rising, coming, in the making.
– OPPOSITES unfavourable.

promote v. **1 upgrade**, give promotion to, elevate, advance, move up. **2 encourage**, further, advance, foster, develop, contribute to, boost, stimulate. **3 advertise**, publicize, give publicity to, beat/bang the drum for, market, merchandise; informal push, plug, hype.
– OPPOSITES demote, obstruct.

promotion n. **1 upgrading**, preferment, elevation, advancement, step up (the ladder). **2 encouragement**, furtherance,

p

furthering, advancement, contribution to, fostering, boosting, stimulation. **3 advertising**, marketing, publicity, propaganda; informal hard sell, plug, hype, puff.

prompt v. **1 induce**, make, move, motivate, lead, dispose, persuade, incline, encourage, stimulate, prod, impel, spur on, inspire. **2 give rise to**, bring about, cause, occasion, result in, lead to, elicit, produce, precipitate, trigger, spark off, provoke. **3 remind**, cue, feed, help out, jog someone's memory.
– OPPOSITES deter.
•adj. **quick**, swift, rapid, speedy, fast, expeditious, direct, immediate, instant, early, punctual, in good time, on time.
– OPPOSITES slow, late.
•adv. **exactly**, precisely, sharp, on the dot, dead, punctually; informal bang on; N. Amer. informal on the button, on the nose.

promptly adv. **1 punctually**, on time; informal on the dot, bang on; Brit. informal spot on; N. Amer. informal on the button, on the nose. **2 without delay**, straight/right away, at once, immediately, now, as soon as possible, quickly, swiftly, rapidly, speedily, fast; informal pronto, asap.
– OPPOSITES late.

prone adj. **1 susceptible**, vulnerable, subject, open, liable, given, predisposed, likely, disposed, inclined, apt. **2 lying face down**, on your stomach/front, lying flat, lying down, horizontal, prostrate.

pronounce v. **1 say**, enunciate, articulate, utter, voice, sound, vocalize, get your tongue round. **2 declare**, proclaim, judge, rule, decree, ordain.

pronounced adj. **noticeable**, marked, strong, conspicuous, striking, distinct, prominent, unmistakable, obvious.
– OPPOSITES slight.

proof n. **evidence**, verification, corroboration, demonstration, authentication, confirmation, certification, documentation.
•adj. **resistant**, immune, unaffected, impervious.

prop n. **1 pole**, post, support, upright, brace, buttress, stay, strut. **2 mainstay**, pillar, anchor, support, cornerstone.
•v. **lean**, rest, stand, balance.
◻ **prop up 1 hold up**, shore up, buttress, support, brace, underpin. **2 subsidize**, underwrite, fund, finance.

propaganda n. **information**, promotion, advertising, publicity, disinformation; informal hype.

propel v. **1 move**, power, push, drive. **2 throw**, thrust, toss, fling, hurl, pitch, send, shoot.

proper adj. **1 real**, genuine, actual, true, bona fide; informal kosher. **2 right**, correct, accepted, conventional, established, official, regular, acceptable, appropriate, suitable, apt. **3 formal**, conventional, correct, orthodox, polite, respectable, seemly.
– OPPOSITES wrong, improper.

property n. **1** possessions, belongings, things, effects, stuff, goods; informal gear. **2** building(s), premises, house(s), land; N. Amer. real estate. **3** quality, attribute, characteristic, feature, power, trait, hallmark.

prophecy n. prediction, forecast, prognostication, prognosis, divination.

prophesy v. predict, foretell, forecast, foresee, prognosticate.

prophet, prophetess n. forecaster, seer, soothsayer, fortune teller, clairvoyant, oracle.

proportion n. **1** part, portion, amount, quantity, bit, piece, percentage, fraction, section, segment, share. **2** ratio, distribution, relative amount/number, relationship. **3** balance, symmetry, harmony, correspondence, correlation, agreement. **4** men of huge proportions: size, dimensions, magnitude, measurements, mass, volume, bulk, expanse, extent.

proportional, proportionate adj. corresponding, comparable, in proportion, pro rata, commensurate, equivalent, consistent.
- OPPOSITES disproportionate.

proposal n. scheme, plan, idea, project, programme, motion, proposition, suggestion, submission.

propose v. **1** put forward, suggest, submit, advance, offer, present, move, come up with, nominate, recommend.

2 intend, mean, plan, have in mind, aim.

proposition n. **1** proposal, scheme, plan, project, idea, programme. **2** task, job, undertaking, venture, activity, affair.

proprietor, proprietress n. owner, possessor, holder, householder, master, mistress, landowner, landlord, landlady, shopkeeper.

prosecute v. charge, take to court, take legal action against, sue, try, bring to trial, put on trial, put in the dock, indict; N. Amer. impeach.
- OPPOSITES defend.

prospect n. likelihood, hope, expectation, chance, odds, probability, possibility, promise, outlook, lookout.
• v. search, look, explore, survey, scout, hunt, dowse.

prospective adj. potential, possible, probable, likely, future, eventual, -to-be, soon-to-be, in the making, intending, aspiring, would-be.

prospectus n. brochure, syllabus, curriculum, catalogue, programme, list, schedule.

prosper v. flourish, thrive, do well, bloom, blossom, burgeon, progress, do all right for yourself, get ahead, get on (in the world), be successful; informal go places.
- OPPOSITES fail.

prosperity n. success, affluence, wealth, ease, plenty.
- OPPOSITES hardship, failure.

P

prosperous adj. thriving, flourishing, successful, strong, vigorous, profitable, lucrative, expanding, booming, burgeoning, **affluent**, wealthy, rich, moneyed, well off, well-to-do; informal in the money.
– OPPOSITES ailing, poor.

prostitute n. whore, sex worker, call girl, courtesan; informal working girl; N. Amer. informal hooker, hustler.
•v. **betray**, sacrifice, sell, sell out, debase, degrade, demean, devalue, cheapen, lower, shame, misuse.

protect v. keep safe, keep from harm, guard, defend, shield, save, safeguard, preserve, cushion, insulate, shelter, screen, keep, look after.
– OPPOSITES expose, harm.

protection n. **1** defence, security, safeguard, safety, sanctuary, shelter, refuge, immunity, indemnity. **2** safe keeping, care, charge, guardianship, support, aegis, patronage. **3** barrier, buffer, shield, screen, cushion, bulwark, armour, insulation.

protective adj. **1** protecting, covering, insulated, impermeable, -proof, -resistant.
2 solicitous, careful, caring, defensive, paternal, maternal, overprotective, possessive.

protector n. **1** defender, preserver, guardian, champion, patron, custodian. **2** guard, shield, buffer, cushion, pad, screen.

protest n. **1** objection, complaint, challenge, dissent, demurral, remonstration, fuss, outcry. **2** demonstration, rally, vigil, sit-in, occupation, work-to-rule, stoppage, strike, walkout, mutiny, picket, boycott; informal demo.
•v. **1** object, express opposition, dissent, take issue, take a stand, put up a fight, take exception, complain, express disapproval, disagree, make a fuss, speak out; informal kick up a fuss. **2** insist on, maintain, assert, affirm, announce, proclaim, declare, profess, avow.

protocol n. **etiquette**, convention, formalities, custom, the rules, procedure, ritual, decorum, the done thing.

prototype n. **original**, master, template, pattern, sample.

protract v. prolong, lengthen, extend, draw out, drag out, spin out, stretch out, string out.
– OPPOSITES curtail, shorten.

protracted adj. **prolonged**, extended, long-drawn-out, lengthy, long.
– OPPOSITES short.

proud adj. **1** pleased, glad, happy, delighted, thrilled, satisfied, gratified. **2** *a proud moment*: **pleasing**, gratifying, satisfying, cheering, heartwarming, happy, glorious. **3** arrogant, conceited, vain, self-important, full of yourself, overbearing, bumptious, presumptuous, overweening, haughty, high and mighty;

informal **big-headed**, **too big for your boots**, **stuck-up**.
– OPPOSITES ashamed, humble.

prove v. **show (to be true)**, demonstrate, substantiate, corroborate, verify, validate, authenticate, confirm.
– OPPOSITES disprove.

proverb n. **saying**, adage, saw, maxim, axiom, motto, aphorism, epigram.

provide v. **1 supply**, give, come up with, produce, deliver, donate, contribute; informal fork out, lay out. **2** *he was provided with tools*: **equip**, furnish, issue, supply, fit out, rig out, kit out, arm, provision; informal fix up. **3 offer**, present, afford, give, add, bring, yield, impart, lend. □ **provide for** feed, nurture, nourish, support, maintain, keep, sustain.

provided, **providing** conj. **if**, on condition that, provided that, presuming (that), assuming (that), as long as, with/on the understanding that.

provider n. **supplier**, donor, giver, contributor, source.

province n. **1 territory**, region, state, department, canton, area, district, sector, zone, division. **2 (the provinces) the regions**, the rest of the country, rural areas/districts, the countryside; informal the sticks, the middle of nowhere; N. Amer. informal the boondocks. **3 domain**, area, department, responsibility, sphere, world, realm, field, discipline, territory; informal bailiwick.

provincial adj. **1 local**, small-town, rural, country, outlying, backwoods; informal one-horse. **2 unsophisticated**, parochial, insular, narrow-minded, inward-looking, suburban, small-town; N. Amer. informal corn-fed.
– OPPOSITES cosmopolitan, sophisticated.

provision n. **1** *limited provision for young children*: **facilities**, services, amenities, resource(s), arrangements. **2 (provisions) supplies**, food and drink, stores, groceries, foodstuff(s), rations. **3 term**, requirement, specification, stipulation.

provisional adj. **interim**, temporary, transitional, changeover, stopgap, short-term, fill-in, acting, working.
– OPPOSITES permanent, definite.

provocation n. **goading**, prodding, incitement, harassment, pressure, teasing, taunting, torment; informal hassle, aggravation.

provocative adj. **annoying**, irritating, maddening, galling, insulting, offensive, inflammatory, incendiary, like a red rag to a bull; informal aggravating.

provoke v. **1 arouse**, produce, evoke, cause, give rise to, excite, spark off, touch off, kindle, generate, engender, instigate, result in, lead to, bring on, precipitate, prompt, trigger. **2 goad**, spur, prick, sting, prod, incite, rouse, stimulate. **3 annoy**, anger, enrage, irritate, madden, nettle; Brit. rub up the

P

wrong way; informal aggravate, rile, needle, get/put someone's back up; Brit. informal wind up.
– OPPOSITES allay, appease.

prowess n. **skill**, expertise, mastery, ability, capability, capacity, talent, aptitude, dexterity, proficiency, finesse; informal know-how.
– OPPOSITES inability, ineptitude.

prowl v. **steal**, slink, skulk, sneak, stalk, creep; informal snoop.

proxy n. **deputy**, representative, substitute, delegate, agent, surrogate, stand-in, go-between.

prudent adj. **1 wise**, well judged, sensible, politic, judicious, shrewd, sage, sagacious, far-sighted, canny. **2 cautious**, careful, provident, circumspect, thrifty, economical.
– OPPOSITES unwise, extravagant.

prudish adj. **puritanical**, priggish, prim, moralistic, censorious, strait-laced, Victorian, stuffy; informal goody-goody.
– OPPOSITES permissive.

prune v. **1 cut back**, trim, clip, shear, shorten, thin, shape. **2 reduce**, cut (back/down), pare (down), slim down, trim, downsize, axe, shrink; informal slash.
– OPPOSITES increase.

pry v. **be inquisitive**, poke about/around, ferret about/around, spy, be a busybody; informal stick/poke your nose in/into, be nosy, snoop; Austral./NZ informal stickybeak.

pseudonym n. **pen name**, nom de plume, assumed name, alias, sobriquet, stage name, nom de guerre.

psychiatrist n. **psychotherapist**, psychoanalyst, analyst; informal shrink.

psychic adj. **1 supernatural**, paranormal, other-worldly, metaphysical, extrasensory, magic(al), mystic(al), occult. **2 clairvoyant**, telepathic.
▪ n. **clairvoyant**, fortune teller, medium, spiritualist, telepath, mind-reader.

psychological adj. **1 mental**, emotional, inner, cognitive. **2 (all) in the mind**, psychosomatic, emotional, subjective, subconscious, unconscious.
– OPPOSITES physical.

psychology n. **mind**, mindset, thought processes, way of thinking, mentality, psyche, attitude(s), make-up, character, temperament; informal what makes someone tick.

pub n. (Brit.) **bar**, inn, tavern, hostelry; Brit. public house; informal watering hole; Brit. informal local, boozer; N. Amer. historical saloon.

puberty n. **adolescence**, pubescence, youth, teenage years, teens.

public adj. **1 state**, national, constitutional, civic, civil, official, social, municipal, nationalized. **2 popular**, general, common, communal, collective, shared, joint, universal, widespread. **3 prominent**, well known,

important, leading, eminent, distinguished, celebrated, household, famous; N. Amer. major-league. **4 open (to the public)** communal, available, free, unrestricted.
- OPPOSITES private, secret.
•n. **1 people**, citizens, subjects, electors, electorate, voters, taxpayers, residents, inhabitants, citizenry, population, populace, community, society, country, nation. **2 audience**, spectators, followers, following, fans, devotees, admirers.

WORD LINKS
fear of public places: agoraphobia

publication n. **1 book**, volume, title, opus, tome, newspaper, paper, magazine, periodical, newsletter, bulletin, journal, report. **2 issuing**, publishing, printing, distribution.

publicity n. **1 public attention**, media attention, exposure, glare, limelight, spotlight. **2 promotion**, advertising, propaganda, boost, push; informal hype, ballyhoo, puff, build-up, plug.

publicize v. **1 make known**, make public, announce, broadcast, spread, promulgate, disseminate, circulate, air. **2 advertise**, promote, build up, talk up, push, beat the drum for, boost; informal hype, plug, puff (up).
- OPPOSITES conceal, suppress.

publish v. **1 issue**, bring out, produce, print. **2 make known**,

make public, publicize, announce, broadcast, issue, put out, distribute, spread, promulgate, disseminate, circulate, air.

pudding n. **dessert**, sweet, last course; Brit. informal afters, pud.

puerile adj. **childish**, immature, infantile, juvenile, babyish, silly, inane, fatuous, foolish.
- OPPOSITES mature.

puff n. **1 gust**, blast, flurry, rush, draught, waft, breeze, breath. **2 pull**; informal drag, toke.
•v. **1 breathe heavily**, pant, blow, gasp. **2 smoke**, draw on, drag on, inhale.

pugnacious adj. **combative**, aggressive, antagonistic, belligerent, quarrelsome, argumentative, hostile, truculent.
- OPPOSITES peaceable.

pull v. **1 tug**, haul, drag, draw, tow, heave, jerk, wrench; informal yank. **2 strain**, sprain, wrench, tear. **3 attract**, draw, bring in, pull in, lure, seduce, entice, tempt.
- OPPOSITES push.
•n. **1 tug**, jerk, heave; informal yank. **2 gulp**, draught, drink, swallow, mouthful, slug; informal swig. **3 puff**; informal drag, toke. **4 attraction**, draw, lure, magnetism, fascination, appeal, allure.
□ **pull off** achieve, fulfil, succeed in, accomplish, bring off, carry off, clinch, fix. **pull out** withdraw, resign, leave, retire, step down, bow out, back out, give up; informal quit. **pull through** get better, get well

P

again, improve, recover, rally, come through, recuperate.

pulp n. **1 mush**, mash, paste, purée, slop, slush, mulch. **2 flesh**, marrow, meat.
- v. **mash**, purée, cream, crush, press, liquidize.

pulse n. **1 heartbeat**, heart rate. **2 rhythm**, beat, tempo, pounding, throb, throbbing, thudding, drumming.
- v. **throb**, pulsate, vibrate, beat, pound, thud, thump, drum, reverberate, echo.

pump v. **1 force**, drive, push, inject, suck, draw. **2 inflate**, blow up, fill up, swell, enlarge, distend, expand, dilate, puff up. **3 spurt**, spout, squirt, jet, surge, spew, gush, stream, flow, pour, spill, well, cascade.

punch[1] v. **hit**, strike, thump, jab, smash; informal sock, slug, biff, bop; Brit. informal stick one on, slosh; N. Amer. informal boff, bust; Austral./NZ informal quilt.
- n. **blow**, hit, knock, thump, box, jab, clip; informal sock, slug, biff, bop; N. Amer. informal boff, bust.

punch[2] v. **perforate**, puncture, pierce, prick, hole, spike, skewer.

punctual adj. **on time**, prompt, on schedule, in (good) time; informal on the dot.
- OPPOSITES late.

punctuate v. **break up**, interrupt, intersperse, pepper, sprinkle, scatter.

puncture n. **1 hole**, perforation, rupture, cut, gash, slit, leak. **2 flat tyre**; informal flat.

- v. **prick**, pierce, stab, rupture, perforate, cut, slit, deflate.

pungent adj. **strong**, powerful, pervasive, penetrating, sharp, acid, sour, biting, bitter, tart, vinegary, tangy, aromatic, spicy, piquant, peppery, hot, garlicky.
- OPPOSITES bland, mild.

punish v. **discipline**, penalize, correct, sentence, teach someone a lesson; informal come down on (like a ton of bricks); dated chastise.

punishing adj. **arduous**, demanding, taxing, strenuous, rigorous, stressful, trying, heavy, difficult, tough, exhausting, tiring, gruelling.
- OPPOSITES easy.

punishment n. **penalty**, sanction, penance, discipline, forfeit, sentence.

WORD LINKS
relating to punishment: penal, punitive

punitive adj. **penal**, disciplinary, corrective.

puny adj. **1 small**, weak, feeble, slight, undersized, stunted, underdeveloped; informal weedy. **2 pitiful**, pitiable, miserable, sorry, meagre, paltry; informal pathetic, measly.
- OPPOSITES sturdy.

pupil n. **1 student**, scholar, schoolchild, schoolboy, schoolgirl. **2 disciple**, follower, student, protégé, apprentice, trainee, novice.
- OPPOSITES teacher.

puppet n. **1** marionette, glove puppet, finger puppet. **2** pawn, tool, instrument, cat's paw, poodle, mouthpiece, stooge.

purchase v. **buy**, acquire, obtain, pick up, procure, pay for, invest in; informal get hold of, score.
– OPPOSITES sell.
•n. **1** acquisition, buy, investment, order. **2** grip, grasp, hold, foothold, toehold, anchorage, support, traction, leverage.
– OPPOSITES sale.

pure adj. **1** unadulterated, undiluted, sterling, solid, unalloyed. **2** clean, clear, fresh, sparkling, unpolluted, uncontaminated, untainted. **3** virtuous, moral, good, righteous, honourable, reputable, wholesome, clean, honest, upright, upstanding, exemplary, innocent, chaste, unsullied, undefiled; informal squeaky clean. **4** sheer, utter, absolute, out-and-out, complete, total, perfect.
– OPPOSITES impure, polluted.

purely adv. **entirely**, wholly, exclusively, solely, only, just, merely.

purge v. **1** cleanse, clear, purify, rid, empty, strip, scour. **2** remove, get rid of, eliminate, clear out, sweep out, expel, eject, evict, dismiss, sack, oust, axe, depose, root out, weed out.
•n. **removal**, elimination, expulsion, ejection, exclusion, eviction, dismissal.

purify v. **clean**, cleanse, refine, decontaminate, filter, clear,

freshen, deodorize, sanitize, disinfect, sterilize.

puritanical adj. **moralistic**, puritan, strait-laced, stuffy, prudish, prim, priggish, narrow-minded, censorious, austere, severe, ascetic, abstemious; informal goody-goody, starchy.
– OPPOSITES permissive.

purity n. **1** cleanness, freshness, cleanliness. **2** virtue, morality, goodness, righteousness, piety, honour, honesty, integrity, innocence.

purpose n. **1** motive, motivation, grounds, occasion, reason, point, basis, justification. **2** intention, aim, object, objective, goal, plan, ambition, aspiration. **3** function, role, use. **4** determination, resolution, resolve, steadfastness, single-mindedness, enthusiasm, ambition, motivation, commitment, conviction, dedication.
□ **on purpose** deliberately, intentionally, purposely, wilfully, knowingly, consciously.

purposeful adj. **determined**, resolute, steadfast, single-minded, committed.
– OPPOSITES aimless.

purposely adv. **deliberately**, intentionally, on purpose, wilfully, knowingly, consciously.

purse n. **1** wallet; N. Amer. change purse, billfold. **2** (N. Amer.) handbag, shoulder bag, clutch bag; N. Amer. pocketbook. **3** prize, reward, winnings, stake(s).
•v. **press together**, compress, tighten, pucker, pout.

P

pursue v. **1** follow, run after, chase, hunt, stalk, track, trail, hound. **2** strive for, work towards, seek, search for, aim at/for, aspire to. **3** engage in, be occupied in, practise, follow, conduct, ply, take up, undertake, carry on with, continue, proceed with, apply oneself to.

pursuit n. *a range of leisure pursuits:* activity, hobby, pastime, diversion, recreation, amusement, occupation.

push v. **1** shove, thrust, propel, send, drive, force, prod, poke, nudge, elbow, shoulder, ram, squeeze, jostle. **2** press, depress, hold down, squeeze, operate, activate. **3** urge, press, pressure, pressurize, force, coerce, dragoon, browbeat; informal lean on, twist someone's arm.
– OPPOSITES pull.
• n. **1** shove, thrust, nudge, bump, jolt, prod, poke. **2** *the army's eastward push:* advance, drive, thrust, charge, attack, assault, onslaught, onrush, offensive.

pushy adj. assertive, overbearing, domineering, aggressive, forceful, forward, thrusting, ambitious, overconfident, cocky; informal bossy.

put v. **1** place, set, lay, deposit, position, leave, plant, situate, settle, install; informal stick, dump, park, plonk, pop; N. Amer. informal plunk. **2** express, word, phrase, frame, formulate, render, convey, state.
□ **put across/over** communicate, convey, get across/over,

explain, make clear, spell out.
put off 1 deter, discourage, dissuade, daunt, unnerve, intimidate, scare off; informal turn off. **2** postpone, defer, delay, put back, adjourn, hold over, reschedule, shelve; N. Amer. table; informal put on ice, put on the back burner. **put out 1** annoy, anger, irritate, offend, displease, irk, gall, upset; informal rile, miff. **2** inconvenience, trouble, bother, impose on. **3** extinguish, quench, douse, smother, blow out, snuff out. **4** issue, publish, release, bring out, circulate, publicize, post. **put up 1** accommodate, house, take in, give someone a roof over their head. **2** nominate, propose, put forward, recommend. **3** build, construct, erect, raise. **4** display, pin up, stick up, hang up, post. **5** provide, supply, furnish, give, contribute, donate, pledge, pay; informal cough up, shell out; N. Amer. informal ante up, pony up. **put up with** tolerate, take, stand (for), accept, stomach, swallow, endure, bear; informal abide, lump it; Brit. informal stick; formal brook.

puzzle v. baffle, perplex, bewilder, confuse, mystify, nonplus; informal flummox, stump, beat.
• n. enigma, mystery, paradox, conundrum, poser, riddle, problem.

puzzling adj. baffling, perplexing, bewildering, confusing, complicated, unclear, mysterious, enigmatic.

quaint adj. **1 picturesque**, charming, sweet, attractive, old-fashioned, old-world; Brit. twee. **2 unusual**, curious, eccentric, quirky, bizarre, whimsical, unconventional; informal offbeat.
– OPPOSITES ugly.

quake v. **shake**, tremble, quiver, shudder, sway, rock, wobble, move, heave, convulse.

qualification n. **1 certificate**, diploma, degree, licence, document, warrant. **2 modification**, limitation, reservation, stipulation, alteration, amendment, revision, moderation, mitigation, condition, proviso, caveat.

qualified adj. **1 certified**, certificated, chartered, licensed, professional. **2 limited**, conditional, restricted, contingent, circumscribed, guarded, equivocal, modified, adapted, amended, adjusted, moderated, reduced.
– OPPOSITES wholehearted.

qualify v. **1 be eligible**, meet the requirements, be entitled, be permitted. **2 be certified**, be licensed, pass, graduate, succeed. **3 authorize**, empower, allow, permit, license. **4 modify**, limit, restrict, make conditional, moderate, temper, modulate, mitigate.

quality n. **1 standard**, grade, class, calibre, condition, character, nature, form, rank, value, level. **2 excellence**, superiority, merit, worth, value, virtue, calibre, distinction. **3 feature**, trait, attribute, characteristic, point, aspect, facet, side, property.

quantity n. **amount**, total, aggregate, sum, quota, mass, weight, volume, bulk.

quarrel n. **argument**, disagreement, squabble, fight, dispute, wrangle, clash, altercation, feud, vendetta; Brit. row; informal tiff, slanging match, run-in, spat; Brit. informal bust-up.
– OPPOSITES agreement.
• v. **argue**, fight, disagree, fall out, differ, be at odds, bicker, squabble, cross swords; Brit. row.
– OPPOSITES agree.
◻ **quarrel with** fault, criticize, object to, oppose, take exception to, attack, take issue with, impugn, contradict, dispute, controvert; informal knock.

quarrelsome adj. **argumentative**, disputatious, confrontational, captious, pugnacious, combative, antagonistic, bellicose, belligerent, cantankerous, choleric; Brit. informal stroppy.
– OPPOSITES peaceable.

quarry n. **prey**, victim, object, goal, target, kill, game, prize.

quarter n. **1 district**, area, region, part, side, neighbourhood, precinct, locality, sector, zone, ghetto, community, enclave. **2 source**, direction, place, location. **3** *the servants' quarters:* **accommodation**, lodgings, rooms, chambers, home; informal pad, digs; formal abode, residence, domicile. **4** *riot squads gave no quarter:* **mercy**, leniency, clemency, compassion, pity, charity, sympathy, tolerance.

•v. **accommodate**, house, board, lodge, put up, take in, install, shelter; Military billet.

quash v. **1 cancel**, reverse, rescind, repeal, revoke, retract, countermand, withdraw, overturn, overrule. **2 stop**, put an end to, stamp out, crush, put down, check, curb, nip in the bud, squash, suppress, stifle.

queasy adj. **nauseous**, bilious, sick, ill, unwell, poorly, green about the gills; Brit. off colour.

queen n. **monarch**, sovereign, ruler, head of state, Crown, Her Majesty.

queer adj. **odd**, strange, unusual, funny, peculiar, curious, bizarre, weird, uncanny, freakish, eerie, unnatural, abnormal, anomalous; informal spooky.
– OPPOSITES normal.

quell v. **1 put an end to**, put a stop to, crush, put down, check, crack down on, curb, nip in the bud, squash, quash, subdue, suppress, overcome. **2 calm**, soothe, pacify, settle, quieten, silence, allay, assuage, mitigate, moderate.

query n. **1 question**, enquiry. **2 doubt**, uncertainty, question (mark), reservation.
•v. **1 ask**, enquire, question; Brit. informal quiz. **2 challenge**, question, dispute, doubt, have suspicions about, distrust.
– OPPOSITES accept.

quest n. **1 search**, hunt, pursuance. **2 expedition**, journey, voyage, trek, travels, odyssey, adventure, exploration, search, crusade, mission, pilgrimage.

question n. **1 enquiry**, query, interrogation. **2 doubt**, dispute, argument, debate, uncertainty, reservation. **3 issue**, matter, topic, business, problem, concern, debate, argument, dispute, controversy.
– OPPOSITES answer, certainty.
•v. **1 interrogate**, cross-examine, cross-question, quiz, interview, debrief, examine; informal grill, pump. **2 query**, challenge, dispute, cast aspersions on, doubt, suspect.
□ **out of the question** impossible, impracticable, unfeasible, unworkable, inconceivable, unimaginable, unrealizable, unsuitable; informal not on.

> **WORD LINKS**
> *relating to questions:*
> interrogative

questionable adj. **suspicious**, suspect, dubious, irregular, odd, strange, murky, dark, unsavoury, disreputable; informal funny, fishy, shady, iffy; Brit. informal dodgy.

queue n. row, column, file, chain, string, procession, waiting list; N. Amer. line, wait list.

quick adj. **1** fast, swift, rapid, speedy, brisk, lightning, whirlwind, whistle-stop, breakneck; informal nippy, zippy; literary fleet. **2** hasty, hurried, cursory, perfunctory, desultory, superficial, brief. **3** sudden, instantaneous, instant, immediate, abrupt, precipitate. **4** intelligent, bright, clever, gifted, able, astute, sharp-witted, smart, alert, sharp, perceptive; informal brainy, on the ball.

– OPPOSITES slow, long.

quicken v. **1** speed up, accelerate, step up, hasten, hurry (up). **2** stimulate, excite, arouse, rouse, stir up, activate, whet, inspire, kindle.

quickly adv. **1** fast, swiftly, briskly, rapidly, speedily, at full tilt, at a gallop, at the double, post-haste, hotfoot; informal like (greased) lightning, hell for leather, like blazes, like the wind; Brit. informal like the clappers, like billy-o; N. Amer. informal lickety-split. **2** immediately, directly, at once, straight away, right away, instantly, forthwith; N. Amer. momentarily; informal like a shot, asap, p.d.q., pronto. **3** briefly, fleetingly, briskly, hastily, hurriedly, cursorily, perfunctorily.

quiet adj. **1** silent, still, hushed, noiseless, soundless, mute, dumb, speechless. **2** soft, low, muted, muffled, faint, hushed, whispered, suppressed. **3** peaceful, sleepy, tranquil, calm, still, restful.

– OPPOSITES loud, busy.

· n. silence, still, hush, restfulness, calm, tranquillity, serenity, peace.

quietly adv. **1** silently, noiselessly, soundlessly, inaudibly. **2** softly, faintly, in a low voice, in a whisper, in a murmur, under your breath, in an undertone, sotto voce.

quilt n. duvet, cover(s); Brit. eiderdown; N. Amer. comforter; Austral. trademark Doona.

quirk n. **1** idiosyncrasy, peculiarity, oddity, eccentricity, foible, whim, vagary, habit, characteristic, trait, fad. **2** chance, fluke, freak, anomaly, twist.

quirky adj. eccentric, idiosyncratic, unconventional, unorthodox, unusual, strange, bizarre, peculiar, zany; informal wacky, way-out, offbeat.

– OPPOSITES conventional.

quit v. **1** leave, vacate, exit, depart from. **2** (informal) **resign from**, leave, give up, hand in your notice; informal chuck, pack in. **3** (informal) **give up**, stop, discontinue, drop, abandon, abstain from; informal pack in, leave off.

quite adv. **1** completely, entirely, totally, wholly, absolutely, utterly, thoroughly, altogether. **2** fairly, rather, somewhat, relatively, comparatively, moderately, reasonably; informal pretty.

q

quiz n. **competition**, test of knowledge.
• v. **question**, interrogate, cross-examine, cross-question, interview; informal grill, pump.

quota n. **share**, allocation, allowance, ration, portion, slice, percentage; Brit. informal whack.

quotation n. **1 extract**, quote, citation, excerpt, passage; N. Amer. cite. **2 estimate**, quote, price, tender, bid, costing.

quote v. **1 recite**, repeat, reproduce, retell, echo. **2 mention**, cite, refer to, name, instance, allude to, point out.
• n. see **QUOTATION** 1, 2.

Rr

race¹ n. **1 contest**, competition, event, fixture, heat, trial(s). **2** *the race for naval domination*: **rivalry**, competition, contention, quest.
• v. **1 compete**, contend, run, be pitted against. **2 hurry**, dash, rush, run, sprint, bolt, charge, career, shoot, hurtle, hare, fly, speed, zoom; informal tear, belt.

race² n. **1 ethnic group**, origin, bloodline, stock. **2 people**, nation.

racial adj. **ethnic**, ethnological, race-related, cultural, national, tribal, genetic.

rack n. **frame**, framework, stand, holder, trestle, support, shelf.
• v. **torment**, afflict, torture, agonize, harrow, plague, persecute, trouble, worry.

racket n. **1 noise**, din, hubbub, clamour, uproar, tumult, commotion, rumpus, pandemonium; Brit. row; informal hullabaloo. **2** (informal) **fraud**, swindle,

sharp practice; informal scam, rip-off.

radiant adj. **1 shining**, bright, illuminated, brilliant, gleaming, glowing, ablaze, luminous, lustrous, incandescent, dazzling, shimmering. **2 joyful**, elated, thrilled, overjoyed, jubilant, rapturous, ecstatic, euphoric, in seventh heaven, on cloud nine, delighted, very happy; informal on top of the world, over the moon. – OPPOSITES dark, gloomy.

radiate v. **1 emit**, give off, discharge, diffuse, scatter, shed, cast. **2 shine**, beam, emanate, pour. **3 fan out**, spread out, branch out/off, extend, issue.

radical adj. **1 thorough**, complete, total, comprehensive, exhaustive, sweeping, far-reaching, wide-ranging, extensive, profound, major. **2 fundamental**, basic, deep-seated, essential, structural. **3 revolutionary**, progressive,

reformist, revisionist, progressivist, extreme, fanatical, militant.
– OPPOSITES superficial, minor, conservative.

raffle n. lottery, (prize) draw, sweepstake, sweep, tombola; N. Amer. lotto.

rage n. 1 fury, anger, wrath, outrage, indignation, temper, spleen; formal ire. 2 craze, passion, fashion, taste, trend, vogue, fad, mania; informal thing.
•v. be angry, be furious, be enraged, be incensed, seethe, be beside yourself, rave, storm, fume, spit; informal be livid, be wild, be steamed up.

ragged adj. 1 tattered, torn, ripped, frayed, worn (out), threadbare, scruffy, shabby; informal tatty. 2 jagged, craggy, rugged, uneven, rough, irregular, indented.

raid n. 1 attack, assault, descent, blitz, incursion, sortie, onslaught, storming. 2 robbery, burglary, hold-up, break-in, ram raid; informal smash-and-grab, stick-up; N. Amer. informal heist.
•v. 1 attack, assault, set upon, descend on, swoop on, storm, rush. 2 rob, hold up, break into, plunder, steal from, pillage, loot, ransack; informal stick up.

raider n. robber, burglar, thief, housebreaker, plunderer, pillager, looter, marauder, attacker, assailant, invader.

railing n. fence, fencing, rail's, palisade, balustrade, banister.

rain n. 1 rainfall, precipitation, raindrops, drizzle, mizzle, shower, rainstorm, cloudburst, torrent, downpour, deluge, storm. 2 a rain of hot ash: shower, deluge, flood, torrent, avalanche, flurry, storm, hail.
•v. 1 pour (down), pelt down, tip down, teem down, beat down, lash down, drizzle, spit; informal be chucking it down; Brit. informal bucket down. 2 bombs rained on the city: fall, hail, drop, shower.

> **WORD LINKS**
> relating to rain: pluvial

rainy adj. wet, showery, drizzly, damp, inclement.
– OPPOSITES dry, fine.

rainy adj. wet, showery, drizzly, damp, inclement.
– OPPOSITES dry, fine.

raise v. 1 lift (up), hold aloft, elevate, uplift, hoist, haul up, hitch up; Brit. informal hoick up. 2 increase, put up, push up, up, mark up, inflate; informal hike (up), jack up, bump up. 3 amplify, louden, magnify, intensify, boost, lift, increase. 4 get, obtain, acquire, accumulate, amass, collect, fetch, net, make. 5 bring up, air, present, table, propose, submit, advance, suggest, put forward. 6 give rise to, occasion, cause, produce, engender, elicit, create, result in, lead to, prompt. 7 bring up, rear, nurture, educate.
– OPPOSITES lower, reduce.

rake v. 1 scrape, collect, gather. 2 smooth (out), level, even out, flatten, comb. **3 rummage**, search, hunt, sift, rifle.

rally v. **1 regroup**, reassemble, re-form, reunite, convene, mobilize. **2 recover**, improve, get better, pick up, revive, bounce back, perk up, look up, turn a corner.
• n. **1 (mass) meeting**, gathering, assembly, demonstration, march; informal demo. **2 recovery**, upturn, improvement, comeback, resurgence.

ram v. **1 force**, thrust, plunge, stab, push, sink, dig, stick, cram, jam, stuff. **2 hit**, strike, crash into, collide with, impact, smash into, butt.

ramble v. **1 walk**, hike, tramp, trek, backpack. **2 chatter**, babble, prattle, blather, gabble, jabber, twitter, rattle; Brit. informal witter, chunter, rabbit.

rambling adj. **1 long-winded**, verbose, wordy, prolix, disjointed, disconnected.
2 sprawling, spreading, labyrinthine, maze-like.
– OPPOSITES concise, compact.

ramification n. **consequence**, result, aftermath, outcome, effect, upshot, development, implication.

ramp n. **slope**, bank, incline, gradient, rise, drop.

rampage v. **riot**, run amok, go berserk, storm, charge, tear.
▫ **go on the rampage** riot, go berserk, get out of control, run amok; N. Amer. informal go postal.

rampant adj. **uncontrolled**, unrestrained, unchecked, unbrid-

led, out of control, out of hand, widespread, rife, spreading.
– OPPOSITES controlled.

random adj. **unsystematic**, unmethodical, arbitrary, unplanned, chance, casual, indiscriminate, non-specific, haphazard, stray, erratic, hit-or-miss.
– OPPOSITES systematic.

range n. **1 extent**, limit, reach, span, scope, compass, sweep, area, field, orbit, ambit, horizon, latitude. **2 row**, chain, sierra, ridge, massif. **3 assortment**, variety, diversity, mixture, collection, array, selection, choice.
• v. **1 vary**, fluctuate, differ, extend, stretch, reach, go, run, cover. **2 roam**, wander, travel, journey, rove, traverse, walk, hike, trek.

rank¹ n. **1 position**, level, grade, echelon, class, status, standing. **2 high standing**, blue blood, high birth, nobility, aristocracy. **3 row**, line, file, column, string, train, procession.
• v. **1 classify**, class, categorize, rate, grade, bracket, group, designate, list. **2 line up**, align, order, arrange, dispose, set out, array, range.

rank² adj. **1 abundant**, lush, luxuriant, dense, profuse, vigorous, overgrown; informal jungly. **2 offensive**, nasty, revolting, sickening, obnoxious, foul, fetid, rancid, putrid. **3** rank stupidity: **downright**, utter, out-and-out, absolute, complete, sheer, blatant, arrant, thorough, unqualified.

rankle v. **annoy**, upset, anger, irritate, offend, affront, displease, provoke, irk, vex, pique, nettle, gall; informal rile, miff, peeve, aggravate, hack off; Brit. informal nark; N. Amer. informal tick off.

ransack v. **1 plunder**, pillage, raid, rob, loot, sack, strip, despoil, ravage, devastate. **2 scour**, rifle through, comb, search, turn upside down

ransom n. **pay-off**, payment, sum, price.

rant v. **shout**, sound off, hold forth, go on, fulminate, spout, bluster; informal mouth off.

rap v. **hit**, knock, strike, smack, bang; informal whack, thwack, bash, wallop.

rapid adj. **quick**, fast, swift, speedy, express, expeditious, brisk, lightning, meteoric, whirlwind, sudden, instantaneous, instant, immediate.
– OPPOSITES slow.

rapport n. **affinity**, close relationship, (mutual) understanding, bond, empathy, sympathy, accord.

rare adj. **1 infrequent**, scarce, sparse, few and far between, occasional, limited, isolated, odd, unaccustomed. **2 unusual**, recherché, uncommon, thin on the ground, like gold dust, unfamiliar, atypical. **3 exceptional**, outstanding, unparalleled, peerless, matchless, unique, unrivalled, beyond compare.
– OPPOSITES common, commonplace.

rarely adv. **seldom**, infrequently, hardly (ever), scarcely.
– OPPOSITES often.

raring adj. **eager**, keen, enthusiastic, impatient, longing, desperate; informal dying, itching.

rarity n. **1 infrequency**, scarcity. **2 curiosity**, oddity, collector's item, rare bird, wonder, nonpareil, one of a kind; Brit. informal one-off.

rash[1] n. **1 spots**, eruption, nettlerash, hives. **2** *a rash of articles in the press*: **series**, succession, spate, wave, flood, deluge, torrent, outbreak, epidemic, flurry.

rash[2] adj. **reckless**, impulsive, impetuous, hot-headed, daredevil, madcap, hasty, foolhardy, incautious, precipitate, careless, heedless, thoughtless, unthinking, imprudent, foolish.
– OPPOSITES prudent.

rate n. **1 percentage**, ratio, proportion, scale, standard. **2 charge**, price, cost, tariff, fare, fee, remuneration, payment. **3 speed**, pace, tempo, velocity.
• v. **1 assess**, evaluate, appraise, judge, weigh up, estimate, gauge. **2 merit**, deserve, warrant, be worthy of.

rather adv. **1 sooner**, by preference, by choice, more readily. **2 quite**, a bit, a little, fairly, slightly, somewhat, relatively, comparatively; informal pretty.

ratify v. **confirm**, approve, sanction, endorse, agree to, accept, uphold, authorize, formalize, sign.

r

rating n. grade, classification, ranking, position, category, assessment, evaluation, mark, score.

ratio n. proportion, relationship, rate, percentage, fraction, correlation.

ration n. 1 allowance, allocation, quota, share, portion, helping. 2 *the garrison ran out of rations:* **supplies**, provisions, food, stores.
▸v. control, limit, restrict, conserve.

rational adj. logical, reasoned, sensible, reasonable, realistic, cogent, intelligent, shrewd, common-sense, sane, sound.

rationale n. reason(s), thinking, logic, grounds, sense.

rationalize v. 1 justify, explain (away), account for, defend, vindicate, excuse. 2 streamline, reorganize, modernize, update, trim, hone, simplify, downsize, prune.

rattle v. 1 clatter, clank, knock, clunk, clink, jangle, tinkle. 2 unnerve, disconcert, disturb, fluster, shake, perturb, throw, discomfit; informal faze.

raucous adj. 1 harsh, strident, screeching, piercing, shrill, grating, discordant, dissonant, noisy, loud, cacophonous. 2 rowdy, noisy, boisterous, roisterous, wild.
– OPPOSITES soft, quiet.

ravage v. lay waste, devastate, ruin, destroy, wreak havoc on.

rave v. 1 rant, rage, lose your temper, storm, fume, shout; informal fly off the handle, hit the roof; Brit. informal go spare; N. Amer. informal flip your wig. 2 enthuse, go into raptures, wax lyrical, rhapsodize, sing the praises of, acclaim, eulogize, extol; informal ballyhoo.
– OPPOSITES criticize.

raw adj. 1 uncooked, fresh, natural. 2 unprocessed, untreated, unrefined, crude, natural. 3 inexperienced, new, untrained, untried, untested, callow, green; informal wet behind the ears. 4 sore, red, painful, tender, chafed.
– OPPOSITES cooked, processed.

ray n. beam, shaft, stream, streak, flash, glimmer, flicker, spark.

raze v. destroy, demolish, tear down, pull down, knock down, level, flatten, bulldoze, wipe out, lay waste.

reach v. 1 extend, stretch, outstretch, thrust, stick, hold. 2 arrive at, get to, come to, end up at. 3 *the temperature reached 75°:* attain, get to, rise to, fall to, sink to, drop to; informal hit. 4 *ministers reached an agreement:* achieve, work out, draw up, put together, negotiate, thrash out, hammer out. 5 contact, get in touch with, get through to, get, speak to; informal get hold of.
▸n. 1 grasp, range, stretch, capabilities, capacity. 2 jurisdiction, authority, influence, power, scope, range, compass, ambit.

react v. **respond**, act in response, reply, answer, behave.

reaction n. **1 response**, answer, reply, rejoinder, retort, riposte; informal comeback. **2 backlash**, counteraction.

reactionary adj. **right-wing**, conservative, traditionalist, conventional, diehard.
– OPPOSITES radical, progressive.

read v. **1 peruse**, study, scrutinize, look through, pore over, run your eye over, cast an eye over, leaf through, scan. **2 understand**, make out, make sense of, decipher, interpret, construe. **3 register**, record, display, show, indicate.

> WORD LINKS
> *ability to read:* literacy;
> *inability to read:* illiteracy

readable adj. **1 legible**, decipherable, clear, intelligible, comprehensible. **2 enjoyable**, entertaining, interesting, absorbing, gripping, enthralling, engrossing; informal unputdownable.
– OPPOSITES illegible.

readily adv. **1 willingly**, unhesitatingly, ungrudgingly, gladly, happily, eagerly. **2 easily**, without difficulty.

readiness n. **willingness**, eagerness, keenness, enthusiasm, alacrity.
□ **in readiness** (at the) ready, prepared, available, on hand, accessible, handy.

reading n. **1 perusal**, study, scanning. **2 learning**, scholarship, education, erudition. **3 recital**, recitation, performance. **4 lesson**, passage, excerpt. **5 interpretation**, understanding, explanation, analysis, construction.

ready adj. **1 prepared**, equipped, all set, organized, primed; informal fit, psyched up, geared up. **2 completed**, finished, prepared, organized, arranged, done, fixed. **3** *he's always ready to help:* **willing**, prepared, pleased, inclined, disposed, eager, keen, happy, glad; informal game. **4** *a ready supply of food:* **(easily) available**, accessible, handy, close/near at hand, to/on hand, convenient, within reach, near, at your fingertips; informal on tap. **5** *a ready answer:* **prompt**, quick, swift, speedy, fast, immediate, unhesitating.
• v. **prepare**, organize, gear up; informal psych up.

real adj. **1 actual**, true, factual, non-fictional, historical, material, physical, tangible, concrete. **2 genuine**, authentic, bona fide, proper, true; informal pukka, kosher. **3 sincere**, genuine, true, unfeigned, heartfelt. **4 complete**, utter, thorough, absolute, total, prize, perfect; Brit. informal right, proper.
– OPPOSITES imaginary, false.

realism n. **1 pragmatism**, practicality, common sense, level-headedness. **2 authenticity**, accuracy, fidelity, truthfulness, verisimilitude.

r

realistic adj. **1 practical**, pragmatic, matter-of-fact, down-to-earth, sensible, commonsensical, rational, level-headed; informal no-nonsense. **2 achievable**, attainable, feasible, practicable, reasonable, sensible, workable; informal doable.
3 authentic, accurate, true to life, lifelike, truthful, faithful, natural, naturalistic.
– OPPOSITES unrealistic.

reality n. **1 the real world**, real life, actuality, corporeality.
2 fact, actuality, truth.
3 authenticity, verisimilitude, fidelity, truthfulness, accuracy.
– OPPOSITES fantasy.

realization n. **1 awareness**, understanding, comprehension, consciousness, appreciation, recognition, discernment.
2 fulfilment, achievement, accomplishment, attainment.

realize v. **1 register**, perceive, understand, grasp, comprehend, see, recognize, take in; informal tumble to; Brit. informal twig. **2 fulfil**, achieve, accomplish, make happen, bring to fruition, bring about/off, actualize. **3 make**, clear, gain, earn, return, produce. **4 be sold for**, fetch, go for, make, net.

really adv. **1 in (actual) fact**, actually, in reality, in truth.
2 genuinely, truly, certainly, honestly, undoubtedly, unquestionably.

realm n. **1 kingdom**, country, land, state, nation, territory, dominion, empire, monarchy, principality. **2 the realm of academia**: **domain**, sphere, area, field, world, province.

reap v. **1 harvest**, cut, pick, gather, garner. **2 receive**, obtain, get, derive, acquire, secure, realize.

rear[1] n. **back (part)**, hind part, end, tail (end), back (end); Nautical stern.
•adj. **back**, end, rearmost, hind, last.
– OPPOSITES front.

rear[2] v. **1 bring up**, care for, look after, nurture, parent; N. Amer. raise. **2 breed**, raise, keep, grow, cultivate. **3 houses reared up on either side**: **rise**, tower, soar, loom.

reason n. **1 cause**, ground(s), basis, rationale, motive, explanation, justification, defence, vindication, excuse, apologia. **2 rationality**, logic, cognition, reasoning, intellect, thought, understanding; formal ratiocination. **3 sanity**, mind, mental faculties, senses, wits; informal marbles.
•v. **calculate**, conclude, reckon, think, judge, deduce, infer, surmise; informal figure.
◻ **reason out** work out, think through, make sense of, get to the bottom of, puzzle out; informal figure out. **reason with** talk round, bring round, persuade, prevail on, convince.

┌─────────────────────────┐
│ WORD LINKS   │
│ *relating to reason:* rational │
└─────────────────────────┘

reasonable adj. **1** sensible, rational, logical, fair, just, equitable, intelligent, wise, level-headed, practical, realistic, sound, valid, commonsensical, tenable, plausible, credible, believable. **2** practicable, sensible, appropriate, suitable. **3 fairly good**, acceptable, satisfactory, average, adequate, fair, tolerable, passable; informal OK. **4 inexpensive**, affordable, moderate, low, cheap, within your means.

reassure v. **put someone's mind at rest**, encourage, hearten, buoy up, cheer up, comfort, soothe.
– OPPOSITES alarm.

rebate n. **partial refund**, partial repayment, discount, deduction, reduction.

rebel n. **1 revolutionary**, insurgent, insurrectionist, mutineer, guerrilla, terrorist, freedom fighter. **2 nonconformist**, dissenter, dissident, maverick.
– OPPOSITES loyalist, conformist.
•v. **revolt**, mutiny, riot, rise up, take up arms.
•adj. **1 rebellious**, insurgent, revolutionary, mutinous. **2 defiant**, disobedient, insubordinate, subversive, rebellious, nonconformist, maverick.
– OPPOSITES loyal, obedient.
□ **rebel against** defy, disobey, kick against, challenge, oppose, resist.

rebellion n. **1 revolt**, uprising, insurrection, mutiny, revolution, insurgence. **2 defiance**, dis-

obedience, insubordination, subversion, resistance.
– OPPOSITES compliance.

rebellious adj. **1 rebel**, insurgent, mutinous, revolutionary. **2 defiant**, disobedient, insubordinate, unruly, mutinous, obstreperous, recalcitrant, intractable; Brit. informal bolshie.
– OPPOSITES loyal, obedient.

rebound v. **1 bounce (back)**, spring back, ricochet, boomerang. **2 backfire**, misfire, come back on.

rebuff v. **reject**, turn down, spurn, refuse, decline, snub, slight, dismiss, brush off.
– OPPOSITES accept.
•n. **rejection**, snub, slight, refusal, spurning; informal brush-off, kick in the teeth, slap in the face.

rebuke v. **reprimand**, reproach, scold, admonish, reprove, chastise, upbraid, berate, take to task; informal tell off; Brit. informal tick off; N. Amer. informal chew out; formal castigate.
•n. **reprimand**, reproach, scolding, admonition; informal telling-off, dressing-down; Brit. informal ticking-off.
– OPPOSITES praise.

recalcitrant adj. **uncooperative**, intractable, insubordinate, defiant, rebellious, wilful, wayward, headstrong, self-willed, contrary, perverse, difficult, awkward; Brit. informal bloody-minded, bolshie, stroppy; formal refractory.
– OPPOSITES amenable.

r

recall v. **1 remember**, recollect, call to mind, think back on/to, reminisce about. **2 remind someone of**, bring to mind, call up, conjure up, evoke. **3 call back**, order home, withdraw.
– OPPOSITES forget.
•n. **recollection**, remembrance, memory.

recede v. **1 retreat**, go back/down/away, withdraw, ebb, subside. **2 diminish**, lessen, dwindle, fade, abate, subside.
– OPPOSITES advance, grow.

receive v. **1 be given**, be presented with, be awarded, be sent, be in receipt of, get, obtain, gain, acquire, be paid. **2 hear**, listen to, respond to, react to. **3 experience**, sustain, undergo, meet with, suffer, bear.
– OPPOSITES give, send.

recent adj. **new**, the latest, current, fresh, modern, late, contemporary, up to date, up to the minute.
– OPPOSITES old.

recently adv. **not long ago**, a little while back, just now, newly, freshly, of late, lately, latterly.

reception n. **1 response**, reaction, treatment. **2 party**, function, social occasion, celebration, get-together, gathering, soirée; N. Amer. levee; informal do.

receptive adj. **open-minded**, responsive, amenable, well disposed, flexible, approachable, accessible.
– OPPOSITES unresponsive.

recess n. **1 alcove**, bay, niche, nook, corner. **2 break**, adjournment, interlude, interval, rest, holiday, vacation.

recession n. **downturn**, depression, slump, slowdown.
– OPPOSITES boom.

recipe n. *a recipe for success:* **formula**, prescription, blueprint.

reciprocal adj. **mutual**, common, shared, give-and-take, joint, corresponding, complementary.

reciprocate v. **requite**, return, give back.

recital n. **1 performance**, concert, recitation, reading. **2 report**, account, listing, catalogue, litany.

recite v. **1 quote**, say, speak, read aloud, declaim, deliver, render. **2 recount**, list, detail, reel off, relate, enumerate.

reckless adj. **rash**, careless, thoughtless, heedless, precipitate, impetuous, impulsive, irresponsible, foolhardy, devil-may-care.
– OPPOSITES cautious.

reckon v. **1 calculate**, compute, work out, figure, count (up), add up, total, tally; Brit. tot up. **2 include**, count, regard as, look on as, consider, judge, think of as, deem, rate. **3 think**, believe, be of the opinion, suppose, assume. □ **reckon on/with** take into account, take into consideration, bargain for/on, anticipate, foresee, be prepared for, consider.

r

reckoning n. **calculation**, estimation, computation, working out, addition, count.

reclaim v. **1 get back**, claim back, recover, retrieve, recoup. **2 save**, rescue, redeem, salvage.

recline v. **lie**, lie down/back, lean back, relax, loll, lounge, sprawl, stretch out.

recluse n. **hermit**, ascetic, eremite, loner, lone wolf; *historical* anchorite.

recognition n. **1 identification**, recollection, remembrance. **2 acknowledgement**, acceptance, admission, confession. **3 appreciation**, gratitude, thanks, congratulations, credit, commendation, acclaim, acknowledgement.

recognize v. **1 identify**, place, know, put a name to, remember, recall, recollect; *Scottish & N. English* ken. **2 acknowledge**, accept, admit, concede, confess, realize. **3 pay tribute to**, appreciate, be grateful for, acclaim, commend.

recoil v. **1 draw back**, jump back, pull back, flinch, shy away, shrink (back), blench. **2 feel revulsion**, feel disgust, shrink from, wince at.

recollect v. **remember**, recall, call to mind, think of, think back to, reminisce about.
– OPPOSITES forget.

recollection n. **memory**, recall, remembrance, impression, reminiscence.

recommend v. **1 advocate**, endorse, commend, suggest, put

forward, propose, nominate, put up, speak favourably of, put in a good word for, vouch for; *informal* plug. **2 advise**, counsel, urge, exhort, enjoin, prescribe, argue for, back, support.

recommendation n. **1 advice**, counsel, guidance, suggestion, proposal. **2 commendation**, endorsement, good word, testimonial, tip; *informal* plug.

reconcile v. **1 reunite**, bring (back) together, pacify, appease, placate, mollify; *formal* conciliate. **2** *reconciling his religious beliefs with his career:* **make compatible**, harmonize, square, make congruent, balance. **3 settle**, resolve, sort out, smooth over, iron out, mend, remedy, heal, rectify; *informal* patch up. **4** *they had to reconcile themselves to drastic losses:* **accept**, resign yourself to, come to terms with, learn to live with, get used to, make the best of.

reconnoitre v. **survey**, explore, scout (out), find out the lie of the land, investigate, examine, scrutinize, inspect, observe, take a look at, patrol; *informal* recce, check out.

reconsider v. **rethink**, review, revise, re-evaluate, reassess, have second thoughts, change your mind.

reconstruct v. **rebuild**, remake, recreate, restore, reassemble, remodel, revamp, renovate.

record n. **1 account**, document, data, file, dossier, evidence, report, annals, archive, chronicle,

minutes, transactions, proceedings, transcript, certificate, deed, register, log. **2 disc**, recording, album, LP, single.
•v. **1 write down**, take down, note, jot down, put down on paper, document, enter, log, minute, register. **2 indicate**, register, show, display. **3 film**, photograph, tape, tape-record, video-record, videotape.

recount v. **tell**, relate, narrate, describe, report, relay, convey, communicate, impart.

recover v. **1 get better**, improve, rally, recuperate, convalesce, revive, be on the mend, get back on your feet, pick up, heal, bounce back, pull through. **2 retrieve**, regain, get back, recoup, reclaim, repossess, recapture. **3 salvage**, save, rescue, retrieve.
– OPPOSITES deteriorate.

recovery n. **1 improvement**, recuperation, convalescence, rally, revival. **2 retrieval**, repossession, reclamation, recapture.
– OPPOSITES relapse.

recreation n. **1 pleasure**, leisure, relaxation, fun, enjoyment, entertainment, amusement, diversion. **2 pastime**, hobby, leisure activity.
– OPPOSITES work.

recruit v. **1 enlist**, call up, conscript; US draft. **2 muster**, form, raise, mobilize. **3 hire**, employ, take on, enrol, sign up, engage.
– OPPOSITES demobilize.
•n. **1 conscript**; US draftee; N. Amer. informal yardbird. **2 new-**

comer, trainee, initiate, joiner, beginner, novice.

rectify v. **correct**, (put) right, sort out, deal with, amend, remedy, repair, fix, make good, resolve, settle; informal patch up.

recur v. **happen again**, reoccur, repeat (itself), come back, return, reappear.

recycle v. **reuse**, reprocess, reclaim, recover, salvage.

red adj. **1 scarlet**, vermilion, ruby, cherry, cerise, cardinal, carmine, crimson, maroon, magenta, burgundy, claret. **2 flushed**, blushing, pink, rosy, florid, ruddy. **3 auburn**, Titian, chestnut, carroty, ginger.

redeem v. **1 save**, deliver from sin, absolve. **2 retrieve**, regain, recover, get back, reclaim, repossess, buy back. **3 exchange**, convert, trade in, cash in.

redolent adj. **evocative**, suggestive, reminiscent.

redress v. **rectify**, correct, right, compensate for, make amends for, remedy, make good.
•n. **compensation**, reparation, restitution, recompense, repayment, amends.

reduce v. **1 lessen**, make smaller, lower, decrease, diminish, minimize, shrink, narrow, cut, curtail, contract, shorten, downsize; informal chop. **2 bring down**, make cheaper, lower, mark down, slash, discount. **3 he reduced her to tears**: **bring to**, bring to the point of, drive to.
– OPPOSITES increase.

reduction n. **1 lessening**, lowering, decrease, diminution, cut, cutback, downsizing. **2 discount**, deduction, cut.

redundancy n. **dismissal**, lay-off, sacking, discharge, unemployment.

redundant adj. **unnecessary**, not required, unneeded, surplus (to requirements), superfluous. □ **make redundant** dismiss, lay off, discharge, give someone their notice; informal sack, fire.

reel v. **1 stagger**, lurch, sway, rock, stumble, totter, wobble, teeter. **2 go round (and round)**, whirl, spin, revolve, swirl, twirl, turn, swim.

refer v. **pass**, direct, hand on/ over, send on, transfer, entrust, assign. □ **refer to 1** mention, allude to, touch on, speak of/about, talk of/about, write about, comment on, point out, call attention to. **2** apply to, relate to, pertain to, be relevant to, concern, be connected with. **3** consult, turn to, look at, have recourse to.

referee n. **umpire**, judge, adjudicator, arbitrator; informal ref.

reference n. **1 mention**, allusion, quotation, comment, remark. **2 source**, citation, authority, credit. **3 testimonial**, recommendation, character reference, credentials.

referendum n. **(popular) vote**, ballot, poll, plebiscite.

refine v. **1 purify**, filter, distil, process, treat. **2 improve**,
perfect, polish (up), hone, fine-tune.

refined adj. **1 purified**, processed, treated. **2 cultivated**, cultured, polished, elegant, sophisticated, urbane, polite, gracious, well bred. **3 discriminating**, discerning, fastidious, exquisite, impeccable, fine.
– OPPOSITES crude, coarse.

reflect v. **1 mirror**, send back, throw back, echo. **2 indicate**, show, display, demonstrate, be evidence of, evince, reveal, betray. **3 think**, consider, review, mull over, ponder, contemplate, deliberate, ruminate, meditate, muse, brood; formal cogitate.

reflection n. **1 image**, likeness. **2 indication**, display, demonstration, manifestation, expression, evidence. **3 thought**, consideration, contemplation, deliberation, pondering, rumination, meditation, musing; formal cogitation.

reform v. **1 improve**, better, ameliorate, correct, rectify, restore, revise, refine, revamp, adapt, redesign, reconstruct, reorganize. **2 mend your ways**, change for the better, turn over a new leaf.
• n. **improvement**, amelioration, refinement, rectification, restoration, adaptation, revision, redesign, revamp, reconstruction, reorganization.

refrain v. **abstain**, desist, hold back, stop yourself, forbear, avoid; informal swear off.

r

refresh v. **1 reinvigorate**, revitalize, revive, rejuvenate, restore, energize, enliven, perk up, brace, freshen, wake up, breathe new life into; informal buck up. **2** refresh your memory: **jog**, stimulate, prompt, prod.

refreshing adj. **1 invigorating**, revitalizing, reviving, bracing, fortifying, enlivening, stimulating, exhilarating, energizing. **2** a refreshing change of direction: **welcome**, stimulating, fresh, new, imaginative, innovative.

refreshment n. **food and drink**, snacks, titbits; informal nibbles.

refuge n. **1 shelter**, protection, safety, security, asylum, sanctuary. **2 place of safety**, shelter, haven, sanctuary, sanctum, retreat, bolt-hole, hiding place.

refugee n. **asylum seeker**, fugitive, displaced person, exile, émigré.

refund v. **repay**, give back, return, pay back, reimburse, compensate, recompense.
‣ n. **repayment**, reimbursement, compensation, rebate.

refurbish v. **renovate**, recondition, rehabilitate, revamp, overhaul, restore, redecorate, upgrade, refit; informal do up.

refusal n. **non-acceptance**, no, rejection, rebuff; informal knockback, thumbs down.

refuse[1] v. **1 decline**, turn down, say no to, reject, spurn, rebuff; informal pass up, knock back. **2 withhold**, deny.
– OPPOSITES accept.

refuse[2] n. **rubbish**, waste, litter; N. Amer. garbage, trash; informal dreck, junk.

refute v. **1 disprove**, prove wrong, rebut, explode, debunk, discredit, invalidate; informal shoot full of holes. **2 deny**, reject, repudiate, rebut, contradict.

regain v. **recover**, get back, win back, recoup, retrieve, repossess, take back, retake, recapture, reconquer.

regal adj. **royal**, kingly, queenly, princely, majestic.

regard v. **1 consider**, look on, view, see, think of, judge, deem, estimate, assess, reckon, rate. **2 look at**, contemplate, eye, gaze at, stare at, observe, view, study, scrutinize.
‣ n. **1 consideration**, heed, care, concern, thought, notice, attention. **2** doctors are held in high regard: **esteem**, respect, admiration, approval, honour, estimation. **3** (fixed) **look**, gaze, stare, observation, contemplation, study, scrutiny. **4** he sends his regards: **best wishes**, greetings, respects, compliments.

regarding prep. **concerning**, as regards, with/in regard to, with respect to, with reference to, relating to, respecting, re, about, apropos, on the subject of, in connection with, vis-à-vis.

regardless adv. **anyway**, anyhow, in any case, nevertheless, nonetheless, despite everything, even so, all the same, in any event, come what may.

□ **regardless of** irrespective of, without reference to, without consideration of, discounting, ignoring, notwithstanding, no matter.

regime n. **1 government**, administration, leadership, rule, authority, control, command. **2 system**, arrangement, scheme, policy, method, course, plan, programme.

region n. **district**, province, territory, division, area, section, sector, zone, belt, quarter.

regional adj. **1 geographical**, territorial. **2 local**, provincial, district, parochial, zonal.
– OPPOSITES national.

register n. **1 list**, roll, roster, index, directory, catalogue, inventory. **2 record**, chronicle, log, ledger, archive, annals, files.
•v. **1 record**, enter, file, lodge, write down, submit, report, note, minute, log. **2 enrol**, put your name down, enlist, sign on/up, apply. **3 indicate**, read, record, show. **4 display**, show, express, exhibit, betray, reveal.

regret v. **1 be sorry about**, feel contrite about, feel remorse for, rue, repent of. **2 mourn**, grieve for/over, weep over, sigh over, lament, bemoan.
– OPPOSITES welcome.
•n. **1 remorse**, contrition, repentance, compunction, ruefulness, self-reproach, pangs of conscience. **2 sadness**, sorrow, disappointment, unhappiness, grief.

regrettable adj. **unfortunate**, unwelcome, sorry, woeful, disappointing, reprehensible, deplorable, disgraceful.

regular adj. **1 uniform**, even, consistent, constant, unchanging, unvarying, fixed. **2 frequent**, repeated, continual, recurrent, periodic, constant, perpetual, numerous. **3 usual**, normal, customary, habitual, routine, typical, accustomed, established.
– OPPOSITES erratic, occasional, unusual.

regulate v. **1 control**, adjust, balance, set, synchronize. **2 police**, supervise, monitor, be responsible for, control, manage, direct, govern.

regulation n. **1 rule**, order, directive, act, law, by-law, statute, dictate, decree. **2 control**, policing, supervision, superintendence, monitoring, governance, management, administration, responsibility.

rehabilitate v. **1 reintegrate**, readapt; N. Amer. informal rehab. **2 reinstate**, restore, bring back, pardon, absolve, exonerate, forgive; formal exculpate. **3 recondition**, restore, renovate, refurbish, revamp, overhaul, redevelop, rebuild, reconstruct.

rehearsal n. **practice**, trial performance, read-through, run-through, drill, training, coaching; informal dry run.

rehearse v. **1 prepare**, practise, read through, run through/over, go over. **2 train**, drill, prepare,

r

coach. **3** list, enumerate, itemize, detail, spell out, catalogue, recite, repeat, go over, run through, recap.

reign v. **1** be king/queen, sit on the throne, wear the crown, be supreme, rule. **2** *chaos reigned:* prevail, exist, be present, be the case, occur, be rife, be rampant, be the order of the day.
•n. **rule**, sovereignty, monarchy, dominion, control.

rein v. **restrain**, check, curb, constrain, hold back/in, keep under control, regulate, restrict, control, curtail, limit.
□ **free rein** freedom, a free hand, leeway, latitude, flexibility, liberty, independence, licence, room to manoeuvre, carte blanche. **keep a tight rein on** regulate, discipline, control, keep in line.

reinforce v. **1** strengthen, fortify, bolster up, shore up, buttress, prop up, underpin, brace, support, boost. **2** augment, increase, add to, supplement, boost, top up.

reinforcement n. **1** strengthening, fortification, bolstering, shoring up, buttressing. **2** *we need reinforcements:* **additional troops**, auxiliaries, reserves, support, backup, help.

reinstate v. **restore**, put back, bring back, reinstitute, reinstall, re-establish.

reiterate v. **repeat**, restate, recapitulate, recap, go over, rehearse.

reject v. **1** turn down, refuse, decline, say no to, spurn; *informal* pass up, give the thumbs down to. **2** rebuff, spurn, shun, snub, cast off/aside, discard, abandon, desert, turn your back on, cold-shoulder; *informal* give someone the brush-off.
– OPPOSITES accept, welcome.
•n. **second**, discard, misshape, faulty item, cast-off.

rejoice v. be happy, be glad, be delighted, celebrate, make merry; *informal* be over the moon.
– OPPOSITES mourn.
□ **rejoice in** delight in, enjoy, revel in, glory in, relish, savour.

rejoin v. **return to**, be reunited with, join again, reach again, regain.

rejuvenate v. **revive**, revitalize, regenerate, breathe new life into, revivify, reanimate, resuscitate, refresh, reawaken; *informal* give a shot in the arm to, pep up, buck up.

relapse v. **deteriorate**, degenerate, lapse, slip back, slide back, regress, revert, retrogress.
– OPPOSITES improve.

relate v. **tell**, recount, narrate, report, describe, recite, rehearse.
□ **relate to 1** connect with, associate with, link with, ally with, couple with. **2** apply to, concern, pertain to, have a bearing on, involve. **3** identify with, get on (well) with, feel sympathy with, have a rapport wit, empathize with, understand; *informal* hit it off with.

related adj. connected, interconnected, associated, linked, allied, corresponding, analogous, parallel, comparable, equivalent.

relation n. **1 connection**, relationship, association, link, tie-in, correlation, correspondence, parallel. **2 relative**, family member, kinsman, kinswoman; (**relations**) family, kin, kith and kin, kindred. **3** *our relations with Europe*: **dealings**, communication, relationship, connections, contact, interaction.

relationship n. **1 connection**, relation, association, link, correlation, correspondence, parallel. **2 family ties**, kinship, affinity, common ancestry. **3 romance**, affair, love affair, liaison, amour, fling.

relative adj. **1 comparative**, respective, comparable. **2 proportionate**, in proportion, commensurate, corresponding.
– OPPOSITES disproportionate.
•n. **relation**, member of the family, kinsman, kinswoman; (**relatives**) family, kin, kith and kin, kindred.

relax v. **1 rest**, loosen up, ease up/off, slow down, de-stress, unbend, unwind, put your feet up, take it easy; informal chill out; N. Amer. informal hang loose, decompress. **2 loosen**, slacken, unclench, weaken, lessen. **3 moderate**, temper, ease, loosen, lighten, dilute, weaken, reduce, decrease; informal let up on.
– OPPOSITES tense, tighten.

relaxation n. **recreation**, enjoyment, amusement, entertainment, fun, pleasure, leisure.

relay n. **broadcast**, transmission, showing, feed.
•v. **pass on**, hand on, transfer, repeat, communicate, send, transmit, circulate.

release v. **1 free**, set free, turn loose, let go/out, liberate, discharge. **2 untie**, undo, unfasten, loose, let go, unleash. **3 make public**, make known, issue, put out, publish, broadcast, circulate, launch, distribute.
– OPPOSITES imprison.

relegate v. **downgrade**, demote, lower, put down, move down.
– OPPOSITES upgrade, promote.

relent v. **1 change your mind**, do a U-turn, back-pedal, back down, give way/in, capitulate; Brit. do an about-turn. **2 ease**, slacken, let up, abate, drop, die down, lessen, decrease, subside, weaken, tail off.

relentless adj. **1 persistent**, unfaltering, unremitting, unflagging, untiring, unwavering, dogged, single-minded, tireless, indefatigable. **2 harsh**, cruel, remorseless, unrelenting, merciless, pitiless, implacable, inexorable, unforgiving, unbending, unyielding.

relevant adj. **pertinent**, applicable, apposite, material, apropos, to the point, germane.

reliable adj. **dependable**, trustworthy, good, safe, authentic,

r

faithful, genuine, sound, true, loyal, unfailing; *humorous* trusty.
– OPPOSITES unreliable.

reliance n. **1 dependence**, need. **2 trust**, confidence, faith, belief, conviction.

relic n. **artefact**, historical object, antiquity, remnant, vestige, remains.

relief n. **1 respite**, remission, interruption, variation, diversion; *informal* let-up. **2 alleviation**, relieving, palliation, soothing, easing, lessening, mitigation. **3 help**, aid, assistance, charity, succour. **4 replacement**, substitute, deputy, reserve, cover, stand-in, supply, locum, understudy.

relieve v. **1 alleviate**, mitigate, ease, counteract, dull, reduce. **2 replace**, take over from, stand in for, fill in for, substitute for, deputize for, cover for. **3 free**, release, exempt, excuse, absolve, let off.
– OPPOSITES aggravate.

relieved adj. **glad**, thankful, grateful, pleased, happy, easy/easier in your mind, reassured.
– OPPOSITES worried.

religion n. **faith**, belief, worship, creed, church, sect, denomination, cult.

> WORD LINKS
> *study of religion:* divinity, theology

religious adj. **1 devout**, pious, reverent, godly, God-fearing, churchgoing. **2 spiritual**, theological, scriptural, doctrinal,

ecclesiastical, church, holy, divine, sacred. **3 scrupulous**, conscientious, meticulous, punctilious, strict, rigorous.
– OPPOSITES atheistic, secular.

relinquish v. **1 renounce**, resign, give up/away, hand over, let go of. **2 leave**, resign from, stand down from, bow out of, give up; *informal* quit, chuck.
– OPPOSITES retain.

relish n. **1 enjoyment**, gusto, delight, pleasure, glee, appreciation, enthusiasm. **2 condiment**, sauce, dressing.
– OPPOSITES distaste.
•v. **enjoy**, delight in, love, adore, take pleasure in, rejoice in, appreciate, savour, revel in, luxuriate in, glory in.
– OPPOSITES dislike.

reluctance n. **unwillingness**, disinclination, hesitation, wavering, vacillation, doubts, second thoughts, misgivings.

reluctant adj. **unwilling**, disinclined, unenthusiastic, resistant, opposed, hesitant, loath.
– OPPOSITES willing, eager.

rely v.
□ **rely on** depend on, count on, bank on, be dependent on, be sure of, have faith in, trust in; *informal* swear by; *N. Amer. informal* figure on.

remain v. **1 continue**, endure, last, abide, carry on, persist, stay around, survive, live on. **2 stay**, stay behind, stay put, wait behind, be left, hang on; *informal* hang around/round. **3 he**

remained calm: **continue to be,** stay, keep.

remainder n. rest, balance, residue, others, remnant(s), leftovers, surplus, extra, excess.

remains pl. n. **1** remainder, residue, rest, remnant(s), leftovers, scraps, debris, detritus. **2** antiquities, relics, artefacts. **3** corpse, body, carcass, bones; Medicine cadaver.

remark v. **comment,** say, observe, mention, reflect; formal opine.
•n. **comment,** statement, utterance, observation, reflection.

remarkable adj. **extraordinary,** exceptional, outstanding, notable, striking, memorable, unusual, conspicuous, momentous.
– OPPOSITES ordinary.

remedy n. **1 treatment,** cure, medicine, medication, medicament, drug. **2 solution,** answer, cure, fix, antidote, panacea.
•v. **put right,** set right, rectify, solve, sort out, straighten out, resolve, correct, repair, mend, fix.

remember v. **1 recall,** call to mind, recollect, think of, reminisce about, look back on. **2 memorize,** retain, learn off by heart, get off pat. **3 bear in mind,** be mindful of, take into account. **4 commemorate,** pay tribute to, honour, salute, pay homage to.
– OPPOSITES forget.

remembrance n. **1 recollection,** reminiscence, recall. **2 commemoration,** memory, recognition.

remind v. **jog someone's memory,** prompt.
□ **remind someone of** make someone think of, cause someone to remember, put someone in mind of, call to mind, evoke.

reminiscent adj. **similar to,** comparable with, evocative of, suggestive of, redolent of.

remiss adj. **negligent,** neglectful, irresponsible, careless, thoughtless, heedless, lax, slack, slipshod, lackadaisical; N. Amer. derelict; informal sloppy.
– OPPOSITES careful.

remit n. **area of responsibility,** sphere, orbit, scope, ambit, province, brief, instructions, orders; informal bailiwick.
•v. **1 send,** dispatch, forward, hand over, pay. **2 pardon,** forgive, excuse.

remnant n. **remains,** remainder, leftovers, offcut, residue, rest.

remonstrate v. **protest,** complain, object, take issue, argue, expostulate.

remorse n. **regret,** guilt, contrition, repentance, shame.

remorseful adj. **sorry,** regretful, contrite, repentant, penitent, guilt-ridden, conscience-stricken, chastened, self-reproachful.
– OPPOSITES unrepentant.

remote adj. **1 isolated,** far-off, faraway, distant, out of the way,

off the beaten track, secluded, lonely, inaccessible; N. Amer. in the backwoods; informal in the middle of nowhere. **2** *a remote possibility:* **unlikely**, improbable, doubtful, dubious, faint, slight, slim, small, slender. **3 aloof**, distant, detached, withdrawn, unforthcoming, unapproachable, unresponsive, unfriendly, unsociable, introspective, introverted; informal stand-offish.
– OPPOSITES close.

removal n. **1 taking away**, withdrawal, abolition. **2 dismissal**, ejection, expulsion, ousting, deposition; informal sacking, firing. **3 move**, transfer, relocation.

remove v. **1 take off**, take away, move, take out, pull out, withdraw, detach, undo, unfasten, disconnect. **2 dismiss**, discharge, get rid of, eject, expel, oust, depose, unseat; informal sack, fire, kick out. **3 abolish**, withdraw, eliminate, get rid of, do away with, stop, cut; informal axe.
– OPPOSITES attach, insert.

renaissance n. **revival**, renewal, resurrection, reawakening, re-emergence, rebirth, reappearance, resurgence.

render v. **1 make**, cause to be/become, leave, turn. **2 give**, provide, supply, furnish, contribute. **3 act**, perform, play, depict, portray, interpret, represent, draw, paint, execute.

rendezvous n. **meeting**, appointment, assignation; informal date; literary tryst.
•v. **meet**, come together, gather, assemble.

renegade n. **traitor**, defector, deserter, turncoat, rebel, mutineer.
•adj. **1 treacherous**, traitorous, disloyal, treasonous, rebel, mutinous. **2 apostate**, heretic, heretical, dissident.
– OPPOSITES loyal.

renege v. **default on**, fail to honour, go back on, break, back out of, withdraw from, retreat from, backtrack on, break your word/promise.
– OPPOSITES honour.

renew v. **1 resume**, return to, take up again, come back to, begin again, restart, recommence, continue (with), carry on (with). **2 reaffirm**, repeat, reiterate, restate. **3 revive**, regenerate, revitalize, reinvigorate, restore, resuscitate. **4 renovate**, restore, refurbish, revamp, remodel, modernize; informal do up; N. Amer. informal rehab.

renounce v. **1 give up**, relinquish, abandon, surrender, waive, forego, desist from, keep off; informal say goodbye to. **2 reject**, repudiate, deny, abandon, wash your hands of, turn your back on, disown, spurn, shun.

renovate v. **modernize**, restore, refurbish, revamp, recondition, rehabilitate, update, upgrade, refit; informal do up; N. Amer. informal rehab.

renown n. **fame**, distinction, eminence, illustriousness, prominence, repute, reputation, prestige, acclaim, celebrity, notability.

renowned adj. **famous**, well known, celebrated, famed, eminent, distinguished, acclaimed, illustrious, prominent, great, esteemed.
– OPPOSITES unknown.

rent n. **hire charge**, rental, payment.
•v. **1 hire**, lease, charter. **2 let (out)**, lease (out), hire (out), charter (out).

repair v. **1 mend**, fix (up), put/set right, restore (to working order), overhaul, renovate; informal patch up. **2 rectify**, make good, (put) right, correct, make up for, make amends for, compensate for, redress.
•n. **1 restoration**, mending, overhaul, renovation. **2 mend**, darn, patch. **3** in good repair: **condition**, working order, state, shape, fettle; Brit. informal nick.

repay v. **1 reimburse**, refund, pay back, recompense, compensate, remunerate, settle up with. **2** he repaid her kindness: **reciprocate**, return, requite, reward.

repeal v. **cancel**, abolish, reverse, rescind, revoke, annul, quash.
– OPPOSITES enact.
•n. **cancellation**, abolition, reversal, rescinding, annulment.

repeat v. **1 say again**, restate, reiterate, go/run through again, recapitulate, recap. **2 recite**, quote, parrot, regurgitate, echo; informal trot out. **3 do again**,

redo, replicate, duplicate.
•n. **repetition**, replication, duplicate.

repeated adj. **recurrent**, frequent, persistent, continual, incessant, constant, regular, periodic, numerous, (very) many.
– OPPOSITES occasional.

repeatedly adv. **frequently**, often, again and again, over and over (again), time and (time) again, many times, persistently, recurrently, constantly, continually, regularly; N. Amer. oftentimes.

repel v. **1 fight off**, repulse, drive back, force back, beat back, hold off, ward off, fend off, keep at bay; Brit. see off. **2 revolt**, disgust, repulse, sicken, nauseate, turn someone's stomach; informal turn off; N. Amer. informal gross out.
– OPPOSITES attract.

repellent adj. **1 revolting**, repulsive, disgusting, repugnant, sickening, nauseating, stomach-turning, vile, nasty, foul, awful, horrible, dreadful, terrible, obnoxious, loathsome, offensive, objectionable, abhorrent, despicable, reprehensible, contemptible, odious, hateful; N. Amer. vomitous; informal ghastly, horrid, gross; literary noisome. **2 impermeable**, impervious, resistant, -proof.

repent v. **feel remorse**, regret, be sorry, rue, reproach yourself, be ashamed, feel contrite, be penitent, be remorseful.

repentant adj. **penitent**, contrite, regretful, rueful,

remorseful, apologetic, chastened, ashamed, shamefaced.
– OPPOSITES impenitent.

repercussion n. **consequence**, result, effect, outcome, reverberation, backlash, aftermath, fallout.

repertoire n. **collection**, range, repertory, list, store, stock, repository, supply.

repetition n. **1 reiteration**, restatement, retelling. **2 repetitiousness**, repetitiveness, tautology.

repetitive, repetitious adj. **recurring**, recurrent, repeated, unvaried, unchanging, routine, mechanical, automatic, monotonous, boring; informal samey.
– OPPOSITES varied.

replace v. **1 put back**, return, restore. **2 take the place of**, succeed, take over from, supersede, stand in for, substitute for, deputize for; informal step into someone's shoes/boots. **3 substitute**, exchange, change, swap.

replacement n. **substitute**, stand-in, fill-in, locum, understudy, relief, cover, proxy, surrogate.

replenish v. **1 refill**, top up, fill up, recharge; N. Amer. freshen. **2 stock up**, restock, restore, replace.
– OPPOSITES empty.

replica n. **copy**, model, duplicate, reproduction, dummy, imitation, facsimile.

reply v. **respond**, answer, write back, rejoin, retort, riposte, counter, come back.
•n. **answer**, response, rejoinder, retort, riposte; informal comeback.

report v. **1 communicate**, announce, divulge, disclose, reveal, relay, describe, narrate, delineate, detail, document, give an account of, make public, publish, broadcast, proclaim, publicize. **2 inform on**; informal shop, tell on, squeal on, rat on; Brit. informal grass on. **3** *I reported for duty:* **present yourself**, arrive, turn up, clock in; informal show up.
•n. **1 account**, record, minutes, proceedings, transcript. **2 news**, information, word, intelligence. **3 story**, account, article, piece, item, column, feature, bulletin, dispatch, communiqué. **4 rumour**, whisper; informal buzz. **5 bang**, crack, explosion, boom.

reporter n. **journalist**, correspondent, newsman, newswoman, columnist; Brit. pressman; informal hack, stringer, journo.

reprehensible adj. **deplorable**, disgraceful, discreditable, despicable, blameworthy; culpable, wrong, bad, shameful, dishonourable, inexcusable, unforgivable, indefensible, unjustifiable.
– OPPOSITES praiseworthy.

represent v. **1 stand for**, symbolize, personify, epitomize, typify, embody, illustrate, exemplify. **2 depict**, portray, render, picture, delineate, show, illustrate. **3 appear for**, act for, speak on behalf of.

representation n. **1 portrayal**, depiction, delineation, presentation, rendition. **2 likeness**, painting, drawing, picture, illustration, sketch, image, model, figure, statue.

representative adj. **1 typical**, archetypal, characteristic, illustrative, indicative. **2 symbolic**, emblematic.
– OPPOSITES atypical.
• n. **1 spokesperson**, spokesman, spokeswoman, agent, official, mouthpiece. **2 salesman**, commercial traveller, agent, negotiator; informal rep.
3 deputy, substitute, stand-in, proxy, delegate, ambassador, emissary.

repress v. **1 suppress**, quell, quash, subdue, put down, crush, extinguish, stamp out, defeat, contain. **2 oppress**, subjugate, tyrannize. **3 restrain**, hold back/in, suppress, keep in check, control, curb, stifle, bottle up; informal button up, keep the lid on.
– OPPOSITES express.

repression n. **1 suppression**, quashing, subduing, crushing, stamping out. **2 oppression**, subjugation, suppression, tyranny, authoritarianism, despotism. **3 restraint**, suppression, control, curbing, stifling.

repressive adj. **oppressive**, authoritarian, despotic,
tyrannical, dictatorial, fascist, autocratic, totalitarian, un-democratic.

reprieve v. **pardon**, spare, amnesty; informal let off (the hook).
• n. **pardon**, stay of execution, amnesty.

reprimand v. **rebuke**, reproach, scold, admonish, reprove, chastise, upbraid, berate, take to task, castigate; informal tell off; Brit. informal tick off; N. Amer. informal chew out.
– OPPOSITES praise.
• n. **rebuke**, reproach, scolding, admonition; informal telling-off, dressing-down, carpeting; Brit. informal ticking-off.

reprisal n. **retaliation**, counter-attack, comeback, revenge, vengeance, retribution, requital; informal a taste of your own medicine.

reproachful adj. **disapproving**, reproving, critical, censorious, disparaging, withering, accusatory, admonitory.
– OPPOSITES approving.

reproduce v. **1 copy**, duplicate, replicate, photocopy, xerox, photostat, print. **2 repeat**, replicate, recreate, redo, simulate, imitate, emulate, mimic. **3 breed**, procreate, propagate, multiply, proliferate.

reproduction n. **1 print**, copy, reprint, duplicate, facsimile, photocopy; trademark Xerox. **2 breeding**, procreation, propagation, proliferation.

r

repudiate v. **1 reject**, renounce, disown, abandon, give up, turn your back on, cast off, lay aside, wash your hands of; formal forswear; literary forsake. **2 deny**, refute, contradict, controvert, rebut, dispute, dismiss, brush aside; formal gainsay.
– OPPOSITES embrace.

repugnant adj. **abhorrent**, revolting, repulsive, repellent, disgusting, offensive, objectionable, vile, foul, nasty, loathsome, sickening, nauseating, hateful, detestable, execrable, abominable, monstrous, appalling, unsavoury, unpalatable.
– OPPOSITES pleasant.

repulsive adj. **disgusting**, revolting, foul, nasty, obnoxious, sickening, nauseating, stomach-churning, vile; informal ghastly, gross, horrible; literary noisome.
– OPPOSITES attractive.

reputable adj. **well thought of**, highly regarded, respected, respectable, of (good) repute, prestigious, established, reliable, dependable, trustworthy.
– OPPOSITES untrustworthy.

reputation n. **name**, good name, character, repute, standing, stature, position, renown, esteem, prestige.

request n. **1 appeal**, entreaty, plea, petition, application, demand, call, solicitation. **2 requirement**, wish, desire, choice.
•v. **ask for**, appeal for, call for, seek, solicit, plead for, beg for, apply for, put in for, demand,

petition for, sue for, implore, entreat; literary beseech.

require v. **1 need**, have need of, be short of, want, desire, lack, miss. **2 necessitate**, demand, call for, involve, entail, take. **3 demand**, insist on, call for, ask for, expect. **4 order**, instruct, command, enjoin, oblige, compel, force.

requirement n. **need**, necessity, prerequisite, stipulation, demand, want, essential.

requisition n. **1 order**, request, call, application, claim, demand; Brit. indent. **2 appropriation**, commandeering, seizure, confiscation, expropriation.
•v. **1 commandeer**, appropriate, take over, take possession of, occupy, seize, confiscate, expropriate. **2 request**, order, call for, demand.

rescue v. **1 save**, free, set free, release, liberate, deliver. **2 retrieve**, recover, salvage.
•n. **saving**, rescuing, release, freeing, liberation, deliverance.

research n. **investigation**, experimentation, testing, analysis, fact-finding, examination, scrutiny.
•v. **investigate**, study, enquire into, look into, probe, explore, analyse, examine, scrutinize.

resemblance n. **similarity**, likeness, similitude, correspondence, congruence, conformity, comparability, parallel.
– OPPOSITES dissimilarity.

resemble v. **look like**, be similar to, remind someone of, take after, approximate to, smack of, correspond to, echo, mirror, parallel.
– OPPOSITES differ from.

resent v. **begrudge**, feel aggrieved at/about, feel bitter about, grudge, be resentful of, take exception to, object to, take amiss, take offence at.
– OPPOSITES welcome.

resentful adj. **aggrieved**, indignant, irritated, piqued, put out, in high dudgeon, dissatisfied, disgruntled, discontented, offended, bitter, jaundiced, envious, jealous; informal miffed, peeved; Brit. informal narked; N. Amer. informal sore.

resentment n. **bitterness**, indignation, irritation, pique, dissatisfaction, disgruntlement, discontentment, acrimony, rancour.

reservation n. **1 doubt**, qualm, scruple; (**reservations**) misgivings, scepticism, unease, hesitation, objection. **2 reserve**, enclave, sanctuary, territory, homeland.

reserve v. **1 put aside**, set aside, keep (back), save, hold back, keep in reserve, earmark, retain. **2 book**, order, arrange for, secure, engage, hire.
•n. **1 stock**, store, supply, stockpile, pool, hoard, cache, fund. **2 reinforcements**, extras, auxiliaries. **3 national park**, sanctuary, preserve, reservation. **4 shyness**, diffidence, timidity,

taciturnity, inhibition, reticence, detachment, aloofness, distance, remoteness. **5** she trusted him without reserve: **reservation**, qualification, condition, limitation, hesitation, doubt.
•adj. **substitute**, stand-in, relief, replacement, fallback, spare, extra.

reserved adj. **1 uncommunicative**, reticent, unforthcoming, aloof, cool, undemonstrative, unsociable, unfriendly, quiet, silent, taciturn, withdrawn, secretive, shy, retiring, diffident, timid, introverted; informal stand-offish. **2 booked**, taken, spoken for, prearranged.
– OPPOSITES outgoing.

reservoir n. **1 lake**, pool, pond, basin. **2 receptacle**, container, holder, tank. **3 stock**, store, stockpile, reserve(s), supply, bank, pool.

reside v. **1 live**, lodge, stay, occupy, inhabit; formal dwell, be domiciled. **2** power resides with the president: **be vested in**, be bestowed on, be conferred on, be in the hands of.

residence n. **home**, house, address, quarters, lodgings; informal pad; formal dwelling, abode, domicile.

resident n. **inhabitant**, local, citizen, native, householder, homeowner, occupier, tenant; humorous denizen.

residue n. **remainder**, rest, remnant(s), surplus, extra, excess, remains, leftovers.

resign v. **1 leave**, give notice, stand down, step down; informal quit, pack in. **2 give up**, leave, vacate, renounce, relinquish, surrender.

resignation n. *he accepted his fate with resignation*: **patience**, forbearance, stoicism, fortitude, fatalism, acceptance.

resigned adj. **patient**, long-suffering, uncomplaining, forbearing, stoical, philosophical, fatalistic.

resilient adj. **1 flexible**, pliable, supple, durable, hard-wearing, stout, strong, sturdy, tough. **2 strong**, tough, hardy, quick to recover, buoyant, irrepressible.

resist v. **1 withstand**, be proof against, combat, weather, endure, be resistant to, keep out. **2 oppose**, fight against, object to, defy, kick against, obstruct. **3 refrain from**, abstain from, forbear from, desist from, not give in to, restrain yourself from.

resistance n. **1 opposition**, hostility, struggle, fight, battle, stand, defiance. **2 immunity**, defences.

resistant adj. **1 impervious**, immune, invulnerable, proof, unaffected. **2 opposed**, averse, hostile, inimical, against; informal anti.
– OPPOSITES vulnerable.

resolute adj. **determined**, purposeful, resolved, adamant, single-minded, firm, unswerving, unwavering, steadfast, staunch, stalwart, unfaltering,

indefatigable, tenacious, strong-willed, unshakeable.
– OPPOSITES half-hearted.

resolution n. **1 intention**, decision, intent, aim, plan, commitment, pledge, promise. **2 motion**, proposal, proposition. **3 determination**, purpose, purposefulness, resolve, single-mindedness, firmness, will power, strength of character. **4 solution**, answer, end, settlement, conclusion.

resolve v. **1 settle**, sort out, solve, fix, straighten out, deal with, put right, rectify; informal hammer out, thrash out. **2 determine**, decide, make up your mind. **3 vote**, rule, decide formally, agree.
• n. **determination**, purpose, resolution, single-mindedness; informal guts.

resort n. **option**, alternative, choice, possibility, hope, measure, step, recourse, expedient. □ **resort to** fall back on, have recourse to, turn to, make use of, avail yourself of.

resound v. **echo**, reverberate, ring, boom, thunder, rumble, resonate.

resounding adj. **1 reverberating**, resonating, echoing, ringing, sonorous, deep, rich. **2** *a resounding success*: **enormous**, huge, very great, tremendous, terrific, colossal, emphatic, outstanding, remarkable, phenomenal.

resource n. **1 facility**, amenity, aid, help, support. **2 initiative**, resourcefulness, enterprise, ingenuity, inventiveness. **3** *we lack resources:* **assets**, funds, wealth, money, capital, supplies, materials, stores, stocks, reserves.

resourceful adj. **ingenious**, enterprising, inventive, creative, clever, talented, able, capable.

respect n. **1** esteem, regard, high opinion, admiration, reverence, deference, honour. **2** *the report was accurate in every respect:* **aspect**, regard, feature, way, sense, particular, point, detail. **3** (**respects**) regards, compliments, greetings, best/good wishes.
- OPPOSITES contempt.
- v. **1** esteem, admire, think highly of, have a high opinion of, look up to, revere, honour.
2 show consideration for, have regard for, observe, be mindful of, be heedful of.
3 abide by, comply with, follow, adhere to, conform to, act in accordance with, obey, observe, keep (to).
- OPPOSITES despise, disobey.

respectable adj. **1** reputable, upright, honest, honourable, trustworthy, decent, good, well bred, clean-living. **2** *fairly good,* decent, fair-sized, reasonable, moderately good, large, sizeable, considerable.
- OPPOSITES disreputable.

respectful adj. deferential, reverent, dutiful, polite, well mannered, civil, courteous, gracious.
- OPPOSITES rude.

respective adj. separate, personal, own, particular, individual, specific, special.

respite n. rest, break, breathing space, interval, lull, pause, time out, relief; informal breather, let-up.

respond v. **1** answer, reply, write back, come back, rejoin, retort, riposte, counter. **2** react, reciprocate, retaliate.

response n. **1** answer, reply, rejoinder, retort, riposte; informal comeback. **2** reaction, reply, retaliation; informal comeback.
- OPPOSITES question.

responsibility n. **1** duty, task, function, job, role, onus; Brit. informal pigeon. **2** blame, fault, guilt, culpability, liability, accountability, answerability. **3** trustworthiness, (common) sense, maturity, reliability, dependability. **4** *managerial responsibility:* **authority,** control, power, leadership.

responsible adj. **1** in charge of, in control of, at the helm of, accountable for, liable for. **2** accountable, answerable, to blame, guilty, culpable, blameworthy, at fault, in the wrong. **3** trustworthy, sensible, mature, reliable, dependable, levelheaded, stable.
- OPPOSITES irresponsible.

responsive adj. reactive, receptive, amenable, flexible, open to suggestions, forthcoming.

rest[1] v. **1** relax, ease up/off, let up, slow down, have/take a

r

break, unbend, unwind, take it
easy, put your feet up; informal
take five, have/take a breather,
chill out. **2** *her hands rested on
the rail:* lie, be laid, repose, be
placed, be positioned, be sup-
ported by. **3 support**, prop (up),
lean, lay, set, stand, position,
place, put.
•n. **1 relaxation**, repose, leisure,
time off; informal lie-down.
2 break, breathing space, interval, interlude, intermission, time
off/out, respite, lull, pause;
informal breather. **3 stand**, base,
holder, support, rack, frame,
shelf.

rest² n. **remainder**, residue,
balance, others, remnant(s),
surplus, excess.

restful adj. **relaxing**, quiet, calm,
tranquil, soothing, peaceful,
leisurely, undisturbed, untroubled.
- OPPOSITES exciting.

restless adj. **1 uneasy**, ill at ease,
fidgety, edgy, tense, worked up,
nervous, nervy, agitated,
anxious; informal jumpy, jittery,
twitchy, uptight. **2** *a restless
night:* **sleepless**, wakeful, fitful,
broken, disturbed, troubled, unsettled.

restoration n. **1 reinstatement**, reinstitution, re-
establishment, reimposition,
return. **2 repair**, renovation,
mending, refurbishment, recon-
ditioning, rehabilitation, rebuilding, reconstruction; N. Amer.
informal rehab.

restore v. **1 reinstate**, bring
back, reinstitute, reimpose, reinstall, re-establish. **2** *he restored
it to its rightful owner:* **return**,
give back, hand back. **3 repair**,
fix, mend, refurbish, recondition, rehabilitate, renovate, revamp, rebuild; informal do up;
N. Amer. informal rehab. **4 reinvigorate**, revitalize, revive, refresh,
energize, freshen.

restrain v. **control**, check, hold
in check, curb, suppress, repress, contain, rein back/in,
smother, stifle, bottle up; informal
keep the lid on.

restrained adj. **1 self-
controlled**, sober, steady, unemotional, undemonstrative.
2 muted, soft, discreet, subtle,
quiet, unobtrusive, unostentatious, understated, tasteful.
- OPPOSITES impetuous.

restraint n. **1 constraint**, check,
control, restriction, limitation,
curtailment, rein, brake, deterrent. **2 self-control**, self-
discipline, control, moderation,
judiciousness. **3 subtlety**, taste,
discretion, discrimination.

restrict v. **1 limit**, keep within
bounds, regulate, control,
moderate, cut down, curtail.
2 hinder, interfere with,
impede, hamper, obstruct,
block, check, curb.

restricted adj. **1 cramped**,
confined, constricted, small,
narrow, tight. **2 limited**, controlled, regulated, reduced.

restriction n. **limitation**, constraint, control, regulation,

result → retract

check, curb, reduction, diminution, curtailment.

result n. **consequence**, outcome, upshot, sequel, effect, reaction, repercussion.
– OPPOSITES cause.
• v. **follow**, ensue, develop, stem, spring, arise, derive, proceed; (**result from**) be caused by, be brought about by, be produced by, originate in.
□ **result in** end in, culminate in, lead to, trigger, cause, bring about, occasion, effect, give rise to, produce.

resume v. **restart**, recommence, begin again, start again, reopen, renew, return to, continue with, carry on with.
– OPPOSITES suspend, abandon.

résumé n. **summary**, precis, synopsis, abstract, outline, abridgement, overview.

resumption n. **restart**, recommencement, reopening, continuation, renewal, return, revival.

resurgence n. **renewal**, revival, renaissance, recovery, comeback, reawakening, resurrection, reappearance, re-emergence.

resurrect v. **revive**, restore, regenerate, revitalize, breathe new life into, reinvigorate, resuscitate, rejuvenate, re-establish, relaunch.

retain v. **keep (possession of)**, keep hold of, hang on to, maintain, preserve, conserve.

retaliate v. **fight back**, hit back, respond, react, reply, reciprocate, counter-attack, get back at someone, pay someone back; informal get your own back.

retaliation n. **revenge**, vengeance, reprisal, retribution, repayment, response, reaction, reply, counter-attack.

retard v. **delay**, slow down/up, hold back/up, postpone, detain, decelerate, hinder, impede, check.
– OPPOSITES accelerate.

reticent adj. **uncommunicative**, unforthcoming, unresponsive, tight-lipped, quiet, taciturn, silent, reserved.
– OPPOSITES expansive.

retire v. **1 give up work**, stop work, be pensioned off; informal be put out to grass. **2 withdraw**, go away, exit, leave, take yourself off, absent yourself. **3 go to bed**, call it a day; informal turn in, hit the hay/sack.

retiring adj. **1 departing**, outgoing. **2 shy**, diffident, self-effacing, unassuming, unassertive, reserved, reticent, quiet, timid, modest.
– OPPOSITES incoming, outgoing.

retort v. **answer**, reply, respond, return, counter, riposte, retaliate.
• n. **answer**, reply, response, counter, rejoinder, riposte, retaliation; informal comeback.

retract v. **1 pull in**, pull back, draw in. **2 take back**, withdraw, recant, disavow, disclaim, repudiate, renounce, reverse,

r

revoke, rescind, go back on, backtrack on; formal abjure.

retreat v. withdraw, retire, draw back, pull back/out, fall back, give way, give ground.
- OPPOSITES advance.
•n. **1 withdrawal**, retirement, pullback, flight. **2 refuge**, haven, sanctuary, hideaway, hideout, hiding place; informal hidey-hole.

retribution n. punishment, penalty, your just deserts, revenge, reprisal, requital, retaliation, vengeance, an eye for an eye (and a tooth for a tooth), tit for tat, nemesis.

retrieve v. get back, bring back, recover, recapture, regain, recoup, salvage, rescue.

retrograde adj. for the worse, regressive, retrogressive, negative, downhill, backward(s), unwelcome.

retrospect n.
□ **in retrospect** looking back, on reflection, in/with hindsight.

return v. **1 go back**, come back, arrive back, come home. **2 recur**, reoccur, repeat itself, reappear. **3 give back**, hand back, pay back, repay, restore, put back, replace, reinstall, reinstate.
- OPPOSITES leave.
•n. **1 recurrence**, reoccurrence, repeat, reappearance. **2 replacement**, restoration, reinstatement, restitution. **3 yield**, profit, gain, revenue, interest, dividend.

revamp v. renovate, redecorate, refurbish, remodel, refashion, redesign, restyle; informal do up, give something a facelift, give something a makeover, vamp up; Brit. informal tart up.

reveal v. **1 disclose**, make known, make public, broadcast, publicize, circulate, divulge, tell, let slip/drop, give away/out, blurt out, release, leak, bring to light, lay bare, unveil; informal let on. **2 show**, display, exhibit, unveil, uncover.
- OPPOSITES conceal, hide.

revel v. celebrate, make merry; informal party, live it up, whoop it up, paint the town red.
•n. **2 celebration**, festivity, jollification, merrymaking, party; informal rave, shindig, bash; Brit. informal rave-up; N. Amer. informal wingding, blast.
□ **revel in** enjoy, delight in, love, like, adore, take pleasure in, relish, lap up, savour; informal get a kick out of.

revelation n. disclosure, announcement, report, admission, confession, divulging, giving away/out, leak, betrayal, publicizing.

revelry n. celebration(s), parties, festivity, jollification, merrymaking, carousal, roistering, fun and games; informal partying.

revenge n. retaliation, retribution, vengeance, reprisal, recrimination, an eye for an eye

(and a tooth for a tooth),
redress.
– OPPOSITES forgiveness.
• v. **avenge**, exact retribution for,
take reprisals for, get redress
for, make someone pay for;
informal get your own back for.

revenue n. **income**, takings,
receipts, proceeds, earnings,
profit(s), gain, yield.
– OPPOSITES expenditure.

reverberate v. **resound**, echo,
resonate, ring, boom, rumble.

revere v. **respect**, admire, think
highly of, esteem, venerate,
look up to, be in awe of.
– OPPOSITES despise.

reverence n. **high esteem**, high
regard, great respect, honour,
veneration, homage, admiration, appreciation, deference.
– OPPOSITES scorn.

reverent adj. **reverential**,
respectful, admiring, devoted,
devout, awed, deferential.

reversal n. **1 turnaround**, turnabout, about-face, volte-face,
change of heart, U-turn, back-
tracking; Brit. about-turn.
2 swap, exchange, change,
interchange, switch. **3 alteration**, overturning, overthrow,
disallowing, overriding, overrul-
ing, veto, revocation. **4 setback**,
upset, failure, misfortune, mishap, disaster, blow, disappointment, adversity, hardship,
affliction, vicissitude, defeat.

reverse v. **1 back**, move back/
backwards. **2 turn upside
down**, turn over, upend, invert,

turn back to front. **3 swap
(round)**, change (round), exchange, switch (round), trans-
pose. **4 alter**, change, overturn,
overthrow, disallow, override,
overrule, veto, revoke.
• adj. **backward(s)**, inverted,
transposed, opposite.
• n. **1 opposite**, contrary, converse, inverse, antithesis. **2 setback**, reversal, upset, failure,
misfortune, mishap, disaster,
blow, disappointment, adversity, hardship, affliction, vicissitude, defeat. **3 other side**, back,
underside, flip side.
– OPPOSITES front.

revert v. **return**, go back, change
back, default, relapse.

review n. **1 analysis**, evaluation,
assessment, appraisal, examination, investigation, enquiry,
probe, inspection, study. **2 reconsideration**, reassessment,
re-evaluation, reappraisal.
3 criticism, critique, write-up,
assessment, commentary.
• v. **1 survey**, study, research,
consider, analyse, examine,
scrutinize, explore, look into,
probe, inspect, inspect, assess, evaluate, appraise, weigh
up; informal size up. **2 reconsider**,
re-examine, reassess, re-
evaluate, reappraise, rethink.

reviewer n. **critic**, commentator, judge.

revise v. **1 reconsider**, review,
re-examine, reassess, re-
evaluate, reappraise, rethink,
change, alter, modify. **2 amend**,
correct, edit, rewrite, redraft,

r

rephrase, rework. **3** (Brit.) **go over**, reread, memorize, cram; informal bone up on; Brit. informal swot up (on), mug up (on).

revision n. **1** alteration, adaptation, editing, rewriting, redrafting, correction, updating. **2 reconsideration**, review, re-examination, reassessment, re-evaluation, reappraisal, rethink, change, modification.

revitalize v. reinvigorate, re-energize, boost, regenerate, revive, revivify, rejuvenate, reanimate, resuscitate, refresh, stimulate, breathe new life into; informal give a shot in the arm to, pep up, buck up.

revival n. **1 improvement**, rallying, turn for the better, upturn, upswing, resurgence. **2 comeback**, re-establishment, reintroduction, restoration, reappearance, resurrection, rebirth.
– OPPOSITES downturn.

revive v. **1** resuscitate, bring round, bring back to consciousness; informal give the kiss of life to. **2 reinvigorate**, revitalize, refresh, energize, reanimate. **3** reviving old traditions: **reintroduce**, re-establish, restore, resurrect, bring back.

revoke v. cancel, repeal, rescind, reverse, annul, nullify, void, invalidate, countermand, retract, withdraw, overrule, override; formal abrogate.

revolt v. **1** rebel, rise up, take to the streets, riot, mutiny. **2 disgust**, sicken, nauseate, turn someone's stomach, put off, offend; informal turn off; N. Amer. informal gross out.
• n. **rebellion**, revolution, insurrection, mutiny, uprising, riot, insurgence, coup (d'état).

revolting adj. disgusting, sickening, nauseating, stomach-turning, repulsive, repugnant, hideous, nasty, foul, offensive; N. Amer. vomitous; informal ghastly, horrid, gross.
– OPPOSITES attractive, pleasant.

revolution n. **1 rebellion**, revolt, insurrection, mutiny, uprising, rising, riot, insurgence, coup (d'état). **2 dramatic change**, sea change, metamorphosis, transformation, innovation, reorganization, restructuring; informal shake-up; N. Amer. informal shakedown. **3 turn**, rotation, circle, spin, orbit, circuit, lap.

revolutionary adj. **1 rebellious**, rebel, insurgent, rioting, mutinous, renegade. **2 new**, novel, original, unusual, unconventional, unorthodox, newfangled, innovatory, modern, state-of-the-art, futuristic, pioneering.
• n. **rebel**, insurgent, mutineer, insurrectionist, agitator.

revolutionize v. transform, shake up, turn upside down, restructure, reorganize, transmute, metamorphose; humorous transmogrify.

revolve v. **1 go round**, turn round, rotate, spin. **2 circle**, travel, orbit.

revulsion n. **disgust**, repulsion, abhorrence, repugnance, nausea, horror, aversion, abomination, distaste.
– OPPOSITES delight.

reward n. **award**, honour, decoration, bonus, premium, bounty, present, gift, payment, recompense, prize; informal payoff.
•v. **recompense**, pay, remunerate.
– OPPOSITES punish.

rewarding adj. **satisfying**, gratifying, pleasing, fulfilling, enriching, illuminating, worthwhile, productive, fruitful.

rhetoric n. **1 oratory**, eloquence, command of language, way with words. **2 wordiness**, verbosity, grandiloquence, bombast, pomposity, extravagant language, purple prose, turgidity; informal hot air.

rhetorical adj. **1** *a rhetorical device:* **stylistic**, oratorical, linguistic, verbal. **2 extravagant**, grandiloquent, high-flown, bombastic, grandiose, pompous, pretentious, overblown, turgid, flowery; informal highfalutin.

rhyme n. **poem**, verse, ode; (**rhymes**) poetry, doggerel.

rhythm n. **1 beat**, cadence, tempo, time, pulse. **2 metre**, measure, pattern.

rich adj. **1 wealthy**, affluent, moneyed, well off, well-to-do, prosperous; informal loaded, well heeled, made of money.
2 sumptuous, opulent, luxurious, lavish, gorgeous, splendid, magnificent, costly, expensive, fancy, palatial; informal plush; Brit. informal swish; N. Amer. informal swank. **3** *a garden rich in flowers:* **well stocked**, well provided, abounding, crammed, packed, teeming, bursting. **4** *a rich supply:* **plentiful**, abundant, copious, ample, profuse, lavish, liberal, generous. **5 fertile**, productive, fruitful, fecund. **6 creamy**, fatty, heavy, full-flavoured. **7** *rich colours:* **strong**, deep, full, intense, vivid, brilliant.
– OPPOSITES poor, plain.

riches pl. n. **money**, wealth, funds, cash, means, assets, capital, resources; informal bread, loot; Brit. informal dosh, brass, lolly; N. Amer. informal bucks.

richly adv. **1 sumptuously**, opulently, luxuriously, lavishly, gorgeously, splendidly, magnificently. **2** *the reward she richly deserves:* **fully**, amply, well, thoroughly, completely, wholly, totally, entirely, absolutely, utterly.

rid v. **clear**, free, purge, empty, strip.
□ **get rid of** dispose of, throw away/out, clear out, discard, scrap, dump, bin, jettison, expel, eliminate; informal chuck (away), ditch, junk; Brit. informal get shot of; N. Amer. informal trash.

riddle n. puzzle, conundrum, brain-teaser, problem, question, poser, enigma, mystery.

ride v. **1** sit on, mount, control, manage, handle. **2** travel, move, proceed, drive, cycle, trot, canter, gallop.
▸n. **trip**, journey, drive, run, excursion, outing, jaunt, lift; informal spin.

ridicule n. mockery, derision, laughter, scorn, scoffing, jeering.
– OPPOSITES respect.
▸v. mock, deride, laugh at, heap scorn on, jeer at, make fun of, scoff at, satirize, caricature, parody.

ridiculous adj. laughable, absurd, ludicrous, risible, comical, funny, hilarious, amusing, farcical, silly, stupid, idiotic, preposterous.
– OPPOSITES sensible.

rife adj. widespread, general, common, universal, extensive, ubiquitous, endemic, inescapable.

rifle v. **1** rummage, search, hunt, forage. **2** burgle, rob, steal from, loot, raid, plunder, ransack.

rift n. **1** crack, split, breach, fissure, fracture, cleft, crevice, opening. **2** disagreement, estrangement, breach, split, schism, quarrel, falling-out, conflict, feud; Brit. row; Brit. informal bust-up.

rig[1] v. **1** equip, kit out, fit out, supply, furnish, provide, arm. **2** dress, clothe, attire, robe, garb, get up; informal doll up. **3** he will rig up a shelter: set up, erect, assemble, put together, whip up, improvise, contrive; Brit. informal knock up.

rig[2] v. manipulate, engineer, distort, misrepresent, pervert, tamper with, falsify, fake; informal fix; Brit. informal fiddle.

right adj. **1** just, fair, equitable, proper, good, upright, righteous, virtuous, moral, ethical, principled, honourable, honest, lawful, legal. **2** correct, unerring, accurate, exact, precise, valid; Brit. informal spot on. **3** suitable, appropriate, fitting, apposite, apt, correct, proper, desirable, preferable, ideal. **4** opportune, advantageous, favourable, convenient, good, lucky, fortunate. **5** right-hand; Nautical starboard; Heraldry dexter.
– OPPOSITES wrong, left.
▸adv. **1** completely, fully, totally, absolutely, utterly, thoroughly, quite. **2** exactly, precisely, directly, immediately, just, squarely, dead; informal (slap) bang, smack, plumb. **3** correctly, accurately, perfectly.
– OPPOSITES wrong, badly.
▸n. **1** goodness, righteousness, virtue, integrity, propriety, probity, morality, truth, honesty, honour, justice, fairness, equity. **2** entitlement, prerogative, privilege, liberty, authority, power, licence, permission, dispensation, leave, due.
– OPPOSITES wrong.
▸v. remedy, rectify, retrieve, fix, resolve, sort out, settle, square,

straighten out, correct, repair, mend, redress.

□ **right away** at once, straight away, (right) now, this (very) minute, this instant, immediately, instantly, directly, forthwith, without further ado, promptly, quickly, without delay, asap, as soon as possible; N. Amer. in short order; informal straight off, pronto.

righteous adj. **good**, virtuous, upright, upstanding, decent, ethical, principled, moral, honest, honourable, blameless.
– OPPOSITES wicked.

rightful adj. **1 legal**, lawful, real, true, proper, correct, recognized, genuine, authentic, acknowledged, approved, valid, bona fide; informal legit, kosher. **2 deserved**, merited, due, just, right, fair, proper, fitting, appropriate, suitable.
– OPPOSITES wrongful.

right-wing adj. **conservative**, rightist, reactionary, traditionalist, conventional.
– OPPOSITES left-wing.

rigid adj. **1 stiff**, hard, taut, firm, inflexible, unbendable, unyielding, inelastic. **2** *a rigid routine:* **fixed**, set, firm, inflexible, invariable, hard and fast, cast-iron, strict, stringent, rigorous, uncompromising, intransigent.
– OPPOSITES flexible.

rigorous adj. **1 meticulous**, conscientious, punctilious, careful, scrupulous, painstaking, exact, precise, accurate, particular,

strict. **2 strict**, stringent, rigid, inflexible, draconian, intransigent, uncompromising. **3** *rigorous conditions:* **harsh**, severe, bleak, extreme, demanding.
– OPPOSITES slapdash, lax.

rim n. **edge**, brim, lip, border, side, margin, brink, boundary, perimeter, circumference, limits, periphery.

rind n. **skin**, peel, zest, integument.

ring[1] n. **1 circle**, band, halo, disc. **2 arena**, enclosure, amphitheatre, bowl. **3 gang**, syndicate, cartel, mob, band, circle, organization, association, society, alliance, league.
•v. **surround**, circle, encircle, enclose, hem in, confine, seal off.

ring[2] v. **1 chime**, sound, peal, toll, clang, bong; literary knell. **2 resound**, reverberate, resonate, echo. **3 telephone**, phone (up), call (up); informal give someone a buzz; Brit. informal give someone a bell, get on the blower to.

rinse v. **wash (out)**, clean, cleanse, bathe, dip, drench, splash, swill, sluice.

riot n. **disorder**, disturbance, lawlessness, upheaval, uproar, commotion, free-for-all, uprising, insurrection.
•v. **(go on the) rampage**, run wild, run amok, run riot, go berserk; informal raise hell.

riotous adj. **1 unruly**, rowdy, disorderly, uncontrollable, unmanageable, undisciplined,

uproarious, tumultuous, violent, wild, lawless, anarchic. **2 boisterous**, lively, loud, noisy, unrestrained, uninhibited, uproarious; Brit. informal rumbustious.
– OPPOSITES peaceful.

rip v. **tear**, pull, wrench, snatch, drag, pluck; informal yank.

ripe adj. **1 mature**, full grown, fully developed. **2** *ripe for development*: **ready**, fit, suitable, right. **3** *the time is ripe*: **opportune**, advantageous, favourable, auspicious, good, right.
– OPPOSITES immature.

ripen v. **mature**, mellow, develop.

riposte n. **retort**, counter, rejoinder, sally, return, answer, reply, response; informal comeback.

rise v. **1 climb**, come up, arise, ascend, mount, soar. **2 loom**, tower, soar. **3 go up**, increase, soar, shoot up, surge, leap, jump, rocket, escalate, spiral. **4 get higher**, grow, increase, become louder, swell, intensify. **5 stand up**, get to your feet, get up, jump up, leap up, stir, bestir yourself.
– OPPOSITES fall, descend, drop.
•n. **1 increase**, hike, leap, upsurge, upswing, climb. **2 raise**, increase, increment. **3 slope**, incline, hill, elevation, acclivity.

risk n. **1 chance**, uncertainty, unpredictability, instability, insecurity. **2 possibility**, chance, probability, likelihood, danger, peril, threat, menace, prospect.
•v. **endanger**, jeopardize,

imperil, hazard, gamble (with), chance, put at risk, put on the line.

risky adj. **dangerous**, hazardous, perilous, unsafe, insecure, precarious, touch-and-go, treacherous, uncertain, unpredictable; informal dicey.

rite n. **ceremony**, ritual, ceremonial, custom, service, observance, liturgy, worship, office.

ritual n. **ceremony**, rite, act, practice, custom, tradition, convention, formality, protocol.
•adj. **ceremonial**, prescribed, set, conventional, traditional, formal.

rival n. **opponent**, opposition, challenger, competitor, contender, adversary, antagonist, enemy; literary foe.
– OPPOSITES ally.
•v. **match**, compare with, compete with, vie with, equal, emulate, measure up to, touch; informal hold a candle to.
•adj. *rival candidates*: **competing**, opposing, in competition.

rivalry n. **competition**, contention, opposition, conflict, feuding; informal keeping up with the Joneses.

river n. **1 stream**, brook, watercourse, rivulet, tributary; Scottish & N. English burn; N. English beck; S. English bourn; N. Amer. & Austral./NZ creek. **2** *a river of molten lava*: **stream**, torrent, flood, deluge, cascade.

> **WORD LINKS**
> *relating to rivers:* fluvial

r

riveting adj. **fascinating**, gripping, engrossing, intriguing, absorbing, captivating, enthralling, compelling, spellbinding, mesmerizing; informal unputdownable.
– OPPOSITES boring.

road n. **1 street**, thoroughfare, roadway, highway, lane; Brit. motorway. **2** *the road to recovery*: **way**, path, route, course.

roam v. **wander**, rove, ramble, drift, walk, traipse, range, travel, tramp, trek; informal cruise.

roar v. **bellow**, yell, shout, thunder, bawl, howl, scream, cry, bay; informal holler.

roaring adj. **blazing**, burning, flaming.

rob v. **1 burgle**, steal from, hold up, break into, raid, loot, plunder, pillage; informal mug; N. Amer. burglarize. **2 cheat**, swindle, defraud; informal do out of, con out of.

robber n. **burglar**, thief, housebreaker, mugger, shoplifter, raider, looter.

robbery n. **burglary**, theft, stealing, housebreaking, shoplifting, embezzlement, fraud, hold-up, raid; informal mugging, smash-and-grab, stick-up; N. Amer. heist.

robe n. **1 cloak**, kaftan, djellaba, wrap, mantle, cape; N. Amer. wrapper. **2** *ceremonial robes*: **garb**, vestments, regalia, finery.

robot n. **machine**, automaton, android; informal bot, droid.

robust adj. **1 strong**, vigorous, sturdy, tough, powerful, solid, rugged, hardy, strapping, healthy, (fighting) fit, hale and hearty. **2 durable**, resilient, tough, hard-wearing, long-lasting, sturdy, strong.
– OPPOSITES frail, fragile.

rock[1] n. **boulder**, stone, pebble.

rock[2] v. **1 move to and fro**, sway, see-saw, roll, pitch, plunge, toss, lurch. **2 stun**, shock, stagger, astonish, startle, surprise, shake, take aback, throw, unnerve, disconcert.

rocky[1] adj. **stony**, pebbly, shingly, rough, bumpy, craggy, mountainous.

rocky[2] adj. **unsteady**, shaky, unstable, wobbly, tottery, rickety.
– OPPOSITES steady, stable.

rod n. **bar**, stick, pole, baton, staff, shaft, strut, rail, spoke.

rogue n. **scoundrel**, rascal, good-for-nothing, wretch, villain, criminal, lawbreaker; informal crook.

role n. **1 part**, character. **2 capacity**, position, function, job, post, office, duty, responsibility.

roll v. **1 turn over and over**, spin, rotate, revolve, wheel, trundle, bowl. **2 flow**, run, course, stream, pour, trickle. **3 wind**, coil, fold, curl, twist. **4 rock**, sway, reel, list, pitch, plunge, lurch, toss.
• n. **1 cylinder**, tube, scroll, reel, spool, bobbin. **2 turn**, rotation, revolution, spin, whirl. **3 list**, register, directory, record, file,

index, catalogue, inventory.
4 *a roll of thunder:* **rumble**, reverberation, echo, boom, clap, crack.

romance n. **1 love affair**, relationship, liaison, courtship, attachment, amour. **2 story**, tale, legend, fairy tale. **3 mystery**, glamour, excitement, exoticism, mystique, appeal, allure, charm.

romantic adj. **1 loving**, amorous, passionate, tender, affectionate; *informal* lovey-dovey. **2 sentimental**, hearts-and-flowers; *informal* slushy, schmaltzy; *Brit. informal* soppy. **3 idyllic**, picturesque, fairy-tale, beautiful, lovely, charming, pretty. **4 idealistic**, unrealistic, fanciful, impractical, head-in-the-clouds, starry-eyed, utopian, rose-tinted.
– OPPOSITES unsentimental, realistic.
•n. **idealist**, sentimentalist, dreamer, fantasist.
– OPPOSITES realist.

romp v. **play**, frolic, frisk, gambol, skip, prance, caper, cavort.

room n. **1 space**, headroom, legroom, area, expanse, extent. **2** *there's very little room for manoeuvre:* **scope**, opportunity, capacity, leeway, latitude, freedom.

roomy adj. **spacious**, capacious, sizeable, generous, big, large, extensive, voluminous, ample; *formal* commodious.
– OPPOSITES cramped.

root n. **1 source**, origin, cause, reason, basis, foundation,

bottom, seat. **2** *his Irish roots:* **origins**, beginnings, family, birth, heritage.
•v. **rummage**, hunt, search, rifle, delve, forage, dig, poke.
□ **root out** eradicate, eliminate, weed out, destroy, wipe out, stamp out, abolish, end, put a stop to.

rope n. **cord**, cable, line, hawser, string.

roster n. **schedule**, list, register, agenda, calendar; *Brit.* rota.

rosy adj. **1 pink**, roseate, reddish, glowing, healthy, fresh, radiant, blooming, blushing, flushed, ruddy. **2 promising**, optimistic, auspicious, hopeful, encouraging, favourable, bright, golden.
– OPPOSITES pale, bleak.

rot v. **1 decay**, decompose, disintegrate, crumble, perish. **2 go bad**, go off, spoil, moulder, putrefy, fester. **3 deteriorate**, degenerate, decline, decay, go to seed, go downhill; *informal* go to pot, go to the dogs.
•n. **decay**, decomposition, mould, mildew, blight, canker.

rotate v. **1 revolve**, go round, turn (round), spin, gyrate, whirl, twirl, swivel, circle, pivot. **2 alternate**, take turns, change, switch, interchange, exchange, swap.

rotation n. **1 revolving**, turning, spinning, gyration, circling. **2 turn**, revolution, orbit, spin. **3 sequence**, succession, alternation, cycle.

r

rotten adj. **1 decaying**, mouldy, bad, off, decomposing, spoiled, putrid, rancid, festering, fetid. **2 corrupt**, unprincipled, dishonest, dishonourable, unscrupulous, untrustworthy, immoral; informal crooked; Brit. informal bent.
– OPPOSITES fresh.

rough adj. **1 uneven**, irregular, bumpy, stony, rocky, rugged, rutted, pitted. **2 coarse**, bristly, scratchy, prickly, shaggy, hairy, bushy. **3 dry**, leathery, weatherbeaten, chapped, calloused, scaly. **4 gruff**, hoarse, harsh, rasping, husky, throaty, gravelly. **5 violent**, aggressive, belligerent, pugnacious, boisterous, rowdy, disorderly, unruly, riotous. **6 boorish**, loutish, oafish, brutish, coarse, crude, uncouth, vulgar, unrefined, unladylike, ungentlemanly, uncultured. **7 turbulent**, stormy, squally, tempestuous, violent, heavy, choppy. **8 preliminary**, hasty, quick, sketchy, cursory, basic, crude, rudimentary, raw, unpolished, incomplete, unfinished. **9 approximate**, inexact, imprecise, vague, estimated; N. Amer. informal ballpark.
– OPPOSITES smooth, gentle, calm, exact.
•n. **sketch**, draft, outline, mock-up.

round adj. **circular**, spherical, globular, cylindrical.
•n. **1 ball**, sphere, globe, orb, circle, disc, ring, hoop. **2** *a policeman on his rounds:* **circuit**, beat, route, tour. **3 stage**, level, heat,

game, bout, contest. **4 succession**, sequence, series, cycle.
•v. **go round**, travel round, skirt, circumnavigate, orbit.
□ **round off** finish off, crown, cap, top, conclude, close, end. **round up** gather together, herd together, muster, marshal, rally, assemble, collect, group; N. Amer. corral.

roundabout adj. **circuitous**, indirect, meandering, serpentine, tortuous, oblique, circumlocutory.
– OPPOSITES direct.

roundly adv. **1 vehemently**, emphatically, fiercely, forcefully, severely, plainly, frankly, candidly. **2 utterly**, completely, thoroughly, decisively, conclusively, heavily, soundly.

rouse v. **1 wake (up)**, awaken, arouse; Brit. informal knock up. **2 wake up**, awake, come to, get up, rise, bestir yourself. **3 stir up**, excite, galvanize, electrify, stimulate, inspire, move, inflame, agitate, goad, provoke, prompt, whip up.

rousing adj. **stirring**, inspiring, exciting, stimulating, moving, electrifying, invigorating, energizing, exhilarating.

rout n. **defeat**, beating, retreat, flight; informal licking, hammering, thrashing, pasting, drubbing.
– OPPOSITES victory.
•v. **defeat**, beat, conquer, vanquish, crush, put to flight, drive off, scatter; informal lick, hammer, clobber, thrash.

r

route n. **way**, course, road, path, direction.

routine n. **1 procedure**, practice, pattern, drill, regime, programme, schedule, plan. **2 act**, performance, number, turn, piece; informal spiel, patter.
•adj. **1 standard**, regular, customary, normal, usual, ordinary, typical, everyday. **2 boring**, tedious, monotonous, humdrum, run-of-the-mill, pedestrian, predictable, hackneyed, unimaginative, unoriginal, banal, trite.
– OPPOSITES unusual.

row¹ n. **1 line**, column, file, queue, procession, chain, string, succession; informal crocodile. **2 tier**, line, rank, bank.
□ **in a row** consecutively, in succession, running, straight; informal on the trot.

row² (Brit.) n. **1 argument**, quarrel, squabble, fight, dispute, altercation, falling-out; informal tiff, run-in, slanging match, spat; Brit. informal bust-up. **2 din**, noise, racket, uproar, hubbub, rumpus; informal hullabaloo.
•v. **argue**, quarrel, squabble, bicker, fight, fall out, disagree, have words; informal scrap.

rowdy adj. **unruly**, disorderly, riotous, undisciplined, uncontrollable, ungovernable, disruptive, obstreperous, out of control, rough, wild, boisterous, uproarious, noisy, loud; Brit. informal rumbustious.
– OPPOSITES peaceful.

royal adj. **regal**, kingly, queenly, princely, sovereign.

rub v. **1 massage**, knead, stroke, pat. **2 apply**, smear, spread, work in. **3 chafe**, scrape, pinch.
□ **rub out** erase, delete, remove, obliterate, expunge.

rubbish n. **1 refuse**, waste, litter, scrap, detritus, debris, dross; N. Amer. garbage, trash; informal dreck, junk. **2 nonsense**, gibberish, claptrap, garbage; informal baloney, tripe, drivel, bilge, bunk, piffle, twaddle, poppycock, gobbledegook; Brit. informal codswallop, cobblers, tosh.

rude adj. **1 ill-mannered**, bad-mannered, impolite, discourteous, uncivil, impertinent, insolent, impudent, disparaging, abusive, curt, brusque, offhand. **2 vulgar**, coarse, smutty, dirty, filthy, crude, lewd, obscene, risqué; informal blue; Brit. informal near the knuckle.
– OPPOSITES polite.

rudimentary adj. **1 basic**, elementary, fundamental, essential. **2 primitive**, crude, simple, unsophisticated, rough (and ready), makeshift. **3 vestigial**, undeveloped, incomplete.

rudiments pl. n. **basics**, fundamentals, essentials, first principles, foundations; informal nuts and bolts, ABC.

rueful adj. **regretful**, apologetic, sorry, remorseful, shamefaced, sheepish, hangdog, contrite, repentant, penitent, conscience-stricken, self-reproachful, sorrowful, sad.

ruffle v. **1 disarrange**, tousle, dishevel, rumple, mess up; N. Amer. informal muss up. **2 disconcert**, unnerve, fluster, agitate, upset, disturb, discomfit, put off, perturb, unsettle; informal faze, throw, get to.
– OPPOSITES smooth.

rugged adj. **1 rough**, uneven, bumpy, rocky, stony, pitted. **2 robust**, durable, sturdy, strong, tough, resilient. **3 well built**, burly, strong, muscular, muscly, brawny, strapping, tough, hardy, robust, sturdy, solid; informal hunky. **4** *his rugged features*: **strong**, craggy, roughhewn, manly, masculine.
– OPPOSITES smooth, delicate.

ruin n. **1 disintegration**, decay, disrepair, dilapidation, destruction, demolition, devastation. **2** *the ruins of a church*: **remains**, remnants, fragments, rubble, debris, wreckage. **3 downfall**, collapse, defeat, undoing, failure. **4 bankruptcy**, insolvency, penury, destitution, poverty.
• v. **1 spoil**, wreck, blight, shatter, dash, scotch, mess up; informal screw up; Brit. informal scupper. **2 bankrupt**, make insolvent, impoverish, pauperize, wipe out, break, cripple, bring someone to their knees. **3 destroy**, devastate, lay waste, ravage, raze, demolish, wreck, wipe out, flatten.

ruined adj. derelict, dilapidated, tumbledown, ramshackle, decrepit, falling to pieces, crumbling, decaying, disintegrating, in ruins.

ruinous adj. **1 disastrous**, devastating, catastrophic, calamitous, crippling, crushing, damaging, destructive, harmful, costly. **2 extortionate**, exorbitant, excessive, skyhigh, outrageous, inflated; Brit. over the odds; informal steep.

rule n. **1 regulation**, ruling, directive, order, law, statute, ordinance. **2 procedure**, practice, protocol, convention, norm, routine, custom, habit. **3 principle**, precept, standard, axiom, truth, maxim. **4 government**, jurisdiction, command, power, dominion, control, administration, sovereignty, leadership.
• v. **1 govern**, preside over, control, lead, dominate, run, head, administer. **2 reign**, be on the throne, be in power, govern. **3 decree**, order, pronounce, judge, adjudge, ordain, decide, determine, find.
▢ **as a rule** usually, in general, normally, ordinarily, customarily, for the most part, on the whole, by and large, mostly, commonly, typically.
rule out exclude, eliminate, disregard, preclude, prohibit, prevent, disallow.

ruler n. **leader**, sovereign, monarch, potentate, king, queen, emperor, empress, prince, princess, crowned head, head of state, president, premier, governor.
– OPPOSITES subject.

r

ruling n. **judgement**, decision, adjudication, finding, verdict, pronouncement, resolution, decree, injunction.

•adj. **1 governing**, controlling, commanding, supreme. **2 main**, chief, principal, major, dominating, consuming; informal number-one.

rummage v. **search**, hunt, root about/around, ferret about/around, fish about/around, dig, delve, go through, explore, sift through, rifle through.

rumour n. **gossip**, hearsay, talk, tittle-tattle, speculation, word, report, story, whisper; informal the grapevine, the word on the street, the buzz.

run v. **1 sprint**, race, dart, rush, dash, hasten, hurry, scurry, scamper, gallop, jog, trot. **2 flee**, take flight, make off, take off, take to your heels, bolt, make your getaway, escape; informal beat it, clear off/out, scram, leg it; Brit. informal scarper. **3 extend**, stretch, reach, continue. **4 flow**, pour, stream, gush, flood, cascade, roll, course, glide, spill, trickle, drip, dribble, leak. **5 be in charge of**, manage, direct, control, head, govern, supervise, superintend, oversee, organize, coordinate. **6** *it's expensive to run a car:* **maintain**, keep, own, possess, have, use, operate. **7** *I left the engine running:* **operate**, function, work, go.
•n. **1 jog**, sprint, dash, gallop, trot. **2 route**, journey, circuit, round, beat. **3 drive**, ride, turn, trip, excursion, outing, jaunt; informal spin, tootle. **4 series**, succession, sequence, string, streak, spate. **5 enclosure**, pen, coop. **6** *a ski run:* **slope**, track, piste; N. Amer. trail.

□ **run down 1 run over**, knock down/over, hit. **2 criticize**, denigrate, belittle, disparage, deprecate, find fault with; informal put down, knock, bad-mouth; Brit. informal rubbish, slag off. **run into 1 collide with**, hit, strike, crash into, smash into, plough into, ram. **2 meet (by chance)**, run across, chance on, stumble on, happen on; informal bump into. **3 experience**, encounter, meet with, be faced with, be confronted with. **run out 1 be used up**, dry up, be exhausted, be finished, peter out. **2 expire**, end, terminate, finish, lapse. **run over 1 overflow**, spill over, brim over. **2 exceed**, go over, overshoot, overreach. **3 review**, repeat, run through, go over, reiterate, recapitulate, look over, read through; informal recap on. **run over run down**, knock down/over, hit.

runaway n. **fugitive**, refugee, truant, absconder, deserter.

rundown n. **summary**, synopsis, precis, run-through, recap, review, overview, briefing, sketch, outline; informal lowdown.

run down adj. **1 dilapidated**, tumbledown, ramshackle, derelict, crumbling, neglected, uncared-for. **2 unwell**, ill, poorly, unhealthy, peaky, tired, drained, exhausted, worn out, below par, washed out; Brit. off colour; informal under the weather; Brit. informal off; Austral./NZ informal crook.

runner n. **1 athlete**, sprinter, hurdler, racer, jogger. **2 messenger**, courier, errand boy; informal gofer.

running n. **1 administration**, management, organization, coordination, orchestration, handling, direction, control, supervision. **2 operation**, working, function, performance. •adj. **1 flowing**, gushing, rushing, moving. **2 in succession**, in a row, in sequence, consecutively, straight, together; informal on the trot.

runny adj. **liquid**, liquefied, fluid, melted, molten, watery, thin. – OPPOSITES solid, thick.

rupture n. & v. **break**, fracture, crack, burst, split, fissure, breach.

rural adj. **country**, rustic, bucolic, pastoral, agricultural, agrarian. – OPPOSITES urban.

ruse n. **ploy**, stratagem, tactic, scheme, trick, gambit, dodge, subterfuge, machination, wile; Brit. informal wheeze.

rush v. **1 hurry**, dash, run, race, sprint, bolt, dart, gallop, career, charge, shoot, hurtle, hare, fly, speed, zoom, scurry, scuttle, scamper, hasten; informal tear, belt, pelt, scoot, zip, whip, hotfoot it; Brit. informal bomb. **2 gush**, pour, surge, stream, course, cascade. **3 attack**, charge, storm. •n. **1 dash**, run, sprint, dart, bolt, charge, scramble. **2 hustle and bustle**, commotion, hubbub, hurly-burly, stir. **3 charge**, onslaught, attack, assault.

rushed adj. **hasty**, fast, speedy, quick, swift, rapid, hurried.

rust v. **corrode**, oxidize, tarnish.

rustic adj. **1 rural**, country, pastoral, bucolic, agricultural, agrarian; literary Arcadian. **2 plain**, simple, homely, unsophisticated, rough, crude. – OPPOSITES urban. •n. **peasant**, countryman, countrywoman, bumpkin, yokel, country cousin; N. Amer. informal hillbilly, hayseed, hick.

rustle v. **1 swish**, whoosh, whisper, sigh. **2 steal**, thieve, take, abduct, kidnap.

rut n. **1 furrow**, groove, trough, ditch, hollow, pothole, crater. **2 boring routine**, humdrum existence, groove, dead end.

ruthless adj. **merciless**, pitiless, cruel, heartless, hard-hearted, cold-hearted, cold-blooded, harsh, callous. – OPPOSITES merciful.

r

sabotage n. vandalism, wrecking, destruction, damage, obstruction, disruption; Brit. informal a spanner in the works.
•v. **vandalize**, wreck, damage, destroy, incapacitate, obstruct, disrupt, spoil, ruin, undermine; Brit. informal throw a spanner in the works.

sack n. bag, pouch, pocket, pack.
•v. (informal) **dismiss**, discharge, lay off, make redundant, let go, throw out; informal fire, give someone the sack; Brit. informal give someone their cards.
□ **the sack** (informal) dismissal, discharge, redundancy; informal the boot, the axe, the heave-ho, the push.

sacred adj. **1** holy, hallowed, blessed, consecrated, sanctified. **2 religious**, spiritual, devotional, church, ecclesiastical.
– OPPOSITES secular, profane.

sacrifice n. **1** offering, gift, oblation. **2** surrender, giving up, abandonment, renunciation, forfeiture.
•v. **1** offer up, immolate. **2** give up, forgo, abandon, renounce, relinquish, cede, surrender, forfeit.

sacrilege n. desecration, profanity, blasphemy, irreverence, disrespect.

sad adj. **1** unhappy, sorrowful, depressed, downcast, miserable, down, despondent, wretched, glum, gloomy, doleful, melancholy, mournful, woebegone, forlorn, heartbroken; informal blue, down in the mouth, down in the dumps. **2 tragic**, unhappy, miserable, wretched, sorry, pitiful, pathetic, heartbreaking, heart-rending. **3 unfortunate**, regrettable, sorry, deplorable, lamentable, pitiful, shameful, disgraceful.
– OPPOSITES happy, cheerful.

sadden v. depress, dispirit, deject, dishearten, grieve, discourage, upset, get down.

saddle v. burden, encumber, lumber, land, impose something on.

sadness n. unhappiness, sorrow, dejection, depression, misery, despondency, gloom, gloominess, wretchedness, melancholy.

safe adj. **1** secure, protected, sheltered, guarded, out of harm's way. **2 unharmed**, unhurt, uninjured, unscathed, all right, fine, well, in one piece, out of danger, safe and sound. **3 cautious**, circumspect, prudent, careful, unadventurous, conservative. **4 harmless**,

innocuous, non-toxic, non-poisonous.
– OPPOSITES dangerous, harmful.

safeguard n. **protection**, defence, buffer, provision, security, cover, insurance.
•v. **protect**, preserve, conserve, save, secure, shield, guard, keep safe.
– OPPOSITES jeopardize.

safety n. **1 welfare**, well-being, protection, security. **2 shelter**, sanctuary, refuge.

sag v. **1 sink**, slump, loll, flop, crumple. **2 dip**, droop, bulge, bag.

saga n. **1 epic**, legend, (folk) tale, romance, narrative, myth. **2 story**, tale, yarn.

sage n. **wise man/woman**, philosopher, scholar, guru, prophet, mystic.

sail v. **1 voyage**, travel, navigate, cruise. **2 set sail**, put to sea, leave, weigh anchor. **3 steer**, pilot, captain; informal skipper. **4 glide**, drift, float, flow, sweep, skim, coast, flit, scud.

sailor n. **seaman**, seafarer, mariner, yachtsman, yachtswoman, hand; informal old salt, matelot, Jack Tar.

saintly adj. **holy**, godly, pious, religious, devout, spiritual, virtuous, righteous, good, pure.
– OPPOSITES ungodly.

sake n. **1** for the sake of clarity: **purpose(s)**, reason(s). **2** for her son's sake: **benefit**, advantage, good, well-being, welfare.

salary n. **pay**, wages, earnings, payment, remuneration, fee(s), stipend, income.

sale n. **1 selling**, dealing, trading. **2 deal**, transaction, bargain.
– OPPOSITES purchase.

salty adj. **salt**, salted, saline, briny, brackish.

salubrious adj. **pleasant**, agreeable, nice, select, high-class; Brit. upmarket; informal posh, classy; Brit. informal swish.

salute n. **tribute**, testimonial, homage, honour, celebration (of), acknowledgement (of).
•v. **pay tribute to**, pay homage to, honour, celebrate, acknowledge, take your hat off to.

salvage v. **rescue**, save, recover, retrieve, reclaim.

salvation n. **1 redemption**, deliverance. **2 lifeline**, means of escape, saviour.
– OPPOSITES damnation, ruin.

same adj. **1 identical**, selfsame, very same. **2 matching**, identical, alike, carbon-copy, twin, indistinguishable, interchangeable, corresponding, equivalent, parallel, like, comparable, similar, homogeneous.
– OPPOSITES another, different.
□ **the same** unchanging, unvarying, unvaried, consistent, uniform.

sample n. **1 specimen**, example, snippet, swatch, taste, taster. **2 cross section**, sampling, selection.
•v. **try (out)**, taste, test, put to

S

the test, appraise, evaluate; informal check out.

sanctimonious adj. **self-righteous**, holier-than-thou, pious, moralizing, smug, superior, priggish, hypocritical, insincere; informal goody-goody.

sanction n. **1 penalty**, punishment, deterrent, restriction, embargo, ban, prohibition, boycott. **2 authorization**, consent, leave, permission, authority, dispensation, assent, acquiescence, agreement, approval, endorsement, blessing; informal the thumbs up, the OK, the green light.
– OPPOSITES prohibition.
•v. **authorize**, permit, allow, endorse, approve, accept, back, support; informal OK.
– OPPOSITES prohibit.

sanctuary n. **1 refuge**, haven, oasis, shelter, retreat, bolt-hole, hideaway. **2 safety**, protection, shelter, immunity, asylum. **3 reserve**, wildlife reserve, park.

sane adj. **1 of sound mind**, in your right mind, compos mentis, lucid, rational, balanced, normal; informal all there. **2 sensible**, practical, realistic, prudent, reasonable, rational, level-headed, commonsensical.
– OPPOSITES mad, foolish.

sanguine adj. **optimistic**, hopeful, buoyant, positive, confident, cheerful, bullish; informal upbeat.
– OPPOSITES gloomy.

sanity n. **1 mental health**, reason, rationality, stability, lucidity, sense, wits, mind. **2 sense**,

good sense, common sense, wisdom, prudence, rationality.

sap n. **juice**, secretion, fluid, liquid.
•v. **erode**, wear away/down, deplete, reduce, lessen, undermine, drain, bleed.

sarcasm n. **irony**, derision, mockery, ridicule, scorn.

sarcastic adj. **ironic**, sardonic, derisive, scornful, contemptuous, mocking, caustic, scathing, trenchant, acerbic.

sardonic adj. **mocking**, cynical, scornful, derisive, sneering, scathing, caustic, trenchant, cutting, acerbic.

satanic adj. **diabolical**, fiendish, devilish, demonic, ungodly, hellish, infernal, wicked, evil, sinful.
– OPPOSITES godly.

satire n. **parody**, burlesque, caricature, irony, lampoon, skit; informal spoof, take-off, send-up.

satirical adj. **mocking**, ironic, sardonic, critical, irreverent, disparaging, disrespectful.

satirize v. **mock**, ridicule, deride, make fun of, parody, lampoon, caricature, take off, criticize; informal send up, take the mickey out of.

satisfaction n. **contentment**, content, pleasure, gratification, fulfilment, enjoyment, happiness, pride.

satisfactory adj. **adequate**, all right, acceptable, good enough, sufficient, reasonable, competent, fair, decent, average, passable, fine, in order, up to scratch, up to the mark.

satisfy v. **1 fulfil**, gratify, meet, fill, indulge, appease, assuage, quench, slake, satiate. **2 convince**, assure, reassure, put someone's mind at rest. **3 comply with**, meet, fulfil, answer, conform to, measure up to, come up to.
– OPPOSITES frustrate.

saturate v. **1 soak**, drench, wet through. **2 flood**, glut, oversupply, overfill, overload.

saturated adj. **1 soaked**, soaking (wet), wet through, sopping (wet), sodden, dripping, wringing wet, drenched, soaked to the skin. **2 waterlogged**, flooded, boggy, awash.
– OPPOSITES dry.

sauce n. **relish**, condiment, ketchup, dip, dressing, jus, coulis, gravy.

saunter v. **stroll**, amble, wander, meander, walk; informal mosey, tootle; formal promenade.

savage adj. **1 vicious**, brutal, cruel, sadistic, ferocious, fierce, violent, barbaric, bloodthirsty, merciless, pitiless. **2 untamed**, wild, feral, undomesticated. **3** *a savage attack on the government*: **fierce**, blistering, scathing, searing, stinging, devastating, withering, virulent, vitriolic.
– OPPOSITES mild, tame.
• n. **brute**, beast, monster, barbarian, sadist, animal.
• v. **maul**, attack, lacerate, claw, bite, tear to pieces.

save v. **1 rescue**, set free, free, liberate, deliver, redeem. **2 preserve**, keep, protect, safeguard, salvage, retrieve, reclaim, rescue. **3 put aside**, set aside, put by, keep, conserve, retain, store, hoard, stockpile; informal squirrel away. **4 prevent**, avoid, forestall, spare, stop, obviate, avert.

saving n. **1 reduction**, cut, decrease, economy. **2 (savings)** nest egg, capital, assets, funds, resources, reserves.

saviour n. **rescuer**, liberator, deliverer, champion, protector, redeemer.

savour v. **relish**, enjoy, appreciate, delight in, revel in, luxuriate in.
• n. **smell**, aroma, fragrance, scent, perfume, bouquet, taste, flavour, tang, smack.

savoury adj. **salty**, spicy, tangy, piquant.
– OPPOSITES sweet.
• n. **canapé**, hors d'oeuvre, appetizer, titbit.

say v. **1 speak**, utter, voice, pronounce. **2 declare**, state, announce, remark, observe, mention, comment, note, add. **3 recite**, repeat, utter, deliver, perform. **4 indicate**, show, read.
• n. **influence**, sway, weight, voice, input.

saying n. **proverb**, maxim, aphorism, axiom, expression, phrase, formula, slogan, catchphrase.

scale n. **1 hierarchy**, ladder, ranking, pecking order, order,

spectrum. **2 ratio**, proportion. **3 extent**, size, scope, magnitude, dimensions, range, breadth, degree.
•v. **climb**, ascend, clamber up, scramble up, shin (up), mount; N. Amer. shinny (up).

scaly adj. **dry**, flaky, scurfy, rough, scabrous.

scan v. **1 study**, examine, scrutinize, inspect, survey, search, scour, sweep, watch. **2 glance through**, look through, have a look at, run your eye over, cast your eye over, flick through, browse through, leaf through, thumb through.

scandal n. **1 gossip**, rumour(s), slander, libel, aspersions, muckraking; informal dirt. **2** *it's a scandal that the hospital has closed:* **disgrace**, outrage, sin, (crying) shame.

scandalous adj. **1 disgraceful**, shocking, outrageous, monstrous, criminal, wicked, shameful, appalling, deplorable, inexcusable, intolerable, unforgivable, unpardonable. **2 discreditable**, disreputable, dishonourable, improper, unseemly, sordid. **3 scurrilous**, malicious, slanderous, libellous, defamatory.

scant adj. **little**, little or no, minimal, limited, negligible, meagre, insufficient, inadequate.
– OPPOSITES abundant, ample.

scanty adj. **1 meagre**, scant, minimal, limited, modest, restricted, sparse, tiny, small, paltry, negligible, scarce, in short supply, thin on the ground, few and far between; informal measly, piddling, mingy, pathetic. **2 skimpy**, revealing, short, brief, low-cut.
– OPPOSITES ample, plentiful.

scapegoat n. **whipping boy**, Aunt Sally; informal fall guy; N. Amer. informal patsy.

scar n. **1 mark**, blemish, disfigurement, discoloration, pockmark, pit, lesion, cicatrix. **2** *psychological scars:* **trauma**, damage, injury.
•v. **disfigure**, mark, blemish, discolour, mar, spoil.

scarce adj. **in short supply**, scant, scanty, inadequate, lacking, meagre, sparse, hard to come by, at a premium, few and far between, thin on the ground, rare.
– OPPOSITES plentiful.

scarcely adv. **1 hardly**, barely, only just. **2 rarely**, seldom, infrequently, not often, hardly ever; informal once in a blue moon.

scarcity n. **shortage**, dearth, lack, undersupply, insufficiency, paucity, poverty, deficiency, inadequacy, unavailability, absence.

scare v. **frighten**, startle, alarm, terrify, unnerve, worry, intimidate, terrorize, cow; informal freak out; Brit. informal put the wind up; N. Amer. informal spook.
•n. **fright**, shock, start, turn, jump.

s

scared adj. **frightened**, afraid, fearful, nervous, panicky, terrified; informal in a cold sweat; N. Amer. informal spooked.

scary adj. (informal) **frightening**, terrifying, hair-raising, spine-chilling, blood-curdling, eerie, sinister; informal creepy, spine-tingling, spooky.

scathing adj. **withering**, blistering, searing, devastating, fierce, ferocious, savage, severe, stinging, biting, cutting, virulent, vitriolic, scornful, bitter, harsh.
– OPPOSITES mild.

scatter v. **1 spread**, sprinkle, distribute, strew, disseminate, sow, throw, toss, fling. **2 disperse**, break up, disband, separate, dissolve.
– OPPOSITES gather, assemble.

scavenge v. **search**, hunt, look, forage, rummage, root about/around, grub about/around.

scenario n. **1 plot**, outline, storyline, framework, screenplay, script. **2 situation**, chain of events, course of events.

scene n. **1 location**, site, place, position, spot, locale. **2 background**, setting, context, milieu, backdrop. **3 incident**, event, episode, happening, proceeding. **4 view**, vista, outlook, panorama, landscape, scenery. **5** she made a scene: **fuss**, exhibition of yourself, performance, tantrum, commotion, disturbance, row; informal to-do; Brit. informal carry-on. **6** the political scene: **arena**, stage, sphere, world, milieu, realm. **7 clip**,

section, segment, part, sequence, extract.

scenery n. **1 landscape**, countryside, country, terrain, setting, surroundings, environment. **2 set**, setting, backdrop.

scenic adj. **picturesque**, pretty, attractive, beautiful, charming, impressive, striking, spectacular, breathtaking, panoramic.

scent n. **1 smell**, fragrance, aroma, perfume, savour, odour. **2 perfume**, fragrance, eau de toilette, toilet water, eau de cologne. **3 spoor**, trail, track.
•v. **smell**, nose out, detect, pick up, sense.

scented adj. **perfumed**, sweet-smelling, fragranced, fragrant, aromatic.

sceptic n. **cynic**, doubter, unbeliever, doubting Thomas.

sceptical adj. **dubious**, doubtful, doubting, cynical, distrustful, suspicious, disbelieving, unconvinced.
– OPPOSITES certain, convinced.

scepticism n. **doubt**, a pinch of salt, disbelief, cynicism, distrust, suspicion, incredulity. **s**

schedule n. **plan**, programme, timetable, scheme, agenda, diary, calendar, itinerary.
•v. **arrange**, organize, plan, programme, timetable, set up, line up; N. Amer. slate.

scheme n. **1 plan**, project, programme, strategy, stratagem, tactic; Brit. informal wheeze. **2 plot**, intrigue, conspiracy, ruse, ploy, stratagem,

manoeuvre, subterfuge, machinations; informal racket, scam.
• v. **plot**, conspire, intrigue, connive, manoeuvre, plan.

scheming adj. **cunning**, crafty, calculating, devious, conniving, wily, sly, tricky, artful.
– OPPOSITES ingenuous, honest.

schism n. **division**, split, rift, breach, rupture, break, separation, severance, chasm, gulf, disagreement.

scholar n. **academic**, intellectual, learned person, man/woman of letters, authority, expert; informal egghead; N. Amer. informal pointy-head.

scholarly adj. **learned**, educated, erudite, academic, well read, intellectual, literary, highbrow.
– OPPOSITES uneducated, illiterate.

scholarship n. **1 learning**, knowledge, erudition, education, academic study. **2 grant**, award, endowment; Brit. bursary.

school n. **1 college**, academy, alma mater. **2 department**, faculty, division. **3 tradition**, approach, style, way of thinking, persuasion, creed, credo, doctrine, belief, opinion, point of view.
• v. **train**, teach, tutor, coach, instruct, drill.

WORD LINKS
relating to schools: scholastic

science n. *the science of criminology:* **subject**, discipline, field, branch of knowledge, body of knowledge, area of study.

scientific adj. **1 technological**, technical, evidence-based, empirical. **2 systematic**, methodical, organized, ordered, exact, rigorous, precise, accurate, mathematical.

scintillating adj. **brilliant**, dazzling, exciting, exhilarating, stimulating, sparkling, lively, vivacious, vibrant, animated, effervescent, witty, clever.
– OPPOSITES dull, boring.

scoff v. **sneer**, jeer, laugh; (**scoff at**) mock, deride, ridicule, dismiss, belittle; informal pooh-pooh.

scoop n. **spoon**, ladle, dipper.
□ **scoop out 1** hollow out, gouge out, dig, excavate. **2** remove, take out, spoon out, scrape out. **scoop up** pick up, gather up, lift, take up, snatch up, grab.

scope n. **1 extent**, range, breadth, reach, sweep, span, area, sphere, realm, compass, orbit, ambit, terms of reference, remit. **2 opportunity**, freedom, latitude, leeway, capacity, room (to manoeuvre).

scorch v. **1 burn**, sear, singe, char, blacken, discolour.
2 dry up, parch, wither, shrivel, desiccate.

scorching adj. **hot**, red-hot, blazing, flaming, fiery, burning, blistering, searing; informal boiling, baking, sizzling.
– OPPOSITES freezing, mild.

score n. **1** result, outcome, total, tally, count. **2** rating, grade, mark, percentage.
•v. **1** get, gain, chalk up, achieve, make, record, rack up, notch up; *informal* bag, knock up. **2 arrange**, set, adapt, orchestrate, write, compose. **3 scratch**, cut, notch, incise, scrape, nick, gouge.
□ **score out/through** cross out, strike out, delete, put a line through, obliterate.

scorn n. **contempt**, derision, disdain, mockery, sneering.
– OPPOSITES admiration, respect.
•v. **1 deride**, treat with contempt, mock, scoff at, sneer at, jeer at, laugh at. **2 spurn**, rebuff, reject, ignore, shun, snub.
– OPPOSITES admire, respect.

scornful adj. **contemptuous**, derisive, withering, mocking, sneering, jeering, scathing, snide, disparaging, supercilious, disdainful.
– OPPOSITES admiring.

scour[1] v. **scrub**, rub, clean, polish, buff, shine, burnish, grind, abrade.

scour[2] v. **search**, comb, hunt through, rummage through, look high and low in, ransack, turn upside-down.

scourge n. **affliction**, bane, curse, plague, menace, evil, misfortune, burden, blight, cancer, canker.

scout n. **1 lookout**, outrider, spy. **2** reconnaissance, reconnoitre, survey, exploration, search; *informal* recce; *Brit. informal* shufti.
•v. **1** *I scouted around for some logs:* **search**, look, hunt, ferret around, root around, nose around. **2** *a patrol was sent to scout out the area:* **reconnoitre**, explore, inspect, investigate, spy out, survey, scan, study; *informal* check out, case.

scowl v. **glower**, frown, glare, grimace, lour, look daggers.
– OPPOSITES smile.

scramble v. **1 clamber**, climb, crawl, claw your way, scrabble, struggle; *N. Amer.* shinny. **2 muddle**, confuse, mix up, jumble (up), disarrange, disorganize, disorder, disturb, mess up.
•n. **1 clamber**, climb. **2** *the scramble for a seat:* **struggle**, jostle, scrimmage, scuffle, tussle, free-for-all, jockeying, competition, race.

scrap n. **1 fragment**, piece, bit, snippet, oddment, remnant, morsel, sliver. **2** *not a scrap of evidence:* **bit**, shred, speck, iota, particle, ounce, jot. **3 waste**, rubbish, refuse, debris; *N. Amer.* garbage, trash; *informal* junk.
•v. **1 throw away**, throw out, dispose of, get rid of, discard, dispense with, bin, decommission, break up, demolish; *informal* chuck (away/out), ditch, dump, junk; *Brit. informal* get shot of; *N. Amer. informal* trash. **2 abandon**, drop, abolish, withdraw, do away with, put an end to, cancel, axe; *informal* ditch, dump, junk.
– OPPOSITES keep.

scrape v. **1 rub**, scratch, scour, grind, sand, sandpaper, abrade,

S

file. **2 grate**, creak, rasp, scratch. **3 graze**, scratch, scuff, rasp, skin, cut, lacerate, bark, chafe.
‣n. **1 grating**, creaking, rasp, scratch. **2 graze**, scratch, abrasion, cut, laceration, wound.

scratch v. scrape, abrade, graze, score, scuff, skin, cut, lacerate, bark, chafe.
‣n. **abrasion**, graze, scrape, cut, laceration, wound, mark, line.
◻ **up to scratch** good enough, up to the mark, up to standard, up to par, satisfactory, acceptable, adequate, passable, sufficient, all right; informal OK.

scream v. & n. shriek, screech, yell, howl, bawl, yelp, squeal, wail, squawk.

screen n. **1 partition**, divider, windbreak. **2 display**, monitor, visual display unit. **3 mesh**, net, netting. **4 buffer**, protection, shield, shelter, guard.
‣v. **1 partition**, divide, separate, curtain. **2 conceal**, hide, veil, shield, shelter, shade, protect. **3** *all blood is screened for the virus*: check, test, examine, investigate, vet; informal check out. **4 show**, broadcast, transmit, televise, put out, air.

screw n. **1 bolt**, fastener. **2 propeller**, rotor.
‣v. **1 tighten**, turn, twist, wind. **2 fasten**, secure, fix, attach. **3** (informal) **extort**, force, extract, wrest, wring, squeeze; informal bleed.
◻ **screw up 1** wrinkle, pucker, crumple, crease, furrow, contort, distort, twist. **2** (informal)

wreck, ruin, destroy, damage, spoil, mess up; informal louse up, foul up; scupper.

scribble v. scrawl, scratch, dash off, jot (down), doodle, sketch.
‣n. scrawl, squiggle(s), jottings, doodle, doodlings.

script n. **1 handwriting**, writing, hand. **2 text**, screenplay, libretto, score, lines, dialogue, words.

scrounge v. beg, borrow; informal cadge, sponge, bum, touch someone for; N. Amer. informal mooch; Austral./NZ informal bludge.

scrounger n. beggar, parasite, cadger; informal sponger, freeloader; N. Amer. informal mooch; Austral./NZ informal bludger.

scrub v. **1 brush**, scour, rub, clean, cleanse, wash. **2** (informal) **abandon**, scrap, drop, cancel, call off, axe; informal ditch, dump, junk.

scruffy adj. shabby, worn, down at heel, ragged, tattered, mangy, dirty, untidy, unkempt, bedraggled, messy, dishevelled, ill-groomed; informal tatty.
– OPPOSITES smart.

scruples pl. n. qualms, compunction, hesitation, reservations, second thoughts, doubt(s), misgivings, uneasiness, reluctance.

scrupulous adj. careful, meticulous, painstaking, thorough, assiduous, sedulous, attentive, conscientious, punctilious, searching, close, rigorous, strict.
– OPPOSITES careless.

scrutinize v. **examine**, inspect, survey, study, look at, peruse, investigate, explore, probe, enquire into, go into, check.

sculpture n. **carving**, statue, statuette, figure, figurine, effigy, bust, head, model.

scum n. **film**, layer, covering, froth, filth, dross, dirt.

scupper v. (Brit. informal) **ruin**, wreck, destroy, sabotage, torpedo, spoil.

scurrilous adj. **defamatory**, slanderous, libellous, scandalous, insulting, offensive, abusive, malicious; informal bitchy.

sea n. **1 ocean**, waves; informal the drink; Brit. informal the briny; literary the deep. **2** *a sea of roofs:* **expanse**, stretch, area, tract, sweep, carpet, mass.
• adj. **marine**, ocean, oceanic, maritime, naval, nautical.
☐ **at sea** confused, perplexed, puzzled, baffled, mystified, bemused, bewildered, nonplussed, dumbfounded, at a loss, lost; informal flummoxed, fazed.

seal n. **1 sealant**, adhesive, mastic. **2 emblem**, symbol, insignia, badge, crest.
• v. **1 stop up**, seal up, cork, stopper, plug, make watertight. **2 clinch**, secure, settle, conclude, complete, finalize, confirm.
☐ **seal off** close off, shut off, cordon off, fence off, isolate.

seam n. **1 join**, stitching, joint. **2 layer**, stratum, vein, lode.

seaman n. **sailor**, seafarer, mariner, boatman, hand, merchant seaman.
– OPPOSITES landlubber.

sear v. **1 scorch**, burn, singe, char, dry up, wither. **2 flash-fry**, seal, brown.

search v. **1 hunt**, look, seek, forage, look high and low, ferret about, root about, rummage. **2** *he searched the house:* **look through**, scour, go through, sift through, comb, turn upside down, ransack, rifle through; Austral./NZ informal fossick through. **3 examine**, inspect, check, frisk.
• n. **hunt**, look, quest, examination, exploration.

searching adj. **penetrating**, piercing, probing, keen, shrewd, sharp, intent.

seaside n. **coast**, shore, seashore, beach, sand, sands.

season n. **period**, time, time of year, spell, term.
• v. **flavour**, add salt/pepper to, spice.

seasoned adj. **experienced**, practised, well versed, knowledgeable, established, veteran, hardened.
– OPPOSITES inexperienced.

seasoning n. **flavouring**, salt and pepper, herbs, spices, condiments.

seat n. **1 chair**, bench, stool; (**seats**) seating. **2 headquarters**, base, centre, nerve centre, hub, heart, location, site. **3 residence**, ancestral home, mansion.

•v. **1 position**, put, place, ensconce, install, settle. **2 have
room for**, contain, take, sit,
hold, accommodate.

secluded adj. **sheltered**, private,
concealed, hidden, unfrequent-
ed, sequestered, tucked away,
remote, isolated, off the beaten
track.

second[1] adj. **1 next**, following,
subsequent. **2 additional**, extra,
alternative, another, spare,
backup; N. Amer. alternate.
3 secondary, subordinate,
subsidiary, lesser, inferior.
– OPPOSITES first.
•n. **assistant**, attendant, helper,
aide, supporter, auxiliary,
second in command, number
two, deputy, understudy; informal
sidekick.
•v. **support**, vote for, back,
approve, endorse.

second[2] n. **moment**, bit, little
while, instant, flash; informal sec,
jiffy; Brit. informal mo, tick.

secondary adj. **1 less important**, subordinate, lesser, minor,
peripheral, incidental, subsidiary, ancillary. **2 accompanying**,
attendant, concomitant, consequential, resulting, resultant.
– OPPOSITES primary, main.

second-hand adj. **used**, old,
worn, pre-owned, nearly new,
handed-down, hand-me-down,
cast-off.
– OPPOSITES new, direct.
•adv. **indirectly**; informal on the
grapevine.
– OPPOSITES directly.

secondly adv. **furthermore**, also,
moreover, second, in the second
place, next.

secrecy n. **confidentiality**, privacy, mystery, concealment,
stealth.

secret adj. **1 confidential**, top
secret, classified, undisclosed,
unknown, private, under wraps;
informal hush-hush. **2 hidden**,
concealed, disguised,
camouflaged. **3 clandestine**,
covert, undercover, underground, surreptitious, stealthy,
cloak-and-dagger, furtive, conspiratorial.
– OPPOSITES public, open.
□ **in secret** secretly, in private,
behind closed doors, under
cover, furtively, stealthily, on
the quiet, covertly; formal sub
rosa.

secretive adj. **uncommunicative**, secret, unforthcoming,
playing your cards close to your
chest, reticent, tight-lipped.
– OPPOSITES open, communicative.

secretly adv. **in secret**, in private,
privately, behind closed doors,
under cover, furtively, stealthily,
on the quiet, covertly.

sect n. **group**, cult, denomination, order, splinter group,
faction, camp.

sectarian adj. **factional**, separat-
ist, partisan, doctrinaire,
dogmatic, illiberal, intolerant,
bigoted, narrow-minded.

section n. **1 part**, bit, portion,
segment, compartment,

s

module, element, unit. **2 passage**, subsection, chapter, subdivision, clause. **3 department**, area, division.

sector n. **1 part**, branch, arm, division, area, department, field, sphere. **2 district**, quarter, section, zone, region, area, belt.

secular adj. **non-religious**, lay, temporal, civil, worldly, earthly, profane.
– OPPOSITES sacred, religious.

secure adj. **1 fastened**, fixed, secured, done up, closed, shut, locked. **2 safe**, protected, safe and sound, out of harm's way, in safe hands, invulnerable, undamaged, unharmed. **3** *his position as leader was secure*: **certain**, assured, settled, stable, not at risk. **4 unworried**, at ease, relaxed, happy, confident.
– OPPOSITES loose, insecure.
▪v. **1 fasten**, close, shut, lock, bolt, chain, seal. **2 obtain**, acquire, gain, get, get hold of, come by; *informal* land.

security n. **1 safety**, protection. **2 safety measures**, safeguards, surveillance, defence, policing. **3 guarantee**, collateral, surety, pledge, bond.

sedate[1] v. **tranquillize**, put under sedation, drug.

sedate[2] adj. **1 slow**, steady, dignified, unhurried, relaxed, measured, leisurely, slow-moving, easy, gentle. **2 calm**, placid, tranquil, quiet, uneventful, staid, boring, dull.
– OPPOSITES fast, exciting.

sediment n. dregs, grounds, lees, residue, deposit, silt.

seduce v. **1 attract**, allure, lure, tempt, entice, beguile, inveigle, manipulate. **2 have your (wicked) way with**, take advantage of.

seductive adj. **tempting**, inviting, enticing, alluring, beguiling, attractive.

see v. **1 discern**, detect, perceive, spot, notice, catch sight of, glimpse, make out, pick out, distinguish, spy; *informal* clap eyes on, clock; *literary* behold, espy, descry. **2 watch**, look at, view, catch. **3 inspect**, view, look round, tour, survey, examine, scrutinize. **4 understand**, grasp, comprehend, follow, realize, appreciate, recognize, work out, fathom; *informal* get, latch on to, tumble to, figure out; *Brit. informal* twig, suss (out). **5** *see what he's up to*: **find out**, discover, learn, ascertain, determine, establish. **6** *see that no harm comes to him*: **ensure**, make sure/certain, see to it, take care, mind. **7** *I see trouble ahead*: **foresee**, predict, forecast, prophesy, anticipate, envisage. **8 consult**, confer with, talk to, have recourse to, call in, turn to. **9 go out with**, date, take out, be involved with; *informal* go steady with; *dated* court.
□ **see to** attend to, deal with, see about, take care of, look after, sort out, organize, arrange.

seed n. **pip**, stone, kernel.

seek v. 1 search for, try to find, look for, be after, hunt for. 2 ask for, request, solicit, call for, appeal for, apply for. 3 try, attempt, endeavour, strive, work, do your best.

seem v. appear (to be), have the appearance/air of being, give the impression of being, look, sound, come across as, strike someone as.

seep v. ooze, trickle, exude, drip, dribble, flow, leak, drain, bleed, filter, percolate, soak.

seethe v. 1 teem, swarm, boil, swirl, churn, surge, bubble, heave. 2 be angry, be furious, be enraged, rage, be incensed, be beside yourself, boil, rant, fume; informal be livid, foam at the mouth.

segment n. piece, bit, section, part, portion, division, slice, wedge.

segregate v. separate, set apart, keep apart, isolate, quarantine, partition, divide, discriminate against.
– OPPOSITES integrate.

seize v. 1 grab, grasp, snatch, take hold of, clutch, grip. 2 capture, take, overrun, occupy, conquer, take over. 3 confiscate, impound, commandeer, requisition, appropriate, expropriate, sequestrate. 4 kidnap, abduct, take captive, take prisoner, take hostage, hijack; informal snatch.
– OPPOSITES release.

seizure n. 1 capture, takeover, annexation, invasion, occupa-

tion. 2 confiscation, appropriation, expropriation, sequestration. 3 kidnap, abduction, hijack. 4 convulsion, fit, spasm, paroxysm.

seldom adv. rarely, infrequently, hardly (ever), scarcely (ever); informal once in a blue moon.
– OPPOSITES often.

select v. choose, pick (out), single out, opt for, decide on, settle on, sort out, take, adopt.
•adj. 1 choice, prime, hand-picked, top-quality, first-class; informal top-flight. 2 exclusive, elite, privileged, wealthy; informal posh.
– OPPOSITES inferior.

selection n. 1 choice, pick, option, preference. 2 range, array, diversity, variety, assortment, mixture. 3 anthology, assortment, collection, assemblage, miscellany, medley.

selective adj. discerning, discriminating, exacting, demanding, particular; informal choosy, picky.
– OPPOSITES indiscriminate.

self-centred adj. egocentric, egotistic, self-absorbed, self-obsessed, self-seeking, self-serving, narcissistic, vain, inconsiderate, thoughtless; informal looking after number one.

self-confidence n. self-assurance, assurance, confidence, composure, aplomb, poise, sangfroid.

self-conscious adj. embarrassed, uncomfortable, uneasy,

ill at ease, nervous, awkward, shy, diffident, timid.
– OPPOSITES confident.

selfish adj. **egocentric**, egotistic, self-centred, self-absorbed, self-obsessed, self-seeking, wrapped up in yourself, mean, greedy; informal looking after number one.
– OPPOSITES unselfish, altruistic.

selfless adj. **unselfish**, altruistic, considerate, compassionate, kind, noble, generous, magnanimous, ungrudging.
– OPPOSITES selfish, inconsiderate.

self-righteous adj. **sanctimonious**, holier-than-thou, pious, self-satisfied, smug, priggish, complacent, moralizing, superior, hypocritical; informal goody-goody.
– OPPOSITES humble.

sell v. **put up for sale**, put on the market, auction (off), trade in, deal in, retail, market, traffic in, peddle, hawk.
– OPPOSITES buy.

seller n. **vendor**, dealer, retailer, trader, merchant, agent, hawker, pedlar, purveyor, supplier, stockist.
– OPPOSITES buyer.

semblance n. **(outward) appearance**, air, show, facade, front, veneer, guise, pretence.

seminar n. **1 conference**, symposium, meeting, convention, forum, summit. **2 study group**, workshop, tutorial, class.

send v. **1 dispatch**, post, mail, email, consign, forward, transmit, convey, communicate, broadcast, radio. **2 propel**, project, eject, deliver, discharge, spout, fire, shoot, release, throw, fling, cast, hurl. **3** *you're sending me crazy:* **make**, drive, turn.
– OPPOSITES receive.
□ **send for** call, summon, ask for, request, order. **send up** (informal) satirize, ridicule, make fun of, parody, lampoon, mock, caricature, imitate, ape; informal take off, spoof, take the mickey out of.

send-off n. **farewell**, goodbye, adieu, leave-taking, departure.

senior adj. **1 older**, elder. **2 superior**, higher-ranking, more important; N. Amer. ranking.
– OPPOSITES junior, subordinate.

sensation n. **1 feeling**, sense, perception, impression. **2 commotion**, stir, uproar, furore, scandal, impact; informal splash, to-do.

sensational adj. **1 shocking**, scandalous, fascinating, exciting, thrilling, interesting, dramatic, momentous, historic, newsworthy. **2 overdramatized**, melodramatic, exaggerated, sensationalist, graphic, explicit, lurid; informal shock-horror, juicy. **3** (informal) **gorgeous**, stunning, wonderful, superb, excellent, first-class; informal great, terrific, tremendous, fantastic, fabulous, out of this world; Brit. informal smashing.
– OPPOSITES dull, unremarkable.

s

sense n. **1 feeling**, faculty, awareness, sensation, recognition, perception. **2 appreciation**, awareness, understanding, comprehension. **3 wisdom**, common sense, wit, reason, intelligence, judgement, brain(s), sagacity; informal gumption, nous, horse sense, savvy; Brit. informal loaf; N. Amer. informal smarts. **4 purpose**, point, use, value, advantage, benefit. **5 meaning**, definition, denotation, nuance, drift, gist, thrust, tenor, message.
– OPPOSITES stupidity.
•v. **detect**, feel, observe, notice, recognize, pick up, be aware of, distinguish, make out, perceive, discern, divine, intuit; informal catch on to.

senseless adj. **pointless**, futile, useless, needless, meaningless, absurd, foolish, insane, stupid, idiotic, mindless, illogical.
– OPPOSITES sensible.

sensible adj. **practical**, realistic, responsible, reasonable, commonsensical, rational, logical, sound, no-nonsense, level-headed, down-to-earth, wise.
– OPPOSITES foolish.

sensitive adj. **1** *she's sensitive to changes in temperature*: **responsive to**, reactive to, sensitized to, aware of, conscious of, susceptible to, affected by, vulnerable to. **2 delicate**, fragile, tender, sore. **3 tactful**, careful, thoughtful, diplomatic, delicate, subtle, kid-glove. **4 touchy**, oversensitive, hypersensitive,

easily offended, thin-skinned, defensive, paranoid, neurotic. **5 difficult**, delicate, tricky, awkward, problematic, ticklish, controversial, emotive.
– OPPOSITES insensitive, resilient.

sensitivity n. **1 responsiveness**, sensitiveness, reactivity, susceptibility. **2 tact**, diplomacy, delicacy, subtlety, understanding. **3 touchiness**, oversensitivity, hypersensitivity, defensiveness. **4 delicacy**, trickiness, awkwardness, ticklishness.

sensual adj. **1 physical**, carnal, bodily, fleshly, animal. **2 passionate**, sexual, physical, tactile, hedonistic.
– OPPOSITES spiritual.

sensuous adj. **1 rich**, sumptuous, luxurious. **2 voluptuous**, sexy, seductive, luscious, lush, ripe.

sentence n. **1 judgement**, ruling, decision, verdict. **2** *a long sentence*: **punishment**, prison term; informal time, stretch.
•v. **condemn**, doom, punish, convict.

sentiment n. **1 view**, feeling, attitude, thought, opinion, belief. **2 sentimentality**, emotion, tenderness, softness; informal schmaltz; Brit. informal soppiness.

sentimental adj. **1 nostalgic**, emotional, affectionate, loving, tender. **2 mawkish**, over-emotional, romantic, hearts-and-flowers; Brit. twee; informal schmaltzy, corny; Brit. informal soppy; N. Amer. informal sappy.

separate adj. **1 unconnected,** unrelated, different, distinct, discrete, detached, divorced, disconnected, independent. **2 set apart,** detached, cut off, segregated, isolated, free-standing, self-contained.
•v. **1 disconnect,** detach, disengage, uncouple, split, sunder, sever. **2 partition,** divide, stand between, come between, keep apart, isolate, section off. **3 part (company),** go their separate ways, split up, disperse, scatter. **4 split up,** break up, part, become estranged, divorce.
– OPPOSITES unite, join.

separately adv. **individually,** one by one, one at a time, singly, severally, apart, independently, alone, by yourself, on your own.

separation n. **1 disconnection,** splitting, division, breaking-up. **2 break-up,** split, estrangement, divorce; Brit. informal bust-up.

septic adj. **infected,** festering, suppurating, putrid, putrefying, poisoned; Medicine purulent.

sequel n. **continuation,** further episode, follow-up.

sequence n. **1 succession,** order, course, series, chain, train, progression, chronology, pattern, flow. **2 excerpt,** clip, extract, section.

serene adj. **calm,** composed, tranquil, peaceful, placid, untroubled, relaxed, at ease, unperturbed, unruffled, unworried; N. Amer. centered; informal together, unflappable.
– OPPOSITES agitated.

series n. **succession,** sequence, string, chain, run, round, spate, wave, rash, course, cycle, row.

serious adj. **1 solemn,** earnest, grave, sombre, unsmiling, stern, grim, humourless, stony, dour, poker-faced, long-faced. **2 important,** significant, momentous, weighty, far-reaching, consequential. **3 intellectual,** highbrow, heavy-weight, deep, profound, literary, learned, scholarly; informal heavy. **4** a serious injury: **severe,** grave, bad, critical, acute, terrible, dire, dangerous, grievous. **5 sincere,** earnest, genuine, wholehearted, committed, resolute, determined.
– OPPOSITES light-hearted, trivial, minor.

sermon n. **address,** homily, talk, speech, lecture.

servant n. **attendant,** domestic, maid, housemaid, retainer, flunkey, minion, slave, lackey, drudge; informal skivvy.

serve v. **1 work for,** obey, do the bidding of. **2** this job serves the community: **benefit,** help, assist, aid, make a contribution to. **3** he served a six-month apprentice-ship: **carry out,** perform, do, fulfil, complete, discharge, spend. **4 present,** give out, distribute, dish up, provide, supply. **5 attend to,** deal with, see to, assist, help, look after. **6** a saucer serving as an ashtray: **act as,** function as, do duty.

service n. **1 work,** employment, labour. **2** he has done us a service:

favour, kindness, good turn, helping hand. **3 ceremony**, ritual, rite, sacrament. **4 overhaul**, check, maintenance, servicing, repair. **5** *a range of local services:* **amenity**, facility, resource, utility. **6 (armed) forces**, military, army, navy, air force.
•v. **overhaul**, check, go over, maintain, repair.

serviceable adj. **1 in working order**, working, functioning, operational, usable, workable, viable. **2 functional**, utilitarian, sensible, practical, hardwearing, durable, tough, robust.

session n. **1 meeting**, sitting, assembly, conclave; N. Amer. & NZ caucus. **2 period**, time, term.

set[1] v. **1 put (down)**, place, lay, deposit, position, settle, leave, stand, plant; informal stick, dump, park, plonk, pop. **2 fix**, embed, insert, mount. **3** *set the table:* **lay**, prepare, arrange. **4** *he set us some work:* **assign**, allocate, give, allot. **5 arrange**, schedule, fix (on), decide on, settle on, choose, agree on, determine, designate, appoint, name, specify, stipulate. **6 adjust**, regulate, synchronize, calibrate, put right, correct. **7 solidify**, harden, stiffen, thicken, gel, cake, congeal, coagulate, clot.
□ **set off/out** set out, start out, sally forth, leave, depart, embark, set sail; informal hit the road.
set up 1 erect, put up, construct, build. **2 establish**, start, begin, institute, found, create.

3 arrange, organize, fix (up), schedule, timetable, line up.

set[2] n. **1 series**, collection, group, batch, arrangement, array, assortment, selection. **2 group**, circle, crowd, crew, band, fraternity, company, ring, camp, school, clique, faction; informal gang, bunch.

set[3] adj. **1 fixed**, established, scheduled, specified, appointed, arranged, settled, decided, agreed, predetermined, hard and fast, unvarying, unchanging, invariable, rigid, inflexible. **2 ready**, prepared, organized, equipped, primed; informal geared up, psyched up.
– OPPOSITES variable, unprepared.

setback n. **problem**, difficulty, hitch, complication, upset, blow; informal glitch, hiccup.
– OPPOSITES breakthrough.

setting n. **surroundings**, position, situation, environment, background, backdrop, spot, place, location, locale, site, scene.

settle v. **1 resolve**, sort out, clear up, end, fix, work out, iron out, set right, reconcile; informal patch up. **2 put in order**, sort out, tidy up, arrange, organize, order, clear up, straighten out. **3 decide on**, set, fix, agree on, name, establish, arrange, choose, pick. **4** *I've settled the bill:* **pay**, square, clear. **5 make your home**, set up home, take up residence, put down roots, establish yourself, live, move to. **6** *a drink will settle your nerves:* **calm**, quieten,

s

quiet, soothe, relax. **7** land, come to rest, alight, perch.

settlement n. **1** agreement, deal, arrangement, conclusion, resolution, understanding, pact. **2** community, colony, outpost, encampment, post, village.

settler n. colonist, frontiersman, pioneer, immigrant, newcomer, incomer.

sever v. **1** cut off, chop off, detach, separate, amputate. **2** cut (through), rupture, split, pierce. **3** break off, discontinue, suspend, end, cease, dissolve.
– OPPOSITES join.

several adj. some, a number of, a few, various, assorted.

severe adj. **1** acute, very bad, serious, grave, critical, dire, dangerous, life-threatening. **2** severe storms: fierce, violent, strong, powerful, intense, forceful. **3** cold, freezing, icy, arctic, harsh, bitter. **4** severe criticism: harsh, scathing, sharp, strong, fierce, savage, devastating, withering. **5** a severe expression: stern, dour, grim, forbidding, disapproving, unsmiling, unfriendly, sombre, stony, cold, frosty. **6** plain, simple, austere, spartan, unadorned, stark, clinical, uncluttered, minimalist, functional.
– OPPOSITES minor, gentle, mild.

sew v. stitch, tack, seam, hem, embroider.

sex n. **1** sexual intercourse, lovemaking, making love, sexual relations, mating, copulation;

formal fornication, coitus. **2** gender.

> **WORD LINKS**
> *relating to sexual activity:* carnal

sexuality n. **1** sensuality, sexiness, seductiveness, eroticism, physicality, sexual appetite, passion, desire, lust. **2** sexual orientation, sexual preference, leaning, persuasion.

sexy adj. **1** sexually attractive, seductive, desirable, alluring; informal fanciable; Brit. informal fit; N. Amer. informal foxy. **2** erotic, sexually explicit, titillating, naughty, X-rated, rude, pornographic, crude; informal raunchy, steamy; euphemistic adult.

shabby adj. **1** run down, scruffy, dilapidated, in disrepair, ramshackle, tumbledown, dingy; Brit. informal grotty. **2** scruffy, old, worn out, threadbare, ragged, frayed, tattered, battered, faded, moth-eaten, the worse for wear; informal tatty; N. Amer. informal raggedy. **3** mean, unkind, unfair, shameful, shoddy, unworthy, contemptible, despicable, discreditable, ignoble; informal rotten.
– OPPOSITES smart.

shack n. hut, cabin, shanty, lean-to, shed, hovel; Scottish bothy.

shackle v. **1** chain, fetter, manacle, secure, tie (up), bind, tether, hobble, put in chains, clap in irons, handcuff. **2** restrain, restrict, limit, constrain, handicap, hamstring, hamper,

s

hinder, impede, obstruct, inhibit.

shade n. **1** shadow, shadiness, shelter, cover. **2** colour, hue, tone, tint, tinge. **3** nuance, gradation, degree, difference, variation, variety, nicety, subtlety, undertone, overtone. **4** little, bit, trace, touch, modicum, tinge; informal tad, smidgen. **5** blind, curtain, screen, cover, covering, awning, canopy.
– OPPOSITES light.
•v. cast a shadow over, shadow, shelter, cover, screen.

shadow n. **1** silhouette, outline, shape, contour, profile. **2** shade, darkness, twilight, gloom.
•v. follow, trail, track, stalk, pursue; informal tail, keep tabs on.

shady adj. **1** shaded, shadowy, dim, dark, sheltered, leafy. **2** (informal) suspicious, suspect, questionable, dubious, irregular, underhand; informal fishy, murky; Brit. informal dodgy; Austral./NZ informal shonky.
– OPPOSITES bright, honest.

shaft n. **1** pole, stick, rod, staff, shank, handle, stem. **2** a shaft of light: ray, beam, gleam, streak, pencil. **3** tunnel, passage, hole, bore, duct, well, flue, vent.

shake v. **1** vibrate, tremble, quiver, quake, shiver, shudder, judder, wobble, rock, sway, convulse. **2** jiggle, joggle, jerk, agitate; informal wiggle, waggle. **3** brandish, wave, flourish, swing, wield. **4** upset, distress, disturb, unsettle, disconcert, discompose, unnerve, throw off

balance, agitate, fluster, shock, alarm, scare, worry; informal rattle.
•n. judder, trembling, quivering, quake, tremor, shiver, shudder, wobble.

shaky adj. **1** unsteady, unstable, rickety, wobbly; Brit. informal wonky. **2** faint, dizzy, lightheaded, giddy, weak, wobbly, in shock. **3** unreliable, untrustworthy, questionable, dubious, doubtful, tenuous, suspect, flimsy, weak; informal iffy; Brit. informal dodgy.
– OPPOSITES steady, stable.

shallow adj. superficial, trivial, facile, insubstantial, lightweight, empty, trifling, surface, skin-deep, frivolous, foolish, silly.
– OPPOSITES profound.

sham n. pretence, fake, act, simulation, fraud, lie, counterfeit, humbug.
•adj. fake, pretended, feigned, simulated, false, artificial, bogus, insincere, affected, make-believe; informal pretend, put-on, phoney.
– OPPOSITES genuine.
•v. pretend, fake, malinger; informal put it on; Brit. informal swing the lead.

shambles pl. n. **1** chaos, muddle, jumble, confusion, disorder, havoc. **2** mess, pigsty; informal disaster area; Brit. informal tip.

shame n. **1** guilt, remorse, contrition. **2** humiliation, embarrassment, indignity, loss of face, mortification, disgrace, dishonour, discredit, ignominy, disrepute, infamy, scandal. **3** *it's a shame she never married*: pity, sad thing, bad luck; informal crime, sin.

– OPPOSITES pride, honour.

•v. **1 disgrace**, dishonour, discredit, blacken, drag through the mud. **2 humiliate**, embarrass, humble, take down a peg or two, cut down to size; informal show up.

– OPPOSITES honour.

shamefaced adj. **ashamed**, abashed, sheepish, guilty, contrite, sorry, remorseful, repentant, penitent, regretful, rueful, apologetic; informal with your tail between your legs.

– OPPOSITES unrepentant.

shameful adj. **1 disgraceful**, deplorable, despicable, contemptible, discreditable, unworthy, reprehensible, shabby, shocking, scandalous, outrageous, abominable, atrocious, appalling, inexcusable, unforgivable. **2 embarrassing**, mortifying, humiliating, ignominious.

– OPPOSITES admirable.

shameless adj. **flagrant**, blatant, barefaced, overt, undisguised, brazen, unconcealed, unabashed, unashamed, unblushing, unrepentant.

shape n. **1 form**, appearance, configuration, structure, contours, lines, outline, silhouette, profile. **2 guise**, likeness, semblance, form, appearance, image. **3 condition**, health, trim, fettle, order; Brit. informal nick.

•v. **1 form**, fashion, make,

mould, model. **2** *events which shaped the course of her life*: **determine**, form, influence, affect.

shapeless adj. **1 formless**, amorphous, unformed, indefinite. **2 baggy**, saggy, ill-fitting, oversized, unstructured, badly cut.

shapely adj. **well proportioned**, curvaceous, voluptuous, full-figured, attractive, sexy; informal curvy.

share n. **portion**, part, division, quota, allowance, ration, allocation; informal cut, slice; Brit. informal whack.

•v. **1 split**, divide, go halves on; informal go fifty-fifty on. **2 apportion**, divide up, allocate, portion out, measure out, carve up; Brit. informal divvy up. **3 participate**, take part, play a part, be involved, have a hand.

sharp adj. **1 keen**, razor-edged, sharpened, well honed. **2 intense**, acute, severe, agonizing, excruciating, stabbing, shooting, searing. **3 tangy**, piquant, acidic, acid, sour, tart, pungent, vinegary. **4 cold**, chilly, brisk, icy, bitter, biting, keen, penetrating. **5 harsh**, bitter, cutting, caustic, scathing, barbed, spiteful, hurtful, unkind, cruel, malicious. **6** *a sharp increase*: **sudden**, abrupt, unexpected, rapid, steep. **7 astute**, intelligent, bright, incisive, keen, quick-witted, shrewd, canny, perceptive, smart, quick; informal on the ball, quick on the uptake; N. Amer. informal heads-up.

s

- **OPPOSITES** blunt, mild.
- adv. **precisely**, exactly, prompt, promptly, punctually; informal on the dot; N. Amer. informal on the button.

sharpen v. **hone**, whet, strop, grind, file.

shatter v. **1 smash**, break, splinter, crack, fracture, fragment, disintegrate. **2 destroy**, wreck, ruin, dash, crush, devastate, demolish, torpedo, scotch; informal do for, put paid to; Brit. informal scupper.

shave v. **1 cut off**, crop, trim, barber. **2 plane**, pare, whittle, scrape, shear.

sheath n. **covering**, cover, case, casing, sleeve, scabbard.

shed[1] n. **hut**, lean-to, outhouse, outbuilding, cabin, shack.

shed[2] v. **1 drop**, scatter, spill. **2 throw off**, cast off, discard, slough off, moult. **3 take off**, remove, discard, climb out of, slip out of; Brit. informal peel off. **4** the moon shed a faint light: **cast**, radiate, emit, give out.

sheen n. **shine**, lustre, gloss, patina, burnish, polish, shimmer.

sheer adj. **1 utter**, complete, absolute, total, thorough, pure, downright, out-and-out, unqualified, unmitigated, unalloyed. **2 steep**, abrupt, sharp, precipitous, vertical. **3 thin**, fine, gauzy, diaphanous, transparent, see-through, flimsy, filmy, translucent.

sheet n. **1 layer**, covering, blanket, coat, film, veneer, crust, skin, surface, stratum. **2 pane**, panel, slab, plate, piece. **3 page**, leaf, folio. **4** a sheet of water: **expanse**, area, stretch, sweep.

shell n. **1 pod**, hull, husk. **2 body**, case, casing, framework, hull, fuselage, hulk.
- v. **1 pod**, hull, husk; N. Amer. shuck. **2 bombard**, fire on, attack, bomb, blitz.

shelter n. **1 protection**, cover, shade, safety, security, refuge. **2 sanctuary**, refuge, home, haven, safe house.
- **OPPOSITES** exposure.
- v. **1 protect**, shield, screen, cover, shade, defend, cushion, guard, insulate, cocoon. **2 take shelter**, take refuge, take cover; informal hole up.
- **OPPOSITES** expose.

sheltered adj. **1 shady**, shaded, protected, still, tranquil. **2 protected**, cloistered, isolated, secluded, cocooned, insulated, secure, safe, quiet.

shelve v. **postpone**, put off, delay, defer, put back, reschedule, hold over/off, put to one side, suspend, stay, mothball; N. Amer. put over, table; informal put on ice, put on the back burner.

shepherd v. **usher**, steer, herd, lead, take, escort, guide, conduct, marshal, walk.

shield n. **protection**, guard, defence, cover, screen, shelter.
- v. **protect**, guard, defend, cover, screen, shade, shelter.
- **OPPOSITES** expose.

shift v. **1 move**, transfer, transport, switch, relocate, reposition, rearrange. **2** *the wind shifted:* **veer**, alter, change, turn.
•n. **1 change**, alteration, adjustment, variation, modification, revision, reversal, U-turn. **2 stint**, stretch, spell.

shimmer v. **glint**, glisten, twinkle, sparkle, flash, gleam, glow, glimmer, wink.
•n. **glint**, twinkle, sparkle, flash, gleam, glow, glimmer, lustre, glitter.

shine v. **1 beam**, gleam, radiate, glow, glint, glimmer, sparkle, twinkle, glitter, glisten, shimmer, flash. **2 polish**, burnish, buff, rub up, brush, clean. **3 excel**, stand out.
•n. **polish**, gleam, gloss, lustre, sheen, patina.

shiny adj. **glossy**, bright, glassy, polished, gleaming, satiny, lustrous.
– OPPOSITES matt.

ship n. **boat**, vessel, craft.
•v. **deliver**, send, dispatch, transport, carry, distribute.

WORD LINKS
relating to ships: maritime, nautical

shirk v. **evade**, dodge, avoid, get out of, sidestep, shrink from, shun, skip, neglect; informal duck (out of), cop out of; Brit. informal skive off; N. Amer. informal cut.

shiver v. **tremble**, quiver, shake, shudder, quake.
•n. **shudder**, twitch, start.

shock[1] n. **1 blow**, upset, surprise, revelation, bolt from the blue, rude awakening, eye-opener. **2 fright**, scare, start; informal turn. **3 trauma**, collapse, breakdown, post-traumatic stress disorder. **4 vibration**, reverberation, shake, jolt, impact, blow.
•v. **appal**, horrify, outrage, scandalize, disgust, traumatize, distress, upset, disturb, stun, rock, shake.
– OPPOSITES delight.

shock[2] n. **mass**, mane, mop, thatch, head, bush, tangle, cascade, halo.

shocking adj. **appalling**, horrifying, horrific, dreadful, awful, terrible, scandalous, outrageous, disgraceful, abominable, atrocious, disgusting, distressing, upsetting, disturbing, startling.

shoddy adj. **poor-quality**, inferior, second-rate, tawdry, jerry-built, cheapjack, gimcrack; informal tatty.

shoot v. **1 gun down**, mow down, pick off, hit, wound, injure, kill. **2 fire**, open fire, snipe, let fly, bombard, shell, discharge, launch. **3 race**, speed, flash, dash, rush, hurtle, streak, whizz, zoom, career, fly; informal belt, tear, zip, whip; Brit. informal bomb; N. Amer. informal hightail it, barrel. **4 film**, photograph, record.
•n. **sprout**, bud, runner, tendril, offshoot, cutting.

s

shop n. **store**, retail outlet, boutique, emporium, department store, supermarket, hypermarket, superstore, chain store; N. Amer. mart.

shore n. **seashore**, beach, sand(s), shoreline, coast; literary littoral.

short adj. **1 small**, little, petite, tiny, diminutive, elfin; Scottish wee; informal pint-sized, knee-high to a grasshopper. **2 concise**, brief, succinct, to the point, compact, pithy, abridged, abbreviated, condensed. **3 brief**, fleeting, short-lived, momentary, passing, lightning, quick, rapid, cursory. **4 scarce**, scant, meagre, sparse, insufficient, deficient, inadequate, lacking. **5 curt**, sharp, abrupt, blunt, brusque, terse, offhand.
– OPPOSITES tall, long, plentiful.
•adv. she stopped short: **abruptly**, suddenly, sharply, all of a sudden, unexpectedly, without warning.
□ **short of** deficient in, lacking, in need of, low on, short on, missing; informal strapped for, pushed for, minus.

shortage n. **scarcity**, dearth, poverty, insufficiency, deficiency, inadequacy, famine, lack, deficit, shortfall.
– OPPOSITES abundance.

shortcoming n. **fault**, defect, flaw, imperfection, deficiency, limitation, failing, drawback, weakness, weak point.
– OPPOSITES strength.

shorten v. **abbreviate**, abridge, condense, contract, compress, reduce, shrink, diminish, cut (down), trim, pare (down), prune, curtail, truncate.
– OPPOSITES lengthen.

shortly adv. **soon**, presently, in a little while, at any moment, in a minute, in next to no time, before long, by and by; N. Amer. momentarily; informal anon, any time now, in a jiffy; Brit. informal in a mo.

shot n. **1 report**, crack, bang, blast; **(shots)** gunfire, firing. **2 the winning shot: stroke**, hit, strike, kick, throw. **3 marksman**, markswoman, shooter. **4 photograph**, photo, snap, snapshot, picture, print, slide, still.

shoulder v. **1 take on (yourself)**, undertake, accept, assume, bear, carry. **2 push**, shove, thrust, jostle, force, bulldoze, bundle.

shout v. **yell**, cry (out), call (out), roar, howl, bellow, bawl, raise your voice; informal holler.
– OPPOSITES whisper.
•n. **yell**, cry, call, roar, howl, bellow, bawl; informal holler.

shove v. **push**, thrust, propel, drive, force, ram, knock, elbow, shoulder, jostle.

show v. **1 be visible**, be seen, be in view, be obvious. **2 display**, exhibit, put on show, put on display, put on view. **3 he showed his frustration: manifest**, exhibit, reveal, convey, communicate, make known, express, make

plain, make obvious, disclose, evince, betray. **4 demonstrate**, explain, describe, illustrate, teach, instruct. **5 prove**, demonstrate, confirm, substantiate, corroborate, verify, bear out. **6** *she showed them to their seats:* escort, accompany, take, conduct, lead, usher, guide, direct.
– OPPOSITES conceal.
•n. **1 display**, array, sight, spectacle. **2 exhibition**, display, fair, exposition, festival, parade; N. Amer. exhibit. **3 programme**, broadcast, presentation, production. **4 appearance**, outward appearance, image, pretence, (false) front, guise, pose, affectation, semblance.
☐ **show off 1** (informal) put on airs, put on an act, swank, strut, grandstand, posture, draw attention to yourself. **2 display**, show to advantage, exhibit, demonstrate, parade, draw attention to, flaunt. **show up 1** be visible, be obvious, be seen, be revealed, appear. **2** (informal) turn up, appear, arrive, come, get here/there, put in an appearance, materialize. **3** (informal) humiliate, embarrass, shame, put someone to shame, mortify. **4 expose**, reveal, make obvious, highlight, emphasize, draw attention to.

showdown n. **confrontation**, clash, face-off.

shower n. **1 fall**, drizzle, sprinkling, flurry. **2 volley**, hail, salvo, barrage.
•v. **1 rain**, fall, hail. **2 deluge**, flood, inundate, swamp, overwhelm, snow under.

show-off n. (informal) **exhibitionist**, extrovert, poser, poseur, swaggerer, self-publicist.

showy adj. **ostentatious**, flamboyant, gaudy, garish, brash, vulgar, loud, fancy, ornate; informal flash, flashy.
– OPPOSITES restrained.

shred n. **1 tatter**, ribbon, rag, fragment, sliver, snippet, remnant. **2 scrap**, bit, speck, particle, ounce, jot, crumb, fragment, grain, drop, trace.
•v. **grate**, cut up, tear up.

shrewd adj. **astute**, sharp, smart, intelligent, clever, canny, perceptive; informal on the ball.
– OPPOSITES stupid.

shriek v. & n. **scream**, screech, squeal, squawk, roar, howl, shout, yelp; informal holler.

shrill adj. **high-pitched**, piercing, high, sharp, ear-piercing, ear-splitting, penetrating.

shrink v. **1 get smaller**, contract, diminish, lessen, reduce, decrease, dwindle, decline, fall off. **2 recoil**, shy away, flinch, be averse, be afraid, hesitate.
– OPPOSITES expand, increase.

shrivel v. **wither**, shrink, wilt, dry up, dehydrate, parch, frazzle.

shroud n. **covering**, cover, cloak, mantle, blanket, layer, cloud, veil, winding sheet.
•v. **cover**, envelop, veil, cloak, blanket, screen, conceal, hide, mask, obscure.

s

shudder v. **shake**, shiver, tremble, quiver, judder.
•n. **shake**, shiver, tremor, trembling, quivering, judder, vibration.

shuffle v. **1 shamble**, hobble, limp, drag your feet. **2 mix (up)**, rearrange, jumble (up), re-organize.

shun v. **avoid**, steer clear of, give a wide berth to, have nothing to do with; informal freeze out; Brit. informal send to Coventry.
– OPPOSITES welcome.

shut v. **close**, pull to, push to, slam, fasten, put the lid on, lock, secure.
– OPPOSITES open.
□ **shut down** close (down), cease trading; informal fold. **shut up** be quiet, keep quiet, stop talking, hold your tongue; informal keep mum, pipe down, belt up.

shuttle v. **commute**, run, ply, go/travel back and forth, ferry.

shy adj. **bashful**, diffident, timid, reserved, introverted, retiring, self-effacing, withdrawn.
– OPPOSITES confident.
□ **shy away from** flinch, recoil, hang back, be loath, be reluctant, baulk at, be unwilling, be disinclined, hesitate.

sick adj. **1 ill**, unwell, poorly, ailing, indisposed, out of sorts; informal under the weather, laid up; Austral./NZ informal crook. **2 nauseous**, queasy, bilious, green about the gills. **3** I'm sick of this music: **fed up**, bored, tired, weary, jaded. **4** (informal)

macabre, tasteless, ghoulish, morbid, black, gruesome, perverted, cruel.
– OPPOSITES well.
□ **be sick** (Brit.) vomit, heave, retch; informal puke (up), throw up, spew (up); N. Amer. informal barf, upchuck.

sicken v. **1 nauseate**, make sick, turn someone's stomach, disgust, revolt, repel, appal; N. Amer. informal gross out. **2 fall ill**, become infected, be stricken.

sickening adj. **nauseating**, stomach-turning, repulsive, revolting, disgusting, offensive, off-putting, distasteful, obscene, gruesome, grisly; N. Amer. informal gross.

sickly adj. **1 unhealthy**, in poor health, delicate, frail, weak. **2 pale**, wan, pasty, sallow, pallid, ashen, anaemic. **3 sentimental**, mawkish, cloying, sugary, slushy, saccharine; informal slushy, schmaltzy, cheesy, corny; Brit. informal soppy.
– OPPOSITES healthy.

sickness n. **1 illness**, disease, ailment, infection, malady, infirmity; informal bug, virus; Brit. informal lurgy. **2 nausea**, biliousness, queasiness, vomiting, retching; informal throwing up, puking.

side n. **1 edge**, border, verge, boundary, margin, rim, fringe(s), flank, bank, perimeter, extremity, periphery, limit(s). **2 district**, quarter, area, region, part, neighbourhood, sector, zone. **3 surface**, face. **4 point of**

view, viewpoint, perspective, opinion, standpoint, position, outlook, slant, angle, aspect, facet. **5 faction**, camp, bloc, party, wing. **6 team**, squad, line-up.
- OPPOSITES centre, end.
• adj. **1 lateral**, wing, flanking. **2 subordinate**, secondary, minor, peripheral, incidental, subsidiary.
- OPPOSITES front, central.
□ **side with** support, take someone's part, stand by, back, be loyal to, defend, champion, ally yourself with.

sidetrack v. **distract**, divert, deflect, draw away.

sideways adv. **1 to the side**, laterally. **2 edgewise**, edgeways, side first, end on.
• adj. **1 lateral**, sideward, on the side, side to side. **2 indirect**, oblique, sidelong, surreptitious, furtive, covert, sly.

sift v. **1 sieve**, strain, screen, filter. **2** *we sift out unsuitable applications:* **separate out**, filter out, sort out, weed out, get rid of, remove. **3** *sifting through the data:* **search**, look, examine, inspect, scrutinize.

sigh v. **1 breathe (out)**, exhale, groan, moan. **2 rustle**, whisper, murmur.

sight n. **1 eyesight**, vision, eyes. **2 view**, glimpse, glance, look. **3 landmark**, place of interest, monument, spectacle, marvel, wonder.
• v. **glimpse**, catch sight of, see,

spot, spy, make out, pick out, notice, observe.

> **WORD LINKS**
> *relating to sight:* optical, visual

sign n. **1 indication**, signal, symptom, pointer, suggestion, intimation, mark, manifestation, demonstration, token. **2 warning**, omen, portent, threat, promise. **3 notice**, board, placard, signpost. **4 symbol**, figure, emblem, device, logo, character.
• v. **1 write your name on**, autograph, initial, countersign. **2 endorse**, validate, agree to, approve, ratify, adopt. **3 write**, inscribe, pen.

signal n. **1 gesture**, gesticulation, sign, wave, cue, indication, warning, prompt, reminder. **2 indication**, sign, symptom, hint, pointer, clue, demonstration, evidence, proof.
• v. **1 gesture**, gesticulate, sign, indicate, motion, wave, beckon, nod. **2** *his death signals the end of an era:* **mark**, signify, mean, indicate, be a sign of, be evidence of.

significance n. **importance**, import, consequence, seriousness, gravity, weight, magnitude.

significant adj. **1 notable**, noteworthy, remarkable, important, of consequence, momentous. **2 large**, considerable, sizeable, appreciable, conspicuous, obvious, sudden. **3 meaningful**, expressive, eloquent, suggestive, knowing, telling.

s

signify v. **mean**, denote, designate, represent, symbolize, stand for.

silence n. **1 quietness**, quiet, still, stillness, hush, tranquillity, peace, peacefulness. **2 failure to speak**, dumbness, muteness, reticence, taciturnity.
– OPPOSITES noise, loquacity.
•v. **1 quieten**, quiet, hush, still, muffle. **2 gag**, muzzle, censor.

silent adj. **1 quiet**, still, hushed, noiseless, soundless, inaudible. **2 speechless**, quiet, unspeaking, dumb, mute, taciturn, uncommunicative, tight-lipped. **3 unspoken**, wordless, tacit, unvoiced, unexpressed, implied, implicit, understood.
– OPPOSITES audible, loquacious.

silhouette n. **outline**, contour(s), profile, form, shape.
•v. **outline**, define.

silly adj. **1 foolish**, stupid, inane, feather-brained, bird-brained, frivolous, immature, childish, empty-headed, scatterbrained; informal dotty, scatty. **2 unwise**, imprudent, thoughtless, foolish, stupid, unintelligent, rash, reckless, foolhardy, irresponsible, hare-brained; informal crazy, barmy; Brit. informal daft. **3** he brooded about silly things: **trivial**, trifling, petty, small, insignificant, unimportant.
– OPPOSITES sensible.

similar adj. **alike**, like, much the same, comparable, corresponding, equivalent, parallel, analogous, kindred; informal much of a muchness.
– OPPOSITES different, dissimilar.

similarity n. **resemblance**, likeness, comparability, correspondence, parallel, equivalence, uniformity.

similarly adv. **likewise**, comparably, correspondingly, in the same way, by the same token.

simmer v. **1 boil gently**, cook gently, bubble, stew, poach. **2 seethe**, fume, smoulder.

simple adj. **1 straightforward**, easy, uncomplicated, uninvolved, undemanding, elementary; informal child's play, a cinch, a piece of cake, like falling off a log. **2 clear**, plain, lucid, straightforward, unambiguous, understandable, comprehensible, accessible; informal user-friendly. **3 plain**, unadorned, basic, unsophisticated, no-frills, classic, understated, uncluttered, restrained. **4 unpretentious**, unsophisticated, ordinary, unaffected, unassuming, natural, straightforward.
– OPPOSITES difficult, complex, ornate.

simplicity n. **1 straightforwardness**, ease. **2 clarity**, plainness, lucidity, intelligibility, comprehensibility, accessibility. **3 austerity**, plainness, spareness, clean lines. **4 plainness**, modesty, naturalness.
– OPPOSITES complexity.

simplify v. **make simpler**, clarify, put into words of one

syllable, streamline; informal dumb down.
- OPPOSITES complicate.

simply adv. **1 straightforwardly**, directly, clearly, plainly, intelligibly, lucidly, unambiguously. **2 plainly**, soberly, unfussily, without clutter, classically. **3 merely**, just, purely, solely, only.

simulate v. **1 feign**, pretend, fake, affect, put on. **2 replicate**, reproduce, imitate, mimic.

simultaneous adj. **concurrent**, happening at the same time, contemporaneous, coinciding, coincident, synchronized.
- OPPOSITES separate.

simultaneously adv. **at the same time**, at one and the same time, at once, concurrently, (all) together, in unison, in concert, in chorus.

sin n. **1 wrong**, act of wickedness, transgression, crime, offence, misdeed; old use trespass. **2 wickedness**, wrongdoing, evil, immorality, iniquity, vice, crime.
- OPPOSITES virtue.
• v. **transgress**, do wrong, misbehave, err, go astray; old use trespass.

sincere adj. **1 heartfelt**, wholehearted, profound, deep, true, honest, earnest, fervent. **2 honest**, genuine, truthful, direct, frank, candid; informal straight, on the level, upfront; N. Amer. informal on the up and up.

sincerely adv. **genuinely**, honestly, really, truly, truthfully, wholeheartedly, earnestly.

sincerity n. **genuineness**, honesty, truthfulness, integrity, directness, openness, candour.

sinful adj. **immoral**, wicked, (morally) wrong, evil, bad, iniquitous, ungodly, irreligious, sacrilegious.
- OPPOSITES virtuous.

sing v. **1 chant**, trill, intone, croon, chorus. **2 trill**, warble, chirp, chirrup, cheep.

singe v. **scorch**, burn, sear, char.

singer n. **vocalist**, songster, songstress, soloist, chorister, cantor.

single adj. **1 sole**, one, lone, solitary, unaccompanied, alone. **2 individual**, separate, particular, distinct. **3 unmarried**, unwed, unattached, free.
- OPPOSITES double, multiple.
□ **single out** select, pick out, choose, decide on, target, earmark, mark out, separate out, set apart.

single-handed adv. **by yourself**, alone, on your own, solo, unaided, unassisted, without help.

single-minded adj. **determined**, committed, unswerving, unwavering, resolute, purposeful, devoted, dedicated, uncompromising, tireless, tenacious, persistent, dogged.
- OPPOSITES half-hearted.

singly adv. **one by one**, one at a time, one after the other, individually, separately.
- OPPOSITES together.

s

sinister adj. **1 menacing**, threatening, forbidding, baleful, frightening, alarming, disturbing, ominous. **2 evil**, wicked, criminal, nefarious, villainous; informal shady.
– OPPOSITES innocent.

sink v. **1 submerge**, founder, capsize, go down, be engulfed. **2 scuttle**, scupper. **3 fall**, drop, descend, plunge, plummet, slump. **4 embed**, insert, drive, plant.
– OPPOSITES float, rise.

sinner n. **wrongdoer**, evildoer, transgressor, miscreant, offender, criminal; old use trespasser.

sip v. **drink**, taste, sample, nip. • n. **mouthful**, swallow, drink, drop, dram, nip; informal swig.

sit v. **1 take a seat**, sit down, be seated, perch, ensconce yourself, flop; informal take the load off your feet; Brit. informal take a pew. **2 be placed**, be positioned, be situated, be set, rest, stand, perch. **3 be in session**, meet, be convened. **4** *she sits on the tribunal*: **serve on**, have a seat on, be a member of.
– OPPOSITES stand.

site n. **location**, place, position, situation, locality, whereabouts. • v. **place**, put, position, situate, locate.

situation n. **1 circumstances**, state of affairs, affairs, state, condition, case, predicament, plight. **2 location**, position, spot, site, setting, environment.

3 post, position, job, employment.

size n. **dimensions**, measurements, proportions, magnitude, largeness, area, expanse, breadth, width, length, height, depth.
□ **size up** (informal) assess, appraise, get the measure of, judge, take stock of, evaluate; Brit. informal suss out.

sizeable adj. **large**, substantial, considerable, respectable, significant, goodly.
– OPPOSITES small.

sizzle v. **crackle**, fizzle, sputter, hiss, spit.

sketch n. **drawing**, outline, draft, diagram, design, plan; informal rough. • v. **draw**, make a drawing of, pencil, rough out, outline.

sketchy adj. **incomplete**, patchy, fragmentary, scrappy, cursory, perfunctory, scanty, vague, inadequate, insufficient.
– OPPOSITES detailed.

skilful adj. **expert**, accomplished, skilled, masterly, talented, deft, dexterous, handy; informal mean, crack, ace; N. Amer. informal crackerjack.
– OPPOSITES incompetent.

skill n. **expertise**, accomplishment, skilfulness, mastery, talent, deftness, dexterity, prowess, competence, artistry.
– OPPOSITES incompetence.

skim v. **1** *skim off the fat*: **remove**, scoop off, separate. **2 glide**, move lightly, slide, sail, skate.

3 *she skimmed through the paper:* glance, flick, flip, leaf, thumb, scan, run your eye over.

skin n. **1** hide, pelt, fleece. **2** peel, rind. **3** film, layer, membrane, crust, covering, coating.
–v. **1** peel, pare. **2** graze, scrape, abrade, bark, rub raw, chafe.

> **WORD LINKS**
> *relating to the skin:* cutaneous;
> *branch of medicine concerning the skin:* dermatology

skinny adj. thin, underweight, scrawny, bony, gaunt, emaciated, skeletal, wasted, pinched, spindly, gangly; informal anorexic.

skip v. **1** caper, prance, trip, dance, bound, bounce, gambol. **2** omit, leave out, miss out, dispense with, pass over, skim over, disregard; informal give something a miss.

skirt v. **1** go round, walk round, circle. **2** border, edge, flank, line. **3** *he skirted round the subject:* avoid, evade, sidestep, dodge, pass over, gloss over; informal duck.

skull n. cranium.

> **WORD LINKS**
> *relating to the skull:* cranial

sky n. literary the heavens, the firmament, the ether, the (wide) blue yonder.

> **WORD LINKS**
> *relating to the sky:* celestial

slab n. piece, block, hunk, chunk, lump, cake, tablet, brick, panel, plate, sheet.

slack adj. **1** limp, loose. **2** sagging, flabby, flaccid, loose, saggy. **3** sluggish, slow, quiet, slow-moving, flat, depressed, stagnant. **4** lax, negligent, careless, slapdash, slipshod; informal sloppy.
– OPPOSITES taut, firm.
•v. (Brit. informal) idle, shirk, be lazy, be indolent, waste time, lounge about; Brit. informal skive; N. Amer. informal goof off.

slam v. bang, thump, crash, smash, plough, run, bump, collide with, hit, strike, ram; N. Amer. impact.

slanderous adj. defamatory, denigratory, disparaging, libellous, pejorative, false, misrepresentative, scurrilous, scandalous, malicious.

slant v. **1** slope, tilt, incline, be at an angle, tip, lean, dip, pitch, shelve, list, bank. **2** bias, distort, twist, skew, weight.
•n. **1** slope, incline, tilt, gradient, pitch, angle, camber. **2** point of view, viewpoint, standpoint, stance, angle, perspective, approach, view, attitude, position, bias, spin.

slap v. smack, strike, hit, cuff, clip, spank; informal whack.
•n. smack, blow, cuff, clip, spank; informal whack.

slash v. **1** cut, gash, slit, lacerate, knife. **2** (informal) reduce, cut, lower, bring down, mark down.
•n. cut, gash, slit, laceration, incision, wound.

slaughter v. **1** kill, butcher, cull, put down. **2** massacre, murder,

s

butcher, kill, exterminate, wipe out, put to death, execute; literary slay.

• n. **massacre**, (mass) murder, (mass) killing, (mass) execution, extermination, carnage, bloodshed, bloodletting, bloodbath; literary slaying.

slave n. servant, lackey, drudge; Brit. informal skivvy, dogsbody; historical serf, vassal.
– OPPOSITES master.
• v. **toil**, labour, sweat, work like a Trojan/dog, work your fingers to the bone; informal sweat blood, slog away; Brit. informal graft.

WORD LINKS
like a slave: servile

slavery n. enslavement, servitude, serfdom, bondage, captivity.
– OPPOSITES freedom.

sleazy adj. **1 corrupt**, immoral, ignoble, dishonourable. **2 squalid**, seedy, seamy, sordid, insalubrious.

sleek adj. **1 smooth**, glossy, shiny, shining, lustrous, silken, silky. **2 streamlined**, elegant, graceful.
– OPPOSITES scruffy.

sleep n. nap, doze, siesta, cat-nap; informal snooze, forty winks, shut-eye; Brit. informal kip; literary slumber.
• v. **be asleep**, doze, take a siesta, take a nap, catnap; informal snooze, get some shut-eye; Brit. informal kip; literary slumber.
– OPPOSITES wake up.

□ **go to sleep** fall asleep, get to sleep; informal drop off, nod off, drift off, crash out, flake out; N. Amer. informal sack out.

WORD LINKS
causing sleep: sedative, soporific

sleepy adj. **1 drowsy**, tired, somnolent, heavy-eyed; informal dopey. **2 quiet**, peaceful, tranquil, placid, slow-moving, dull, boring.
– OPPOSITES awake, alert.

slender adj. **1 slim**, lean, willowy, svelte, lissom, graceful, slight, thin, skinny. **2 faint**, remote, tenuous, fragile, slim, small, slight.
– OPPOSITES plump, strong.

slice n. **1 piece**, portion, slab, wedge, rasher, sliver, wafer. **2 share**, part, portion, tranche, percentage, proportion, allocation; informal cut, whack.
• v. **cut**, carve, divide.

slick adj. **1 efficient**, smooth, smooth-running, polished, well organized, well run, streamlined. **2 glib**, polished, assured, self-assured, smooth-talking, plausible; informal smarmy.
• v. **smooth**, plaster, sleek, grease, oil, gel.

slide v. glide, slip, slither, skim, skate, skid, slew.

slight adj. **1 small**, tiny, minute, negligible, insignificant, minimal, remote, slim, faint. **2 slim**, slender, delicate, dainty, fragile.
– OPPOSITES large, plump.
• v. **insult**, snub, rebuff, spurn,

s

give someone the cold shoulder, cut (dead), take no notice of, scorn, ignore.
•n. **insult**, affront, snub, rebuff; informal put-down, slap in the face.

slightly adv. **a little**, a bit, somewhat, faintly, vaguely, a shade.
– OPPOSITES very.

slim adj. **1 slender**, lean, thin, willowy, sylphlike, svelte, lissom, slight, trim. **2** *a slim chance*: **slight**, small, slender, faint, remote.
– OPPOSITES fat.
•v. **lose weight**, diet, go on a diet; N. Amer. slenderize.

slimy adj. **slippery**, slithery, greasy, sticky, viscous; informal slippy.

sling v. **1 hang**, suspend, string, swing. **2** (informal) **throw**, toss, fling, hurl, cast, pitch, lob, flip; informal chuck, heave, bung.

slip v. **1 slide**, skid, slither, fall (over), lose your balance, lose your footing, tumble. **2 creep**, steal, sneak, slide, sidle, slope, slink, tiptoe.
•n. **1 false step**, slide, skid, fall, tumble. **2 mistake**, error, blunder, gaffe, oversight, miscalculation, omission, lapse; informal slip-up, boo-boo, howler; Brit. informal boob, clanger, bloomer; N. Amer. informal goof, blooper.
□ **slip up** (informal) make a mistake, blunder, get something wrong, miscalculate, make an error, err; informal make a booboo; Brit. informal boob, drop a clanger; N. Amer. informal goof up.

slippery adj. **1 slithery**, greasy, oily, icy, glassy, smooth, slimy, wet; informal slippy. **2 sneaky**, sly, devious, crafty, cunning, tricky, evasive, scheming, unreliable, untrustworthy; informal shady, shifty; Brit. informal dodgy; Austral./NZ informal shonky.

slit n. **1 cut**, incision, split, slash, gash. **2 opening**, gap, chink, crack, aperture, slot.
•v. **cut**, slash, split open, slice open.

slither v. **slide**, slip, glide, wriggle, crawl, skid.

sliver n. **splinter**, shard, chip, flake, shred, scrap, shaving, paring, piece, fragment.

slobber v. **drool**, slaver, dribble, salivate.

slogan n. **catchphrase**, catchline, motto, jingle; N. Amer. informal tag line.

slope n. **tilt**, pitch, slant, angle, gradient, incline, inclination, fall, camber; N. Amer. grade.
•v. **tilt**, slant, incline, lean, drop/fall away, descend, shelve, camber, rise, ascend, climb.

sloping adj. **slanting**, leaning, inclined, angled, cambered, tilted.
– OPPOSITES level.

sloppy adj. **1 runny**, watery, liquid, mushy; informal gloopy. **2 careless**, slapdash, slipshod, disorganized, untidy, slack, slovenly; informal slap-happy.

slot n. **1 aperture**, slit, crack, hole, opening. **2 time**, spot, period, niche, space; informal window.
•v. **insert**, slide, fit, put, place.

s

slovenly adj. **1 scruffy**, untidy, messy, unkempt, ill-groomed, dishevelled, bedraggled, rumpled, frowzy. **2 careless**, slapdash, slipshod, haphazard, hit-or-miss, untidy, messy, negligent, lax, lackadaisical, slack; informal sloppy, slap-happy.
– OPPOSITES tidy, careful.

slow adj. **1 unhurried**, leisurely, steady, sedate, measured, ponderous, sluggish, plodding. **2 lengthy**, time-consuming, long-drawn-out, protracted, prolonged, gradual. **3 stupid**, unintelligent, obtuse; informal dense, dim, thick, slow on the uptake, dumb, dopey; Brit. informal dozy.
– OPPOSITES fast, quick.
•v. **1 reduce speed**, go slower, decelerate, brake. **2 hold back**, hold up, delay, retard, set back, check, curb.
– OPPOSITES accelerate.

slowly adv. **1 unhurriedly**, without hurrying, steadily, at a leisurely pace, at a snail's pace. **2 gradually**, bit by bit, little by little, slowly but surely, step by step.
– OPPOSITES quickly.

sluggish adj. **lethargic**, listless, lacking in energy, lifeless, inactive, slow, torpid, enervated.
– OPPOSITES vigorous.

slum n. **hovel**; (**slums**) ghetto, shanty town.

slump v. **1 sit heavily**, flop, collapse, sink; informal plonk yourself. **2 fall**, plummet, tumble, collapse, drop; informal crash, nosedive.
•n. **1 fall**, drop, tumble, downturn, downswing, slide, decline, decrease; informal nosedive. **2 recession**, decline, depression, slowdown.
– OPPOSITES rise, boom.

slur v. **mumble**, speak unclearly, garble.
•n. **insult**, slight, slander, smear, allegation, imputation.

sly adj. **1 cunning**, crafty, clever, wily, artful, tricky, scheming, devious, underhand, sneaky. **2 roguish**, mischievous, impish, playful, wicked, arch, knowing. **3 surreptitious**, furtive, stealthy, covert.
– OPPOSITES open, straightforward.

smack n. **slap**, blow, cuff, clip, spank; informal whack.
•v. **slap**, strike, hit, cuff, clip, spank; informal whack.
•adv. (informal) **exactly**, precisely, straight, right, directly, squarely, dead, plumb; informal slap, bang; N. Amer. informal smack dab.

small adj. **1 little**, tiny, short, petite, diminutive, elfin, miniature, mini, minute, toy, baby, undersized, poky, cramped; Scottish wee; informal teeny, tiddly, pintsized; Brit. informal titchy. **2 slight**, minor, unimportant, trifling, trivial, insignificant, inconsequential, negligible, inappreciable; informal piffling.
– OPPOSITES big, large.

smarmy adj. (informal) **unctuous**, ingratiating, slick, oily, greasy, obsequious, sycophantic, fawning; informal slimy.

smart adj. **1 well dressed**, well turned out, stylish, chic, fashionable, modish, elegant, dapper; N. Amer. trig; informal natty, snappy. **2** *a smart restaurant:* **fashionable**, stylish, high-class, exclusive, chic, fancy; Brit. upmarket; N. Amer. high-toned; informal trendy, classy, swanky; Brit. informal swish; N. Amer. informal swank. **3** (informal) **clever**, bright, intelligent, quick-witted, shrewd, astute, perceptive; informal brainy, quick on the uptake. **4** *a smart pace:* **brisk**, quick, fast, rapid, lively, energetic, vigorous; informal cracking.
– OPPOSITES scruffy, stupid.
•v. **1 sting**, burn, tingle, prickle, hurt. **2** *she smarted at the accusation:* **feel hurt**, feel upset, take offence, feel aggrieved, feel indignant, be put out.

smash v. **1 break**, shatter, splinter, crack; informal bust. **2** *he smashed into a wall:* **crash**, smack, slam, plough, run, bump, hit, strike, ram, collide with; N. Amer. impact.
•n. **crash**, collision, accident; N. Amer. wreck; informal pile-up; Brit. informal shunt.

smattering n. **bit**, little, modicum, touch, soupçon, rudiments, basics; informal smidgen, smidge, tad.

smear v. **1 spread**, rub, daub, slap, cover, coat, smother, plaster. **2 smudge**, streak, mark. **3 sully**, tarnish, blacken, drag through the mud, damage,

defame, malign, slander, libel;
•n. **1 streak**, smudge, daub, dab, spot, patch, blotch, mark; informal splodge. **2 accusation**, lie, untruth, slur, slander, libel, defamation.

smell n. **1 odour**, aroma, fragrance, scent, perfume, bouquet, nose. **2 stink**, stench, reek; Brit. informal pong, whiff.
•v. **1 scent**, sniff, get a sniff of, detect. **2 stink**, reek; Brit. informal pong, hum.

> **WORD LINKS**
> relating to the sense of smell:
> olfactory

smelly adj. **foul-smelling**, stinking, reeking, rank, fetid, malodorous, pungent; literary noisome.

smile v. **beam**, grin (from ear to ear), smirk, simper, leer.
– OPPOSITES frown.
•n. **beam**, grin, smirk, simper, leer.

smirk v. **sneer**, simper, snigger, leer, grin.

smitten adj. **1 struck down**, laid low, suffering, affected, afflicted. **2 infatuated**, besotted, in love, obsessed, head over heels, enamoured, captivated, enchanted, under someone's spell; informal bowled over, swept off your feet.

smoke v. **1 smoulder**; old use reek. **2 puff on**, draw on, pull on, inhale; informal drag on.
•n. **fumes**, exhaust, gas, vapour, smog.

smoky adj. **smoke-filled**, sooty, smoggy, hazy, foggy, murky, thick; Brit. informal fuggy.

smooth adj. **1 even**, level, flat, plane, unwrinkled, glassy, glossy, silky, polished. **2 creamy**, fine, velvety. **3 calm**, still, tranquil, undisturbed, unruffled, even, flat, like a millpond. **4 steady**, regular, uninterrupted, unbroken, easy, effortless, trouble-free. **5 suave**, urbane, sophisticated, polished, debonair, courteous, gracious, persuasive, glib, slick, smooth-tongued; informal smarmy.
– OPPOSITES uneven, rough.
• v. **1 flatten**, level (out/off), even out/off, press, roll, iron, plane. **2 ease**, facilitate, expedite, help, assist, aid, pave the way for.
– OPPOSITES roughen, hinder.

smother v. **1 suffocate**, asphyxiate, stifle, choke. **2 extinguish**, put out, snuff out, douse, stamp out. **3 smear**, daub, spread, cover, plaster. **4 she smothered a giggle: stifle**, muffle, strangle, suppress, hold back, fight back, swallow, conceal.

smudge n. **streak**, smear, mark, stain, blotch, blob, dab; informal splotch, splodge.
• v. **streak**, mark, dirty, soil, blotch, blacken, smear, blot, daub, stain; informal splotch, splodge.

smug adj. **self-satisfied**, conceited, complacent, superior, pleased with yourself.

snack n. **light meal**, sandwich, refreshments, nibbles, titbit(s); informal bite (to eat).

snag n. **complication**, difficulty, catch, hitch, obstacle, pitfall, problem, setback, disadvantage, drawback.
• v. **catch**, hook, tear.

snake n. **serpent**.
• v. the road snakes inland: **twist**, wind, meander, zigzag, curve.

snap v. **1 break**, fracture, splinter, split, crack; informal bust. **2 bark**, snarl, growl, retort; informal jump down someone's throat.
• n. **photograph**, picture, photo, shot, snapshot, print, slide.

snare n. **trap**, gin, wire, net, noose.
• v. **trap**, catch, net, bag, ensnare, hook.

snatch v. **1 grab**, seize, take hold of, take, pluck, grasp at, clutch at. **2 steal**, take, thieve, make off with; informal swipe, nab, lift; Brit. informal nick, pinch, whip. **3 kidnap**, abduct, take as hostage.

sneak v. **creep**, slink, steal, slip, slide, sidle, tiptoe, pad.

sneaking adj. **1 secret**, private, hidden, concealed, unvoiced, unexpressed. **2 a sneaking suspicion: niggling**, nagging, insidious, lingering, persistent.

sneaky adj. **sly**, crafty, cunning, wily, scheming, devious, deceitful, underhand.

sneer v. **1 smirk**, snigger, curl your lip. **2 scoff**, laugh, scorn,

disdain, be contemptuous, mock, ridicule, deride, jeer, jibe.
• n. **1 smirk**, snigger. **2 jeer**, jibe, insult; informal dig.

sniff v. **1 inhale**, snuffle. **2 smell**, scent, get a whiff of.
• n. **1 snuffle**, snort. **2 smell**, scent, whiff, lungful.
□ **sniff out** (informal) detect, find, discover, bring to light, track down, dig up, root out, uncover, unearth.

snigger v. & n. **giggle**, titter, snicker, chortle, laugh, sneer, smirk.

snippet n. **piece**, bit, scrap, fragment, particle, shred, excerpt, extract.

snivel v. **sniffle**, snuffle, whimper, whine, weep, cry; Scottish greet; informal blubber; Brit. informal grizzle.

snobbish, **snobby** adj. **elitist**, superior, supercilious, arrogant, condescending, pretentious, affected; informal snooty, high and mighty, la-di-da, stuck-up; Brit. informal toffee-nosed.

snoop v. (informal) **pry**, spy, be a busybody, poke your nose into, root about, ferret about; informal be nosy; Austral. informal stickybeak.

snub v. **rebuff**, spurn, cold-shoulder, cut (dead), ignore, insult, slight; informal freeze out; N. Amer. informal stiff.
• n. **rebuff**, slap in the face; informal brush-off, put-down.

snug adj. **1 cosy**, comfortable, warm, sheltered, secure; informal

comfy. **2 tight**, skintight, close-fitting, figure-hugging.
– OPPOSITES loose.

snuggle v. **nestle**, curl up, huddle (up), cuddle up, nuzzle, settle; N. Amer. snug down.

soak v. **1 dip**, immerse, steep, submerge, douse, marinate, souse. **2 drench**, wet through, saturate. **3** *water soaked through the carpet:* **permeate**, penetrate, impregnate, percolate, seep, spread. **4 absorb**, suck up, blot, mop up.

soaking adj. **drenched**, wet (through), soaked (through), sodden, soggy, waterlogged, saturated, sopping, dripping, wringing.
– OPPOSITES parched.

soar v. **1 rise**, ascend, climb. **2 glide**, plane, float, hover. **3 increase**, escalate, shoot up, spiral, rocket; informal go through the roof, skyrocket.
– OPPOSITES plummet.

sob v. **weep**, cry, snivel, whimper; Scottish greet; informal blubber; Brit. informal grizzle.

sober adj. **1 clear-headed**, teetotal, abstinent, dry; informal on the wagon. **2 serious**, solemn, sensible, staid, sedate, quiet, dignified, grave, level-headed, down-to-earth. **3 sombre**, subdued, restrained, austere, severe, drab, plain, dark.
– OPPOSITES drunk.

so-called adj. **supposed**, alleged, presumed, inappropriately named, ostensible, reputed, self-styled.

sociable adj. friendly, amicable, affable, companionable, gregarious, cordial, warm, genial.
– OPPOSITES unfriendly.

social adj. **1 communal**, community, collective, general, popular, civil, public, civic. **2 recreational**, leisure, entertainment.
•n. **party**, gathering, function, get-together, celebration; informal do.

socialize v. interact, converse, be sociable, mix, mingle, get together, meet, fraternize, consort; informal hobnob, hang out.

society n. **1 the community**, the (general) public, the people, the population, civilization, humankind, mankind, the world at large. **2 an industrial society**: culture, community, civilization, nation. **3 high society**: polite society, the upper classes, the gentry, the elite, the smart set, the beau monde; informal the upper crust. **4 club**, association, group, circle, institute, guild, lodge, league, union, alliance. **5 company**, companionship, fellowship, friendship.

> WORD LINKS
> study of society: sociology

sofa n. settee, couch, divan, chaise longue, chesterfield.

soft adj. **1 mushy**, squashy, pulpy, squishy, doughy, spongy, springy, elastic, pliable, pliant; informal gooey; Brit. informal squidgy. **2 swampy**, marshy, boggy, muddy, squelchy.
3 smooth, velvety, fleecy, downy, furry, silky, silken. **4 dim**, low, faint, subdued, muted, subtle. **5 quiet**, low, gentle, faint, muted, subdued, muffled, hushed, whispered. **6 lenient**, easy-going, tolerant, forgiving, forbearing, indulgent, liberal, lax.
– OPPOSITES hard, firm, harsh.

soften v. the compensation should soften the blow: ease, alleviate, relieve, soothe, take the edge off, cushion, lessen, diminish, blunt, deaden.

soggy adj. mushy, squashy, pulpy, slushy, squelchy, swampy, marshy, boggy, soaking, wet, saturated, drenched; Brit. informal squidgy.

soil¹ n. **1 earth**, dirt, clay, ground, loam. **2 territory**, land, region, country, domain, dominion.

soil² v. dirty, stain, smear, smudge, spoil, foul.

soldier n. fighter, trooper, serviceman/woman, warrior; US GI; Brit. informal squaddie.

> WORD LINKS
> relating to soldiers: military

sole adj. only, one, single, solitary, lone, unique, exclusive.

solely adv. only, simply, purely, just, merely, uniquely, exclusively, entirely, wholly, alone.

solemn adj. **1 dignified**, ceremonial, stately, formal, majestic, imposing, splendid, magnificent, grand. **2 serious**, grave, sober, sombre, unsmiling, stern, grim, dour, humourless.

3 sincere, earnest, honest, genuine, firm, heartfelt, whole-hearted, sworn.
- OPPOSITES frivolous, light-hearted.

solicit v. **1 ask for**, request, seek, apply for, put in for, call for, beg for, plead for. **2 ask**, approach, appeal to, lobby, petition, importune, call on, press.

solid adj. **1 hard**, rock-hard, rigid, firm, solidified, set, frozen, compact, compressed, dense. **2** *solid gold*: **pure**, unadulterated, genuine. **3 well built**, sound, substantial, strong, sturdy, durable, stout. **4 well founded**, valid, sound, logical, authoritative, convincing, cogent. **5** *solid support*: **unanimous**, united, consistent, undivided.
- OPPOSITES liquid, flimsy, untenable.

solidarity n. **unanimity**, unity, agreement, team spirit, accord, harmony, consensus; formal concord.

solidify v. **harden**, set, thicken, stiffen, congeal, cake, freeze, ossify, fossilize, petrify.
- OPPOSITES liquefy.

solitary adj. **1 lonely**, unaccompanied, by yourself, on your own, alone, friendless, unsociable, withdrawn, reclusive; N. Amer. lonesome. **2 isolated**, remote, lonely, out of the way, in the back of beyond, outlying, off the beaten track, secluded; N. Amer. in the backwoods. **3 single**, lone, sole, only, one, individual.
- OPPOSITES sociable.

solitude n. **loneliness**, solitariness, isolation, seclusion, privacy, peace.

solution n. **1 answer**, result, resolution, key, explanation. **2 mixture**, blend, emulsion, compound.

solve v. **answer**, resolve, work out, puzzle out, fathom, decipher, decode, clear up, straighten out, get to the bottom of, unravel, explain; informal figure out, crack; Brit. informal suss out.

sombre adj. **1 dark**, drab, dull, dingy, restrained, sober, funereal. **2 solemn**, earnest, serious, grave, sober, unsmiling, gloomy, sad, mournful, melancholy, lugubrious, cheerless.
- OPPOSITES bright, cheerful.

somehow adv. **one way or another**, no matter how, by fair means or foul, by hook or by crook, come what may.

sometimes adv. **occasionally**, from time to time, now and then, every so often, once in a while, on occasion, at times, off and on.

song n. **air**, strain, ditty, chant, number, track, melody, tune.

sonorous adj. **resonant**, rich, full, round, booming, deep, clear, mellow, strong, resounding, reverberant.

soon adv. **shortly**, presently, in the near future, before long, in a little while, in a minute, in a moment; Brit. informal in a tick.

s

sooner adv. **1** earlier, before now. **2** rather, preferably, given the choice.

soothe v. **1** calm (down), pacify, comfort, hush, quiet, settle (down), appease, mollify; Brit. quieten (down). **2** ease, alleviate, relieve, take the edge off, allay, lessen, reduce.
– OPPOSITES agitate, aggravate.

soothing adj. relaxing, restful, calm, calming, tranquil, peaceful.

sophisticated adj. **1** advanced, state-of-the-art, the latest, up-to-the-minute, cutting-edge, complex. **2** worldly, worldly-wise, experienced, cosmopolitan, urbane, cultured, cultivated, polished, refined.
– OPPOSITES crude, naive.

sophistication n. worldliness, experience, urbanity, culture, polish, refinement, elegance, style, poise, finesse, savoir faire.

sordid adj. **1** sleazy, seedy, seamy, unsavoury, tawdry, cheap, disreputable, discreditable, ignominious, shameful, wretched, despicable. **2** squalid, slummy, dirty, filthy, shabby, scummy; informal scuzzy; Brit. informal grotty.
– OPPOSITES respectable.

sore adj. **1** painful, hurting, aching, throbbing, smarting, stinging, inflamed, sensitive, tender, raw, wounded, injured. **2** (N. Amer. informal) upset, angry, annoyed, cross, disgruntled, dissatisfied, irritated; informal aggravated,

miffed, peeved; Brit. informal narked; N. Amer. informal ticked off.

sorrow n. **1** sadness, unhappiness, misery, despondency, regret, despair, desolation, heartache, grief. **2** the sorrows of life: trouble, difficulty, problem, woe, affliction, trial, tribulation, misfortune.
– OPPOSITES joy.

sorry adj. **1** regretful, apologetic, remorseful, contrite, repentant, rueful, penitent, guilty, shame-faced, ashamed. **2** he felt sorry for her: full of pity, sympathetic, compassionate, moved, concerned. **3** I was sorry to hear about the accident: sad, sorrowful, distressed.
– OPPOSITES glad, unrepentant.

sort n. type, kind, variety, class, category, style, form, genre, species, breed, make, model, brand.
•v. **1** classify, class, group, organize, arrange, order, grade, catalogue. **2** the problem was soon sorted out: resolve, settle, solve, fix, work out, straighten out, deal with, put right, set right, rectify, iron out.

soul n. **1** spirit, psyche, (inner) self. **2** feeling, emotion, passion, animation, intensity, warmth, energy, vitality, spirit.

sound¹ n. **1** noise, din, racket, row, resonance, reverberation. **2** utterance, cry, word, noise, peep.
– OPPOSITES silence.
•v. **1** make a noise, resonate, resound, reverberate, go off,

ring, chime, ping. **2** *sound the horn:* **blow**, blast, toot, ring, use, operate, activate, set off. **3 appear**, look (like), seem, give every indication of being, strike someone as.

> **WORD LINKS**
> *relating to sound:* acoustic, sonic

sound² adj. **1 healthy**, in good condition/shape, fit, hale and hearty, in fine fettle, undamaged, unimpaired. **2 well built**, solid, substantial, strong, sturdy, durable, stable, intact. **3 well founded**, valid, reasonable, logical, weighty, authoritative, reliable. **4 reliable**, dependable, trustworthy, fair, good. **5 solvent**, debt-free, in the black, in credit, creditworthy, secure. **6 deep**, undisturbed, uninterrupted, untroubled, peaceful.
– **OPPOSITES** unhealthy, unsafe.

sour adj. **1 acid**, acidic, tart, bitter, sharp, vinegary, pungent. **2 bad**, off, turned, curdled, rancid, high, fetid. **3 embittered**, resentful, jaundiced, bitter, cross, crabby, crotchety, cantankerous, bad-tempered, disagreeable, unpleasant; *informal* grouchy.
– **OPPOSITES** sweet, fresh.
•v. **spoil**, mar, damage, harm, impair, upset, poison, blight.

source n. **1 spring**, wellspring, wellhead, origin. **2 origin**, derivation, starting point, start, beginning, fountainhead, root, author, originator.

souvenir n. **memento**, keepsake, reminder, memorial, trophy.

sovereign n. **ruler**, monarch, potentate, overlord, king, queen, emperor, empress, prince, princess.
•adj. **autonomous**, independent, self-governing, self-determining, non-aligned, free.

sovereignty n. **1 power**, rule, supremacy, dominion, jurisdiction, ascendancy, domination, authority, control. **2 autonomy**, independence, self-rule, self-government, home rule, self-determination, freedom.

sow v. **plant**, scatter, disperse, strew, broadcast, seed.

space n. **1 room**, capacity, latitude, margin, leeway, play, elbow room, clearance. **2 area**, expanse, stretch, sweep, tract. **3 gap**, interval, opening, aperture, cavity, niche, interstice. **4 blank**, gap, box. **5 period**, span, time, duration, stretch, course, interval, gap. **6 outer space**, deep space, the universe, the galaxy, the solar system.
•v. **position**, arrange, range, array, spread, lay out, set.

spacious adj. **roomy**, capacious, commodious, voluminous, sizeable, generous.
– **OPPOSITES** cramped.

span n. **1 extent**, length, width, reach, stretch, spread, distance, range. **2 period**, space, time, duration, course,

s

interval.
- v. **1 bridge**, cross, traverse, pass over. **2 last**, cover, extend, spread over.

spare adj. **1 extra**, supplementary, additional, second, other, alternative, emergency, reserve, backup, relief, substitute; N. Amer. alternate. **2 surplus**, superfluous, excess, leftover, redundant, unnecessary, unwanted; informal going begging. **3** *your spare time:* **free**, leisure, unoccupied. **4 slender**, lean, willowy, svelte, lissom, thin, skinny, gaunt, lanky, spindly.
- v. **1 afford**, manage, part with, give, provide, do without. **2 pardon**, let off, forgive, have mercy on, reprieve, release, free.

sparing adj. **thrifty**, economical, frugal, careful, prudent, cautious.
– OPPOSITES lavish, extravagant.

spark n. **flash**, glint, twinkle, flicker, flare.
- v. *the arrest sparked off riots:* **cause**, give rise to, occasion, bring about, start, precipitate, prompt, trigger (off), provoke, stimulate, stir up.

sparkle v. & n. **glitter**, glint, glisten, twinkle, flicker, flash, shimmer.

sparkling adj. **1 effervescent**, fizzy, carbonated, aerated. **2 brilliant**, dazzling, scintillating, exciting, exhilarating, stimulating, invigorating, vivacious, lively, vibrant.
– OPPOSITES still, dull.

sparse adj. **scant**, scanty, scattered, scarce, infrequent, few and far between, meagre, paltry, limited, in short supply.
– OPPOSITES abundant.

spartan adj. **austere**, harsh, hard, frugal, rigorous, strict, severe, ascetic, self-denying, abstemious, bleak, bare, plain.
– OPPOSITES luxurious.

spate n. **series**, succession, run, cluster, string, rash, epidemic, outbreak, wave, flurry.

speak v. **1 talk**, converse, communicate, chat, have a word, gossip, commune, say something; informal chew the fat. **2 say**, utter, state, declare, voice, express, pronounce, articulate, enunciate, verbalize. **3 give a speech**, talk, lecture, hold forth; informal spout, sound off.

speaker n. **speech-maker**, lecturer, talker, orator, spokesperson, spokesman/woman, reader, commentator, broadcaster, narrator.

special adj. **1 exceptional**, unusual, remarkable, out of the ordinary, outstanding, unique. **2 distinctive**, distinct, individual, particular, specific, peculiar. **3 momentous**, significant, memorable, important, historic, red-letter.
– OPPOSITES ordinary, general.

specialist n. **expert**, authority, pundit, professional, connoisseur, master, maestro; informal buff.

speciality n. **strength**, strong point, forte, métier, strong suit, party piece, pièce de résistance, claim to fame.

species n. **type**, kind, sort, breed, strain, variety, class, classification, category.

specific adj. **1 particular**, set, specified, fixed, determined, distinct, definite. **2 detailed**, explicit, express, clear-cut, unequivocal, precise, exact.
– OPPOSITES general, vague.

specification n. *a shelter built to their specifications:* **instruction**, guideline, parameter, stipulation, requirement, condition, order, detail.

specify v. **state**, name, identify, define, set out, itemize, detail, list, enumerate, spell out, stipulate, lay down.

specimen n. **sample**, example, model, instance, illustration, demonstration.

spectacle n. **1 display**, show, pageantry, performance, exhibition, pomp and circumstance, extravaganza, spectacular. **2 sight**, vision, scene, prospect, picture.

spectacular adj. **impressive**, magnificent, splendid, dazzling, sensational, stunning, dramatic, outstanding, memorable, unforgettable, striking, picturesque, eye-catching, breathtaking, glorious; informal out of this world.
– OPPOSITES dull, unimpressive.

spectator n. **watcher**, viewer, observer, onlooker, bystander, witness.

spectre n. **ghost**, phantom, apparition, spirit, wraith, presence; informal spook.

speculate v. **1 conjecture**, theorize, hypothesize, guess, surmise, wonder, muse. **2 gamble**, venture, wager, invest, play the market.

speculative adj. **1 conjectural**, suppositional, theoretical, hypothetical, tentative, unproven, unfounded, groundless, unsubstantiated. **2 risky**, hazardous, unsafe, uncertain, unpredictable; informal chancy.

speech n. **1 speaking**, talking, verbal communication, conversation, dialogue, discussion. **2 diction**, elocution, articulation, enunciation, pronunciation, delivery, words. **3 talk**, address, lecture, discourse, oration, presentation, sermon. **4 language**, parlance, tongue, idiom, dialect, vernacular; informal lingo.

> **WORD LINKS**
> *relating to speech:* oral, phonetic, phonic

speechless adj. **lost for words**, dumbstruck, struck dumb, tongue-tied, inarticulate, mute, dumb, voiceless, silent.

speed n. **1 rate**, pace, tempo, momentum, velocity; informal lick. **2 rapidity**, swiftness, promptness, alacrity, briskness, haste, hurry; old use celerity.
– OPPOSITES slowness.
▸v. **1 hurry**, rush, dash, race, sprint, career, shoot, hurtle,

s

hare, fly, zoom, hasten; informal tear, belt, pelt; Brit. informal bomb. **2** *a holiday will speed his recovery:* **hasten**, accelerate, advance, further, promote, boost, stimulate, aid, assist, facilitate.
– OPPOSITES slow, hinder.
□ **speed up** hurry up, accelerate, go faster, get a move on, put a spurt on, pick up speed; informal step on it.

speedy adj. **fast**, swift, quick, rapid, expeditious, prompt, immediate, brisk, hasty, hurried, precipitate, rushed.
– OPPOSITES slow.

spell¹ v. **signal**, signify, mean, amount to, add up to, constitute.
□ **spell out** explain, make clear, clarify, specify, detail.

spell² n. **1 charm**, incantation, magic formula, curse; N. Amer. hex; (**spells**) magic, sorcery, witchcraft. **2 influence**, charm, magnetism, charisma, magic.
□ **put a spell on** bewitch, enchant, entrance, curse, jinx; N. Amer. hex.

spell³ n. **1 period**, time, interval, season, stretch, run; Brit. informal patch. **2 bout**, fit, attack.

spellbound adj. **enthralled**, fascinated, rapt, riveted, transfixed, gripped, captivated, bewitched, enchanted, mesmerized, hypnotized.

spend v. **1 pay out**, expend, disburse; informal lay out, blow, splurge. **2 pass**, occupy, fill, take up, while away.

sphere n. **1 globe**, ball, orb, bubble. **2** *his sphere of influence:* **area**, field, compass, orbit, range, scope, extent. **3 domain**, realm, province, field, area, territory, arena, department.

spice n. **1 seasoning**, flavouring, condiment. **2 excitement**, interest, colour, piquancy, zest, an edge.

spicy adj. **hot**, tangy, peppery, piquant, spiced, highly seasoned, pungent.
– OPPOSITES bland.

spike n. **prong**, pin, barb, point, skewer, stake, spit.

spill v. **1 knock over**, tip over, upset, overturn. **2 overflow**, brim over, run over, pour, slop, slosh, splash, leak.

spin v. **1 revolve**, rotate, turn, go round, whirl, twirl, gyrate. **2** *she spun round to face him:* **whirl**, wheel, turn, swing, twist, swivel, pivot.
•n. **1 rotation**, revolution, turn, whirl, twirl, gyration. **2 slant**, angle, twist, bias. **3 trip**, jaunt, outing, excursion, journey, drive, ride, run, turn; informal tootle.

spine n. **1 backbone**, spinal column, back. **2 needle**, quill, barb, bristle, spike, prickle, thorn.

> WORD LINKS
> relating to the spine: vertebral

spiral adj. **coiled**, helical, curling, winding, twisting.
•n. **coil**, curl, twist, whorl, scroll, helix, corkscrew.

• v. *smoke spiralled up*: **coil**, wind, swirl, twist, snake.

spirit n. **1 soul**, psyche, inner self, mind. **2 ghost**, phantom, spectre, apparition, presence. **3 mood**, frame/state of mind, humour, temper, morale, esprit de corps. **4 ethos**, essence, atmosphere, mood, feeling, climate. **5 enthusiasm**, energy, verve, vigour, dynamism, dash, sparkle, exuberance, gusto, fervour, zeal, fire, passion; informal get-up-and-go.
– OPPOSITES body, flesh.

spirited adj. **lively**, energetic, enthusiastic, vigorous, dynamic, passionate; informal feisty, gutsy; N. Amer. informal peppy.
– OPPOSITES apathetic, lifeless.

spiritual adj. **1 inner**, mental, psychological, incorporeal, non-material. **2 religious**, sacred, divine, holy, devotional.
– OPPOSITES physical, secular.

spit v. **expectorate**, hawk; Brit. informal gob.
• n. **spittle**, saliva, sputum, slobber, dribble.

spite n. **malice**, malevolence, ill will, vindictiveness, meanness, nastiness; informal bitchiness, cattiness.
• v. **upset**, hurt, wound.
– OPPOSITES please.
□ **in spite of** despite, notwithstanding, regardless of, in defiance of, in the face of.

spiteful adj. **malicious**, malevolent, vindictive, vengeful, mean, nasty, hurtful, mischievous, cruel, unkind; informal bitchy, catty.
– OPPOSITES benevolent.

splash v. **1 sprinkle**, spatter, splatter, spray, shower, wash, squirt, slosh, slop. **2 wash**, break, lap, pound. **3 paddle**, wade, wallow.

splendid adj. **1 magnificent**, sumptuous, grand, imposing, superb, spectacular, resplendent, rich, lavish, ornate, gorgeous, glorious, dazzling, handsome, beautiful; informal plush; Brit. informal swish. **2** (informal) **excellent**, wonderful, marvellous, superb, glorious, lovely, delightful, first-class; informal super, great, amazing, fantastic, terrific, tremendous; Brit. informal smashing, brilliant.
– OPPOSITES simple, modest, inferior.

splendour n. **magnificence**, sumptuousness, grandeur, resplendence, richness, glory, majesty.
– OPPOSITES simplicity.

splinter n. **sliver**, chip, shard, fragment, shred; Scottish skelf.
• v. **shatter**, smash, break into smithereens, fracture, split, crack, disintegrate.

split v. **1 break**, cut, burst, snap, crack, splinter, fracture, rupture, come apart. **2 tear**, rip, slash, slit. **3 share**, divide up, distribute, dole out, parcel out, carve up, slice up, apportion. **4 fork**, divide, branch, diverge. **5** *the band split up last year*: **break up**,

s

separate, part, part company, go their separate ways.
- OPPOSITES join, unite, converge.
- n. **1 crack**, fissure, cleft, crevice, break, fracture, breach. **2 rip**, tear, cut, rent, slash, slit. **3 division**, rift, breach, schism, rupture, separation, estrangement. **4 break-up**, split-up, separation, parting, estrangement, rift.
- OPPOSITES merger.

spoil v. **1 damage**, ruin, impair, blemish, disfigure, blight, deface, harm, destroy, wreck. **2** *rain spoiled my plans*: **upset**, mess up, ruin, wreck, undo, sabotage, scotch, torpedo; informal muck up, screw up, do for; Brit. informal scupper. **3 overindulge**, pamper, indulge, mollycoddle, cosset, wait on someone hand and foot. **4 go bad**, go off, go rancid, turn, go sour, rot, decompose, decay, perish.
- OPPOSITES improve, enhance.

spoilsport n. **killjoy**, dog in the manger, misery; informal wet blanket, party-pooper.

spoken adj. **verbal**, oral, vocal, unwritten, word-of-mouth.

spokesperson, **spokesman**, **spokeswoman** n. **representative**, voice, mouthpiece, agent, official; informal spin doctor.

sponsor n. **backer**, patron, promoter, benefactor, supporter, contributor.
- v. **finance**, fund, subsidize, back, promote, support, contribute to; N. Amer. informal bankroll.

spontaneous adj. **1 unplanned**, unpremeditated, impulsive, impromptu, spur-of-the-moment, unprompted; informal off-the-cuff. **2 natural**, uninhibited, relaxed, unselfconscious, unaffected.

sporadic adj. **occasional**, infrequent, irregular, periodic, scattered, patchy, isolated, odd, intermittent, spasmodic, fitful, desultory, erratic, unpredictable.
- OPPOSITES frequent, continuous.

sport n. **game**, physical recreation.
- v. **wear**, have on, dress in, show off, parade, flaunt.

sporting adj. **sportsmanlike**, generous, considerate, fair; Brit. informal decent.

sporty adj. (informal) **athletic**, fit, active, energetic.

spot n. **1 mark**, patch, dot, fleck, smudge, smear, stain, blotch, splash; informal splotch, splodge. **2 pimple**, pustule, blackhead, boil, blemish; informal zit; Scottish informal blob; (**spots**) acne, rash. **3 place**, site, position, situation, setting, location, venue.
- v. **see**, notice, observe, catch sight of, detect, make out, discern, recognize, identify, locate; Brit. informal clock; literary espy, descry.

spotless adj. **clean**, pristine, immaculate, shining, shiny, gleaming, spick and span.
- OPPOSITES filthy.

spotlight → spurious

spotlight n. **attention**, glare of publicity, limelight, public eye.

spotted adj. **spotty**, dotted, polka-dot, freckled, mottled.

spotty adj. **1 polka-dot**, spotted, dotted. **2** (Brit.) **pimply**, pimpled, acned; Scottish informal plooky.

spouse n. **partner**, husband, wife, mate, consort; informal better half; Brit. informal other half.

sprawl v. **stretch out**, lounge, loll, slump, flop, slouch.

spray v. **1 shower**, sprinkle, jet, squirt, mist, spume, foam, froth, spindrift. **2 aerosol**, vaporizer, atomizer, sprinkler.
•v. **1 sprinkle**, dribble, drizzle, water, soak, douse, drench. **2 spout**, jet, gush, spurt, shoot, squirt.

spread v. **1 lay out**, open out, unfurl, unroll, roll out, straighten out, fan out, stretch out, extend. **2** the landscape spread out below: **extend**, stretch, sprawl. **3 scatter**, strew, disperse, distribute. **4 circulate**, broadcast, put about, publicize, propagate, repeat. **5 travel**, move, be borne, sweep, diffuse, reproduce, be passed on, be transmitted. **6 smear**, daub, plaster, apply, rub.
•n. **1 expansion**, proliferation, dissemination, diffusion, transmission, propagation. **2 span**, width, extent, stretch, reach.

spree n. **bout**, orgy; informal binge, splurge.

spring v. **leap**, jump, bound, vault, hop.
•n. **springiness**, bounce, resilience, elasticity, flexibility, stretch, stretchiness, give.
□ **spring from** originate from, have its origins in, derive from, arise in, stem from, emanate from, evolve from.

WORD LINKS
relating to the season of spring: vernal

sprinkle v. **splash**, trickle, drizzle, spray, shower, drip, scatter, strew, dredge, dust.

sprint v. **run**, race, rush, dash, bolt, fly, charge, shoot, speed; informal hotfoot it, leg it.
– OPPOSITES stroll.

sprout v. **1 germinate**, put/send out shoots, bud. **2 spring**, come up, grow, develop, appear.

spruce adj. **neat**, well groomed, well turned out, well dressed, smart, trim, dapper; informal natty, snazzy.
– OPPOSITES dishevelled.
□ **spruce up** smarten up, tidy up, clean, groom; informal do up, titivate; Brit. informal tart up; N. Amer. informal gussy up.

spur n. **stimulus**, incentive, encouragement, inducement, impetus, motivation.
– OPPOSITES disincentive.
•v. **stimulate**, encourage, prompt, prod, impel, motivate, move, galvanize, inspire, drive.
– OPPOSITES discourage.

spurious adj. **bogus**, fake, false, fraudulent, sham, artificial,

imitation, simulated, feigned; informal phoney.
– OPPOSITES genuine.

spurn v. reject, rebuff, scorn, turn down, treat with contempt, disdain, look down your nose at; informal turn your nose up at.
– OPPOSITES welcome, accept.

spurt v. squirt, shoot, jet, erupt, gush, pour, stream, pump, surge, spew, course, well, spring, burst, spout.
•n. squirt, jet, gush, stream, rush, surge, flood, cascade, torrent.

spy n. agent, mole, plant; N. Amer. informal spook.
•v. notice, observe, see, spot, sight, catch sight of, glimpse, make out, discern, detect.
□ **spy on** observe, keep under surveillance, eavesdrop on, watch, bug.

spying n. espionage, intelligence gathering, surveillance, infiltration.

squabble n. quarrel, disagreement, row, argument, dispute, wrangle, clash, altercation; informal tiff, set-to, run-in, scrap, dust-up; Brit. informal barney, ding-dong.
•v. quarrel, row, argue, bicker, disagree; informal scrap.

squad n. 1 team, crew, gang, force. 2 detachment, detail, unit, platoon, battery, troop, patrol, squadron, commando.

squalid adj. 1 dirty, filthy, dingy, grubby, grimy, wretched, miserable, mean, seedy, shabby, sordid, insalubrious; Brit. informal grotty. 2 improper, sordid, unseemly, unsavoury, sleazy, cheap, base, low, corrupt, dishonest, dishonourable, disreputable, discreditable, contemptible, shameful.
– OPPOSITES clean.

squander v. waste, throw away, misuse, misspend, fritter away, spend like water; informal blow, run through, splurge, pour down the drain.
– OPPOSITES save.

square n. piazza, plaza, quadrangle.
•adj. level, even, drawn, equal, tied, level pegging; informal even-steven(s).

squash v. 1 crush, squeeze, mash, pulp, flatten, compress, distort, pound, trample. 2 force, ram, thrust, push, cram, jam, stuff, pack, squeeze, wedge.

squeak n. & v. peep, cheep, squeal, tweet, yelp, whimper.

squeeze v. 1 compress, press, crush, squash, pinch, nip, grasp, grip, clutch. 2 extract, press, force, express. 3 force, thrust, cram, ram, jam, stuff, pack, wedge, press, push, squash, crush, crowd, force your way.
•n. 1 press, pinch, nip, grasp, grip, clutch, hug. 2 crush, jam, squash, congestion.

squirm v. 1 wriggle, wiggle, writhe, twist, slither, fidget, twitch, toss and turn. 2 wince, shudder.

squirt v. **1 spurt**, shoot, spray, jet, erupt, gush, rush, pump, surge, stream, spew, well, issue, emanate. **2 splash**, spray, shower, sprinkle.

stab v. **knife**, run through, skewer, spear, gore, spike, impale.
• n. **1** a stab of pain: **twinge**, pang, throb, spasm, cramp, prick. **2** (informal) **attempt**, try, endeavour, effort; informal go, shot, crack, bash.

stability n. **1 firmness**, solidity, steadiness. **2 balance (of mind)**, (mental) health, sanity, reason. **3 strength**, durability, lasting nature, permanence.

stable adj. **1 firm**, solid, steady, secure. **2 well balanced**, well adjusted, of sound mind, compos mentis, sane, normal, rational, reasonable, sensible. **3** a stable relationship: **secure**, solid, strong, steady, firm, sure, steadfast, established, enduring, lasting.
– OPPOSITES unstable.

stack n. **heap**, pile, mound, mountain, pyramid, tower.
• v. **1 heap (up)**, pile (up), assemble, put together, collect. **2 load**, fill (up), pack, charge, stuff, cram, stock.

staff n. **1 employees**, workers, workforce, personnel, human resources, manpower, labour. **2 stick**, stave, pole, rod.
• v. **man**, people, crew, work, operate.

stage n. **1 phase**, period, juncture, step, point, level. **2 part**, section, portion, stretch, leg, lap, circuit. **3 platform**, dais, stand, rostrum, podium.

stagger v. **1 lurch**, reel, sway, teeter, totter, stumble. **2 amaze**, astound, astonish, surprise, stun, confound, daze, take aback; informal flabbergast; Brit. informal knock for six.

stagnant adj. **1 still**, motionless, standing, stale, dirty, brackish. **2 inactive**, sluggish, slow-moving, static, flat, depressed, moribund, dead, dormant.
– OPPOSITES flowing.

staid adj. **sedate**, respectable, serious, steady, conventional, traditional, unadventurous, set in your ways, sober, formal, stuffy, stiff; informal starchy, stick-in-the-mud.
– OPPOSITES frivolous.

stain v. **1 discolour**, soil, mark, spot, spatter, splatter, smear, splash, smudge, begrime. **2 colour**, tint, dye, paint.
• n. **1 mark**, spot, blotch, smudge, smear. **2 blemish**, taint, blot, smear, slur, stigma.

stake¹ n. **post**, pole, stick, spike, upright, support, cane.

stake² n. **1 bet**, wager, ante. **2 share**, interest, investment, involvement, concern.
• v. **bet**, wager, lay, put on, gamble, risk.

stale adj. **1 old**, past its best, off, dry, hard, musty, mouldy, rancid. **2 stuffy**, musty, fusty, stagnant. **3 overused**, hackneyed, tired, worn out, overworked,

S

threadbare, banal, clichéd, trite, unimaginative, uninspired, flat; informal old hat; N. Amer. played out.

– OPPOSITES fresh.

stalemate n. deadlock, impasse, stand-off, gridlock.

stalk v. **1** trail, follow, shadow, track, go after, hunt; informal tail. **2** strut, stride, march, flounce, storm, stomp, sweep.

stall n. **1** stand, table, counter, booth, kiosk. **2** pen, coop, sty, corral, enclosure, compartment.
•v. **1** delay, play for time, procrastinate, hedge, drag your feet, filibuster, stonewall. **2** hold off, stave off, keep at bay, evade, avoid.

stalwart adj. staunch, loyal, faithful, committed, devoted, dedicated, dependable, reliable.

– OPPOSITES disloyal.

stamina n. endurance, staying power, energy, toughness, determination, tenacity, perseverance, grit.

stammer v. stutter, stumble over your words, hesitate, falter, pause, splutter.

stamp v. **1** trample, step, tread, tramp, stomp, stump, clump, crush, squash, flatten. **2** imprint, print, impress, punch, inscribe, emboss.
•n. mark, hallmark, sign, seal, sure sign, smack, savour, air.
□ **stamp out** put an end to, end, stop, crush, put down, curb, quell, suppress, extinguish, stifle, abolish, get rid of,

eliminate, eradicate, destroy, wipe out.

stance n. **1** posture, body position, pose, attitude. **2** attitude, opinion, standpoint, position, approach, policy, line.

stand v. **1** rise, get to your feet, get up, pick yourself up. **2** be situated, be located, be positioned, be sited. **3** put, set, erect, place, position, prop, install, arrange; informal park. **4** remain in force, remain in operation, hold, hold good, apply, be the case, exist, prevail. **5** withstand, endure, bear, put up with, take, cope with, handle, sustain, resist, stand up to. **6** (informal) put up with, endure, tolerate, accept, take, abide, stand for, support, countenance; formal brook.

– OPPOSITES sit, lie down.

•n. **1** attitude, stance, opinion, standpoint, position, approach, policy, line. **2** opposition, resistance. **3** base, support, platform, stage, dais, rest, plinth, tripod, rack, trivet. **4** stall, counter, booth, kiosk.
□ **stand by 1** wait, be prepared, be ready for action, be on full alert, wait in the wings. **2** support, stick with/by, remain loyal to, stand up for, back up, defend, stick up for. **3** abide by, keep (to), adhere to, hold to, stick to, observe, comply with. **stand for** mean, be short for, represent, signify, denote, symbolize. **stand in** deputize, act, substitute, fill in, take over,

cover, hold the fort, step into the breach, replace, relieve.

stand out be noticeable, be visible, be obvious, be conspicuous, stick out, attract attention; *informal* stick/stand out a mile, stick/stand out like a sore thumb.

standard n. **1 quality**, level, calibre, merit, excellence. **2 guideline**, norm, yardstick, benchmark, gauge, measure, criterion, guide, touchstone, model, pattern. **3 principle**, ideal; (**standards**) morals, code of behaviour, ethics. **4 flag**, banner, ensign, colour(s).
•adj. **1 normal**, usual, average, typical, stock, common, ordinary, customary, conventional, established. **2 definitive**, classic, recognized, accepted, approved, authoritative.
– OPPOSITES unusual, special.

standing n. **1 status**, ranking, position, reputation, stature. **2 prestige**, rank, eminence, seniority, repute, stature, esteem, importance, account.

staple adj. **main**, principal, chief, major, primary, leading, foremost, first, most important, predominant, dominant, basic, prime; *informal* number-one.

star n. **1 heavenly body**, celestial body. **2 principal**, leading lady/man, lead, hero, heroine. **3 celebrity**, superstar, famous name, household name, leading light, VIP, personality, luminary; *informal* celeb, big shot, megastar.
•adj. **1 outstanding**, exceptional,

2 top, leading, greatest, foremost, major, pre-eminent.

WORD LINKS
relating to stars: astral, stellar;
study of stars: astronomy

stare v. **gaze**, gape, goggle, glare, ogle, peer; *informal* gawk; *Brit. informal* gawp.

stark adj. **1 sharp**, sharply defined, crisp, distinct, clear, clear-cut. **2 desolate**, bare, barren, empty, bleak, dreary, depressing, grim.
– OPPOSITES indistinct, ornate.
•adv. **stark naked: completely**, totally, utterly, absolutely, entirely, wholly, fully, quite, altogether, thoroughly.

start v. **1 begin**, commence, get under way, get going, go ahead, make a start; *informal* kick off, get the ball rolling, get the show on the road. **2 come into being**, begin, arise, originate, develop. **3 establish**, set up, found, create, bring into being, institute, initiate, inaugurate, introduce, open, launch. **4 activate**, switch/turn on, start up, fire up, boot up. **5 flinch**, jerk, jump, twitch, wince.
– OPPOSITES end, finish, stop.
•n. **1 beginning**, commencement, inception, onset, inauguration, dawn, birth, emergence; *informal* kick-off. **2 lead**, head start, advantage. **3 jerk**, twitch, spasm, jump.
– OPPOSITES end.

startle v. **surprise**, frighten, scare, alarm, shock, give

s

someone a fright, make someone jump.

starving adj. **hungry**, undernourished, malnourished, starved, ravenous, famished.
– OPPOSITES full.

state[1] n. **1 condition**, shape, position, situation, circumstances, state of affairs, predicament, plight. **2 country**, nation, land, kingdom, realm, power, republic. **3 government**, parliament, administration, regime. **4 state of anxiety**, panic, fluster; informal flap, tizzy.

state[2] v. **express**, voice, utter, put into words, declare, announce, make known, put across/over, communicate, air.

stately adj. **dignified**, majestic, ceremonious, courtly, imposing, solemn, regal, grand.
– OPPOSITES undignified.

statement n. **declaration**, expression, affirmation, assertion, announcement, utterance, communication, bulletin, communiqué.

static adj. **1 unchanged**, fixed, stable, steady, unchanging, unvarying, constant. **2 stationary**, motionless, immobile, unmoving, still, at a standstill.
– OPPOSITES variable, dynamic.

station n. **1 establishment**, base, camp, post, depot, mission, site, facility, installation. **2 office**, depot, base, headquarters. **3 channel**, wavelength.

•v. **base**, post, establish, deploy, garrison.

stationary adj. **static**, parked, motionless, immobile, still, stock-still, at a standstill, at rest.
– OPPOSITES moving.

stature n. **1 height**, size, build. **2 reputation**, repute, standing, status, position, prestige, distinction, eminence, prominence, importance.

status n. **1 standing**, rank, position, level, place. **2 prestige**, kudos, cachet, standing, stature, esteem, image, importance, authority, fame.

staunch[1] adj. **stalwart**, loyal, faithful, committed, devoted, dedicated, reliable.
– OPPOSITES disloyal, unfaithful.

staunch[2] v. **stem**, stop, halt, check, curb; N. Amer. stanch.

stay v. **1 remain (behind)**, wait, linger, stick, be left, hold on, hang on; informal hang around; Brit. informal hang about; old use tarry. **2 continue (to be)**, remain, keep, carry on being. **3 visit**, stop (off/over), holiday, lodge; N. Amer. vacation.
– OPPOSITES leave.

•n. **visit**, stop, stopover, break, holiday; N. Amer. vacation; literary sojourn.

steady adj. **1 stable**, firm, fixed, secure. **2 still**, motionless, static, stationary, unmoving. **3** a steady gaze: **fixed**, intent, unwavering, unfaltering. **4** steady breathing: **constant**, consistent, regular, even, rhythmic.

5 continuous, continual, unceasing, ceaseless, perpetual, unremitting, endless. **6 regular**, settled, firm, committed, long-term.
- **OPPOSITES** unstable, shaky, fluctuating.
- v. **1 stabilize**, hold steady, brace, support, balance, rest. **2 calm**, soothe, quieten, compose, settle, subdue, quell.

steal v. **1 take**, thieve, help yourself to, pilfer, embezzle; informal swipe, lift, filch; Brit. informal nick, pinch, knock off; N. Amer. informal heist. **2 plagiarize**, copy, pirate; informal rip off, lift, pinch, crib; Brit. informal nick. **3 creep**, sneak, slink, slip, glide, tiptoe, slope.

> **WORD LINKS**
> compulsion to steal: kleptomania

stealth n. **furtiveness**, secretiveness, secrecy, surreptitiousness.

stealthy adj. **furtive**, secretive, secret, surreptitious, sneaky, sly.
- **OPPOSITES** open.

steep adj. **1 sheer**, precipitous, abrupt, sharp, perpendicular, vertical. **2** a steep increase: **sharp**, sudden, dramatic, precipitate.
- **OPPOSITES** gentle, gradual.

steeped adj.
- □ **steeped in** imbued with, filled with, permeated with, suffused with, soaked in, pervaded by.

steer v. **guide**, direct, manoeuvre, drive, pilot, navigate.

stem[1] n. **stalk**, shoot, trunk.
- □ **stem from** come from, arise from, originate from, have its origins in, spring from, derive from.

stem[2] v. **stop**, staunch, halt, check, curb; N. Amer. stanch.

stench n. **stink**, reek; Brit. informal niff, pong, whiff; N. Amer. informal funk; literary miasma.

step n. **1 pace**, stride, footstep, footfall, tread, tramp. **2 stair**, tread; **(steps)** stairs, staircase, flight of stairs. **3 action**, act, course of action, measure, move, operation, procedure. **4 advance**, development, move, movement, breakthrough. **5 stage**, level, grade, rank, degree, phase.
- v. **walk**, move, tread, pace, stride.
- □ **step down** resign, stand down, give up your post/job, bow out, abdicate; informal quit. **step in** intervene, become involved, intercede. **step up** increase, intensify, strengthen, escalate, speed up, accelerate; informal up, crank up.

stereotype n. **conventional idea**, standard image, cliché, formula.
- v. **typecast**, pigeonhole, conventionalize, categorize, label, tag.

sterile adj. **1 unproductive**, infertile, unfruitful, barren. **2 hygienic**, clean, pure, uncontaminated, sterilized, disinfected, germ-free, antiseptic.
- **OPPOSITES** fertile.

sterilize v. **1 disinfect**, fumigate, decontaminate, sanitize, clean, cleanse, purify. **2 neuter**, castrate, spay, geld; N. Amer. & Austral. alter; Brit. informal doctor.
– OPPOSITES contaminate.

stern adj. **1 unsmiling**, frowning, serious, severe, forbidding, grim, unfriendly, austere, dour. **2 strict**, severe, stringent, harsh, drastic, hard, tough, extreme, draconian.
– OPPOSITES genial, lax.

stick[1] n. **1 branch**, twig, switch. **2 walking stick**, cane, staff, crutch. **3 post**, pole, cane, stake, rod.

stick[2] v. **1 thrust**, push, insert, jab, poke, dig, plunge. **2 pierce**, penetrate, puncture, prick, stab. **3 adhere**, cling. **4** stick the stamp there: **attach**, fasten, affix, fix, paste, glue, gum, tape. **5 jam**, get jammed, catch, get caught, get trapped. **6** (Brit. informal) **tolerate**, put up with, take, stand, stomach, endure, bear, abide.
□ **stick out 1 protrude**, jut (out), project, stand out, extend, poke out, bulge. **2 be conspicuous**, be obvious, stand out, leap out; informal stick out a mile. **stick to abide by**, keep, adhere to, hold to, comply with, fulfil, stand by. **stick up for support**, take someone's side, take someone's part, side with, stand by, stand up for, defend.

sticky adj. **1 adhesive**, self-adhesive, gummed. **2 tacky**, gluey, gummy, treacly,

glutinous, viscous; informal gooey. **3 humid**, muggy, close, sultry, steamy, sweaty, sweltering, oppressive. **4 awkward**, difficult, tricky, ticklish, delicate, embarrassing, sensitive; informal hairy.
– OPPOSITES dry, fresh, cool.

stiff adj. **1 rigid**, hard, firm, inelastic, unyielding, brittle. **2 thick**, firm, viscous, semi-solid. **3 aching**, achy, painful, arthritic; informal creaky. **4 formal**, reserved, wooden, forced, strained, stilted; informal starchy, uptight. **5** stiff penalties: **harsh**, severe, heavy, stringent, drastic, draconian; Brit. swingeing. **6** they put up a stiff resistance: **vigorous**, determined, strong, spirited, resolute, tenacious, dogged, stubborn. **7 difficult**, hard, arduous, tough, strenuous, laborious, exacting, tiring, demanding. **8 strong**, potent, alcoholic.
– OPPOSITES flexible, soft, limp.

stifle v. **1 smother**, check, restrain, keep back, hold back, hold in, withhold, choke back, muffle, suppress, curb. **2 suppress**, quash, quell, put an end to, put down, stop, extinguish, stamp out, crush, subdue, repress. **3 suffocate**, smother, asphyxiate, choke.

stigma n. **shame**, disgrace, dishonour, ignominy, humiliation, stain, taint.
– OPPOSITES honour,.

still adj. **1 motionless**, unmoving, stock-still, immobile, rooted to the spot, transfixed, static,

stationary. **2 quiet**, silent, calm, peaceful, serene, windless, noiseless, undisturbed, flat, smooth, like a millpond.
– OPPOSITES moving, noisy.
• adv. **1 even now**, yet. **2 nevertheless**, nonetheless, all the same, even so, but, however, despite that, in spite of that.
• v. **quieten**, quiet, silence, hush, calm, settle, pacify, subdue.

stimulate v. **encourage**, prompt, motivate, trigger, spark, spur on, galvanize, fire, inspire, excite; N. Amer. light a fire under.
– OPPOSITES discourage.

stimulating adj. **thought-provoking**, interesting, inspiring, inspirational, lively, exciting, provocative.
– OPPOSITES uninspiring, boring.

stimulus n. **motivation**, encouragement, impetus, prompt, spur, inducement, incentive, inspiration, fillip; informal shot in the arm.
– OPPOSITES deterrent.

sting n. **1 prick**, wound, injury. **2 pain**, pricking, smarting, soreness, hurt, irritation.
• v. **1 prick**, wound. **2 smart**, burn, hurt, be irritated, be sore. **3** the criticism stung her: **upset**, wound, hurt, distress, pain, mortify.

stink v. **reek**, smell.
• n. **stench**, reek; Brit. informal pong; N. Amer. informal funk.

stint n. **spell**, stretch, turn, session, term, time, shift, tour of duty.

stipulate v. **specify**, set out, lay down, demand, require, insist on.

stir v. **1 mix**, blend, beat, whip, whisk, fold in; N. Amer. muddle. **2 move**, get up, get out of bed, rise, rouse yourself, bestir yourself. **3 disturb**, rustle, shake, move, agitate. **4** the war stirred him to action: **spur**, drive, rouse, prompt, propel, motivate, encourage, urge, impel, provoke, goad.
• n. **commotion**, disturbance, fuss, excitement, sensation; informal to-do, hoo-ha.

stock n. **1 merchandise**, goods, wares. **2 store**, supply, stockpile, reserve, hoard, cache, bank. **3 animals**, livestock, beasts, flocks, herds. **4 descent**, ancestry, origin(s), lineage, birth, extraction, family, blood, pedigree.
• adj. **usual**, routine, predictable, set, standard, staple, customary, familiar, conventional, traditional, stereotyped, clichéd, hackneyed, unoriginal, formulaic.
– OPPOSITES unusual, original.
• v. **sell**, carry, keep (in stock), offer, supply, provide, furnish.

stockpile n. **stock**, store, supply, collection, reserve, hoard, cache; informal stash.
• v. **store up**, amass, accumulate, store (up), stock up on, hoard, cache, collect, lay in, put away, put/set aside, put by, stow away, save; informal salt away, stash away.

s

stocky adj. **thickset**, sturdy, heavily built, chunky, burly, strapping, brawny, solid, heavy, hefty, beefy.
– OPPOSITES slender.

stomach n. **1 abdomen**, middle, belly, gut, paunch; informal tummy, insides, pot, spare tyre. **2 appetite**, taste, inclination, desire, wish.
•v. **tolerate**, put up with, take, stand, endure, bear; informal hack, abide; Brit. informal stick.

> WORD LINKS
> relating to the stomach: gastric

stone n. **1 rock**, pebble, boulder. **2 gem**, gemstone, jewel; informal rock, sparkler. **3 kernel**, seed, pip, pit.

> WORD LINKS
> relating to stone: lapidary

stoop v. **bend**, lean, crouch, bow, duck.

stop v. **1 end**, halt, finish, terminate, wind up, bring to a stop/halt, discontinue, cut short, interrupt, nip in the bud, shut down. **2** he stopped smoking: **cease**, refrain from, discontinue, desist from, break off, give up, abandon, cut out; informal quit, pack in; Brit. informal jack in. **3 pull up**, draw up, come to a stop/halt, come to rest, pull in/over. **4** the music stopped: **come to an end**, draw to a close, end, cease, halt, finish, be over, conclude. **5 prevent**, obstruct, impede, block, bar, preclude, dissuade from.

– OPPOSITES start, begin, continue.
•n. **1 halt**, end, finish, cessation, close, conclusion, termination, standstill. **2 break**, stopover, stop-off, stay, visit; literary sojourn. **3 stopping place**, station, halt.

store n. **1 stock**, supply, stockpile, hoard, cache, reserve, bank, pool; informal stash. **2 storeroom**, storehouse, repository, stockroom, depot, depository, warehouse. **3** ship's stores: **supplies**, provisions, stocks, food, rations, materials, equipment, hardware. **4 shop**, emporium, (retail) outlet, boutique, department store, supermarket, hypermarket, superstore, megastore; N. Amer. mart.
•v. **keep**, stockpile, stock up with, lay in, set aside, put aside, put away/by, save, collect, accumulate, amass, hoard; informal squirrel away, salt away, stash.
– OPPOSITES use, discard.

storehouse n. **warehouse**, depository, repository, store, storeroom, depot.

storm n. **1 tempest**, squall, gale, hurricane, tornado, cyclone, typhoon, thunderstorm, rainstorm, monsoon, hailstorm, snowstorm, blizzard. **2 uproar**, outcry, fuss, furore, rumpus, trouble; informal to-do, hoo-ha, ructions, stink; Brit. informal row.
•v. **1 stride**, march, stomp, stamp, stalk, flounce, fling. **2 attack**, charge, rush, swoop on.

stormy adj. **1 blustery**, squally, windy, gusty, blowy, thundery, wild, violent, rough, foul. **2 angry**, heated, fierce, furious, passionate, acrimonious.
– OPPOSITES calm, peaceful.

story n. **1 tale**, narrative, account, history, anecdote, saga; informal yarn. **2 plot**, storyline, scenario. **3 news**, report, item, article, feature, piece. **4 rumour**, whisper, allegation, speculation, gossip.

stout adj. **1 fat**, big, plump, portly, rotund, dumpy, corpulent, thickset, burly, bulky; informal tubby; Brit. informal podgy; N. Amer. informal zaftig, corn-fed. **2 strong**, sturdy, solid, tough, durable, hard-wearing. **3 determined**, vigorous, forceful, spirited, committed, brave, fearless, valiant, gallant, bold, plucky; informal gutsy.
– OPPOSITES thin, flimsy.

straight adj. **1 direct**, linear, unswerving, undeviating. **2 level**, even, in line, aligned, square, vertical, upright, perpendicular, horizontal. **3 in order**, tidy, neat, shipshape, spick and span, orderly, organized, arranged, sorted out, straightened out. **4 honest**, direct, frank, candid, truthful, sincere, forthright, straightforward, plain-spoken, blunt, unambiguous; informal upfront. **5 undiluted**, neat, pure; N. Amer. informal straight up.
– OPPOSITES winding, crooked.
•adv. **1 right**, directly, squarely, full; informal smack, (slap) bang;

N. Amer. informal smack dab. **2 frankly**, directly, candidly, honestly, forthrightly, plainly, point-blank, bluntly, flatly; Brit. informal straight up. **3 logically**, rationally, clearly, lucidly, coherently, cogently.
□ **straight away** at once, right away, (right) now, this/that (very) minute, this/that instant, immediately, instantly, directly, forthwith, then and there; N. Amer. in short order; informal straight off, pronto; N. Amer. informal lickety-split.

straighten v. **1 put straight**, adjust, put in order, arrange, rearrange, tidy, neaten. **2** we must straighten this out with him: **put right**, sort out, clear up, settle, resolve, rectify, remedy; informal patch up.

straightforward adj. **1 uncomplicated**, easy, simple, plain sailing, elementary, undemanding. **2 honest**, frank, candid, open, truthful, sincere, on the level, forthright, plain-speaking, direct; informal upfront; N. Amer. informal on the up and up.
– OPPOSITES complicated, devious.

strain[1] v. **1 overtax**, overwork, overextend, overreach, overdo it, exhaust, wear out; informal knacker, knock yourself out. **2 injure**, damage, pull, wrench, twist, sprain. **3 sieve**, sift, filter, screen.
•n. **1 tension**, tightness, tautness. **2 injury**, sprain, wrench, twist. **3 pressure**, demands,

s

burdens, stress; informal hassle. **4 stress**, (nervous) tension, exhaustion, fatigue, pressure, overwork.

strain² n. **variety**, kind, type, sort, breed, genus.

strained adj. **1 awkward**, tense, uneasy, uncomfortable, edgy, difficult, troubled. **2 forced**, unnatural, artificial, insincere, false, affected, put-on.

strait n. **1 channel**, sound, narrows, stretch of water. **2 (straits) difficulty**, trouble, crisis, mess, predicament, plight; informal hot water, jam, hole, fix, scrape.

strand n. **thread**, filament, fibre, length.

stranded adj. **1 shipwrecked**, wrecked, marooned, grounded, aground, beached. **2 helpless**, abandoned, forsaken, left high and dry, left in the lurch.

strange adj. **1 unusual**, odd, curious, peculiar, funny, queer, bizarre, weird, uncanny, surprising, unexpected, anomalous, atypical; informal fishy. **2 unfamiliar**, unknown, new, novel. – OPPOSITES ordinary, familiar.

stranger n. **newcomer**, new arrival, visitor, guest, outsider, foreigner.

strangle v. **throttle**, choke, garrotte, asphyxiate.

strap n. **belt**, tie, band, thong. •v. **tie**, lash, secure, fasten, bind, make fast, truss.

strapping adj. **big**, strong, well built, brawny, burly, muscular; informal beefy.

strategic adj. **planned**, calculated, deliberate, tactical, judicious, prudent, shrewd.

strategy n. **plan**, grand design, game plan, policy, programme, scheme.

stray v. **1 wander off**, go astray, get separated, get lost, drift away. **2 digress**, deviate, wander, get sidetracked, go off at a tangent, get off the subject. •adj. **1 homeless**, lost, abandoned, feral. **2** *a stray bullet*: **random**, chance, freak, unexpected, isolated.

streak n. **1 band**, line, strip, stripe, vein, slash, ray, smear. **2 element**, vein, strain, touch. **3 period**, spell, stretch, run; Brit. informal patch. •v. **1 stripe**, band, fleck, smear, mark. **2 race**, speed, flash, shoot, dash, rush, hurtle, whizz, zoom, career, fly; informal belt, tear, zip, whip; Brit. informal bomb; N. Amer. informal barrel.

stream n. **1 brook**, rivulet, tributary; Scottish & N. English burn; N. English beck; S. English bourn; N. Amer. & Austral./NZ creek. **2 jet**, flow, rush, gush, surge, torrent, flood, cascade. **3 succession**, series, string. •v. **1 flow**, pour, course, run, gush, surge, flood, cascade, spill. **2 pour**, surge, flood, swarm, pile, crowd.

streamlined adj. **1 aerodynamic**, smooth, sleek, elegant. **2 efficient**, smooth-running, well run, well oiled, slick.

street n. road, thoroughfare, avenue, drive, boulevard, lane; N. Amer. highway.

strength n. **1 power**, muscle, might, brawn, muscularity, robustness, sturdiness, vigour, stamina. **2 fortitude**, resilience, spirit, backbone, courage, bravery, pluck, grit; informal guts. **3** strength of feeling: **intensity**, vehemence, force, depth. **4** the strength of their argument: **force**, weight, power, persuasiveness, soundness, cogency, validity. **5 strong point**, advantage, asset, forte, aptitude, talent, skill, speciality.
– OPPOSITES weakness.

strengthen v. **1 make strong**, make stronger, build up, harden, toughen. **2 grow strong**, grow stronger, gain strength, intensify, pick up. **3 reinforce**, support, back up, bolster, authenticate, confirm, substantiate, corroborate.
– OPPOSITES weaken.

strenuous adj. **1 difficult**, arduous, hard, tough, taxing, demanding, exacting, exhausting, tiring, gruelling, back-breaking; Brit. informal knackering. **2 vigorous**, energetic, forceful, strong, spirited, intense, determined, resolute, dogged.
– OPPOSITES easy, half-hearted.

stress n. **1 strain**, pressure, (nervous) tension, worry, anxiety, trouble, difficulty; informal hassle. **2 emphasis**, importance, weight, accent, accentuation.
• v. **1 emphasize**, draw attention to, underline, underscore, point up, highlight, accentuate. **2 over-stretch**, overtax, pressurize, pressure, push to the limit, worry, harass; informal hassle.
– OPPOSITES play down.

stressful adj. **demanding**, trying, taxing, difficult, hard, tough, fraught, traumatic, tense, frustrating.
– OPPOSITES relaxing.

stretch v. **1 expand**, give, be elastic, be stretchy, be tensile. **2 pull (out)**, draw out, extend, lengthen, elongate, expand. **3 bend**, strain, distort, exaggerate, embellish. **4** she stretched out her arm: **reach out**, hold out, extend, straighten (out). **5** I stretched out on the sofa: **lie down**, recline, lean back, sprawl, lounge, loll. **6 extend**, spread, continue, go on.
– OPPOSITES shorten, contract.
• n. **1 expanse**, area, tract, belt, sweep, extent. **2 period**, time, spell, run, stint, session, shift.

strict adj. **1 precise**, exact, literal, faithful, accurate, careful, scrupulous, meticulous, punctilious. **2 stringent**, rigorous, severe, harsh, hard, stern, rigid, tough, uncompromising, authoritarian, firm. **3** in strict confidence: **absolute**, utter, complete, total.
– OPPOSITES loose, liberal.

stride v. & n. **step**, pace, march.

strife n. **conflict**, friction, discord, disagreement, dissension, dispute, argument, quarrelling.
– OPPOSITES peace.

strike v. **1 hit**, slap, smack, thump, punch, beat, bang; informal clout, wallop, belt, whack, thwack, bash, clobber, bop, biff; Austral./NZ informal quilt. **2 crash into**, collide with, hit, run into, bump into, smash into; N. Amer. impact. **3 occur to**, come to (mind), dawn on someone, hit, spring to mind, enter your head. **4** *you strike me as intelligent:* **seem to**, appear to, give someone the impression of being. **5 take industrial action**, go on strike, down tools, walk out.
•n. **1 industrial action**, walkout. **2 attack**, assault, bombing.

striking adj. **1 noticeable**, obvious, conspicuous, visible, distinct, marked, unmistakable, strong, remarkable. **2 impressive**, imposing, magnificent, spectacular, breathtaking, marvellous, wonderful, stunning, sensational, dramatic.
– OPPOSITES unremarkable.

string n. **1 twine**, cord, yarn, thread. **2 series**, succession, chain, sequence, run, streak. **3 queue**, procession, line, file, column, convoy, train, cavalcade. **4 (strings) conditions**, qualifications, provisions, provisos, caveats, stipulations, riders, limitations, restrictions; informal catches.
•v. **hang**, suspend, sling, stretch, run, thread, loop, festoon.

stringent adj. **strict**, firm, rigid, rigorous, severe, harsh, tough, tight, exacting, demanding.
– OPPOSITES lax.

strip¹ v. **1 undress**, strip off, take your clothes off, disrobe. **2 dismantle**, disassemble, take to bits/pieces, take apart. **3 empty**, clear, clean out, plunder, rob, burgle, loot, pillage, ransack, sack.

strip² n. **(narrow) piece**, band, belt, ribbon, slip, shred, stretch.

strive v. **try (hard)**, attempt, endeavour, aim, make an effort, exert yourself, struggle, do your best, do all you can, do your utmost, labour, work, toil, strain; informal go all out, give it your best shot.

stroke n. **1 blow**, hit, slap, smack, thump, punch. **2 movement**, action, motion. **3 mark**, line. **4 thrombosis**, embolism, seizure; dated apoplexy.
•v. **caress**, fondle, pat, pet, touch, rub, massage, soothe.

stroll v. & n. **walk**, amble, wander, meander, ramble, promenade, saunter; informal mosey.

strong adj. **1 powerful**, sturdy, robust, athletic, fit, tough, rugged, strapping, well built, muscular, brawny, lusty, healthy. **2 forceful**, determined, spirited, assertive, self-assertive, tough, formidable, strong-minded, redoubtable; informal gutsy, feisty. **3 secure**, solid, well built, durable, hard-wearing, heavy-duty, tough, sturdy, well made, long-lasting. **4** *a strong supporter:* **keen**, passionate, fervent, zealous, enthusiastic, eager, dedicated, loyal. **5** *strong feelings:* **intense**, vehement,

passionate, ardent, fervent, deep-seated. **6 forceful**, compelling, powerful, convincing, persuasive, sound, valid, cogent, well founded. **7 intense**, bright, brilliant, vivid, vibrant, dazzling, glaring. **8 highly flavoured**, mature, ripe, piquant, tangy, spicy. **9 concentrated**, undiluted. **10 alcoholic**, intoxicating, hard, stiff.
– OPPOSITES weak, gentle, mild.

stronghold n. **1 fortress**, fort, castle, citadel, garrison. **2** *a Tory stronghold:* **bastion**, centre, hotbed.

structure n. **1 building**, edifice, construction, erection. **2 construction**, organization, system, arrangement, framework, form, formation, shape, composition, anatomy, make-up.
•v. **arrange**, organize, design, shape, construct, build.

struggle v. **1 strive**, try hard, endeavour, make every effort, exert yourself, do your best, do your utmost. **2 fight**, battle, grapple, wrestle, scuffle.
•n. **1 striving**, endeavour, effort, exertion, campaign, battle, drive, push. **2 fight**, scuffle, brawl, tussle, fracas; informal bust-up, set-to. **3** *a power struggle:* **contest**, competition, fight, clash, rivalry, friction, feuding, conflict.

strut v. **swagger**, prance, parade, stride, sweep, flounce; N. Amer. informal sashay.

stubborn adj. **1 obstinate**, headstrong, wilful, strong-willed, pig-headed, mulish, inflexible, uncompromising, unbending, unyielding, obdurate, intractable, recalcitrant; informal stiff-necked. **2 indelible**, permanent, persistent, tenacious, resistant.

stuck adj. **1 fixed**, fastened, attached, glued, pinned. **2 jammed**, immovable. **3 baffled**, beaten, at a loss; informal stumped, up against a brick wall.

student n. **1 undergraduate**, scholar, pupil, schoolchild, schoolboy, schoolgirl. **2 trainee**, apprentice, probationer, novice, learner.

studio n. **workshop**, workroom, atelier.

studious adj. **scholarly**, academic, bookish, intellectual, erudite, learned, donnish; informal brainy.

study n. **1 learning**, education, schooling, scholarship, tuition, research. **2 investigation**, enquiry, research, examination, analysis, review, survey. **3 office**, workroom, studio.
•v. **1 work**, revise; informal swot, cram, mug up. **2 learn**, read up on, be taught. **3 investigate**, research, inquire into, look into, examine, analyse, survey. **4 scrutinize**, examine, inspect, consider, regard, look at, observe, watch, survey.

stuff n. **1 material**, substance, fabric, matter. **2 items**, articles, objects, goods, belongings, possessions, effects,

paraphernalia; informal gear, kit, things, bits and pieces, odds and ends; Brit. informal clobber.
• v. 1 fill, pack, pad, upholster. 2 shove, thrust, push, ram, cram, squeeze, force, jam, pack, pile.

stuffing n. padding, wadding, filling, packing.

stuffy adj. 1 airless, close, musty, stale, unventilated. 2 staid, sedate, sober, priggish, strait-laced, conformist, conservative, old-fashioned; informal straight, starchy, fuddy-duddy.
– OPPOSITES airy.

stumble v. 1 trip, lose your balance, lose your footing, slip. 2 stagger, totter, blunder, hobble.
□ stumble across/on find, chance on, happen on, light on, come across/upon, discover, unearth, encounter; informal dig up.

stump v. (informal) baffle, perplex, puzzle, confound, defeat, put at a loss; informal flummox, fox, throw, floor.

stun v. 1 daze, stupefy, knock out, lay out. 2 astound, amaze, astonish, dumbfound, stupefy, stagger, shock, take aback; informal flabbergast, knock sideways.

stunning adj. beautiful, lovely, glorious, wonderful, marvellous, magnificent, superb, sublime, spectacular, fine, delightful; informal fantastic, terrific, tremendous, sensational, heavenly, divine, gorgeous, fabulous, awesome.
– OPPOSITES ordinary.

stunt n. feat, exploit, trick.

stunted adj. small, undersized, underdeveloped, diminutive.

stupid adj. 1 unintelligent, dense, obtuse, foolish, idiotic, slow, simple-minded, brainless, mindless; informal thick, dim, dumb, dopey, dozy, moronic, cretinous; Brit. informal daft. 2 foolish, silly, senseless, idiotic, ill-advised, ill-considered, un-wise, nonsensical, ludicrous, ridiculous, laughable, fatuous, asinine, lunatic; informal crazy, half-baked, cockeyed, hare-brained, crackbrained; Brit. informal potty.
– OPPOSITES intelligent, sensible.

sturdy adj. 1 strapping, well built, muscular, strong, hefty, brawny, powerful, solid, burly; informal beefy. 2 robust, strong, well built, solid, stout, tough, durable, long-lasting, hard-wearing.
– OPPOSITES feeble.

stutter v. stammer, stumble, falter, hesitate.

style n. 1 manner, way, technique, method, methodology, approach, system, mode. 2 flair, elegance, stylishness, chic, taste, grace, poise, polish, sophistication, suavity, urbanity; informal class. 3 kind, type, variety, sort, design, pattern, genre. 4 fashion, trend, vogue, mode.
• v. design, fashion, tailor, cut.

stylish adj. fashionable, modern, up to date, modish, smart, sophisticated, elegant, chic,

dapper, dashing; informal trendy, natty; N. Amer. informal kicky, tony.
– OPPOSITES unfashionable.

subdue v. **conquer**, defeat, vanquish, overcome, overwhelm, crush, beat, subjugate, suppress.

subdued adj. **1 sombre**, downcast, sad, dejected, depressed, gloomy, despondent. **2 hushed**, muted, quiet, low, soft, faint, muffled, subtle, indistinct, dim, unobtrusive.
– OPPOSITES cheerful, loud, bright.

subject n. **1 theme**, subject matter, topic, issue, thesis, question, concern. **2 branch of study**, discipline, field. **3 citizen**, national, resident, taxpayer, voter.
•v. **expose to**, submit to, treat with, put through.
□ **subject to** conditional on, contingent on, dependent on.

subjective adj. **personal**, individual, emotional, biased, intuitive.
– OPPOSITES objective.

submerge v. **1 go under (water)**, dive, sink, plunge, plummet. **2 immerse**, dip, plunge, duck, dunk. **3** the farmland was submerged: **flood**, deluge, swamp, overwhelm, inundate.

submission n. **1 yielding**, capitulation, surrender, resignation, acceptance, consent, compliance, acquiescence, obedience, subjection, subservience, servility. **2 proposal**, suggestion, proposition, tender,

presentation. **3 argument**, assertion, contention, statement, claim, allegation.
– OPPOSITES defiance.

submissive adj. **compliant**, yielding, acquiescent, passive, obedient, dutiful, docile, pliant, tractable, biddable, malleable, meek, unassertive; informal under someone's thumb.

submit v. **1 yield**, give in/way, back down, cave in, capitulate, surrender, acquiesce. **2** he refused to submit to their authority: **be governed by**, abide by, comply with, accept, be subject to, agree to, consent to, conform to. **3 put forward**, present, offer, tender, propose, suggest, enter, put in, send in. **4 contend**, assert, argue, state, claim, allege.
– OPPOSITES resist.

subordinate adj. **inferior**, junior, lower-ranking, lower, supporting.
•n. **junior**, assistant, second (in command), number two, deputy, aide, underling, minion.
– OPPOSITES superior, senior.

subscribe v. **contribute**, donate, give, pay.
□ **subscribe to** support, endorse, agree with, accept, go along with.

subscription n. **membership fee**, dues, annual payment, charge.

subsequent adj. **following**, ensuing, succeeding, later, future, coming, to come, next.
– OPPOSITES previous.

s

subsequently adv. later (on), at a later date, afterwards, in due course, following this/that, eventually; formal thereafter.

subside v. **1** abate, let up, quieten down, calm, slacken (off), ease (up), relent, die down, diminish, decline. **2** recede, ebb, fall, go down, get lower. **3** sink, settle, cave in, collapse, give way.
– OPPOSITES intensify, rise.

subsidiary adj. subordinate, secondary, subservient, supplementary, peripheral, auxiliary.
– OPPOSITES principal.
•n. branch, division, subdivision, derivative, offshoot.

subsidize v. finance, fund, support, contribute to, give money to, underwrite, sponsor; informal shell out for; N. Amer. informal bankroll.

subsidy n. finance, funding, backing, support, grant, sponsorship, allowance, contribution, handout.

substance n. **1** material, compound, matter, stuff. **2** significance, importance, import, validity, foundation. **3** content, subject matter, theme, message, essence. **4** wealth, fortune, riches, affluence, prosperity, money, means.

substantial adj. **1** considerable, real, significant, important, major, valuable, useful, sizeable, appreciable. **2** sturdy, solid, stout, strong, well built, durable, long-lasting, hard-wearing.
– OPPOSITES insubstantial.

substitute n. replacement, deputy, relief, proxy, reserve, surrogate, cover, stand-in, understudy; informal sub.
•v. **1** exchange, swap, use instead of, use as an alternative to, use in place of, replace with. **2** I found someone to substitute for me: deputize for, stand in for, cover for, fill in for, take over from.

subtle adj. **1** understated, muted, subdued, delicate, soft, low-key, toned-down. **2** gentle, slight, gradual. **3** a subtle distinction: fine, fine-drawn, nice, tenuous.
– OPPOSITES gaudy, crude.

suburban adj. **1** residential, commuter-belt. **2** dull, boring, uninteresting, conventional, ordinary, unsophisticated, provincial, parochial, bourgeois, middle-class.

subversive adj. disruptive, troublemaking, insurrectionary, seditious, dissident.
•n. troublemaker, dissident, agitator, renegade.

succeed v. **1** triumph, achieve success, be successful, do well, flourish, thrive; informal make it, make the grade. **2** be successful, turn out well, work (out), be effective; informal come off, pay off. **3** replace, take over from, follow, supersede.
– OPPOSITES fail, precede.

success n. **1** victory, triumph. **2** prosperity, affluence, wealth, riches, opulence. **3** best-seller,

sell-out, winner, triumph; informal hit, smash, sensation.
– OPPOSITES failure.

successful adj. **1 prosperous**, affluent, wealthy, rich, famous, eminent, top, respected. **2 flourishing**, thriving, booming, buoyant, profitable, moneymaking, lucrative.

succession n. **sequence**, series, progression, chain, string, train, line, run.

successive adj. **consecutive**, in a row, sequential, in succession, running; informal on the trot.

succinct adj. **concise**, short (and sweet), brief, compact, condensed, crisp, laconic, terse, to the point, pithy.
– OPPOSITES verbose.

succulent adj. **juicy**, moist, luscious, soft, tender, choice, mouth-watering, appetizing, flavoursome, tasty, delicious; informal scrumptious, scrummy.
– OPPOSITES dry.

succumb v. **yield**, give in/way, submit, surrender, capitulate, cave in, fall victim.
– OPPOSITES resist.

suck v. **sip**, sup, slurp, drink, siphon.

sudden adj. **unexpected**, unforeseen, immediate, instantaneous, instant, precipitous, abrupt, rapid, swift, quick.

suddenly adv. **all of a sudden**, all at once, abruptly, swiftly, unexpectedly, without warning, out of the blue.
– OPPOSITES gradually.

sue v. **take legal action**, go to court, take to court, litigate.

suffer v. **1 hurt**, ache, be in pain, be in distress, be upset, be miserable. **2** *he suffers from asthma:* **be afflicted by**, be affected by, be troubled with, have. **3 undergo**, experience, be subjected to, receive, sustain, endure, face, meet with.

suffering n. **hardship**, distress, misery, adversity, pain, agony, anguish, trauma, torment, torture, hurt, affliction.
– OPPOSITES pleasure, joy.

sufficient adj. & det. **enough**, adequate, plenty of, ample.
– OPPOSITES inadequate.

suggest v. **1 propose**, put forward, recommend, advocate, advise. **2 indicate**, lead someone to the belief, give the impression, demonstrate, show. **3 hint**, insinuate, imply, intimate.

suggestion n. **1 proposal**, proposition, recommendation, advice, counsel, hint, tip, clue, idea. **2 hint**, trace, touch, suspicion, ghost, semblance, shadow, glimmer. **3 insinuation**, hint, implication.

suggestive adj. **1 redolent**, evocative, reminiscent, characteristic, indicative, typical. **2 provocative**, titillating, sexual, sexy, risqué, **indecent**, indelicate, improper, unseemly, smutty, dirty.

suit n. **1 outfit**, ensemble. **2 legal action**, lawsuit, (court) case,

s

action, (legal/judicial) proceedings, litigation.
- v. **1 look attractive on**, look good on, become, flatter. **2 be convenient for**, be acceptable to, be suitable for, meet the requirements of; informal fit. **3** *recipes suited to students:* be appropriate, tailor, fashion, adjust, adapt, modify, fit, gear, design.

suitable adj. **1 acceptable**, satisfactory, convenient. **2 appropriate**, apposite, apt, fitting, fit, suited, tailor-made, in keeping, ideal; informal right up someone's street. **3 proper**, right, seemly, decent, appropriate, fitting, correct, due.
- OPPOSITES unsuitable.

suite n. apartment, flat, rooms.

sullen adj. surly, sulky, morose, resentful, moody, grumpy, bad-tempered, unsociable, uncommunicative, unresponsive.
- OPPOSITES cheerful.

sum n. **1 amount**, quantity, price, charge, fee, cost. **2 total**, sum total, grand total, tally, aggregate. **3 entirety**, totality, total, whole, beginning and end. **4 calculation**, problem; (**sums**) arithmetic, mathematics; Brit. informal maths; N. Amer. informal math.
□ **sum up** summarize, make/give a summary of, encapsulate, put in a nutshell, precis, outline, recapitulate, review, recap.

summarize v. **sum up**, abridge, condense, outline, put in a nutshell, precis.

summary n. synopsis, precis, résumé, abstract, outline, rundown, summing-up, overview.

summit n. **1 (mountain) top**, peak, crest, crown, apex, tip, cap, hilltop. **2 meeting**, conference, talk(s).
- OPPOSITES base.

summon v. **1 send for**, call for, request the presence of, ask, invite. **2 convene**, call, assemble, rally, muster, gather together. **3 summons**, subpoena.

sumptuous adj. lavish, luxurious, opulent, magnificent, resplendent, gorgeous, splendid; informal plush; Brit. informal swish.
- OPPOSITES plain.

sun n. sunshine, sunlight, daylight, light, warmth.

> **WORD LINKS**
>
> *relating to the sun:* solar

sundry adj. various, varied, miscellaneous, assorted, mixed, diverse, diversified, several, numerous, many, manifold, multifarious, multitudinous; literary divers.

sunny adj. **1 bright**, sunlit, clear, fine, cloudless. **2 cheerful**, cheery, happy, bright, merry, bubbly, jolly, good-natured, good-tempered, optimistic, upbeat.
- OPPOSITES dull, cloudy.

sunrise n. dawn, crack of dawn, daybreak, break of day, first light, early morning; N. Amer. sunup.

sunset n. nightfall, twilight, dusk, evening; N. Amer. sundown.

superb adj. **excellent**, first-class, outstanding, marvellous, wonderful, splendid, admirable, fine, exceptional, glorious; informal great, fantastic, fabulous, terrific, super, awesome, ace; Brit. informal brilliant, smashing.
– OPPOSITES poor, unimpressive.

supercilious adj. **arrogant**, haughty, conceited, disdainful, overbearing, pompous, condescending, superior, patronizing, imperious, proud, snobbish, smug, scornful, sneering; informal high and mighty, snooty, stuck-up.

superficial adj. **1** surface, exterior, external, outer, slight. **2** cursory, perfunctory, casual, sketchy, desultory, token, slapdash, offhand, rushed, hasty, hurried. **3** apparent, seeming, outward, ostensible, cosmetic, slight. **4** facile, shallow, flippant, empty-headed, trivial, frivolous, silly, inane.
– OPPOSITES deep, thorough.

superfluous adj. **surplus**, redundant, unneeded, unnecessary, excess, extra, (to) spare, remaining, unused, left over, waste.
– OPPOSITES necessary.

superhuman adj. **extraordinary**, phenomenal, prodigious, stupendous, exceptional, immense, heroic, Herculean.

superior adj. **1** senior, higher-ranking, higher. **2** better, finer, higher quality, top-quality, choice, select, prime, excellent. **3** condescending, supercilious, patronizing, haughty, disdainful, lordly, snobbish; informal high and mighty, snooty, toffee-nosed.
– OPPOSITES junior, inferior.
• n. **manager**, chief, supervisor, senior, controller, foreman; informal boss.
– OPPOSITES subordinate.

superiority n. **supremacy**, advantage, lead, dominance, primacy, ascendancy, eminence.

supernatural adj. **1** paranormal, psychic, magic, magical, occult, mystic, mystical. **2** ghostly, phantom, spectral, other-worldly, unearthly.

supersede v. **replace**, take the place of, take over from, succeed, supplant.

supervise v. **oversee**, be in charge of, superintend, preside over, direct, manage, run, look after, be responsible for, govern, keep an eye on, observe, monitor, mind.

supervisor n. **manager**, director, overseer, controller, superintendent, governor, chief, head, foreman; informal boss; Brit. informal gaffer.

supple adj. **1** lithe, lissom, willowy, flexible, agile, acrobatic, nimble. **2** pliable, flexible, soft, bendy, workable, stretchy, springy.
– OPPOSITES stiff, rigid.

supplement n. **1** extra, add-on, accessory, adjunct. **2** surcharge, addition, increase, increment. **3** appendix,

s

addendum, postscript, addition, coda. **4 pull-out**, insert.
•v. **add to**, augment, increase, boost, swell, amplify, enlarge, top up.

supplementary adj. **additional**, supplemental, extra, more, further, add-on, subsidiary, auxiliary, ancillary.

supply v. **1 provide**, give, furnish, equip, contribute, donate, grant, confer, dispense. **2 satisfy**, meet, fulfil, cater for.
•n. **1 stock**, store, reserve, reservoir, stockpile, hoard, cache, fund, bank. **2** *we're running out of supplies:* **provisions**, stores, rations, food, necessities.

support v. **1 hold up**, bear, carry, prop up, keep up, brace, shore up, underpin, buttress, reinforce. **2 provide for**, maintain, sustain, keep, take care of, look after. **3 stand by**, defend, back, stand/stick up for, take someone's side, side with. **4 back up**, substantiate, bear out, corroborate, confirm, verify. **5 help**, aid, assist, contribute to, back, subsidize, fund, finance; N. Amer. informal bankroll. **6 back**, champion, favour, be in favour of, advocate, encourage, promote, endorse, espouse.
– OPPOSITES contradict, oppose.
•n. **1 pillar**, post, prop, upright, brace, buttress, foundation, underpinning. **2 encouragement**, friendship, backing, endorsement, help, assistance, comfort. **3 contributions**,

donations, money, subsidy, funding, funds, finance, capital.

supporter n. **1 advocate**, backer, adherent, promoter, champion, defender, upholder, campaigner. **2 contributor**, donor, benefactor, sponsor, backer, patron, subscriber, wellwisher. **3 fan**, follower, enthusiast, devotee, admirer.

supportive adj. **encouraging**, caring, sympathetic, reassuring, understanding, concerned, helpful.

suppose v. **1 assume**, presume, surmise, expect, imagine, dare say, take it, take as read, suspect, guess, conjecture. **2 hypothesize**, postulate, posit.

supposed adj. **alleged**, reputed, rumoured, claimed, purported.

supposition n. **belief**, conjecture, speculation, assumption, presumption, inference, theory, hypothesis, feeling, idea, notion, guesswork.

suppress v. **1 subdue**, crush, quell, quash, squash, stamp out, crack down on, clamp down on, put an end to. **2 restrain**, repress, hold back, control, stifle, smother, check, keep in check, curb, contain, bottle up. **3 censor**, keep secret, conceal, hide, hush up, gag, withhold, cover up, stifle.
– OPPOSITES encourage, reveal.

supremacy n. **control**, power, rule, sovereignty, dominance, superiority, predominance, primacy, dominion, authority, mastery, ascendancy.

supreme adj. **1** highest, chief, head, top, foremost, principal, superior, premier, first, prime. **2 extraordinary**, remarkable, phenomenal, exceptional, outstanding, incomparable, unparalleled. **3** *the supreme sacrifice*: **ultimate**, greatest, highest, extreme, final, last.
– OPPOSITES subordinate.

sure adj. **1** certain, positive, convinced, confident, definite, satisfied, persuaded, assured, free from doubt. **2 guaranteed**, unfailing, infallible, unerring, foolproof, certain, reliable, dependable, trustworthy, trusty; informal sure-fire.
– OPPOSITES uncertain, unlikely.

surface n. **1** outside, exterior, top, side, finish. **2 outward appearance**, facade, veneer.
– OPPOSITES inside, interior.
•v. **1 come to the surface**, come up, rise. **2 emerge**, arise, appear, come to light, crop up, materialize, spring up.

surge n. **1 gush**, rush, outpouring, stream, flow. **2** *a surge in demand*: **increase**, rise, growth, upswing, upsurge, escalation, leap.
•v. **1 gush**, rush, stream, flow, burst, pour, cascade, spill, sweep, roll. **2 increase**, rise, grow, leap.

surly adj. **sullen**, sulky, moody, morose, unfriendly, unpleasant, scowling, unsmiling, bad-tempered, grumpy, gruff, churlish, ill-humoured.
– OPPOSITES friendly.

surmise v. **guess**, conjecture, suspect, deduce, infer, conclude, theorize, speculate, assume, presume, suppose, understand, gather.

surmount v. **overcome**, prevail over, triumph over, beat, vanquish, conquer, get the better of.

surpass v. **excel**, exceed, transcend, outdo, outshine, outstrip, outclass, eclipse, improve on, top, trump, cap, beat, better, outperform.

surplus n. **excess**, surfeit, superfluity, oversupply, glut, remainder, residue, remains, leftovers.
– OPPOSITES dearth.
•adj. **excess**, leftover, unused, remaining, extra, additional, spare, superfluous, redundant, unwanted, unneeded, dispensable.
– OPPOSITES insufficient.

surprise n. **1 astonishment**, amazement, wonder, bewilderment, disbelief. **2 shock**, bolt from the blue, bombshell, revelation, rude awakening, eye-opener.
•v. **1 astonish**, amaze, startle, astound, stun, stagger, shock, take aback; informal bowl over, floor, flabbergast; Brit. informal knock for six. **2 take by surprise**, catch unawares, catch off guard, catch red-handed.

s

surprised adj. **astonished**, amazed, astounded, startled, stunned, staggered, nonplussed, shocked, taken aback, dumbfounded, speechless, thunderstruck; informal bowled over, flabbergasted.

surprising adj. **unexpected**, unforeseen, astonishing, amazing, startling, astounding, staggering, incredible, extraordinary.

surrender v. **1 give up**, give yourself up, give in, cave in, capitulate, concede (defeat), submit, lay down your arms/weapons. **2 give up**, relinquish, renounce, cede, abdicate, forfeit, sacrifice, hand over, turn over, yield.
– OPPOSITES resist.
•n. **1 capitulation**, submission, yielding. **2 relinquishing**, renunciation, abdication, resignation.

surreptitious adj. **secret**, secretive, stealthy, clandestine, sneaky, sly, furtive, covert.
– OPPOSITES blatant.

surround v. **encircle**, enclose, encompass, ring, hem in, confine, cut off, besiege, trap.

surrounding adj. **neighbouring**, enclosing, nearby, near, local, adjoining, adjacent.

surroundings pl. n. **environment**, setting, background, backdrop, vicinity, locality, habitat.

surveillance n. **observation**, scrutiny, watch, view, inspection, supervision, spying, espionage.

survey v. **1 look at**, look over, view, contemplate, regard, gaze at, stare at, eye, scrutinize, examine, inspect, scan, study, assess, appraise, take stock of; informal size up. **2 interview**, question, canvass, poll, investigate, research.
•n. **1 study**, review, overview, examination, inspection, assessment, appraisal. **2 poll**, investigation, enquiry, study, probe, questionnaire, census, research.

survive v. **1 remain alive**, live, sustain yourself, pull through, hold out, make it. **2 continue**, remain, persist, endure, live on, persevere, abide, go on, carry on. **3 outlive**, outlast, remain alive after.

susceptible adj. **impressionable**, credulous, gullible, innocent, ingenuous, naive, easily led, defenceless, vulnerable.
□ **susceptible to** liable to, prone to, subject to, inclined to, predisposed to, open to, vulnerable to, an easy target for.
– OPPOSITES immune, resistant.

suspect v. **1 have a suspicion**, have a feeling, feel, be inclined to think, fancy, reckon, guess, conjecture, surmise, have a hunch, fear. **2 doubt**, distrust, mistrust, have misgivings about, have qualms about, be suspicious of, be sceptical about.
•adj. **suspicious**, dubious, doubtful, untrustworthy; informal fishy, funny; Brit. informal dodgy.

suspend v. **1 adjourn**, interrupt, break off, cut short, discontinue;

N. Amer. table. **2 exclude**, debar, remove, expel, eject, rusticate. **3 hang**, sling, string, swing, dangle.

suspense n. tension, uncertainty, doubt, anticipation, excitement, anxiety, strain.

suspicion n. **1 intuition**, feeling, impression, inkling, hunch, fancy, notion, idea, theory, premonition; informal gut feeling. **2 misgiving**, doubt, qualm, reservation, hesitation, scepticism.
– OPPOSITES trust.

suspicious adj. **1 doubtful**, unsure, dubious, wary, chary, sceptical, mistrustful. **2 suspect**, dubious, unsavoury, disreputable; informal shifty, shady; Brit. informal dodgy. **3** suspicious circumstances: **strange**, odd, questionable, irregular, funny, doubtful, mysterious; informal fishy.
– OPPOSITES trusting, innocent.

sustain v. **1 comfort**, help, assist, encourage, support, give strength to, buoy up. **2 continue**, carry on, keep up, keep alive, maintain, preserve. **3 nourish**, feed, nurture, keep alive. **4 suffer**, experience, undergo, receive. **5 confirm**, corroborate, substantiate, bear out, prove, authenticate, back up, uphold.

sustained adj. **continuous**, ongoing, steady, continual, constant, prolonged, persistent, non-stop, perpetual, relentless.
– OPPOSITES sporadic.

sustenance n. nourishment, food, nutrition, provisions, rations; informal grub, chow; Brit. informal scoff; literary viands; dated victuals.

swagger v. **strut**, parade, stride, prance; informal sashay.

swallow v. eat, drink, gulp down, consume, devour, put away, quaff, slug; informal swig, swill, down; Brit. informal scoff.

swamp n. **marsh**, bog, fen, quagmire, morass.
•v. **1 flood**, inundate, deluge, fill. **2** fans swamped her website with messages: **overwhelm**, engulf, snow under, overload, inundate, deluge.

swap v. **exchange**, trade, barter, switch, change, replace.

swarm n. **1 hive**, flock. **2 crowd**, horde, mob, throng, mass, army, herd, pack.
•v. **flock**, crowd, throng, surge, stream.

swathe v. **wrap**, envelop, bandage, cover, shroud, drape, wind, enfold.

sway v. **1 swing**, shake, undulate, move to and fro. **2 stagger**, wobble, rock, lurch, reel, roll. **3 influence**, affect, manipulate, bend, mould.
•n. **1 swing**, roll, shake, undulation. **2 power**, rule, government, sovereignty, dominion, control, jurisdiction, authority.

swear v. **1 promise**, vow, pledge, give your word, undertake, guarantee. **2 insist**, declare, proclaim, assert, maintain, emphasize, stress. **3 curse**, blaspheme, use bad language; informal cuss, eff and blind.

swearing n. **bad language**, cursing, blaspheming, obscenities, expletives, swear words; informal effing and blinding, four-letter words.

sweat v. **1 perspire**, drip with sweat. **2 work**, labour, toil, slog, slave, work your fingers to the bone.

> WORD LINKS
> *causing sweating:* sudorific

sweep v. **brush**, clean (up), clear (up).

sweeping adj. **1 extensive**, wide-ranging, broad, comprehensive, far-reaching, thorough, radical. **2 wholesale**, blanket, general, unqualified, indiscriminate, oversimplified.
– OPPOSITES limited.

sweet adj. **1 sugary**, sweetened, sugared, honeyed, syrupy, sickly, cloying. **2 fragrant**, aromatic, perfumed. **3 musical**, melodious, dulcet, tuneful, soft, harmonious, silvery, mellifluous. **4 likeable**, appealing, engaging, amiable, pleasant, agreeable, kind, nice, thoughtful, considerate, delightful, lovely. **5 cute**, lovable, adorable, endearing, charming, winsome.
– OPPOSITES sour, savoury, disagreeable.
• n. (Brit.) **1 confectionery**, bonbon; N. Amer. candy; old use sweetmeat. **2 dessert**, pudding; Brit. informal afters, pud.

sweeten v. **1 make sweet**, add sugar to, sugar. **2 mollify**, placate, soothe, soften up, pacify, appease, win over.

sweetheart n. **lover**, love, girlfriend, boyfriend, beloved, beau; informal steady, squeeze; literary swain.

swell v. **1 expand**, bulge, distend, inflate, dilate, bloat, blow up, puff up, balloon, fatten, fill out. **2 grow**, enlarge, increase, expand, rise, escalate, multiply, proliferate, snowball, mushroom.
– OPPOSITES shrink, decrease.

swelling n. **bump**, lump, bulge, protuberance, protrusion, distension.

swerve v. **veer**, deviate, diverge, weave, zigzag, change direction; Sailing tack.

swift adj. **fast**, rapid, quick, speedy, expeditious, prompt, brisk, immediate, instant, hasty, hurried, sudden, abrupt.
– OPPOSITES slow, leisurely.

swindle v. **defraud**, cheat, trick, dupe, deceive, fool, hoax, hoodwink, bamboozle; informal fleece, do, con, diddle, rip off, take for a ride, pull a fast one on, put one over on; N. Amer. informal stiff.
• n. **fraud**, trick, deception, cheat, racket, sharp practice; informal con, fiddle, diddle, rip-off.

swindler n. **fraudster**, fraud, (confidence) trickster, cheat, rogue, charlatan, impostor, hoaxer; informal con man, shark, hustler, phoney, crook.

swing v. **1 sway**, move back and forth, oscillate, wave, rock, swivel, pivot, turn, rotate. **2 brandish**, wave, flourish, wield. **3 curve**, bend, veer, turn, bear, wind, twist, deviate, slew. **4 change**, fluctuate, waver, seesaw.
•n. **1 oscillation**, sway, wave. **2 change**, move, turnaround, turnabout, reversal, fluctuation, variation.

swirl v. **whirl**, eddy, billow, spiral, twist, twirl, circulate, revolve, spin.

switch n. **1 button**, lever, control. **2 change**, move, shift, transition, transformation, reversal, turnaround, U-turn, changeover, transfer, conversion.
•v. **1 change**, shift; informal chop and change. **2 exchange**, swap, interchange, change round, rotate.

swollen adj. **distended**, bulging, inflated, dilated, bloated, puffed up, puffy, tumescent, inflamed.

swoop v. **dive**, descend, pounce, sweep down, plunge, drop down.

sycophant n. **toady**, creep, flatterer; informal bootlicker, yes-man.

sycophantic adj. **obsequious**, servile, subservient, grovelling, toadying, fawning, ingratiating, unctuous; informal smarmy, bootlicking.

symbol n. **1 representation**, token, sign, emblem, figure, image, metaphor, allegory. **2 sign**, character, mark, letter. **3 logo**, emblem, badge, stamp, trademark, crest, insignia, coat of arms, seal, device, monogram, hallmark, motif.

symbolic adj. **1 emblematic**, representative, typical, characteristic, symptomatic. **2 figurative**, metaphorical, allegorical.
– OPPOSITES literal.

symbolize v. **represent**, stand for, be a sign of, denote, signify, mean, indicate, convey, express, embody, epitomize, encapsulate, personify.

symmetrical adj. **regular**, uniform, consistent, even, equal, balanced, proportional.

sympathetic adj. **1 compassionate**, caring, concerned, understanding, sensitive, supportive, empathetic, kindhearted, warm-hearted. **2 likeable**, pleasant, agreeable, congenial, companionable.
– OPPOSITES unsympathetic.

sympathize v. **commiserate**, show concern, offer condolences; (**sympathize with**) pity, feel sorry for, feel for, identify with, understand, relate to.

sympathy n. **compassion**, care, concern, commiseration, pity, condolence.
– OPPOSITES indifference.

symptom n. **indication**, indicator, manifestation, sign, mark, feature, trait, clue, hint, warning, evidence, proof.

s

symptomatic adj. **indicative**, characteristic, suggestive, typical, representative, symbolic.

synthesis n. **combination**, union, amalgam, blend, mixture, compound, fusion, composite, alloy.

synthetic adj. **artificial**, fake, imitation, mock, simulated, man-made, manufactured; informal pretend.
– OPPOSITES natural.

system n. **1 structure**, organization, arrangement, order, network; informal set-up. **2 method**, methodology, modus operandi, technique, procedure, means, way, scheme, plan, policy, programme, formula, routine. **3 (the system) the establishment**, the administration, the authorities, the powers that be, bureaucracy, officialdom.

systematic adj. **structured**, methodical, organized, orderly, planned, regular, routine, standardized, standard, logical, coherent, consistent.
– OPPOSITES disorganized.

Tt

table n. **chart**, diagram, figure, graphic, graph, plan, list.

tablet n. **1 slab**, stone, panel, plaque, plate, sign. **2 pill**, capsule, lozenge, pastille, drop. **3 bar**, cake, slab, brick, block.

taboo n. **prohibition**, proscription, veto, ban, interdict.
•adj. **forbidden**, prohibited, vetoed, banned, proscribed, outlawed, off limits, beyond the pale, unmentionable, unspeakable; informal no go.
– OPPOSITES acceptable.

tacit adj. **implicit**, understood, implied, inferred, hinted, suggested, unspoken, unstated, unsaid, unexpressed, unvoiced, taken for granted, taken as read.
– OPPOSITES explicit.

tack n. **pin**, nail, staple, rivet.
•v. **pin**, nail, staple, fix, fasten, attach, secure.
□ **tack something on** add, append, attach, join on, tag on.

tackle n. **1 equipment**, apparatus, kit, implements, paraphernalia; informal gear, clobber. **2 interception**, challenge, block, attack.
•v. **1 deal with**, take care of, attend to, see to, handle, manage, get to grips with, address. **2 confront**, face up to, take on, challenge, attack, grab, struggle with, intercept, block, stop, bring down, floor, fell; informal have a go at.

tacky[1] adj. **sticky**, wet, gluey, viscous, gummy; informal gooey.

s
t

tacky² adj. **tawdry**, tasteless, kitsch, vulgar, crude, garish, gaudy, trashy, cheap; informal cheesy; Brit. informal naff.
- OPPOSITES tasteful.

tactful adj. **diplomatic**, discreet, considerate, sensitive, understanding, thoughtful, delicate, judicious, subtle.

tactic n. **1 scheme**, plan, manoeuvre, method, trick, ploy. **2 (tactics) strategy**, policy, campaign, game plan, planning, manoeuvres, logistics.

tactical adj. **calculated**, planned, strategic, prudent, politic, diplomatic, judicious, shrewd.

tactless adj. **insensitive**, inconsiderate, thoughtless, indelicate, undiplomatic, indiscreet, unsubtle, inept, gauche, blunt.

tag n. **label**, ticket, badge, mark, tab, sticker, docket.
•v. **label**, mark, ticket, identify, flag, indicate.

tail n. **rear**, end, back, extremity, bottom.
- OPPOSITES head, front.
•v. (informal) **follow**, shadow, stalk, trail, track, keep under surveillance.

tailor n. **outfitter**, couturier, costumier, dressmaker, fashion designer.
•v. **customize**, adapt, adjust, modify, change, convert, alter, mould, gear, fit, shape, tune.

WORD LINKS
relating to tailoring: sartorial

taint v. **1 contaminate**, pollute, adulterate, infect, blight, spoil,

soil, ruin. **2 tarnish**, sully, blacken, stain, blot, damage.

take v. **1** *she took his hand:* **grasp**, get hold of, grip, clasp, clutch, grab. **2** *he took an envelope from his pocket:* **remove**, pull, draw, withdraw, extract, fish. **3 capture**, seize, catch, arrest, apprehend, take into custody, carry off, abduct. **4 steal**, remove, appropriate, make off with, pilfer, purloin; informal filch, swipe, snaffle; Brit. informal pinch, nick. **5** *take four from the total:* **subtract**, deduct, remove, discount; informal knock off, minus. **6 occupy**, use, utilize, fill, hold, reserve, engage; informal bag. **7 write**, note (down), jot (down), scribble, scrawl, record, register, document, minute. **8 bring**, carry, bear, transport, convey, move, transfer, shift, ferry; informal cart, tote. **9 escort**, accompany, help, assist, show, lead, guide, see, usher, convey. **10 travel on/by**, journey on, go via, use. **11** *I can't take much more:* **endure**, bear, tolerate, stand, put up with, abide, stomach, accept, allow, countenance, support, shoulder; formal brook.
- OPPOSITES give, add.
□ **take after** resemble, look like, remind someone of. **take apart** dismantle, take to pieces, disassemble, break up. **take in 1** deceive, delude, hoodwink, mislead, trick, dupe, fool, cheat, defraud, swindle; informal con. **2** comprehend, understand, grasp, follow, absorb; informal get. **take off 1** become airborne,

t

take to the air, leave the ground, lift off, blast off. **2** succeed, do well, become popular, catch on, prosper, flourish. **take on 1** compete against, oppose, challenge, confront, face. **2** engage, hire, employ, sign up. **3** undertake, accept, assume, shoulder, acquire. **take over** assume control of, take charge of, take command of, seize, hijack, commandeer. **take up 1** begin, start, commence, engage in, practise. **2** consume, fill, absorb, use, occupy. **3** resume, recommence, restart, carry on, continue, pick up, return to. **4** accept, say yes to, agree to, adopt.

takeover n. **buyout**, purchase, acquisition, amalgamation, merger.

takings pl. n. **proceeds**, returns, receipts, earnings, winnings, pickings, spoils, profit, gain, income, revenue.

tale n. **story**, narrative, anecdote, account, history, legend, fable, myth, saga; *informal* yarn.

talent n. **flair**, aptitude, facility, gift, knack, technique, bent, ability, forte, genius, brilliance.

talented adj. **gifted**, skilful, accomplished, brilliant, expert, consummate, able, proficient; *informal* ace.
– OPPOSITES inept.

talk v. **1** speak, chat, chatter, gossip, jabber, prattle; *informal* yak; *Brit. informal* natter, rabbit. **2** *they were able to talk in peace*: **converse**, communicate, speak (to one another), confer, consult, negotiate, parley; *informal* have a confab.
• n. **1** chatter, gossip, prattle, jabbering; *informal* yak; *Brit. informal* nattering. **2** **conversation**, chat, discussion, tête-à-tête, heart-to-heart, dialogue; *informal* confab, gossip. **3** (**talks**) **negotiations**, discussions, conference, summit, meeting, consultation, dialogue. **4** **lecture**, speech, address, discourse, oration, presentation, report, sermon.

talkative adj. **chatty**, garrulous, loquacious, voluble, communicative; *informal* mouthy.
– OPPOSITES taciturn.

tall adj. **1** *a tall man*: **big**, large, huge, giant, lanky, gangling. **2** *tall buildings*: **high**, big, lofty, towering, sky-high, gigantic, colossal.
– OPPOSITES short, low.

tally n. **running total**, count, record, reckoning, register, account, roll.
• v. **correspond**, agree, accord, concur, coincide, match, fit, be consistent, conform, equate, parallel; *informal* square.
– OPPOSITES disagree.

tame adj. **1** **domesticated**, docile, trained, gentle, mild, pet. **2** **unexciting**, uninteresting, uninspiring, uninspired, dull, bland, flat, pedestrian, humdrum, boring.
– OPPOSITES wild.
• v. **1** **domesticate**, break in, train. **2** *she learned to tame her emotions*: **subdue**, curb,

control, calm, master, moderate, discipline, overcome.

tamper v. **interfere**, meddle, monkey around, tinker, fiddle; informal mess about; Brit. informal muck about.

tangible adj. **real**, actual, physical, solid, palpable, material, substantial, concrete, visible, definite, perceptible, discernible.
– OPPOSITES abstract, theoretical.

tangle v. **entangle**, snarl, catch, entwine, twist, knot, mat.
• n. **1 snarl**, mass, knot, mesh. **2 muddle**, jumble, mix-up, confusion, shambles.

tank n. **container**, receptacle, vat, cistern, repository, reservoir, basin.

tantalize v. **tease**, torment, torture, tempt, entice, lure, beguile, excite, fascinate, titillate, intrigue.

tantrum n. **fit of temper**, fit of rage, outburst, pet, paroxysm, frenzy; informal paddy, wobbly; N. Amer. informal hissy fit.

tap[1] n. **valve**, stopcock; N. Amer. faucet, spigot.
• v. **1 bug**, wiretap, monitor, eavesdrop on. **2 draw on**, exploit, milk, mine, use, utilize, turn to account.

tap[2] v. **knock**, rap, strike, beat, pat, drum.

tape n. **1 binding**, ribbon, string, braid, band. **2 cassette**, recording, video.
• v. **1 bind**, stick, fix, fasten, secure, attach. **2 record**, tape-record, video.

taper v. **narrow**, thin (out), come to a point, attenuate.
– OPPOSITES thicken.
□ **taper off** decrease, lessen, dwindle, diminish, reduce, decline, die down, peter out, wane, ebb, slacken (off), fall off, let up, thin out.

target n. **1 objective**, goal, aim, mark, end, plan, intention, aspiration, ambition. **2 victim**, butt, recipient, focus, object, subject.
• v. **1 pick out**, single out, earmark, fix on, attack, aim at, fire at. **2** a product targeted at women: **aim**, direct, level, intend, focus.

tariff n. **1 tax**, duty, toll, excise, levy, charge, rate, fee. **2 price list**, menu.

tarnish v. **1 discolour**, rust, oxidize, corrode, stain, dull, blacken. **2 sully**, blacken, stain, blemish, ruin, disgrace, mar, damage, harm, drag through the mud.
• n. **discoloration**, oxidation, rust, verdigris.

tart[1] n. **pastry**, flan, quiche, tartlet, vol-au-vent, pie.

tart[2] (informal) v. **1 dress up**, smarten up; informal doll yourself up, titivate yourself. **2 decorate**, renovate, refurbish, redecorate, smarten up; informal do up, fix up.

tart[3] adj. **1 sour**, sharp, acidic, zesty, tangy, piquant. **2 scathing**, sharp, biting, cutting, sarcastic, hurtful, spiteful.
– OPPOSITES sweet, kind.

t

task n. **job**, duty, chore, charge, assignment, detail, mission, engagement, occupation, undertaking, exercise.

taste n. **1** flavour, savour, relish, tang, smack. **2** mouthful, morsel, drop, bit, sip, nip, touch, soupçon, dash. **3** *a taste for adventure*: **liking**, love, fondness, fancy, desire, penchant, partiality, inclination, appetite, stomach, palate, thirst, hunger. **4** *his first taste of opera*: **experience**, impression, exposure to, contact with, involvement with. **5** judgement, discrimination, discernment, refinement, elegance, grace, style. **6** sensitivity, decorum, propriety, etiquette, nicety, discretion.
•v. **1** *I tasted the wine*: **sample**, test, try, savour. **2** *he could taste blood*: **perceive**, discern, make out, distinguish.

WORD LINKS
relating to the sense of taste: gustatory

tasteful adj. **stylish**, refined, cultured, elegant, smart, chic, exquisite.
– OPPOSITES tasteless.

tasteless adj. **1** flavourless, bland, insipid, unappetizing, watery, weak, thin. **2** vulgar, crude, tawdry, garish, gaudy, loud, trashy, showy, ostentatious, cheap; *informal* flash, tacky, kitsch; *Brit. informal* naff. **3** crude, indelicate, uncouth, crass, tactless, undiplomatic, indiscreet, inappropriate, offensive.
– OPPOSITES tasty, tasteful.

tasty adj. **delicious**, palatable, luscious, mouth-watering, delectable, appetizing, tempting; *informal* yummy, scrumptious, moreish.
– OPPOSITES bland.

taunt n. **jeer**, jibe, sneer, insult, barb; *informal* dig, put-down; **(taunts)** teasing, provocation, goading, derision, mockery.
•v. **jeer at**, sneer at, scoff at, poke fun at, make fun of, get at, insult, tease, torment, ridicule, deride, mock; *N. Amer.* ride; *informal* rib, needle.

taut adj. **tight**, stretched, rigid, flexed, tensed.
– OPPOSITES slack.

tawdry adj. **gaudy**, flashy, showy, garish, loud, tasteless, vulgar, trashy, cheapjack, shoddy, shabby, gimcrack; *informal* rubbishy, tacky, kitsch.
– OPPOSITES tasteful.

tax n. **duty**, excise, customs, dues, levy, tariff, toll, tithe, charge.
•v. **strain**, stretch, overburden, overload, overwhelm, try, wear out, exhaust, sap, drain, weary, weaken.

WORD LINKS
relating to tax: fiscal

teach v. **educate**, instruct, school, tutor, inform, coach, train, drill.

WORD LINKS
relating to teaching: educational

teacher n. **educator**, tutor, instructor, schoolteacher, master, mistress, schoolmarm, governess, coach, trainer, lecturer, professor, don, guide, mentor, guru.

team n. group, squad, company, party, crew, troupe, band, side, line-up; informal bunch, gang.
- v. *ankle boots teamed with jeans*: **match**, coordinate, complement, pair up.
□ **team up** join (forces), collaborate, work together, unite, combine, cooperate, link, ally, associate, club together.

tear v. **1 rip**, split, pull, pull apart, pull to pieces, shred, rupture, sever. **2 lacerate**, cut (open), gash, slash, scratch, hack, pierce, stab. **3 snatch**, grab, seize, rip, wrench, wrest, pull, pluck; informal yank.
- n. **rip**, hole, split, slash, slit, ladder, snag.

tearful adj. **1 close to tears**, emotional, upset, distressed, sad, unhappy, in tears, crying, weeping, sobbing, snivelling; informal weepy, blubbing; formal lachrymose. **2 emotional**, upsetting, distressing, sad, heartbreaking, sorrowful, poignant, moving, touching, tear-jerking.
- OPPOSITES cheerful.

tease v. make fun of, laugh at, deride, mock, ridicule, guy, make a monkey (out) of, taunt, bait, goad, pick on; informal take the mickey out of, rag, have on, pull someone's leg; Brit. informal wind up.

technical adj. **1 practical**, scientific, technological, high-tech.

2 specialist, specialized, scientific, complex, complicated, esoteric.

technique n. **1 method**, approach, procedure, system, way, manner, means, strategy. **2 skill**, ability, proficiency, expertise, artistry, craftsmanship, adroitness, deftness, dexterity.

tedious adj. boring, dull, monotonous, repetitive, unrelieved, unvaried, uneventful, lifeless, uninteresting, unexciting, uninspiring, lacklustre, dreary, soul-destroying; informal deadly; N. Amer. informal dullsville.
- OPPOSITES exciting.

teenager n. adolescent, youth, young person, minor, juvenile; informal teen.

teetotal adj. abstinent, abstemious, sober, dry; informal on the wagon.

telephone n. phone, handset, receiver; informal blower; N. Amer. informal horn.
- v. **phone**, call, dial; Brit. ring (up); informal call up, give someone a buzz, get on the blower to; Brit. informal give someone a bell, give someone a tinkle; N. Amer. informal get someone on the horn.

television n. TV; informal the small screen; Brit. informal telly, the box; N. Amer. informal the tube.

tell v. **1** *why didn't you tell me?* **inform**, notify, let know, make aware, acquaint with, advise, put in the picture, brief, fill in, alert, warn; informal clue in/up.

t

2 *she told the story slowly:* **relate**, recount, narrate, report, recite, describe, sketch. **3 instruct**, order, command, direct, charge, enjoin, call on, require. **4** *it was hard to tell what he meant:* **ascertain**, determine, work out, make out, deduce, discern, perceive, see, identify, recognize, understand, comprehend; *informal* figure out; *Brit. informal* suss out. **5** *he couldn't tell one from the other:* **distinguish**, differentiate, discriminate. **6** *the strain began to tell on him:* **take its toll**, leave its mark, affect.

telling adj. **revealing**, significant, weighty, important, meaningful, influential, striking, potent, powerful, compelling.
– OPPOSITES insignificant.

temper n. **1** *he walked out in a temper:* **rage**, fury, fit of pique, tantrum, bad mood, pet, sulk, huff; *Brit. informal* strop, paddy; *N. Amer. informal* hissy fit. **2** *a display of temper:* **anger**, fury, rage, annoyance, irritation, pique, petulance; *Brit. informal* stroppiness. **3** *she struggled to keep her temper:* **composure**, self-control, self-possession, calm, good humour; *informal* cool.
•v. *their idealism is tempered with realism:* **moderate**, modify, modulate, mitigate, alleviate, reduce, weaken, lighten, soften.
◻ **lose your temper** get angry, fly into a rage, erupt; *informal* go mad, go bananas, have a fit, see red, fly off the handle, blow your top, hit the roof, lose your rag;

Brit. informal go spare, throw a wobbly.

temperament n. **character**, nature, disposition, personality, make-up, constitution, temper.

temperamental adj. **volatile**, excitable, emotional, unpredictable, hot-headed, quick-tempered, impatient, touchy, moody, sensitive, highly strung.
– OPPOSITES placid.

tempestuous adj. **turbulent**, wild, stormy, violent, emotional, passionate, impassioned, fiery, intense, uncontrolled, unrestrained.
– OPPOSITES calm.

temple n. **place of worship**, shrine, sanctuary, church, cathedral, mosque, synagogue, mandir, gurdwara.

temporarily adv. **1 for the time being**, for the moment, for now, for the present, provisionally, pro tem, in the interim. **2 briefly**, for a short time, momentarily, fleetingly.
– OPPOSITES permanently.

temporary adj. **1 provisional**, short-term, interim, makeshift, stopgap, acting, fill-in, stand-in, caretaker. **2 brief**, short-lived, momentary, fleeting, passing, ephemeral.
– OPPOSITES permanent, lasting.

tempt v. **entice**, persuade, convince, inveigle, induce, cajole, coax, lure, attract, appeal to, tantalize, whet the appetite of, seduce; *informal* sweet-talk.
– OPPOSITES discourage, deter.

temptation n. **1 desire**, urge, itch, impulse, inclination. **2 lure**, allure, enticement, attraction, draw, pull.

tempting adj. **enticing**, alluring, attractive, appealing, inviting, seductive, beguiling, fascinating, mouth-watering.
– OPPOSITES uninviting.

tenable adj. **defensible**, justifiable, supportable, sustainable, arguable, able to hold water, reasonable, rational, sound, viable, plausible, credible, believable, conceivable.
– OPPOSITES untenable.

tenacious adj. **persevering**, persistent, determined, dogged, strong-willed, indefatigable, tireless, resolute, patient, purposeful, unflagging, staunch, steadfast, untiring, unwavering, unswerving, unshakeable; formal pertinacious.

tenant n. **occupant**, resident, inhabitant, leaseholder, lessee, lodger; Brit. occupier.

tend¹ v. **be inclined**, be apt, be disposed, be prone, be liable, be likely, have a tendency.

tend² v. **look after**, take care of, minister to, attend to, see to, watch over, keep an eye on, mind, protect, guard.
– OPPOSITES neglect.

tendency n. **inclination**, propensity, proclivity, proneness, aptness, likelihood, bent, leaning, liability.

tender¹ adj. **1** a gentle, tender man: **caring**, kind, kind-hearted, soft-hearted, compassionate, sympathetic, warm, gentle, mild, benevolent. **2** a tender kiss: **affectionate**, fond, loving, romantic, emotional; informal lovey-dovey. **3 soft**, succulent, juicy, melt-in-the-mouth. **4 sore**, sensitive, inflamed, raw, painful, hurting, aching, throbbing. **5** the tender age of fifteen: **young**, youthful, impressionable, inexperienced; informal wet behind the ears.
– OPPOSITES hard-hearted, callous, tough.

tender² v. **offer**, proffer, put forward, present, propose, suggest, advance, submit, hand in.
•n. **bid**, offer, quotation, quote, estimate, price.

tense adj. **1 taut**, tight, rigid, stretched, strained, stiff. **2 anxious**, nervous, on edge, edgy, strained, stressed, ill at ease, uneasy, restless, worked up, keyed up, overwrought, jumpy, nervy; informal a bundle of nerves, jittery, twitchy, uptight. **3 nerve-racking**, stressful, anxious, worrying, fraught, charged, strained, nail-biting.
– OPPOSITES relaxed, calm.
•v. **tighten**, tauten, flex, contract, brace, stiffen.
– OPPOSITES relax.

tension n. **1 tightness**, tautness, rigidity, pull. **2 strain**, stress, anxiety, pressure, worry, nervousness, jumpiness, edginess, restlessness, suspense, uncertainty. **3 strained relations**,

t

tentative adj. 1 *a tentative arrangement:* **provisional**, unconfirmed, preliminary, exploratory, experimental. 2 *a few tentative steps:* **hesitant**, uncertain, cautious, timid, hesitating, faltering, shaky, unsteady, halting.
– OPPOSITES definite, confident.

tenuous adj. **slight**, insubstantial, flimsy, weak, doubtful, dubious, questionable, suspect, vague, nebulous, hazy.
– OPPOSITES convincing.

tepid adj. 1 **lukewarm**, warmish. 2 **unenthusiastic**, apathetic, half-hearted, indifferent, cool, lukewarm, uninterested.

term n. 1 **word**, expression, phrase, name, title, designation, label, description. 2 *the terms of the contract:* **condition**, stipulation, specification, provision, proviso, restriction, qualification. 3 **period**, length of time, spell, stint, duration, stretch, run, session.
▪ v. **call**, name, entitle, title, style, designate, describe as, dub, label, tag.

terminal adj. 1 **incurable**, untreatable, inoperable, fatal, lethal, mortal, deadly. 2 **final**, last, concluding, closing, end.
▪ n. 1 **station**, last stop, end of the line, depot; Brit. terminus. 2 **workstation**, VDU, visual display unit.

terminate v. **bring to an end**, end, bring to a close, close, conclude, finish, stop, wind up,
discontinue, cease, cut short, abort, axe; informal pull the plug on.
– OPPOSITES begin.

terminology n. **phraseology**, terms, expressions, words, language, parlance, vocabulary, nomenclature, usage, idiom, jargon; informal lingo.

terrain n. **land**, ground, territory, topography, landscape, countryside, country.

terrestrial adj. **earthly**, worldly, mundane, earthbound.

terrible adj. 1 *a terrible crime:* **dreadful**, awful, appalling, horrific, horrible, horrendous, atrocious, monstrous, sickening, heinous, vile, gruesome, unspeakable. 2 *terrible pain:* **severe**, extreme, intense, excruciating, agonizing, unbearable. 3 *a terrible film:* **very bad**, dreadful, awful, frightful, atrocious, execrable; informal pathetic, pitiful, useless, lousy, appalling; Brit. informal chronic.
– OPPOSITES minor, slight, excellent.

terrific adj. 1 **tremendous**, huge, massive, gigantic, colossal, mighty, considerable; informal mega, whopping; Brit. informal ginormous. 2 (informal) **marvellous**, wonderful, sensational, outstanding, superb, excellent, first-rate, dazzling, out of this world, breathtaking; informal great, fantastic, fabulous, super, ace, wicked, awesome; Brit. informal brilliant.

terrify v. **frighten**, horrify, petrify, scare, strike terror into, paralyse, transfix.

territory n. **1 region**, area, enclave, country, state, land, dependency, colony, dominion. **2** *mountainous territory*: **terrain**, land, ground, countryside.

terror n. **fear**, dread, horror, fright, alarm, panic, shock.

terrorize v. **persecute**, victimize, torment, tyrannize, intimidate, menace, threaten, bully, browbeat, scare, frighten, terrify, petrify; Brit. informal put the frighteners on.

terse adj. **brief**, short, to the point, concise, succinct, crisp, pithy, incisive, laconic, elliptical, brusque, abrupt, curt, clipped, blunt.
– **OPPOSITES** long-winded, polite.

test n. **1 trial**, experiment, check, examination, assessment, evaluation, appraisal, investigation. **2 exam**, examination; N. Amer. quiz.
•v. **try out**, trial, put through its paces, experiment with, check, examine, assess, evaluate, appraise, investigate, sample.

testify v. **swear**, attest, give evidence, state on oath, declare, assert, affirm.

testimonial n. **reference**, letter of recommendation, commendation.

testimony n. **evidence**, sworn statement, attestation, affidavit, statement, declaration, assertion.

testing adj. **difficult**, challenging, tough, hard, demanding, taxing, stressful.
– **OPPOSITES** easy.

text n. **1 book**, work, textbook. **2** *the pictures relate well to the text*: **words**, content, body, wording, script, copy.

textiles pl. n. **fabrics**, cloths, materials.

texture n. **feel**, touch, appearance, finish, surface, grain, consistency.

thank v. **express your gratitude to**, say thank you to, show your appreciation to.

thankful adj. **grateful**, relieved, pleased, glad.

thankless adj. **unenviable**, difficult, unpleasant, unrewarding, unappreciated, unrecognized, unacknowledged.
– **OPPOSITES** rewarding.

thanks pl. n. **gratitude**, appreciation, acknowledgement, recognition, credit.
☐ **thanks to** as a result of, owing to, due to, because of, through, on account of, by virtue of.

thaw v. **melt**, unfreeze, defrost, soften, liquefy.
– **OPPOSITES** freeze.

theatre n. **1 playhouse**, auditorium, amphitheatre. **2 acting**, the stage, drama, dramaturgy, show business; informal showbiz. **3** *a lecture theatre*: **hall**, room, auditorium.

theatrical adj. **1 stage**, dramatic, thespian, show-business; informal showbiz. **2 exaggerated**, ostentatious, stagy, melodramatic, showy, affected, overdone; informal hammy.

theft n. **robbery**, stealing, larceny, shoplifting, burglary, embezzlement, raid, hold-up; informal smash-and-grab; N. Amer. informal heist.

theme n. **1 subject**, topic, argument, idea, thrust, thread, motif, keynote. **2 melody**, tune, air, motif, leitmotif.

theoretical adj. **hypothetical**, speculative, academic, conjectural, suppositional, notional, unproven.
– OPPOSITES actual.

theory n. **1 hypothesis**, thesis, conjecture, supposition, speculation, postulation, proposition, premise, opinion, view, belief, contention. **2** modern economic theory: **ideas**, concepts, philosophy, ideology, thinking, principles.

therapeutic adj. **healing**, curative, remedial, medicinal, restorative, health-giving.

therapist n. **psychologist**, psychotherapist, analyst, psychoanalyst, psychiatrist, counsellor; informal shrink.

therapy n. **1 treatment**, remedy, cure. **2** he's currently in therapy: **psychotherapy**, psychoanalysis, counselling.

therefore adv. **consequently**, because of that, for that reason, that being the case, so, as a result, hence, accordingly.

thesis n. **1 theory**, contention, argument, proposal, proposition, premise, assumption, supposition, hypothesis. **2 dissertation**, essay, paper, treatise, composition, study; N. Amer. theme.

thick adj. **1 broad**, wide, deep, stout, bulky, hefty, chunky, solid, plump. **2** the station was thick with people: **crowded**, full, packed, teeming, seething, swarming, crawling, crammed, thronged, bursting at the seams, solid, overflowing; informal jampacked, chock-a-block, stuffed; Austral./NZ informal chocker. **3 plentiful**, abundant, profuse, luxuriant, bushy, rich, riotous, exuberant, rank, rampant, dense; informal jungly. **4 semi-solid**, firm, stiff, heavy, viscous, gelatinous. **5** thick fog: **dense**, heavy, opaque, impenetrable, soupy, murky.
– OPPOSITES thin, slender, sparse.

thicken v. **stiffen**, condense, solidify, set, gel, congeal, clot, coagulate.

thief n. **robber**, burglar, housebreaker, shoplifter, pickpocket, mugger, kleptomaniac; informal crook.

thieve v. **steal**, take, purloin, help yourself to, snatch, pilfer, embezzle, misappropriate; informal rob, swipe, nab, lift; Brit. informal pinch, knock off; N. Amer. informal heist.

thin adj. **1 narrow**, fine, attenuated. **2 lightweight**, light, fine, delicate, flimsy, diaphanous,

gauzy, gossamer, sheer, filmy, transparent, see-through.
3 slim, lean, slender, willowy, svelte, sylphlike, spare, slight, skinny, underweight, scrawny, scraggy, bony, gaunt, emaciated, skeletal, lanky, spindly, gangly; informal anorexic.
4 watery, weak, runny, sloppy.
– OPPOSITES thick, broad, fat.
• v. **1 dilute**, water down, weaken. **2** *the crowds thinned out*: disperse, dissipate, scatter.
– OPPOSITES thicken.

thing n. **1 object**, article, item, artefact, commodity; informal doodah, whatsit; Brit. informal gubbins. **2 (things) belongings**, possessions, stuff, property, worldly goods, goods and chattels, effects, paraphernalia, bits and pieces, luggage, baggage; informal gear, junk; Brit. informal clobber. **3 (things) equipment**, apparatus, gear, kit, tackle, stuff, implements, tools, utensils, impedimenta, accoutrements.

think v. **1 believe**, be of the opinion, be of the view, be under the impression, expect, imagine, anticipate, suppose, guess, fancy; informal reckon, figure. **2** *his family was thought to be rich*: **consider**, judge, hold, reckon, deem, presume, estimate, regard as, view as.
3 ponder, reflect, deliberate, consider, meditate, contemplate, muse, ruminate, brood; formal cogitate. **4** *she thought of all the visits she had made*: **recall**, remember, recollect, call to

mind, imagine, picture, visualize, envisage.
□ **think up** devise, dream up, come up with, invent, create, concoct, make up, hit on; informal cook up.

thinker n. **intellectual**, philosopher, scholar, sage, ideologist, theorist, intellect, mind; informal brain.

thinking adj. **intelligent**, sensible, reasonable, rational, logical, analytical, thoughtful.
• n. **reasoning**, idea(s), theory, thoughts, philosophy, beliefs, opinion(s), view(s).

thirst n. *his thirst for knowledge*: **craving**, desire, longing, yearning, hunger, hankering, eagerness, lust, appetite; informal yen, itch.
□ **thirst for** crave, want, covet, desire, hunger for, lust after, hanker after, wish for, long for.

thirsty adj. **longing for a drink**, dry, dehydrated; informal parched, gasping.

thorn n. prickle, spike, barb, spine.

thorny adj. **1 prickly**, spiky, barbed, spiny, sharp. **2 problematic**, tricky, ticklish, delicate, controversial, awkward, difficult, knotty, tough, complicated, complex, involved, intricate, vexed; informal sticky.

thorough adj. **1** *a thorough investigation*: **rigorous**, in-depth, exhaustive, minute, detailed, close, meticulous, methodical, careful, complete, comprehensive. **2** *he's slow but thorough*: **meticulous**, scrupulous,

t

assiduous, conscientious, painstaking, punctilious, methodical, careful. **3 utter**, downright, absolute, complete, total, out-and-out, real, perfect, proper; Brit. informal right; Austral./NZ informal fair.
- OPPOSITES superficial, cursory.

thought n. **1 idea**, notion, opinion, view, impression, feeling, theory. **2 thinking**, contemplation, musing, pondering, consideration, reflection, rumination, deliberation, meditation; formal cogitation. **3 have you no thought for others? consideration**, understanding, regard, sensitivity, care, compassion, sympathy.

thoughtful adj. **1 pensive**, reflective, contemplative, musing, meditative, ruminative, introspective, philosophical, preoccupied, in a brown study. **2 considerate**, caring, attentive, understanding, sympathetic, solicitous, concerned, helpful, obliging, accommodating, kind, compassionate.
- OPPOSITES thoughtless.

thoughtless adj. **1 inconsiderate**, uncaring, insensitive, uncharitable, unkind, tactless, undiplomatic, indiscreet, careless. **2 unthinking**, heedless, careless, unmindful, absent-minded, injudicious, ill-advised, ill-considered, imprudent, unwise, foolish, silly, stupid, reckless, rash, precipitate, negligent, neglectful, remiss.
- OPPOSITES thoughtful.

thrash v. **1 hit**, beat, strike, batter, thump, hammer, pound; informal belt. **2 he was thrashing around in pain: flail**, writhe, thresh, jerk, toss, twist, twitch.

thread n. **1 cotton**, yarn, fibre, filament. **2 train of thought**, drift, direction, theme, tenor.
•v. she threaded her way between the tables: **weave**, inch, squeeze, navigate, negotiate.

threadbare adj. **worn**, old, holey, moth-eaten, mangy, ragged, frayed, tattered, decrepit, shabby, scruffy; informal tatty, the worse for wear.

threat n. **1 threatening remark**, warning, ultimatum. **2 a possible threat to aircraft: danger**, peril, hazard, menace, risk. **3 the company faces the threat of liquidation: possibility**, chance, probability, likelihood, risk.

threaten v. **1 menace**, intimidate, browbeat, bully, terrorize. **2 endanger**, jeopardize, imperil, put at risk. **3 herald**, bode, warn of, presage, foreshadow, indicate, point to, be a sign of, signal.

threshold n. **1 doorstep**, entrance, entry, gate, portal. **2 start**, beginning, commencement, brink, verge, dawn, inception, day one, opening, debut.

thrifty adj. **frugal**, economical, sparing, careful with money, provident, prudent, abstemious, parsimonious, penny-pinching.
- OPPOSITES extravagant.

thrill n. **excitement**, stimulation, pleasure, tingle; informal buzz, kick; N. Amer. informal charge.
- OPPOSITES boredom.
- v. **excite**, stimulate, arouse, rouse, inspire, delight, exhilarate, intoxicate, stir, electrify, move; informal give someone a buzz/kick; N. Amer. informal give someone a charge.
- OPPOSITES bore.

thrilling adj. **exciting**, stimulating, stirring, action-packed, rip-roaring, gripping, electrifying, riveting, fascinating, dramatic, hair-raising.
- OPPOSITES boring.

thrive v. **flourish**, prosper, burgeon, bloom, blossom, do well, advance, succeed, boom.
- OPPOSITES decline, wither.

thriving adj. **flourishing**, prospering, growing, developing, blooming, healthy, successful, booming, profitable; informal going strong.
- OPPOSITES declining.

throb v. **pulsate**, beat, pulse, palpitate, pound, thud, thump, drum, judder, vibrate, quiver.
- n. **pulsation**, beat, pulse, palpitation, pounding, thudding, thumping, drumming, juddering, vibration, quivering.

throng n. **crowd**, horde, mass, army, herd, flock, drove, swarm, sea, troupe, pack; informal bunch, gaggle, gang.
- v. **1** pavements thronged with tourists: **fill**, crowd, pack, cram, jam. **2** visitors thronged round

him: **flock**, crowd, cluster, mill, swarm, congregate, gather.

throttle v. **choke**, strangle, garrotte.

through prep. **1** by means of, by way of, by dint of, via, using, thanks to, by virtue of, as a result of, as a consequence of, on account of, owing to. **2** throughout, for the duration of, until/to the end of, all.

throughout prep. **1** all over, in every part of, everywhere in. **2** all through, for the duration of, for the whole of, until the end of, all.

throw v. **1** hurl, toss, fling, pitch, cast, lob, launch, bowl; informal chuck, heave, sling, bung. **2** he threw the door open: **push**, thrust, fling, bang. **3** cast, send, give off, emit, radiate, project. **4** disconcert, unnerve, fluster, ruffle, put off, throw off balance, unsettle, confuse; informal rattle, faze.
- n. **lob**, toss, pitch, bowl.
- □ **throw away/out** discard, dispose of, get rid of, scrap, dump, jettison; informal chuck (away/out), ditch, bin, junk; Brit. informal get shot of. **throw out** expel, eject, evict, drive out, force out, oust, remove, get rid of, depose, topple, unseat, overthrow; informal boot out, kick out; Brit. informal turf out.

thrust v. **1** shove, push, force, plunge, stick, drive, ram, lunge. **2** fame had been thrust on him: **force**, foist, impose, inflict.
- n. **1** shove, push, lunge, poke.

2 advance, push, drive, attack, assault, onslaught, offensive. **3 force**, propulsion, power, impetus. **4 gist**, substance, drift, message, import, tenor.

thug n. ruffian, hooligan, bully boy, hoodlum, gangster, villain; informal tough, bruiser, heavy; Brit. informal rough, bovver boy; N. Amer. informal hood, goon.

thump v. **1 hit**, beat, punch, strike, smack, batter, pummel; informal whack, wallop, bash, biff, clobber, clout; Brit. informal slosh; N. Amer. informal slug. **2 throb**, pound, beat, thud, hammer.

thunder n. rumble, boom, roar, pounding, crash, reverberation. •v. **1 rumble**, boom, roar, pound, crash, resound, reverberate. **2** *'Answer me!' he thundered:* **shout**, roar, bellow, bark, bawl.

thwart v. foil, frustrate, forestall, stop, check, block, prevent, defeat, impede, obstruct, derail, snooker; informal put paid to, do for, stymie; Brit. informal scupper. – OPPOSITES help.

ticket n. **1 pass**, authorization, permit, token, coupon, voucher. **2 label**, tag, sticker, tab, slip, docket.

tickle v. **1 stroke**, pet. **2 stimulate**, interest, appeal to, amuse, entertain, divert, please, delight.

tide n. **1 current**, flow, stream, ebb. **2** *the tide of history:* **course**, movement, direction, trend, current, drift, run.

tidy adj. **1** *a tidy room:* **neat**, in good order, orderly, well kept,

in apple-pie order, shipshape, spick and span, spruce, uncluttered, straight. **2** *a tidy person:* **organized**, neat, methodical, meticulous, systematic. – OPPOSITES untidy. •v. **put in order**, clear up, sort out, straighten (up), clean up, spruce up, smarten up.

tie v. **1 bind**, tie up, tether, hitch, strap, truss, fetter, rope, make fast, moor, lash. **2 do up**, lace, knot. **3 restrict**, restrain, limit, tie down, constrain, cramp, hamper, handicap, hamstring, encumber, shackle. **4 link**, connect, couple, relate, join, marry. **5 draw**, be equal, be even. •n. **1 lace**, string, cord, fastening. **2 bond**, connection, link, relationship, attachment, affiliation. **3 restriction**, constraint, curb, limitation, restraint, hindrance, encumbrance, handicap, obligation, commitment. **4 draw**, dead heat.

tier n. **1 row**, rank, bank, line, layer, level. **2 grade**, gradation, echelon, rung on the ladder.

tight adj. **1 firm**, secure, fast. **2 taut**, rigid, stiff, tense, stretched, strained, clenched. **3 close-fitting**, narrow, figure-hugging, skintight; informal sprayed on. **4** *a tight mass of fibres:* **compact**, compressed, dense, solid. **5 small**, tiny, narrow, limited, restricted, confined, cramped, constricted. **6** *tight security:* **strict**, rigorous, stringent, tough. – OPPOSITES slack, loose.

tighten v. **1** stretch, tauten, strain, stiffen, tense. **2 strengthen**, increase, make stricter.

– OPPOSITES loosen, slacken.

tilt v. slope, tip, lean, list, bank, slant, incline, pitch, cant, angle.
•n. slope, list, camber, gradient, bank, slant, incline, pitch, cant, bevel, angle.

timber n. **1** wood; N. Amer. lumber. **2 beam**, spar, plank, batten, lath, board, joist, rafter.

time n. **1** moment, point (in time), occasion, instant, juncture, stage. **2** *he worked there for a time*: while, spell, stretch, stint, interval, period, length of time, duration, phase. **3** era, age, epoch, aeon, period, years, days.
•v. **schedule**, arrange, set, organize, fix, book, line up, timetable, plan; N. Amer. slate.
□ **all the time** constantly, around the clock, day and night, (morning, noon, and night), (day in, day out), always, without a break, ceaselessly, endlessly, incessantly, perpetually, permanently, continuously, continually, eternally; informal 24-7. **at times** occasionally, sometimes, from time to time, now and then, every so often, once in a while, on occasion, off and on, at intervals, periodically.

> **WORD LINKS**
> *relating to time*: chronological, temporal

timeless adj. lasting, enduring, classic, ageless, permanent, perennial, abiding, unchanging, unvarying, never-changing, eternal, everlasting.
– OPPOSITES ephemeral.

timely adj. **opportune**, well timed, convenient, appropriate, expedient, seasonable, propitious.
– OPPOSITES ill-timed.

timetable n. schedule, programme, agenda, calendar, diary.
•v. **schedule**, arrange, programme, organize, fix, time, line up; Brit. diarize; N. Amer. slate.

timid adj. fearful, afraid, faint-hearted, timorous, nervous, scared, frightened, shy, diffident.
– OPPOSITES bold.

tinge v. tint, colour, stain, shade, wash.
•n. **1** tint, colour, note, shade, tone, hue. **2 trace**, note, touch, suggestion, hint, flavour, element, streak, suspicion, soupçon.

tingle v. prickle, prick, sting, itch, tickle.
•n. **prickle**, pricking, tingling, sting, itch, pins and needles.

tinker v. fiddle, play about, mess about, adjust, try to mend; Brit. informal muck about.

tint n. **1** shade, colour, tone, hue, tinge, cast, flush, blush. **2 dye**, colourant, colouring, wash.
•v. **dye**, colour, tinge.

tiny adj. minute, minuscule, microscopic, very small, mini, diminutive, miniature, baby, toy, dwarf; Scottish wee; informal teeny, tiddly; Brit. informal titchy.
– OPPOSITES huge.

t

tip[1] n. **1 point**, end, extremity, head, spike, prong, nib. **2 peak**, top, summit, apex, crown, crest, pinnacle.
• v. **cap**, top, crown, surmount.

tip[2] v. **1 overturn**, turn over, topple (over), fall (over), keel over, capsize, roll over. **2 lean**, tilt, list, slope, bank, slant, incline, pitch, cant. **3 pour**, empty, drain, dump, discharge, decant.
• n. (Brit.) **dump**, rubbish dump, landfill site.

tip[3] n. **1 gratuity**, baksheesh, present, gift, reward. **2 piece of advice**, suggestion, word of advice, pointer, hint; informal wrinkle.

tirade n. **diatribe**, harangue, rant, attack, polemic, broadside, fulmination, tongue-lashing; informal blast.

tire v. **1 get tired**, weaken, flag, droop. **2 fatigue**, tire out, exhaust, wear out, drain, weary, enervate; informal knock out, take it out of; Brit. informal knacker.

tired adj. **1 exhausted**, worn out, weary, fatigued, ready to drop, drained, enervated; informal all in, dead beat, shattered, done in; Brit. informal knackered, whacked; N. Amer. informal pooped, tuckered out; Austral./NZ informal stonkered. **2** I'm tired of him: **fed up with**, weary of, bored with/by, sick (and tired) of; informal up to here with. **3 hackneyed**, overused, stale, clichéd, predictable, unimaginative, unoriginal, dull, boring; informal corny.
– OPPOSITES energetic, fresh.

tiresome adj. **1 wearisome**, laborious, wearing, tedious, boring, monotonous, dull, uninteresting, unexciting, humdrum, routine. **2 troublesome**, irksome, vexatious, irritating, annoying, exasperating, trying; informal aggravating, pesky.
– OPPOSITES interesting, pleasant.

tiring adj. **exhausting**, wearying, taxing, draining, hard, arduous, strenuous, onerous, gruelling; informal killing; Brit. informal knackering.

title n. **1 heading**, label, inscription, caption, subheading, legend. **2 name**, designation, form of address, rank, office, position; informal moniker, handle. **3** an Olympic title: **championship**, crown, first place.

toast v. **drink (to) the health of**, salute, honour, pay tribute to; old use pledge.

toddle v. **totter**, teeter, wobble, falter, waddle, stumble.

together adv. **1 with each other**, in conjunction, jointly, in cooperation, in collaboration, in partnership, in combination, in league, side by side; informal in cahoots. **2 simultaneously**, at the same time, at once, concurrently, as a group, in unison, in chorus.
– OPPOSITES separately.
• adj. (informal) **level-headed**, well adjusted, sensible, practical, realistic, mature, stable, full of common sense, well organized, efficient, methodical,

self-confident, self-assured; informal unflappable.

toil v. **1 work**, labour, slave, strive; informal slog, beaver; Brit. informal graft. **2 struggle**, drag yourself, trudge, slog, plod; N. Amer. informal schlep.
•n. **hard work**, labour, exertion, slaving, drudgery, effort, (blood, sweat, and tears); informal slog, elbow grease; Brit. informal graft; old use travail.

toilet n. **lavatory**, WC, (public) convenience, cloakroom, powder room, latrine, privy, urinal; N. Amer. bathroom, washroom, rest room, men's/ladies' room, comfort station; Brit. informal loo, bog, the Ladies, the Gents; N. Amer. informal can, john; Austral./ NZ informal dunny.

token n. **1 symbol**, sign, emblem, badge, representation, indication, mark, expression, demonstration. **2 memento**, souvenir, keepsake, reminder. **3 voucher**, coupon, note.
•adj. **token resistance: symbolic**, nominal, perfunctory, slight, minimal, superficial.

tolerable adj. **1 bearable**, endurable, supportable, acceptable. **2 fairly good**, fair, passable, adequate, all right, acceptable, satisfactory, average, run-of-the-mill, mediocre, middling, ordinary, unexceptional; informal OK, so-so, no great shakes.
– OPPOSITES intolerable.

tolerance n. **1 toleration**, acceptance, open-mindedness, broad-mindedness, forbearance, patience, charity, understanding, lenience. **2 endurance**, resilience, resistance, immunity.

tolerant adj. **open-minded**, forbearing, broad-minded, liberal, unprejudiced, unbiased, patient, long-suffering, understanding, charitable, lenient, easy-going, indulgent, permissive.

tolerate v. **1 allow**, permit, condone, accept, swallow, countenance; formal brook. **2** *he couldn't tolerate her moods any longer:* **endure**, put up with, bear, take, stand, support, stomach, abide; Brit. informal stick.

toll¹ n. **1 charge**, fee, payment, levy, tariff, tax. **2 number**, count, tally, total, sum. **3** *the toll on the environment has been high:* **harm**, damage, injury, detriment, adverse effect, cost, price, loss.

toll² v. **ring**, sound, clang, chime, strike, peal.

tomb n. **burial chamber**, vault, crypt, catacomb, sepulchre, mausoleum, grave.

WORD LINKS
relating to a tomb: sepulchral

tone n. **1 sound**, timbre, voice, colour, tonality, intonation, inflection, modulation. **2 mood**, air, feel, flavour, note, attitude, character, spirit, vein. **3 shade**, colour, hue, tint, tinge.
•v. **harmonize**, go, blend, coordinate, team, match, suit, complement.

t

□ **tone down** moderate, modify, temper, soften, modulate, lighten, subdue.

tonic n. stimulant, boost, restorative, refresher, fillip; informal shot in the arm, pick-me-up, bracer.

too adv. 1 excessively, overly, unduly, immoderately, inordinately, unreasonably, extremely, very. 2 also, as well, in addition, into the bargain, besides, moreover, furthermore.

tool n. implement, utensil, instrument, device, apparatus, gadget, appliance, machine, contrivance, contraption; informal gizmo.

tooth n. fang, tusk; informal gnasher.

> **WORD LINKS**
> relating to teeth: dental

top n. 1 summit, peak, pinnacle, crest, crown, brow, head, tip, apex, apogee. 2 lid, cap, cover, stopper, cork. 3 *he was at the top of his career*: height, peak, pinnacle, zenith, culmination, climax, prime.
– OPPOSITES bottom, base.
• adj. 1 highest, topmost, uppermost. 2 foremost, chief, leading, principal, pre-eminent, greatest, best, finest, elite, premier, prime, superior, select, five-star, grade A. 3 maximum, greatest, utmost.
– OPPOSITES lowest, minimum.
• v. 1 exceed, surpass, go beyond, better, beat, outstrip, outdo, outshine, eclipse, transcend, cap. 2 lead, head, be at

the top of. 3 *mousse topped with cream*: cover, cap, coat, finish, garnish.
□ **top up** fill, refill, refresh, freshen, replenish, recharge, resupply.

topic n. subject, theme, issue, matter, point, question, concern, argument, thesis.

topical adj. current, up to date, up to the minute, contemporary, recent, relevant, in the news.
– OPPOSITES out of date.

topple v. 1 fall, tumble, tip, overbalance, overturn, keel over, lose your balance. 2 knock over, upset, push over, tip over, upend. 3 overthrow, oust, unseat, overturn, bring down, defeat, get rid of, dislodge, eject.

torment n. agony, suffering, torture, pain, anguish, misery, distress, trauma.
• v. 1 torture, afflict, rack, harrow, plague, haunt, distress, agonize. 2 tease, taunt, bait, provoke, harass, bother, persecute; informal needle.

torn adj. 1 ripped, rent, cut, slit, ragged, tattered. 2 wavering, vacillating, irresolute, dithering, uncertain, unsure, undecided, in two minds.

tornado n. whirlwind, cyclone, typhoon, storm, hurricane; N. Amer. informal twister.

torrent n. 1 *a torrent of water*: flood, deluge, spate, cascade, rush. 2 *a torrent of abuse*: outburst, outpouring, stream, flood, volley, barrage, tide.
– OPPOSITES trickle.

tortuous adj. **1 twisting**, winding, zigzag, sinuous, snaky, meandering, serpentine.
2 convoluted, complicated, complex, labyrinthine, involved, Byzantine, lengthy.
– OPPOSITES straight.

torture n. **1 abuse**, ill-treatment, mistreatment, maltreatment, persecution, cruelty, atrocity.
2 torment, agony, suffering, pain, anguish, misery, distress, heartbreak, trauma.
‑v. **1 abuse**, ill-treat, mistreat, maltreat, persecute. **2 torment**, rack, afflict, harrow, plague, distress, trouble.

toss v. **1 throw**, hurl, fling, sling, pitch, lob, launch; informal heave, chuck, bung. **2** he tossed a coin: **flip**, flick, spin. **3 pitch**, lurch, rock, roll, plunge, reel, sway.

total adj. **1 entire**, complete, whole, full, combined, aggregate, gross, overall. **2 utter**, complete, absolute, thorough, perfect, downright, out-and-out, outright, sheer, unmitigated, unqualified, unalloyed.
– OPPOSITES partial.
‑n. **sum**, aggregate, whole, entirety, totality.
‑v. **1 add up to**, amount to, come to, run to, make. **2** he totalled up his score: **add**, count, reckon, tot up, compute, work out.

totalitarian adj. **autocratic**, undemocratic, one-party, dictatorial, tyrannical, despotic, fascist, oppressive, authoritarian, absolutist.
– OPPOSITES democratic.

totally adv. **completely**, entirely, wholly, thoroughly, fully, utterly, absolutely, perfectly, unreservedly, unconditionally, downright.
– OPPOSITES partly.

touch v. **1 contact**, meet, brush, graze, come up against, be in contact with, border, abut.
2 feel, pat, tap, stroke, fondle, caress, pet, handle. **3** sales touched £20,000: **reach**, attain, come to, make, rise to, soar to; informal hit. **4 compare with**, be on a par with, equal, match, rival, measure up to, better, beat; informal hold a candle to.
5 handle, hold, pick up, move, use, meddle with, play about with, fiddle with, interfere with, tamper with, disturb. **6 affect**, move, stir, make an impression on.
‑n. **1 tap**, pat, contact, stroke, caress. **2 skill**, expertise, dexterity, deftness, adroitness, adeptness, ability, talent, flair, facility, proficiency, knack. **3 trace**, bit, suggestion, suspicion, hint, scintilla, tinge, dash, taste, spot, drop, dab, soupçon. **4** the gas lights are a nice touch: **detail**, feature, point, element, addition. **5** are you in touch with him? **contact**, communication, correspondence.
□ **touch on** refer to, mention, comment on, remark on, bring up, raise, broach, allude to, cover, deal with.

WORD LINKS
relating to touch: tactile

t

touching adj. **moving**, affecting, heart-warming, emotional, emotive, poignant, sad, tear-jerking.

touchy adj. **1 sensitive**, over-sensitive, hypersensitive, easily offended, thin-skinned, highly strung, tense, irritable, tetchy, testy, crotchety, peevish, querulous, bad-tempered, petulant; informal snappy, ratty; N. Amer. informal cranky. **2 delicate**, sensitive, tricky, ticklish, embarrassing, awkward, difficult, contentious, controversial.

tough adj. **1 durable**, strong, resilient, sturdy, rugged, solid, stout, robust, hard-wearing, long-lasting, heavy-duty, well built, made to last. **2 chewy**, leathery, gristly, stringy, fibrous. **3 strict**, stern, severe, stringent, rigorous, hard, firm, hard-hitting, uncompromising. **4** the training was pretty tough: **difficult**, hard, strenuous, onerous, gruelling, exacting, arduous, demanding, taxing, tiring, exhausting, punishing. **5** tough questions: **difficult**, hard, knotty, thorny, tricky.
– OPPOSITES weak, lenient, easy.
•n. **ruffian**, thug, hoodlum, hooligan, bully boy; informal heavy, bruiser; Brit. informal yob.

toughen v. **1 strengthen**, fortify, reinforce, harden, temper, anneal. **2** measures to toughen up discipline: **make stricter**, make more severe, stiffen, tighten up.

tour n. **1 trip**, excursion, journey, expedition, jaunt, outing, trek. **2** a tour of the factory: **visit**, inspection, walkabout.
•v. **travel round**, visit, explore, holiday in, go round.

tourist n. **holidaymaker**, traveller, sightseer, visitor, backpacker, globetrotter, tripper; N. Amer. vacationer.
– OPPOSITES local.

tournament n. **competition**, contest, championship, meeting, event.

tow v. **pull**, haul, drag, draw, tug, lug.

tower v. **soar**, rise, rear, overshadow, overhang, hang over, dominate.

town n. **city**, metropolis, conurbation, municipality; Brit. borough; Scottish burgh.
– OPPOSITES country.

> **WORD LINKS**
> relating to towns: urban, municipal

toxic adj. **poisonous**, dangerous, harmful, injurious, noxious, pernicious, deadly, lethal.
– OPPOSITES harmless.

toy n. **plaything**, game.
•adj. **model**, imitation, replica, miniature.
▫ **toy with 1** think about, consider, flirt with, entertain the possibility of; informal kick around. **2** fiddle with, play with, fidget with, twiddle, finger.

trace v. **1 track down**, find, discover, detect, unearth, turn up, hunt down, ferret out, run to ground. **2 draw**, outline, mark.
•n. **1 sign**, mark, indication,

track n. **1 path**, footpath, lane, trail, route, way. **2 course**, racecourse, racetrack, velodrome; Brit. circuit. **3** *the tracks of a fox:* **traces**, marks, prints, footprints, trail, spoor. **4** *the railway tracks:* **rail**, line. **5 song**, recording, number, piece.
- v. **follow**, trail, pursue, shadow, stalk; informal tail.
□ **track down** discover, find, detect, hunt down, unearth, uncover, turn up, dig up, ferret out, run to ground.

trade n. **1 dealing**, buying and selling, commerce, traffic, business. **2 occupation**, work, craft, job, career, profession, business, line (of work), métier.
- v. **1 deal**, do business, bargain, negotiate, traffic, buy and sell, merchandise. **2** *I traded the car for a newer model:* **swap**, exchange, barter, part-exchange.

WORD LINKS
relating to trade: mercantile

trader n. **dealer**, merchant, buyer, seller, vendor, purveyor, supplier, trafficker.

tradition n. **custom**, practice, convention, ritual, observance, way, usage, habit, institution, unwritten law; formal praxis.

traditional adj. **customary**, long-established, time-honoured, classic, wonted, accustomed, standard, regular, normal, conventional, habitual, ritual, age-old.

tragedy n. **disaster**, calamity, catastrophe, cataclysm, misfortune, adversity.

tragic adj. **1 disastrous**, calamitous, catastrophic, cataclysmic, devastating, terrible, dreadful, awful, appalling, horrendous, fatal. **2 sad**, unhappy, pathetic, moving, distressing, painful, harrowing, heart-rending, sorry.
– OPPOSITES fortunate, happy.

trail n. **1** *a trail of clues:* **series**, string, chain, succession, sequence. **2 track**, spoor, path, scent, traces, marks, signs, prints, footprints. **3 path**, way, footpath, track, route.
- v. **1 drag**, sweep, be drawn, dangle. **2** *roses trailed over the banks:* **hang**, droop, fall, spill, cascade. **3 follow**, pursue, track, shadow, stalk, hunt; informal tail. **4 lose**, be down, be behind, lag behind.

train v. **1 instruct**, teach, coach, tutor, school, educate, prime, drill, ground. **2 study**, learn, prepare, take instruction. **3 exercise**, work out, get into shape, practise. **4 aim**, point, direct, level, focus.
- n. **chain**, string, series, set, sequence, succession, course.

trainer n. **coach**, instructor, teacher, tutor, handler.

trait n. **characteristic**, attribute, feature, quality, habit, mannerism, idiosyncrasy, peculiarity.

evidence, clue, vestige, remains, remnant. **2 bit**, touch, hint, suggestion, suspicion, shadow, dash, tinge; informal smidgen, tad.

t

traitor n. **betrayer**, back-stabber, double-crosser, renegade, Judas, quisling, fifth columnist, turncoat, defector; *informal* snake in the grass.

tramp v. **trudge**, plod, stamp, trample, lumber, trek, walk, slog, hike; *informal* traipse; *N. Amer. informal* schlep.
 •n. **1 vagrant**, vagabond, homeless person, down-and-out, traveller, drifter; *N. Amer.* hobo; *N. Amer. informal* bum. **2 tread**, step, footstep, footfall. **3 trek**, walk, hike, slog, march, roam, ramble; *N. Amer. informal* schlep.

trample v. **tread**, stamp, walk, squash, crush, flatten.

trance n. **daze**, stupor, hypnotic state, dream, reverie.

tranquil adj. **peaceful**, calm, restful, quiet, still, serene, relaxing, undisturbed.
 – OPPOSITES busy, excitable.

tranquillizer n. **sedative**, barbiturate, calmative, narcotic, opiate; *informal* downer.
 – OPPOSITES stimulant.

transaction n. **deal**, bargain, agreement, undertaking, arrangement, negotiation, settlement.

transcend v. **go beyond**, rise above, exceed, surpass, excel, outstrip.

transfer v. **move**, take, bring, shift, convey, remove, carry, transport, relocate.

transform v. **change**, alter, convert, revolutionize, overhaul, reconstruct, rebuild, reorganize, rearrange, rework.

transformation n. **change**, alteration, conversion, metamorphosis, revolution, overhaul, reconstruction, rebuilding, reorganization, rearrangement, reworking.

transient adj. **transitory**, temporary, short-lived, short-term, ephemeral, impermanent, brief, short, momentary, fleeting, passing.
 – OPPOSITES permanent.

transition n. **change**, passage, move, transformation, conversion, metamorphosis, alteration, changeover, shift, switch.

transitional adj. **1** *a transitional period*: **intermediate**, interim, changeover, changing, fluid, unsettled. **2** *a transitional government*: **interim**, temporary, provisional, pro tem, acting, caretaker.

translate v. **interpret**, convert, render, put, change, express, decipher, reword, decode, gloss, explain.

translation n. **interpretation**, rendition, conversion, change, alteration, adaptation.

transmission n. **1 transfer**, communication, passing on, conveyance, dissemination, spread, circulation, relaying. **2 broadcasting**, televising, airing. **3 broadcast**, programme, show.

transmit v. **1 transfer**, communicate, pass on, hand on, convey, impart, channel, carry, relay, dispatch, disseminate, spread, circulate. **2 broadcast**, send out, air, televise.

transparent adj. **1 clear**, translucent, limpid, crystal clear, crystalline, pellucid. **2 see-through**, sheer, filmy, gauzy, diaphanous. **3 obvious**, blatant, unambiguous, unequivocal, clear, plain, apparent, unmistakable, manifest, conspicuous, patent.
– OPPOSITES opaque, obscure.

transport v. **convey**, carry, take, transfer, move, shift, send, deliver, bear, ship, ferry; informal cart.
• n. **conveyance**, carriage, delivery, shipping, freight, shipment, haulage.

trap n. **1 snare**, net, mesh, gin; N. Amer. deadfall. **2 trick**, ploy, ruse, deception, subterfuge; informal set-up.
• v. **1 snare**, entrap, capture, catch, ambush. **2 confine**, cut off, corner, shut in, pen in, hem in, imprison. **3 trick**, dupe, deceive, fool, hoodwink.

trash n. **1** (N. Amer.) **rubbish**, refuse, waste, litter, junk; N. Amer. garbage. **2** (informal) **nonsense**, rubbish, trivia, pulp fiction, pap; informal drivel.

trauma n. **1 shock**, upheaval, distress, stress, strain, pain, anguish, suffering, upset, ordeal. **2 injury**, damage, wound.

traumatic adj. **disturbing**, shocking, distressing, upsetting, painful, agonizing, hurtful,

stressful, devastating, harrowing.

travel v. **journey**, tour, take a trip, voyage, go sightseeing, globetrot, backpack, trek.
• n. **travelling**, journeys, expeditions, trips, tours, excursions, voyages, treks, wanderings, jaunts.

traveller n. **tourist**, tripper, holidaymaker, sightseer, globetrotter, backpacker, passenger, commuter; N. Amer. vacationer.

treacherous adj. **1 traitorous**, disloyal, unfaithful, duplicitous, deceitful, false, back-stabbing, double-crossing, two-faced, untrustworthy, unreliable, apostate, renegade. **2 dangerous**, hazardous, perilous, unsafe, precarious, risky; informal dicey, hairy.
– OPPOSITES loyal, faithful.

tread v. **1 walk**, step, stride, pace, march, tramp, plod, stomp, trudge. **2 crush**, flatten, press down, squash, trample on, stamp on.
• n. **step**, footstep, footfall, tramp.

treason n. **treachery**, disloyalty, betrayal, sedition, subversion, mutiny, rebellion.

treasure n. **1 riches**, valuables, jewels, gems, gold, silver, precious metals, money, cash, wealth, fortune. **2 masterpiece**, gem, pearl, jewel.
• v. **cherish**, hold dear, prize, set great store by, value greatly.

treasury n. **storehouse**, repository, treasure house, exchequer, fund, mine, bank, coffers, purse.

t

treat v. **1 behave towards**, act towards, use, deal with, handle. **2** *police are treating the fires as arson*: **regard**, consider, view, look on, put down as. **3 deal with**, tackle, handle, discuss, explore, investigate. **4 tend**, nurse, attend to, give medical attention to. **5 cure**, heal, remedy. **6** *he treated her to lunch*: **buy**, take out for, stand, give, pay for, entertain, wine and dine; informal foot the bill for. **7** *the crowd was treated to a superb display*: **entertain with**, regale with, fete with.
•n. **1 celebration**, entertainment, amusement, surprise. **2 present**, gift, titbit, delicacy, luxury, indulgence, extravagance; informal goody. **3 pleasure**, delight, thrill, joy.

treatment n. **1 behaviour**, conduct, handling, management, dealings. **2 medical care**, therapy, nursing, ministrations, medication, medicament, drugs. **3 discussion**, handling, investigation, exploration, consideration, study, analysis.

treaty n. **agreement**, settlement, pact, deal, entente, concordat, accord, protocol, compact, convention; formal concord.

tree n.

> **WORD LINKS**
> *relating to trees*: arboreal

trek n. **journey**, trip, expedition, safari, hike, march, tramp, walk.

tremble v. **shake**, quiver, shudder, judder, vibrate, wobble, rock, move, sway.

tremendous adj. **1 huge**, enormous, immense, colossal, massive, prodigious, stupendous; informal whopping, astronomical; Brit. informal ginormous. **2 excellent**, first-class, outstanding, marvellous, wonderful, splendid, superb, admirable; informal great, fantastic, fabulous, terrific, super, awesome, ace; Brit. informal brilliant, smashing.

trench n. **ditch**, channel, trough, excavation, furrow, rut, conduit.

trend n. **1 tendency**, movement, drift, swing, shift, course, current, direction, inclination, leaning. **2 fashion**, vogue, style, mode, craze, mania, rage; informal fad, thing.

trespass v. **intrude**, encroach, invade, enter without permission.

trial n. **1 case**, lawsuit, hearing, tribunal, litigation, proceedings. **2 test**, experiment, pilot study, examination, check, assessment, audition, evaluation, appraisal; informal dry run. **3 trouble**, affliction, ordeal, tribulation, difficulty, problem, misfortune, mishap.

tribe n. **ethnic group**, people, family, clan, race, dynasty, house, nation.

tribunal n. **court**, board, panel, committee.

tribute n. **accolade**, praise, commendation, salute,

testimonial, homage, congratulations, compliments, plaudits.
– OPPOSITES criticism.

trick n. **1 stratagem**, ploy, ruse, scheme, device, manoeuvre, dodge, subterfuge, swindle, fraud; informal con, set-up, scam, sting. **2 practical joke**, hoax, prank; informal leg-pull, spoof, put-on. **3 knack**, skill, technique, secret, art.
• v. **deceive**, delude, hoodwink, mislead, take in, dupe, fool, gull, cheat, defraud, swindle; informal con, diddle, take for a ride, pull a fast one on; N. Amer. informal sucker.

trickle v. **dribble**, drip, ooze, leak, seep, spill, exude, percolate.
– OPPOSITES pour, gush.
• n. **dribble**, drip, thin stream, rivulet.

tricky adj. **1 difficult**, awkward, problematic, delicate, ticklish, sensitive; informal sticky. **2 cunning**, crafty, wily, devious, sly, scheming, calculating, deceitful.
– OPPOSITES straightforward.

trifle n. **triviality**, thing of no consequence, bagatelle, inessential, nothing, technicality; (**trifles**) trivia, minutiae.

trifling adj. **trivial**, unimportant, insignificant, inconsequential, petty, minor, of no account, footling, incidental; informal piffling.
– OPPOSITES important.

trigger v. **start**, set off, initiate, spark (off), activate, touch off, provoke, precipitate, prompt,

stir up, cause, give rise to, lead to, set in motion, bring about.

trim v. **1 cut**, crop, bob, shorten, clip, snip, shear, dock, lop off, prune, shave, pare. **2 decorate**, adorn, ornament, embellish, edge, border, fringe.
• n. **1 decoration**, ornamentation, adornment, embellishment, border, edging, piping, fringe, frill. **2 haircut**, cut, clip, snip.
• adj. **1 neat**, tidy, orderly, uncluttered, well kept, well maintained, immaculate, spick and span, spruce, dapper. **2 slim**, slender, lean, sleek, willowy.
– OPPOSITES untidy.
□ **in trim** fit, in good health, in fine fettle, slim, in shape.

trimming n. **1 decoration**, ornamentation, adornment, borders, edging, piping, fringes, frills. **2** (**trimmings**) **accompaniments**, extras, frills, accessories, accoutrements, trappings, paraphernalia.

trio n. **threesome**, three, triumvirate, triad, troika, trinity, trilogy.

trip v. **1 stumble**, lose your footing, catch your foot, slip, fall (down), tumble. **2 skip**, dance, prance, bound, spring, scamper.
• n. **1 excursion**, outing, jaunt, holiday, break, visit, tour, journey, expedition, drive, run; informal spin. **2 stumble**, slip, fall, misstep.

triple adj. **threefold**, tripartite, three-way, three times, treble.

triumph n. **1 victory**, win, conquest, success, achievement.

t

2 jubilation, exultation, elation, delight, joy, happiness, glee, pride, satisfaction.
– OPPOSITES defeat, disappointment.
•v. **win**, succeed, come first, be victorious, carry the day, prevail.
– OPPOSITES lose.
□ **triumph over** defeat, beat, conquer, trounce, vanquish, overcome, overpower, overwhelm, get the better of; informal lick.

triumphant adj. **1 victorious**, successful, winning, conquering. **2 jubilant**, exultant, celebratory, elated, joyful, delighted, gleeful, proud, cock-a-hoop.
– OPPOSITES defeated, despondent.

trivial adj. **unimportant**, insignificant, inconsequential, minor, of no account, of no importance, petty, trifling, footling, negligible; informal piffling.
– OPPOSITES important, significant.

troop n. **1 group**, party, band, gang, body, company, troupe, crowd, squad, unit. **2 (troops)** soldiers, armed forces, soldiery, servicemen, servicewomen.
•v. **walk**, march, file, flock, crowd, throng, stream, swarm.

trophy n. **1 cup**, medal, prize, award. **2 souvenir**, memento, keepsake, spoils, booty.

tropical adj. **hot**, sweltering, humid, sultry, steamy, sticky, oppressive, stifling.
– OPPOSITES cold.

trot v. **run**, jog, scuttle, scurry, bustle, scamper.

trouble n. **1 difficulty**, problems, bother, inconvenience, worry, anxiety, distress, stress, agitation, harassment, unpleasantness; informal hassle. **2** she poured out all her troubles: **problem**, misfortune, difficulty, trial, tribulation, woe, grief, heartache, misery, affliction, suffering. **3** he's gone to a lot of trouble: **bother**, inconvenience, fuss, effort, exertion, labour, work. **4 nuisance**, bother, inconvenience, irritation, problem, trial, pest; informal headache, pain, drag. **5** you're too gullible, that's your trouble: **shortcoming**, weakness, failing, fault. **6 disease**, illness, sickness, ailment, complaint, problem, disorder, disability. **7 malfunction**, failure, breakdown. **8 disturbance**, disorder, unrest, fighting, scuffles, breach of the peace.
•v. **1 worry**, bother, concern, disturb, upset, agitate, distress, perturb, annoy, nag, prey on someone's mind; informal bug. **2 afflict**, burden, suffer from, be cursed with. **3** I'm sorry to trouble you: **inconvenience**, bother, impose on, disturb, put out, disoblige; informal hassle.

troublesome adj. **1 annoying**, irritating, exasperating, maddening, infuriating, bothersome, tiresome, nagging, difficult, awkward; N. Amer. informal pesky. **2 difficult**, awkward, uncooperative, rebellious, unmanageable, unruly, obstreperous, disruptive, disobedient, naughty, recalcitrant.

truant n. absentee; Brit. informal skiver; Austral./NZ informal wag.
□ **play truant** stay away from school, truant; Brit. informal skive (off), bunk off; N. Amer. informal play hookey; Austral./NZ informal play the wag.

truce n. ceasefire, armistice, cessation of hostilities, peace.

true adj. **1** correct, truthful, accurate, right, verifiable, the case; formal veracious. **2** genuine, authentic, real, actual, bona fide, proper, legitimate; informal kosher. **3** sincere, genuine, real, unfeigned, heartfelt. **4** loyal, faithful, constant, devoted, trustworthy, reliable, dependable, staunch. **5** *a true reflection*: accurate, faithful, telling it like it is, realistic, factual, lifelike.
– OPPOSITES false, untrue.

trumpet v. proclaim, announce, declare, noise abroad, shout from the rooftops.

trunk n. **1** stem, bole, stock, stalk. **2** torso, body. **3** proboscis, nose, snout. **4** chest, box, crate, coffer, portmanteau, case.

trust n. confidence, belief, faith, certainty, assurance, conviction, credence, reliance.
•v. **1** have faith in, have (every) confidence in, believe in, put your hopes/faith on. **2** rely on, depend on, bank on, count on, be sure of. **3** hope, expect, take it, assume, presume. **4** entrust,

consign, commit, give, hand over, turn over, assign.
– OPPOSITES distrust, mistrust.

trusting adj. trustful, unsuspecting, unquestioning, naive, innocent, childlike, ingenuous, wide-eyed, credulous, gullible, easily taken in.
– OPPOSITES distrustful, suspicious.

trustworthy adj. reliable, dependable, honest, as good as your word, above suspicion; informal on the level.
– OPPOSITES unreliable.

truth n. **1** accuracy, correctness, authenticity, veracity, verity, truthfulness. **2** fact(s), reality, real life, actuality.
– OPPOSITES lies, fiction, falsehood.

truthful adj. true, accurate, correct, factual, faithful, reliable.
– OPPOSITES deceitful, untrue.

try v. **1** attempt, endeavour, make an effort, exert yourself, strive, do your best, do your utmost, aim, seek; informal have a go/shot/crack/stab, go all out. **2** test, put to the test, sample, taste, inspect, investigate, examine, appraise, evaluate, assess; informal check out. **3** *she tried his patience*: tax, strain, test, stretch, sap, drain, exhaust, wear out.
•n. attempt, effort, endeavour; informal go, shot, crack, stab, bash.

trying adj. **1** stressful, taxing, demanding, difficult, challenging, frustrating, fraught; informal hellish. **2** annoying, irritating, exasperating, maddening, infuriating, tiresome, troublesome, irksome, vexatious.

tuck v. **push**, insert, slip, thrust, stuff, stick, cram; informal pop.

tug v. **1** he tugged at her sleeve: **pull**, pluck, tweak, twitch, jerk, catch hold of; informal yank. **2** **drag**, pull, lug, draw, haul, heave, tow, trail.

tuition n. **instruction**, teaching, coaching, tutoring, tutelage, lessons, education, schooling, training.

tumble v. **1** fall over, fall down, topple over, go head over heels, lose your balance, take a spill, trip (up), stumble. **2** oil prices tumbled: **plummet**, plunge, dive, nosedive, drop, slump, slide; informal crash.
– OPPOSITES rise.

tumour n. **cancer**, growth, lump, malignancy; Medicine carcinoma, sarcoma.

WORD LINKS
branch of medicine concerning tumours: oncology

tune n. **melody**, air, strain, theme, song, jingle, ditty.
•v. **attune**, adapt, adjust, regulate.

tunnel n. **underground passage**, underpass, subway, shaft, burrow, hole, warren, labyrinth.
•v. **dig**, burrow, mine, bore, drill.

turbulent adj. **tempestuous**, stormy, unstable, unsettled, tumultuous, chaotic, anarchic, lawless.
– OPPOSITES peaceful.

turmoil n. **confusion**, upheaval, turbulence, tumult, disorder, disturbance, ferment, chaos, mayhem.
– OPPOSITES peace, order.

turn v. **1** go round, revolve, rotate, spin, roll, circle, wheel, whirl, twirl, gyrate, swivel, pivot. **2** change direction, change course, make a U-turn, turn about/round, wheel round. **3** bend, curve, wind, meander, twist, snake, zigzag. **4** he turned pale: **become**, go, grow, get. **5** (go) sour, go off, curdle, become rancid, go bad, spoil.
•n. **1** rotation, revolution, spin, whirl, twirl, gyration, swivel. **2** bend, corner, junction, twist, dog-leg; Brit. hairpin bend. **3** opportunity, chance, say, stint, time, try; informal go, shot, stab, crack. **4** she did me some good turns: **service**, deed, act, favour, kindness.
□ **turn down 1** reject, spurn, rebuff, refuse, decline. **2** reduce, lower, decrease, lessen, mute. **turn into 1** become, develop into, turn out to be, be transformed into, change into, metamorphose into. **2** convert, change, transform, make, adapt, modify. **turn off/out** switch off, shut off, put off, extinguish, deactivate; informal kill, cut. **turn on** switch on, put on, start up, activate, trip. **turn out 1** come, be present, attend, appear, turn up, arrive, assemble, gather; informal show up. **2** transpire, emerge, come to light, become apparent. **3** happen, occur, come

about, develop, work out, come out, end up; informal pan out.

turn up 1 be found, be discovered, be located, reappear. **2** arrive, appear, present yourself; informal show (up). **3** present itself, occur, happen, crop up. **4** increase, raise, amplify, intensify. **5** discover, uncover, unearth, find, dig up, expose.

turning n. **junction**, turn-off, side road, exit; N. Amer. turnout.

turning point n. **watershed**, critical moment, decisive moment, moment of truth, crossroads, crisis.

turnout n. **1 attendance**, audience, house, congregation, crowd, gate, gathering. **2 outfit**, clothing, dress, garb, attire, ensemble; informal get-up.

turnover n. **1 gross revenue**, income, yield, sales, business. **2** staff turnover: **rate of replacement**, change, movement.

tutor n. **teacher**, instructor, coach, educator, lecturer, trainer, mentor.
• v. **teach**, instruct, educate, school, coach, train, drill.

twig n. **stick**, sprig, shoot, offshoot, stem, branchlet.

twilight n. **1 dusk**, sunset, sundown, nightfall, evening, close of day. **2 half-light**, semidarkness, gloom.

> WORD LINKS
> resembling twilight: crepuscular

twin n. **duplicate**, double, carbon copy, likeness, mirror image, replica, lookalike, clone, match, pair; informal spitting image, dead ringer.
• adj. **1 matching**, identical, paired. **2 twofold**, double, dual, related, connected, parallel, complementary.
• v. **combine**, join, link, couple, pair.

twinge n. **pain**, spasm, ache, throb, cramp, stitch, pang.

twinkle v. & n. **glitter**, sparkle, shine, glimmer, shimmer, glint, gleam, glisten, flicker, flash, wink.

twist v. **1 crumple**, crush, buckle, mangle, warp, deform, distort, contort. **2 sprain**, wrench, turn, rick, crick. **3** she twisted her hair round her finger: **wind**, twirl, coil, curl, wrap. **4** the wires were twisted together: **intertwine**, interlace, weave, plait, braid, coil, wind. **5** the road twisted and turned: **wind**, bend, curve, turn, meander, weave, zigzag, snake.
• n. **bend**, curve, turn, zigzag, dog-leg.

twitch v. **jerk**, convulse, have a spasm, quiver, tremble, shiver, shudder.
• n. **spasm**, convulsion, quiver, tremor, shiver, shudder, tic.

tycoon n. **magnate**, mogul, businessman, captain of industry, industrialist, financier, entrepreneur; informal, derogatory fat cat.

type n. **1 kind**, sort, variety, class, category, set, genre, species, order, breed, ilk. **2 print**,

t

typeface, characters, lettering, font; Brit. fount.

typical adj. **1 representative**, characteristic, classic, quintessential, archetypal. **2 normal**, average, ordinary, standard, regular, routine, run-of-the-mill, conventional, unremarkable; informal bog-standard.
– OPPOSITES unusual, exceptional.

typify v. **epitomize**, exemplify, characterize, embody, be representative of, personify, symbolize.

tyranny n. **despotism**, absolute power, autocracy, dictatorship, totalitarianism, fascism, oppression, repression, subjugation, enslavement.

tyrant n. **dictator**, despot, autocrat, authoritarian, oppressor, slave-driver, martinet, bully.

Uu

ubiquitous adj. **everywhere**, omnipresent, all over the place, all-pervasive, universal, worldwide, global.
– OPPOSITES rare.

ugly adj. **1 unattractive**, unsightly, ill-favoured, hideous, plain, unprepossessing, horrible, ghastly, repellent, grotesque; N. Amer. homely; Brit. informal no oil painting. **2 unpleasant**, nasty, disagreeable, alarming, dangerous, perilous, threatening, menacing, hostile, ominous, sinister.
– OPPOSITES beautiful.

ulterior adj. **underlying**, undisclosed, undivulged, concealed, hidden, covert, secret, unapparent.
– OPPOSITES overt.

ultimate adj. **1 eventual**, final, concluding, terminal, end.

2 fundamental, basic, primary, elementary, absolute, central, crucial, essential. **3 best**, ideal, greatest, quintessential, supreme.

ultimately adv. **1 eventually**, in the end, in the long run, at length, finally, in time, one day. **2 fundamentally**, basically, primarily, essentially, at heart, deep down.

umpire n. **referee**, judge, line judge, linesman, adjudicator, arbitrator, moderator; informal ref.

unable adj. **incapable**, powerless, impotent, inadequate, incompetent, unqualified, unfit.

unacceptable adj. **unsatisfactory**, inadmissible, inappropriate, unsuitable, undesirable, unreasonable, insupportable,

intolerable, objectionable, distasteful; informal out of order.
- OPPOSITES satisfactory.

unanimous adj. **in agreement**, of one mind, in accord, united, undivided, with one voice.
- OPPOSITES split.

unarmed adj. **defenceless**, unprotected, unguarded.

unassuming adj. **modest**, self-effacing, diffident, humble, meek, reserved, unobtrusive, unostentatious, unpretentious, unaffected, natural.

unauthorized adj. **unofficial**, unsanctioned, unaccredited, unlicensed, unwarranted, unapproved, disallowed, prohibited, banned, forbidden, outlawed, illegal, illicit, proscribed.
- OPPOSITES official.

unaware adj. **ignorant**, oblivious, unconscious, unwitting, unsuspecting, uninformed, unenlightened, innocent; informal in the dark.
- OPPOSITES aware.

unbelievable adj. **incredible**, inconceivable, unthinkable, unimaginable, unconvincing, farfetched, implausible, improbable; informal hard to swallow.

unbiased adj. **impartial**, unprejudiced, neutral, non-partisan, disinterested, detached, dispassionate, objective, even-handed, fair.

unborn adj. **expected**, embryonic, fetal, in utero.

unbroken adj. **1 undamaged**, unharmed, unscathed, un-

touched, sound, intact, whole. **2 uninterrupted**, continuous, endless, constant, unremitting, ongoing. **3 unbeaten**, undefeated, unsurpassed, unrivalled, unmatched, supreme.

uncanny adj. **1 eerie**, unnatural, unearthly, other-worldly, ghostly, strange, abnormal, weird; informal creepy, spooky. **2** *an uncanny resemblance:* **striking**, remarkable, extraordinary, exceptional, incredible.

uncertain adj. **1** *the effects are uncertain:* **unknown**, debatable, open to question, in doubt, in the balance, up in the air, unpredictable, unforeseeable, undetermined; informal iffy. **2** *he was uncertain about the decision:* **unsure**, doubtful, dubious, undecided, irresolute, hesitant, vacillating, vague, unclear, ambivalent, in two minds.
- OPPOSITES certain, sure.

unclear adj. **uncertain**, unsure, unsettled, up in the air, in doubt, ambiguous, equivocal, indefinite, vague, mysterious, obscure, hazy, nebulous.
- OPPOSITES clear, evident.

uncomfortable adj. **1 painful**, awkward, lumpy, confining, cramped. **2 uneasy**, ill at ease, awkward, nervous, tense, edgy, restless, embarrassed, anxious; informal rattled, twitchy.
- OPPOSITES comfortable, relaxed.

uncommon adj. **unusual**, abnormal, rare, atypical, exceptional, unconventional,

u

unfamiliar, strange, extraordinary, peculiar, scarce, few and far between, isolated, infrequent.

unconditional adj. **unquestioning**, unqualified, unreserved, unlimited, unrestricted, wholehearted, complete, total, entire, full, absolute, unequivocal.

unconscious adj. **1 knocked out**, senseless, comatose, inert, stunned; informal out cold, out for the count. **2 subconscious**, instinctive, involuntary, uncontrolled, subliminal; informal gut. **3 unaware**, oblivious, ignorant, in ignorance, heedless.
– OPPOSITES aware.

uncouth adj. **uncivilized**, uncultured, rough, coarse, crude, loutish, boorish, rude, discourteous, disrespectful, bad-mannered, ill-bred.
– OPPOSITES civilized.

uncover v. **1 expose**, reveal, lay bare, unwrap, unveil, strip. **2 discover**, detect, come across, stumble on, chance on, find, turn up, unearth, dig up.

under prep. **1 below**, beneath, underneath. **2 less than**, lower than, below. **3 subordinate to**, answerable to, responsible to, subject to, junior to, inferior to.
– OPPOSITES above, over.

undercover adj. **secret**, covert, clandestine, underground, surreptitious, furtive, cloak-and-dagger, stealthy; informal hush-hush.
– OPPOSITES overt.

underestimate v. **underrate**, undervalue, miscalculate, misjudge, do an injustice to.
– OPPOSITES overestimate.

undergo v. **experience**, go through, submit to, face, be subjected to, receive, endure, brave, bear, withstand, weather.

underground adj. **1 subterranean**, buried, sunken. **2 secret**, clandestine, surreptitious, covert, undercover, closet, cloak-and-dagger, resistance, subversive.
▪ n. **metro**; N. Amer. **subway**; Brit. informal **tube**.

underline v. **1 underscore**, mark, pick out, emphasize, highlight. **2 emphasize**, stress, highlight, accentuate, accent, focus on, spotlight.

underlying adj. **fundamental**, basic, primary, central, essential, principal, elementary, initial.

undermine v. **weaken**, diminish, reduce, impair, mar, spoil, ruin, damage, sap, shake, threaten, subvert, compromise, sabotage.
– OPPOSITES strengthen.

understand v. **1 comprehend**, grasp, take in, see, apprehend, follow, make sense of, fathom; informal work out, figure out, make head or tail of, get; Brit. informal twig, suss. **2 know**, realize, recognize, acknowledge, appreciate, be aware of, be conscious of. **3 believe**, gather, take it, hear (tell), notice, see, learn.

u

understandable adj. **1** comprehensible, intelligible, clear, plain, unambiguous, transparent, straightforward, explicit, coherent. **2** unsurprising, expected, predictable, inevitable, reasonable, acceptable, logical, rational, normal, natural, justifiable, excusable, pardonable, forgivable.
– OPPOSITES incomprehensible.

understanding n. **1** comprehension, grasp, mastery, appreciation, knowledge, awareness, skill, expertise, proficiency; informal know-how. **2** intellect, intelligence, brainpower, judgement, insight, intuition, acumen, sagacity, wisdom; informal nous. **3** belief, perception, view, conviction, feeling, opinion, intuition, impression. **4** sympathy, compassion, pity, feeling, concern, consideration, kindness, sensitivity, decency, goodwill. **5** agreement, arrangement, deal, bargain, settlement, pledge, pact.
– OPPOSITES ignorance.
• adj. sympathetic, compassionate, sensitive, considerate, kind, thoughtful, tolerant, patient, forbearing, lenient, forgiving.

understate v. play down, underrate, underplay, trivialize, minimize, diminish, downgrade, brush aside, gloss over.
– OPPOSITES exaggerate.

undertake v. **1** set about, embark on, go about, engage in, take on, be responsible for, get down to, get to grips with,

tackle, attempt; informal have a go at. **2** promise, pledge, vow, give your word, swear, guarantee, contract, give an assurance, commit yourself.

undertaker n. funeral director; N. Amer. mortician.

undertaking n. **1** enterprise, venture, project, campaign, scheme, plan, operation, endeavour, effort, task. **2** promise, pledge, agreement, oath, covenant, vow, commitment, guarantee, assurance.

underwater adj. submerged, sunken, undersea, submarine.

underwear n. underclothes, undergarments, underthings, lingerie; informal undies; Brit. informal smalls.

underwrite v. sponsor, support, back, insure, indemnify, subsidize, pay for, finance, fund; N. Amer. informal bankroll.

undesirable adj. unpleasant, disagreeable, nasty, unwelcome, unwanted, unfortunate.
– OPPOSITES pleasant.

undo v. **1** unfasten, unbutton, unhook, untie, unlace, unlock, unbolt, loosen, detach, free, open. **2** cancel, reverse, overrule, overturn, repeal, rescind, countermand, revoke, annul, invalidate, negate. **3** ruin, undermine, overturn, scotch, sabotage, spoil, impair, mar, destroy, wreck; informal blow; Brit. informal scupper.
– OPPOSITES fasten.

undoubtedly adv. doubtless, indubitably, unquestionably,

u

indisputably, undeniably, incontrovertibly, without (a) doubt, clearly.

undue adj. **excessive**, immoderate, intemperate, inordinate, disproportionate, uncalled for, unnecessary, unwarranted, unjustified, unreasonable, inappropriate, unmerited, unsuitable, improper.
– OPPOSITES appropriate.

unearth v. **1** dig up, excavate, exhume, disinter, root out. **2** *I unearthed an interesting fact:* **discover**, find, come across, hit on, bring to light, expose, turn up.

uneasy adj. **1** worried, anxious, troubled, disturbed, nervy, tense, edgy, on edge, apprehensive, fearful, uncomfortable, unsettled, ill at ease; informal jittery. **2** *an uneasy peace:* **tense**, awkward, strained, fraught, precarious, unstable, insecure.
– OPPOSITES calm.

unemployed adj. **jobless**, out of work, unwaged, redundant, laid off, on benefit; Brit. signing on; N. Amer. on welfare; Brit. informal on the dole, resting.

uneven adj. **1** bumpy, rough, lumpy, stony, rocky, rutted. **2** irregular, crooked, lopsided, askew, asymmetrical. **3** inconsistent, variable, fluctuating, irregular, erratic, patchy, fitful.
– OPPOSITES flat, regular.

unfair adj. **1** unjust, prejudiced, biased, discriminatory, one-sided, unequal, uneven, unbalanced, partisan. **2** undeserved,

unmerited, unreasonable, unjustified; Brit. informal out of order. **3** unsporting, dirty, underhand, dishonourable, dishonest.
– OPPOSITES just, justified.

unfasten v. undo, open, disconnect, untie, unbutton, unzip, loosen, free, unlock, unbolt.

unfit adj. **1** *the film is unfit for children:* **unsuitable**, inappropriate, not designed. **2** *unfit for duty:* **incapable of**, not up to, not equal to, unequipped, inadequate, unprepared; informal not cut out for. **3** unhealthy, out of condition/shape, debilitated.
– OPPOSITES suitable, healthy.

unfold v. **1** open out, spread out, flatten, straighten out, unroll, unfurl. **2** develop, evolve, happen, take place, occur.

unfortunate adj. **1** unlucky, hapless, ill-starred, star-crossed, wretched, poor, pitiful; informal down on your luck. **2** unwelcome, disadvantageous, unfavourable, unlucky, adverse, unpromising, inauspicious. **3** regrettable, inappropriate, unsuitable, tactless, injudicious.
– OPPOSITES lucky.

unfriendly adj. **hostile**, disagreeable, antagonistic, aggressive, unpleasant, surly, uncongenial, inhospitable, unneighbourly, unwelcoming, unsociable, cool, cold, aloof, distant; informal stand-offish.

ungainly adj. **awkward**, clumsy, graceless, inelegant, gawky, gauche, uncoordinated.
– OPPOSITES graceful.

u

unhappy adj. **1 sad**, miserable, sorrowful, dejected, despondent, disconsolate, morose, heartbroken, down, dispirited, downhearted, depressed, melancholy, mournful, gloomy, glum; informal down in the mouth, fed up, blue. **2** *I was very unhappy with the service:* **dissatisfied**, displeased, discontented, disappointed, disgruntled. **3 unfortunate**, unlucky, ill-starred, ill-fated, doomed; informal jinxed.
– OPPOSITES happy, pleased.

unhealthy adj. **1 harmful**, detrimental, destructive, injurious, damaging, noxious, poisonous. **2 sick**, poorly, ill, unwell, unfit, ailing, weak, frail, infirm, washed out, run down. **3 abnormal**, morbid, macabre, twisted, unwholesome, warped, depraved, unnatural; informal sick.

uniform adj. **1 constant**, consistent, steady, invariable, unchanging, stable, static, regular, fixed, even. **2 identical**, matching, similar, equal, same, like, consistent.
– OPPOSITES variable.
• n. **costume**, outfit, suit, ensemble, livery, regalia; informal get-up, rig, gear.

unify v. **unite**, combine, bring together, join, merge, fuse, amalgamate, coalesce, consolidate.
– OPPOSITES separate.

uninteresting adj. **boring**, dull, unexciting, tiresome, tedious, dreary, lifeless, humdrum,
colourless, bland, insipid, banal, dry.
– OPPOSITES exciting.

union n. **1 unification**, joining, merger, fusion, amalgamation, coalition, combination, synthesis, blend. **2 association**, league, guild, confederation, federation.
– OPPOSITES separation.

unique adj. **1 distinctive**, individual, special, particular, specific, idiosyncratic, single, sole, lone, unrepeated, solitary, exclusive; informal one-off. **2 remarkable**, special, notable, unequalled, unparalleled, unmatched, unsurpassed, incomparable.
– OPPOSITES common.

unit n. **1 component**, part, section, segment, element, module, constituent, subdivision. **2 quantity**, measure, denomination. **3 group**, detachment, contingent, division, cell, faction, department, office, branch.

unite v. **1 unify**, join, link, connect, combine, amalgamate, fuse, weld, bond, bring together. **2 join together**, join forces, combine, band together, ally, cooperate, collaborate, work together, team up. **3 merge**, mix, blend, mingle, combine.
– OPPOSITES divide.

unity n. **1 union**, unification, integration, amalgamation, coalition, federation, confederation. **2 harmony**, accord, cooperation, collaboration, agreement,

u

consensus, solidarity. **3 one-ness**, singleness, wholeness, uniformity, homogeneity.
– OPPOSITES disunity.

universal adj. general, common, widespread, ubiquitous, comprehensive, global, worldwide, international.

universally adv. always, without exception, by everyone, in all cases, everywhere, worldwide, globally, internationally, commonly, generally.

universe n. cosmos, macrocosm, space, infinity, nature, all existence.

> WORD LINKS
> relating to the universe: cosmic

unkind adj. unpleasant, disagreeable, nasty, mean, cruel, vicious, spiteful, malicious, callous, unsympathetic, uncharitable, hard-hearted, harsh, heartless, cold-hearted; informal bitchy, catty.

unknown adj. **1** undisclosed, unrevealed, secret, undetermined, undecided. **2** unexplored, uncharted, unmapped, undiscovered, untravelled. **3** unidentified, unnamed, anonymous, nameless. **4** obscure, unfamiliar, unheard of, unsung, minor, undistinguished.
– OPPOSITES familiar.

unlikely adj. improbable, doubtful, dubious, questionable, unconvincing, implausible, far-fetched, unrealistic, incredible, unbelievable, inconceivable.
– OPPOSITES probable, likely.

unload v. unpack, empty, clear, remove, offload.

unlucky adj. **1** unfortunate, hapless, luckless, down on your luck, unsuccessful, ill-fated, ill-starred, jinxed. **2** unfavourable, inauspicious, unpropitious, ominous.
– OPPOSITES lucky, fortunate.

unnatural adj. **1** abnormal, unusual, uncommon, extraordinary, strange, unorthodox, exceptional, irregular, untypical. **2** artificial, man-made, synthetic. **3** affected, artificial, stilted, forced, false, fake, insincere, contrived, mannered, self-conscious; informal put on, phoney.
– OPPOSITES natural.

unnecessary adj. unneeded, inessential, not required, uncalled for, unwarranted, dispensable, optional, extraneous, expendable, redundant.

unpleasant adj. **1** an unpleasant situation: disagreeable, distressing, nasty, horrible, terrible, awful, dreadful, invidious, objectionable. **2** an unpleasant man: unlikeable, unlovable, disagreeable, bad-tempered, unfriendly, rude, impolite, obnoxious, nasty, spiteful, mean, objectionable, annoying, irritating. **3** unappetizing, unpalatable, unsavoury, unappealing, disgusting, revolting, nauseating, sickening.
– OPPOSITES pleasant, agreeable.

unpopular adj. disliked, friendless, unloved, unwelcome,

u

avoided, ignored, rejected, shunned, out of favour.

unravel v. **1** untangle, disentangle, separate out, unwind, untwist. **2 solve**, resolve, clear up, puzzle out, get to the bottom of, explain, clarify; informal figure out.
– OPPOSITES entangle.

unreal adj. **imaginary**, fictitious, pretend, make-believe, made-up, dreamed-up, mock, false, illusory, mythical, fanciful, hypothetical, theoretical; informal phoney.

unrest n. **disturbance**, trouble, turmoil, disruption, disorder, chaos, anarchy, dissatisfaction, dissent, strife, agitation, protest, rebellion, uprising, rioting.
– OPPOSITES peace.

unsafe adj. **1 dangerous**, risky, hazardous, high-risk, treacherous, insecure, unsound, harmful, injurious, toxic. **2 unreliable**, open to doubt, questionable, doubtful, dubious, suspect; informal iffy; Brit. informal dodgy.
– OPPOSITES safe.

unsatisfactory adj. **disappointing**, displeasing, inadequate, unacceptable, poor, bad, substandard, weak, mediocre, not up to par, defective, deficient; informal leaving a lot to be desired.

unscrupulous adj. **dishonest**, deceitful, devious, underhand, unethical, immoral, shameless, exploitative, corrupt, unprincipled, dishonourable,

disreputable; informal crooked, shady.

unsettle v. **disturb**, disconcert, unnerve, upset, disquiet, perturb, alarm, dismay, trouble, bother, agitate, fluster, ruffle, shake (up), throw; informal rattle, faze.

unsightly adj. **unattractive**, ugly, unprepossessing, hideous, horrible, repulsive, revolting, offensive, grotesque.
– OPPOSITES attractive.

unsociable adj. **unfriendly**, uncongenial, unneighbourly, unapproachable, introverted, reserved, withdrawn, retiring, aloof, distant, remote, detached; informal stand-offish.

unstable adj. **1 unsteady**, rocky, wobbly, rickety, shaky, unsafe, insecure, precarious. **2 changeable**, volatile, variable, fluctuating, irregular, unpredictable, erratic. **3 unbalanced**, of unsound mind, mentally ill, deranged, demented, disturbed, unhinged.
– OPPOSITES steady, firm.

unsuccessful adj. **1 failed**, abortive, ineffective, fruitless, profitless, unproductive, vain, futile. **2 unprofitable**, loss-making.

unsuitable adj. **1 inappropriate**, ill-suited, inapposite, inapt, unacceptable, unfitting, incompatible, out of place, out of keeping, incongruous, unseemly. **2** *an unsuitable moment*: **inopportune**, badly

u

timed, unfortunate, difficult, infelicitous.
– OPPOSITES appropriate.

unsure adj. **1 undecided**, uncertain, irresolute, dithering, in two minds, in a quandary, dubious, doubtful, sceptical, unconvinced. **2 unconfident**, unassertive, insecure, hesitant, diffident, anxious, apprehensive.
– OPPOSITES sure, certain.

untangle v. disentangle, unravel, unsnarl, straighten out, untwist, unknot, sort out.

unthinkable adj. **unimaginable**, inconceivable, unbelievable, incredible, implausible, out of the question, impossible, unconscionable, unreasonable.

untidy adj. **1 disordered**, messy, disorganized, cluttered, in chaos, haywire, in disarray, disorderly, topsy-turvy, at sixes and sevens, jumbled; informal higgledy-piggledy. **2 scruffy**, dishevelled, unkempt, messy, rumpled, bedraggled.
– OPPOSITES neat, tidy.

untoward adj. unexpected, unforeseen, surprising, unusual, inappropriate, inconvenient, unwelcome, unfavourable, adverse, unfortunate, infelicitous.

untrue adj. false, invented, made up, fabricated, concocted, trumped up, erroneous, wrong, incorrect, inaccurate.
– OPPOSITES true, correct.

unusual adj. **1** an unusual sight: **uncommon**, abnormal, atypical, unexpected, surprising, un-

familiar, different, strange, odd, curious, extraordinary, unorthodox, unconventional, peculiar, queer, unwonted; informal weird, offbeat. **2** a man of unusual talent: **remarkable**, extraordinary, exceptional, particular, outstanding, notable, noteworthy, distinctive, striking, significant, special, unique, unparalleled, prodigious.
– OPPOSITES common.

unwarranted adj. **1 unjustified**, indefensible, inexcusable, unforgivable, unpardonable, uncalled for, unnecessary, unjust, groundless. **2 unauthorized**, unsanctioned, unapproved, uncertified, unlicensed, illegal, unlawful, illicit, illegitimate, criminal, actionable.
– OPPOSITES justified.

unwieldy adj. awkward, unmanageable, unmanoeuvrable, cumbersome, clumsy, massive, heavy, hefty, bulky.

unwilling adj. **1 reluctant**, unenthusiastic, hesitant, resistant, grudging, involuntary, forced. **2** he was unwilling to go: **disinclined**, reluctant, averse, loath, not in the mood; (**be unwilling to do something**) baulk at, demur at, shy away from, flinch from, shrink from, have qualms about, have misgivings about, have reservations about.
– OPPOSITES willing.

upbeat adj. **cheerful**, optimistic, cheery, positive, confident, hopeful, sanguine, bullish, buoyant.
– OPPOSITES pessimistic.

u

upbringing n. childhood, early life, formative years, teaching, instruction, rearing.

update v. **1** modernize, upgrade, improve, overhaul. **2** brief, bring up to date, inform, fill in, tell, notify, keep posted; informal clue in, put in the picture, bring/keep up to speed.

upgrade v. improve, modernize, update, reform.
– OPPOSITES downgrade.

upheaval n. disturbance, disruption, trouble, turbulence, disorder, confusion, turmoil.

uphill adj. **1** upward, rising, ascending, climbing. **2** difficult, hard, tough, demanding, arduous, taxing, exacting, stiff, gruelling, onerous.
– OPPOSITES downhill.

uphold v. **1** confirm, endorse, sustain, approve, support, back (up). **2** maintain, sustain, continue, preserve, protect, keep, hold to, keep alive, keep going.
– OPPOSITES oppose.

upkeep n. **1** maintenance, repair(s), servicing, care, preservation, conservation, running. **2 (financial)** support, maintenance, keep, subsistence, care.

uplifting adj. inspiring, stirring, inspirational, rousing, moving, touching, affecting, cheering, heartening, encouraging.

upper adj. **1** higher, superior, top. **2** senior, superior, higher-level, higher-ranking, top.
– OPPOSITES lower.

upper-class adj. aristocratic, noble, patrician, titled, blue-blooded, high-born, elite; Brit. county; informal upper-crust, top-drawer; Brit. informal posh.

upright adj. **1** vertical, perpendicular, plumb, straight (up), erect, on end, on your feet. **2** honest, honourable, upstanding, respectable, high-minded, law-abiding, worthy, righteous, decent, good, virtuous, principled.
– OPPOSITES flat, horizontal.

uprising n. rebellion, revolt, insurrection, mutiny, revolution, insurgence, rioting, coup.

uproar n. **1** commotion, disturbance, rumpus, disorder, confusion, chaos, tumult, mayhem, pandemonium, bedlam, noise, din, clamour, hubbub, racket; Brit. row; informal hullabaloo. **2** outcry, furore, fuss, commotion, hue and cry, rumpus; Brit. row; informal hullabaloo, stink, ructions.
– OPPOSITES calm.

upset v. **1** distress, trouble, perturb, dismay, sadden, grieve, disturb, unsettle, disconcert, disquiet, worry, bother, agitate, fluster, throw, ruffle, unnerve, shake. **2** knock over, overturn, upend, tip over, topple, spill. **3** disrupt, interfere with, disturb, throw into confusion, mess up.
– OPPOSITES calm.
• n. **1** distress, trouble, dismay, disquiet, worry, bother, agitation, hurt, grief. **2** a stomach

u

upset: **disorder**, complaint, ailment, illness, sickness; informal **bug**; Brit. informal **lurgy**.
• adj. **1 distressed**, troubled, perturbed, dismayed, disturbed, unsettled, disconcerted, worried, bothered, anxious, agitated, flustered, ruffled, unnerved, shaken, saddened, grieved; informal **cut up**, **choked**; Brit. informal **gutted**. **2** *an upset stomach:* **disturbed**, unsettled, queasy, bad, poorly; informal **gippy**.
– OPPOSITES calm.

upside down adj. **1 upturned**, upended, wrong side up, overturned, inverted, capsized. **2 in disarray**, in disorder, jumbled up, in a muddle, untidy, disorganized, in chaos, in confusion, topsy-turvy, at sixes and sevens; informal **higgledy-piggledy**.

up to date adj. **1 modern**, contemporary, the latest, state-of-the-art, new, up-to-the-minute, advanced. **2 informed**, up to speed, in the picture, in touch, au fait, conversant, familiar, knowledgeable, acquainted.
– OPPOSITES out of date, old-fashioned.

urban adj. **town**, city, municipal, metropolitan, built-up, inner-city, suburban.
– OPPOSITES rural.

urge v. **1 encourage**, exhort, press, entreat, implore, call on, appeal to, beg, plead with. **2 advise**, counsel, advocate, recommend.
• n. *his urge to travel:* **desire**, wish, need, compulsion, longing, yearning, hankering, craving, hunger, thirst; informal **yen**, **itch**.

urgent adj. **1 pressing**, acute, dire, desperate, critical, serious, grave, intense, crying, burning, compelling, extreme, high-priority, life-and-death.

usage n. **1** *energy usage:* **consumption**, use. **2** *the usage of equipment:* **use**, utilization, operation, manipulation, running, handling. **3 language**, expression, phraseology, parlance, idiom.

use v. **1 utilize**, employ, avail yourself of, work, operate, wield, ply, apply, put into service. **2 exercise**, employ, bring into play, practise, apply. **3 take advantage of**, exploit, manipulate, take liberties with, impose on, abuse, capitalize on, profit from, trade on; milk; informal **cash in on**, **walk all over**. **4** *we have used up our funds:* **consume**, get/go through, exhaust, deplete, expend, spend.
• n. **1 utilization**, application, employment, operation, manipulation. **2 exploitation**, manipulation, abuse. **3** *what is the use of that?* **advantage**, benefit, good, point, object, purpose, sense, reason, service, utility, help, gain, avail, profit, value, worth.

used adj. **second-hand**, pre-owned, nearly new, old, worn, hand-me-down, cast-off.
▫ **used to** accustomed to, no stranger to, familiar with, at

home with, in the habit of, experienced in, versed in, conversant with, acquainted with.

useful adj. **1** *a useful tool:* **functional**, practical, handy, convenient, utilitarian, serviceable, of service; informal nifty. **2** *a useful experience:* **beneficial**, advantageous, helpful, worthwhile, profitable, rewarding, productive, constructive, valuable, fruitful.
– OPPOSITES useless.

useless adj. **1** futile, pointless, to no avail, vain, to no purpose, unavailing, hopeless, ineffectual, fruitless, unprofitable, unproductive, abortive. **2** (informal) **incompetent**, inept, ineffective, incapable, inadequate, hopeless, bad; informal a dead loss.
– OPPOSITES useful, beneficial.

usher v. **escort**, accompany, take, show, see, lead, conduct, guide.
• n. **guide**, attendant, escort.

usual adj. **normal**, customary, accustomed, wonted, habitual, routine, regular, standard, typical, established, set, stock, conventional, traditional, expected, familiar.
– OPPOSITES exceptional.

usually adv. **normally**, generally, habitually, customarily, routinely, typically, ordinarily, commonly, as a rule, in general, more often than not, mainly, mostly.

utensil n. **implement**, tool, instrument, device, apparatus, gadget, appliance, contrivance, contraption; informal gizmo.

utility n. **usefulness**, use, benefit, value, advantage, help, practicality, effectiveness, service.

utilize v. **use**, employ, avail yourself of, press into service, bring into play, deploy, draw on, exploit.

utmost adj. **greatest**, highest, maximum, most, extreme, supreme, paramount.

utter[1] adj. **complete**, total, absolute, thorough, perfect, downright, out-and-out, outright, sheer, arrant, positive, prize, pure, unmitigated, unadulterated, unqualified, unalloyed.

utter[2] v. **say**, speak, voice, mouth, express, articulate, pronounce, enunciate, emit, let out, give, produce.

utterance n. **remark**, comment, statement, observation, declaration, pronouncement.

u

Vv

vacancy n. opening, position, post, job, opportunity.

vacant adj. **1** empty, unoccupied, not in use, free, available, unfilled, uninhabited, untenanted; informal up for grabs. **2** blank, expressionless, unresponsive, emotionless, impassive, vacuous, empty, glazed.
– OPPOSITES full, occupied.

vacate v. **1** leave, move out of, evacuate, quit, depart from. **2** resign from, leave, stand down from, give up, bow out of, relinquish, retire from; informal quit.
– OPPOSITES occupy.

vacation n. holiday, trip, tour, break, leave, time off, recess.

vagrant n. tramp, drifter, down-and-out, beggar, itinerant, wanderer; N. Amer. hobo; N. Amer. informal bum.

vague adj. **1** indistinct, indefinite, indeterminate, unclear, ill-defined, hazy, fuzzy, misty, blurry, out of focus, shadowy, obscure. **2** imprecise, rough, approximate, inexact, non-specific, ambiguous, hazy, uncertain. **3** absent-minded, forgetful, dreamy, abstracted; informal with your head in the clouds, scatty, not with it.
– OPPOSITES clear, definite.

vaguely adv. **1** slightly, a little, a bit, somewhat, rather, in a way, faintly, obscurely; informal sort of. **2** absent-mindedly, abstractedly, vacantly.

vain adj. **1** conceited, narcissistic, proud, arrogant, boastful, cocky, egotistical, immodest; informal big-headed. **2** futile, useless, pointless, ineffective, unavailing, fruitless, unproductive, unsuccessful, failed, abortive.
– OPPOSITES modest, successful.
□ in vain unsuccessfully, to no avail, to no purpose, fruitlessly.

valiant adj. brave, courageous, plucky, intrepid, heroic, gallant, bold, fearless, daring, unafraid, unflinching, undaunted, doughty, indomitable, stout-hearted; informal game, gutsy.
– OPPOSITES cowardly.

valid adj. **1** well founded, sound, reasonable, rational, logical, justifiable, defensible, cogent, credible, forceful. **2** legally binding, lawful, official, in force, in effect.

validate v. ratify, endorse, approve, agree to, accept, authorize, legalize, legitimize, warrant, license, certify, recognize.

valley n. dale, vale, hollow, gully, gorge, ravine, canyon, rift; Brit. combe; Scottish glen.

v

valuable adj. **1 precious**, costly, high-priced, expensive, dear, priceless. **2 useful**, helpful, beneficial, advantageous, invaluable, productive, worthwhile, worthy, important.
– OPPOSITES worthless.

valuables pl. n. **precious items**, costly items, prized possessions, treasures.

value n. **1 price**, cost, worth, market price. **2 worth**, usefulness, advantage, benefit, gain, profit, good, help. **3 (values) principles**, ethics, morals, standards, code of behaviour.
–v. **1 evaluate**, assess, estimate, appraise, price. **2 think highly of**, have a high opinion of, rate highly, esteem, set great store by, respect.
– OPPOSITES despise.

vanish v. **disappear**, be lost to sight, become invisible, recede from view, fade (away), evaporate, melt away, end, cease to exist.
– OPPOSITES appear.

vanity n. **conceit**, narcissism, self-love, self-admiration, egotism, pride, arrogance, boastfulness, cockiness; informal big-headedness.
– OPPOSITES modesty.

variable adj. **changeable**, shifting, fluctuating, irregular, inconstant, inconsistent, fluid, unstable; informal up and down.
– OPPOSITES constant.

variant n. **variation**, version, form, alternative, adaptation, alteration, modification.
–adj. **alternative**, other, different, divergent.

variation n. **1** regional variations: **difference**, dissimilarity, disparity, contrast, discrepancy, imbalance. **2** there was little variation from the pattern: **deviation**, variance, divergence, departure, fluctuation, change, alteration, modification.

varied adj. **diverse**, assorted, miscellaneous, mixed, sundry, wide-ranging, disparate, heterogeneous, motley.

variety n. **1 diversity**, variation, diversification, change, difference. **2 assortment**, miscellany, range, array, collection, selection, mixture, medley. **3 sort**, kind, type, class, category, style, form, make, model, brand, strain, breed.
– OPPOSITES uniformity.

various adj. **diverse**, different, differing, varied, assorted, mixed, sundry, miscellaneous, disparate, heterogeneous, motley.

varnish n. & v. **lacquer**, shellac, japan, enamel, glaze, polish.

vary v. **1 differ**, be dissimilar, disagree, be at variance. **2 fluctuate**, rise and fall, go up and down, change, alter, shift, swing.

vast adj. **huge**, extensive, broad, wide, boundless, enormous, immense, great, massive, colossal, gigantic, mammoth, giant, mountainous; informal mega, whopping.
– OPPOSITES tiny.

V

vault¹ n. **1 cellar**, basement, crypt, undercroft, catacomb, burial chamber. **2 strongroom**, safe deposit.

vault² v. **jump**, leap, spring, bound, clear.

veer v. **turn**, swerve, swing, weave, wheel, change direction, change course, deviate.

vehement adj. **passionate**, forceful, ardent, impassioned, heated, spirited, urgent, fervent, fierce, strong, forcible, powerful, emphatic, vigorous, intense, earnest, keen, enthusiastic, zealous.
– OPPOSITES mild.

vehicle n. **1 means of transport**, transportation, conveyance. **2 channel**, medium, means, agent, instrument, mechanism, organ, apparatus.

WORD LINKS
relating to vehicles: automotive

veil n. **covering**, screen, curtain, mantle, cloak, mask, blanket, shroud, canopy, cloud, pall.
•v. **cover**, surround, swathe, enfold, envelop, conceal, hide, obscure, screen, shield, cloak, blanket, shroud.

vein n. **1 blood vessel**, capillary. **2 layer**, seam, lode, stratum, deposit.

WORD LINKS
relating to veins: vascular, venous

velocity n. **speed**, pace, rate, tempo, rapidity.

veneer n. **1 surface**, lamination, layer, overlay, facing, covering, finish, exterior. **2 facade**, front, show, outward display, appearance, impression, semblance, guise, mask, pretence, cover, camouflage.

vengeance n. **revenge**, retribution, retaliation, requital, reprisal, an eye for an eye.
– OPPOSITES forgiveness.

venomous adj. **poisonous**, toxic, dangerous, deadly, lethal, fatal.
– OPPOSITES harmless.

vent n. **outlet**, inlet, opening, aperture, hole, gap, orifice, space, duct, flue, shaft, well, passage, airway.
•v. **let out**, release, pour out, utter, express, air, voice.

ventilate v. **air**, aerate, oxygenate, freshen, cool.

venture n. **enterprise**, undertaking, project, scheme, operation, endeavour, speculation.
•v. **1 put forward**, advance, proffer, offer, air, suggest, volunteer, submit, propose. **2 dare**, be so bold as, presume, have the audacity, have the nerve, take the liberty of.

verbal adj. **oral**, spoken, word-of-mouth, stated, said, unwritten.

verbose adj. **wordy**, loquacious, garrulous, talkative, voluble, long-winded, lengthy, prolix, circumlocutory, rambling.
– OPPOSITES succinct.

verdict n. **judgement**, adjudication, decision, finding, ruling, sentence.

v

verge n. **1 edge**, border, margin, side, brink, rim, lip, fringe, boundary, perimeter. **2** *I was on the verge of tears*: **brink**, threshold, edge, point.
□ **verge on** approach, border on, be close/near to, resemble, be tantamount to, tend towards, approximate to.

verify v. **confirm**, prove, substantiate, corroborate, back up, bear out, justify, support, uphold, testify to, validate, authenticate.
– OPPOSITES refute.

versatile adj. **1** *a versatile player*: **adaptable**, flexible, all-round, multi-talented, resourceful. **2** *a versatile device*: **adjustable**, adaptable, multi-purpose, all-purpose.

verse n. **1 poetry**, lyrics. **2 poem**, lyric, rhyme, ditty, limerick. **3 stanza**, canto.

version n. **1 account**, report, statement, description, record, story, rendering, interpretation, explanation, understanding, reading, impression, side. **2 edition**, translation, impression. **3 type**, sort, kind, form, equivalent, variety, variant, design, model, style.

vertical adj. **upright**, erect, perpendicular, plumb, on end, standing.
– OPPOSITES flat, horizontal.

very adv. **extremely**, exceedingly, exceptionally, extraordinarily, tremendously, immensely, acutely, singularly, decidedly, highly, remarkably, really; informal awfully, terribly, seriously, mega, ultra; Brit. informal well, dead, jolly; N. Amer. informal real, mighty.
– OPPOSITES slightly.

vessel n. **1 boat**, ship, craft. **2 container**, receptacle, basin, bowl, pan, pot, jug.

vestige n. **remnant**, fragment, remains, echo, trace, mark, legacy, reminder.

vet v. **check up on**, screen, investigate, examine, scrutinize, inspect, look over, assess, evaluate, appraise; informal check out.

veteran n. **old hand**, past master, doyen, doyenne; informal old-timer; N. Amer. informal vet.
– OPPOSITES novice.
• adj. **long-serving**, seasoned, old, hardened, practised, experienced; informal battle-scarred.

veto n. **rejection**, dismissal, prohibition, proscription, embargo, ban, interdict.
• v. **reject**, turn down, throw out, dismiss, prohibit, forbid, proscribe, disallow, embargo, ban, rule out; informal kill, give the thumbs down to.
– OPPOSITES approve.

viable adj. **feasible**, workable, practicable, practical, realistic, achievable, attainable; informal doable.
– OPPOSITES impracticable.

vibrant adj. **1 spirited**, lively, energetic, vigorous, dynamic, passionate, fiery; informal feisty.

V

2 vivid, bright, striking, brilliant, glowing, strong, rich.
- OPPOSITES lifeless, pale.

vibrate v. **shake**, tremble, shiver, quiver, shudder, throb, pulsate.

vice n. **1 immorality**, wrongdoing, wickedness, evil, iniquity, villainy, corruption, misconduct, sin, depravity. **2 fault**, failing, flaw, defect, shortcoming, weakness, deficiency, foible, frailty.
- OPPOSITES virtue.

vicious adj. **1 brutal**, ferocious, savage, violent, ruthless, merciless, heartless, callous, cruel, cold-blooded, inhuman, barbaric, bloodthirsty. **2 malicious**, spiteful, vindictive, venomous, cruel, bitter, acrimonious, hostile, nasty; informal catty.
- OPPOSITES gentle.

victim n. **sufferer**, injured party, casualty, fatality, loss, survivor.

victimize v. **persecute**, pick on, bully, abuse, discriminate against, exploit, take advantage of; informal have it in for.

victorious adj. **triumphant**, conquering, vanquishing, winning, champion, successful.
- OPPOSITES unsuccessful.

victory n. **success**, triumph, conquest, win, coup; informal walkover.
- OPPOSITES defeat, loss.

vie v. **compete**, contend, struggle, fight, battle, jockey.

view n. **1 outlook**, prospect, panorama, vista, scene, scenery, landscape. **2 opinion**, viewpoint, belief, judgement, thinking, notion, idea, conviction, persuasion, attitude, feeling, sentiment. **3** *the church came into view*: **sight**, perspective, vision, visibility.
• v. **1 look at**, observe, eye, gaze at, contemplate, regard, scan, survey, inspect, scrutinize; informal check out; N. Amer. informal eyeball. **2 consider**, regard, look on, see, perceive, judge, deem, reckon.

viewer n. **watcher**, spectator, onlooker, observer; **(viewers)** audience, crowd.

vigilant adj. **watchful**, observant, attentive, alert, eagle-eyed, on the lookout, on your guard; informal beady-eyed.
- OPPOSITES inattentive.

vigorous adj. **1 robust**, healthy, hale and hearty, strong, sturdy, fit, hardy, tough, energetic, lively, active. **2 strenuous**, powerful, forceful, spirited, determined, aggressive, passionate; informal punchy, feisty.
- OPPOSITES weak, feeble.

vigorously adv. **strenuously**, strongly, powerfully, forcefully, energetically, heartily, all out, fiercely, hard; informal like mad; Brit. informal like billy-o.

vigour n. **health**, strength, robustness, energy, life, vitality, spirit, passion, determination, dynamism, drive; informal oomph, get-up-and-go.
- OPPOSITES lethargy.

vile adj. foul, nasty, unpleasant, bad, horrid, repulsive, disgusting, hateful, nauseating; informal gross.
– OPPOSITES pleasant.

villain n. criminal, lawbreaker, offender, felon, miscreant, wrongdoer, rogue, scoundrel, reprobate; informal crook, baddy.

vindicate v. 1 acquit, clear, absolve, exonerate; informal let off. 2 justify, warrant, substantiate, confirm, corroborate, prove, defend, support, back, endorse.
– OPPOSITES incriminate.

vintage adj. 1 high-quality, quality, choice, select, superior. 2 classic, ageless, timeless, old, antique, historic.

violate v. 1 contravene, breach, infringe, break, transgress, disobey, defy, flout, disregard, ignore. 2 desecrate, profane, defile, degrade, debase, damage, vandalize, deface, destroy.
– OPPOSITES respect.

violation n. 1 contravention, breach, infringement, transgression, defiance, flouting, disregard. 2 desecration, defilement, damage, vandalism, destruction.

violence n. 1 brutality, savagery, cruelty, barbarity. 2 force, power, strength, might, ferocity, intensity, vehemence.

violent adj. 1 brutal, vicious, savage, rough, aggressive, threatening, fierce, ferocious, bloodthirsty. 2 powerful, forceful, hard, sharp, smart, strong,

vigorous, mighty, hefty. 3 intense, extreme, strong, powerful, fierce, unbridled, uncontrollable, ungovernable, consuming, passionate.
– OPPOSITES gentle, mild.

virtual adj. effective, near (enough), essential, practical, to all intents and purposes, in all but name, implied, unacknowledged.

virtually adv. effectively, all but, more or less, practically, almost, nearly, close to, verging on, just about, as good as, essentially, to all intents and purposes.

virtue n. 1 goodness, righteousness, morality, integrity, dignity, rectitude, honour, probity. 2 good point, good quality, strong point, asset, forte, attribute, strength, merit, advantage, benefit; informal plus.
– OPPOSITES vice.

visible adj. observable, perceptible, noticeable, detectable, discernible, in sight, in view, on display, evident, apparent, manifest, plain.

vision n. 1 eyesight, sight, observation, eyes, view, perspective. 2 apparition, spectre, phantom, ghost, wraith, manifestation, hallucination, illusion, mirage. 3 dream, reverie, plan, hope, fantasy, pipe dream. 4 imagination, creativity, inventiveness, inspiration, intuition, perception, insight.

> **WORD LINKS**
> *relating to vision:* visual, optic

V

visit v. **call on**, go to see, look in on, stay with, holiday with, stop by, drop by; informal pop/drop in on, look up.
•n. **(social) call**, stay, stopover, trip, holiday, vacation; literary sojourn.

visitor n. **1 guest**, caller, company. **2 tourist**, traveller, holidaymaker, tripper, vacationer, sightseer.

vista n. **view**, scene, prospect, panorama, sight, scenery, landscape.

visual adj. **1 optical**, ocular. **2 visible**, observable, perceptible, discernible.

visualize v. **envisage**, conjure up, picture, call to mind, see, imagine, dream up.

vital adj. **1 essential**, critical, crucial, indispensable, all-important, imperative, mandatory, high-priority, key, life-and-death. **2 lively**, energetic, active, sprightly, spirited, vivacious, exuberant, dynamic, vigorous; informal full of beans.
– OPPOSITES unimportant.

vitality n. **life**, energy, spirit, vivacity, exuberance, dynamism, vigour, passion, drive; informal get-up-and-go.

vivid adj. **1 bright**, colourful, brilliant, radiant, vibrant, strong, bold, deep, intense, rich, warm. **2 graphic**, realistic, lifelike, faithful, authentic, striking, evocative, arresting, colourful, dramatic, memorable, powerful, stirring, moving, haunting.
– OPPOSITES dull, vague.

vocal adj. **1 spoken**, said, voiced, uttered, articulated, oral. **2 vociferous**, outspoken, forthright, plain-spoken, blunt, frank, candid, passionate, vehement, vigorous.

vocation n. **calling**, life's work, mission, purpose, profession, occupation, career, job, employment, trade, craft, line (of work).

vogue n. **fashion**, trend, fad, fancy, craze, rage, enthusiasm, passion.

voice n. **opinion**, view, feeling, wish, desire, vote.
•v. **express**, communicate, declare, state, vent, utter, say, speak, articulate, air; informal come out with.

> WORD LINKS
> relating to the human voice:
> vocal

void n. **vacuum**, emptiness, nothingness, blankness, (empty) space, gap, cavity, chasm, gulf.
•adj. **1 empty**, vacant, blank, bare, clear, free. **2 invalid**, null (and void), ineffective, worthless.
– OPPOSITES full, valid.

volatile adj. **1 unpredictable**, temperamental, capricious, fickle, impulsive, emotional, excitable, turbulent, erratic, unstable. **2** a volatile situation: **tense**, strained, fraught, uneasy, uncomfortable, charged, explosive, inflammatory, turbulent.
– OPPOSITES stable.

v

volley n. **barrage**, cannonade, battery, bombardment, salvo, burst, storm, hail, shower, deluge, torrent.

volume n. **1 book**, publication, tome, work, title. **2 capacity**, mass, bulk, extent, size, dimensions. **3 quantity**, amount, mass, bulk, measure. **4 loudness**, sound, amplification.

voluntarily adv. **of your own free will**, of your own volition, by choice, by preference, spontaneously, willingly, readily, freely.

voluntary adj. **1 optional**, discretionary, at your discretion, elective, non-compulsory. **2 unpaid**, unsalaried, for free, honorary.
– OPPOSITES compulsory.

volunteer v. **1 offer**, tender, proffer, put forward, put up, venture. **2 offer your services**, present yourself, make yourself available, come forward.

vomit v. **be sick**, spew, heave, retch, gag; informal throw up, puke; N. Amer. informal barf.

vote n. **1 ballot**, poll, election, referendum, plebiscite, show of hands. **2 (the vote) suffrage**, franchise, voting rights.

WORD LINKS
study of trends in voting: psephology

voucher n. **coupon**, token, ticket, pass, chit, slip, stub, docket; Brit. informal chitty.

vow n. **promise**, pledge, oath, bond, covenant, commitment, word (of honour).
•v. **promise**, pledge, swear, undertake, make a commitment, give your word, guarantee.

voyage n. **journey**, trip, cruise, passage, sail, crossing, expedition, odyssey.

vulgar adj. **1 rude**, crude, dirty, filthy, smutty, naughty, indecent, obscene, coarse, risqué; informal blue. **2 tasteless**, crass, tawdry, ostentatious, flamboyant, showy, gaudy, garish; informal flash, tacky. **3 impolite**, ill-mannered, boorish, uncouth, unsophisticated, unrefined.
– OPPOSITES tasteful.

vulnerable adj. **1 in danger**, in peril, in jeopardy, at risk, unprotected, undefended, unguarded, open to attack, exposed, defenceless, an easy target. **2 helpless**, weak, sensitive, thin-skinned.
– OPPOSITES invulnerable.

v

Ww

waddle v. **toddle**, totter, wobble, shuffle.

wag v. **1 swing**, swish, switch, sway, shake; *informal* **waggle**. **2 shake**, wave, wiggle, flourish, brandish.

wage n. **pay**, salary, stipend, fee, remuneration, income, earnings.
• v. **engage in**, carry on, conduct, execute, pursue, prosecute, proceed with.

wail n. & v. **howl**, cry, bawl, moan, groan, yowl, whine, lament.

wait v. **1** *we waited in the airport:* **stay (put)**, remain, rest, stop, linger, loiter; *old use* tarry. **2** *she had to wait until her bags arrived:* **stand by**, hold back, bide your time, mark time, kill time, waste time, kick your heels, twiddle your thumbs; *informal* hold on, hang around, sit tight.
• n. **delay**, hold-up, interval, interlude, pause, break, suspension, stoppage, halt, interruption, lull, gap.

waiter, **waitress** n. **server**, steward, stewardess, attendant, butler, servant; *N. Amer.* waitperson.

waive v. **1 give up**, abandon, renounce, relinquish, surrender, sacrifice, turn down.

2 disregard, ignore, overlook, set aside, forgo.

wake¹ v. **awake**, waken, wake up, stir, come to, come round, rouse.
• n. **vigil**, watch, funeral.

wake² n. **backwash**, slipstream, trail, path, track.
□ **in the wake of** in the aftermath of, after, subsequent to, following, as a result of, as a consequence of, on account of, because of.

walk v. **1 stroll**, saunter, amble, trudge, plod, hike, tramp, trek, march, stride, troop, wander, ramble, promenade, traipse; *informal* mosey, hoof it. **2 accompany**, escort, guide, show, see, take, usher.
• n. **1 ramble**, hike, tramp, march, stroll, promenade, constitutional, turn. **2 gait**, step, stride, tread. **3 path**, pathway, footpath, track, walkway, promenade, footway, pavement, trail, towpath.

walker n. **rambler**, hiker, trekker, stroller, pedestrian.

wall n. **fortification**, rampart, barricade, bulwark, partition.

wallet n. **purse**, case, pouch, holder; *N. Amer.* billfold, pocketbook.

wallow v. **1 roll**, loll about, lie around, splash about.

2 luxuriate, bask, take pleasure, take satisfaction, indulge (yourself), delight, revel, glory.

wan adj. **pale**, ashen, white, grey, anaemic, colourless, waxen, pasty, peaky, sickly, washed out, ghostly.

wander v. **1 stroll**, amble, saunter, walk, potter, ramble, meander, roam, range, drift; informal traipse, mosey. **2 stray**, depart, diverge, deviate, digress, drift, get sidetracked.

wane v. **decline**, diminish, decrease, dwindle, shrink, tail off, ebb, fade, lessen, peter out, fall off, recede, slump, weaken, wither, evaporate, die out.
– OPPOSITES grow.

want v. **desire**, wish for, hope for, fancy, care for, like, long for, yearn for, crave, hanker after, hunger for, thirst for, cry out for, covet; informal have a yen for, be dying for.
•n. **1 lack**, absence, non-existence, dearth, deficiency, inadequacy, insufficiency, paucity, shortage, scarcity. **2 need**, austerity, privation, deprivation, poverty, destitution. **3** *her wants would be taken care of:* **wish**, desire, demand, longing, fancy, craving, need, requirement; informal yen.

wanting adj. **deficient**, inadequate, lacking, insufficient, imperfect, flawed, unsound, substandard, inferior, second-rate.

wanton adj. **deliberate**, wilful, malicious, gratuitous, un-provoked, motiveless, arbitrary, unjustifiable, senseless.

war n. **1 conflict**, warfare, combat, fighting, action, bloodshed, fight, campaign, hostilities. **2 campaign**, crusade, battle, fight, struggle.
– OPPOSITES peace.
•v. **fight**, battle, combat, wage war, take up arms, feud, quarrel, struggle, contend, wrangle, cross swords.

WORD LINKS

relating to war: martial;
engaged in a war: belligerent

ward n. **1 room**, department, unit, area. **2 district**, constituency, division, quarter, zone, parish. **3 dependant**, charge, protégé.

warden n. **1 superintendent**, caretaker, porter, steward, custodian, watchman, concierge, doorman, commissioner. **2 prison officer**, guard, jailer, warder, keeper; informal screw.

warehouse n. **storeroom**, depot, depository, stockroom; informal lock-up.

wares pl. n. **goods**, merchandise, products, produce, stock, commodities.

warfare n. **fighting**, war, combat, conflict, action, hostilities.

warm adj. **1** *a warm kitchen:* **hot**, cosy, snug. **2** *a warm day:* **balmy**, summery, sultry, hot, mild, temperate. **3** *warm water:* **tepid**, lukewarm, heated. **4** *a warm sweater:* **thick**, chunky,

w

thermal, woolly. **5** *a warm welcome:* **friendly**, cordial, amiable, genial, kind, pleasant, fond, welcoming, hospitable, hearty.
– OPPOSITES cold, chilly.

warmth n. **1 heat**, cosiness, snugness. **2 friendliness**, amiability, geniality, cordiality, kindness, tenderness, fondness.

warn v. **1 inform**, notify, tell, alert, apprise, make someone aware, remind; *informal* tip off. **2 advise**, exhort, urge, counsel, caution.

warning n. **1 (advance) notice**, alert, hint, signal, sign, alarm bells; *informal* a tip-off. **2 caution**, notification, information, exhortation, advice. **3 omen**, premonition, foreboding, prophecy, prediction, forecast, token, portent, signal, sign. **4** *his sentence is a warning to other drunk drivers:* **example**, deterrent, lesson, caution, message, moral. **5 reprimand**, caution, remonstrance, admonition, censure; *informal* dressing-down, talking-to, telling-off.

warp v. **1 buckle**, twist, bend, distort, deform, curve, bow, contort. **2 corrupt**, twist, pervert, deprave.

warrant n. **1 authorization**, order, writ, mandate, licence, permit, summons. **2 voucher**, chit, slip, ticket, coupon, pass.
•v. **1 justify**, deserve, vindicate, call for, sanction, permit, authorize, excuse, account for, legitimate, support, license, merit, qualify for, rate.

2 guarantee, promise, affirm, swear, vouch, vow, pledge, undertake, declare, testify.

warranty n. **guarantee**, assurance, promise, commitment, undertaking, pledge, agreement, covenant.

warrior n. **fighter**, soldier, serviceman, combatant.

wary adj. **1 cautious**, careful, circumspect, on your guard, chary, alert, on the lookout, attentive, heedful, watchful, vigilant, observant. **2** *we are wary of strangers:* **suspicious**, chary, leery, careful, distrustful.
– OPPOSITES inattentive, trustful.

wash v. **1 clean yourself**, bathe, shower. **2 clean**, cleanse, scrub, wipe, shampoo, launder, lather, sluice, swill, douse, swab, disinfect. **3** *she washed off the blood:* **remove**, expunge, eradicate, sponge off, scrub off, wipe off, rinse off. **4 splash**, lap, dash, break, beat, surge, ripple, roll.
•n. **1 laundry**, washing. **2 backwash**, wake, trail, path.
◻ **wash away** erode, abrade, wear away, eat away.

waste v. **1 squander**, misspend, misuse, fritter away, throw away, lavish, dissipate; *informal* blow, splurge. **2** *she is wasting away:* **grow weak**, grow thin, wilt, fade, deteriorate.
– OPPOSITES conserve.
•adj. **1 unwanted**, excess, superfluous, left over, scrap, unusable, unprofitable. **2 uncultivated**, barren, desert, arid, bare, desolate.

•n. **1 misuse**, misapplication, abuse, extravagance, lavishness. **2 rubbish**, refuse, litter, debris, junk, sewage, effluent; N. Amer. garbage, trash. **3 (wastes) desert**, wasteland, wilderness, emptiness, wilds.

wasteful adj. prodigal, profligate, uneconomical, extravagant, lavish, excessive, imprudent, improvident, spendthrift.
– OPPOSITES frugal.

watch v. **1 observe**, view, look at, eye, gaze at, peer at, contemplate, inspect, scrutinize, scan; informal check out, get a load of, recce, eyeball. **2 spy on**, keep in sight, keep under surveillance, track, monitor, tail; informal keep tabs on, stake out. **3 guard**, mind, protect, look after, keep an eye on, take care of, shield, defend.
– OPPOSITES ignore.
•n. **1 wristwatch**, timepiece, chronometer. **2 guard**, vigil, lookout, observation, surveillance.

watchdog n. ombudsman, monitor, scrutineer, inspector, supervisor.

watchful adj. observant, alert, vigilant, attentive, aware, sharp-eyed, eagle-eyed, on the look-out, wary, cautious, careful.

water v. **1 sprinkle**, moisten, dampen, wet, spray, splash, hose, douse. **2 salivate**, become wet, moisten.
□ **water down 1** dilute, thin (out), weaken, adulterate.

2 tone down, temper, mitigate, moderate, soften, tame.

WORD LINKS
relating to water: aquatic, aqueous

waterfall n. falls, cascade, cataract, rapids.

watertight adj. **1 impermeable**, impervious, (hermetically) sealed, waterproof. **2 indisputable**, unquestionable, incontrovertible, irrefutable, unassailable, foolproof, sound, flawless, conclusive.
– OPPOSITES leaky.

wave v. **1 flap**, wag, shake, swish, swing, brandish, flourish, wield. **2 ripple**, flutter, undulate, stir, flap, sway, shake, quiver. **3 gesture**, signal, beckon, motion.
•n. **1 signal**, sign, motion, gesture. **2 breaker**, roller, comber, boomer, ripple; (**waves**) swell, surf. **3** *a wave of planning applications:* spate, surge, flow, flood, stream, torrent. **4** *a wave of emotion:* surge, rush, tide, upsurge, sudden feeling.

waver v. **1** *the candlelight wavered:* flicker, quiver. **2** *his voice wavered:* falter, wobble, tremble, quaver. **3 hesitate**, dither, be irresolute, be undecided, vacillate, blow hot and cold; Brit. haver, hum and haw; informal shilly-shally, sit on the fence.

way n. **1 method**, process, procedure, technique, system, plan, strategy, scheme, means, mechanism, approach. **2 manner**, style, fashion, mode. **3** *I've changed my ways:* **practice**, wont, habit, custom, convention, routine, trait, attribute, peculiarity, idiosyncrasy, conduct, behaviour. **4 route**, course, direction, track, path, access, gate, exit, entrance, door. **5 distance**, length, stretch, journey. **6** *April is a long way away:* **time**, stretch, term, span, duration. **7 direction**, bearing, course, orientation, line, tack. **8** *in some ways, he may be better off:* **respect**, regard, aspect, facet, sense, detail, point, particular. **9** *the country is in a bad way:* **state**, condition, situation, circumstances, position, predicament, plight; *informal* shape.

□ **give way 1** yield, back down, surrender, concede defeat, give in, submit; *informal* throw in the towel/sponge, cave in. **2** collapse, give, cave in, fall in, come apart, crumple.

waylay v. **1 ambush**, hold up, attack, pounce on; *informal* mug. **2 accost**, detain, intercept; *informal* buttonhole.

wayward adj. **wilful**, headstrong, stubborn, obstinate, perverse, contrary, disobedient, undisciplined, rebellious, defiant, recalcitrant, unruly, wild; *formal* refractory.

weak adj. **1 feeble**, frail, delicate, fragile, infirm, ailing, debilitated, decrepit, exhausted, enervated; *informal* weedy. **2 inadequate**, poor, defective,

faulty, deficient, imperfect, substandard. **3 unconvincing**, tenuous, implausible, unsatisfactory, poor, inadequate, lame, feeble, flimsy, hollow; *informal* pathetic. **4** *a weak bridge:* **fragile**, rickety, insubstantial, wobbly, unstable, ramshackle, jerry-built, shoddy. **5 spineless**, craven, cowardly, timid, irresolute, indecisive, ineffectual, meek, tame, soft, faint-hearted; *informal* yellow, gutless. **6** *a weak voice:* **indistinct**, muffled, muted, hushed, faint, low. **7 watery**, dilute, diluted, watered down, thin, tasteless.
– OPPOSITES strong.

weaken v. **1 enfeeble**, debilitate, incapacitate, sap, tire, exhaust. **2 decrease**, dwindle, diminish, wane, ebb, subside, peter out, fizzle out, tail off, decline, falter. **3 impair**, undermine, compromise, lessen.
– OPPOSITES strengthen, bolster.

weakness n. **1 frailty**, feebleness, fragility, delicacy, debility, incapacity, decrepitude; *informal* weediness. **2 fault**, flaw, defect, deficiency, failing, shortcoming, imperfection, Achilles heel. **3** *a weakness for champagne:* **fondness**, liking, partiality, love, penchant, predilection, inclination, taste. **4 timidity**, cravenness, cowardliness, indecision, irresolution, ineffectuality, ineffectiveness, impotence.

wealth n. **1 affluence**, prosperity, riches, means, fortune, money, cash, capital, treasure,

finance; informal wherewithal, dough, bread. **2 abundance**, profusion, plethora, mine, store; informal lot, load, mountain, stack, ton; Brit. informal shedload.
– OPPOSITES poverty, dearth.

wealthy adj. **rich**, affluent, moneyed, well off, well-to-do, prosperous; informal well heeled, rolling in it, made of money, loaded, flush.
– OPPOSITES poor.

wear v. **1 be dressed in**, be clothed in, have on, sport. **2 bear**, have, show, display, exhibit, give, put on, assume. **3 erode**, abrade, rub away, grind away, wash away, crumble (away), eat away (at). **4 last**, endure, hold up, bear up.
• n. **1 use**, service, value; informal mileage. **2 clothes**, garments, dress, attire, garb, wardrobe; informal get-up, gear, togs; Brit. informal kit, clobber. **3 damage**, friction, abrasion, erosion.
□ **wear off** fade, diminish, lessen, dwindle, decrease, wane, peter out, fizzle out, pall, disappear, vanish. **wear out 1** deteriorate, become worn, fray, become threadbare. **2** tire out, fatigue, weary, exhaust, drain, sap, enervate; informal whack, poop, shatter, do in; Brit. informal knacker.

wearing adj. **tiring**, exhausting, wearying, fatiguing, enervating, draining, sapping, demanding, exacting, taxing, gruelling, punishing.

weary adj. **1 tired**, worn out, exhausted, fatigued, sapped, spent, drained; informal done in, ready to drop, shattered, bushed; Brit. informal knackered, whacked; N. Amer. informal pooped. **2 tiring**, exhausting, fatiguing, enervating, draining, sapping, demanding, taxing, arduous, gruelling.
– OPPOSITES energetic.

weather n. **conditions**, climate, elements, forecast, outlook.
• v. **survive**, come through, ride out, pull through, withstand, endure, rise above; informal stick out.

weave¹ v. **1 entwine**, lace, twist, knit, braid, plait. **2 invent**, make up, fabricate, construct, create, spin.

weave² v. *he had to weave his way through the crowds:* **thread**, wind, wend, dodge, zigzag.

web n. **1 mesh**, net, lattice, lace-work, gauze, gossamer. **2 network**, nexus, complex, tangle, chain.

wedded adj. **1 married**, matrimonial, marital, conjugal, nuptial. **2** *he is wedded to his work:* **dedicated**, devoted, attached, fixated.

wedding n. **marriage (service)**, nuptials, union.

wedge n. **triangle**, segment, slice, section, chunk, lump, slab, hunk, block, piece.
• v. **squeeze**, cram, jam, ram, force, push, shove; informal stuff, bung.

W

weep v. cry, shed tears, sob, snivel, whimper, wail, bawl, keen; Scottish greet; informal boo-hoo, blub.

weigh v. **1 measure the weight of**, put on the scales. **2 have a weight of**, tip the scales at. **3** *he weighed up the possibilities:* **consider**, contemplate, think about, mull over, chew over, reflect on, ruminate over, muse on, assess, examine, review, explore, take stock of. **4** *they need to weigh benefit against risk:* **balance**, evaluate, compare, juxtapose, contrast.

weight n. **1 mass**, heaviness, load, burden. **2 influence**, force, leverage, sway, pull, power, authority; informal clout. **3 burden**, load, millstone, trouble, worry. **4** *the weight of the evidence is against him:* **most**, bulk, majority, preponderance, body, lion's share.

weird adj. **1 uncanny**, eerie, unnatural, supernatural, unearthly, other-worldly, ghostly, mysterious, strange, abnormal, unusual; informal creepy, spooky, freaky. **2 bizarre**, odd, curious, strange, quirky, outlandish, eccentric, unconventional, unorthodox, idiosyncratic, surreal, crazy, absurd, grotesque, peculiar; informal wacky, freaky; N. Amer. informal wacko.
– OPPOSITES normal, conventional.

welcome n. greeting, salutation, reception, hospitality, the red carpet.

• v. **1 greet**, salute, receive, meet, usher in. **2 be pleased by**, be glad about, approve of, applaud, appreciate, embrace.
– OPPOSITES resent.

• adj. **pleasing**, good, agreeable, encouraging, gratifying, heartening, promising, favourable, pleasant.

weld v. fuse, bond, stick, join, attach, seal, splice, melt, solder.

welfare n. **1 well-being**, health, comfort, security, safety, protection, success, interest, good. **2 social security**, benefit, public assistance, pension, credit, support, sick pay, unemployment benefit; Brit. informal the dole.

well¹ adv. **1 satisfactorily**, nicely, correctly, fittingly, suitably, appropriately. **2 skilfully**, ably, competently, proficiently, adeptly, deftly, expertly, excellently. **3** *they speak well of him:* **admiringly**, highly, approvingly, favourably, appreciatively, warmly, enthusiastically, in glowing terms.
– OPPOSITES badly.

• adj. **1 healthy**, fine, fit, robust, strong, vigorous, blooming, thriving, in fine fettle; informal in the pink. **2 satisfactory**, all right, fine, in order, as it should be, acceptable; informal OK, hunky-dory.
– OPPOSITES unwell, unsatisfactory.

□ **as well** too, also, in addition, into the bargain, besides, furthermore, moreover, to boot.

w

well → whisk

well² n. borehole, spring, waterhole, shaft.
- v. flow, spill, stream, gush, roll, cascade, flood, spout, burst, issue.

well built adj. sturdy, strapping, brawny, burly, hefty, muscular, strong, rugged; informal hunky, beefy.
- OPPOSITES puny.

well known adj. **1** familiar, popular, common, everyday, established. **2** famous, famed, prominent, notable, renowned, distinguished, eminent, illustrious, acclaimed.
- OPPOSITES unknown.

wet adj. **1** damp, moist, soaked, drenched, saturated, sopping, dripping, soggy, waterlogged, squelchy. **2** rainy, pouring, teeming, showery, drizzly. **3** sticky, tacky.
- v. dampen, moisten, sprinkle, spray, splash, soak, saturate, flood, douse, drench.
- OPPOSITES dry.

wharf n. quay, pier, dock, berth, landing, jetty, harbour, dockyard.

wheel v. **1** push, trundle, roll. **2** gulls wheeled overhead: turn, go round, circle, orbit.

wheeze v. gasp, whistle, hiss, rasp, croak, pant, cough.

whereabouts n. location, position, site, situation, spot, point, home, address, neighbourhood.

while n. we chatted for a while: time, spell, stretch, stint, span, interval, period; Brit. informal patch.
- v. tennis helped to while away the time: pass, spend, occupy, use up, kill.

whim n. impulse, urge, notion, fancy, inclination, caprice, vagary.

whimper v. whine, cry, sob, moan, snivel, wail, groan; Brit. informal grizzle.

whimsical adj. fanciful, playful, mischievous, waggish, quaint, curious, droll, eccentric, quirky, idiosyncratic, unconventional.

whine v. **1** wail, whimper, cry, mewl, moan, howl, yowl; informal grizzle. **2** complain, grouse, grouch, grumble, moan, carp; informal gripe, bellyache, whinge.

whip n. lash, scourge, strap, belt.
- v. **1** flog, lash, flagellate, cane, belt, thrash, beat; informal tan someone's hide. **2** whisk, beat. **3** rouse, stir up, excite, galvanize, electrify, stimulate, inspire, fire up, inflame, provoke.

whirl v. rotate, circle, wheel, turn, revolve, orbit, spin, twirl, pirouette, gyrate.

whirlpool n. eddy, vortex, maelstrom.

whirlwind n. tornado, hurricane, typhoon, cyclone, vortex; N. Amer. informal twister.
- adj. rapid, lightning, headlong, impulsive, breakneck, meteoric, sudden, swift, fast, quick, speedy.

whisk v. **1** speed, hurry, rush, sweep, hurtle, shoot. **2** pull, snatch, pluck, tug, jerk; informal whip, yank. **3** whip, beat, mix.

w

•n. *an egg whisk:* **beater**, mixer, blender.

whisper v. **murmur**, mutter, mumble, speak softly, breathe, say sotto voce.
•n. **1 murmur**, mutter, mumble, low voice, undertone.
2 rumour, story, report, gossip, speculation, suggestion, hint; *informal* buzz.
– OPPOSITES shout.

white adj. **pale**, pallid, wan, ashen, chalky, pasty, peaky, washed out, ghostly, deathly.

whole adj. **1 entire**, complete, full, unabridged, uncut. **2 intact**, in one piece, unbroken, undamaged, flawless, unmarked, perfect.
– OPPOSITES incomplete.
•n. **1 entity**, unit, body, ensemble. **2** *the whole of the year:* **all**, every part, the lot, the sum.
□ **on the whole** overall, all in all, all things considered, for the most part, in the main, in general, by and large, normally, usually, almost always, typically, ordinarily.

wholehearted adj. **unqualified**, unreserved, unconditional, complete, full, total, absolute.
– OPPOSITES half-hearted.

wholesale adj. **extensive**, widespread, large-scale, wideranging, comprehensive, total, mass, indiscriminate, sweeping.
– OPPOSITES partial.

wholesome adj. **1 healthy**, health-giving, good, nutritious, nourishing, natural, organic.
2 moral, ethical, good, clean,

virtuous, pure, innocent, chaste, uplifting, edifying.

wholly adv. **completely**, totally, absolutely, entirely, fully, thoroughly, utterly, downright, in every respect; *informal* one hundred per cent.

wicked adj. **1 evil**, sinful, immoral, wrong, bad, iniquitous, corrupt, base, vile, villainous, criminal, nefarious; *informal* crooked. **2 mischievous**, playful, naughty, impish, roguish, puckish, cheeky.
– OPPOSITES virtuous.

wide adj. **1 broad**, extensive, spacious, vast, spread out. **2 comprehensive**, ample, broad, extensive, wide-ranging, large, exhaustive, all-inclusive, expansive, all-embracing, encyclopedic, catholic. **3 off target**, off the mark, inaccurate.
– OPPOSITES narrow.

widen v. **broaden**, open up/out, expand, extend, enlarge.

widespread adj. **general**, extensive, universal, common, global, worldwide, omnipresent, ubiquitous, across the board, predominant, prevalent, rife, broad.
– OPPOSITES limited.

width n. **breadth**, thickness, span, diameter, girth.

wield v. **1 brandish**, flourish, wave, swing, use, employ, handle. **2** *he wields enormous power:* **exercise**, exert, hold, maintain, command, control.

wife n. **spouse**, partner, mate, consort, bride; *informal* better half, missus; Brit. informal other half.

WORD LINKS
very fond of your wife: uxorious

wild adj. **1** untamed, undomesticated, feral, fierce, ferocious, savage. **2 uncultivated**, native, indigenous. **3** uninhabited, unpopulated, uncultivated, rugged, rough, inhospitable, desolate, barren. **4 stormy**, squally, tempestuous, turbulent, blustery. **5 uncontrolled**, unrestrained, undisciplined, unruly, rowdy, disorderly, riotous, out of control, unbridled. **6** *a wild scheme:* **foolish**, ridiculous, ludicrous, stupid, foolhardy, idiotic, madcap, absurd, silly, impractical, impracticable, unworkable; informal crazy, crackpot. **7** *a wild guess:* **random**, arbitrary, haphazard, uninformed.
- OPPOSITES tame, cultivated, calm, disciplined.

wilderness n. wilds, wastes, desert, wasteland.

wiles pl. n. tricks, ruses, ploys, schemes, dodges, manoeuvres, subterfuges, guile, artfulness, cunning.

wilful adj. **1** deliberate, intentional, premeditated, planned, conscious, calculated. **2 headstrong**, strong-willed, obstinate, stubborn, pigheaded, recalcitrant; Brit. informal bloody-minded, bolshie.
- OPPOSITES accidental.

will n. **1 determination**, strength of character, resolve, single-mindedness, drive, commitment, dedication, doggedness, tenacity, staying power. **2** *they stayed against their will:* **desire**, wish, preference, inclination, intention. **3** *it was God's will:* **wish**, desire, decision, choice, decree, command.
-v. **1 want**, wish, please, see fit, think fit/best, like, choose, prefer. **2 decree**, order, ordain, command.

willing adj. **1 ready**, prepared, disposed, inclined, minded, happy, glad, pleased, agreeable, amenable; informal game. **2 readily given**, ungrudging.
- OPPOSITES reluctant.

willingly adv. **voluntarily**, of your own free will, of your own accord, readily, without reluctance, ungrudgingly, cheerfully, happily, gladly, with pleasure.
- OPPOSITES reluctantly.

willingness n. **readiness**, inclination, will, wish, desire.
- OPPOSITES reluctance.

wilt v. **1 droop**, sag, become limp, flop. **2 languish**, flag, droop, become listless, fade.
- OPPOSITES flourish.

wily adj. **shrewd**, clever, sharp, astute, canny, smart, crafty, cunning, artful, sly, scheming, calculating, devious; informal foxy.
- OPPOSITES naive.

win v. **1 come first**, be victorious, carry/win the day, come out on top, succeed, triumph, prevail. **2 earn**, gain, secure, collect, pick up, walk away/off with,

W

carry off; informal land, net, bag, scoop.
- OPPOSITES lose.
•n. **victory**, triumph, conquest.
- OPPOSITES defeat.

wince v. grimace, pull a face, flinch, blench, start.

wind¹ n. **1 breeze**, current of air, gale, hurricane, gust, draught; informal blow; literary zephyr. **2 breath**; informal puff.

wind² v. **1 twist (and turn)**, bend, curve, loop, zigzag, weave, snake. **2 wrap**, furl, entwine, lace. **3 coil**, roll, twist, twine.
□ **wind up 1** conclude, bring to an end/close, terminate; informal wrap up. **2** close (down), dissolve, put into liquidation.

windfall n. bonanza, jackpot, pennies from heaven, godsend.

windy adj. **breezy**, blowy, fresh, blustery, gusty, wild, stormy, squally.
- OPPOSITES still.

wing n. **1 part**, section, side, annexe, extension. **2 faction**, camp, caucus, arm, branch, group, section, set.
•v. **1 fly**, glide, soar. **2 wound**, graze, hit.

wink v. **1 blink**, flutter, bat. **2 sparkle**, twinkle, flash, glitter, gleam, shine, scintillate.

winner n. victor, champion, conqueror, medallist; informal champ, top dog.
- OPPOSITES loser.

winning adj. **1 victorious**, successful, triumphant, undefeated, conquering, first, top. **2 engaging**, charming, appealing, endearing, sweet, cute, winsome, attractive, prepossessing, fetching, disarming, captivating.

winnings pl. n. prize money, gains, booty, spoils, proceeds, profits, takings, purse.

wintry adj. bleak, cold, chilly, frosty, freezing, icy, snowy, arctic, glacial, bitter, raw; informal nippy; Brit. informal parky.
- OPPOSITES warm.

wipe v. rub, mop, sponge, swab, clean, dry, polish. **2** he wiped off the marks: rub off, clean off, remove, erase, efface.

wisdom n. **1 understanding**, intelligence, sagacity, sense, common sense, shrewdness, astuteness, judgement, prudence, circumspection, logic, rationale, soundness, advisability. **2 knowledge**, learning, erudition, scholarship, philosophy, lore.
- OPPOSITES folly.

wise adj. sage, sagacious, intelligent, clever, learned, knowledgeable, enlightened, astute, smart, shrewd, sharp-witted, canny, knowing, sensible, prudent, discerning, perceptive.
- OPPOSITES foolish.

wish v. want, desire, feel inclined, feel like, care, choose, please, think fit.
•n. **1 desire**, longing, yearning, whim, craving, hunger, hope, aspiration, aim, ambition, dream; informal hankering, yen.

2 *her parents' wishes:* **request**, requirement, bidding, instruction, direction, demand, order, command, want, desire, will.
□ **wish for** desire, want, hope for, covet, dream of, long for, yearn for, crave, hunger for, aspire to, set your heart on, seek, fancy, hanker after; informal have a yen for.

wistful adj. **nostalgic**, yearning, longing, forlorn, melancholy, sad, mournful, pensive, reflective, contemplative.

wit n. **1** *he needed all his wits to escape:* **intelligence**, shrewdness, astuteness, cleverness, canniness, sense, judgement, acumen, insight, brains, mind; informal nous. **2 wittiness**, humour, drollery, repartee, badinage, banter, wordplay, jokes, witticisms, quips, puns. **3 comedian**, humorist, comic, joker; informal wag.

witch n. **sorceress**, enchantress, hex.

witchcraft n. **sorcery**, (black) magic, wizardry, spells, incantations, necromancy, Wicca.

withdraw v. **1 remove**, extract, pull out, take out, take back. **2 abolish**, cancel, lift, set aside, end, stop, remove, reverse, revoke, rescind, repeal, annul. **3 retract**, take back, go back on, recant, repudiate, renounce, back down, climb down, backtrack, back-pedal, do a U-turn, eat your words. **4 retreat**, pull out of, evacuate, quit, leave. **5 retire**, retreat, adjourn,

decamp, leave, depart, absent yourself; formal repair.
– OPPOSITES insert, enter.

withdrawal n. **1 removal**, abolition, cancellation, discontinuation, termination, elimination. **2 departure**, pull-out, exit, exodus, evacuation, retreat.

withdrawn adj. **introverted**, unsociable, inhibited, uncommunicative, unforthcoming, quiet, reticent, reserved, retiring, private, reclusive, distant, shy, timid.
– OPPOSITES outgoing.

wither v. **1 shrivel (up)**, dry up, wilt, droop, go limp, fade, perish. **2 waste (away)**, shrivel (up), shrink, atrophy. **3 diminish**, dwindle, shrink, lessen, fade, wane, evaporate, disappear.
– OPPOSITES thrive.

withering adj. **scornful**, contemptuous, scathing, stinging.

withhold v. **1 hold back**, keep back, refuse to give, retain, hold on to, hide, conceal, keep secret; informal sit on. **2 suppress**, repress, hold back, fight back, choke back, control, check, restrain, contain.
– OPPOSITES release.

withstand v. **resist**, weather, survive, endure, cope with, stand, tolerate, bear, defy, brave, hold out against.

witness n. **observer**, onlooker, eyewitness, spectator, viewer, watcher, bystander, passer-by.
▸ v. **1 see**, observe, watch, view,

w

notice, spot, be present at, attend. **2 countersign**, sign, endorse, validate.

witty adj. **humorous**, amusing, droll, funny, comic, jocular, sparkling, scintillating, entertaining, clever, quick-witted.

wizard n. **1 sorcerer**, warlock, magus, (black) magician, enchanter. **2 genius**, expert, master, virtuoso, maestro, marvel; informal hotshot, whizz-kid; Brit. informal dab hand; N. Amer. informal maven.

wobble v. **1 rock**, sway, see-saw, teeter, jiggle, shake. **2 teeter**, totter, stagger, lurch, waddle. **3** *her voice wobbled*: **tremble**, shake, quiver, quaver, waver.

wobbly adj. **1 unsteady**, unstable, shaky, rocky, rickety, unsafe, precarious; informal wonky. **2 shaky**, quivery, weak, unsteady; informal like jelly.
– OPPOSITES stable.

woe n. **1 misery**, sorrow, distress, sadness, unhappiness, heartache, heartbreak, despair, adversity, misfortune, disaster, suffering, hardship. **2** *financial woes*: **trouble**, difficulty, problem, trial, tribulation, misfortune, setback, reverse.
– OPPOSITES joy.

woeful adj. **1 sad**, unhappy, sorrowful, miserable, gloomy, doleful, plaintive, wretched. **2 dreadful**, awful, terrible, atrocious, disgraceful, deplorable, hopeless, lamentable; informal rotten, appalling, pathetic,

pitiful, lousy, abysmal, dire; Brit. informal duff, chronic.
– OPPOSITES cheerful, excellent.

woman n. **lady**, female; Scottish & N. English lass; Irish colleen; informal chick; N. Amer. informal sister, dame, broad; Austral./NZ informal sheila; literary damsel.

> WORD LINKS
> *relating to women*: female, feminine;
> *branch of medicine concerning women*: gynaecology;
> *hatred of women*: misogyny

womanly adj. **1 feminine**, female. **2 voluptuous**, curvaceous, shapely, ample, buxom, full-figured; informal curvy, busty.
– OPPOSITES manly, boyish.

wonder n. **1 awe**, admiration, fascination, surprise, astonishment, amazement. **2** *the wonders of nature*: **marvel**, miracle, phenomenon, sensation, spectacle, beauty, curiosity.
•v. **1 ponder**, think about, meditate on, reflect on, muse on, speculate about, conjecture, be curious about. **2 marvel**, be amazed, be astonished, stand in awe, be dumbfounded; informal be flabbergasted.

wonderful adj. **marvellous**, magnificent, superb, glorious, sublime, lovely, delightful; informal super, great, fantastic, terrific, tremendous, sensational, fabulous, awesome, magic, wicked; Brit. informal smashing, brilliant; N. Amer. informal peachy, dandy, neat; Austral./NZ informal beaut, bonzer.

woo v. **1 pay court to**, pursue, chase; dated court, romance, seek the hand of. **2 seek**, pursue, curry favour with, try to win, try to attract, try to cultivate. **3 entice**, tempt, coax, persuade, wheedle, seduce; informal sweet-talk.

wood n. **1 timber**, planks, logs; N. Amer. lumber. **2 forest**, woodland, trees, copse, coppice, grove; Brit. spinney.

> WORD LINKS
> relating to wood: **ligneous**

wooded adj. **forested**, afforested, tree-covered; literary sylvan.

wooden adj. **1 wood**, timber. **2 stilted**, stiff, unnatural, awkward, flat, clumsy, graceless, inelegant. **3 expressionless**, impassive, poker-faced, emotionless, blank, vacant, unresponsive, lifeless.

wool n. **fleece**, hair, coat.

woolly adj. **1 woollen**, wool. **2 fleecy**, shaggy, hairy, fluffy. **3 vague**, ill-defined, hazy, unclear, fuzzy, indefinite, confused, muddled.

word n. **1 term**, name, expression, designation. **2 remark**, comment, observation, statement, utterance. **3 script**, lines, lyrics, libretto. **4** I give you my **word**: promise, assurance, guarantee, undertaking, pledge, vow, oath, bond. **5 talk**, conversation, chat, tête-à-tête, heart-to-heart, one-to-one, discussion; informal confab. **6** there's no word from the hospital: **news**, information, communication, intelligence, message, report, communiqué, dispatch, bulletin; literary tidings.
-v. **phrase**, express, put, couch, frame, formulate, style.

> WORD LINKS
> relating to words: **verbal, lexical**

wording n. **phrasing**, phraseology, language, words, expression, terminology.

wordy adj. **long-winded**, verbose, lengthy, rambling, garrulous, voluble; informal windy; Brit. informal waffly.
– OPPOSITES succinct.

work n. **1 labour**, toil, slog, drudgery, exertion, effort, industry; informal grind, sweat; Brit. informal graft; old use travail. **2 employment**, job, post, position, situation, occupation, profession, career, vocation, calling. **3 tasks**, jobs, duties, assignments, projects, chores. **4 composition**, piece, creation, opus; (**works**) oeuvre, canon.
– OPPOSITES leisure.
-v. **1 labour**, toil, exert yourself, slave (away); informal slog (away), beaver away; Brit. informal graft. **2 be employed**, have a job, earn your living, do business. **3 function**, go, run, operate. **4 operate**, use, handle, control, run, manipulate. **5 succeed**, turn out well, go as planned, get results, be effective; informal come off, pay off, do the trick. **6 achieve**, accomplish, bring about, produce, perform.
– OPPOSITES rest, fail.

□ **work out 1** calculate, compute, reckon up, determine. **2** understand, comprehend, puzzle out, sort out, make sense of, get to the bottom of, make head or tail of, unravel, decode, decipher; informal figure out; Brit. informal suss out. **3** devise, formulate, draw up, put together, develop, construct, arrange, organize, contrive, concoct.

worker n. employee, member of staff, workman, labourer, hand, operator, operative, agent, wage-earner, breadwinner, proletarian.

workshop n. **1** workroom, studio, factory, works, plant, industrial unit. **2** study group, discussion group, seminar, forum, class.

world n. **1** earth, globe, planet, sphere. **2** sphere, society, circle, arena, milieu, province, domain, preserve, realm, field. **3** (**the world**) everyone, people, mankind, humankind, humanity, the public, all and sundry.

worldly adj. **1** earthly, terrestrial, temporal, mundane, mortal, human, material, physical. **2** sophisticated, experienced, worldly-wise, knowledgeable, knowing, enlightened, mature, seasoned, cosmopolitan, urbane, cultured.
– OPPOSITES spiritual, naive.

worldwide adj. global, international, intercontinental, universal, ubiquitous.
– OPPOSITES local.

worn adj. **shabby**, worn out, threadbare, in tatters, falling to pieces, ragged, frayed, motheaten, scruffy, having seen better days.
– OPPOSITES new, smart.

worried adj. **anxious**, troubled, bothered, concerned, uneasy, fretful, agitated, nervous, edgy, tense, apprehensive, fearful, afraid, frightened; Brit. informal in a stew, in a flap.
– OPPOSITES carefree.

worry v. **1** be anxious, be concerned, fret, agonize, brood, panic, lose sleep, get worked up; informal get in a flap, get in a state. **2** trouble, make anxious, disturb, distress, upset, concern, unsettle, perturb, scare, prey on someone's mind; informal bug, get to.
• n. **1** anxiety, distress, concern, unease, disquiet, nerves, agitation, edginess, tension, apprehension, fear, misgiving. **2** problem, cause for concern, nuisance, pest, trial, trouble, bane, bugbear; informal pain, headache, hassle.

worsen v. **1** aggravate, add to, intensify, increase, compound, magnify, heighten, inflame, exacerbate. **2** deteriorate, degenerate, decline; informal go downhill.
– OPPOSITES improve.

worship n. **1** reverence, veneration, adoration, glorification, exaltation, devotion, praise, thanksgiving, homage, honour. **2** service, rite, prayer, praise, devotion, observance.

•v. **1 revere**, pray to, pay homage to, honour, adore, venerate, praise, glorify, exalt. **2 love**, cherish, treasure, hold dear, esteem, adulate, idolize, deify, hero-worship, lionize; informal put on a pedestal.

worth n. **1 value**, price, cost, valuation, estimate. **2 benefit**, good, advantage, use, value, virtue, desirability, sense.

worthless adj. **1 valueless**, of no value; informal trashy. **2 useless**, pointless, meaningless, senseless, inconsequential, ineffective, ineffectual, fruitless, unproductive, unavailing, valueless. **3 good-for-nothing**, ne'er-do-well, useless, despicable, contemptible, degenerate; informal no-good, lousy.
– OPPOSITES valuable, useful.

worthwhile adj. **valuable**, useful, of service, beneficial, rewarding, advantageous, positive, helpful, profitable, gainful, fruitful, productive, constructive, effective.

worthy adj. **good**, righteous, virtuous, moral, ethical, upright, respectable, upstanding, high-minded, principled, reputable, decent.
– OPPOSITES disreputable.
•n. **dignitary**, personage, grandee, VIP, notable, pillar of society, luminary, leading light; informal bigwig.

would-be adj. **aspiring**, budding, promising, prospective, potential, hopeful, keen, eager, ambitious; informal wannabe.

wound n. **1 injury**, cut, gash, laceration, graze, scratch, abrasion, puncture, lesion; Medicine trauma. **2 insult**, blow, slight, offence, affront, hurt, damage, injury.
•v. **1 injure**, hurt, harm, lacerate, cut, graze, gash, stab, slash. **2** her words wounded him: **hurt**, offend, affront, distress, grieve, pain.

wrap v. **1 enclose**, enfold, envelop, encase, cover, fold, wind, swathe, bundle, swaddle. **2 pack**, package, parcel up, bundle (up), gift-wrap.
•n. **shawl**, stole, cloak, cape, mantle, scarf.

wrath n. **anger**, rage, temper, fury, outrage, spleen, resentment, (high) dudgeon, indignation; literary ire.
– OPPOSITES happiness.

wreath n. **garland**, circlet, chaplet, crown, festoon, lei, ring, loop, circle.

wreathe v. **1 festoon**, garland, drape, cover, deck, decorate, ornament, adorn. **2 spiral**, coil, loop, wind, curl, twist, snake.

wreck n. **1 shipwreck**, sunken ship, hull. **2 wreckage**, debris, ruins, remains, burnt-out shell.
•v. **1 destroy**, break, demolish, crash, smash up, write off; N. Amer. informal trash, total. **2 ruin**, spoil, disrupt, undo, put a stop to, frustrate, blight, crush, dash, destroy, scotch, shatter, devastate, sabotage; informal mess up, screw up, put paid to, stymie; Brit. informal scupper.

w

wrench v. **1 tug**, pull, jerk, wrest, heave, twist, force, prise; N. Amer. pry; informal yank. **2 sprain**, twist, turn, strain, rick, crick.

wrestle v. **grapple**, fight, struggle, scuffle, tussle, brawl; informal scrap.

wretched adj. **1 miserable**, unhappy, sad, heartbroken, griefstricken, distressed, desolate, devastated, disconsolate, downcast, dejected, depressed, melancholy, forlorn. **2 harsh**, hard, grim, difficult, poor, pitiful, piteous, pathetic, tragic, miserable, bleak, cheerless, hopeless, sorry, sordid; informal crummy.
- OPPOSITES cheerful, comfortable.

wriggle v. **squirm**, writhe, wiggle, thresh, flounder, flail, twitch, twist and turn, snake, worm.
□ **wriggle out of** avoid, shirk, dodge, evade, sidestep, escape; informal duck.

wrinkle n. **crease**, fold, pucker, line, crinkle, furrow, ridge, groove; informal crow's feet.
•v. **crease**, pucker, gather, crinkle, crumple, rumple, ruck up, scrunch up.

write v. **1 put in writing**, put down, jot down, note (down), take down, record, inscribe, sign, scribble, scrawl, pen, pencil. **2 compose**, draft, think up, formulate, compile, pen, dash off, produce. **3 correspond**, communicate, get in touch,

keep in contact; informal drop someone a line.

writer n. **author**, wordsmith; informal scribbler, scribe, penpusher, hack.

writhe v. **squirm**, wriggle, thrash, flail, toss, twist.

writing n. **1 handwriting**, hand, script, calligraphy, lettering, print, printing; informal scribble, scrawl. **2 written work**, compositions, books, publications, papers, articles, essays, oeuvre.

WORD LINKS

study of handwriting:
graphology

---

wrong adj. **1 incorrect**, mistaken, erroneous, inaccurate, wide of the mark, inexact, imprecise; informal off beam, out. **2 inappropriate**, unsuitable, ill-advised, ill-considered, illjudged, unwise, infelicitous; informal out of order. **3 bad**, dishonest, illegal, unlawful, illicit, criminal, corrupt, unethical, immoral, wicked, sinful, iniquitous, nefarious, reprehensible; informal crooked. **4 amiss**, awry, out of order, not right, defective, faulty.
- OPPOSITES right, correct.
•adv. **incorrectly**, wrongly, inaccurately, erroneously, mistakenly.
•n. **1 immorality**, sin, wickedness, evil, illegality, unlawfulness, crime, corruption, villainy, dishonesty, injustice, misconduct, transgression. **2 misdeed**,

w

offence, injury, crime, transgression, sin, injustice, outrage, atrocity.
- **OPPOSITES** right.
- v. **mistreat**, ill-use, ill-treat, do an injustice to, abuse, harm, hurt, injure.

wrongdoer n. **offender**, lawbreaker, criminal, felon, delinquent, villain, culprit, evil-doer, sinner, transgressor, malefactor, miscreant, rogue, scoundrel; informal crook, wrong 'un.

yank v. & n. (informal) **jerk**, pull, tug, wrench.

yardstick n. **standard**, measure, gauge, scale, guide, guideline, indicator, test, touchstone, barometer, criterion, benchmark.

yarn n. **thread**, cotton, wool, fibre, filament.

yawning adj. **gaping**, wide, cavernous, deep, huge, vast.

yearly adv. **annually**, once a year, per annum, each/every year.

yearn v. **long**, pine, crave, desire, want, wish, hanker, covet, hunger, thirst, ache; informal itch.

yell v. **shout**, cry out, howl, wail, scream, shriek, screech, yelp, squeal, roar, bawl; informal holler.

yellow adj. **golden**, gold, blonde, fair, flaxen, lemon, primrose, mustard.

yes adv. **certainly**, very well, of course, by all means, sure, all right, absolutely, indeed, affirmative, agreed, roger; Scottish &

N. English aye; informal yeah, yep; Brit. informal righto.
- **OPPOSITES** no.

yield v. **1 produce**, bear, give, provide, afford, return, bring in, earn, realize, generate, deliver, pay out. **2 surrender**, capitulate, submit, admit defeat, back down, give in, cave in, raise the white flag, throw in the towel, give up the struggle.
- **OPPOSITES** withhold, resist.
- n. **profit**, gain, return, dividend, earnings.

yob, yobbo n. (Brit. informal) **lout**, thug, hooligan, tearaway, vandal, ruffian, troublemaker; Austral. larrikin; informal tough, bruiser, yahoo; Brit. informal lager lout; Scottish informal ned.

yokel n. **rustic**, bumpkin, peasant, provincial; N. Amer. informal hayseed, hillbilly, hick.

young adj. **1 youthful**, juvenile, junior, adolescent, teenage, in your salad days. **2 immature**, childish, inexperienced, naive, green, wet behind the ears. **3** a

young industry: **new**, fledgling, developing, budding, in its infancy, emerging, in the making.
- OPPOSITES old, mature.
- n. **offspring**, progeny, family, babies, litter, brood.

youngster n. **child**, teenager, adolescent, youth, juvenile, minor, junior, boy, girl; Scottish & N. English lass, lassie; informal lad, kid, whippersnapper, teen.

youth n. **1 early years**, teens, adolescence, boyhood, girlhood, childhood, minority.
2 young man, boy, juvenile, teenager, adolescent, junior, minor; informal lad, kid.

youthful adj. **young**, boyish, girlish, fresh-faced, young-looking, spry, sprightly, vigorous, active.
- OPPOSITES elderly.

Zz

zany adj. **eccentric**, odd, unconventional, bizarre, weird, mad, crazy, comic, madcap, quirky, idiosyncratic; informal wacky, oddball, off the wall; Brit. informal daft; N. Amer. informal kooky.
- OPPOSITES conventional.

zeal n. **enthusiasm**, passion, ardour, fervour, fervency, fire, devotion, gusto, vigour, energy, vehemence, intensity, eagerness, fanaticism.
- OPPOSITES apathy.

zealot n. **fanatic**, enthusiast, extremist, radical, diehard, activist, militant.

zealous adj. **ardent**, fervent, passionate, impassioned, enthusiastic, devoted, committed, dedicated, eager, keen, avid, vehement, intense, fierce, fanatical.
- OPPOSITES apathetic.

zenith n. **high point**, crowning point, height, top, acme, peak, pinnacle, apex, apogee, crown, crest, summit, culmination, climax.
- OPPOSITES nadir.

zero n. **nought**, nothing, nil, 0; informal zilch; old use naught.

zest n. **enthusiasm**, gusto, relish, appetite, eagerness, keenness, zeal, passion, energy, liveliness.

zigzag v. **twist**, meander, snake, wind, weave, swerve.

zone n. **area**, sector, section, belt, stretch, region, territory, district, quarter, neighbourhood.

zoom v. (informal) **hurry**, rush, dash, race, speed, sprint, career, shoot, hurtle, hare, fly; informal tear, belt, whizz; Brit. informal bomb.

y

z